Harcourt

Orlando Austin Chicago New York Toronto London San Diego

Visit *The Learning Site!*
www.harcourtschool.com

2007 Edition

Printed in the United States of America

ISBN 0-15-352225-9

4 5 6 7 8 9 10 032 10 09 08 07

Senior Author

Evan M. Maletsky
Professor of Mathematics
Montclair State University
Upper Montclair, New Jersey

Mathematics Advisor

Tom Roby
Associate Professor of Mathematics
California State University
Hayward, California

Authors

Angela Giglio Andrews
Math Teacher, Scott School
Naperville District #203
Naperville, Illinois

Jennie M. Bennett
Houston Independent School District
Houston, Texas

Grace M. Burton
Professor, Watson School of Education
University of North Carolina at Wilmington
Wilmington, North Carolina

Lynda A. Luckie
K-12 Mathematics Coordinator
Gwinnett County Public Schools
Lawrenceville, Georgia

Joyce C. McLeod
Visiting Professor
Rollins College
Winter Park, Florida

Vicki Newman
Classroom Teacher
McGaugh Elementary School
Los Alamitos Unified School District
Seal Beach, California

Tom Roby
Associate Professor of Mathematics
California State University
Hayward, California

Janet K. Scheer
Executive Director
Create A Vision
Foster City, California

Program Consultants and Specialist

Janet S. Abbott
Mathematics Consultant
California

Elsie Babcock
Director, Mathematics and Science Center
Mathematics Consultant
Wayne Regional Educational Service Agency
Wayne, Michigan

William J. Driscoll
Professor of Mathematics
Department of Mathematical Sciences
Central Connecticut State University
New Britain, Connecticut

Lois Harrison-Jones
Education and Management Consultant
Dallas, Texas

Rebecca Valbuena
Language Development Specialist
Stanton Elementary School
Glendora, California

UNIT 1 CHAPTERS 1–4 Understand Whole Numbers and Operations

Technology Link

Harcourt Mega Math: *Chapter 1, p. 2; Chapter 2, pp. 21, 32; Chapter 3, p. 48; Chapter 4, p. 65*
The Harcourt Learning Site: www.harcourtschool.com
Multimedia Math Glossary: www.harcourtschool.com/mathglossary

UNIT WRAPUP

UNIT 2
CHAPTERS 5–7

Time, Data, and Graphing

5

6

Technology Link

Harcourt Mega Math: *Chapter 5, pp. 99, 104; Chapter 6, p. 122; Chapter 7, p. 136*
The Harcourt Learning Site:
www.harcourtschool.com
Multimedia Math Glossary:
www.harcourtschool.com/mathglossary

Is your favorite color red, blue, or yellow?

SUSIE'S SURVEY DATA	
Color	Votes
Red	𝍸 𝍸
Blue	𝍸 𝍸 I
Yellow	𝍸 III

7 ANALYZE AND GRAPH DATA 134

UNIT WRAPUP

UNIT 3 Multiplication and Division Facts

CHAPTERS 8–9

8 PRACTICE MULTIPLICATION AND DIVISION FACTS 162

Technology Link

Harcourt Mega Math: *Chapter 8, pp. 168, 173; Chapter 9, p. 185*

The Harcourt Learning Site:
www.harcourtschool.com

Multimedia Math Glossary:
www.harcourtschool.com/mathglossary

9 ALGEBRA USE MULTIPLICATION AND DIVISION FACTS 182

UNIT WRAPUP

UNIT 4
CHAPTERS 10–12

Multiply by 1- and 2-Digit Numbers

Technology Link

Harcourt Mega Math: *Chapter 10, p. 219; Chapter 11, p. 236; Chapter 12, pp. 253, 260*
The Harcourt Learning Site: www.harcourtschool.com
Multimedia Math Glossary: www.harcourtschool.com/mathglossary

MULTIPLY BY 2-DIGIT NUMBERS 250

UNIT WRAPUP

UNIT 5

CHAPTERS 13–16

Divide by 1- and 2-Digit Divisors

Technology Link

Harcourt Mega Math: *Chapter 13, pp. 279, 282; Chapter 14, p. 303; Chapter 15, p. 320; Chapter 16, p. 348*

The Harcourt Learning Site: **www.harcourtschool.com**

Multimedia Math Glossary: **www.harcourtschool.com/mathglossary**

15 DIVIDE BY 2-DIGIT DIVISORS 314

16 NUMBER THEORY 334

UNIT WRAPUP

UNIT 6 Geometry and Algebra

CHAPTERS 17–20

Technology Link

Harcourt Mega Math: *Chapter 17, pp. 365, 370; Chapter 18, p. 385; Chapter 19, p. 407; Chapter 20, p. 429*
The Harcourt Learning Site:
www.harcourtschool.com
Multimedia Math Glossary:
www.harcourtschool.com/mathglossary

19 MOTION GEOMETRY 396

20 ALGEBRA EXPLORE NEGATIVE NUMBERS AND GRAPHING 418

UNIT WRAPUP

UNIT 7 Fractions and Probability

CHAPTERS 21–23

21 UNDERSTAND FRACTIONS 444

22 ADD AND SUBTRACT FRACTIONS AND MIXED NUMBERS 466

OUTCOMES AND PROBABILITY 488

UNIT WRAPUP

Technology Link

Harcourt Mega Math: *Chapter 21, p. 449; Chapter 22, p. 482; Chapter 23, pp. 490, 496, 498*

The Harcourt Learning Site:
www.harcourtschool.com

Multimedia Math Glossary:
www.harcourtschool.com/mathglossary

UNIT 8
CHAPTERS 24–27

Measurement and Decimals

24 CUSTOMARY MEASUREMENT 516

25 METRIC MEASUREMENT 538

Harcourt Mega Math: *Chapter 24, p. 522; Chapter 25, p. 541; Chapter 26, pp. 566, 568; Chapter 27, p. 590*
The Harcourt Learning Site: www.harcourtschool.com
Multimedia Math Glossary: www.harcourtschool.com/mathglossary

UNDERSTAND DECIMALS 558

ADD AND SUBTRACT DECIMALS 582

UNIT WRAPUP

UNIT 9 Perimeter, Area, and Volume

CHAPTERS 28–30

28 PERIMETER OF PLANE FIGURES 610

29 AREA OF PLANE FIGURES 626

Technology Link

Harcourt Mega Math: *Chapter 29, p. 631; Chapter 30, pp. 644, 648*

The Harcourt Learning Site:
www.harcourtschool.com

Multimedia Math Glossary:
www.harcourtschool.com/mathglossary

Why Learn Math?

Building Success Now

You use time concepts when you plan your after-school activities. ▼

▲ You measure weight and capacity when you cook.

You compare, add, and subtract numbers in scores when you play or watch your favorite sport. ▶

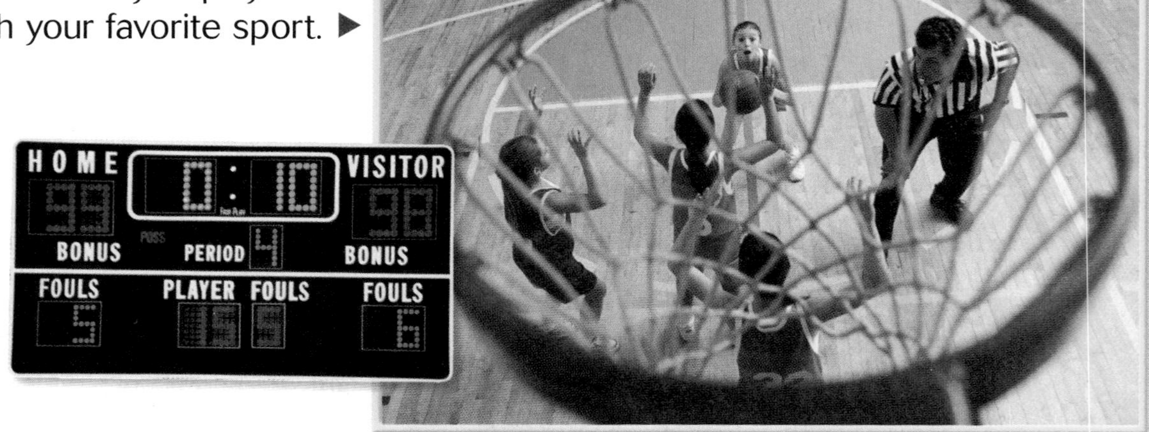

You will use the mathematics that you learn in **Harcourt Math** every day. The skills you learn will help you **build success** both now and in the future.

Building Success for the Future

◀ If you become a filmmaker, you will use time and measurement concepts as you shoot and piece together movie scenes.

If you become an architect, you will add and subtract fractions and decimals as you plan your next project. ▼

▲ If you become a marine biologist, you will use mathematics in studying and reporting on ocean animals.

Have a great year and enjoy learning Math!

PRACTICE WHAT YOU LEARN

It's in the Bag

PROJECT In each unit of this book, you will do a project that will help you practice the math skills you have learned. Make the Fold-n-Hold bag to hold some of these projects.

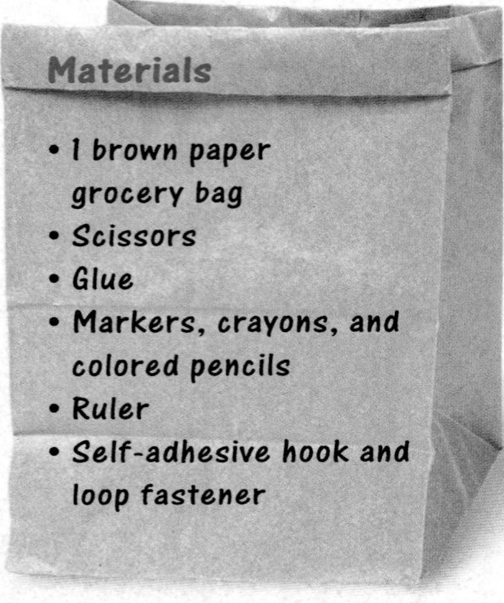

Materials
• 1 brown paper grocery bag
• Scissors
• Glue
• Markers, crayons, and colored pencils
• Ruler
• Self-adhesive hook and loop fastener

Directions

1. Lay the bag in front of you with the bottom side up. Fold the bag in half. The open end of the bag that is folded over will be the closure flap. (*Picture A*)
2. Unfold the bag. Cut down each side of the closure flap to where you folded the bag in half and then cut across. (*Picture B*)
3. Fold the end of the closure flap down 1 inch. Unfold and cut the corners off on a diagonal. Glue the fold down.
4. Attach a square of hook fastener on the underside of the closure flap. Fold the bottom of the bag under. Attach a 7-inch strip of loop fastener to the front of the pouch part of the bag. (*Picture C*)
5. Label the top closure flap *Fold-n-Hold* and the back of the pocket *My Math Projects*. Close the bag and decorate with markers, crayons, or colored pencils.

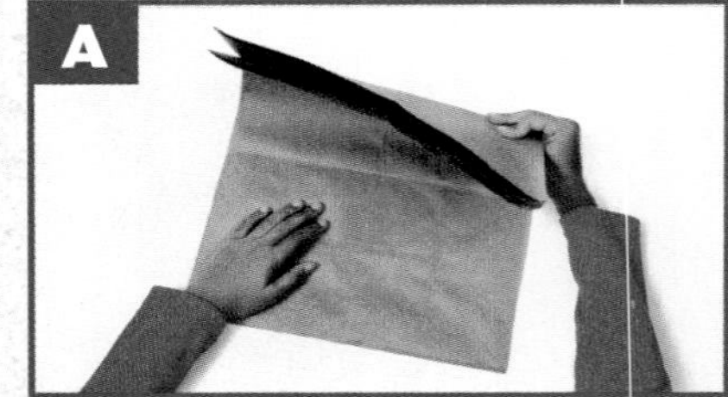

SHOW WHAT YOU LEARN

Taking a test is one way to show what you've learned. Being a good test taker is like being a good problem solver. When you answer test questions, you are solving problems.

Each time you take a test, remember to:

- Listen carefully to your teacher's instructions.
- Read all the directions.
- Pay attention to where and how to mark the test.
- Read the problems carefully.
- If you don't understand a problem, read it again.
- Mark or write your answers clearly.
- Answer questions you are sure about first.
- Work quickly but carefully.
- If you finish early, go back and check your work.
- Relax and do the best that you can.

GETTING READY!

Addition Strategies

Use counting on, make a ten, doubles, and doubles plus one to find a sum mentally and to practice addition facts.

COUNT ON

12 + 3 = ▢

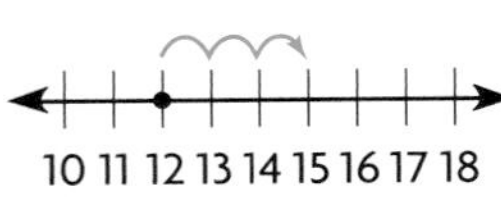

Start with the greater addend. Say 12. Count on 3. 13, 14, 15 The sum is 15.

So, 12 + 3 = 15.

MAKE A TEN

8 + 5 = ▢

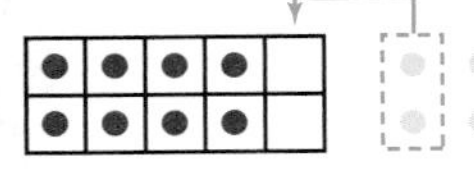

Move 2 counters to fill the ten frame. 8 + 2 = 10 There are 3 more counters to add. 10 + 3 = 13

So, 8 + 5 = 13.

DOUBLES

6 + 6 = ▢

When the addends are the same, you are adding doubles.

So, 6 + 6 = 12.

DOUBLES PLUS ONE

6 + 7 = ▢

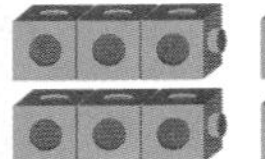

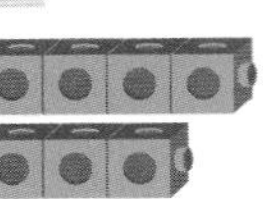

Think: 6 + 7 is 1 more than 6 + 6.

Add the doubles. 6 + 6 = 12

Then add one more. 12 + 1 = 13

So, 6 + 7 = 13.

▶ Practice

Find the sum. Name the strategy you used.

1. 8 + 9 **2.** 7 + 4 **3.** 5 + 5 **4.** 9 + 3

5. 10 + 2 **6.** 2 + 7 **7.** 10 + 10 **8.** 9 + 1

9. 5 + 9 **10.** 5 + 4 **11.** 7 + 7 **12.** 7 + 8

13. $\begin{array}{r} 3 \\ +4 \\ \hline \end{array}$ **14.** $\begin{array}{r} 6 \\ +1 \\ \hline \end{array}$ **15.** $\begin{array}{r} 9 \\ +9 \\ \hline \end{array}$ **16.** $\begin{array}{r} 6 \\ +5 \\ \hline \end{array}$

17. $\begin{array}{r} 8 \\ +6 \\ \hline \end{array}$ **18.** $\begin{array}{r} 8 \\ +3 \\ \hline \end{array}$ **19.** $\begin{array}{r} 10 \\ +9 \\ \hline \end{array}$ **20.** $\begin{array}{r} 10 \\ +3 \\ \hline \end{array}$

Subtraction Strategies

Use counting back to find a difference mentally and to practice subtraction facts.

COUNT BACK

13 − 3 = ■

9 10 11 12 13 14 15 16 17

So, 13 − 3 = 10.

Start with the first number.
Say 13. Count back 3.
12, 11, 10
The difference is 10.

Addition and subtraction are inverse, or opposite, operations. You can use addition facts to recall subtraction facts.

17 − 9 = ■

8 + 9 = 17

FACT FAMILIES

15 − 7 = ■

Think: 7 + ■ = 15

Think about fact families. Remember how numbers are related.

7, 8, 15

8 + 7 = 15 7 + 8 = 15

15 − 8 = 7 15 − 7 = 8

15 in all

8 red 7 blue

So, 15 − 7 = 8.

▶ Practice

Find the difference. Name the strategy you used.

1. 9 − 8 **2.** 12 − 2 **3.** 20 − 10 **4.** 11 − 6

5. 5 − 1 **6.** 16 − 9 **7.** 13 − 6 **8.** 9 − 1

9. 17 − 8 **10.** 14 − 7 **11.** 13 − 9 **12.** 8 − 2

13. 11 − 3 **14.** 16 − 8 **15.** 10 − 6 **16.** 15 − 6

17. 5 − 3 **18.** 6 − 3 **19.** 17 − 9 **20.** 10 − 2

CHAPTER 1

Place Value and Number Sense

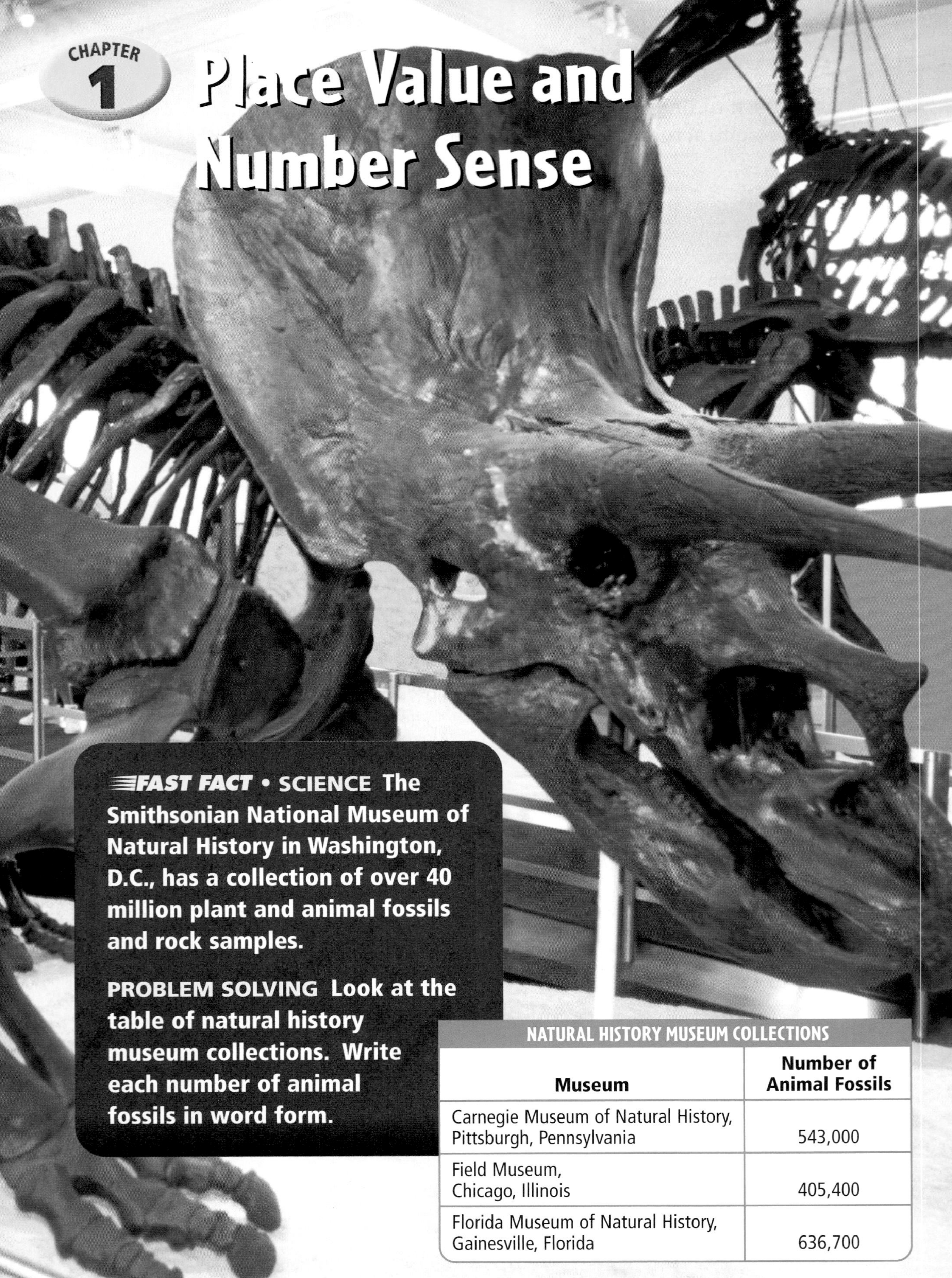

FAST FACT • SCIENCE The Smithsonian National Museum of Natural History in Washington, D.C., has a collection of over 40 million plant and animal fossils and rock samples.

PROBLEM SOLVING Look at the table of natural history museum collections. Write each number of animal fossils in word form.

NATURAL HISTORY MUSEUM COLLECTIONS

Museum	Number of Animal Fossils
Carnegie Museum of Natural History, Pittsburgh, Pennsylvania	543,000
Field Museum, Chicago, Illinois	405,400
Florida Museum of Natural History, Gainesville, Florida	636,700

CHECK WHAT YOU KNOW

Use this page to help you review and remember important skills needed for Chapter 1.

READ AND WRITE NUMBERS TO THOUSANDS

Write each word form in standard form.

1. ninety
2. one hundred eighty-four
3. nine hundred seventy
4. two thousand, seventy
5. six thousand, three hundred forty-nine
6. six thousand, seven

BENCHMARK NUMBERS

Estimate the number of beads in each jar.

Jar A has 10 beads.

Jar B has 50 beads.

7. 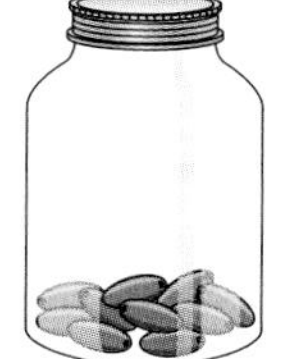

10 or 50?

8. 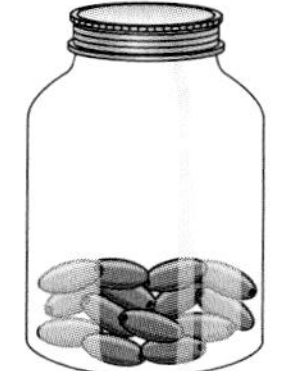

25 or 50?

9. 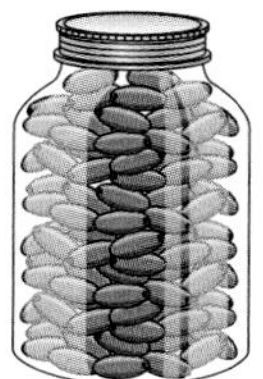

50 or 100?

10. 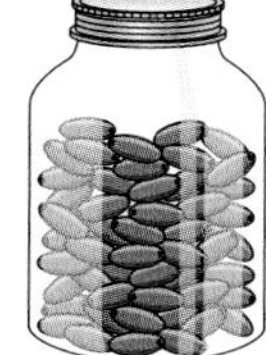

20 or 70?

VOCABULARY POWER

REVIEW

digit [di′jət] *noun*

One meaning of *digit* is "a finger or toe." What is the mathematical meaning of *digit*? Write a sentence using *digit* to show your understanding of the word.

PREVIEW

period

millions

benchmark

www.harcourtschool.com/mathglossary

LESSON 1

Understand Place Value

Quick Review

1. 55 − 10
2. 21 + 10
3. 877 − 100
4. 163 + 100
5. 3,218 + 1,000

Learn

IT'S DEEP! The deepest-living starfish was collected from a depth of 24,881 feet in the western Pacific Ocean in 1962.

What is the value of the digit 2 in 24,881?

Remember

A digit is one of the ten symbols 0, 1, 2, 3, 4, 5, 6, 7, 8, or 9 used to write numbers.

Ten thousands	Thousands	Hundreds	Tens	Ones
2	4,	8	8	1
$2 \times 10,000$	$4 \times 1,000$	8×100	8×10	1×1
20,000	4,000	800	80	1

Think: Multiply the digit by its place value to find the value of each digit.

So, the value of the digit 2 is 20,000.

MATH IDEA The value of a digit depends on its place-value position in the number.

Changing a given digit in a number changes the value of the number.

More Practice: Harcourt Mega Math Fraction Action, *Number Line Mine,* Level A

Examples

- **A** 58,937 to 59,937 increased by 1,000
- **B** 58,937 to 68,937 increased by 10,000
- **C** 58,937 to 88,937 increased by 30,000
- **D** 58,937 to 57,937 decreased by 1,000
- **E** 58,937 to 48,937 decreased by 10,000
- **F** 58,937 to 28,937 decreased by 30,000

- Which digit in the number 13,872 would be changed to form 19,872? How would the value of 13,872 change?

▲ The Japan Marine Science and Technology Center's *Shinkai 6500* collects ocean data from any depth down to 21,325 feet.

Check

1. **Explain** how to find the value of the digit 7 in the number 76,308.

Write the value of the digit 4 in each number.

2. 27,345
3. 74,960
4. 83,412
5. 14,873

Compare the digits to find the change in value.

6. 8,947 to 3,947
7. 82,756 to 82,716
8. 14,583 to 16,583

Practice and Problem Solving

Extra Practice, page 14, Set A

Write the value of the digit 8 in each number.

9. 53,489
10. 97,806
11. 86,239
12. 68,391

Compare the digits to find the change in value.

13. 62,895 to 32,895
14. 93,714 to 99,714
15. 38,047 to 38,097
16. 49,807 to 49,207
17. 51,386 to 11,386
18. 29,471 to 29,671

Change the value of the number by the given amount.

19. 37,842 increased by 1,000
20. 37,842 decreased by 1,000
21. 63,172 increased by 600
22. 24,597 increased by 4,000
23. 71,408 decreased by 20,000
24. 52,496 decreased by 70

Complete.

25. $24{,}180 = 20{,}000 + \blacksquare + 100 + 80$
26. $5{,}2\blacksquare6 = 5{,}000 + 200 + 30 + 6$
27. **NUMBER SENSE** In a 4-digit number, the first two digits are both 2. The sum of the ones and tens digits is 14. What numbers are possible?
28. **Write About It** If you add a ten thousands digit that is 2 times the ones digit to the number 2,794, what is the new number? Explain.

Mixed Review and Test Prep

For 29–30, find the missing number.

29. $60 - \blacksquare = 20$
30. $\blacksquare - 5 = 39$
31. Draw a plane figure that has four sides of equal length.
32. $78 + 63$
33. **TEST PREP** Find the missing number. 318, 324, 330, ■, 342

   A 334 **B** 336 **C** 338 **D** 340

LESSON 2

Place Value Through Hundred Thousands

Learn

EARTH TO MOON The least distance from the Earth to the moon is 225,792 miles.

To show this number, a column for hundred thousands has to be added to the place-value chart.

PERIOD

THOUSANDS			ONES		
Hundreds	Tens	Ones	Hundreds	Tens	Ones
2	2	5,	7	9	2

Each group of three digits is called a **period**. Commas separate the periods. Each period has ones, tens, and hundreds in it. The number 225,792 has two periods, *ones* and *thousands*.

MATH IDEA Place-value and period names help you read and write numbers.

Standard Form: 225,792

Word Form: two hundred twenty-five thousand, seven hundred ninety-two

Expanded Form: 200,000 + 20,000 + 5,000 + 700 + 90 + 2

Examples

Standard Form	Word Form	Expanded Form
A 40,915	forty thousand, nine hundred fifteen	40,000 + 900 + 10 + 5
B 607,304	six hundred seven thousand, three hundred four	600,000 + 7,000 + 300 + 4

Quick Review

Write the place value of the digit 3.

1. 49,031
2. 35,477
3. 2,386
4. 693
5. 83,904

VOCABULARY

period

Check

1. **Explain** how its period helps you identfiy the place value of the digit 9 in 952,700. In 1969, the *Apollo 11* astronauts traveled 952,700 miles.

Write each number in two other forms.

2. two hundred five thousand, sixty-one
3. 916,359

Practice and Problem Solving

Extra Practice, page 14, Set B

Write each number in two other forms.

4. three hundred thousand, ninety-six
5. four hundred sixteen thousand, two hundred ten
6. 40,705
7. 60,000 + 3,000 + 40 + 8

Complete.

8. 52,376 = fifty-two __?__, three hundred __?__ = ■ + 2,000 + 300 + 70 + ■
9. 90,000 + ■ + 80 = 90,58■ = ninety thousand, five __?__ eighty

Write the value of the blue digit.

10. 534,908
11. 980,571
12. 143,296
13. 278,105
14. 357,841
15. 493,560
16. 782,046
17. 609,428
18. If five hundred thousand, twenty-six is increased by three thousand, what is the new number in standard form?
19. I am 900 more than the greatest possible 4-digit even number that can be made using the digits 1, 4, 2, 5. What number am I?
20. Write the word form of the number that is 1,000 more than 23,548.

Mixed Review and Test Prep

21. 325 − ■ = 194
22. ■ − 75 = 896
23. Round 615 to the nearest hundred.
24. 35 + ■ = 66 + 35
25. TEST PREP Find the sum.

    417 + 89 + 123

    A 519 C 619
    B 529 D 629

LESSON 3

Place Value Through Millions

Quick Review

What is the value of the digit 4?

1. 54,190 **2.** 3,427

3. 243,018 **4.** 8,934

5. 648

VOCABULARY

millions

Learn

READ ALL ABOUT IT! Newspapers keep people informed of local, national, and world events. The first newspaper was written in Germany in the 1600s.

Look at this story. It contains about 200 words. If there are 5 stories of this size on one page, about how many words are on the page?

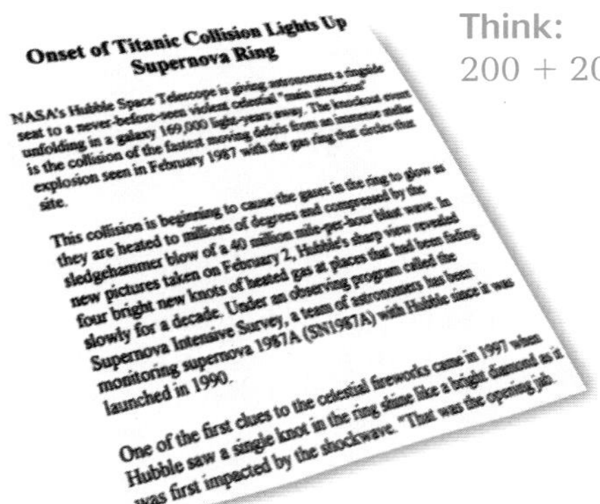

Onset of Titanic Collision Lights Up Supernova Ring

NASA's Hubble Space Telescope is giving astronomers a ringside seat to a never-before-seen violent celestial "main attraction" unfolding in a galaxy 169,000 light-years away. The knockout event is the collision of the fastest moving debris from an immense stellar explosion seen in February 1987 with the gas ring that circles the site.

This collision is beginning to cause the gases in the ring to glow as they are heated to millions of degrees and compressed by the sledgehammer blow of a 40 million mile-per-hour blast wave. In new pictures taken on February 2, Hubble's sharp view revealed four bright new knots of heated gas at places that had been fading slowly for a decade. Under an observing program called the Supernova Intensive Survey, a team of astronomers has been monitoring supernova 1987A (SN1987A) with Hubble since it was launched in 1990.

One of the first clues to the celestial fireworks came in 1997 when Hubble saw a single knot in the ring shine like a bright diamond as it was first impacted by the shockwave. "That was the opening jab.

Think:
200 + 200 + 200 + 200 + 200 = 1,000

So, there are about 1,000 words on a page.

With 1,000 words on a page,
10 pages have 10,000 words.
100 pages have 100,000 words.
1,000 pages have 1,000,000 words.

The period to the left of *thousands* is ***millions***.

PERIOD

MILLIONS			THOUSANDS			ONES		
Hundreds	**Tens**	**Ones**	**Hundreds**	**Tens**	**Ones**	**Hundreds**	**Tens**	**Ones**
		1,	0	0	0,	0	0	0

Write: 1,000,000 **Read:** one million

One million is a large number. If you read 100 words a minute, it would take you almost 7 days nonstop to read 1,000,000 words.

More About Millions

You can use place value and period names to help you read and write numbers in the millions.

The world's largest ball of twine is found in Cawker City, Kansas. As of September 2001, it contained over 83,264,496 inches of twine.

▲ The ball of twine weighs 17,320 pounds. That's more than the weight of 6 cars!

Look at this number on the place-value chart.

PERIOD

MILLIONS			THOUSANDS			ONES		
Hundreds	Tens	Ones	Hundreds	Tens	Ones	Hundreds	Tens	Ones
	8	3,	2	6	4,	4	9	6

Standard Form: 83,264,496

Word Form: eighty-three million, two hundred sixty-four thousand, four hundred ninety-six

Expanded Form: 80,000,000 + 3,000,000 + 200,000 + 60,000 + 4,000 + 400 + 90 + 6

Examples

Standard Form	Word Form	Expanded Form
A 54,060,900	fifty-four million, sixty thousand, nine hundred	50,000,000 + 4,000,000 + 60,000 + 900
B 100,207,054	one hundred million, two hundred seven thousand, fifty-four	100,000,000 + 200,000 + 7,000 + 50 + 4

Check

1. **Tell** how many periods an 8-digit number has.

Write the value of the blue digit.

2. 7,943,120
3. 8,450,203
4. 68,549,227

Write each number in word form.

5. 57,643,120
6. 16,452,003
7. 608,049,227

LESSON CONTINUES

Practice and Problem Solving

Extra Practice, page 14, Set C

Write the value of the blue digit.

8. 7,534,908 **9.** 98,745,300 **10.** 142,980,871

11. 4,371,568 **12.** 36,420,156 **13.** 512,604,397

Write each number in word form.

14. 5,769,042 **15.** 882,831,001 **16.** 42,168,339

Use place value to find each missing number. Explain.

17. 6,758,324; 6,768,324; ■; 6,788,324

18. 9,537,461; 9,537,561; ■; 9,537,761

19. 2,408,693; 2,409,694; ■; 2,411,696

20. 4,657,839; 4,657,939; ■; 4,658,139

21. Write the word form of the number that is 10,000,000 more than 5,670,891.

22. Write 12,097,341 in expanded form.

23. Write 8,000,000 + 100,000 + 70,000 + 3,000 + 900 + 50 + 6 in word form.

Complete.

24. 7,523,■46 = 7,000,000 + 500,000 + 20,000 + 3,000 + 800 + 40 + 6

25. 7,903,264 = seven _?_ , nine hundred three _?_ , two hundred sixty-four

26. **? What's the Question?** Mrs. Diaz wrote the number 46,152,780. The answer is 6,000,000. What is the question?

27. What number is twice the value of the ten thousands digit in 423,008?

28. ***FAST FACT*** • **SCIENCE** Saturn takes about 10,760 days to orbit the sun. Is it correct to read this number as ten million, seven hundred sixty? Explain.

29. **What's the Error?** Carl said that 24,613,351 is one million more than 14,613,351. Describe his error.

30. **Vocabulary Power** What does the *place value* of a digit tell you? How does switching the positions of the digits in the number 52 affect that number's value?

Mixed Review and Test Prep

31. 714 + 836

32. 854 − 138

33. 42 ÷ 7

34. 8 × 4

35. The sum of two numbers is 15. The difference is 3. What are the numbers?

36. What is the place value of the digit 6 in 36,280? (p. 2)

37. Write two hundred thousand, eighty-six in standard form. (p. 4)

38. **TEST PREP** Bobby has 87 basketball cards. He has 13 more than Jeff. How many cards does Jeff have?

A 71 **B** 74 **C** 95 **D** 100

39. **TEST PREP** Choose the rule that best describes the pattern.

1, 7, 13, 19, 25

F Add 6.

G Add 5.

H Add 4.

J Add 3.

Problem Solving Thinker's Corner

ROMAN NUMERALS Our *numeration system* uses Arabic numerals, or digits (0, 1, 2, . . .), to write numbers. The Romans used the symbols in this chart to name numbers.

I	V	X	L	C	D	M
1	5	10	50	100	500	1,000

A Add when the symbols are alike or when the symbols' values decrease from left to right. A numeral cannot be added more than three times in a row.

LXIII = 63

50 + 10 + 1 + 1 + 1 = 63

B Subtract when a symbol's value is less than the value of the symbol to its right.

XIX = 19

IX represents 10 − 1 = 9

10 + 9 = 19

Write the Roman numerals as Arabic numerals.

1. XIV
2. XXXIX
3. XLI
4. XC
5. LXVIII
6. **REASONING** Find the missing numbers. III, VI, IX, XII, ■, ■, XXI.
7. Write 35, 44, and 62 as Roman numerals.

LESSON 4

Benchmark Numbers

Quick Review

1. 20 + 20
2. 12 + 12
3. 400 + 400
4. 80 + 80
5. 30 + 30 + 30

VOCABULARY

benchmark

Learn

SIZE IT UP! For a number to have meaning, it should be related to something you already know.

The Washington Monument is 555 feet tall. That is about the same as 25 two-story houses stacked on top of each other.

MATH IDEA A **benchmark** is a known number of things that helps you understand the size or amount of a different number of things.

You can use a benchmark when you are estimating a number of items that would take a long time to count.

Examples

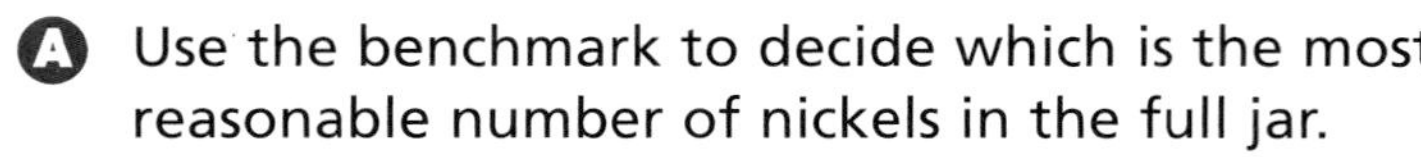

A Use the benchmark to decide which is the most reasonable number of nickels in the full jar.

100 1,000 10,000

Benchmark: 500 nickels

The full jar holds about 2 times the benchmark amount.

$2 \times 500 = 1{,}000$

500 nickels

The most reasonable number of nickels in the full jar is 1,000.

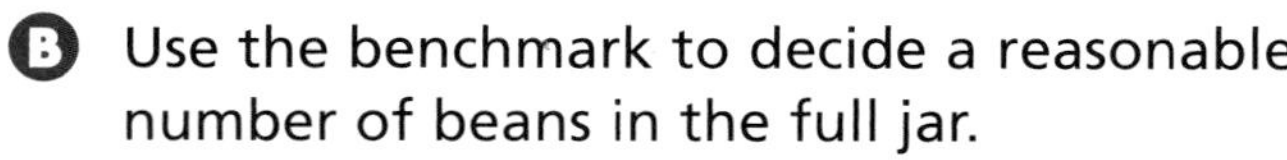

B Use the benchmark to decide a reasonable number of beans in the full jar.

Benchmark: 50 beans

The full jar holds about 8 times the benchmark amount.

$8 \times 50 = 400$

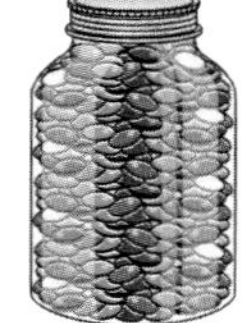

50 beans

A reasonable number of beans in the jar is 400.

• In Example B, why is 4,000 not a reasonable number?

Check

1. **Explain** whether the number of students in your class is a good benchmark for the number of students in your school.

Use the benchmark to decide which is the more reasonable number.

2. beads in the jar

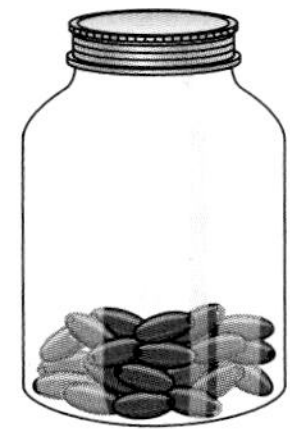

20 beads

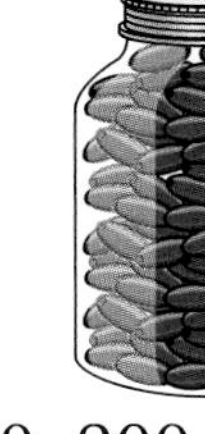

80, 200, or 800

3. gallons of water in the tank

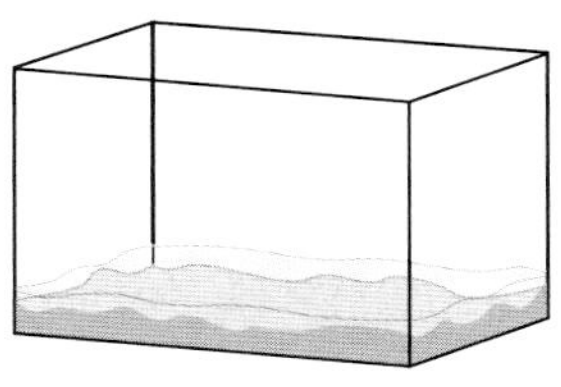

20 gallons

40; 200; or 2,000

Practice and Problem Solving

Extra Practice, page 14, Set D

Use the benchmark to decide which is the more reasonable number.

4. pretzel sticks in the jar

50, 250, or 500

5. beads in the vase

200; 400; or 2,000

6. Emily has 6 dolls and Dana has 11. If Laura has 8 more dolls than Emily and Dana combined, how many dolls does Laura have?

7. **Write About It** Explain when you would use a benchmark number.

Mixed Review and Test Prep

8. 78 + 9
9. 746 + 24
10. 5 × 5
11. 532 − 40
12. **TEST PREP** Which is the missing addend for 18 + ■ = 26?
   A 4 **B** 5 **C** 8 **D** 9

LESSON 5

Problem Solving Skill
Use a Graph

UNDERSTAND | PLAN | SOLVE | CHECK

Quick Review

1. 210 + 37
2. 364 − 122
3. 97 + 103
4. 527 + 81
5. 2,230 − 1,023

Remember

A pictograph is a graph that uses pictures to show and compare information.

PRIZED PETS Betty, Marcia, and Ed want to know which pets are the most popular in the United States. Betty thinks cats are the most popular pets. Marcia thinks dogs are the most popular. Ed's choice is fish. Where can you find the information to see who is correct?

You can use a graph that compares the estimated numbers of kinds of pets in the United States.

Look at the pictograph. Cats are shown with the most symbols, 7. Since each symbol stands for 10,000,000 pets, there are about 70 million pet cats.

So, Betty is correct. Cats are the most popular pets in the United States.

Talk About It

- About how many pets are dogs?
- The number of reptiles is shown with one half of a symbol. About how many pets are reptiles?
- **What if** the number of reptiles were about 15 million? How many symbols would be used?

Problem Solving Practice

USE DATA There are more than 62,000,000 pet dogs in the United States. The graph shows how some of their birthdays were celebrated.

DOG BIRTHDAY CELEBRATIONS

Special treat	
Cake	
New toy	
New bone	
Trip to the park	

Key: Each = about 1 million celebrations.

1. Find the number of dogs who got birthday cake. How did you find this number?
2. What celebration happened the least number of times?

USE DATA For 3–4, use the cat food sales graph.

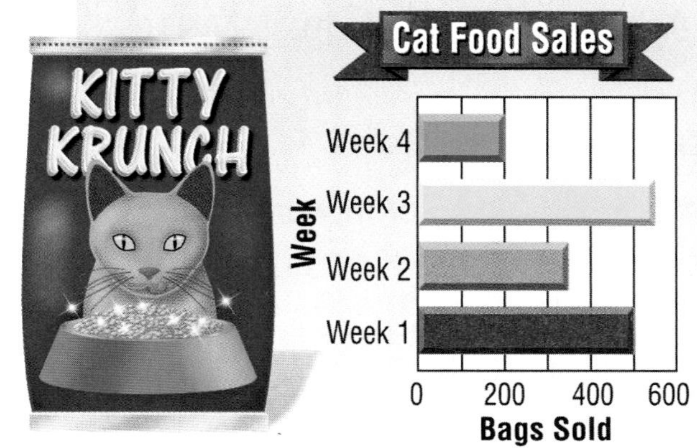

3. During which week were the most bags of cat food sold?
   A Week 1 **C** Week 3
   B Week 2 **D** Week 4
4. In which weeks were fewer than 500 bags of cat food sold?
   F Weeks 1, 2
   G Weeks 1, 4
   H Weeks 2, 4
   J Weeks 1, 3

Mixed Applications

5. The hour hand on the clock is between 8 and 9. The minute hand is pointing to 7. What time is it?
6. ALGEBRA Tom is 4 years younger than Jan but 2 years older than Sue. If Jan is 15, how old is Sue?
7. In two hours 639 people rode to the top of the Sears Tower. During the first hour 257 people went to the top. How many people rode to the top during the second hour?
8. **REASONING** Yvonne arrived at the party after Irma. Diana arrived before Irma but after Ann. In what order did they arrive at the party?
9. I am less than 80 and greater than 60. The sum of my digits is 8. I am odd. What number am I?
10. Gloria spent $5.08 for milk and eggs. The eggs cost $1.49. How much did the milk cost?

Extra Practice

Set A (pp. 2–3)

Write the value of the digit 6 in each number.

1. 7,056
2. 15,608
3. 60,789
4. 16,340

Set B (pp. 4–5)

Write each number in two other forms.

1. 482,907
2. 500,128
3. 961,542
4. 271,964

Write the value of the blue digit.

5. 137,568
6. 739,062
7. 561,342
8. 906,723
9. 354,781
10. 827,910
11. 269,415
12. 478,536

Set C (pp. 6–9)

Write each number in word form.

1. 68,247,311
2. 8,601,824
3. 3,714,069
4. 742,093,758

Write the value of the blue digit.

5. 13,749,568
6. 4,739,062
7. 397,561,342
8. 458,906,723
9. 8,675,309
10. 474,613,351
11. 100,560,214
12. 265,976,284
13. Write the word form of the number that is 10,000,000 more than 6,021,849.

Set D (pp. 10–11)

Use the benchmark to decide which is the more reasonable number.

1. table tennis balls in bucket B

A

10 balls

B

100; 1,000; or 10,000

2. sunflower seeds in bird feeder B

A

300 seeds

B

600; 3,000; or 30,000

Review/Test

CHECK VOCABULARY AND CONCEPTS

Choose the best term from the box.

benchmark
million
period

1. You can use the number of students in your class as a _?_ to help you find the number of students in your grade. (p. 10)
2. Each group of three digits is called a _?_. (p. 4)

CHECK SKILLS

Write each number in two other forms. (pp. 4–9)

3. 20,000 + 80 + 3
4. 200,057
5. 4,902,746
6. 48,360,105

Write the value of the blue digit. (pp. 2–9)

7. 8,451
8. 29,710
9. 652,700
10. 4,136,729

11. Which is the most reasonable number of beads in the full jar, 70, 350, or 700? (p. 10)

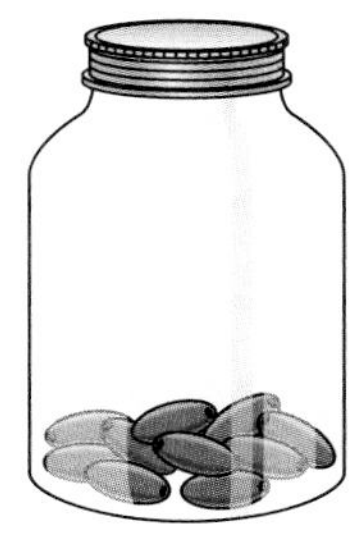

10 beads

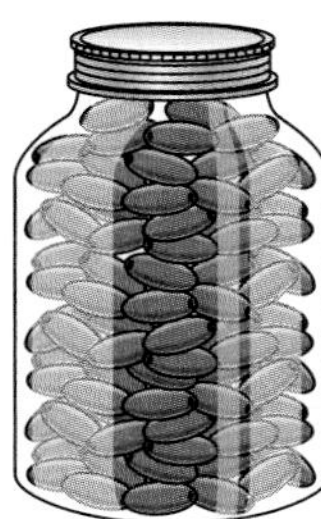

12. Which is the most reasonable number of gallons of water in barrel B, 3, 30, or 300? (p. 10)

A
10 gallons

B

CHECK PROBLEM SOLVING

For 13–15, use the graph. (pp. 12–13)

13. Which animals have lifespans longer than 20 years?
14. About how many years does the grizzly bear live?
15. About how many years longer does the Asian elephant live than the grizzly bear?

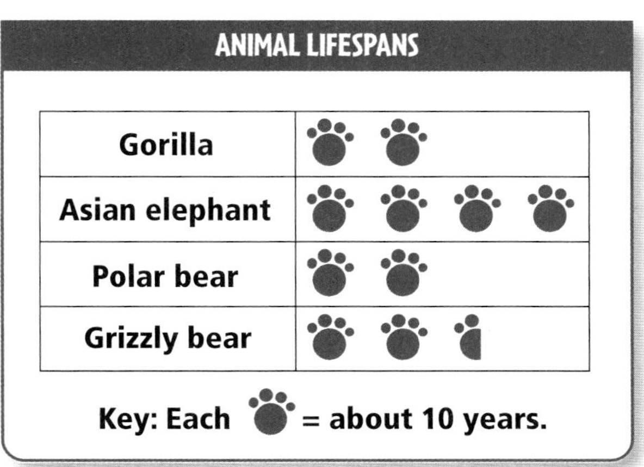

ANIMAL LIFESPANS

Gorilla	
Asian elephant	
Polar bear	
Grizzly bear	

Key: Each = about 10 years.

Standardized Test Prep

NUMBER SENSE, CONCEPTS, AND OPERATIONS

1. How is five hundred nineteen thousand, three hundred eight written in standard form?

A 519,300

B 519,308

C 519,380

D 590,308

TIP **Eliminate choices.** See item 2. Think about the symbols used for comparing numbers. The choices + and ÷ are operation signs, so you can eliminate them.

2. Which symbol makes the following true?

5,278 ● 5,728

F >

G <

H +

J ÷

3. Which is the value of the digit 8 in 183,614?

A 8,000

B 10,000

C 80,000

D 800,000

4. **Explain It** A football stadium has 30 sections of seats. Each section can seat about 1,000 people. About how many people can be seated in the whole stadium? Explain your thinking.

MEASUREMENT

5. Look at the clock.

Which clock below shows the same time?

F

H

G

J

6. Which is the perimeter of Lu's rectangular garden?

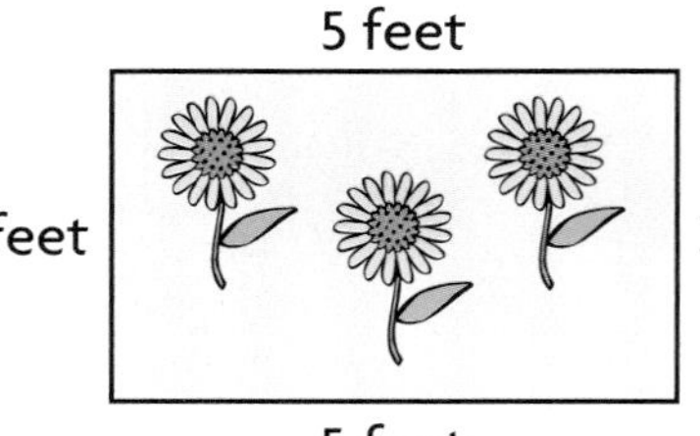

A 16 feet

B 15 feet

C 10 feet

D 6 feet

7. **Explain It** Which unit would you use to measure the length of a butterfly: inch, foot, yard, or mile? Explain how you decided.

GEOMETRY AND SPATIAL SENSE

8. Which shaded angle is greater than a right angle?

F
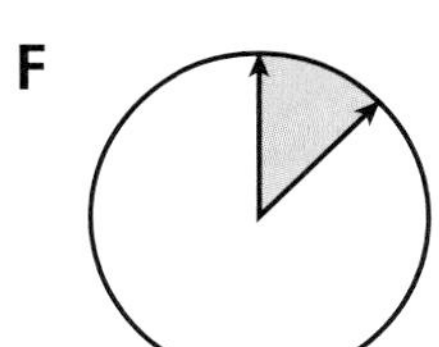

G
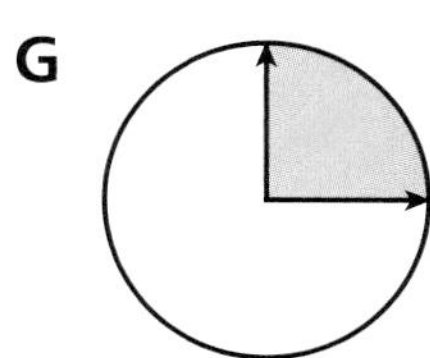

H
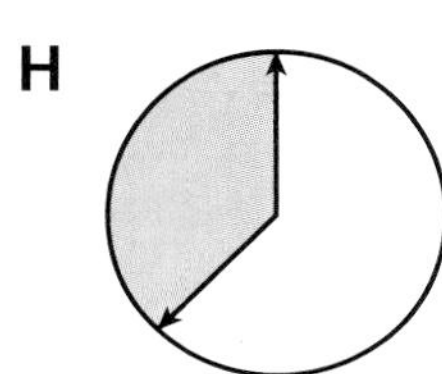

J
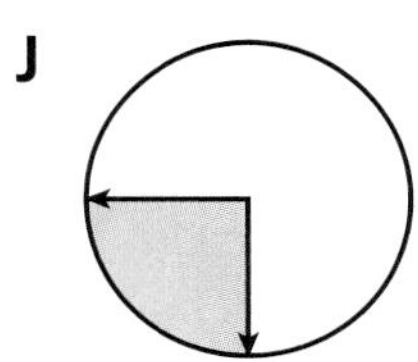

9. Which letter has a line of symmetry?

A **G**   C **M**

B **J**   D **Z**

10. **Explain It** How are the two figures pictured below alike? How are they different?

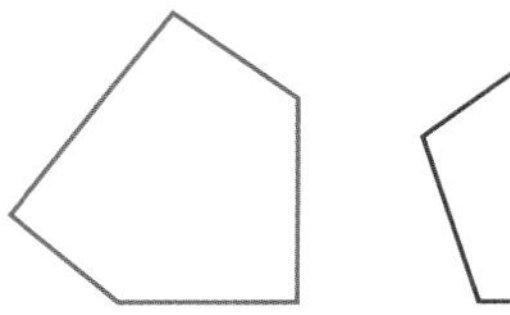

DATA ANALYSIS AND PROBABILITY

11. Mina, Alan, and Jeff collected empty cans for their class. The pictograph below shows the results.

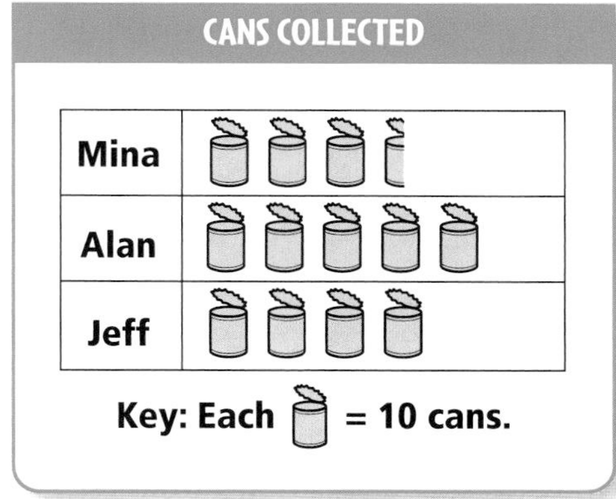

How many more cans did Alan collect than Mina?

F 50   **H** 15

G 35   **J** 10

12. Suppose a person picks one card without looking. What are the possible outcomes?

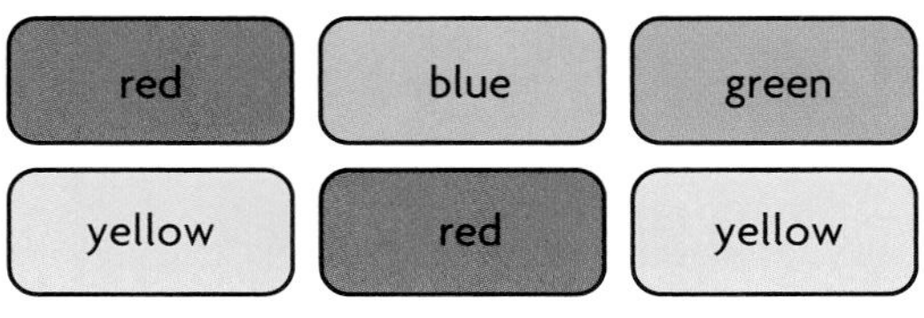

A red, blue, green

B red, yellow, blue, green

C red, blue, yellow

D red, blue, green, yellow, red, yellow

13. **Explain It** Chris rolled two cubes, each numbered 1 through 6. If he adds the numbers, is it *impossible, unlikely, likely,* or *certain* that he will get a sum less than 2? Explain your thinking.

CHAPTER 2

Compare and Order Whole Numbers

FAST FACT • SOCIAL STUDIES The Cumberland Gap National Historical Park is one of the 5 largest national historical parks in the United States. It is located where the borders of Virginia, Tennessee, and Kentucky meet.

PROBLEM SOLVING List the 5 largest national historical parks and their areas from least to greatest, and tell which parks have the least and the greatest areas.

LARGEST NATIONAL HISTORICAL PARKS

Park	Location	Area (in acres)
Cumberland Gap	Virginia, Tennessee, Kentucky	20,454
Jean Lafitte	Louisiana	20,020
Chaco Culture	New Mexico	33,974
Chesapeake and Ohio Canal	Maryland, West Virginia, Washington, D.C.	19,237
Klondike Gold Rush	Alaska, Washington	13,191

CHECK WHAT YOU KNOW

Use this page to help you review and remember important skills needed for Chapter 2.

PLACE VALUE

Write the value of the blue digit.

1. 24,638 **2.** 1,002 **3.** 4,991 **4.** 2,856,311

5. 2,307 **6.** 53,692 **7.** 9,356,888 **8.** 4,090,483

ROUND TO TENS AND HUNDREDS

Round each number to the nearest ten and to the nearest hundred.

9. 764 **10.** 996 **11.** 857 **12.** 305

13. 5,892 **14.** 5,306 **15.** 9,976 **16.** 6,431

ORDER NUMBERS TO THOUSANDS

Write the numbers in order from *least* to *greatest*.

17. 684; 680; 689 **18.** 540; 504; 603 **19.** 394; 359; 349

20. 6,809; 6,098; 6,890 **21.** 3,564; 3,278; 3,782 **22.** 4,037; 4,370; 3,407

Write the numbers in order from *greatest* to *least*.

23. 8,093; 9,803; 9,380 **24.** 1,763; 1,637; 7,163 **25.** 1,527; 1,257; 2,751

VOCABULARY POWER

REVIEW

thousand [thou′zənd] *noun*

The word *thousand* comes from a combination of old Germanic words for *swollen (teue)* and *hundred (hundt)*. Does calling a thousand a "swollen hundred" make sense? Why or why not?

PREVIEW

round

www.harcourtschool.com/mathglossary

LESSON 1

Compare Numbers

Quick Review

Write the value of the blue digit.

1. 19,563 **2.** 68,320

3. 134,578 **4.** 78,904

5. 479,813

Learn

RIVER RUN The Missouri River is 2,315 miles long, and the Mississippi River is 2,348 miles long. Which river is longer?

One Way Use a number line to compare the lengths of the rivers. Compare 2,315 and 2,348.

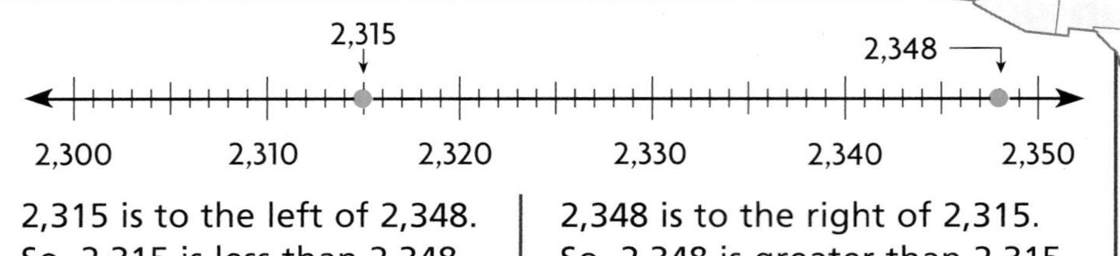

2,315 is to the left of 2,348.
So, 2,315 is less than 2,348.

2,315 < 2,348

2,348 is to the right of 2,315.
So, 2,348 is greater than 2,315.

2,348 > 2,315

Remember

< means "is less than."
> means "is greater than."
= means "is equal to."

So, the Mississippi River is longer.

Another Way Use base-ten blocks to compare numbers. Compare 348 and 362.

Compare the values of the blocks in each place-value position from left to right. Keep comparing until the values are different.

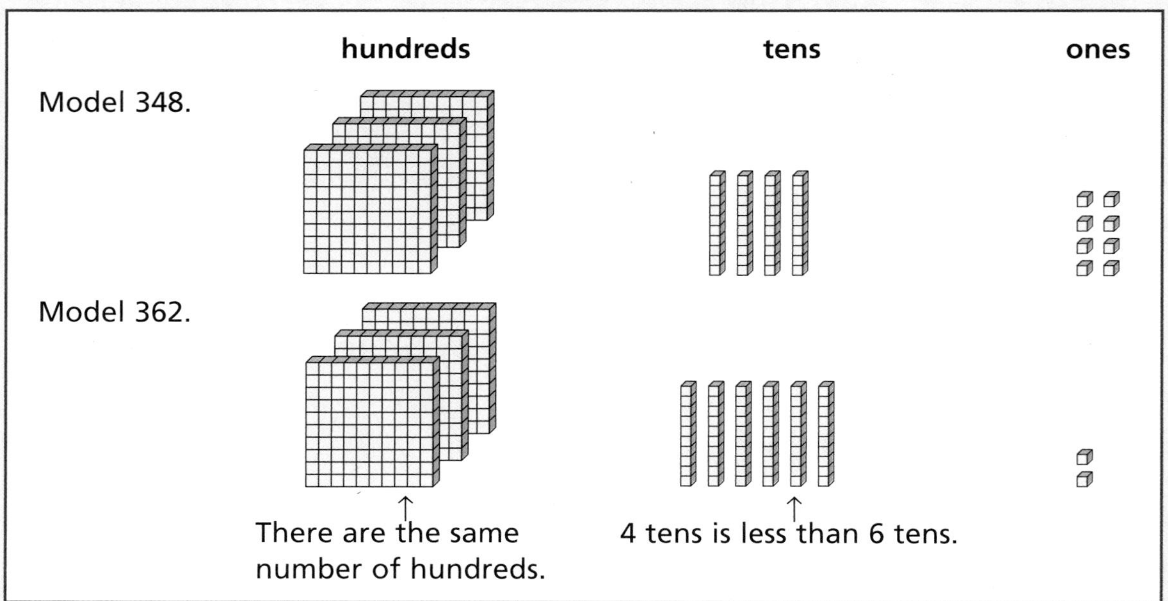

So, 348 < 362.

Compare Using Place Value

A place-value chart can help you compare two numbers by comparing the digits in each place-value position.

Compare 2,340,083 and 2,331,760.

MILLIONS			THOUSANDS			ONES		
Hundreds	Tens	Ones	Hundreds	Tens	Ones	Hundreds	Tens	Ones
		2,	3	4	0,	0	8	3
		2,	3	3	1,	7	6	0

Example

STEP 1

Start with the first place on the left.
Compare the millions.

2,340,083
↓ 2 = 2
2,331,760

There are the same number of millions.

STEP 2

Compare the hundred thousands.

2,340,083
↓ 3 = 3
2,331,760

There are the same number of hundred thousands.

STEP 3

Compare the ten thousands.

2,340,083
↓ 4 > 3
2,331,760

4 ten thousands are greater than 3 ten thousands.

So, 2,340,083 > 2,331,760.

MATH IDEA To compare numbers, start at the left and compare the digits in each place-value position until the digits differ.

Technology Link

More Practice: Harcourt Mega Math The Number Games, *Tiny's Think Tank,* Level I; Fraction Action, *Number Line Mine,* Level B

Check

1. Make a model or draw a picture to compare 1,358 and 1,427 using base-ten blocks.

Compare using the number line. Write the greater number.

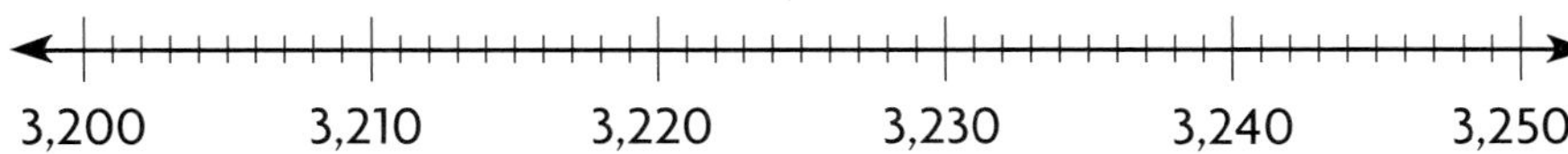

2. 3,224 or 3,242
3. 3,218 or 3,240
4. 3,234 or 3,229

Compare. Write <, >, or = for each ●.

5. 2,346 ● 2,338
6. 521,878 ● 52,878
7. 52,457 ● 67,623
8. 254,908 ● 254,908
9. 9,531 ● 4,631
10. 478,765 ● 479,112

LESSON CONTINUES

Practice and Problem Solving

Extra Practice, page 34, Set A

Compare using the number line. Write the greater number.

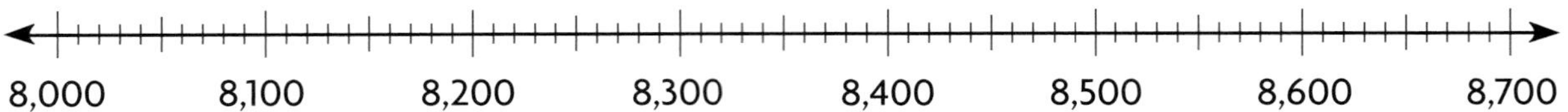

11. 8,110 or 8,340
12. 8,600 or 8,060
13. 8,413 or 8,314

Compare. Write <, >, or = for each ●.

14. 2,475 ● 2,475
15. 13,056 ● 13,156
16. 255,136 ● 25,116
17. 301,876 ● 3,018,760
18. 1,670 ● 1,670
19. 410,000 ● 414,000
20. 3,911,067 ● 3,911,007
21. 439,503,209 ● 350,320,943
22. 5,000,371 ● 500,371
23. 82,245,235 ● 82,245,535

Find all of the digits that can replace each ■.

24. 9■7,536 < 957,549
25. 423,■96,517 < 423,695,815
26. 84,41■,811 < 84,413,604
27. 24,■62 > 24,701

Are the two numbers equivalent? Write *equivalent* or *not equivalent*.

28. 153,890 and one hundred fifty-three thousand, eight hundred ninety
29. 2,000,000 + 400,000 + 50,000 + 600 + 7 and 2,450,670
30. thirty-eight million, forty-nine and 30,000,000 + 8,000,000 + 40 + 9

USE DATA For 31–33, use the table.

31. Which river is longer, Amazon or Nile?
32. Which Asian river has a length greater than 3,500 miles?
33. **Write a problem** that compares two rivers from the World Rivers table.

WORLD RIVERS		
River	Continent	Length (mi)
Amazon	South America	4,000
Chang	Asia	3,964
Huang	Asia	3,395
Nile	Africa	4,160

34. **Vocabulary Power** When you *compare* two items, you tell how they are alike and different. What do you do when you compare two numbers? Give an example.
35. **REASONING** Which is greater, the number that is 1,000 less than 13,495, or the number that is 10,000 less than 23,495?

36. Chris and his father drove 876 miles on a weekend. They drove 416 miles of that on Sunday. Did they drive farther on Saturday or on Sunday?

37. **What's the Error?** Sarah said that 6,850 is greater than 48,500 because $6 > 4$. Describe her error. Tell which number is greater.

Mixed Review and Test Prep

Write the value of the digit 4. (p. 4)

38. 241,389 **39.** 759,486

40. Write the number that is 1,000,000 greater than 99,036,871. (p. 6)

41. Write 1,034,506 in word form. (p. 6)

42. Complete. (p. 4)
$40{,}000 + ■ + 50 = 40{,}850$

43. **TEST PREP** Which is the standard form of $50{,}000{,}000 + 30{,}000 + 4$? (p. 6)

A 15,304,000 **C** 50,030,004
B 15,034,000 **D** 50,300,400

44. **TEST PREP** Which is the value of the change from 34,891 to 36,891? (p. 2)

F 20,000 **H** 2,000
G 200 **J** 200,000

Problem Solving — Thinker's Corner

ALGEBRAIC THINKING You can use what you know about $<$, $>$, and $=$ to describe other number relationships.

$\neq$ means "is not equal to."
$\leq$ means "is less than or equal to."
$\geq$ means "is greater than or equal to."

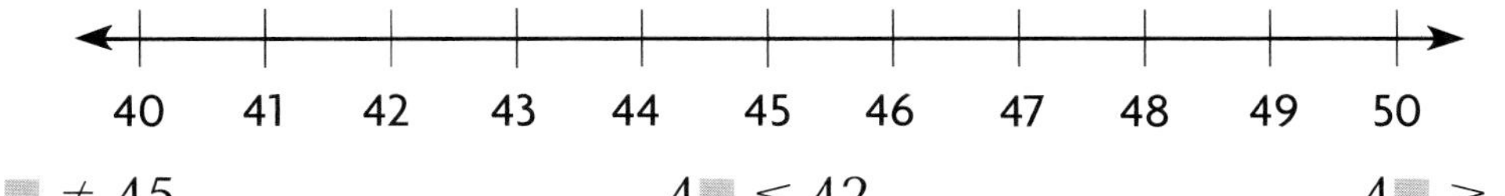

$4■ \neq 45$

40, 41, 42, 43, 44, 46, 47, 48, and 49 are *not equal to* 45.

So, you can replace ■ with 0, 1, 2, 3, 4, 6, 7, 8, or 9.

$4■ \leq 42$

40, 41, and 42 are *less than or equal to* 42.

So, you can replace ■ with 0, 1, or 2.

$4■ \geq 47$

47, 48, and 49 are *greater than or equal to* 47.

So, you can replace ■ with 7, 8, or 9.

Find all of the digits that can replace each ■.

1. $360 \neq 36■$ **2.** $52■ \leq 525$ **3.** $4{,}■15 \geq 4{,}715$

4. $17{,}6■8 \leq 17{,}648$ **5.** $8{,}396 \neq 8{,}39■$ **6.** $29{,}024 \geq 29{,}0■4$

LESSON 2

Order Numbers

Quick Review

Compare. Write <, >, or = for each ●.

1. 17,094 ● 10,749
2. 23,516 ● 32,651
3. 7,892 ● 7,892
4. 9,513 ● 15,390
5. 86,413 ● 84,316

Learn

LOTS OF LAND The map shows the land area, in square miles, of Illinois, Iowa, and Wisconsin. Place the states in order from least to greatest land area.

One Way Use a number line to show the order.

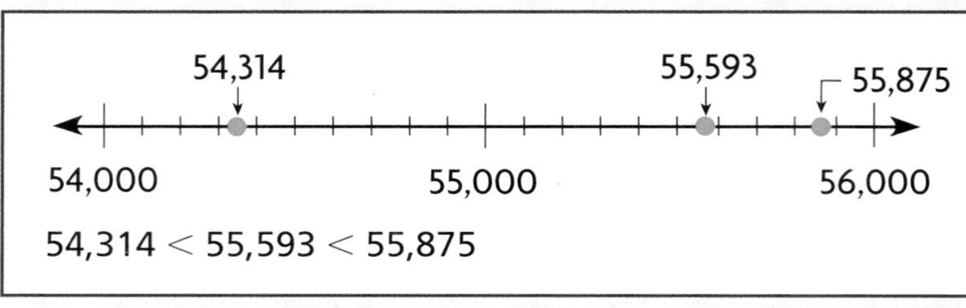

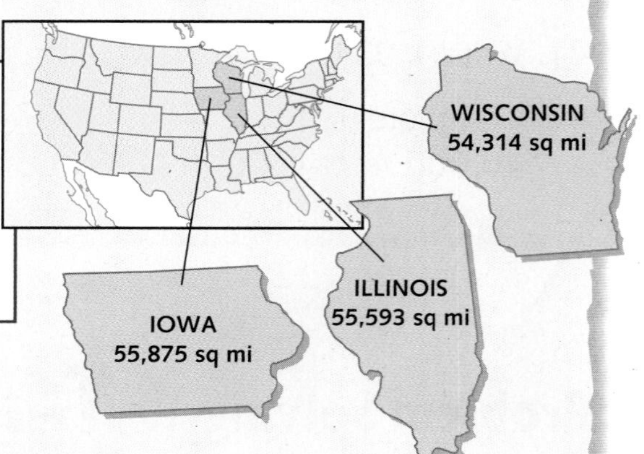

So, the order is Wisconsin, Illinois, Iowa.

Another Way Use place value to order numbers. Order 437,243; 469,872; and 435,681 from least to greatest.

STEP 1

Start with the first place on the left. Compare the hundred thousands.

437,243
↓
469,872 $4 = 4$
↓
435,681

There are the same number of hundred thousands.

STEP 2

Compare the ten thousands.

437,243
↓
469,872 $3 < 6$
↓
435,681

Since $3 < 6$, 469,872 is the greatest.

STEP 3

Compare the thousands digits in the other two numbers.

437,243
↓ $5 < 7$
435,681

So, the order from least to greatest is 435,681; 437,243; 469,872.

- Explain how you would order 68,195; 681,095; and 61,958 from least to greatest.

Use Models

New York, Virginia, and Massachusetts all have coastlines on the Atlantic Ocean. Use base-ten blocks to model the numbers in the table and place the states in order from longest to shortest coastline.

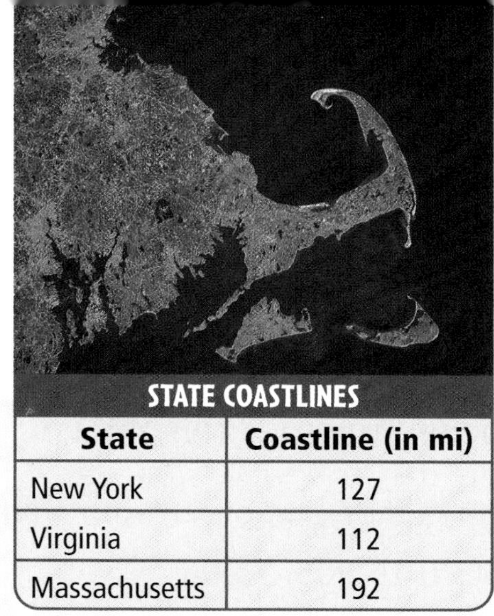

STATE COASTLINES

State	Coastline (in mi)
New York	127
Virginia	112
Massachusetts	192

Example Compare.

Model the three numbers using base-ten blocks. Then compare the values of the blocks in each place-value position from left to right.

New York	Virginia	Massachusetts
127	112	192

STEP 1

Compare the hundreds.

There are the same number of hundreds.

STEP 2

Compare the tens.

The model for 192 has the most tens, so it is the greatest number.

STEP 3

Compare the tens in 127 and 112.

The model for 127 has more tens, so it is greater than 112.

So, the states in order from longest to shortest coastline are Massachusetts, New York, Virginia.

Check

1. **Draw** a picture of base-ten blocks to show how to order 2,617; 2,716; and 2,672 from *least* to *greatest*.

Write the numbers in order from *least* to *greatest*.

2. 7,969; 7,964; 7,975

7,950 7,955 7,960 7,965 7,970 7,975 7,980

3. 9,131; 9,155; 9,138

9,130 9,135 9,140 9,145 9,150 9,155 9,160

Write the numbers in order from *greatest* to *least*.

4. 35,000; 35,225; 34,350

5. 870,000; 877,000; 807,000

Practice and Problem Solving

Extra Practice, page 34, Set B

Write the numbers in order from *least* to *greatest*.

6. 12,139; 12,117; 12,109; 12,123

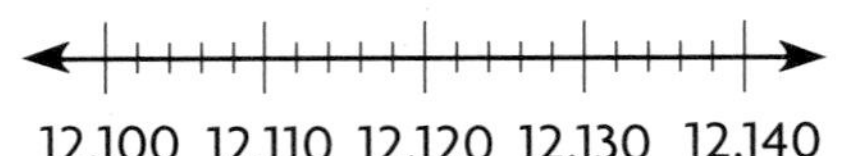

7. 36,397; 36,457; 36,384; 36,419

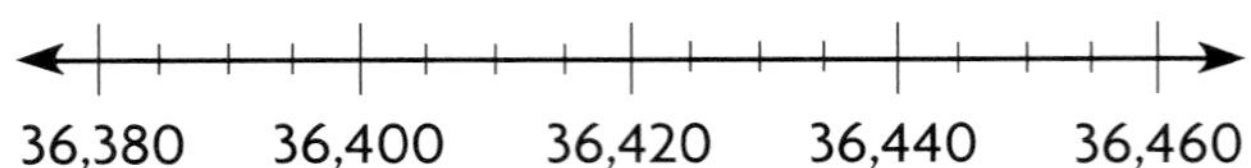

8. 190,209; 191,210; 190,201

9. 1,234,410; 1,234,402; 1,434,320

Write the numbers in order from *greatest* to *least*.

10. 16,432; 16,905; 7,906

11. 119,234; 119,819; 1,119,080

12. Order the numbers in the box from greatest to least. Then, underline the numbers greater than 625,000 and less than 650,000.

648,279	**628,341**	**642,978**
682,437	**624,879**	**612,443**

For 13–14, write the number represented by each letter. Then, write the *greatest* and *least* numbers.

13.

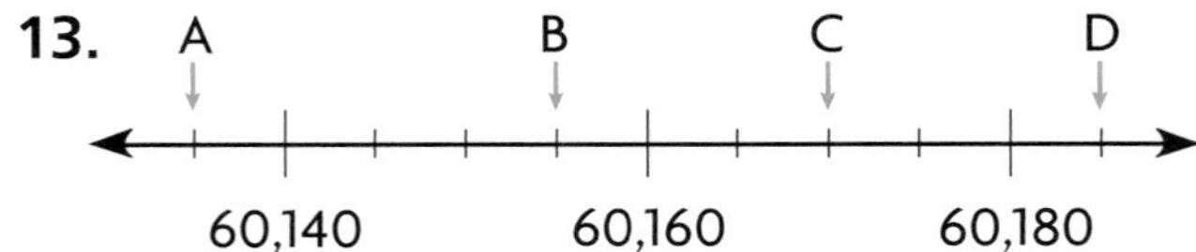

14.

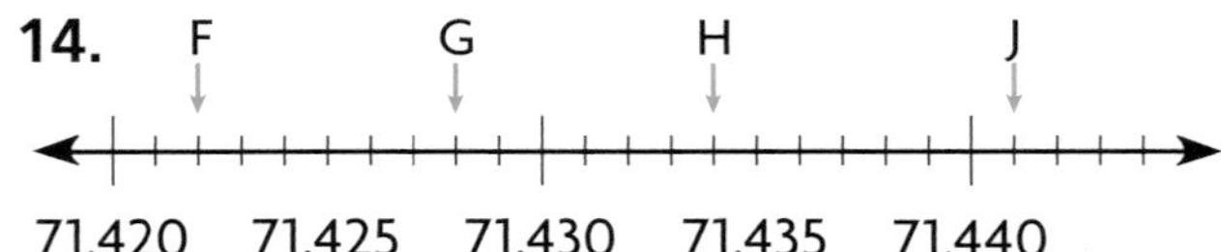

Write all of the digits that can replace each ■.

15. $358 < 3\blacksquare 3 < 370$

16. $1{,}012 < 1{,}\blacksquare 20 < 1{,}200$

17. $5{,}328 < \blacksquare{,}680 < 5{,}690$

18. $82{,}913 < 8\blacksquare{,}086 < 83{,}096$

19. $4{,}526{,}109 > 4{,}526{,}\blacksquare 17 > 4{,}526{,}010$

20. $3{,}942{,}687 > 3{,}942{,}6\blacksquare 3 > 3{,}942{,}670$

21. I am a number between 149,900 and 150,000. My tens digit is 7 more than my ones digit. The sum of my tens and ones digits is 9. What number am I?

22. **What's the Error?** Paul ordered the populations of three states from least to greatest. His work is shown below. Describe his error. Write the states in the correct order.

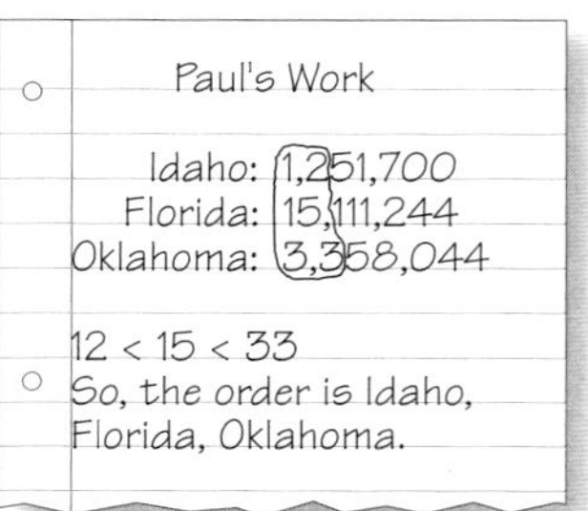
Paul's Work

Idaho: 1,251,700
Florida: 15,111,244
Oklahoma: 3,358,044

12 < 15 < 33
So, the order is Idaho, Florida, Oklahoma.

23. Jamal and his mom left for the store at 11:40 A.M. They arrived back home at 1:00 P.M. How long were they gone?

24. **Write a problem** comparing three or more numbers. Use facts from your science book.

USE DATA For 25–27, use the table.

25. Name the Great Lakes in order from greatest area to least area.

26. Which lakes have areas greater than Lake Erie's area?

27. Which lakes have areas less than 10,000 square miles?

AREAS OF THE GREAT LAKES (in square miles)	
Lake	**Area**
Erie	9,910
Huron	23,000
Michigan	22,300
Ontario	7,340
Superior	31,700

Mixed Review and Test Prep

Find the sum or difference.

28. $398 + 571$

29. $890 - 231$

30. $700 - 103$

31. $651 + 362$

32. Two different 6-digit numbers each have three 8's and three 7's. No two digits next to each other are the same. Write the numbers in standard form. (p. 4)

33. **TEST PREP** Which is the value of the digit 5 in 54,287? (p. 2)
   - **A** 5
   - **B** 50
   - **C** 5,000
   - **D** 50,000

34. **TEST PREP** Which is the value of the digit 3 in 13,720,980? (p. 6)
   - **F** 3,000
   - **G** 30,000
   - **H** 3,000,000
   - **J** 30,000,000

Problem Solving Thinker's Corner

PICO, CENTRO, NADA In Venezuela, people play a number game called *Pico, Centro, Nada.*

Think of a 2-digit number. Have your partner try to guess the number. With each incorrect guess, give one of these clues:

- *Pico* means that one digit is correct, but it's in the wrong place.
- *Centro* means that one digit is correct, and it's in the correct place.
- *Nada* means that neither digit is correct.

1. When one number for each player is found, work together to compare the numbers using $<$, $>$, or $=$.

2. When four numbers have been found, list the numbers in order from *least* to *greatest*.

LESSON 3

Problem Solving Strategy
Make a Table

PROBLEM Mt. Rainier, in Washington, is 14,410 ft tall; Mt. Whitney, in California, is 14,494 ft tall; Mt. Bear, in Alaska, is 14,831 ft tall; and Colorado's Mt. Elbert is 14,433 ft tall. Which mountains are taller than Mt. Elbert?

Quick Review

Write the greater number.

1. 4,861 or 40,810

2. 17,092 or 7,920

3. 5,614 or 51,462

4. 32,811 or 37,112

5. 300,020 or 30,200

UNDERSTAND

- What are you asked to find?
- What information will you use?
- Is there any information you will not use? Explain.

PLAN

- What strategy can you use to solve the problem?
  You can *make a table* to organize the information to find the mountains that are taller than Mt. Elbert.

SOLVE

- How can you use the strategy to solve the problem?
  Compare the heights. Place the mountains in the table from the tallest mountain to the shortest. Mt. Bear and Mt. Whitney are taller than Mt. Elbert.

U.S. MOUNTAINS

Name	Height (in feet)
Mt. Bear	14,831
Mt. Whitney	14,494
Mt. Elbert	14,433
Mt. Rainier	14,410

CHECK

- How can you decide if your answer is correct?

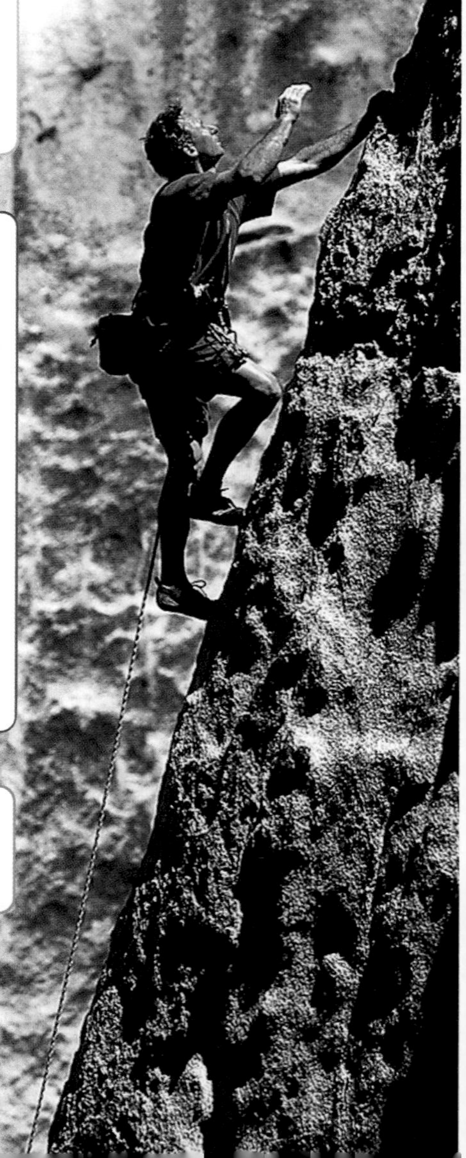

Mt. McKinley, in Alaska, is the tallest U.S. mountain peak, at 20,320 ft. It is taller than 30,000 new pencils placed end to end. ▶

Problem Solving Practice

1. **What if** University Peak, in Alaska, is added to the table? Its height is 14,470 ft. Make a new table ordering the heights from the tallest mountain to the shortest.

USE DATA For 2–5, make a table to solve.

An author wrote four books about hiking. *Hike for Life* sold 390,457 copies; *Safe Hiking* sold 256,749 copies; *Tricky Trails* sold 354,216 copies; and 391,752 copies of *Miles a Day* were sold.

Strategies

Draw a Diagram or Picture
Make a Model or Act It Out
Make an Organized List
Find a Pattern
Make a Table or Graph
Predict and Test
Work Backward
Solve a Simpler Problem
Write an Equation
Use Logical Reasoning

Problem Solving

2. Which book sold the most copies?

3. Which book sold the fewest copies?

4. **What if** *Safe Hiking* had sold 385,485 copies? Which book would have sold the fewest copies?
   - **A** *Miles a Day*
   - **B** *Tricky Trails*
   - **C** *Safe Hiking*
   - **D** *Hike for Life*

5. Which book sold about the same number of copies as *Miles a Day*?
   - **F** *Hiking World*
   - **G** *Tricky Trails*
   - **H** *Safe Hiking*
   - **J** *Hike for Life*

Mixed Strategy Practice

6. Delta County holds its fair every two years. The twenty-sixth fair was in 1948. In what year was the 50th Delta County Fair held?

7. **What's the Question?** Pat has 5 more posters than Bill. Bill has 8 posters. Roger has 4 fewer posters than Pat. The answer is 9 posters.

USE DATA For 8–10, use the table.

8. If Lenny continues to increase his number of pull-ups by the same amount each day, how many pull-ups will he complete on Saturday?

9. Lenny did 84 pull-ups for the week. How many pull-ups did he do Friday through Sunday?

10. How many pull-ups would Lenny complete if he did 8 pull-ups each day for 7 days? 10 pull-ups?

Lenny's Exercise Plan

Day	Number of Pull-Ups
Monday	6
Tuesday	8
Wednesday	10
Thursday	12

LESSON 4 Round Numbers

Quick Review

Tell whether the number is closer to 100 or 200.

1. 98 **2.** 172

3. 145 **4.** 159

5. 120

VOCABULARY

round

Learn

NEW NEIGHBORS In 2000, an average of 70,817 immigrants came to the United States each month. A reporter wants to **round** this number to the nearest thousand to make it easier to understand. What is this number rounded to the nearest thousand?

One Way

Use a number line to round numbers.

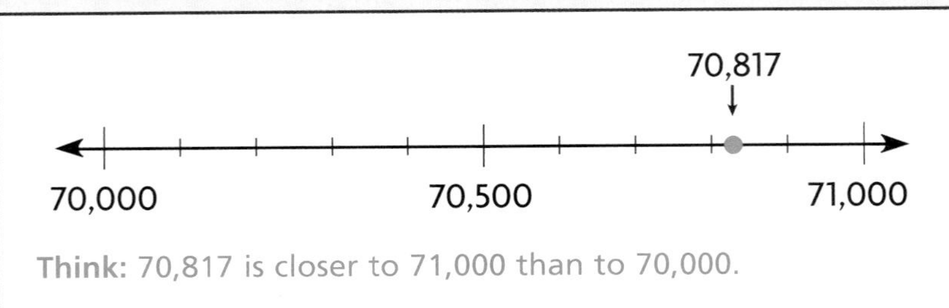
70,817
70,000
70,500
71,000
Think: 70,817 is closer to 71,000 than to 70,000.

So, 70,817 rounded to the nearest thousand is 71,000.

Another Way

Use these rules to round numbers.

To round a number:

- Find the place to which you want to round.
- Look at the digit to its right.
- If the digit is *less than 5,* the digit in the rounding place stays the same.
- If the digit is *5 or more,* the digit in the rounding place increases by 1.
- Change all digits to the right of the rounding place to zero.

Round 70,817 to the nearest ten thousand.

70,817 is between 70,000 and 80,000.

place to be rounded → 70,817 ← Look at the thousands digit.

Since 0 is less than 5, the digit 7 stays the same. So, 70,817 rounded to the nearest ten thousand is 70,000.

Round Greater Numbers

Immigrants from all over the world bring their native languages to the United States. The table shows a recent year's data about languages most often used at home, other than English.

LANGUAGES OTHER THAN ENGLISH SPOKEN IN THE U.S.	
Language	**Number of People**
Spanish	17,339,000
French	1,702,000
German	1,547,000
Italian	1,309,000
Chinese	1,249,000

Round the number of people who speak German to the nearest

hundred thousand. 1,547,000 → 1,500,000

ten thousand. 1,547,000 → 1,550,000

Examples

A Round 17,339,000 to the nearest million.

17,339,000 is between 17,000,000 and 18,000,000.

place to be rounded ↓ 17,339,000 Look at the hundred thousands digit.

Since 3 is less than 5, the digit 7 stays the same. So, 17,339,000 rounded to the nearest million is 17,000,000.

B Round 17,339,000 to the nearest ten thousand.

17,339,000 is between 17,330,000 and 17,340,000.

place to be rounded ↓ 17,339,000 Look at the thousands digit.

Since 9 is greater than 5, the digit 3 is increased by 1. So, 17,339,000 rounded to the nearest ten thousand is 17,340,000.

- When rounding, you change some digits to zero. Explain how you know which digits to change.

Check

1. **Explain** how to round 99,999 to the nearest ten thousand.

2. **Find** the least and greatest numbers that round to 600,000.

Round each number to the nearest thousand.

3. 16,822
4. 895,104
5. 4,286,531
6. 9,104,523

Round each number to the place value of the blue digit.

7. 98,749
8. 167,403
9. 317,482
10. 1,247,962

LESSON CONTINUES

Practice and Problem Solving

Extra Practice, page 34, Set C

Round each number to the nearest thousand.

11. 64,385 **12.** 37,179 **13.** 82,435 **14.** 93,798

15. 399,999 **16.** 8,365,700 **17.** 1,438,607 **18.** 2,513,986

Round each number to the place value of the blue digit.

19. 529,999 **20.** 154,879 **21.** 1,943,672 **22.** 2,837,486

23. 667,841 **24.** 725,639 **25.** 453,602 **26.** 375,926

27. 6,385,837 **28.** 7,384,609 **29.** 9,645,408 **30.** 12,647,813

31. 5,476,301 **32.** 14,358,900 **33.** 41,683,205 **34.** 62,591,073

35. Describe all the numbers that, when rounded to the nearest thousand, are 312,000.

36. Which number rounds to sixteen million, eight hundred thousand: 16,864,381 or 16,849,268?

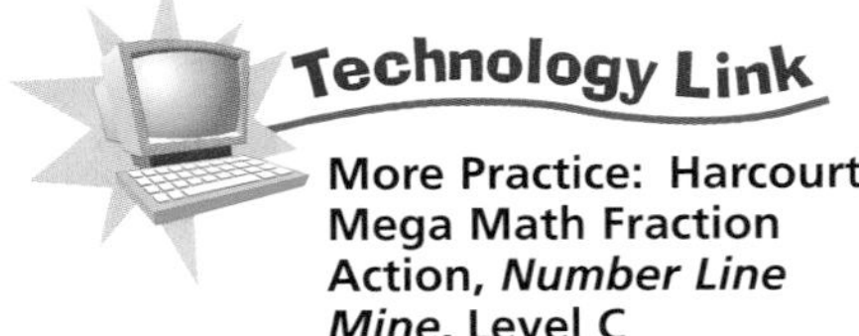

Technology Link

More Practice: Harcourt Mega Math Fraction Action, *Number Line Mine,* Level C

37. On the place-value chart, my thousands period is seventy-four. My ones period is 500 + 20 + 3. My millions digit is 3 times my ones digit. What number am I? Round me to the nearest hundred thousand.

USE DATA For 38–41, use the table.

38. Which state had a little more than 100,000 immigrants admitted?

39. Which state's number of immigrants has the digit 7 in the hundreds place?

40. Is the number of immigrants admitted to Florida closer to 98,000 or 99,000?

41. Write the number that is 50,000 greater than the number of immigrants admitted to New York.

IMMIGRANTS ADMITTED, 2000

State	Immigrants
Michigan	16,773
New York	106,061
Florida	98,391

42. **REASONING** Write a number that never repeats a digit and rounds to 7,000,000.

43. **Write About It** Explain how to round 994,685 to the nearest hundred thousand.

44. **FAST FACT • SOCIAL STUDIES** In 2000, a total of 133,362 people immigrated to the United States from Europe. Round this number to the nearest thousand.

45. Rico's mother arrived at the school 15 minutes after the bus left. She arrived at 3:05 P.M. At what time did the bus leave the school?

Mixed Review and Test Prep

46. Write eighteen thousand, five hundred seventy in standard form. (p. 4)

47. What number is 100 greater than the sum of 418 and 975?

48. Use word form to write the number that is 1,000 greater than 99,756. (p. 4)

49. Which number is greater, 568,413 or 568,143? (p. 20)

50. Write 150,210 in word form. (p. 4)

51. Write 5,000,000 + 2,000 + 10 + 4 in standard form. (p. 6)

52. **TEST PREP** Which number, when subtracted from 800, gives a difference greater than 200?
A 423 **B** 609 **C** 612 **D** 742

53. **TEST PREP** Which number is between 476,891 and 674,198? (p. 24)
F 468,981 **H** 676,819
G 647,918 **J** 746,189

Problem Solving LINKUP . . . to Reading

STRATEGY • COMPARE When you **compare** two or more things, you look at how they are alike. When you **contrast** two or more things, you look at how they are different.

Look at the chart below. The chart compares and contrasts information about 5 deserts. Can you think of other ways to compare and contrast the deserts?

COMPARE	CONTRAST
The Kalahari and the Sahara are located in Africa.	The Australian Desert is the only desert located in Australia.
All have areas greater than 500,000 sq km.	The Sahara is larger than the other 4 deserts put together.

DESERTS OF THE WORLD

Desert	Location	Area (in sq km)
Kalahari	Africa	520,000
Gobi	Asia	1,036,000
Arabian	Asia	1,300,000
Australian	Australia	3,800,000
Sahara	Africa	9,000,000

1. Look at the areas of the Arabian Desert and the Gobi Desert. How do they compare? How do they contrast?

2. Round each area to the nearest million. Compare and contrast the numbers. How does this change the data?

Extra Practice

Set A (pp. 20–23)

Compare. Write <, >, or = for each ●.

1. 2,310 ● 2,340
2. 25,050 ● 23,050
3. 22,790 ● 22,790
4. 130,290 ● 130,230
5. 365,280 ● 361,792
6. 12,941 ● 115,226
7. 47,569 ● 47,650
8. 594,031 ● 594,010
9. 731,598 ● 703,892
10. Casey has 3,500 stickers, Joanie has 3,573 stickers, and Emil has 3,432 stickers. Who has the most stickers?

USE DATA For 11–12, use the table.

11. Which plane traveled the greatest distance?
12. A plane called *Streak* flew a distance of 6,156 miles. Is this greater than or less than *Silver's* distance?

FLIGHT DISTANCES

Name of Plane	Distance Traveled (in miles)
Flying Eagle	5,987
Max 7	6,251
Silver	6,076
Flight Machine	5,872

Set B (pp. 24–27)

Write the numbers in order from *least* to *greatest*.

1. 13,069; 13,960; 13,609
2. 76,214; 74,612; 76,421
3. 160,502; 160,402; 163,500
4. 7,450,343; 7,429,203; 7,492,393

Write the numbers in order from *greatest* to *least*.

5. 37,456; 34,567; 37,654
6. 49,325; 49,852; 49,538
7. 560,898; 560,908; 560,890
8. 2,864,305; 2,648,509; 2,986,413

Set C (pp. 30–33)

Round each number to the place value of the blue digit.

1. 512,399
2. 238,299
3. 942,310
4. 251,003
5. 499,210
6. 9,449,390
7. 3,215,007
8. 1,924,308
9. 4,957,021
10. Which number rounds to three million, nine hundred ninety thousand: 3,985,762 or 3,958,617?

Review/Test

✓ CHECK VOCABULARY AND CONCEPTS

Choose the best term from the box.

greatest
least
rounded
5 or more
less than 5

1. To compare numbers, you can use a number line or start with the _?_ place-value position. (p. 20)
2. The number 7,950,614 _?_ to the nearest million is 8,000,000. (p. 30)
3. When rounding, if the digit to the right of the rounding place is _?_, the digit in the rounding place increases by one. (p. 30)

✓ CHECK SKILLS

Compare. Write $<$, $>$, or $=$ for each ●. (pp. 20–23)

4. 15,980 ● 15,754
5. 34,980 ● 3,690
6. 780,256 ● 783,130
7. 1,895,006 ● 1,392,950
8. 282,700 ● 2,308,030
9. 562,026 ● 562,026
10. Write 25,908; 25,616; and 25,972 in order from *least* to *greatest*. (pp. 24–27)
11. Write 3,791,808; 3,759,204; and 3,090,910 in order from *greatest* to *least*. (pp. 24–27)

Round each number to the place value of the blue digit. (pp. 30–33)

12. 105,219
13. 983,050
14. 4,591,203
15. 7,948,033
16. 6,839,032
17. 871,094
18. 3,217,849
19. 7,981,936
20. 17,340,206
21. 34,761,502
22. 29,457,863
23. 58,732,141

✓ CHECK PROBLEM SOLVING

Solve. (pp. 28–29)

24. City A's population is 342,653. City B has 451,321 people; and City C has 353,308 people. Make a table that lists the cities in order from least to greatest population. Which cities' populations are greater than 345,000?
25. In a recent year, a statewide festival's total attendance was 746,982. Round 746,982 to the nearest hundred thousand, ten thousand, and thousand. Which of these rounded amounts is closest to the actual attendance?

Standardized Test Prep

NUMBER SENSE, CONCEPTS, AND OPERATIONS

1. Mira made a table to show the attendance at a film festival over a period of 4 years.

FILM FESTIVAL ATTENDANCE	
Year	**Number of People**
2000	513
2001	975
2002	500
2003	397

How many more people attended in 2001 than in 2000?

A 462 **C** 562

B 472 **D** 1,488

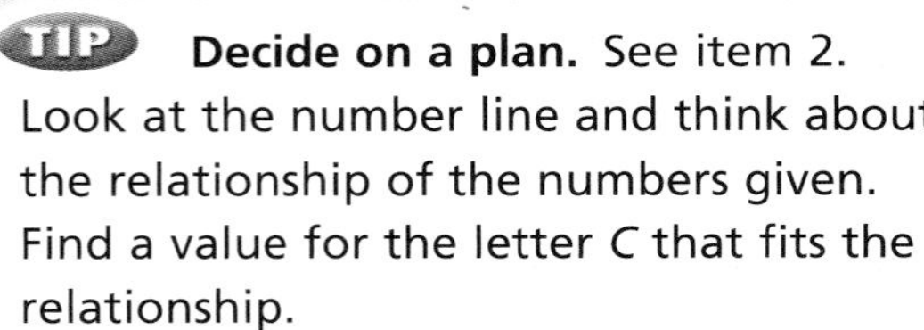

TIP **Decide on a plan.** See item 2. Look at the number line and think about the relationship of the numbers given. Find a value for the letter *C* that fits the relationship.

2. Which number is represented by the letter *C* on the number line?

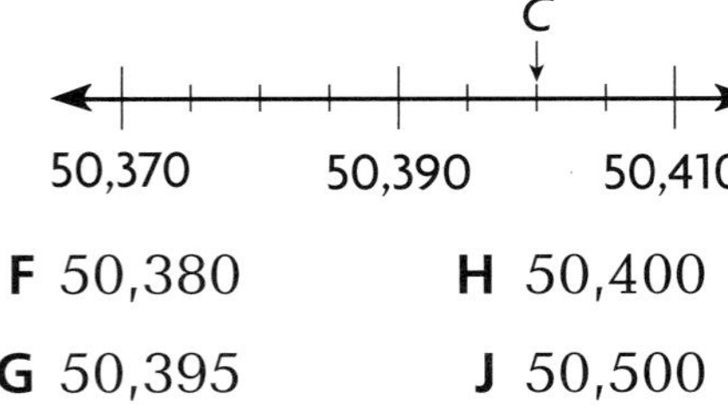

F 50,380 **H** 50,400

G 50,395 **J** 50,500

3. Explain It Explain how knowing the number of pennies in one jar can help you estimate the number of pennies in a second jar that is four times as large. Give an example.

MEASUREMENT

4. Which unit of measure would be the **most** appropriate to determine the capacity of a bathtub?

A cups

B pints

C quarts

D gallons

5. This thermometer shows the temperature at 7:00 A.M.

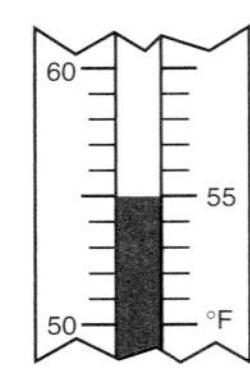

The temperature rose 5 degrees by 11:00 A.M. What did the thermometer read then?

F 55°F

G 60°F

H 62°F

J 64°F

6. Which appears to be a right angle?

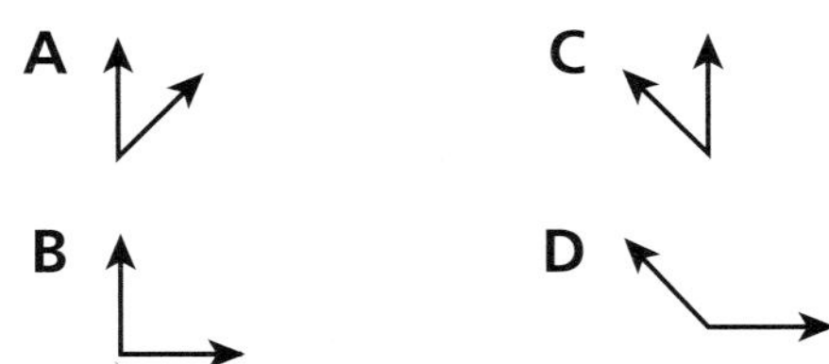

7. Explain It Describe a situation involving money in which an exact answer is needed and one in which an estimate will do. Explain your thinking.

 GEOMETRY AND SPATIAL SENSE

8. The shape of which sign contains only right angles?

F 

H 

G 

J 

9. Which figures appear to be similar?

A 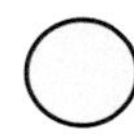 

B 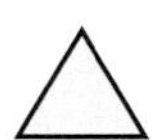

C 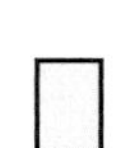 

D 

10. Explain It Kathy is planning to build this fence around her garden.

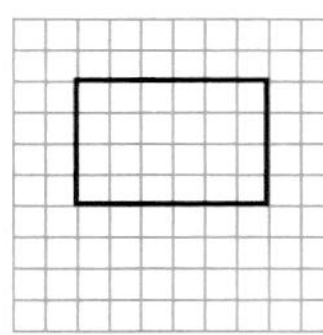

= 1 foot

How many feet of fencing will she need? Explain how you decided.

 ALGEBRAIC THINKING

11. José's class members made a bar graph to show their favorite fruits.

Which of the following could be used to determine how many more votes oranges got than pears?

F $8 - 2 = \blacksquare$

G $\blacksquare - 2 = 8$

H $8 + 2 = \blacksquare$

J $\blacksquare - 8 = 2$

12. Which means the same as this sentence?

Three times five equals fifteen.

A $3 \times 5 + 15$

B $3 \times 5 = 15$

C $3 \times 5 - 15$

D $3 \times 5 = 3 \times 5$

13. Explain It Describe a rule for this pattern. Then describe the missing figure.

     ? 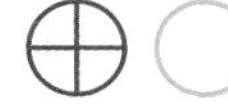

Add and Subtract Whole Numbers

FAST FACT • SCIENCE
Insects are part of a group of animals called arthropods (ARTH•ruh•pahdz). Arthropods also include crustaceans (krus•TAY•shuhnz) and arachnids (uh•RAK•nidz). Spiders are different from insects. One difference is that insects have six legs and spiders have eight legs.

PROBLEM SOLVING **Using the circle graph, tell how many more types of insects there are than arachnids.**

ARTHROPODS

Crustaceans: 40,000 types
crabs
lobsters
shrimps
crayfish

Arachnids: 70,000 types
spiders
scorpions
mites
ticks

Insects: 750,000 types
grasshoppers
termites
flies
beetles

Garden spider

CHECK WHAT YOU KNOW

Use this page to help you review and remember important skills needed for Chapter 3.

ROUND NUMBERS

Round each number to the nearest thousand.

1. 61,335 **2.** 222,606 **3.** 99,707 **4.** 45,384 **5.** 869,530

Round each number to the place value of the blue digit.

6. 589,005 **7.** 344,940 **8.** 402,196 **9.** 121,067 **10.** 321,500

11. 1,752,621 **12.** 12,919,940 **13.** 1,161,969 **14.** 88,947,024 **15.** 72,009,304

TWO-DIGIT ADDITION AND SUBTRACTION

Find the sum or difference.

16. $13 + 24$ **17.** $58 - 29$ **18.** $36 - 14$ **19.** $52 + 11$ **20.** $78 - 43$

21. $73 - 19$ **22.** $65 + 36$ **23.** $42 + 68$ **24.** $90 - 28$ **25.** $81 + 26$

26. 23 + 37 + 42 = ■ **27.** 42 + 31 + 63 = ■

28. 87 − 59 = ■ **29.** 64 − 29 = ■

VOCABULARY POWER

REVIEW

round [round] *verb*

In mathematics, the word *round* can be used to mean "find the nearest value of a number based on a given place value." How else is *round* used in mathematics?

www.harcourtschool.com/mathglossary

LESSON 1

Use Mental Math Strategies

Quick Review

Write the number that is one thousand more.

1. 1,350
2. 7,802
3. 15,927
4. 23,618
5. 42,678

Learn

THINK IT THROUGH Sometimes you don't need paper and pencil to compute. Use these strategies to help you compute mentally.

One Way *Break Apart* Strategy

You can break apart numbers to add the tens and ones separately.

Examples

A Find the sum. 58 + 26

Think: 58 = 50 + 8
26 = 20 + 6

Add the tens. 50 + 20 = 70

Add the ones. 8 + 6 = 14

Add the sums. 70 + 14 = 84

So, 58 + 26 = 84.

B Find the difference. 46 − 25

Think: 46 = 40 + 6
25 = 20 + 5

Subtract the tens. 40 − 20 = 20

Subtract the ones. 6 − 5 = 1

Add the differences. 20 + 1 = 21

So, 46 − 25 = 21.

More Examples

C Find the sum. 39 + 48

30 + 40 = 70

9 + 8 = 17

70 + 17 = 87

D Find the difference. 97 − 52

90 − 50 = 40

7 − 2 = 5

40 + 5 = 45

- Explain how to use this strategy to find 62 + 29.

More Strategies

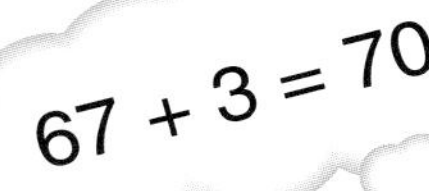

24 − 3 = 21

70 + 21 = 91

Another Way *Make a Ten* Strategy

You can change one number to a multiple of 10 and then adjust the other number.

Subtraction is easier if the number you are subtracting is a multiple of 10. If you increase the number you are subtracting, you must add the same amount to adjust the answer.

Examples

E Find the sum. 67 + 24

$67 + 3 = 70$ Think: Add 3 to 67 to get 70.

$24 - 3 = 21$ Subtract 3 from 24 to adjust the sum.

$70 + 21 = 91$ Add 70 + 21.

F Find the difference. 186 − 29

$29 + 1 = 30$ Think: Add 1 to 29 to get 30.

$186 + 1 = 187$ Add 1 to 186 to adjust the difference.

$187 - 30 = 157$ Subtract 187 − 30.

- What if you subtract 4 from 24 in Example E? How could you find 67 + 24 mentally?

You also can adjust the sum or difference after changing one number.

More Examples

G Find the difference. 75 − 38

$38 + 2 = 40$

$$\begin{array}{r} 75 \\ -\ 40 \\ \hline 35 \\ +\ 2 \\ \hline 37 \end{array}$$

Add 2 to 35 to adjust the sum.

H Find the sum. 284 + 476

$284 + 6 = 290$

$$\begin{array}{r} 290 \\ +\ 476 \\ \hline 766 \\ -\ 6 \\ \hline 760 \end{array}$$

Subtract 6 from 766 to adjust the difference.

Check

1. **Explain** how to find 83 − 37 mentally.
2. **Write** an addition problem. Find the sum by breaking the numbers apart.

LESSON CONTINUES

For 3–10, add or subtract mentally. Tell the strategy you used.

3. 85 − 17	**4.** 72 + 28	**5.** 83 − 19	**6.** 95 + 28
7. 68 + 25	**8.** 52 − 27	**9.** 74 + 32	**10.** 76 − 28

Practice and Problem Solving

Extra Practice, page 58, Set A

For 11–22, add or subtract mentally. Tell the strategy you used.

11. 78 − 15	**12.** 16 + 28	**13.** 26 − 12	**14.** 47 + 23
15. 27 + 48	**16.** 75 − 36	**17.** 38 + 85	**18.** 91 − 66
19. 62 − 29	**20.** 34 + 58	**21.** 44 − 17	**22.** 63 + 39

Find the sum or difference.

23. 168 − 59	**24.** 249 + 87	**25.** 216 + 79	**26.** 152 − 75
27. 261 + 88	**28.** 431 − 232	**29.** 441 + 263	**30.** 284 − 192
31. 758 − 453	**32.** 576 − 391	**33.** 713 + 428	**34.** 674 + 332

USE DATA For 35–38, use the table.

35. Which animal has a length of about 60 feet?

36. How many feet longer is the blue whale than the crocodile?

37. Which two animals have the greatest difference in length? Which have the least difference?

38. **What's the Question?** The answer is 90 feet.

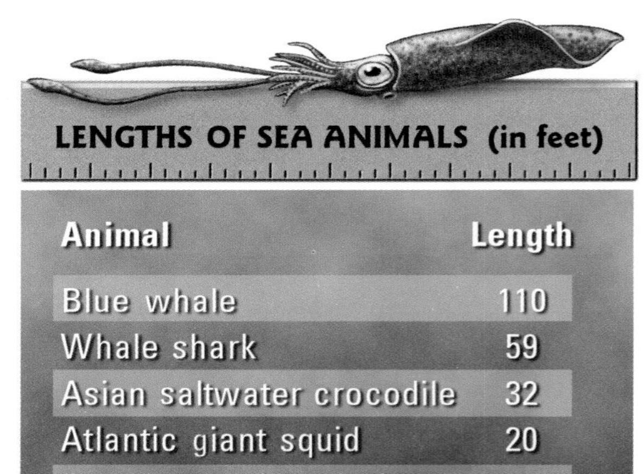

LENGTHS OF SEA ANIMALS (in feet)

Animal	Length
Blue whale	110
Whale shark	59
Asian saltwater crocodile	32
Atlantic giant squid	20
Japanese spider crab	9

39. On Friday, there were 2,999 people at the aquarium. On Saturday, there were 1,465 people. Use mental math to find how many people were at the aquarium during the two days. Explain your strategy.

40. ***FAST FACT*** • **SCIENCE** The Central Florida Zoo covers 109 acres. The National Zoo, in Washington, D.C., covers 163 acres. If the Central Florida Zoo bought another 55 acres for expansion, which zoo would be larger? How much larger?

41. Rex has 6 horses, 10 cows, 5 goats, and 4 cars. He puts the cows, goats, and cars in the barn. How many of his animals are in the barn?

42. Lisa's dog weighs 45 pounds. Reggie's dog weighs 27 pounds. How much more does Lisa's dog weigh than Reggie's dog?

Mixed Review and Test Prep

43. Write the numbers from greatest to least: 2,567; 2,763; 189,576; 187,487; 189,875. (p. 24)

44. Round 5,789,132 to the nearest hundred thousand. (p. 30)

Compare. Write <, >, or = for each ●.

45. 8,567 ● 9,087 (p. 20)

46. 8,237,958 ● 8,549,788 (p. 20)

47. **TEST PREP** Maria has 5 dimes, 1 nickel, and 3 pennies in her pocket. How much money does she have?

A 58¢ **B** 52¢ **C** 48¢ **D** 45¢

48. **TEST PREP** Which of the following is NOT true?

F $8 + 10 = 10 + 8$

G $12 + 3 = 11 + 4$

H $8 + 1 = 2 + 7$

J $7 + 9 = 6 + 8$

Problem Solving Thinker's Corner

COMPATIBLE NUMBERS Two numbers that add up to sums like 10 or 100 are **compatible numbers.** Compatible numbers make mental math easy.

The Order Property of Addition says that numbers can be added in any order and the sum remains the same. Use the Order Property of Addition to add compatible numbers.

HINT: These pairs of compatible numbers have a sum of 100.

10 and 90
20 and 80
30 and 70
40 and 60
50 and 50

Find the sum. $68 + 230 + 32 + 170$

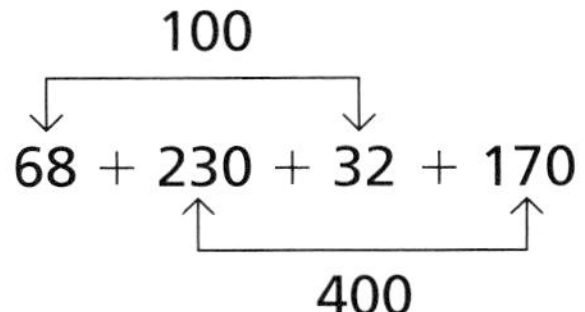

HINT: Look for compatible numbers.

$$68 + 230 + 32 + 170 = 68 + 32 + 230 + 170$$
$$= 100 + 400 = 500$$

So, the sum is 500.

Use compatible numbers to find each sum.

1. $175 + 25 + 61 + 39 =$ ■

2. $82 + 18 + 60 + 40 =$ ■

3. $78 + 250 + 122 + 48 =$ ■

4. $302 + 168 + 32 + 175 =$ ■

LESSON 2

Estimate Sums and Differences

Quick Review

Round to the greatest place value.

1. 460 **2.** 742
3. 1,927 **4.** 4,381
5. 19,570

 **Learn**

PET POWER The table shows the results of a survey by the North Adams Animal Shelter. About how many people have either dogs or cats, but not both?

PET HOUSEHOLDS

Pet	Number
Cat only	34,221
Dog only	38,899
Cat & dog	6,520
Tropical fish	4,872
Bird	1,036

One Way Use rounding.

Estimate. 34,221 + 38,899

Round each number to the nearest thousand.

$$\begin{array}{rcr} 34{,}221 & \rightarrow & 34{,}000 \\ +\ 38{,}899 & \rightarrow & +\ 39{,}000 \\ & & 73{,}000 \end{array}$$

So, about 73,000 people have either dogs or cats.

Another Way Use front-end estimation.

Estimate. 34,221 + 38,899

Add the value of the front digits.

$$\begin{array}{rcr} 34{,}221 & \rightarrow & 30{,}000 \\ +\ 38{,}899 & \rightarrow & +\ 30{,}000 \\ & & 60{,}000 \end{array}$$

So, about 60,000 people have either dogs or cats.

- Which way, rounding or front-end estimation, do you think gives an estimate that is closer to the actual sum? Explain.

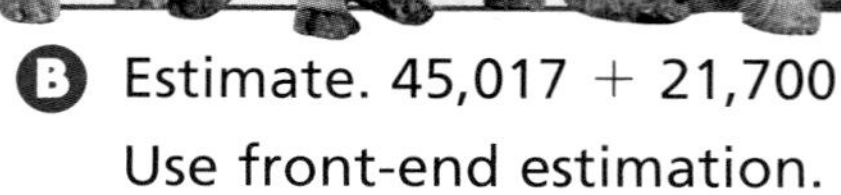

Examples

 Estimate. 5,372 + 1,497

Round each number to the nearest hundred.

$$\begin{array}{rcr} 5{,}372 & \rightarrow & 5{,}400 \\ +\ 1{,}497 & \rightarrow & +\ 1{,}500 \\ & & 6{,}900 \end{array}$$

The sum is about 6,900.

B Estimate. 45,017 + 21,700

Use front-end estimation.

$$\begin{array}{rcr} 45{,}017 & \rightarrow & 40{,}000 \\ +\ 21{,}700 & \rightarrow & +\ 20{,}000 \\ & & 60{,}000 \end{array}$$

The sum is about 60,000.

Estimate Differences

You can use rounding or front-end estimation to estimate the difference of whole numbers.

One Way Use rounding.

Estimate. 86,017 − 35,572

Round to the nearest ten thousand.

$$\begin{array}{r} 86{,}017 \\ -\ 35{,}572 \\ \hline \end{array} \rightarrow \begin{array}{r} 90{,}000 \\ -\ 40{,}000 \\ \hline 50{,}000 \end{array}$$

So, the difference is about 50,000.

Another Way Use front-end estimation.

Estimate. 4,892 − 1,431

Subtract the value of the front digits.

$$\begin{array}{r} 4{,}892 \\ -\ 1{,}431 \\ \hline \end{array} \rightarrow \begin{array}{r} 4{,}000 \\ -\ 1{,}000 \\ \hline 3{,}000 \end{array}$$

So, the difference is about 3,000.

Once you have found an estimate, you can adjust it to make it *closer to* the actual sum or difference.

More Examples

C Estimate. 7,593 − 3,145

Round to the nearest thousand.

$$\begin{array}{r} 7{,}593 \\ -\ 3{,}145 \\ \hline 4{,}448 \end{array} \rightarrow \begin{array}{r} 8{,}000 \\ -\ 3{,}000 \\ \hline 5{,}000 \end{array}$$

Find a closer estimate by rounding to the nearest hundred.

$$\begin{array}{r} 7{,}593 \\ -\ 3{,}145 \\ \hline 4{,}448 \end{array} \rightarrow \begin{array}{r} 7{,}600 \\ -\ 3{,}100 \\ \hline 4{,}500 \end{array}$$

So, a closer estimate is 4,500.

D Estimate. 22,720 + 34,378

Add the value of the front digits.

$$\begin{array}{r} 22{,}720 \\ +\ 34{,}378 \\ \hline 57{,}098 \end{array} \rightarrow \begin{array}{r} 20{,}000 \\ +\ 30{,}000 \\ \hline 50{,}000 \end{array}$$

Find a closer estimate by including the value of the remaining digits.

2,720 + 4,378 is about 7,000.

50,000 + 7,000 = 57,000

So, a closer estimate is 57,000.

Check

1. **Explain** why a front-end estimate of a sum will never be greater than the actual sum.

Estimate the sum or difference by using rounding.

2. $\begin{array}{r} 279 \\ +645 \\ \hline \end{array}$

3. $\begin{array}{r} 7{,}939 \\ -\ 4{,}209 \\ \hline \end{array}$

4. $\begin{array}{r} 65{,}461 \\ +\ 23{,}780 \\ \hline \end{array}$

5. $\begin{array}{r} 47{,}813 \\ -\ 25{,}379 \\ \hline \end{array}$

LESSON CONTINUES

Estimate the sum or difference by using front-end estimation.

6. $\begin{array}{r} 257 \\ -123 \\ \hline \end{array}$

7. $\begin{array}{r} 1{,}936 \\ +\ 7{,}483 \\ \hline \end{array}$

8. $\begin{array}{r} \$13{,}024 \\ +\ \$58{,}417 \\ \hline \end{array}$

9. $\begin{array}{r} 90{,}111 \\ -\ 23{,}187 \\ \hline \end{array}$

Adjust the estimate to make it closer to the exact sum or difference.

10. 9,876 + 6,291 = 16,167
Estimate: 10,000 + 6,000 = 16,000

11. 87,908 − 33,110 = 54,798
Estimate: 90,000 − 30,000 = 60,000

Practice and Problem Solving

Extra Practice, page 58, Set B

Estimate the sum or difference by using rounding.

12. $\begin{array}{r} 123 \\ +381 \\ \hline \end{array}$

13. $\begin{array}{r} \$40{,}717 \\ +\ \$74{,}910 \\ \hline \end{array}$

14. $\begin{array}{r} 28{,}183 \\ -\ 12{,}275 \\ \hline \end{array}$

15. $\begin{array}{r} 8{,}600 \\ -\ 4{,}908 \\ \hline \end{array}$

Estimate the sum or difference by using front-end estimation.

16. $\begin{array}{r} 9{,}584 \\ -\ 6{,}102 \\ \hline \end{array}$

17. $\begin{array}{r} 8{,}037 \\ +\ 4{,}047 \\ \hline \end{array}$

18. $\begin{array}{r} 71{,}234 \\ -\ 12{,}736 \\ \hline \end{array}$

19. $\begin{array}{r} \$96{,}254 \\ +\ \$15{,}224 \\ \hline \end{array}$

Adjust the estimate to make it closer to the exact sum or difference.

20. 4,962 − 1,852 = 3,110
Estimate: 5,000 − 2,000 = 3,000

21. 51,099 + 45,724 = 96,823
Estimate: 50,000 + 50,000 = 100,000

22. 8,482 + 6,079 = 14,561
Estimate: 8,000 + 6,000 = 14,000

23. 38,852 − 16,487 = 22,365
Estimate: 40,000 − 20,000 = 20,000

USE DATA For 24–26, use the table.

24. About how many golden retrievers and cocker spaniels are registered in all?

25. About how many more German shepherds than poodles are there?

26. About how many beagles and poodles are registered in all?

27. **REASONING** Write two numbers that have an estimated sum of 1,000,000. Use the digits 1, 2, 3, 4, 5, and 6 in each number.

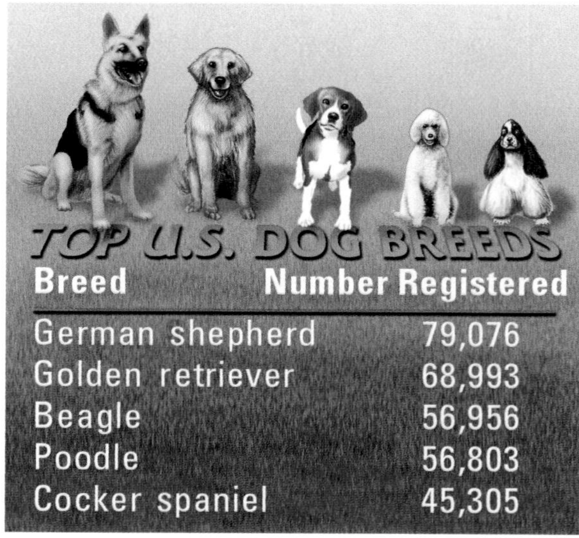

TOP U.S. DOG BREEDS

Breed	Number Registered
German shepherd	79,076
Golden retriever	68,993
Beagle	56,956
Poodle	56,803
Cocker spaniel	45,305

28. **Write About It** Write a problem that you can solve by using the estimate 7,000 + 5,000 = 12,000.

29. John and Sara both estimated the sum 5,512 + 2,501. John rounded and got 9,000. Sara used front-end estimation and got 7,000. Which estimate do you think is closer to the exact sum? Explain.

30. **Vocabulary Power** When we say that two things are *different,* we mean that they are unlike in some way. What does finding the *difference* between two numbers show about those numbers?

Mixed Review and Test Prep

31. Order 26,812; 8,261; 28,612; and 28,599 from *greatest* to *least.* (p. 24)

32. Which number is greater, 827,156 or 826,156? (p. 20)

33. Which number is greater, 92,745 or 92,740? (p. 20)

34. What is 200,000 + 50,000 + 3,000 + 20 + 7 in standard form? (p. 4)

35. TEST PREP Which is two hundred eighty-six in expanded form? (p. 2)

A 200 + 68
B 280 + 6
C 200 + 80 + 6
D 2,000 + 800 + 6

36. TEST PREP Which is 32,851 rounded to the nearest hundred? (p. 30)

F 30,000
G 32,000
H 32,900
J 33,900

Problem Solving Thinker's Corner

CLOSER ESTIMATES Another way to estimate is to find two estimates that an exact sum is *between.*

About how many Maine coon and Siamese cats are registered in the United States?

TOP REGISTERED PEDIGREE CAT BREEDS	
Breed	**Number**
Persian	25,524
Maine coon	4,539
Siamese	2,131

STEP 1

Find an ***underestimate,*** or an estimate that is a little *less than* the exact sum, by rounding *down* to the next hundred.

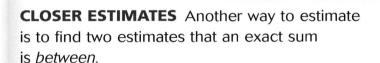

4,539 → 4,500
\+ 2,131 → + 2,100
6,600 ← underestimate

STEP 2

Find an ***overestimate,*** or an estimate that is a little *more than* the exact sum, by rounding *up* to the next hundred.

4,539 → 4,600
\+ 2,131 → + 2,200
6,800 ← overestimate

So, the actual sum 4,539 + 2,131 is *between* 6,600 and 6,800.

Find an underestimate and an overestimate for each sum.

1. 6,576 + 3,990
2. 2,849 + 17,365
3. 35,909 + 40,498

LESSON 3

Add and Subtract to 4-Digit Numbers

Quick Review

1. 460 + 218
2. 355 − 145
3. 175 + 250
4. 796 − 445
5. 804 + 257

Learn

GREAT LAKES! The area of Lake Erie is 9,910 square miles. The area of Lake Ontario is 7,340 square miles. What is the combined area of the two lakes? What is the difference in their areas?

Example 1

Find the sum. 9,910 + 7,340

Estimate. 10,000 + 7,000 = 17,000

STEP 1	STEP 2	STEP 3	STEP 4
Add the ones.	Add the tens.	Add the hundreds. Regroup 12 hundreds.	Add the thousands.
9,910 +7,340 0	9,910 +7,340 50	1 9,910 +7,340 250	1 9,910 +7,340 17,250

So, the combined area of the two lakes is 17,250 square miles. The answer is close to the estimate, so 17,250 is reasonable.

Technology Link

More Practice: Harcourt Mega Math The Number Games, *Tiny's Think Tank,* Levels B and C

Example 2

Find the difference. 9,910 − 7,340

Estimate. 10,000 − 7,000 = 3,000

STEP 1	STEP 2	STEP 3	STEP 4
Subtract the ones.	Regroup hundreds. Subtract the tens.	Subtract the hundreds.	Subtract the thousands.
9, 9 1 0 − 7, 3 4 0 0	8 11 9, 9 1 0 − 7, 3 4 0 7 0	8 11 9, 9 1 0 − 7, 3 4 0 5 7 0	8 11 9, 9 1 0 − 7, 3 4 0 2, 5 7 0

So, the difference in their areas is 2,570 square miles.
The answer is close to the estimate, so 2,570 is reasonable.

Check

1. **Explain** how you know when it is not necessary to regroup in subtraction.

Find the sum or difference. Estimate to check.

2. $\begin{array}{r} 899 \\ +267 \\ \hline \end{array}$

3. $\begin{array}{r} 674 \\ -406 \\ \hline \end{array}$

4. $\begin{array}{r} 8{,}902 \\ -5{,}730 \\ \hline \end{array}$

5. $\begin{array}{r} 9{,}201 \\ +\ 1{,}321 \\ \hline \end{array}$

Practice and Problem Solving

Extra Practice, page 58, Set C

Find the sum or difference. Estimate to check.

6. $\begin{array}{r} 798 \\ -127 \\ \hline \end{array}$

7. $\begin{array}{r} \$3{,}204 \\ -\$2{,}413 \\ \hline \end{array}$

8. $\begin{array}{r} 409 \\ 762 \\ +805 \\ \hline \end{array}$

9. $\begin{array}{r} 5{,}762 \\ 5{,}243 \\ +1{,}111 \\ \hline \end{array}$

10. $\begin{array}{r} 2{,}409 \\ +5{,}762 \\ \hline \end{array}$

11. $\begin{array}{r} 5{,}320 \\ -1{,}375 \\ \hline \end{array}$

12. $\begin{array}{r} 9{,}862 \\ -7{,}361 \\ \hline \end{array}$

13. $\begin{array}{r} \$3{,}228 \\ +\$4{,}228 \\ \hline \end{array}$

14. 409 + 952

15. \$1,124 + \$1,525 + \$1,651 + \$4,176

16. 6,230 − 4,651

17. 1,987 + 936

For 18–19, find the missing digit.

18. $\begin{array}{r} 2{,}90\blacksquare \\ -1{,}894 \\ \hline 1{,}007 \end{array}$

19. $\begin{array}{r} 3{,}486 \\ +\blacksquare{,}964 \\ \hline 9{,}450 \end{array}$

USE DATA For 20–21, use the map.

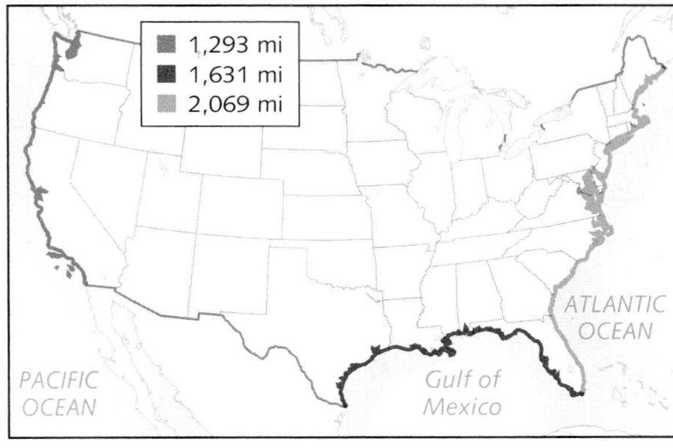

20. The lengths of which two coastlines have a sum of about 4,000 miles? Find the actual sum.

21. About how many miles long are all the United States coastlines shown?

Mixed Review and Test Prep

For 22–23, round to the nearest hundred. (p. 30)

22. 563

23. 712

24. $\begin{array}{r} 562 \\ +\ 349 \\ \hline \end{array}$

25. $\begin{array}{r} 736 \\ -\ 472 \\ \hline \end{array}$

26. **TEST PREP** Which has the same sum as 43 + 25? (p. 40)

A 40 + 22
B 48 + 30
C 40 + 28
D 38 + 20

LESSON 4

Subtract Across Zeros

Learn

ON THE MOVE Scientists track animals to find how far they migrate. A humpback whale migrated about 7,100 miles in a year. A green sea turtle migrated 1,315 miles. About how much farther did the whale migrate than the turtle?

Quick Review

1. 900 − 600
2. 1,000 − 500
3. 200 − 50
4. 500 − 250
5. 600 − 175

Example

Find the difference. 7,100 − 1,315

Estimate. 7,000 − 1,000 = 6,000

STEP 1 Subtract the ones. Regroup 1 hundred as 9 tens 10 ones. $\begin{array}{r} 7,100 \\ -1,315 \\ \hline 5 \end{array}$	**STEP 2** Subtract the tens. $\begin{array}{r} 7,100 \\ -1,315 \\ \hline 85 \end{array}$
STEP 3 Subtract the hundreds. Regroup 7 thousands as 6 thousands 10 hundreds. $\begin{array}{r} 7,100 \\ -1,315 \\ \hline 785 \end{array}$	**STEP 4** Subtract the thousands. $\begin{array}{r} 7,100 \\ -1,315 \\ \hline 5,785 \end{array}$

So, the humpback whale migrated about 5,785 miles farther than the green sea turtle. Since 5,785 is close to the estimate of 6,000, the answer is reasonable.

- In Step 1, why is it necessary to regroup 1 hundred?

Check

1. **Explain** how to regroup 40,000 to subtract 7,165.

Find the difference. Estimate to check.

2. 400 − 287

3. 3,700 − 1,692

4. \$300 − \$163

5. 2,100 − 594

Practice and Problem Solving

Extra Practice, page 58, Set D

Find the difference. Estimate to check.

6. 4,001 − 3,090

7. 6,008 − 4,009

8. \$3,005 − \$1,978

9. 5,004 − 859

10. 5,700 − 4,190

11. 7,001 − 3,090

12. 5,200 − 3,087

13. 8,600 − 6,123

14. 3,000 − 2,218

15. 8,000 − 2,319

16. 9,008 − 4,899

17. 1,000 − 919

Compare. Write <, >, or = for each ●.

18. 3,000 − 2,541 ● 4,200 − 3,756

19. 2,000 − 1,008 ● 2,100 − 1,097

20. One seal weighs 130 kilograms more than a second seal. If the second seal weighs 179 kilograms, how much does the first seal weigh?

21. An arctic tern flew 10,230 miles to Antarctica. A sea turtle swam 1,400 miles to South America. How much farther did the arctic tern migrate than the sea turtle?

22. A male walrus at the zoo weighs 1,390 kilograms. A female walrus weighs 268 kilograms less. How much do they weigh together?

23. **? What's the Error?** Quan subtracted 9,910 from 23,000 and got 12,090. Describe and correct his error.

Mixed Review and Test Prep

24. 2,624 + 2,981 (p. 48)

25. 6,422 + 8,600 (p. 48)

26. Write four million, two hundred seventy-six thousand, one hundred three in standard form. (p. 6)

27. Order 100,430; 100,562; 99,650 from *greatest* to *least*. (p. 24)

28. **TEST PREP** The rectangular box for David's turtle is 90 cm long and 56 cm wide. How much shorter is the width than the length?

A 146 cm
B 94 cm
C 65 cm
D 34 cm

LESSON 5

Choose a Method

Learn

THINK BIG! In the United States, the two largest states are Alaska and Texas. What is the combined area in square miles of the two states?

Quick Review

1. 263 − 44
2. 630 − 463
3. 32 + 28 + 12
4. 23 + 17 + 41
5. 854 − 392

Example 1

Estimate. Then choose a method of computation.

600,000 + 300,000 = 900,000

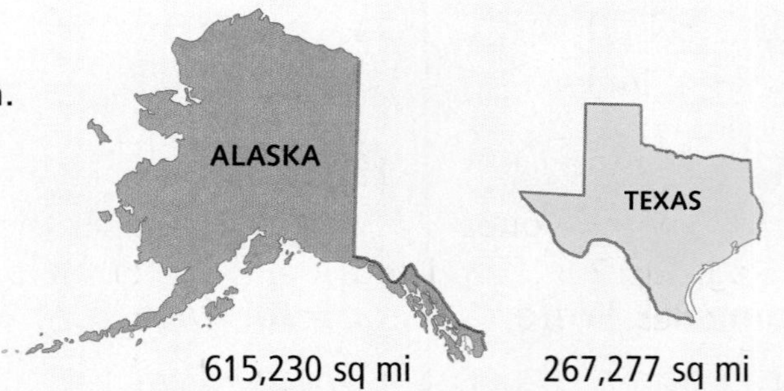

615,230 sq mi 267,277 sq mi

USE PAPER AND PENCIL Find the sum.

615,230 + 267,277

STEP 1

Add the ones and tens. Regroup 10 tens as 1 hundred 0 tens.

$$\begin{array}{r} \scriptstyle 1 \\ 615{,}230 \\ +267{,}277 \\ \hline 07 \end{array}$$

STEP 2

Add the hundreds and thousands. Regroup 12 thousands as 1 ten thousand 2 thousands.

$$\begin{array}{r} \scriptstyle 1\ \ 1 \\ 615{,}230 \\ +267{,}277 \\ \hline 2{,}507 \end{array}$$

STEP 3

Add the ten thousands.

$$\begin{array}{r} \scriptstyle 1\ \ 1 \\ 615{,}230 \\ +267{,}277 \\ \hline 82{,}507 \end{array}$$

STEP 4

Add the hundred thousands.

$$\begin{array}{r} \scriptstyle 1\ \ 1 \\ 615{,}230 \\ +267{,}277 \\ \hline 882{,}507 \end{array}$$

USE A CALCULATOR Find the sum.

6 1 5 2 3 0 +

2 6 7 2 7 7 Enter =

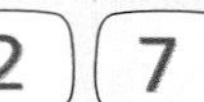

882507

So, Alaska and Texas have a combined area of 882,507 square miles. The answer is close to the estimate of 900,000, so 882,507 is reasonable.

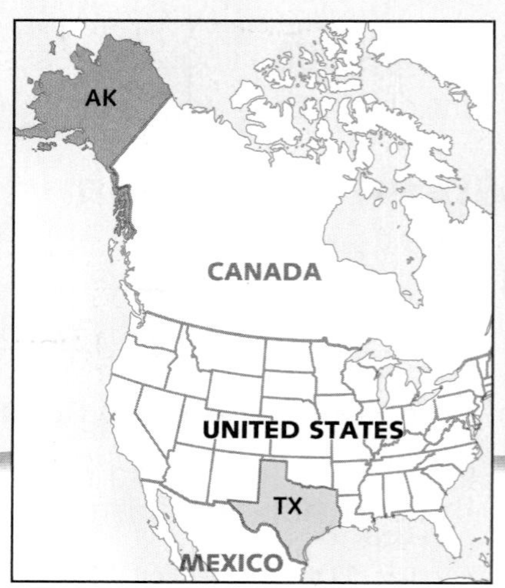

MENTAL MATH Is mental math a good choice for finding the sum of these numbers?

Subtract Greater Numbers

Matterhorn Peak in Colorado is 12,264 feet high. Mt. McKinley in Alaska is 20,320 feet high. How much higher is Mt. McKinley than Matterhorn Peak?

▲ Mt. McKinley, North America's highest mountain, is located in Denali National Park in Alaska.

Example 2

Estimate. Then choose a method to compute.

20,000 − 12,000 = 8,000

USE PAPER AND PENCIL Find the difference.

20,320 − 12,264

STEP 1

Subtract the ones.
Regroup 2 tens as 1 ten 10 ones.

```
        1 10
  2 0, 3 2 0
− 1 2, 2 6 4
            6
```

STEP 2

Subtract the tens and hundreds.
Regroup 3 hundreds 1 ten as 2 hundreds 11 tens.

```
         11
       2  1 10
  2 0, 3  2  0
− 1 2, 2  6  4
       0  5  6
```

STEP 3

Subtract the thousands and ten thousands.
Regroup 2 ten thousands 0 thousands as 1 ten thousand 10 thousands.

```
              11
  1 10     2   1 10
  2  0,    3   2  0
− 1  2,    2   6  4
     8,    0   5  6
```

USE A CALCULATOR Find the difference.

2 0 3 2 0 − 1 2 2 6 4 Enter =

20320−12264
= 8056

So, Mt. McKinley is 8,056 feet higher than Matterhorn Peak. The answer is close to the estimate of 8,000, so 8,056 is reasonable.

Check

1. **Explain** which method you would use to compute the sum of 7,890,040 and 2,109,060.

Find the sum or difference. Write the method you used to compute.

2. $98,634 − $62,512

3. 437,702 + 58,093

4. 500,600 − 263,710

5. 261,710 + 172,542

LESSON CONTINUES

Practice and Problem Solving

Extra Practice, page 58, Set E

Find the sum or difference. Write the method you used to compute.

6. $\begin{array}{r} \$983{,}368 \\ -\ \$261{,}125 \\ \hline \end{array}$ **7.** $\begin{array}{r} 51{,}237 \\ +\ 28{,}802 \\ \hline \end{array}$ **8.** $\begin{array}{r} 200{,}000 \\ +\ 134{,}902 \\ \hline \end{array}$ **9.** $\begin{array}{r} 265{,}710 \\ +\ 137{,}942 \\ \hline \end{array}$

10. $\begin{array}{r} 412{,}533 \\ +\ 283{,}056 \\ \hline \end{array}$ **11.** $\begin{array}{r} 584{,}201 \\ -\ 493{,}557 \\ \hline \end{array}$ **12.** $\begin{array}{r} \$784{,}200 \\ +\ \$\ \ 35{,}220 \\ \hline \end{array}$ **13.** $\begin{array}{r} 80{,}702 \\ -\ 60{,}698 \\ \hline \end{array}$

14. $\begin{array}{r} \$761{,}357 \\ -\ \$572{,}326 \\ \hline \end{array}$ **15.** $\begin{array}{r} 546{,}071 \\ +\ 291{,}503 \\ \hline \end{array}$ **16.** $\begin{array}{r} 63{,}200 \\ -\ 22{,}050 \\ \hline \end{array}$ **17.** $\begin{array}{r} 268{,}412 \\ +\ \ \ 37{,}287 \\ \hline \end{array}$

18. $33{,}333 + 214{,}142 + 527{,}998$

19. $211{,}500 + 201{,}943 + 14{,}159$

Compare. Write <, >, or = for each ●.

20. $637{,}124 - 215{,}275$ ● $784{,}725 - 398{,}419$

21. $323{,}125 + 125{,}362$ ● $342{,}125 + 125{,}362$

22. $211{,}345 + 467{,}311$ ● $200{,}457 + 478{,}199$

23. Find the difference of 723,503 and 500,497.

24. Find the sum of 864,235 and 252,214.

25. Find the difference of 974,210 and 473,689.

26. Find the sum of 670,000 and 220,925.

Find the missing digit.

27. $\begin{array}{r} 43\blacksquare{,}257 \\ -\ 253{,}019 \\ \hline 186{,}238 \end{array}$ **28.** $\begin{array}{r} 278{,}269 \\ +\ 921{,}57\blacksquare \\ \hline 1{,}199{,}843 \end{array}$ **29.** $\begin{array}{r} 156{,}217 \\ +\ \blacksquare 32{,}368 \\ \hline 788{,}585 \end{array}$ **30.** $\begin{array}{r} 461{,}335 \\ -\ 31\blacksquare{,}288 \\ \hline 149{,}047 \end{array}$

31. In 2002, a theater spent \$112,840 on equipment. In 2003, \$97,560 was spent. What was the total amount spent? Was more money spent in 2002 or 2003?

32. The play *Clue* had 47,250 performances. The play *The Mousetrap* had 18,872 performances. How many more performances were given of the play *Clue*?

▲ **This outdoor theater is located in Wolf Trap National Park for the Performing Arts, in Vienna, Virginia.**

33. Lori wrote a number that is thirty-one thousand, five hundred twenty-three greater than 17,996. What number did she write?

34. **Write a problem** using the data. There are 479,743 people in Wyoming and 609,331 people in Alaska.

35. Kyle got on the elevator on the fourth floor. He went down 2 floors and then up 6 floors and got off. On which floor did Kyle get off the elevator?

36. Mr. Randall sold 1,285 wooden cutouts at his crafts booth. He has 298 left. How many cutouts did Mr. Randall have to start with?

Mixed Review and Test Prep

USE DATA For 37–38, use the table. (p. 52)

FALL FOLIAGE FESTIVAL ATTENDANCE		
Day	**2003**	**2004**
Thursday	13,789	15,034
Friday	23,681	27,950
Saturday	34,625	41,393

37. What was the total attendance at the festival in 2003 for all 3 days?

38. How many more people attended the festival in 2004 than in 2003?

39. Which is less: 315,731 or 351,731? (p. 20)

40. How many people are between the fifth and twelfth in line for a movie?

41. **TEST PREP** What is five million, twenty-five thousand, ten in standard form? (p. 6)

A 5,025,100 **C** 525,210
B 5,025,010 **D** 525,100

42. **TEST PREP** Which is the difference? (p. 52)

489,211 − 16,179

F 451,389 **H** 497,230
G 473,032 **J** 505,390

Problem Solving Thinker's Corner

CLUSTERING

Baseball stadiums seat tens of thousands of fans. Look at the data in the table. Notice that the numbers cluster, or gather, around 50,000. You can use this fact to help you estimate the total number of seats in the stadiums.

BASEBALL STADIUM SEATING CAPACITIES	
Team	**Capacity**
Atlanta Braves	50,062
Baltimore Orioles	48,876
Cincinnati Reds	52,953
Milwaukee Brewers	53,192
Minnesota Twins	48,678
Montreal Expos	46,500
Pittsburgh Pirates	47,687
St. Louis Cardinals	49,738

1. Estimate the number of seats in the 3 stadiums with the greatest number of seats.
2. Estimate the number of seats in the 3 stadiums with the least number of seats.
3. Compare your totals. Explain why there is no difference between your totals.

LESSON 6

Problem Solving Skill
Estimate or Find Exact Answers

UNDERSTAND → PLAN → SOLVE → CHECK

Quick Review

Compare. Write <, >, or = for each ●.

1. 1,374 ● 1,367
2. 3,549 ● 4,539
3. 8,632 ● 8,632
4. 5,046 ● 5,406
5. 4,573 ● 4,357

FANS IN THE STANDS The table shows five games ranked by attendance.

BASEBALL GAME ATTENDANCE		
Rank	**Attendance**	**Team**
1	80,227	Montreal vs. Colorado
2	78,672	San Francisco vs. Los Angeles
3	74,420	Detroit vs. Cleveland
4	73,163	St. Louis vs. Cleveland
5	72,470	Philadelphia vs. Colorado

MATH IDEA Whether you need an exact answer or an estimate depends on the situation.

Examples

A About how many people attended a game played by Colorado?

Estimate to find the number of people.

$$\begin{array}{rcr} 80{,}227 & \rightarrow & 80{,}000 \\ +72{,}470 & \rightarrow & +70{,}000 \\ & & \hline 150{,}000 \end{array}$$

So, about 150,000 people attended.

B How many more people attended the Detroit game than the Philadelphia game?

Subtract to find an exact answer.

$$\begin{array}{r} 74{,}420 \\ -72{,}470 \\ \hline 1{,}950 \end{array}$$

(regrouping marks: 3, 13, 3, 12)

So, 1,950 more people attended.

Talk About It

- Tell whether you need an estimate or an exact answer to find how many more people attended the Montreal game than the Philadelphia game.

Problem Solving Practice

For 1–2, tell whether an estimate or an exact answer is needed. Solve.

1. Brianne bought a baseball hat and a pennant. How much change will she get from $20?
2. About how much money does Andy need to buy a baseball bat and baseball at the park?
3. The stadium shop sold 70 bats and 120 hats during the first game and 82 bats and 96 hats during the second game. Which question requires an exact calculation to answer?

   A Did the shop sell more bats or more hats?

   B About how many more hats than bats were sold during the second game?

   C How many hats were sold in all?

   D Did the shop sell more than 150 bats?

4. Which expression would be best to use to estimate by rounding the total cost of 2 hats and 2 bats?

   F $15 + $15 + $25 + $25

   G $10 + $10 + $10 + $10

   H $10 + $10 + $20 + $20

   J $20 + $20 + $20 + $20

Mixed Applications

5. At a college, 1,825 students signed up to play an indoor sport, and 2,984 signed up for an outdoor sport. Write an expression to show how many students signed up for a sport.
6. Of the students enrolled at the college, 1,408 are from Alabama, 1,450 are from Florida, and 1,230 are from Louisiana. Which of these states do the most students come from?
7. There are 9,470 students who live on campus. If there are 11,652 students in all, how many students do not live on campus?
8. In the football stadium, there are 66,322 seats. There are 2,974 people watching a practice game. How many seats are empty?
9. The School of Science bought a new telescope for $8,376. Write the number in word form.
10. **Write a problem** in which you need to find an estimated sum or difference.

Extra Practice

Set A (pp. 40–43)

Add or subtract mentally. Tell the strategy you used.

1. $98 + 46$
2. $109 - 94$
3. $246 + 176$
4. $64 - 23$
5. $346 + 79$
6. $169 - 104$

Set B (pp. 44–47)

Estimate the sum or difference by using rounding.

1. $\begin{array}{r} 16{,}453 \\ -11{,}019 \\ \hline \end{array}$
2. $\begin{array}{r} 678{,}401 \\ +259{,}345 \\ \hline \end{array}$
3. $\begin{array}{r} 27{,}645 \\ -10{,}067 \\ \hline \end{array}$

Estimate the sum or difference by using front-end estimation.

4. $\begin{array}{r} 85{,}103 \\ -76{,}495 \\ \hline \end{array}$
5. $\begin{array}{r} 405{,}501 \\ +570{,}201 \\ \hline \end{array}$
6. $\begin{array}{r} 854{,}633 \\ +941{,}053 \\ \hline \end{array}$

Set C (pp. 48–49)

Find the sum or difference. Estimate to check.

1. $\begin{array}{r} 625 \\ +292 \\ \hline \end{array}$
2. $\begin{array}{r} 9{,}004 \\ -5{,}762 \\ \hline \end{array}$
3. $\begin{array}{r} 2{,}435 \\ +2{,}576 \\ \hline \end{array}$
4. $941 - 701$
5. $1{,}241 + 1{,}367 + 495$
6. $9{,}204 - 4{,}352$

Set D (pp. 50–51)

Find the difference. Estimate to check.

1. $\begin{array}{r} 8{,}000 \\ -4{,}934 \\ \hline \end{array}$
2. $\begin{array}{r} 6{,}001 \\ -\quad 638 \\ \hline \end{array}$
3. $\begin{array}{r} 9{,}040 \\ -3{,}401 \\ \hline \end{array}$
4. $\begin{array}{r} 2{,}000 \\ -1{,}764 \\ \hline \end{array}$
5. $\begin{array}{r} 1{,}600 \\ -1{,}041 \\ \hline \end{array}$
6. $\begin{array}{r} 4{,}006 \\ -1{,}706 \\ \hline \end{array}$
7. $\begin{array}{r} 3{,}900 \\ -1{,}461 \\ \hline \end{array}$
8. $\begin{array}{r} 7{,}060 \\ -1{,}515 \\ \hline \end{array}$

Set E (pp. 52–55)

Find the sum or difference. Write the method you used to compute.

1. $\begin{array}{r} 11{,}420 \\ +92{,}780 \\ \hline \end{array}$
2. $\begin{array}{r} 496{,}140 \\ +328{,}628 \\ \hline \end{array}$
3. $\begin{array}{r} 46{,}709 \\ -13{,}456 \\ \hline \end{array}$
4. $\begin{array}{r} 950{,}275 \\ -450{,}550 \\ \hline \end{array}$

Review/Test

CHECK VOCABULARY AND CONCEPTS

Choose the best term from the box.

estimate
front-end estimation
rounding

1. You use _?_ when you add the front digit of each addend to get an estimate. (pp. 44–47)
2. Sometimes you need an exact answer, while at other times, all you need is an _?_. (pp. 56–57)

CHECK SKILLS

Add or subtract mentally. Tell the strategy you used. (pp. 40–43)

3. $43 - 27$
4. $54 + 37$
5. $89 + 17$
6. $92 - 43$
7. $65 + 49$

Estimate the sum or difference. (pp. 44–47)

8. 32,895 + 27,982
9. $34,698 − $11,683
10. 53,625 − 24,219
11. 93,863 + 68,410
12. 538,195 + 273,982
13. $4,669 − $1,028
14. 7,516 − 2,495
15. 853,467 − 387,410

Find the sum or difference. (pp. 48–55)

16. 258 + 784
17. 925 − 378
18. 8,586 − 455
19. 7,448 − 1,737
20. 5,000 + 3,718
21. 35,276 − 22,865
22. 784,109 − 426,545
23. 30,019 − 12,645

CHECK PROBLEM SOLVING

Write whether an estimate or an exact answer is needed. Solve. (pp. 56–57)

24. The school cafeteria served 115 cartons of whole milk, 78 cartons of chocolate milk, and 35 cartons of orange juice. About how many drinks were served?

25. Ellie will win a prize if she sells 400 boxes of cookies this year. If she sold 113 in January, 107 in February, and 68 in March, how many more boxes does she need to sell to win a prize?

Standardized Test Prep

NUMBER SENSE, CONCEPTS, AND OPERATIONS

1. Mike had $4,200. He bought a motorcycle for $3,275 and a leather jacket for $799. How much does Mike have left?

   A $4,074 C $136

   B $226 D $126

TIP **Understand the problem.** See item 2. Use the details in the question. Look for a 4 in the tens place, and then compare the numbers to 620.

2. Which number is **greater than** 620 and has a 4 in the tens place?

   F 540

   G 604

   H 640

   J 654

3. **Explain It** The table below shows some data about the Brooklyn Bridge.

BROOKLYN BRIDGE	
Description	**Length (in feet)**
Total length	5,989
Length of river span	1,596
Length of one cable	3,579

About how much longer is the total length of the bridge than one of the cables? Use rounding or front-end estimation. Explain how you decided.

MEASUREMENT

4. What is the perimeter of the figure below?

   A 4 units C 8 units

   B 6 units D 12 units

5. Sue is meeting her friend in Miami 9 days after October 17. On what date is Sue meeting her friend?

October						
Sun	Mon	Tue	Wed	Thu	Fri	Sat
			1	2	3	4
5	6	7	8	9	10	11
12	13	14	15	16	17	18
19	20	21	22	23	24	25
26	27	28	29	30	31	

   F October 9

   G October 18

   H October 24

   J October 26

6. **Explain It** What is the length of the nail below to the nearest centimeter?

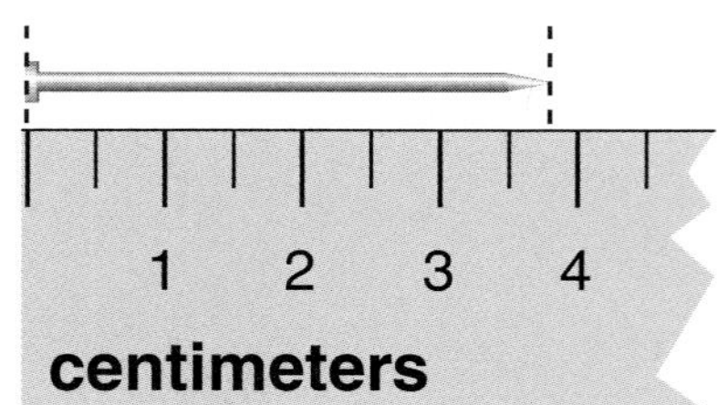

Explain how you decided.

GEOMETRY AND SPATIAL SENSE

7. Which solid has the **greatest** number of faces?

A 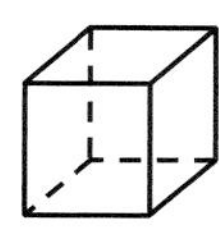

C 

B 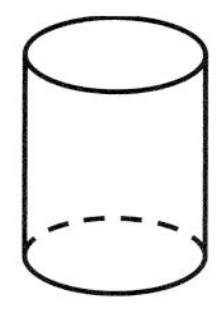

D 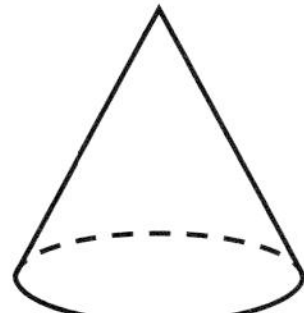

8. Which shape has at least one line of symmetry?

F 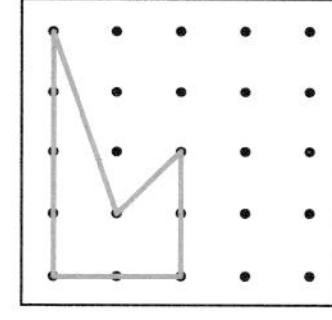

H 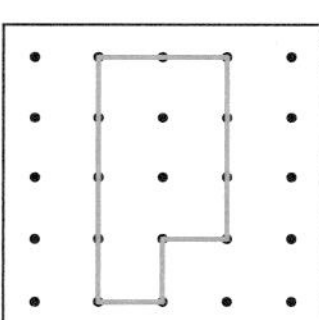

G 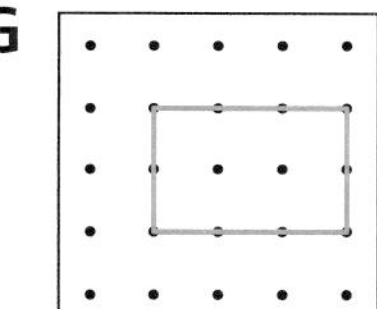

J 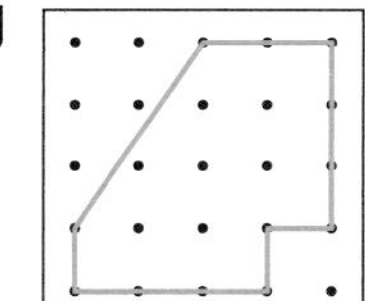

9. **Explain It** José plotted 3 points on the coordinate grid. What is the ordered pair of the point José needs to plot to make a square? Explain your thinking.

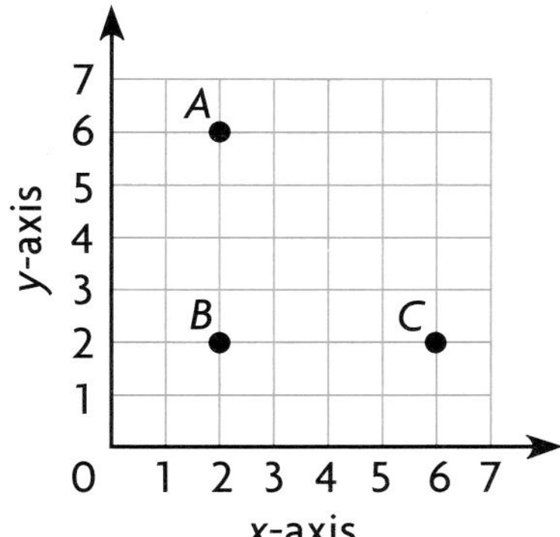

DATA ANALYSIS AND PROBABILITY

10. A dart is thrown, and it hits the dartboard. What are the possible outcomes?

A 1, 2, 3

B 1, 10, 100

C 1, 10, 50, 500

D 10; 100; 1,000

11. Jan made the graph below to show her weekly assignments.

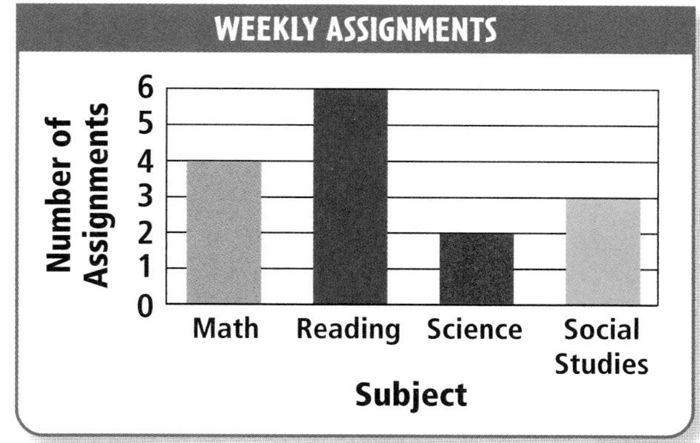

In which subject did Jan get the **fewest** homework assignments?

F math

G reading

H social studies

J science

12. **Explain It** The graph below shows the number of students who attended Depauw Elementary each year.

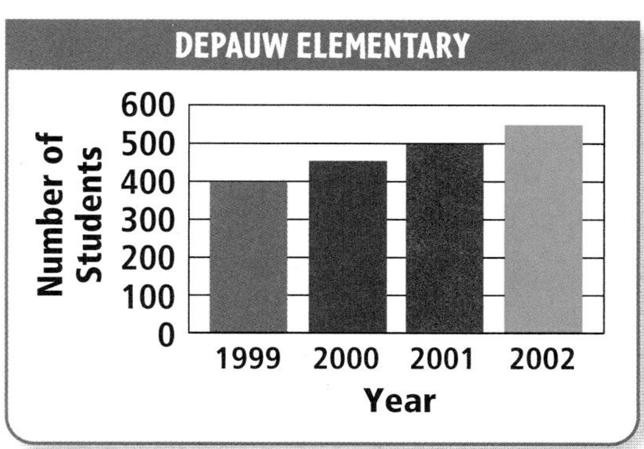

If the trend continued, about how many students attended in 2003? Explain your thinking.

CHAPTER 4

Algebra: Use Addition and Subtraction

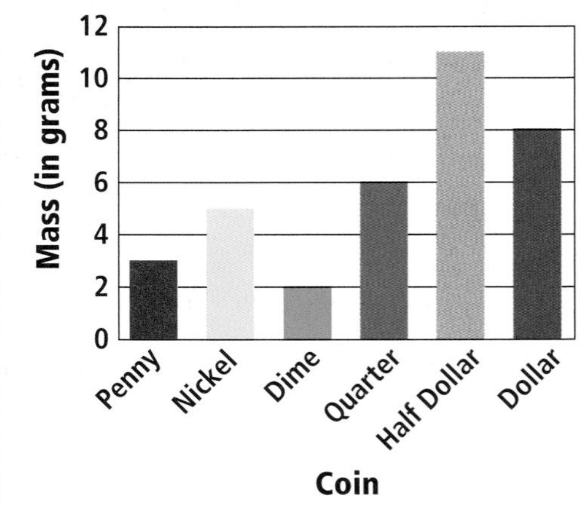

FAST FACT • SOCIAL STUDIES On April 2, 1792, Congress created the United States Mint. The United States Mint's primary mission is to produce enough coins for people to use. It produces six coins of different values, sizes, and masses.

PROBLEM SOLVING The mass of one dime plus the mass of what other coin is equal to the mass of one dollar?

CHECK WHAT YOU KNOW

Use this page to help you review and remember important skills needed for Chapter 4.

MISSING ADDENDS

Find the missing number.

1. $\blacksquare + 4 = 12$
2. $6 + \blacksquare = 14$
3. $\blacksquare + 5 = 12$
4. $9 + \blacksquare = 15$
5. $7 + \blacksquare = 16$
6. $7 + \blacksquare = 10$
7. $8 + \blacksquare = 16$
8. $\blacksquare + 9 = 19$
9. $9 + \blacksquare = 17$

FACT FAMILIES

Copy and complete each number sentence.

10. $5 + 2 = \blacksquare$
    $7 - 2 = \blacksquare$
11. $6 + 3 = \blacksquare$
    $9 - 3 = \blacksquare$
12. $8 + 1 = \blacksquare$
    $9 - 1 = \blacksquare$
13. $7 + 6 = \blacksquare$
    $13 - 7 = \blacksquare$
14. $9 + 5 = \blacksquare$
    $14 - 9 = \blacksquare$
15. $7 + 8 = \blacksquare$
    $15 - 8 = \blacksquare$
16. $8 + 8 = \blacksquare$
    $16 - 8 = \blacksquare$
17. $4 + 7 = \blacksquare$
    $11 - 4 = \blacksquare$

NUMBER PATTERNS

Write the next three possible numbers in the pattern.

18. 10, 20, 30, 40, ■, ■, ■
19. 25, 30, 35, 40, ■, ■, ■
20. 30, 26, 22, 18, ■, ■, ■
21. 99, 88, 77, 66, ■, ■, ■

VOCABULARY POWER

REVIEW

equal [ē´kwəl] *adjective*

In mathematics, the word *equal* is used to describe amounts with the same value. Common related words include *equality, equalize,* and *unequaled.* How are the meanings of these words related to the mathematical meaning of *equal*?

PREVIEW

expression
variable
equation
Commutative Property
Associative Property
Identity Property

www.harcourtschool.com/mathglossary

LESSON 1

Expressions

Quick Review

Add 15 to each number.

1. 460 **2.** 523

3. 196 **4.** 837

5. 728

VOCABULARY

expression

variable

Learn

FANCY FLOWERS Sue had 12 flowers. Lily gave her 4 more flowers. Sue gave her teacher 3 of her flowers. How many does she have left?

You can write an expression to find the number of flowers Sue has left.

An **expression** has numbers and operation signs. It does not have an equal sign.

Think: 12 flowers plus 4 flowers, minus 3 flowers

↓ ↓ ↓ ↓ ↓

(12 + 4) − 3

Find the value of $(12 + 4) - 3$.

$(12 + 4) - 3$ Add 12 and 4.

↓

$16 - 3$ Subtract 3 from 16.

↓

13

So, $(12 + 4) - 3$ is 13. Sue has 13 flowers left.

Parentheses tell which operation to do first. Expressions with the same numbers and operations can have different values, depending on where you place parentheses.

Examples

A Find the value of $(9 - 5) + 2$.

$(9 - 5) + 2$ Subtract 5 from 9.

↓

$4 + 2$ Add 4 and 2.

↓

6

So, the value of $(9 - 5) + 2$ is 6.

B Find the value of $9 - (5 + 2)$.

$9 - (5 + 2)$ Add 5 and 2.

↓

$9 - 7$ Subtract 7 from 9.

↓

2

So, the value of $9 - (5 + 2)$ is 2.

- How is Example A different from Example B?

Expressions with Variables

Fergus planted 3 rows in his garden in the morning. In the afternoon, he planted some more rows. What expression can you write to show the total number of rows he planted?

You can use a variable to show the number of rows he planted in the afternoon. A **variable** is a letter or symbol that represents any number you don't know.

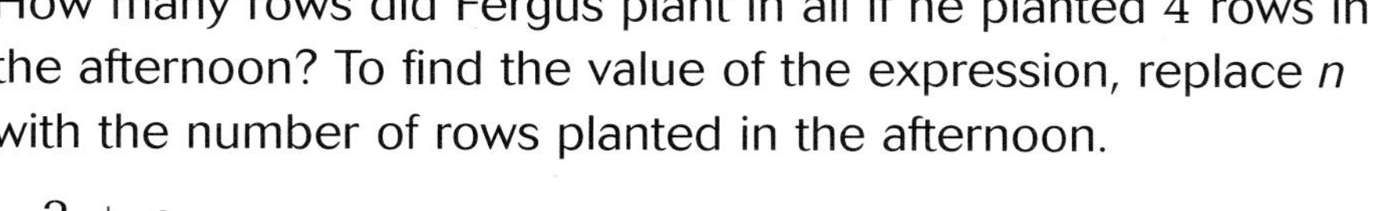

3 rows planted in the morning plus some more rows planted

$$3 + n$$

So, the expression showing the total number of rows is $3 + n$.

How many rows did Fergus plant in all if he planted 4 rows in the afternoon? To find the value of the expression, replace n with the number of rows planted in the afternoon.

$3 + n$

$3 + 4$ ← Replace n with 4 since he planted 4 rows in the afternoon.

↓

7

So, Fergus planted 7 rows in all.

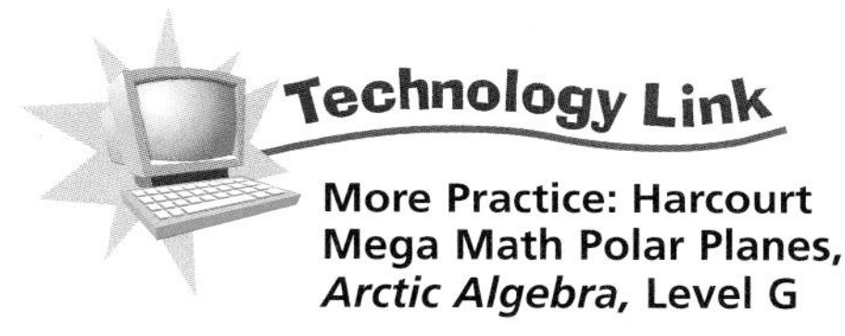

More Practice: Harcourt Mega Math Polar Planes, *Arctic Algebra*, Level G

More Examples

C Find the value of $9 - c$ if $c = 2$.

$9 - c$ Replace c with 2.

↓

$9 - 2$ Subtract 2 from 9.

↓

7

So, the value of the expression is 7.

D Find the value of $8 + (m - 2)$ if $m = 6$.

$8 + (m - 2)$ Replace m with 6.

↓

$8 + (6 - 2)$ Subtract 2 from 6.

↓

$8 + 4$ Add 8 and 4.

↓

12

So, the value of the expression is 12.

Check

1. **Explain** when you need to use a variable when writing an expression.

LESSON CONTINUES

Write an expression.

2. Eight people were at the party, then 7 more arrived.

3. Mike had 21 toy cars. He gave 4 of them to a friend, then got 5 more.

Write an expression. Choose a variable for the unknown. Tell what the variable represents.

4. There were 22 students in the class, but some were absent.

5. Chris had 18 cards. Then he bought some more, but lost 7.

Find the value of each expression.

6. $5 + 2 + 6$

7. $(8 - 7) + 1$

8. $6 - (3 + 2)$

Find the value of each expression if $g = 6$.

9. $g + 9$

10. $(g - 4) + 7$

11. $5 + (12 - g)$

Practice and Problem Solving

Extra Practice, page 82, Set A

Write an expression.

12. The class collected 15 bags of trash, then collected 12 more bags.

13. A room had 25 desks. Five desks were added, then 3 were removed.

Write an expression. Choose a variable for the unknown. Tell what the variable represents.

14. Susan had 24 stamps. She used some of the stamps to mail letters.

15. There were 4 pizzas at the party, then people ate 3 of them and ordered some more.

16. Nancy had 23 books. Her dad bought some books and gave Nancy all but 3 of them.

17. Carly starts with 37 pieces of candy. She gives one piece to each student in her class, and one to each of her 2 brothers.

Find the value of each expression.

18. $17 - 9 - 6$

19. $(25 - 10) + 8$

20. $(62 - 40) + 31$

Find the value of each expression if $a = 12$ and $b = 7$.

21. $50 - a$

22. $a + 10$

23. $(b + 6) + a$

Write words to match each expression.

24. $14 + 9$

25. $c + (8 - 4)$

26. $80 - (47 - g)$

27. **Vocabulary Power** The word *operation* is from a Latin word meaning "work." How do operations such as addition or subtraction "work" on numbers?

28. **? What's the Error?** David said that the value of $40 - (d + 16)$ is 40 if $d = 16$. Describe and correct his error.

29. A teacher donated 35 folders, 17 books, and 45 pencils to the school carnival. How many items did the teacher donate?

30. What whole numbers can k and m be if the expression $30 - (k + m)$ has a value of 25?

Mixed Review and Test Prep

For 31–32, use the graph.

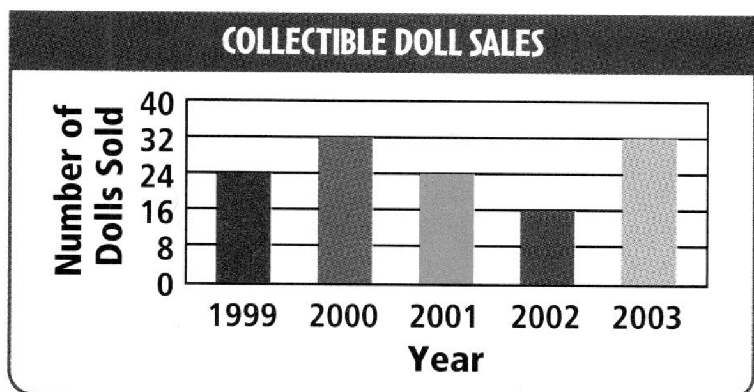

31. How many more dolls were sold in 2000 than in 2002?

32. What was the total number of dolls sold in the years 1999 to 2003?

33. Natalie read three books. One book had 368 pages, another had 331 pages, and the last book had 373 pages. Order the books from greatest number of pages to least number of pages. (p. 24)

34. **TEST PREP** If 256 people attended the 5:00 P.M. showing of a movie and 324 people attended the 7:30 P.M. showing of the movie, how many people attended the movie? (p. 48)

A 680 **C** 570

B 580 **D** 500

35. **TEST PREP** Which gives the same number whether it is rounded to the nearest thousand or to the nearest ten thousand? (p. 30)

F 56,037

G 49,411

H 64,348

J 50,485

Problem Solving LINKUP. . . to Health

The Food Guide Pyramid is a chart showing the food groups and the recommended number of servings from each group.

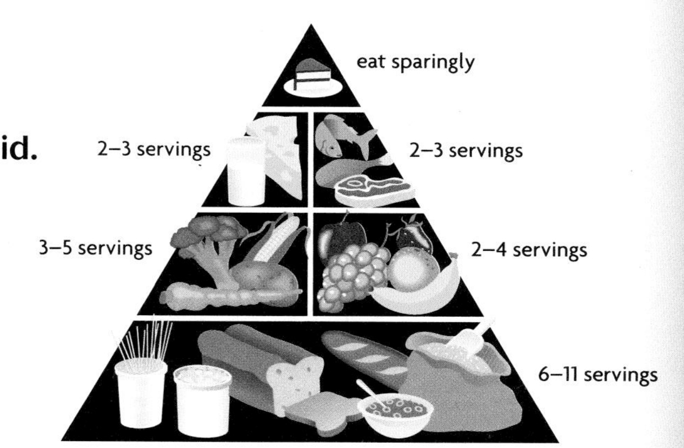

USE DATA For 1–2, use the Food Guide Pyramid.

1. Andy ate 2 servings from the breads and cereals group for breakfast. He had another 3 servings at lunch, and some for dinner. Did he have more than the lowest recommended number of servings if he had 3 servings at dinner? Explain.

2. What expression could you write for the highest recommended number of servings from the vegetable group minus some number of servings of broccoli?

LESSON

2 Addition Properties

Quick Review

1. 2 + (3 + 6)
2. 14 − (6 + 7)
3. (13 − 8) + 5
4. (22 + 17) − 22
5. 30 − (19 − 11)

VOCABULARY

Commutative Property
Associative Property
Identity Property

Learn

COIN COLLECTORS Lynda and her brother Bill collect quarters and half dollars. Lynda has 32 quarters and 20 half dollars. Bill has the same number of coins in his collection. If he has 20 quarters, how many half dollars does he have?

Lynda's coins		Bill's coins
32 quarters + 20 half dollars		20 quarters + ■ half dollars
↓ ↓ ↓		↓ ↓ ↓
32 + 20	=	20 + ■

Numbers can be added in any order and the sum will be the same. This is called the Order Property, or **Commutative Property**.

Since 32 + 20 = 20 + 32, then ■ = 32.

So, Bill has 32 half dollars.

There are two other addition properties you can use when you add.

The Grouping Property, or **Associative Property**, states that the way addends are grouped does not change the sum.

(14 + 25) + 45 = 14 + (25 + 45)
↓ ↓
39 + 45 = 14 + 70
↓ ↓
84 = 84

The Zero Property, or **Identity Property**, states that when you add zero to any number, the sum is that number.

56 + 0 = 56
0 + 56 = 56

Examples Evaluate the expression.

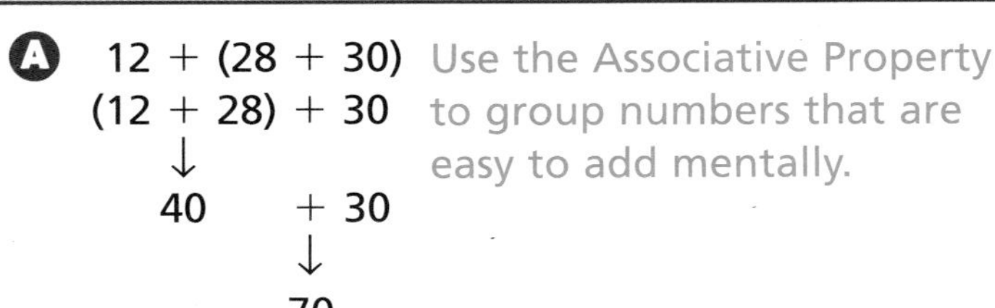

A 12 + (28 + 30) Use the Associative Property to group numbers that are easy to add mentally.
(12 + 28) + 30
↓
40 + 30
↓
70

B 16 + 9 + 4 Use the Commutative Property to change the order of numbers.
16 + 4 + 9
↓
20 + 9
↓
29

Check

1. **Explain** how the Commutative Property and the Associative Property are alike and how they are different.

Find the missing number, and tell which addition property you used.

2. $\blacksquare + 32 = 32$
3. $14 + 8 = 8 + \blacksquare$
4. $(4 + 9) + 5 = 4 + (\blacksquare + 5)$
5. $7 + 4 = \blacksquare + 7$
6. $0 + \blacksquare = 80$
7. $\blacksquare + (3 + 5) = (7 + 3) + 5$

Practice and Problem Solving

Extra Practice, page 82, Set B

Find the missing number, and tell which addition property you used.

8. $12 + 64 = \blacksquare + 12$
9. $14 = 0 + \blacksquare$
10. $(23 + 17) = (\blacksquare + 23)$
11. $90 + \blacksquare = 90$
12. $(1 + 17) + 1 = \blacksquare + (17 + 1)$
13. $(4 + 9) + \blacksquare = 4 + (9 + 1)$

Change the order or group the addends so that you can add them mentally. Find the sum. Tell which property you used.

14. $17 + 40 + 3$
15. $34 + 46 + 7$
16. $13 + 30 + 70$
17. $23 + 12 + 77 + 12$
18. $800 + 347 + 3 + 200$
19. $1{,}500 + 1{,}500 + 1{,}490$
20. Write 3 different expressions that show the amount of money you have if you have a quarter, a dime, and a nickel.
21. **Write About It** Explain why you might want to change the order or grouping of addends when finding a sum.
22. Which expression has a greater value: $18 - (19 - 17)$ or $17 + (19 - 18)$? Explain.

Mixed Review and Test Prep

For 23–24, find the value of each expression if $c = 17$. (p. 64)

23. $c + 19 - 15$
24. $50 - (c + 2)$
25. Order the numbers 7,969; 7,964; and 7,975 from least to greatest. (p. 24)
26. $4{,}900 - 3{,}244$ (p. 48)
27. **TEST PREP** Which number makes this statement true? (p. 24)

$$436{,}251 < \blacksquare < 526{,}251$$

A 536,251
B 526,251
C 436,251
D 456,251

LESSON

3 Equations

Quick Review

1. $17 + 35 = \square$
2. $24 + \square = 42$
3. $56 - 27 = \square$
4. $49 - \square = 31$
5. $\square + 58 = 96$

VOCABULARY

equation

Learn

GOOD VIBRATIONS Richard had 12 CDs in his collection. He got some more CDs for his birthday. Now he has a total of 15 CDs. What equation can you write to show this?

An **equation** is a number sentence stating that two amounts are equal.

12 CDs plus some CDs equals 15 CDs.

$$\begin{array}{ccccc} \downarrow & \downarrow & \downarrow & \downarrow & \downarrow \\ 12 & + & c & = & 15 \end{array}$$

So, the equation is $12 + c = 15$. The variable c represents the number of CDs Richard received for his birthday.

Examples Write an equation. Choose a variable for the unknown.

A 5 tickets plus some extra tickets are 45 tickets. Let t stand for the number of extra tickets.

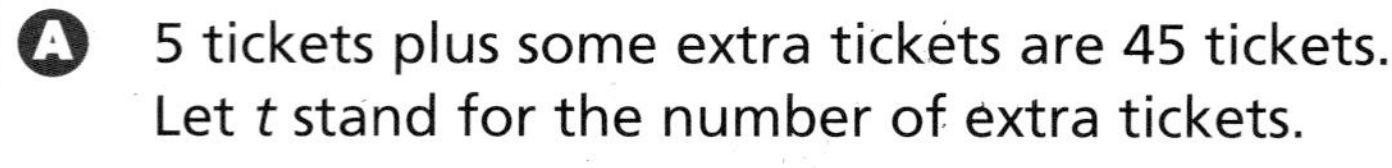

5 + the number of extra tickets = 45

$$\begin{array}{ccc} \downarrow & \downarrow & \downarrow \\ 5\ + & t & = 45 \end{array}$$

The equation is $5 + t = 45$.

B There are some students. Eight students leave. Now there are 24 students. Let n stand for the beginning number of students.

the beginning number of students − 8 = 24

$$\begin{array}{ccc} \downarrow & \downarrow & \downarrow \\ n & -\ 8 & = 24 \end{array}$$

The equation is $n - 8 = 24$.

- **REASONING** How would you write the equation in Example B if there were only 18 students left?

MATH IDEA You can use a variable to represent an unknown number when writing either equations or expressions.

Solve Equations Mentally

How many CDs did Richard receive for his birthday?

An equation is true if the values on both sides of the equal sign are equal. You solve an equation when you find the value of a variable that makes the equation true. You can solve this equation using mental math.

$12 + c = 15$ — **Think:** 12 plus what number equals 15?

$c = 3$

Check: $12 + 3 \stackrel{?}{=} 15$ — Replace c with 3.

$15 = 15$ ✓ — The equation is true. The value of c is 3.

So, Richard received 3 CDs for his birthday.

More Examples Solve the equation.

C $6 + m = 10$ — **Think:** 6 plus what number equals 10?

$m = 4$

Check: $6 + 4 \stackrel{?}{=} 10$ — Replace m with 4.

$10 = 10$ ✓ — The equation is true.

So, the value of m is 4.

D $g - 8 = 3$ — **Think:** What number minus 8 equals 3?

$g = 11$

Check: $11 - 8 \stackrel{?}{=} 3$ — Replace g with 11.

$3 = 3$ ✓ — The equation is true.

So, the value of g is 11.

Check

1. **Explain** how you know when the value of a variable in an equation is correct.

Write an equation. Choose a variable for the unknown. Tell what the variable represents.

2. There are some boxes of cereal on a shelf. Pauline takes 3 boxes. Now there are 12 boxes on the shelf.
3. There are 15 apples on the table. Five of them are red and the others are green.

Solve the equation by using mental math. Check your solution.

4. $b + 7 = 17$
5. $d - 4 = 8$
6. $5 = 4 + r$
7. $22 - m = 10$
8. $6 = n - 7$
9. $12 + w = 14$

LESSON CONTINUES

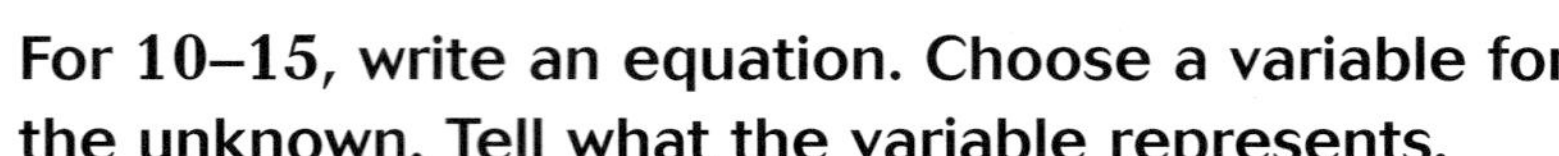

Practice and Problem Solving

Extra Practice, page 82, Set C

For 10–15, write an equation. Choose a variable for the unknown. Tell what the variable represents.

10. There are 25 sodas in a machine. Mr. Lee adds some sodas. Now there are 42 sodas.

11. Randy had 10 pieces of string. He gave some away. Now he has 3 pieces of string.

12. There are 35 crayons in a box. Four are red. The rest are other colors.

13. Mira added 12 pennies to a jar of pennies. Now there are 74 pennies in the jar.

14. Joe had 115 CDs. Kate gave him some more. Now Joe has 118 CDs.

15. Javier has 420 points. He has 30 fewer points than Maria.

Solve the equation by using mental math. Check your solution.

16. $x + 12 = 17$

17. $8 + p = 14$

18. $q - 7 = 0$

19. $20 - c = 11$

20. $2 = 7 - m$

21. $15 = z + 5$

22. $3 + k = 3$

23. $13 - g = 12$

24. $n - 10 = 1$

Write words to match the equation.

25. $c + 5 = 19$

26. $8 - m = 4$

27. $45 = 13 + g$

USE DATA For 28–29, use the table.

CLASSROOM CD COLLECTION	
Type of Music	**Number of CDs**
Classical	12
Jazz	11
World Music	3
Popular	7

28. Write an equation, using the variable n, to show the total number of classical and jazz CDs.

29. The classroom had some popular CDs and then got 4 more. Write an equation to show the number of popular CDs it had originally. Tell what the variable represents.

30. The zoo has 20 animals in its ape exhibit. There are 8 gorillas, 7 chimpanzees, and the rest are orangutans and gibbons. Could there be 2 orangutans and 4 gibbons? Explain.

31. **What's the Question?** Kathy has 8 pets: 2 dogs, 3 cats, and some birds. She used the equation $5 + n = 8$. The answer is $n = 3$.

32. A post office sold 2,567 stamps on Monday and 1,614 stamps on Tuesday. How many more stamps were sold on Monday than on Tuesday?

33. ***FAST FACT*** • **SCIENCE** Music CDs were introduced in 1982. Nine years later, for the first time, more CDs than audiocassettes were sold. Write an equation to find what year this happened.

Mixed Review and Test Prep

34. Heath had 24 comic books. He gave 6 to Sam and then bought 3 more. Write an expression to show how many comic books Heath has now. (p. 64)

35. $1,463 + 2,896$ (p. 48)

36. $6,000 - 4,756$ (p. 50)

For 37–38, find the value of the expression if $c = 12$. (p. 64)

37. $c + 7$

38. $18 - (c + 1)$

39. TEST PREP Which is 1,000 more than 35,921? (p. 2)

A 45,921
B 34,921
C 36,921
D 44,921

40. TEST PREP Which property of addition does this equation show? (p. 68)

$12 + (45 + 28) = (12 + 45) + 28$

F Commutative
G Identity
H Zero
J Associative

Problem Solving Thinker's Corner

EQUATIONS ON A NUMBER LINE

Sometimes you can use a number line to solve an equation.

Solve $16 + n = 22$.

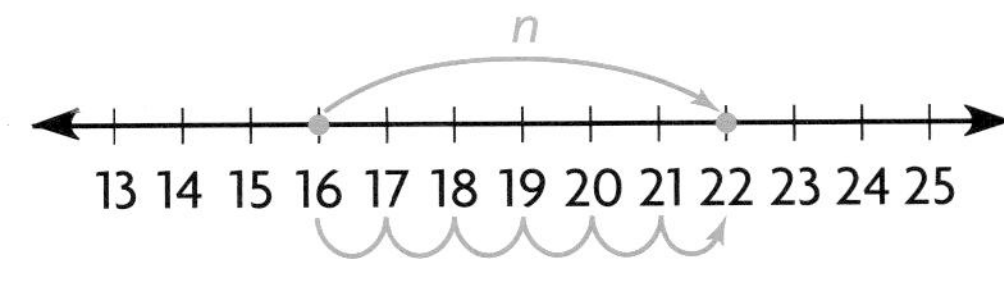

- Draw a number line and plot 16 and 22.
- Count the number of spaces from 16 to 22. This number is the value of n.
- $n = 6$

Check: $16 + 6 \stackrel{?}{=} 22$ Replace n with 6.
$22 = 22$ ✓ The equation is true.

So, the value of n is 6.

Solve $37 - m = 30$.

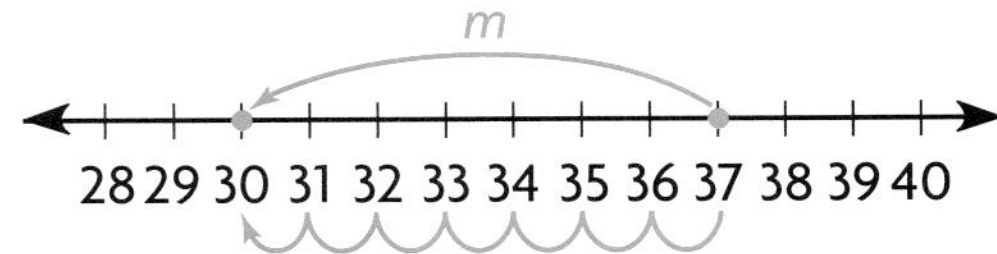

- Draw a number line and plot 30 and 37.
- Count the number of spaces from 37 to 30. This number is the value of m.
- $m = 7$

Check: $37 - 7 \stackrel{?}{=} 30$ Replace m with 7.
$30 = 30$ ✓ The equation is true.

So, the value of m is 7.

Use a number line to solve the equation. Check your solution.

1. $c + 25 = 30$ **2.** $23 + m = 28$ **3.** $g - 4 = 41$ **4.** $24 = x - 8$

5. $24 = y + 15$ **6.** $17 - b = 13$ **7.** $38 + a = 49$ **8.** $32 = 39 - d$

LESSON 4

Patterns: Find a Rule

Quick Review

Add 4 to each number.

1. 4 **2.** 6

3. 10 **4.** 14

5. 24

Learn

NUMBER CRUNCHER When Mr. Wiley puts the number 12 into a number machine, the number 15 comes out. When he puts in 18, out comes 21, and when he puts in 24, out comes 27. What number comes out when he puts 30 into the machine?

INPUT	OUTPUT
12	15
18	21
24	27
30	■

HINT: Look for a pattern to help you find a rule.

Pattern: Each output is 3 more than the input.

Rule: Add 3.

Input: 30 *Output*: 33

So, when Mr. Wiley puts in 30, the number 33 is the output.

You can write an equation to show the rule. Use variables to show the input and output.

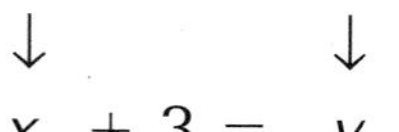

input **output**

↓ ↓

$x + 3 = y$

Think of the equation as a rule. To find the value of y, add 3 to x.

Examples Find a rule. Write the rule as an equation. Use the equation to extend the pattern.

A

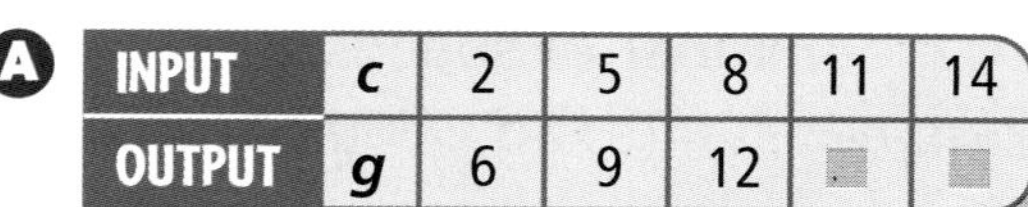

INPUT	c	2	5	8	11	14
OUTPUT	g	6	9	12	■	■

Rule: Add 4.

$c + 4 = g$

Test your rule on each pair of numbers in the table.

$c + 4 = g$ $c + 4 = g$

$11 + 4 = 15$ $14 + 4 = 18$

So, the next two numbers are 15 and 18.

B

INPUT	k	37	24	18	12	6
OUTPUT	m	31	18	12	■	■

Rule: Subtract 6.

$k - 6 = m$

Test your rule on each pair of numbers in the table.

$k - 6 = m$ $k - 6 = m$

$12 - 6 = 6$ $6 - 6 = 0$

So, the next two numbers are 6 and 0.

Check

1. **Explain** why it is important to test the rule with all the numbers in the table.

Find a rule. Write the rule as an equation. Use the equation to extend the pattern.

2.

INPUT	x	6	15	18	23	28
OUTPUT	y	13	22	25	■	■

3.

INPUT	s	43	32	21	11	7
OUTPUT	t	37	26	15	■	■

Practice and Problem Solving

Extra Practice, page 82, Set D

Find a rule. Write the rule as an equation. Use the equation to extend the pattern.

4.

INPUT	b	68	56	45	34	23	12
OUTPUT	c	57	45	34	23	■	■

5.

INPUT	d	39	47	55	60	67	75
OUTPUT	f	26	34	42	47	■	■

6.

INPUT	w	12	19	28	37	49	54
OUTPUT	z	■	■	48	57	69	74

7.

INPUT	r	15	30	20	37	28	43
OUTPUT	s	■	■	35	52	43	58

Use the rule and equation to make an input/output table.

8. Add 8. $x + 8 = y$
9. Subtract 6. $h - 6 = j$
10. Add 12. $t + 12 = w$
11. Subtract 9. $f - 9 = g$
12. Subtract 10. $r - 10 = s$
13. Add 21. $c + 21 = d$
14. Subtract 14. $k - 14 = m$
15. Add 24. $a + 24 = b$
16. The arena collects the same service charge for each ticket purchased. The total price for a $20 ticket is $22, and the price for a $25 ticket is $27. What is the total price for two $30 tickets?
17. **Write a problem** using a rule shown in this table. Then solve your problem to find the missing number.

INPUT	OUTPUT
c	g
$15	$8
$18	$11
$24	$17
$40	■

Mixed Review and Test Prep

18. $8,503 - 5,927$ (p. 48)
19. $7,768 + 4,309$ (p. 48)

Write the value of the blue digit. (p. 4)

20. 345,687
21. 982,521
22. TEST PREP Which is true? (p. 20)

A $5,341 > 5,431$
B $6,236 = 6,226$
C $4,357 < 4,135$
D $3,964 > 3,694$

LESSON

5 Balance Equations

Quick Review

Write the total amount of money.

1. 1 nickel
2. 1 nickel, 3 pennies
3. 1 dime, 1 nickel
4. 2 nickels, 4 pennies
5. 1 dime, 3 nickels, 1 penny

Learn

IT'S ALL THE SAME Amounts on both sides of an equal sign have the same value. What happens when you add the same amount to both sides of an equation?

Marisha and Tony each have 1 nickel. Marisha gets 1 dime from Mrs. Maria, and Tony gets 2 nickels. Do they have the same amount? Use coins to model the problem.

Activity

MATERIALS: coins, workmat

- Divide your workmat into two parts. Think of each side of the workmat as one side of an equation.
- Place 1 nickel on each side. Then add 1 dime to the left side. Place 2 nickels on the right side.

Marisha's money	Tony's money

- Compare the total value of the coins on each side. Are the values equal?

So, Tony and Marisha have the same amount of money.

Remember

In an equation, the left side and the right side are equal. Both sides have the same value.

Left Side ↓ Right Side ↓

$6 + 3 = 9$

- Now remove a nickel from each side. What are the values? Are both sides equal? Explain.
- **What if** you added a nickel to one side and 4 pennies to the other side? Would both sides be equal?

MATH IDEA If you add the same amount to, or subtract the same amount from, both sides of a true equation, the values on both sides are still equal and the equation is still true.

Add or Subtract Equal Amounts

This is a true equation because the values on both sides are equal.

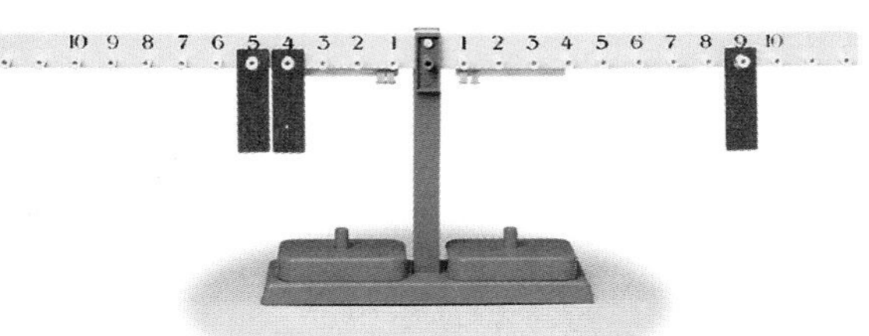

$$\begin{array}{ccc} 5 + 4 & = & 9 \\ \downarrow & & \downarrow \\ 9 & = & 9 \end{array}$$

What if you add 3 to the left side of the equation? Does adding 3 to the right side of the equation keep the equation true?

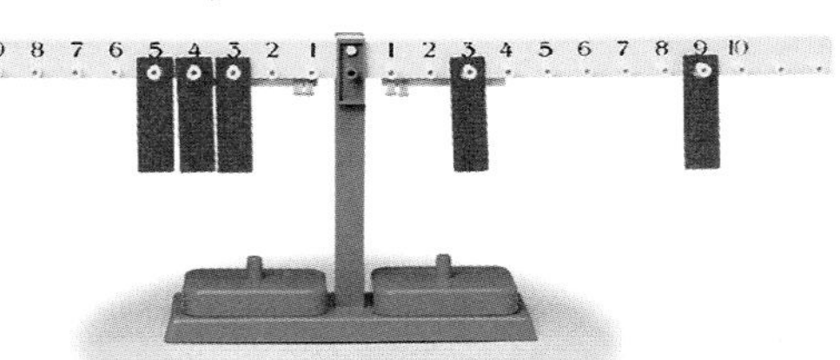

$5 + 4 = 9$

Add 3 to the left side. → $5 + 4 + 3 = 9 + 3$ ← Add 3 to the right side.

$12 = 12$ ← Compare both sides.

So, adding 3 to both sides keeps this equation true.

Examples

A

$9 + 8 = 17$

Add 7 to the left side. → $9 + 8 + 7 = 17 + 7$ ← Add 7 to the right side.

$24 = 24$ ← Compare both sides.

B

$46 = 15 + 31$

Subtract 14 from the left side. → $46 - 14 = 15 + 31 - 14$ ← Subtract 14 from the right side.

$32 = 32$ ← Compare both sides.

Check

1. **Explain** what you have to do to both sides of an equation to keep the equation true.

Tell whether the equations are true. Write *yes* or *no*. Explain.

2. 2 nickels + 3 nickels = 5 dimes

3. 1 dime − 1 nickel = 5 pennies

LESSON CONTINUES

Practice and Problem Solving

Extra Practice, page 82, Set E

Tell whether the equations are true. Write *yes* or *no*. Explain.

4. 1 quarter − 2 dimes = 5 pennies

5. 1 quarter = 2 dimes + 1 nickel

6. 2 nickels + 4 nickels = 5 dimes

7. 2 dimes − 3 nickels = 5 pennies

8. 2 dimes + 2 nickels = 1 dime + 4 nickels

9. 1 quarter − 1 dime = 1 dime + 1 nickel

10. 2 dimes + 4 nickels = 1 quarter + 5 pennies

11. 1 dime + 10 pennies = 1 dime + 2 nickels

Complete to make the equation true.

12. 2 nickels + 1 dime + 3 pennies = 4 nickels + __?__

13. 2 dimes + 3 nickels = 1 quarter + __?__

14. 2 nickels + 1 dime − 4 pennies = 3 nickels + __?__

15. 2 dimes + 2 nickels = 1 quarter + __?__

16. 5 nickels + 3 pennies = 2 dimes + __?__

17. 1 dime + 2 nickels = 1 quarter − __?__

18. 1 nickel + 1 dime + 6 pennies = 4 nickels + __?__

19. 3 dimes + 3 nickels = 1 quarter + __?__

20. $15 + 3 = 15 + \blacksquare$

21. $8 + 1 = \blacksquare + 8$

22. $8 + 2 + \blacksquare = 10 + 4$

23. $10 + 9 - \blacksquare = 19 - 8$

24. $20 - \blacksquare = 15 + 5 - 1$

25. $7 + 10 = \blacksquare + 5 + 2$

26. $15 - 8 = 14 - \blacksquare$

27. $7 + 9 = \blacksquare + 8$

28. $10 + 2 + \blacksquare = 6 + 8$

29. $11 + 6 - \blacksquare = 19 - 5$

30. **? What's the Error?** Stacey made this model. Describe her error. What must Stacey do to make the values equal?

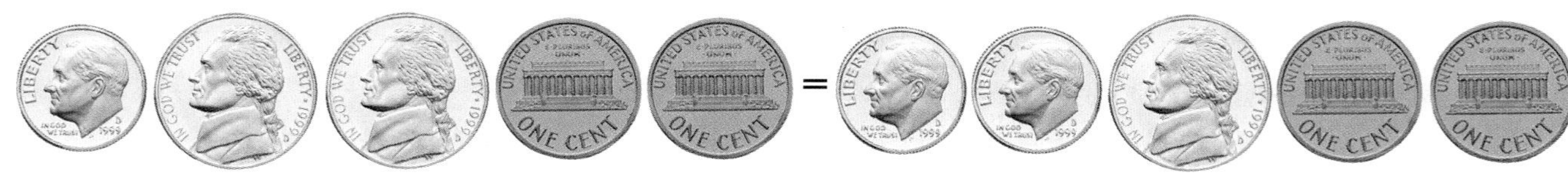

31. Bob has 23 colored pencils, 37 markers, and 25 notepads in a box. How many items are in Bob's box?

32. Carin had \$14. Her mother gave her \$2. She spent \$3 on lunch. How much money did she have then?

33. Phan and Li each had 55¢. Mr. Lee gave Phan 4 coins and Li 2 coins. Could they still have the same amount of money? Explain.

34. Karen had 3 times as many coins as Jon. Could Jon have more money than Karen? Explain.

Mixed Review and Test Prep

For 35–36, use the graph.

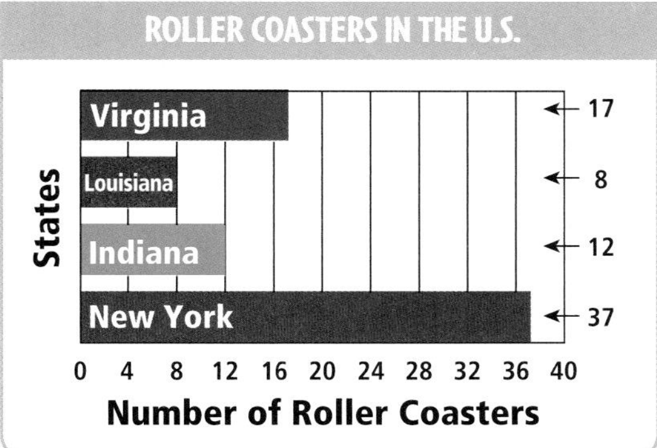

35. Complete: __?__ has 5 fewer roller coasters than __?__ has.

36. There are 576 roller coasters in the United States. How many roller coasters are there in the states not listed on the graph?

37. Each row and column in the table has the same sum. Find the missing numbers.

112	157	164
213	A	159
108	215	B

38. **TEST PREP** Which is five hundred five thousand, fifty-two in standard form? (p. 4)

A 5,052 **C** 505,052
B 55,052 **D** 5,005,052

39. **TEST PREP** Which is the solution for this equation?

$$14 - c = 6$$

F $c = 6$ **H** $c = 12$
G $c = 8$ **J** $c = 20$

Problem Solving Thinker's Corner

MONEY PUZZLES Use the clues to find the combination and order of bills or coins.

1. ◯ ◯ ◯ ◯

- The value of the first coin is 13¢ more than the total of the others.
- The third and fourth coins have the same value.

2. ▭ ▭ ▭ ▭

- The total value is an odd number less than $30.
- The value of the last bill is 4 times the value of the second.

LESSON 6

Problem Solving Strategy
Act It Out

Quick Review

1. $6 + 8 + \blacksquare = 19$
2. $7 + 2 + \blacksquare = 18$
3. $5 + \blacksquare + 4 = 16$
4. $\blacksquare + 3 + 8 = 17$
5. $4 + \blacksquare + 6 = 15$

PROBLEM Sally and Sam are top chess players. Sally won 8 games. Sam won 2 games and then won 6 more. The next day Sally won 3 more games. How many more wins does Sam need to be tied with Sally?

UNDERSTAND

- What are you asked to find?
- What information will you use?
- Is there any information you will not use? If so, what?

PLAN

- What strategy can you use?
  Act it out to show how many wins Sam needs to tie with Sally. Use counters to model the number of games Sally won and Sam won.

SOLVE

- How can you use the strategy to solve the problem?
  Use a workmat and counters to model the number of games each person won.

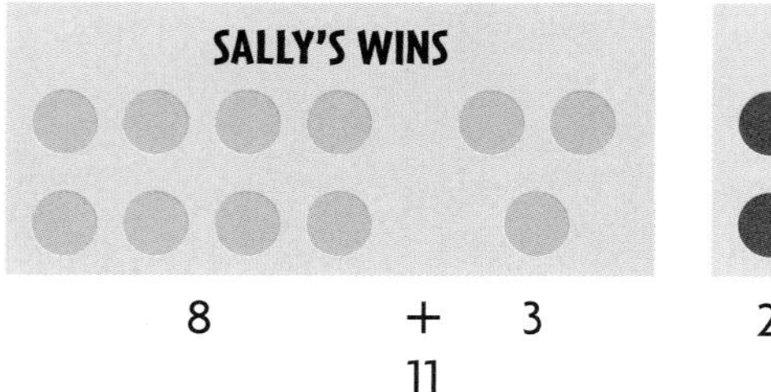

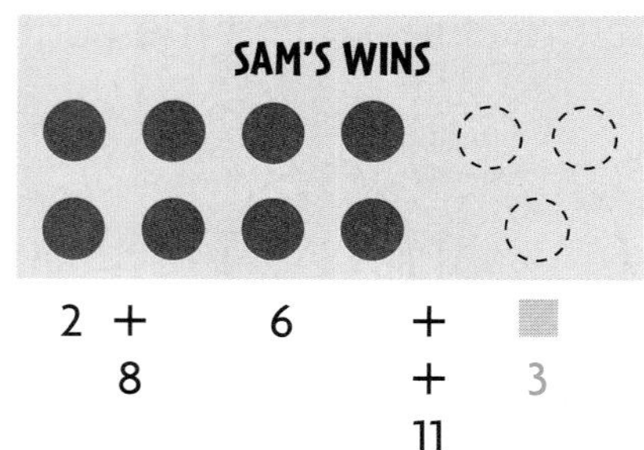

8 + 3
11

2 + 6 + ■
8 + 3
11

Use the model to show the number of games won. Then write an equation to show the model:
$8 + 3 = 2 + 6 + 3$

So, Sam needs to win 3 more games.

CHECK

- How can you check that your answer is correct?

Problem Solving Practice

Act it out to solve.

1. **What if** Sam wins 5 more chess games after he ties with Sally? If Sam and Sally end up winning the same number of games, how many more chess games will Sally win after the tie?

2. Bart had 6 checkers and found 7 more. Jenny has 8 checkers. How many more checkers will she need so that she and Bart have the same number of checkers?

Strategies

- Draw a Diagram or Picture
- **Make a Model or Act It Out**
- Make an Organized List
- Find a Pattern
- Make a Table or Graph
- Predict and Test
- Work Backward
- Solve a Simpler Problem
- Write an Equation
- Use Logical Reasoning

Problem Solving

3. Stacey gave 8 pens to Dan. Now she has 15 pens. Which equation best describes this?
   A $n - 8 = 15$ **C** $n + 8 = 15$
   B $15 - 8 = n$ **D** $n + 15 = 2$

4. Lisa had 7 tapes. Mike gave her some more. Now she has 12 tapes. Which equation best describes this?
   F $7 - t = 12$ **H** $12 - t = 19$
   G $7 + t = 12$ **J** $t - 7 = 12$

5. **What's the Error?** John has captured 9 chess pieces. Carol has captured 4 chess pieces and has taken 3 more. Carol acts it out and decides she needs to capture 5 more pieces to have the same number as John. Describe her error. Write the correct answer.

Mixed Strategy Practice

6. Ben is cooking hamburgers at a picnic. He bought 7 packages of hamburger buns. If each package holds 8 buns, how many buns did he get?

7. Kris has 3 quarters. Zach has an equal amount of money in dimes and nickels. Zach has 9 coins. How many dimes does Zach have? How many nickels does he have?

8. A game has 24 squares. Each square is red or black. The number of red squares is 2 times the number of black squares. How many squares of each color are there?

9. Heather has 6 pencils and borrows 4 more. John has 10 pencils. If John gives away 2 pencils, what must Heather do to have the same number?

Extra Practice

Set A (pp. 64–67)

Find the value of each expression if $c = 30$.

1. $186 + c + 10$
2. $(96 - c) + 3$
3. $c + (34 - 10)$
4. $467 - (103 + c)$
5. $(4{,}765 - 3{,}041) + c$
6. $6{,}741 - (c + 1{,}231)$

Set B (pp. 68–69)

Find the missing number, and tell which addition property you used.

1. ▒ + 45 = 45 + 17
2. 34 + ▒ = 34
3. (1 + 6) + 7 = 1 + (▒ + 7)
4. ▒ + 89 = 89
5. 9 + (▒ + 5) = (9 + 8) + 5
6. 130 + 79 = 79 + ▒

Set C (pp. 70–73)

1. There are 17 book bags in a room. Some bags are picked up and now 7 are left. Write an equation. Choose a variable for the unknown. Tell what the variable represents.

Solve the equation by using mental math. Check your solution.

2. $14 - c = 7$
3. $13 = m + 4$
4. $\$8 + g = \$20$
5. $21 = 6 + k$
6. $a + \$5 = \$14$
7. $4 = 16 - m$

Set D (pp. 74–75)

Find a rule. Write the rule as an equation. Use the equation to extend the pattern.

1.

INPUT	*r*	12	20	31	45	65
OUTPUT	*s*	9	17	28	▒	▒

2.

INPUT	*w*	18	26	42	65	86
OUTPUT	*v*	▒	▒	49	72	93

3.

INPUT	*x*	54	41	29	15	6
OUTPUT	*y*	66	53	41	▒	▒

4.

INPUT	*d*	87	74	63	45	27
OUTPUT	*f*	▒	▒	49	31	13

Set E (pp. 76–79)

Complete to make the equation true.

1. 2 dimes + 2 nickels + 3 pennies = 7 nickels − __?__
2. 1 quarter + 4 dimes = 2 quarters + 1 dime + __?__
3. 5 + 7 = 7 + ▒
4. 26 − ▒ = 15 + 5

CHAPTER 4

Review/Test

CHECK VOCABULARY AND CONCEPTS

Choose the best term from the box.

equation
expression
variable

1. A letter or symbol that stands for an unknown number is a __?__. (p. 65)
2. An __?__ combines numbers and operations but does not have an equal sign. (p. 64)

CHECK SKILLS

Find the value of each expression if $g = 108$. (pp. 64–67)

3. $g - (20 + 12)$
4. $251 + g + 289$
5. $44{,}876 - (317 - g)$
6. $(240 + 52) - g$
7. $485 - (g + 93)$
8. $g + (169 - 47)$

Find the missing number, and tell which addition property you used. (pp. 68–69)

9. $\blacksquare + 9 = 9 + 6$
10. $(2 + 1) + \blacksquare = 2 + (1 + 3)$
11. $0 + \blacksquare = 55$

Solve the equation by using mental math. (pp. 70–73)

12. $x + 8 = 14$
13. $23 - k = 11$
14. $9 = 15 - n$

15. Joaquin had 50 sports banners. He traded 32 of his banners for 15 new banners. Write an expression. How many banners does he have left? (pp. 64–67)

16. 36 flowers minus some flowers equals 24 flowers. Write an equation. Choose a variable for the unknown. Tell what the variable represents. (pp. 70–73)

17. Complete to make the equation true. (pp. 76–79)

    5 dimes + 2 nickels =
    3 dimes + __?__ + 5 pennies

18. Find a rule. Write the rule as an equation. Extend the pattern. (pp. 74–75)

INPUT	c	47	54	62	84	96
OUTPUT	k	56	■	71	93	■

CHECK PROBLEM SOLVING

For 19–20, act it out to solve. (pp. 80–81)

19. Karl and Erik worked on a project. Karl worked 8 hours. Together they worked 14 hours. How many hours did Erik work?

20. There were 23 members in Troop 102. Some new members joined, and now there are 30 members. How many new members joined?

Standardized Test Prep

NUMBER SENSE, CONCEPTS, AND OPERATIONS

1. Andy made this chart of the number of tickets sold at the spring concert.

CONCERT TICKETS SOLD	
Day	**Number**
Thursday	2,104
Friday	2,459
Saturday	3,066
Sunday	3,006
Monday	2,495

Which statement is true?

A More tickets were sold on Monday than on Saturday.

B Fewer tickets were sold on Saturday than on Sunday.

C The most tickets were sold on Friday.

D The fewest tickets were sold on Thursday.

2. Mt. McKinley, the tallest mountain in the United States, is 20,320 feet tall. Mt. Everest, the tallest mountain in the world, is 29,035 feet tall. How much taller is Mt. Everest than Mt. McKinley?

F 9,715 feet　　**H** 8,715 feet

G 9,285 feet　　**J** 8,285 feet

3. **Explain It** Which is a more reasonable number of marbles in the full jar, 50 or 500? Explain your thinking.

10 marbles

GEOMETRY AND SPATIAL SENSE

4. Which figure shows intersecting lines?

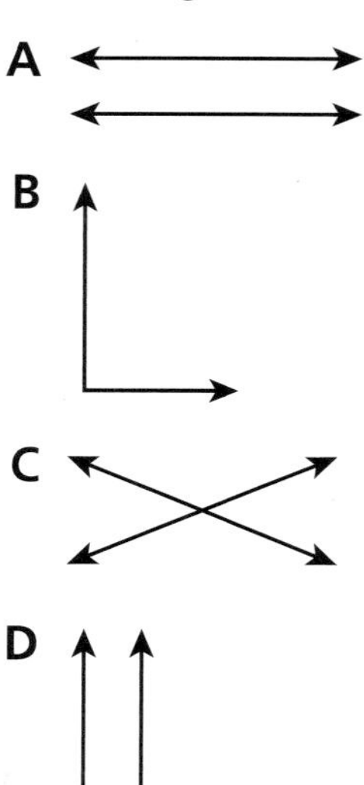

5. How many sides do the 5 squares below have?

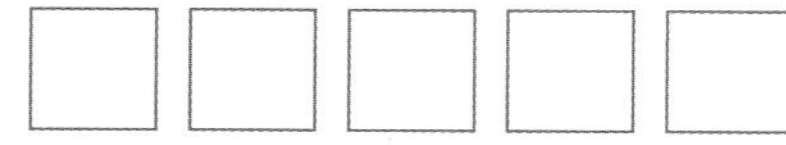

F 10

G 15

H 20

J 25

TIP **Look for important words.**
See item 6. An important word is *vertices.* Also important are the given shape names. Determine how many vertices each shape has.

6. **Explain It** Ella wants to draw a plane figure that has no vertices. Which shape should Ella draw? Write *circle, square, rectangle,* or *triangle.* Explain how you decided.

ALGEBRAIC THINKING

7. Angela has saved $85 to buy a new bike. Let m represent the amount she still needs to buy the bike. Which expression shows how much the new bike costs?

A $m + 85$

B $m - 85$

C $m \times 85$

D $m \div 85$

8. Use the number line to solve $26 + x = 33$.

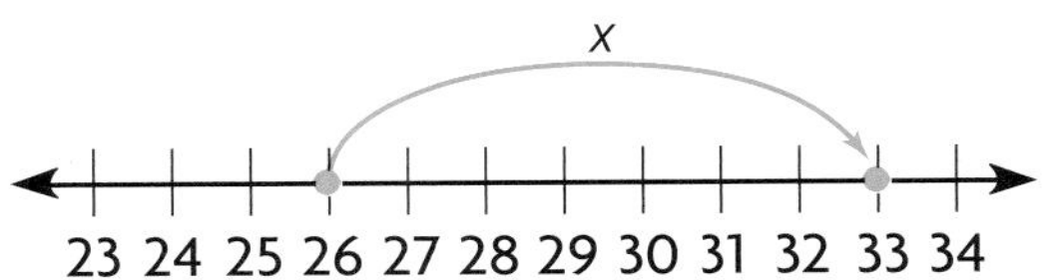

F $x = 1$

G $x = 7$

H $x = 26$

J $x = 33$

9. **Explain It** Use the equation $m + 11 = p$ to extend the pattern in the table.

INPUT	OUTPUT
m	*p*
9	20
22	33
45	56
60	71
73	■
88	■
123	■

Explain how you found the missing numbers.

DATA ANALYSIS AND PROBABILITY

10. If the pointer on this spinner is spun 30 times, which color will the pointer probably land on the **greatest** number of times?

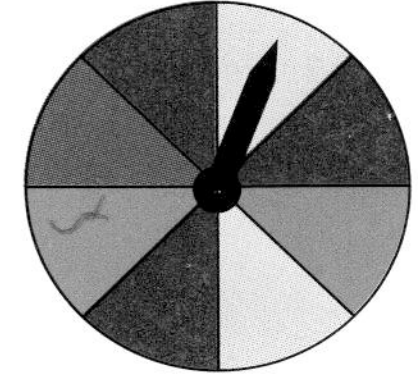

A red

B blue

C green

D yellow

11. Which is the median age in the table below?

AGES OF DOGS (in years)					
Dog	Bo	Fifi	Fido	Max	Jet
Age	4	1	6	3	5

F 6

G 5

H 4

J 3

12. **Explain It** Chris is making his lunch for school. He can have a cheese or turkey sandwich, and either an apple, an orange, or a banana.

How many different lunch combinations are possible? Make a list to show how you decided.

IT'S IN THE BAG

Ring Place-Value Strip

PROJECT Make a place-value strip to practice place-value concepts reading greater numbers.

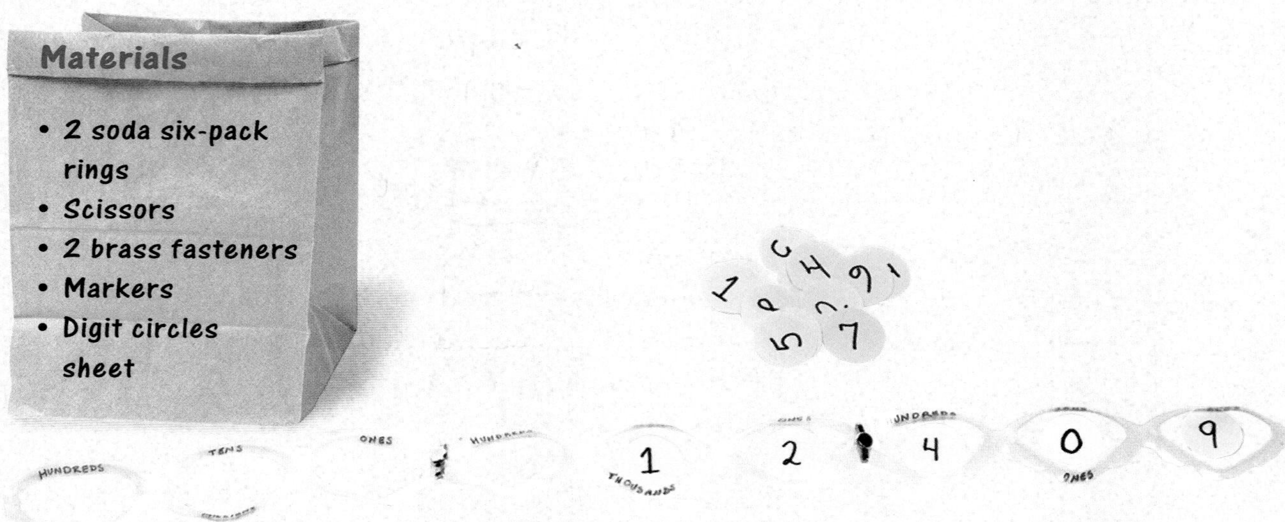

Directions

1. Cut 2 six-pack rings down the middle lengthwise to form 4 three-ring strips. *(Picture A)*

2. Connect two of the strips together by overlapping one end of each strip and punching through them with a brass fastener. Repeat to connect a third strip, making one long nine-ring strip. *(Picture B)*

3. Write *ONES* above the first ring on the right, *TENS* above the second ring, and *HUNDREDS* above the third ring. Write the period name for these first three places—*ONES*. Repeat this for the next 6 rings, and include the period names on each set of 3 rings. *(Picture C)*

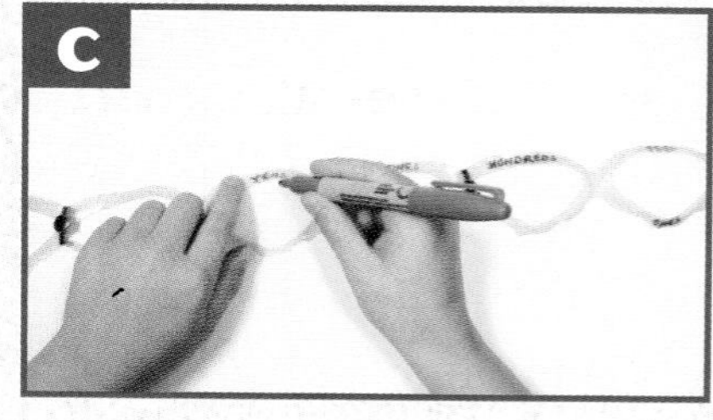

4. Work with a partner. Lay your place-value strip across your desk. As your partner reads a number, put digit circles in the proper place-value rings of your strip to show the number. You also can put digit circles in your partner's strip, and have your partner read the number.

Challenge

Other Bases

The decimal number system is a *base-ten* system because each place value is ten times the place value to the right. The system uses the digits 0, 1, 2, 3, 4, 5, 6, 7, 8, and 9.

Numbers also can be written in bases other than base ten. In the *base-five* system, for example, each place value is five times the place value to the right. That system uses the digits 0, 1, 2, 3, and 4.

These are the first four place values for number positions in base-ten and base-five systems.

Base-ten place value	1,000	100	10	1
Base-five place value	125	25	5	1

The value of a number depends on the number system in which the number is written. To find the base-ten number that is equivalent to a base-five number, multiply each digit by its base-five place value and then add.

What is the base-ten number that is equivalent to the base-five number 143?

STEP 1 Find the value of each digit by multiplying the digit by its place value.

Base-five place value	125	25	5	1
Digit		**1**	**4**	**3**

The value of the digit **1** is $1 \times 25 =$ **25**.
The value of the digit **4** is $4 \times 5 =$ **20**.
The value of the digit **3** is $3 \times 1 =$ **3**.

STEP 2 Add the values.

25 + 20 + 3 = 48

So, the base-ten number that is equivalent to the base-five number 143 is 48.

Use the place-value chart above to write the base-ten number that is equivalent to each base-five number.

1. 22 **2.** 404 **3.** 1214 **4.** 4302

Use the place-value chart below for base-two numbers to write the base-ten number that is equivalent to each base-two number.

5. 11 **6.** 110

7. 1011 **8.** 1100

Base-two place value	8	4	2	1

UNIT 1

Study Guide and Review

VOCABULARY

Choose the best term from the box.

1. A known number of things that helps you understand the size or amount of a different number of things is a __?__. (p. 10)
2. A symbol or letter that stands for an unknown number is a __?__. (p. 65)
3. A part of a number sentence that combines numbers and operations but does not have an equal sign is an __?__. (p. 64)

benchmark
equation
expression
variable

STUDY AND SOLVE

Chapter 1

Write the value of a digit.

Write the value of the blue digit.

4,359,687

The digit 5 is in the ten-thousands position.

So, the digit 5 has a value of 50,000.

Write the value of the blue digit. (pp. 2–9)

4. 62,422
5. 382,755
6. 7,405,699
7. 1,469,302
8. 841,977,302
9. 354,821,638

Chapter 2

Compare and order numbers.

Order 6,824; 8,643; and 6,834 from *least* to *greatest*.

6,824 ↓ $8 > 6$ 8,643 ↓ $8 > 6$ 6,834	6,824 ↓ $8 = 8$ 6,834	6,824 ↓ $2 < 3$ 6,834
8,643 is the greatest number.	There are the same number of hundreds.	$6{,}824 < 6{,}834$

So, $6{,}824 < 6{,}834 < 8{,}643$.

Write $<$, $>$, or $=$ for each ●. (pp. 20–23)

10. 6,260 ● 6,620
11. 4,920 ● 4,290
12. 68,750 ● 68,750
13. 14,211 ● 4,321
14. 1,800,234 ● 1,801,254
15. Order the numbers 78,994; 87,497; and 78,499 from *least* to *greatest*. (pp. 24–27)

Chapter 3

Estimate and find sums and differences.

Find the difference.

$$\begin{array}{r} 5{,}000 \\ -3{,}567 \\ \hline 1{,}433 \end{array}$$

(Regrouping shown: 4 10 10 10, with 9 9 above the middle tens.)

- Regroup when needed.
- Subtract the ones.
- Subtract the tens.
- Subtract the hundreds.
- Subtract the thousands.

Find the sum or difference. Estimate to check. (pp. 44–55)

16. $\begin{array}{r} 99{,}452 \\ -\ 6{,}803 \\ \hline \end{array}$

17. $\begin{array}{r} 132{,}741 \\ +104{,}458 \\ \hline \end{array}$

18. $\begin{array}{r} 13{,}000 \\ -10{,}687 \\ \hline \end{array}$

19. $\begin{array}{r} 400{,}561 \\ +592{,}625 \\ \hline \end{array}$

Chapter 4

Write expressions and equations that contain variables.

20 cups minus some cups plus 3 cups

$$(20 - c) + 3$$

Parentheses are used for $20 - c$ since some cups, c, were removed before 3 cups were added.

Write an expression or equation for each. Choose a variable for the unknown. (pp. 64–67, 70–73)

20. Sandy had 5 cards. She gave some away.
21. Shanti had some stamps. She gave 23 to Penny. Shanti has 71 stamps left.

Solve equations mentally.

Solve the equation.

$12 + c = 20$ Think: 12 plus what number equals 20?

$c = 8$

Check: $12 + 8 = 20$ Replace c with 8.

$20 = 20$ ✓ The equation is true.

The value of c is 8.

Solve the equation by using mental math. Check your solution. (pp. 70–73)

22. $m - 4 = 11$
23. $g + 9 = 13$
24. $12 = 24 - r$
25. $8 = 5 + w$

PROBLEM SOLVING PRACTICE (pp. 56–57, 80–81)

26. Mr. Miller has written 157 pages of a book. He wants the book to have about 550 pages. About how many more pages does he need to write? Tell whether an exact answer or estimate is needed, and solve.
27. Jack and Mary are playing a game. Jack has 7 cards and picks up 1 card from the unused stack. Mary has 5 cards. How many more cards does Mary need to have the same number as Jack?

PERFORMANCE ASSESSMENT

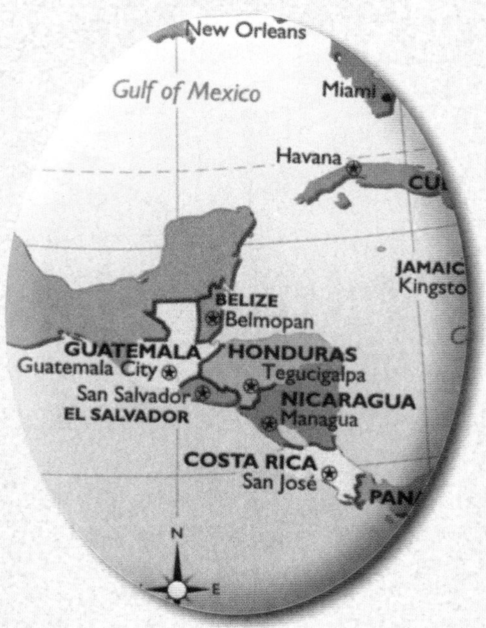

TASK A • POPULATION STUDY

The students in Maria's class are writing reports on Central American countries. Maria reads in an almanac that the population of El Salvador is about 6,123,000; the population of Honduras is about 6,250,000; the population of Costa Rica is about 3,711,000; and the population of Nicaragua is about 4,813,000.

a. Make a table to organize the population data for the four countries.

b. Describe the order in which you listed the populations. Where is Nicaragua on your list?

c. Maria read that the population of Panama is about 2,800,000. She thought that this number was probably rounded to the nearest hundred thousand. Describe the numbers that could represent the actual population of Panama. Where would you list Panama in your table?

TASK B • BUYING A COMPUTER

The Stockwells saved $1,900 to buy a computer, monitor, and printer. The table shows the cost of items they might choose.

Computer		Monitor		Printer	
Brand A	$1,029	15-inch	$239	ink jet	$289
Brand B	$1,179	17-inch	$379	laser jet	$429

a. Estimate to find one possible choice of computer, monitor, and printer the Stockwells could buy with the money they have. Then find the actual total cost of these items.

b. How much of the $1,900 will be left if they purchase the items you suggested?

c. Suppose the Stockwells decide to start a new savings account to buy software. They put $100 in the account. They take out $45 to buy a new game and then put in $20. Write an expression to find the amount of money remaining in the account. Then find the value of the expression.

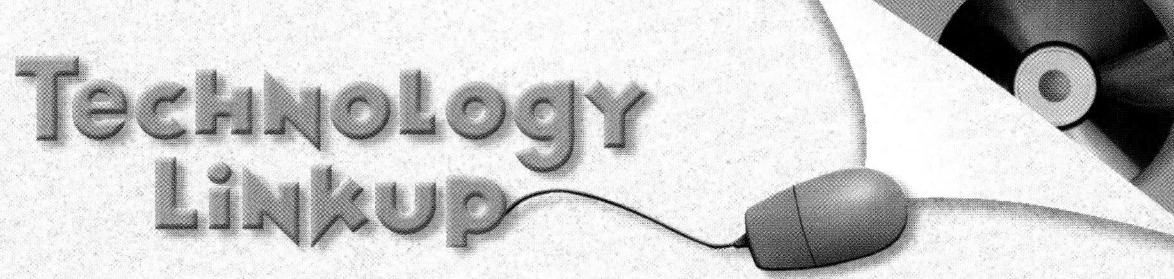

Order Numbers

There are 16,549,000 forested acres of land in Florida. North Carolina has 19,278,000 forested acres, Virginia has 15,858,000 forested acres, and Alabama has 21,974,000 forested acres. Place the states in order from greatest to least amount of forested land.

	A	B	C
1	Florida	16,549,000	
2	North Carolina	19,278,000	
3	Virginia	15,858,000	
4	Alabama	21,974,000	

You can use a spreadsheet program to order a list of data.

- Enter the data in two columns on a spreadsheet and highlight them all.
- Click *Data*. Then click *Sort*.
- You can then select the column by which to sort. To sort the list of data by number of acres, select *Column B*.
- Select whether you want to sort the list into *ascending* or *descending* order. To order from greatest to least, select *descending*.
- The list then will be sorted from greatest to least.

	A	B	C
1	Alabama	21,974,000	
2	North Carolina	19,278,000	
3	Florida	16,549,000	
4	Virginia	15,858,000	

So, the states in order from greatest to least amount of forested land are Alabama, North Carolina, Florida, Virginia.

Practice and Problem Solving

Use a spreadsheet program to order the numbers.

1. Mark's class collected 140 cans during Week 1, 134 cans during Week 2, and 143 cans during Week 3. During which week did his class collect the most cans?

2. North Carolina has 301 miles of coastline. Louisiana has 397 miles, and Texas has 367 miles of coastline. Which of these states has the shortest coastline?

GO ON-LINE **Multimedia Math Glossary** www.harcourtschool.com/mathglossary

Vocabulary Power Look up *digit* in the Multimedia Math Glossary. Write a problem that can be answered by ordering three 4-digit numbers.

▲ The Mississippi River begins as a brook, 20 feet wide, at the outlet of Lake Itasca, Minnesota.

PROBLEM SOLVING ON LOCATION in Minnesota

LAKES

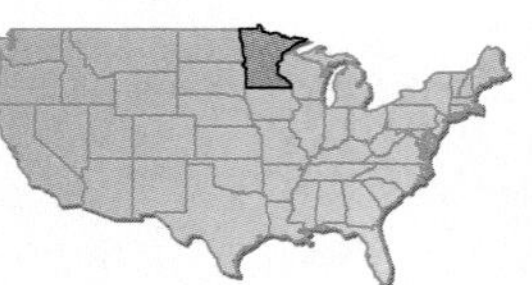

Minnesota is called "the land of 10,000 lakes," but it actually has more than 15,000 lakes.

SIZES OF MINNESOTA LAKES	
Lake	**Size (in acres)**
Cass Lake	15,596
Lake Mille Lacs	132,516
Lake Minnetonka	14,004
Lake Vermilion	40,557
Lake Winnibigoshish	58,544
Leech Lake	111,527
Otter Tail Lake	13,725
Upper Red Lake	107,832

USE DATA For 1–5, use the table.

1. **REASONING** Which two lakes are closest in size? What is the difference in their sizes?
2. What is the difference in size between the largest and the smallest lake?
3. To which place would you have to round the sizes of Lake Winnibigoshish and Leech Lake to get the same number?
4. Tom caught some perch while fishing on Lake Vermilion. He can catch 5 more perch before reaching the daily limit of 20. Write an equation, using a variable, that shows this. Solve the equation.
5. **STRETCH YOUR THINKING** Lower Red Lake is about 44,168 acres larger than Upper Red Lake. Write an expression that shows the total size of these two connected lakes.

PARKS

The 2,348-mile-long Mississippi River begins in Minnesota, where it flows from Lake Itasca. You can visit the headwaters of the Mississippi River in Itasca State Park. The Mississippi River travels past 10 states on its journey south to the Gulf of Mexico.

USE DATA For 1–5, use the table.

1. Put the states in order from *least* to *greatest* population. Which state has the third greatest population?
2. If you round the population of each state to the nearest thousand, for which states will the populations increase by 1 in the thousands place?
3. Write the population of Minnesota in expanded form.
4. **What if** some people, *p*, move to Illinois? What expression can you write to show the number of people who would live there then?
5. How many more people live in Tennessee than in Louisiana?

POPULATIONS OF STATES THAT BORDER THE MISSISSIPPI RIVER

State	Population
Arkansas	2,551,373
Illinois	12,128,370
Iowa	2,869,413
Kentucky	3,960,825
Louisiana	4,372,035
Minnesota	4,775,508
Mississippi	2,768,619
Missouri	5,468,338
Tennessee	5,483,535
Wisconsin	5,250,446

Lake Vermilion is the sixth largest lake in Minnesota. ▶

CHAPTER 5

Understand Time

Steam locomotive

FAST FACT • SOCIAL STUDIES The first United States railroad company, the Baltimore & Ohio Railroad, was founded in 1827. Since then, railroads have been built across the United States. The line graph below shows how the number of miles of railroad line in the U.S. has changed over time.

PROBLEM SOLVING During which two-decade period was the increase in miles of railroad line the greatest?

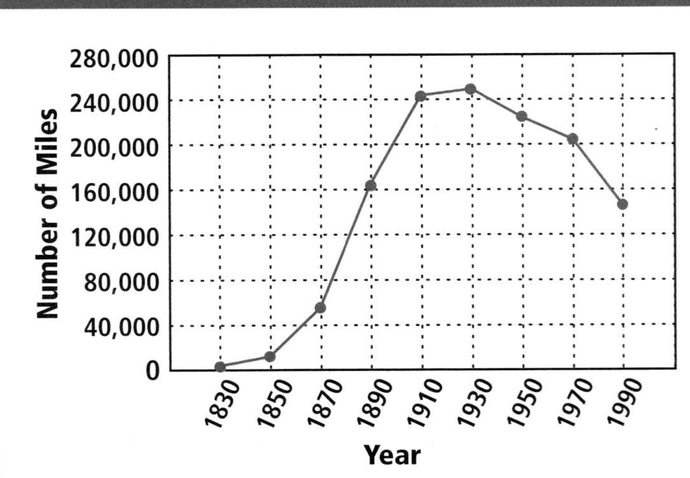

CHECK WHAT YOU KNOW

Use this page to help you review and remember important skills needed for Chapter 5.

TIME TO THE MINUTE

Write the time.

1. 

2. 

3. 

4. 

Write the time in words.

5. 

6. 

7. 

8. 

USE A CALENDAR

For 9–12, use the calendar.

NOVEMBER						
Sun	Mon	Tue	Wed	Thu	Fri	Sat
					1	2
3	4	5	6	7	8	9
10	11	12	13	14	15	16
17	18	19	20	21	22	23
24	25	26	27	28	29	30

9. What day of the week is November 14?

10. What is the date of the third Tuesday in November?

11. If you circled all of the dates for Saturdays and Sundays in November, how many dates would be circled?

12. If soccer practices are on Mondays and Wednesdays, how many soccer practices will there be in November?

VOCABULARY POWER

REVIEW

minute [mi′nət] *noun*

During the American Revolution there was a group of Patriots called the Minutemen. What does this name tell you about how fast these men could get ready for a battle?

PREVIEW

seconds

elapsed time

century

decade

GO ON-LINE **www.harcourtschool.com/mathglossary**

LESSON 1

Telling Time

Quick Review

Name the time that is 15 minutes before each time.

1. 1:00 **2.** 11:30 **3.** 2:15

4. 5:45 **5.** 7:00

VOCABULARY

seconds (sec)

Learn

ON TIME? This morning, Aaron's family will take a ride on the Tweetsie Railroad. The train leaves at eleven o'clock. Aaron's family is in the station waiting room. The time right now is shown on the clock. Has Aaron's family missed the train?

The time on the clock is 10:48, or 12 minutes before 11:00. So, Aaron's family has not missed the train.

In 1992 Locomotive #12, owned by the Tweetsie Railroad in Blowing Rock, N.C., was listed in the National Register of Historic Places. ▼

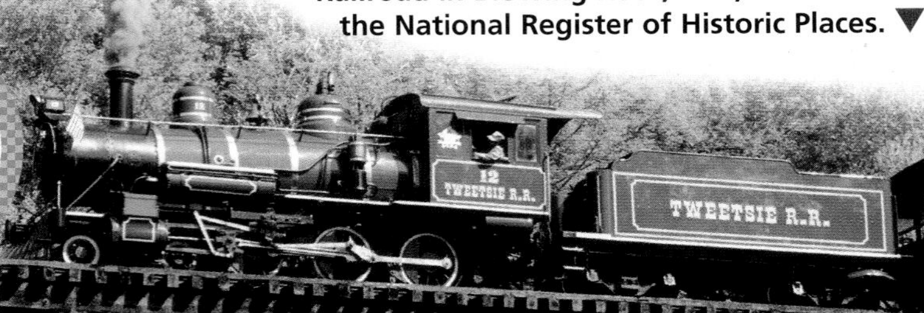

Examples

A

Read or write this time as:

- 9:50
- 50 minutes after nine
- 10 minutes before ten

B

Read or write this time as:

- 2:24 and 16 seconds
- 24 minutes 16 seconds after two
- 44 seconds before 2:25

Use what you know about units of time to estimate how long an activity will last.

- What activities can you do in about 1 second? in about 1 minute? in about 5 minutes?

UNITS OF TIME
60 **seconds (sec)** = 1 minute (min)
60 minutes = 1 hour (hr)
24 hours = 1 day

Check

1. **Explain** how to find the number of seconds in 2 minutes.

Write the time as shown on a digital clock.

2. 38 minutes after six
3. 16 minutes before two
4. 19 minutes after four

Practice and Problem Solving

Extra Practice, page 108, Set A

Write the time as shown on a digital clock.

5. 17 minutes after four

6. 10 minutes before five

7. 13 minutes before seven

Write the time shown on the clock in 2 different ways.

8.

9.

10.

11.

12.

13.

Write the letter of the unit used to measure the time.

a. days **b.** hours **c.** minutes **d.** seconds

14. to blink your eyes

15. to eat breakfast

16. from sunrise to sunset

17. How many minutes are in 3 hours 25 minutes?

18. How many seconds are in 4 minutes 12 seconds?

19. Your friend is planning to pick you up at the train station. You need to tell him the arrival time of your train. Should you be accurate to the nearest day, hour, minute, or second? Explain.

20. Normally, a person blinks 1 time about every 6 seconds. About how many times does a person blink in 30 seconds? About how many times does a person blink in 1 minute?

Mixed Review and Test Prep

21. Write three hundred sixty-five thousand, eight hundred forty-two in standard form. (p. 4)

Find the missing number. (p. 76)

22. $16 + \blacksquare = (11 + 5)$

23. $14 + \blacksquare = 7 + 7 + 6$

24. Lowell School has 513 students. There are 284 girls. How many fewer boys than girls are there? (p. 48)

25. **TEST PREP** Wendy's bank has 7 quarters, 11 dimes, 16 nickels, and 37 pennies in it. How much is in her bank?

A \$3.57 **B** \$3.77 **C** \$4.02 **D** \$4.27

LESSON 2

Elapsed Time

Learn

START TO FINISH Trail Elementary School is having a Cultural Fair. Use the schedule to find how long the fair will last.

Elapsed time is the time that passes from the start to the end of an activity. You can use a clock to count forward from the starting time to the ending time.

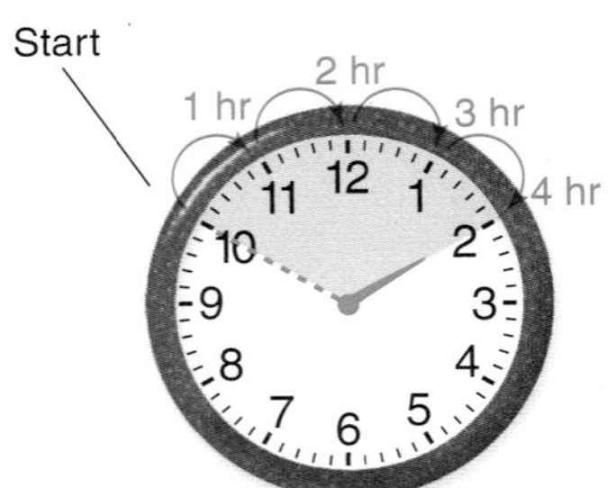

Think: From 10:00 A.M. to 2:00 P.M., 4 full hours have passed.

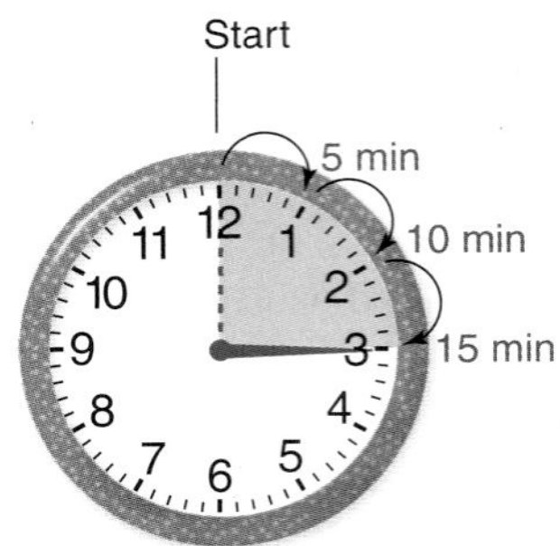

Think: From 2:00 P.M. to 2:15 P.M., 15 minutes have passed.

So, the fair will last 4 hr 15 min.

Example 1

A karate presentation has been added at 2:30 P.M. If it lasts 35 minutes, at what time will it end?

One Way

Count forward on a clock.

Another Way

Use addition.

$$\begin{array}{r} 2 \text{ hr } 30 \text{ min} \\ + \quad 35 \text{ min} \\ \hline 2 \text{ hr } 65 \text{ min} \end{array}$$

Think: 60 min = 1 hr

So, 2 hr + 1 hr + 5 min = 3 hr 5 min.

Both ways show that the karate presentation will end at 3:05 P.M.

Quick Review

Write the time, using A.M. or P.M.

1. when you wake up
2. when you get to school
3. when you eat lunch
4. when the sun sets
5. when you go to bed

VOCABULARY

elapsed time

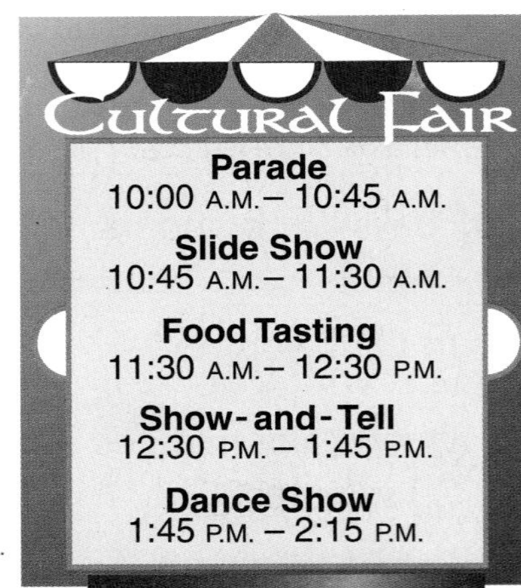

Cultural Fair

Parade	10:00 A.M.– 10:45 A.M.
Slide Show	10:45 A.M.– 11:30 A.M.
Food Tasting	11:30 A.M.– 12:30 P.M.
Show-and-Tell	12:30 P.M. – 1:45 P.M.
Dance Show	1:45 P.M. – 2:15 P.M.

Remember

A.M. means "before noon."
P.M. means "after noon."

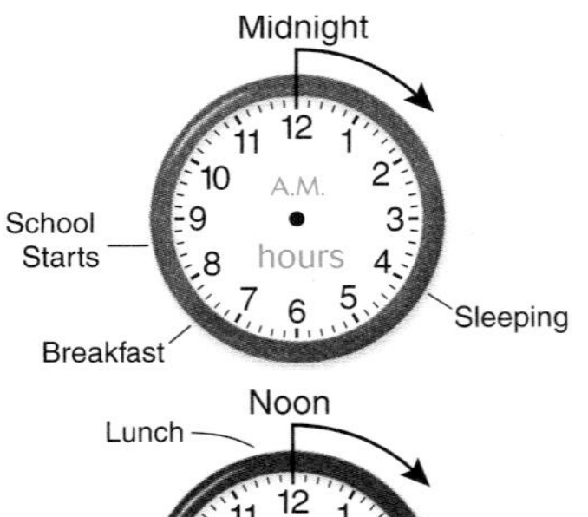

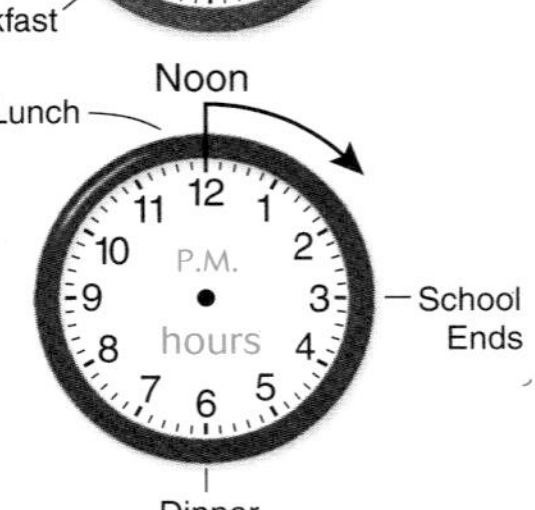

Example 2

The principal wants to move the dance show to 10:15 A.M. The parade must end by 10:10 A.M. The parade will last 45 minutes. Find the start time of the parade.

One Way

Count backward on a clock.

Another Way

Use subtraction.

Think: 1 hr = 60 min
Rename 10 hr 10 min
as 9 hr 70 min.
60 min + 10 min = 70 min

$$\begin{array}{r} \overset{9}{\cancel{10}} \text{ hr } \overset{70}{\cancel{10}} \text{ min} \\ - \quad 45 \text{ min} \\ \hline 9 \text{ hr } 25 \text{ min} \end{array}$$

The parade should start at 9:25 A.M.

- Rana's mom can attend only the slide show and the food tasting. Will she be at school for more or less than 2 hours? Explain.

Technology Link

More Practice: Harcourt Mega Math, The Number Games, *Tiny's Think Tank*, Level D

Check

1. **Explain** how to find the elapsed time from the beginning of the slide show to the end of show-and-tell at the Cultural Fair. Use the data on page 98.

Find the elapsed time.

2. **start:** 9:30 A.M.
   end: 4:50 P.M.

3. **start:** 11:10 A.M.
   end: 2:45 P.M.

4. **start:** 1:20 P.M.
   end: 9:05 P.M.

USE DATA For 5–6, use the movie schedule.

5. At what time does each movie end?

6. Can you see all the movies in one day? Why or why not?

7. The movie *In a Flash* is 90 minutes long and ends at 9:10 P.M. What time does it begin?

MOVIE SCHEDULE	
Storm at Sea	1:15 P.M.
Eagle's Flight	2:35 P.M.
Mountain Journey	4:30 P.M.
Race to the Finish	6:05 P.M.

LESSON CONTINUES

Practice and Problem Solving

Extra Practice, page 108, Set B

Find the elapsed time.

8. **start:** 7:35 A.M. **end:** 2:15 P.M.
9. **start:** 9:10 A.M. **end:** 11:53 A.M.
10. **start:** 7:45 P.M. **end:** 1:10 A.M.
11. **start:** 11:35 A.M. **end:** 3:10 P.M.
12. **start:** 6:40 A.M. **end:** 10:17 A.M.
13. **start:** 4:25 P.M. **end:** 12:38 A.M.

Copy and complete the tables.

	START TIME	END TIME	ELAPSED TIME
14.	10:50 A.M.	■	3 hr 5 min
16.	■	2:30 P.M.	2 hr 40 min
18.	10:45 A.M.	2:22 P.M.	■

	START TIME	END TIME	ELAPSED TIME
15.	■	9:42 P.M.	4 hr 30 min
17.	8:12 A.M.	■	6 hr 33 min
19.	4:50 P.M.	8:05 P.M.	■

20. **? What's the Error?** Jim says the elapsed time from 7:35 A.M. to 9:45 P.M. is 2 hr 10 min. Describe his error. Write the correct answer.

21. Mark spends 3 hours doing chores and eating meals. He wants to visit friends for 4 hours, shop for 2 hours, read for 3 hours, and sleep for 10 hours. Will Mark be able to do everything in one day? Explain.

22. Use the flight schedule. How many minutes longer is the flight from Atlanta to Boston than the flight from Miami to Atlanta?

KELLY'S FLIGHT SCHEDULE	
Miami, FL, to Atlanta, GA	**Atlanta, GA, to Boston, MA**
LEAVES: 10:30 A.M.	LEAVES: 1:40 P.M.
ARRIVES: 12:18 P.M.	ARRIVES: 4:18 P.M.

23. **FAST FACT • SOCIAL STUDIES** Look at the table to the right. The 1896 Olympic marathon distance was 40,000 meters. Since 1924, the distance has been 2,195 meters longer. What is the total distance that Carlos and Josia ran? How much faster were their times than Spiridon's?

OLYMPIC MARATHONS		
Year	**Name**	**Time**
1896	Spiridon Loues	2 hr 58 min 50 sec
1984	Carlos Lopes	2 hr 9 min 21 sec
1996	Josia Thugwane	2 hr 12 min 36 sec
2000	Gezahgne Abera	2 hr 10 min 11 sec

24. **Write a problem** about how much time it might take to get to school in the morning. Include beginning and ending times. Compare your elapsed time with your classmates' times.

USE DATA For 25–27, use the schedule.

25. At about what time does each flight arrive in New York City?

26. If Ms. Lane needs to be in New York City for a 3:30 P.M. meeting, on which airline can she fly?

27. Mr. Wright arrived in New York at about 4:15 P.M. At what time did he leave Miami?

FLIGHTS FROM MIAMI, FL, TO NEW YORK CITY, NY

Each flight lasts about 2 hours and 45 minutes.

Airline	Departure Time
Airline A	9:05 A.M.
Airline B	11:10 A.M.
Airline C	1:30 P.M.
Airline D	2:45 P.M.

Mixed Review and Test Prep

Write the value of the blue digit. (pp. 2–6)

28. 45,623

29. 83,238

30. 172,908

31. 2,498,762

32. **TEST PREP** 27 + 35 + 118 (p. 40)
   A 160 **B** 170 **C** 179 **D** 180

33. **TEST PREP** Ryan had 32 baseball cards. Ken gave Ryan 18 cards. Ryan gave 5 of those cards to Tran. Choose an expression for the number of cards Ryan has now. (p. 64)
   F 32 − (18 − 5) **H** 32 + (18 + 5)
   G 32 + (18 − 5) **J** 32 − (18 + 5)

Problem Solving LINKUP . . . to Reading

STRATEGY • USE GRAPHIC AIDS Graphic aids are tables, time lines, maps, and diagrams that organize information so it is easy to read. Use the weather map to answer the questions.

1. Name the types of information shown on the map.

2. Use the compass rose to find the cities with rain that are east of Chicago.

3. Today is November 21. Eight days ago, Seattle and Minneapolis were 9 degrees warmer than shown. Name the date 8 days ago, and give the temperatures in both cities.

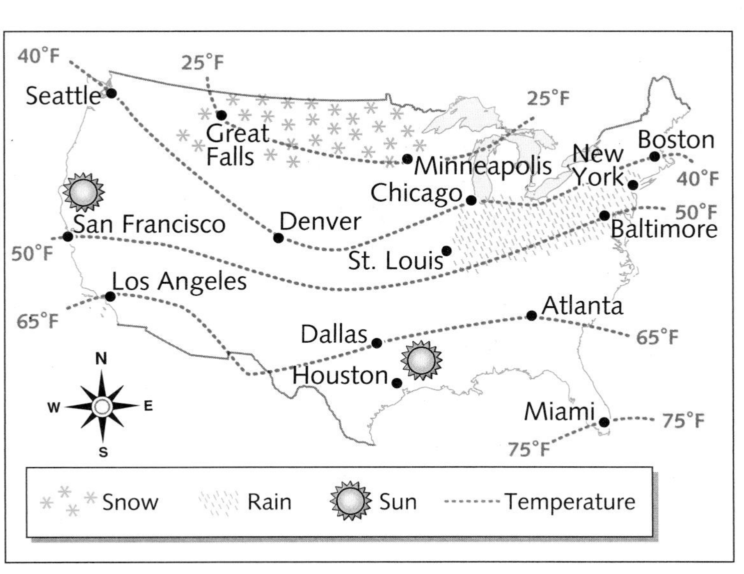

LESSON 3

Problem Solving Skill
Sequence Information

UNDERSTAND | PLAN | SOLVE | CHECK

Quick Review

Add 1 hour 40 minutes to each time.

1. 2:15 P.M. **2.** 9:25 A.M.

3. 4:13 P.M. **4.** 7:35 A.M.

5. 8:20 A.M.

PLAN YOUR DAY Sanjay plans to write a report about his visit to a wild animal park. He *must* see both movies and the alligator show. He will be at the park from 8:30 A.M. to 2:30 P.M. and will have lunch from 11:30 to noon. How can Sanjay schedule his day to complete these activities?

One way to sequence information is to arrange the data in order of importance.

To help you use time wisely, things that must be done should be at the top of the list. Things you could do another day should go closer to the bottom.

Things I must do:
- movie about endangered animals
- movie about rainforests
- alligator show
- lunch 11:30 - noon

Things I want to do:
- bird show
- dolphin feeding
- animal behavior

Sanjay completed his schedule as shown.

- In what other way could Sanjay plan his activities? Explain.

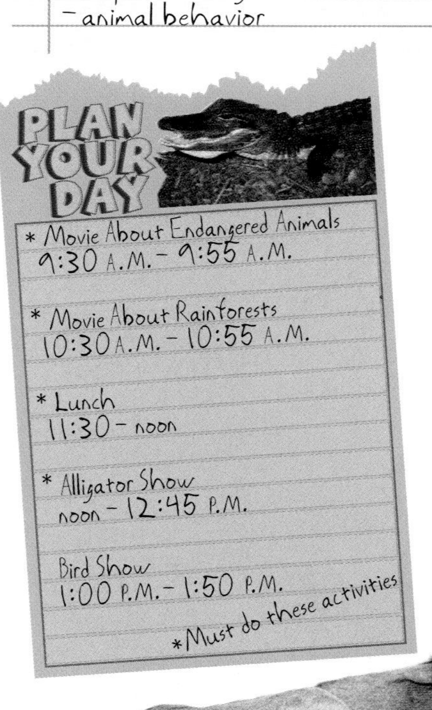
PLAN YOUR DAY

* Movie About Endangered Animals
9:30 A.M. - 9:55 A.M.

* Movie About Rainforests
10:30 A.M. - 10:55 A.M.

* Lunch
11:30 - noon

* Alligator Show
noon - 12:45 P.M.

Bird Show
1:00 P.M. - 1:50 P.M.

*Must do these activities

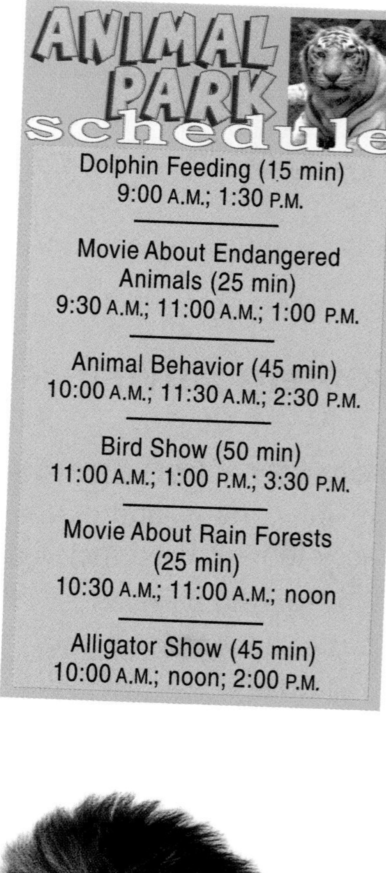
ANIMAL PARK schedule

Dolphin Feeding (15 min)
9:00 A.M.; 1:30 P.M.

Movie About Endangered Animals (25 min)
9:30 A.M.; 11:00 A.M.; 1:00 P.M.

Animal Behavior (45 min)
10:00 A.M.; 11:30 A.M.; 2:30 P.M.

Bird Show (50 min)
11:00 A.M.; 1:00 P.M.; 3:30 P.M.

Movie About Rain Forests (25 min)
10:30 A.M.; 11:00 A.M.; noon

Alligator Show (45 min)
10:00 A.M.; noon; 2:00 P.M.

Problem Solving Practice

USE DATA For 1–4, use the schedule and the information below.

Evelyn has movie theater gift certificates. She will be at the theater from noon to 5:30 P.M., and she really wants to see one new movie.

MOVIE SCHEDULE	
Movie	**Playing Times**
Safari	12:20–2:30; 2:30–4:40
Gentle Journey	12:40–3:10; 2:30–5:00
Lions New!	12:40–3:00; 2:40–5:00
Wild Adventures	11:30–2:30; 2:40–5:40
Raging River New!	12:20–2:40; 2:50–5:10
Whale Wonders	2:50–4:55; 3:20–5:25

1. How would you schedule Evelyn's afternoon?
2. Which movie is longer, *Lions* or *Safari*?
3. Which movies would Evelyn be able to watch?
   A *Raging River, Wild Adventures*
   B *Safari, Wild Adventures*
   C *Safari, Raging River*
   D *Lions, Gentle Journey*
4. Which two movies are the same length?
   F *Safari, Whale Wonders*
   G *Gentle Journey, Lions*
   H *Wild Adventures, Gentle Journey*
   J *Lions, Raging River*

Mixed Applications

USE DATA For 5–6, use the table and the information below.

Amy is planning a surprise party for her friend. She wants the party to last less than 4 hours. The table shows the activities she would like to include. The stars indicate activities that must be done.

Activity	Time
*Eat lunch and cake	30 min
*Open presents	45 min
*Go swimming	1 hr 30 min
Play charades	1 hr 30 min
Play volleyball	1 hr 15 min

5. Can the party include all of the starred activities? Why or why not?
6. Can the party include all of the activities? How would you plan the surprise party? Make a schedule.
7. Raul bought a tennis racket for $40.50 and 3 cans of tennis balls for $3.00 each. He had $7.37 left. How much money did he have before this purchase?
8. One hundred twelve students try out for the Youth Orchestra. If 42 boys and 34 girls are chosen, how many students are not chosen?
9. **Write a problem** about elapsed time, using the movie schedule above.

LESSON 4

Elapsed Time on a Calendar

Learn

TIME AFTER TIME The school play, *Time Trek,* will be presented on March 7. Rehearsals will begin on February 25. There are 8 rehearsals. There will be 1 rehearsal each day. There will be no rehearsals on Saturday or Sunday. Find the day and date of the last rehearsal.

To find the elapsed time, count the number of days. Start counting with February 25.

FEBRUARY						
Sun	Mon	Tue	Wed	Thu	Fri	Sat
					1	2
3	4	5	6	7	8	9
10	11	12	13	14	15	16
17	18	19	20	21	22	23
24	25	26	27	28		

MARCH						
Sun	Mon	Tue	Wed	Thu	Fri	Sat
					1	2
3	4	5	6	7	8	9
10	11	12	13	14	15	16
17	18	19	20	21	22	23
24/31	25	26	27	28	29	30

So, Wednesday, March 6, is the last rehearsal.

- Will the rehearsals last for more than or less than one week? by how many days?

Tito practices his voice exercises every day for 4 weeks. Using the fact 1 week = 7 days, you can say that Tito practices his voice exercises for 4 × 7 days, or 28 days.

- **What if** Tito continues to practice his voice exercises for 9 more weeks? How many more days does he practice?

More Practice: Harcourt Mega Math, The Number Games, *Tiny's Think Tank,* Level E

Quick Review

What day of the week is 9 days

1. after Monday?
2. before Sunday?
3. after Thursday?
4. before Friday?
5. before Tuesday?

VOCABULARY

century **decade**

Remember

Units of Time
1 week = 7 days
1 year = 12 months
1 year = about 52 weeks
1 year = 365 days
1 leap year = 366 days

Century or Decade

Ford's Theatre in Washington, D.C., opened in 1863. The theater was 1 century 4 decades 1 year old in 2004. How old, in years, was the theater in 2004?

1 **century** = 100 years

1 **decade** = 10 years

▲ **Ford's Theatre, Washington, D.C.**

Example

You can multiply to change from a larger unit of time to a smaller unit of time.

1 decade is 10 years, so 4 decades is 4 × 10 years, or 40 years.

$$\begin{aligned} \text{1 century} &= 100 \text{ years} \\ \text{4 decades} &= +\ \ 40 \text{ years} \\ &\ \ \ \ 140 \text{ years} \end{aligned}$$

1 century 4 decades 1 year is 140 years + 1 year.

So, the theater was 141 years old in 2004.

Check

1. **Explain** how to find the number of decades in a century.

USE DATA For 2–3, use the calendars here and on page 104.

2. Report cards were mailed on March 15. They will be mailed again in 9 weeks. On what date will report cards be mailed?
3. In a leap year, February has 29 days instead of 28. How long is it from February 24 to March 4 in a regular year? in a leap year?

APRIL						
Sun	Mon	Tue	Wed	Thu	Fri	Sat
	1	2	3	4	5	6
7	8	9	10	11	12	13
14	15	16	17	18	19	20
21	22	23	24	25	26	27
28	29	30				

MAY						
Sun	Mon	Tue	Wed	Thu	Fri	Sat
			1	2	3	4
5	6	7	8	9	10	11
12	13	14	15	16	17	18
19	20	21	22	23	24	25
26	27	28	29	30	31	

Find the missing number.

4. 5 weeks = ■ days
5. 800 years = ■ centuries
6. 7 decades = ■ years
7. 2 years = ■ months
8. 3 decades = ■ years
9. 7 weeks = ■ days

LESSON CONTINUES ▶

Practice and Problem Solving

Extra Practice, page 108, Set C

USE DATA For 10–13, use the calendars.

September						
Sun	Mon	Tue	Wed	Thu	Fri	Sat
			1	2	3	4
5	6	7	8	9	10	11
12	13	14	15	16	17	18
19	20	21	22	23	24	25
26	27	28	29	30		

October						
Sun	Mon	Tue	Wed	Thu	Fri	Sat
					1	2
3	4	5	6	7	8	9
10	11	12	13	14	15	16
17	18	19	20	21	22	23
24/31	25	26	27	28	29	30

Come and see
The Old Time Theatre Exhibit
September 2 to October 9

10. The exhibit is from September 2 through October 9. About how many weeks will the exhibit last?

11. The exhibit began advertising 2 months before it came to town. In what month did it begin advertising?

12. Cliff bought a ticket 5 weeks before the last day of the exhibit. On what day and date did Cliff buy his ticket?

13. The next exhibit will begin 2 weeks 2 days after October 9. What is the opening day and date of the new exhibit?

Find the missing number.

14. 2 years 3 weeks = about ■ weeks

15. 5 centuries 3 decades = ■ decades

16. 3 centuries 4 decades = ■ years

17. 6 decades 7 years = ■ years

18. About how many years is 4 decades 52 weeks?

19. What year was 1 century 2 decades before 1913?

20. What year was 2 centuries 3 decades after 1728?

21. What year was 1 century 4 decades 3 years after 1789?

22. Liz left on a trip May 23 and returned on June 7. Bridget left on a trip June 4 and returned on June 22. Whose trip was longer? How much longer?

23. Joel has read 134 pages in his whale book. He has 153 more pages to read. Write a number sentence using *n* to show how many pages are in the book.

24. **Write About It** Explain how to find two dates. The first is 10 days after October 6. The second is 2 weeks after the first. What are the two dates?

25. **Vocabulary Power** The abbreviation P.M. comes from two Latin words, *post* and *meridiem*. Together, the words mean "after noon" in Latin. How can this help you remember which hours are P.M.?

USE DATA For 26–27, use the calendars on page 106.

26. If today is September 12, what date and day of the week is 11 days from now?

27. **PATTERNS** Look at the dates in any of the columns of one of the calendars. Describe the pattern.

Mixed Review and Test Prep

28. Round 853,902 to the nearest hundred thousand. (p. 30)

29. Add 64,217 and 36,371. (p. 52)

30. Find the sum of 37,954 and the number 10,000 greater than 82,149. (p. 52)

31. Find the value of the expression $92 + (35 + 6)$. (p. 64)

32. $34{,}000 - 9{,}651$ (p. 50)

33. $81{,}643 + 27{,}285$ (p. 52)

34. **TEST PREP** $3 \times \blacksquare = 6 \times 5$
   A 1   C 5
   B 3   D 10

35. **TEST PREP** $943 + \blacksquare = 8{,}352$ (p. 76)
   F 7,409   H 8,409
   G 8,295   J 9,295

Problem Solving LINKUP . . . to Science

A time line shows the order of events. Events are listed by date, from the earliest to the latest. This time line shows some of the events in the history of the United States space program.

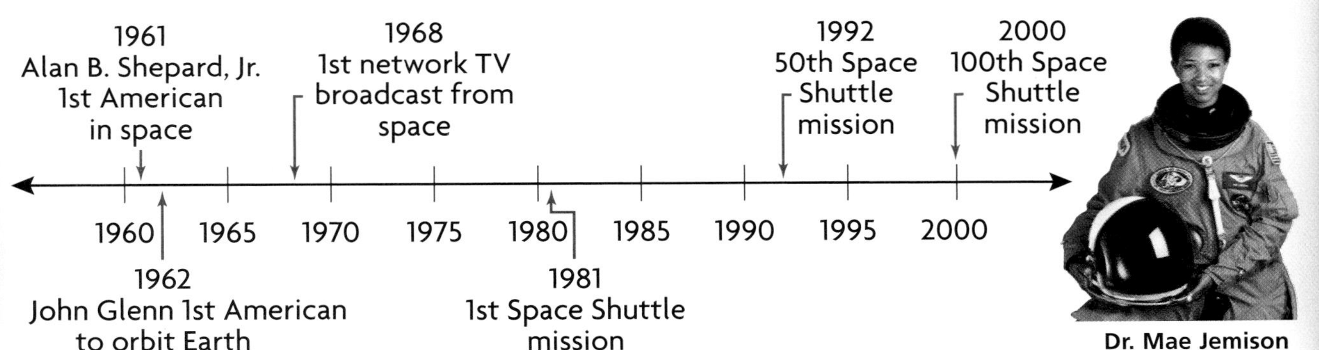

Dr. Mae Jemison

For 1–4, use the time line.

1. How many decades passed between the first American in space and the first Space Shuttle mission?

2. How many years before 2000 was the first network TV broadcast from space?

3. Dr. Mae Jemison, born in 1956, was a mission specialist on the fiftieth Space Shuttle mission. What birthday did she have in the year of this flight?

4. **REASONING** John Glenn returned to space after his seventy-seventh birthday, in 1998. What birthday did he have in the year he first orbited the Earth?

Extra Practice

Set A (pp. 96–97)

Write the time shown on the clock in two different ways.

1. 

2. 

3. 

Write the time as shown on a digital clock.

4. 11 minutes before one

5. 4 minutes after eight

6. 37 minutes before two

Set B (pp. 98–101)

Find the elapsed time.

1. **start:** 9:20 A.M.
end: 12:07 P.M.

2. **start:** 11:50 P.M.
end: 6:35 A.M.

3. **start:** 5:35 P.M.
end: 1:58 A.M.

Copy and complete the tables.

	START TIME	END TIME	ELAPSED TIME
4.	9:05 A.M.	11:35 A.M.	■
6.	■	2:23 P.M.	46 minutes
8.	3:35 P.M.	■	5 hr 17 min

	START TIME	END TIME	ELAPSED TIME
5.	■	5:35 P.M.	1 hr 45 min
7.	10:40 A.M.	■	1 hr 50 min
9.	9:20 A.M.	12:35 P.M.	■

Set C (pp. 104–107)

For 1–2, use the calendars.

1. Today is October 19. Janice has 3 weeks to train for the marathon. What is the date of the marathon?

2. A road race is scheduled 16 days after the 1st Thursday in November. What is the date of the road race?

3. What year was 3 centuries 8 decades before 1999?

October

Sun	Mon	Tue	Wed	Thu	Fri	Sat
		1	2	3	4	5
6	7	8	9	10	11	12
13	14	15	16	17	18	19
20	21	22	23	24	25	26
27	28	29	30	31		

November

Sun	Mon	Tue	Wed	Thu	Fri	Sat
					1	2
3	4	5	6	7	8	9
10	11	12	13	14	15	16
17	18	19	20	21	22	23
24	25	26	27	28	29	30

Review/Test

✓ CHECK VOCABULARY AND CONCEPTS

Choose the best term from the box.

second decade century

1. A _?_ is 100 years. (p. 105)
2. A _?_ is 10 years. (p. 105)

✓ CHECK SKILLS

Write the time in two different ways. (pp. 96–97)

3. 

4. 

5. 

Find the elapsed time. (pp. 98–101)

6. start: 8:22 A.M.
   end: 5:09 P.M.
7. start: 3:18 P.M.
   end: 11:59 P.M.
8. start: 8:43 P.M.
   end: 3:33 A.M.
9. start: 7:26 A.M.
   end: 9:12 A.M.

Find the missing number. (pp. 104–107)

10. 6 weeks 5 days = ■ days
11. 4 decades 8 years = ■ years
12. 3 centuries 7 decades = ■ years
13. 1 year 27 weeks = about ■ weeks

✓ CHECK PROBLEM SOLVING

14. Use the table to make a schedule for Sharon between 10:30 A.M. and 3:00 P.M. (pp. 102–103)

THINGS TO DO	
Activity	**Time**
Violin practice	1 hr
* Haircut	1:30 P.M.–2:00 P.M.
* Homework	45 min
Movie	12:30 P.M.–2:20 P.M.
Lunch	30 min

*Starred activities must be done.

15. The county fair will be open for two weeks. If the fair ends on September 27, on what date will it open? (pp. 104–107)

September						
Sun	Mon	Tue	Wed	Thu	Fri	Sat
1	2	3	4	5	6	7
8	9	10	11	12	13	14
15	16	17	18	19	20	21
22	23	24	25	26	27	28
29	30					

Standardized Test Prep

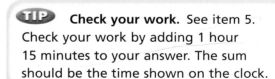

NUMBER SENSE, CONCEPTS, AND OPERATIONS

1. A new magazine sold 3,196 subscriptions during the month of June and 2,962 subscriptions during the month of July. What was the total number of subscriptions sold during these two months?

   A 10,158

   B 6,158

   C 5,158

   D 4,158

2. What is the **greatest** 4-digit number that can be made with these cards?

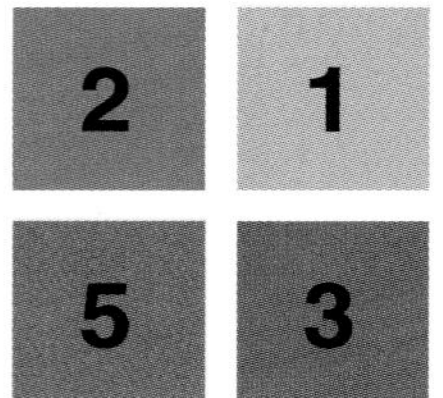

   F 1,253

   G 3,521

   H 5,231

   J 5,321

3. **Explain It** Venus has a diameter of 12,104 kilometers. Mars has a diameter of 6,794 kilometers. How much greater is the diameter of Venus than the diameter of Mars? Explain your reasoning.

MEASUREMENT

4. Which of the following tells how much the apples weigh?

   A 1 ounce

   B 10 ounces

   C 1 pound

   D 10 pounds

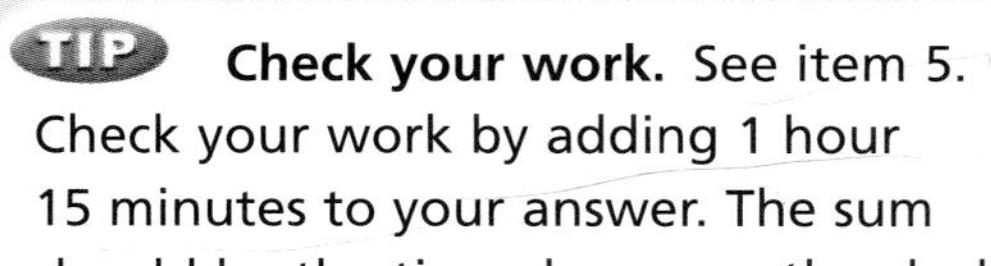

Check your work. See item 5. Check your work by adding 1 hour 15 minutes to your answer. The sum should be the time shown on the clock.

5. Mia has been at swim practice for 1 hour and 15 minutes. This clock shows the present time. At what time did Mia start practice?

   F 4:25

   G 4:20

   H 3:25

   J 3:20

6. **Explain It** What is the best estimate to describe the length of a new pencil? Write 7 *pounds*, 7 *miles*, or 7 *inches*. Explain how you decided.

ALGEBRAIC THINKING

7. Sasha has a new job. She earns $3 on Monday. Each day after that, she earns $3 more than the day before. How much will Sasha earn on Friday?

MONEY EARNED				
Mon	**Tue**	**Wed**	**Thu**	**Fri**
$3	$6	■	■	■

A $9

B $10

C $12

D $15

8. Jack has 45 marbles. Let n represent the number of marbles Jack gives to a friend. Which expression represents how many marbles Jack has left?

F $45 + n$

G $45 - n$

H $45 \div n$

J $45 \times n$

9. **Explain It** Alicia wants to buy a new bike that costs $99. She has saved $58. Let m represent the amount she still needs to buy the bike. What equation could she write to find how much money she still needs? Explain how you can check your answer.

GEOMETRY AND SPATIAL SENSE

10. Which figures appear to be congruent?

A

B

C

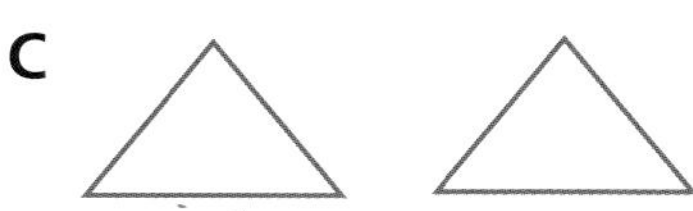

D

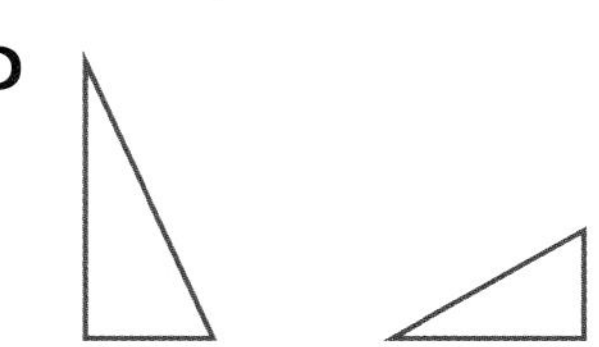

11. Look at the sign below.

Which figure shows the sign turned 180°?

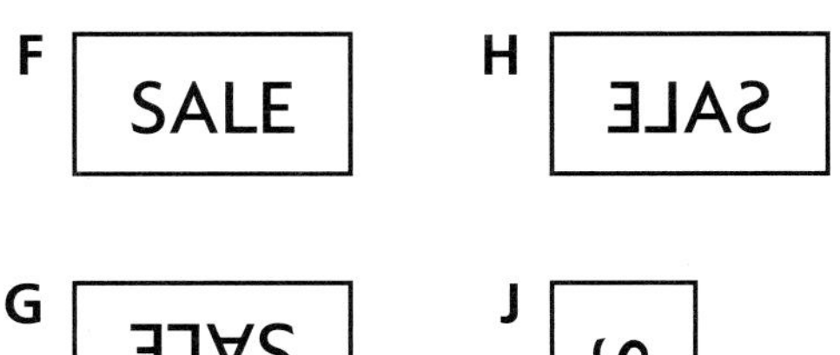

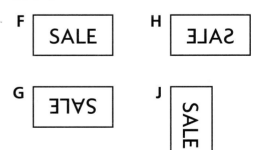

12. **Explain It** Juan says that the lower case letter t appears to be made from parallel line segments. Sue says it appears to be made from perpendicular line segments. Who is correct? How do you know?

t

CHAPTER 6 Collect and Organize Data

FAST FACT • SCIENCE The waters around the Florida Keys are home to more than 6,000 species of marine plants and animals.

PROBLEM SOLVING The tally table lists the 5 most frequently sighted types of fish in the Florida Keys and shows how many of each type a diver saw during one dive. Make a bar graph of the data and order the types of fish from most to least seen.

FISH SEEN DURING ONE DIVE

Type of Fish	Number Seen
Blue tang	卌 卌 卌 III
Stoplight parrotfish	卌 IIII
Yellowtail snapper	卌 卌 II
Bluehead	III
Sergeant major	卌 I

CHECK WHAT YOU KNOW

Use this page to help you review and remember important skills needed for Chapter 6.

READ PICTOGRAPHS

For 1–4, use the pictograph.

RUNNING CLUB MEMBERS	
Third grade	🏃🏃½🏃
Fourth grade	🏃🏃🏃🏃🏃🏃
Fifth grade	🏃🏃🏃🏃½🏃

Key: Each 🏃 = 2 members.

1. How many members of the Running Club are in fourth grade?
2. If 5 more third graders joined the Running Club, how many symbols would there be for third grade?
3. What is the total number of members in the Running Club?
4. How many fifth-grade members are in the Running Club?

TALLIES TO FREQUENCY TABLES

For 5–7, use the table.

SCHOOL FRUIT STAND	
Week	Pieces of Fruit Sold
1	𝍸 𝍸 |||
2	𝍸
3	𝍸 ||||
4	𝍸 ||

5. Use the tally table to make a frequency table.
6. How many pieces of fruit were sold in Weeks 1 and 2?
7. How many more pieces of fruit were sold in Weeks 1 and 2 than in Weeks 3 and 4?

VOCABULARY POWER

REVIEW

data [dā′tə] *noun*

Data is information collected about people or things from which conclusions can be drawn. There are many different ways to show the collected data. Describe some of the ways that data can be displayed.

PREVIEW

survey	**range**
frequency	**outlier**
cumulative frequency	**stem-and-leaf plot**
mean	**stem**
mode	**leaf**
median	**scale**
line plot	**interval**

www.harcourtschool.com/mathglossary

Collect and Organize Data

Learn

TAKE YOUR PICK You are taking a **survey** when you ask different people the same questions and record their answers. Follow these rules to get the information you want:

- Make the questions clear and simple.
- Ask each person the questions only once.
- Use tally marks to record each person's answer, or response.

Jason and Susie each wrote a question to find the class's favorite color for School Spirit Day decorations. Compare the results of their surveys.

Quick Review

1. 315 + 70
2. 817 − 209
3. 257 + 43
4. 1,000 − 430
5. 15 + 25 + 16 + 24

VOCABULARY

survey **frequency**
cumulative frequency

Remember

In a tally table, tally marks are used to record data. The tally marks 𝍸| stand for 6.

Is your favorite color red, blue, or yellow?

SUSIE'S SURVEY DATA	
Color	Votes
Red	𝍸 𝍸
Blue	𝍸 𝍸 |
Yellow	𝍸 |||

What is your favorite color?

JASON'S SURVEY DATA

Color	Votes
Yellow	|||
Green	𝍸 𝍸
Blue	𝍸 |
Red	𝍸 |
Orange	||||

Both surveys ask about favorite colors, but Jason's allows more color choices. His survey allows any colors, such as orange or green. Susie's question allows only 3 color choices.

Frequency Tables

A frequency table helps you organize the data from a tally table. The **frequency** is the number of times a response occurs. The **cumulative frequency** is a running total of the frequencies.

LOGGERHEAD TURTLE NESTS FOUND	
Day	Tally
May 11	||||
May 12	𝍸	
May 13	𝍸 ||||
May 14	𝍸	

These tables show the numbers of loggerhead sea turtle nests found in four days on Fort Lauderdale Beach, Florida. Use them to find the day when the most turtle nests were found, and the total number of nests found.

LOGGERHEAD TURTLE NESTS FOUND		
Day	Frequency (Number of Nests Found)	Cumulative Frequency
May 11	4	4
May 12	6	10
May 13	9	19
May 14	6	25

← $4 + 6 = 10$
← $10 + 9 = 19$
← $19 + 6 = 25$ ← Total number of turtle nests found

May 13 had the greatest frequency, so May 13 was the day that the most turtle nests were found. The total number of nests found was 25.

MATH IDEA Tables can be used to collect, organize, and display data.

Check

1. **Write** a survey question, with choices, to find your classmates' favorite type of pizza.

Use Jason's and Susie's survey results on page 114. Tell whether each statement is *true* or *false*. Explain.

2. Susie's data show that more students prefer blue than red.
3. Jason's data show that red is the students' favorite color.

For 4–6, use this frequency table.

4. How many slices were sold in Hour 2?
5. By the end of Hour 3, how many slices had been sold?
6. How many more slices were sold in Hour 1 than Hour 4?

Pizza Slices Sold		
Hour	Frequency	Cumulative Frequency
1	16	16
2	20	36
3	12	48
4	9	57

LESSON CONTINUES

Practice and Problem Solving

Extra Practice, page 130, Set A

Gina asked her friends, "What is your favorite kind of party?" She put the data in a table.

FAVORITE KIND OF PARTY	
Party	**Votes**
Bowling	7
Skating	8
Movie	4
Pool	5

For 7–9, use the table to tell whether each statement is *true* or *false*. Explain.

7. Gina's data show that more friends prefer a bowling party than a pool party.
8. Gina's data show that a pool party is the least favorite choice.
9. Gina's data show that a skating party is the favorite party of the greatest number of her friends.
10. Copy the party table and add a cumulative frequency column. How many friends did Gina survey?
11. Write a survey question to find favorite fruits. Survey your classmates. Make a tally table and a frequency table for your data.
12. **Write About It** Write a problem using this data: Rosa buys four items priced at $27, $12, $15, and $32.

For 13–15, use the table.

SKATING TICKETS SOLD		
Day	**Tickets Sold**	**Cumulative Frequency**
Tuesday	5	■
Wednesday	■	23
Thursday	10	■
Friday	■	45

13. Copy and complete the table. How many tickets were sold on Wednesday?
14. How many tickets were sold during the 4 days?
15. On which two days were the most tickets sold?
16. Nancy planted a 4-year-old tree in the park in 1988. How old will the tree be in 2010?
17. Mrs. Barker was 34 years old in 1998. How old was she in 1979?

For 18–20, use the bar graph.

18. Which cookie is the students' favorite?
19. How many more students chose chocolate chip cookies than raisin cookies?
20. **REASONING** How many students were surveyed in all?

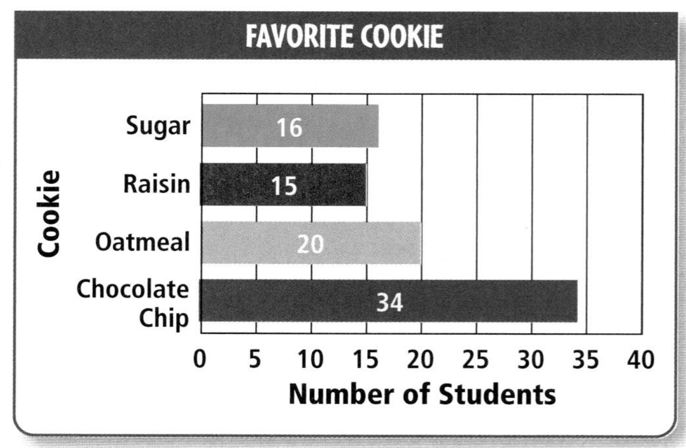

For 21–23, use the table.

21. How many bottles of juice were sold Monday and Tuesday?

22. How many more bottles of juice were sold on Thursday than Tuesday?

23. How many bottles of juice were sold in all?

JOE'S JUICE STAND		
Day	**Frequency**	**Cumul Frequen**
Monday	140	140
Tuesday	197	337
Wednesday	259	596
Thursday	238	834

Mixed Review and Test Prep

24. Round 56,341 to the nearest ten thousand. (p. 30)

25. Which is greater, 1,364,217 or 1,436,217? (p. 20)

26. Subtract 40,135 from 56,091. (p. 52)

27. Find the missing number in the pattern: 56,410; 45,410; ■; 23,410; 12,410. Describe the pattern. (p. 74)

28. Find the sum of 25,984 and the number that is 10,000 greater than 31,092. (p. 52)

29. Find the value of the expression $(56 - 39) + 48$. (p. 64)

30. $80,000 - 4,705$ (p. 50)

31. $67,813 + 14,589$ (p. 52)

32. TEST PREP $10 \times ■ = 8 \times 5$

- **A** 3
- **B** 4
- **C** 5
- **D** 6

33. TEST PREP $2,890 + 3,678 + 4,722$ (p. 48)

- **F** 9,180
- **G** 10,290
- **H** 11,180
- **J** 11,290

Problem Solving Thinker's Corner

Taking a survey is a good way to predict how people will vote in an election. A random survey is one where each voter has the same chance of being surveyed. A survey that is not random may ask the same question of a group of people with similar interests.

Angela and Paul are running for class president. Angela has promised more computer time if elected, and Paul has a lot of friends in the band.

KIM
Computer Club Members
Who would you vote for?
Angela 9 votes
Paul 1 vote

TOSHIO
Band Members
Who would you vote for?
Angela 2 votes
Paul 8 votes

SETH
Students at Lunch
Who would you vote for?
Angela 14 votes
Paul 20 votes

Use the survey results to answer each question.

1. Which group of people was probably chosen at random?
2. Explain why you think Kim's results were different from Seth's.
3. Who do you think will win the election? Tell why you think this.

Mean, Median, and Mode

Quick Review

1. 3 + 4 + 4 + 5
2. 16 ÷ 4
3. 2 + 3 + 5 + 5 + 6
4. 20 ÷ 5
5. 4 + 5 + 8 + 9

VOCABULARY

mean **mode**
median

Mr. Humphrey's class went whale watching. The table shows how many whales the students saw on the trip. Find the mean number of whale sightings.

The **mean** is the average of a set of numbers, and is found by dividing the sum of a set of numbers by the number of addends.

Activity 1

MATERIALS: connecting cubes

STEP 1

Make stacks of cubes to model the number of whales each student saw.

STEP 2

Rearrange the stacks so that they are equal. The mean is the number in each stack.

WHALE SIGHTINGS

Student	Number of Whales
Joni	3
Pablo	4
Emma	1
Mitchell	4
Chad	3

So, the mean number of whales is 3 whales.

You also can use paper and pencil to find the mean of a data set.

Example

Some students saw dolphins. Jennifer saw 3 dolphins, Leon saw 5, Kari saw 5, and Josh saw 7. Find the mean number of dolphins.

STEP 1

Add all of the numbers in the data set.

3 + 5 + 5 + 7 = 20

STEP 2

Divide the sum by the number of addends. The quotient is the mean.

20 ÷ 4 = 5

So, the mean number of dolphins is 5 dolphins.

- How is rearranging the stacks of cubes like dividing?
- Travis saw 2 dolphins and Sheri saw 2 dolphins. Include the data in the example above. Then, find the mean.

Finding Mode and Median

Mr. Alber's class recorded the high temperatures for the first 11 days of October. Find the mode and median of the data.

OCTOBER HIGH TEMPERATURES (in degrees Fahrenheit)											
Date	1	2	3	4	5	6	7	8	9	10	11
Temp.	65	62	62	62	65	60	59	59	57	58	60

Activity 2

MATERIALS: index cards

STEP 1

Find the mode.

Write the 11 temperatures on index cards. Sort the cards by numbers. The **mode** is the number that occurs most often. There may be more than one mode, or there may be no mode.

57 58 59
60 62 65

STEP 2

Find the median.

Order the index cards from least to greatest. Turn one card over on each end. Keep doing this, moving toward the middle, until only one number is showing. That number is the **median**, or middle number.

?

• What is the mode of the data? What is the median?

Example

Find the median of the data set.

Order the data from least to greatest.

2, 3, 4, 4, 4, 6, 6, 7, 7, 7

↑ ↑
middle numbers

Points Scored by Mia						
Points	**2**	**3**	**4**	**5**	**6**	**7**
Frequency	**1**	**1**	**3**	**0**	**2**	**3**

When a data set has two middle numbers, the median is the mean of the two numbers.

STEP 1

Add the two middle numbers.

$6 + 4 = 10$

STEP 2

Then, divide the sum by 2.

$10 \div 2 = 5$

So, the median of the data is 5.

LESSON CONTINUES

Check

1. **Explain** how to find the mode and mean of the data in the Example at the bottom of page 119.

Find the mean, median, and mode.

2.

STRAWBERRIES PICKED					
Day	1	2	3	4	5
Baskets	5	7	6	4	3

3.

KITTENS BORN						
Litter	1	2	3	4	5	6
Kittens	3	5	5	6	3	2

Find the median.

4.

SCIENCE TEST SCORES					
Test	1	2	3	4	5
Score	88	95	67	86	95

5.

SHELLS COLLECTED							
Day	Sun	Mon	Tue	Wed	Thu	Fri	Sat
Shells	31	17	18	15	19	23	31

Practice and Problem Solving

Extra Practice, page 130, Set B

Find the mean, median, and mode.

6.

POINTS SCORED					
Game	1	2	3	4	5
Points	12	12	7	9	10

7.

ALLIGATORS SIGHTED						
Day	1	2	3	4	5	6
Alligators	4	2	4	4	2	2

Find the median.

8.

STUDENTS' HEIGHTS (in inches)					
Student	Ann	Bob	Carl	Dan	Ed
Height	54	53	56	54	55

9.

SWIM TEAM				
Age	9	10	11	12
Frequency	4	3	2	2

10. **What's the Error?** Jim says the median of the data below is 220 and the mode is 170. Describe his error and write the correct median and mode.

PLAY TICKETS SOLD					
Week	1	2	3	4	5
Tickets	150	170	220	160	220

11. **REASONING** Carol scored 89, 88, 93, 88, 85, and 93 on six tests. After she took the seventh test, the mode was 93. Find the median of the seven scores.

12. **Write About It** Record the high temperatures for your city for a one-week period and put the data in a table. Find the median and the mode.

13. **Vocabulary Power** The words *mean* and *median* both come from the same root word and originally meant the same thing. Explain how today's meanings of the mean and median of a set of data are different.

14. **ESTIMATION** The summer temperature in Scottsdale, Arizona, can be 104°F. The summer temperature in Anchorage, Alaska, can be 65°F. About how much warmer could it be in Scottsdale than in Anchorage?

15. The boat taking Mr. Humphrey's class leaves at 9:40 A.M. The trip lasts 3 hours and 15 minutes. What time will the class return from the trip?

Mixed Review and Test Prep

For 16–17, write $<$ or $>$ for each ●. (p. 48)

16. $7,500 - 1,000$ ● $7,400$

17. $8,395$ ● $7,059 + 1,300$

For 18–22, find the sum or difference. (p. 48)

18. $549 + 301$

19. $287 + 109 + 91$

20. $867 - 329$

21. $506 - 207$

22. $8,467 + 1,212$

23. **TEST PREP** Mr. Key is traveling for 832 miles. He has driven 453 miles so far. How many more miles does he have to drive? (p. 48)

A 379 **C** 479
B 389 **D** 1,285

24. **TEST PREP** Which equation shows the Associative Property of Addition? (p. 68)

F $35 + 6 = 6 + 35$
G $(35 + 6) + 18 = 35 + (6 + 18)$
H $35 + 0 = 35$
J $35 + 6 + 18 = 59$

Problem Solving Thinker's Corner

MORE ABOUT MODE The mode often is used when dealing with groups of objects which are not numbers. Look at the Favorite Marine Animal table. Dolphin received the most responses, so dolphin represents the mode.

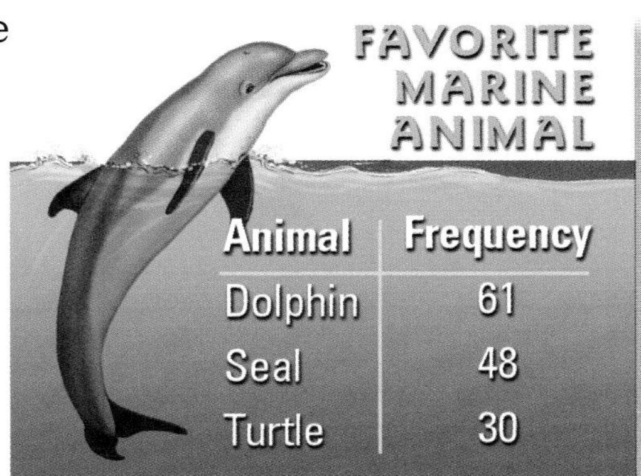

FAVORITE MARINE ANIMAL

Animal	Frequency
Dolphin	61
Seal	48
Turtle	30

Find the mode.

1.

VOTES FOR CLASS PRESIDENT			
Student	Tammy	Kevin	Janice
Frequency	9	13	1

2.

BATS OBSERVED			
Type	Brown	Red	Indiana
Frequency	15	7	5

LESSON

3 Read Line Plots

Learn

"X" MARKS THE SPOT A graph that shows the frequency of data along a number line is called a **line plot**. This line plot shows the number of runs Corey batted in during one baseball season.

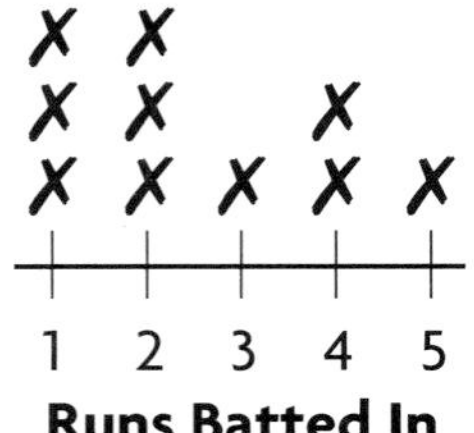

Runs Batted In by Corey

The three X's above the 2 on the line plot show that Corey batted in 2 runs in 3 different games.

You can use a line plot to find the range. The **range** is the difference between the greatest and the least values in a set of data.

$5 - 1 = 4$ The range is 4.

Look at the line plot of the number of brothers and sisters. Most of the data form a cluster, or group, from 0 to 3. The value 7 is called an outlier. An **outlier** is a value separated from the rest of the data.

Check

1. **Explain** how a line plot and a tally table are alike.

For 2–3, use the library line plot.

2. What is the range of the data?
3. What value would be considered an outlier? Explain.

Quick Review

1. 480 + 120
2. 61 + 59
3. 100 − 43
4. 1,000 − 350
5. 165 + 135

VOCABULARY

line plot **range**
outlier

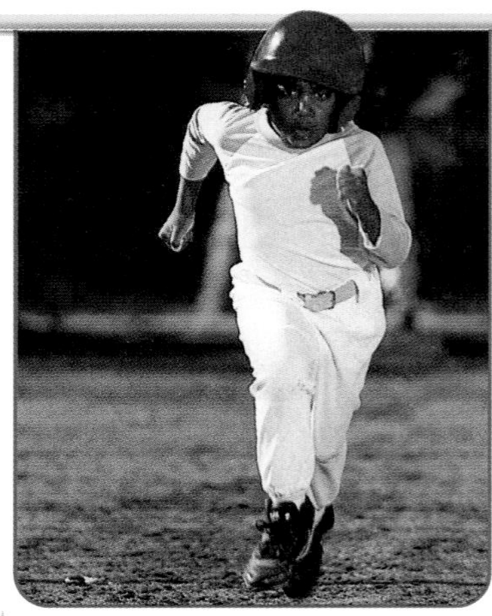

Technology Link

More Practice: Harcourt Mega Math The Number Games, *ArachnaGraph*, Levels E and F

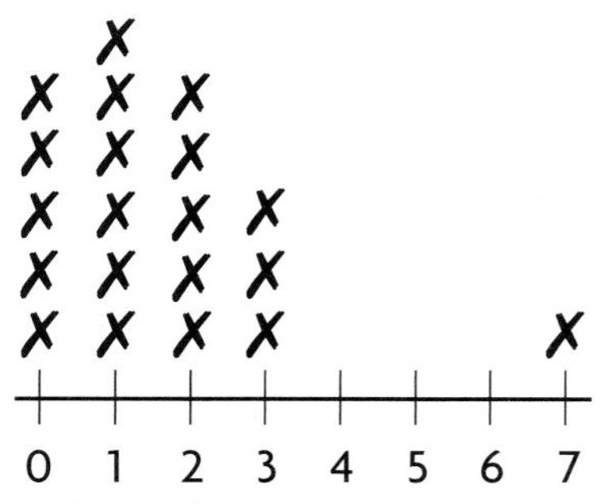

Number of Brothers and Sisters

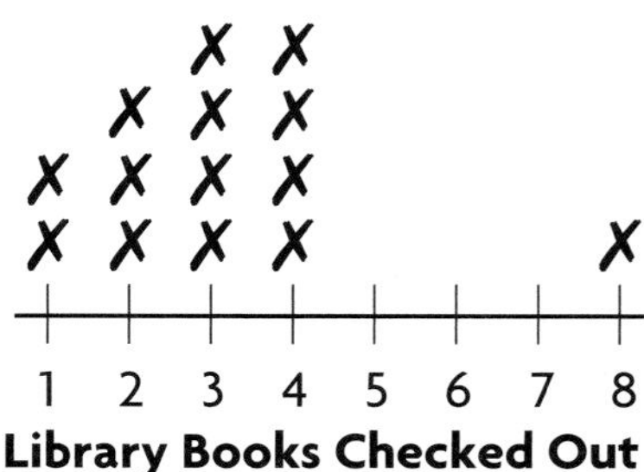

Library Books Checked Out

Practice and Problem Solving
Extra Practice, page 130, Set C

For 4–6, use the first line plot.

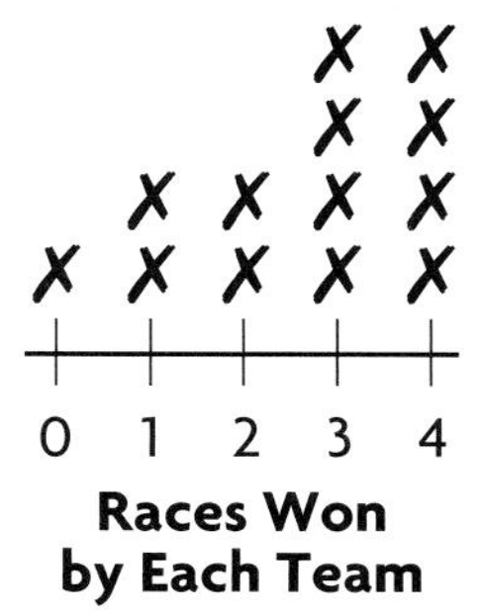

Races Won by Each Team

4. How many teams won three races? How many races is that in all?
5. How many teams are shown? How do you know?
6. How many races were won in all?

For 7–9, use the second line plot.

7. Each X in this line plot stands for one player. What do the numbers on the line plot stand for?
8. What value would be considered an outlier? Explain.
9. What is the range of the number of free-throw baskets made? What is the median?

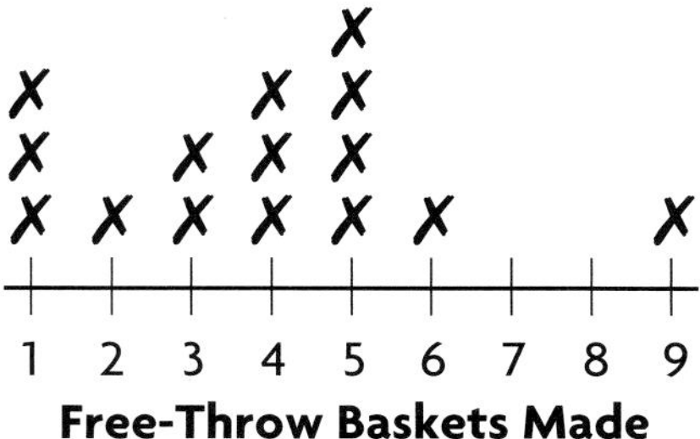

Free-Throw Baskets Made

For 10–12, use this table.

JUICE PACKS BOUGHT	
Juice Packs	Students
0	I
1	II
2	II
3	IIII

10. Make a line plot of the data. Find the mean, median, mode, and range of the number of juice packs bought.
11. **REASONING** Find the total number of juice packs the students bought.
12. How many students bought juice packs?
13. Jackie worked in the garden for 25 min. Then she walked the dog for 15 min. If she started at 11:30 A.M., what time did she finish?
14. **? What's the Question?** Molly has n nickels. She gives 14 to her brother. The answer is $n - 14$.

Mixed Review and Test Prep

Round to the nearest thousand. (p. 30)

15. 75,391
16. 148,569
17. Write a number greater than 23,487 and less than 23,847. (p. 24)
18. 378 + (813 − 72) (p. 64)
19. **TEST PREP** What is 1,276 subtracted from 1,493? (p. 48)
    - **A** 216
    - **B** 217
    - **C** 223
    - **D** 769

LESSON 4

Make Stem-and-Leaf Plots

Quick Review

1. 330 + 50 + 200
2. 75 + 9
3. 47 + 16
4. 80 − 45
5. 66 − 38

VOCABULARY

stem-and-leaf plot

stem

leaf

LIVE CORAL There are more than 50 different known corals in the Florida Keys. Use the data for the number of different corals seen by 9 divers to make a stem-and-leaf plot.

NUMBER OF DIFFERENT CORALS SEEN								
13	21	26	17	34	29	34	30	11

A **stem-and-leaf-plot** shows groups of data arranged by place value.

The coral reef off of the Florida Keys is the only living coral reef in the continental United States. ▶

Example 1

STEP 1

Group the data by the tens digits.

10:	13	17	11
20:	21	26	29
30:	34	34	30

STEP 2

Order the tens digits in a column from least to greatest to form the stems. Draw a line to the right of the stems.

1 |
2 |
3 |

Each tens digit is called a **stem**.

STEP 3

Write each ones digit to the right of its tens digit.

1	3 7 1
2	1 6 9
3	4 4 0

Each ones digit is called a **leaf**.

STEP 4

Order the leaves from least to greatest. Include a title, labels, and a key to show what each stem and leaf represents.

Number of Different Corals Seen

Stem	Leaves
1	1 3 7
2	1 6 9
3	0 4 4

2|1 = 21 corals.

Since the stem-and-leaf plot organizes data in order of place value, you can use it to find the median of a set of data.

Example 2 Use the stem-and-leaf plot to find the median.

Begin by crossing off the least leaf and the greatest leaf on the plot.

Keep crossing off pairs of leaves that are the least and greatest until only one leaf remains. That number is the median. If two leaves remain, the median is the mean of those leaves.

So, the median number of corals seen is 26.

Number of Different Corals Seen

Stem	Leaves
1	~~1~~ 3 7
2	1 6 9
3	0 4 ~~4~~

Check

1. **Explain** how you could find the median in Example 2 if another diver had seen 32 corals.

For 2–3, use the stem-and-leaf plot of the different fish spotted in the Florida Keys.

2. What are the least and greatest numbers of different fish spotted?

3. What is the mode? the median?

Number of Different Fish Spotted

Stem	Leaves
2	0 0 1
3	3 6 6 8 9
4	4 5 7 8
5	2

2|0 = 20 fish.

Practice and Problem Solving

Extra Practice, page 130, Set D

For 4–6, use the stem-and-leaf plot of miniature golf scores.

4. Which digits are stems?

5. What is the mode? the median?

6. What are the lowest and highest miniature golf scores? What is the range?

Miniature Golf Scores

Stem	Leaves
2	8
3	0 5 5 7
4	1 2 2 4 8
5	0 0 1 3 3 3 7

3|5 = 35.

For 7–8, use the stem-and-leaf plot of Kay's bowling scores.

7. Write all of the scores shown on this stem-and-leaf plot.

8. What is the median of Kay's bowling scores?

Kay's Bowling Scores

Stem	Leaves
10	0 3 8
11	0 4 5 6
12	3 7

10|0 = 100.

9. The heights of Mr. Jin's students are 53, 48, 55, 49, 49, 51, 55, 57, 57, 59, 54, 55, and 48 inches. Make a stem-and-leaf plot of these data. Find the median and the mode of the heights.

10. Josie is making a pictograph with a key in which each symbol stands for 5 students. How many symbols stand for 20 students? 25 students?

11. **Write About It** Explain the difference between stems and leaves on a stem-and-leaf plot.

Mixed Review and Test Prep

12. 15,982 + 16,775 (p. 52)

13. 3,901 + 2,881 (p. 48)

14. Write an expression using the variable *n* for a number of cards minus 8 cards. (p. 64)

15. Order 86,962; 86,923; 85,816 from *least* to *greatest*. (p. 24)

16. **TEST PREP** Choose the number that does *not* round to 8,600. (p. 30)

A 8,596 **C** 8,547
B 8,623 **D** 8,647

LESSON 5

Compare Graphs

Quick Review

1. 349 + 690
2. 921 − 487
3. 14 + ■ + 6 = 38
4. 3 × 4
5. 5 × 8

VOCABULARY

scale interval

Learn

RAISE THE BAR Graphs A and B show the same data. However, the graphs look different.

The **scale** of a graph is a series of numbers placed at fixed, or equal, distances. Both graphs have a scale of 0–50. The highest value of the scale should be greater than the greatest value of the data.

The **interval** of a graph is the difference between two numbers on the scale. Graph A's scale has an interval of 5. Graph B's scale has an interval of 10.

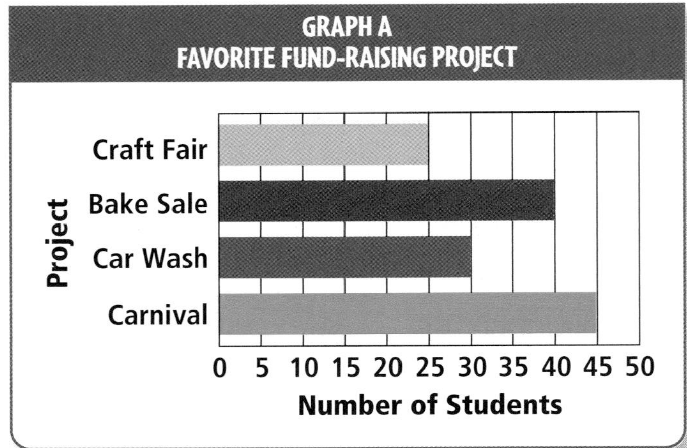

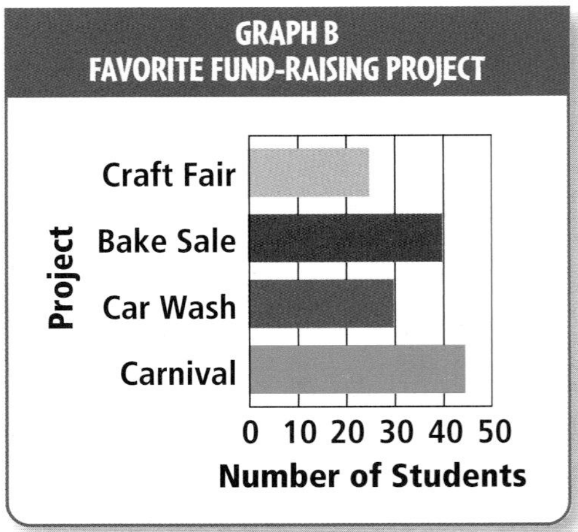

• Why is it easier to compare the bars in Graph A?

Check

1. **Explain** why the lengths of the bars in Graph A and the lengths of the bars in Graph B are different.

For 2–3, explain how the length of the bars would change in Graph B above.

2. if the interval were 20
3. if the interval were 2

Practice and Problem Solving

Extra Practice, page 130, Set E

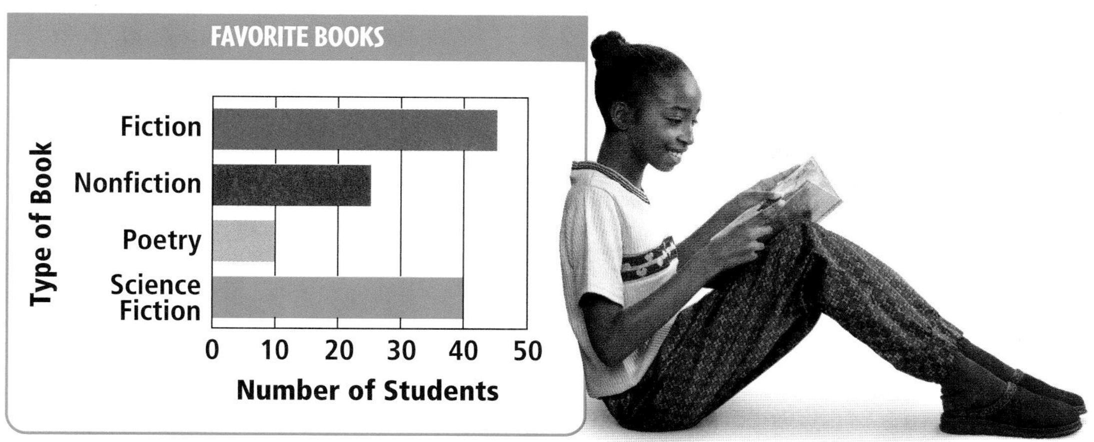

For 4–7, explain how the lengths of the bars would change in the graph above.

4. if the interval were 1

5. if the interval were 2

6. if the interval were 20

7. if the interval were 25

8. What is the mode of the data in the graph above?

9. What is the scale of the graph above?

For 10–13, choose 5, 10, or 100 as the most reasonable interval for each set of data. Explain your choice.

10. 5, 16, 20, 11, 15

11. 15, 31, 48, 30, 69

12. 100, 200, 200, 450, 500, 300

13. 32, 50, 89, 60, 101

For 14–16, use the graph above.

14. Make a new graph with an interval of 5. Explain how the length of the bars changed.

15. **Write a problem** with an answer of 25, using the data from the graph.

16. **REASONING** Josef's choice had 15 more votes than nonfiction. Zoe's choice had the fewest votes. Ali's choice was different from Josef's and Zoe's, but it was not fiction. What did each student choose?

Mixed Review and Test Prep

17. Write eight hundred seventy-two thousand, one hundred six in standard form. (p. 4)

18. $\begin{array}{r} 6{,}000 \\ -1{,}753 \\ \hline \end{array}$ (p. 50)

19. $\begin{array}{r} 4{,}000 \\ -\ 2{,}995 \\ \hline \end{array}$ (p. 50)

20. Find the value of $(36 - 12) + 14$. (p. 64)

21. TEST PREP Choose the equation that best fits these words: Nine eggs plus some more eggs are 12 eggs. (p. 70)

A $9 - n = 12$ **C** $9 + n = 12$

B $12 + 9 = n$ **D** $12 + n = 9$

LESSON 6

Problem Solving Strategy
Make a Graph

Quick Review

1. 2 × 3 **2.** 4 × 3
3. 7 × 3 **4.** 8 × 3
5. 10 × 3

PROBLEM You can determine the age of a fish by its scales, which have growth rings like trees. Each ring represents 1 year. The life span of a French angelfish is about 14 years, and the life span of a queen parrotfish is about 5 years. The life span of a queen triggerfish is about 12 years, and the life span of a coney is about 4 years. Which two fish have the greatest difference in life spans?

UNDERSTAND

- What are you asked to find?
- What information will you use?
- Is there any information you will not use? If so, what?

PLAN

- What strategy can you use to solve the problem?
  You can *make a graph* to help you see the information easily.

SOLVE

- What graph or plot can you make to help you solve the problem?

  You can make a pictograph to compare the life spans of the fish.

  On the graph, the French angelfish has the greatest number of symbols, so its life span is the longest. The coney has the least number of symbols, so its life span is the shortest.

  So, the French angelfish and the coney have the greatest difference in life spans.

LIFE SPANS OF FISH

Type of Fish	Life Span (in years)
French angelfish	🐟🐟🐟🐟🐟🐟🐟
Queen parrotfish	🐟🐟 half 🐟
Queen triggerfish	🐟🐟🐟🐟🐟🐟
Coney	🐟🐟

Key: Each 🐟 = 2 years.

CHECK

- How can you check to see whether your graph is correct?

Problem Solving Practice

1. **What if** you wanted to add the bonefish to your pictograph? The bonefish has a life span of about 10 years. How many symbols would you use on your pictograph for this fish?

2. ***FAST FACT*** • **SCIENCE** The maximum length of a neon goby is 5 cm. For a reef butterflyfish it is 15 cm, for a striped parrotfish it is 35 cm, and for a purple reeffish it is 10 cm. Make a pictograph of the data. Then find the median.

Strategies

- Draw a Diagram or Picture
- Make a Model or Act It Out
- Make an Organized List
- Find a Pattern
- **Make a Table or Graph**
- Predict and Test
- Work Backward
- Solve a Simpler Problem
- Write an Equation
- Use Logical Reasoning

Problem Solving

For 3–4 use the table.

3. How many trees were planted by Tate School?

   A 20 **C** 24
   B 23 **D** 25

4. How many more trees did Tate School plant in 2001 than in 2002?

   F 2 **H** 4
   G 3 **J** 5

TREES PLANTED BY TATE SCHOOL

Year	Number of Trees
2001	𝍸 |||
2002	𝍸	
2003	𝍸 𝍸

Mixed Strategy Practice

5. Henri found that 986 people went to a movie on Friday, 1,453 people went on Saturday, and 1,622 went on Sunday. How many people went to the movie in all?

6. Each of the 24 students is playing either basketball or volleyball. If 4 students switched from basketball to volleyball, there would be an equal number playing each sport. How many students are playing volleyball?

7. There are 57 shirts. Twenty of them are blue and the others are yellow. Write an equation using the variable y to show this.

8. Ben has 3 times as many marbles as Jon. Together they have between 18 and 25 marbles. How many marbles might Jon have?

9. Carmen bought a shirt for $14.99. She bought a sweater for $25.39. Estimate to the nearest dollar the amount that Carmen spent.

10. The product of two numbers is 36. Their sum is 13. What are the numbers? What is their difference?

CHAPTER 6

Extra Practice

Set A (pp. 114–117)

Use the frequency table.

1. During which hour were the most cups of juice sold?
2. How many total cups of juice were sold?

CUPS OF JUICE SOLD AT THE FESTIVAL

Hour	Frequency	Cumulative Frequency
1	15	15
2	26	41
3	28	69
4	19	88

Set B (pp. 118–121)

Find the mean, median, and mode.

1. **CARS WASHED**

Hour	1	2	3	4
Cars	6	4	3	7

2. **MOVIES SEEN IN THE SUMMER**

Student	Ed	Sue	Bob	Jan	Ann
Movies	7	6	9	4	4

Set C (pp. 122–123)

Use the line plot.

1. How many total prizes were won?
2. Find the range, the mode(s), and the median, of the number of prizes won.

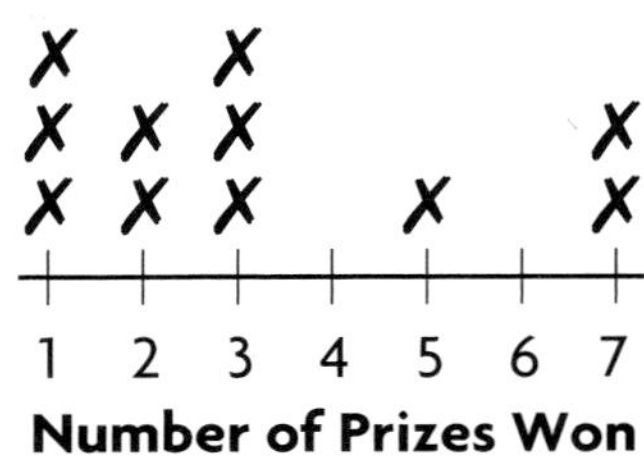

Set D (pp. 124–125)

Use the stem-and-leaf plot.

1. What is the mode? What is the median?
2. Find the lowest score and the highest score. What is the range?

Spelling Test Scores

Stem	Leaves
7	1 4 4 6 6
8	2 2 3 5 8 8
9	2 2 4 4 4 4

Set E (pp. 126–127)

Use the graph.

1. What is the scale of the graph? What is the interval?
2. How would the bars change if the interval were 10? if it were 3?

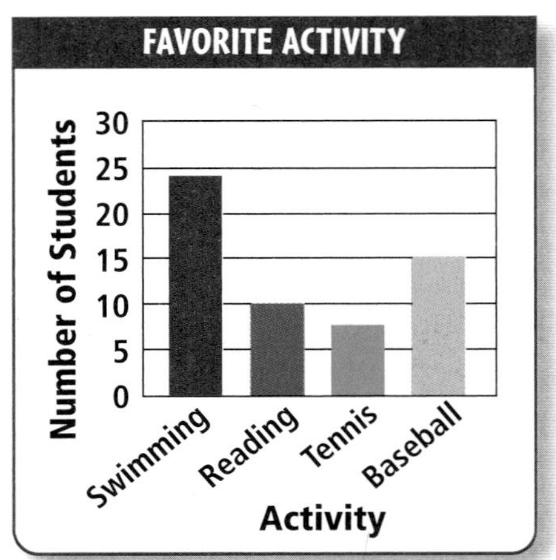

CHAPTER 6

Review/Test

✓ CHECK VOCABULARY AND CONCEPTS

Choose the best term from the box.

stem-and-leaf plot
line plot
survey

1. You are taking a _?_ when you ask several people the same questions and record their answers. (p. 114)
2. A _?_ shows groups of data arranged by place value. (p. 124)

✓ CHECK SKILLS

For 3–4, use the frequency table. (pp. 114–117)

3. Copy and complete the cumulative frequency table at the right. How many cans were collected in all?
4. How many more cans were collected in Weeks 1 and 2 than in Week 4?

CANS OF FOOD COLLECTED

Week	Frequency	Cumulative Frequency
1	10	■
2	12	■
3	14	■
4	18	■

For 5–6, use the table. (pp. 118–123)

5. Make a line plot of Laura's test scores.
6. What is the median and mode of Laura's test scores? What is the range?

LAURA'S TEST SCORES

Test	1	2	3	4	5	6	7
Score	86	90	95	84	94	86	92

7. Josh went on a four-day fishing trip. He caught 8 fish the first day, 4 fish the second day, 7 fish the third day, and 5 fish the fourth day. What is the mean for the number of fish Josh caught?

✓ CHECK PROBLEM SOLVING

For 8–10, use the table. (pp. 128–129)

8. The table shows the number of games won by a hockey team from 2000 to 2003. Use the data in the table to make a bar graph. Decide on a scale and interval to use, and label your graph.
9. Between which two years did the number of games won increase the most?
10. How many games did the Sharks win in all from 2000 to 2003?

SHARKS' WIN RECORD

Year	Games Won
2000	35
2001	40
2002	30
2003	44

CHAPTERS 1–6

Standardized Test Prep

NUMBER SENSE, CONCEPTS, AND OPERATIONS

1. Which number sentence shows the Commutative Property of Addition?

A $(4 + 3) + 2 = 4 + (3 + 2)$

B $2 + 7 = 7 + 2$

C $6 + 0 = 6$

D $5 + 1 = 3 + 3$

TIP **Understand the problem.**
See item 2. Read the problem carefully to make sure you understand what it is asking. Then think about the steps you will need to take to solve the problem.

2. The table below shows the costs of three vacations taken by the Rodriguez family. The family budget for the three vacations was $9,500.

VACATION COSTS	
Vacation Spot	**Cost**
Ft. Lauderdale, FL	$2,150
Myrtle Beach, SC	$3,285
Maui, HI	$4,010

How much of the budget did the family NOT spend?

F $18,945 **H** $550

G $9,445 **J** $55

3. **Explain It** Denzel spent $18 on groceries. He paid with a $50 bill. Explain how Denzel can ESTIMATE how much change he should receive.

MEASUREMENT

4. Sam left his house at 9:40. He arrived at the mall 1 hour 30 minutes later. Which clock shows the time Sam arrived at the mall?

A

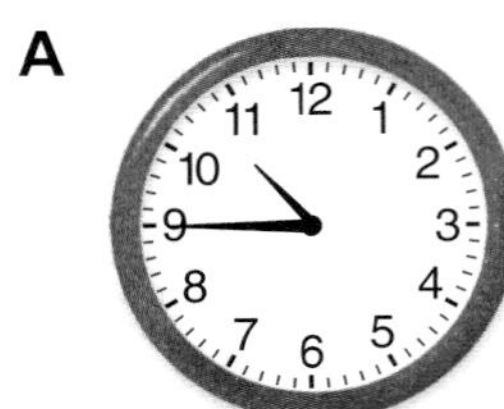

C

B

D

5. Frank's birthday is July 3. Karen's birthday is 2 weeks 4 days after Frank's. What is the date of Karen's birthday?

July						
Sun	Mon	Tue	Wed	Thu	Fri	Sat
		1	2	3	4	5
6	7	8	9	10	11	12
13	14	15	16	17	18	19
20	21	22	23	24	25	26
27	28	29	30	31		

F July 3 **H** July 17

G July 7 **J** July 21

6. **Explain It** There are 365 days in most years. Tell how old you are, and explain how you could ESTIMATE the number of days that have passed since you were born.

ALGEBRAIC THINKING

7. Julio planted a garden. The first year he put 3 tulips in his garden. Each year after that, Julio added 5 more tulips. In which year will his garden have 23 tulips?

A fourth year

B fifth year

C sixth year

D seventh year

8. Which number sentence shows that three plus a number equals nine?

F $3 + 9 = n$

G $9 + 3 = n$

H $3 + n = 9$

J $3 + n = 10$

9. **Explain It** Harold chose a number and then used a rule to make a new number. He did this several times, using the same rule. The table below shows his results. What rule could Harold have used?

INPUT	OUTPUT
c	*g*
2	8
6	12
3	9
10	16

Explain how you decided.

DATA ANALYSIS AND PROBABILITY

10. Which line plot shows the same data as the table below?

VIDEO RENTALS	
Day	**Number of Videos**
1	IIII
2	II
3	卌 II
4	卌
5	III

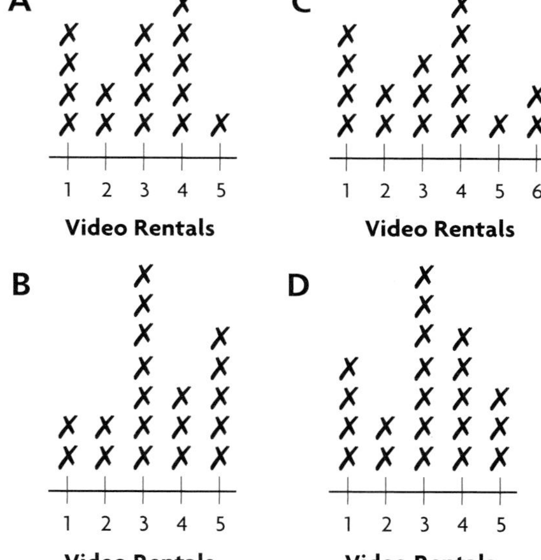

11. Amy is making a bar graph using the data below.

2, 2, 4, 8, 10, 14, 6, 6, 12

Which interval is the **most** reasonable for Amy to use?

F 2

G 10

H 20

J 100

12. **Explain It** What is the mean of the data below?

2, 1, 6, 9, 7

Explain how you found the answer.

Analyze and Graph Data

FAST FACT • SCIENCE Lightning flashes occur somewhere on Earth more than 100 times every second. Scientists measure the number of lightning flashes during storms.

PROBLEM SOLVING The bar graph shows the greatest number of lightning flashes per square mile measured in each of 8 states during a storm. About how many lightning flashes were measured in Maryland? Were more lightning flashes measured during a storm in Tennessee or during one in North Carolina?

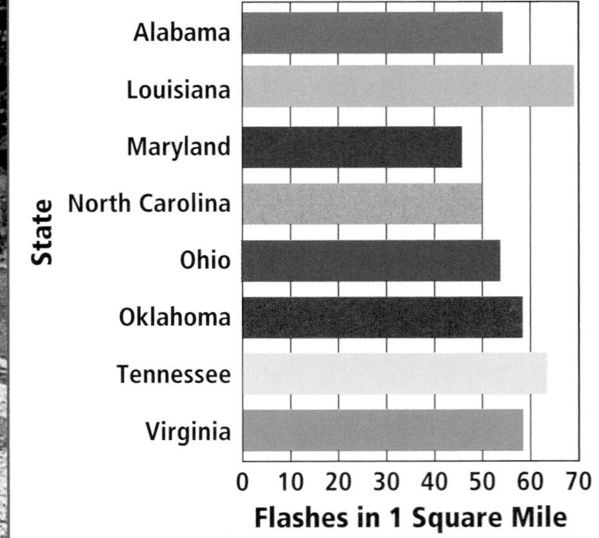

CHECK WHAT YOU KNOW

Use this page to help you review and remember important skills needed for Chapter 7.

PARTS OF A GRAPH

For 1–3, use the first bar graph.

1. What is the title of this graph?
2. What label would you place at the bottom?
3. What label would you place at the left side?

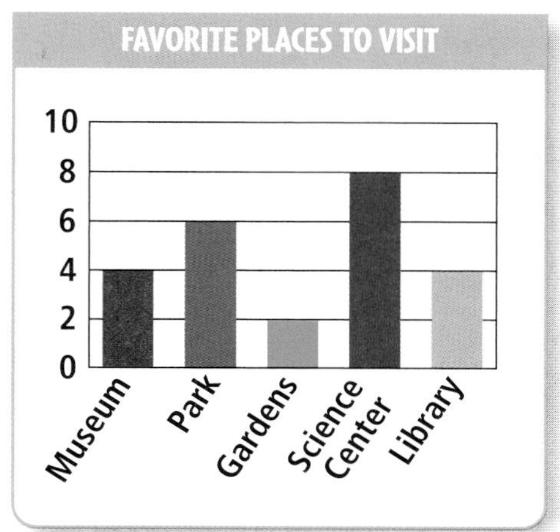

READ BAR GRAPHS

For 4–7, use the second bar graph.

4. Which way of going to school is used by the most students?
5. How many students ride to school in a car?
6. How many students were surveyed for this bar graph?
7. How many students go to school by car or by bicycle?

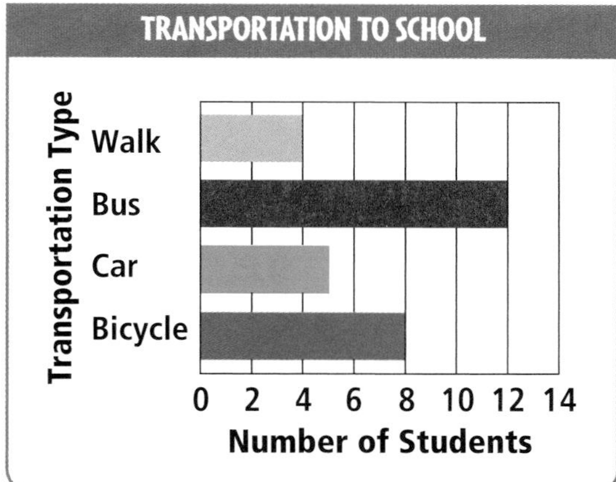

VOCABULARY POWER

REVIEW

graph [graf] *noun*

The word *graph* comes from the Greek word *graphein,* which means "to write." To the Greeks, writings also included drawings, carvings, and scratchings. How do these meanings relate to pictographs?

PREVIEW

double-bar graph
line graph
trends
circle graph

www.harcourtschool.com/mathglossary

LESSON 1

Make Bar and Double-Bar Graphs

Quick Review

Compare. Write $<$, $>$, or $=$ for each ●.

1. 77 ● 61 **2.** 43 ● 59

3. 22 ● 91 **4.** 66 ● 37

5. 85 ● 58

VOCABULARY

double-bar graph

Explore

Double-bar graphs are used to compare similar kinds of data. Make a double-bar graph that shows the data from the table.

Activity

MATERIALS: bar-graph pattern, two different-colored crayons

STEP 1

Decide on a title, labels, and a scale for the graph. For these data, use a scale of 0–16 with an interval of 4.

MONTHLY SNOWFALL (in inches)

City	Jan	Feb	Mar
Chicago	11	8	7
Cleveland	12	12	10

STEP 2

Make the graph. Use one color for Chicago and another color for Cleveland. Make a key to show which color stands for each city.

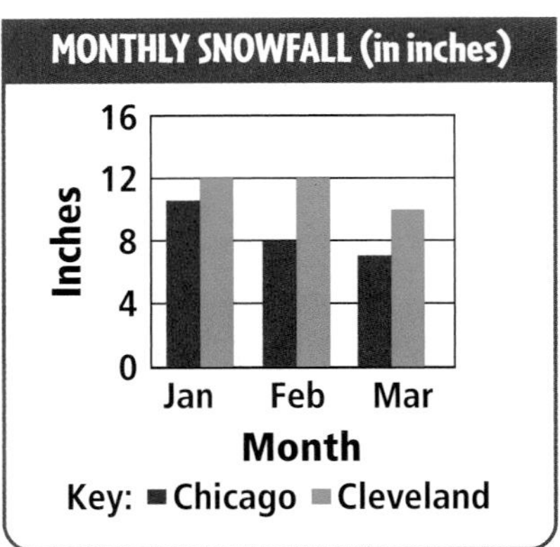

Technology Link

More Practice: Harcourt Mega Math The Number Games, *ArachnaGraph*, Level D

What scale and interval should I use for my Favorite Winter Activity graph?

- What does the graph show about the monthly snowfall in Chicago and Cleveland?

Try It

- Use the table to make a double-bar graph comparing the data for boys and girls.

FAVORITE WINTER ACTIVITY

Activity	Boys	Girls
Sledding	77	60
Ice-skating	35	78
Skiing	75	70

Connect

The data from the "Favorite Winter Activity" table on page 136 are shown in the two bar graphs below. The same labels, intervals, and scales are used for both graphs. A key is not needed when the data are graphed separately.

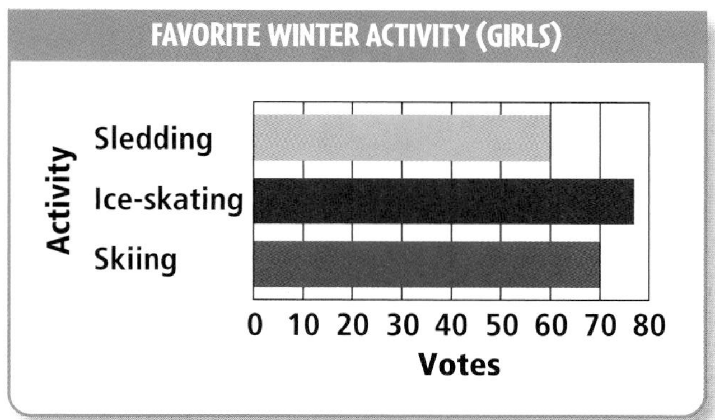

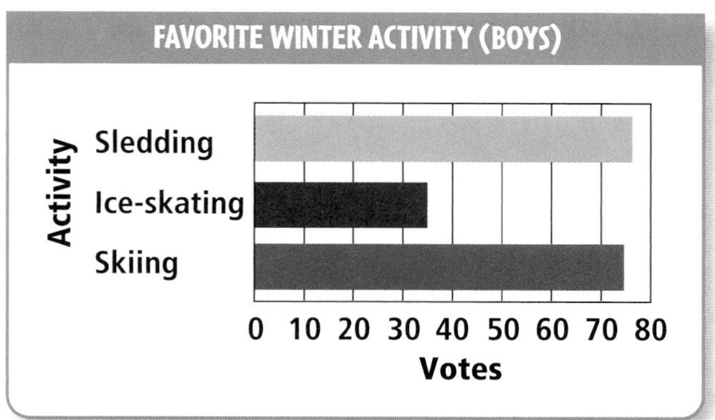

Practice and Problem Solving

For 1–4, use the table.

FAVORITE WINTER OLYMPIC EVENT		
Event	**Third Graders**	**Fifth Graders**
Bobsledding	17	15
Ski jumping	14	16
Figure skating	9	10

1. Make a bar graph for each grade to compare the data for the two classes.

2. Make a double-bar graph to compare the data for the two classes.

3. Which graph makes it easier to compare the data for the two classes? Explain.

4. **REASONING** Conduct a survey to determine fourth graders' favorite events. Make a triple-bar graph using the data and the table above. What is the total number of third, fourth, and fifth graders surveyed?

5. ***FAST FACT*** **• SOCIAL STUDIES** During the 2002 Winter Olympics, the United States won 10 gold medals, 13 silver medals, and 11 bronze medals. Germany won 12 gold, 16 silver, and 7 bronze medals. Make a double-bar graph to show the data.

Mixed Review and Test Prep

6. Which is greater, 314,689 or 341,869? (p. 20)

7. Round 415,906 to the nearest ten thousand. (p. 30)

8. What is the value of 6 in the number 48,602,751? (p. 6)

9. What is 13,847 subtracted from 23,005? (p. 52)

10. **TEST PREP** What is the sum of 415,903 and 58,769? (p. 52)

A 463,662 **C** 474,672
B 464,572 **D** 474,772

LESSON 2

Read Line Graphs

Learn

READ BETWEEN THE LINES You can show how data change over a period of time by using a **line graph**.

Quick Review

1. 34 − 12
2. 76 − 45
3. 66 − 23
4. 98 − 53
5. 81 − 48

VOCABULARY

line graph **trends**

Example 1

Look at the graph. The line connecting the points shows the changes in snowfall amounts for each month. What is the snowfall amount for December?

STEP 1

Find the line labeled December. Follow that line up to the point (•).

STEP 2

Follow that line to the scale on the left to locate the snowfall amount for December.

So, the snowfall amount for December is 30 inches.

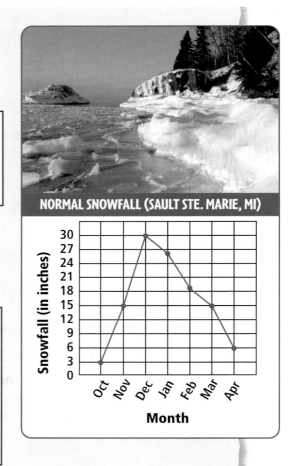

NORMAL SNOWFALL (SAULT STE. MARIE, MI)

Snowfall (in inches): 0, 3, 6, 9, 12, 15, 18, 21, 24, 27, 30

Month: Oct, Nov, Dec, Jan, Feb, Mar, Apr

Example 2

Find the range of the data.

STEP 1

Look at the graph to find the greatest value and the least value.

30 inches ←greatest value

3 inches ←least value

STEP 2

Subtract the least value from the greatest value to find the range.

$$\begin{array}{r} 30 \\ -\ 3 \\ \hline 27 \end{array}$$

So, the range for the snowfall amounts is 27 inches.

In the Ski Club Membership line graph, you can see **trends**, or areas where the data increase, decrease, or stay the same over time. An increase in membership is seen between 2003 and 2004.

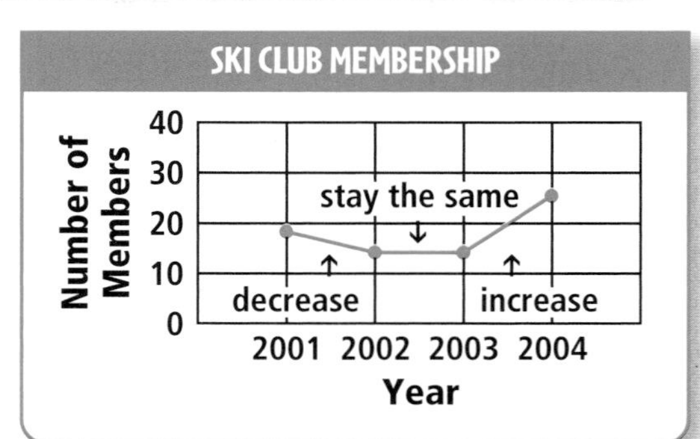

Check

For 1–4, use the line graph at the right.

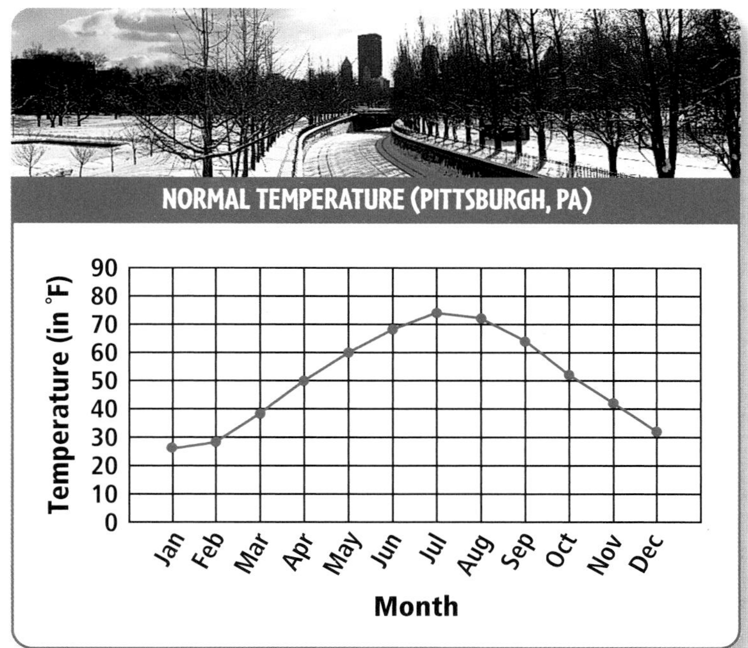

1. **Name** the two months on the line graph between which the normal temperature increases from 39°F to 50°F.
2. What is the lowest normal temperature for Pittsburgh?
3. What month has the highest normal temperature?
4. Compare the February temperature to the June temperature.

Practice and Problem Solving

Extra Practice, page 150, Set A

For 5–7, use the line graph at the right.

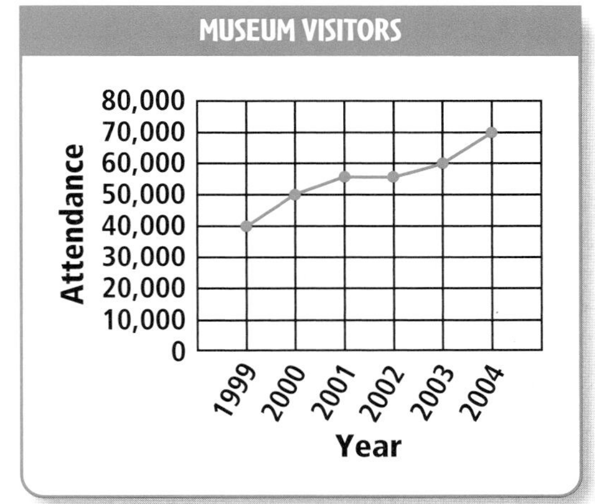

5. How many people visited the museum in the year with the lowest attendance?
6. About how many people visited the museum from 1999 through 2004?
7. Between which two years did the attendance stay about the same?
8. **Write a problem** using the temperature data for Pittsburgh, PA.
9. **REASONING** A set of 3 numbers has the sum 110. The median of the numbers is 40. The range is 30. What are the numbers?

Mixed Review and Test Prep

10. 35,842 − 18,764 = ■ (p. 52)
11. Which is greater, 46,731 or 46,781? (p. 20)
12. Find the mode of 2, 2, 3, 4, 6, 6, 7, 7, 9, 11, 11, 11. (p. 118)
13. Find the median of 2, 4, 7, 6, 9, 8, 10, 11, 5, 4, 6, 9, 9. (p. 118)
14. **TEST PREP** Find the sum.
    37,870 + 29,602 (p. 52)
    - A 56,472
    - B 57,472
    - C 67,472
    - D 67,572

LESSON 3

Make Line Graphs

Quick Review

1. 200 − 33 **2.** 100 − 53
3. 400 − 47 **4.** 500 − 68
5. 300 − 81

MATERIALS
line graph pattern

Explore

LIGHTNING DISTANCE Have you ever wondered how far away a strike of lightning is from you? You can count seconds to find the distance. Use the Distance from Lightning table at the right to make a line graph.

DISTANCE FROM LIGHTNING

Distance (in mi)	Time Until Thunder Is Heard (in sec)
1	5
2	10
3	15
4	20

Activity 1

STEP 1

Choose a scale and an interval. Write the scale numbers along the left side of the graph. Write the labels and title on the graph.

STEP 2

Plot a point to show each distance and the number of seconds until the thunder is heard. Connect the points from left to right.

DISTANCE FROM LIGHTNING

Time Until Thunder Is Heard (in sec): 0, 5, 10, 15, 20, 25
Distance (in mi): 1, 2, 3, 4

Try It

- You also can determine the distance lightning is from you in kilometers. Every three seconds equals one kilometer. Make a line graph of the data. Be sure to title and label your graph. Choose an appropriate interval and scale.

DISTANCE FROM LIGHTNING

Distance (in km)	Time Until Thunder Is Heard (in sec)
1	3
2	6
3	9
4	12

Connect

Each point on a line graph can be described by the horizontal and vertical labels. The first point on the graph at the right can be described as Monday and 1 cm.

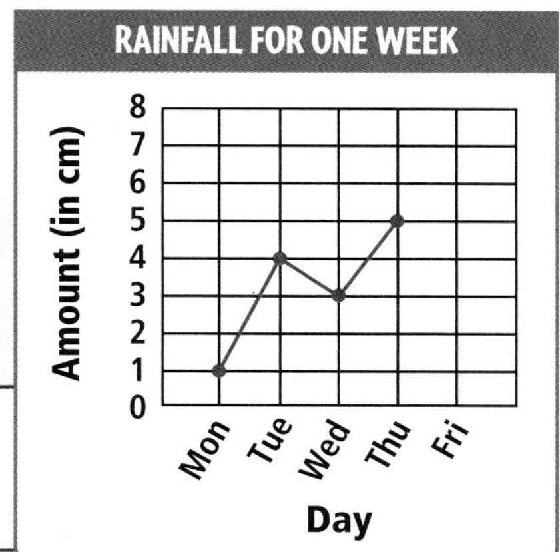

Activity 2

Graph a point on the line graph for Friday and 2 cm.

STEP 1

Copy the graph. Find Friday on the horizontal scale and go up until you reach 2 cm on the vertical scale.

STEP 2

Plot a point on your graph where the horizontal and vertical scales meet. Then connect the point for Thursday to the point for Friday.

Practice and Problem Solving

For 1–2, make a line graph.

1.

STEVE'S PLANT					
Week	1	2	3	4	5
Height (in inches)	1	2	3	4	5

2.

LEON'S PLANT					
Week	1	2	3	4	5
Height (in inches)	0	1	3	5	6

3. Copy the graph. Graph the following points: Monday and 4 cm, Tuesday and 3 cm, Wednesday and 5 cm, Thursday and 1 cm, and Friday and 0 cm.

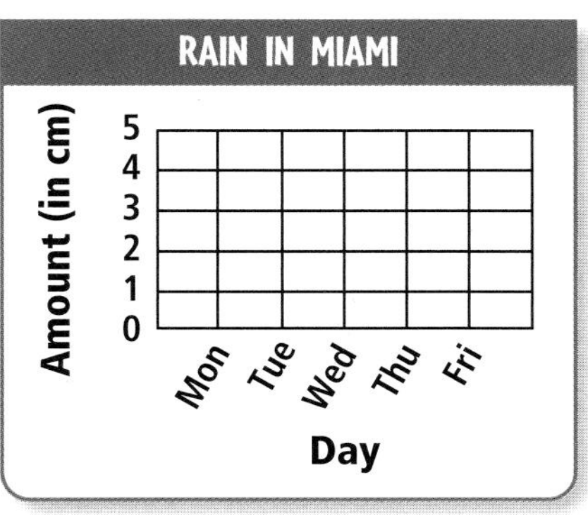

4. Look at the graph from Exercise 3. Is the rain total for Monday through Friday greater than or less than 10 cm?

5. **Write About It** Explain how you can describe a point on a line graph.

Mixed Review and Test Prep

6. Which is greater, 1,238 or 1,543 − 308? (p. 48)

7. Round 744,478 to the nearest thousand. (p. 30)

8. Find 100,000 more than 2,843,715. (p. 6)

9. 4,951 − 3,729 (p. 48)

10. **TEST PREP** Which expression shows 5 less than a number, x? (p. 64)

A $5 - x$
B $x - 5$
C $x + 5$
D $x - 5 - x$

LESSON 4

Make Circle Graphs

Quick Review

1. 23 + 77
2. 66 + 34
3. 116 + 84
4. 155 + 45
5. 175 + 125

VOCABULARY

circle graph

MATERIALS 5 sheets of paper, circle graph pattern, markers, scissors, tape

Explore

FAVORITE SEASON In a survey, Carol asked 200 students at Lincoln Elementary to name their favorite season.

You can use a bar graph to make a circle graph. A **circle graph** shows data as a whole made up of different parts.

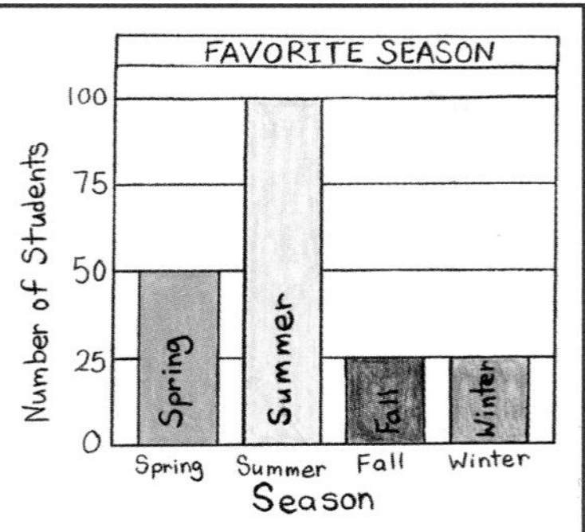

Activity 1

STEP 1

Copy the bar graph. Write a label on each bar.

STEP 2

Cut out each bar from your graph. Tape the ends of the bars together, without overlapping, to form a circle.

STEP 3

Place your circle on a sheet of paper and trace around it. Mark where each bar begins and ends around the circle.

STEP 4

Mark the center of the traced circle. Then draw a radius from each of the points you marked on the circle.

STEP 5

Color the sections of the circle. Label each section, and title your circle graph.

Try It

a. Use the data to make a bar graph. Then use your bar graph to make a circle graph.

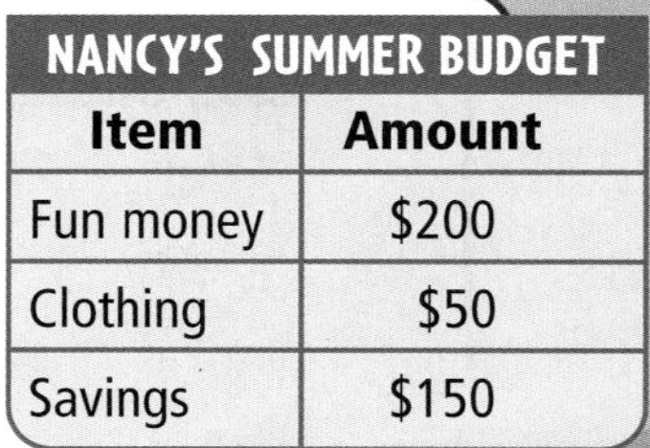

NANCY'S SUMMER BUDGET	
Item	**Amount**
Fun money	$200
Clothing	$50
Savings	$150

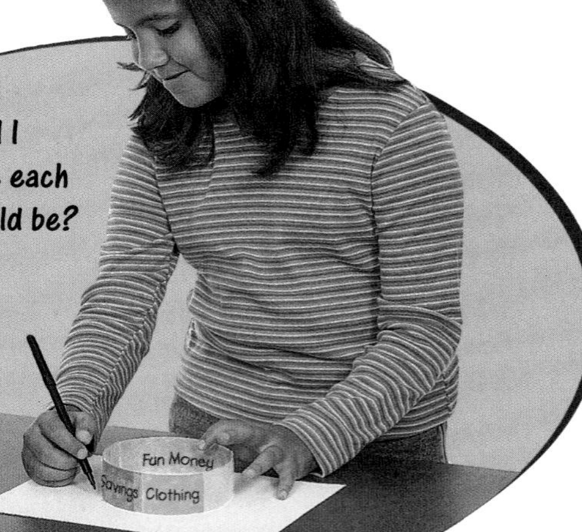

Connect

You can use a circle graph pattern to make a circle graph.

FAVORITE RAINY DAY ACTIVITY	
Activity	**Number of Students**
Read	1
Television	5
Video games	4

Activity 2

Make a circle graph.

STEP 1

Add to find the number of students in the data. Since the number of students is 10, use a circle graph pattern divided into ten equal sections.

STEP 2

Use a different color for each activity. Shade 1 section for the number of students who like to read. Shade 5 sections for the number of students who like to watch television. Shade 4 sections for the number of students who like to play video games.

STEP 3

Label each activity on your graph. Then title your graph.

Practice and Problem Solving

For 1–2, make a circle graph.

1.

CLASS ELECTION	
Student	**Number of Votes**
Tom	30
Phillip	60
Alice	10

2.

RHONDA'S ALLOWANCE	
Activity	**Amount**
Movies	$5
Snack	$2
Skating	$3

3. What does the whole circle in Exercise 1 represent?

4. What does the whole circle in Exercise 2 represent?

5. Pauline spent $4 of her $10 allowance on books. She saved the rest. How would you show this in a circle graph?

Mixed Review and Test Prep

6. Compare. 3,842,000 ● 3,842,100 (p. 20)

7. Find the elapsed time. Start: 8:22 a.m. End: 12:45 p.m. (p. 98)

8. Find the value. $92 + (41 - 28)$ (p. 64)

9. $37{,}000 - 8{,}952$ (p. 50)

10. **TEST PREP** Which expression has a value of 33? (p. 64)

A $(32 + 11) - 10$ **C** $(18 - 6) + 15$
B $42 + (11 - 10)$ **D** $32 - (6 + 15)$

LESSON 5

Choose an Appropriate Graph

Quick Review

Find the mode.

1. 4, 3, 6, 5, 4

2. 6, 6, 12, 8, 9, 13

3. 11, 12, 14, 15, 17

4. 4, 7, 7, 8, 8, 8

5. 1, 9, 5, 5, 9, 4

Learn

NATURE NAP Some animals sleep most of the day, and others hardly sleep at all. Look at how Cindy, Joe, and Elayna showed the data in the table. Which graph or plot works best for the data?

HOURS OF SLEEP

Animal	Hours of Sleep in a Day
Giraffe	4
Raccoon	13
Squirrel	14
Bear	8

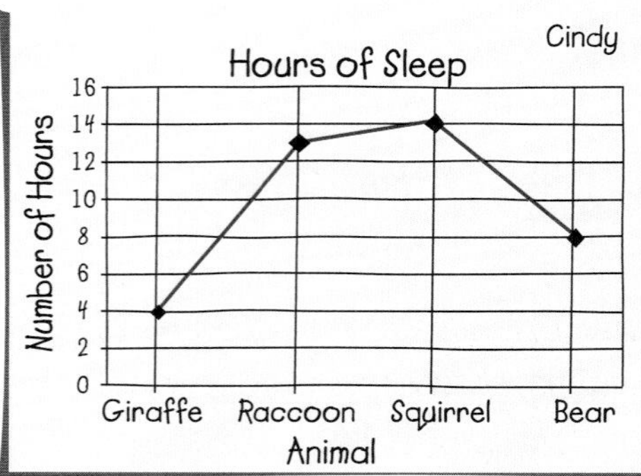

A line graph is used to show changes over time.

Joe

Hours of Sleep

Stem	Leaves
0	4 8
1	3 4

A stem-and-leaf plot arranges data by place value.

Elayna

Hours of Sleep

Number of Hours: 0, 2, 4, 6, 8, 10, 12, 14, 16

Giraffe, Raccoon, Squirrel, Bear

Animal

A bar graph is used to compare data about different groups.

The data show the number of hours different kinds of animals sleep each day. The data do not show changes over time, and some important information is not shown by the stem-and-leaf plot. So, Elayna's bar graph is best for displaying the data.

- Would a circle graph be good for the data? Explain.

Line Plot or Line Graph

The kind of graph you choose usually depends on the type of information that you want to show.

Elsa recorded her science test scores each week for nine weeks. She displayed the data in two different ways.

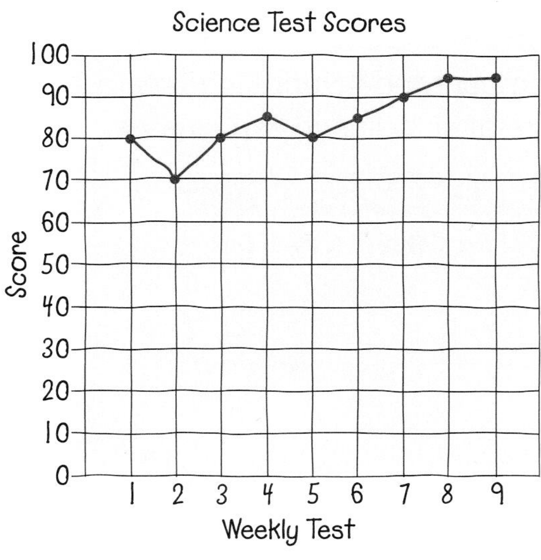

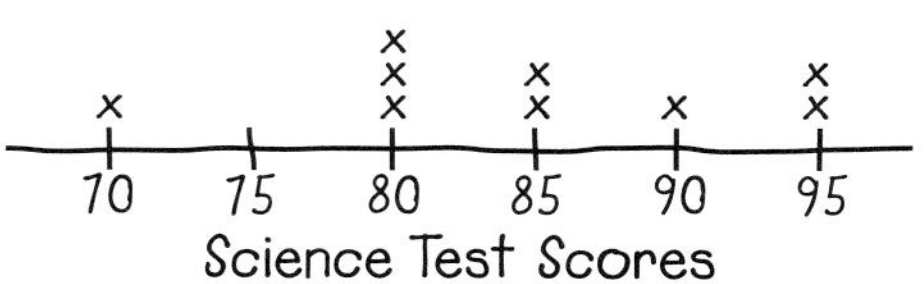

Elsa's line plot shows all the scores, but the line graph also shows the week each test was taken.

- **REASONING** Which display is better for finding how many times Elsa got an 80 on a science test? Explain.

Check

1. **Choose** which display Elsa should use to show how her science scores have improved. Explain your choice.

2. **Explain** the differences in the types of information shown in a stem-and-leaf plot, a bar graph, a circle graph, and a line graph.

For 3–6, write the kind of graph or plot you would choose.

3. to compare the speeds of five different animals

4. to show the total votes in an election

5. to show the weekly math grades of your classmates

6. to show your heights each year since birth

7. Lyn found that there were 9 cars, 4 vans, 6 bikes, and 1 bus on a street. Would a circle graph or a line graph be a better choice for Lyn's data?

8. The temperature was recorded each hour from 6 A.M. to 6 P.M. Would a bar graph or a line graph be a better choice to show the data?

9. **Write About It** Explain which display would be easier to use to find the median and mode of Elsa's scores.

LESSON CONTINUES

Practice and Problem Solving

Extra Practice, page 150, Set B

For 10–17, write the kind of graph or plot you would choose.

10. to compare the favorite subjects of students in two fourth-grade classes

11. to show the number of soccer goals scored by all team members

12. to keep a record of plant growth

13. to show monthly temperatures

14. to show the favorite sports of students in fourth grade

15. to compare the favorite ice cream flavors of students in two classes

16.

CLASS TEST SCORES				
79	83	91	88	94
96	85	77	81	92

17.

NUMBER OF NEW STUDENTS				
	Sep	Oct	Nov	Dec
2003	31	11	10	6
2004	18	22	2	10

For 18–21, use the graph and the plot.

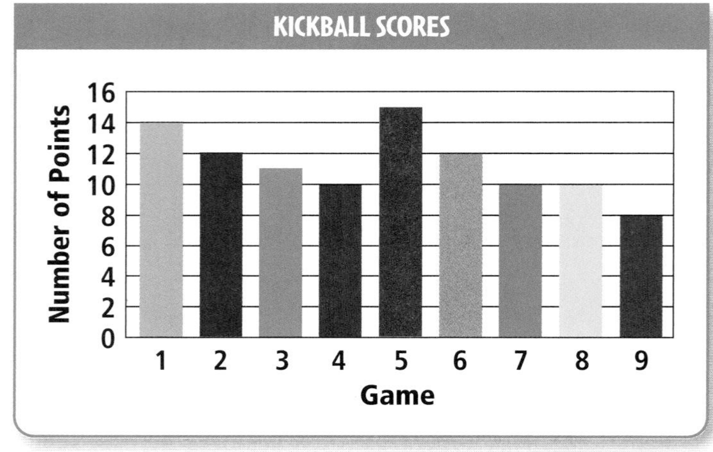

18. Which display shows how many points the team scored in the third game?

19. In which game did the team score more points than in the first game? How many more points were scored?

20. What is the median of the team's scores? What is the mode?

21. In how many games did the team score more than 10 points?

22. **What's the Error?** To look for trends, Frank made a line plot of the number of hours he slept each night for a week. Describe his error. Tell which display he should have made.

23. Collect data about the languages spoken by students in your class. Choose the best graph to display your data. Make the graph.

24. **Vocabulary Power** *Line graphs* and *line plots* have similar names but show data in different ways. Tell how the line in each type of display is used to show the data.

25. **Write About It** Write a question and survey 20 students. Choose and make an appropriate display for the data. Tell why you chose that kind of display.

26. **NUMBER SENSE** The least two-digit number that rounds to 100 is 50. What is the least three-digit number that rounds to 1,000? What is the greatest four-digit number that rounds to 1,000?

27. A total of 2,615 concert tickets were sold Monday–Wednesday. If 543 tickets were sold Monday and 876 tickets were sold Tuesday, how many more tickets were sold on Wednesday than Tuesday?

Mixed Review and Test Prep

28. $\begin{array}{r} 16{,}083 \\ +\ 8{,}564 \\ \hline \end{array}$ (p. 52)

29. $\begin{array}{r} 60{,}004 \\ -46{,}937 \\ \hline \end{array}$ (p. 50)

30. 34,985 − 12,607 (p. 52)

31. Write an expression using the variable *y* to show 25 beads minus some beads. (p. 64)

32. **TEST PREP** Which is greater than 11,463 and less than 11,600? (p. 24)

A 11,375 **C** 11,552
B 11,459 **D** 11,673

33. **TEST PREP** Cheri's class has 5 cages with 3 hamsters in each cage. How many hamsters does her class have?

F 8 **G** 9 **H** 12 **J** 15

Problem Solving Thinker's Corner

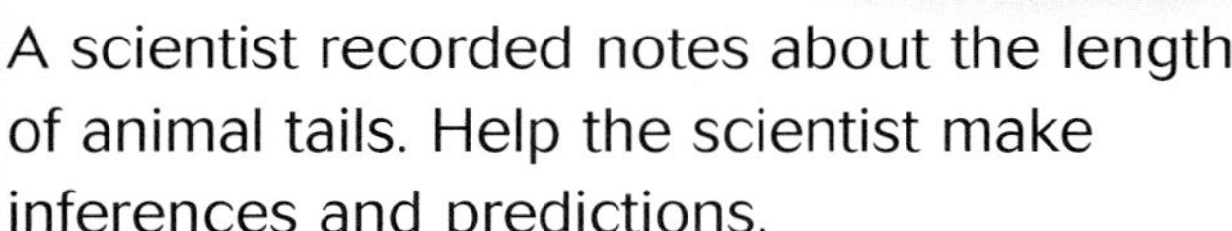

A scientist recorded notes about the length of animal tails. Help the scientist make inferences and predictions.

When you make an **inference**, you draw conclusions based on information you have.

When you make a **prediction**, you guess what might happen based on information you have.

1. Use the notes to make inferences and to complete the table.
2. Predict what the length of a baby African elephant's tail will be when the elephant is full-grown.
3. Tell why you made the prediction you did.

Notes

A. The tails of the red kangaroo, giraffe, and African buffalo are the same length.

B. The Asian elephant's tail is eight inches longer than the African elephant's tail.

C. The leopard's tail is four inches shorter than the Asian elephant's tail.

LENGTHS OF MAMMAL TAILS

Mammal	Length (in inches)
?	51
?	43
?	59
?	43
?	43
?	55

LESSON 6

Problem Solving Skill
Draw Conclusions

UNDERSTAND › PLAN › SOLVE › CHECK

Quick Review

Compare. Write <, >, or = for each ●.

1. 34 ● 43
2. 91 ● 77
3. 145 ● 181
4. 293 ● 293
5. 1,980 ● 2,001

RAINY SEASON Bangladesh is located in Asia on the Indian Ocean. Sometimes the weather is very dry, and sometimes there are heavy rains. During the rainy—or monsoon—season, people often use waterways instead of roads for transportation.

You can use a graph to compare data. Use the data and what you know to answer questions and draw conclusions.

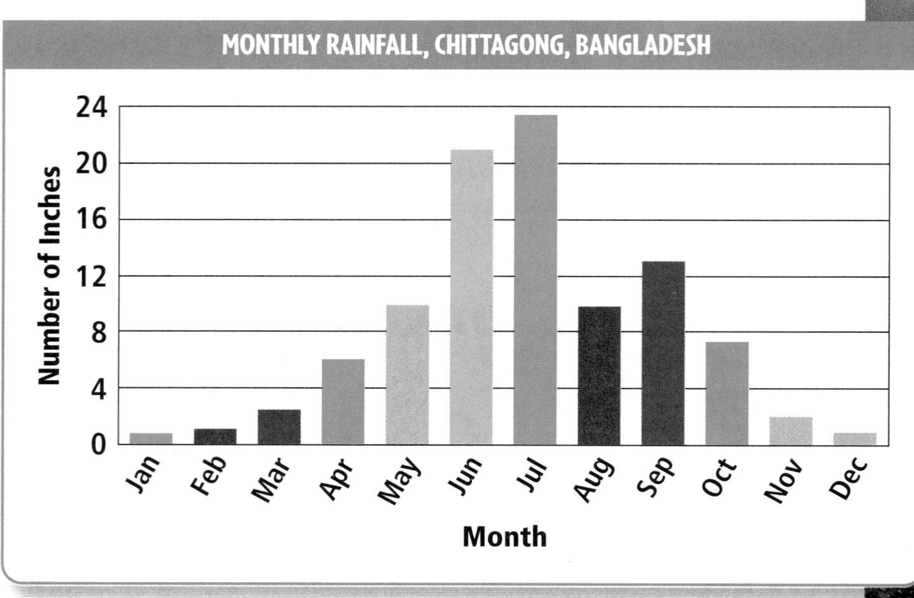

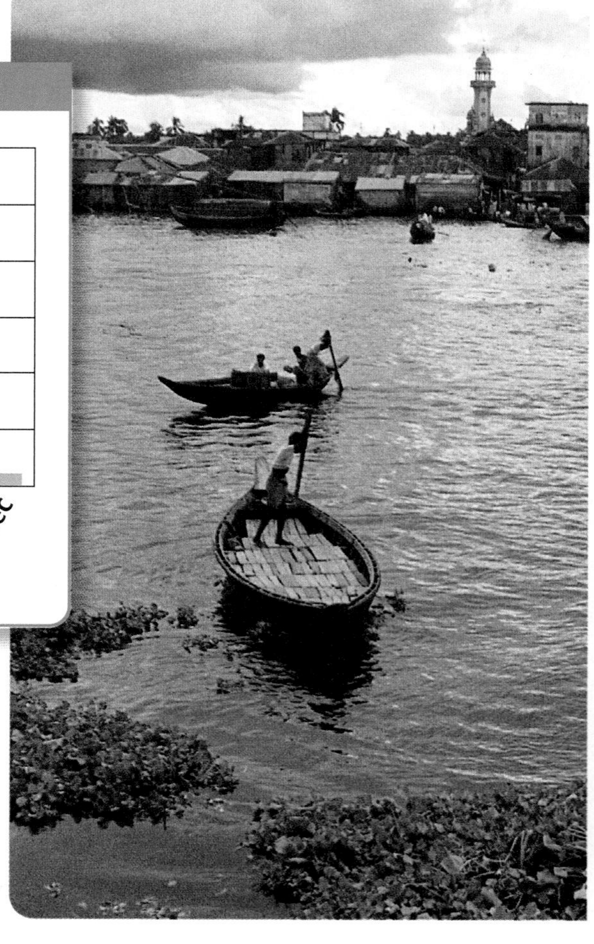

Which months of the year do you think make up the monsoon season?

Monsoon season is a time of very heavy rains. From April to October, Bangladesh usually receives over 5 inches of rain each month. During June and July, monthly rainfall can be greater than 20 inches.

So, June and July probably make up the monsoon season in Bangladesh.

• Estimate the yearly rainfall in Chittagong.

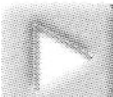

Problem Solving Practice

For 1–4, use the graph on page 148.

1. In which two months does Bangladesh receive the most rainfall?
2. In which two months does Bangladesh receive the least rainfall?
3. During which months are the roads in Bangladesh likely to be flooded?
4. Make a double-bar graph to compare the monthly rainfall in Chittagong with the monthly rainfall in your town.

For 5–6, use the graph.

Jennifer made a line graph to show the snowfall from November to February.

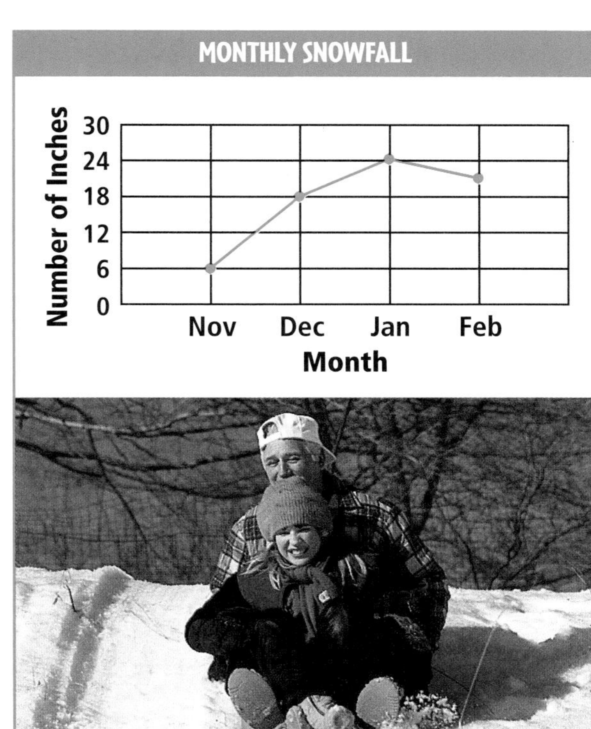

5. Which conclusion can you NOT make about the data?
   - **A** More snow fell in January than in February.
   - **B** The snowfall decreased from November to February.
   - **C** Six more inches of snow fell in January than in December.
   - **D** Eighteen inches of snow fell in December.
6. How many total inches of snow fell?
   - **F** 64 inches
   - **G** 65 inches
   - **H** 66 inches
   - **J** 69 inches

Mixed Applications

7. Mrs. Porter wants to buy one sticker for each of her 32 students. If stickers come in packs of 10, how many packs of stickers will she need to buy? Explain.
8. **REASONING** Write an expression with a value of 893, using only addition and subtraction, but do not use 3, 8, or 9 as digits.
9. Mr. Milo is taking a trip of 731 miles. He travels 458 miles on Saturday and completes the trip on Sunday. How many fewer miles did he travel on Sunday?
10. **? What's the Question?** Look at the Monthly Snowfall line graph. The answer is 18.

Extra Practice

Set A (pp. 138–139)

For 1–5, use the graph.

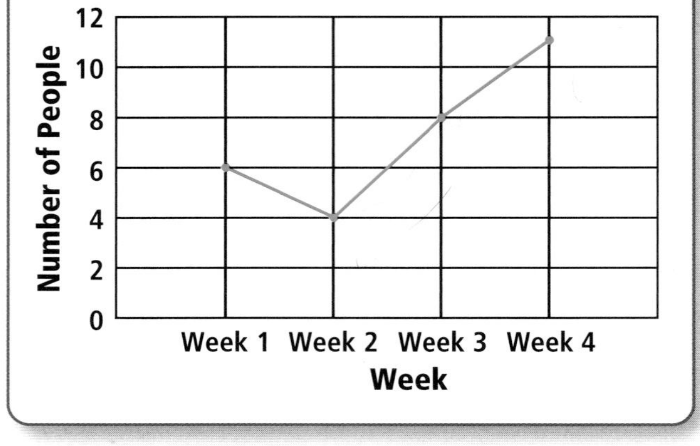

1. During which week were the most people at the meeting? the fewest?
2. During which weeks were more than 6 people at the meeting?
3. How many people were present during the third week?
4. Between which two weeks was there the greatest increase in the number of people at the meeting?
5. If 12 more people attended the meeting in July than in June, how many people attended in July?

Set B (pp. 144–147)

For 1–4, write the kind of graph or plot you would choose.

1. to show your weights each year since birth
2. to show favorite sports seasons
3. to show this week's science test scores of your classmates
4. to show the kinds of movies watched by your classmates
5. Mr. Cason surveyed his students to find out their favorite activities. He organized the data in a table. What is the best graph or plot to show the data? Make the graph or plot.
6. Mrs. Varga recorded the attendance of the Parkview bowling league for 5 weeks. She organized the data in a table. What is the best graph or plot to show the data? Make the graph or plot.

FAVORITE ACTIVITIES

	Board Game	Playground	Movie	Puzzle
Boys	7	9	4	2
Girls	5	7	2	3

LEAGUE ATTENDANCE

Week	1	2	3	4	5
Members	29	21	27	30	24

Review/Test

CHECK VOCABULARY AND CONCEPTS

Choose the best term from the box.

double-bar graph
line graph
line plot
stem-and-leaf plot

1. A graph that uses a line to show how something changes over a period of time is a _?_. (p. 138)
2. A graph used to compare similar kinds of data is called a _?_. (p. 136)

CHECK SKILLS

For 3–4, use the line graph. (pp. 138–139)

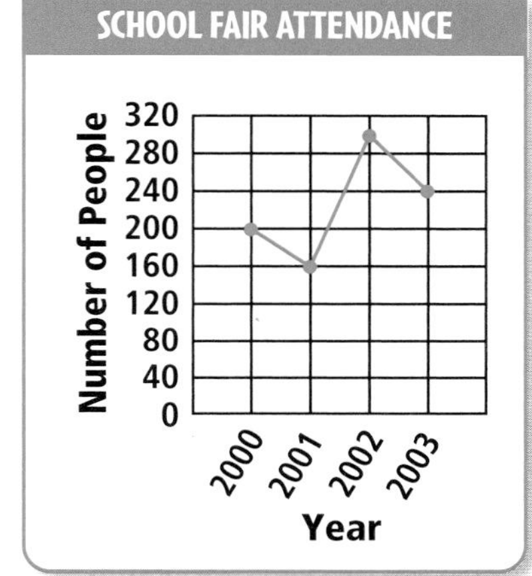

3. The line graph shows how many people attended the school fair each year for 4 years. In which years was the attendance fewer than 240 people?
4. What is the total number of people who attended during the 4 years?

For 5–8, write the kind of graph or plot you would choose. (pp. 144–147)

5. to compare the favorite movies of two classes
6. to record the height of a tree during six months
7. to compare the favorite ice cream flavors of your classmates
8. to record students' scores on a recent history test

CHECK PROBLEM SOLVING

For 9–10, use the Favorite Animals frequency table. (pp. 136–137, 148–149)

9. Make a double-bar graph to compare the data of the first-grade and third-grade classes.
10. Can you conclude that more first-grade students like dogs and horses than do third-grade students? Explain.

FAVORITE ANIMALS

Animal	First-Grade Students	Third-Grade Students
Cat	3	5
Dog	7	9
Fish	2	7
Horse	9	6

Standardized Test Prep

MEASUREMENT

1. Ed got a haircut on June 8. He will get his hair cut again in 6 weeks.

June						
Sun	Mon	Tue	Wed	Thu	Fri	Sat
		1	2	3	4	5
6	7	8	9	10	11	12
13	14	15	16	17	18	19
20	21	22	23	24	25	26
27	28	29	30			

July						
Sun	Mon	Tue	Wed	Thu	Fri	Sat
				1	2	3
4	5	6	7	8	9	10
11	12	13	14	15	16	17
18	19	20	21	22	23	24
25	26	27	28	29	30	31

When will Ed get his hair cut again?

A June 15 **C** July 8

B July 6 **D** July 20

2. Erica went to the movies. Previews started at 3:20 P.M. The previews lasted 15 minutes, and the movie ended at 5:30 P.M. How long was the movie?

F 2 hours 15 minutes

G 2 hours

H 1 hour 55 minutes

J 1 hour 5 minutes

3. **Explain It** Tony is shopping for a rack to hold his CD collection. Should he estimate the number of CDs he has, or should he count them to find the exact number? Explain your answer.

GEOMETRY AND SPATIAL SENSE

TIP **Get the information you need.** See item 4. Look for a relationship among the 3 figures. Then look at the answer choices and choose the figure that does NOT match this relationship.

4. Which figure does NOT belong with the 3 figures below?

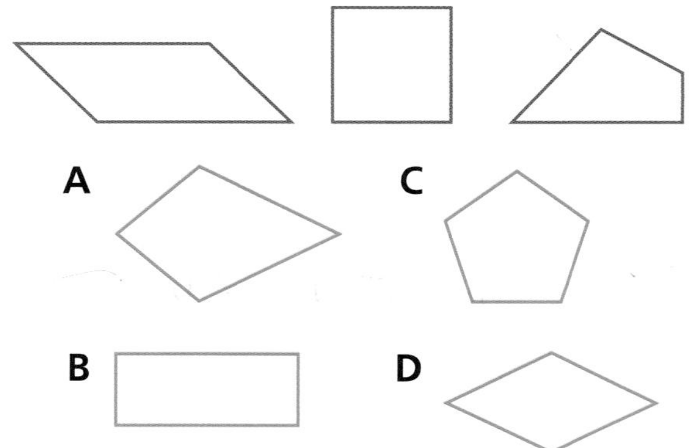

5. Which angle appears to be an obtuse angle?

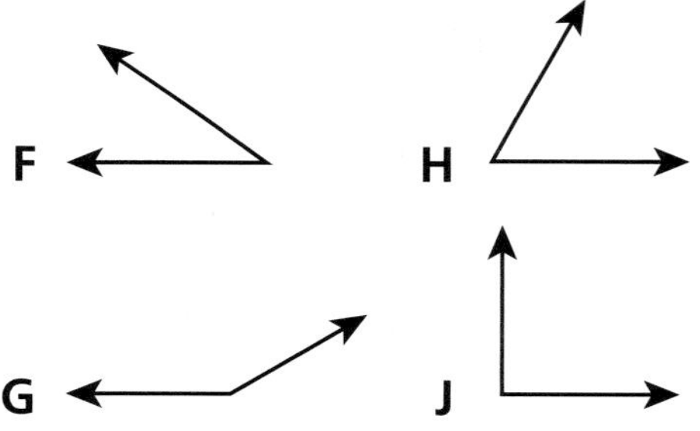

6. **Explain It** Mrs. Vasquez packed some dishes in a box to send to her daughter. What solid figure does the box represent? How many faces does this solid figure have?

FRAGILE

Explain how you decided.

ALGEBRAIC THINKING

7. Which of the following could the equation below represent?

$$b + 7 = 9$$

A Nine more than some number equals seven.

B Seven times some number equals nine.

C Seven less than some number equals nine.

D Seven more than some number equals nine.

8. Which rule could describe the pattern below?

7, 17, 27, 37, 47, 57, 67

F Add 10.

G Subtract 10.

H Multiply by 10.

J Divide by 10.

9. **Explain It** The table below shows the number of visitors to Micanopy, Florida, over a four-month period.

VISITORS TO MICANOPY	
Month	**Number of People**
January	1,130
February	811
March	1,635
April	1,706

Write an equation that could be used to find how many people visited Micanopy in January and February. Use p for the variable. Explain your answer.

DATA ANALYSIS AND PROBABILITY

10. Mia made a line graph to show car sales from April to July.

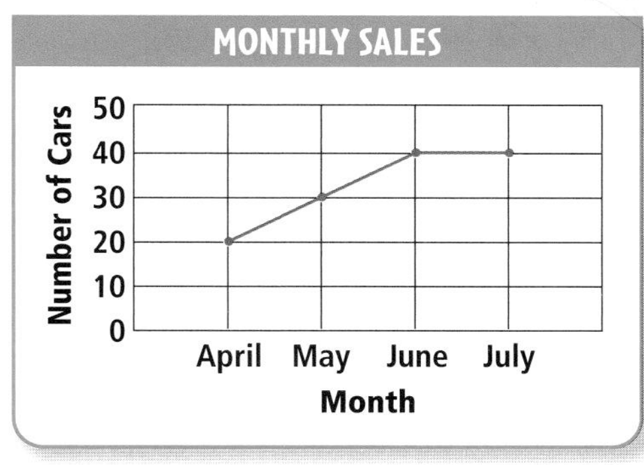

Which conclusion can you make about the data?

A More cars were sold in April than in May.

B Car sales increased from April to June.

C Twenty more cars were sold in May than in June.

D Car sales in April and July were the same.

11. Mark invites 6 friends to a party. Their ages are 6, 7, 8, 8, 9, and 10. What is the median age?

F 50 **G** 8 **H** 4 **J** 3

12. **Explain It** Make a graph that shows the data from the table below.

TIME WORKED (in hours)			
Worker	**Mon**	**Tue**	**Wed**
Mr. Ramirez	6	7	10
Mrs. Allen	3	8	11

Name the kind of graph you used to display the data. Explain your choice of graph.

IT'S IN THE BAG

Gold Medal Graphing

PROJECT Make a "gold medal" to collect and organize data and to practice time concepts.

Materials

- *Scissors and hole punch*
- *Gold or yellow card-stock*
- *3 feet of ribbon*
- *Markers*
- *Chenille stick*
- *Brass fastener*
- *2 foam pieces*
- *Glue*
- *Graphing and time sheets*

Directions

1. Cut out two 5-inch-diameter circles from the card-stock, and each of the graph circles. Put these in a stack, with the card-stock circles on the top and bottom, and tie them together with a chenille stick. *(Picture A)*

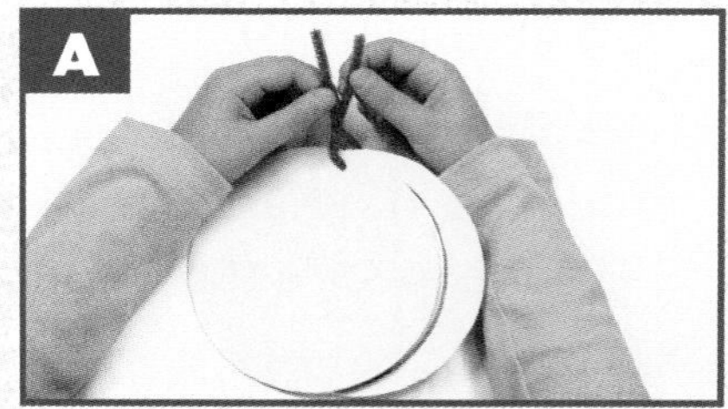

2. Insert the ribbon through a loop in the chenille stick and tie the ends to fit over your head. *(Picture B)*

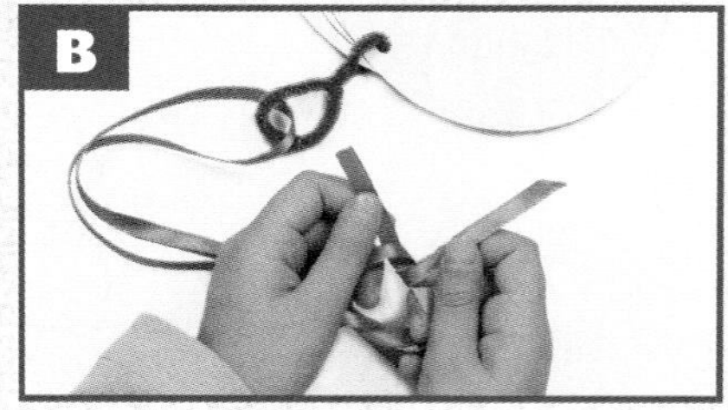

3. Cut out the clock face and attach the foam pieces to the center of the clock by using the brass fastener. Glue the completed clock to the back of your medal. *(Picture C)*

4. Complete the line plot, stem-and-leaf plot, and circle graph in your medal by collecting data from 10 of your classmates.

5. On the clock, show the time that school begins in the morning. Then, using the data from your stem-and-leaf plot, model the times at which your classmates must leave for school in order to be on time.

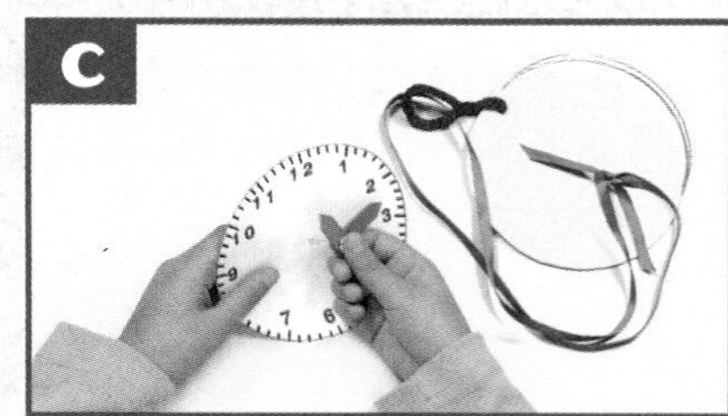

Challenge

Time Zones

The continental United States is divided into four time zones. Look at the map. When moving from one time zone to the next, there is a difference of 1 hour.

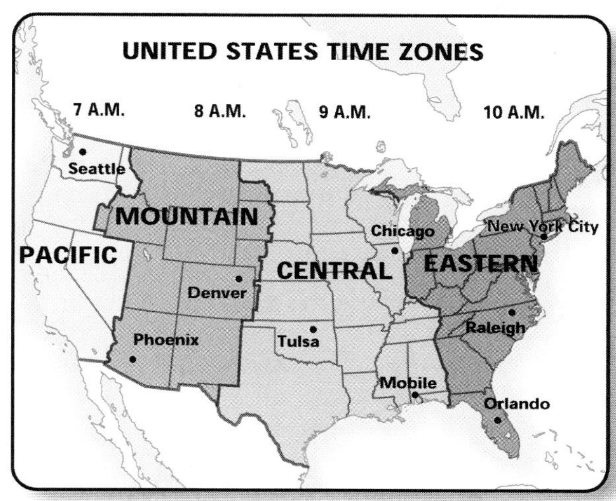

Examples

A What time is it in Raleigh, North Carolina, when it is 8:00 A.M. in Phoenix, Arizona?

Raleigh, North Carolina, is in the eastern time zone. Phoenix, Arizona, is in the mountain time zone. The difference between the mountain time zone and the eastern time zone is 2 hours.

So, it is 10:00 A.M. in Raleigh, North Carolina.

B What time is it in the Pacific time zone when it is 8:00 P.M. in the central time zone?

CENTRAL	5 P.M.	6 P.M.	7 P.M.	8 P.M.
PACIFIC	3 P.M.	4 P.M.	5 P.M.	■

From the central time zone to the Pacific time zone the pattern is subtract 2 hours.

So, it is 6 P.M. in the Pacific time zone when it is 8 P.M. in the central time zone.

Try It

For 1–4, use the map or a pattern to solve.

1. What time is it in the central time zone when it is 8:00 P.M. in the Pacific time zone?
2. What is the time difference between New York City and Denver?
3. If it is 2 P.M. in Orlando, what time is it in Mobile?
4. If it is 8:30 P.M. in Tulsa, what time is it in Seattle?

Find the next time for each pattern.

5. 12:00 P.M., 2:00 P.M., 4:00 P.M., ■
6. 3:15 P.M., 6:15 P.M., 9:15 P.M., ■

UNIT 2

Study Guide and Review

VOCABULARY

Choose the best term from the box.

1. A __?__ is 100 years. A __?__ is 10 years. (pp. 104–107)

2. In a set of data that is ordered from least to greatest, the number in the middle is the __?__. (pp. 118–121)

cumulative frequency
median
mode
century
decade

STUDY AND SOLVE

Chapter 5

Read and write time. Write the elapsed time.

Find the elapsed time.

- Count ahead one hour at a time from 10:45 A.M. to 2:45 P.M., or 4 hours.
- Count ahead one minute at a time from 2:45 P.M. to 2:52 P.M., or 7 minutes.

Start Time **End Time**

So, the elapsed time is 4 hours 7 minutes.

3. Write the time shown on the clock two ways. Include seconds. (pp. 96–97)

Find the elapsed time. (pp. 98–101)

4. **start:** 8:15 A.M.
end: 6:48 P.M.

5. If a movie started at 11:50 A.M. and was 2 hours 18 minutes long, at what time did the movie end?

Chapter 6

Use cumulative frequency tables.

How many pies were sold on Day 1 and Day 2?

PIES SOLD AT ART FESTIVAL

Day	Frequency	Cumulative Frequency
1	16	16
2	23	39
3	14	53
4	24	77
5	19	96

So, 39 pies were sold on Day 1 and Day 2.

For 6–9, use the cumulative frequency table. (pp. 114–123)

6. How many pies were sold on the first day?

7. How many more pies were sold on Day 2 than Day 1?

8. What was the total number of pies sold at the end of 5 days?

9. What are the median and range of the number of pies sold?

Interpret graphs using a variety of scales.

How would the heights of the bars on the graph change if the interval were 5?

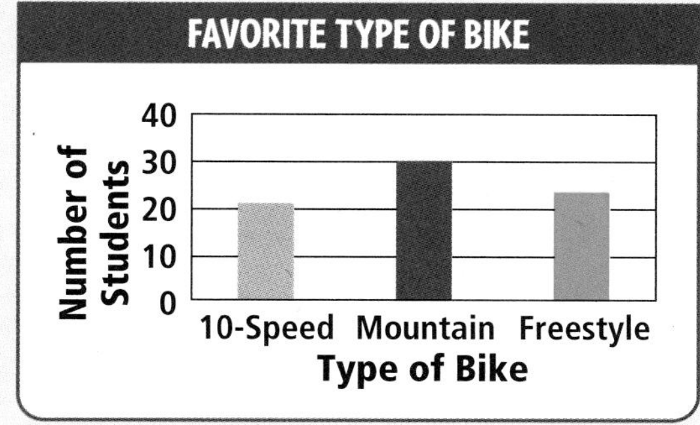

The bars would be taller if the interval were 5.

For 10–13, choose 5, 10, or 100 as the most reasonable interval for each set of data. (pp. 126–127)

10. 0, 50, 100, 100

11. 25, 30, 50, 75, 80

12. 5, 15, 20, 30, 35

13. 100, 150, 200, 200, 350

14. Use the bar graph at the left. How would the heights of the bars on the graph change if the interval were 20?

Chapter 7

Choose an appropriate graph.

Choose a graph to compare the number of red folders sold by two stores in one week.

A line graph shows changes over time. | A bar graph compares different groups of data.

A bar graph would be the better display since two groups of data are being compared.

Write the kind of graph or plot you would choose. (pp. 144–147)

15. to show the test scores of everyone in a class

16. to show a jogger's time at each mile on a 3-mile run

17. to compare the favorite sports of fourth-grade boys and girls

PROBLEM SOLVING PRACTICE

Solve. (pp. 102–103,128–129, 148–149)

18. Use the table to make a schedule for Beth from 1:00–4:00 P.M. The schedule must include lunch.

ACTIVITY	TIME
Watch video	1 hour 45 minutes
Lunch	45 minutes
Ride bike	45 minutes
Play board game	30 minutes

19. Make a graph of the data in the table. Between which two years did sales increase the most?

YEAR	SALES
1997	$250
1998	$180
1999	$220
2000	$270

PERFORMANCE ASSESSMENT

TASK A • TIME FOR FUN

Daniel and his family went to the airport to meet his cousin, Michael, who was coming for a visit. Michael's plane was scheduled to arrive at 9:35 A.M. It arrived 10 minutes late.

a. The family stopped for a quick snack and then drove for 1 hour and 45 minutes to get back to Daniel's house. Draw a clock face to show the time you think they arrived at Daniel's house.

b. The boys want to plan an afternoon of activities to last 4 hours. The table shows the activities they would like to include. There is a star next to the activities they definitely want to include. What other activities would they be able to add?

c. Make a schedule for the boys' afternoon. Give the starting time, ending time, and elapsed time of each activity.

Afternoon Activities

Activity	Time
Hiking	1 hr 15 min
*Lunch	30 min
Swimming	1 hr
*Car Show	1 hr 15 min
Fishing	45 min

TASK B • FAVORITE ACTIVITIES

Caroline took a survey of the favorite after-school activities of some of her classmates. She asked the students this question, "Would you rather go bike riding, play soccer, or play a video game?"

FAVORITE AFTER-SCHOOL ACTIVITY		
Activity	**Boys**	**Girls**
Bike Riding	卌 卌 ||||	卌 卌 卌 卌 |
Playing Soccer	卌 卌 卌 ||	卌 卌 卌 |||
Playing Video Game	卌 卌 卌 |	卌 |||

a. Did Caroline ask a good survey question? Why or why not?

b. Caroline recorded the results of her survey in the table. Make a plot or graph Caroline could use to display the data.

c. Write a question your classmates could answer by looking at the graph or plot you drew.

Make Graphs

A survey was conducted to find the favorite colors of 100 fourth graders. Twenty-three voted for red, 36 for blue, 12 for yellow, 18 for green, and 11 for purple. Make a bar graph to display these results.

You can use a spreadsheet program to make a bar graph.

- Enter the data in two rows on a spreadsheet and highlight them all.

	A	B	C	D	E
1	Red	Blue	Yellow	Green	Purple
2	23	36	12	18	11
3					
4					

- Click *Insert*. Then click *Chart*.
- Choose a chart type: Column or Bar for a bar graph, Line for a line graph, or Pie for a circle graph.
- A window will show a preview of the graph.
- Fill in the labels for the graph:

  Chart title: Favorite Colors
  Category (X) axis: Color
  Value (Y) axis: Number of Students

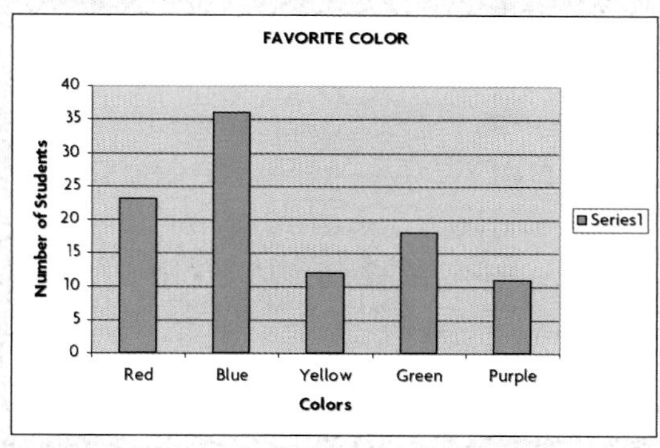

- Insert the graph on the spreadsheet with the data.
- Click *Finish* to view the completed graph.

Practice and Problem Solving

Use a spreadsheet program to make a bar graph of the number of children going to camp.

CHILDREN GOING TO CAMP					
Week	1	2	3	4	5
Children	88	74	68	80	77

1. For which week is the bar on the graph the shortest? What does this show?
2. During which weeks are there *more than* 75 children going to camp?
3. **Write About It** Explain how you can use the bar graph to find the week when the median number of children are going to camp.

GO ON-LINE **Multimedia Math Glossary**
www.harcourtschool.com/mathglossary
Vocabulary Power Look up *bar graph* in the Multimedia Math Glossary. Write a problem that can be answered using the example shown in the glossary.

PROBLEM SOLVING ON LOCATION in Oklahoma

▲ The Osage reservation is one of the largest in the state, covering almost 1,500,000 acres in north-central Oklahoma.

NATIVE AMERICAN RESERVATIONS

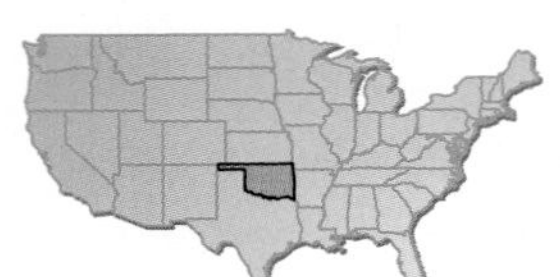

Oklahoma is home to more than 250,000 people of Native American descent. Some of them live on the many Native American reservations across the state.

OKLAHOMA NATIVE AMERICAN RESERVATIONS	
Reservation	**Size (in acres)**
Wichita	80,000
Otoe-Missouria	21,000
Cheyenne-Arapaho	81,000
Choctaw	132,000
Seminole	36,000

The table shows the size of 5 major reservations in Oklahoma.

USE DATA For 1–7, use the table.

1. Make a graph to compare the sizes of the reservations. Explain your choice of graph.
2. What scale and interval did you use in your graph? Explain your choices.
3. What is the range of the sizes of the reservations?
4. What is the difference in size between the Choctaw reservation and the Seminole reservation?
5. Which reservation is 60,000 acres smaller than the Cheyenne-Arapaho reservation?
6. Which 2 reservations have a combined area of 116,000 acres?
7. Would a line graph be a good way to display the data in the table? Why or why not?

RED EARTH MUSEUM

The Red Earth Museum, in Oklahoma City, reaches more than 300,000 people per year with its educational programs and exhibitions. The *Oklahoma Indian* program lets students explore the history and culture of the 40 Native American tribes of Oklahoma.

▲ **The Red Earth Museum is the largest museum in the country dedicated exclusively to Native American arts and culture.**

The table shows how many students attended the *Oklahoma Indian* program over 5 weeks.

EDUCATIONAL PROGRAMS	
Week	**Number of Students**
1	58
2	59
3	63
4	39
5	41

USE DATA For 1–4, use the table.

1. What kind of graph would be best for displaying the data in the table? Explain your answer.
2. What is the range of the data? How would the range change if 34 students had attended the program in Week 4?
3. Between which two consecutive weeks was there the greatest increase in the number of students attending the program?
4. **Write About It** Write a problem that uses the data in the table. Then solve your problem.
5. The museum is open from 9:00 A.M. to 5:00 P.M., Tuesday through Friday, from 9:00 A.M. to 6:00 P.M. on Saturday, and from 11:00 A.M. to 6:00 P.M. on Sunday. How many hours is the museum open each week?
6. *Oklahoma Indian* begins at 11:00 A.M. and lasts for one hour. A program called *Native Homes* begins immediately after *Oklahoma Indian* and lasts for 45 minutes. What time does *Native Homes* end?

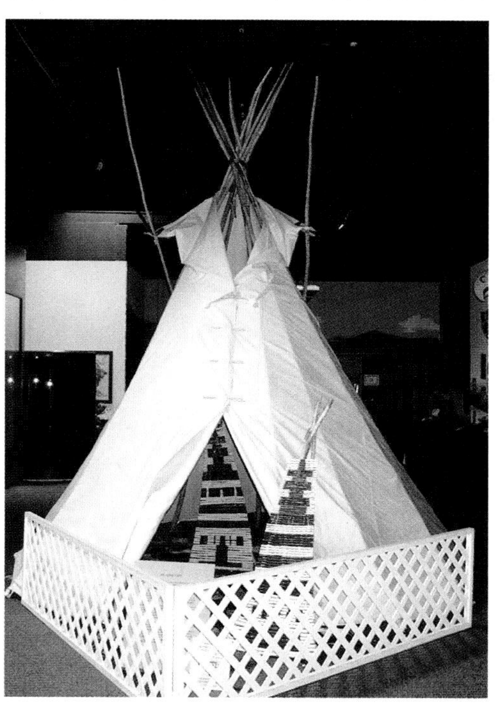

CHAPTER 8

Practice Multiplication and Division Facts

FAST FACT • SOCIAL STUDIES The New York Philharmonic was the first symphony orchestra in the United States. It was founded in 1842.

PROBLEM SOLVING Look at the seating plan for an orchestra. If each brass player needs 2 pieces of music, how many pieces of music are needed for this section? If 2 woodwind players share a music stand, how many stands are needed for this section?

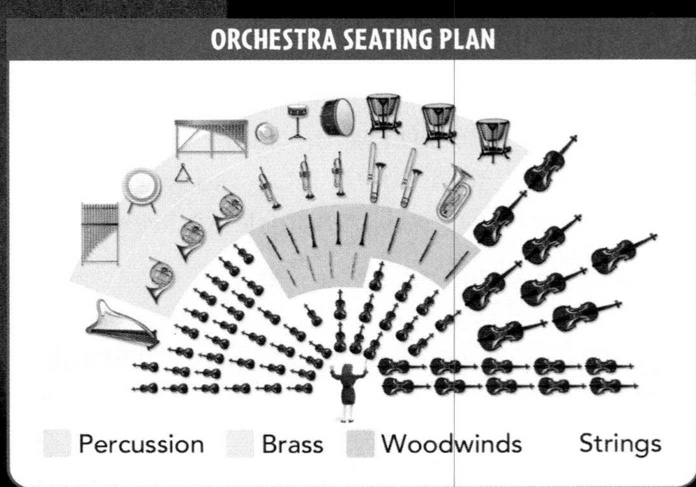

Check What You Know

Use this page to help you review and remember important skills needed for Chapter 8.

MEANING OF MULTIPLICATION

Use the array to find the value of each expression.

1\.

■ rows of ■ = ■

■ × ■ = ■

2\. 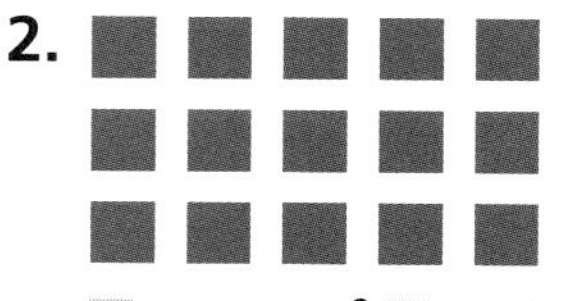

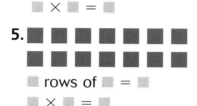

■ rows of ■ = ■

■ × ■ = ■

3\. 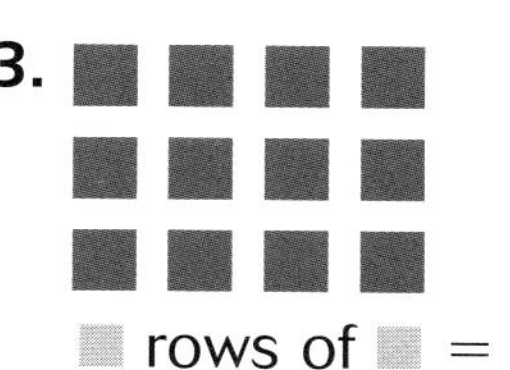

■ rows of ■ = ■

■ × ■ = ■

4\. 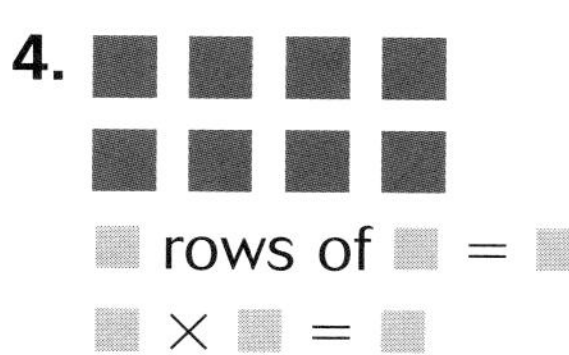

■ rows of ■ = ■

■ × ■ = ■

5\.

■ rows of ■ = ■

■ × ■ = ■

6\. 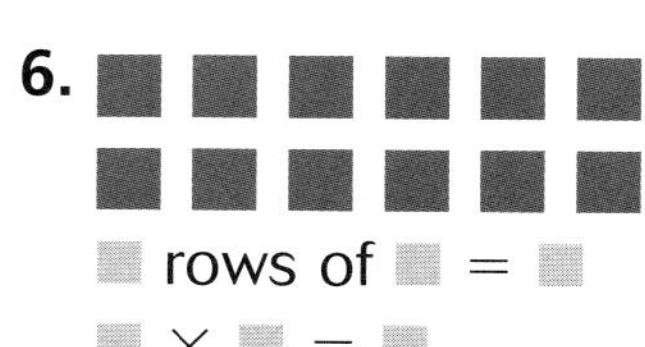

■ rows of ■ = ■

■ × ■ = ■

MEANING OF DIVISION

Answer the questions for each picture.

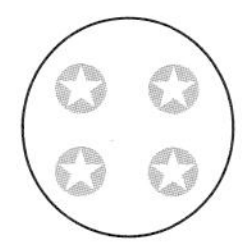 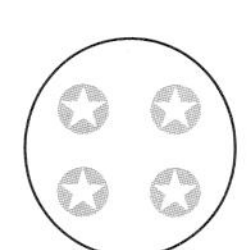 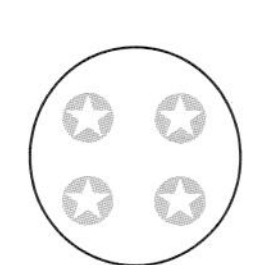

7. How many counters are there in all?
8. How many equal groups are there?
9. How many are there in each group?

10. How many counters are there in all?
11. How many equal groups are there?
12. How many are there in each group?

Vocabulary Power

REVIEW

factor [fak′tər] *noun*

A *factor* is a number that is multiplied by another number to find a product. *Ingredient* is a synonym for *factor*. Describe how a factor is an ingredient in a multiplication problem.

PREVIEW

inverse operations
fact family
multiple
Identity Property
Zero Property
Commutative Property
Associative Property

GO ON-LINE **www.harcourtschool.com/mathglossary**

LESSON 1

Algebra: Relate Multiplication and Division

Quick Review

1. 2×6
2. 4×3
3. 4×4
4. 8×2
5. 5×4

VOCABULARY

inverse operations

fact family

Learn

HALFTIME NOTES The band played 6 songs during the halftime of the football game. Each song was 3 minutes long. How long did the band play?

$6 \times 3 = n$

$\downarrow$

$6 \times 3 = 18$

$18 = n$

So, the band played for 18 minutes.

The band played for 18 minutes at another football game. Each song was 3 minutes long. How many songs did the band play?

$18 \div 3 = n$

6	×	3	=	18,	so	18	÷	3	=	6
↓		↓		↓		↓		↓		↓
factor		factor		product		dividend		divisor		quotient

$n = 6$

So, the band played 6 songs.

MATH IDEA Multiplication and division by the same number are opposite operations, or **inverse operations**. One operation undoes the other.

A set of related multiplication and division equations using the same numbers is a **fact family**.

$6 \times 3 = 18$ $18 \div 3 = 6$

$3 \times 6 = 18$ $18 \div 6 = 3$

← fact family for 3, 6, 18

Check

1. **Explain** why you can use multiplication to find $24 \div 4$.

Find the value of the variable. Write a related equation.

2. $2 \times 4 = n$ **3.** $12 \div 3 = x$ **4.** $28 \div 4 = y$ **5.** $5 \times 3 = z$

Practice and Problem Solving

Extra Practice, page 178, Set A

Find the value of the variable. Write a related equation.

6. $16 \div 2 = n$ **7.** $20 \div 4 = b$ **8.** $3 \times 4 = y$ **9.** $5 \times 4 = c$

10. $6 \times 3 = p$ **11.** $6 \times 5 = n$ **12.** $36 \div 4 = a$ **13.** $27 \div 3 = y$

14. $b \div 4 = 8$ **15.** $18 \div n = 2$ **16.** $y \times 4 = 40$ **17.** $8 \times n = 24$

Write the fact family for each set of numbers.

18. 2, 3, 6 **19.** 4, 7, 28 **20.** 3, 7, 21

21. Name 2 fact families that have only two equations. Explain.

USE DATA For 22–24, use the table.

22. Michael collected baseball cards for 3 months. He collected 44 cards in the first month and 29 cards in the second month. How many cards did Michael collect in the third month?

23. Michael collected the same number of soccer cards in each of 4 weeks. How many soccer cards did he collect each week?

24. What is the total number of cards Michael collected?

MICHAEL'S CARD COLLECTION

Sport	Number Collected
Football	64
Soccer	28
Baseball	110
Basketball	35

25. **Write About It** Explain how you can use multiplication to solve a division problem. Give an example.

Mixed Review and Test Prep

For 26–29, find the sum or difference. (p. 48)

26. $3{,}542 + 1{,}869 + 5{,}273$

27. $8{,}600 - 4{,}237$

28. $3{,}189 - 1{,}814$

29. $2{,}509 + 1{,}487 + 4{,}375$

30. **TEST PREP** What is seven hundred five in standard form? (p. 4)

A 75
B 705
C 7,005
D 7,500

LESSON 2

Multiply and Divide Facts Through 5

Quick Review

1. 6×2
2. $12 \div 2$
3. 5×3
4. $15 \div 3$
5. $6 \div 3$

Learn

PUT IT IN REVERSE! Mrs. Frazier asked her students to use models to show that division is the inverse of multiplication. This is how her students showed that division is the inverse of multiplication.

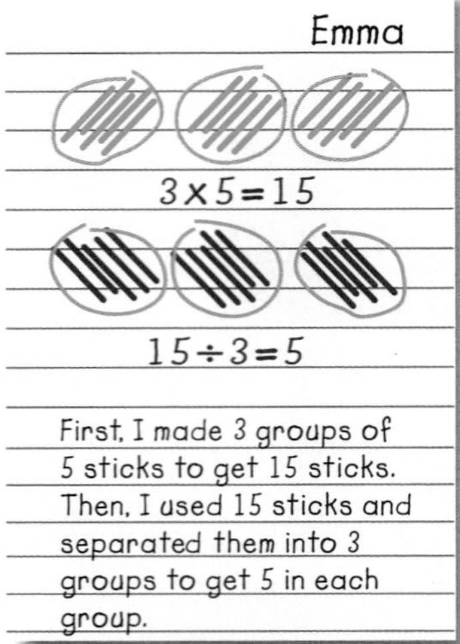

Emma
3x5=15
15÷3=5
First, I made 3 groups of 5 sticks to get 15 sticks. Then, I used 15 sticks and separated them into 3 groups to get 5 in each group.

Blake

0 1 2 3 4 5 6 7 8 9

3x3=9

0 1 2 3 4 5 6 7 8 9

9÷3=3

I started at 0 and made jumps of 3 on a number line to land at 9. Then, starting at 9 I took jumps of 3 back to 0.

Carlos

5x4=20

20÷4=5

I made 5 rows of 4 blocks to make 20 blocks. Then I divided the 20 blocks into 4 columns to get 5 in each column.

Latoya

→ To multiply, I looked across row 6 and down column 4 to find the product 24.

→ To divide, I found 24 by looking down column 4. Then I looked left to find the quotient.

6x4=24,

so 24÷4=6.

×	0	1	2	3	4	5	6	7	8	9
0	0	0	0	0	0	0	0	0	0	0
1	0	1	2	3	4	5	6	7	8	9
2	0	2	4	6	8	10	12	14	16	18
3	0	3	6	9	12	15	18	21	24	27
4	0	4	8	12	16	20	24	28	32	36
5	0	5	10	15	20	25	30	35	40	45
6	0	6	12	18	24	30	36	42	48	54

- Which model do you like the best? Explain.

Check

1. **Draw** a model that shows the inverse operation of 5×6. Then write the related equation.

Write a related multiplication or division equation.

2. $10 \div 2 = 5$

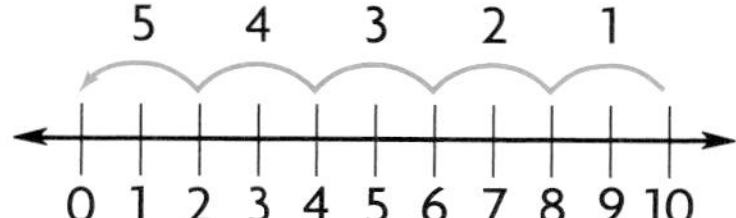

3. $4 \times 4 = 16$

4. $4 \times 3 = 12$

Practice and Problem Solving

Extra Practice, page 178, Set B

Write a related multiplication or division equation.

5. $2 \times 6 = 12$

6. $2 \times 3 = 6$

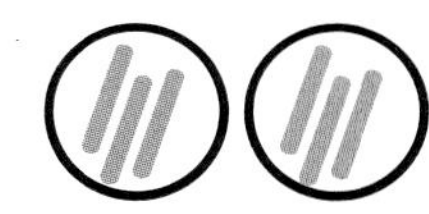

7. $4 \times 2 = 8$

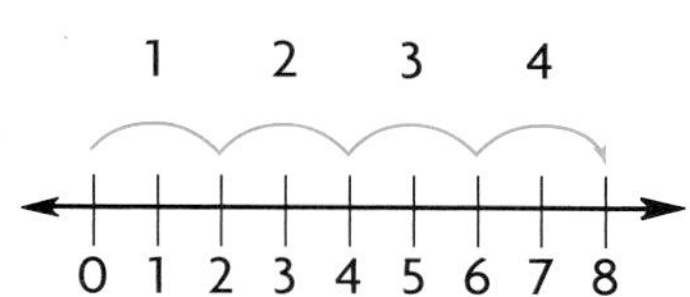

Find the product or quotient.

8. $14 \div 2$
9. 5×5
10. 5×7
11. $32 \div 4$
12. $28 \div 4$
13. 4×8
14. $36 \div 4$
15. 3×0
16. $8 \div 2$
17. 2×5

ALGEBRA Find the value of the variable.

18. $4 \times 2 = 8$, so $4 \times 2 \times 2 = n$.

19. $5 \times 5 = 25$, so $(5 \times 5) + 10 = a$.

20. $45 \div 5 = 9$, so $(45 \div 5) \times 2 = b$.

21. $3 \times 4 = 12$, so $3 \times 4 \times 2 = n$.

22. There are 16 friends bowling. The same number of friends are bowling in each of 4 lanes. How many friends are bowling in each lane?

23. Felipe's remote-controlled car travels 2 feet forward and then 2 feet back. If Felipe's car does this twice, what is the total distance the car will have traveled?

24. **Write a problem** using division that you can solve by using the multiplication equation $7 \times 5 = 35$.

Mixed Review and Test Prep

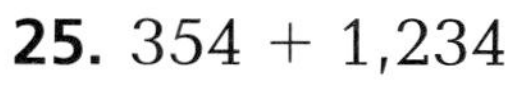

25. $354 + 1,234$ (p. 48)

26. $586 + 4,821$ (p. 48)

27. Round 8,754 to the nearest hundred. (p. 30)

28. Round 14,842 to the nearest thousand. (p. 30)

29. **TEST PREP** At the store, Martha bought corn for \$1.19, an onion for \$0.35, and lettuce for \$0.89. How much change did she receive from \$5.00?

A \$2.43
B \$2.57
C \$2.87
D \$7.43

LESSON 3

Multiply and Divide Facts Through 10

Quick Review

1. 5×6
2. $30 \div 6$
3. 4×7
4. 7×3
5. $25 \div 5$

Learn

DIVIDE AND CONQUER You can break apart numbers to make them easier to multiply. Find the product of 6 and 8.

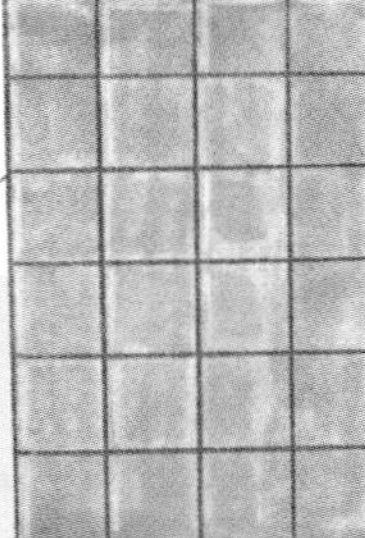

Activity

MATERIALS: centimeter grid paper

What is 6×8?

STEP 1

Draw a rectangular array that is 6 units wide and 8 units long. Think of the area as 6×8.

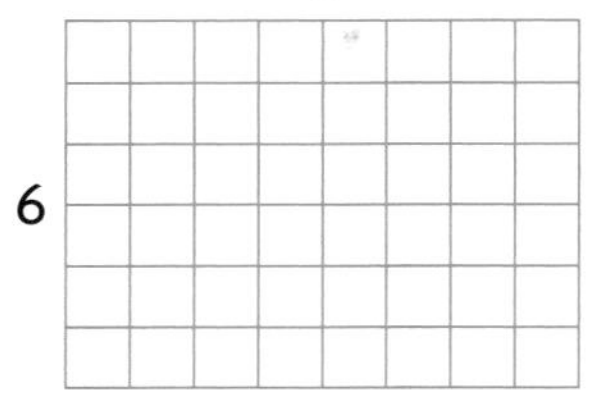

STEP 2

Cut apart the array to make two smaller arrays for products you know.

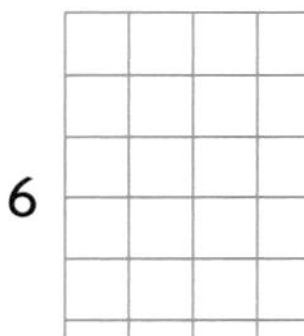

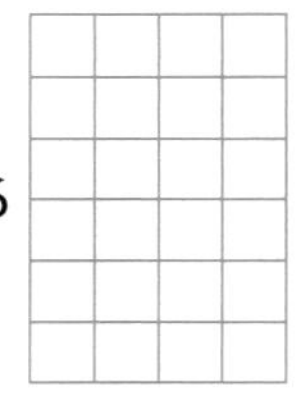

The factor 8 is now 4 plus 4.

STEP 3

Find the sum of the products of the two smaller arrays.

$6 \times 4 = 24$

$6 \times 4 = 24$

$24 + 24 = 48$

So, $6 \times 8 = 48$.

- What two smaller arrays can you make if you cut equal parts of the 6×8 array horizontally?
- Use grid paper to find 8×10.

MATH IDEA If you forget a multiplication fact, you can break apart one of the factors into products you know.

Technology Link

More Practice: Harcourt Mega Math, The Number Games, *Up, Up, and Array,* Levels C and G

More Strategies

Strategies can help you learn the multiplication and division facts that you do not know.

×	0	1	2	3	4	5	6	7	8	9	10
0	0	0	0	0	0	0	0	0	0	0	0
1	0	1	2	3	4	5	6	7	8	9	10
2	0	2	4	6	8	10	12	14	16	18	20
3	0	3	6	9	12	15	18	21	24	27	30
4	0	4	8	12	16	20	24	28	32	36	40
5	0	5	10	15	20	25	30	35	40	45	50
6	0	6	12	18	24	30	36	42	48	54	60
7	0	7	14	21	28	35	42	49	56	63	70
8	0	8	16	24	32	40	48	56	64	72	80
9	0	9	18	27	36	45	54	63	72	81	90
10	0	10	20	30	40	50	60	70	80	90	100

↑ Facts to memorize

Think of the inverse operation.

What is $36 \div 9$?

Think: $4 \times 9 = 36$

So, $36 \div 9 = 4$.

Use the Order Property.

What is 8×5?

Think: $5 \times 8 = 40$

So, $8 \times 5 = 5 \times 8 = 40$.

Use a pattern.

What is 6×9?

Think: $6 \times 5 = 30$, so I can count on from 30 by 6 for the remaining 4 times.

Count: 30 . . . 36, 42, 48, 54.

So, $6 \times 9 = 54$.

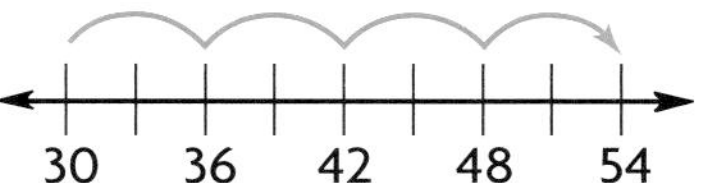

Use the *break apart* strategy.

What is 7×6?

Think: $6 = 2 + 4$

$7 \times 2 = 14$ and $7 \times 4 = 28$,
$7 \times 6 = 14 + 28$

So, $7 \times 6 = 42$.

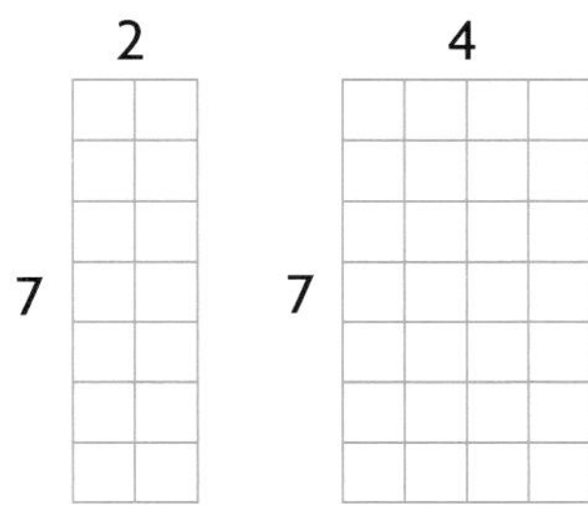

Check

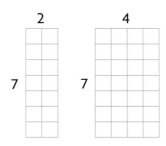

1. **Explain** how breaking apart numbers can help you find the product of greater numbers.

Find the product or quotient. Show the strategy you used.

2. 9×6 **3.** 3×10 **4.** 6×6 **5.** $42 \div 6$ **6.** $72 \div 9$

LESSON CONTINUES

Practice and Problem Solving

Extra Practice, page 178, Set C

Show how the arrays can be used to find the product.

7. What is 9×8?

$9 \times 4 = ■$

$9 \times 4 = ■$

$9 \times 8 = ■ + ■$

So, $9 \times 8 = ■$.

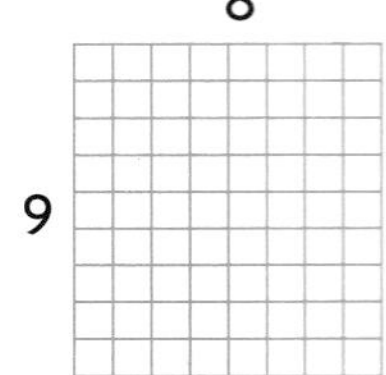

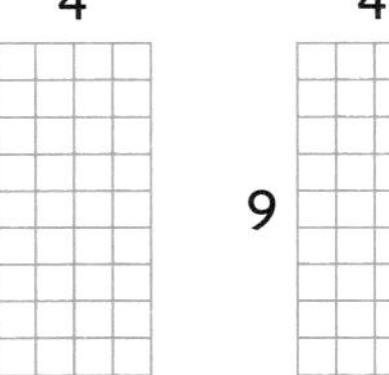

8. What is 7×9?

$7 \times 3 = ■$

$7 \times 3 = ■$

$7 \times 3 = ■$

$7 \times 9 = ■ + ■ + ■$

So, $7 \times 9 = ■$.

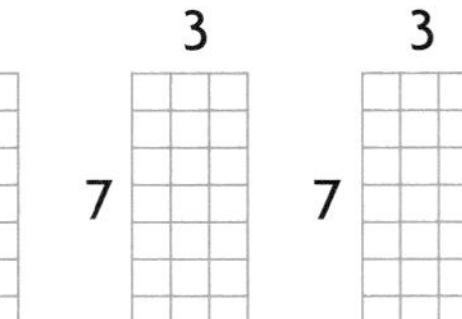

Find the product or quotient. Show the strategy you used.

9. 5×9 **10.** 4×9 **11.** 4×6

12. 9×9 **13.** 8×8 **14.** 10×7

15. 9×7 **16.** 7×8 **17.** 8×9

18. $48 \div 6$ **19.** $72 \div 8$ **20.** $48 \div 8$

21. $70 \div 10$ **22.** $54 \div 6$ **23.** $63 \div 9$

ALGEBRA **Find the missing factor.**

24. $■ \times 6 = 60$ **25.** $7 \times ■ = 49$ **26.** $■ \times 9 = 81$

For 27–30, look for patterns in the Facts of Nine table.

27. How does the pattern of the tens digits in the products relate to the pattern of the first factors?

28. How does each product relate to the second factor?

29. Explain how you can use the patterns you found to find 9×9 without the table.

30. **What's the Error?** Gwyn used the *break apart* strategy to solve 8×9. Describe her error. Show a correct way to use the strategy.

$8 \times 3 = 24$ and $8 \times 3 = 24$

$24 + 24 = 48$

Facts of Nine
$1 \times 9 = 9$
$2 \times 9 = 18$
$3 \times 9 = 27$
$4 \times 9 = 36$
$5 \times 9 = 45$
$6 \times 9 = 54$
$7 \times 9 = 63$
$8 \times 9 = 72$
$9 \times 9 = 81$

31. Sandra shared some jacks equally with Maria and Tom. There were 2 jacks left. Maria got 11 jacks. How many jacks did Sandra have to start?

32. **Vocabulary Power** The word *inverse* means "opposite in effect." Describe how multiplication and division are inverse operations. Give an example.

Mixed Review and Test Prep

33. Write six hundred seventy thousand, fifty-four in standard form. (p. 4)

34. Write 5,241,211 in expanded form. (p. 6)

35. Order 111, 456, and 237 from greatest to least. (p. 24)

36. Order 35,314; 34,919; and 35,335 from least to greatest. (p. 24)

37. $\begin{array}{r} 47{,}345 \\ +24{,}399 \\ \hline \end{array}$ (p. 52)

38. $\begin{array}{r} 90{,}260 \\ -18{,}435 \\ \hline \end{array}$ (p. 52)

39. **TEST PREP** In batting practice, Ellie hit 10 balls in a row before getting a strike. Then she hit 12 balls, then 16 balls. How many balls did she hit altogether? (p. 40)

A 10 **B** 22 **C** 26 **D** 38

40. **TEST PREP** At the art fair, May bought 2 rings for $3.50 each. She also bought a picture for $7.50 and a drink for $1.25. How much money did May spend at the art fair?

F $8.75 **G** $12.25 **H** $15.75 **J** $17.75

Problem Solving LINKUP . . . to Art

The Romans often covered floors with small colored tiles made of material such as marble or stone. The picture shows part of a Roman floor. Works of art done in this style are known as *mosaics*.

You can use what you know about multiplying to find the total number of tiles you would need to make a design to cover part of your desk.

1. Draw a section of the design shown or make your own design with pattern blocks.
2. Record the number of each of the different shapes you used in your design.
3. Write a multiplication sentence to find the total number of each shape of tile you would need if you made 8 designs like the one you drew.

LESSON
4

HANDS
ON

Multiplication Table Through 12

Quick Review

1. 9 × 6
2. 8 × 5
3. 63 ÷ 9
4. 7 × 7
5. 54 ÷ 6

VOCABULARY

multiple

MATERIALS blank multiplication table through 12

Explore

Use strategies and patterns to learn new facts. Make your own multiplication table for the facts from 0 through 12.

Activity

THE ELEVENS

Complete the column for 11 to 10 × 11. Use break-apart numbers to find 11 × 11 and 12 × 11.

Think:

10 × 11 = 110
1 × 11 = 11
11 × 11 = 110 + 11
So, 11 × 11 = 121.

10 × 11 = 110
2 × 11 = 22
12 × 11 = 110 + 22
So, 12 × 11 = 132.

Complete the row for 11.

THE TWELVES

Complete the column for 12 to 10 × 12. Use break-apart numbers to find 12 × 12.

Think:

10 × 12 = 120
2 × 12 = 24
12 × 12 = 120 + 24
So, 12 × 12 = 144.

Complete the row for 12.

×	0	1	2	3	4	5	6	7	8	9	10	11	12
0	0	0	0	0	0	0	0	0	0	0	0		
1	0	1	2	3	4	5	6	7	8	9	10		
2	0	2	4	6	8	10	12	14	16	18	20		
3	0	3	6	9	12	15	18	21	24	27	30		
4	0	4	8	12	16	20	24	28	32	36	40		
5	0	5	10	15	20	25	30	35	40	45	50		
6	0	6	12	18	24	30	36	42	48	54	60		
7	0	7	14	21	28	35	42	49	56	63	70		
8	0	8	16	24	32	40	48	56	64	72	80		
9	0	9	18	27	36	45	54	63	72	81	90		
10	0	10	20	30	40	50	60	70	80	90	100		
11													
12													

I found the row for
8 and the column
for 11. What's
the product?

- Explain how you can use the multiplication table to find 99 ÷ 11.

Try It

Use your multiplication table to find the product.

a. 8 × 11 **b.** 3 × 11 **c.** 4 × 12

Connect

A **multiple** is the product of a given number and another whole number. Look at the row or the column for 6 in the table on page 172. Find the multiples of 6 shown in the table.

So, 6, 12, 18, 24, 30, 36, 42, 48, 54, 60, 66, and 72 are all multiples of 6.

- What are the multiples of 11 shown in the table?
- What pattern do you see in the multiples for 11?

Technology Link

More Practice: Harcourt Mega Math, The Number Games, *Up, Up, and Array,* Levels D and H and Fraction Action, *Number Line Mine,* Level D

Practice and Problem Solving

Use the multiplication table to find the product or quotient.

1. 1×12 **2.** 2×10 **3.** 3×11 **4.** 4×12

5. 5×9 **6.** 6×10 **7.** 7×11 **8.** 8×12

9. $120 \div 12$ **10.** $88 \div 11$ **11.** $90 \div 10$ **12.** $144 \div 12$

13. $110 \div 11$ **14.** $121 \div 11$ **15.** $100 \div 10$ **16.** $132 \div 11$

ALGEBRA **Find the value of the variable.**

17. $r \times 12 = 120$ **18.** $11 \times n = 121$ **19.** $100 \div s = 10$ **20.** $p \div 11 = 7$

21. **REASONING** The first six multiples of 12 are 12, 24, 36, 48, 60, and 72. What are the next six multiples?

22. Rosa collected 3 dozen eggs and Peter collected 7 dozen. How many eggs did they collect altogether?

23. ***FAST FACT*** **• MUSIC** A piano keyboard has 88 keys. If an octave is 8 keys, how many octaves does a piano keyboard have?

24. **What's the Question?** The answer is that one factor is 11 and the product is 132.

Mixed Review and Test Prep

For 25–26, find the value of the expression. (p. 64)

25. $(15 - 9) + 3$

26. $(27 + 2) - 12$

27. What is three hundred seventy-two thousand, twenty-five in standard form? (p. 4)

28. How much time elapses between 11:30 A.M. and 1:05 P.M.? (p. 98)

29. **TEST PREP** Angel had \$310. He spent \$27. How much does Angel have left? (p. 50)

A \$273 **C** \$293
B \$283 **D** \$383

LESSON 5

Multiplication Properties

Quick Review

1. 4×3
2. 9×9
3. 10×8
4. 7×5
5. 12×4

VOCABULARY

Identity Property
Zero Property
Commutative Property
Associative Property

Learn

Properties of multiplication can help you find products of two or more factors.

Properties

The **Identity Property** states that the product of 1 and any number is that number.

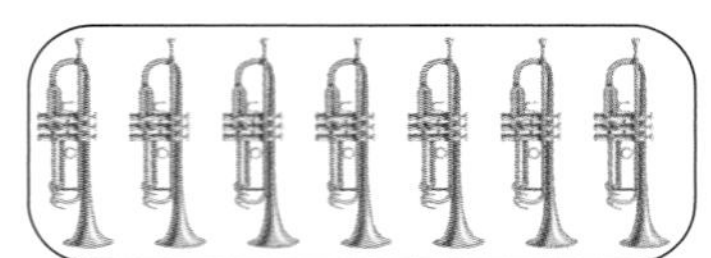

$1 \times 7 = 7$

The **Zero Property** states that the product of 0 and any number is 0.

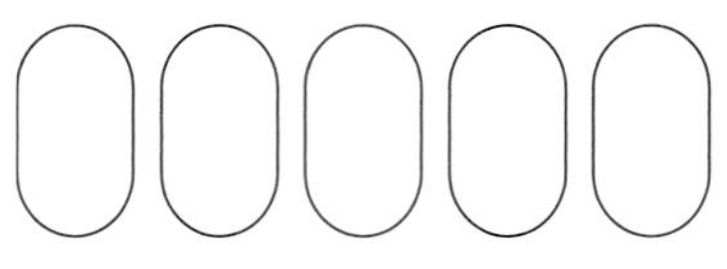

$5 \times 0 = 0$

The **Commutative Property** states that you can multiply two factors in any order and get the same product.

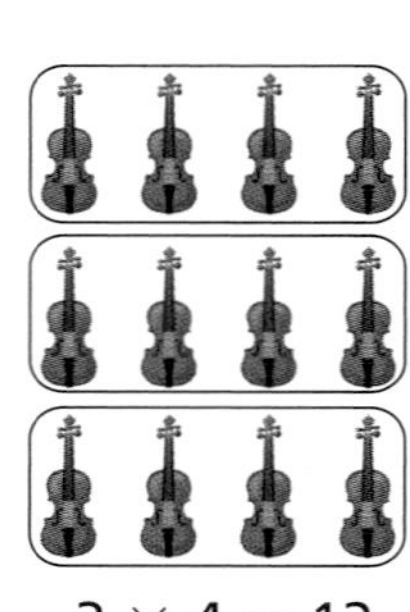

$3 \times 4 = 12$

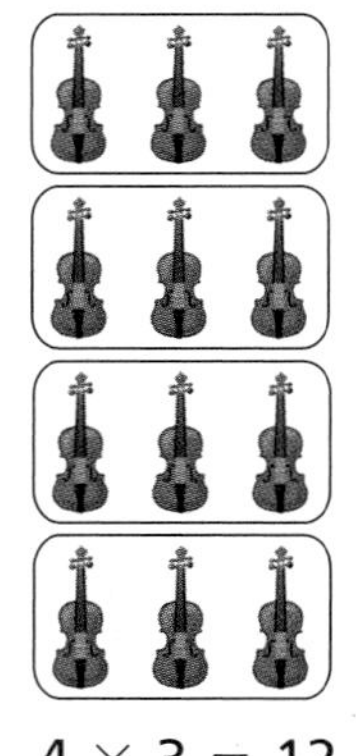

$4 \times 3 = 12$

The **Associative Property** states that you can group factors in different ways and get the same product. Use parentheses to group the factors you multiply first.

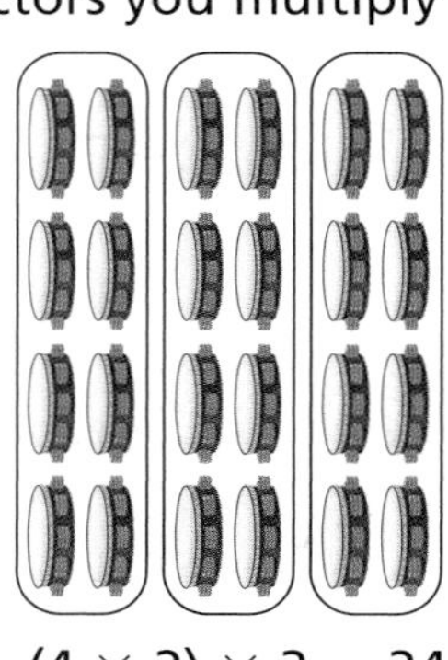

$(4 \times 2) \times 3 = 24$

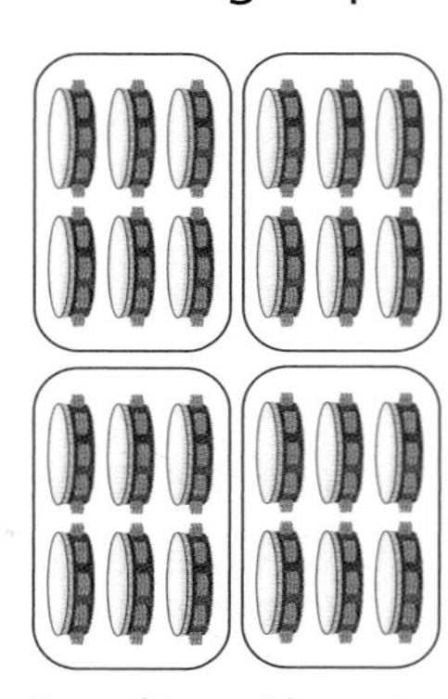

$4 \times (2 \times 3) = 24$

- Explain how to find 8×6 if you know that $6 \times 8 = 48$.

Check

1. **Name** two ways you can group $2 \times 5 \times 3$ to find the product. Are the products the same? Explain.

Find the missing number. Name the property you used.

2. $\blacksquare \times 1 = 12$
3. $9 \times \blacksquare = 0$
4. $(6 \times 2) \times 5 = 6 \times (\blacksquare \times 5)$

Practice and Problem Solving

Extra Practice, page 178, Set D

Find the missing number. Name the property you used.

5. ■ × 11 = 11
6. 7 × 3 = ■ × 7
7. (4 × 2) × 2 = ■ × (2 × 2)
8. 0 = ■ × 5
9. 8 × 5 = 5 × ■
10. ■ × 3 = 3
11. ■ × (3 × 3) = (6 × 3) × 3
12. 9 × 10 = 10 × ■
13. (5 × 3) × ■ = 5 × (3 × 2)

Show two ways to group by using parentheses.
Find the product.

14. 5 × 2 × 3
15. 9 × 1 × 5
16. 3 × 2 × 6
17. 9 × 0 × 12
18. 2 × 2 × 3
19. 5 × 2 × 5
20. 4 × 3 × 4
21. 2 × 2 × 6

Write the missing number for each ■. Then find the product.

22. 8 × 4 = 4 × ■
23. 2 × 9 = ■ × 2
24. ■ × 3 = 3 × 5
25. 6 × ■ = 5 × 6

ALGEBRA Write <, >, or = for each ●.

26. 1 × (4 × 7) ● 7 × (4 × 1)
27. 3 × (3 × 2) ● (9 × 1) × 4
28. 10 × (3 × 1) ● 3 × (3 × 2)
29. 1 × 2 × 3 ● 3 × 1 × 2
30. 2 × (2 × 5) ● (2 × 3) × 5
31. 9 × (2 × 3) ● 3 × (6 × 2)

32. Which multiplication property would you use to find 356 × 1? Explain and write the product.

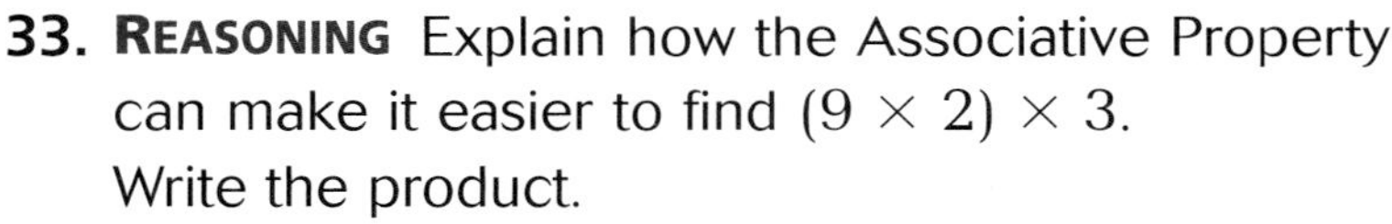

33. **REASONING** Explain how the Associative Property can make it easier to find (9 × 2) × 3. Write the product.

34. Emanuel practices the guitar 3 hours each week. Lois practices the piano 5 hours each week. How many more hours does Lois practice in 4 weeks than Emanuel?

Mixed Review and Test Prep

35. 3,005 (p. 48)
 2,354
 +1,789

36. 4,569 (p. 48)
 2,382
 +4,375

37. 43,259 (p. 52)
 −18,513

38. 2,674 (p. 52)
 −1,003

39. **TEST PREP** Josh wants to pick 108 apples. So far, he has counted 5 dozen. How many more dozen apples does he need to meet his goal? (p. 172)

A 2 B 3 C 4 D 5

Problem Solving Skill
Choose the Operation

UNDERSTAND PLAN SOLVE CHECK

Find the product.

1. 3 × (5 × 2)
2. (4 × 3) × 6
3. (2 × 6) × 3
4. 2 × 5 × 6
5. 8 × 2 × 3

OPERATION PRECIPITATION Study the problems. Use the chart to help you choose the operation needed to solve each problem.

Add	Join groups of different sizes
Subtract	Take away or compare groups
Multiply	Join equal-size groups
Divide	Separate into equal-size groups or find how many in each group

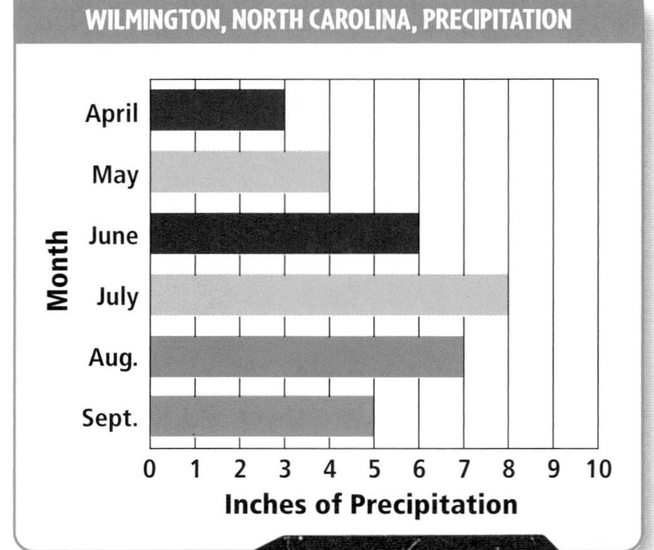

A. What if Wilmington gets the same amount of rainfall for the next 5 months as in September? What would be the total rainfall for these 5 months?

B. About how much rain fell each week in May?

C. How much more rain fell in May through July than in August and September?

D. What is the total amount of rainfall for Wilmington from April through September?

- Solve Problems A–D. Tell the operation you used.
- What two different operations could you use to solve Problem A? to solve Problem B?

Talk About It

- What words in the box at the top of the page help you decide which operation to use for each of Problems A–D?

Problem Solving Practice

Solve. Name the operation or operations you used.

1. During the past 9 weeks, the school chorus practiced a total of 36 hours. If they practiced the same number of hours each week, how many hours did they practice each week?

2. The cafeteria served 124 school lunches. There were a total of 11 pizzas cut into 12 slices each. If each student received 1 slice, how many slices were left?

3. Mrs. Ling ordered 12 pizzas cut into 8 slices each. How many slices did she order?

4. Mr. Davis cut a sheet cake into 6 rows of 8 pieces. How many pieces of cake are there in all?

Choose the letter of the correct answer.

Before the concert, Michele sold 12 large umbrellas. Each umbrella was shared by 4 people. How many people used the umbrellas?

5. Which expression could you use to solve the problem?

   A $12 \div 4$ **C** 12×4
   B $12 - 4$ **D** $12 + 4$

6. How many people used the umbrellas?

   F 4 **G** 8 **H** 16 **J** 48

Mixed Applications

USE DATA For 7–10, use the table.

7. Ben buys 2 board games and 4 books. How much change does he get from $5.00?

8. Tyler bought 3 tapes and 2 books. How much did he spend at the sale?

9. **Write a problem** using the information in the table.

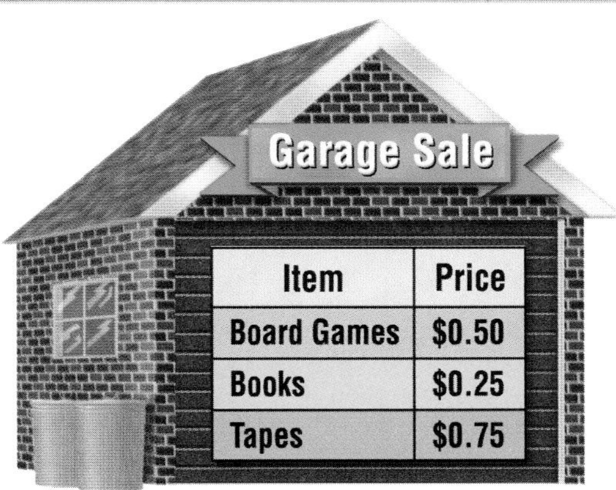

Item	Price
Board Games	$0.50
Books	$0.25
Tapes	$0.75

10. Caro bought 2 tapes, a book, and a board game. Chad bought 4 tapes. How much more did Chad spend then Caro?

11. A train left Oakville at 7:45 A.M. It arrived in Bay City at 1:10 P.M. How long was the train trip?

Extra Practice

Set A (pp. 164–165)

Find the value of the variable. Write a related equation.

1. $15 \div 3 = c$ **2.** $7 \times 4 = b$ **3.** $4 \times 5 = k$ **4.** $27 \div 9 = y$

5. $24 \div 3 = a$ **6.** $2 \times 6 = n$ **7.** $8 \times 4 = d$ **8.** $25 \div 5 = z$

Write the fact family for each set of numbers.

9. 3, 4, 12 **10.** 4, 6, 24 **11.** 2, 9, 18 **12.** 3, 7, 21

Set B (pp. 166–167)

Find the product or quotient.

1. 7×3 **2.** 8×4 **3.** 5×6 **4.** 4×4

5. $5 \div 5$ **6.** $36 \div 4$ **7.** $27 \div 3$ **8.** $12 \div 4$

9. 9×2 **10.** 5×4 **11.** 7×5 **12.** 5×8

13. $20 \div 5$ **14.** $16 \div 8$ **15.** $24 \div 4$ **16.** $45 \div 9$

Set C (pp. 168–171)

1. For 7×6, draw one array to show the expression. Next, use the break-apart strategy and draw two arrays that could be used to solve the problem.

Find the product or quotient. Show the strategy you used.

2. 7×4 **3.** 8×9 **4.** 6×6 **5.** 9×4

6. $55 \div 5$ **7.** $36 \div 6$ **8.** $27 \div 9$ **9.** $60 \div 5$

10. 9×11 **11.** 12×4 **12.** 7×7 **13.** 7×8

14. $54 \div 6$ **15.** $48 \div 8$ **16.** $63 \div 9$ **17.** $64 \div 8$

Set D (pp. 174–175)

Find the missing number. Name the property you used.

1. $(4 \times 3) \times 3 = \blacksquare \times (3 \times 3)$ **2.** $0 = 7 \times \blacksquare$ **3.** $1 \times \blacksquare = 12$

4. $9 \times 4 = \blacksquare \times 9$ **5.** $3 \times (\blacksquare \times 8) = (3 \times 1) \times 8$ **6.** $6 \times \blacksquare = 8 \times 6$

Review/Test

✓ CHECK VOCABULARY AND CONCEPTS

Choose the best term from the box.

inverse
fact family
Associative Property
quotient
Commutative Property

1. The _?_ states that when the grouping of factors is changed, the product remains the same. (p. 174)
2. Multiplication and division by the same number are opposite, or _?_, operations. One operation undoes the other. (p. 164)
3. A set of related multiplication and division sentences using the same numbers is a _?_. (p. 164)

✓ CHECK SKILLS

Find the value of the variable. Write a related equation. (pp. 164–165)

4. $18 \div 3 = n$ **5.** $6 \times 7 = a$ **6.** $y \div 4 = 5$ **7.** $9 \times c = 63$

Write a related division equation. (pp. 166–167)

8. $3 \times 5 = 15$ **9.** $3 \times 3 = 9$ **10.** $4 \times 2 = 8$

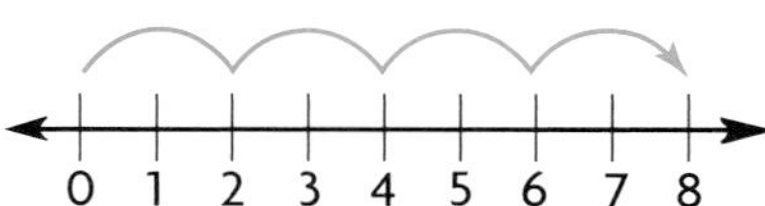

Find the product or quotient. (pp. 168–173)

11. 4×7 **12.** $18 \div 3$ **13.** $56 \div 8$ **14.** 9×8 **15.** 12×5

16. $144 \div 12$ **17.** 8×11 **18.** 10×9 **19.** $48 \div 6$ **20.** $121 \div 11$

Find the missing number. Name the property you used. (pp. 174–175)

21. $8 \times (■ \times 3) = (8 \times 4) \times 3$ **22.** $■ \times 9 = 0$ **23.** $11 = ■ \times 1$

✓ CHECK PROBLEM SOLVING

Solve. Write the operation or operations you used. (pp. 176–177)

24. For a class field trip, 42 students went to a museum. If the museum takes groups of 7 students, how many groups were there?

25. Jack wants 6 packs of cards. If a store sells 1 pack of cards for $3 and a set of 6 packs of cards for $15, how much money will he save if he buys the set?

Standardized Test Prep

NUMBER SENSE, CONCEPTS, AND OPERATIONS

1. The Lunch Stop charges the following prices for sandwiches and drinks.

LUNCH STOP MENU PRICES	
Item	**Price**
Tuna sandwich	\$3
Chicken sandwich	\$4
Tomato salad	\$2
Mineral water	\$1
Cola	\$1

Pablo bought a chicken sandwich and a bottle of mineral water. How much change did he receive from \$10?

A \$3 **C** \$5

B \$4 **D** \$6

2. Which group of people could NOT equally share 8 pennies?

F 2 people **H** 6 people

G 4 people **J** 8 people

3. Explain It Parking Lot A at the airport has 4,508 cars parked in spaces. Parking Lot B has 6,916 cars parked in spaces. ESTIMATE the number of cars that are parked in the two lots. Tell how you found your answer.

ALGEBRAIC THINKING

4. What is the value of the variable in the following statement?

$3 \times 2 = 6$, so $(3 \times 2) + 8 = a$.

A 48 **C** 13

B 14 **D** 2

5. George has 5 fish in his fish tank. His friend Ellie has 5 more fish in her tank. Let n represent the number of fish Ellie has. Which expression could be used to find the number of fish in Ellie's tank?

F $5 + 5 = n$

G $5 - 5 = n$

H $5 \times 5 = n$

J $5 \div 5 = n$

6. Explain It Carol bought some beads to make jewelry. In January she bought 1 package of beads. Each month after that, she bought double the number that she had bought the month before.

CAROL'S BEADS	
Month	**Number of Packages**
January	1
February	2
March	4
April	■
May	■
June	■

How many packages of beads did Carol buy in June? Explain how you decided.

DATA ANALYSIS AND PROBABILITY

7. What does the circle graph represent?

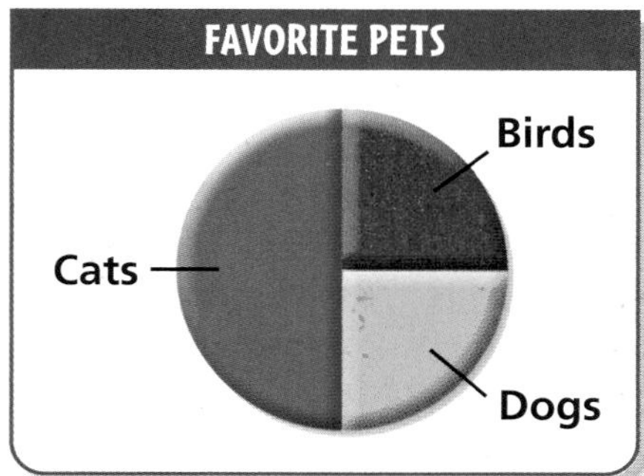

A The total number of votes for dogs.

B The total number of votes for cats.

C The total number of votes for birds.

D The total number of votes for favorite pet.

8. What is the median of the data in the table below?

RUNS SCORED

Player	Ed	Kim	Suki	Bob
Runs	5	2	7	3

F 17 H 4

G 8 J 1

9. **Explain It** If the pointer on this spinner is spun 25 times, which number will the pointer probably land on the **least** number of times?

Explain your thinking.

GEOMETRY AND SPATIAL SENSE

TIP **Look for important words.** See item 10. An important word is NOT. Three of the answer choices are true statements about plane figures. You are to find the one that is NOT true.

10. Which statement is NOT true?

A A square has 4 sides and 4 angles.

B A pentagon has 5 sides and 5 angles.

C A triangle has 3 sides and 4 angles.

D A rectangle has 4 sides and 4 angles.

11. Which solid figure has the faces shown?

F cylinder

G cube

H cone

J sphere

12. **Explain It** Name another object that would belong with the objects below.

Explain how you decided.

CHAPTER 9

Algebra: Use Multiplication and Division Facts

FAST FACT

SOCIAL STUDIES Cookie jars came into common use in the United States during the Great Depression. Today, these jars are popular collectibles. There is even a Cookie Jar Museum in Lemont, Illinois, where over 2,000 jars are displayed!

PROBLEM SOLVING Look at the drawing of the shelves. Suppose you have 12 cat cookie jars you want to display, with an equal number of jars on each of 3 shelves. Write and solve an equation to show the number of jars on each shelf. Then copy and complete the drawing.

CHECK WHAT YOU KNOW

Use this page to help you review and remember important skills needed for Chapter 9.

MULTIPLICATION AND DIVISION FACTS

Find the product or quotient.

1. 6×10 **2.** 4×12 **3.** 5×6 **4.** 3×9

5. 8×2 **6.** 7×8 **7.** 9×9 **8.** 5×11

9. $49 \div 7$ **10.** $63 \div 7$ **11.** $45 \div 5$ **12.** $54 \div 6$

FIND A RULE

Write a rule for each table. Copy and complete each table.

13.

Bags	2	3	4	5	6
Apples	12	18	■	■	■

14.

Octopus	2	3	4	5	6
Arms	16	24	■	■	■

15.

Tricycles	3	4	5	6	7	8
Wheels	9	12	15	■	■	■

16.

Dimes	2	3	4	5	6	7
Nickels	4	6	8	■	■	■

17.

Birds	5	6	7	8	9
Wings	10	12	■	■	■

18.

Dogs	4	5	6	7	8
Paws	16	20	■	■	■

VOCABULARY POWER

REVIEW

equation [i•kwā′zhən] *noun*

The meaning of *equation* is rooted in the Latin word *aequus* for "level." Think of what a seesaw or balance scale is like. Explain how an equation is related to a seesaw or balance scale.

PREVIEW

order of operations

www.harcourtschool.com/mathglossary

LESSON 1

Expressions

Quick Review

1. 12 − (4 + 1)
2. 17 − (5 − 2)
3. 35 − (3 − 1)
4. (17 − 7) + 10
5. (50 − 20) + 5

Learn

PLENTY OF PAGES Tyler collects comic books. He displays his collection in 3 binders, with 10 comic books in each. On a trip to the store, Tyler bought 2 new comic books. How many comic books does he have in his collection now?

You can write an expression to find the number of comic books in Tyler's collection.

Think: (3 binders × 10 comic books in each binder) + 2 new comic books

↓ ↓ ↓

(3 × 10) + 2

Find the value of (3 × 10) + 2.

(3 × 10) + 2	Do what is in parentheses first.
↓	Multiply 3 and 10.
30 + 2	Then add 30 and 2.
↓	
32	

So, Tyler has 32 comic books in his collection.

Remember

An *expression* is part of a number sentence that has numbers and operation signs but does not have an equal sign.

Examples Write an expression. Then find the value of the expression.

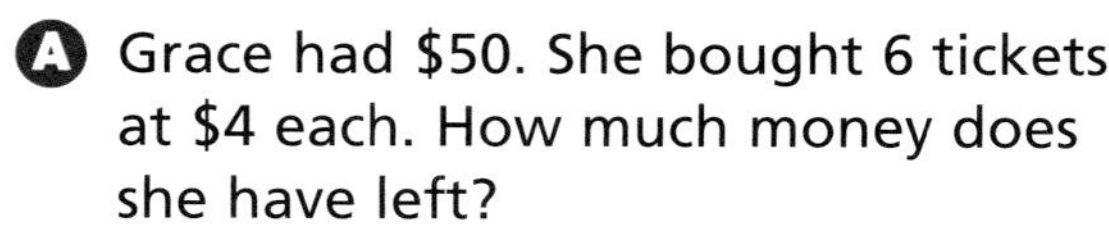

A Grace had $50. She bought 6 tickets at $4 each. How much money does she have left?

$50 minus (6 tickets at $4 each)

↓ ↓

50 − (6 × 4)

50 − (6 × 4)	Find the value.
↓	
50 − 24	
↓	
26	

So, Grace has $26 left.

B John had 15 rocks in his collection. He divided his rocks into 3 boxes. How many rocks are in each box?

15 rocks divided into 3 boxes

↓ ↓

15 ÷ 3

15 ÷ 3	Find the value.
↓	
5	

So, there are 5 rocks in each box.

Check

More Practice: Harcourt Mega Math Ice Station Exploration, *Arctic Algebra,* Level H

1. **Explain** where you would place the parentheses so that $8 \times 6 - 3$ has a value of 24.

Find the value of the expression.

2. $(4 \times 6) - 2$
3. $24 \div 3$
4. $(54 \div 9) - 1$
5. $(8 \times 9) + 7$

Write an expression to match the words.

6. Eric divided 45 stickers equally among 9 pages.
7. Lauren had $8 and then worked 4 hours for $5 each hour.

Practice and Problem Solving

Extra Practice, page 200, Set A

Find the value of the expression.

8. $(26 - 6) \div 2$
9. $46 + (15 \div 3)$
10. $8 \times (7 + 2)$
11. $(3 \times 6) + 12$
12. $35 \div 5 \times 9$
13. $(14 - 2) \times 5$
14. $99 - (12 \times 8)$
15. $(2 \times 9) + 2$

Write the words to match the expression.

16. $27 \div 3$
17. $9 \times (4 - 1)$
18. 8×7
19. $(6 \div 2) \times 5$

For 20–21, write an expression to match the words. Then find the value of the expression.

20. Lily had 15 postcards. She gave away 8 and then bought 2 more. How many cards does she have now?
21. There are 6 rows with 5 desks in each row and 2 desks not in rows. How many desks are there in all?
22. **FAST FACT • SOCIAL STUDIES** The Library of Congress has the largest comic book collection in the United States, containing about 100,000 pieces. It is growing by about 200 issues each month. About how many more issues will the library have in 3 months?

Mixed Review and Test Prep

Write <, >, or = for each ●. (p. 20)

23. 1,945 ● 1,899
24. 34,785 ● 34,885

Find the product. (p. 172)

25. 5×12
26. 11×12
27. $8 \times (3 \times 2)$ (p. 174)

28. **TEST PREP** A new movie began advertising 3 months before its opening. The movie opened on July 4. In which month did advertising begin? (p. 104)

A March
B April
C May
D June

LESSON 2

Order of Operations

Quick Review

1. $81 \div 9$
2. 8×9
3. $65 + 22$
4. $98 - 12$
5. $3 + (7 - 4)$

VOCABULARY

order of operations

MATERIALS calculator

Explore

Miguel and Jill are looking at Miguel's cookie jar collection. He has 20 jars and wants to put 8 jars on each of 2 shelves. How many jars will not be on shelves?

$$20 - 8 \times 2$$

Activity 1

- Try solving the problem by performing the operations in order from left to right. What do you get?
- Try solving the problem by subtracting first and then multiplying. What do you get?
- Try solving the problem by multiplying first and then subtracting. What do you get?

When solving problems with more than one operation, you need to know what operation to do first. A special set of rules, called the **order of operations**, can be used to solve expressions with more than one operation.

First, perform any operations in parentheses.
Next, multiply and divide from left to right.
Then, add and subtract from left to right.

STEP 1

$20 - 8 \times 2$ ↓ $20 - 16$ There are no parentheses, so multiply from left to right.

STEP 2

$20 - 16$ ↓ 4 Then subtract.

So, 4 cookie jars will not be on shelves.

Try It

Use the order of operations to find the value of each expression.

a. $(9 \times 3) + 8$ **b.** $1 + 6 \times 7$

c. $(16 + 4) \div 2$ **d.** $54 \div 9 - 3$

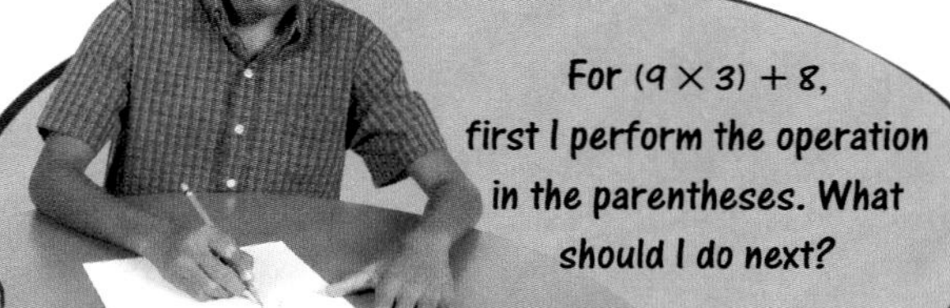

For (9 × 3) + 8, first I perform the operation in the parentheses. What should I do next?

Connect

You can use a calculator that follows the order of operations to help you solve problems. Not all calculators follow the order of operations.

Example Evaluate $5 + 6 \times 3$ with a calculator.

Follows Order of Operations

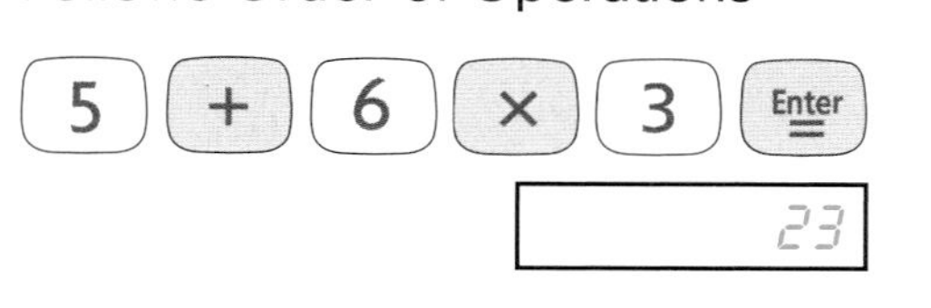

Does Not Follow Order of Operations

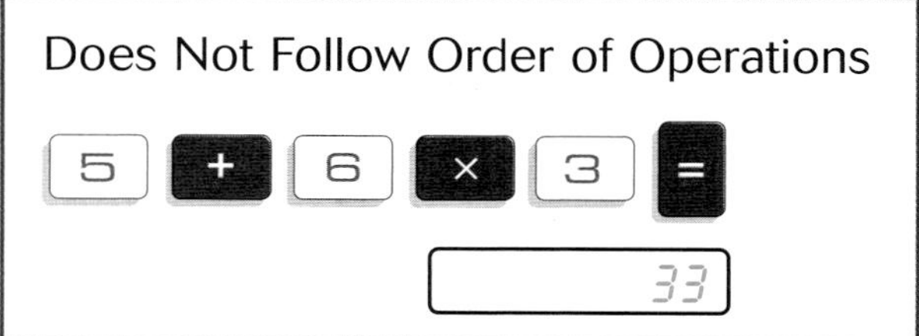

- Use a calculator to find the value of $8 + 32 \div 4 + 2$. Then use paper and pencil and the order of operations to find the value.
- Does your calculator follow the order of operations? Explain.

Practice and Problem Solving

Write *correct* if the operations are listed in the correct order. If not, write the correct order of operations.

1. $(9 + 3) \times 4$ Multiply, add
2. $2 \times (3 + 4)$ Add, multiply
3. $27 - (14 \div 2)$ Subtract, divide
4. $(23 - 11) \div 4 + 2$ Divide, subtract, add

Follow the order of operations to find the value of each expression.

5. $95 - 8 \times 2$
6. $32 + 5 \times 7$
7. $63 \div 9 + 45$
8. $(30 - 6) \div 3$
9. $81 + (54 \div 6)$
10. $(28 - 16) \times 4$
11. $13 + (36 \div 4)$
12. $5 \times (23 - 18) + 7$
13. $(78 - 16) + 12 \div 3$
14. A calculator displays 91 as the value of $9 + 4 \times 7$. Does the calculator follow the order of operations? Explain.
15. **Write About It** Explain why you need to use the order of operations when finding the value of an expression with more than one operation.

Mixed Review and Test Prep

16. What is the value of the digit 8 in 98,745,021? (p. 6)
17. Write three million, seven hundred eight thousand, two hundred sixty-five in standard form. (p. 6)
18. **TEST PREP** Ken scored 8, 7, 10, 6, and 8 on five quizzes. What is the median score of the five quizzes? (p. 119)

   A 6 **C** 8
   B 7 **D** 10

LESSON 3

Expressions and Equations with Variables

Quick Review

Solve for *r*.

1. $6 + r = 16$ **2.** $7 + 5 = r$

3. $r + 8 = 17$ **4.** $r - 5 = 9$

5. $23 - r = 21$

Learn

LET IT SNOW Carly bought a snowdome in each state she visited on vacation. She visited Michigan, Indiana, and Ohio. Each snowdome cost the same amount in all three states. What expression can you write to find the amount she spent?

You can use a variable to represent the price of each snowdome.

3 snowdomes × price of each snowdome
↓ ↓
$3 \times s$

The variable *s* stands for the price of each snowdome.

Suppose Carly paid \$4 for each snowdome. To find the value of the expression, replace *s* with the price of each snowdome.

$3 \times s$
↓
3×4 Replace *s* with 4 since she paid \$4 for each snowdome.
↓
12

So, Carly spent \$12 for 3 snowdomes.

Remember

- A *variable* can stand for any number.
- An *equation* is a number sentence that shows two amounts are equal.

Examples On vacation, Alex bought some \$3 magnets. His sister, Mia, spent \$8 on some keychains.

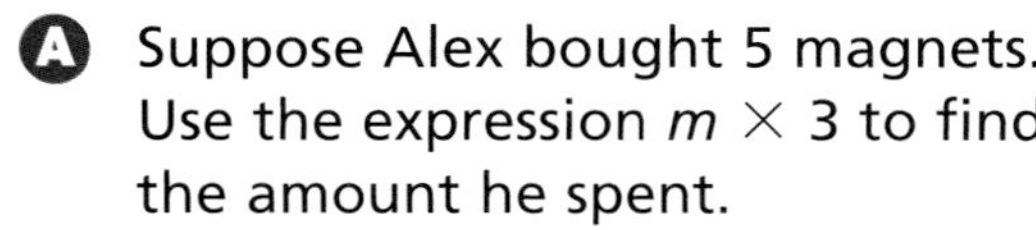

A Suppose Alex bought 5 magnets. Use the expression $m \times 3$ to find the amount he spent.

$m \times 3$ Replace *m* with 5.
↓
5×3 Evaluate the expression.
↓
15

So, Alex spent \$15 for 5 magnets.

B Suppose Mia bought 4 keychains. Use the expression $8 \div k$ to find the amount she spent on each keychain.

$8 \div k$ Replace *k* with 4.
↓
$8 \div 4$ Evaluate the expression.
↓
2

So, Mia spent \$2 on each keychain.

Equations with Variables

A toy maker has 18 boxes of snowdomes to ship to 3 souvenir shops. Each shop will get the same number of boxes. What equation can you write to show this?

18 boxes divided equally among 3 shops is a number of boxes.

$18 \div 3 \quad = \quad t$ ← t is the number of boxes shipped to each shop.

So, the equation is $18 \div 3 = t$.

If the missing information changes, the equation changes.

Examples

A 18 boxes divided equally among a number of shops is 6 boxes.

$18 \div s \quad = \quad 6$ ← s is the number of shops.

The equation is $18 \div s = 6$.

B A number of boxes divided equally among 3 shops is 6 boxes.

$n \div 3 \quad = \quad 6$ ← n is the number of boxes.

The equation is $n \div 3 = 6$.

You can solve equations by using mental math.

Examples

A

$9 \times g = 63$

$g = 7$

Think: 9 times what number equals 63?

Check: $9 \times 7 \stackrel{?}{=} 63$ — Replace g with 7.

$63 = 63$ ✓ — The equation is true. The value of g is 7.

B

$48 \div n = 8$

$n = 6$

Think: 48 divided by what number equals 8?

Check: $48 \div 6 \stackrel{?}{=} 8$ — Replace n with 6.

$8 = 8$ ✓ — The equation is true. The value of n is 6.

Check

1. **Explain** how to write an equation that shows that 5 shelves, with the same number of books on each shelf, is 25 books.

Find the value of the expression.

2. $4 \times p$ if $p = 7$
3. $5 \times w$ if $w = 7$
4. $16 \div g$ if $g = 4$
5. $54 \div x$ if $x = 6$

LESSON CONTINUES

Write an equation for each. Choose a variable for the unknown. Tell what the variable represents.

6. Some cans of soda for each of 6 people is a total of 12 cans of soda.

7. 32 dogs divided equally among a number of walkers is 4 dogs each.

Use mental math to solve each equation. Check your work.

8. $21 = a \times 7$ **9.** $48 \div c = 6$ **10.** $27 \div b = 3$ **11.** $h \times 5 = 25$

Practice and Problem Solving

Extra Practice, page 200, Set B

Find the value of the expression.

12. $9 \times z$ if $z = 7$ **13.** $9 \times d$ if $d = 9$ **14.** $56 \div n$ if $n = 8$ **15.** $96 \div x$ if $x = 12$

Write an expression that matches the words.

16. 7 times a number of pages, p, in an album

17. 4 times the number of magnets, m, on a refrigerator

18. 36 keys divided by a number of keychains, k

19. a number of postcards, p, times 8 stacks

Match the expression with the words.

20. $(36 \div n) - 4$ **21.** $48 \div s$ **22.** $25 + (c \times 3)$ **23.** $6 \times g$

a. forty-eight divided by a number, s

b. twenty-five plus the product of c times three

c. six times a number, g

d. the quotient of thirty-six divided by n minus four

Write an equation for each. Choose a variable for the unknown. Tell what the variable represents.

24. A number of cars divided equally among 6 rows is 9 cars in each row.

25. Some pencils in each of 5 boxes is a total of 50 pencils.

26. 8 students in each of 8 groups is the total number of students.

27. A number of ice cubes divided equally among 7 glasses is 5 ice cubes.

Use mental math to solve each equation. Check your work.

28. $77 \div y = 11$ **29.** $m \times 6 = 36$ **30.** $12 \times k = 60$ **31.** $81 \div x = 9$

USE DATA For 32–33, use the table.

32. Ming and 4 of his friends ate some hot dogs. They spent $20. Write an equation to show the number of hot dogs they ate.

33. In the first hour, the concession stand collected a total of $36 just for burgers. Write an equation to show the total number of burgers sold.

Burgers & Bites

Food/Item	Cost
Burger	$3
Hot Dog	$2
Soda	$1

34. **What's the Error?** Julio claims that $5 \times y$ is 10 if $y = 5$. Describe his error. Write the correct answer.

35. Erin has 5 quarters in each of 4 stacks. Tyra has 8 quarters in each of 3 stacks. How much more money does Tyra have than Erin?

Mixed Review and Test Prep

For 36–37, write a related division equation. (p. 164)

36. $6 \times 9 = 54$

37. $9 \times 11 = 99$

38. $3,894 - 2,085$ (p. 48)

39. $185 - 165$ (p. 40)

40. $22,509 + 4,946$ (p. 52)

41. **TEST PREP** In the parking lot, there are 8 rows with 12 spaces in each. Cars are parked in 13 spaces. How many more cars can park in the parking lot? (p. 172)

A 66
B 72
C 83
D 96

Problem Solving Thinker's Corner

VALUABLE PLATES Write an expression using the numbers in each license plate. Copy the numbers in order from left to right. Place parentheses and operation signs (+, −, ×, or ÷) to make the expression equal the given value.

1. 

Value: 52

2. 

Value: 81

3. 

Value: 20

4. 

Value: 69

5. 

Value: 19

6. Stars Fell On 546 129 Alabama

Value: 6

Problem Solving Strategy
Work Backward

Quick Review

1. $3 \times n = 27$
2. $n \div 3 = 5$
3. $36 \div n = 9$
4. $5 \times n = 30$
5. $5 + n = 9 \times 8$

PROBLEM Tony had some dimes in his bank. He added 7 nickels and then had a total of 75¢. How much money did Tony have in dimes?

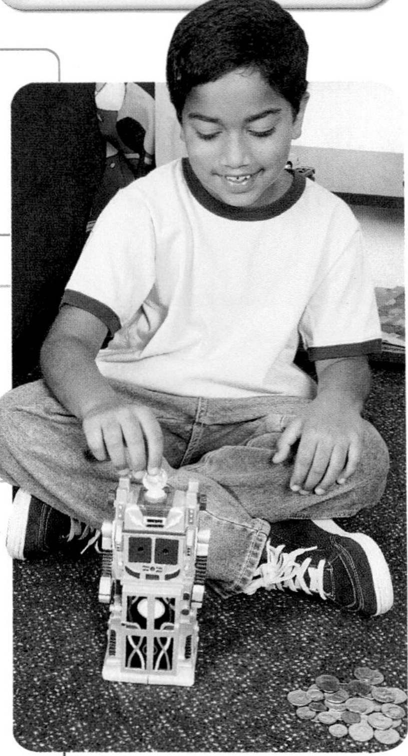

UNDERSTAND

- What are you asked to find?
- What information will you use?
- Is there information you will not use? Explain.

PLAN

- What strategy can you use to solve the problem?

You can write an equation with a variable. Then solve the equation by *working backward.*

SOLVE

- How can you solve the problem?

Write an equation. Let d represent the amount of money in dimes.

$d + (7 \times 5) = 75$ ← 75¢ in all
↑ amount in dimes

To find the value of d, work backward.

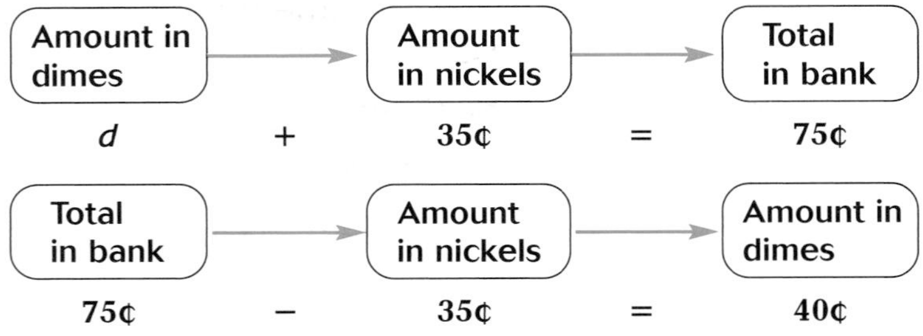

So, the variable, d, has a value of 40. Tony had 40¢ in dimes.

CHECK

- What other strategies could you use to solve the problem? Explain.

Problem Solving Practice

Write an equation and work backward to solve.

1. **What if** Tony had a total of 85¢ after adding 7 nickels? How much would Tony have in dimes?

2. Sid had 5 trading cards. Then his mother gave him some packages with 8 cards in each package. Sid now has 37 cards. How many packages did his mother give him?

Strategies

- Draw a Diagram or Picture
- Make a Model or Act It Out
- Make an Organized List
- Find a Pattern
- Make a Table or Graph
- Predict and Test
- **Work Backward**
- Solve a Simpler Problem
- Write an Equation
- Use Logical Reasoning

Problem Solving

Joey and Nicole are playing a board game. In the first three turns, Joey moves 6 spaces forward, 3 back, and 4 forward. Nicole moves 5 spaces forward, 1 back, and 5 forward.

3. Who is ahead in the game?
   - **A** Joey
   - **B** Nicole
   - **C** Lucy
   - **D** They are on the same space.

4. How many spaces apart are Joey and Nicole's playing pieces?
   - **F** 2 spaces
   - **G** 3 spaces
   - **H** 4 spaces
   - **J** 5 spaces

Mixed Strategy Practice

5. The Snack Bar at the local skating rink uses 8 lemons for every 2 quarts of lemonade. How many lemons are used to make 8 quarts of lemonade?

6. Ty had some money in his coin bank. He put 3 dimes and 7 pennies in the bank and now has $1.17. How much money was in the bank to begin with?

7. On Sunday, the Snack Bar sold 341 drinks. On Monday, 85 drinks were sold in the morning and 163 in the afternoon. How many more drinks were sold on Sunday than on Monday?

8. Taylor had 127 baseball cards. He gave 18 cards to Felisha. Felisha then gave Taylor some cards. Taylor then had a total of 114 cards. How many cards did Felisha give Taylor?

9. Sally's dance lesson begins at 4:25 P.M. and lasts for 1 hr 15 min. What time does her lesson end?

10. **Write a problem** involving coins that can be solved using the strategy *work backward*. Then solve the problem.

LESSON 5

Balance Equations

Quick Review

1. 8×2 **2.** 5×4

3. 3×4 **4.** $6 \div 3$

5. $21 \div 7$

Learn

IS IT EQUAL? In this activity, you will multiply both sides of an equation by the same number to test if both sides stay equal to each other.

Activity

MATERIALS: coins, pieces of paper

Make a workmat.

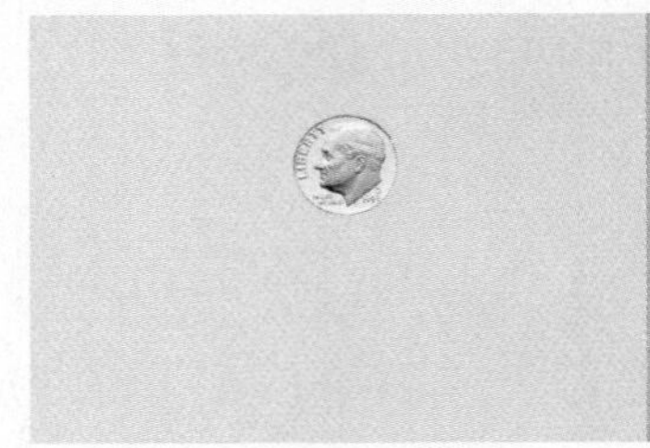

$1 \times 10¢$ $2 \times 5¢$

Each side of the workmat represents one side of an equation.

Place 1 dime on the left side and 2 nickels on the right side.

- Compare the two sides. Are the values of the coins equal? Explain.
- Multiply the total value of the coins on each side by 4. Compare the two sides. Are the values still equal? Explain.

$4 \times 10¢$ $4 \times (2 \times 5¢)$

- **What if** you multiply the total value of the coins on one side by 4 and the total value of the coins on the other side by 2? Will the total values of the two sides still be equal? Explain.

Multiply or Divide Both Sides

Use the workmat. Decide if both sides stay equal.

a. Left side: 10 pennies; right side: 2 nickels; multiply both sides by 3.

b. Left side: 10 pennies; right side: 2 nickels; divide both sides by 2.

MATH IDEA When you multiply or divide both sides of an equation by the same number, the two sides stay equal.

Examples

Multiply or divide both sides of the equation by the given number. Find the values.

A $6 = 6$; multiply by 2.

$$6 = 6$$
$$6 \times 2 = 6 \times 2 \leftarrow \text{Multiply by 2.}$$
$$12 = 12$$

B $12 = 2 \times 6$; multiply by 4.

$$12 = 2 \times 6$$
$$12 \times 4 = (2 \times 6) \times 4 \leftarrow \text{Multiply by 4.}$$
$$48 = 12 \times 4$$
$$48 = 48$$

C $(3 + 5) = (1 + 7)$; divide by 2.

$$(3 + 5) = (1 + 7)$$
$$(3 + 5) \div 2 = (1 + 7) \div 2 \leftarrow \text{Divide by 2.}$$
$$8 \div 2 = 8 \div 2$$
$$4 = 4$$

D $(3 \times 3) = (27 \div 3)$; divide by 9.

$$(3 \times 3) = (27 \div 3)$$
$$(3 \times 3) \div 9 = (27 \div 3) \div 9 \leftarrow \text{Divide by 9.}$$
$$9 \div 9 = 9 \div 9$$
$$1 = 1$$

Check

1. **Explain** why the values of the sides stay equal when you multiply both sides of the equation $(4 + 5) = (6 + 3)$ by the number 3.

Multiply or divide both sides by the given number. Find the new value.

2. $10 = 10$; divide both sides by 5.

3. $6 = 2 \times 3$; multiply both sides by 8.

LESSON CONTINUES

Practice and Problem Solving

Extra Practice, page 200, Set C

Multiply or divide both sides by the given number. Find the new value.

4. 3 nickels = 3 nickels; multiply both sides by 4.

5. 1 dime 2 pennies = 2 nickels 2 pennies; multiply both sides by 5.

6. 2 nickels = 1 dime; multiply both sides by 7.

7. 5 pennies = 1 nickel; multiply both sides by 6.

8. $9 = 3 \times 3$; divide both sides by 9.

9. $8 = 2 \times 4$; divide both sides by 8.

10. $4 \times 3 = 12$; multiply both sides by 5.

11. $12 = 3 \times 4$; multiply both sides by 7.

12. $(4 + 2) = (2 \times 3)$; divide both sides by 3.

13. $(2 + 6) = (2 \times 4)$; divide both sides by 4.

14. $(3 + 7) = (2 \times 5)$; divide both sides by 2.

15. $(8 + 4) = (6 \times 2)$; divide both sides by 2.

USE DATA For 16–19, use the graph.

16. How many more apple pies are baked than coconut pies?

17. The bakery has an order for 40 apple pies. Are there enough pies baked to fill the order? Explain.

18. Mrs. Holiday wants 24 peach pies for a picnic. How many more peach pies does the bakery need to make?

19. The museum bought all the coconut pies for a party. How many pies did the museum buy?

20. **What if** you divide both sides of the equation $(4 + 2) = (42 \div 7)$ by 2? Are the values of the sides of the equation still equal?

21. **What's the Error?** Jan claims that if you multiply the left side of $5 = 5$ by 3 and the right side by 2, the equation will stay equal. What is her error?

22. Ian invited 10 friends bowling. Each friend bowled 3 games. Ian bowled 2 games. Write an expression to show how many games were bowled.

23. There were 12 rows of plants. Each row had 4 flowers. Mr. Williams picked 3 flowers. Write an expression to show how many flowers are in the garden now.

24. There are 18 boxes. There are twice as many large boxes as small boxes. How many large boxes are there? How many small boxes are there?

Mixed Review and Test Prep

25. Write 800,000 + 40,000 + 300 + 9 in standard form. (p. 4)

26. 123 + 656 (p. 40)

27. 2,389 − 921 (p. 48)

28. Denise has 3 cases of pens. Each case has 6 boxes. Each box has 2 pens. How many pens does she have? (p. 174)

29. (p. 48)

$$\begin{array}{r} 2{,}173 \\ +3{,}584 \\ \hline \end{array}$$

30. (p. 48)

$$\begin{array}{r} 9{,}314 \\ -6{,}763 \\ \hline \end{array}$$

31. **TEST PREP** A local station is showing a movie that begins at 7:00 P.M. It is 90 minutes long. At what time will it end? (p. 98)

A 5:00 P.M. **C** 8:00 P.M.
B 6:30 P.M. **D** 8:30 P.M.

Problem Solving LINKUP ... to Reading

STRATEGY • CAUSE AND EFFECT Sometimes one action has an effect on another action. The **cause** is the reason something happens. The **effect** is the result.

Study Karen's party plans on the clipboard.

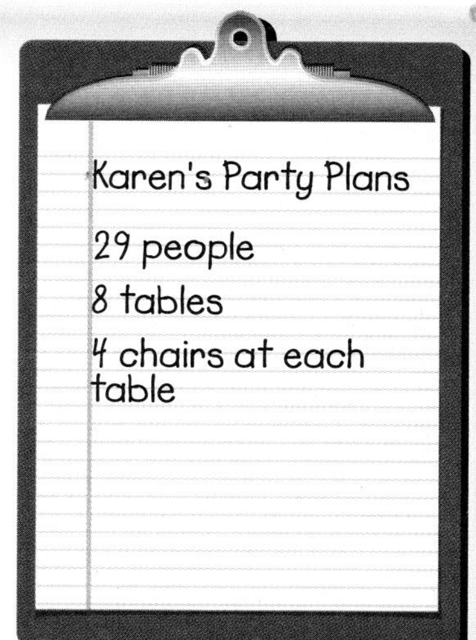

What if 4 more people come to Karen's party? Will this change her party plans?

Karen can make a table to help her plan.

CAUSE	EFFECT
4 more people come to the party.	There are more people at the party than I planned for.

Use the table to solve 1–3.

1. How many people are coming to the party?

2. What will happen because more people are coming?

3. Does she have enough chairs? Explain.

4. Felix bought 7 packs of water with 6 bottles in each pack for the fourth-grade field trip. He drank 2 bottles. If 38 students are going on the trip, will there be enough water? Make a table to solve.

LESSON 6

Patterns: Find a Rule

Quick Review

1. 12 ÷ 3
2. 9 ÷ 3
3. 14 ÷ 7
4. 16 ÷ 4
5. 27 ÷ 9

Learn

INPUT/OUTPUT The Math Factory sorts numbers into boxes. Use the input/output table to find what number comes out when 45 is put into the machine.

INPUT	OUTPUT
25	5
30	6
35	7
40	8
45	■

HINT: Look for a pattern to help you find a rule.

Pattern: Each output is the input divided by 5.

Rule: Divide by 5.

← *Input:* 45   *Output:* 45 ÷ 5 = 9

So, when you put in 45, the Math Factory puts out 9.

You can write an equation to show the rule. Use variables to show the input and output.

input ↓ **output** ↓

$x \div 5 = y$

Think of the equation as a rule. To find the value of *y*, divide *x* by 5.

Examples

A Find a rule.
Write the rule as an equation.

INPUT	*n*	3	4	5	6
OUTPUT	*t*	18	24	30	36

Test your rule on each pair of numbers in the table.

Rule: Multiply by 6.

$n \times 6 = t$

B Find a rule.
Write the rule as an equation.
Use the equation to find the next two numbers in the pattern.

INPUT	*p*	72	63	54	45	36	27
OUTPUT	*r*	8	7	6	5	■	■

Rule: Divide by 9.

$p \div 9 = r$ $p \div 9 = r$

$36 \div 9 = 4$ $27 \div 9 = 3$

The next two numbers in the pattern are 4 and 3.

Check

1. **Explain** why it is important to test a rule with all the number pairs in the table.

Find a rule. Write the rule as an equation.

2.

INPUT	x	21	28	35	42
OUTPUT	y	3	4	5	6

3.

INPUT	s	8	9	10	11
OUTPUT	t	40	45	50	55

Practice and Problem Solving

Extra Practice, page 200, Set D

Find a rule. Write the rule as an equation. Find the missing numbers.

4.

INPUT	b	12	11	9	7	■	■	■
OUTPUT	c	24	22	18	14	12	8	4

5.

INPUT	d	16	32	48	64	80	96
OUTPUT	f	2	4	6	8	■	■

6.

INPUT	w	■	■	6	8	10	12
OUTPUT	z	24	48	72	96	120	144

7.

INPUT	r	6	12	18	24	30	36
OUTPUT	s	■	■	6	8	10	12

Use the rule and the equation to make an input/output table.

8. Divide by 11. $x \div 11 = y$

9. Multiply by 4. $h \times 4 = j$

10. Divide by 10. $t \div 10 = w$

11. Multiply by 8. $f \times 8 = g$

12. Multiply by 7. $r \times 7 = s$

13. Divide by 6. $c \div 6 = d$

14. Multiply by 3. $k \times 3 = m$

15. Divide by 12. $a \div 12 = b$

16. The first three inputs in the Number Cruncher are 48, 44, and 40. The first three outputs are 12, 11, and 10. Find a rule. Then write the rule as an equation and extend the pattern to find the next two output numbers.

17. **Vocabulary Power** *Variable* was first used to describe the changes, or shades, in the color of early clothing made from speckled fur. How does a change in the value of an input variable affect the value of an output variable?

Mixed Review and Test Prep

18. 34,578 + 27,916 (p. 52)

19. 98,521 − 85,769 (p. 52)

20. Over the weekend, the Garden Shop sold 9,754 plants in all. It sold 4,675 plants on Friday and 1,987 plants on Saturday. How many plants did the Garden Shop sell on Sunday? (p. 48)

21. What is 12,784 written in expanded form? (p. 4)

22. **TEST PREP** Which is **not** true? (p. 20)

A $6{,}431 > 6{,}341$
B $6{,}236 = 6{,}236$
C $6{,}357 < 6{,}135$
D $6{,}964 > 6{,}694$

Extra Practice

Set A (pp. 184–185)

Find the value of the expression.

1. $4 \times 5 + 2$
2. $100 - (8 \times 5)$
3. $56 \div 7 + 20$
4. $13 + (5 \times 6)$
5. $(12 + 8) \div 4$
6. $(27 \div 3) \times 7$
7. $85 - (3 \times 7)$
8. $50 + (72 \div 9)$

Write an expression to match the words.

9. There were 3 shelves with 7 footballs each. Lin took 4 footballs out to the field.
10. The 5 cases of puppy food each contain 10 bags. Kate placed 6 extra bags next to the cases.

Set B (pp. 188–191)

Find the value of the expression.

1. $12 \times h$ if $h = 3$
2. $36 \div s$ if $s = 9$
3. $8 \times y$ if $y = 7$
4. $24 \div m$ if $m = 4$

Write an equation for each. Choose a variable for the unknown. Tell what the variable represents.

5. 4 boxes with 3 games in each box are the total number of games.
6. 25 people in some cars are 5 people in each car.

Set C (pp. 194–197)

Multiply or divide both sides by the given number. Find the new value.

1. $(3 + 1) = (2 \times 2)$; multiply both sides by 5.
2. $(5 + 7) = (4 \times 3)$; divide both sides by 6.

Set D (pp. 198–199)

Find a rule. Write the rule as an equation. Find the missing number.

1.

INPUT	OUTPUT
b	*c*
18	9
14	7
10	5
6	■

2.

INPUT	OUTPUT
d	*f*
2	6
4	12
6	18
8	■

3.

INPUT	OUTPUT
w	*z*
■	54
8	72
10	90
12	108

4.

INPUT	OUTPUT
r	*s*
33	■
27	9
24	8
21	7

Review/Test

CHECK CONCEPTS

1. Explain which operation to do first to find the value of $2 + (3 \times 4)$. How do you know? (pp. 186–187)

2. Write an expression you could use to find the number of quarters that have the same value as any number of dollars. (pp. 188–191)

CHECK SKILLS

Find the value of the expression. (pp. 184–187)

3. $(18 \div 3) + 2$
4. $6 \times 7 - 5$
5. $63 \div 7 - 9$
6. $25 + (4 \times 6)$
7. $(32 - 8) \div 8$
8. $7 - (72 \div 12)$
9. $45 - (7 \times 6)$
10. $(8 \times 9) + 21$

Write an equation for each. Choose a variable for the unknown. Tell what the variable represents. (pp. 188–191)

11. A number of books divided by 9 readers is 18 books.

12. \$42 divided by a number of people is \$6.

Multiply or divide both sides by the given number. Find the new value. (pp. 194–197)

13. $6 = (2 \times 3)$; multiply both sides by 9.

14. $(6 \times 2) = (4 + 8)$; divide both sides by 3.

Find a rule. Write the rule as an equation. Find the missing number. (pp. 198–199)

15.

INPUT	OUTPUT
a	*b*
4	28
5	35
8	56
■	63

16.

INPUT	OUTPUT
x	*y*
72	9
56	7
40	5
48	■

17.

INPUT	OUTPUT
m	*n*
4	■
5	55
7	77
9	99

18.

INPUT	OUTPUT
q	*r*
144	12
132	11
120	10
■	9

CHECK PROBLEM SOLVING

Write an equation and work backward to solve. (pp. 192–193)

19. Tommy had 3 nickels. Angela gave him some quarters. Now he has 90¢. How much money does Tommy have in quarters?

20. Jack had some dimes. He spent 4 dimes on candy and had 30¢ left over. How many dimes did Jack have before buying the candy?

Standardized Test Prep

NUMBER SENSE, CONCEPTS, AND OPERATIONS

1. Which of these facts is NOT related to the others?

A $6 \times 4 = 24$ **C** $24 \div 8 = 3$

B $24 \div 6 = 4$ **D** $24 \div 4 = 6$

2. Which operations can be used in the circles below to find the smallest possible result?

$1 \bullet 5 \bullet 1$

F $\times$ and $\div$

G $\times$ and $-$

H $+$ and $\div$

J $+$ and $-$

3. Explain It Tom's Toy Store is having a sale. The table below shows the regular and sale prices of several items.

TOM'S TOY STORE		
Item	**Regular Price**	**Sale Price**
Puzzle	$5.99	$3.19
Board Game	$7.29	$5.95
Computer Game	$8.79	$6.25
Stuffed Animal	$4.19	$3.89

Fred bought a board game, a puzzle, and a computer game at the sale prices. He said he saved about $3.00 compared to buying the same items at the regular prices. Jenny said that Fred saved about $7.00. Who do you agree with? Explain your thinking.

MEASUREMENT

4. The members of the Cohen family went to the beach for a vacation. They left on August 10 and returned 2 weeks 6 days later. On which day and date did they return home?

August						
Sun	Mon	Tue	Wed	Thu	Fri	Sat
1	2	3	4	5	6	7
8	9	10	11	12	13	14
15	16	17	18	19	20	21
22	23	24	25	26	27	28
29	30	31				

A Tuesday, August 17

B Monday, August 23

C Tuesday, August 24

D Monday, August 30

5. Which is the **best** unit of measure for the capacity of this soup pot?

F milliliter

G meter

H liter

J gram

6. Explain It Mrs. Alvarez has a square box lid that measures 1 foot 4 inches on each side. She wants to glue a braid all around the edge of the lid. Should Mrs. Alvarez estimate how much braid she needs, or should she measure to find the length required? Explain your answer.

GEOMETRY AND SPATIAL SENSE

7. Which shape does NOT have a line of symmetry?

A

C 

B

D 

TIP **Eliminate choices.** See item 8. Think about the meanings of *similar* and *congruent*. More than one pair of figures is similar, but only one pair is NOT congruent.

8. Which pair of figures is similar but NOT congruent?

F 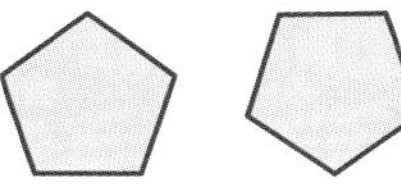

G 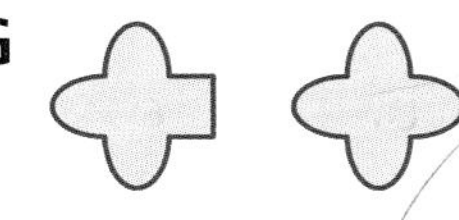

H 

J 

9. **Explain It** What is the ordered pair for the Science Museum?

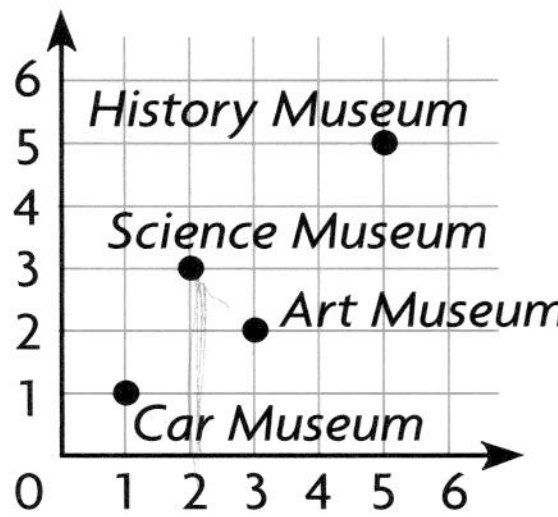

Explain how you decided.

ALGEBRAIC THINKING

10. Which expression matches the words below?

six times the number of books, b, on a bookshelf

A $6 + b$

B $b - 6$

C $6 \times b$

D $6 \div b$

11. Lauren is paid $3 for each hour she watches her little sister. She was paid $12. Let h represent the number of hours Lauren watched her sister. Which equation below could be used to find the total number of hours Lauren watched her sister?

F $\$3 + h = \$12$

G $\$3 \times h = \$12$

H $\$3 - h = \$12$

J $\$3 \div h = \$12$

12. **Explain It** What are the missing numbers in the table below?

INPUT	OUTPUT
x	y
18	9
20	10
22	11
24	12
26	13
28	14
30	
32	

Explain how you decided.

IT'S IN THE BAG

Math First-Aid Kit

PROJECT Make a first-aid kit to help you study basic facts and write algebraic expressions.

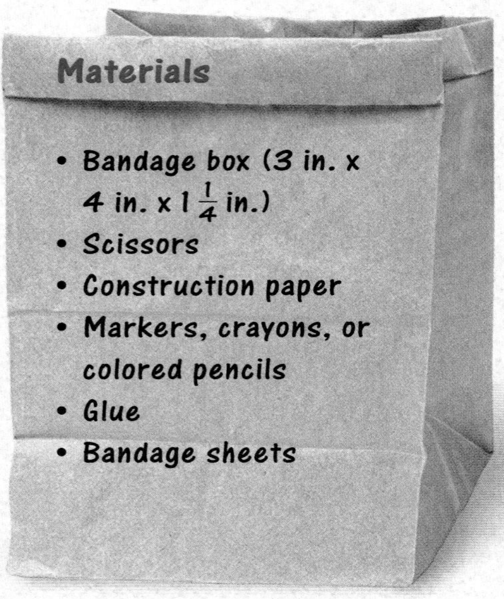

Materials

- Bandage box (3 in. x 4 in. x $1\frac{1}{4}$ in.)
- Scissors
- Construction paper
- Markers, crayons, or colored pencils
- Glue
- Bandage sheets

Directions

1. Color and then cut out the bandages. *(Picture A)*

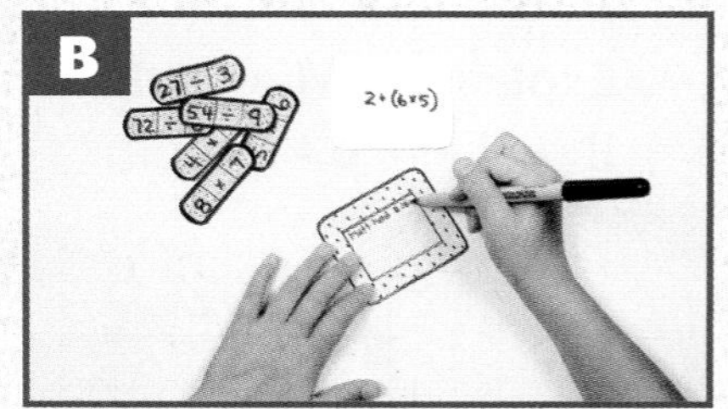

2. On the small bandages, write basic facts. On the larger bandages, write word problems and the matching expression. Write the answer or the expression for the problems on the back of the bandages. *(Picture B)*

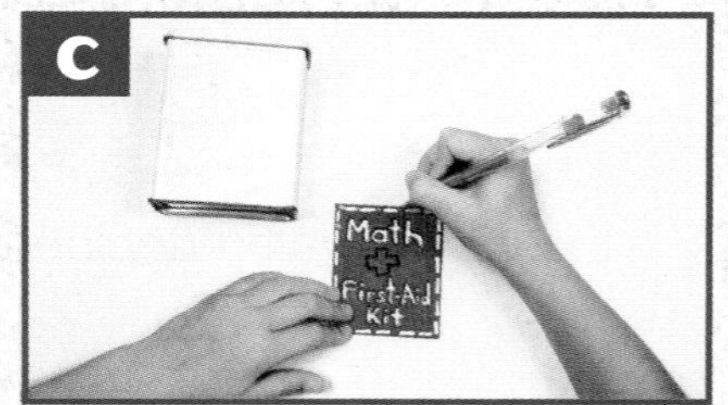

3. Cover and decorate the bandage box. Label the box *Math First-Aid Kit. (Picture C)*

4. With a partner, take turns quizzing each other by using the bandages.

Challenge

Predict Patterns

Patterns are all around us. They can be found in nature, architecture, music, art, language, and mathematics.

Emily is using square tiles to continue a pattern.

She can predict how many tiles will be in her next design by finding a rule. Look at the table below.

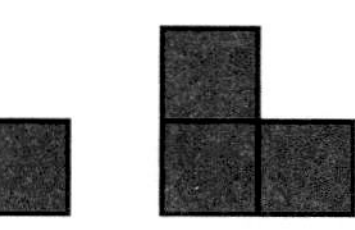
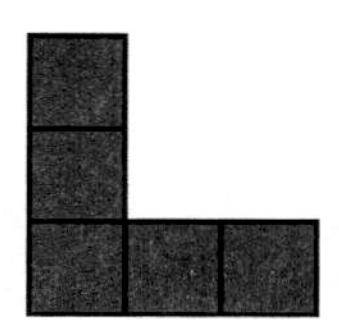

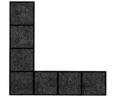

DESIGN	PATTERN DESCRIPTION	NUMBER OF TILES
	The 1st design has 1 tile in its base and 0 tiles on top.	1
	The 2nd design has 2 tiles in its base and 1 tile on top.	3
	The 3rd design has 3 tiles in its base and 2 tiles on top.	5
	The 4th design has 4 tiles in its base and 3 tiles on top.	7
n	**Rule:** The number of tiles on top is 1 less than the number of tiles in the base. The nth design has n tiles in its base and $n - 1$ tiles on top.	$n + (n - 1)$

If $n = 5$, then $5 + (5 - 1)$ gives the number of tiles in the 5th design.

- How can you predict the number of tiles for any design in the pattern?

Try It

Predict the number of objects in the 5th design of each pattern. Draw a picture to show how the pattern will look.

1.

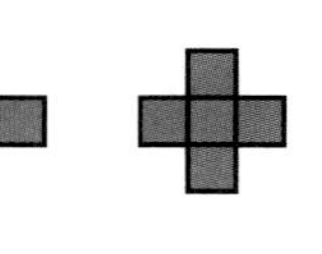

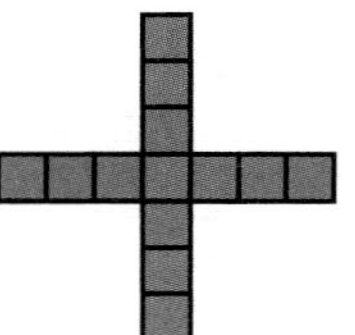

2.

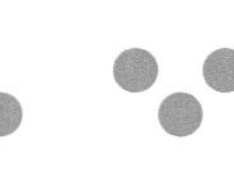
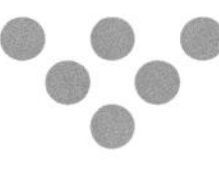
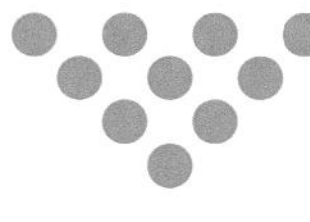

Study Guide and Review

VOCABULARY

Choose the best term from the box.

inverse
Associative Property
Commutative Property
fact family

1. Multiplication and division by the same number undo each other. They are _?_ operations. (p. 164)
2. The _?_ states that when the grouping of factors is changed, the product remains the same. (p. 174)

STUDY AND SOLVE

Chapter 8

Write related multiplication and division facts.

Find the value of n. Write a related multiplication or division equation.

$28 \div 4 = n$

Multiplication: $4 \times 7 = 28$ (4 → factor, 7 → factor, 28 → product)

Division: $28 \div 4 = 7$ (28 → dividend, 4 → divisor, 7 → quotient)

$4 \times 7 = 28$ is related to $28 \div 4 = 7$.

So, the value of n is 7.

Find the value of the variable. Write a related multiplication or division equation. (pp. 164–165, 166–173)

3. $88 \div 11 = y$
4. $9 \times 6 = h$
5. $3 \times 5 = s$
6. $18 \div 6 = n$
7. $90 \div 10 = p$
8. $6 \times 8 = a$
9. $8 \times 10 = x$
10. $144 \div 12 = b$
11. $72 \div 8 = t$
12. $6 \times 7 = k$

Use the properties of multiplication to find products.

Commutative Property

You can multiply the factors in any order and get the same product.

$3 \times 4 = 12$ $4 \times 3 = 12$

Find the missing number. Name the property you used. (pp. 174–175)

13. $(3 \times 2) \times 9 = \blacksquare \times (2 \times 9)$
14. $9 \times 8 = \blacksquare \times 9$
15. $\blacksquare \times 1 = 7$
16. $0 = 12 \times \blacksquare$
17. $8 \times (5 \times 2) = (8 \times \blacksquare) \times 2$

Chapter 9

Write expressions for words. Find the values of expressions.

Erika had 12 pencils. Then she bought 3 more packs with 5 pencils in each pack.

$12 + (3 \times 5)$ • Write an expression for the number of pencils.

$12 + 15$ • Multiply the number of pencils that Erika bought.

27 • Find the value of the expression.

So, Erika now has 27 pencils.

Write an expression. Then find the value. (pp. 184–185)

18. Mary bought 4 bows for \$3 each and then spent \$6 on tape. How much did she spend in all?

19. Robin had 50¢. She gave away 2 dimes. How much money does she have now?

Write expressions with variables.

8 times the number of people, *m*

8 times the number of people → $8 \times m$

• Choose an operation.
• Write the expression.

Write an expression that matches the words. (pp. 188–191)

20. 7 times the number of people, *p*, in a room

21. \$60 divided by the number of equally-sized bank accounts, *b*

Find a rule to extend the pattern.

INPUT	*d*	5	6	8	9	10
OUTPUT	*e*	10	12	16	18	■

Pattern: Each output, *e*, is the input, *d*, multiplied by 2.
Rule: Multiply by 2.

So, when the input is 10 the output is 10×2, or 20.

Find a rule. Write the rule as an equation. Find the missing numbers. (pp. 198–199)

22.

INPUT	*s*	72	60	48	24
OUTPUT	*t*	6	5	4	■

23.

INPUT	*d*	3	5	8	12
OUTPUT	*e*	■	35	56	84

PROBLEM SOLVING PRACTICE

Solve. (pp. 176, 192)

24. Toni earns \$2 baby-sitting and \$4 mowing lawns each week. If she works for 8 weeks, how much money will she earn? Name the operation or operations you used.

25. Charlie had 12¢. His father gave him some nickels, and now he has 47¢. Write an equation to find how many nickels Charlie's father gave him.

PERFORMANCE ASSESSMENT

TASK A • OUTDOOR GAMES

After school 36 students play outdoor games. The students are divided into teams. There are at least 2 players on a team, and all the teams have the same number of players.

a. Draw arrays to show two different ways 36 students can be divided into teams of equal size.

b. Write a multiplication sentence and a division sentence for each array you drew. Explain how the sentences you wrote show that division is the inverse of multiplication.

c. Suppose 4 more students want to play the outdoor games. Will the teams be able to stay the same size as before, or will different-sized teams need to be formed?

TASK B • WORK IT OUT

After school and on weekends, Nicole and her sister Amy earn spending money. Nicole takes some of her neighbors' dogs for walks and Amy mows lawns.

a. Nicole earns $2 for each dog she walks. Write an expression to find the number of dollars she will earn for walking any number of dogs. (Use *d* to represent the number of dogs.) Then use the expression you wrote to find out how much Nicole will earn if she walks 4 dogs.

b. Amy made this input/output table to help her know how much money (*m*) she will earn for mowing different numbers of lawns (*l*). How much does Amy earn for each lawn she mows? Write an equation that describes a rule for the table.

INPUT	OUTPUT
l	*m*
1	6
2	12
3	18
4	24

c. Nicole and Amy want to buy a CD that costs $16. What is one way they can earn $16 together? Tell how many dogs Nicole would have to walk and how many lawns Amy would have to mow.

Calculator • Evaluate Expressions

Jamie wants to buy some magazines that cost $6 each. She is also buying a book for $17. What is the total cost if she buys the book plus 3 magazines? 4 magazines?

If m represents the number of magazines Jamie buys, then the expression $6 \times m + 17$ will give the total cost.

What is the value of the expression $6 \times m + 17$ when $m = 3$ and when $m = 4$?

 **Use the TI-15 Opl and Op2 keys to evaluate the expression.**

STEP 1 Press these keys to enter the expression.

STEP 2 Find the value when $m = 3$.

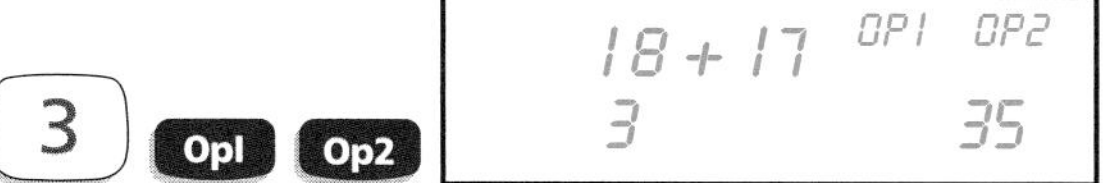

The value is 35.

STEP 3 Find the value when $m = 4$.

The value is 41.

So, Jamie will spend $35 if she buys the book plus 3 magazines. She will spend $41 if she buys the book plus 4 magazines.

TIP Before entering a new problem, clear the stored operations.

Practice and Problem Solving

Use the Opl and Op2 keys to find the value of the expression.

1. $a \times 16 + 35$ if $a = 1, 2, 3, 4$
2. $y \div 15 - 17$ if $y = 300, 570, 630$
3. $b \times 72 + 115$ if $b = 16, 25, 39, 43$
4. $d \div 32 + 46$ if $d = 2{,}080; 3{,}008$
5. **Write a problem** using an expression with a variable and two operations. Then give two values for the variable.

GO ON-LINE **Multimedia Math Glossary**
www.harcourtschool.com/mathglossary

Vocabulary Power Look up *expression* in the Multimedia Math Glossary. How is a number expression similar to an expression with variables? How is it different? Give an example of each type of expression.

TIDE POOLS

Tide pools are pools that form where the ocean meets the land. Tide pools provide homes for many small ocean plants and animals.

▲ Every year, visitors come to Virginia Beach to swim, surf, and beachcomb.

For 1–3, write an equation with a variable that matches each statement. Tell what the variable represents. Find the value of the variable.

1. 5 arms on each of some starfish are 35 arms.
2. Some arms on each of 10 starfish are 60 arms.
3. 12 blue crabs divided equally among 3 tide pools is the number of blue crabs in each pool.
4. Suppose you see 4 fiddler crabs in each of 4 tide pools and 5 fiddler crabs in each of 2 tide pools. How many fiddler crabs have you seen in all? Write an equation you can use to solve the problem.

Most kinds of starfish, or sea stars, have between 5 and 10 "arms." ▶

5. The table shows the number of tentacles on 1 to 5 octopods. Find a rule. Write the rule as an equation, and complete the table.

INPUT	OUTPUT
o	***t***
1	8
2	16
3	24
4	32
5	

BOTTLENOSE DOLPHINS

Bottlenose dolphins are the most common kind of dolphin found along the coast of the United States from Cape Cod to the Gulf of Mexico. You can often see bottlenose dolphins if you visit the beaches of Virginia.

1. A baby dolphin is called a calf. A calf eats 4 times each hour during the first week of life. How many times does it eat in 8 hours during this time?

2. Dolphins travel in groups called pods. The average pod size is 7 dolphins. If Madeleine spotted 3 pods from the beach, about how many dolphins did she see?

3. Bottlenose dolphins swim about 5 miles per hour. At this speed, how long will it take a dolphin to swim the 40 miles from Newport News to Virginia Beach?

4. Bottlenose dolphins regularly dive to depths of 10 to 150 feet. If a dolphin dives 10 feet in its first dive and 30 feet in its second dive, how many times as far did it dive the second time as the first time?

5. Dolphins eat fish, squid, and crustaceans. A 300-pound dolphin eats around 12 pounds of food each day. About how much food does a 300-pound dolphin eat in 5 days? in a week?

6. There are about 67,000 bottlenose dolphins in the U.S. Gulf of Mexico and 11,700 in the U.S. waters of the western North Atlantic. How many dolphins is this in all? How many more are in the Gulf of Mexico?

A dolphin opens its ▶ blowhole and starts to breathe out under water. When it jumps out of the water, the dolphin breathes in and then closes the blowhole.

CHAPTER 10

Multiply by 1-Digit Numbers

FAST FACT • SCIENCE Manatees in Florida spend most of their time eating and resting. An average adult manatee can eat up to 108 pounds of vegetation daily.

PROBLEM SOLVING About how many hours would an adult manatee spend eating during the month of October? How much vegetation could it eat during one week of that month?

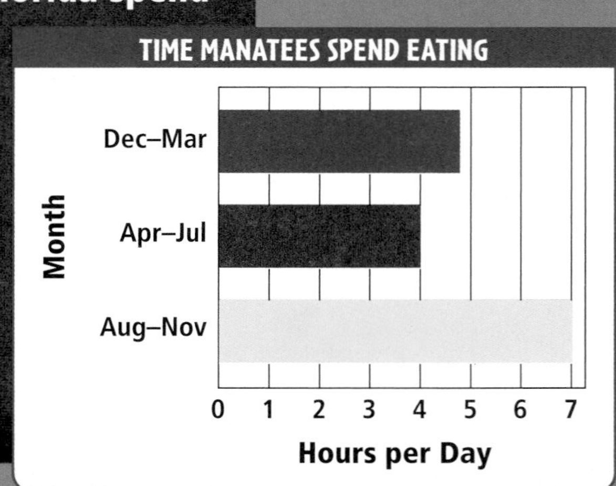

CHECK WHAT YOU KNOW

Use this page to help you review and remember important skills needed for Chapter 10.

MODEL MULTIPLICATION

Write a multiplication sentence for the model.

1. 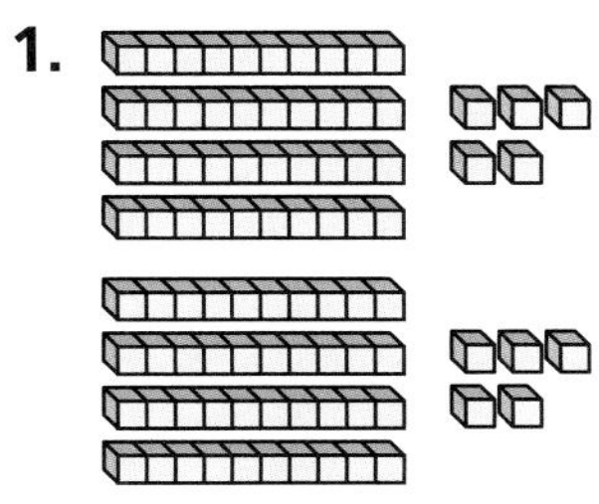

2.

3.

4.

5.

6.

MULTIPLICATION FACTS

Find each product.

7. $\begin{array}{r} 5 \\ \times 6 \\ \hline \end{array}$

8. $\begin{array}{r} 8 \\ \times 3 \\ \hline \end{array}$

9. $\begin{array}{r} 9 \\ \times 5 \\ \hline \end{array}$

10. $\begin{array}{r} 9 \\ \times 8 \\ \hline \end{array}$

11. $\begin{array}{r} 9 \\ \times 7 \\ \hline \end{array}$

12. $\begin{array}{r} 2 \\ \times 6 \\ \hline \end{array}$

13. $\begin{array}{r} 7 \\ \times 4 \\ \hline \end{array}$

14. $\begin{array}{r} 3 \\ \times 5 \\ \hline \end{array}$

VOCABULARY POWER

REVIEW

multiplication [mul•tə•plə•kā′shən] *noun*

Multiplication and *multivitamin* begin with *multi.* Think of words that begin with *multi,* and look at their definitions. What do these words have in common?

PREVIEW

compatible numbers

www.harcourtschool.com/mathglossary

LESSON 1

Mental Math: Multiplication Patterns

Quick Review

1. $6 \times 7 = ■$ **2.** $8 \times 6 = ■$

3. $5 \times 9 = ■$ **4.** $9 \times 8 = ■$

5. $8 \times 7 = ■$

Learn

FOUND MONEY Kim is saving for a trip to see the manatees. She is wrapping pennies to take to the bank and has wrapped 7 rolls. Each roll has 50 pennies. How many pennies has she wrapped?

Example

Multiply.

$$\begin{array}{r} 50 \\ \times\ 7 \\ \hline 350 \end{array}$$

Think: $7 \times 5 = 35$
$7 \times 5 \text{ tens} = 35 \text{ tens}$
$7 \times 50 = 350$

So, Kim has wrapped 350 pennies.

Use mental math to multiply greater numbers when you know basic facts and patterns.

More Examples

A
$7 \times 2 = 14$
$7 \times 20 = 140$
$7 \times 200 = 1,400$
$7 \times 2,000 = 14,000$

B
$5 \times 8 = 40$
$5 \times 80 = 400$
$5 \times 800 = 4,000$
$5 \times 8,000 = 40,000$

MATH IDEA As the number of zeros in a factor increases, the number of zeros in the product increases.

Check

1. **Explain** how to use a basic fact and a pattern to find $7 \times 5,000$.

Use mental math to complete.

2. $3 \times 2 = 6$
$3 \times 20 = 60$
$3 \times 200 = ■$
$3 \times 2,000 = ■$

3. $4 \times 4 = 16$
$4 \times 40 = ■$
$4 \times 400 = ■$
$4 \times 4,000 = ■$

4. $2 \times 6 = ■$
$2 \times 60 = ■$
$2 \times 600 = ■$
$2 \times 6,000 = ■$

5. $5 \times 2 = ■$
$5 \times 20 = ■$
$5 \times 200 = ■$
$5 \times 2,000 = ■$

Practice and Problem Solving

Extra Practice, page 230, Set A

Use mental math to complete.

6. $8 \times 6 = ■$
$8 \times 60 = ■$
$8 \times 600 = ■$
$8 \times 6{,}000 = ■$

7. $4 \times 3 = ■$
$4 \times 30 = ■$
$4 \times 300 = ■$
$4 \times 3{,}000 = ■$

8. $6 \times 5 = ■$
$6 \times 50 = ■$
$6 \times 500 = ■$
$6 \times 5{,}000 = ■$

9. $5 \times 4 = ■$
$5 \times 40 = ■$
$5 \times 400 = ■$
$5 \times 4{,}000 = ■$

Use mental math. Write the basic fact and use a pattern to find the product.

10. 6×400 **11.** $7 \times 4{,}000$ **12.** 3×600 **13.** 5×600

14. $7 \times 60{,}000$ **15.** 6×90 **16.** $3 \times 7{,}000$ **17.** $3 \times 30{,}000$

ALGEBRA Find the value of *n*.

18. $5 \times 40{,}000 = n$ **19.** $n = 2 \times 3{,}000$ **20.** $6 \times n = 4{,}200$ **21.** $8 \times 6{,}000 = n$

22. $n = 7 \times 5{,}000$ **23.** $3 \times n = 2{,}700$ **24.** $5 \times n = 25{,}000$ **25.** $8 \times n = 72{,}000$

USE DATA Copy and complete each table.

26. 1 roll = 40 nickels

Number of Rolls	1	2	3	4	5	6
Number of Nickels	40	80	■	■	■	■

27. 1 roll = 50 dimes

Number of Rolls	1	2	3	4	5	6
Number of Dimes	50	100	■	■	■	■

28. Micah and his family have been saving for the manatee trip for two years. They have three \$100 bills, six \$20 bills, and five \$10 bills. How much money have they saved?

29. **What's the Error?** Renee has 20 rolls of pennies. Each roll has 50 pennies. Renee calculates that she has 100 pennies. Describe her error. Write the correct answer.

30. **Write About It** What is $80{,}000 \times 7$? Explain how you found the answer.

Mixed Review and Test Prep

31. 12×12 (p. 172) **32.** $8 \times 2 \times 5$ (p. 174)

33. Wendy's karate class begins at 11:40 A.M. and lasts 1 hour 50 minutes. When does Wendy's class end? (p. 98)

34. Evaluate $4 \times (8 - 2)$. (p. 184)

35. **TEST PREP** Which operation can you place in the expression below to get the least possible value? (p. 184)

$$(1 + 7) \bullet 2$$

A $+$ **C** $-$
B $\div$ **D** $\times$

LESSON

2 Estimate Products

Quick Review

Round to the nearest hundred.

1. 572 **2.** 921
3. 1,726 **4.** 2,135
5. 5,834

VOCABULARY
compatible numbers

Learn

BIG SQUEEZE The Farmers Market ordered 249 quarts of orange juice and sold it by the cup. There are 4 cups in a quart. About how many cups of juice were sold?

You can estimate 4×249.

One Way Use rounding.

STEP 1
Round the greater factor to the nearest hundred.
$4 \times 249 \rightarrow 4 \times 200$

STEP 2
Use basic facts and patterns.
$4 \times 2 = 8$
$4 \times 20 = 80$
$4 \times 200 = 800$

Another Way Use **compatible numbers**.

Compatible numbers are numbers that are easy to compute mentally.

STEP 1
4×249
↓
4×250
Think: 4×25 is easy to compute mentally.

STEP 2
Multiply.
If $4 \times 25 = 100$
Then $4 \times 250 = 1{,}000$

So, both 800 cups and 1,000 cups are reasonable estimates of the amount of orange juice sold.

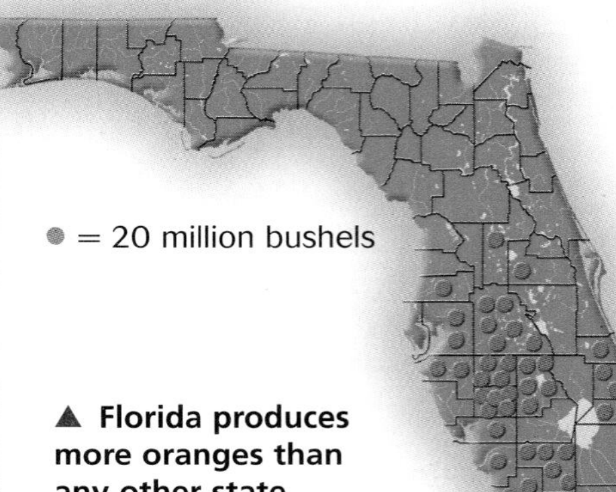

▲ Florida produces more oranges than any other state.

More Examples Estimate the products.

A
$63 \times 7 \rightarrow 60 \times 7 = 420$

B
$2{,}479 \times 3 \rightarrow 2{,}500 \times 3 = 7{,}500$

C
$\$5.82 \times 6 \rightarrow \$6 \times 6 = \$36$

Check

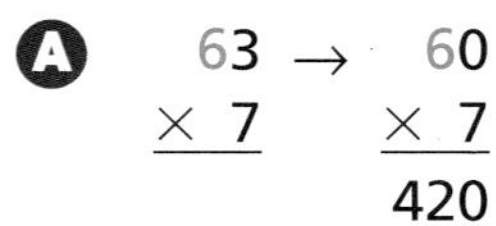

1. **Explain** how you can tell if the estimated products in Examples B and C are greater than or less than the exact products.

Estimate the product. Choose the method.

2. 6×23
3. 9×507
4. $3 \times 8{,}126$
5. $4 \times \$57.63$

Practice and Problem Solving

Extra Practice, page 230, Set B

Estimate the product. Choose the method.

6. 187×4
7. 87×6
8. 764×5
9. 679×4
10. $\$11.89 \times 6$
11. 247×8
12. 389×7
13. $\$6.24 \times 7$
14. 8×26
15. $5 \times \$65.13$
16. 4×749
17. $9 \times 1{,}789$
18. $3 \times \$19.85$
19. 4×341
20. $7 \times \$812.15$
21. $2 \times 6{,}789$

ALGEBRA Choose two factors from the box for each estimated product ■ × ▲.

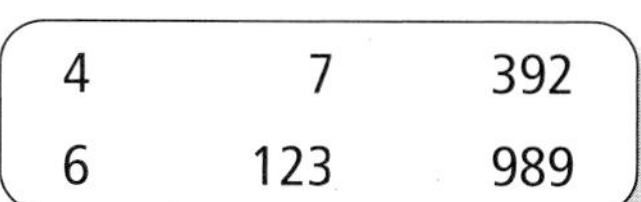

4	7	392
6	123	989

22. 1,600
23. 600
24. 7,000
25. 2,400

USE DATA For 26–27, use the graph.

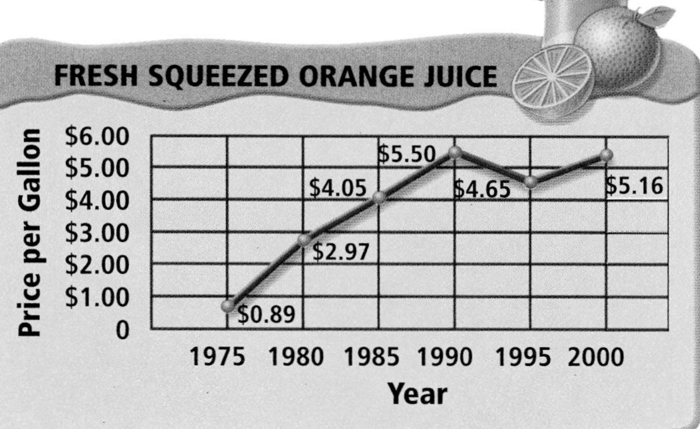

26. In 1980, was $8 enough to buy 3 gallons of juice? Explain your thinking.
27. Six gallons of orange juice cost about $12 in 1978. How much more did the same amount of juice cost in 2000?
28. **FAST FACT • SCIENCE** Each Florida orange tree produces about 5 bushels of oranges each year. A bushel of oranges weighs about 56 pounds. How many pounds of oranges will 2 orange trees produce in a year?

Mixed Review and Test Prep

29. Write <, >, or = for ●. (p. 20)
107,216 ● 170,206
30. What is the median for 23, 23, 15, 27, and 40? (p. 119)
31. Round 2,678,213 to the nearest hundred thousand. (p. 30)
32. **TEST PREP** What are the missing numbers in this pattern? (p. 74)
101, 131, 161, ■, ■, 251
   - **A** 181, 191
   - **B** 191, 211
   - **C** 191, 221
   - **D** 207, 231

LESSON 3

Multiply 2-Digit Numbers

Quick Review

1. $7 \times 40 = ■$
2. $30 \times 4 = ■$
3. $8 \times 60 = ■$
4. $20 \times 5 = ■$
5. $6 \times 500 = ■$

MATERIALS base-ten blocks

Learn

VERY BERRY Last year at the Strawberry Festival, 24 people entered the strawberry shortcake-eating contest. This year, three times that many people entered the contest. How many people entered the strawberry shortcake-eating contest this year?

Find 3×24.
Estimate. $3 \times 25 = 75$

HANDS ON

Activity

Make a model and use regrouping to find the product.

STEP 1

Model 3 groups of 24.

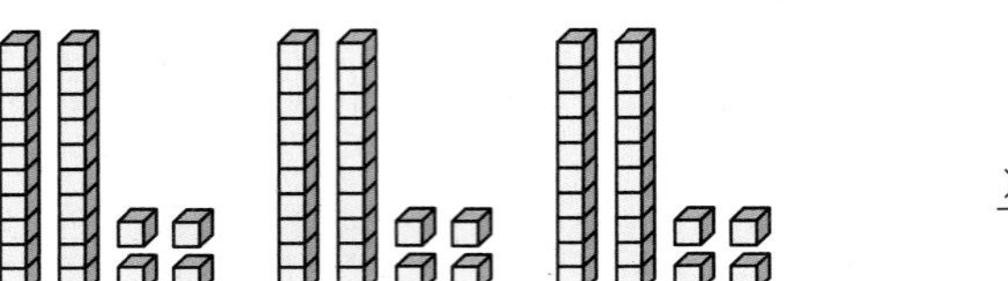

$$\begin{array}{r} 24 \\ \times\ 3 \\ \hline \end{array}$$

STEP 2

Multiply the ones.
3×4 ones $= 12$ ones
Regroup the ones.

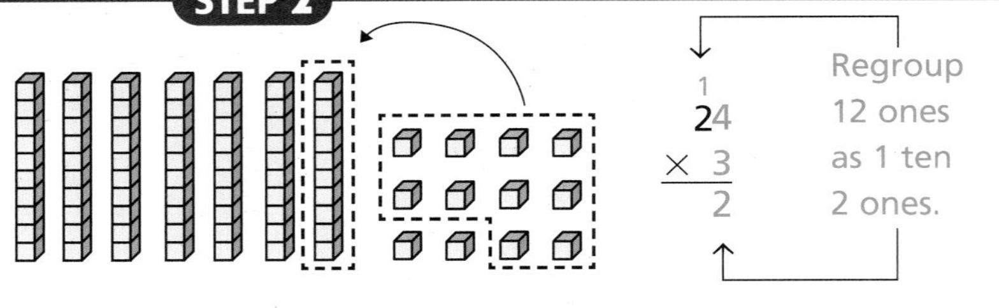

$$\begin{array}{r} \overset{1}{2}4 \\ \times\ 3 \\ \hline 2 \end{array}$$

Regroup 12 ones as 1 ten 2 ones.

STEP 3

Multiply the tens.
3×2 tens $= 6$ tens
Add the regrouped ten.

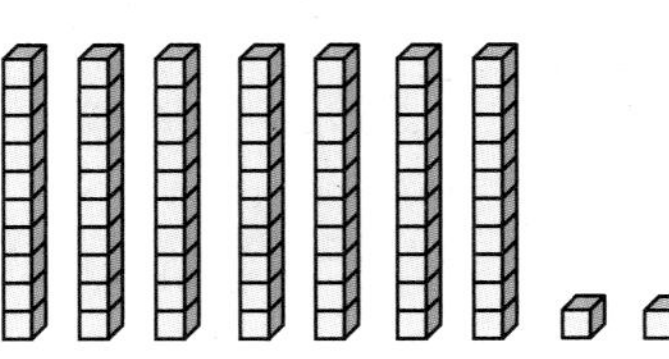

$$\begin{array}{r} \overset{1}{2}4 \\ \times\ 3 \\ \hline 72 \end{array}$$

So, 72 people entered the strawberry shortcake-eating contest. Since 72 is close to the estimate of 75, it is reasonable.

- Make a model and use regrouping to find the product 4×35.

Two Ways to Multiply

You can pick your own strawberries at the festival. If there are 16 pints of strawberries in a box, how many pints are in 5 boxes?

Find 5×16.

Technology Link

More Practice: Harcourt Mega Math The Number Games, *Up, Up, and Array,* Level J

One Way Use partial products.

STEP 1 Multiply the ones.

$$\begin{array}{r} 16 \\ \times\ 5 \\ \hline 30 \end{array} \longleftarrow 5 \times 6$$

STEP 2 Multiply the tens.

$$\begin{array}{r} 16 \\ \times\ 5 \\ \hline 30 \\ 50 \\ \hline \end{array} \longleftarrow 5 \times 10$$

STEP 3 Add the products.

$$\begin{array}{r} 16 \\ \times\ 5 \\ \hline 30 \\ +50 \\ \hline 80 \end{array}$$

Another Way Use regrouping.

STEP 1 Multiply the ones.

$$\begin{array}{r} \scriptstyle 3 \\ 16 \\ \times\ 5 \\ \hline 0 \end{array}$$

STEP 2 Multiply the tens.

$$\begin{array}{r} \scriptstyle 3 \\ 16 \\ \times\ 5 \\ \hline 80 \end{array}$$

So, there are 80 pints of strawberries in 5 boxes.

More Examples

Partial Products

A
$$\begin{array}{r} 42 \\ \times\ 7 \\ \hline 14 \\ +\ 280 \\ \hline 294 \end{array}$$

B
$$\begin{array}{r} 89 \\ \times\ 3 \\ \hline 27 \\ +\ 240 \\ \hline 267 \end{array}$$

Regrouping

C
$$\begin{array}{r} \scriptstyle 1 \\ 23 \\ \times\ 5 \\ \hline 115 \end{array}$$

D
$$\begin{array}{r} \scriptstyle 4 \\ 58 \\ \times\ 6 \\ \hline 348 \end{array}$$

Check

1. **Explain** how to find 4×58 by using either regrouping or the partial products method.

Find the product. Estimate to check.

2. 3×43
3. 6×51
4. 4×24
5. 5×38
6. 7×16

Practice and Problem Solving

Extra Practice, page 230, Set C

Find the product. Estimate to check.

7. 46×2 **8.** 57×4 **9.** 39×7 **10.** 82×4 **11.** 27×3

12. 62×4 **13.** 48×5 **14.** 59×3 **15.** 36×6 **16.** 74×8

17. 93×3 **18.** 35×7 **19.** 67×4 **20.** 81×5 **21.** 49×6

22. 6×43 **23.** 9×62 **24.** 5×84 **25.** 7×49 **26.** 4×73

Find the missing factor.

27. $5 \times$ ■ $= 230$ **28.** $4 \times$ ■ $= 304$ **29.** ■ $\times 37 = 222$

Compare. Write $<$, $>$, or $=$ for each ●.

30. 8×37 ● 5×79 **31.** 6×27 ● 3×54 **32.** 9×58 ● 5×98

USE DATA For 33–35 and 37–38, use the table.

33. A large bowl holds 8 cups of fresh strawberries. How many calories are there in the bowl of fresh strawberries? (HINT: 1 pint = 2 cups)

34. Chef Marie tops her strawberry pie with 20 whole strawberries. She made 10 pies for the Strawberry Festival. About how many seeds are on top of Chef Marie's pies?

35. There are 26 students in Cindy's fourth grade class. About how many pounds of berries, on average, did Cindy's class eat during the last year?

36. **What's the Error?** Cory says that $7 \times 52 = 354$. Describe Cory's error and find the correct product.

37. **Write a problem** that uses one of the Berry Facts and involves multiplying a 2-digit number by a 1-digit number.

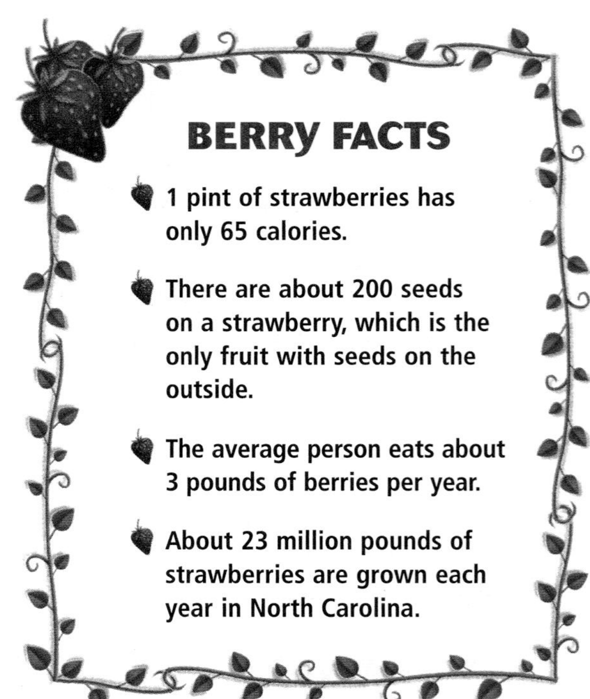

BERRY FACTS
1 pint of strawberries has only 65 calories.
There are about 200 seeds on a strawberry, which is the only fruit with seeds on the outside.
The average person eats about 3 pounds of berries per year.
About 23 million pounds of strawberries are grown each year in North Carolina.

38. **What's the Question?** Olivia ate 1 pint of strawberries. Gabe and Matt shared 2 pints of strawberries. The answer is 195 calories.

39. Mrs. Kuwana bought 12 packages with 8 buns in each package for a neighborhood party. How many packages of 10 hot dogs each will she need for all hot dogs to have a bun and no buns left over?

40. Juan bought 5 boxes of cookies with 24 in a box, and Sara bought 3 boxes of cookies with 48 in a box. Explain how to find out who got more cookies.

Mixed Review and Test Prep

41. $23 + 48$ (p. 40)

42. $39 - 16$ (p. 40)

43. Round 3,270,516 to the nearest hundred thousand. (p. 30)

44. Find the value of the expression. $42 - (25 + 17)$ (p. 64)

45. Joy's room measures 3 yards by 4 yards. Find the number of square yards of carpet she'll need to cover the floor. Explain your thinking.

46. **TEST PREP** Carson walked his neighbor's 3 dogs for 3 days. He earned $2 per dog each day. How much money did Carson earn? (p. 174)

A $20
B $18
C $16
D $12

Problem Solving LINKUP . . . to Reading

ANALOGIES

An analogy shows a relationship between words or ideas.

Arm is to body as branch is to tree.

Product is to × as sum is to +.

▲ is to 3 as ■ is to 4.

Complete each analogy.

1. 2×14 is to [base-ten blocks: 2 tens 8 ones] as 3×21 is to _?_.
2. Factor is to multiplication as addend is to _?_.
3. 14 ones is to 1 ten 4 ones as 14 tens is to _?_.
4. Add is to subtract as multiply is to _?_.
5. 2×38 is to $(2 \times 30) + (2 \times 8)$ as 3×45 is to _?_.

TIP Find the relationship between the first pair. Then show the same relationship between the second pair.

LESSON 4

Multiply 3- and 4-Digit Numbers

Quick Review

1. 4×800
2. 600×7
3. $3,000 \times 5$
4. $9 \times 8,000$
5. $6 \times 1,200$

Learn

ON THE GO Kurt and his family are traveling from Palatka, Florida, to Tampa, Florida, on vacation. They will drive 156 miles to get to Tampa and will drive home on the same route. How many miles will they drive in all?

Find 2×156. Estimate. $2 \times 150 = 300$

Example 1

STEP 1

Multiply the ones.

2×6 ones $= 12$ ones

Regroup the ones.

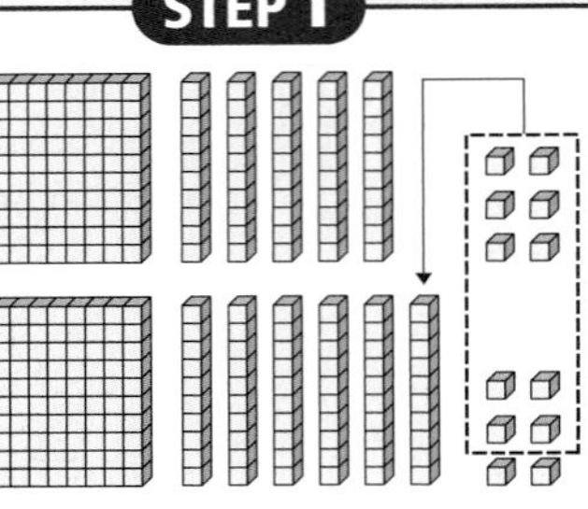

$$\begin{array}{r} {}^{1} \\ 156 \\ \times 2 \\ \hline 2 \end{array}$$

Regroup the 12 ones as 1 ten 2 ones.

STEP 2

Multiply the tens.

2×5 tens $= 10$ tens

Add the regrouped ten.

Regroup the tens.

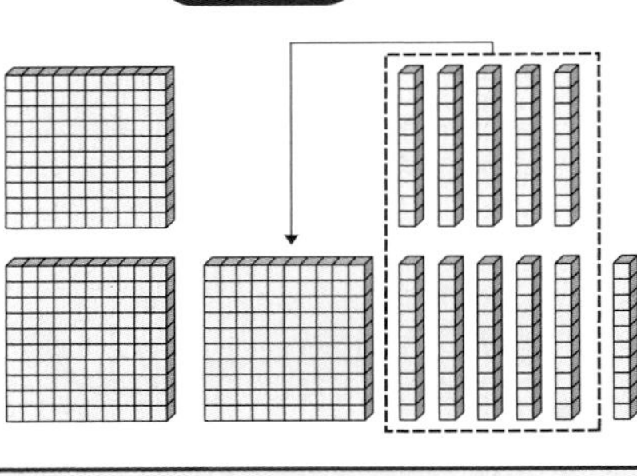

$$\begin{array}{r} {}^{1}{}^{1} \\ 156 \\ \times 2 \\ \hline 12 \end{array}$$

Regroup the 11 tens as 1 hundred 1 ten.

STEP 3

Multiply the hundreds.

2×1 hundred $= 2$ hundreds

Add the regrouped hundred.

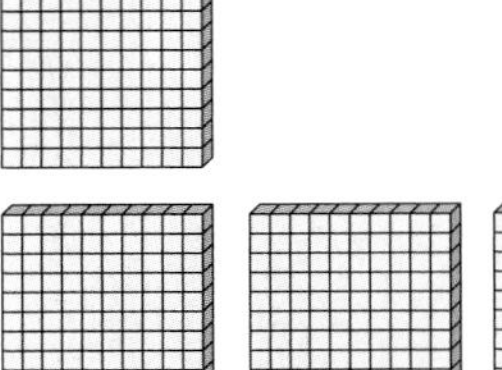

$$\begin{array}{r} {}^{1}{}^{1} \\ 156 \\ \times 2 \\ \hline 312 \end{array}$$

So, they will travel 312 miles in all. Since 312 is close to the estimate of 300, it is reasonable.

Multiply 4-Digit Numbers

While on vacation, Kurt enjoyed riding a roller coaster at a theme park. The roller coaster can carry 1,276 riders every hour. How many people can ride the roller coaster in 3 hours?

Find $3 \times 1,276$.
Estimate. $3 \times 1,300 = 3,900$

Example 2

STEP 1 Multiply the ones.

$$\begin{array}{r} {}^{1}\\ 1,276 \\ \times \quad 3 \\ \hline 8 \end{array}$$

STEP 2 Multiply the tens.

$$\begin{array}{r} {}^{21}\\ 1,276 \\ \times \quad 3 \\ \hline 28 \end{array}$$

STEP 3 Multiply the hundreds.

$$\begin{array}{r} {}^{21}\\ 1,276 \\ \times \quad 3 \\ \hline 828 \end{array}$$

STEP 4 Multiply the thousands.

$$\begin{array}{r} {}^{21}\\ 1,276 \\ \times \quad 3 \\ \hline 3,828 \end{array}$$

So, 3,828 people can ride the roller coaster in 3 hours.
Since 3,828 is close to the estimate of 3,900, it is reasonable.

More Examples

A
$$\begin{array}{r} {}^{11}\\ 234 \\ \times \quad 3 \\ \hline 702 \end{array}$$

B
$$\begin{array}{r} {}^{31}\\ 852 \\ \times \quad 6 \\ \hline 5,112 \end{array}$$

C
$$\begin{array}{r} {}^{2\ \ 1}\\ 2,814 \\ \times \quad 3 \\ \hline 8,442 \end{array}$$

D
$$\begin{array}{r} {}^{6\ 42}\\ 3,964 \\ \times \quad 7 \\ \hline 27,748 \end{array}$$

Check

1. **Explain** how you record the 28 ones when you multiply 4 by 7 in Example D.

Find the product. Estimate to check.

2. $\begin{array}{r} 136 \\ \times \quad 5 \\ \hline \end{array}$
3. $\begin{array}{r} 254 \\ \times \quad 2 \\ \hline \end{array}$
4. $\begin{array}{r} 321 \\ \times \quad 3 \\ \hline \end{array}$
5. $\begin{array}{r} 125 \\ \times \quad 9 \\ \hline \end{array}$
6. $\begin{array}{r} 2,371 \\ \times \quad 5 \\ \hline \end{array}$
7. $\begin{array}{r} 1,843 \\ \times \quad 9 \\ \hline \end{array}$
8. $\begin{array}{r} 3,655 \\ \times \quad 7 \\ \hline \end{array}$
9. $\begin{array}{r} 2,792 \\ \times \quad 3 \\ \hline \end{array}$
10. 3×437
11. $6 \times 2,317$
12. 7×173
13. $5 \times 2,533$

LESSON CONTINUES

Practice and Problem Solving

Extra Practice, page 230, Set D

Find the product. Estimate to check.

14. 241×2 **15.** 632×4 **16.** 318×3 **17.** 653×5

18. $4,714 \times 6$ **19.** $7,105 \times 8$ **20.** $1,479 \times 2$ **21.** $2,935 \times 3$

22. 2×825 **23.** 7×402 **24.** 4×973 **25.** 8×531

26. $2 \times 3,322$ **27.** $5 \times 4,861$ **28.** $3 \times 2,507$ **29.** $8 \times 4,619$

Multiply. Then add to find the product.

30. 3×472
$(3 \times 400) + (3 \times 70) + (3 \times 2)$

31. $3 \times 1,509$
$(3 \times 1,000) + (3 \times 500) + (3 \times 9)$

Compare. Write <, >, or = for each ●.

32. 4×326 ● 3×467 **33.** 8×199 ● 5×321 **34.** $2 \times 3,750$ ● $3 \times 2,500$

35. 5×272 ● 6×231 **36.** 7×408 ● 6×476 **37.** $4 \times 7,424$ ● $8 \times 3,695$

USE DATA For 38–40, use the graph.

38. During which months was the average high temperature greater than 80°?

39. Name the month in which the average high temperature increased from below 90°F to above 90°F.

40. Which month had about the same average high temperature as February?

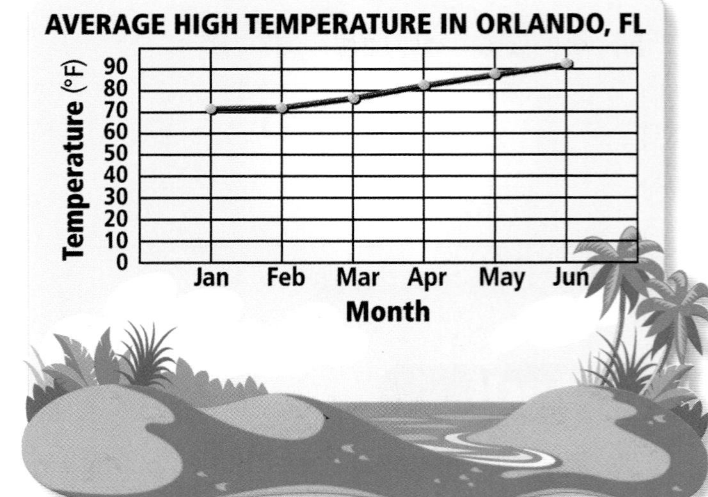

41. **? What's the Question?** Jamal, Tim, and Lisa each brought 4 rolls of film on their vacation. They can take 36 pictures with each roll. The answer is 432 pictures.

42. The theme park tickets for Tom and his 2 sisters cost $27 each. His parents' tickets cost $36 each. How much did the family's tickets cost?

43. **REASONING** Can two different multiplication problems have the same estimated product? Explain.

44. **What's the Error?** Jeff made an error in his multiplication. Describe his error, and explain how to find the correct answer.

Jeff

```
   2
2,206
×    4
8,884
```

45. Find the missing numbers on Keisha's paper. Explain your thinking.

Keisha

```
 4,623
×    ■
36,9■4
```

Mixed Review and Test Prep

46. $\begin{array}{r} 6{,}899 \\ +2{,}267 \\ \hline \end{array}$ (p. 48)

47. $\begin{array}{r} 8{,}902 \\ -5{,}730 \\ \hline \end{array}$ (p. 48)

48. Find the value of $2 \times (3 + 6)$. (p. 184)

49. $6 \times 5{,}000$ (p. 214)

Find the product. Name the property you used. (p. 174)

50. 9×1

51. $(3 \times 3) \times 4$

52. **TEST PREP** Which coordinates describe the location of the tree?

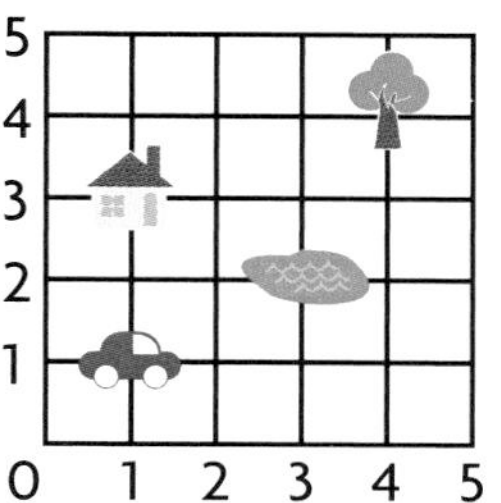

A (1,1) **B** (4,4) **C** (1,3) **D** (3,2)

Problem Solving Thinker's Corner

VISUAL THINKING Chris is drawing a picture to help him find the product 3×146.

He drew 146 by using a large square for a hundred, bars for tens, and small squares for ones.

1. Copy and complete Chris's drawing to show 3×146. What is the product?
2. What if you show 3×246? How would your picture change?

Make drawings to find the products.

3. 3×423 **4.** 341×5 **5.** 4×209

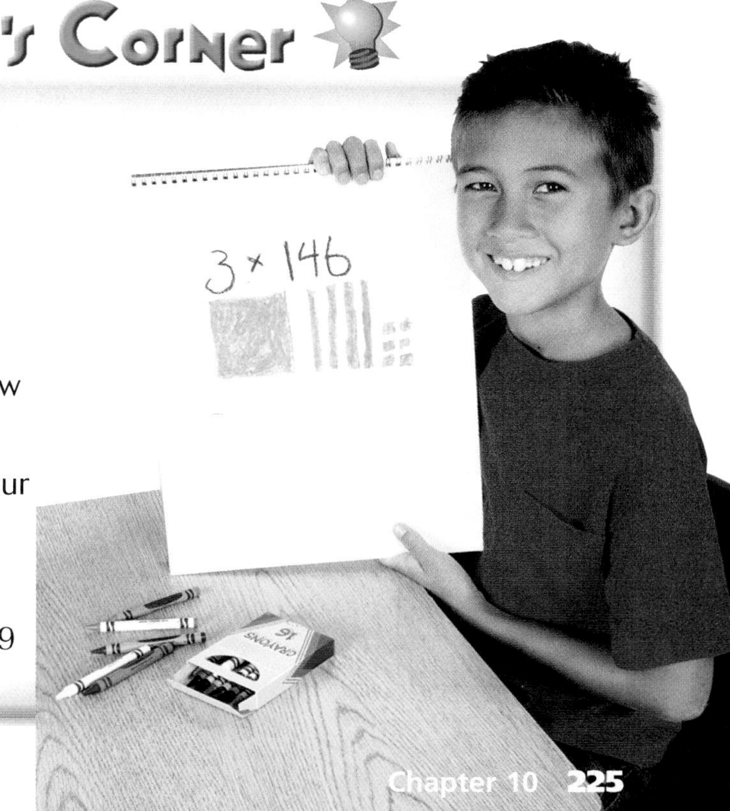

LESSON 5

Multiply with Zeros

Quick Review

1. 3 × 200
2. 4 × 6,000
3. 2 × 15,000
4. 7 × 20 × 20
5. 5 × 60 × 300

Learn

TREE TALK The Talking Tree Trail has 7 talking trees. The trees have recorded messages that tell about the trees, the trail, and the forest. Suppose there are 1,005 visitors to the trail in June. If each visitor listens to all of the messages, how many times are the messages heard?

Find $7 \times 1{,}005$.
Estimate. $7 \times 1{,}000 = 7{,}000$

▲ The Talking Tree Trail is located in Holmes Educational State Forest, North Carolina.

Example

STEP 1

Multiply the ones.
Regroup the ones.

$$\begin{array}{r} \scriptstyle 3 \\ 1{,}005 \\ \times \quad 7 \\ \hline 5 \end{array}$$

Regroup 35 ones as 3 tens 5 ones.

STEP 2

Multiply the tens.
Add the regrouped tens.

$$\begin{array}{r} \scriptstyle 3 \\ 1{,}005 \\ \times \quad 7 \\ \hline 35 \end{array}$$

STEP 3

Multiply the hundreds.

$$\begin{array}{r} \scriptstyle 3 \\ 1{,}005 \\ \times \quad 7 \\ \hline 035 \end{array}$$

STEP 4

Multiply the thousands.

$$\begin{array}{r} \scriptstyle 3 \\ 1{,}005 \\ \times \quad 7 \\ \hline 7{,}035 \end{array}$$

So, the messages are heard 7,035 times. Since 7,035 is close to the estimate of 7,000, it is reasonable.

More Examples

A

$$\begin{array}{r} \scriptstyle 5 \\ 5{,}070 \\ \times \quad 8 \\ \hline 40{,}560 \end{array}$$

B

$$\begin{array}{r} \$24.08 \\ \times \quad 4 \\ \hline \end{array} \rightarrow \begin{array}{r} \scriptstyle 1\ 3 \\ 2408 \\ \times \quad 4 \\ \hline \$96.32 \end{array}$$

Multiply amounts of money the same way you multiply whole numbers. Write the product in dollars and cents.

Check

1. **Explain** why there is a 5 above the hundreds place in Example A.

Find the product. Estimate to check.

2. 460×8
3. 208×7
4. $1,509 \times 3$
5. $\$60.30 \times 2$
6. $7,200 \times 5$

Practice and Problem Solving

Extra Practice, page 230, Set E

Find the product. Estimate to check.

7. 290×6
8. $1,005 \times 8$
9. $4,080 \times 7$
10. $6,011 \times 3$
11. $\$98.04 \times 5$

12. 5×704
13. 6×670
14. $8 \times 5,007$
15. $4 \times 8,090$
16. $8 \times 6,750$

Find the product. Estimate to check.

17. $(2 \times 403) \times 4$
18. $(3 \times \$20.08) \times 7$
19. $(8 \times 5,007) \times 6$
20. $(5 \times \$46.70) \times 3$
21. $(2 \times 8,040) \times 5$
22. $(6 \times \$37.90) \times 9$

23. **USE DATA** Justin hiked to the top of Mt. Mitchell, NC, which has an elevation that is 3 times the elevation at the Talking Tree Trail. How high is Mt. Mitchell?

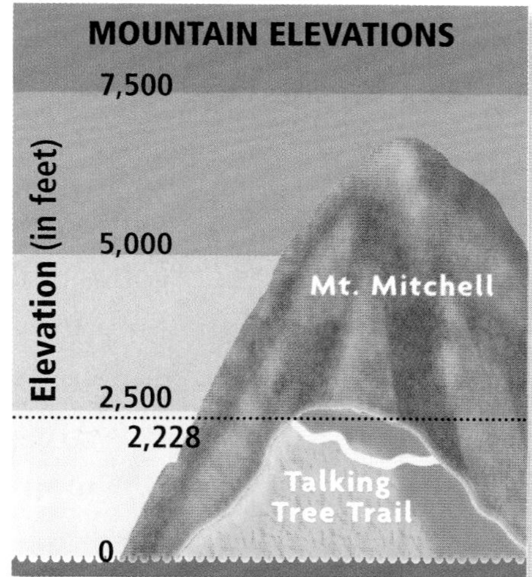

24. **Vocabulary Power** The prefix *re-* when added to a root word can mean "again," as in *rerun* ("to run again"). How does this information help you understand what *regroup* means?

25. Mountain cabins are available to rent for \$170 a night during the summer or \$140 a night during the winter. You want to rent a cabin for 6 nights. How much less would your stay cost during the winter than during the summer?

Mixed Review and Test Prep

26. On Tuesday, Sara's flute lesson is from 4:50 P.M. to 5:20 P.M. and her piano lesson is from 6:00 P.M. to 6:45 P.M. How many minutes does Sara spend in lessons? (p. 98)

27. Write 56,730 in expanded form. (p. 4)

28. **TEST PREP** Which time is 12 minutes before 3:00? (p. 96)

A 1:48 **B** 2:30 **C** 2:48 **D** 2:50

LESSON 6

Problem Solving Strategy
Write an Equation

Quick Review

Find the value of *n*.

1. $5 \times 5 = 20 + n$

2. $10 \times n = 32 - 2$

3. $85 - 12 = 70 + n$

4. $n \div 6 = 19 - 11$

5. $12 \times n = 100 - 4$

PROBLEM Rinata uses her computer to find information on the Internet for her project on dolphins. Each month of Internet service costs $15.95. What is the total cost for Rinata to have Internet service for 6 months?

UNDERSTAND

- What are you asked to find?
- What information will you use?
- Is there any information you will not use?

PLAN

- What strategy can you use to find the answer?
  You can *write an equation*. An equation can show how the facts in the problem are related.

SOLVE

- How can you use the strategy to find the answer?
  You can *write an equation* that uses n for the product. Then multiply to find the product.

number of months		**cost per month**		**total cost of Internet service**
↓		↓		↓
6	×	$15.95	=	n
		$95.70	=	n

So, it costs $95.70 for 6 months of service.

CHECK

- Look back at the problem. Does the answer make sense for the problem? Explain.

Problem Solving Practice

For 1–3, write an equation and solve.

1. **What if** Internet access costs $19.95 per month? How much would it cost Rinata to have Internet access for 5 months?
2. Leon bought 4 books about sea life that cost $12.45 each. How much did he spend?
3. Ms. Davies allows her computer class 25 minutes each day to try new computer programs. How many minutes is this in 5 days?

Strategies

- Draw a Diagram or Picture
- Make a Model or Act It Out
- Make an Organized List
- Find a Pattern
- Make a Table or Graph
- Predict and Test
- Work Backward
- Solve a Simpler Problem
- **Write an Equation**
- Use Logical Reasoning

Adam ran a 10-mile race at a pace of 7 minutes per mile. How many minutes did it take Adam to complete the race?

4. What equation can you use to help you answer the question?

   A $10 \times 7 = n$
   B $7 \times 5 = n$
   C $10 = 7 \times n$
   D $7 = 10 \times n$

5. What solution answers the question?

   F 55 minutes
   G 60 minutes
   H 70 minutes
   J 75 minutes

Mixed Strategy Practice

6. Four students are standing in line. Jane is standing 2 meters behind Kara and 1 meter in front of Chrissy. Chrissy is standing an equal distance between Kara and Paul. How far away is the first student standing from the last?

7. A computer lab has 8 rows of computers. Each row has 4 computers. There are also 4 computers grouped in the center of the room. How many computers are in the lab?

8. Karen left her house at the time shown on the clock. She arrived at Kaitlyn's house 15 minutes later. They spent 30 minutes eating lunch and then took a 15-minute walk. At what time did they finish their walk?

9. Jason took 3 courses while attending camp at a sea life park. The total cost for the 3 courses was $138.33. Use the chart to find the cost of the "Get All Wet!" course.

Sea Life Camp

Course	Cost
Wild Animals	$52.98
Predators and Prey..	$45.75
Get All Wet!	?

Extra Practice

Set A (pp. 214–215)

Use mental math to complete.

1. $3 \times 5 = $ ■
$3 \times 50 = $ ■
$3 \times 500 = $ ■

2. $4 \times 8 = $ ■
$4 \times 80 = $ ■
$4 \times 800 = $ ■

3. $2 \times 7 = $ ■
$2 \times 70 = $ ■
$2 \times 700 = $ ■
$2 \times 7{,}000 = $ ■

4. $5 \times 9 = $ ■
$5 \times 90 = $ ■
$5 \times 900 = $ ■
$5 \times 9{,}000 = $ ■

5. Ruiz has four \$20 bills and three \$5 bills. How much money does he have?

Set B (pp. 216–217)

Estimate the product. Choose the method.

1. $\begin{array}{r} 728 \\ \times \quad 7 \\ \hline \end{array}$ **2.** $\begin{array}{r} 219 \\ \times \quad 8 \\ \hline \end{array}$ **3.** $\begin{array}{r} 704 \\ \times \quad 4 \\ \hline \end{array}$ **4.** $\begin{array}{r} 237 \\ \times \quad 4 \\ \hline \end{array}$ **5.** $\begin{array}{r} 590 \\ \times \quad 4 \\ \hline \end{array}$ **6.** $\begin{array}{r} 814 \\ \times \quad 6 \\ \hline \end{array}$

7. About how many weeks are in 4 years 4 weeks?

Set C (pp. 218–221)

Find the product. Estimate to check.

1. $\begin{array}{r} 18 \\ \times\ 3 \\ \hline \end{array}$ **2.** $\begin{array}{r} 27 \\ \times\ 5 \\ \hline \end{array}$ **3.** $\begin{array}{r} 58 \\ \times\ 4 \\ \hline \end{array}$ **4.** $\begin{array}{r} 83 \\ \times\ 7 \\ \hline \end{array}$ **5.** $\begin{array}{r} 64 \\ \times\ 9 \\ \hline \end{array}$ **6.** $\begin{array}{r} 47 \\ \times\ 6 \\ \hline \end{array}$

Set D (pp. 222–225)

Find the product. Estimate to check.

1. $\begin{array}{r} 403 \\ \times \quad 7 \\ \hline \end{array}$ **2.** $\begin{array}{r} 783 \\ \times \quad 2 \\ \hline \end{array}$ **3.** $\begin{array}{r} 3{,}991 \\ \times \qquad 4 \\ \hline \end{array}$ **4.** $\begin{array}{r} \$8.61 \\ \times \qquad 6 \\ \hline \end{array}$ **5.** $\begin{array}{r} \$11.74 \\ \times \qquad 5 \\ \hline \end{array}$ **6.** $\begin{array}{r} 2{,}668 \\ \times \qquad 6 \\ \hline \end{array}$

7. Mr. Jones bought 4 boxes of brushes for his students to use. Each box has 125 brushes. How many brushes did he buy?

Set E (pp. 226–227)

Find the product. Estimate to check.

1. $7 \times \$78.07$ **2.** $5 \times \$1{,}054$ **3.** $6 \times \$69.03$ **4.** $8 \times 2{,}007$

5. Amanda earns \$12.70 each week baby-sitting for her cousin. How much does she earn in 4 weeks?

Review/Test

CHECK VOCABULARY AND CONCEPTS

Choose the best term from the box.

compatible numbers
round
estimate

1. You can _?_ to find a number that is close to an exact amount. (p. 216)
2. Numbers that are easy to compute mentally are called _?_. (p. 216)

CHECK SKILLS

Use mental math to complete. (pp. 214–215)

3. $5 \times 6 = \blacksquare$
   $5 \times 60 = \blacksquare$
   $5 \times 600 = \blacksquare$
4. $3 \times 7 = \blacksquare$
   $3 \times 70 = \blacksquare$
   $3 \times 700 = \blacksquare$
5. $4 \times 3 = \blacksquare$
   $4 \times 30 = \blacksquare$
   $4 \times 300 = \blacksquare$
   $4 \times 3{,}000 = \blacksquare$
6. $2 \times 8 = \blacksquare$
   $2 \times 80 = \blacksquare$
   $2 \times 800 = \blacksquare$
   $2 \times 8{,}000 = \blacksquare$

Estimate the product. Choose the method. (pp. 216–217)

7. 5×294
8. 5×66
9. 3×834
10. $6 \times \$5.36$

Find the product. Estimate to check. (pp. 218–221, 222–225, 226–227)

11. 45×5
12. $1{,}068 \times 6$
13. 42×4
14. 863×3
15. $3{,}122 \times 2$
16. 56×3
17. $3{,}897 \times 5$
18. $3{,}045 \times 9$
19. $\$8.21 \times 4$
20. $\$10.96 \times 8$
21. $\$7.50 \times 3$
22. $\$38.05 \times 7$

CHECK PROBLEM SOLVING

Solve. (pp. 228–229)

23. Carmen buys 8 magazines. Each magazine sells for $3.28. How much does Carmen spend on magazines?
24. There are 500 sheets of paper in each package. How many sheets of paper are in 9 packages?
25. In its orbit, the Space Shuttle travels about 286 miles every minute. How far does it travel in 5 minutes?

Standardized Test Prep

NUMBER SENSE, CONCEPTS, AND OPERATIONS

1. Mike made a table to compare the lengths of some birds.

LENGTHS OF BIRDS	
Bird	**Length (in feet)**
Swift	$\frac{6}{12}$
Canary	$\frac{5}{12}$
Robin	$\frac{10}{12}$
Winter Wren	$\frac{3}{12}$

Which bird has the **greatest** length?

A Swift

B Canary

C Robin

D Winter Wren

2. About $\frac{29}{100}$ of the Earth's surface is land. Which of the following has the same value as $\frac{29}{100}$?

F 0.02

G 0.29

H 0.71

J 2.90

3. **Explain It** Two of the longest rivers in the world are the Amazon River and the Chang River. The Amazon is 4,000 miles long. What other information do you need in order to find out how much longer the Amazon River is than the Chang River? Explain your thinking.

MEASUREMENT AND GEOMETRY

4. Sarah is 4 feet 5 inches tall. How many inches tall is she?

1 foot = 12 inches

A 20 inches

B 45 inches

C 48 inches

D 53 inches

Check your work.
See item 5. Check your work by adding 15 minutes to your answer. The sum should be the time shown on the clock.

5. Albert has been doing his homework for 15 minutes. This clock shows the present time. At what time did Albert start his homework?

F 4:00

G 4:05

H 5:00

J 5:05

6. **Explain It** Which measure is the best estimate to describe the length of the toy car?

Choose the best estimate. Write 2 *inches*, 2 *miles*, or 2 *pounds*. Explain how you decided.

ALGEBRAIC THINKING

7. The average temperature during April in Miami, Florida, is 75° Fahrenheit. The average temperature in April in Asheville, North Carolina, is 56° Fahrenheit. Let *d* represent the difference in the average temperatures.

   Which equation below can be used to find the difference between the average temperatures in Miami and Asheville in April?

   A $d = 75 + 56$

   B $d = 75 - 56$

   C $d = 75 \times 56$

   D $d = 75 \div 56$

8. An artist painted 8 pictures. He sold 2 of the pictures and then painted more. Which expression below **best** represents the number of pictures the artist has?

   F $(p + 8) - 2$

   G $(p - 8) + 2$

   H $(8 - 2) + p$

   J $(8 - p) + 2$

9. **Explain It** This table represents the cost of pens at a school store. Copy and complete the table.

PEN COSTS					
Number of Pens	1	2	3	4	5
Cost	\$2	\$4	\$6		

   Explain how the cost of the pens changes as the number of pens changes.

DATA ANALYSIS AND PROBABILITY

10. The ages of the students in the Science Club are 11, 12, 11, 12, 12, 14, and 13. What is the range of their ages?

    A 2

    B 3

    C 4

    D 5

11. The fourth graders at Walker Elementary School voted for their favorite lunch food. The bar graph below shows the results.

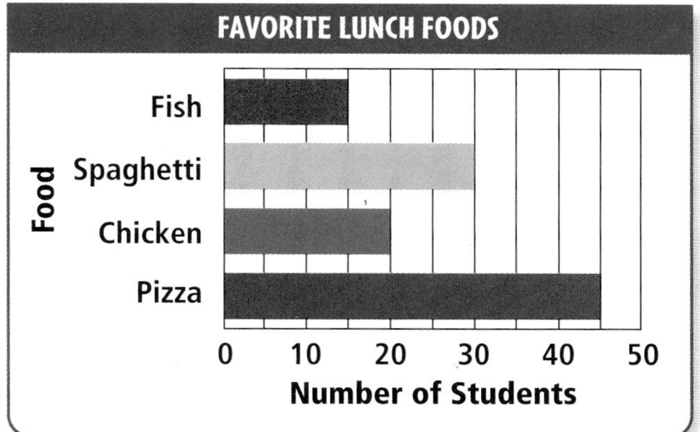

    How many more students voted for pizza than for chicken and fish combined?

    F 5

    G 10

    H 35

    J 75

12. **Explain It** Lynn has a red shirt, a blue shirt, a green shirt, black pants, and a brown skirt in her closet. List all the possible combinations to find the number of outfits she can make. Explain your thinking.

CHAPTER 11

Multiply by Tens

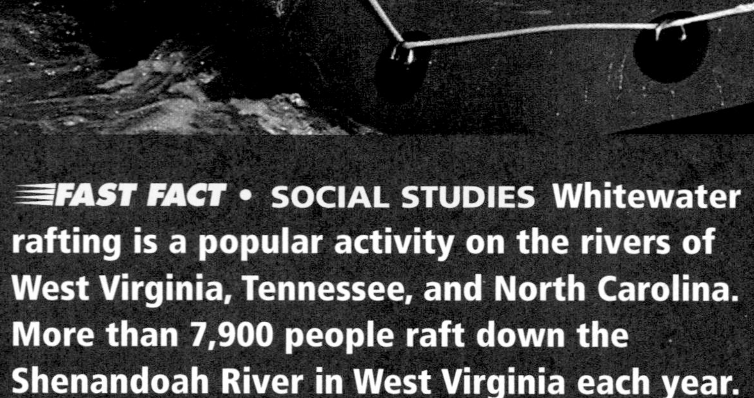

FAST FACT • SOCIAL STUDIES Whitewater rafting is a popular activity on the rivers of West Virginia, Tennessee, and North Carolina. More than 7,900 people raft down the Shenandoah River in West Virginia each year.

PROBLEM SOLVING Rafters must meet a minimum weight requirement in order to raft safely. The table shows the minimum weights needed. If there are 7 people in a raft who meet the minimum requirement, what is the least amount of weight a raft on each river will carry?

MINIMUM RAFTING WEIGHT REQUIREMENTS (per person)

River	Weight
Shenandoah River, WV Class I–III	50 pounds
Upper Pigeon River, TN Class III–IV	70 pounds
Nantahala River, NC Class II–III	60 pounds

CHECK WHAT YOU KNOW

Use this page to help you review and remember important skills needed for Chapter 11.

MULTIPLY BY TENS, HUNDREDS, AND THOUSANDS

Multiply.

1. 3×900 **2.** 4×40 **3.** $2 \times 6{,}000$ **4.** 5×20

5. $8 \times 2{,}000$ **6.** 7×300 **7.** 9×50 **8.** $6 \times 1{,}000$

9. $\begin{array}{r} 10 \\ \times\ 9 \\ \hline \end{array}$ **10.** $\begin{array}{r} 5{,}000 \\ \times\ \ \ 3 \\ \hline \end{array}$ **11.** $\begin{array}{r} 900 \\ \times\ \ 2 \\ \hline \end{array}$ **12.** $\begin{array}{r} 600 \\ \times\ \ 5 \\ \hline \end{array}$

MODEL MULTIPLICATION

Use the base-ten blocks to find the product.

13. $\begin{array}{r} 14 \\ \times\ 3 \\ \hline \end{array}$ **14.** $\begin{array}{r} 25 \\ \times\ 2 \\ \hline \end{array}$

15. $\begin{array}{r} 27 \\ \times\ 2 \\ \hline \end{array}$ **16.** $\begin{array}{r} 17 \\ \times\ 3 \\ \hline \end{array}$

17. $\begin{array}{r} 12 \\ \times\ 5 \\ \hline \end{array}$

VOCABULARY POWER

REVIEW

product [prä′dəkt] *noun*

A product is the result of putting things together. For example, a toy is a product from a toy factory. How is a product such as a toy like a product in multiplication? Explain.

PREVIEW

Distributive Property

www.harcourtschool.com/mathglossary

LESSON 1

Mental Math: Multiplication Patterns

Quick Review

1. 5×10 **2.** 8×20
3. 7×500 **4.** 9×600
5. $3,000 \times 4$

Learn

CROSS-COUNTRY Luis and his family drove from New York City to the Grand Canyon. They drove for a total of 50 hours at an average speed of 50 miles per hour. About how far did they drive?

Multiply. 50×50

Use a basic fact and a pattern.

Factors		Product
5×5	=	25
5×50	=	250
50×50	=	2,500
↑ 1 zero ↑ 1 zero		↑ 2 zeros

Think: Use the basic fact $5 \times 5 = 25$. Look for a pattern of zeros.

So, Luis and his family drove about 2,500 miles.

- What do you notice about the pattern of zeros in the factors and the products?

▲ The Grand Canyon is located in northern Arizona and surrounds 277 miles of the Colorado River.

Examples Use a basic fact and a pattern to find the product.

A	B	C
$4 \times 1 = 4$	$7 \times 6 = 42$	$6 \times 5 = 30$
$4 \times 10 = 40$	$70 \times 60 = 4,200$	$60 \times 5 = 300$
$4 \times 100 = 400$	$70 \times 600 = 42,000$	$60 \times 50 = 3,000$
$4 \times 1,000 = 4,000$	$70 \times 6,000 = 420,000$	$600 \times 50 = 30,000$

MATH IDEA Basic facts and patterns can be used to help you find products when you multiply by multiples of 10, 100, or 1,000.

Technology Link

More Practice: Harcourt Mega Math The Number Games, *Tiny's Think Tank,* Level K

Check

1. **Explain** why the products in Example C have more zeros than the factors.

Use a basic fact and a pattern to find the products.

2. 9×10
9×100
$9 \times 1{,}000$

3. 6×60
60×60
600×60

4. 8×50
80×50
800×50

5. 30×9
300×90
$300 \times 9{,}000$

Practice and Problem Solving

Extra Practice, page 246, Set A

Use a basic fact and a pattern to find the product.

6. 80×600
7. 700×500
8. 60×30
9. 50×20
10. $80 \times 1{,}200$
11. $100 \times 1{,}000$
12. $300 \times 5{,}000$
13. $8 \times 3{,}000{,}000$
14. $\begin{array}{r} 90 \\ \times\ 6 \\ \hline \end{array}$
15. $\begin{array}{r} 8{,}000 \\ \times\ \ 60 \\ \hline \end{array}$
16. $\begin{array}{r} 40 \\ \times 30 \\ \hline \end{array}$
17. $\begin{array}{r} 600 \\ \times\ 12 \\ \hline \end{array}$

ALGEBRA Find the value of n.

18. $n \times 800 = 7{,}200$
19. $80 \times n = 720{,}000$
20. $8{,}000 \times n = 40{,}000$
21. $7{,}000 \times 10 = n$

22. On Tori's vacation, her dad drove about 60 miles per hour for 6 hours each day. About how far did he drive in 5 days?

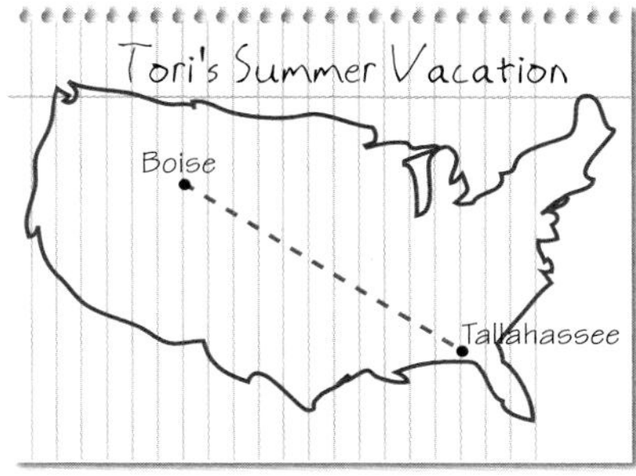

23. Kim exercised 6 minutes one week, 9 minutes the second week, 12 minutes the third week, and 15 minutes the fourth week. If this pattern continues, how long will she exercise in the sixth week?

24. **What's the Error?** Describe Sheldon's error. Write the correct answer.

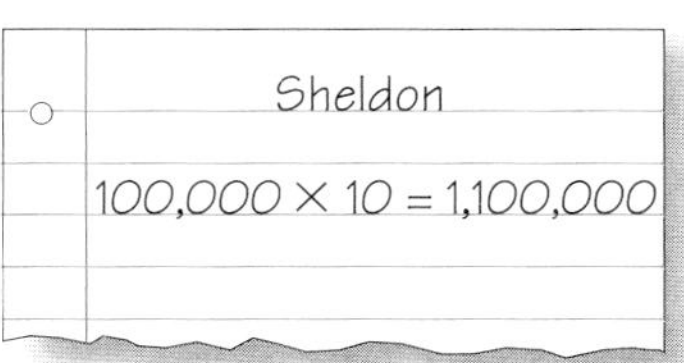

Mixed Review and Test Prep

25. Dana went to camp for 3 weeks. She returned home July 31. When did she leave for camp? (p. 104)

JULY						
Sun	Mon	Tue	Wed	Thu	Fri	Sat
				1	2	3
4	5	6	7	8	9	10
11	12	13	14	15	16	17
18	19	20	21	22	23	24
25	26	27	28	29	30	31

26. $6{,}470 - 3{,}587$ (p. 50)

27. Compare. Write $<$, $>$, or $=$ for the ●. (p. 52)
$15{,}970 - 10{,}820$ ● $80{,}700 - 75{,}812$

28. $3 \times \$25.62$ (p. 222)

29. **TEST PREP** What is the range for 2, 3, 2, 6, 5? (p. 122)

A 2 **B** 3 **C** 4 **D** 5

LESSON 2

The Distributive Property

Quick Review

Write each number in expanded form.

1. 62 **2.** 57

3. 23 **4.** 14

5. 77

VOCABULARY

Distributive Property

MATERIALS grid paper, different-color markers

Explore

Cora and Mark are planting a flower garden. They want to plant 8 rows with 22 sunflowers in each row. How many sunflowers will they have in their garden?

You can use the Distributive Property to solve the problem. The **Distributive Property** states that multiplying a sum by a number is the same as multiplying each addend by the number and then adding the products.

Activity 1 Multiply. 8×22

You can make a model and use the Distributive Property to find the product.

STEP 1

Outline a rectangle that is 8 units wide and 22 units long. Think of the area as the product.

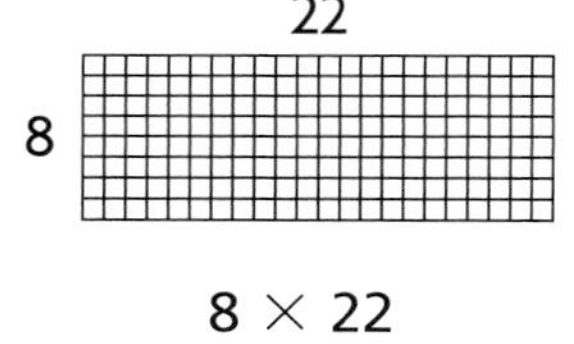

8×22

STEP 2

Break apart the rectangle by counting 20 units from the left and drawing a line.

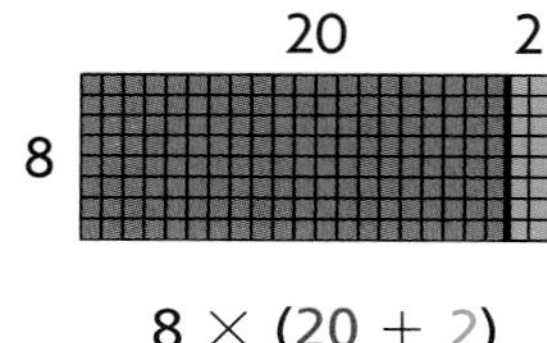

$8 \times (20 + 2)$

STEP 3

Use the Distributive Property to show the sum of two products. Multiply what is in the parentheses first. Add the partial products.

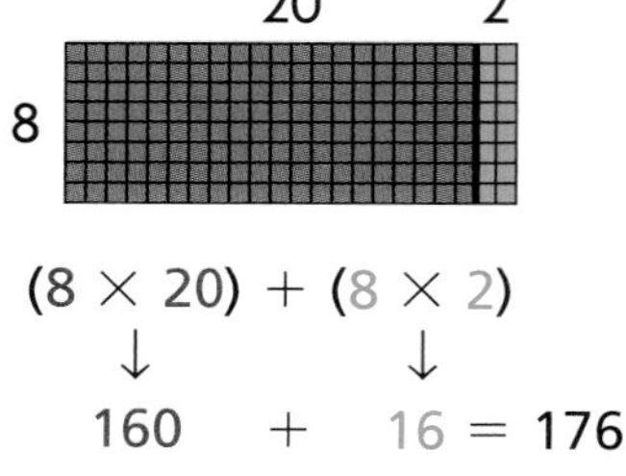

$(8 \times 20) + (8 \times 2)$

$\downarrow \qquad \downarrow$

$160 + 16 = 176$

So, they will have 176 sunflowers.

Try It

Make a model and use the Distributive Property to find the product.

a. 6×18 **b.** 5×27

c. 7×34

I am multiplying 6 × 18. What do I do next?

Connect

You can use the Distributive Property to multiply by multiples of 10.

Activity 2 Multiply. 20×13

STEP 1

Show the model.
Break apart the model by counting over 10 units from the left and drawing a line.

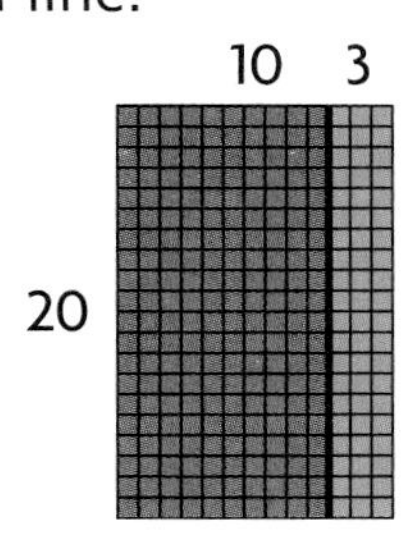

$20 \times 13 = 20 \times (10 + 3)$

STEP 2

Use the Distributive Property to show the sum of two products. Multiply what is in parentheses first. Add the partial products.

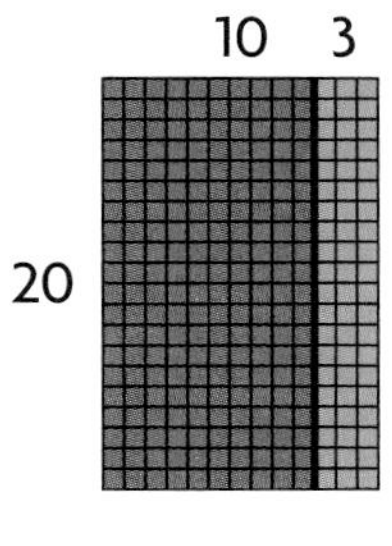

$(20 \times 10) + (20 \times 3)$

$\downarrow \qquad \downarrow$

$200 + 60 = 260$

So, 20×13 is 260.

Practice and Problem Solving

Use a model and the Distributive Property to find the product.

1. 7×37 **2.** 20×15 **3.** 10×13 **4.** 30×22 **5.** 20×26

6. 50×34 **7.** 40×93 **8.** 60×48 **9.** 70×52 **10.** 40×16

11. **Write About It** Explain how to find 20×82.

12. Kyle's Nursery planted 30 rows of trees with 35 trees in each row. This is 50 trees fewer than last year. How many trees did the nursery plant last year?

Mixed Review and Test Prep

13. The rule is *add 4*. Use the rule and input 5 to find the output. (p. 74)

14. Corey bought 3 CDs that each cost \$15.88. How much change did he receive from \$50.00? (p. 222)

15. Order 23,465; 32,465; 23,645; and 23,456 from least to greatest. (p. 24)

16. **TEST PREP** $(48 \div 8) - 2$ (p. 184)

A 8 **B** 6 **C** 4 **D** 2

LESSON 3

Multiply by Tens

Quick Review

1. 4 × 10
2. 4 × 100
3. 4 × 1,000
4. 5 × 10
5. 5 × 100

Learn

ROUNDUP At the roundup, 30 ranchers each herded 52 cows. How many cows were herded in all?

Example Multiply. 30 × 52

STEP 1

Multiply by the ones. Place a zero in the ones place.

$$\begin{array}{r} 52 \\ \times 30 \\ \hline 0 \end{array} \leftarrow 0 \text{ ones} \times 52$$

STEP 2

Multiply by the tens.

$$\begin{array}{r} 52 \\ \times 30 \\ \hline 1{,}560 \end{array} \leftarrow 3 \text{ tens} \times 52$$

So, the ranchers herded 1,560 cows.

MATH IDEA When you multiply a whole number by a multiple of 10, the digit in the ones place of the product is always a zero.

Check

1. **Tell** how many zeros are in the product of 18 and 20. How many zeros are in the product of 12 and 50? Explain how you can tell before you multiply.

Find the product.

2. $\begin{array}{r} 12 \\ \times 10 \\ \hline \end{array}$ 3. $\begin{array}{r} 18 \\ \times 30 \\ \hline \end{array}$ 4. $\begin{array}{r} 28 \\ \times 20 \\ \hline \end{array}$ 5. $\begin{array}{r} 32 \\ \times 40 \\ \hline \end{array}$ 6. $\begin{array}{r} 47 \\ \times 30 \\ \hline \end{array}$

7. $\begin{array}{r} 46 \\ \times 40 \\ \hline \end{array}$ 8. $\begin{array}{r} 91 \\ \times 20 \\ \hline \end{array}$ 9. $\begin{array}{r} 55 \\ \times 60 \\ \hline \end{array}$ 10. $\begin{array}{r} 72 \\ \times 30 \\ \hline \end{array}$ 11. $\begin{array}{r} 33 \\ \times 30 \\ \hline \end{array}$

Practice and Problem Solving

Extra Practice, page 246, Set B

Find the product.

12. 16×10
13. 19×20
14. 34×40
15. 27×30
16. 48×50
17. 55×70
18. 78×80
19. 84×60
20. 34×50
21. 99×90
22. 45×50
23. 93×30
24. 56×20
25. 45×40
26. 87×30
27. 20×14
28. 30×24
29. 26×40
30. 36×50
31. 20×52
32. 70×39
33. 52×80
34. 50×54
35. 69×70
36. 90×18

Find the missing digits.

37. ■0 × 40 = 400
38. 20 × ■0 = 600
39. ■7 × 40 = 680
40. 53 × ■0 = 3,180
41. 4■ × 50 = 2,250
42. 77 × 3■ = 2,■10

USE DATA For 43–45, use the bar graph.

43. How many shows does each person do in 20 weeks?
44. How many shows does Carrie do in 50 weeks?
45. In 30 weeks, how many more shows does Jake do than Floyd?
46. **Vocabulary Power** *Multiple* means "more than one." For example, you can make multiple copies of a story. Explain how multiple copies are like a multiple of a number like 10.

47. **Write a problem** that can be solved by multiplying by a multiple of 10 using data from the bar graph.
48. **ALGEBRA** Mr. Cano wrote the expression ▲ × 80 = 64,000. Find the value of ▲.

Mixed Review and Test Prep

49. $23,426 + 2,213$ (p. 52)
50. $6,124 - 4,750$ (p. 52)
51. Find the median for the data: 40, 82, 27, 39, and 52. (p. 118)
52. In what place-value position is the 7 in 7,324,980? (p. 6)
53. **TEST PREP** $(3 \times 4) \times 2 = n$ (p. 174)
    - **A** $n = 8$
    - **B** $n = 12$
    - **C** $n = 14$
    - **D** $n = 24$

LESSON 4

Estimate Products

Quick Review

1. 20 × 40
2. 3 × 200
3. 50 × 30
4. 6 × 600
5. 80 × 30

Learn

SPLISH SPLASH Lauren's class is going whitewater rafting. The trip costs $112 per student. If Lauren has 24 classmates, about how much will it cost the class to go rafting?

Example Estimate. 24 × $112

STEP 1

Round each factor.

$$\begin{array}{r}\$112\\ \times\ 24\\ \hline\end{array} \rightarrow \begin{array}{r}\$100\\ \times\ 20\\ \hline\end{array}$$

STEP 2

Multiply.

$$\begin{array}{r}\$100\\ \times\ 20\\ \hline \$2{,}000\end{array}$$

So, it will cost about $2,000 for Lauren's class to go rafting.

- Will the actual cost be greater than or less than $2,000? Explain.

More Examples

A

$$\begin{array}{r}73\\ \times 42\\ \hline\end{array} \rightarrow \begin{array}{r}70\\ \times 40\\ \hline 2{,}800\end{array}$$

B

$$\begin{array}{r}254\\ \times\ 65\\ \hline\end{array} \rightarrow \begin{array}{r}300\\ \times\ 70\\ \hline 21{,}000\end{array}$$

Remember

To round a number:

- Find the place to which you want to round. Look at the digit to its right.
- If the digit is less than 5, the digit in the rounding place stays the same.
- If the digit is 5 or greater, the digit in the rounding place increases by 1.

Check

1. **Explain** how you can estimate the product 52 × 168.

Round each factor. Estimate the product.

2. $\begin{array}{r}18\\ \times 29\\ \hline\end{array}$
3. $\begin{array}{r}389\\ \times\ 64\\ \hline\end{array}$
4. $\begin{array}{r}\$45\\ \times\ 12\\ \hline\end{array}$
5. $\begin{array}{r}\$259\\ \times\ \ 41\\ \hline\end{array}$
6. $\begin{array}{r}52\\ \times 27\\ \hline\end{array}$
7. $\begin{array}{r}76\\ \times 31\\ \hline\end{array}$
8. $\begin{array}{r}410\\ \times\ 78\\ \hline\end{array}$
9. $\begin{array}{r}197\\ \times\ 16\\ \hline\end{array}$

Practice and Problem Solving

Extra Practice, page 246, Set C

Round each factor. Estimate the product.

10. $\$19 \times 12$ **11.** 278×33 **12.** $\$548 \times 45$ **13.** 38×27 **14.** 32×61

15. 419×72 **16.** 78×36 **17.** 64×67 **18.** 219×23 **19.** 634×55

20. 527×34 **21.** 56×39 **22.** 67×46 **23.** 915×32 **24.** 742×44

25. 13×85 **26.** 76×852 **27.** $\$49 \times 24$ **28.** 90×412 **29.** $18 \times \$319$

Estimate to compare. Write <, >, or = for each ●.

30. 20×132 ● 3,000 **31.** 13,000 ● 26×645 **32.** 49×42 ● 1,800

USE DATA For 33–34, use the table.

33. The table shows the average number of apples in each size bag and the number of bags sold. Estimate the number of apples sold for each of the bag sizes.

34. The fourth-grade students at Oak Elementary School are taking 8 large bags of apples to eat on their rafting trip. Estimate the total number of apples they are taking.

Bags of Apples Sold

Bags	Average Number of Apples	Number of Bags Sold
Small	11	27
Medium	18	21
Large	26	12

35. ***FAST FACT*** • **SOCIAL STUDIES** Each month the average person in the United States uses about 46 pounds of paper. Estimate the amount of paper used by the average person in the United States in 1 year.

36. **Write About It** Explain how you would estimate the product 16×934.

Mixed Review and Test Prep

37. $2,357 + 4,987$ (p. 48)

38. $6,998 - 4,736$ (p. 48)

39. Write the time that is 1 hour 50 minutes later. (p. 98)

40. $7 \times (2 \times 3) = n$ (p. 174)

41. **TEST PREP** There are 4 stacks of 20 baseball cards and 5 other baseball cards that are not in a stack. Which expression shows the total number of baseball cards? (p. 184)

A $(5 \times 20) + 4$
B $(4 \times 20) + 5$
C $(20 \times 5) + 4$
D $(4 \times 5) + 20$

LESSON 5

Problem Solving Strategy
Solve a Simpler Problem

Quick Review

1. 6×20
2. 30×20
3. 9×30
4. 40×30
5. 30×500

PROBLEM Ms. Alexander is buying art supplies for the 148 fourth-grade students at her school. She estimates that each student will use 50 sheets of drawing paper during the school year. How many sheets of drawing paper should she buy?

UNDERSTAND

- What are you asked to find?
- What information will you use?
- Is there any information you will not use? Explain.

PLAN

- What strategy can you use to solve the problem?

You can find the product 50×148 by breaking apart 148 into numbers that are easier to multiply and then *solving the simpler problem.*

$$\begin{array}{r} 148 \\ \times\ 50 \\ \hline \end{array}$$

SOLVE

- How can you use the strategy to solve the problem?

Rewrite 148 as $100 + 40 + 8$, multiply each addend by 50, and add the partial products.

$$\begin{array}{lr l} 148 = 100 + 40 + 8 & & \\ \times\ 50 & 50 & \leftarrow 50 \times (100 + 40 + 8) \\ \hline & 400 & \leftarrow 50 \times 8 \\ & 2{,}000 & \leftarrow 50 \times 40 \\ & +\ 5{,}000 & \leftarrow 50 \times 100 \\ \cline{2-2} & 7{,}400 & \end{array}$$

So, Ms. Alexander should buy 7,400 sheets of paper.

CHECK

- What other strategy could you use to solve the problem?

Problem Solving Practice

Break the problem into simpler parts and solve.

1. **What if** there were 62 fourth-grade students in an art class? About how many sheets of paper would be needed for the year?

2. There were 37 students in a summer art class. Each student made 50 drawings. How many drawings did they make?

Strategies

Draw a Diagram or Picture
Make a Model or Act It Out
Make an Organized List
Find a Pattern
Make a Table or Graph
Predict and Test
Work Backward
Solve a Simpler Problem
Write an Equation
Use Logical Reasoning

Problem Solving

The art teacher bought 3,300 crayons. She gave 20 crayons to each of the 157 students in her classes. How many crayons did she give to the students?

3. Which expression can you use to help you answer the question?
   A $3{,}300 \times (100 + 50 + 7)$
   B $20 \times (3{,}000 + 300)$
   C $20 \times (100 + 50 + 7)$
   D $157 + 20$

4. Which shows the total number of crayons the teacher gave her students?
   F 3,240 crayons
   G 3,140 crayons
   H 3,014 crayons
   J 2,904 crayons

Mixed Strategy Practice

USE DATA For 5–6, use the bar graph.

5. How many books did Mr. Matthew's class, Mr. Stevens's class, and Miss Kelsie's class read altogether?

6. **What's the Question?** The difference in the number of books read is 75 books.

7. Julia takes ballet after gymnastics. Gymnastics begins at 3:30 P.M. and lasts 1 hour 15 minutes. It takes 10 minutes to walk to ballet class. At what time does Julia get to ballet?

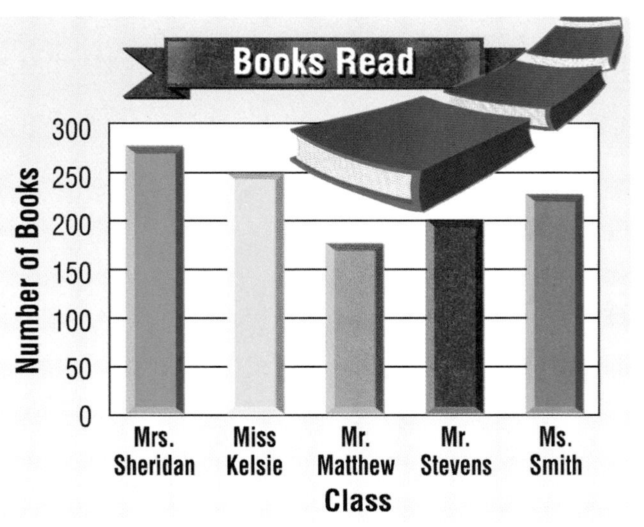

8. The ninth-grade English teacher asked her students to write a poem 125 words long. There are 80 students in her classes. About how many words will the teacher read?

9. Mr. James bought 30 pieces of chalk for each classroom. There are 15 classrooms on the second floor and 22 on the first floor. How many pieces of chalk did Mr. James buy?

Extra Practice

Set A (pp. 236–237)

Use a basic fact and patterns to find the product.

1. 90×500 **2.** $40 \times 8{,}000$ **3.** 90×30 **4.** 700×200

5. 80×60 **6.** $7{,}000 \times 200$ **7.** 800×50 **8.** 300×10

Find the value of *n*.

9. $10{,}000 \times n = 500{,}000$ **10.** $7{,}000 \times 7{,}000 = n$ **11.** $n \times 50 = 10{,}000$

12. $900 \times 12{,}000 = n$ **13.** $n \times 250{,}000 = 6{,}250{,}000$ **14.** $80 \times n = 320{,}000$

Set B (pp. 240–241)

Find the product.

1. 11×20 **2.** 45×30 **3.** 18×40 **4.** 25×30 **5.** 62×50

6. 43×20 **7.** 32×60 **8.** 17×50 **9.** 65×30 **10.** 84×40

11. 73×40 **12.** 21×70 **13.** 19×20 **14.** 55×30 **15.** 47×80

16. 24×20 **17.** 64×40 **18.** 16×30 **19.** 12×80 **20.** 38×60

21. Erin swims 25 laps a day. How many laps is this in 30 days?

Set C (pp. 242–243)

Round each factor. Estimate the product.

1. 13×22 **2.** 479×48 **3.** $\$73 \times 18$ **4.** 529×11 **5.** 91×27

6. $\$87 \times 61$ **7.** 52×48 **8.** 734×52 **9.** $\$618 \times 37$ **10.** 129×23

11. 32×79 **12.** 43×57 **13.** 89×531 **14.** 93×271 **15.** 32×197

16. 18×39 **17.** 58×129 **18.** 72×489 **19.** $21 \times \$625$ **20.** 42×385

Review/Test

CHECK CONCEPTS

1. Explain how a basic fact and a pattern can help you find the product 60×400. (pp. 236–237)
2. Make a model and use the Distributive Property to find the product 30×17. (pp. 238–239)

CHECK SKILLS

Use a basic fact and a pattern to find the product. (pp. 236–237)

3. 20×900
4. 500×600
5. $9{,}000 \times 60$
6. 300×700

Find the product. (pp. 240–241)

7. 66×30
8. 44×60
9. 22×90
10. 75×80
11. 73×40
12. 36×30
13. 52×20
14. 64×50
15. 24×50
16. 86×20
17. 19×40
18. 93×70

Round each factor. Estimate the product. (pp. 242–243)

19. 222×48
20. 252×14
21. 931×56
22. 79×68

CHECK PROBLEM SOLVING

For 23–25, break the problem into simpler parts and solve. (pp. 244–245)

23. A choir has 98 members and needs to buy 20 sheets of music for each member. How many sheets do they need to buy?
24. The Toy Warehouse has 248 shelves. Each shelf has 16 cases of toys. How many cases are on the shelves?
25. Kevin is reading a series of books. Each book has 155 pages, and there are 25 books in the series. How many total pages will Kevin have read when he completes the series?

Standardized Test Prep

NUMBER SENSE, CONCEPTS, AND OPERATIONS

1. Mr. Wong has 60 packages of drawing paper. Each package has 200 sheets of paper. How many sheets of paper are there?

   A 120

   B 260

   C 12,000

   D 120,000

2. The table below shows the number of callers who pledged money to a public TV station.

PUBLIC TV FUND DRIVE	
Pledge Amount	**Number of Callers**
$10	29
$50	11
$100	9

   Which is the **best** estimate for how much money was pledged to the station in all?

   F about $3,800 **H** about $1,800

   G about $2,800 **J** about $1,000

3. **Explain It** The first box contains 15 straws. Find the **best** estimate for the number of straws in the second box. Explain how you decided.

GEOMETRY AND SPATIAL SENSE

4. Which piece will fit in the design below with no gaps or overlaps?

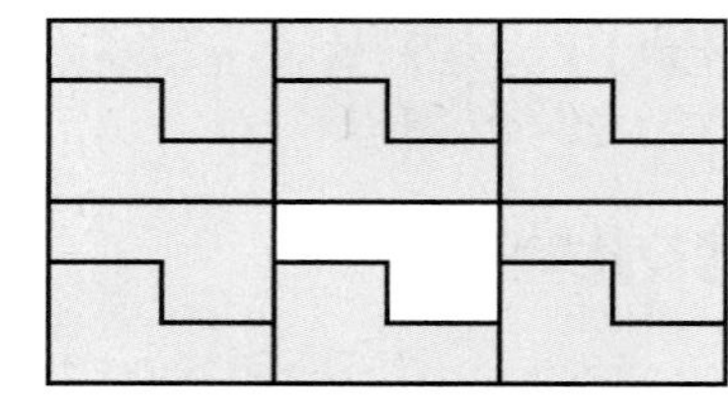

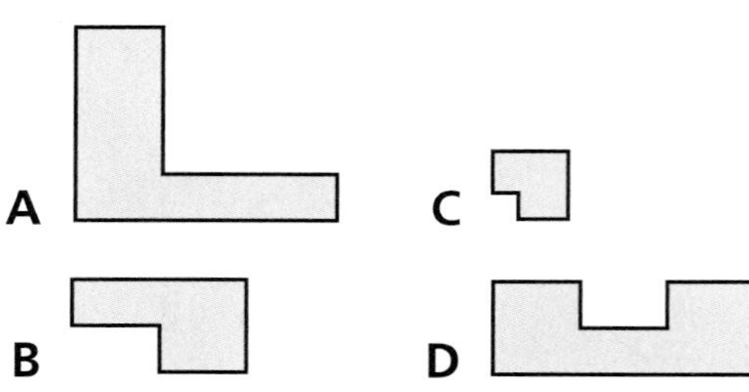

5. Which set of coordinates **best** describes the location of the Hot Dog Hut?

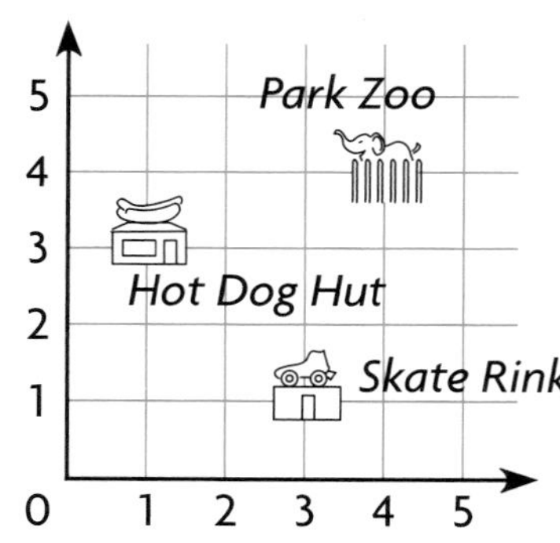

   F (1,3) **H** (4,2)

   G (3,1) **J** (5,2)

6. **Explain It** Which term describes the lines below?

   Write *parallel*, *perpendicular*, *intersecting*, or *acute*. Explain your thinking.

ALGEBRAIC THINKING

7. Which number sentence comes next in the pattern below?

$7 \times 1 = 7$

$7 \times 10 = 70$

$7 \times 100 = 700$

$7 \times 1{,}000 = 7{,}000$

A $5 \times 1{,}000 = 5{,}000$

B $7 \times 1{,}000 = 7{,}000$

C $7 \times 10{,}000 = 70{,}000$

D $7{,}000 \times 100 = 700{,}000$

8. Lisa has some dimes. Three times the number of dimes she has is less than 8. Which of the following could be used to find how many dimes Lisa has?

F $3 + n = 8$

G $3 \times n = 8$

H $3 \times n < 8$

J $3 \times n > 8$

TIP **Get the information you need.**
See item 9. Look for the relationship of each number to the number that comes after it. Think of a rule that matches this relationship.

9. **Explain It** Find a rule for this pattern.

10, 20, 40, 80, 160, 320, 640, ▢

Explain how to use your rule to find the next number in the pattern.

DATA ANALYSIS AND PROBABILITY

10. The table below shows the ages of several members of the movie club.

MOVIE CLUB MEMBERS

Person	Age (in years)
Fred	10
Pablo	11
Joni	10
Luisa	10
Beth	12

Which is the mode of their ages?

A 10 **C** 12

B 11 **D** 53

11. Which **best** describes the chance of the pointer landing on red on this spinner?

F least likely

G most likely

H impossible

J certain

12. **Explain It** The Smith family members made a circle graph to show their monthly budget.

MONTHLY BUDGET

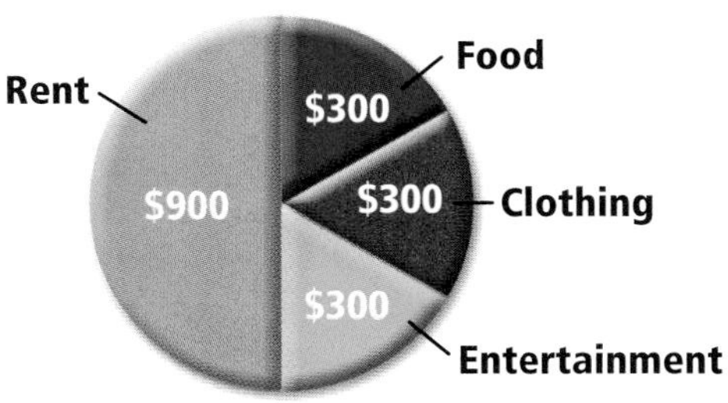

How much more does the Smith family spend on rent than on food and clothing? Explain your thinking.

CHAPTER 12

Multiply by 2-Digit Numbers

FAST FACT • SOCIAL STUDIES The *Greetings from America* stamp set, introduced in early 2002, represents each of the 50 states. The postage rate to mail a letter then was 34 cents. Before 1863, postage rates were based on the number of sheets in a letter and the distance it was traveling. Beginning in 1863, rates became based on weight only.

PROBLEM SOLVING Look at the graph. How much did a book of 20 stamps cost at the end of 2002? How much more did a book of 20 stamps cost in 2002 than in 1982?

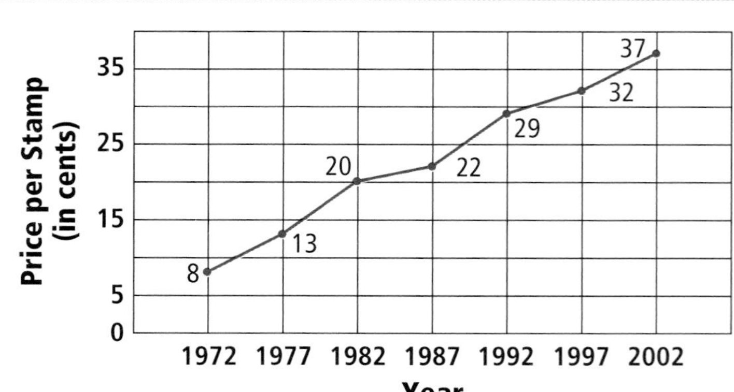

Check What You Know

Use this page to help you review and remember important skills needed for Chapter 12.

Estimate Products

Estimate the product.

1. 12×9
2. 14×6
3. 21×8
4. 18×5
5. 272×3
6. 350×7
7. 649×4
8. 212×7
9. 322×9
10. 817×2
11. 444×3
12. $9{,}145 \times 2$
13. $4 \times 2{,}781$
14. 5×550
15. $6 \times 7{,}317$
16. 4×385

Multiply by 1-Digit Numbers

Find the product. Estimate to check.

17. 12×6
18. 43×4
19. 39×3
20. 61×5
21. 35×7
22. 25×5
23. 125×2
24. 163×3
25. 350×3
26. 100×5
27. 49×7
28. 101×9

Vocabulary Power

REVIEW

money [mə´nē] *noun*

Money comes from the Latin *moneta*, meaning "mint" or "coinage." List three synonyms you can think of for *money*. Use each word in a sentence.

PREVIEW

multistep problem

www.harcourtschool.com/mathglossary

LESSON 1

Multiply 2-Digit Numbers

Quick Review

1. 3 × 12 **2.** 2 × 25
3. 2 × 31 **4.** 2 × 40
5. 2 × 32

Learn

TOTALLY TOMATOES Mr. Henson grows tomatoes. There are 35 plants on each tray. Mr. Henson has 88 trays. How many tomato plants does he have in all?

Example 1

Multiply. 35 × 88
↓ ↓
Estimate. 40 × 90 = 3,600

You can use place value and regrouping to find 35 × 88.

STEP 1

Think of 35 as 3 tens 5 ones. Multiply by 5 ones.

```
  4
  88
 ×35
 440  ← 5 × 88
```

STEP 2

Multiply by 3 tens, or 30.

```
  2
  4
  88
 ×35
  440
 2640  ← 30 × 88
```

STEP 3

Add the products.

```
   2
   4
   88
  ×35
  440
+2 640
 3,080
```

So, there are 3,080 tomato plants. Since 3,080 is close to the estimate of 3,600, the answer is reasonable.

More Examples

```
   2
   7
   29
  ×38
  232  ← 8 × 29
 +870  ← 30 × 29
1,102
```

B

```
    3
    1
   $55
  × 62
   110  ← 2 × 55
+3 300  ← 60 × 55
$3,410
```

• Explain how you know in which place to begin when you multiply by 2-digit numbers.

Find Products

The greenhouse has 45 bags of potting soil. Each bag has enough soil to pot 29 plants. How many plants can be potted?

Example 2

Multiply. 45 × 29

↓ ↓

Estimate. 50 × 30 = 1,500

One Way

Colleen used regrouping to find the product.

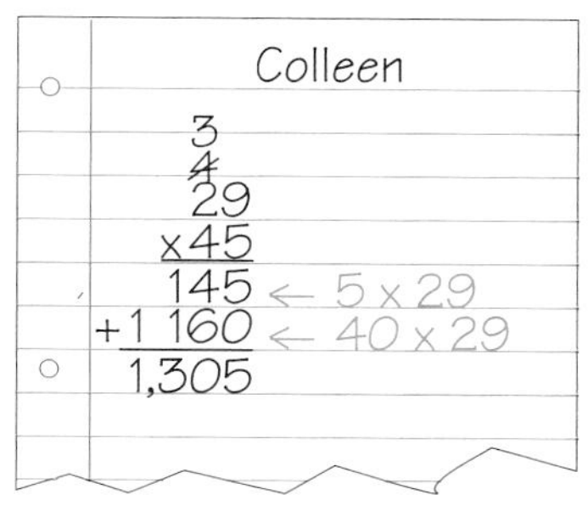

Another Way

Brad used partial products.

Brad

```
   29
  x45
   45  ← 5 x 9
  100  ← 5 x 20
  360  ← 40 x 9
 +800  ← 40 x 20
1,305
```

So, there is enough soil to pot 1,305 plants. Since 1,305 is close to the estimate of 1,500, the answer is reasonable.

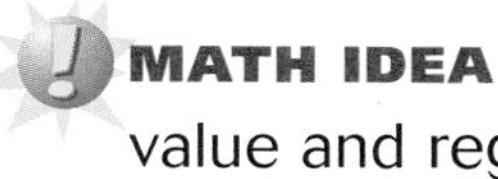

MATH IDEA You can find products using place value and regrouping or you can use the partial products method.

- Explain why the second partial product is always greater than the first partial product when you multiply two 2-digit numbers.

Technology Link

More Practice: Harcourt Mega Math, The Number Games, *Up, Up, and Array*, Level K

Check

1. **Explain** how the partial products method of finding products is different from the regrouping method.

Choose either method to find the product. Estimate to check.

2. 37×22
3. 54×31
4. 42×26
5. 78×41
6. $\$23 \times 34$
7. 67×14
8. 93×76
9. 82×47
10. 51×79
11. 38×64

LESSON CONTINUES

Practice and Problem Solving

Extra Practice, page 264, Set A

Choose either method to find the product. Estimate to check.

12. $\begin{array}{r} 44 \\ \times 35 \\ \hline \end{array}$
13. $\begin{array}{r} 67 \\ \times 14 \\ \hline \end{array}$
14. $\begin{array}{r} \$63 \\ \times\ 42 \\ \hline \end{array}$
15. $\begin{array}{r} 81 \\ \times 22 \\ \hline \end{array}$
16. $\begin{array}{r} 72 \\ \times 59 \\ \hline \end{array}$
17. $\begin{array}{r} \$38 \\ \times\ 29 \\ \hline \end{array}$
18. $\begin{array}{r} 76 \\ \times 45 \\ \hline \end{array}$
19. $\begin{array}{r} 68 \\ \times 79 \\ \hline \end{array}$
20. $\begin{array}{r} 97 \\ \times 65 \\ \hline \end{array}$
21. $\begin{array}{r} 82 \\ \times 35 \\ \hline \end{array}$
22. $\begin{array}{r} 52 \\ \times 17 \\ \hline \end{array}$
23. $\begin{array}{r} 69 \\ \times 42 \\ \hline \end{array}$
24. $\begin{array}{r} \$53 \\ \times\ 74 \\ \hline \end{array}$
25. $\begin{array}{r} 22 \\ \times 85 \\ \hline \end{array}$
26. $\begin{array}{r} \$71 \\ \times\ 61 \\ \hline \end{array}$

27. 51×28
28. 38×17
29. 23×14
30. 61×51
31. $41 \times \$16$
32. $61 \times \$87$
33. 74×11
34. $76 \times \$68$
35. 14×65
36. 38×55
37. 46×34
38. 63×59

MENTAL MATH Write the missing product.

39. $20 \times 16 = 320$, so $20 \times 17 = ■$.
40. $45 \times 28 = 1{,}260$, so $45 \times 29 = ■$.
41. $13 \times 50 = 650$, so $13 \times 49 = ■$.
42. $45 \times 17 = 765$, so $45 \times 16 = ■$.

Copy and complete.

43. $\begin{array}{rl} 45 & \\ \times 72 & \\ \hline 10 & \leftarrow ■ \times ■ \\ 80 & \leftarrow ■ \times ■ \\ 350 & \leftarrow ■ \times ■ \\ +2\ 800 & \leftarrow ■ \times ■ \\ \hline 3{,}240 & \end{array}$

44. $\begin{array}{rl} 23 & \\ \times 98 & \\ \hline 24 & \leftarrow ■ \times ■ \\ 160 & \leftarrow ■ \times ■ \\ 270 & \leftarrow ■ \times ■ \\ +1\ 800 & \leftarrow ■ \times ■ \\ \hline 2{,}254 & \end{array}$

45. **ALGEBRA** Find the missing numbers. Explain.

$\begin{array}{r} 35 \\ \times 6■ \\ \hline 1■5 \\ +2\ 100 \\ \hline 2{,}275 \end{array}$

46. **What's the Error?** Describe Emilia's error. Write the correct answer.

Emilia

$\begin{array}{r} 64 \\ \times\ 43 \\ \hline 192 \\ +256 \\ \hline 448 \end{array}$

47. **Vocabulary Power** *Partial* means "relating to a part rather than a whole." How does this meaning relate to a partial product when multiplying 2-digit numbers?

48. **REASONING** Is 12×22 greater than or less than 200? Explain.

USE DATA For 49–50, use the graph.

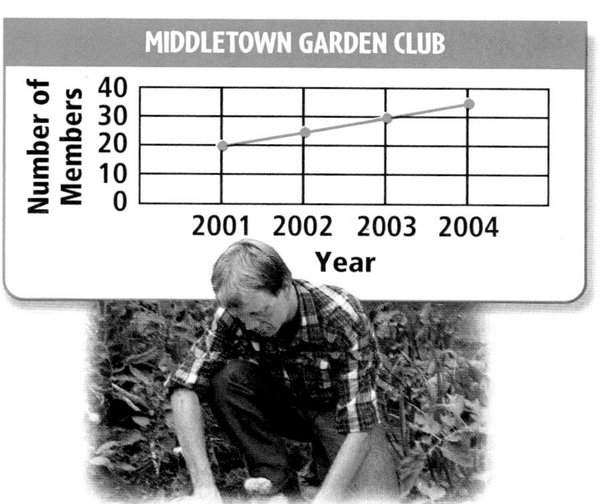

49. Grace and her father belong to a garden club. How many more members were there in 2004 than in 2001?

50. Each member pays $32 in dues each year. How much more was paid in dues in 2004 than in 2002?

51. Ellie rides her bike 22 miles each week for exercise. What is the total number of miles Ellie rides in a year?

Mixed Review and Test Prep

52. $9{,}213 \times 6$ (p. 222)

53. 942×5 (p. 222)

54. One load of laundry in a washing machine uses 49 gallons of water. Mr. Porter washed 17 loads of laundry last month. How much water did he use? (p. 252)

55. What is the median? 18, 19, 19, 26, 28, 35, 35, 40, 42 (p. 118)

56. **TEST PREP** Al has 14 rows of stamps. Each row has 9 stamps. Al's brother has 56 stamps. How many stamps does Al have? (p. 218)

A 94 **B** 126 **C** 182 **D** 443

57. **TEST PREP** Mr. Konrad has 56 tulip bulbs. He plants them in 8 rows with the same number in each row. How many bulbs are in each row? (p. 168)

F 10 **G** 9 **H** 8 **J** 7

Problem Solving LINKUP . . . to Science

NETWORKS A **network** is a system of parts that are connected. For example, computers in an office that are connected are part of a network.

This diagram shows a network of paths. Each path has a value.

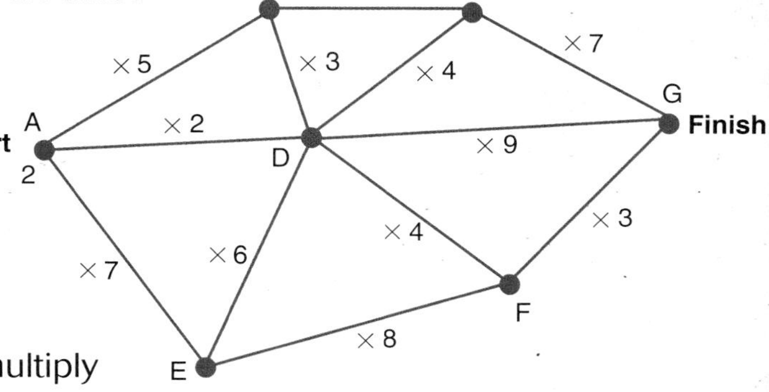

For 1–2, follow these steps.

a. Find a path from **Start** to **Finish.**
b. Begin at Start with the number 2.
c. As you move from letter to letter, multiply your results by the number along the path.

1. Name a path that has a product greater than 500.

2. Name a path that has a product less than 100.

LESSON 2

Multiply 3-Digit Numbers

Quick Review

1. 9 × 40
2. 10 × 30
3. 5 × 50
4. 7 × 20
5. 6 × 200

Learn

WISH YOU WERE HERE Gulfside Gift Shop ordered 36 boxes of postcards to sell. There are 124 postcards in each box. How many postcards does the gift shop have to sell?

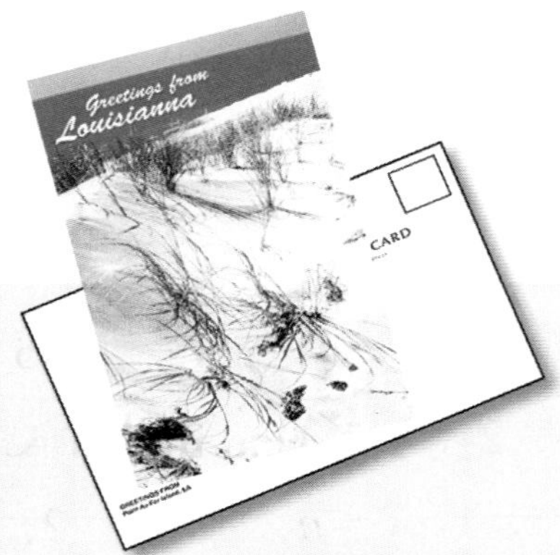

Example

Multiply. 36 × 124

Estimate. 40 × 120 = 4,800

STEP 1

Multiply by the ones.

```
  12
  124
×  36
  744  ← 6 × 124
```

STEP 2

Multiply by the tens.

```
  1
  12
  124
×  36
  744
 3720  ← 30 × 124
```

STEP 3

Add the products.

```
   1
   12
   124
 ×  36
   744
+3 720
 4,464
```

So, Gulfside Gift Shop has 4,464 postcards to sell. Since 4,464 is close to the estimate of 4,800, the answer is reasonable.

More Examples

A

```
     1
   204
 ×  41
   204  ← 1 × 204
+8 160  ← 40 × 204
 8,364
```

B

```
     5
   109
 ×  60       These zeros
                can be
   000  ← omitted.
+6 540  ← 60 × 109
 6,540
```

C

```
      1
      31
    $562
  ×   35
   2 810  ← 5 × 562
+16 860  ← 30 × 562
$19,670
```

Check

1. **Explain** what happened to the regrouped digit, 5, in Example B when the 0 was multiplied by 60.

Find the product. Estimate to check.

2. 237×21 **3.** $\$103 \times 29$ **4.** 187×35 **5.** 417×72 **6.** 532×20

Practice and Problem Solving

Extra Practice, page 264, Set B

Find the product. Estimate to check.

7. 888×22 **8.** $\$794 \times 25$ **9.** 204×41 **10.** 437×70 **11.** $\$837 \times 21$

12. 357×41 **13.** $\$627 \times 30$ **14.** 904×86 **15.** $\$790 \times 32$ **16.** 252×53

17. 23×256 **18.** 52×236 **19.** $85 \times \$299$ **20.** $80 \times \$567$ **21.** 50×108

ALGEBRA Find the value for n that makes the equation true.

22. $20 \times 543 = n$ **23.** $30 \times 147 = n$ **24.** $80 \times 209 = n$

25. $n \times 276 = 2{,}760$ **26.** $n \times 900 = 54{,}000$ **27.** $n \times 500 = 40{,}000$

USE DATA For 28–29, use the graph.

28. Medium fruit baskets sold for $16. What was the total value of sales in December for medium baskets?

29. Small fruit baskets sold for $7. How much more did Fruit Galore make on sales of small fruit baskets in December than in November?

30. Maya bought 12 postcards that cost 57 cents each. How much did Maya spend?

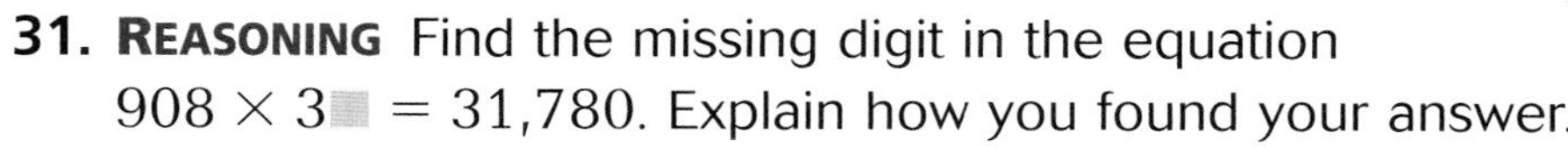

31. **REASONING** Find the missing digit in the equation $908 \times 3\blacksquare = 31{,}780$. Explain how you found your answer.

Mixed Review and Test Prep

32. $3{,}447 + 1{,}725$ (p. 48) **33.** $4{,}007 - 1{,}341$ (p. 50)

34. $60 + (8{,}420 - 1{,}650)$ (p. 64)

35. Compare. Write <, >, or = for ●. (p. 20)
2,076,355 ● 2,085,325

36. **TEST PREP** Peter is 8 years older than Mark. If Mark is 29 years old, how old is Peter? (p. 64)

A 21 years old
B 27 years old
C 31 years old
D 37 years old

LESSON 3

Choose a Method

Quick Review

1. 80 × 100
2. 30 × 40
3. 90 × 70
4. 80 × 600
5. 40 × 700

Learn

FOREIGN EXCHANGE In the United States, the dollar is used. In Venezuela, the bolivar is used. When Elena visited her grandparents in Venezuela last year, one dollar was equal to 1,432 bolivars. If Elena spent 42 dollars on gifts, how many bolivars did she spend?

Example

Multiply. 42 × 1,432

Estimate. 40 × 1,400 = 56,000

Then choose a method of computation that will be useful for the numbers given.

Use Paper and Pencil. Find the product. 42 × 1,432 = ■

STEP 1

Multiply by the ones.

$$\begin{array}{r} 1{,}432 \\ \times \quad 42 \\ \hline 2\,864 \end{array} \leftarrow 2 \times 1{,}432$$

STEP 2

Multiply by the tens.

$$\begin{array}{r} {}^{1\,1} \\ 1{,}432 \\ \times \quad 42 \\ \hline 2\,864 \\ 57\,280 \end{array} \leftarrow 40 \times 1{,}432$$

STEP 3

Add the products.

$$\begin{array}{r} {}^{1\,1} \\ 1{,}432 \\ \times \quad 42 \\ \hline 2\,864 \\ +57\,280 \\ \hline 60{,}144 \end{array}$$

So, Elena spent 60,144 bolivars. Since 60,144 is close to the estimate of 56,000, the answer is reasonable.

More Examples

 **Use Mental Math**

40 × 5,025 = ■

Think: 40 × 5,000 = 200,000
and 40 × 25 = 1,000

So, 40 × 5,025 = 201,000.

 **Use a Calculator**

24 × $3,701 = ■

2 4 × 3 7 0 1 =

88'824.

Estimate to check:
20 × 4,000 = 80,000

So, 24 × $3,701 = $88,824.

 **MATH IDEA** You can find a product by using paper and pencil, a calculator, or mental math. Look at the numbers in the problem before you choose a method.

Check

1. **Explain** when you might choose mental math instead of paper and pencil.

Find the product. Estimate to check. Write the method you used.

2. $\begin{array}{r} 152 \\ \times\ 11 \\ \hline \end{array}$

3. $\begin{array}{r} \$31 \\ \times\ 22 \\ \hline \end{array}$

4. $\begin{array}{r} 1{,}700 \\ \times\ \ \ 5 \\ \hline \end{array}$

5. $\begin{array}{r} \$317 \\ \times\ 72 \\ \hline \end{array}$

6. $\begin{array}{r} 5{,}502 \\ \times\ 24 \\ \hline \end{array}$

Practice and Problem Solving

Extra Practice, page 264, Set C

Find the product. Estimate to check. Write the method you used.

7. $\begin{array}{r} 434 \\ \times\ 28 \\ \hline \end{array}$

8. $\begin{array}{r} \$287 \\ \times\ \ \ 7 \\ \hline \end{array}$

9. $\begin{array}{r} 56 \\ \times\ 60 \\ \hline \end{array}$

10. $\begin{array}{r} \$504 \\ \times\ 31 \\ \hline \end{array}$

11. $\begin{array}{r} 7{,}200 \\ \times\ \ \ 8 \\ \hline \end{array}$

? What's the Error? Exercises 12–15 show 4 different common errors. Describe each error and correct it.

12. $\begin{array}{r} 1{,}274 \\ \times\ \ \ 67 \\ \hline 8\ 918 \\ +\ 7\ 644 \\ \hline 16{,}562 \end{array}$

13. $\begin{array}{r} 5{,}782 \\ \times\ \ \ 88 \\ \hline 40\ 646 \\ +\ 406\ 460 \\ \hline 447{,}106 \end{array}$

14. $\begin{array}{r} 2{,}500 \\ \times\ \ \ 32 \\ \hline 500 \\ +\ 7\ 500 \\ \hline 8{,}000 \end{array}$

15. $\begin{array}{r} 4{,}306 \\ \times\ \ \ 39 \\ \hline 38\ 754 \\ +\ 129\ 180 \\ \hline 157{,}834 \end{array}$

16. A magazine company has 9,822 customers. Each customer is sent 2 issues each month. How many magazines does the company send each year?

17. Elena bought some stamps that cost 70 cents and some postcards that cost 55 cents. She spent $5. How many of each did she buy?

18. **FAST FACT • HEALTH** The recommended serving of water for the average person is 8 glasses a day. How many glasses would that be in a week? in 30 days?

19. **REASONING** Find the product. Explain your method. $\begin{array}{r} 684 \\ \times\ 306 \\ \hline \end{array}$

Mixed Review and Test Prep

Find the product. (p. 240)

20. $\begin{array}{r} 42 \\ \times 20 \\ \hline \end{array}$

21. $\begin{array}{r} 57 \\ \times 30 \\ \hline \end{array}$

22. The river cruise began at 9:15 A.M. and ended at 2:50 P.M. How long was the cruise? (p. 98)

23. $19 \times 27 = n$ (p. 252)

24. **TEST PREP** What year is 2 centuries 1 decade after 1927? (p. 104)

A 1937
B 2027
C 2037
D 2137

LESSON 4

Practice Multiplication Using Money

Quick Review

1. 3 × 72
2. 4 × 49
3. 2 × 96
4. 3 × 86
5. 3 × 93

Learn

BIKE BONANZA Bill owns a bike shop. Last month at his bike sale, Bill sold 24 bikes for $75.99 each. How much did he collect on the sale of these bikes?

Example

Multiply. 24 × $75.99

Estimate. 20 × $80 = $1,600

Multiply money the way you multiply whole numbers.

Technology Link

More Practice: Harcourt Mega Math, The Number Games, *Buggy Bargains*, Level J

STEP 1

Multiply the ones.

```
  233
  7599
×   24
 30396 ←4 × 7,599
```

STEP 2

Multiply the tens.

```
  111
  233
  7599
×   24
 30396
151980 ←20 × 7,599
```

STEP 3

Add the products.

```
   111
   233
   7599
 ×   24
  30396
+151980
 182376
```

STEP 4

Write the answer in dollars and cents. The product is $1,823.76.

So, Bill took in $1,823.76. Since $1,823.76 is close to the estimate of $1,600, the answer is reasonable.

More Examples

A

```
      1
      4
  $4,006
×     27
  28 042 ←7 × 4,006
+80 120  ←20 × 4,006
$108,162
```

B

```
      3
      2
   $5.09
×     43
   15 27 ←3 × 509
 +203 60 ←40 × 509
 $218.87 ←Add decimal point
           and dollar sign.
```

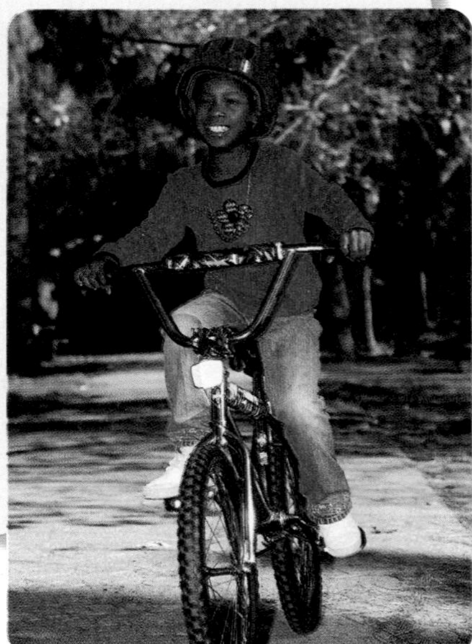

Check

1. **Explain** how you know where to put the decimal point in a money problem.

Find the product. Estimate to check.

2. $\$892 \times 37$
3. $\$5,637 \times 51$
4. $\$25.68 \times 21$
5. $\$2,015 \times 24$
6. $\$48.03 \times 39$

Practice and Problem Solving

Extra Practice, page 264, Set D

Find the product. Estimate to check.

7. $\$1,735 \times 43$
8. $\$0.97 \times 68$
9. $\$37.45 \times 28$
10. $\$2.56 \times 81$
11. $\$1,505 \times 79$

12. $3 \times \$2,954$ 13. $56 \times \$8,221$ 14. $20 \times \$1,076$ 15. $31 \times \$2.25$ 16. $48 \times \$126$

17. $29 \times \$4,151$ 18. $72 \times \$1,407$ 19. $68 \times \$7,521$ 20. $99 \times \$9,998$ 21. $55 \times \$30.63$

ALGEBRA Find the number for n that makes the equation true.

22. $45 \times \$236 = n$ 23. $36 \times \$2,087 = n$ 24. $93 \times \$47 = n$ 25. $68 \times \$795 = n$

26. $24 \times n = \$24,000$ 27. $80 \times n = \$72,000$ 28. $12 \times n = \$1,440$

USE DATA For 29–32, use the table.

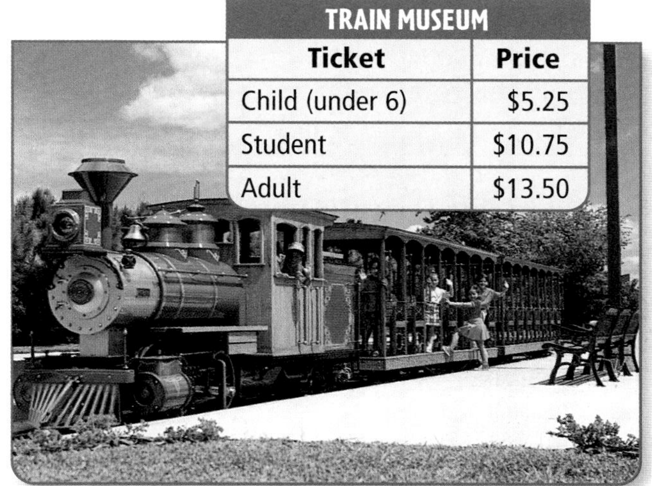

TRAIN MUSEUM	
Ticket	Price
Child (under 6)	$5.25
Student	$10.75
Adult	$13.50

29. How much will Train Museum tickets cost for 25 students?

30. How much more are two adult tickets than two student tickets?

31. Bradley has $15. Can he buy a student ticket and a book that costs $4.50? Explain.

32. **Write a problem** about buying tickets for more than 1 adult and more than 1 student who visit the museum. Show the solution.

Mixed Review and Test Prep

33. $7,805 + 2,678$ (p. 48)

34. $2,900 - 407$ (p. 50)

35. $50,225 + 23,186$ (p. 52)

36. $25,030 - 21,089$ (p. 52)

37. $84,582 + 37,329$ (p. 52)

38. **TEST PREP** Rachel scored 15 points and then some more points. By the end of the basketball game, she had scored 32 points. Which equation describes the situation? (p. 70)

A $15 - p = 32$
B $15 + p = 32$
C $32 + 15 = p$
D $p - 15 = 32$

LESSON 5

Problem Solving Skill
Multistep Problems

UNDERSTAND | PLAN | SOLVE | CHECK

Quick Review

1. 4×217
2. 2×340
3. 2×497
4. 3×526
5. 3×705

VOCABULARY
multistep problem

REACH YOUR GOAL The soccer players sold bottles of water to earn money for equipment. They charged $2.25 for each bottle of water. They sold 52 bottles on Saturday and 45 bottles on Sunday. How much money did they collect?

MATH IDEA Sometimes it takes more than one step to solve a problem. To solve **multistep problems**, decide *what* the steps are and *in what order* you should do them.

Example

To find how much money the soccer players collected, multiply the total number of bottles sold by $2.25.

STEP 1

Add to find the total number of bottles sold.

$$\begin{array}{r l} 52 & \leftarrow \text{bottles sold on Saturday} \\ +45 & \leftarrow \text{bottles sold on Sunday} \\ \hline 97 & \end{array}$$

The players sold 97 bottles of water.

STEP 2

Multiply to find the amount of money collected.

$$\begin{array}{r l} \$2.25 & \leftarrow \text{price for each bottle} \\ \times \quad 97 & \leftarrow \text{total number of bottles} \\ \hline \$218.25 & \end{array}$$

So, the players collected $218.25.

Talk About It

- Could you use the equation $(52 + 45) \times \$2.25 = n$ to solve the problem? Explain.
- Would you get the same answer if you first multiplied $52 \times \$2.25$ and $45 \times \$2.25$ and then added the two products? Explain.

Problem Solving Practice

1. **What if** the soccer players had charged $3.25 for each bottle of water they sold? How much more money would they have collected?

2. The soccer coach bought 12 new uniforms for $17.25 each and 6 soccer balls for $8.25 each. How much did he spend in all?

USE DATA For 3–4, use the table.

During soccer season, Darren's Snack Bar sells lunches. Darren kept this record of the number of items sold at last Saturday's game.

DARREN'S SNACK BAR - *Specials*

Item	Price	Number Sold
Fruit Salad	$2.59	33
Turkey Sandwich	$5.87	29
Veggie Sandwich	$4.38	18
Chicken Soup	$1.39	15
Chocolate Pie	$1.21	12

3. Which equation can you use to find the amount of money Darren took in from the sale of fruit salads and turkey sandwiches?
   A $\$2.59 + \$5.87 = n$
   B $(\$2.59 \times 33) + (\$5.87 \times 29) = n$
   C $(\$2.59 \times 33) - (\$5.87 \times 29) = n$
   D $(\$2.59 + \$5.87) \times (33 + 29) = n$

4. How much more money did Darren take in from the sale of fruit salads than from the sale of veggie sandwiches?
   F $4.37 more
   G $4.43 more
   H $6.63 more
   J $17.43 more

Mixed Applications

5. Mrs. Ling had a bucket of crayons. She gave 14 crayons to each of 21 students. If 131 crayons were left in the bucket, how many crayons were there to start?

6. Norman spent $15.00 on a pizza and 2 salads. The pizza cost twice as much as the 2 salads. What was the price of each item?

7. Tommy and Helen were playing a game. First Helen picked a number and added 4. Then she multiplied by 6. Last she subtracted 3. The result was 51. What number did Helen pick?

8. Harry, Eli, Macy, and Sandy are standing in line at the movies. Harry is just behind Eli. Macy is between Harry and Sandy. Who is first in line?

9. Band members practice from 3:00 P.M. to 5:00 P.M. twice a week. For how many hours do they practice in 4 weeks?

10. **Write a problem** that requires more than two steps to solve. Show the solution.

Extra Practice

Set A (pp. 252–255)

Choose a method to find the product. Estimate to check.

1. 71×64
2. $\$29 \times 23$
3. 92×33
4. 89×16
5. 46×96
6. 14×36
7. 22×81
8. $\$45 \times 15$
9. 93×39
10. 45×67

Set B (pp. 256–257)

Find the product. Estimate to check.

1. $\$226 \times 65$
2. 547×53
3. 924×38
4. 839×22
5. 409×28
6. 91×682
7. $59 \times \$474$
8. 47×567
9. 38×106
10. 35×750

Set C (pp. 258–259)

Find the product. Estimate to check. Write the method you used.

1. 325×4
2. $9{,}234 \times 9$
3. 805×66
4. $\$3{,}782 \times 21$
5. $7{,}760 \times 48$
6. $76 \times 6{,}432$
7. $4 \times 1{,}210$
8. $26 \times 7{,}031$
9. 37×108
10. $18 \times 5{,}160$

Set D (pp. 260–261)

Find the product. Estimate to check.

1. $\$19 \times 66$
2. $\$74 \times 76$
3. $\$805 \times 45$
4. $\$1{,}249 \times 64$
5. $\$3.95 \times 25$
6. $\$57 \times 20$
7. $\$8{,}019 \times 50$
8. $\$454 \times 18$
9. $\$7.68 \times 90$
10. $\$56.10 \times 32$

11. Lily bought 15 tickets to a concert. Each ticket cost \$27.75. How much did she spend?

12. The swim team sold shirts for a fund-raiser. If the team members sold 68 shirts for \$12.95 each, how much did they raise?

Review/Test

CHECK VOCABULARY AND CONCEPTS

Choose the best term from the box.

multistep problem
estimate
partial products
ones

1. A _?_ requires two or more steps to find the solution. (p. 262)
2. To check whether your answer is reasonable, compare the answer to the _?_. (p. 252)
3. When multiplying by two-digit numbers, you add the _?_ to get the final product. (p. 253)

CHECK SKILLS

Find the product. Estimate to check. (pp. 252–261)

4. 39×16
5. 54×33
6. $\$143 \times 62$
7. 472×73
8. 92×58
9. $\$0.61 \times 29$
10. $2{,}303 \times 67$
11. $8{,}845 \times 53$
12. 67×82
13. $\$297 \times 34$
14. $9{,}709 \times 36$
15. $\$62.11 \times 85$
16. 604×55
17. 253×31
18. $\$43.26 \times 41$
19. $\$7{,}132 \times 18$
20. $5{,}853 \times 24$
21. 77×46
22. 935×25
23. 720×99

CHECK PROBLEM SOLVING

Solve. (pp. 262–263)

24. Josh plays on a bowling team. There are 13 players. If 5 players scored an average of 145 each and 8 players scored an average of 134 each, what is the average total score of the team?
25. The deli ordered 25 boxes of napkins. Each box holds 275 napkins. How many more napkins would the store have gotten if there had been 29 boxes?

Standardized Test Prep

NUMBER SENSE, CONCEPTS, AND OPERATIONS

 **Decide on a plan.**

See item 1. Think about which operation would be needed to solve the problem. Then find the expression that shows it.

1. Eagle Elementary School has 3 fourth-grade classes. There are 22 students in each class. Which expression could be used to find the number of fourth-grade students in Eagle Elementary School?

   A $22 + 3$ **C** 22×3

   B $22 - 3$ **D** $22 \div 3$

2. Which multiplication fact could you use to help you find $60 \div 12$?

   F $12 \times 60 = 720$

   G $2 \times 30 = 60$

   H $6 \times 10 = 60$

   J $12 \times 5 = 60$

3. **Explain It** The graph shows the number of used cars sold for 4 weeks.

USED CAR LOT	
Week	**Number of Cars Sold**
1	4
2	6
3	4
4	5

   About how many cars does the used car lot sell in 12 weeks? Explain your answer.

MEASUREMENT

4. Jenny wants to know the temperature outside. Which tool should she use?

   A Ruler

   B  Thermometer

   C Bathroom scale

   D  Measuring cup

5. Which of these would be **best** to measure the length of a desk?

   F Centimeter ruler

   G  Thermometer

   H  Balance

   J 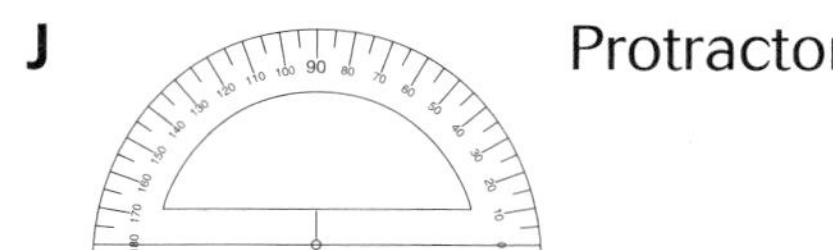 Protractor

6. **Explain It** About how many pounds does the kitten weigh?

   Explain your thinking.

GEOMETRY AND SPATIAL SENSE

7. Which triangle appears to have one right angle?

A

B

C

D

8. Which shapes have the same perimeter?

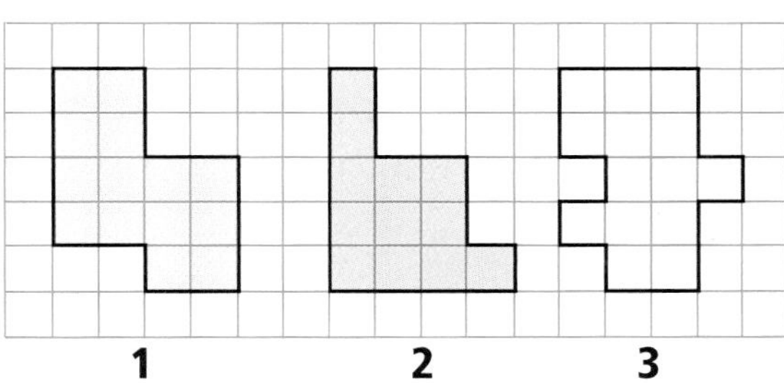

F 1 and 2

G 1 and 3

H 2 and 3

J 1, 2, and 3

9. **Explain It** Marla has a solid figure. It has six flat faces. Four faces are rectangles. Two faces are squares. What is the name of Marla's solid figure? Write *cone*, *cylinder*, *cube*, or *rectangular prism*. Explain how you decided.

DATA ANALYSIS AND PROBABILITY

10. The line graph shows the number of students who bought school lunches during one school week.

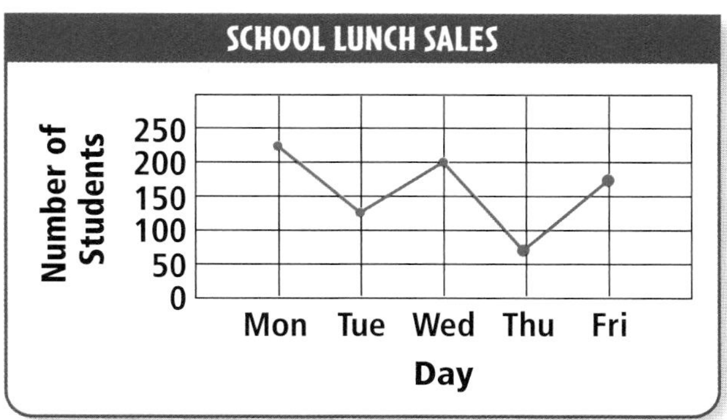

On which day did the **greatest** number of students buy lunch?

A Monday

B Tuesday

C Thursday

D Friday

11. If one card is picked without looking, which number is **most likely** to be picked?

3	1	4	2	4	1	4	4

F 1 **H** 3

G 2 **J** 4

12. **Explain It** Mr. Ramirez asked a group of fourth-graders to choose their favorite subject. Math got 8 votes, science got 12 votes, and social studies got 5 votes. Make a graph to display the data. Tell why you chose the graph you did.

IT'S IN THE BAG

Magnetic Multiplication

PROJECT Practice multiplying by using magnetic numbers kept in a metal box.

Materials

- 1 small metal box
- 1 roll of $\frac{1}{2}$ inch magnetic tape
- Markers (1 permanent)
- Number strip sheet
- Colored paper
- Glue
- Scissors
- Ruler

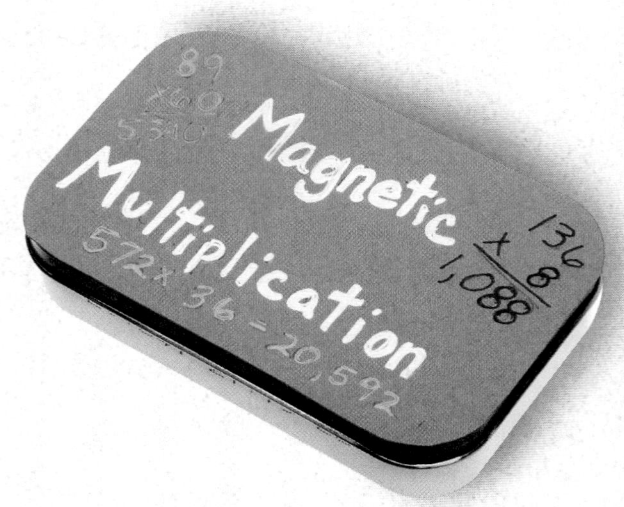

Directions

1. Cut out number strips. Attach each strip to the sticky side of the magnetic tape.

2. Cut along the lines to make magnetic tiles. Put all the tiles into the deep side of the metal box. *(Picture A)*

3. Turn the box so it is vertical. Inside the lid measure up $\frac{1}{2}$ inch from the bottom, and draw a horizontal line with a permanent marker. Measure up 1 inch from that line, and draw another horizontal line. Use markers and a sheet of colored paper to title and decorate the outside of the lid. *(Picture B)*

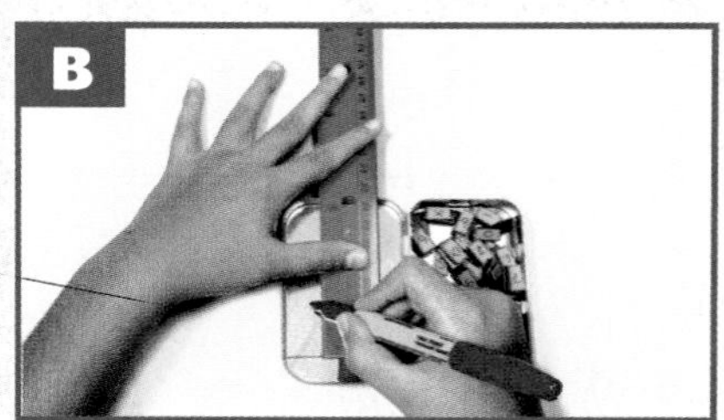

4. Pick numbers out of the box to make the two factors of your multiplication problem. Don't forget the X sign. Place your problem above the top line drawn on the lid. Work the problems in the lid as you would on paper. With a partner, take turns giving each other problems to solve. *(Picture C)*

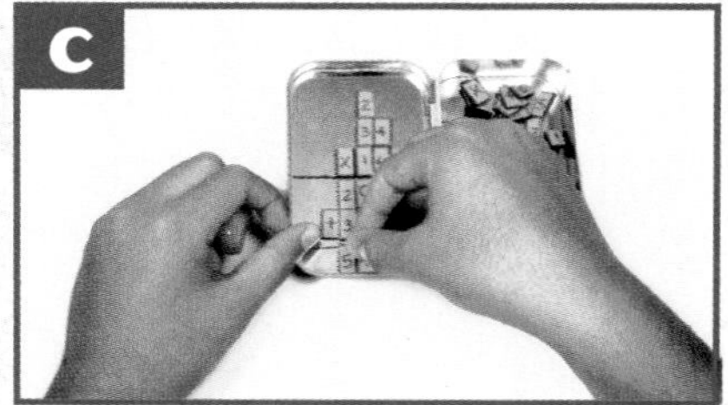

Challenge

Mental Multiplication

Hammond's Instruments has trumpets on sale. If Jim's family pays $99 a month for 5 months, how much will the trumpet cost in all?

Here are two ways to use the Distributive Property to find products.

Find 5×99.

One Way Use addition.

Think: $99 is $90 plus $9.

$$\begin{aligned} 5 \times 99 &= 5 \times (90 + 9) \\ &= (5 \times 90) + (5 \times 9) \\ &= 450 + 45 \\ &= 495 \end{aligned}$$

Another Way Use subtraction.

Think: $99 is $1 less than $100.

$$\begin{aligned} 5 \times 99 &= 5 \times (100 - 1) \\ &= (5 \times 100) - (5 \times 1) \\ &= 500 - 5 \\ &= 495 \end{aligned}$$

So, the trumpet will cost $495.

More Examples

A 8×74

Think: 74 is 70 plus 4.

$$\begin{aligned} 8 \times 74 &= 8 \times (70 + 4) \\ &= (8 \times 70) + (8 \times 4) \\ &= 560 + 32 \\ &= 592 \end{aligned}$$

B 3×146

Think: 146 is 4 less than 150.

$$\begin{aligned} 3 \times 146 &= 3 \times (150 - 4) \\ &= (3 \times 150) - (3 \times 4) \\ &= 450 - 12 \\ &= 438 \end{aligned}$$

Try It

Use the Distributive Property to find each product.

1. 5×49	**2.** 2×85	**3.** $7 \times \$25$	**4.** 78×3	**5.** 8×99
6. 8×17	**7.** 58×6	**8.** $2 \times \$39$	**9.** 29×9	**10.** $\$65 \times 3$
11. 197×8	**12.** $7 \times \$49$	**13.** 598×9	**14.** $\$59 \times 4$	**15.** $4 \times \$146$

Study Guide and Review

VOCABULARY

Choose the best term from the box.

compatible numbers
Distributive Property
estimate

1. Numbers that are easy to compute mentally are __?__. (p. 216)
2. The __?__ states that multiplying a sum by a number is the same as multiplying each addend in the sum by the number and then adding the products. (p. 238)

STUDY AND SOLVE

Chapter 10

Write products of multidigit numbers multiplied by one-digit numbers.

$$\begin{array}{r} \scriptstyle 2\,3 \\ 259 \\ \times \quad 4 \\ \hline 1{,}036 \end{array}$$

- Multiply the ones. 4 × 9 = 36 Regroup.
- Multiply the tens. 4 × 5 = 20 Regroup.
- Multiply the hundreds. 4 × 2 = 8

Multiply. (pp. 218–227)

3. 61×2
4. 398×5
5. $2{,}608 \times 4$
6. $5{,}312 \times 3$
7. $\begin{array}{r} 406 \\ \times \quad 9 \\ \hline \end{array}$
8. $\begin{array}{r} 2{,}060 \\ \times \quad 6 \\ \hline \end{array}$
9. $\begin{array}{r} \$63.32 \\ \times \quad 8 \\ \hline \end{array}$
10. $\begin{array}{r} \$70.86 \\ \times \quad 7 \\ \hline \end{array}$

Chapter 11

Multiply by tens.

$$\begin{array}{r} 72 \\ \times\ 40 \\ \hline 2{,}880 \end{array}$$

- Multiply by the ones. 0 ones × 72 = 0 Place a zero in the ones place.
- Multiply by the tens. 4 tens × 72 = 2,880

Find the product. (pp. 240–241)

11. 15×10
12. 26×20
13. 74×30
14. 51×40
15. $\begin{array}{r} 92 \\ \times 60 \\ \hline \end{array}$
16. $\begin{array}{r} 49 \\ \times 50 \\ \hline \end{array}$
17. $\begin{array}{r} 33 \\ \times 80 \\ \hline \end{array}$
18. $\begin{array}{r} 67 \\ \times 70 \\ \hline \end{array}$

Chapter 12

Multiply two-digit numbers.

$$\begin{array}{r l} {}^{1}72 & \\ \times 46 & \\ \hline 432 & \leftarrow 6 \times 72 \\ +2\,880 & \leftarrow 40 \times 72 \\ \hline 3{,}312 & \end{array}$$

- Multiply the ones.
- Multiply the tens.
- Add the products.

Find the product. (pp. 252–255)

19. 84×68

20. 93×48

21. 705×27

22. 259×65

23. 51×24

24. 895×39

Multiply greater numbers.

$$\begin{array}{r l} {}^{2\ \ 4}5{,}407 & \\ \times \quad 61 & \\ \hline 5\,407 & \leftarrow 1 \times 5{,}407 \\ +324\,420 & \leftarrow 60 \times 5{,}407 \\ \hline 329{,}827 & \end{array}$$

- Multiply the ones.
- Multiply the tens.
- Add the products.

Find the product. (pp. 256–259)

25. $5{,}904 \times 64$

26. $6{,}007 \times 81$

27. $8{,}753 \times 26$

28. $1{,}098 \times 79$

29. $\$65.09 \times 75$

30. $\$72.16 \times 52$

PROBLEM SOLVING PRACTICE

Solve. (pp. 228–229, 244–245, 262–263)

31. There were 246 people at the arcade and each person won 20 tickets. How many total tickets were won? Use a simpler problem to solve.

32. Martina walks 15 minutes in the morning, 15 minutes in the afternoon, and 45 minutes in the evening. If she walks every day for 30 days, for how many minutes will she walk?

33. Chris borrowed 6 history videos to watch for homework. Each video was 75 minutes long. Write an equation to show how long it would take to watch all the videos. Solve.

34. Mr. Uri bought shirts for his daughter's basketball team. There were 14 girls on the team. Each shirt cost $12.48. How much did Mr. Uri spend on the shirts?

PERFORMANCE ASSESSMENT

TASK A • FISH STORY

Andy received an aquarium for his birthday.
He read these directions for setting up the aquarium.

- Add between 7 and 10 pounds of gravel.
- Add 4 or 5 plants.
- Add your choice of fish.

Andy has saved $35.00 to buy gravel, plants, and fish for the aquarium. He wants to have at least two of each kind of fish he chooses.

AQUARIUM SUPPLIES	
Supply	**Price**
Gravel	$0.65 per pound
Plants	$3.25 each

FISH FOR SALE	
Fish	**Price Per Fish**
Tetra	$1.79
Platy	$2.19
Molly	$2.99

a. Estimate a total cost for gravel and plants. Then use estimation to make a list of the numbers and kinds of fish that Andy could buy so that supplies and fish together cost $35.00 or less.

b. What is the actual total cost of the items you chose?

c. Explain how you can use multiplication to help you solve this problem.

TASK B • SPEED WRITING

MATERIALS: stopwatch or clock with second hand

This task is a contest to see who can write the fastest.

a. With a partner timing you, write the word *math* as many times as you can in one minute. Then count and record the number of times you wrote *math*.

b. If you continued to write at this rate, how many times could you write the word *math* in 30 minutes? How many times could you write the word *math* in 2 hours?

c. Use what you found out in part b to explain how to predict the number of times you could write the word *multiply* in 45 minutes.

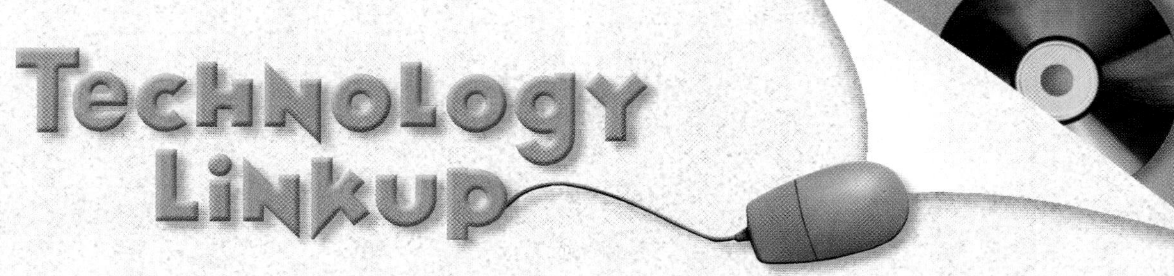

Calculator • Number Patterns

Steve makes a number pattern. His rule is: add 17 and then multiply by 3. The first number in the pattern is 1. What are the next three numbers in the pattern?

Use the TI-15 calculator to extend number patterns.

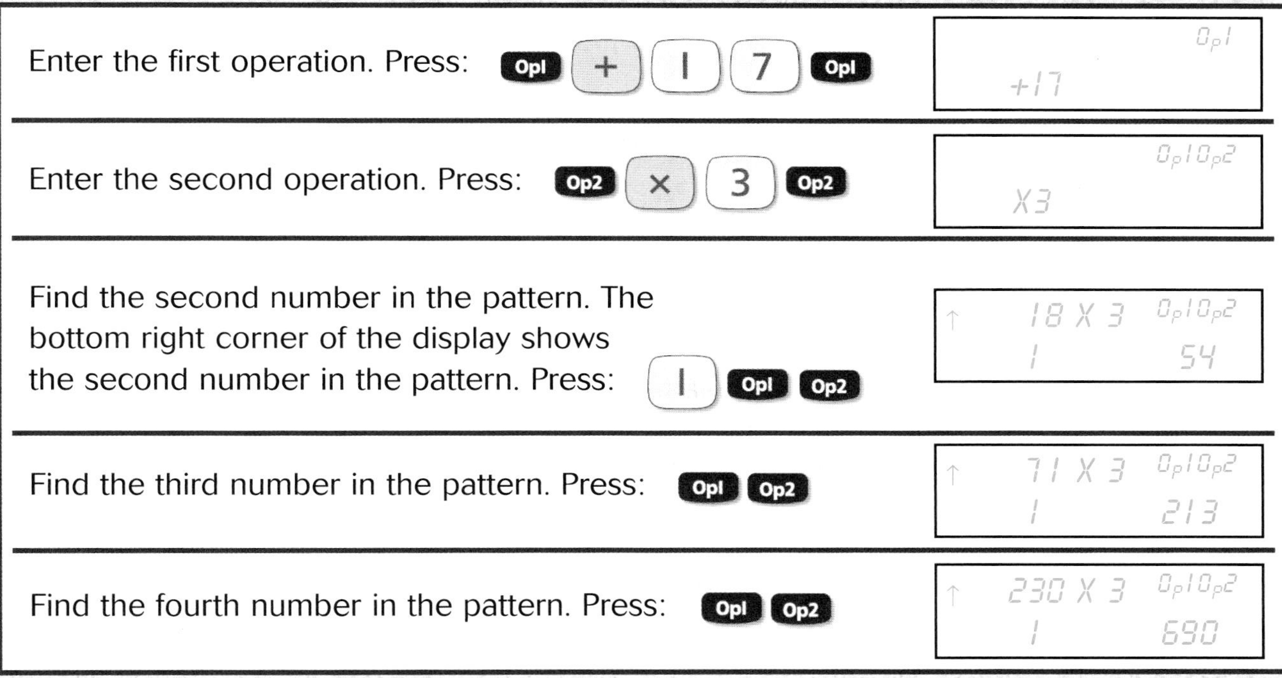

Enter the first operation. Press: Opl + 1 7 Opl
Opl
+17
Enter the second operation. Press: Op2 × 3 Op2
Op1Op2
X3
Find the second number in the pattern. The bottom right corner of the display shows the second number in the pattern. Press: 1 Opl Op2
18 X 3 Op1Op2
1 54
Find the third number in the pattern. Press: Opl Op2
71 X 3 Op1Op2
1 213
Find the fourth number in the pattern. Press: Opl Op2
230 X 3 Op1Op2
1 690

So, the next three numbers in the pattern are 54, 213, and 690.

Try It

Use the TI-15 keys to find the next three numbers in the pattern.

1. **rule:** add 7 and then multiply by 2
   first number: 2
2. **rule:** subtract 30 and then divide by 4
   first number: 1,000
3. **Write a problem** that uses a rule for a pattern. Include two operations. List the first five numbers in your pattern.

TIP Before entering a new rule, clear the stored operations.

GO ON-LINE **Multimedia Math Glossary**
www.harcourtschool.com/mathglossary
Vocabulary Power Look up *multistep problem* in the Multimedia Math Glossary. Write a problem that can be answered by using the example.

PROBLEM SOLVING ON LOCATION

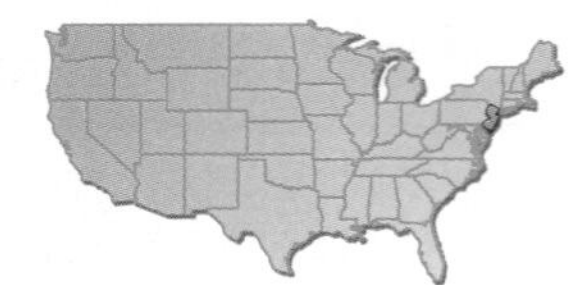

in New Jersey

HIKING AND BIKING

New Jersey is the fifth-smallest state in the United States. The scenery in New Jersey includes mountains, valleys, rivers, and beaches. There are outdoor activities for people of all ages.

▲ **Preserved sand dunes near the New Jersey shore**

1. Leslie, Joanne, and Will plan to hike for 3 hours in Allamuchy State Park. Each of them brings 8 ounces of water for each hour they plan to hike. Write an equation you can use to show how much water they bring altogether. Solve the equation.

2. José rides his bike on the Old Mine Road in the Delaware Water Gap. He bikes at an average speed of 19 miles per hour. Will it take him more or less than 2 hours to bike the 37-mile round trip trail? Explain how you know.

3. The members of the Outdoor Club are hiking in High Point State Park. They average a speed of 3 miles per hour. They would like to hike a total of 16 hours over two days. Will they be able to complete 50 miles of hiking? Explain how you know.

4. Wawayanda State Park is one of the best places to go mountain biking. Suppose mountain bikes can be rented for $5.25 per hour or $20 per day. If you want to ride a mountain bike for 3 hours, would it be less expensive to rent by the hour or by the day? Explain how you know.

CANOEING AND ROCK CLIMBING

Canoeing and rock climbing are also popular outdoor activities in New Jersey.

1. Visitors like to canoe on the Delaware River in the Delaware Water Gap. What if 2-hour canoe rentals cost $35 and a group of visitors rents 8 canoes for 2 hours? Write an equation you can use to find the total cost. What is the total cost?

2. Cindy leads a group on a trip along Cedar Swamp Creek. There are 3 people in each of 19 canoes. Cindy is alone in her canoe. Write an equation you can use to find the number of people in all. Solve the equation.

USE DATA For 3–5, use the table.

3. Two good climbs in the Delaware Water Gap are called Heights of Madness and Morning Sickness. If the rental shop rents 54 pairs of rock-climbing shoes and 45 backpacks, how much will it collect in rental fees?

RENTAL EQUIPMENT

Item	Price
rock-climbing shoes	$6
backpack	$8
sleeping bag	$10

4. How much will it cost a family of four if each member rents rock-climbing shoes, a backpack, and a sleeping bag?

5. Suppose the shop clerk collects $320 from a group in rental fees for rock-climbing shoes, backpacks, and sleeping bags. What is one possible group of items that might have been rented?

▼ **The Delaware River makes an S-shaped curve between New Jersey and Pennsylvania. This area is known as the Delaware Water Gap.**

CHAPTER 13 Understand Division

BEROE'S MIGRATION

Source: Sea Turtle Survival League

Months	Distance Swum
July–Aug	800 km
Sept–Oct	200 km
Nov–Dec	400 km

FAST FACT • SCIENCE Atlantic green turtles migrate hundreds, sometimes thousands, of kilometers between their feeding grounds and nesting beaches.

PROBLEM SOLVING The table shows the approximate number of kilometers that Beroe, an Atlantic green turtle, swam from July to December of 2001. About how many kilometers did Beroe swim each week during November and December?

Atlantic green turtle

CHECK WHAT YOU KNOW

Use this page to help you review and remember important skills needed for Chapter 13.

DIVISION FACTS

Write the division fact that each picture represents.

1. 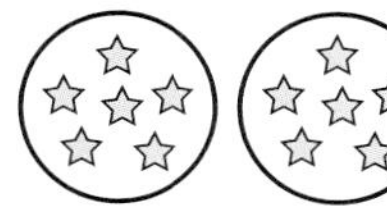  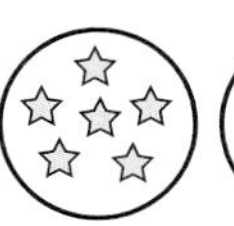

2. 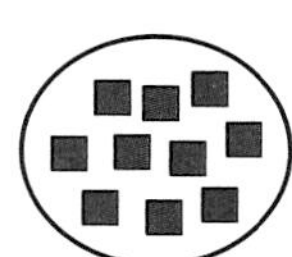 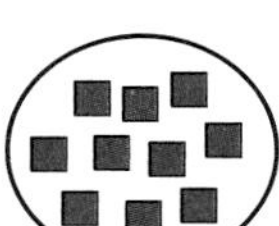

3. 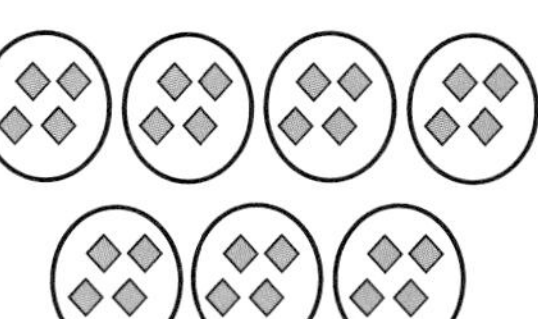

4.  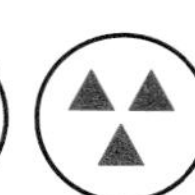 

5. 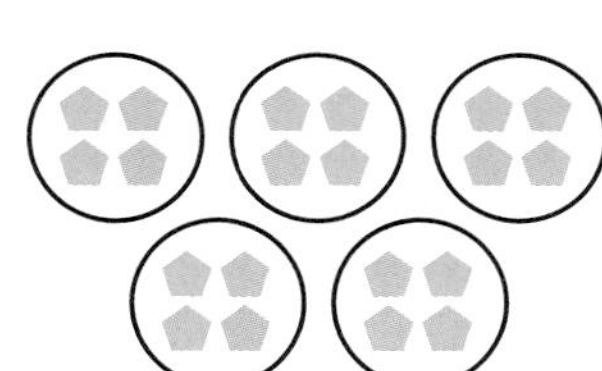

6. 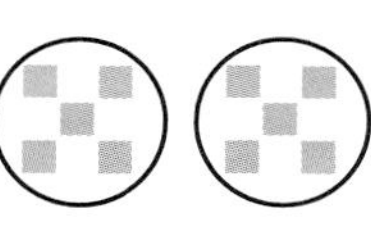

FIND THE QUOTIENT

Find the quotient.

7. 30 ÷ 5	**8.** 28 ÷ 7	**9.** 72 ÷ 9	**10.** 54 ÷ 6
11. 48 ÷ 8	**12.** 24 ÷ 3	**13.** 14 ÷ 2	**14.** 36 ÷ 9
15. 12 ÷ 4	**16.** 81 ÷ 9	**17.** 40 ÷ 8	**18.** 42 ÷ 6

VOCABULARY POWER

REVIEW

quotient [kwō′shənt] *noun*

Quotient contains the root word *quot,* meaning "how many." Think about what the quotient is in a division problem. Use this information to write a definition for *quotient.*

PREVIEW

remainder

www.harcourtschool.com/mathglossary

LESSON 1

Divide with Remainders

Quick Review

1. 8×4
2. $15 \div 3$
3. 3×7
4. 6×4
5. $32 \div 4$

VOCABULARY

remainder

Learn

MODEL IT! Rico has 19 model airplanes to put on some shelves. What is the greatest number of airplanes that he can put on each of 3 shelves? How many airplanes will be left over?

Sometimes a number cannot be divided evenly. The amount left over is called the **remainder.**

HANDS ON

Activity

MATERIALS: counters

Make a model to divide 19 by 3. Write $19 \div 3$ or $3\overline{)19}$.

STEP 1

Use 19 counters. Write: $3\overline{)19}$

STEP 2

Draw three circles. Divide the 19 counters into 3 equal groups.

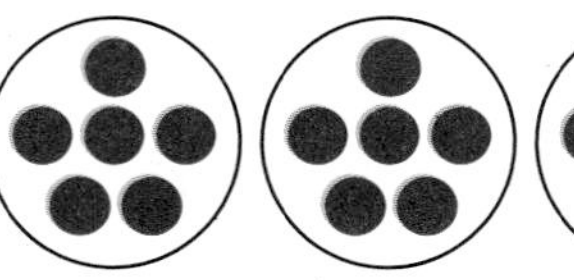

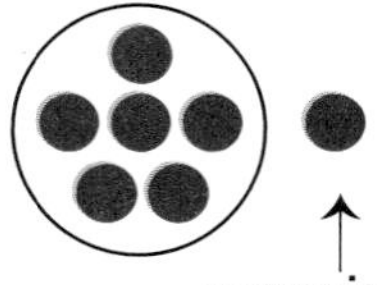

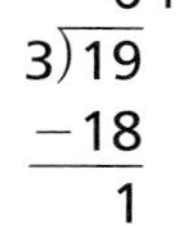

remainder

Record:

$$\begin{array}{r} 6 \text{ r}1 \\ 3\overline{)19} \\ -18 \\ \hline 1 \end{array}$$

The quotient is 6. The remainder is 1.
So, $19 \div 3 = 6$ r1.

So, Rico can put 6 airplanes on each shelf. There will be 1 airplane left over.

MATH IDEA The remainder is a number that is less than the divisor.

Check

1. **Explain** why the answer could not be 5 r4 for the model in the activity.

Make a model, record, and solve.

2. $15 \div 2$ **3.** $20 \div 3$ **4.** $22 \div 4$ **5.** $37 \div 6$

Practice and Problem Solving

Extra Practice, page 290, Set A

Make a model, record, and solve.

6. $29 \div 3$ **7.** $35 \div 4$ **8.** $57 \div 8$ **9.** $45 \div 6$

Divide. You may wish to use counters.

10. $13 \div 4$ **11.** $65 \div 7$ **12.** $30 \div 4$ **13.** $39 \div 5$

14. $3\overline{)28}$ **15.** $4\overline{)37}$ **16.** $5\overline{)42}$ **17.** $5\overline{)49}$

18. $23 \div 4$ **19.** $75 \div 8$ **20.** $29 \div 4$ **21.** $53 \div 7$

22. $2\overline{)17}$ **23.** $5\overline{)22}$ **24.** $6\overline{)47}$ **25.** $4\overline{)26}$

26. $8\overline{)44}$ **27.** $4\overline{)19}$ **28.** $3\overline{)28}$ **29.** $7\overline{)38}$

30. Summer camp has 49 campers. If the campers are divided into 5 equal groups, how many campers are in each group? How many are left over?

31. ***FAST FACT*** • **SPORTS** Sammy Sosa hit a record-setting 20 home runs in June 1998. If there were 4 weeks in June, what is the average number of home runs he hit each week?

32. I am an even, 4-digit number that has more ones than tens. My thousands digit is the quotient $9 \div 3$ and my tens digit is the sum of 3 and 3. I have no hundreds. What number am I?

33. **What's the Error?** Bryan made this model for $4\overline{)23}$. Describe his error. Draw a correct model.

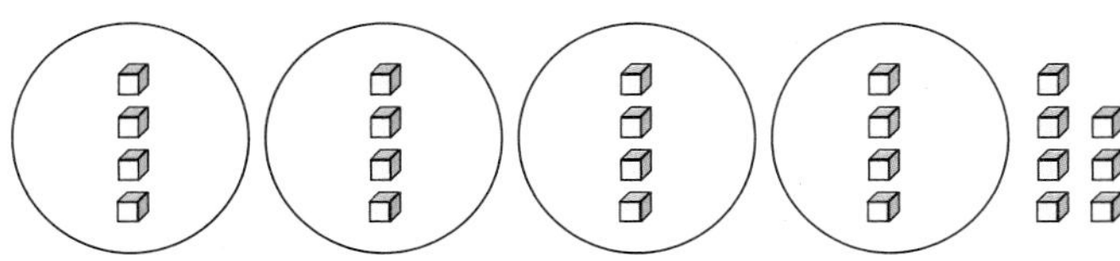

Technology Link

More Practice: Harcourt Mega Math The Number Games, *Up, Up, and Array*, Level L

Mixed Review and Test Prep

Compare. Use < or > for each ●. (p. 168)

34. 9×3 ● 6×4

35. $42 \div 7$ ● $56 \div 8$

36. 328×4 (p. 222) **37.** 295×3 (p. 222)

38. **TEST PREP** The model castle has 2 floors with 14 doors on each floor, 3 floors with 12 doors on each floor, and 1 floor with 10 doors. How many doors are in the castle? (p. 262)

A 36 **C** 74
B 41 **D** 89

LESSON 2

Model Division

Quick Review

1. 4×3
2. $20 \div 5$
3. $12 \div 2$
4. 3×6
5. $16 \div 4$

MATERIALS
base-ten blocks

Explore

TAKE A LOOK! The Berkshire Museum has pictures of 48 extinct animals in 3 different rooms. Each room has the same number of pictures. How many pictures are in each room?

Activity 1

Divide 48 into 3 equal groups. Write $48 \div 3$ or $3\overline{)48}$.
Make a model to show how many are in each group.

STEP 1 Show 48 as 4 tens 8 ones. Draw circles to make 3 equal groups.

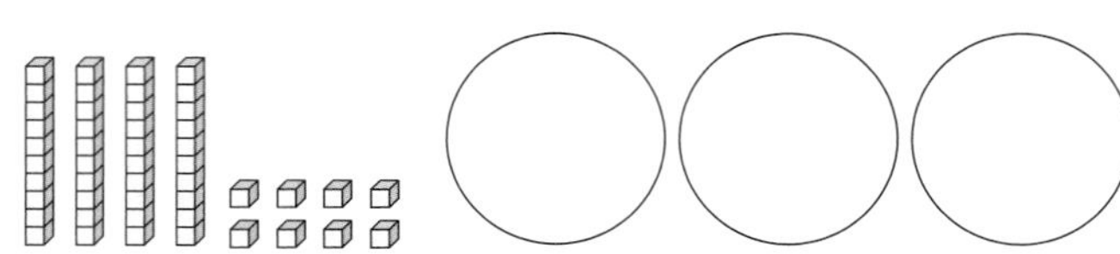

STEP 2 Place an equal number of tens into each group.

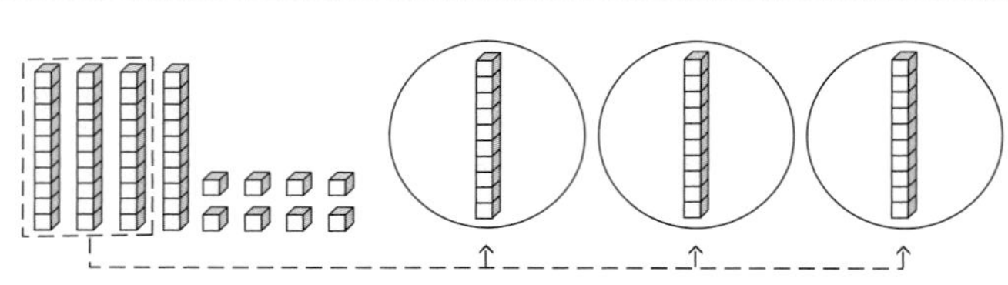

STEP 3 Regroup 1 ten 8 ones as 18 ones. Place an equal number of ones into each group.

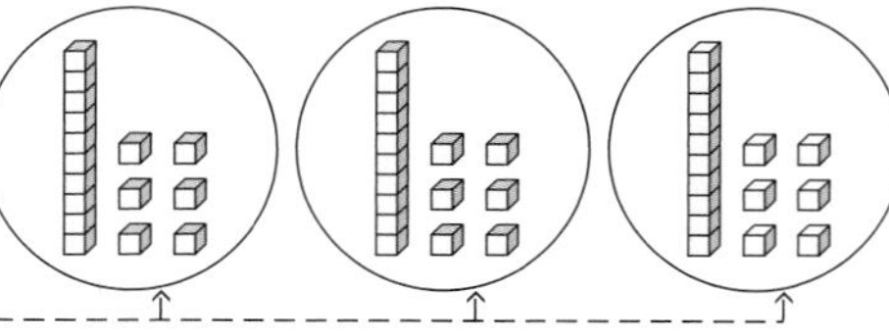

So, there are 16 pictures in each room.

- How many groups did you make?
- How many are in each group?

Try It

Model. Tell how many are in each group.

a. $26 \div 2$ **b.** $42 \div 3$ **c.** $64 \div 4$

We have modeled 26. How many circles should we draw to show 26 ÷ 2?

Connect

Activity 2

Here is a way to record division. Divide 57 by 2.

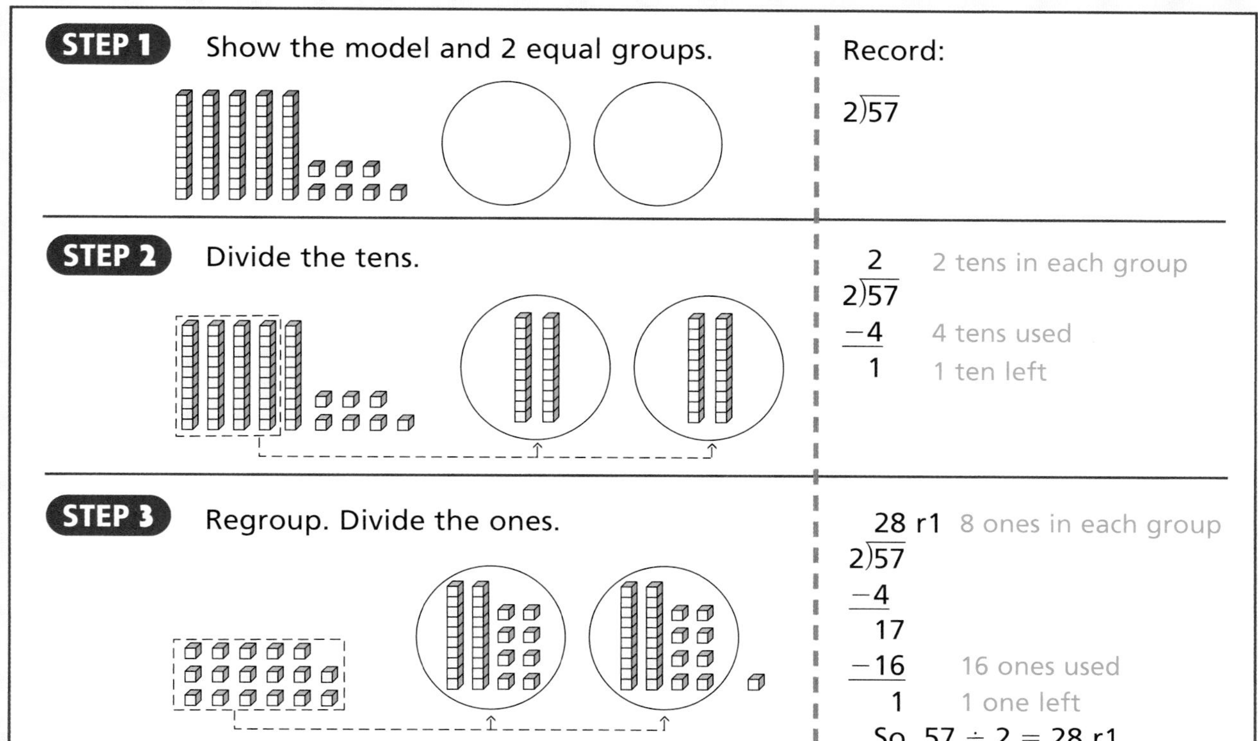

STEP 1 Show the model and 2 equal groups.
Record:
2)57
STEP 2 Divide the tens.
2
2)57
−4
1
2 tens in each group
4 tens used
1 ten left
STEP 3 Regroup. Divide the ones.
28 r1
2)57
−4
17
−16
1
8 ones in each group
16 ones used
1 one left
So, 57 ÷ 2 = 28 r1.

Read: 57 divided by 2 equals 28 remainder 1.

Practice and Problem Solving

Make or draw a model. Record and solve.

1. $35 \div 2$ **2.** $45 \div 3$ **3.** $49 \div 4$ **4.** $47 \div 2$ **5.** $72 \div 6$

6. $7\overline{)88}$ **7.** $3\overline{)56}$ **8.** $6\overline{)78}$ **9.** $5\overline{)66}$ **10.** $4\overline{)72}$

11. **What's the Error?** Emily made this model for $3\overline{)42}$. Describe her error. Draw a correct model.

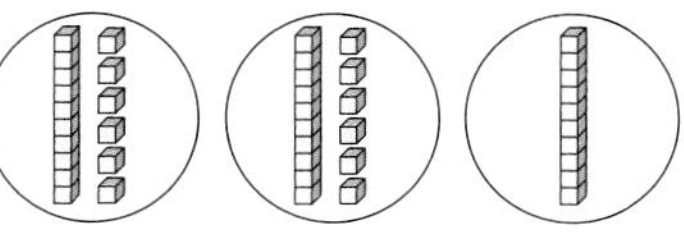

Mixed Review and Test Prep

12. $1{,}909 - 287$ (p. 48)

13. 136×9 (p. 222)

14. $9\overline{)81}$ (p. 168)

15. $2{,}368 + 7{,}416$ (p. 48)

16. **TEST PREP** What time is 2 hours 45 minutes later than 9:35? (p. 98)

A 10:15 **B** 11:35 **C** 12:20 **D** 1:45

LESSON 3

Division Procedures

Quick Review

1. 7×7
2. 3×3
3. 7×4
4. 5×9
5. 8×6

Learn

TINY HATCHLINGS Volunteers are responsible for watching turtle nests on the beach. There are 96 nests. If there are 7 volunteers, how many nests does each volunteer watch? How many nests are left over?

Example

Divide 96 by 7. Write $96 \div 7$ or $7\overline{)96}$.

STEP 1

Divide the 9 tens.

$$\begin{array}{r} 1 \\ 7\overline{)96} \\ -7 \\ \hline 2 \end{array}$$

Divide. $9 \div 7$
Multiply. 1×7
Subtract. $9 - 7$
Compare. $2 < 7$

The difference, 2, must be less than the divisor, 7.

STEP 2

Bring down the 6 ones.

$$\begin{array}{r} 1 \\ 7\overline{)96} \\ -7\downarrow \\ \hline 26 \end{array}$$

STEP 3

Divide the 26 ones.

$$\begin{array}{r} 13 \text{ r5} \\ 7\overline{)96} \\ -7\downarrow \\ \hline 26 \\ -21 \\ \hline 5 \end{array}$$

Divide. $26 \div 7$
Multiply. 3×7
Subtract. $26 - 21$
Compare. $5 < 7$

Write the remainder next to the quotient.

So, each volunteer watches 13 nests. There are 5 nests left over to assign to a new volunteer.

MATH IDEA The order of division is as follows: divide, multiply, subtract, and compare. This order is repeated until the division is complete.

- When you compare, what must you do if the difference is equal to or greater than the divisor?

Technology Link

More Practice: Harcourt Mega Math The Number Games, *Up, Up, and Array,* Level M

Divide and Check

What if there were 5 volunteers? How many nests would each volunteer watch if there were 6 volunteers?

Solve the problems by dividing. Then check your answers. To check your answer, you can compute: (divisor × quotient) + remainder = dividend.

Examples

 **A** 5 volunteers watching 96 nests

Divide	CHECK	
19 r1	19	quotient
$5\overline{)96}$	× 5	divisor
−5↓	95	
46	+ 1	remainder
−45	96	dividend
1		

So, each volunteer would watch 19 nests and 1 nest would be left over.

B 6 volunteers watching 96 nests

Divide	CHECK	
16	16	quotient
$6\overline{)96}$	× 6	divisor
−6↓	96	
36	+ 0	remainder
−36	96	dividend
0		

So, each volunteer would watch 16 nests and no nests would be left over.

- Why is the remainder zero in Example B?

Check

1. **Explain** why you can use multiplication to check a division problem.

Divide and check.

2. $4\overline{)58}$ 3. $3\overline{)65}$ 4. $5\overline{)84}$ 5. $5\overline{)79}$ 6. $7\overline{)99}$

7. $39 \div 2$ 8. $84 \div 6$ 9. $62 \div 4$ 10. $95 \div 8$ 11. $55 \div 3$

Use multiplication to check each answer.

12. $78 \div 6 = 13$ 13. $93 \div 7 = 13$ r2 14. $52 \div 3 = 17$ r1 15. $64 \div 5 = 12$ r4

16. Compare each remainder in Exercises 2–5 with the divisor. Why is the remainder always less than the divisor?

LESSON CONTINUES

Practice and Problem Solving

Extra Practice, page 290, Set B

Divide and check.

17. $4\overline{)84}$ **18.** $4\overline{)51}$ **19.** $7\overline{)52}$ **20.** $2\overline{)46}$

21. $3\overline{)89}$ **22.** $5\overline{)67}$ **23.** $8\overline{)90}$ **24.** $3\overline{)76}$

25. $7\overline{)81}$ **26.** $6\overline{)93}$ **27.** $2\overline{)65}$ **28.** $8\overline{)91}$

29. $4\overline{)56}$ **30.** $4\overline{)59}$ **31.** $6\overline{)88}$ **32.** $5\overline{)69}$

33. $93 \div 8$ **34.** $73 \div 4$ **35.** $94 \div 3$ **36.** $87 \div 5$

Use multiplication to check each answer.

37. $57 \div 4 = 14$ r1 **38.** $85 \div 7 = 12$ r1 **39.** $39 \div 3 = 13$ **40.** $82 \div 7 = 11$ r5

Complete.

41. $(6 \times 12) + 3 = 75$, so $75 \div 6 = 12$ r■ **42.** $(3 \times 25) + 2 = 77$, so ■ $\div 3 = 25$ r2

43. $(6 \times 14) + 3 = 87$, so $87 \div 6 =$ ■ r3 **44.** $(5 \times 13) + 0 = 65$, so $65 \div$ ■ $= 13$

45. $(3 \times 14) + 1 = 43$, so $43 \div 3 = 14$ r■ **46.** $(4 \times 15) + 2 = 62$, so ■ $\div 4 = 15$ r2

ALGEBRA Let d = divisor and q = quotient. Find the value of each variable.

47. $97 \div 5 = 19$ r2
$(d \times q) + 2 = 97$

48. $97 \div 7 = 13$ r6
$(d \times q) + 6 = 97$

49. $97 \div 9 = 10$ r7
$(d \times q) + 7 = 97$

50. $97 \div 6 = 16$ r1
$(d \times q) + 1 = 97$

51. $97 \div 8 = 12$ r1
$(d \times q) + 1 = 97$

52. $97 \div 4 = 24$ r1
$(d \times q) + 1 = 97$

USE DATA For 53–56, use the graph.

53. REASONING Ms. Juanita put the Thursday and Friday volunteers into equal groups for training classes. Each class had 8 members. How many classes did Ms. Juanita need? Explain.

54. The Monday and Tuesday volunteers meet for lunch. Each table seats 4 people. How many tables are needed for the volunteers?

55. What's the Question? The answer is 25 volunteers.

56. Write a problem that requires division, using the data in the graph.

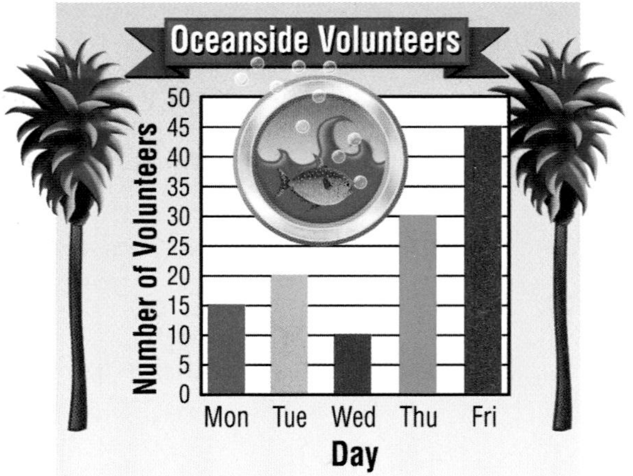

57. Jeremy has 37 pictures of his classmates. He wants to arrange them into groups of 6. How many groups can he make? How many pictures will be left over?

58. **Vocabulary Power** *Remain* means "to be a part not taken or used up." How does this information help you understand what a remainder is?

Mixed Review and Test Prep

59. $\begin{array}{r} 1{,}650 \\ -\ 938 \\ \hline \end{array}$ (p. 48)

60. $\begin{array}{r} 1{,}879 \\ +2{,}548 \\ \hline \end{array}$ (p. 48)

61. $\begin{array}{r} 27 \\ \times 19 \\ \hline \end{array}$ (p. 252)

62. $4\overline{)65}$ (p. 278)

63. Which numbers are missing in the pattern? 12, 24, ■, 48, 60, ■, 84 (p. 172)

64. $20 \times 15 = 300$, so $20 \times 16 =$ ■. (p. 252)

65. **TEST PREP** If 4 boxes have 60 books, how many books are in each box? (p. 218)

A 14
B 15
C 64
D 240

USE DATA For 66, use the graph.

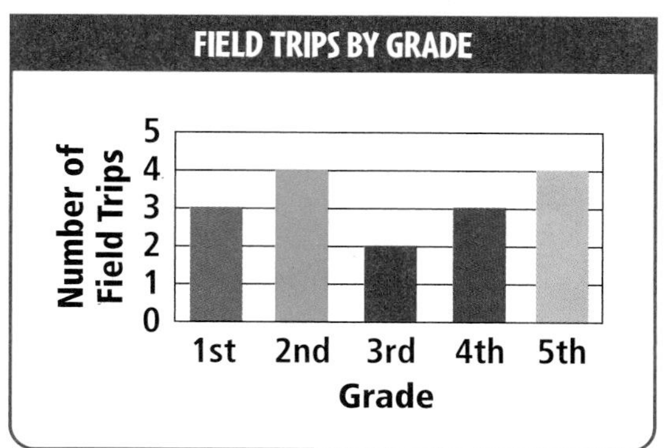

66. **TEST PREP** The principal at Meade School is planning 2 times as many field trips next year. How many field trips are being planned? (p. 218)

F 17 **G** 20 **H** 30 **J** 32

Problem Solving Thinker's Corner

REASONING Miranda has a collection of jungle cats and sea animals. She has 13 jungle cats and 11 sea animals. She wants to display them on some shelves.

- Each shelf will have the same number of items.
- No shelf can have all jungle cats or all sea animals.

Decide how many shelves Miranda needs. Use models or draw a diagram to help you.

1. How many shelves will Miranda need?
2. How many jungle cats and sea animals will be on each shelf?
3. Draw a diagram to show your answer.

LESSON 4

Problem Solving Strategy
Predict and Test

Quick Review

1. $20 \div 4$
2. $18 \div 3$
3. $9\overline{)18}$
4. $32 \div 8$
5. $5\overline{)51}$

PROBLEM There were 81 students visiting a museum. When they were placed in equal groups, 3 students were left over. If groups had between 10 and 15 students, how many groups were formed? How many students were in each group?

UNDERSTAND

- What are you asked to find?
- What information will you use?
- Is there any information you will not use? If so, what?

PLAN

- What strategy can you use to solve the problem?
  You can use the strategy *predict and test*.

SOLVE

- How can you use the strategy to solve the problem?
  Predict divisors. Divide to test each prediction.

NUMBER OF GROUPS		THE REMAINDER	
Predict	**Test**	**Compare to 3**	**Does it check?**
5	$81 \div 5 = 16$ r1	$1 < 3$	No
6	$81 \div 6 = 13$ r3	$3 = 3$	Yes
7	$81 \div 7 = 11$ r4	$4 > 3$	No
8	$81 \div 8 = 10$ r1	$1 < 3$	No
9	$81 \div 9 = 9$	$0 < 3$	No
10	$81 \div 10 = 8$ r1	$1 < 3$	No

So, there were 6 groups with 13 students in each group.

CHECK

- How can you check that your answer is correct?

Problem Solving Practice

Predict and test to solve.

1. **What if** there were 86 students touring the museum? After equal groups of between 15 and 20 were formed, 1 student was left over. How many groups were formed? How many students were in each group?

2. Eileen spent $16.50 at the gift shop. She bought 2 gifts. One of them cost $2.50 more than the other. How much was each gift?

Strategies

- Draw a Diagram or Picture
- Make a Model or Act It Out
- Make an Organized List
- Find a Pattern
- Make a Table or Graph
- **Predict and Test**
- Work Backward
- Solve a Simpler Problem
- Write an Equation
- Use Logical Reasoning

Problem Solving

Suppose you have 35 clay pots. You place an equal number of pots on tables and put 2 pots on the floor. Each table can hold up to 15 pots.

3. How many tables are holding the pots?
   A 2
   B 3
   C 15
   D 35

4. How many pots are on each table?
   F 10
   G 11
   H 12
   J 14

Mixed Strategy Practice

USE DATA For 5–7, use the schedule.

ART CAMP SCHEDULE

CERAMICS	9:00 AM - 10:30 AM
PAINTING	10:30 AM - 11:30 AM
LUNCH	11:30 AM - 12:30 PM
PHOTOGRAPHY	12:30 PM - 1:45 PM
WEARABLE ART	1:45 PM - 3:00 PM

5. It takes Alex 30 minutes to go to or from her home and camp. If she arrives for the start of classes and completes them all, how much time has elapsed when she returns home?

6. **What's the Question?** The elapsed time is 2 hours and 15 minutes.

7. In which of the 4 classes do the campers spend the most time? the least time?

8. **Write About It** If 5 students share some sheets of paper equally, would there ever be more than 4 sheets left over? Explain how you know.

9. Describe a possible pattern in the table.

Number	15	22	25	30
Answer	60	88	100	120

10. Before the game, four soccer players ran a practice drill. Sue finished after Jeremy. Emma finished before Jeremy but after Mark. Who finished first?

LESSON 5

Mental Math: Division Patterns

Quick Review

1. 3 × 20
2. 24 ÷ 3
3. 2 × 40
4. 18 ÷ 2
5. 3 × 300

Learn

EXTREME FUN Best Sports Shop orders 1,800 skateboards for 3 of its stores to share equally. How many skateboards will each store get?

Example

Find 1,800 ÷ 3.

Use basic facts and patterns to find quotients mentally.

dividend		divisor		quotient
18	÷	3	=	6
180	÷	3	=	60
1,800	÷	3	=	600
↑↑ two zeros				two zeros ↑↑

So, each store will get 600 skateboards.

MATH IDEA As the number of zeros in the dividend increases, the number of zeros in the quotient also increases.

More Examples

A
40 ÷ 8 = 5 Think: 5 × 8 = 40
400 ÷ 8 = 50
4,000 ÷ 8 = 500

B
70 ÷ 10 = 7 Think: 7 × 10 = 70
700 ÷ 10 = 70
7,000 ÷ 10 = 700

- In Example A, why is there one more zero in the dividend than in the quotient?

Check

1. **Tell** how many zeros are in the quotient 72,000 ÷ 9 and in the quotient 40,000 ÷ 8.

Use a basic division fact and patterns to write each quotient.

2. a. 560 ÷ 7 **b.** 5,600 ÷ 7	**3. a.** 540 ÷ 6 **b.** 5,400 ÷ 6	**4. a.** 200 ÷ 5 **b.** 2,000 ÷ 5	**5. a.** 8,000 ÷ 8 **b.** 80,000 ÷ 8

Practice and Problem Solving

Extra Practice, page 290, Set C

Use a basic division fact and patterns to write each quotient.

6. a. 270 ÷ 3 **b.** 2,700 ÷ 3	**7. a.** 630 ÷ 9 **b.** 6,300 ÷ 9	**8. a.** 300 ÷ 5 **b.** 3,000 ÷ 5	**9. a.** 4,000 ÷ 10 **b.** 40,000 ÷ 10

Divide mentally. Write the basic division fact and the quotient.

10. 450 ÷ 9	**11.** 210 ÷ 7	**12.** 160 ÷ 8	**13.** 180 ÷ 9
14. 2,800 ÷ 4	**15.** 3,600 ÷ 9	**16.** 15,000 ÷ 3	**17.** 48,000 ÷ 6

ALGEBRA Write the value of n.

18. $420 \div 7 = n$	**19.** $n \div 9 = 30$	**20.** $350 \div n = 50$
21. $4{,}800 \div 8 = n$	**22.** $24{,}000 \div n = 8{,}000$	**23.** $72{,}000 \div 9 = n$

USE DATA Use the pictograph for 24–27.

★BEST Sports Shop

TYPE	NUMBER ON SHELF
TENNIS BALLS	● ● ● ● ● ●
BASEBALLS	● ● ●
GOLF BALLS	● ● ● ● ●
BASKETBALLS	● ● ● ●
EACH ● = 100 BALLS	

24. Each can of tennis balls holds 3 balls. How many cans of tennis balls does the shop have?

25. If golf balls are sold in packages of 4 and each can of tennis balls holds 3 balls, how many more cans of tennis balls does the store have than packages of golf balls?

26. **Write a problem** about the data in the pictograph that can be solved by using a basic division fact and patterns.

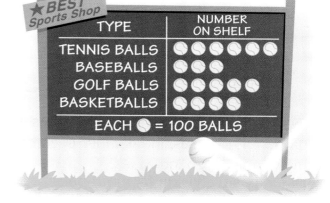

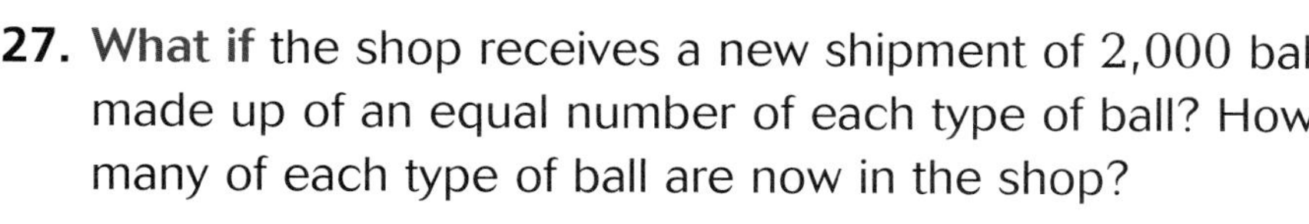

27. **What if** the shop receives a new shipment of 2,000 balls, made up of an equal number of each type of ball? How many of each type of ball are now in the shop?

Mixed Review and Test Prep

28. $\begin{array}{r} 45 \\ \times 27 \\ \hline \end{array}$ (p. 252)

29. $\begin{array}{r} 985 \\ +1{,}307 \\ \hline \end{array}$ (p. 48)

30. Round 61,879 to the nearest hundred. (p. 30)

31. Round 206,714 to the nearest thousand. (p. 30)

32. **TEST PREP** How many faces does a cube have?

A 4 **B** 5 **C** 6 **D** 8

Extra Practice

Set A (pp. 278–279)

Divide. You may wish to use counters.

1. $28 \div 4$
2. $84 \div 9$
3. $37 \div 5$
4. $39 \div 5$
5. $3\overline{)29}$
6. $4\overline{)19}$
7. $5\overline{)42}$
8. $6\overline{)59}$
9. Anton needs 18 pounds of potting soil. The soil comes in 3-pound bags. How many bags will he need?

Set B (pp. 282–285)

Divide and check.

1. $5\overline{)84}$
2. $6\overline{)68}$
3. $2\overline{)47}$
4. $4\overline{)75}$
5. $3\overline{)31}$
6. $95 \div 3$
7. $69 \div 4$
8. $77 \div 6$
9. $58 \div 5$
10. $76 \div 9$

Use multiplication to check each answer.

11. $73 \div 9 = 8$ r1
12. $64 \div 5 = 12$ r4
13. $99 \div 6 = 16$ r3
14. $87 \div 7 = 12$ r3
15. Patty brought 30 cookies to a party. Each of 7 children took the same number of cookies. How many cookies were left over?
16. The school store plans to sell pencils in packages of 5. If there are 83 pencils for sale, how many pencils cannot be sold in a package?

Set C (pp. 288–289)

Use a basic division fact and patterns to write each quotient.

1. $480 \div 6$
 $4{,}800 \div 6$
2. $210 \div 7$
 $2{,}100 \div 7$
3. $320 \div 4$
 $3{,}200 \div 4$
4. $360 \div 6$
 $3{,}600 \div 6$

Write the value of *n*.

5. $36{,}000 \div 6 = n$
6. $n \div 6 = 200$
7. $2{,}800 \div n = 40$
8. $2{,}400 \div 8 = n$
9. $4{,}200 \div 7 = n$
10. $n \div 3 = 900$
11. $560 \div 8 = n$
12. $n \div 7 = 900$
13. The florist ordered 120 daisies. She used the daisies in 6 flower arrangements. How many daisies were in each flower arrangement?
14. The toy factory made 5,400 stuffed bears. If 6 bears fit in a box, how many boxes are needed to ship the bears?

Review/Test

CHECK VOCABULARY AND CONCEPTS

Choose the best term from the box.

divide
quotient
remainder

1. A _?_ is the amount left over when a number cannot be divided evenly. (p. 278)
2. The order of division is _?_, multiply, subtract, and compare. (p. 282)

For 3–6, think of how to model 47 ÷ 3. (pp. 278–281)

3. How many equal groups are needed to model the divisor?
4. Draw the base-ten blocks needed to show the dividend.
5. How many are in each group?
6. How many are left over?

CHECK SKILLS

Divide and check. (pp. 282–285)

7. $3\overline{)23}$
8. $4\overline{)33}$
9. $2\overline{)28}$
10. $6\overline{)72}$
11. $9\overline{)71}$
12. $5\overline{)85}$
13. $4\overline{)65}$
14. $5\overline{)69}$
15. $7\overline{)91}$
16. $6\overline{)79}$
17. $8\overline{)98}$
18. $7\overline{)90}$

Divide mentally. Write the basic division fact and the quotient. (pp. 288–289)

19. 150 ÷ 5
20. 210 ÷ 3
21. 360 ÷ 6
22. 4,500 ÷ 9
23. 5,600 ÷ 8

CHECK PROBLEM SOLVING

Solve. (pp. 286–287)

24. There are 93 students. After equal groups are formed, there are 5 students left over. How many groups are formed? How many students are in each group?
25. Lynn has $73 to spend on CDs. She buys several CDs at the same price and has $3 left over. How many CDs does Lynn buy? How much does each CD cost?

Standardized Test Prep

NUMBER SENSE, CONCEPTS, AND OPERATIONS

1. Which of the following shows $22 \div 3$?

   A 22 dots in each of 3 circles

   B 3 circles, two with 7 dots and one with 8 dots

   C 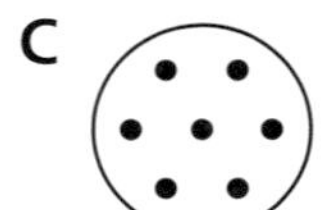 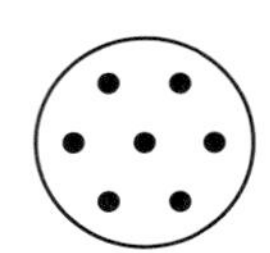 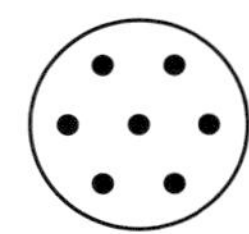

   D  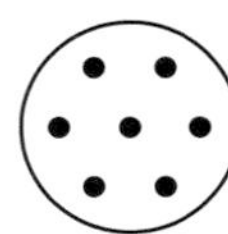 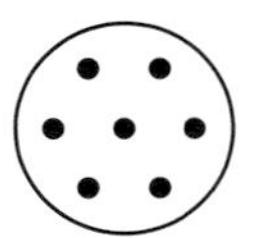

2. The table below shows the number of people who attended a tennis match over a period of three days.

TENNIS MATCH ATTENDANCE	
Day	**Number of People**
Friday	4,471
Saturday	5,396
Sunday	5,904

   About how many people attended on all three days?

   F between 12,000 and 13,000

   G between 13,000 and 14,000

   H between 14,000 and 15,000

   J between 15,000 and 16,000

3. **Explain It** Al is putting 68 photos into an album. Each page holds 6 photos. ESTIMATE how many pages he will need. Explain how you decided.

MEASUREMENT

4. Which is the **best** estimate for the length of a fourth-grader's arm?

   A 2 inches

   B 22 inches

   C 220 inches

   D 22 feet

> **TIP** **Understand the problem.** See item 5. Think of what you know about a *square.* You will have to use what you know about the lengths of the sides in order to find the perimeter.

5. What is the perimeter of the square below?

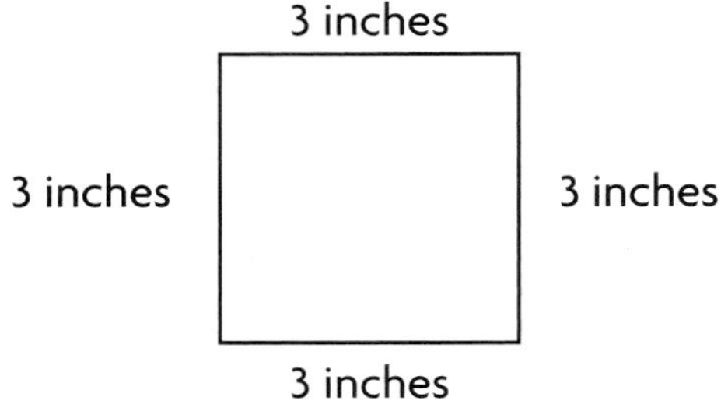

   F 3 inches

   G 6 inches

   H 7 inches

   J 12 inches

6. **Explain It** Tom left his house at about 8:50 A.M. and walked 20 minutes to a friend's house. He left his friend's house at about 11:15 A.M. About how much time did Tom spend at his friend's house? Explain your thinking.

ALGEBRAIC THINKING

7. Which number sentence comes next in the pattern below?

$$25 \div 5 = 5$$
$$250 \div 5 = 50$$
$$2{,}500 \div 5 = 500$$

A $25{,}000 \div 10 = 2{,}500$

B $25{,}000 \div 5 = 5{,}000$

C $25{,}000 \div 1 = 25{,}000$

D $25 \div 5 = 5$

8. Some marbles were shared equally among 4 people. Which expression could be used to describe this situation?

F $m + 4$

G $m - 4$

H $m \times 4$

J $m \div 4$

9. Explain It When a number is put into the machine below, a different number comes out.

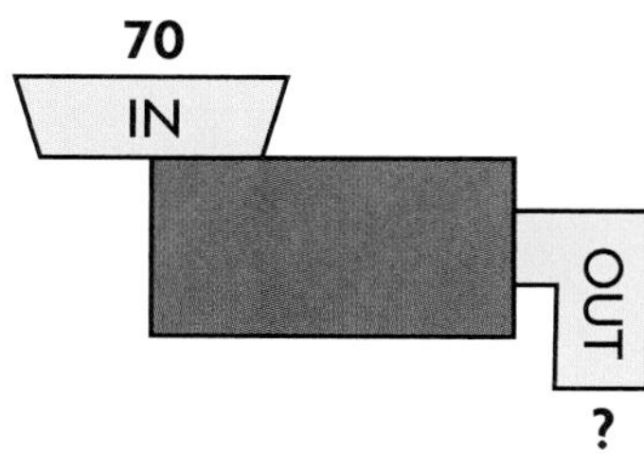

If 14 goes in, 2 comes out.

If 35 goes in, 5 comes out.

If 56 goes in, 8 comes out.

If 70 goes in, what number should come out?

Explain how you decided.

DATA ANALYSIS AND PROBABILITY

10. The bar graph below shows the number of cans collected during the fourth-grade food drive.

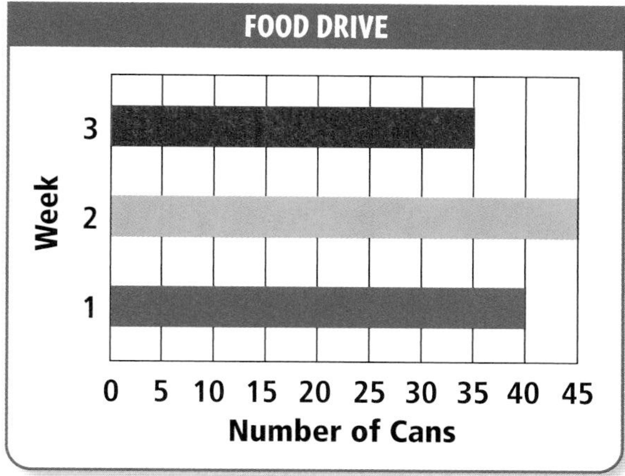

According to the information in the graph, how many total cans were collected during Weeks 1 and 2?

A 35

B 45

C 80

D 85

11. Which kind of graph would be **best** to show the population growth of a city over several years?

F double-bar graph

G stem-and-leaf plot

H line graph

J bar graph

12. Explain It Jim wrote the ages of all his cousins.

Ages: 2, 3, 11, 11, 12, 13, 13, 25, 26

Is the median age of his cousins **greater than, less than,** or **equal to** 12? Explain your thinking.

CHAPTER 14 Divide by 1-Digit Divisors

FAST FACT • SOCIAL STUDIES Hawaiians often welcome visitors to their state with wreaths of flowers called leis (LAYZ). Leis are made from 200 kinds of flowers found in Hawaii.

PROBLEM SOLVING Use the table to find the number of flowers used to make one of each type of lei.

HAWAIIAN LEIS MADE AT ONE SHOP

Type of Lei	Number of Flowers Used	Number of Leis Made
Carnation	350	7
Orchid	375	5
Plumeria	495	9
Rosebud	420	6
Tuberose	320	8

CHECK WHAT YOU KNOW

Use this page to help you review and remember important skills needed for Chapter 14.

PLACE VALUE

Write the value of the blue digit.

1. 394
2. 3,678
3. 2,786
4. 654
5. 5,073

2-DIGIT SUBTRACTION

Find the difference.

6. $\begin{array}{r} 92 \\ -24 \\ \hline \end{array}$
7. $\begin{array}{r} 79 \\ -44 \\ \hline \end{array}$
8. $\begin{array}{r} 66 \\ -29 \\ \hline \end{array}$
9. $\begin{array}{r} 53 \\ -37 \\ \hline \end{array}$
10. $\begin{array}{r} 45 \\ -18 \\ \hline \end{array}$

11. $87 - 56$
12. $38 - 25$
13. $71 - 52$
14. $99 - 73$
15. $64 - 35$

DIVIDE WITH REMAINDERS

Use the model to find the quotient and remainder.

16. 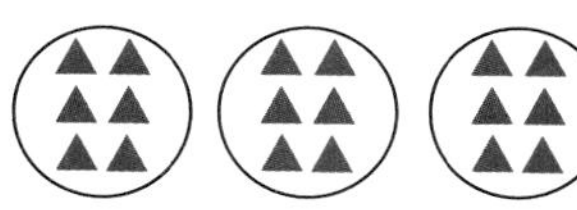

$20 \div 3 = \blacksquare$

17. 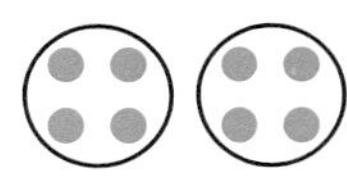 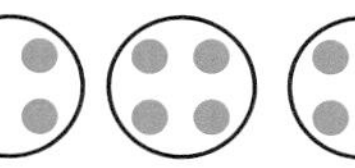

$27 \div 6 = \blacksquare$

18. 

$15 \div 7 = \blacksquare$

19. 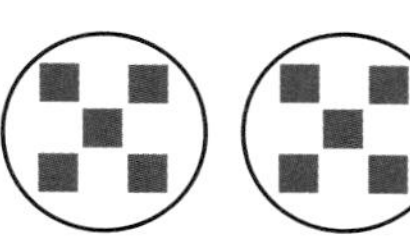 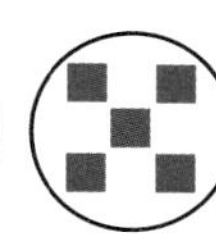 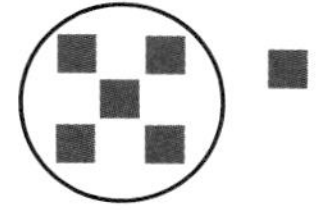

$22 \div 4 = \blacksquare$

VOCABULARY POWER

REVIEW

compatible numbers [kəm•pa′tə•bəl num′bərz] *noun*

Compatible refers to things that can be used together without difficulty. Explain how using compatible numbers can make division easier.

www.harcourtschool.com/mathglossary

LESSON 1

Estimate Quotients

Quick Review

1. 4×7
2. 4×70
3. 4×700
4. $280 \div 4$
5. $2,800 \div 4$

Learn

BIG EATER Kendra and Jamal are researching elephants. They found that a baby elephant eats about 528 pounds of food in a week. About how much does a baby elephant eat in a day?

Estimate. $528 \div 7$

Remember that compatible numbers can be used to estimate quotients.

Use division facts for 7 to find compatible numbers for 528.

Think: $49 \div 7 = 7$ and $56 \div 7 = 8$

So, you can use 490 or 560 for 528.

$490 \div 7$

$560 \div 7$

Think: 528 is between 490 and 560. So, use these compatible numbers as dividends.

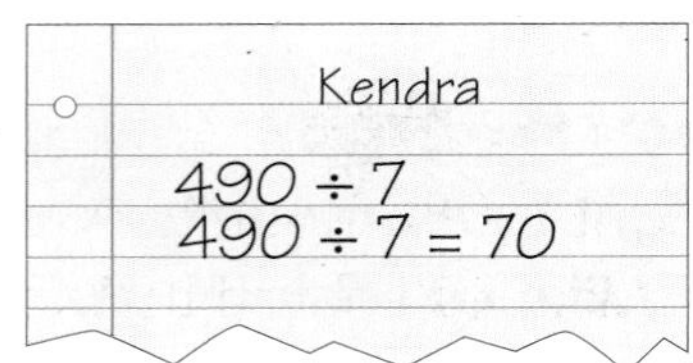

The baby elephant eats about 70 pounds of food each day.

Jamal

$560 \div 7$

$560 \div 7 = 80$

The baby elephant eats about 80 pounds of food each day.

So, both 70 pounds of food and 80 pounds of food are reasonable estimates.

- Would the exact answer be more than or less than 70 pounds? Explain.
- Would the exact answer be closer to 70 or 80?
- Suppose you estimate $346 \div 7$ by rounding the dividend to 300. Is 300 a good choice? Explain.

Check

1. **Explain** how to find compatible numbers to estimate $331 \div 4$.

Choose the letter of the best estimate.

2. $267 \div 7$ **a.** 3 or 4 **b.** 5 or 6 **c.** 30 or 40
3. $348 \div 5$ **a.** 6 or 7 **b.** 40 or 50 **c.** 60 or 70

Practice and Problem Solving

Extra Practice, page 310, Set A

Choose the letter of the best estimate.

4. $242 \div 3$ **a.** 6 or 7 **b.** 8 or 9 **c.** 80 or 90
5. $372 \div 6$ **a.** 60 or 70 **b.** 50 or 60 **c.** 6 or 7
6. $4{,}000 \div 9$ **a.** 400 or 500 **b.** 300 or 400 **c.** 40 or 50

Estimate using compatible numbers.

7. $5\overline{)47}$
8. $9\overline{)59}$
9. $4\overline{)137}$
10. $6\overline{)492}$
11. $8\overline{)444}$
12. $9\overline{)660}$
13. $8\overline{)713}$
14. $9\overline{)6{,}800}$
15. $9\overline{)3{,}150}$
16. $5\overline{)232}$
17. $3\overline{)2{,}720}$
18. $7\overline{)4{,}570}$

Use estimation to tell which quotient is greater.

19. $190 \div 3$ or $165 \div 4$
20. $475 \div 8$ or $365 \div 5$
21. $349 \div 5$ or $703 \div 8$
22. $555 \div 7$ or $303 \div 6$
23. $777 \div 8$ or $888 \div 7$
24. $2{,}000 \div 7$ or $999 \div 2$

25. An elephant family group usually has about 8 members. One part of the savanna has 125 elephants. Another part has 268 elephants. Estimate the difference in the number of family groups found in each part of the savanna.

26. **? What's the Error?** An elephant can eat about 3,080 pounds of food in one week. Mike estimated that an elephant eats about 600 pounds of food in one day. Describe his error. Give a more reasonable estimate.

Mixed Review and Test Prep

27. $13{,}238 - 8{,}179$ (p. 48)

28. $26 \div 9$ (p. 282)

29. Find the product. (p. 174)
$6 \times 4 \times 3$

30. Find the value of n in the equation $18 - 9 = n + 2$. (p. 76)

31. **TEST PREP** Jim started his walk at 11:15 A.M. and stopped at 12:45 P.M. for a 30-minute lunch. Then he walked home. He arrived home at 2:00 P.M. How long did he walk? (p. 98)

A 1 hr 45 min **C** 2 hr 30 min
B 2 hr 15 min **D** 2 hr 45 min

LESSON 2

Place the First Digit

Quick Review

1. 36 ÷ 4
2. 8 × 3
3. 7 × 5
4. 49 ÷ 7
5. 25 ÷ 5

Learn

PAPER PETALS Mrs. Bond ordered 265 sheets of crepe paper to be shared equally among 5 art classes. How many sheets will each class get?

One Way Estimate to place the first digit in the quotient.

Divide 265 by 5. Write 5)265.

STEP 1

Estimate.

Think:

```
  50          60
5)250   or  5)300
```

```
  ■
5)265
```
So, the first digit is in the tens place.

STEP 2

Divide the 26 tens.

```
   5
5)265    Divide. 5)26
 -25     Multiply. 5 × 5
   1     Subtract. 26 − 25
         Compare. 1 < 5
```

STEP 3

Bring down the 5 ones.
Divide the 15 ones.

```
   53
5)265    Divide. 5)15
 -25↓    Multiply. 5 × 3
   15    Subtract. 15 − 15
  -15    Compare. 0 < 5
    0
```

So, each class will get 53 sheets of crepe paper.

Another Way Use place value to place the first digit in the quotient.

Divide 253 by 4. Write 4)253.

STEP 1

Use place value to place the first digit. Look at the hundreds.

4)253 2 < 4, so look at the tens.

```
  ■
4)253
```
25 > 4, so use 25 tens. Place the first digit in the tens place.

STEP 2

Divide the 25 tens.

```
   6
4)253    Divide. 4)25
 -24     Multiply. 4 × 6
   1     Subtract. 25 − 24
         Compare. 1 < 4
```

STEP 3

Bring down the 3 ones.
Divide the 13 ones.

```
   63 r1
4)253    Divide. 4)13
 -24↓    Multiply. 4 × 3
   13    Subtract. 13 − 12
  -12    Compare. 1 < 4
    1
```

Check

1. **Explain** how to use place value to place the first digit in the quotient of 903 ÷ 3.

Tell where to place the first digit. Then divide.

2. $6\overline{)38}$ 3. $4\overline{)81}$ 4. $2\overline{)182}$ 5. $5\overline{)85}$ 6. $6\overline{)771}$

Practice and Problem Solving

Extra Practice, page 310, Set B

Tell where to place the first digit. Then divide.

7. $6\overline{)45}$ 8. $3\overline{)125}$ 9. $5\overline{)558}$ 10. $7\overline{)371}$ 11. $3\overline{)634}$

Divide.

12. $2\overline{)87}$ 13. $4\overline{)189}$ 14. $5\overline{)170}$ 15. $6\overline{)378}$ 16. $3\overline{)801}$

17. $6\overline{)318}$ 18. $4\overline{)239}$ 19. $5\overline{)678}$ 20. $8\overline{)488}$ 21. $7\overline{)917}$

22. 462 ÷ 9 23. 694 ÷ 5 24. 969 ÷ 6 25. 998 ÷ 8 26. 891 ÷ 9

27. Mrs. Williams bought supplies for the art class project. She bought glitter for $2.49, lace for $4.89, and paint for $5.30. How much change did she receive from $20.00?

28. A total of 144 origami figures were on display. The same number of figures were on each of 6 tables. Did each table have 244 figures, 24 figures, or 2 figures? Explain.

29. **Vocabulary Power** When you divide a number, you separate it into equal parts. *Separate* is a synonym of the word *divide*. What other synonyms for *divide* can you think of? List them.

30. **Write About It** Explain how you can decide where to place the first digit in a division problem.

Mixed Review and Test Prep

31. 3 × 3 × 2 (p. 174)

32. 600 − 79 (p. 40)

33. Find the product of 16 and 4. (p. 218)

34. Find the sum. 706 + 552 (p. 40)

35. **TEST PREP** The play started at 7:15 P.M. It lasted 90 minutes and there was a 15-minute intermission. What was the ending time? (p. 98)

- **A** 8:15 P.M.
- **B** 8:45 P.M.
- **C** 9:00 P.M.
- **D** 9:15 P.M.

LESSON 3

Divide 3-Digit Numbers

Quick Review

1. $21 \div 3$
2. 4×2
3. 5×3
4. $35 \div 5$
5. $7\overline{)44}$

Learn

ISLAND ADVENTURE The Aloha Tour Company divided 178 flyers for guided tours equally among 3 resorts. How many flyers did each resort get?

Example

Divide 178 by 3. Write $3\overline{)178}$.

STEP 1

Estimate to place the first digit in the quotient.

Think: $3\overline{)150}$ (50) or $3\overline{)180}$ (60)

$3\overline{)178}$ ■ Place the first digit in the tens place.

STEP 2

Divide the 17 tens.

$$\begin{array}{r} 5 \\ 3\overline{)178} \\ -15 \\ \hline 2 \end{array}$$

Divide. Multiply. Subtract. Compare.

STEP 3

Bring down the 8 ones. Divide the 28 ones.

$$\begin{array}{r} 59 \text{ r1} \\ 3\overline{)178} \\ -15\downarrow \\ \hline 28 \\ -27 \\ \hline 1 \end{array}$$

Divide. Multiply. Subtract. Compare.

STEP 4

To check, multiply the quotient by the divisor. Then add the remainder.

$$\begin{array}{rl} \overset{2}{5}9 & \text{quotient} \\ \times\ 3 & \text{divisor} \\ \hline 177 & \\ +\ \ 1 & \text{remainder} \\ \hline 178 & \text{dividend} \end{array}$$

So, each resort will get 59 flyers, with 1 flyer left over. Since 59 is between 50 and 60, the answer is reasonable.

Hawaii's Kapoloa Falls drop 1,400 feet to the Pololu Valley floor. ▼

More Examples

A

$$\begin{array}{r} \$1.93 \\ 2\overline{)\$3.86} \\ -2 \\ \hline 18 \\ -18 \\ \hline 06 \\ -\ 6 \\ \hline 0 \end{array}$$

Divide money amounts as you divide whole numbers. Write the quotient in dollars and cents.

B

$$\begin{array}{r} 226 \text{ r2} \\ 3\overline{)680} \\ -6 \\ \hline 08 \\ -\ 6 \\ \hline 20 \\ -18 \\ \hline 2 \end{array}$$

- Why are there 3 digits in the quotient of Example B?

Check

1. **Explain** how to find the first digit in the quotient of $324 \div 7$.

Divide and check.

2. $4\overline{)187}$ 3. $2\overline{)453}$ 4. $5\overline{)592}$ 5. $7\overline{)241}$ 6. $6\overline{)687}$

Practice and Problem Solving

Extra Practice, page 310, Set C

Divide and check.

7. $6\overline{)178}$ 8. $4\overline{)472}$ 9. $7\overline{)241}$ 10. $9\overline{)709}$ 11. $3\overline{)470}$

12. $5\overline{)337}$ 13. $2\overline{)\$3.72}$ 14. $8\overline{)697}$ 15. $4\overline{)\$4.68}$ 16. $6\overline{)749}$

17. $7\overline{)\$9.24}$ 18. $9\overline{)530}$ 19. $4\overline{)617}$ 20. $5\overline{)386}$ 21. $8\overline{)\$9.44}$

22. $186 \div 3$ 23. $247 \div 8$ 24. $546 \div 5$ 25. $\$3.02 \div 2$ 26. $614 \div 6$

ALGEBRA **Find the value of $448 \div n$ for each value of n.**

27. $n = 2$ 28. $n = 3$ 29. $n = 4$ 30. $n = 5$ 31. $n = 6$

32. **Mental Math** Which is greater, $345 \div 2$ or $345 \div 3$?

33. Which is greater, $2\overline{)452}$ or $4\overline{)452}$? How much greater?

USE DATA For 34–37, use this information. The Island Tours Theater seats 45 people. There are 210 people on a tour.

34. The tourists are divided into equal groups. If each group has 7 people, how many groups will there be?

35. Each tourist's ticket to the play costs \$8. The tour guide gives the cashier at the window \$1,800. How much change does the guide receive?

36. How many groups of 7 people can watch a play at one time? How many times will the play be performed in order for all the groups to see it?

37. **Write a problem** about Island Tours that requires dividing three-digit numbers.

Mixed Review and Test Prep

38. $7,500 - 896$ (p. 50)

39. $2,300 \times 4$ (p. 222)

40. $6\overline{)83}$ (p. 280)

41. $7\overline{)37}$ (p. 278)

42. **TEST PREP** What is the value of n?
$n + 4 = 15$ (p. 76)

A $n = 60$ **C** $n = 15$
B $n = 19$ **D** $n = 11$

LESSON 4

Zeros in Division

Quick Review

1. $4\overline{)28}$
2. $4\overline{)36}$
3. $7\overline{)63}$
4. $2\overline{)22}$
5. $4\overline{)41}$

Learn

POSTAGE DUE The post office sold 432 stamps in 4 hours. If the same number of stamps were sold each hour, how many stamps were sold each hour?

Example Divide 432 by 4. Write $4\overline{)432}$.

STEP 1

Estimate to place the first digit in the quotient.

Think:

$\begin{array}{r} 100 \\ 4\overline{)400} \end{array}$ or $\begin{array}{r} 200 \\ 4\overline{)800} \end{array}$

$\begin{array}{r} \blacksquare \\ 4\overline{)432} \end{array}$ So, place the first digit in the hundreds place.

STEP 2

Divide the 4 hundreds.

$$\begin{array}{r} 1 \\ 4\overline{)432} \\ \underline{-4} \\ 0 \end{array}$$

STEP 3

Bring down the 3 tens. Divide the 3 tens.

$$\begin{array}{r} 10 \\ 4\overline{)432} \\ \underline{-4\downarrow} \\ 03 \\ \underline{-\ 0} \\ 3 \end{array}$$

$4 > 3$, so write a 0 in the quotient.

STEP 4

Bring down the 2 ones. Divide the 32 ones.

$$\begin{array}{r} 108 \\ 4\overline{)432} \\ \underline{-4} \\ 03 \\ \underline{-\ 0\downarrow} \\ 32 \\ \underline{-32} \\ 0 \end{array}$$

So, the post office sold 108 stamps each hour.

More Examples

A

$$\begin{array}{r} 101 \text{ r1} \\ 5\overline{)506} \\ \underline{-5} \\ 00 \\ \underline{-\ 0} \\ 06 \\ \underline{-\ 5} \\ 1 \end{array}$$

B

$$\begin{array}{r} 130 \\ 6\overline{)780} \\ \underline{-6} \\ 18 \\ \underline{-18} \\ 00 \\ \underline{-\ 0} \\ 0 \end{array}$$

C

$$\begin{array}{r} 104 \text{ r6} \\ 7\overline{)734} \\ \underline{-7} \\ 03 \\ \underline{-\ 0} \\ 34 \\ \underline{-28} \\ 6 \end{array}$$

- Explain what would happen in Example A if you did not write a zero in the tens place of the quotient.
- Explain how you can check the answer in Example C.

Correcting Quotients

The fourth graders collected stamps. They put 4 stamps on each page of an album. The students in Lee Ann's class collected 240 stamps. How many pages did they need?

Look at Lee Ann's paper. Lee Ann divided 240 by 4.

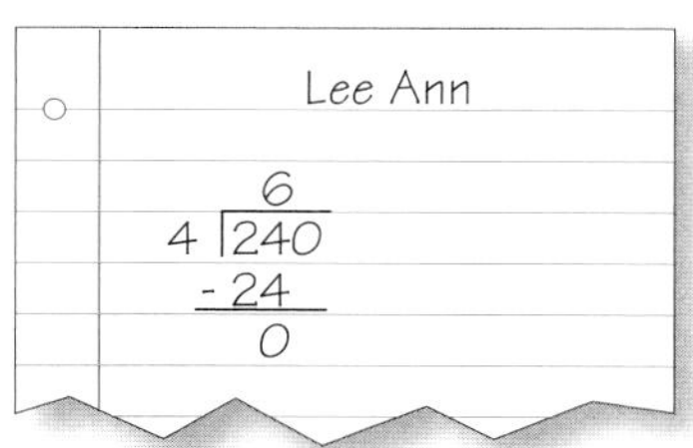

• Describe her error. Write the division correctly.

The students in Craig's class collected 412 stamps. How many pages did they need?

Look at Craig's paper. Craig divided 412 by 4.

Craig

$$\begin{array}{r} 13 \\ 4\overline{)412} \\ -4 \\ \hline 12 \\ -12 \\ \hline 0 \end{array}$$

• Describe his error. Write the division correctly.

MATH IDEA Estimate to decide how many digits should be in the quotient so you do not forget to include zeros.

Technology Link

More Practice: Use Mega Math The Number Games, *Up, Up, and Array,* Level P

Check

1. **Explain** how an estimate could help you remember to write a zero in a quotient.
2. **Explain** how you know if a quotient is reasonable.

Write the number of digits in each quotient.

3. $4\overline{)406}$ 4. $7\overline{)610}$ 5. $5\overline{)309}$ 6. $4\overline{)804}$ 7. $5\overline{)650}$

Divide and check.

8. $5\overline{)800}$ 9. $9\overline{)308}$ 10. $3\overline{)609}$ 11. $3\overline{)305}$ 12. $5\overline{)407}$

LESSON CONTINUES

Practice and Problem Solving

Extra Practice, page 310, Set D

Write the number of digits in each quotient.

13. $8\overline{)818}$ **14.** $6\overline{)510}$ **15.** $3\overline{)207}$ **16.** $4\overline{)600}$ **17.** $5\overline{)405}$

Divide and check.

18. $6\overline{)40}$ **19.** $8\overline{)60}$ **20.** $5\overline{)70}$ **21.** $7\overline{)80}$ **22.** $9\overline{)97}$

23. $5\overline{)405}$ **24.** $4\overline{)240}$ **25.** $6\overline{)243}$ **26.** $7\overline{)636}$ **27.** $8\overline{)706}$

28. $7\overline{)308}$ **29.** $6\overline{)230}$ **30.** $4\overline{)580}$ **31.** $5\overline{)306}$ **32.** $4\overline{)803}$

33. $4\overline{)260}$ **34.** $7\overline{)605}$ **35.** $8\overline{)900}$ **36.** $3\overline{)620}$ **37.** $9\overline{)951}$

38. $402 \div 7$ **39.** $362 \div 9$ **40.** $760 \div 3$ **41.** $860 \div 8$ **42.** $603 \div 6$

43. $361 \div 3$ **44.** $247 \div 8$ **45.** $654 \div 5$ **46.** $421 \div 2$ **47.** $642 \div 6$

ALGEBRA Write +, −, ×, or ÷ for each ●.

48. (35 ● 5) ● 5 = 2 **49.** (9 ● 8) ● 4 = 18 **50.** (36 ● 4) ● 3 = 27

USE DATA For 51–54, use the table.

Toy Company Shipping Costs	
Weight	**Cost per lb**
0–9.99 lb	$0.80
10–19.99 lb	$0.75
20–34.99 lb	$0.70

51. Juan ordered three toys. A board game weighs 4 pounds. A scooter weighs 8 pounds, and a train set weighs 21 pounds. How much did Juan pay to have the toys shipped?

52. **REASONING** Madeleine paid $9.00 in shipping for 4 stuffed animals that weigh 3 pounds each. Did her order weigh 0–9.99 pounds or 10–19.99 pounds?

53. Alex has $4.50. Does he have enough money to pay for shipping on a 5-pound globe? How much will the shipping cost?

54. **What's the Question?** Lucy has $13.00. A toy camera weighs 2 pounds, a doll weighs 3 pounds, and an art kit weighs 3 pounds. She has $6.60 left.

55. **Write About It** Explain how you can decide how many digits will be in a quotient.

56. **FAST FACT • SOCIAL STUDIES** A postal carrier delivers mail to about 500 addresses each day. If a carrier delivers mail for 4 hours, about how many addresses does the carrier deliver to each hour?

57. **What's the Error?** Describe the error and then show the correct way to divide.

$$\begin{array}{r} 5 \text{ r}2 \\ 9\overline{)47} \\ -45 \\ \hline 2 \end{array}$$

58. Yoko takes the train to the city and back 4 times each month. She travels a total of 376 miles. How far away is the city?

59. What is the value of eight $10 bills, six $1 bills, 17 dimes, and 9 pennies?

Mixed Review and Test Prep

For 60–61, write in standard form. (p. 4)

60. seven hundred eleven thousand, forty-five

61. sixty-four thousand, nine hundred fifty-two

62. Write the number that is 10,000 less than two hundred fifty thousand, one hundred sixteen. (p. 52)

63. $\begin{array}{r} 6{,}983 \\ -2{,}094 \\ \hline \end{array}$ (p. 48)

64. $\begin{array}{r} 7{,}682 \\ +6{,}749 \\ \hline \end{array}$ (p. 48)

65. $4 \times \blacksquare = 30 - 2$ (p. 192)

66. $\begin{array}{r} 400 \\ -283 \\ \hline \end{array}$ (p. 40)

67. $\begin{array}{r} 732 \\ -165 \\ \hline \end{array}$ (p. 40)

68. **TEST PREP** Sami has 960 beads in 8 different colors to make jewelry. He has the same number of each color. How many beads of each color does Sami have? (p. 298)

A 100 **B** 110 **C** 120 **D** 130

69. **TEST PREP** Nelson bought 8 pounds of oranges. He paid with $5.00 and got $1.96 change. How much did 1 pound of oranges cost? (p. 300)

F 29¢ **H** 38¢
G 31¢ **J** 42¢

Problem Solving LINKUP ... to Social Studies

On April 3, 1860, the Pony Express began carrying mail between Missouri and California. The riders traveled about 150 miles each day—almost twice as far as a day's travel by stagecoach.

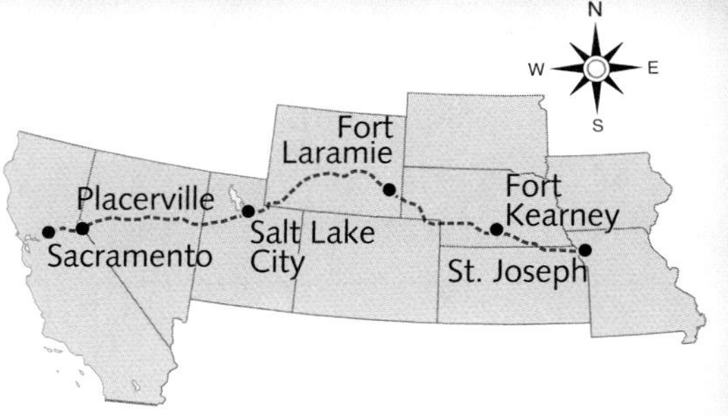

USE DATA **For 1–4, use the information above.**

1. It took the Pony Express riders about 11 days to travel from St. Joseph, Missouri, to Sacramento, California. About how many miles did they travel?

2. A Pony Express rider left Sacramento at 2:45 A.M. and arrived at Placerville at 6:40 A.M. How long did it take the rider to travel to Placerville?

3. One of the longest nonstop rides was made by Buffalo Bill. He rode for about 22 hours at about 15 miles per hour. He used 21 different horses. About how many miles did he ride?

4. **CHALLENGE** The Pony Express carried a total of 34,753 pieces of mail in 308 trips of 2,000 miles each. How many miles did the Pony Express riders travel?

LESSON 5

Choose a Method

Quick Review

1. $3\overline{)63}$
2. $2\overline{)424}$
3. $5\overline{)315}$
4. $4\overline{)884}$
5. $6\overline{)1,806}$

Learn

ROOM AND BOARD For a national gymnastics competition, a total of 1,650 rooms were reserved at 6 hotels. The rooms were divided equally among the hotels. How many rooms were reserved at each hotel?

Choose a method of division that works easily for the numbers given.

Use Paper and Pencil Divide 1,650 by 6. Write $6\overline{)1,650}$.

STEP 1

Estimate to place the first digit in the quotient.

Think:

$$\begin{array}{r}200\\6\overline{)1,200}\end{array} \quad \text{or} \quad \begin{array}{r}300\\6\overline{)1,800}\end{array}$$

$$\begin{array}{r}\blacksquare\\6\overline{)1,650}\end{array}$$

So, place the first digit in the hundreds place.

STEP 2

Divide the 16 hundreds.

$$\begin{array}{r}2\\6\overline{)1,650}\\-1\,2\\\hline 4\end{array}$$

STEP 3

Bring down the 5 tens. Divide the 45 tens.

$$\begin{array}{r}27\\6\overline{)1,650}\\-1\,2\downarrow\\\hline 45\\-42\\\hline 3\end{array}$$

STEP 4

Bring down the 0 ones. Divide the 30 ones.

$$\begin{array}{r}275\\6\overline{)1,650}\\-1\,2\\\hline 45\\-42\downarrow\\\hline 30\\-30\\\hline 0\end{array}$$

So, 275 rooms were reserved at each hotel.

More Examples

A Use Mental Math

2,480 ÷ 4 = ■

Think: 2,400 ÷ 4 = 600
80 ÷ 4 = 20

So, 2,480 ÷ 4 = 620.

B Use a Calculator

7,812 ÷ 5 = ■

7 8 1 2 ÷R 5 = | =1562 R2

So, 7,812 ÷ 5 = 1,562 r2.

MATH IDEA You can divide by using paper and pencil, mental math, or a calculator. Look at the numbers in the problem before you choose a method.

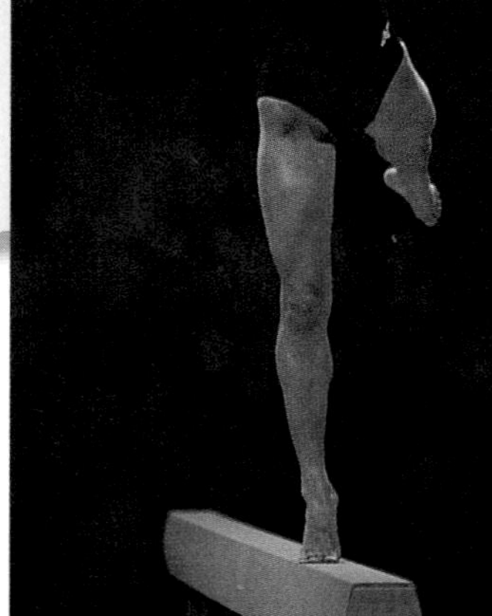

Check

1. **Explain** how looking at the numbers in a problem can help you choose a method to find the quotient.

Divide.

2. $5\overline{)1,440}$ 3. $3\overline{)2,329}$ 4. $8\overline{)17,120}$ 5. $7\overline{)5,030}$ 6. $6\overline{)4,091}$

Practice and Problem Solving

Extra Practice, page 310, Set E

Divide. Write the method you used.

7. $4\overline{)3,420}$ 8. $3\overline{)\$83.70}$ 9. $6\overline{)\$91.20}$ 10. $8\overline{)7,200}$ 11. $2\overline{)1,382}$

12. $5\overline{)185}$ 13. $7\overline{)5,643}$ 14. $9\overline{)398}$ 15. $3\overline{)483}$ 16. $6\overline{)737}$

17. $4\overline{)236}$ 18. $2\overline{)3,892}$ 19. $6\overline{)\$52.14}$ 20. $8\overline{)408}$ 21. $9\overline{)\$61.47}$

22. $7\overline{)3,273}$ 23. $3\overline{)24,090}$ 24. $4\overline{)\$78.04}$ 25. $7\overline{)3,961}$ 26. $5\overline{)20,050}$

27. At the gymnastics meet, there were 276 gymnasts. There was an equal number of gymnasts in each of 4 different events. How many gymnasts were in each event?

28. At the tumbling event, 32 gymnasts each performed for 4 minutes, and 23 gymnasts each performed for 3 minutes. How many minutes did the gymnasts perform in all?

USE DATA For 29–30, use the table.

29. Thao wants to buy 3 pounds of bananas and 2 pounds of coconut. He has \$10.00. Does he have enough money? How much money does Thao need in all?

30. Holly's mother bought 2 pounds of each fruit on the list to make trail mix. How much did she spend on dried fruit?

DRIED FRUIT

Fruit	Cost for Each Pound
Raisins	\$0.97
Bananas	\$1.49
Coconut	\$2.36
Apples	\$3.24

Mixed Review and Test Prep

31. $\begin{array}{r} 238 \\ \times\ \ 6 \\ \hline \end{array}$ (p. 222)

32. $\begin{array}{r} 5,000 \\ -2,198 \\ \hline \end{array}$ (p. 50)

33. $21,000 \div 7$ (p. 288)

34. Reshanda works 27 hours each week at the video store. She earns \$6.50 an hour. How much money does Reshanda earn in 3 weeks? (p. 262)

35. **TEST PREP** Jen has 3 quarters, 2 dimes, 4 nickels, and 1 penny in her pocket. Which combination of coins is possible if Jen pulls 4 coins from her pocket?
   - **A** 4 pennies
   - **B** 3 dimes and 1 nickel
   - **C** 2 pennies and 2 quarters
   - **D** 2 quarters and 2 nickels

LESSON 6

Problem Solving Skill
Interpret the Remainder

UNDERSTAND | PLAN | SOLVE | CHECK

Quick Review

1. $54 \div 6$
2. $8\overline{)64}$
3. $5\overline{)65}$
4. $9\overline{)84}$
5. $7\overline{)220}$

WHAT'S LEFT? Portia and Preston are planning for the school carnival.

When you solve a division problem that has a remainder, the way you interpret the remainder depends on the situation in the problem.

Examples

A Drop the remainder and increase the quotient by 1.

They need 250 cans of soda for the food booth. A carton holds 6 cans of soda. How many cartons of soda will they need to buy?

$$\begin{array}{r} 41 \text{ r}4 \\ 6\overline{)250} \\ -24 \\ \hline 10 \\ -6 \\ \hline 4 \end{array}$$

Since 41 cartons hold less than 250 cans, increase the quotient by 1.

So, they need to buy 42 cartons of soda.

B Drop the remainder.

They have a 250-foot roll of paper to make posters for the carnival. They will cut the roll into 3-foot posters. How many posters will they have?

$$\begin{array}{r} 83 \text{ r}1 \\ 3\overline{)250} \\ -24 \\ \hline 10 \\ -9 \\ \hline 1 \end{array}$$

Drop the remainder. The remainder is not enough for another 3-foot poster.

So, they will have a total of 83 posters.

C Use the remainder as the answer.

Portia made 126 cookies to sell. She divided the cookies into packages of 4 and gave the leftover cookies to her brother. How many cookies did she give her brother?

$$\begin{array}{r} 31 \text{ r}2 \\ 4\overline{)126} \\ -12 \\ \hline 06 \\ -4 \\ \hline 2 \end{array}$$

Use the remainder as the answer.

So, she gave her brother 2 cookies.

Talk About It

- Why isn't 41 cartons of soda the correct answer to the first question?
- Why is the remainder dropped to answer the second question?

Problem Solving Practice

Solve. Then write *a, b,* or *c* to tell how you interpreted the remainder.

a. increase the quotient by 1 **b.** drop the remainder **c.** use the remainder as the answer

1. An 85-inch piece of wire must be cut into 9-inch lengths. How many 9-inch lengths will there be?
2. Dave must pack 55 bottles of juice. Boxes for the bottles hold 8 bottles. How many boxes are needed?
3. Lena has a 50-foot roll of ribbon. She cuts the ribbon into 9-foot pieces to make bows. How many 9-foot pieces will she have?
4. Dora needs to buy pages for her photo album. Each page holds 6 photos. How many pages will she need for 94 photos?
5. Jan's Pillow Factory stuffs each pillow with 3 pounds of duck feathers. Jan has 67 pounds of feathers. How many pounds of feathers will be left over?
6. The Pool Supply Shop had 179 outdoor games. It shipped the same number of games to each of 8 stores. How many outdoor games were left over at the shop?

Mixed Applications

USE DATA For 7–9, use the bar graph.

7. If 900 tickets were sold at the carnival, how many tickets did not get used?
   A 20 **B** 40 **C** 120 **D** 140
8. If each ticket cost 50¢, what was the total spent on snacks?
   F \$50 **G** \$80 **H** \$100 **J** \$120
9. Games and snacks each cost 2 tickets. Sodas were 1 ticket each, and each ride cost 4 tickets. What was the most popular choice?

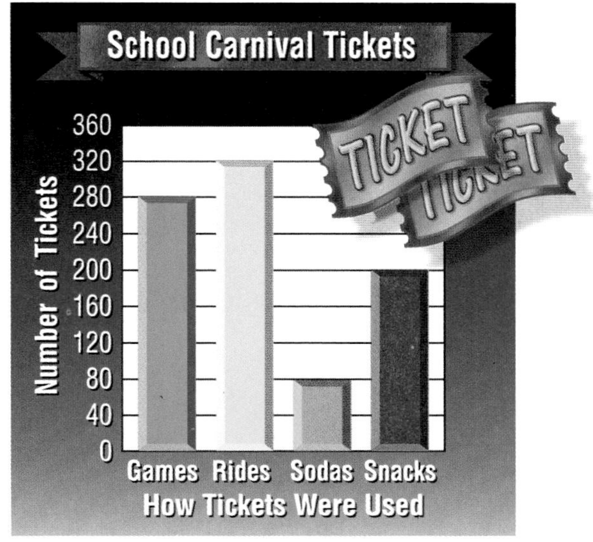

10. A theater has 23 rows of seats. Each row has 15 seats. There are 20 more seats in the balcony. How many seats are in the theater?
11. Nick bought two magazines for \$18.50. The difference in the cost of the magazines was \$2.50. How much did each magazine cost?
12. **Write a problem** in which the solution requires that you increase the quotient by 1.

Problem Solving

Extra Practice

Set A (pp. 296–297)

Estimate using compatible numbers.

1. $48 \div 9$ **2.** $51 \div 7$ **3.** $298 \div 6$ **4.** $359 \div 5$

5. $602 \div 8$ **6.** $183 \div 5$ **7.** $282 \div 4$ **8.** $709 \div 8$

9. $341 \div 6$ **10.** $675 \div 9$ **11.** $193 \div 3$ **12.** $244 \div 9$

Set B (pp. 298–299)

Tell where to place the first digit. Then divide.

1. $3\overline{)242}$ **2.** $8\overline{)679}$ **3.** $2\overline{)469}$ **4.** $5\overline{)412}$ **5.** $7\overline{)887}$

6. $9\overline{)851}$ **7.** $3\overline{)297}$ **8.** $5\overline{)751}$ **9.** $7\overline{)460}$ **10.** $2\overline{)263}$

Set C (pp. 300–301)

Divide and check.

1. $4\overline{)672}$ **2.** $9\overline{)121}$ **3.** $2\overline{)496}$ **4.** $5\overline{)453}$ **5.** $3\overline{)587}$

6. There are 8 swimmers on a team. The swim club has 152 swimmers. How many teams does the swim club have?

Set D (pp. 302–305)

Write the number of digits in each quotient.

1. $5\overline{)709}$ **2.** $8\overline{)650}$ **3.** $4\overline{)407}$ **4.** $5\overline{)360}$ **5.** $7\overline{)620}$

Divide and check.

6. $6\overline{)700}$ **7.** $4\overline{)828}$ **8.** $3\overline{)921}$ **9.** $5\overline{)740}$ **10.** $7\overline{)370}$

11. $570 \div 4$ **12.** $754 \div 8$ **13.** $310 \div 4$ **14.** $890 \div 7$ **15.** $820 \div 4$

Set E (pp. 306–307)

Divide.

1. $9\overline{)2,899}$ **2.** $6\overline{)4,827}$ **3.** $6\overline{)\$31.50}$ **4.** $8\overline{)7,609}$

5. Rashad has 1,386 baseball cards. If he puts an equal number in each of 7 boxes, how many cards are in each box?

Review/Test

CHECK VOCABULARY AND CONCEPTS

Choose the best term from the box.

compatible numbers
remainder
quotient
divisor

1. Numbers that are easy to compute mentally are ?. (p. 296)
2. The way you interpret the ? depends upon the situation in the problem. (p. 308)
3. You can estimate or use place value to place the first digit in a ?. (p. 298)

CHECK SKILLS

Estimate using compatible numbers. (pp. 296–297)

4. $67 \div 8$
5. $84 \div 9$
6. $543 \div 6$
7. $281 \div 9$
8. $207 \div 8$
9. $413 \div 7$
10. $312 \div 4$
11. $429 \div 5$

Tell where to place the first digit. Then divide. (pp. 298–299)

12. $9\overline{)75}$
13. $6\overline{)143}$
14. $4\overline{)346}$
15. $3\overline{)194}$
16. $5\overline{)275}$
17. $473 \div 6$
18. $534 \div 5$
19. $935 \div 3$

Divide. (pp. 300–301)

20. $809 \div 7$
21. $299 \div 8$
22. $124 \div 3$
23. $234 \div 4$
24. $569 \div 5$
25. $831 \div 7$
26. $971 \div 8$
27. $325 \div 3$
28. $\$26.28 \div 6$
29. $3{,}957 \div 2$
30. $4{,}864 \div 6$
31. $\$35.20 \div 8$

CHECK PROBLEM SOLVING

Solve. (pp. 308–309)

32. Tyrone and Jimmy want to build a tree fort. They need 153 feet of lumber. If the lumber comes in 8-foot lengths, how many pieces of lumber do they need?
33. Ling has 231 photos. If she puts 8 photos on a page, how many pages will she need for her photo album?

Standardized Test Prep

NUMBER SENSE, CONCEPTS, AND OPERATIONS

1. Mr. Miller bought 4 packs of pens for grading papers. Each pack has 8 pens. How many pens did Mr. Miller buy?

A 12

B 16

C 20

D 32

2. The table shows the cost of items at Pete's Pet Store. What is the cost for each pound of bird seed?

PETE'S PET STORE	
Item	**Cost**
Bag of cat food	$5.98
Bag of dog food	$5.98
5 pounds of bird seed	$6.45
Dog collar	$3.89
Pack of 3 cat toys	$1.77
Fish aquarium	$15.29

F $6.45

G $2.29

H $1.39

J $1.29

3. **Explain It** The Game Store sold 325 computer games over a period of 6 days. ESTIMATE the number of games sold each day. Explain your thinking.

MEASUREMENT

4. Sandra is going to camp on April 17. The last day of camp is June 30. How many days long is the camp?

April						
Sun	Mon	Tue	Wed	Thu	Fri	Sat
				1	2	3
4	5	6	7	8	9	10
11	12	13	14	15	16	17
18	19	20	21	22	23	24
25	26	27	28	29	30	

May						
Sun	Mon	Tue	Wed	Thu	Fri	Sat
						1
2	3	4	5	6	7	8
9	10	11	12	13	14	15
16	17	18	19	20	21	22
23/30	24/31	25	26	27	28	29

June						
Sun	Mon	Tue	Wed	Thu	Fri	Sat
		1	2	3	4	5
6	7	8	9	10	11	12
13	14	15	16	17	18	19
20	21	22	23	24	25	26
27	28	29	30			

A 75

B 44

C 31

D 30

5. William's computer weighs 16 pounds. How many ounces does it weigh?

1 pound = 16 ounces

F 1 ounce

G 32 ounces

H 256 ounces

J 356 ounces

6. **Explain It** Maude has the following coins and bills in her wallet.

ESTIMATE to the nearest dollar the amount of money Maude has in her wallet. Explain how you decided.

GEOMETRY AND SPATIAL SENSE

7. Carlos wants to write a different number on each face of a cube. How many numbers will he use?

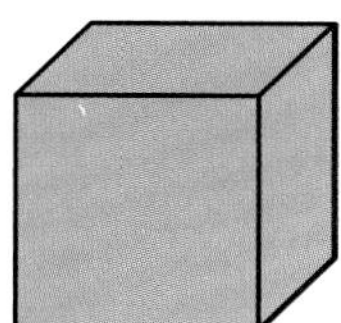

A 3

B 4

C 5

D 6

TIP **Eliminate choices.** See item 8. Think about the number of sides a triangle has. Eliminate the choices that are not multiples of that number. Then determine the answer from the remaining choices.

8. How many sides do 4 triangles have?

F 3

G 4

H 8

J 12

9. **Explain It** Draw a 4-sided shape and name it. Write *square, rectangle, rhombus, trapezoid,* or *other*.

Explain why you named your shape the way you did.

DATA ANALYSIS AND PROBABILITY

10. Bob made a stem-and-leaf plot showing the number of students in several classes in his school.

Class Sizes

Stem	Leaves
1	8 8 9
2	0 1 5 5
3	0 0 0 1

How many classes have 20 or more students?

A 11 **C** 4

B 8 **D** 1

11. On which number is the pointer **most** likely to land?

F 20 **H** 10

G 15 **J** 5

12. **Explain It** The Sharks basketball team's uniforms consist of either a black or a red shirt and either black, red, or white shorts.

How many different uniforms are possible? Explain how you decided.

Divide by 2-Digit Divisors

FAST FACT • SCIENCE Kites were used in ancient China to send messages and to spy on enemies. In modern times, kites have been used as models for the development of the airplane, to gather weather data, and for recreation.

PROBLEM SOLVING A kite tail is not just for decoration. It helps keep the kite steady in the air. A kite tail should be about 7 times the length of the spine. The spine is the vertical length of the center of the kite. Complete the table to find the length of the spine for each type of kite.

KITE TAILS		
Type of Kite	Length of Tail	Length of Spine
Diamond	525 in.	■
Delta	322 in.	■
Sled	252 in.	■
Butterfly	98 in.	■

CHECK WHAT YOU KNOW

Use this page to help you review and remember important skills needed for Chapter 15.

USE COMPATIBLE NUMBERS

Estimate using compatible numbers.

1. $7\overline{)59}$
2. $5\overline{)48}$
3. $9\overline{)38}$
4. $6\overline{)26}$
5. $8\overline{)61}$
6. $7\overline{)54}$
7. $8\overline{)68}$
8. $5\overline{)47}$
9. $4\overline{)35}$
10. $6\overline{)63}$
11. $7\overline{)51}$
12. $9\overline{)76}$
13. $9\overline{)49}$
14. $7\overline{)67}$
15. $5\overline{)38}$

DIVIDE BY 1-DIGIT DIVISORS

Divide.

16. $58 \div 4$
17. $73 \div 5$
18. $37 \div 7$
19. $93 \div 8$
20. $69 \div 9$
21. $43 \div 3$
22. $6\overline{)77}$
23. $7\overline{)46}$
24. $2\overline{)39}$
25. $5\overline{)52}$
26. $8\overline{)74}$
27. $4\overline{)66}$
28. $2\overline{)73}$
29. $3\overline{)88}$
30. $6\overline{)58}$

VOCABULARY POWER

REVIEW

divide [di•vīd′] *verb*

Divide contains the root *vidua,* which means "to separate." Explain what you are separating when you divide in mathematics.

www.harcourtschool.com/mathglossary

LESSON 1

Division Patterns to Estimate

Quick Review

1. 125 ÷ 5
2. 64 ÷ 4
3. 136 ÷ 8
4. 270 ÷ 9
5. 560 ÷ 7

Learn

FLYING HIGH A kite-flying contest had 753 entries from 18 schools. Each school sent in about the same number of entries. About how many entries were there from each school?

You can use basic facts and multiples of 10 to estimate.

Estimate.
753 ÷ 18
↓ ↓
800 ÷ 20

Look for a pattern.
8 ÷ 2 ← **Think:** Use the basic fact 8 ÷ 2.
80 ÷ 20 = 4
800 ÷ 20 = 40

So, there were about 40 entries from each school.

Examples

A	**B**	**C**
6 ÷ 3 = 2 ← basic fact	18 ÷ 6 = 3 ← basic fact	40 ÷ 5 = 8 ← basic fact
60 ÷ 30 = 2	180 ÷ 60 = 3	400 ÷ 50 = 8
600 ÷ 30 = 20	1,800 ÷ 60 = 30	4,000 ÷ 50 = 80
6,000 ÷ 30 = 200	18,000 ÷ 60 = 300	40,000 ÷ 50 = 800

MATH IDEA Basic facts and a pattern can help you estimate quotients.

Check

1. **Explain** how to find the quotient 90,000 ÷ 30 without dividing. Write the number of zeros in the quotient.

Write the numbers you would use to estimate the quotient. Then estimate.

2. 103 ÷ 11
3. 479 ÷ 39
4. 636 ÷ 81
5. 544 ÷ 93

Practice and Problem Solving

Extra Practice, page 330, Set A

Write the numbers you would use to estimate the quotient. Then estimate.

6. $99 \div 18$
7. $450 \div 51$
8. $623 \div 82$
9. $523 \div 47$
10. $94 \div 11$
11. $82 \div 21$
12. $93 \div 33$
13. $184 \div 31$
14. $313 \div 59$
15. $498 \div 55$
16. $813 \div 91$
17. $478 \div 59$

Copy and complete the tables.

	DIVIDEND		DIVISOR		QUOTIENT
18.	80	÷	40	=	■
19.	800	÷	40	=	■
20.	8,000	÷	40	=	■
21.	80,000	÷	40	=	■

	DIVIDEND		DIVISOR		QUOTIENT
22.	50	÷	50	=	■
23.	■	÷	50	=	10
24.	5,000	÷	50	=	■
25.	■	÷	50	=	10,000

26. There are 125 people signed up for a class on making kites. Each group will have 13 people. About how many groups will be formed?

27. Angel arrived at the park at 10:45 A.M. He watched the kite-flying contest and left after 2 hours 35 minutes. At what time did he leave the park?

28. Ms. Lang's class is making kites. Each student needs 280 inches of string. If there are 24 students in the class, how many feet of string will they use? (HINT: 12 inches = 1 foot)

29. Students were given 3 hours to complete their kites. How many minutes is this?

30. The Pittsfield Mets gave away about 12,080 baseball caps in July. About how many caps did they give away each day?

31. **Write About It** Explain how you can use basic facts and a pattern to estimate $72,000 \div 90$.

Mixed Review and Test Prep

Write each number in two other ways. (p. 4)

32. $2,000 + 500 + 40 + 3$

33. seven thousand, sixty

Find the sum or difference. (p. 48)

34. $2,421 + 1,247$

35. $3,631 - 1,485$

36. **TEST PREP** Brenden's team scored 67 points, 83 points, 95 points, and 79 points in their last 4 games. What was the mean number of points scored? (p. 118)

A 71
B 81
C 91
D 101

LESSON 2

Model Division

Quick Review

1. $7\overline{)210}$
2. $9\overline{)45}$
3. $8\overline{)480}$
4. $4\overline{)160}$
5. $123 \div 5$

MATERIALS base-ten blocks

Explore

TEA TIME Ann's Gift Shop has 65 teacups to put on display. Each rack holds 31 cups. How many racks will be filled with teacups? How many teacups will be left over?

Activity 1

Divide. $65 \div 31$

Make a model to divide with a two-digit divisor.

STEP 1

Show 65 as 6 tens 5 ones.

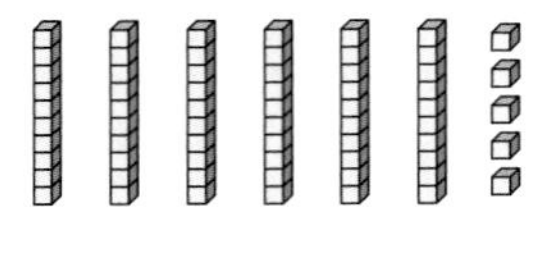

STEP 2

Make 1 group of 31.

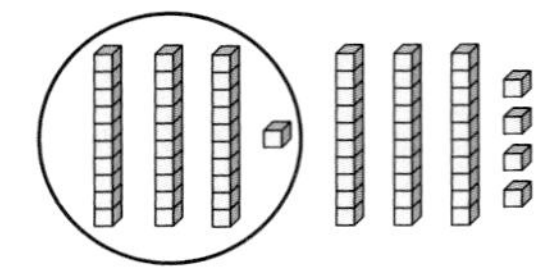

STEP 3

Make 2 groups of 31. Count how many ones are left over.

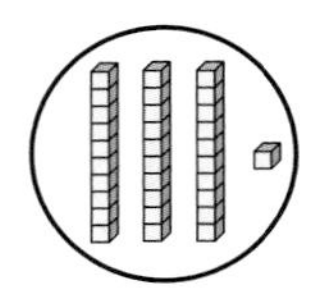

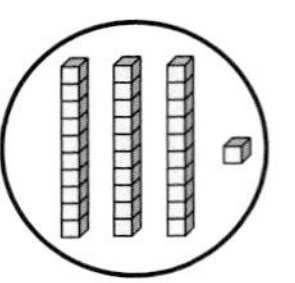

$65 \div 31 = 2$ r3

So, 2 racks will be filled with teacups. There will be 3 teacups left over.

- **Explain** how you can check the quotient and remainder.

Try It

Use base-ten blocks to solve each division problem.

a. $89 \div 22$

b. $76 \div 14$

c. $92 \div 18$

d. $64 \div 12$

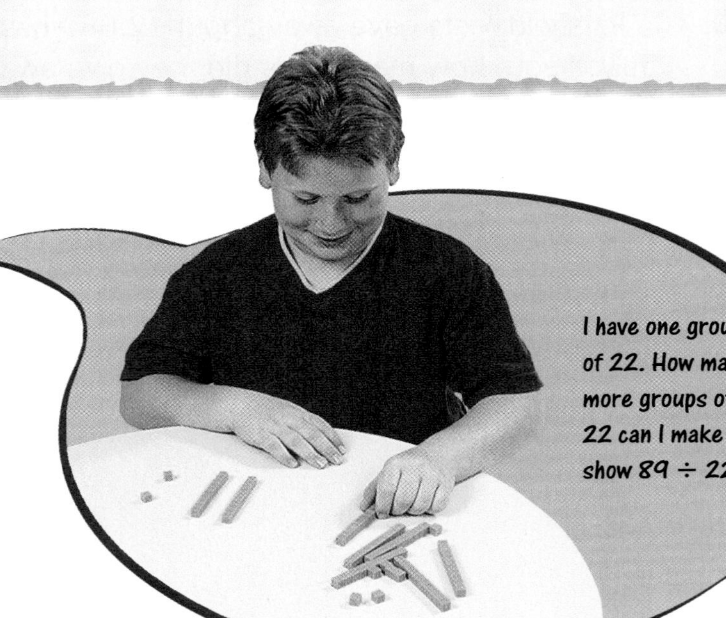

I have one group of 22. How many more groups of 22 can I make to show 89 ÷ 22?

Connect

Activity 2 Here is a way to record division. Divide 65 by 21.

STEP 1 Write the problem 65 ÷ 21.

Model

Record

$21\overline{)65}$

STEP 2 Estimate. 65 ÷ 21

Think: 60 ÷ 20 = 3

Try 3 groups of 21.

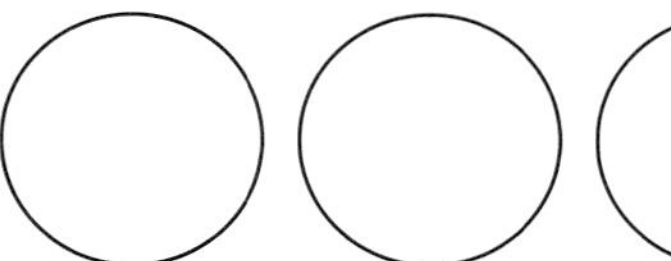

$$\begin{array}{r} 3 \\ 21\overline{)65} \end{array}$$

STEP 3 Make 3 groups of 21.

Multiply. 3 × 21 = 63
Count how many ones are left over.
Subtract. 65 − 63 = 2
Compare. 2 < 21

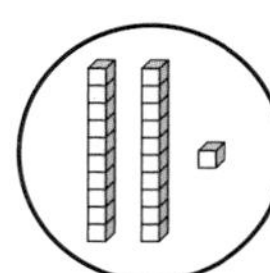

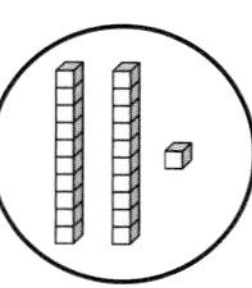

$$\begin{array}{r} 3 \text{ r2} \\ 21\overline{)65} \\ -63 \\ \hline 2 \end{array}$$

Practice and Problem Solving

Make a model to divide.

1. $17\overline{)58}$
2. $18\overline{)77}$
3. $35\overline{)108}$
4. $41\overline{)129}$

Divide. You may use base-ten blocks.

5. 259 ÷ 51
6. 158 ÷ 25
7. 237 ÷ 35
8. 301 ÷ 29
9. Mrs. Ching has 8 boxes of 6 cups. She can display 14 cups on each shelf. How many shelves does Mrs. Ching need for her teacups?
10. **REASONING** There were 6 groups, with 3 tens blocks and 1 ones block in each. What division equation can you write to tell the size of each group?

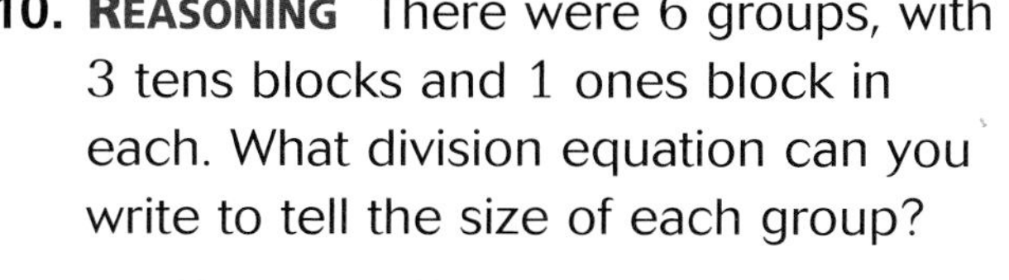

11. **What's the Error?** Silvia made this model for 59 ÷ 14. Describe her error. Draw the correct model.

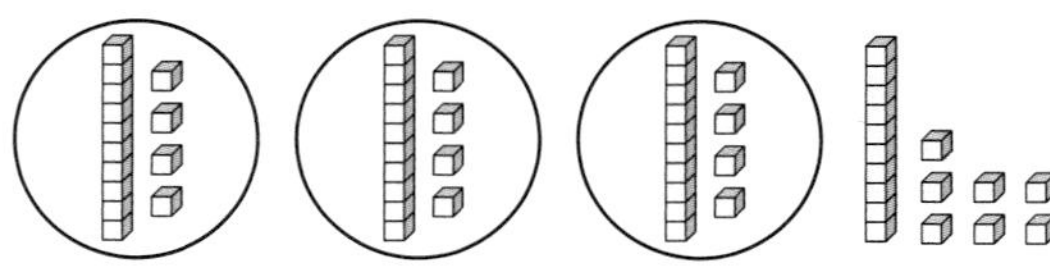

Mixed Review and Test Prep

Compare. Write <, >, or = for each ●. (p. 20)

12. 6,209 ● 6,290
13. 4,873 ● 4,783

Find the elapsed time. (p. 98)

14. **start:** 6:30 A.M. **end:** 2:15 P.M.

15. 36 × 185 (p. 258)
16. **TEST PREP** (47 + 7) ÷ (3 × 3) (p. 186)
    - **A** 9
    - **B** 8
    - **C** 6
    - **D** 4

LESSON 3

Division Procedures

Quick Review

1. 3)96
2. 5)144
3. 7)219
4. 6)512
5. 9)136

Learn

LUNAR PHASES It takes about 27 days for the moon to revolve around the Earth. How many times does the moon revolve around the Earth in 365 days?

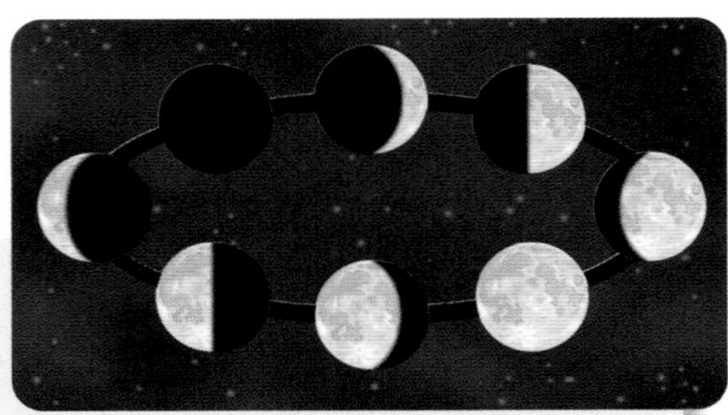

Example

Divide. 365 ÷ 27 or 27)365

STEP 1

Estimate to place the first digit in the quotient.

Think:

```
   10          12
30)300  or  30)360

   ■
27)365   So, place the first
         digit in the tens
         place.
```

STEP 2

Divide 36 tens. Write a 1 in the tens place in the quotient.

```
    1
27)365   Multiply. 27 × 1
  −27    Subtract. 36 − 27
    9    Compare. 9 < 27
```

STEP 3

Bring down the 5 ones. Divide the 95 ones.

```
   13 r14
27)365
  −27↓
    95   Multiply. 27 × 3
   −81   Subtract. 95 − 81
    14   Compare. 14 < 27
```

Write the remainder.

365 ÷ 27 = 13 r14

So, the moon revolves around the Earth 13 times in 365 days.

- What would happen if the difference in Step 2 was greater than the divisor?
- How can you check to see if the answer in Step 3 is correct?

Technology Link

More practice: Harcourt Mega Math The Number Games, *Up, Up, and Array,* Level R

Check

1. **Explain** how an estimate is useful when you divide two-digit numbers.

Divide.

2. 32)972
3. 25)582
4. 12)286
5. 17)365

 Extra Practice, page 330, Set B

Divide.

6. $13\overline{)246}$
7. $20\overline{)483}$
8. $12\overline{)148}$
9. $15\overline{)258}$
10. $11\overline{)201}$
11. $54\overline{)612}$
12. $21\overline{)825}$
13. $34\overline{)749}$
14. $32\overline{)676}$
15. $27\overline{)543}$
16. $41\overline{)784}$
17. $53\overline{)582}$

Complete.

18. $(17 \times 18) + 4 = 310$, so $310 \div 17 = 18$ r■.
19. $(36 \times 20) + 1 = 721$, so ■ $\div 36 = 20$ r1.
20. $(25 \times 31) + 5 = 780$, so $780 \div 25 =$ ■ r5.
21. $(14 \times 30) + 3 = 423$, so $423 \div 14 = 30$ r■.
22. $(40 \times 22) + 8 = 888$, so $888 \div$ ■ $= 22$ r8.
23. $(52 \times 14) + 40 = 768$, so $768 \div$ ■ $= 14$ r40.

USE DATA For 24–26, use the map.

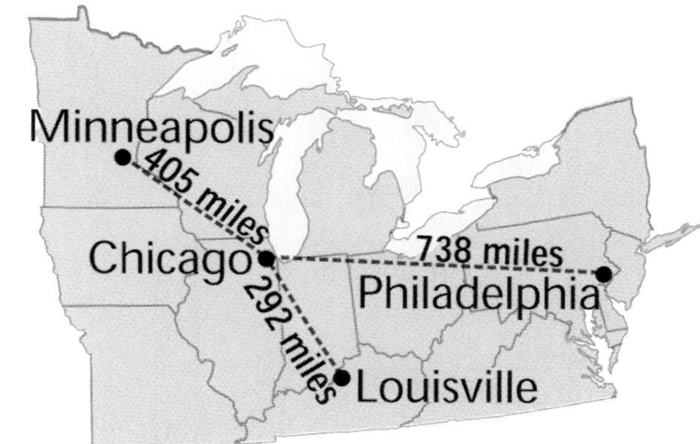

24. The Bensons and the Reeds met in Chicago. The Bensons drove from Minneapolis, and the Reeds drove from Louisville. After a week's stay they drove home. Who drove farther? How much farther?

25. If the average speed of travel was 60 mph, about how long would it take to drive from Chicago to Minneapolis? from Chicago to Louisville?

26. **What's the Question?** Felix and his family drove from Philadelphia to Chicago and back for a vacation. The answer is 1,476 miles.

27. **FAST FACT • SCIENCE** The greatest distance from the Earth to the moon is 251,927 miles, and the least distance is 225,745 miles. How much closer is the moon to the Earth from its least distance?

Mixed Review and Test Prep

Find the sum or difference. (p. 48)

28. 83,204 + 1,423
29. 63,128 − 47,129
30. $20 - (3 \times 2)$ (p. 186)
31. $12 \times 5 \times 7$ (p. 174)

32. **TEST PREP** Joshua travels 23 miles to work and 23 miles home 5 days a week. How many miles does he travel in 4 weeks? (p. 176)

A 920 miles
B 890 miles
C 720 miles
D 690 miles

LESSON 4

Correcting Quotients

Quick Review

1. $20\overline{)800}$
2. $80\overline{)720}$
3. $40\overline{)840}$
4. $25\overline{)150}$
5. $50\overline{)350}$

Learn

THE BAND MARCHES ON! There are 184 band members going to the Cherry Blossom Festival in Washington, D.C. School policy requires a chaperone for every 21 students. How many chaperones are needed?

Since a chaperone is needed for every 21 students, divide 184 by 21.

Example

Divide. $184 \div 21$ or $21\overline{)184}$

Estimate. $180 \div 20 = 9$

STEP 1

Try the estimate, 9.
$21 \times 9 = 189$

$$\begin{array}{r} 9 \\ 21\overline{)184} \\ -189 \\ \hline \end{array}$$

Since $189 > 184$, the estimate is too high.

STEP 2

Try 8.
$21 \times 8 = 168$

$$\begin{array}{r} 8 \\ 21\overline{)184} \\ -168 \\ \hline \end{array}$$

STEP 3

Subtract to find the remainder.

$$\begin{array}{r} 8 \text{ r16} \\ 21\overline{)184} \\ -168 \\ \hline 16 \end{array}$$

Compare. $16 < 21$

There are 8 chaperones, each in charge of 21 students, and 1 more chaperone is needed for the 16 remaining students. So, 9 chaperones are needed.

More Examples

A Divide. $244 \div 27$
Estimate. $240 \div 30 = 8$

Try 8.

$$\begin{array}{r} 8 \\ 27\overline{)244} \\ -216 \\ \hline 28 \end{array}$$

Since $28 > 27$, the estimate is too low.

Try 9.

$$\begin{array}{r} 9 \text{ r1} \\ 27\overline{)244} \\ -243 \\ \hline 1 \end{array}$$

B Divide. $319 \div 84$
Estimate. $320 \div 80 = 4$

Try 4.

$$\begin{array}{r} 4 \\ 84\overline{)319} \\ -336 \\ \hline \end{array}$$

Since $336 > 319$, the estimate is too high.

Try 3.

$$\begin{array}{r} 3 \text{ r67} \\ 84\overline{)319} \\ -252 \\ \hline 67 \end{array}$$

$67 < 84$

Check Estimates

To check if your estimate is too high, too low, or just right, multiply it by the divisor. Then compare the product to the dividend. Subtract if possible.

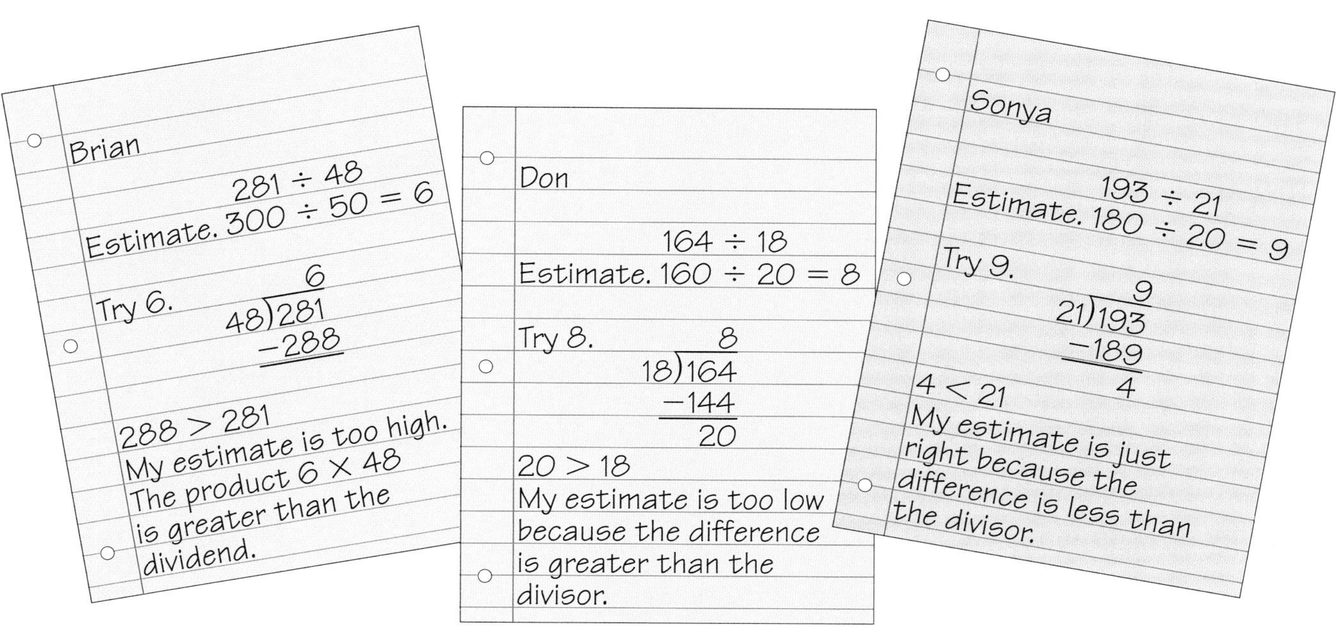

Brian
281 ÷ 48
Estimate. 300 ÷ 50 = 6
Try 6.
6
48)281
−288
288 > 281
My estimate is too high. The product 6 × 48 is greater than the dividend.
Don
164 ÷ 18
Estimate. 160 ÷ 20 = 8
Try 8.
8
18)164
−144
20
20 > 18
My estimate is too low because the difference is greater than the divisor.
Sonya
193 ÷ 21
Estimate. 180 ÷ 20 = 9
Try 9.
9
21)193
−189
4
4 < 21
My estimate is just right because the difference is less than the divisor.

MATH IDEA Sometimes your choice for the first digit of a quotient is not correct. You can correct it by increasing or decreasing the first digit.

- How should Brian and Don correct the quotients shown on their papers above?

Check

1. **Explain** how to correct a quotient.

Write *too high, too low,* or *just right* for each estimate. Then divide.

2. $\begin{array}{r} 8 \\ 27\overline{)257} \end{array}$ 3. $\begin{array}{r} 9 \\ 43\overline{)362} \end{array}$ 4. $\begin{array}{r} 6 \\ 86\overline{)536} \end{array}$ 5. $\begin{array}{r} 9 \\ 51\overline{)462} \end{array}$

Divide.

6. $15\overline{)146}$ 7. $31\overline{)236}$ 8. $75\overline{)536}$ 9. $67\overline{)436}$

LESSON CONTINUES

Practice and Problem Solving

Extra Practice, page 330, Set C

Write *too high, too low,* or *just right* for each estimate. Then divide.

10. $\begin{array}{r} 6 \\ 18\overline{)108} \end{array}$ **11.** $\begin{array}{r} 5 \\ 35\overline{)215} \end{array}$ **12.** $\begin{array}{r} 9 \\ 85\overline{)798} \end{array}$ **13.** $\begin{array}{r} 3 \\ 85\overline{)367} \end{array}$

14. $\begin{array}{r} 10 \\ 22\overline{)221} \end{array}$ **15.** $\begin{array}{r} 9 \\ 45\overline{)369} \end{array}$ **16.** $\begin{array}{r} 25 \\ 36\overline{)853} \end{array}$ **17.** $\begin{array}{r} 5 \\ 79\overline{)487} \end{array}$

Divide.

18. $52\overline{)456}$ **19.** $82\overline{)736}$ **20.** $45\overline{)236}$ **21.** $62\overline{)336}$

22. $79\overline{)238}$ **23.** $86\overline{)528}$ **24.** $68\overline{)596}$ **25.** $81\overline{)377}$

26. $511 \div 42$ **27.** $754 \div 15$ **28.** $875 \div 23$ **29.** $488 \div 37$

30. $647 \div 53$ **31.** $747 \div 24$ **32.** $911 \div 33$ **33.** $939 \div 84$

For 34–36, use what you know about division to find the mystery digits for each problem.

34. $\begin{array}{r} \blacksquare\blacksquare \\ 28\overline{)364} \end{array}$ **35.** $\begin{array}{r} 26 \\ \blacksquare\blacksquare\overline{)702} \end{array}$ **36.** $\begin{array}{r} 5\blacksquare \\ 3\blacksquare\overline{)1,700} \end{array}$

Mystery Digits
0, 1, 2, 3, 4, 7

USE DATA **For 37–40, use the table.**

37. The band director wants the members to march in rows of 14. How many rows will the band have? How many members will not be in a row of 14?

38. The clarinet and flute players need to march together. If the band marches in rows of 14, how many rows of clarinet and flute players will there be?

39. The percussion and trumpet players march in rows with an equal number of players in each row. How many rows could there be? How many players are in each row?

40. **Write a problem** about the marching band, using division.

The Marching Band

Group	Number of Members
Clarinets	24
Flutes	20
Trumpets	12
Percussion	16
Tubas	4
Flags	20

41. Paul had 10 school books, 45 fiction books, 35 nonfiction books, and 78 science fiction books. He gave away 10 fiction books and 15 science fiction books. How many books does he have left?

42. **What's the Error?** First Susan estimated $322 \div 42$ as 8. Then she corrected the quotient by writing 9. Describe her error and tell what she should have written.

43. Vocabulary Power *Estimate* used as a verb means "to give an approximate value." *Estimate* can also be used as a noun. What is the difference when it is used as a noun?

44. Phillip put $5 in a machine that gives change in quarters. How many quarters should Phillip get?

Mixed Review and Test Prep

Find the sum or difference. (p. 48)

45. $\begin{array}{r} 2{,}690 \\ +7{,}421 \\ \hline \end{array}$

46. $\begin{array}{r} 5{,}682 \\ -1{,}900 \\ \hline \end{array}$

Find the product. (p. 174)

47. $2 \times (3 \times 4)$

48. $4 \times (5 \times 2)$

49. TEST PREP If $9 \times n = 72$, what is n? (p. 168)

A 5 **B** 6 **C** 7 **D** 8

50. TEST PREP A group of 52 boys, 67 girls, and 4 teachers are taking a bus trip. If each bus holds 48 people, how many buses will be needed? (p. 320)

F 2 **G** 3 **H** 4 **J** 5

Problem Solving LINKUP . . . to Reading

STRATEGY • SYNTHESIZE INFORMATION
When a problem presents a lot of information, it is helpful to synthesize, or combine, the related facts. You can group the related facts in a table.

Use the graph and the table to find how many rolls Charlie will have of each type of coin.

Synthesize the information by grouping the related facts.

1. How many coins are in a roll of dimes? In a roll of quarters?
2. Copy and complete the table.

COINS	CHARLIE'S COINS	NUMBER OF COINS IN A ROLL	NUMBER OF ROLLS
Pennies	845	50	■
Nickels	164	40	■
Dimes	495	■	■
Quarters	282	■	■

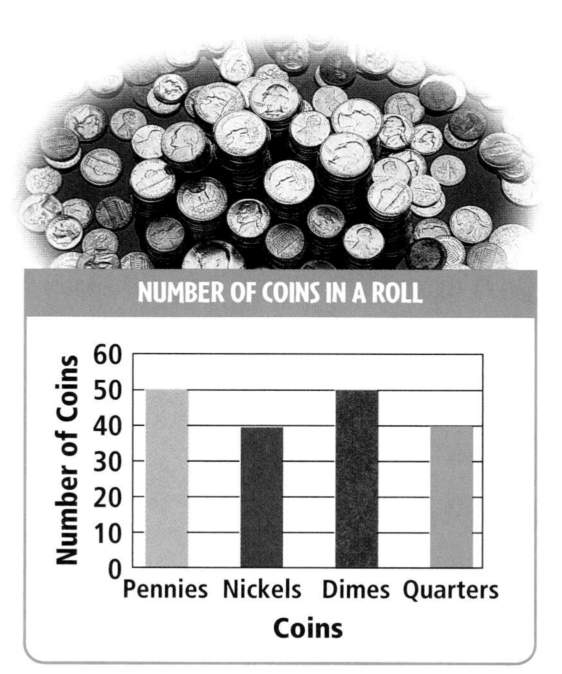

LESSON 5

Problem Solving Skill
Choose the Operation

UNDERSTAND | PLAN | SOLVE | CHECK

Quick Review

1. 12×5
2. $72 \div 8$
3. $17 + 43$
4. $133 - 21$
5. $144 \div 12$

MOVING PICTURES Mr. Regis teaches animation classes. Read problems A–D below. Use the table about the operations and Mr. Regis's notes to help you solve the problems.

Add	• Join groups of different sizes
Subtract	• Take away or compare groups
Multiply	• Join equal-size groups
Divide	• Separate into equal-size groups • Find how many in each group

A How many students are taking animation classes at the art school?

B For Tuesday's class, there are 25 sheets of drawing paper for each student. How many sheets of paper are there in all?

C How many more drawings did Maria's group make than Jerry's group?

D For every second of animation, 12 drawings are needed. How long will Tran's animation last? Will there be any drawings left over? If so, how many?

Art School Sign-Up

Day	Students
Monday	95
Tuesday	123
Thursday	78
Saturday	107

Animation Drawings

Group	Drawings
Jerry	501
Maria	810
Greg	642
Tran	756

Talk About It

- How can you decide which operation or operations to use for each problem?
- Solve Problems A–D.
- What operation or operations did you use in each of Problems A–D?

Problem Solving Practice

Solve. Name the operation or operations you used.

1. Eric took 5 rolls of film with him on vacation. He can take 24 pictures with each roll of film. How many pictures can he take?
2. Eric took 18 pictures in Germany, 28 in France, 13 in Spain, and 11 in Portugal. How many pictures did he take?

Mary took 96 pictures last year. If each roll of film had 24 pictures, how many rolls of film did she use?

3. What operation would you use to solve the problem?
   A multiplication **C** addition
   B division **D** subtraction
4. How many rolls of film did she use?
   F 5 **G** 4 **H** 3 **J** 2

Mixed Applications

USE DATA For 5–7, use the graph.

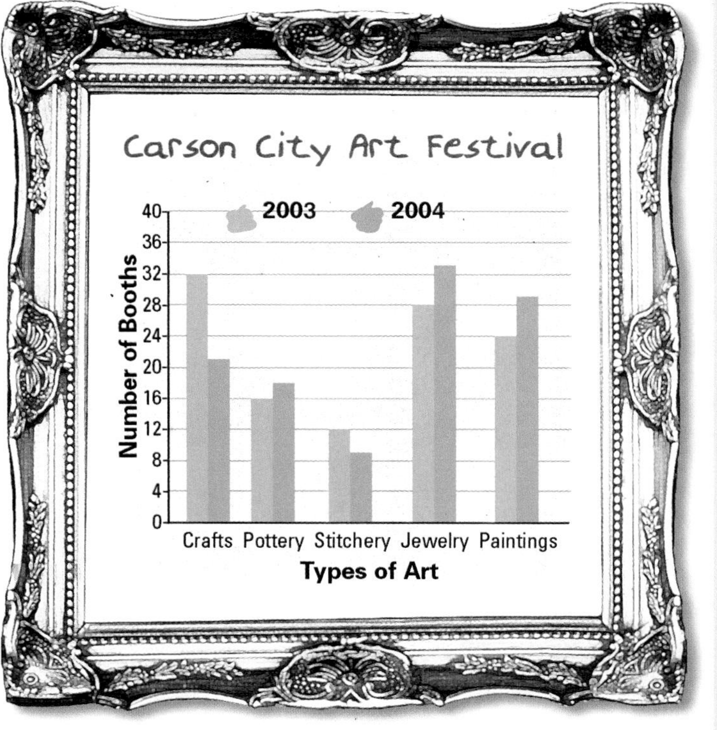

5. In 2004, Jon visited all the pottery, jewelry, and crafts booths. What was the total number of booths he visited?
6. Mr. Marcel spent 10 minutes talking to each booth owner in 2003. How many minutes did Mr. Marcel spend talking to the booth owners? How many hours and minutes is this?
7. In which year were there more booths at the Carson City Art Festival? How many more?
8. There were 265,980 people at a parade in 2003 and 298,125 people at a parade in 2004. Were there more people at the parade in 2003 or 2004? How many more?

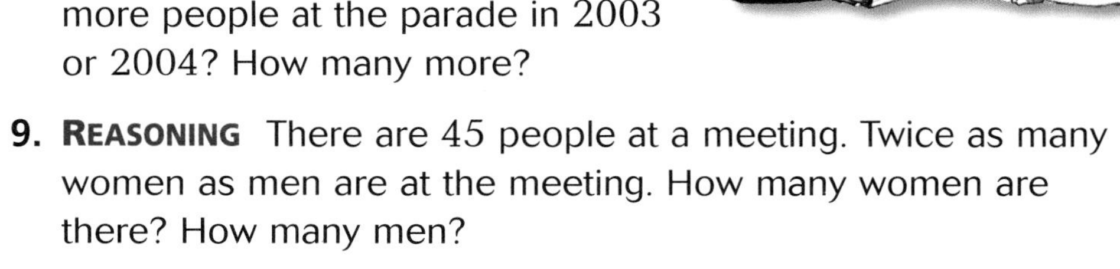

9. **REASONING** There are 45 people at a meeting. Twice as many women as men are at the meeting. How many women are there? How many men?

the Mean

Learn

Quick Review

1. 12 + 11 + 25
2. 9 + 22 + 8
3. 22 + 34 + 5
4. 23 + 17 + 40
5. 36 + 45 + 27 + 9

ON A LEASH Janet earns money walking her neighbor's dogs. Over 4 days she earned $4.75, $3.60, $8.25, and $5.00. What is the mean, or average, amount Janet earned each day?

Example

STEP 1

Add the amounts she earned.

```
  $4.75
  $3.60   4 addends
  $8.25
+ $5.00
 $21.60  ← sum
```

STEP 2

Divide the sum by the number of addends.

```
                  $5.40  ← mean
number →        4)$21.60 ← sum
of addends        −20
                   16
                  −16
                    00
                   − 0
                     0
```

Divide money amounts as you divide whole numbers. Write the quotient in dollars and cents.

So, the mean, or average, amount Janet earned was $5.40 per day.

You can use a calculator to find the mean.
Find the mean of 49, 14, 70, 53, 67, 72, 44, 58, 64, and 59.

4 9 + 1 4 + 7 0 + 5 3 +
6 7 + 7 2 + 4 4 + 5 8 +
6 4 + 5 9 = 550

5 5 0 ÷ 1 0 = 55

So, the mean, or average, is 55.

Check

1. **Explain** in your own words how to find the mean of a set of data.

Write the division problem for finding the mean. Then find the mean.

2. 15, 12, 16, 13
3. 358, 460, 733, 197
4. $26.35, $47.83, $62.29

Practice and Problem Solving

Extra Practice, page 330, Set D

Write the division problem for finding the mean. Then find the mean.

5. 46 37
55 67
93 45
61 91
72 63

6. $5.88 $1.75
$6.49 $4.96
$3.55 $2.15
$8.99 $6.36
$2.53 $8.67
$1.26 $3.69

7. 1,471 680
820 453
325 162
783 573
941 1,071
278

Find the mean.

8. 119, 241, 67, 74, 212, 65, 99, 211, 79, 523

9. 598; 1,045; 822; 971; 400; 84; 2,673; 3,399

10. 2,176; 3,211; 543; 1,287; 753; 970

11. 95, 88, 84, 85, 93, 89

12. 60, 85, 74, 79, 67

13. $3.75, $1.98, $6.75

Find the missing number.

14. 8, 10, 12, ■ Mean is 11.

15. ■, 12, 15, 17, 21 Mean is 15.

USE DATA For 16–18, use the table.

16. Find the average number of points per show the collies won this season.

17. Find the average number of points per show the spaniels won this season.

18. Write < or > to compare the average number of points for collies to the average points for spaniels.

DOG SHOW POINT TOTALS

Show	Collies	Spaniels
1	45	71
2	56	35
3	79	45
4	32	61
5	44	71
6	56	53

19. REASONING For 5–13, look at the least and greatest numbers in the set. Compare these numbers to the mean of the set. What do you notice?

Mixed Review and Test Prep

Write in order from least to greatest. (p. 24)

20. 56; 34; 92; 86; 2; 45

21. 12,543; 12,453; 12,354

22. $903 + 745$ (p. 40)

23. 513×17 (p. 256)

24. TEST PREP Jan has 84 points in a game. Mike has 28 fewer points than Jan. How many points does Mike have? (p. 176)

A 56
B 90
C 102
D 112

Extra Practice

Set A (pp. 316–317)

Write the numbers you would use to estimate the quotient. Then estimate.

1. $832 \div 21$
2. $394 \div 19$
3. $542 \div 38$
4. $407 \div 72$
5. $163 \div 43$
6. $269 \div 56$
7. $658 \div 65$
8. $808 \div 91$
9. Jim wants to make a scrapbook. He can fit 6 baseball cards on each page. He has 123 baseball cards. About how many pages will he need?
10. The 12 members of a scout troop sold 230 buckets of popcorn. About how many buckets of popcorn did each member sell?

Set B (pp. 320–321)

Divide.

1. $12\overline{)645}$
2. $24\overline{)721}$
3. $18\overline{)212}$
4. $34\overline{)310}$
5. $15\overline{)927}$
6. $13\overline{)172}$
7. $26\overline{)525}$
8. $37\overline{)454}$
9. A pen manufacturer packed 718 pens. Each package holds 12 pens. How many packages is this? How many pens are left over?
10. The members of the bicycle club cycled 375 miles in 15 days. If they cycled the same number of miles each day, how many miles did they cycle each day?

Set C (pp. 322–325)

Write *too high, too low,* or *just right* for each estimate. Then divide.

1. $78\overline{)612}$ with estimate 7
2. $34\overline{)312}$ with estimate 8
3. $26\overline{)156}$ with estimate 6
4. $56\overline{)448}$ with estimate 9

Divide.

5. $49\overline{)872}$
6. $63\overline{)917}$
7. $14\overline{)275}$
8. $32\overline{)564}$
9. $25\overline{)743}$
10. $52\overline{)816}$
11. $17\overline{)194}$
12. $21\overline{)836}$

Set D (pp. 328–329)

Find the mean.

1. 58, 89, 77, 93, 64, 45
2. \$4.54, \$3.77, \$5.31
3. 310, 211, 405, 111, 98
4. 22, 35, 19, 47, 56, 73, 62, 42, 39, 16, 26, 55
5. 2,031; 241; 176; 366; 371; 35; 78; 91; 32; 79
6. 974; 2,765; 2,062; 2,235; 687; 1,093

Review/Test

CHECK VOCABULARY AND CONCEPTS

Choose the best term from the box.

divisor
mean
quotient
remainder

1. Multiply the quotient by the _?_ and add the _?_ to the product to check the quotient and remainder of a division problem. (p. 320)
2. The _?_ is the number found by dividing the sum of a set of numbers by the number of addends. (p. 328)

CHECK SKILLS

Write the numbers you would use to estimate the quotient. Then estimate. (pp. 316–317)

3. $623 \div 22$
4. $294 \div 19$
5. $761 \div 37$
6. $82 \div 21$
7. $385 \div 48$
8. $649 \div 52$

Divide. (pp. 318–321)

9. $19\overline{)98}$
10. $25\overline{)237}$
11. $32\overline{)453}$
12. $43\overline{)518}$
13. $27\overline{)394}$
14. $34\overline{)619}$
15. $17\overline{)123}$
16. $56\overline{)767}$

Write *too high, too low,* or *just right* for each estimate. Then divide. (pp. 322–325)

17. $\begin{array}{r} 5 \\ 48\overline{)288} \end{array}$
18. $\begin{array}{r} 4 \\ 35\overline{)175} \end{array}$
19. $\begin{array}{r} 7 \\ 37\overline{)260} \end{array}$
20. $\begin{array}{r} 8 \\ 71\overline{)513} \end{array}$
21. $\begin{array}{r} 8 \\ 52\overline{)468} \end{array}$

Find the mean. (pp. 328–329)

22. 124, 130, 100, 122, 124, 100, 150, 205, 170, 202, 213, 285, 250, 315, 285
23. \$12.20, \$24.56, \$13.20, \$25.60, \$14.75, \$18.32, \$21.48, \$16.81, \$10.79, \$9.83, \$12.50, \$11.48

CHECK PROBLEM SOLVING

Solve. Name the operation or operations you used. (pp. 326–327)

24. Jeremy keeps his stamps in an album. Each sheet in the album holds 18 stamps. How many sheets will he need for 234 new stamps?
25. Mr. Davis is writing a 450-page book. He has written 13 pages each day for 25 days. How many more pages does he need to write?

Standardized Test Prep

NUMBER SENSE, CONCEPTS, AND OPERATIONS

TIP **Look for important words.**

See item 1. The important words are *estimate* and *product*. Estimate each product before you choose the greatest.

1. Estimate each product. Which is the **greatest**?

   A 76×28

   B 67×48

   C 59×31

   D 43×43

2. A whale shark weighs 46,297 pounds. Which digit in the number 46,297 has a place value of ten thousand?

   F 2

   G 4

   H 6

   J 9

3. **Explain It** Last year a group of 612 people went on a tour of Europe on 23 buses. Each bus held about the same number of people. ESTIMATE the number of people on each bus. Explain your thinking.

GEOMETRY AND SPATIAL SENSE

4. For which shape is the dotted line NOT a line of symmetry?

   A

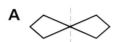

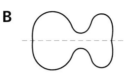

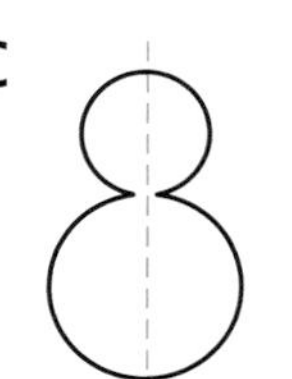

   B

   C

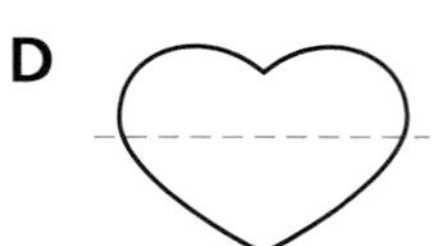

   D

5. Which statement about a square pyramid is true?

   F None of the faces are triangles.

   G All of the faces are circles.

   H Some of the faces are triangles.

   J None of the faces are squares.

6. **Explain It** Compare the figures below.

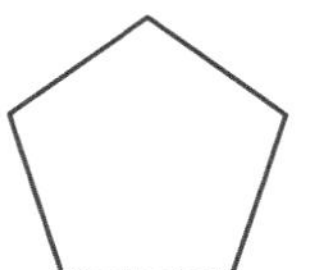

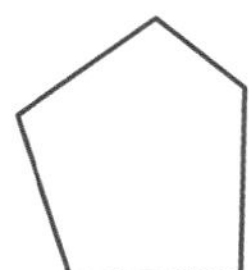

   Explain how they are alike and how they are different.

ALGEBRAIC THINKING

7. Mohammed made the table below to show the number of sports cards in his collection.

SPORTS CARD COLLECTION	
Type of Card	**Number**
Baseball	73
Football	72
Basketball	90
Hockey	29

Which of the following can be used to find how many more baseball cards Mohammed has than hockey cards?

A $73 + 29 = n$

B $73 - 72 = n$

C $73 - 29 = n$

D $73 + n = 100$

8. Which number sentence comes next in the pattern below?

$140 \div 70 = 2$
$1{,}400 \div 70 = 20$
$14{,}000 \div 70 = 200$

F $140{,}000 \div 70 = 2{,}000$

G $1{,}400{,}000 \div 70 = 20{,}000$

H $1{,}400{,}000 \div 20 = 70{,}000$

J $1{,}400{,}000 \div 14 = 100{,}000$

9. **Explain It** Write a rule for the pattern below.

Explain how you decided.

DATA ANALYSIS AND PROBABILITY

10. The ages of the relatives who attended Jamie's party are 24, 18, 39, 12, and 7. What is the mean of their ages?

A 39 **C** 20

B 24 **D** 7

11. The line graph below shows the number of pairs of sneakers sold by The Running Shop for a six-month period.

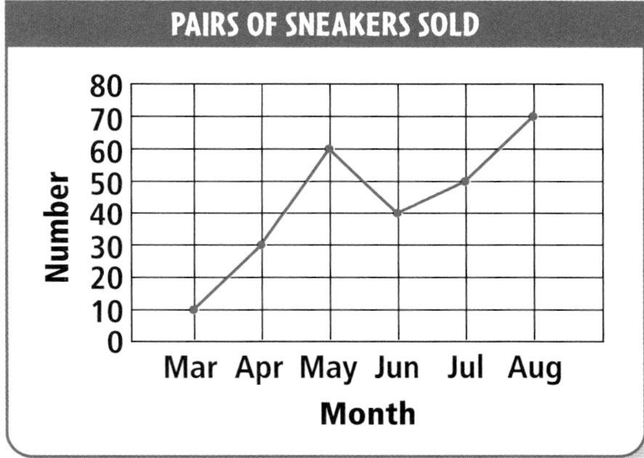

During which month were the **second-fewest** pairs of sneakers sold?

F April **H** June

G May **J** July

12. **Explain It** The table below shows Albert's allowance at different ages.

ALBERT'S ALLOWANCES	
Age	**Amount**
8 years old	\$1.60
9 years old	\$1.80
10 years old	\$2.00

Will Albert's allowance at age 11 be **more than** or **less than** \$2.00? Explain how you know.

CHAPTER 16 Number Theory

FAST FACT • ART Billie Ruth Sudduth was named a Living Treasure by the state of North Carolina in 1997. She is the tenth recipient of the award and first woman to receive this honor. Sudduth uses the Fibonacci Sequence, a famous number pattern, to weave baskets. She uses mathematical relationships to determine the size, the weave, and the line designs of her baskets.

PROBLEM SOLVING Look at the numbers in the Fibonacci Sequence. Explain the number pattern.

Fibonacci 8

NUMBERS IN THE FIBONACCI SEQUENCE

1st	2nd	3rd	4th	5th	6th	7th	8th	9th	10th	11th	12th	13th
1	1	2	3	5	8	13	21	34	55	89	144	233

CHECK WHAT YOU KNOW

Use this page to help you review and remember important skills needed for Chapter 16.

ARRAYS

Use the array to find the product.

1. ■■■■■■ / ■■■■■■ — ▢ × ▢ = ▢
2. ■■■■ / ■■■■ / ■■■■ — ▢ × ▢ = ▢
3. ■■■■■■■■■■■■ — ▢ × ▢ = ▢

MULTIPLICATION FACTS

Find the product.

4. 5×2
5. 4×8
6. 6×2
7. 7×5
8. 9×7
9. 9×6
10. 4×5
11. 6×0
12. 8×5
13. 7×8

MISSING FACTORS

Find the missing factor.

14. $1 \times$ ▢ $= 10$
15. ▢ $\times 3 = 9$
16. ▢ $\times 3 = 27$
17. $12 \times$ ▢ $= 24$
18. $6 \times$ ▢ $= 42$
19. ▢ $\times 4 = 28$
20. $12 \times$ ▢ $= 60$
21. ▢ $\times 9 = 63$

VOCABULARY POWER

REVIEW

pattern [pa′tərn] *noun*

A synonym for the word *pattern* is *order*. Look up the definition of *order*. Explain how *pattern* and *order* are related.

PREVIEW

divisible
prime number
composite number
square number
square root

www.harcourtschool.com/mathglossary

LESSON 1

Divisibility Rules

Quick Review

Find the quotient. Tell if the quotient is *even* or *odd*.

1. 48 ÷ 6 **2.** 63 ÷ 7

3. 20 ÷ 5 **4.** 45 ÷ 9

5. 32 ÷ 4

VOCABULARY

divisible

Learn

AN EVEN COMBINATION A number is **divisible** by another number when the quotient is a whole number and the remainder is zero.

Number	Divisibility Rule
2	The last digit must be even.
3	The sum of the digits must be divisible by 3.
5	The last digit must be 0 or 5.
9	The sum of the digits must be divisible by 9.
10	The last digit must be 0.

Max's locker number is one of these numbers.

425 450 480 486

His locker number is divisible by 2, 3, 5, 9, and 10. Which number is his locker number?

Use divisibility rules to find Max's locker number.

Example

STEP 1

Check for divisibility by 2.
The last digit must be even.

~~425~~ 450 480 486

Cross out 425.

STEP 2

Check for divisibility by 5.
The last digit must be 0 or 5.

~~425~~ 450 480 ~~486~~

Cross out 486.

STEP 3

Check for divisibility by 10.
The last digit must be 0.

~~425~~ 450 480 ~~486~~

450 and 480 are divisible by 10.

STEP 4

Check 450 and 480 for divisibility by 3.
The sum of the digits must be divisible by 3.

$450 \rightarrow 4 + 5 + 0 = 9$ $9 \div 3 = 3$
$480 \rightarrow 4 + 8 + 0 = 12$ $12 \div 3 = 4$

~~425~~ 450 480 ~~486~~

450 and 480 are divisible by 3.

STEP 5

Check 450 and 480 for divisibility by 9.
The sum of the digits must be divisible by 9.

$450 \rightarrow 4 + 5 + 0 = 9$ $9 \div 9 = 1$
$480 \rightarrow 4 + 8 + 0 = 12$ $12 \div 9 = 1 \text{ r}3$

~~425~~ 450 ~~480~~ ~~486~~

Cross out 480.

So Max's locker number is 450, since 450 is the only number divisible by 2, 3, 5, 9, and 10.

Check

1. **Explain** how checking for divisibility by 3 is similar to checking for divisibility by 9. Explain how it is different.

Tell whether the number is divisible by 2, 3, 5, 9, or 10.

2. 96 **3.** 120 **4.** 738 **5.** 4,516 **6.** 9,882

Practice and Problem Solving

Extra Practice, page 350, Set A

Tell whether the number is divisible by 2, 3, 5, 9, or 10.

7. 33 **8.** 65 **9.** 3,750 **10.** 13,467 **11.** 2,130

12. 6,452 **13.** 9,876 **14.** 73,821 **15.** 3,459 **16.** 27,000

REASONING Write *true* or *false* for each statement. Explain.

17. All even numbers are divisible by 10.

18. All numbers that are divisible by 5 are also divisible by 10.

19. All numbers that are divisible by 9 are also divisible by 3.

20. All numbers that are divisible by 3 are also divisible by 9.

21. All numbers that are divisible by 10 are also divisible by 5.

22. All numbers divisible by 2 and 3 are also divisible by 5.

For 23–24, use the locker numbers below.

23. Jen's locker number is shown above. Her locker number is divisible by 3 and 9. Which is her locker number?

24. Dan's locker number is shown above. His locker number is *not* divisible by 2 or 9. Which is his locker number?

25. **Write a problem** with an answer that is divisible by 2, 3, 5, 9, and 10. Show the solution.

26. **Vocabulary Power** Explain how the words *divisible* and *divide* are related.

Mixed Review and Test Prep

27. 567×23 (p. 256)

28. $1{,}789 \times 65$ (p. 258)

29. Order from least to greatest. 1,267,898; 1,278,987; 1,456,892; 1,987 (p. 24)

30. **TEST PREP** James delivers papers in the morning 7 days a week. His route is 26 miles long. How many miles does he travel in 4 weeks? (p. 222)

A 104 miles **C** 286 miles

B 182 miles **D** 728 miles

LESSON 2

Factors and Multiples

Quick Review

1. 5 × ▢ = 50
2. 4 × ▢ = 44
3. 5 × ▢ = 60
4. ▢ × ▢ = 25
5. ▢ × ▢ = 49

Learn

USING PRODUCTS Every whole number has at least two factors—that number and 1.

$1 \times 11 = 11 \qquad 9 \times 1 = 9$

Many numbers can be broken into factors in different ways.

$16 = 4 \times 4 \qquad 16 = 2 \times 8 \qquad 16 = 1 \times 16$

You can use arrays to show the factors of whole numbers.

HANDS ON

Activity **MATERIALS:** square tiles

Make as many arrays as you can that have 36 squares.

1 × 36 = 36

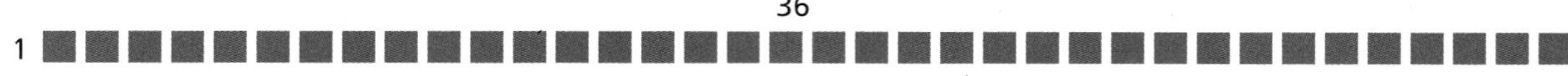

This array has a length of 36 and a width of 1, so 36 and 1 are factors of 36.

2 × 18 = 36

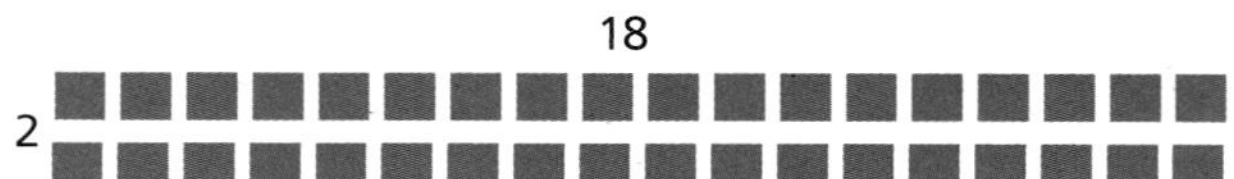

This array has a length of 18 and a width of 2, so 18 and 2 are factors of 36.

3 × 12 = 36

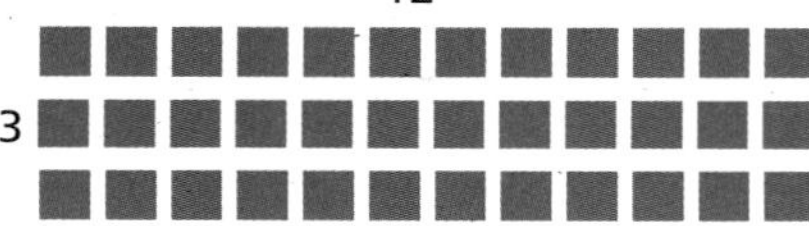

This array has a length of 12 and a width of 3, so 12 and 3 are factors of 36.

4 × 9 = 36

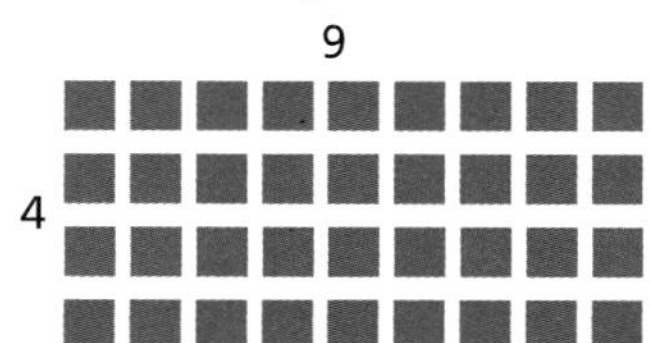

This array has a length of 9 and a width of 4, so 9 and 4 are factors of 36.

6 × 6 = 36

This array has a length of 6 and a width of 6, so 6 and 6 are factors of 36.

So, the factors of 36 are 1, 2, 3, 4, 6, 9, 12, 18, and 36.

- Are there other ways the arrays can be formed and still show the same factors? Explain.

Multiples

Kayla has a piano lesson every seventh day during March. Her first lesson is on March 7. On what other dates in March will she have a piano lesson?

March						
Sun	Mon	Tue	Wed	Thu	Fri	Sat
		1	2	3	4	5
6	7	8	9	10	11	12
13	14	15	16	17	18	19
20	21	22	23	24	25	26
27	28	29	30	31		

The dates of Kayla's lessons are multiples of 7.

A multiple is the product of a given number and another whole number. To find multiples of any number, multiply by the counting numbers 1, 2, 3, 4, and so on. The first four multiples of 7 are shown below.

A multiple of 7 is any product that has 7 as a factor.

So, Kayla will have piano lessons on March 14, 21, and 28.

- What are the first 6 multiples of 4?

You can also make a list or skip-count on a number line to find multiples.

Examples

Make a List	Use a Number Line
First 6 multiples of 10: 10, 20, 30, 40, 50, 60	0 10 20 30 40 50 60
First 6 multiples of 3: 3, 6, 9, 12, 15, 18	0 3 6 9 12 15 18

Check

1. **Explain** how a number line can help you find multiples.

Use arrays to find all the factors of each product.

2. 42 **3.** 54 **4.** 63 **5.** 30

6. 28 **7.** 66 **8.** 45 **9.** 72

List the first 3 multiples of each number.

10. 3 **11.** 5 **12.** 10 **13.** 12

LESSON CONTINUES

Practice and Problem Solving

Extra Practice, page 350, Set B

Use arrays to find all the factors of each product.

14. 10 **15.** 9 **16.** 44 **17.** 21

18. 81 **19.** 40 **20.** 24 **21.** 35

22. 56 **23.** 64 **24.** 48 **25.** 100

List the first 6 multiples of each number.

26. 2 **27.** 9 **28.** 6 **29.** 8

30. 7 **31.** 11 **32.** 4 **33.** 1

Find the missing multiple.

34. ■, 24, 30, 36 **35.** ■, 14, 21, 28 **36.** 8, 16, 24, ■ **37.** 10, 20, ■, 40

38. 12, 15, ■, 21 **39.** 36, ■, 54, 63 **40.** 70, 80, ■, 100 **41.** 22, ■, 44, 55

USE DATA For 42–45, use the table.

TROPICAL FISH SALE	
Fish	**Price**
Angelfish	$3.09
Guppy	$1.89
Goldfish	$0.79
Swordtail	$1.19

42. About how much money will Todd need to buy 6 angelfish? Explain how you decided.

43. Rachel bought 2 goldfish each for her 3 best friends. How much money did she spend?

44. Molly bought 3 swordtails. She paid with a $10 bill. How much change did she receive?

45. Jeremy got $5.00 for his birthday. Can he buy 1 guppy and 2 swordtails? Explain.

46. Use the calendar at the right. Sam's mother filled her car's gasoline tank every eighth day in July, beginning July 8. How many times did she fill her tank in July? On what dates?

July						
Sun	Mon	Tue	Wed	Thu	Fri	Sat
				1	2	3
4	5	6	7	8	9	10
11	12	13	14	15	16	17
18	19	20	21	22	23	24
25	26	27	28	29	30	31

47. Sara wants to make a rectangular design with 24 square tiles. What arrays can she make? Draw a picture and write the factors for each array.

48. Yuri is buying candles to put on a cake. The candles come in boxes of 4. How many boxes of candles will she need to buy in order to have 10 candles on the cake?

49. **REASONING** Can a factor of a number be a multiple of the same number? Explain.

50. **NUMBER SENSE** The product is 32. One factor is 2 times the other factor. What are the factors?

51. **What's the Error?** Brian writes 6, 12, 18, 24, 30 as the factors of 6. Describe his error. Write the correct answer.

52. **Write About It** Liz says she found the factors of 12 in a multiplication table. Explain how she could find the factors for 12.

Mixed Review and Test Prep

53. Find $25 - y$ if $y = 4$ (p. 70)

54. Compare: 75,526 ● 75,562 (p. 20)

55. What is the mode of the data 2, 2, 4, 5, 7, 8, 6, 6, 5, 4, 3, 2? (p. 118)

56. **TEST PREP** 10 decades = ■ (p. 104)

A 110 years **C** 50 years
B 1 century **D** 10 years

57. Write the words to match the expression. $(12 \div 3) \times 8$ (p. 188)

58. **TEST PREP** Kevin earned test scores of 85, 90, 85, 78, 86, 93, and 92. Which is Kevin's median test score? (p. 118)

F 85 **H** 87
G 86 **J** 90

Problem Solving Thinker's Corner

HOT DOG DILEMMA Jasmine is planning a cookout. She wants to serve her guests hot dogs, but doesn't know how many hot dogs and rolls to buy. Hot dogs are sold in packages of 10, and hot dog rolls are sold in packages of 8. How many packages of each will Jasmine need to buy to have the same number of hot dogs and rolls?

Jasmine can use multiples to help solve her dilemma.
She makes two tables.

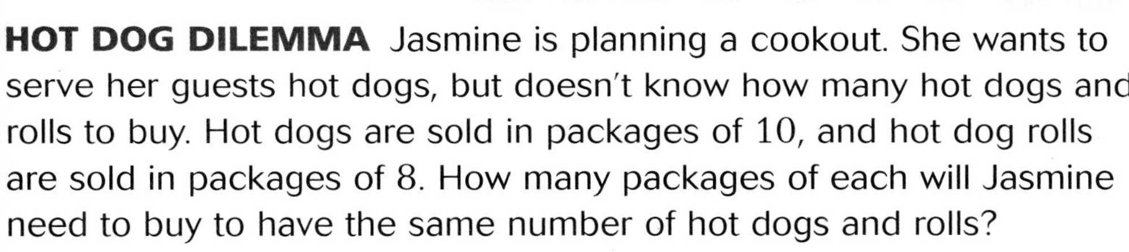

Packages of hot dogs	1	2	3	4	5	6	7	8	9	10
Number of hot dogs	10	20	30	40	50	60				

Packages of rolls	1	2	3	4	5	6	7	8	9	10
Number of rolls	8	16	24	32	40	48				

- Copy and complete the tables. Circle the multiples both tables have in common.
- What is the least number of packages Jasmine needs to buy to have the same number of hot dogs and rolls?

List the first 10 multiples of the numbers in each pair. Circle the multiples they have in common.

1. 3, 4 **2.** 4, 9 **3.** 5, 8 **4.** 2, 6

LESSON

3 Prime and Composite Numbers

Quick Review

1. $5 \times (2 \times 2)$
2. $2 \times (2 \times 4)$
3. $2 \times (3 \times 3)$
4. $(2 \times 5) \times 6$
5. $(3 \times 3) \times 5$

VOCABULARY

prime number

composite number

MATERIALS square tiles

Learn

ALL IN A ROW Julio has 5 model train engines that he wants to arrange in equal rows. How many ways can he arrange them?

HANDS ON Activity 1

Make all the arrays you can with 5 tiles to show all the factors of the number 5.

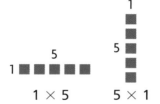

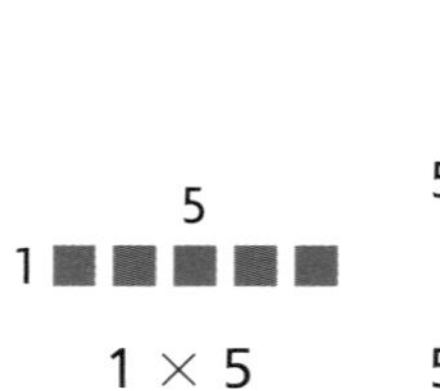

1×5 5×1

So, Julio can arrange the train engines in 2 ways: 1 row of 5 train engines or 5 rows with 1 train engine each.

The number 5 has two factors, 1 and 5. A **prime number** has exactly two factors, 1 and the number itself. So, 5 is a prime number.

HANDS ON Activity 2

Lizette has 12 pots of flowers for her box garden. How many ways can she arrange them in equal rows? Make all the arrays you can with 12 tiles to show all the factors of the number 12.

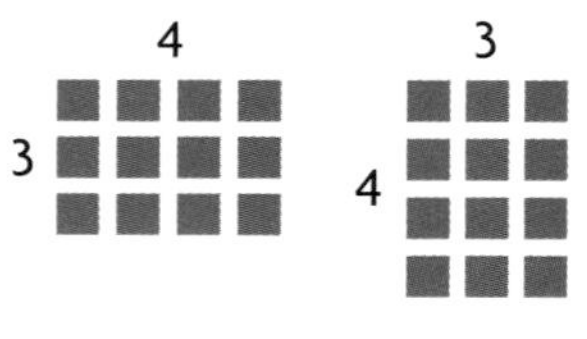

3×4 4×3

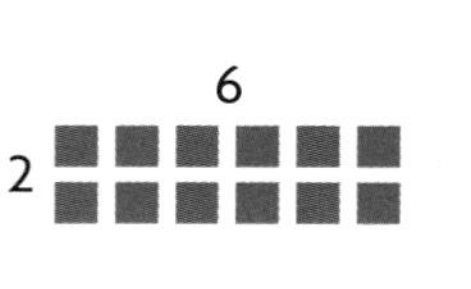

2×6

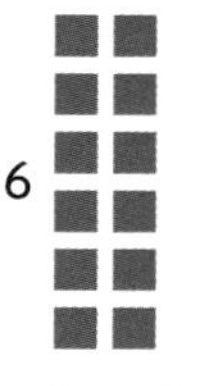

6×2

1×12 12×1

So, Lizette can arrange her pots in 6 different ways.

The factors of 12 are 1, 2, 3, 4, 6, and 12. A **composite number** has more than two factors. So, 12 is a composite number.

Arrays and Factors

The number 1 is neither prime nor composite since it has only one factor, 1.

MATH IDEA You can tell from an array whether a number is prime or composite.

Activity 3

Use square tiles to make all the arrays you can for the numbers 2–11. Make a table like the one below to show the arrays and factors for each number.

Number	Arrays	Factors	Prime or Composite?
2		1, 2	prime
3		1, 3	prime
4		1, 2, 4	composite
5			

- Look at your table. For each number, count the arrays and the factors. How are they related?

Check

1. **Explain** how you can tell whether a number is prime or composite by looking at the factors column of your table.

Make arrays to find the factors. Write *prime* or *composite* for each number.

2. 16 **3.** 27 **4.** 13 **5.** 19 **6.** 21

LESSON CONTINUES

Practice and Problem Solving

Extra Practice, page 350, Set C

Make arrays to find the factors. Write *prime* or *composite* for each number.

7. 31	**8.** 20	**9.** 15	**10.** 29	**11.** 45
12. 17	**13.** 18	**14.** 37	**15.** 22	**16.** 24

Write *prime* or *composite* for each number.

17. 23	**18.** 36	**19.** 47	**20.** 63	**21.** 50
22. 33	**23.** 144	**24.** 132	**25.** 121	**26.** 28
27. 26	**28.** 81	**29.** 41	**30.** 35	**31.** 43

Vincent has some books to stack on a library table. Each stack must have an equal number of books. How many ways can he stack the books found in each box? List the ways.

32.

33.

34.

35.

36. **What's the Error?** Nick listed the first five prime numbers as 2, 3, 7, 11, 13. Describe his error. Write the correct answer.

37. **What's the Question?** Irene listed the factors 1, 2, 4, 8, 16, and 32.

38. **REASONING** Josh is 2 years older than Brianna. Sally is 5 years younger than Josh. Josh is 12 years old. How old are Brianna and Sally?

39. On Monday Ross drew 3 pictures, on Tuesday he drew twice as many, and on Wednesday he drew twice as many pictures as he drew on Tuesday. How many pictures did he draw in all?

40. Lita scored about 90 points on each test. If she took 20 tests, about how many points did she score?

41. In August, Erin has dance lessons every third day. Her first lesson is on August 3. On what dates in August are her other lessons? Which date contains a prime number?

42. **MENTAL MATH** Chelsea bought 10 beads to make a bracelet. She paid $0.12 for each bead. If she gave the sales clerk $2.00, how much change did she receive?

Mixed Review and Test Prep

43. $\begin{array}{r} 4{,}380 \\ +2{,}647 \\ \hline \end{array}$ (p. 48)

44. $\begin{array}{r} 6{,}007 \\ -2{,}150 \\ \hline \end{array}$ (p. 50)

Find the sum or difference. (p. 52)

45. 472,804 + 216,865

46. 28,586 − 10,399

Compare. Write < or > for each ●. (p. 20)

47. 3,840 ● 3,804

48. 6,790 ● 6,970

49. **REASONING** Diane had 2 quarters, a dime, and a nickel. She spent 25¢ for a cookie and 36¢ for an apple. How much money does she have left? (p. 40)

For 50–51, use the graph. (p. 136)

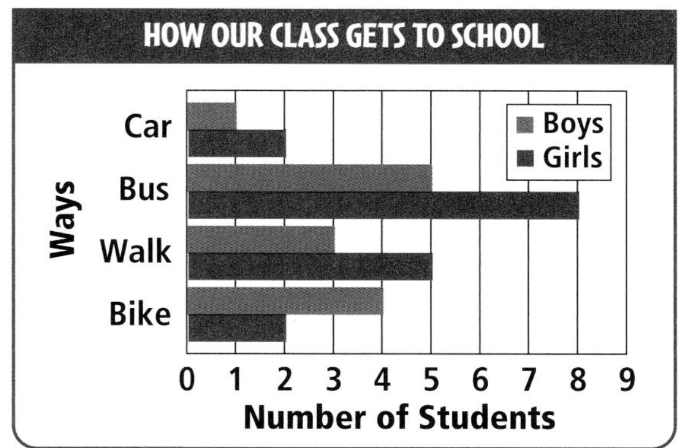

50. **TEST PREP** How many more girls ride a bus than ride a bike to school?

A 5 **B** 6 **C** 10 **D** 15

51. **TEST PREP** In all, how many students are in the class?

F 15 **G** 20 **H** 25 **J** 30

Problem Solving LINKUP . . . to History

Eratosthenes was a Greek mathematician. Around 200 B.C., he invented a method of sifting out the composite numbers, leaving only primes. It is called the Sieve of Eratosthenes.

1	2	3	4	5	6	7	8	9	10
11	12	13	14	15	16	17	18	19	20
21	22	23	24	25	26	27	28	29	30
31	32	33	34	35	36	37	38	39	40
41	42	43	44	45	46	47	48	49	50

Copy the table onto graph paper.

1. Cross out 1. It is neither prime nor composite.
2. Circle 2, 3, 5, and 7. They are all prime. Explain how you know.
3. Cross out all the multiples of 2, 3, 5, and 7. What kind of numbers are they? Explain.
4. Circle the numbers that are not crossed out. How many factors does each have? What kind of numbers are they?
5. Continue the table to 100. List all the prime numbers.
6. **REASONING** Explain why 2 is the only prime number that is even.

LESSON 4

Problem Solving Strategy
Find a Pattern

Quick Review

Find the missing numbers in the pattern.

1. 5, 10, 15, ■, ■, 30
2. 6, 12, 18, ■, ■, 36
3. 2, 10, 3, 15, 4, 20, ■, ■, 6, 30
4. 12, 24, ■, 48, ■, 72
5. 2, 3, 6, 7, 14, 15, 30, ■, ■, 63

PROBLEM In art class, the students are making beaded jewelry. Janis is using red and blue beads to make a necklace. Look for a possible pattern. What colors could the next six beads be?

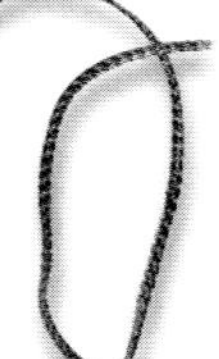

UNDERSTAND

- What are you asked to find?
- What information will you use?
- Is there any information you will not use? Explain.

PLAN

- What strategy can you use to solve the problem?
  You can *find a pattern* in the colors of the beads.

SOLVE

- How can you use the strategy to solve the problem?
  You can write the number of each red bead to see a pattern.

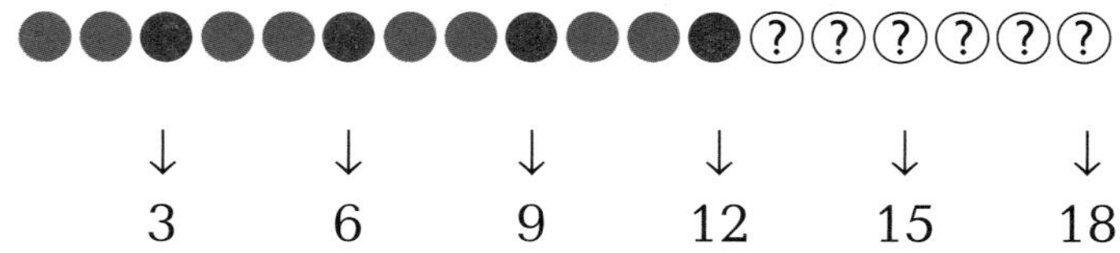

↓ 3 ↓ 6 ↓ 9 ↓ 12 ↓ 15 ↓ 18

So, the next six beads could be blue, blue, red, blue, blue, red.

Pattern: The numbers of the red beads are all multiples of 3. The next multiples of 3 are 15 and 18, so the 15th and 18th beads will be red.

CHECK

- What other strategy could you use?

Problem Solving Practice

Find a pattern to solve.

1. **What if** Janis changes the pattern so that the colors are blue, blue, blue, red? What could the next six beads be?
2. Find a rule. Use your rule to find the missing numbers in the pattern: 72, 63, 54, ■, ■, 27.

Strategies

Draw a Diagram or Picture
Make a Model or Act It Out
Make an Organized List
Find a Pattern
Make a Table or Graph
Predict and Test
Work Backward
Solve a Simpler Problem
Write an Equation
Use Logical Reasoning

Problem Solving

A triangular number is a number that can be shown in an array that looks like a triangle. Look at the pattern of dots. The number of dots used to make each of the triangular arrays shows the first four triangular numbers.

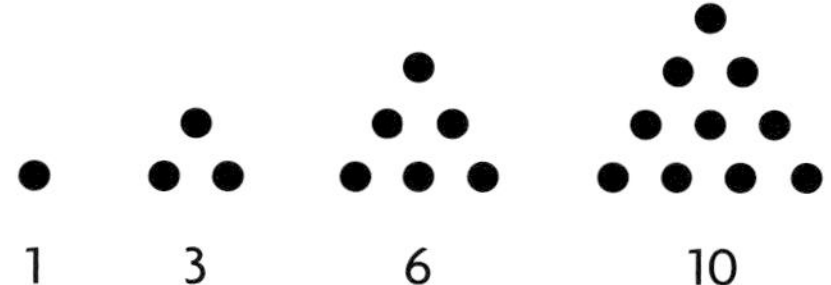

3. How many dots should be in the next drawing?
   A 12 **C** 14
   B 13 **D** 15
4. What are the next two triangular numbers? 1, 3, 6, 10, ■, ■.
   F 12, 15 **H** 15, 21
   G 15, 19 **J** 25, 27

Mixed Strategy Practice

5. Find a rule and extend the pattern.

   1 1
   1 2 1
   1 3 3 1
   1 4 6 4 1
   ■ ■ ■ ■ ■ ■

6. Marina earned $6 per hour for the first 40 hours per week she worked. She earned $9 per hour for any additional hours. If she worked 43 hours in a week, how much did she earn?
7. **ALGEBRA** Edith has a puzzle for her classmates. When she says 12, the answer is 24. When she says 15, the answer is 27. When she says 20, the answer is 32. What is a possible pattern?
8. A furniture store has 6 rows of sofas. Each row has 5 sofas. There are also 4 sofas grouped in the center of the store. How many sofas are in the store?
9. Matthew rode his bicycle to and from school for 20 days. He lives 3 miles from school. How many miles did he ride?
10. **REASONING** Tami wrote the following numbers on the board: 1, 2, 6, 30, 210, ■, ■. Find a rule and predict the next two numbers based on your rule.

LESSON

5 Square Numbers

Quick Review

Write *prime* or *composite*.

1. 2 **2.** 5

3. 18 **4.** 24

5. 45

VOCABULARY

square number

square root

Learn

SQUARE ONE A number that can be modeled with a square array is called a square number.

A **square number** is a number that is the product of any number and itself.

To find some square numbers, start by multiplying 1 by 1.

$1 \times 1 = 1$, so 1 is a square number.

$2 \times 2 = 4$, so 4 is a square number.

$3 \times 3 = 9$, so 9 is a square number.

- Look at the pattern of square numbers in the table. What is the square number for 7×7?

The inverse of a square number is a square root. The **square root** of a number is one of the two equal factors of that number.

$11 \times 11 = 121$, so 11 is the square root of 121.

$12 \times 12 = 144$, so 12 is the square root of 144.

×	1	2	3	4	5	6	7	8	9	10	11	12
1	1	2	3	4	5	6	7	8	9	10	11	12
2	2	4	6	8	10	12	14	16	18	20	22	24
3	3	6	9	12	15	18	21	24	27	30	33	36
4	4	8	12	16	20	24	28	32	36	40	44	48
5	5	10	15	20	25	30	35	40	45	50	55	60
6	6	12	18	24	30	36	42	48	54	60	66	72
7	7	14	21	28	35	42	49	56	63	70	77	84
8	8	16	24	32	40	48	56	64	72	80	88	96
9	9	18	27	36	45	54	63	72	81	90	99	108
10	10	20	30	40	50	60	70	80	90	100	110	120
11	11	22	33	44	55	66	77	88	99	110	121	132
12	12	24	36	48	60	72	84	96	108	120	132	144

▲ **The square numbers form a diagonal line in the multiplication table.**

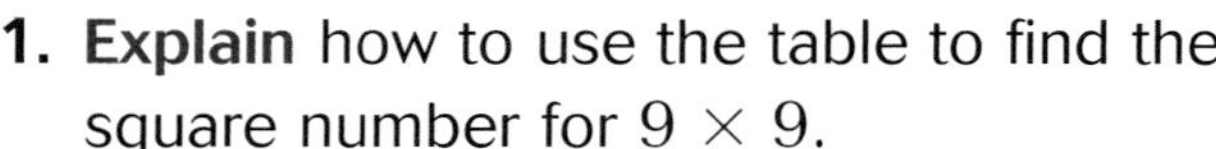

Check

Technology Link

More Practice: Harcourt Mega Math Ice Station Exploration, *Arctic Algebra*, Level P

1. **Explain** how to use the table to find the square number for 9×9.

Name the square number and the square root for each array.

2.

3.

4.

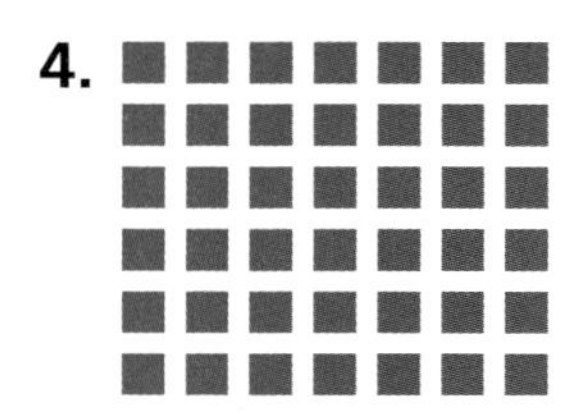

5.

Practice and Problem Solving

Extra Practice, page 350, Set D

Name the square number and the square root for each array.

6.

7. 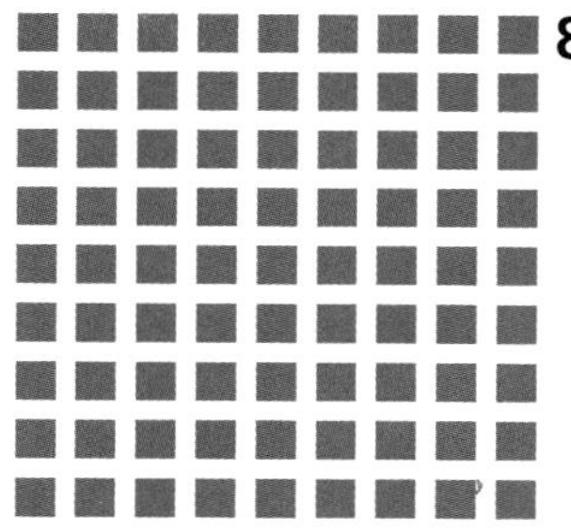

8.

9. 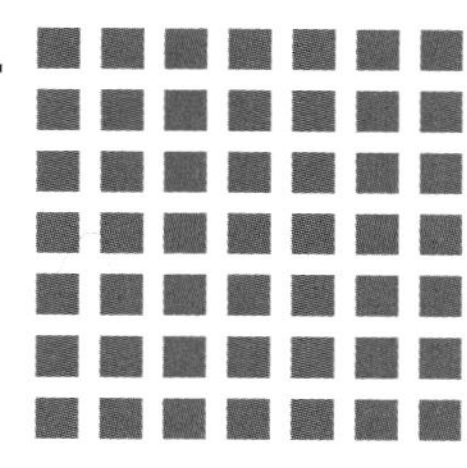

Find the square number.

10. 4×4
11. 6×6
12. 9×9
13. 5×5
14. 3×3
15. 7×7
16. 10×10
17. 1×1

Use the multiplication table to find the square root.

18. 4
19. 144
20. 64
21. 49
22. 25
23. 121
24. 81
25. 9

26. **REASONING** You have bags with 4, 6, 9, 12, 16, 24, and 25 tiles. Which of these bags of tiles can be used to make a square if all the tiles are used? Explain.

27. Becky bought 2 pounds of peaches for \$1.99 per pound and 3 pounds of bananas for \$0.59 per pound. How much did she spend?

28. ***FAST FACT*** • **SCIENCE** The Fibonacci Sequence can be seen in the growth pattern of a plant. This plant began with one stem. It grew for one month and added a new stem in the second month. One month later it added another stem. After six months, the plant had all the stems shown. How many stems will it have next month?

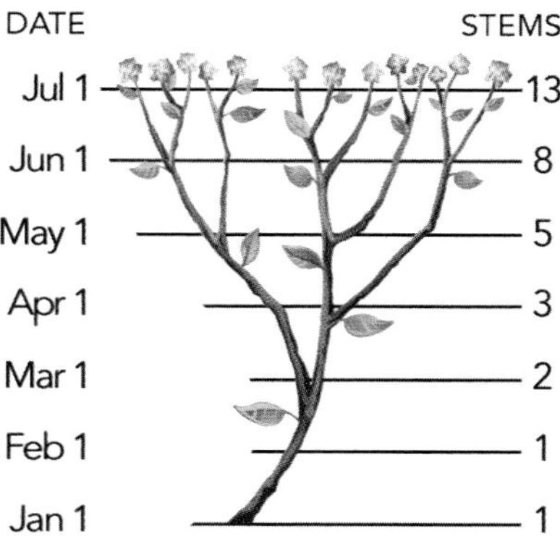

Mixed Review and Test Prep

For 29–30, find the missing number. Name the property you used. (p. 174)

29. $6 \times ■ = 5 \times 6$

30. $■ \times 1 = 10$

31. $32 \div x$ if $x = 8$ (p. 188)

32. $12 + ■ = 9 + 3 + 8$ (p. 76)

33. **TEST PREP** There are 79 children signed up to play baseball. Each team needs 9 players. How many more children are needed so each team will have enough players? (p. 308)

A 3
B 2
C 1
D 0

Extra Practice

Set A (pp. 336–337)

Tell whether the number is divisible by 2, 3, 5, 9, or 10.

1. 82
2. 567
3. 6,292
4. 830
5. 19,244
6. 32,670
7. 421,845
8. 765,949

Set B (pp. 338–341)

Find the factors for each product.

1. 45
2. 56
3. 20
4. 28

List the first 6 multiples of each number.

5. 12
6. 7
7. 3
8. 8
9. David has soccer practice every sixth day of June, beginning June 6. What are the dates of his other practices in June?
10. Leah plans to visit her grandparents every fourth day in May. Her first visit will be May 4. How many times will she visit during May?

Set C (pp. 342–345)

Write *prime* or *composite* for each number.

1. 8
2. 25
3. 39
4. 17
5. 2
6. 84
7. 31
8. 43
9. 72
10. 21
11. 41
12. 16

Set D (pp. 348–349)

Find the square number and the square root for each array.

1. 
2. 
3. 
4. 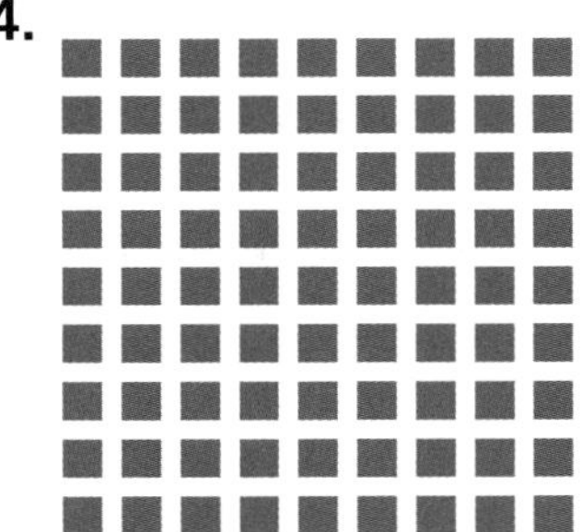
5. Jorge displayed some baseball cards in a square array. His array had 6 cards on each side. How many cards did Jorge display?
6. Adrienne planted a square-shaped rose garden. Did she plant 12, 20, 35, or 64 rose bushes?

Review/Test

CHECK VOCABULARY AND CONCEPTS

Choose the best term from the box.

factor
multiple
prime number
composite number

1. A _?_ has exactly two factors, 1 and the number itself. (p. 342)
2. A product of a given number and another whole number is a _?_. (p. 338)
3. A _?_ has more than two factors. (p. 342)

CHECK SKILLS

Tell whether the number is divisible by 2, 3, 5, 9 or 10. (pp. 336–337)

4. 420
5. 1,245
6. 5,400
7. 60,462

Find the factors for each product. (pp. 338–341)

8. 100
9. 77
10. 12
11. 36

List the first 6 multiples of each number. (pp. 338–341)

12. 6
13. 9
14. 11
15. 10

Write *prime* or *composite* for each number. (pp. 342–345)

16. 9
17. 49
18. 11
19. 39

Name the square number and square root for each array. (pp. 348–349)

20. 
21. 
22.  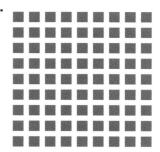
23. 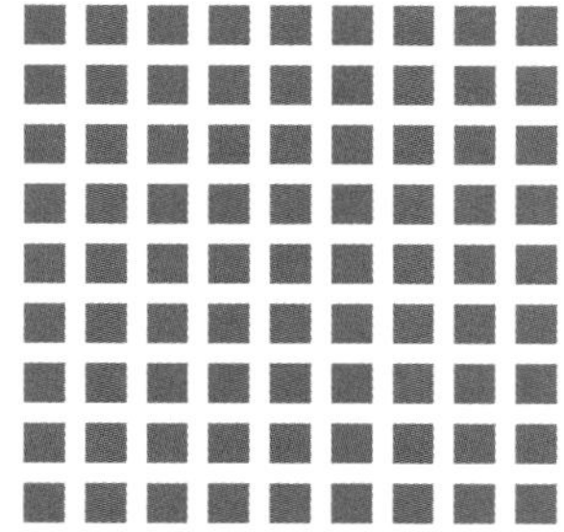

CHECK PROBLEM SOLVING

Solve. (pp. 346–347)

24. Monica does 30 sit-ups every day. From now on, she wants to do 3 more sit-ups than the day before. How many sit-ups will she be doing 8 days from now?
25. Emanuel wrote these numbers on the board: 2, 3, 5, 7, 8, 10, ■, ■. Predict the two missing numbers. Explain.

CHAPTERS 1–16

Standardized Test Prep

NUMBER SENSE, CONCEPTS, AND OPERATIONS

1. The fourth graders are going on a field trip. There are 3 parent volunteers, 3 teachers, and 84 students. How many fourth graders should be put with one of the adults so that each group has an equal number of students?

A 42

B 24

C 16

D 14

2. Alan made a list to show the factors of 6. What is the missing factor?

Factors of 6: 1, 2, ■, 6

F 3

G 4

H 5

J 8

TIP **Decide on a plan.** See item 3. Think of estimation strategies such as *using compatible numbers, using benchmark numbers,* and *rounding,* and decide which strategy would be the best one to use to solve this problem.

3. Explain It Tony works 8 hours a day. If he worked 158 hours last month, about how many days did he work? Name the estimation strategy you used. Explain your thinking.

MEASUREMENT

4. Richard started reading at 1:15. This clock shows the present time.

How long has Richard been reading?

A 35 minutes **C** 50 minutes

B 45 minutes **D** 1 hour 45 minutes

5. Elena made the table below to show the weights of several objects in her classroom.

OBJECTS IN MY CLASSROOM

Object	Weight
Globe	2 pounds 5 ounces
Math book	48 ounces
Dictionary	3 pounds 1 ounce
Plant	80 ounces

Which object is the **heaviest**?

F globe **H** dictionary

G math book **J** plant

6. Explain It Sarah and Bill both measured the length of this crayon.

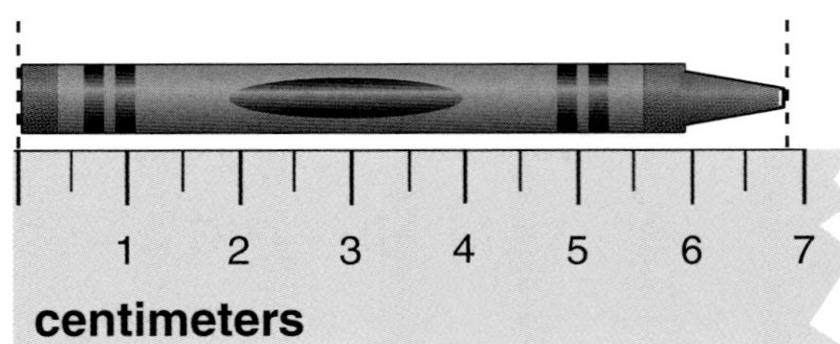

Sarah said that it is about 5 centimeters long. Bill said that it is about 7 centimeters long. Who is correct? Explain your thinking.

GEOMETRY AND SPATIAL SENSE

7. Which figure shows perpendicular lines?

A 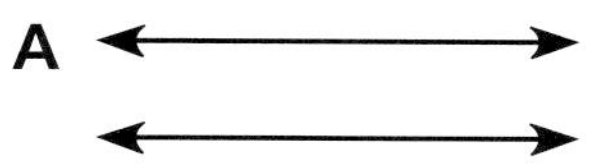

B 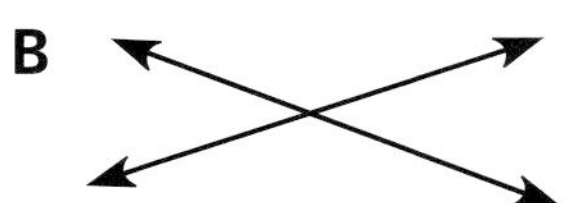

C 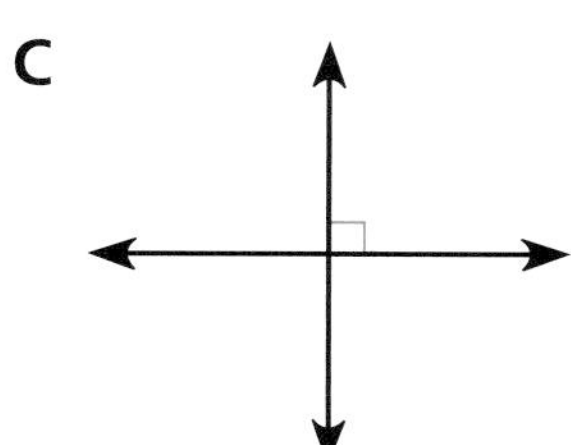

D 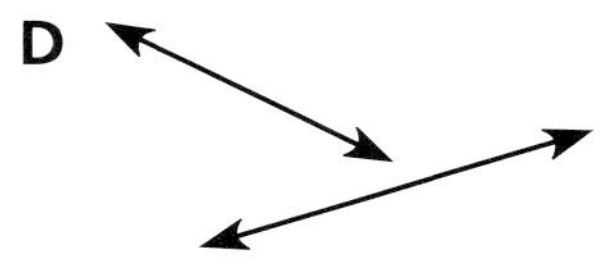

8. What shape is the object below?

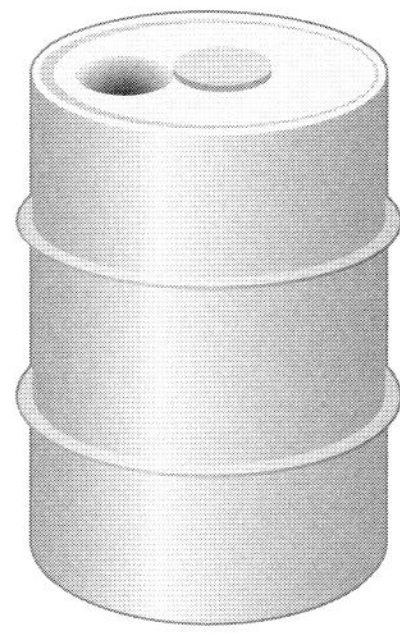

F cube

G rectangular prism

H cylinder

J sphere

9. **Explain It** Draw a figure with 6 equal sides and 6 angles. What is the name of your figure? Explain your thinking.

ALGEBRAIC THINKING

10. Maria is using green and purple squares to make this pattern.

If Maria continues this pattern, what color squares will she use for the next 6 squares?

A green, green, green, purple, purple, purple

B green, green, purple, green, green, purple

C purple, green, purple, purple, green, purple

D green, purple, green, green, purple, green

11. At 2:00 P.M. some people were at a party. Then at 3:00 P.M., 2 more people arrived. Let p represent the number of people at the party at 2:00 P.M. Which expression represents the number of people at the party at 3:00 P.M.?

F $p + 2$

G $p \times 2$

H $p \div 2$

J $p - 2$

12. **Explain It** Look at the table below.

Input	1	2	3	4	5
Output	1	4	9	■	25

What is the missing number? Explain how you decided.

IT'S IN THE BAG

Division Accordion Booklets

PROJECT Make paper accordion booklets to model division problems.

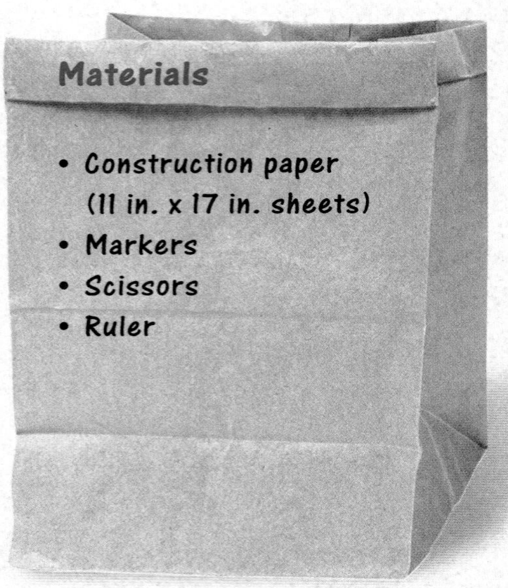

Materials
• Construction paper (11 in. x 17 in. sheets)
• Markers
• Scissors
• Ruler

Directions

1. Read the following sample problem: A florist has 81 daisies to place in 7 vases. If an equal number of daisies are placed in each of the vases, how many daisies will be in each vase?

2. Cut a 3-inch wide strip of construction paper. Add 3 to the divisor of the sample problem. Accordion-fold the strip of construction paper into the resulting number of parts. Write the problem on the first panel and the word *Check* on the last panel. *(Picture A)*

3. On each of the remaining panels, draw a picture to show how many daisies are in each vase. *(Picture B)*

4. On the last panel, check your work. *(Picture C)*

5. Work with a partner to write and solve your own division problems by using accordion booklets.

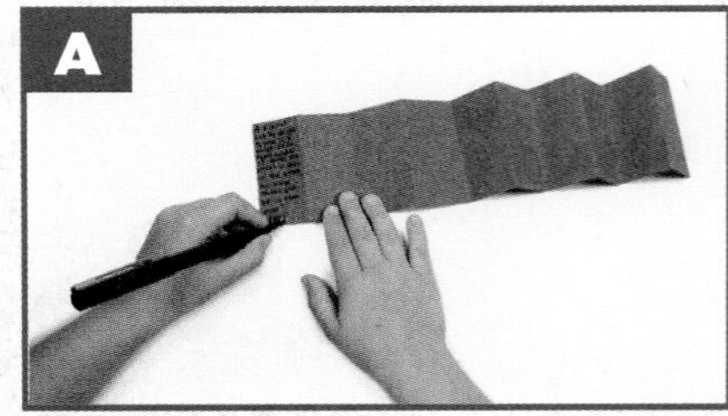

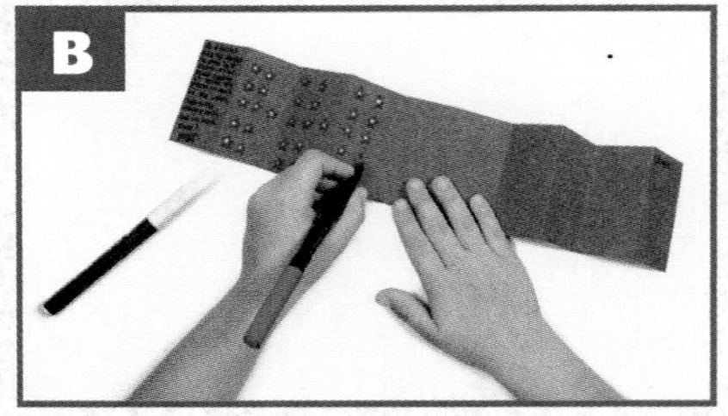

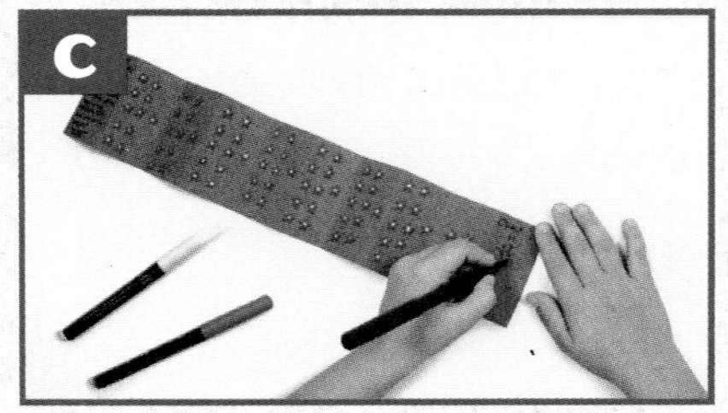

Challenge

Find Prime Factors

Any composite number can be written as a product of prime numbers called **prime factors**. To find the prime factors, make a **factor tree**.

A factor tree for 20 is shown.

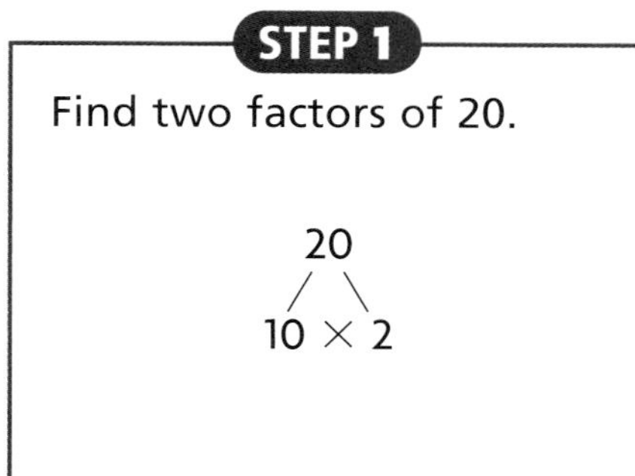

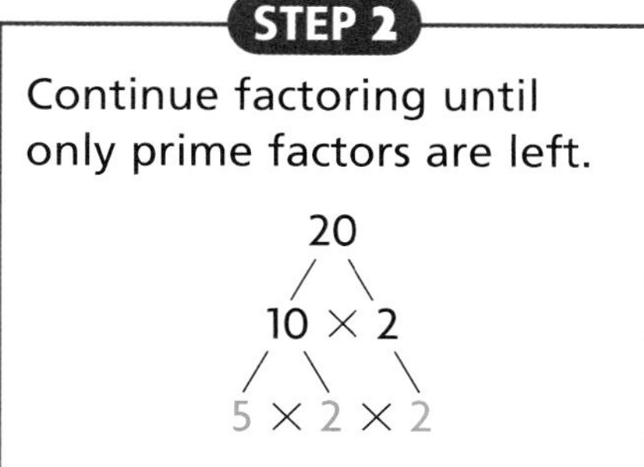

STEP 2
Continue factoring until only prime factors are left.
20
10 × 2
5 × 2 × 2

Record the factors from least to greatest.

So, $20 = 2 \times 2 \times 5$.

Examples

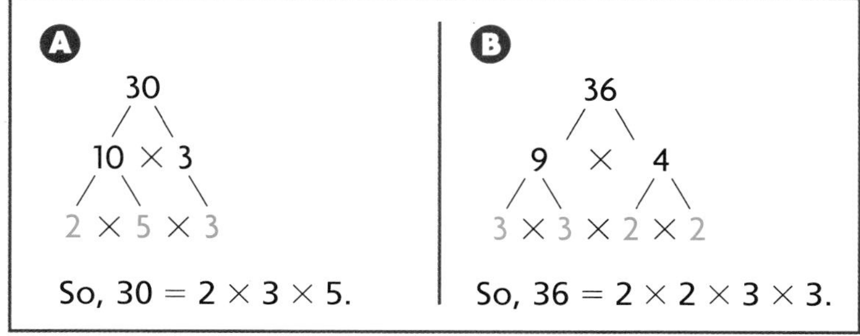

Talk About It

How could you check your answer for Example B?

Try It

Write each as a product of prime factors.

1. 9	**2.** 15	**3.** 24	**4.** 99	**5.** 8
6. 25	**7.** 22	**8.** 40	**9.** 21	**10.** 90
11. 44	**12.** 16	**13.** 48	**14.** 12	**15.** 84
16. 14	**17.** 60	**18.** 10	**19.** 120	**20.** 210

Study Guide and Review

VOCABULARY

1. A _?_ has exactly two factors, 1 and the number itself. (p. 342)

prime number
composite number

STUDY AND SOLVE

Chapter 13

Divide 2-digit numbers.

$$\begin{array}{r} 16 \text{ r3} \\ 4\overline{)67} \\ -4 \\ \hline 27 \\ -24 \\ \hline 3 \end{array}$$

- Divide.
- Multiply.
- Subtract.
- Compare difference with divisor.
- Bring down.
- Repeat as needed.

Check:

$$\begin{array}{r} 16 \\ \times 4 \\ \hline 64 \\ +3 \\ \hline 67 \end{array}$$

Divide and check. (pp. 278–285)

2. $6\overline{)72}$
3. $4\overline{)95}$
4. $3\overline{)76}$
5. $2\overline{)58}$
6. $5\overline{)83}$
7. $7\overline{)96}$
8. $8\overline{)97}$
9. $4\overline{)79}$

Chapter 14

Divide 3- and 4-digit numbers.

$$\begin{array}{r} 39 \text{ r3} \\ 6\overline{)237} \\ -18 \\ \hline 57 \\ -54 \\ \hline 3 \end{array}$$

- Use order of division to find the quotient.
- Repeat the order until the division is complete.

Check:

$$\begin{array}{r} 39 \\ \times 6 \\ \hline 234 \\ +\ \ 3 \\ \hline 237 \end{array}$$

Divide and check. (pp. 298–307)

10. $6\overline{)383}$
11. $2\overline{)\$1.54}$
12. $3\overline{)218}$
13. $5\overline{)4,128}$
14. $7\overline{)2,943}$
15. $8\overline{)\$24.48}$
16. $4\overline{)1,862}$
17. $9\overline{)5,097}$

Chapter 15

Divide with 2-digit divisors.

$$\begin{array}{r} 21 \text{ r11} \\ 16\overline{)347} \\ -32 \\ \hline 27 \\ -16 \\ \hline 11 \end{array}$$

- Divide.
- Multiply.
- Subtract.
- Compare difference with divisor.
- Bring down.
- Repeat as needed.

Check:

$$\begin{array}{r} 21 \\ \times 16 \\ \hline 126 \\ +210 \\ \hline 336 \\ +\ 11 \\ \hline 347 \end{array}$$

Divide. (pp. 318–325)

18. $17\overline{)361}$
19. $64\overline{)904}$
20. $24\overline{)583}$
21. $52\overline{)813}$
22. $31\overline{)843}$
23. $47\overline{)666}$
24. $73\overline{)952}$
25. $28\overline{)898}$

Find the mean of a set of data.

Find the mean.

- Add. \$18 + \$29 + \$110 + \$145 + \$173 = \$475
- Divide. \$475 ÷ 5 = \$95

So, the mean is \$95.

Find the mean. (pp. 328–329)

26. 185, 410, 518, 619

27. 13, 25, 29, 35, 48, 52, 64

28. \$98, \$93, \$89, \$85, \$75, \$80, \$77, \$83, \$72, \$70, \$100, \$110

Chapter 16

Write whether the number is prime or composite.

A **prime number** has exactly two factors.

A **composite number** has more than two factors.

A. 5 has only two factors, 5 and 1. It is prime.
B. 6 has more than 2 factors, 1, 2, 3, and 6. It is composite.

Write *prime* or *composite* for each number. (pp. 342–345)

29. 11	**30.** 27	**31.** 52
32. 72	**33.** 17	**34.** 81
35. 132	**36.** 49	**37.** 31
38. 29	**39.** 72	**40.** 91

PROBLEM SOLVING PRACTICE

Solve. (pp. 286–287, 308–309, 326–327, 346–347)

41. There are 78 flowers. After equal bunches are formed, 3 flowers are left over. How many bunches were formed? How many flowers are in each bunch?

42. This is Hugo's number pattern.
3, 6, 12, 24, 48, 96, ■, ■, ■
Describe his possible pattern. Find the missing numbers.

43. Mia is making costumes. She has 108 yards of cloth. Each costume uses 5 yards of cloth. How many costumes can Mia make? How did you interpret the remainder?

44. The hardware store sold 126 hinges. There were 3 hinges in each package. How many packages of hinges did the hardware store sell? What operation did you use?

PERFORMANCE ASSESSMENT

TASK A • SUMMER VACATION

The Turner family lives in Minneapolis, Minnesota. They are planning to take a family trip this summer. Each family member named a city to visit. The cities and their distances from Minneapolis are shown in the table.

TURNER FAMILY SUMMER VACATION

City	Distance from Minneapolis (in miles)	Miles per Day	Estimated Average Speed (in mph)
Columbus, OH	778	■	■
Detroit, MI	686	■	■
Pittsburgh, PA	886	■	■
Topeka, KS	504	■	■

a. The Turners will travel for 2 days to the city they choose. They will travel the same number of miles on each day of their trip. Copy the table and use this information to complete the "Miles per Day" column.

b. The Turners plan to drive 7 or fewer hours each day. Explain how you could use compatible numbers to estimate the average speed (miles per hour) they will have to drive each day. Then write your estimates in the table.

TASK B • TILE TRIALS

Ryan and Kendra are using square tiles to make rectangular designs for tabletops. Ryan has 20 tiles. Kendra has 19 tiles.

a. How many different 20-tile rectangles can Ryan make? Draw and label the different rectangles.

b. Kendra could make only one rectangle that used all 19 of her tiles. Explain why this is so.

c. Kendra decided to use more tiles. Decide on a number of tiles between 21 and 25. Then find out how many different rectangles can be made with the total number she has. Draw and label the rectangles.

Technology Linkup

Ms. Lee wrote these problems on the board:
1,130 ÷ 125 = ■, 680 ÷ 75 = ■, and 518 ÷ 57 = ■.
Linda says they all have the same quotient.
Greg says they do not. Who is right?

 You can use a calculator to prove that both Linda and Greg are right.

Linda's Method Use the ÷R to divide.	**Greg's Method** Use the ÷ to divide.
Find each quotient.	Find each quotient.
a. 1 1 3 0 ÷R 1 2 5 = =9 R5	**a.** 1 1 3 0 ÷ 1 2 5 = =9.04
b. 6 8 0 ÷R 7 5 = =9 R5	**b.** 6 8 0 ÷ 7 5 = =9.0666667
c. 5 1 8 ÷R 5 7 = =9 R5	**c.** 5 1 8 ÷ 5 7 = =9.0877193

- What do you notice about the whole number parts of Linda's and Greg's quotients?

Practice and Problem Solving

Use ÷R and ÷ to find the quotient in two ways.

1. 356 ÷ 95 **2.** 685 ÷ 103 **3.** 958 ÷ 621 **4.** 1,090 ÷ 55

5. 4,118 ÷ 32 **6.** 62,179 ÷ 33 **7.** 4,092 ÷ 915 **8.** 93,702 ÷ 208

GO ON-LINE **Multimedia Math Glossary** www.harcourtschool.com/mathglossary
Vocabulary Power Look up *remainder* in the Multimedia Math Glossary. Look at the example. Explain which method above you would use to show the remainder.

in Ohio

CLEVELAND METROPARKS ZOO

The Northern Trek area of the Cleveland Metroparks Zoo is home to many cold-climate species such as polar and grizzly bears, Siberian tigers, Bactrian camels, reindeer, and Thorold's deer. The Wolf Wilderness part of this area is home to gray wolves, beavers, and many wetland species.

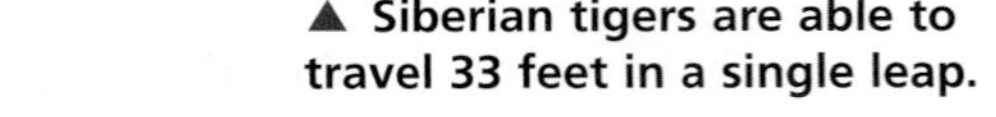

▲ **Siberian tigers are able to travel 33 feet in a single leap.**

1. Twin Siberian tiger cubs Danya and Dasha each weighed 3 pounds at birth. By the time they were a year old, they had grown to weigh 60 times as much! How much did the cubs weigh when they were one year old?

2. If a human baby grew at the same rate as a Siberian tiger, how much would a baby that weighed 7 pounds at birth weigh at one year of age?

3. Wolf packs usually consist of 5 to 8 individuals. If 48 wolves were seen in a forest, about how many packs were seen?

4. Polar bears range in length from 96 to 132 inches. How long is this in feet? (HINT: 12 inches = 1 foot)

5. Research other animals found in the Northern Trek area of the zoo. Write a problem using your data and exchange with a partner to solve.

▼ **The average litter size of the gray wolf is 6 pups.**

▲ **Polar bears are excellent swimmers, often found 100 miles out at sea.**

AUSTRALIAN ADVENTURE

Visitors to the Cleveland Metroparks Zoo can head "down under" at the Australian Adventure exhibit. Koalas can be viewed year-round at Koala Junction, and kangaroos are hopping about at Wallaby Walkabout.

1. An adult kangaroo can leap 27 feet in a single bound. How many feet would a kangaroo leap in 3 bounds?
2. Koalas sleep about 140 hours a week. About how many hours do they sleep per day?
3. A koala eats between 300 and 500 pounds of eucalyptus leaves in a year. Does a koala eat more than or less than two pounds of leaves in a day? Explain how you know.
4. When born, baby kangaroos, or joeys, spend about 235 days in their mother's pouch before they leave for good. About how many weeks is this?
5. **STRETCH YOUR THINKING** Of the 150 species at the Cleveland Metroparks Zoo, 50 are endangered. How many times as many species are not endangered as are endangered? Explain how you found your answer.

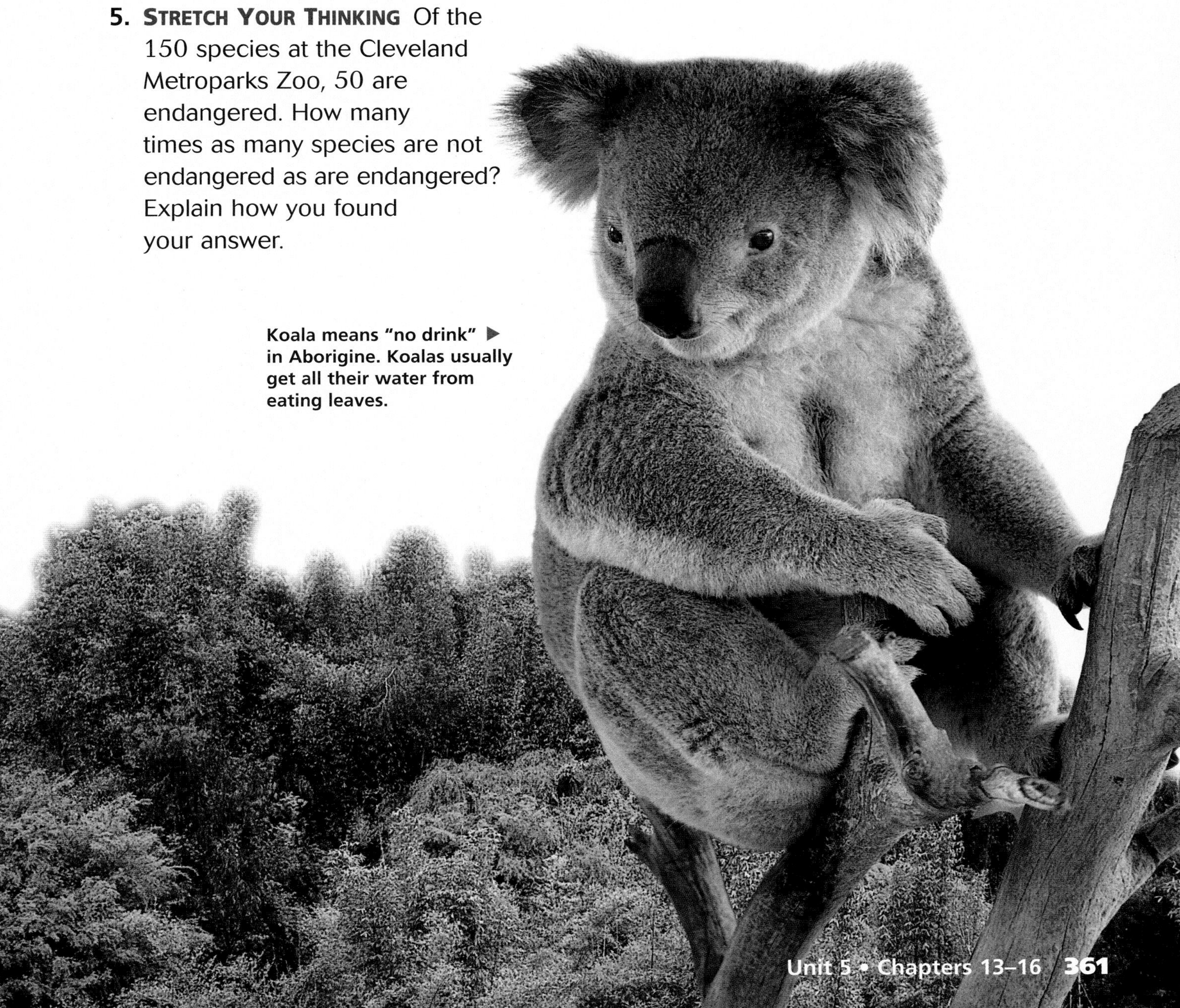

Koala means "no drink" ▶ in Aborigine. Koalas usually get all their water from eating leaves.

Lines, Rays, and Angles

FAST FACT • SOCIAL STUDIES The Ambassador Bridge, between Detroit, Michigan, and Windsor, Ontario, Canada, is the busiest border crossing in North America. About 7,000 trucks cross it each day.

PROBLEM SOLVING Tell what kind of lines and angles you see in the photograph of the bridge.

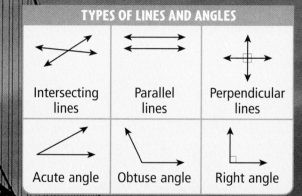

TYPES OF LINES AND ANGLES

Intersecting lines	Parallel lines	Perpendicular lines
Acute angle	Obtuse angle	Right angle

CHECK WHAT YOU KNOW

Use this page to help you review and remember important skills needed for Chapter 17.

IDENTIFY GEOMETRIC FIGURES

Write the name of each figure.

1.

2.

3.

4.

5.

6.

IDENTIFY ANGLES

Tell if each angle is a *right* angle, *greater than* a right angle, or *less than* a right angle.

7.

8. 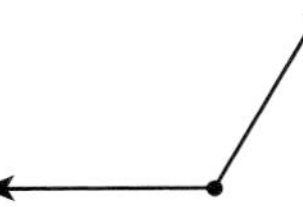

9. 

10.

11. 

12. 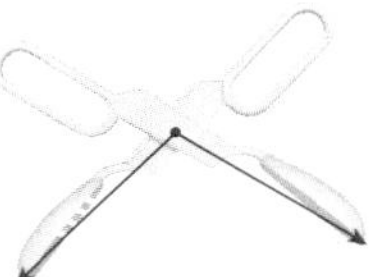

VOCABULARY POWER

REVIEW

geometry [jē•ä′mə•trē] *noun*

Geometry comes from the Greek word for *Earth, Geos*, and from the Greek term, *metros,* "to measure." So, *geometry* means "to measure the Earth." In your own words, tell what the study of geometry includes.

PREVIEW

point	degree (°)
line	right angle
line segment	acute angle
ray	obtuse angle
plane	straight angle
angle	intersecting lines
vertex	parallel lines
protractor	perpendicular lines

www.harcourtschool.com/mathglossary

LESSON 1

Lines and Rays

Quick Review

1. 96 ÷ 9 2. 115 ÷ 33

3. 643 ÷ 50 4. 406 ÷ 20

5. 118 ÷ 25

VOCABULARY

point **ray**
line **plane**
line segment

Learn

GEOMETRY EVERYWHERE! Everywhere you look, you can see points, lines, and rays in nature and in things people make. You can use the following geometric ideas and terms to describe the world around you.

Term and Definition	Draw It	Read It	Write It
A **point** names an exact location in space.	• *A*	point *A*	point *A*
A **line** is a straight path of points that continues without end in both directions. It has no endpoints.	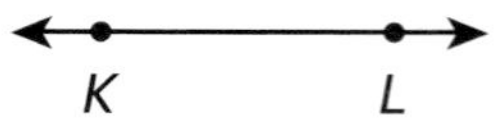	line *KL*	$\overleftrightarrow{KL}$
A **line segment** is part of a line. It has two endpoints and all the points between them. It is the shortest distance between two points.	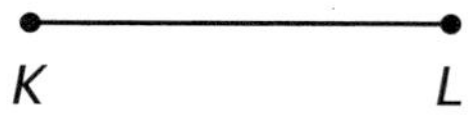	line segment *KL*	$\overline{KL}$
A **ray** is part of a line. It has one endpoint and continues without end in one direction.	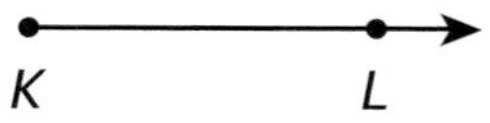	ray *KL*	$\overrightarrow{KL}$
A **plane** is a flat surface of points that continues without end in all directions. A plane is named by at least three points in the plane.	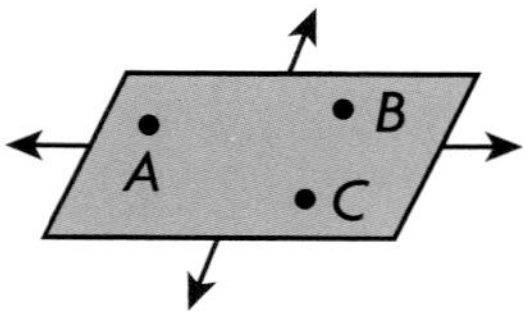	plane *ABC*	plane *ABC*

• Find as many examples of these terms as you can in the photograph. Describe how the definitions of the terms match the figures.

Check

1. **Give** some examples of line segments that you see in your classroom.

Name a geometric term that describes each.

2. side edge of a door
3. sharp tip of a pencil
4. laser beam

Practice and Problem Solving

Extra Practice, page 374, Set A

Name a geometric term that describes each.

5. flagpole
6. parking lot
7. tip of a tack

Draw and label an example of each.

8. line *BC*
9. line segment *PQ*
10. point *G*
11. plane *RST*
12. line *ST*
13. ray *XY*

Draw each line segment with the given length.

14. $\overline{BC}$, 3 cm
15. $\overline{AE}$, 2 in.
16. $\overline{JK}$, $3\frac{1}{2}$ in.
17. $\overline{RS}$, 6 cm

18. **REASONING** Which path is the shortest distance between point *C* and point *D*? Explain how you know.

a. 

b. 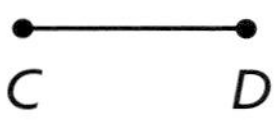

19. Write all the names for the line below.

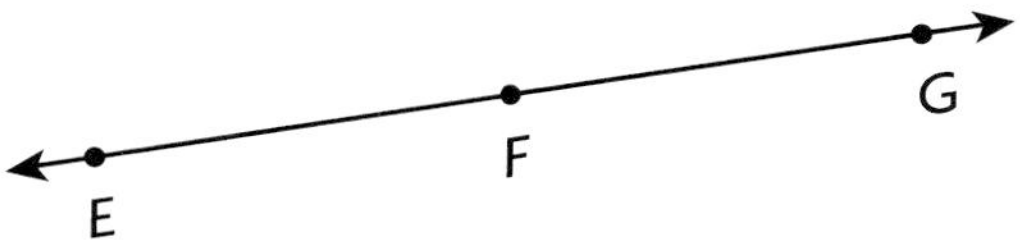

20. For lunch each day, Mia buys a hot meal for $1.75 and milk for $0.50. What is the least number of $1 bills that her mother can give her so she will have enough lunch money for 5 days?

21. Name a geometric term that describes the floor of your classroom.

22. **Write About It** Explain the differences between a line, a ray, and a line segment.

Technology Link

More Practice: Harcourt Mega Math Ice Station Exploration, *Polar Planes,* Level A

Mixed Review and Test Prep

23. 500 − 490 (p. 48)
24. 703 − 585 (p. 48)
25. 6,435 + 797 + 285 (p. 48)
26. Is 15 prime or composite? (p. 342)

27. **TEST PREP** What is the value of the blue digit in 45,678,342? (p. 6)

A 800
B 8,000
C 80,000
D 800,000

LESSON 

2 Measure and Classify Angles

Quick Review

List the factors for each product.

1. 14 **2.** 25
3. 27 **4.** 12
5. 29

VOCABULARY

angle
vertex
protractor
degree (°)
right angle
acute angle
obtuse angle
straight angle

Learn

FROM EVERY ANGLE Two rays with the same endpoint form an **angle**. The endpoint is called the **vertex**.

Draw It	Read It	Write It
ray, A, B, vertex, C, ray	angle *ABC* angle *CBA* angle *B*	$\angle ABC$ $\angle CBA$ $\angle B$

NOTE: The vertex is always the middle letter or the single letter that names the angle.

A **protractor** is a tool used to measure the size of an angle. The unit used for measuring angles is a **degree (°)**. The scale on a protractor is marked from 0° to 180°.

Activity MATERIALS: protractor
Use a protractor to measure angle *ABC*.

STEP 1

Place the center of the protractor on the vertex of the angle.

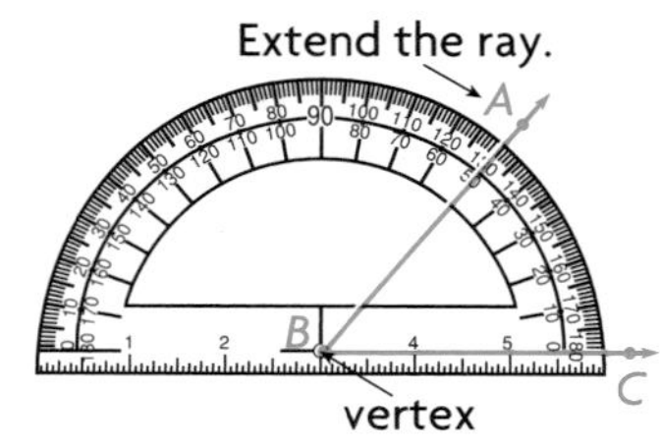

STEP 2

Line up the center point and the 0° mark on the protractor with one ray of the angle.

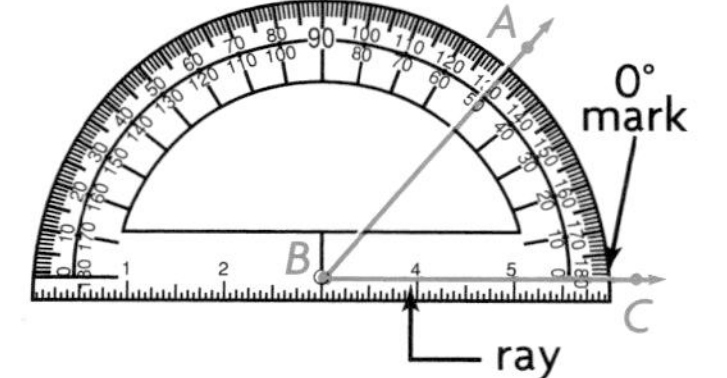

STEP 3

Read the measure of the angle where the other ray passes through the scale. Use the scale that makes sense for the angle size.

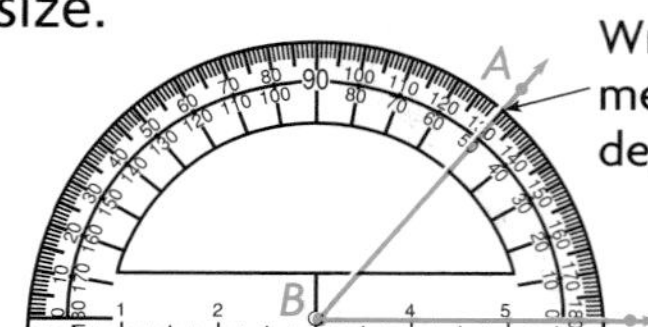

The measure of $\angle ABC = 50°$.

- Trace each angle. Then use a protractor to measure the angle.

a.

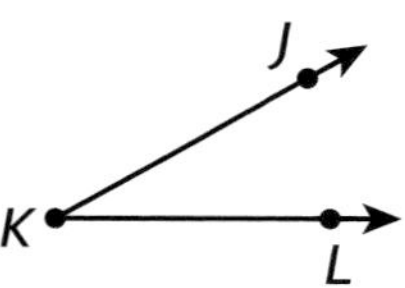

b.

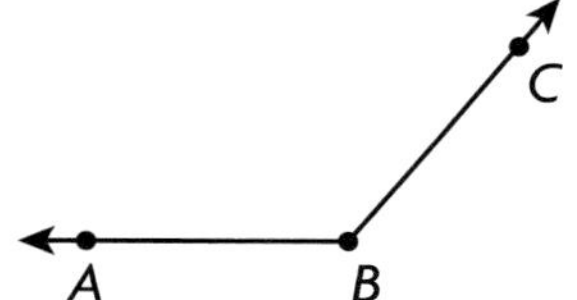

c.

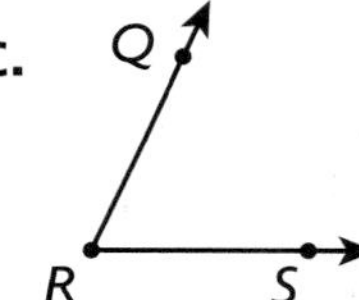

Types of Angles

Activity **MATERIALS:** paper

Make an angle using a sheet of paper. Fold the paper twice to make an angle like this. The angle you made is called a right angle.

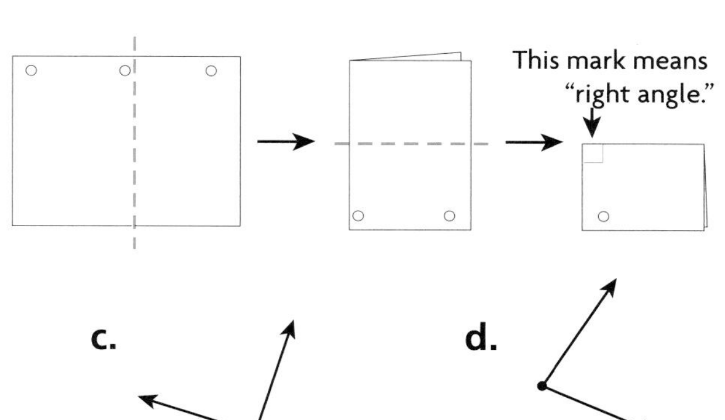

Use the right angle you made to find out which of the following are also right angles. Write *yes* or *no.*

a.

b.

c.

d.

An angle can be classified according to the size of the opening between its rays.

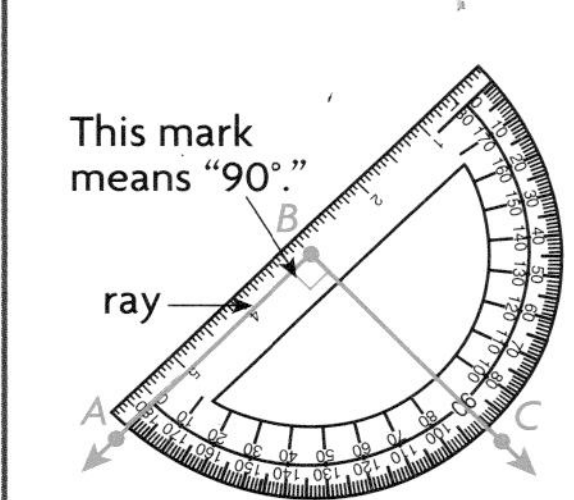

The measure of $\angle B = 90°$.

A **right angle** measures 90°. A right angle forms a square corner.

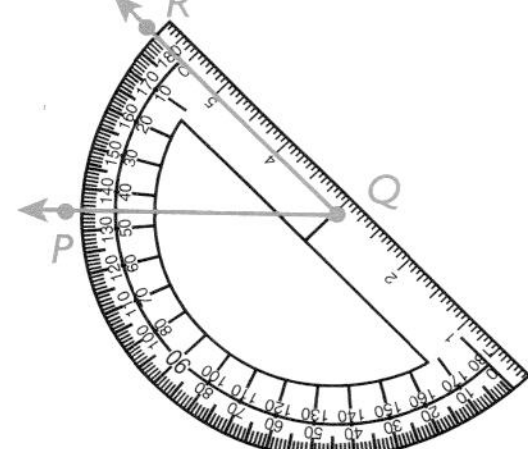

The measure of $\angle Q = 45°$.

An **acute angle** measures greater than 0° and less than 90°.

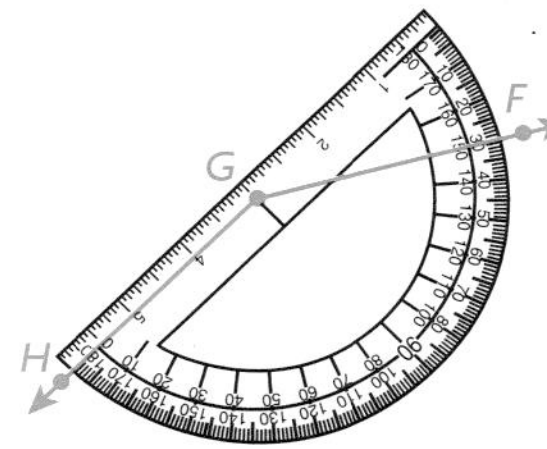

The measure of $\angle G = 150°$.

An **obtuse angle** measures greater than 90° and less than 180°.

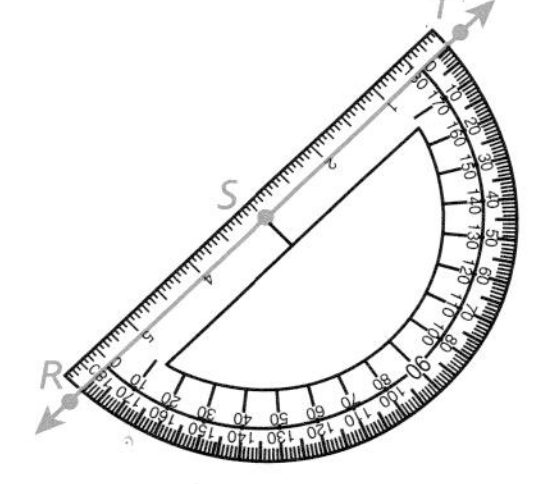

The measure of $\angle S = 180°$.

A **straight angle** measures 180°. A straight angle forms a line.

- Find as many examples as you can of each type of angle in the painting *Three Musicians* by Pablo Picasso. You may trace the angle and use a protractor to measure it.
- Do you always need a protractor to determine whether an angle is acute, obtuse, right, or straight? Explain.

LESSON CONTINUES

Check

1. **Draw** a picture of an object that has a right angle, an acute angle, and a straight angle. Label each angle.

Trace each angle. Use a protractor to measure the angle. Then write *acute, obtuse, right,* or *straight.*

2. 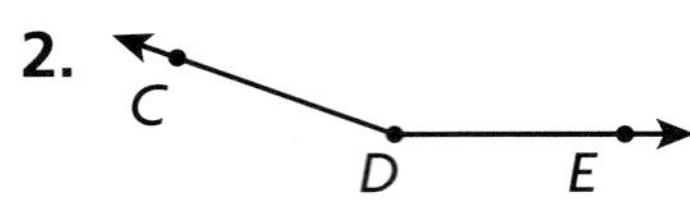

3. 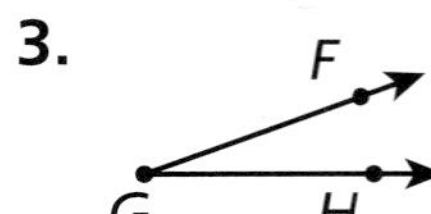

4. 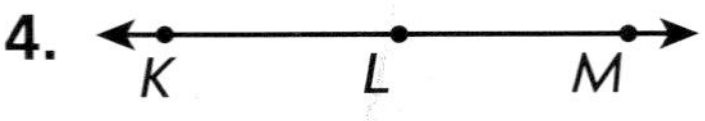

Practice and Problem Solving

Extra Practice, page 374, Set B

Trace each angle. Use a protractor to measure the angle. Then write *acute, obtuse, right,* or *straight.*

5. 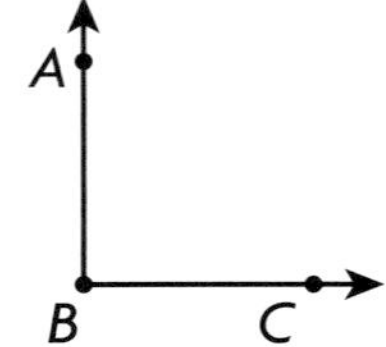

6. 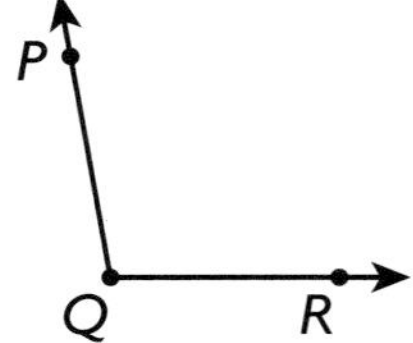

7. 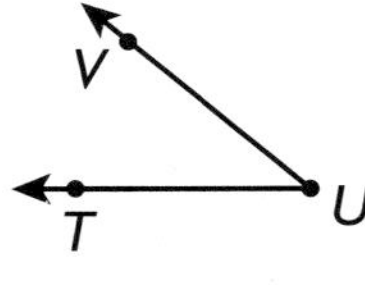

Draw and label an example of each.

8. obtuse angle *RST*
9. acute angle *JKL*
10. right angle *E*

Classify each angle. Write *right, acute, obtuse,* or *straight.*

11. 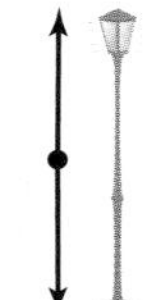

12. 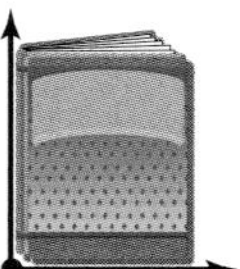

13. 

Write the letter of the phrase that best describes each angle.

14. 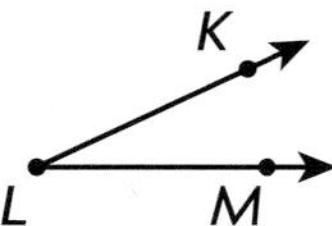

   a. less than 45°
   b. greater than 90°

15. 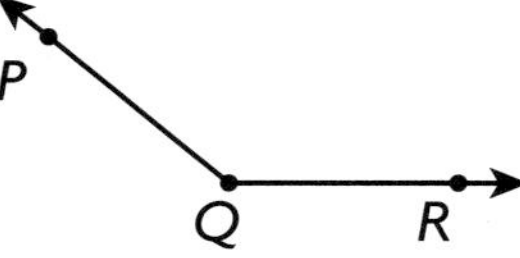

   a. less than 180°
   b. less than 90°

16. 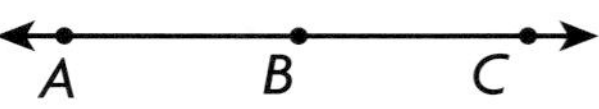

   a. less than 45°
   b. equal to 180°

17. Look at the figure below. Name the figure three different ways.

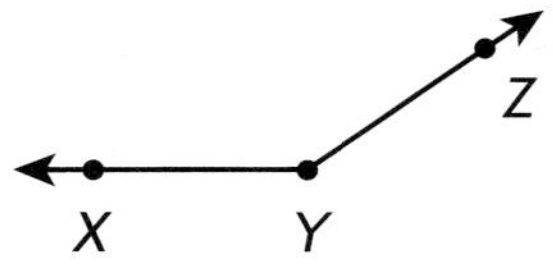

18. **? What's the Error?** Wanda said that the letter *W* has two angles. What error did she make?

19. **REASONING** Use the corner of a sheet of paper to prove or disprove that the three angles in the letter *M* are right angles. M

20. Give a time when the hands on a clock represent each type of angle: acute, obtuse, right, and straight.

21. Suchada spent $15 at the gift shop. Later her father gave her $10 to buy lunch, but she only spent $7. At the end of the day, Suchada had $10. How much money did she have at the beginning of the day?

22. **Vocabulary Power** You use a *scale* to measure weight. Compare and contrast a scale for weight with a protractor scale. How are they alike? How are they different?

Mixed Review and Test Prep

23. $(3 + 4) \times 2$ (p. 184)

24. $1,400 \div 2$ (p. 288)

25. ▒ $\div 8 = 16$ (p. 300)

26. $900 \div 3$ (p. 288)

27. Kim opened a carton of 12 eggs. She put 4 eggs in each of 2 bowls. How many eggs were left in the carton? Write the expression you used. (p. 184)

28. **TEST PREP** What is 745,864 rounded to the nearest ten thousand? (p. 30)

A 700,000 **C** 745,000
B 740,000 **D** 750,000

29. **TEST PREP** It takes Pam 40 minutes to walk home from school. If she left school at 11:45 A.M., what time would she get home? (p. 98)

F 12:10 P.M. **H** 12:25 P.M.
G 12:20 P.M. **J** 12:45 P.M.

Problem Solving

. . . to Art

When architects design houses or buildings, they draw different views by using points, planes, line segments, and angles.

This drawing shows only the front view of a building.

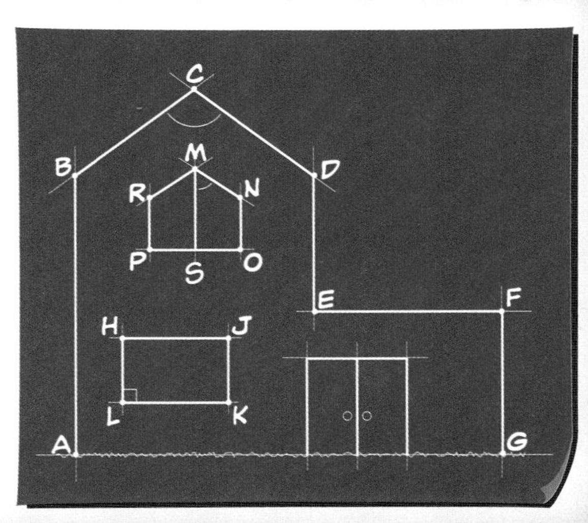

Use the drawing and give an example of each of the following.

1. line segment
2. right angle
3. obtuse angle
4. acute angle
5. point
6. plane

LESSON 3

Line Relationships

Learn

FOLLOW THE LINES Look at the term and definition for each line relationship. Find these same relationships on the road map.

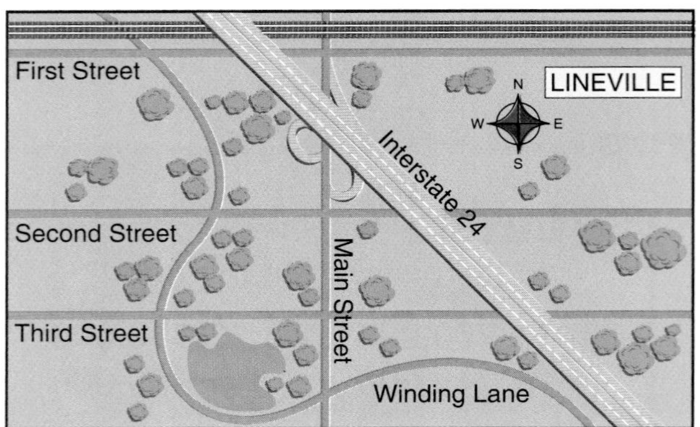

Quick Review

Write *prime* or *composite.*

1. 17 **2.** 6

3. 31 **4.** 45

5. 22

VOCABULARY

intersecting lines

parallel lines

perpendicular lines

Term and Definition	Draw It	Read It	Write It
Intersecting lines are lines that cross each other at exactly one point. They form four angles.	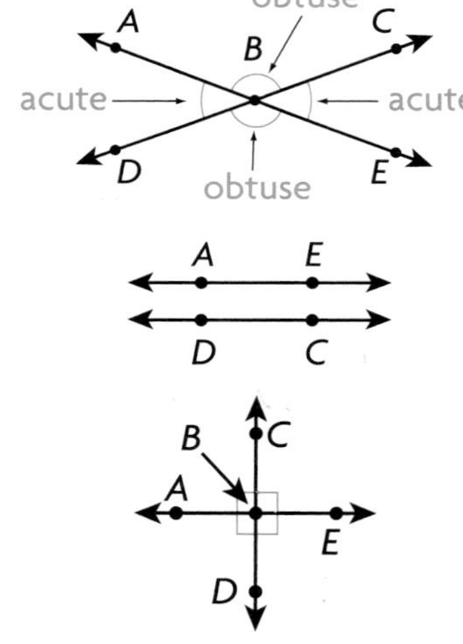	Line *AE* intersects line *DC* at point *B*.	$\overleftrightarrow{AE}$ intersects $\overleftrightarrow{DC}$ at point *B*.
Parallel lines are lines in the same plane that never intersect and are always the same distance apart.		Line *AE* is parallel to line *DC*.	$\overleftrightarrow{AE} \parallel \overleftrightarrow{DC}$
Perpendicular lines are lines that intersect to form four right angles.		Line *AE* is perpendicular to line *DC*.	$\overleftrightarrow{AE} \perp \overleftrightarrow{DC}$

• Which term identifies the relationship between Third Street and Second Street on the map?

Technology Link

More Practice: Harcourt Mega Math Ice Station Exploration, *Polar Planes,* Level C

Check

1. Name two streets on the map that are perpendicular. Name two streets that are intersecting and not perpendicular.

Name any line relationship you see in each figure. Write *intersecting, parallel,* or *perpendicular.*

2. 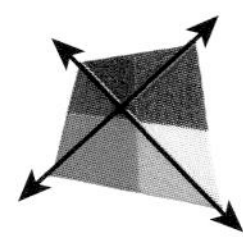

3. 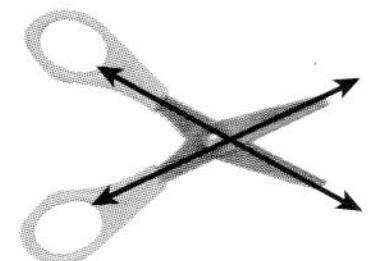

4. 

Practice and Problem Solving

Extra Practice, page 374, Set C

Name any line relationship you see in each figure. Write *intersecting, parallel,* or *perpendicular.*

5. 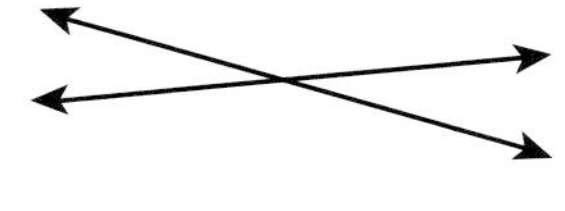

6. 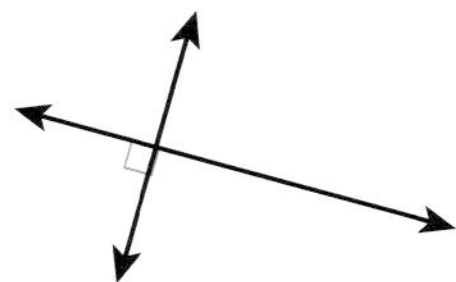

7. 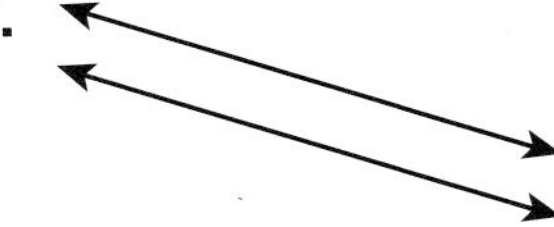

For 8–14, use the drawing at the right.

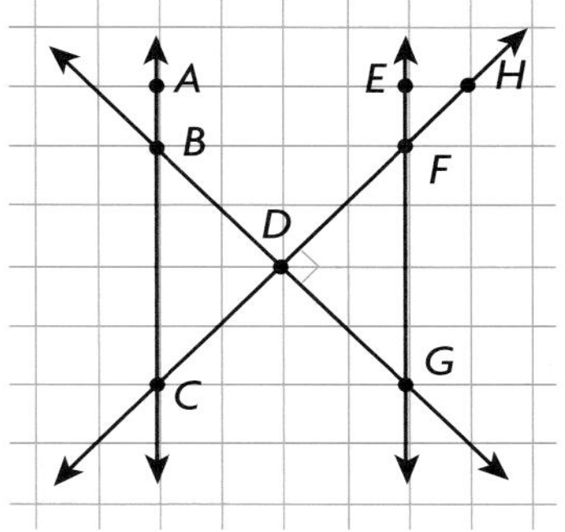

8. Name a right angle.

9. Name two parallel lines.

10. Name an acute angle.

11. Name an obtuse angle.

12. Name four line segments that include point *G*.

13. Name two intersecting lines.

14. Name two perpendicular lines.

Use grid paper to draw each line relationship.

15. perpendicular lines

16. parallel lines

17. intersecting lines

18. The product of two numbers is 45. Their sum is 18. What are the numbers?

19. **Write About It** Explain how you can tell the difference between intersecting lines and parallel lines.

20. **REASONING** Is this statement true or false? "Perpendicular lines are also intersecting lines." Explain your answer.

21. **What's the Error?** Tricia said that all intersecting lines are perpendicular. Explain her error. Include a drawing with your explanation.

Mixed Review and Test Prep

22. 542×6 (p. 222)

23. $804 \div 5$ (p. 302)

24. What are the two missing numbers in the pattern? (p. 346)
20, 18, 16, ▒, 12, 10, ▒, 6

25. $96{,}784 + 8{,}400$ (p. 52)

26. **TEST PREP** In what place is the 9 in 3,902,817? (p. 6)

A thousands
B ten thousands
C hundred thousands
D millions

Problem Solving Strategy
Draw a Diagram

Quick Review

1. 12 + 18 + 9
2. 19 + 21 + 6
3. 8 + 24 + 8
4. 10 + 15 + 23
5. 22 + 8 + 11 + 6

PROBLEM Fairglen Elementary is planning an obstacle course for the school fair. The course will start on the south side of the playground. From the starting point, the course goes 7 units north to the slide. Then it goes 7 units east and 4 units south to the swing set. From the swing set, the course continues 4 units west, 2 units south, and 6 units west to the jungle gym. How long is the course when it crosses its own path?

UNDERSTAND

- What are you asked to find?
- What information will you use?
- Is there any information you will not use? If so, what?

PLAN

- What strategy can you use to solve the problem?
  You can *draw a diagram* to show a map of the obstacle course.

SOLVE

- How can you draw a diagram?
  You can use grid paper. Label your grid *North*, *East*, *South*, and *West*. Follow the directions. Draw line segments to show the course. Label the distances and locations. Then add the units along the path until the path crosses itself.

  So, the obstacle course is 27 units long when it crosses its own path.

North
7
4
West
7
East
4
2
Finish
6
Start
South

CHECK

- How can you check your answer?

Problem Solving Practice

1. **What if** the obstacle course continues from the finish line 3 units north, 7 units east, and then 4 units north? How long is the course when it crosses its own path a third time?

2. Suppose you were given these directions to a museum. On Main Street, go north for 28 miles. Turn right on Highway 33 and go east for 187 miles. How many miles will you travel to the museum?

Strategies

- **Draw a Diagram or Picture**
- Make a Model or Act It Out
- Make an Organized List
- Find a Pattern
- Make a Table or Graph
- Predict and Test
- Work Backward
- Solve a Simpler Problem
- Write an Equation
- Use Logical Reasoning

Problem Solving

***FAST FACT* • SOCIAL STUDIES About one-third of the 1,500 labyrinths in the United States were built in the year 2000. Unlike mazes, labyrinths are walking paths with no dead ends. Study the path of the labyrinth drawing.**

3. How many line segments can you find in the labyrinth from start to finish?

   A 10 line segments
   B 14 line segments
   C 15 line segments
   D 18 line segments

4. What kind of angle is shown by the line segments in the labyrinth?

   F acute angle
   G obtuse angle
   H right angle
   J scalene angle

▲ **The labyrinth at Forestheart Studios, Woodsboro, Maryland, is about 560 feet long.**

Mixed Strategy Practice

5. If Carrie takes one guitar lesson a week, how much will it cost, including book rental, to take four lessons at the store?

Guitar Lesson Fees

1 Lesson	Cost	Book Rental
At home	$10.00	No charge
At store	$7.00	$0.50/week

6. Mr. Ross designs mazes. He made 2 mazes the first week, 3 the second week, and 5 the third week. If Mr. Ross continues this pattern, how many mazes will he make during the fourth week?

7. Zack is showing his brother 90° by using the hour and minute hands on a clock. Name some times he can use to show 90° on a clock.

Extra Practice

Set A (pp. 364–365)

Draw and label an example of each.

1. line segment *DC*
2. point *J*
3. ray *JK*
4. plane *RST*
5. line segment *AB*
6. line *GH*
7. Give some examples of lines that you see every day.
8. Name an object in your classroom that is like a line segment.

Set B (pp. 366–369)

Trace each angle. Use a protractor to measure the angle. Then write *acute, obtuse, right,* or *straight.*

1. 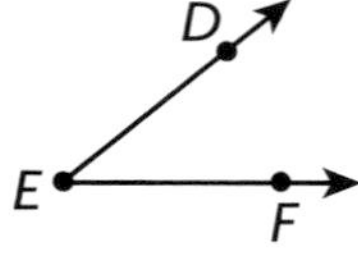

2. 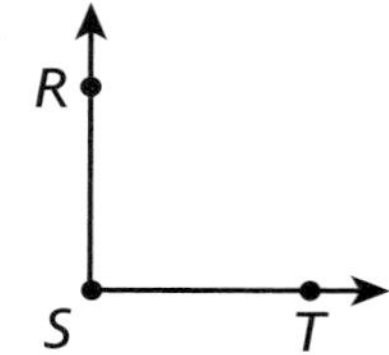

3. 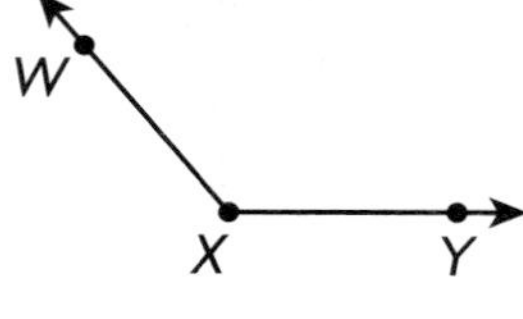

Draw and label an example of each.

4. obtuse angle *MNP*
5. acute angle *B*
6. straight angle *DEF*

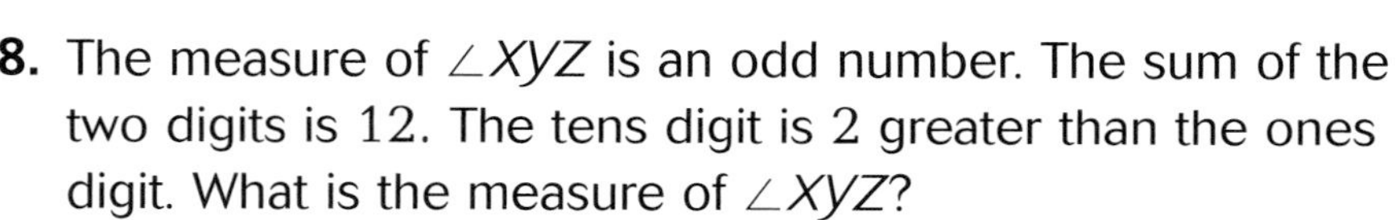

7. The limbs of a tree form angles with the trunk of the tree. Classify angles *A* and *B* in this tree as *acute, obtuse,* or *right.*

8. The measure of $\angle XYZ$ is an odd number. The sum of the two digits is 12. The tens digit is 2 greater than the ones digit. What is the measure of $\angle XYZ$?

Set C (pp. 370–371)

Name any line relationship you see in each figure. Write *intersecting, parallel,* or *perpendicular.*

1. 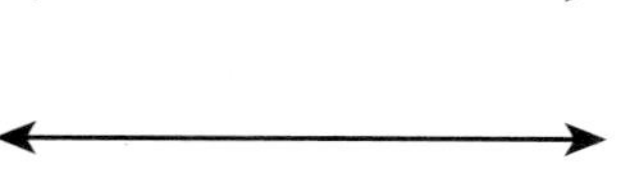

2. 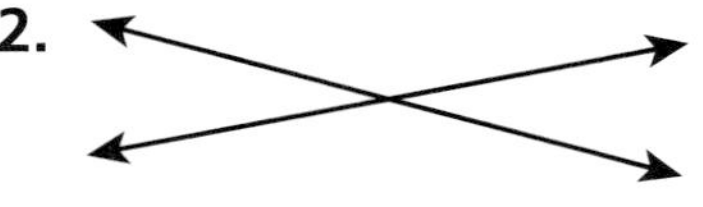

3. 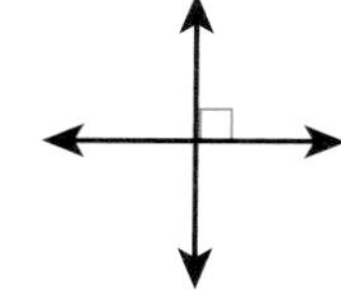

Review/Test

CHECK VOCABULARY AND CONCEPTS

Choose the best term from the box.

angle
degree
line

1. The unit used to measure an angle is called a __?__. (p. 366)
2. Two rays with the same endpoint form an __?__. (p. 366)

CHECK SKILLS

Name the term that describes each. Write *point, plane, line, line segment,* or *ray*. (pp. 364–365)

3. A

4. K

5. M N

6. D C E

Trace each angle. Use a protractor to measure the angle. Then write *acute, obtuse, right,* or *straight*. (pp. 366–369)

7.
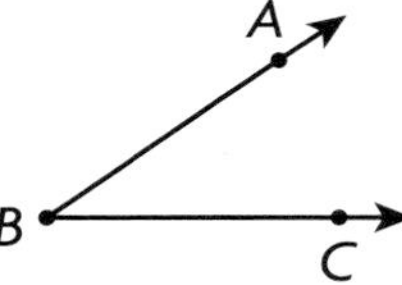

8.
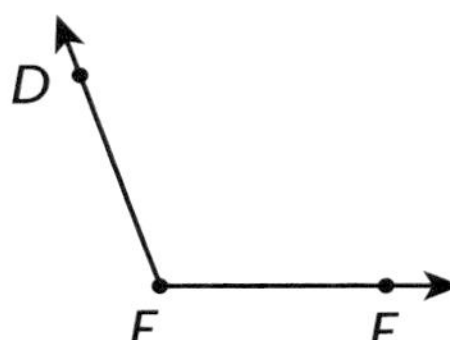

9.
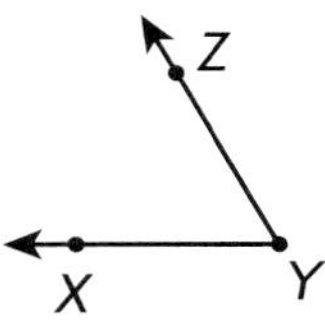

10.

For 11–13, use the drawing at the right. (pp. 370–371)

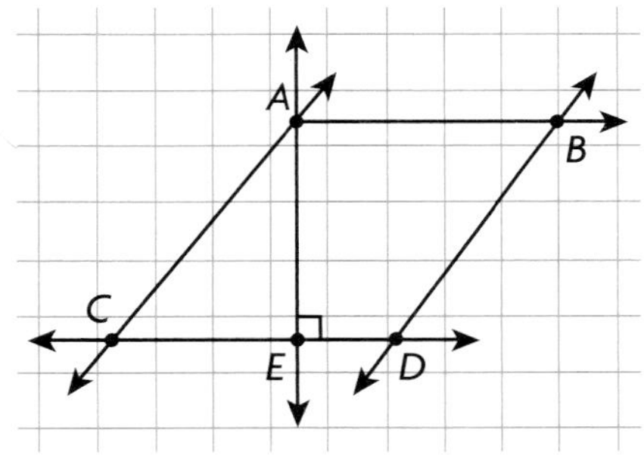

11. Name two parallel lines.
12. Name two intersecting lines.
13. Name two perpendicular lines.

CHECK PROBLEM SOLVING

Solve. (pp. 372–373)

14. Kyle needs directions to Taylor's new house. Taylor drew a map for Kyle to use. Starting from Kyle's house, go 4 blocks south and then 2 blocks west. Turn left. Go 5 more blocks south. Taylor's house is the first house on the right. Draw a diagram of Taylor's map.

15. From her apartment, Ellie walks 5 blocks north and 3 blocks west. Then she turns right and walks 1 more block to the library. How many blocks is the library from Ellie's apartment?

Standardized Test Prep

NUMBER SENSE, CONCEPTS, AND OPERATIONS

1. Which is the **best** estimate for $309 \div 5$?

   A 6 or 7
   B 8 or 9
   C 60 or 70
   D 80 or 90

2. The table shows the number of items sold at the Garden Shop.

NUMBER OF ITEMS SOLD			
Item	**May**	**June**	**July**
Plants	212	238	165
Pots	167	111	67
Potting soil	54	71	82
Hoses	23	31	45

   How many more items were sold in June than July?

   F 451
   G 359
   H 92
   J 5

3. The Nature Store ran a special on orchids. Each orchid sold for \$15. They sold 43 orchids on Sunday, 66 orchids on Monday, and 62 orchids on Tuesday. What were the total sales for the 3 days of the special on orchids?

   A \$171
   B \$1,026
   C \$2,415
   D \$2,565

4. **Explain It** Mr. Hill picked apples. He filled 19 baskets with apples. Each basket contained about 58 apples. ESTIMATE the number of apples he picked. Explain your thinking.

ALGEBRAIC THINKING

5. Which could be the next shape in the pattern?

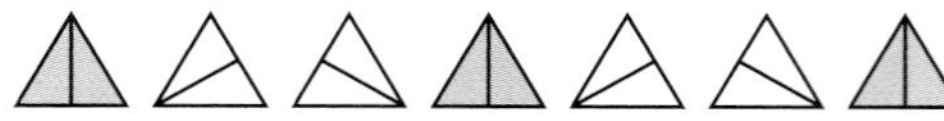

   F
   G
   H
   J

6. Jake is 10 years old. Steve is older than Jake. Let y represent the number of years older Steve is than Jake. Which expression shows how old Steve is?

   A $10 + y$
   B $10 - y$
   C $10 \times y$
   D $10 \div y$

7. **Explain It** Suki is stringing lights in her back yard for a barbecue party. She is using the following pattern.

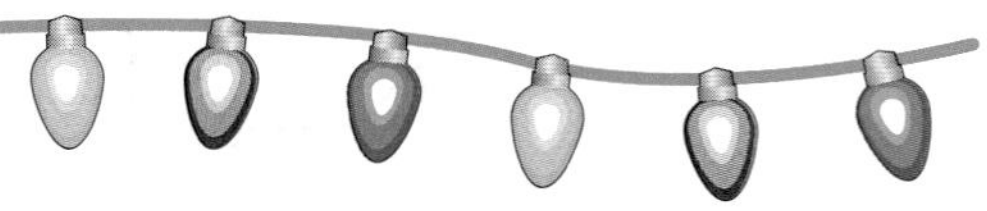

   What color will Suki use for the fifteenth light? Explain your thinking.

DATA ANALYSIS AND PROBABILITY

TIP **Choose the answer.** See item 8. Use the drawing to find the probability for pulling each color. Relate each answer choice to the problem and choose the best answer.

8. Look at the bag of marbles below. Which two colors are **equally likely** to be pulled?

F red and yellow

G red and blue

H blue and yellow

J yellow and green

9. What is the range of 2, 11, 3, 7, 2?

A 2 **C** 11

B 9 **D** 25

10. **Explain It** The circle graph below shows the types of weather for the month of June.

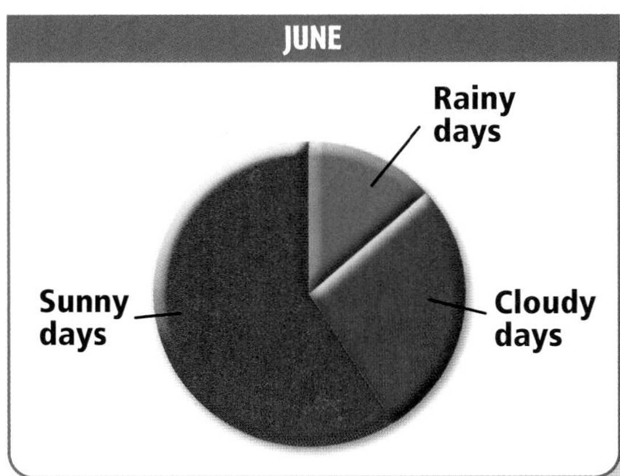

What conclusion can you draw from the data in the graph? Explain your thinking.

MEASUREMENT

11. What is the **best** estimate of the measure of the angle below?

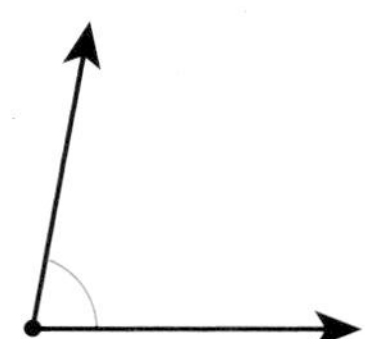

F between 10° and 30°

G between 30° and 45°

H between 45° and 70°

J between 70° and 90°

12. Ryan has soccer practice at 3:00. A bus trip will take 35 minutes. Which bus should Ryan take to get to practice on time?

BUS SCHEDULE	
Bus	**Pick-up Time**
A	2:10
B	2:30
C	2:35
D	2:40

A Bus A **C** Bus C

B Bus B **D** Bus D

13. **Explain It** This clock shows the present time.

If Jane practices the piano for the next 23 minutes, about what time will she be finished? Explain your thinking.

CHAPTER 18

Plane Figures

FAST FACT • SOCIAL STUDIES **Seaside, a planned community in Florida, was modeled after traditional neighborhoods of the 1920s and 1930s. Seaside covers 80 acres along the Gulf of Mexico. People who live there can easily walk or bike to the store or beach. Cottages are built with porches, 3-foot-high white picket fences, and tin roofs.**

PROBLEM SOLVING **What types of plane figures can you see in the photo of Seaside?**

TYPES OF PLANE FIGURES		
triangle	quadrilateral	pentagon
hexagon	octagon	circle

CHECK WHAT YOU KNOW

Use this page to help you review and remember important skills needed for Chapter 18.

CLASSIFY ANGLES

Tell if each angle is *acute, right,* or *obtuse.*

1. 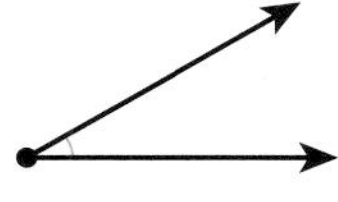
2. 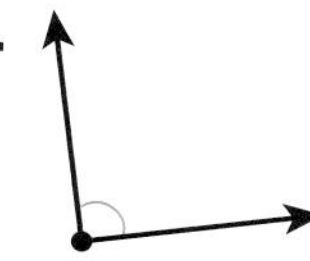
3. 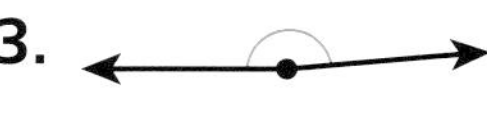
4. 

IDENTIFY PLANE FIGURES

Write the name of each figure.

5. 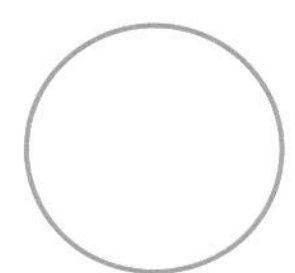
6. 
7. 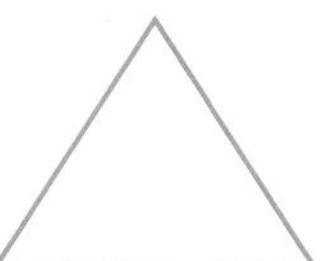
8. 

IDENTIFY QUADRILATERALS

Tell if the polygon is a *quadrilateral* or *not a quadrilateral.*

9. 
10. 
11. 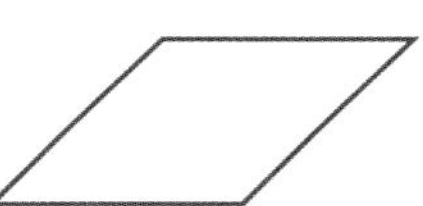
12. 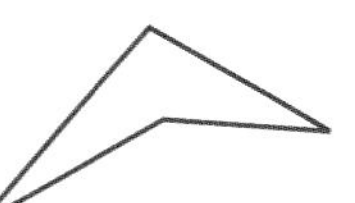

VOCABULARY POWER

REVIEW

acute [ə•kyo͞ot′] *adjective*

Acute comes from the Latin word *acuss,* meaning "needle." A needle is sharp or pointed on one end. How does this information help you define *acute angle*?

PREVIEW

regular polygon	Venn diagram
equilateral triangle	chord
isosceles triangle	diameter
scalene triangle	radius
trapezoid	compass

www.harcourtschool.com/mathglossary

Polygons

Quick Review

Write the number of sides each figure has.

1. **2.** **3.** **4.** **5.**

VOCABULARY

polygon **pentagon**
triangle **hexagon**
quadrilateral **octagon**
regular polygon

SIDES AND ANGLES A **polygon** is a closed plane figure with straight sides. Polygons are named by the number of sides or number of angles they have. Here are some polygons.

triangle	quadrilateral	pentagon	hexagon	octagon
3 sides 3 angles	4 sides 4 angles	5 sides 5 angles	6 sides 6 angles	8 sides 8 angles

In a **regular polygon** all the sides have equal length and all the angles have equal measure.

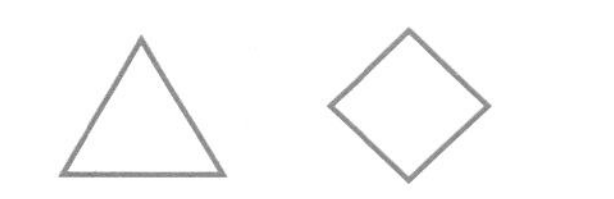

These polygons are regular.

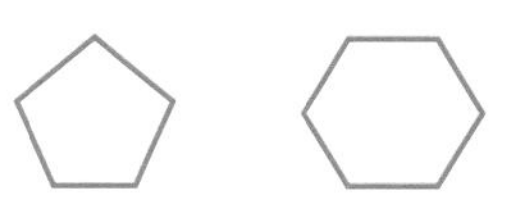

These polygons are not regular.

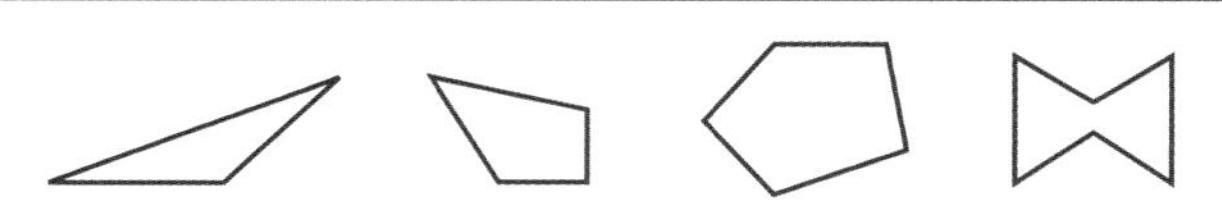

Activity

MATERIALS: dot paper, ruler

Draw a regular triangle.

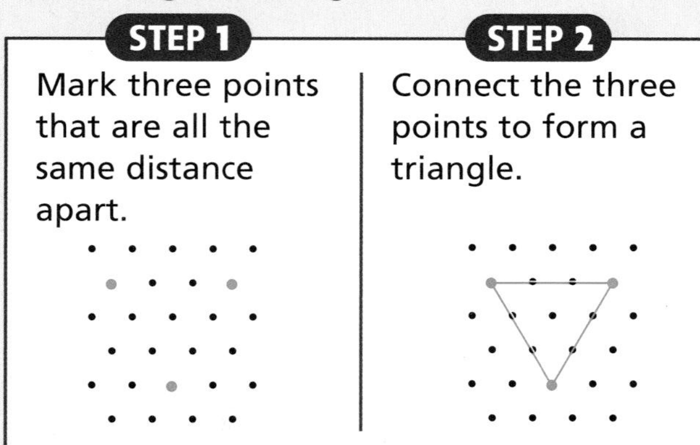

STEP 1 Mark three points that are all the same distance apart.

STEP 2 Connect the three points to form a triangle.

Draw a triangle that is not regular.

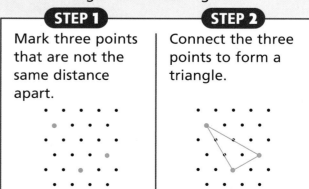

STEP 1 Mark three points that are not the same distance apart.

STEP 2 Connect the three points to form a triangle.

• How are the two triangles alike? How are they different?

Check

1. **Explain** how a polygon that is regular and a polygon that is not regular are different.

Name the polygon. Tell if it appears to be *regular* or *not regular*.

2. 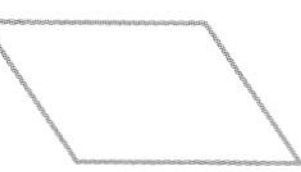
3. 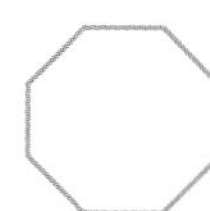
4. 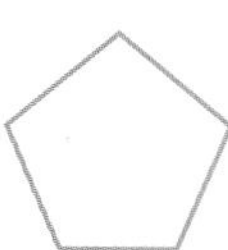
5. 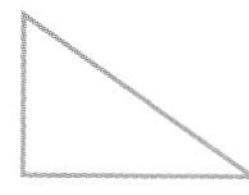

Practice and Problem Solving

Extra Practice, page 392, Set A

Name the polygon. Tell if it appears to be *regular* or *not regular*.

6. 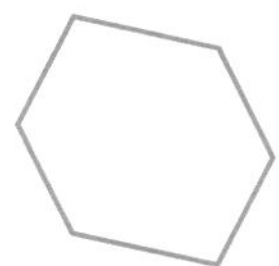
7. 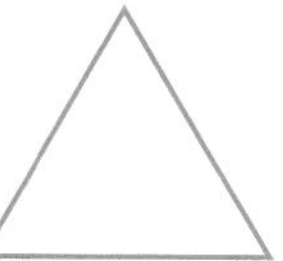
8. 
9. 

Use dot paper to draw each polygon.

10. a pentagon that is not regular
11. a regular triangle
12. a quadrilateral that is not regular
13. a regular hexagon

14. A mosaic has 600 tiles. There are 80 more square tiles than triangular tiles. How many of each tile are there?
15. Draw two regular polygons that have the same shape but are different in size.
16. What types of polygons do you see in the lamp shade?
17. **Write About It** Explain how you can tell what kind of polygon a figure is.

▲ Stained glass lamp by Tiffany Studios

Mixed Review and Test Prep

18. List six multiples of 5. (p. 338)
19. What is the square of 12? (p. 348)
20. Write 38,016 in expanded form. (p. 4)
21. Tell whether 452 is divisible by 2, 3, 5, 9, or 10. (p. 336)
22. TEST PREP What geometric term best describes the stripes in the U.S. Flag? (p. 370)

A parallel lines
B plane
C point
D triangle

LESSON 2

Classify Triangles

Learn

TAKE SIDES Triangles can be classified according to the lengths of their sides or the measures of their angles.

Classify by the lengths of their sides.

A triangle with 3 equal sides is an **equilateral triangle**.

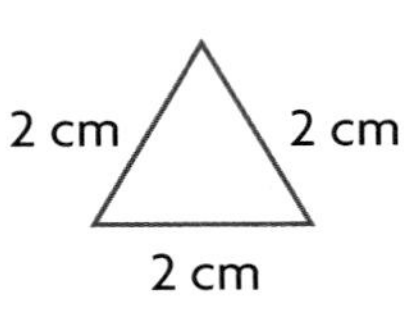

A triangle with 2 equal sides is an **isosceles triangle**.

3 cm 3 cm 2 cm

A triangle with no equal sides is a **scalene triangle**.

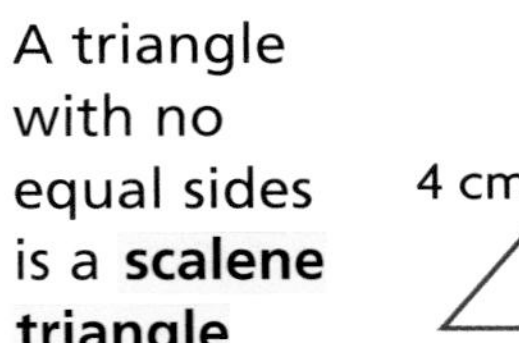

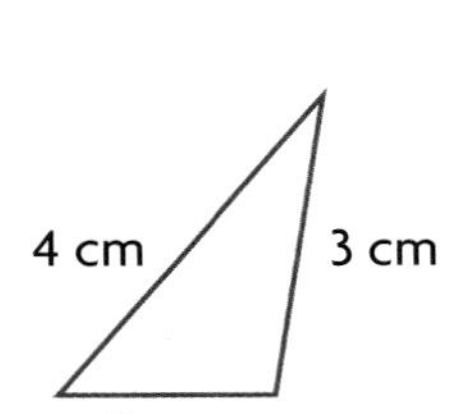

Classify by the measures of their angles.

A triangle that has a right angle is a **right triangle**.

A triangle that has 3 acute angles is an **acute triangle**.

A triangle that has 1 obtuse angle is an **obtuse triangle**.

• The equilateral triangle above is also an acute triangle. Is the scalene triangle above a right, an acute, or an obtuse triangle?

Quick Review

Subtract each from 300.

1. 158 **2.** 238 **3.** 163 **4.** 209 **5.** 179

VOCABULARY

equilateral triangle
isosceles triangle
scalene triangle
right triangle
acute triangle
obtuse triangle

Check

1. Explain the difference between a right, an acute, and an obtuse triangle.

Classify each triangle. Write *isosceles, scalene,* or *equilateral.* Then write *right, acute,* or *obtuse.*

2.

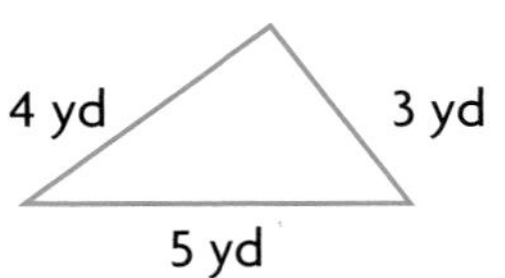

3.

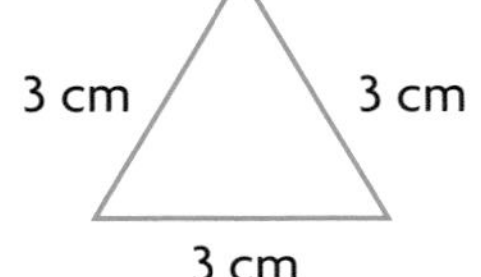

4.

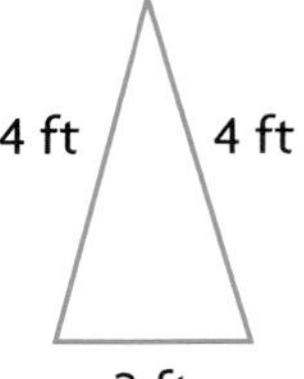

Practice and Problem Solving

Extra Practice, page 392, Set B

Classify each triangle. Write *isosceles, scalene,* or *equilateral.* Then write *right, acute,* or *obtuse.*

5. 3 ft, 7 ft, 9 ft

6. 5 yd, 5 yd, 5 yd

7. 9 cm, 9 cm

8. 8 ft, 6 ft, 4 ft

9.

10.

11.

12.

Classify each triangle by the lengths of its sides. Write *isosceles, scalene,* or *equilateral.*

13. 12 ft, 12 ft, 12 ft
14. 9 cm, 7 cm, 4 cm
15. 13 mm, 13 mm, 8 mm
16. 6 in., 14 in., 14 in.
17. 43 mm, 43 mm, 43 mm
18. 29 yd, 28 yd, 6 yd

Measure the sides of each triangle using a centimeter ruler. Write *isosceles, scalene,* or *equilateral.*

19.

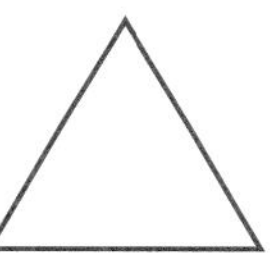

20.

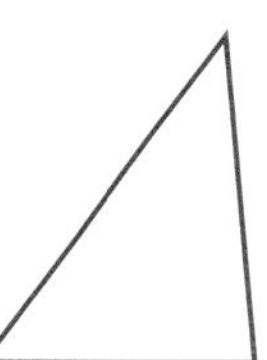

21.

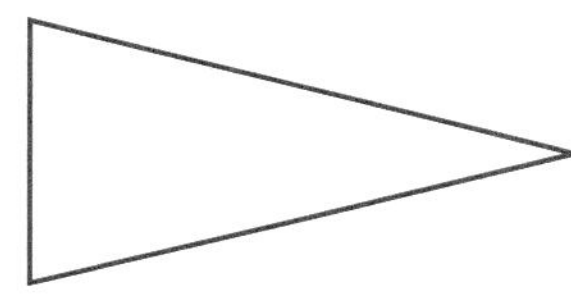

22. I have 3 sides and 3 angles. Only 2 of my angles are acute. What kinds of figures could I be?

23. Draw a triangle with 1 right angle and 2 equal sides that each measure 3 units. Use square dot paper. Name the triangle.

Mixed Review and Test Prep

24. If 5 shelves hold 60 boxes, how many shelves hold 144 boxes? (p. 172)

25. In June, Irma rode her bicycle 8 miles a day for 15 days. How far did Irma ride her bicycle? (p. 218)

26. $7\overline{)362}$ (p. 300)

27. $5\overline{)235}$ (p. 300)

28. TEST PREP What is the median of this set of numbers? (p. 118)
12, 14, 14, 9, 14, 8, 12

A 14 **B** 12 **C** 8 **D** 4

LESSON 3

Classify Quadrilaterals

Learn

CLASSIC LINES A figure with 4 sides and 4 angles is called a quadrilateral. There are many kinds of quadrilaterals. They can be classified by their features.

Activity

MATERIALS: geoboard, rubber bands, dot paper

Copy each quadrilateral on a geoboard. Use dot paper to record your work.

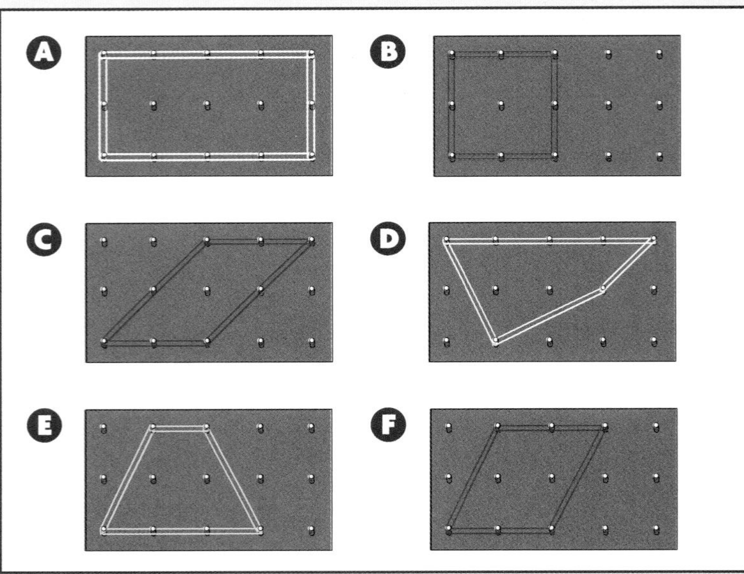

- Which have 2 pairs of parallel sides?
- Which have 4 right angles?
- Which have both pairs of opposite sides equal?
- Which have only 1 pair of parallel sides?
- Which have no pairs of parallel sides?

Quick Review

Name any line relationship you see in each figure.

1.
2.
3.
4.
5. 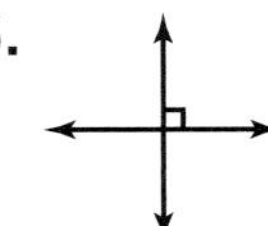

VOCABULARY

parallelogram
rhombus
trapezoid

▲ In 1930, Walter Dorwin Teague designed the No. 2A Beau Brownie camera with an Art Deco theme, using squares and rectangles. It originally cost $5.

Special Quadrilaterals

There are five special types of quadrilaterals: **parallelogram**, square, rectangle, **rhombus**, and **trapezoid**. Each has different features, and some can be classified in more than one way. Use the diagram to help you identify each type of quadrilateral.

The diagram shows that all rectangles are parallelograms and quadrilaterals.

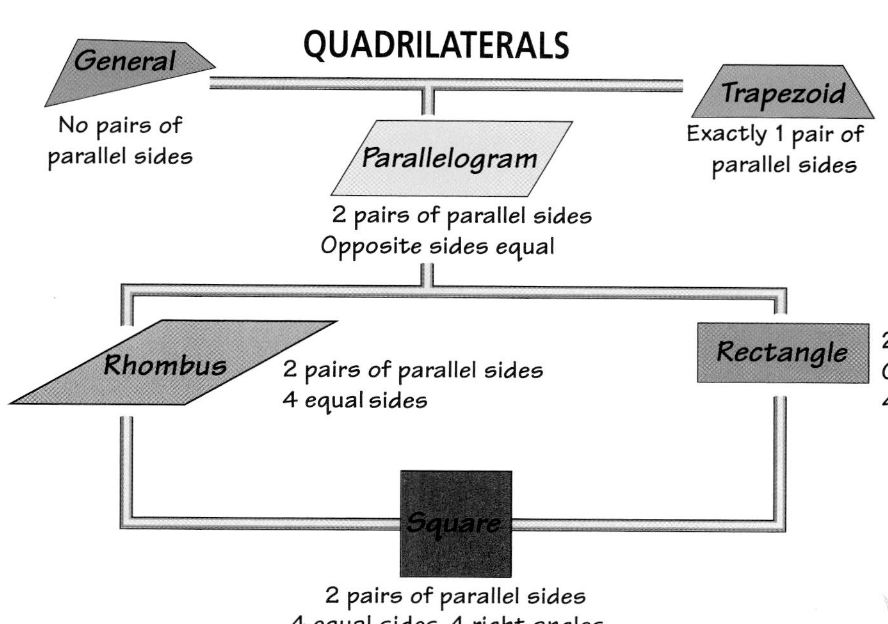

- A parallelogram has 4 equal sides. What figures could it be?

Technology Link

More Practice: Harcourt Mega Math Ice Station Exploration, *Polar Planes*, Level G

Check

1. **Compare and contrast** a trapezoid and a parallelogram.

Classify each figure in as many ways as possible. Write *quadrilateral, parallelogram, rhombus, rectangle, square,* or *trapezoid*.

2.

3.

4.

Draw an example of each quadrilateral.

5. It has 4 equal sides and no right angles.

6. Its opposite sides are parallel and it has 4 right angles.

7. It is a trapezoid with 2 equal sides.

LESSON CONTINUES 

Practice and Problem Solving

Extra Practice, page 392, Set C

Classify each figure in as many ways as possible. Write *quadrilateral, parallelogram, rhombus, rectangle, square,* or *trapezoid.*

8.

9.

10.

11. 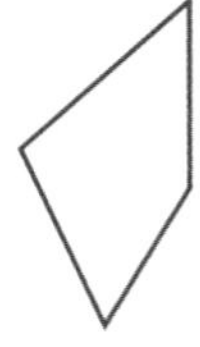

12. 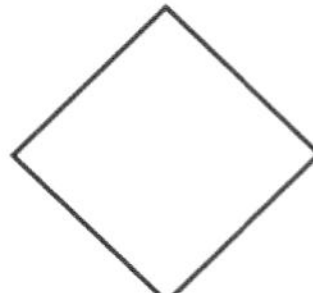

13. 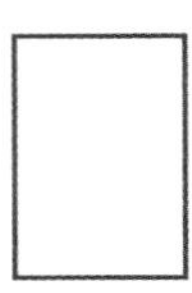

14. 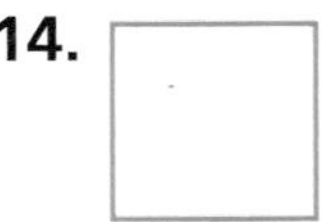

15. 

16. 

Draw an example of each quadrilateral.

17. It has 2 pairs of parallel sides and the opposite sides are equal.

18. The 4 sides are equal and there are 4 right angles.

19. It has exactly 1 pair of parallel sides.

Choose the figure that does not belong. Explain.

20. **a.** 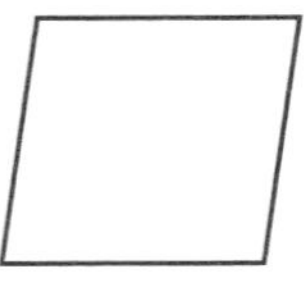 **b.** 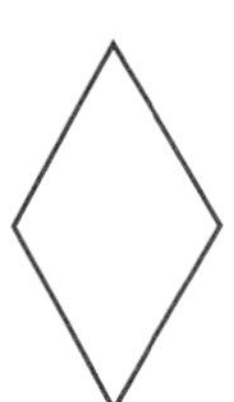 **c.**  **d.** 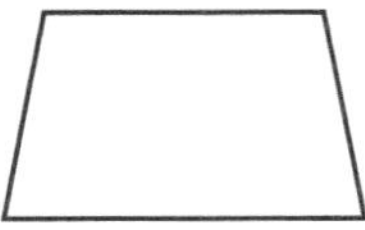

21. **a.** 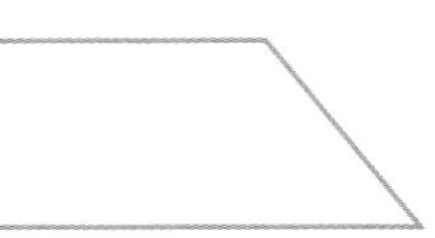 **b.** 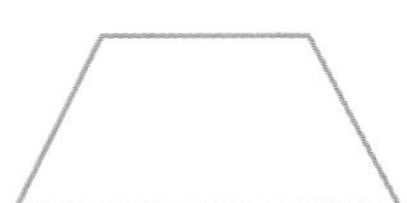 **c.**  **d.** 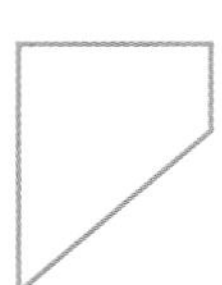

22. **REASONING** Is a square also a rhombus? Explain how you know.

23. I have 4 sides and 4 angles. At least one of my angles is acute. What figures could I be?

24. Draw a square that measures 2 inches on each side. What figures can you make if you draw a line that cuts the square in half?

25. **Write a problem** about a mystery quadrilateral. Give at least three clues that will help identify the quadrilateral.

26. At sunrise the temperature was 72°F. At noon it was 19° warmer. It cooled off 12° in the evening. What was the evening temperature?

27. **Vocabulary Power** The word *rectangle* comes from the words *rectus angulus*, meaning "right angle." How does the meaning relate to a rectangle?

Mixed Review and Test Prep

28. 3×184 (p. 222)

29. $\$7,426 + \$2,915$ (p. 48)

30. $\$5,003 - \$1,879$ (p. 50)

31. $\blacksquare \times 8 = 64$ (p. 168)

32. 7×48 (p. 218)

33. $804 \div \blacksquare = 67$ (p. 320)

34. In September the Reading Club members sold 1,032 movie passes. In October they sold 2,940 passes. In November they sold 125 more than in September. How many passes were sold in all? (p. 48)

35. **TEST PREP** Find the time shown on the clock. (p. 96)

A 4:08
B 4:40
C 8:20
D 8:40

36. **TEST PREP** There are a total of 42 students on 6 teams. Each team has the same number of students. Which equation can be used to find *n*, the number of students on each team? (p. 192)

F $n \times 6 = 42$
G $n \div 6 = 42$
H $6 \times 42 = n$
J $n \times 42 = 6$

Problem Solving LINKUP ... to Reading

STRATEGY • CLASSIFY AND CATEGORIZE
When you *classify* information, you group similar information. When you *categorize*, you name the groups that you have classified.

The diagram on page 385 classifies and categorizes information about quadrilaterals.

For 1–6, use the diagram. Tell if the statement is *true* or *false*. If the statement is false, explain why.

1. All rectangles are squares.
2. All rhombuses are parallelograms.
3. All squares are rectangles.
4. Some trapezoids are parallelograms.
5. Some rhombuses are squares.
6. No trapezoids have 2 pairs of parallel sides.

Problem Solving Strategy
Draw a Diagram

UNDERSTAND | PLAN | SOLVE | CHECK

Quick Review

1. 50 − 10
2. 50 − 1
3. 500 − 100
4. 500 − 1
5. 5,000 − 1,001

VOCABULARY
Venn diagram

PROBLEM Mrs. Stein asked her students to sort these figures into two groups according to how many equal sides each figure has. How can the figures be sorted?

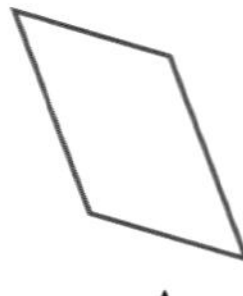
A

B

C

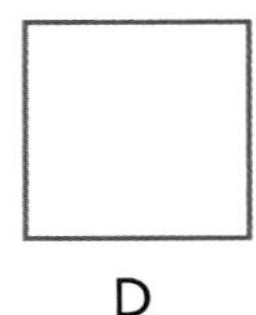
D

E F

UNDERSTAND

- What are you asked to do?
- What information will you use?
- Is there any information you will not use? Explain.

PLAN

- What strategy can you use to solve the problem?
  Draw a diagram to solve the problem.

SOLVE

- What kind of diagram can you make?
  Make a **Venn diagram** showing 2 separate circles to sort the figures. Venn diagrams show relationships among sets of things.

  Label one circle *With 4 Equal Sides*. Put figures B and D in this circle. Label the other circle *Without 4 Equal Sides*. Put figures A, C, E, and F in this circle.

Quadrilaterals

With 4 Equal Sides

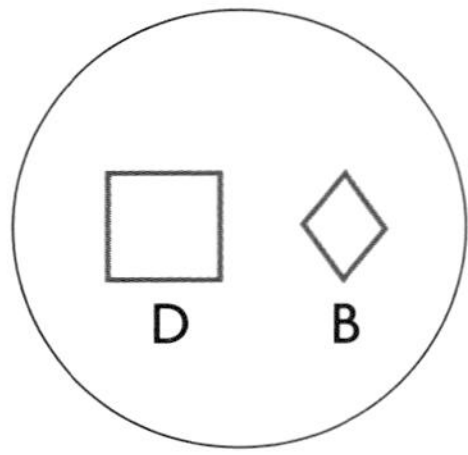

Without 4 Equal Sides

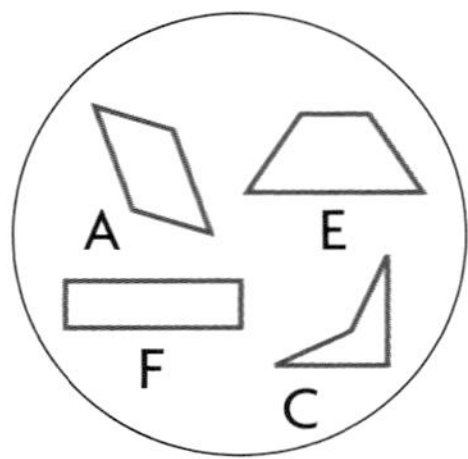

CHECK

- How do you know that the answer is correct?

Problem Solving Practice

Use *draw a diagram* to solve.

1. **What if** Mrs. Stein had asked the students to sort figures A–F into two groups, one with 2 pairs of parallel sides and one with fewer than 2 pairs of parallel sides? Draw a diagram that shows those groupings.

2. Sort these numbers into a Venn diagram showing *Divisible by 2* and *Not Divisible by 2:* 2, 3, 4, 6, 8, 9, 10, 12.

Strategies

- **Draw a Diagram or Picture**
- Make a Model or Act It Out
- Make an Organized List
- Find a Pattern
- Make a Table or Graph
- Predict and Test
- Work Backward
- Solve a Simpler Problem
- Write an Equation
- Use Logical Reasoning

Problem Solving

Look at the Venn diagram. Section B shows what the figures have in common.

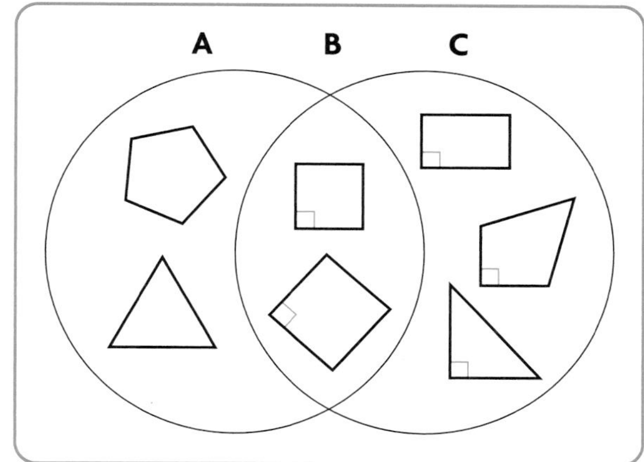

3. Which label best describes the polygons in Section A?
   A regular
   B not regular
   C quadrilaterals
   D not quadrilaterals

4. Which label best describes the polygons in Section B?
   F regular with an acute angle
   G not regular with an acute angle
   H regular with a right angle
   J not regular with a right angle

Mixed Strategy Practice

For 5–6, use the stem-and-leaf plot.

Heights of Jamie's Friends (in inches)

Stem	Leaves
5	7 8 9
6	0 1 1 2 4 5

5. How many of Jamie's friends were measured?

6. What is the mode?

7. Draw a Venn diagram to sort figures A–F on page 388 into these groups: *With Only Right Angles* and *With Other Kinds of Angles.*

8. **Write About It** Describe a rule for this pattern: 1, 2, 4, 8, 16, 32, 64.

9. Draw a trapezoid. What figure would you make if you extended the two non-parallel sides from the endpoints of the shorter side?

10. **REASONING** What is the length of one side of the smallest square that a 12-inch plate will fit into? Draw a picture to prove your answer.

LESSON

5 Circles

Quick Review

1. 305 ÷ 5
2. 805 ÷ 5
3. 608 ÷ 8
4. 506 ÷ 2
5. 708 ÷ 3

VOCABULARY

circle	diameter
center	radius
chord	compass

Learn

ROUND AND ROUND A **circle** is a closed plane figure made up of points that are the same distance from the **center**. A circle can be named by its center.

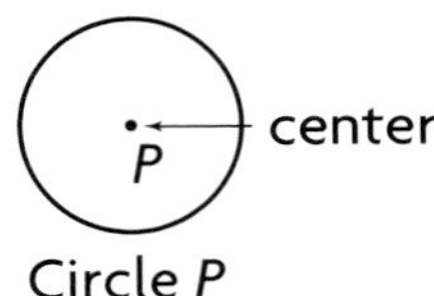

Circle *P*

Other parts of a circle:

A **chord** is a line segment that has its endpoints on the circle.

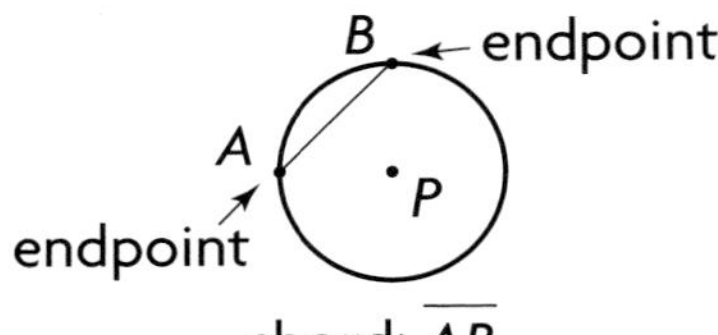

chord: $\overline{AB}$

A **diameter** is a chord that passes through the center.

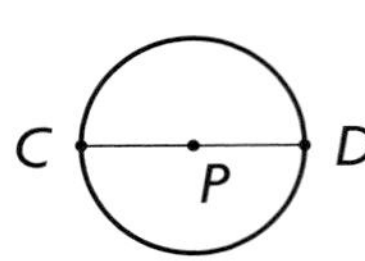

diameter: $\overline{CD}$

A **radius** is a line segment with one endpoint at the center of the circle and the other endpoint on the circle.

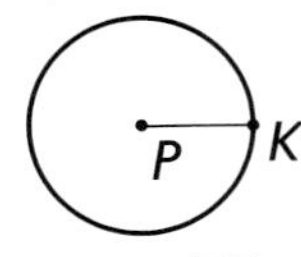

radius: $\overline{PK}$

The radius of a circle is half the length of the diameter.

A **compass** is a tool used to construct circles.

Activity

MATERIALS: compass, ruler

STEP 1

Draw a point to be the center of the circle. Label it with the letter *P*.

STEP 2

Set the compass to the length of the radius you want.

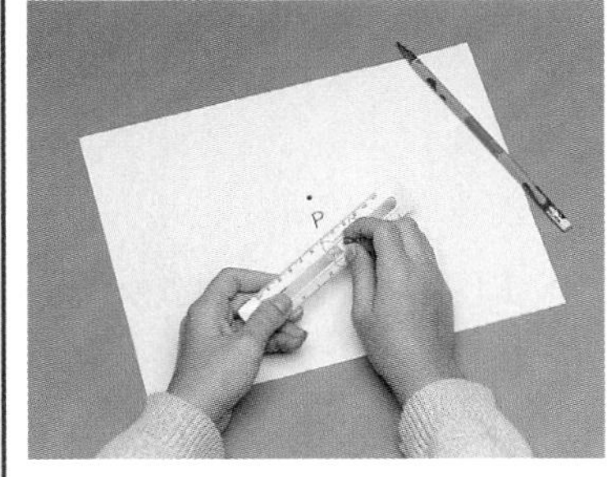

STEP 3

Hold the compass point at point *P*, and move the compass to make the circle.

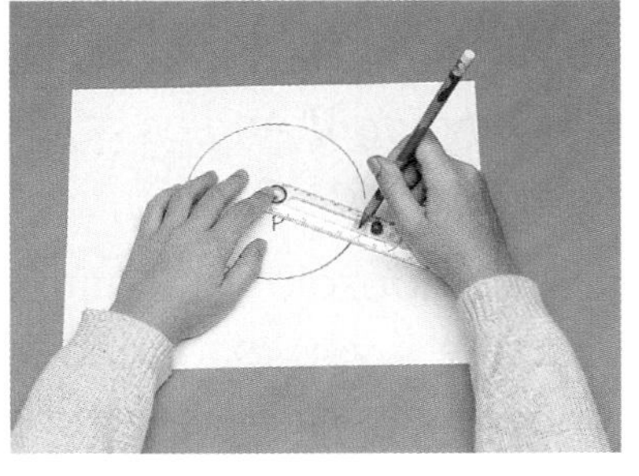

Check

1. **Explain** how you can find the length of the diameter of a circle that has a radius of 3 inches.

Draw circle *P* with a 2-inch radius. Label each of the following.

2. radius: $\overline{PQ}$
3. chord: $\overline{JK}$
4. diameter: $\overline{XY}$

Practice and Problem Solving

Extra Practice, page 392, Set D

For 5–10, use the drawing of circle *M* and a centimeter ruler. Copy and complete the table.

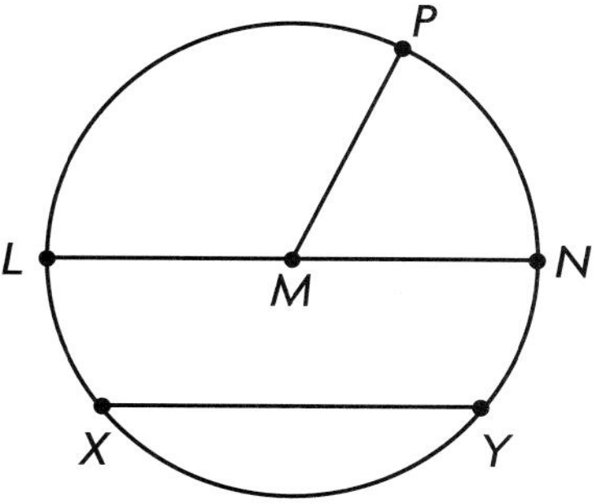

	NAME	PART OF CIRCLE	LENGTH IN CM
5.	$\overline{MP}$	?	■
6.	$\overline{XY}$	?	■
7.	$\overline{MN}$	?	■
8.	$\overline{LN}$	?	■

9. The center of the circle is point _?_.
10. Two points on the circle are _?_ and _?_.
11. Draw a circle with a 3-inch radius. Label the center point *E*. Draw a radius: $\overline{EF}$. Draw a diameter: $\overline{GH}$.

USE DATA For 12–13, use the art at the right.

▼ No-fly Zone

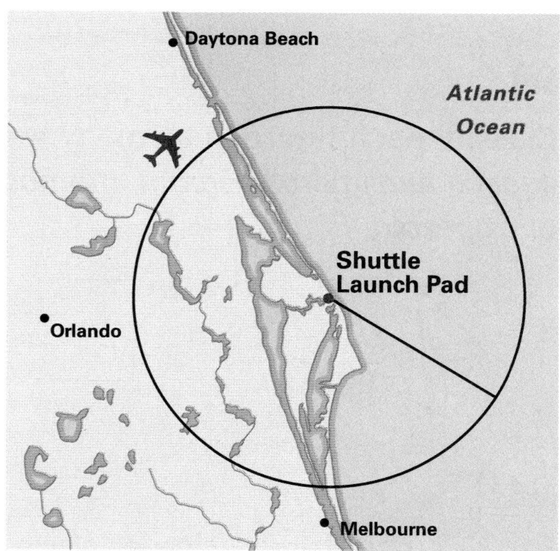

12. **FAST FACT • SCIENCE** In 2001, NASA expanded the "no-fly zone" around the shuttle's launch pad to a radius of 56 kilometers. Find the diameter of the no-fly zone.

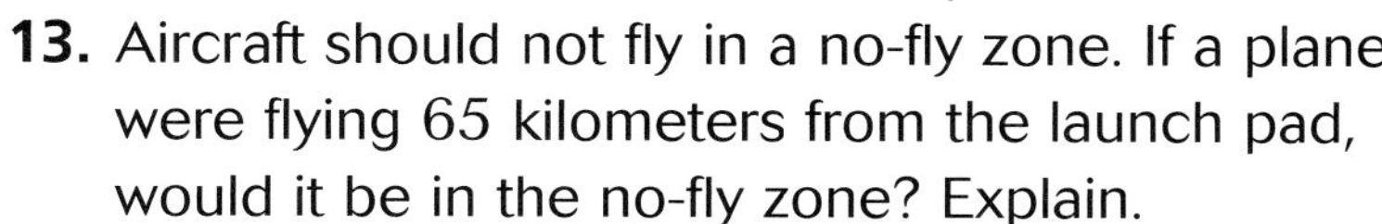

13. Aircraft should not fly in a no-fly zone. If a plane were flying 65 kilometers from the launch pad, would it be in the no-fly zone? Explain.
14. **Write About It** Can the length of a chord be greater than the circle's diameter? Explain.

Mixed Review and Test Prep

15. 7×9 (p. 168)
16. 8×8 (p. 168)
17. Find the value. $24 \times (72 \div 9)$ (p. 184)
18. Find the mean of 2, 4, 7, 2, 10. (p. 118)
19. **TEST PREP** Which of the following is true? (p. 20)
    - **A** $5,126 < 5,216$
    - **B** $5,261 < 5,216$
    - **C** $5,126 > 5,621$
    - **D** $5,216 > 5,612$

Extra Practice

Set A (pp. 380–381)

Name the polygon. Tell if it appears to be *regular* or *not regular*.

1. 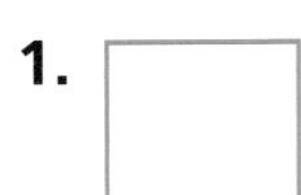
2. 
3. 
4. 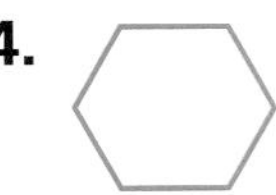

Set B (pp. 382–383)

Classify each triangle. Write *isosceles, scalene,* or *equilateral*. Then write *right, acute,* or *obtuse*.

1. 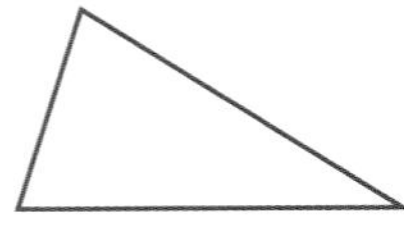
2. 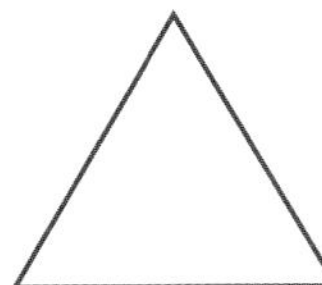
3. 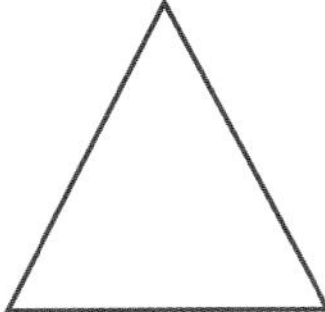
4. 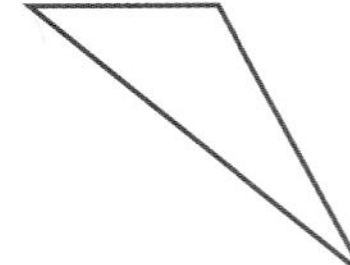

Classify each triangle by the lengths of its sides. Write *isosceles, scalene,* or *equilateral*.

5. 4 feet, 4 feet, 4 feet
6. 8 yards, 10 yards, 7 yards
7. 7 inches, 4 inches, 7 inches

Set C (pp. 384–387)

Classify each figure in as many ways as possible. Write *quadrilateral, parallelogram, rhombus, rectangle, square,* or *trapezoid*.

1. 
2. 
3. 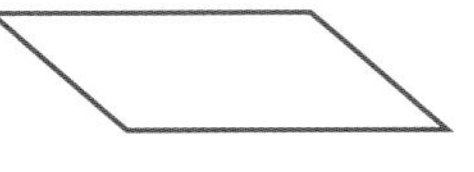
4. 

Set D (pp. 390–391)

For 1–3, use the drawing of circle *P* and a ruler marked in inches.

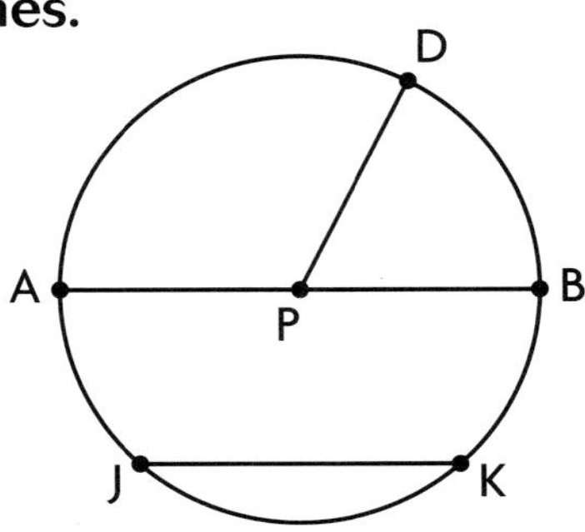

1. The line segment *AB* is a _?_. It measures _?_ inches.
2. The line segment *JK* is a _?_.
3. The line segment *PD* is a _?_. It measures _?_ inch.
4. The radius of one circle is 5 inches longer than the radius of another circle. Together they measure 29 inches. How long is each radius?

Review/Test

CHECK VOCABULARY AND CONCEPTS

Choose the best term from the box.

equilateral
pentagon
rhombus
square

1. A parallelogram with 4 equal sides is a ? or a ?. (p. 385)
2. A triangle that has 3 equal sides is ?. (p. 382)

CHECK SKILLS

Name the polygon. Tell if it appears to be *regular* or *not regular*. (pp. 380–381)

3. 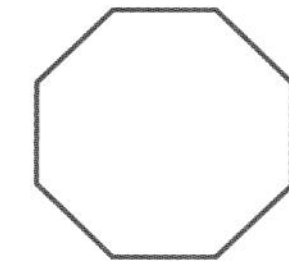

4. 

5. 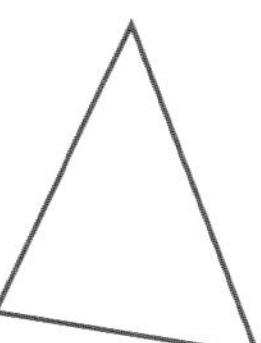

Classify each triangle by the lengths of its sides. Write *isosceles, scalene,* or *equilateral*. (pp. 382–383)

6. 17 ft, 22 ft, 16 ft
7. 5 cm, 5 cm, 5 cm
8. 11 mm, 11 mm, 8 mm

Classify each figure in as many ways as possible. Write *quadrilateral, parallelogram, rhombus, rectangle, square,* or *trapezoid*. (pp. 384–387)

9. 

10. 

11. 

For 12–13, use the drawing of circle *O*. (pp. 390–391)

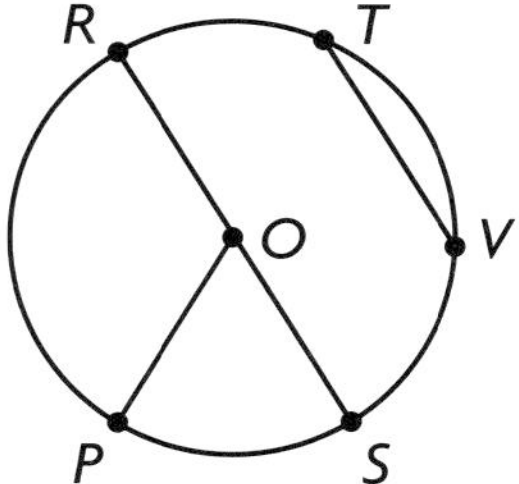

12. Name a chord.
13. Name a radius.

CHECK PROBLEM SOLVING (pp. 388–389)

14. Sort these numbers into a Venn diagram showing *Divisible by 5* and *Not Divisible by 5*: 1, 5, 10, 12, 16, 20, 24.

15. Draw a Venn diagram to sort these figures into two groups: *With Only 2 Equal Sides* and *With 4 Equal Sides.*

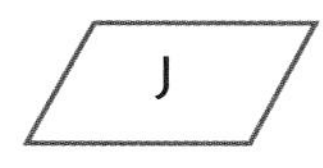

Standardized Test Prep

NUMBER SENSE, CONCEPTS, AND OPERATIONS

1. Each baseball team needs 9 players. So far, 77 children have signed up to play. How many more children are needed for each team to have 9 players?

   A 4

   B 3

   C 2

   D 0

2. Carmen bought 20 rolls of film. She can take 36 photos with each roll. Which operation would be best for finding the total number of photos Carmen can take?

   F addition

   G subtraction

   H multiplication

   J division

3. **Explain It** Jessie wants to buy 4 of the same item. She estimates her total will be about $16. Which item does she want to buy? Explain how you decided.

SPORTS STORE PRICES	
Item	**Cost**
1 can of tennis balls	$4.08
1 pair of running shorts	$17.59
1 pack of golf tees	$2.75
1 baseball	$1.83

GEOMETRY AND SPATIAL SENSE

4. Which geometric term **best** describes the corner of the picture frame?

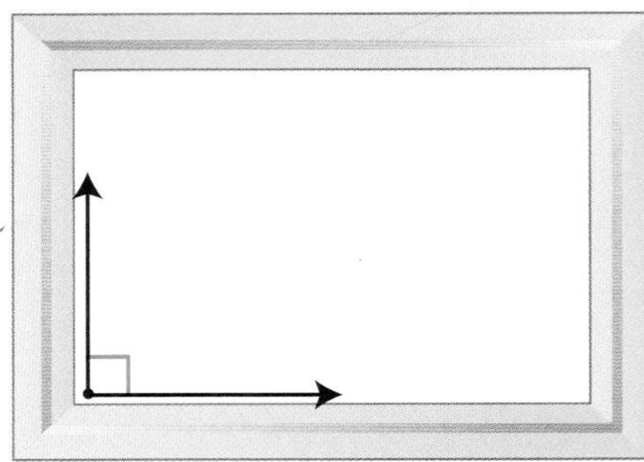

   A ray

   B acute angle

   C right angle

   D line segment

5. Jackie bought the square scarf below.

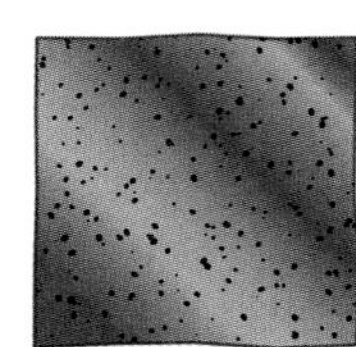

22 inches

   What is the perimeter of the scarf?

   F 22 inches

   G 44 inches

   H 88 inches

   J 484 inches

6. **Explain It** Is the following sentence *true* or *false*?

   "A rectangle is always a rhombus."

   Explain your thinking.

 ALGEBRAIC THINKING

7. What is the value of ■?

$■ + 3 = 10$

$10 - 3 = ■$

A 7

B 4

C 1

D 0

> **TIP** **Decide on a plan.** See item 8. Find a relationship between numbers that follow each other in the pattern. Apply that relationship to determine what number comes next.

8. Chan wrote this number pattern: 1, 3, 5, 7, 9, 11, ■. What could be the next number in the pattern?

F 22

G 14

H 13

J 9

9. **Explain It** Look at the table below.

INPUT	OUTPUT
5	25
8	40
6	30
2	10
■	60
1	5
11	55
9	45

Write a rule. What is the missing number? Explain how you decided.

 DATA ANALYSIS AND PROBABILITY

10. What is the median test score?

Test Scores

Stem	Leaves
7	6 6 8
8	0 8
9	0 0 0 7

A 76

B 80

C 88

D 97

11. What is the **best** title for the graph?

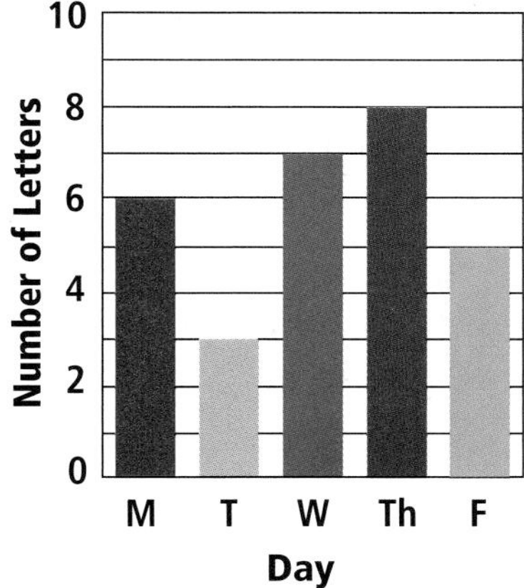

F Days of the Week

G Letters Received

H Shipping Costs

J Number of Days

12. **Explain It** Do you think the number of fourth graders is likely to increase or decrease next year? Explain your thinking.

FOURTH-GRADE STUDENTS AT SPRING LAKE SCHOOL	
When	**Number of Students**
Two years ago	109
Last year	113
This year	120

CHAPTER 19 Motion Geometry

FAST FACT • ART New Orleans, Louisiana, is known for its beautiful iron grillwork. Many of the city's doors, gates, and fences have decorative patterns made from iron. This tradition started more than 200 years ago when artists from the island of Haiti came to New Orleans.

PROBLEM SOLVING Study the grillwork from this home in the Garden District. Then trace the ironwork in the small photo. Draw all its lines of symmetry. What kind of symmetry does it have?

CHECK WHAT YOU KNOW

Use this page to help you review and remember important skills needed for Chapter 19.

IDENTIFY SYMMETRIC FIGURES

Is the blue line a line of symmetry? Write *yes* or *no*.

1.

2. 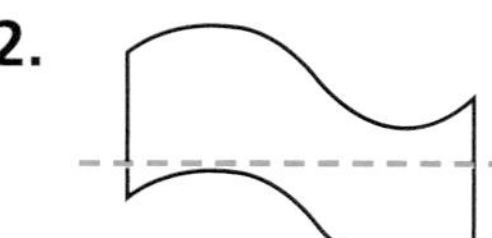

3. 

4. 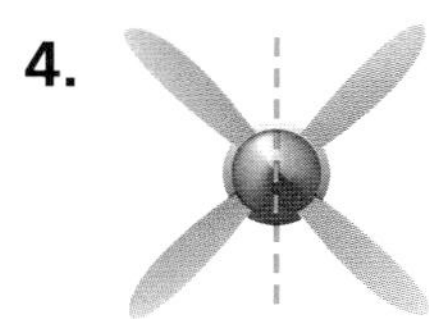

COMPARE FIGURES

Are the figures the same shape and size? Write *yes* or *no*.

5.

6. 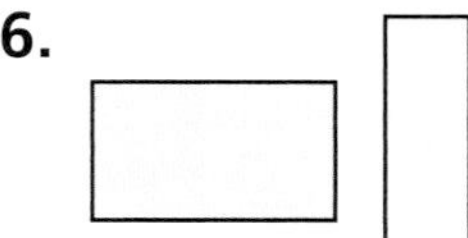

7. 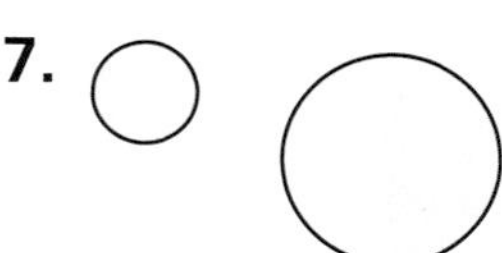

SLIDES, FLIPS, AND TURNS

Tell which kind of motion was used to move each plane figure. Write *slide, flip,* or *turn*.

8. 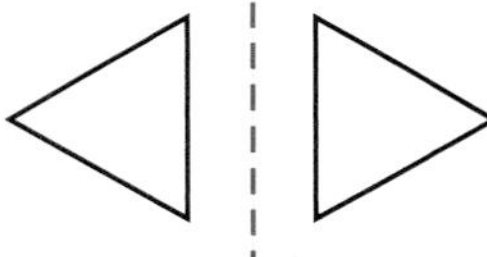

9. 

10. 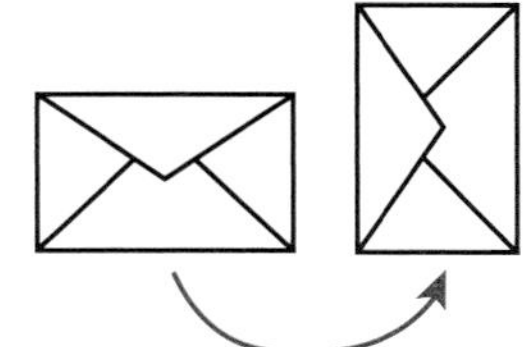

VOCABULARY POWER

REVIEW

slide [slīd] *verb*

To *slide* means "to move smoothly along a surface." A base runner in baseball may slide into home base to score a run. Name other activities in which someone might slide.

PREVIEW

line symmetry
rotational symmetry
congruent
similar
transformation
translation
reflection
rotation
tessellation

www.harcourtschool.com/mathglossary

LESSON 1

Turns and Symmetry

Learn

Turning ray $\overrightarrow{CD}$ around the circle makes angles of different sizes. A complete turn around the circle is 360°.

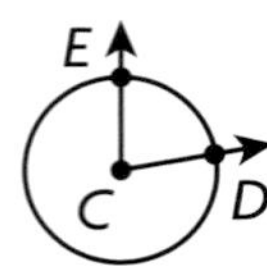

Ray $\overrightarrow{CD}$ can be turned clockwise, the direction clock hands move, or counterclockwise, the direction opposite from the way clock hands move.

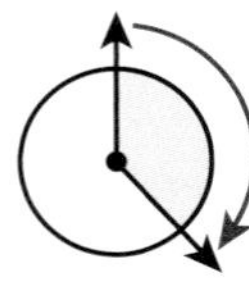
clockwise

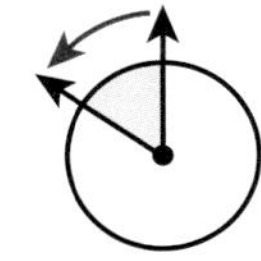
counterclockwise

Quick Review

Name each angle. Write *right, acute, obtuse,* or *straight.*

1. 

2. 

3. 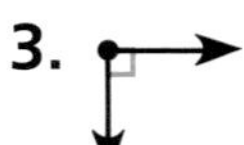

4. 

5. 

VOCABULARY

line symmetry

rotational symmetry

Activity

MATERIALS: 2 strips of paper, paper fastener

Use turns of geostrips to show different angles.

STEP 1

Open the geostrip to form a 90° angle.

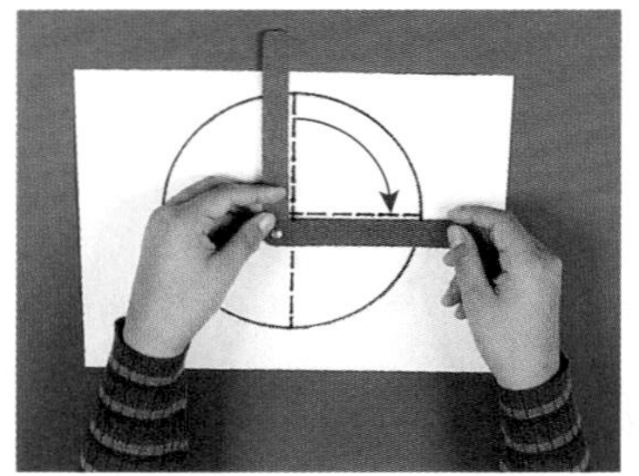

This is a $\frac{1}{4}$, or quarter, turn around a circle.

STEP 2

Now open the geostrip $\frac{1}{4}$ turn more to make a 180° angle.

This is a $\frac{1}{2}$, or half, turn around a circle.

STEP 3

Open your geostrip another $\frac{1}{4}$ turn to make a 270° angle.

This is a $\frac{3}{4}$, or three quarter, turn around a circle.

- Explain how the result of a 270° turn in the clockwise direction can look like the result of a 90° turn in the counterclockwise direction.
- How many $\frac{1}{4}$ turns are the same as a complete turn?

MATH IDEA An angle measure can be related to a complete turn (360°), a $\frac{3}{4}$ turn (270°), a $\frac{1}{2}$ turn (180°), or a $\frac{1}{4}$ turn (90°).

Symmetric Figures

Symmetry can be found all around us—in nature, in art, and in music. A figure can have **line symmetry, rotational symmetry**, or both.

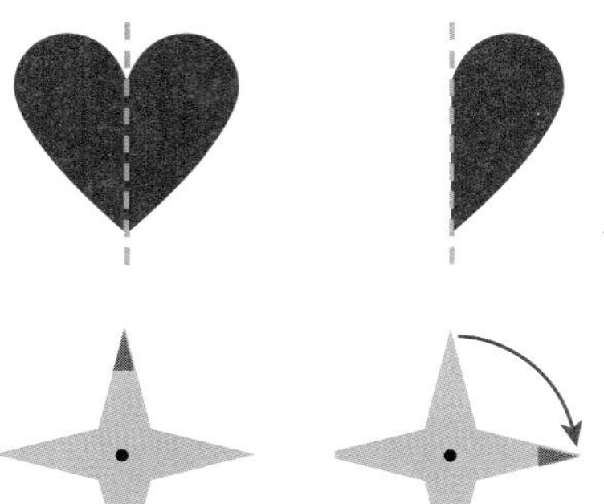

Fold this figure along a line so that its two parts match exactly. It has line symmetry. Some figures can have more than one line of symmetry.

Turn this figure around the center point. It looks the same at each $\frac{1}{4}$ turn. It has rotational symmetry.

▲ **Starfish and sand dollars are examples of regular pentagons found in the ocean.**

- Which of the figures in the photograph has more than one line of symmetry? Which has both line symmetry and rotational symmetry?

Activity **MATERIALS:** grid paper, straightedge, scissors

STEP 1

Draw a square on grid paper. Mark the inside and outside of one corner. Cut out the square.

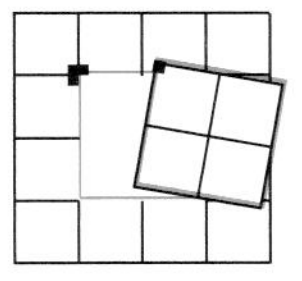

STEP 2

Fold the square in half two times as shown. The center point is the point where both folds meet. Mark this point.

STEP 3

Turn the square $\frac{1}{4}$ turn about its center point. How many times must you turn the square before your marks in the corner line up again?

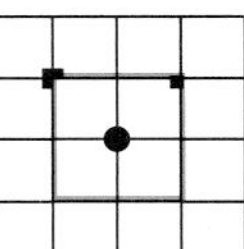

The square must be turned four times.

- How many lines of symmetry does the square have? Draw a picture to explain.

Check

1. **Tell** which of these capital letters does not have line symmetry. Explain how you know.

Tell whether the rays on the circle show a $\frac{1}{4}$, $\frac{1}{2}$, $\frac{3}{4}$, or complete turn.

2. 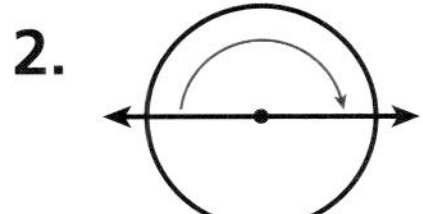

3. 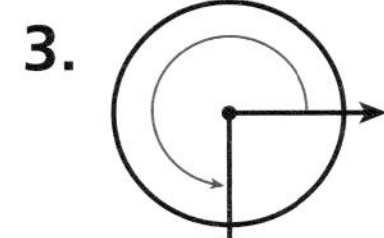

4. 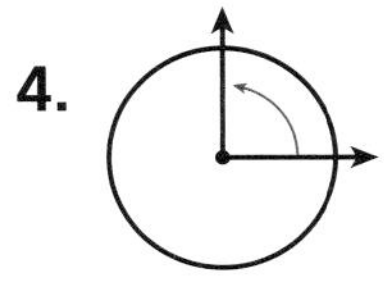

5. 

LESSON CONTINUES ▶

Tell whether the figure has *line symmetry, rotational symmetry,* or *both*.

6. 

7. 

8. 

9. 

Practice and Problem Solving

Extra Practice, page 414, Set A

Tell whether the rays on the circle show a $\frac{1}{4}$, $\frac{1}{2}$, $\frac{3}{4}$, or complete turn.

10. 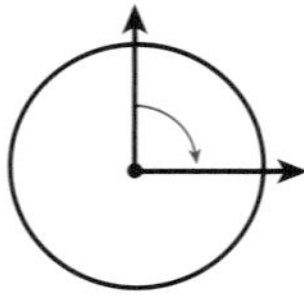

11. 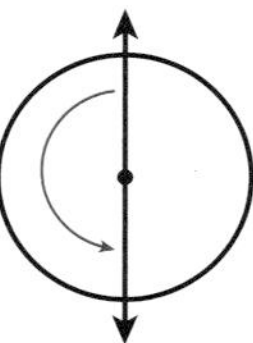

12. 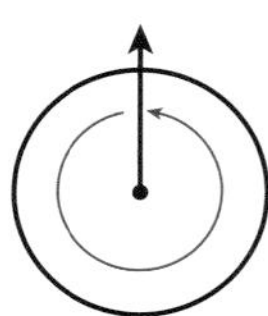

13. 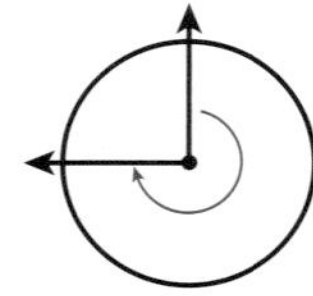

Tell whether the figure has *line symmetry, rotational symmetry,* or *both*.

14. 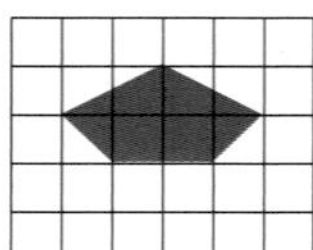

15. 

16. 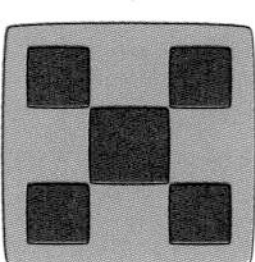

17. 

18. 

19. 

Tell whether the figure has been turned $90°$, $180°$, $270°$, or $360°$.

20. 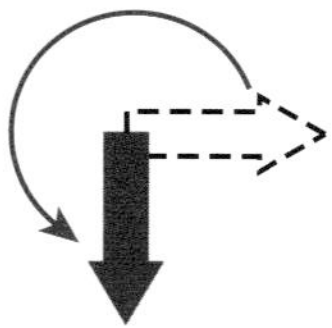

21. 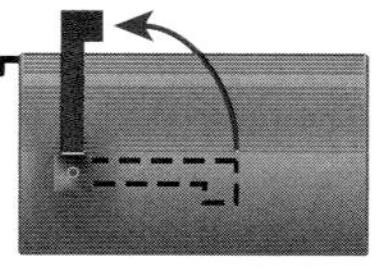

22. 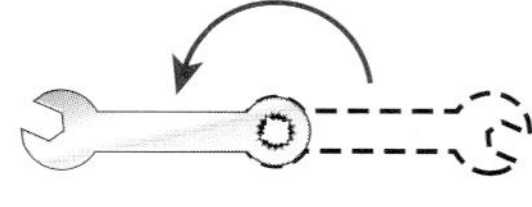

Copy each design on dot paper. Complete each design to show line symmetry.

23. 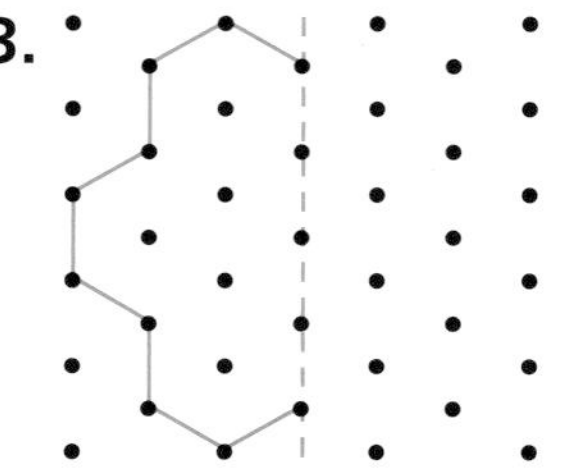

24. 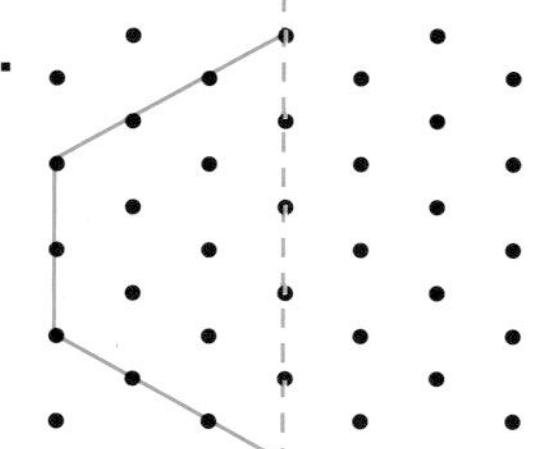

25. 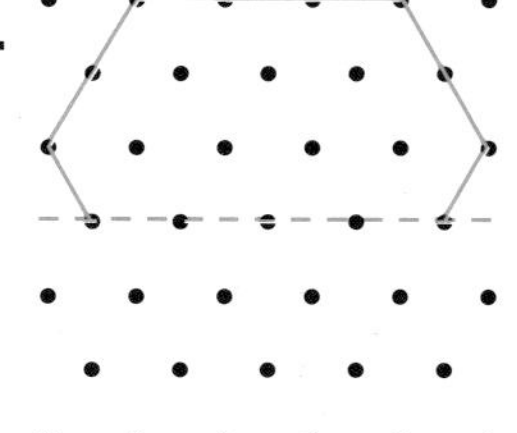

26. Copy the equilateral triangle. Draw all its lines of symmetry. What kind of symmetry does it have?

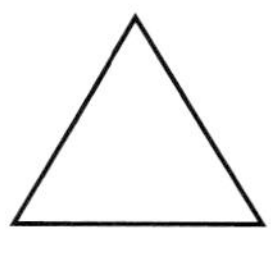

27. Trace the figure at the right. Cut out 8 copies. Use them to design a door with at least 1 line of symmetry.

28. The word BOX has a horizontal line of symmetry. Find two other words that have a horizontal line of symmetry.

29. How many 30° angles can be drawn in a circle without any overlapping? Explain.

30. **What's the Question?** The minute hand on a clock moves from 12 to 4. The answer is 120°.

Mixed Review and Test Prep

31. 56×143 (p. 256)

32. $430 + 178$ (p. 48)

33. What is 32,704 written in expanded form? (p. 4)

34. **TEST PREP** Which is 48 divided by 2? (p. 282)

A 50 **B** 46 **C** 36 **D** 24

35. **TEST PREP** Which property can you use to find $x + 5 = 5 + 2$? (p. 68)

F Associative Property of Addition
G Commutative Property of Addition
H Zero Property
J Distributive Property

Problem Solving LINKUP . . . to Science

FLOWER SYMMETRY Scientists who classify flowers look for lines of symmetry. Flowers having more than one line of symmetry are regular. Flowers having only one line of symmetry are irregular.

regular flower

irregular flower

Tell whether the flower is *regular* or *irregular*.

1. 

2. 

3. 

4. 

LESSON 2

Congruent and Similar Figures

Learn

SAME SHAPE, SAME SIZE Figures that have the same shape and size are **congruent**. Figures do not have to be in the same position to be congruent.

congruent

not congruent

Activity 1 **MATERIALS:** dot paper, rulers, scissors

STEP 1

Copy each pair of figures on dot paper.

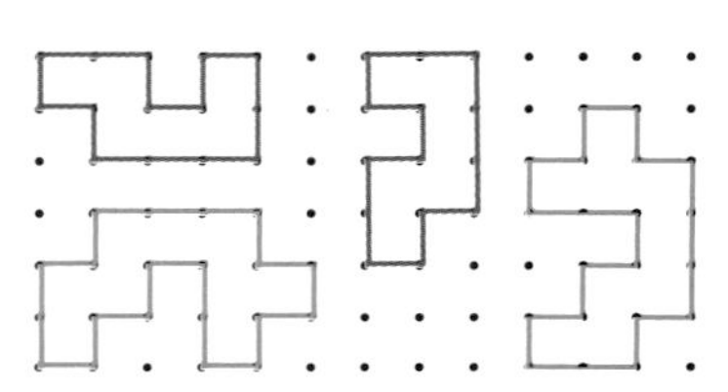

STEP 2

Cut out one in each pair, and move it in any way to check for congruency.

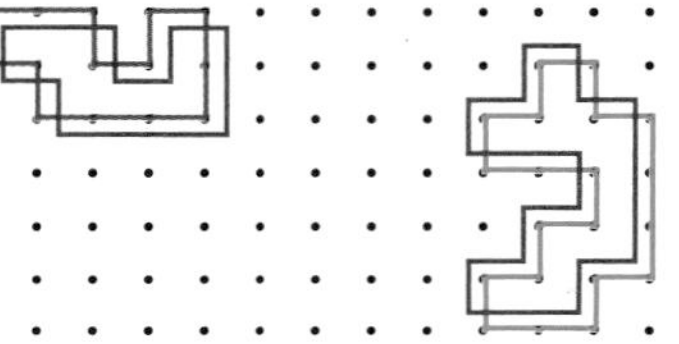

Figures that have the same shape but may have many different sizes are **similar**. When you enlarge or reduce a figure by multiplying or dividing the dimensions by the same number, the new figure is similar to the original figure.

similar

not similar

Activity 2 **MATERIALS:** centimeter dot paper, rulers, scissors

STEP 1

Draw a 2-cm by 2-cm square on dot paper.

STEP 2

Enlarge the square by multiplying the length of each side of the original square by 2.

STEP 3

Reduce the square by dividing the length of each side of the original square by 2.

Quick Review

Are the figures the same shape and size? Write *yes* or *no.*

1.
2.
3.
4.
5.

VOCABULARY

congruent **similar**

▲ The Glass Flowers, Harvard's collection of botanical models, includes 847 life-size models and 3,000 enlarged flowers and plant sections made from glass.

Check

1. **Explain** why two figures that are congruent are also similar.

Tell whether the two figures appear to be *congruent, similar, both,* or *neither.*

2\.

3\.

4\.

Practice and Problem Solving

Extra Practice, page 414, Set B

Tell whether the two figures appear to be *congruent, similar, both,* or *neither.*

5\.

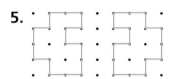

6\.

7\.

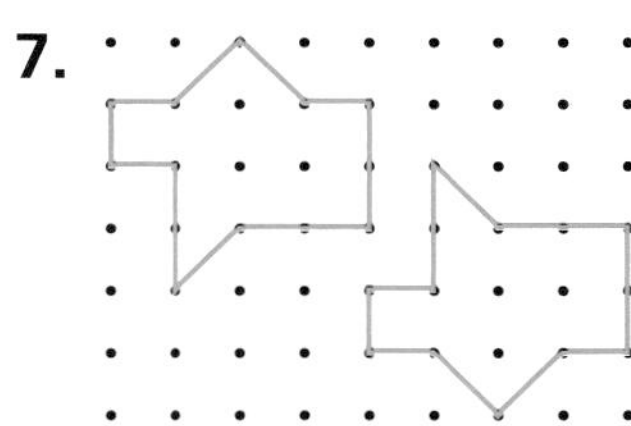

For 8–9, use the quadrilaterals below.

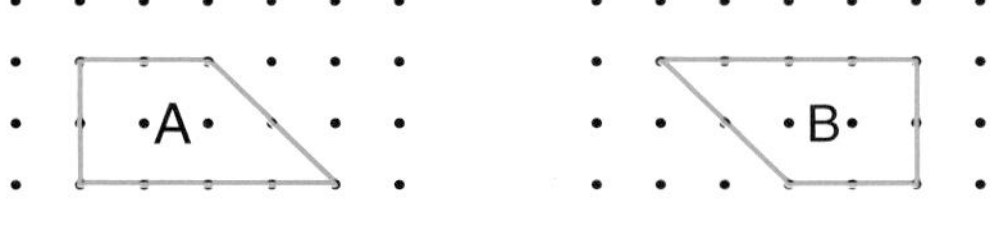

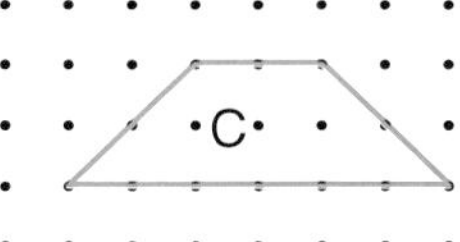

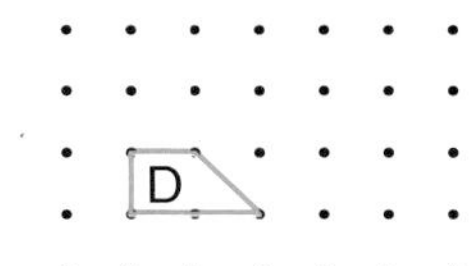

8. Which quadrilateral appears to be congruent to quadrilateral *A*? Explain how you know.

9. Which quadrilateral appears to be similar to, but not congruent to, quadrilateral *A*? Explain how you know.

10. On dot paper, draw two figures that are congruent. Explain how you know.

11. **Write About It** Explain why all squares are similar.

Mixed Review and Test Prep

12. Which letter has line symmetry? Explain how you know. (p. 398)

Z M F P

13. Compare. Write <, >, or = for the ●. (p. 20)

35,406 ● 35,046

Find the value of the variable. (p. 172)

14. $8 \times n = 56$

15. $p \times 5 = 45$

16. **TEST PREP** Which could be the missing number in the pattern? (p. 74)

24, 21, 18, 15, ■ 9, 6, 3

A 11 **C** 13

B 12 **D** 14

LESSON 3

Problem Solving Strategy
Make a Model

Quick Review

Multiply each number by 500.

1. 5 **2.** 20

3. 300 **4.** 900

5. 7,000

PROBLEM Terry is helping decorate a bulletin board about geometry. He wants to make a larger picture of the geometric design at the right. How can he make a model to help him?

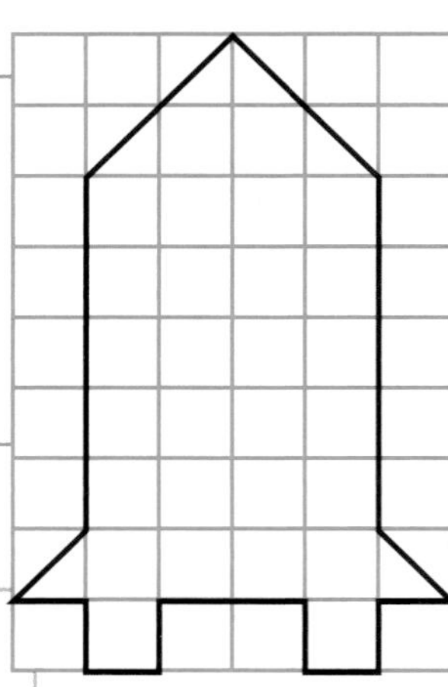

UNDERSTAND

- What are you asked to find?
- What information will you use?
- Is there any information you will not use? If so, what?

PLAN

- What strategy can you use to solve the problem?
  You can *make a model* of the design that is larger than but similar to the one shown here.

SOLVE

- How can you make a model?
  You can use 1-inch grid paper to enlarge the figure. Copy the picture, square by square, to make a larger picture.

CHECK

- How might Terry make an even larger picture?

Problem Solving Practice

For 1–2, make a model to solve.

1. Grant wants to reduce the figure below to put it on a postcard. Use 0.5-centimeter grid paper to help him make a smaller picture.

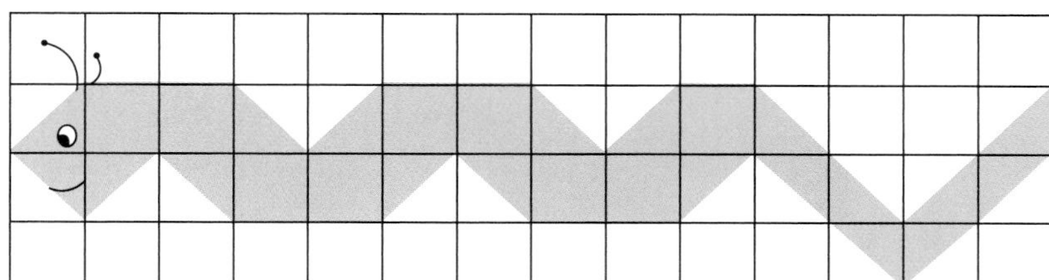

2. **What if** you want to make a larger picture of the figure at the right to put on a poster? Use 1-cm grid paper to help you make a larger picture.

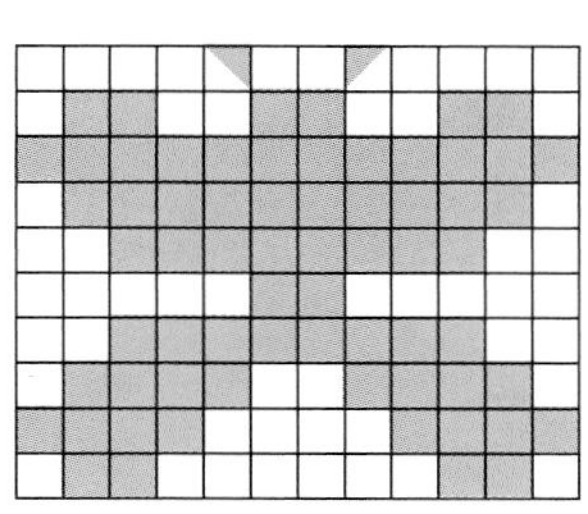

Two squares are 4 units on each side. One square is drawn on 0.5-cm grid paper and the other is on 1-cm grid paper.

3. What is the length of one side of the square on the 0.5-cm grid paper?

A 20 cm
B 10 cm
C 2 cm
D 0.02 cm

4. How many squares on the 0.5-cm grid will fit inside a square on the 1-cm grid without overlapping?

F 2
G 4
H 6
J 8

Strategies

Draw a Diagram or Picture
Make a Model or Act It Out
Make an Organized List
Find a Pattern
Make a Table or Graph
Predict and Test
Work Backward
Solve a Simpler Problem
Write an Equation
Use Logical Reasoning

Mixed Strategy Practice

5. Lizette bought 2 play tickets for \$3.75 each. How much did Lizette spend in all?

6. The sum of two numbers is 23. Their difference is 5. What are the numbers?

7. At a concession stand, Luisa bought a drink for \$0.75, a hot dog for \$1.25, and 3 bags of peanuts for \$0.30 each. She received \$2.10 in change. How much money did she start with?

8. Jack's band had 56 tickets for a concert. Each of the 7 members received the same number of tickets. How many tickets did each member receive?

9. Dennis had 42 marbles. He gave some away and now has 14 marbles. Write an equation that can be used to find how many marbles he gave away.

10. Draw two regular polygons that have the same shape but are different in both size and position.

LESSON 4

Transformations

Quick Review

Tell whether the rays on the circle show a $\frac{1}{4}$, $\frac{1}{2}$, $\frac{3}{4}$, or complete turn.

1. 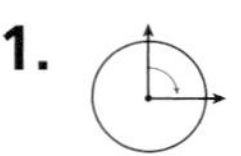
2. 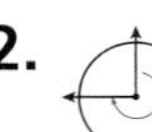
3. 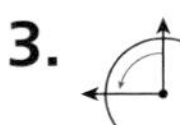
4. 
5.

VOCABULARY

transformation **reflection**
translation **rotation**

Learn

ROTATOR A **transformation** is a movement of a figure. Here are some everyday examples of transformations.

Slide a checker.

Flip a domino.

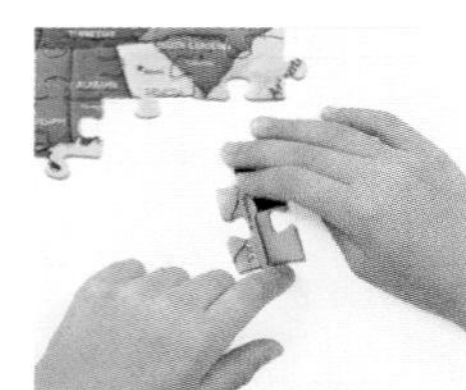
Turn a puzzle piece.

Activity

MATERIALS: dot paper, scissors

You can show transformations of a plane figure by moving it and then tracing it.

STEP 1

Draw a figure on dot paper. Cut it out and trace it. Label your drawing *original.*

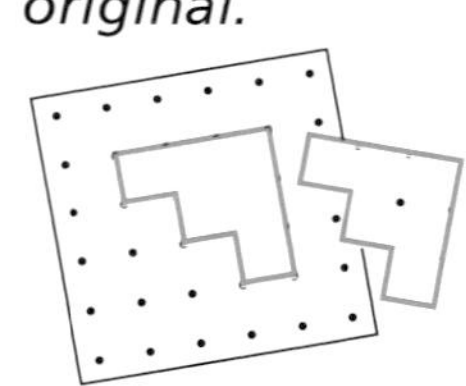

STEP 2

Slide the figure and trace it. Label your drawing *slide.*

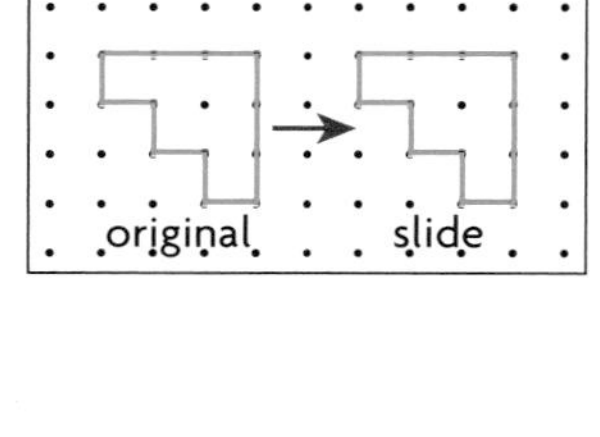

STEP 3

Flip the figure over a line and trace it. Label your drawing *flip.*

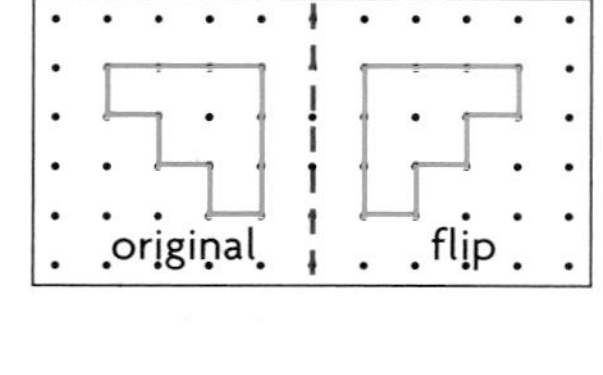

STEP 4

Turn the figure 180° clockwise and trace it. Label your drawing *turn.*

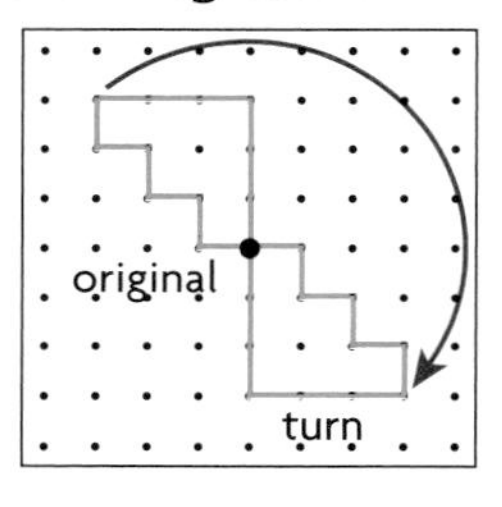

- Describe how your drawing in Step 4 would look if it were rotated 180° counterclockwise. Explain.

Examples

A A slide, or **translation**, moves a figure to a new position along a straight line.

B A flip, or **reflection**, flips a figure over a line.

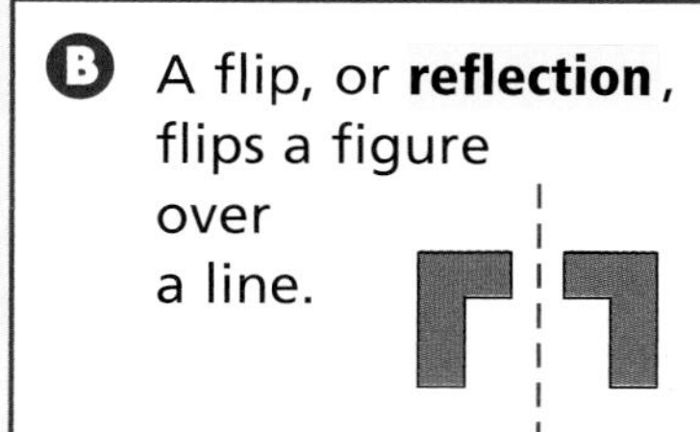

C A turn, or **rotation**, moves a figure around a point.

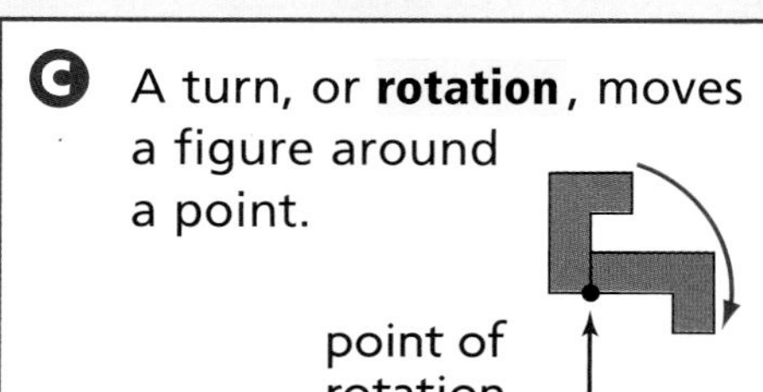

Translations, Reflections, and Rotations

You can use tracing paper to find what moves were used to transform a figure.

Activity **MATERIALS:** tracing paper

Predict how each figure was moved. Trace each figure on the left. Then test your prediction by translating, reflecting, and rotating your tracing to match each figure in its new position.

A
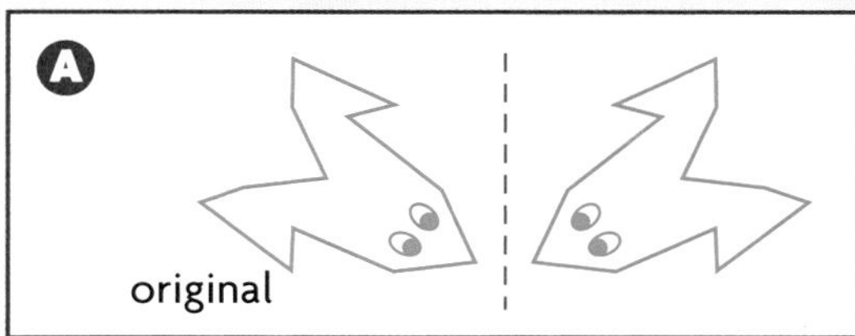

B
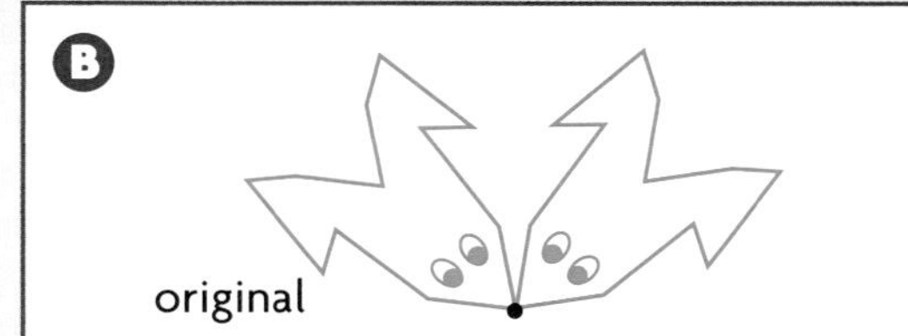

C
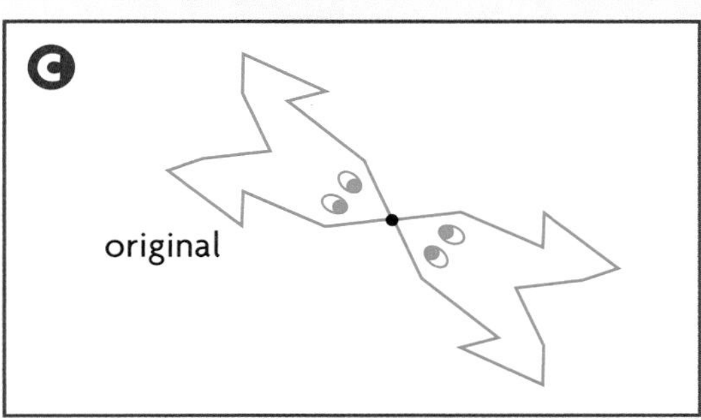

D
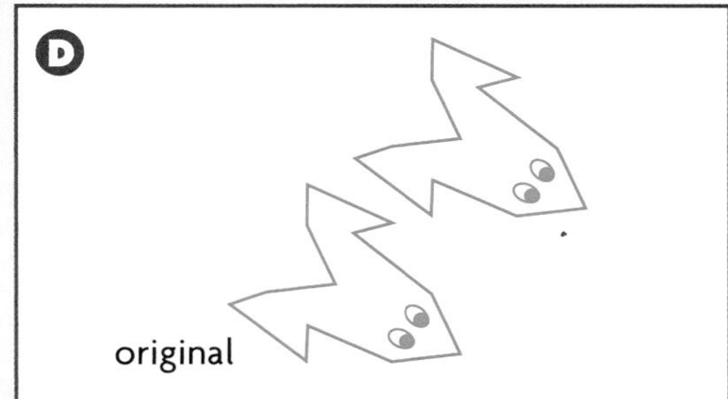

- What transformation did you use to match the figures in A–D?
- How is the original figure in A like the transformed figure? How is it different?
- In B, did you turn your drawing 90° clockwise or 90° counterclockwise to match the transformed figure?

MATH IDEA When you transform a figure, you do not change its shape or size.

Technology Link

More Practice: Harcourt Mega Math Ice Station Exploration, *Polar Planes*, Level M

Check

1. **Explain** how a circle would look if you rotated it 90° counterclockwise.

Tell how each figure was moved. Write *translation, reflection,* or *rotation*.

2. 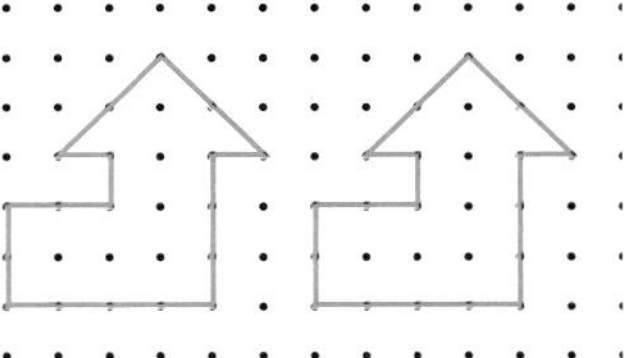

3. 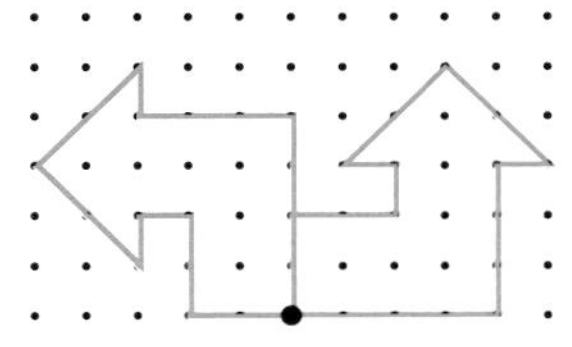

4. 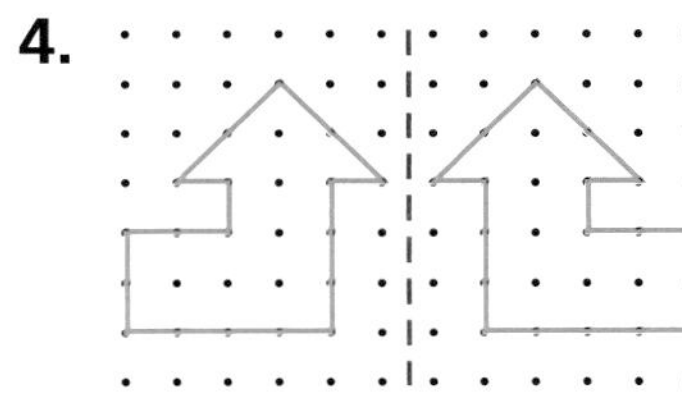

LESSON CONTINUES

Practice and Problem Solving

Extra Practice, page 414, Set C

Tell how each figure was moved. Write *translation, reflection,* or *rotation.*

5. 

6. 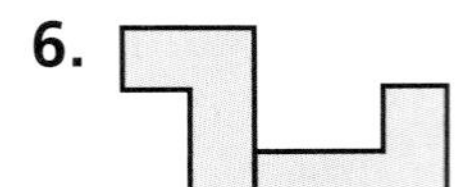

7. 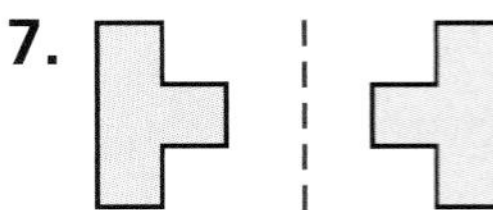

8. 

Copy each figure on dot paper. Then draw figures to show a translation, a reflection, and a rotation of each.

9. 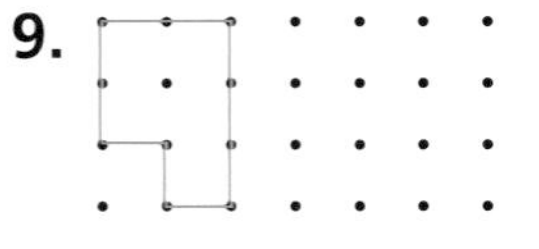

10. 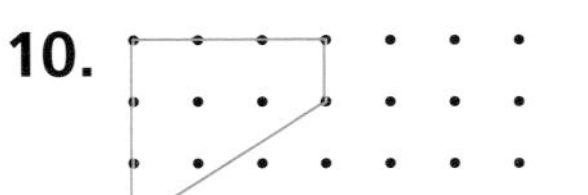

11. 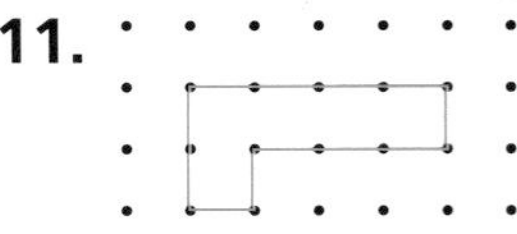

12. 

For 13–15, write the letter of the figure that shows how the figure at the right will look after each transformation.

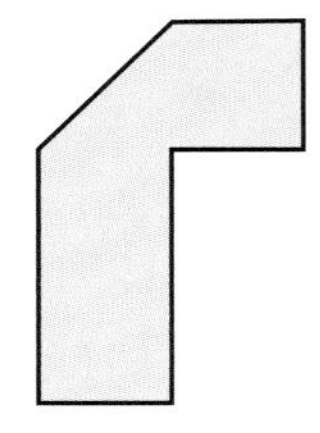

13. translation

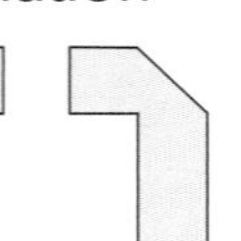

14. reflection

15. rotation

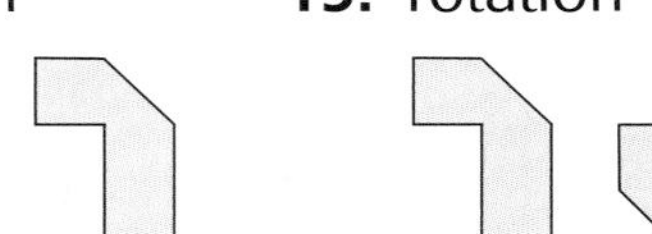

a. b. a. b. a. b.

16. **What's the Question?** George's teacher drew the figures shown at the right. The answer the students gave was reflection.

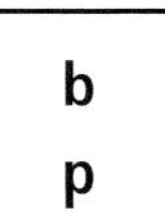

17. Use transformations to find whether or not the two figures shown at the right are congruent. Explain how you know.

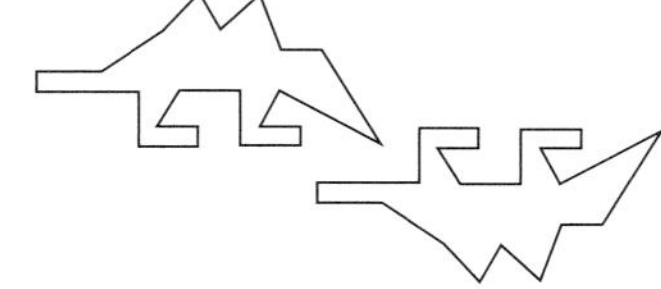

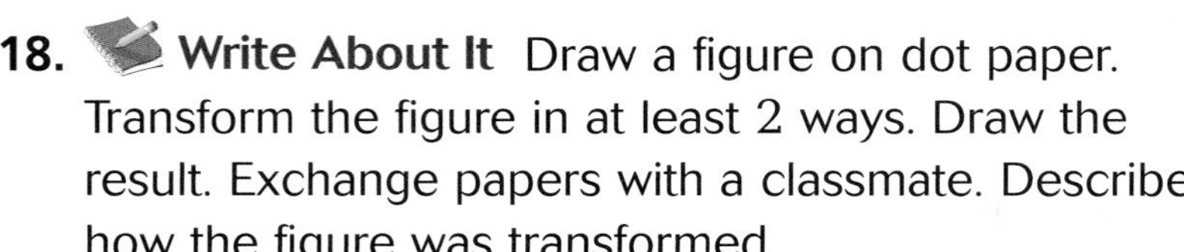

18. **Write About It** Draw a figure on dot paper. Transform the figure in at least 2 ways. Draw the result. Exchange papers with a classmate. Describe how the figure was transformed.

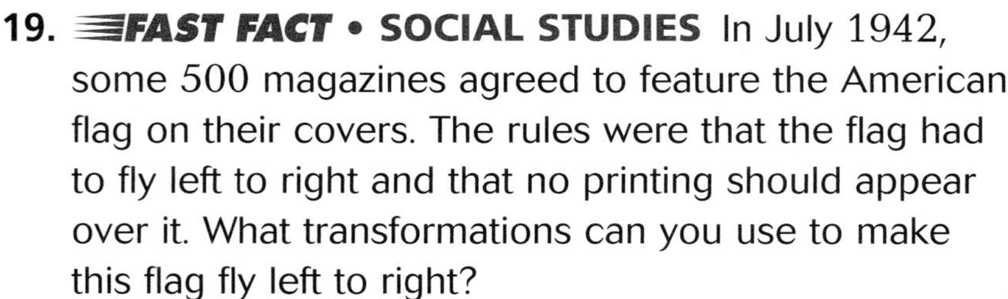

19. **FAST FACT • SOCIAL STUDIES** In July 1942, some 500 magazines agreed to feature the American flag on their covers. The rules were that the flag had to fly left to right and that no printing should appear over it. What transformations can you use to make this flag fly left to right?

This flag is flying right to left.

20. **Vocabulary Power** To rotate *clockwise* means to turn in the same direction as a clock's hands. If the prefix *counter* means "opposite," what direction is *counterclockwise*? Draw an example.

21. Lydia bought tacks for \$3, paper for \$2, and stickers for \$3. Later, Tom gave Lydia \$2. Then Lydia had \$5. How much money did Lydia have before she bought the supplies?

Mixed Review and Test Prep

22. 118×53 (p. 256) 23. $625 \div 5$ (p. 300)

24. Amanda told her mother she would be back in one hour and ten minutes. How many minutes would that be altogether? (p. 98)

25. 7×21 (p. 218) 26. $17\overline{)210}$ (p. 320)

27. Tonya has 45 more pennies than Cari. If Tonya has 139 pennies, how many does Cari have? (p. 40)

28. **TEST PREP** Which is the mean of 88, 84, 75, 60, and 93? (p. 328)

A 80 **C** 87
B 84 **D** 90

29. **TEST PREP** Ms. Sharma bought a book for \$25 and a toy for \$12. How much change should she get from a \$100 bill? (p. 40)

F \$63 **H** \$75
G \$73 **J** \$88

Problem Solving Thinker's Corner

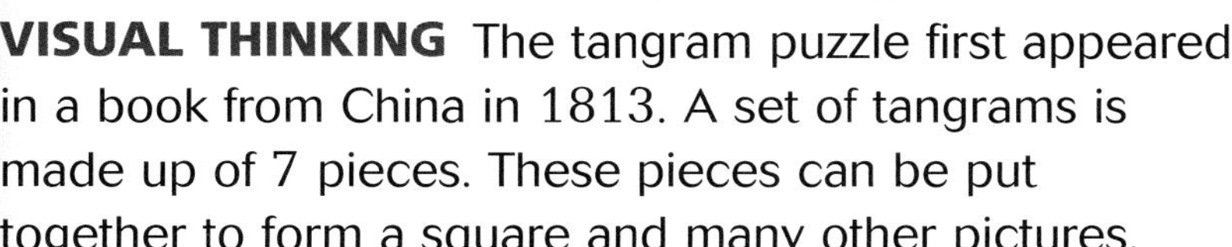

VISUAL THINKING The tangram puzzle first appeared in a book from China in 1813. A set of tangrams is made up of 7 pieces. These pieces can be put together to form a square and many other pictures.

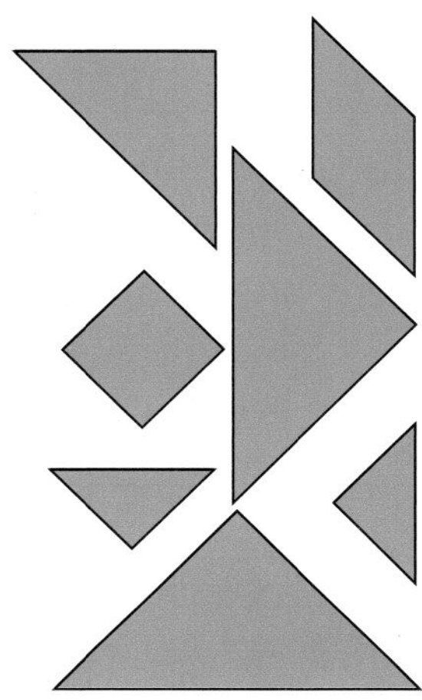

1. Trace the tangram pattern and cut out the pieces. Use all of the pieces to make a square. Describe the transformations you used.

Rearrange your tangram pieces to make the pictures below.

2. 

3.

4. 

LESSON 5

Tessellations

Learn

NO GAPS, NO OVERLAPS The tiles in the terrace of Cà d'Zan in Sarasota, Florida, form a repeating pattern. A pattern of closed figures that covers a surface with no gaps and no overlaps is a **tessellation**, or a tiling pattern.

• Where have you seen tessellations?

Quick Review

Tell how each figure was moved. Write *translation, reflection,* or *rotation.*

1. 2. 3.

4. 5.

VOCABULARY

tessellation

HANDS ON

Activity

MATERIALS: tagboard, construction paper, ruler, scissors

STEP 1

Using tagboard, draw and cut out a triangle that is about the size of an index card.

STEP 2

Trace your triangle and cut out about twenty triangles.

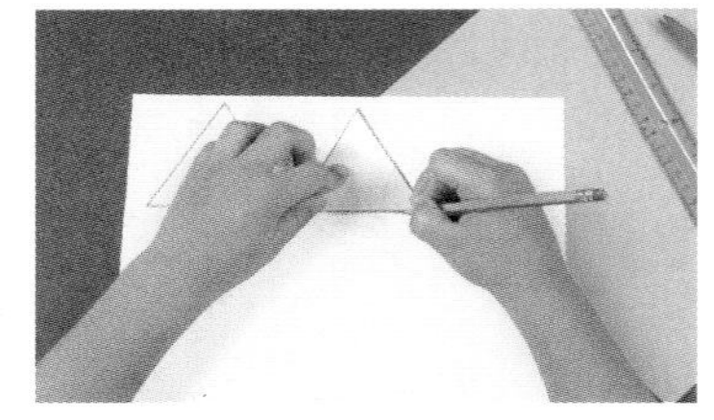

STEP 3

Use your triangles to design a tessellation that covers your desktop.

- Did your classmates' triangles tessellate?
- What transformations did you use to design your tessellation?

You can use one shape or more to make tessellations.

Examples

Will the shape or shapes tessellate?

A

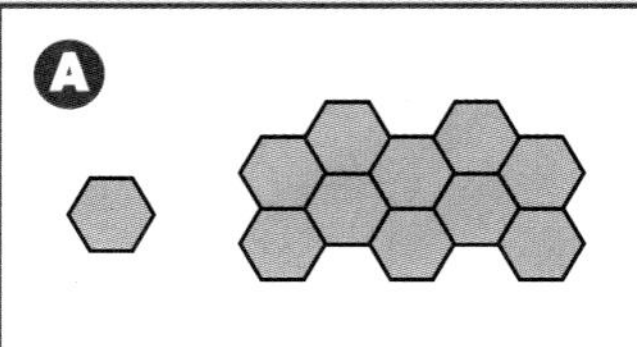

It tessellates.

B

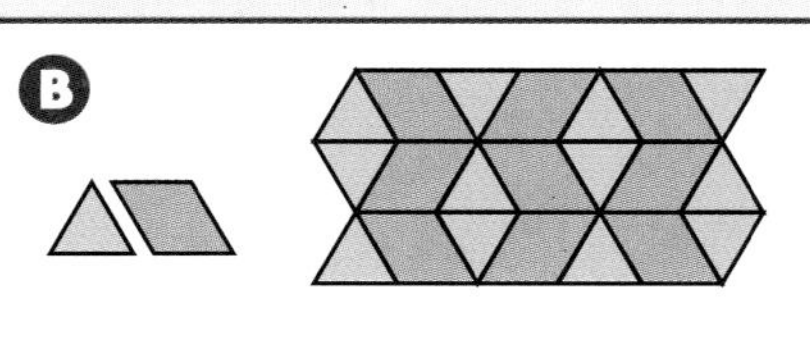

They tessellate.

C

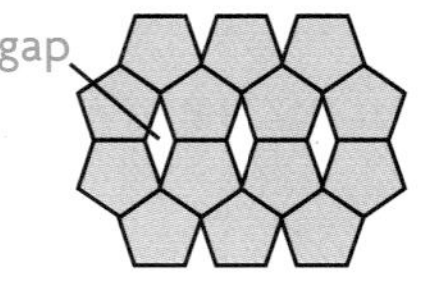

The pentagon does not fit into this gap.

It will not tessellate.

Check

1. **Explain** how you know if a pattern of shapes forms a tessellation.

Trace and cut out several of each figure. Tell if the figure will tessellate. Write *yes* or *no*.

2. 

3. 

4. 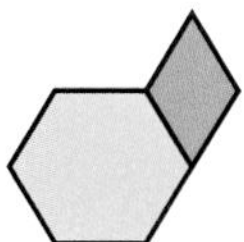

Practice and Problem Solving

Extra Practice, page 414, Set D

Trace and cut out several of each figure. Tell if the figure will tessellate. Write *yes* or *no*.

5. 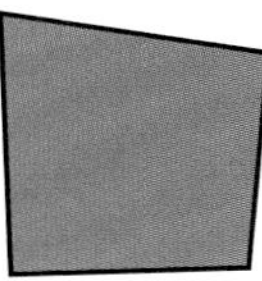

6. 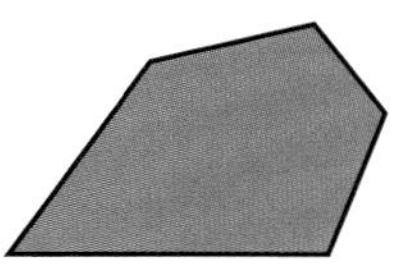

7. 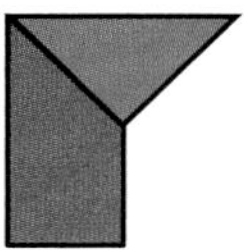

Will these figures tessellate? Write *yes* or *no*.

8. 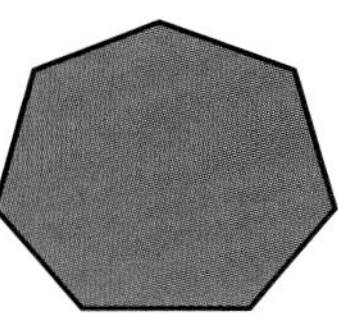

9. 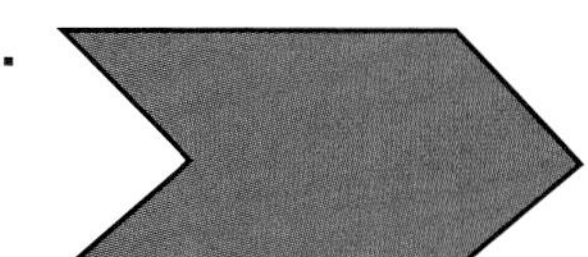

10. 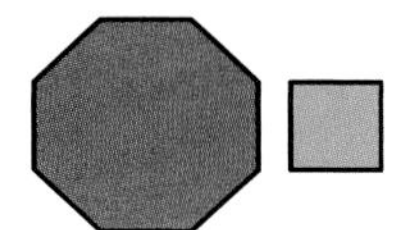

11. Use grid paper to make a tile design that will tessellate. Use one or two shapes in your design. Repeat your design to make a tessellation. Color it to make a pleasing design.

12. **Write About It** Tell whether these shapes will tessellate. Explain how you can check your answer.

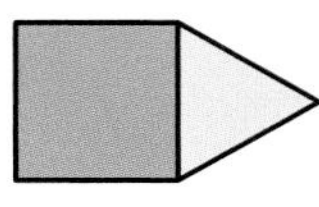

Shape A

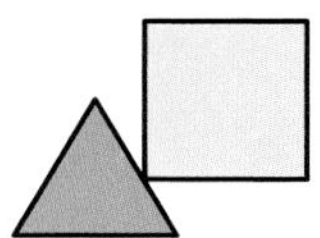

Shape B

13. Do all triangles tessellate? Explain your reasoning.

Mixed Review and Test Prep

14. $348 × 52 (p. 256)

15. 365 ÷ 17 (p. 320)

16. Melinda invited 8 friends to her party. She had 42 party favors. She gave the same number of favors to each friend. How many favors were left over? (p. 278)

17. What is the value of the blue digit in 6,598,253? (p. 6)

18. **TEST PREP** Jim had a ten-dollar bill. He bought 2 books that each cost $3.50. How much does Jim have left? (p. 262)

A $2.00 **C** $4.00
B $3.00 **D** $5.50

LESSON 6

Geometric Patterns

Learn

LOOK AROUND Geometric patterns are used to decorate fabric, ribbon, pottery, quilts, baskets, doors, walls, and buildings. Frieze patterns repeat in one direction. They are often used as ornaments on buildings. Study this frieze pattern. Notice how the figure is reflected over and over.

Quick Review

Write a rule. Find the next 2 possible numbers in the pattern.

1. 22, 20, 18, 16, ■, ■

2. 12, 15, 18, 21, ■, ■

3. 3, 6, 12, 24, ■, ■

4. 48, 42, 36, ■, ■

5. 5, 10, 15, 20, ■, ■

Activity **MATERIALS:** six 1-inch squares of tracing paper, colored pencils

STEP 1

Draw the same simple design on six squares of tracing paper.

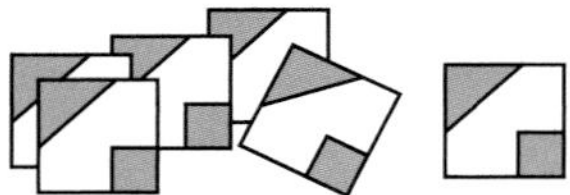

STEP 2

Use transformations to form a repeating pattern with the squares.

- **Describe a pattern shown in Step 2. Then describe the pattern you made.**

MATH IDEA Patterns of geometric figures can be based on color, size, shape, position, or number of figures.

Examples

A Write a rule for the pattern. Draw the next figure.

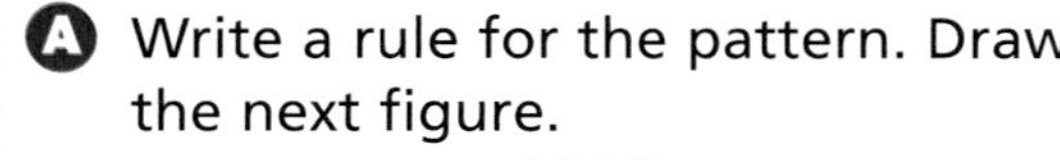

Rule: Increase the number of rows of dots and columns of dots by 1.

So, the next figure is [5 × 5 array of dots].

B Write a rule for the pattern. Draw the missing figure.

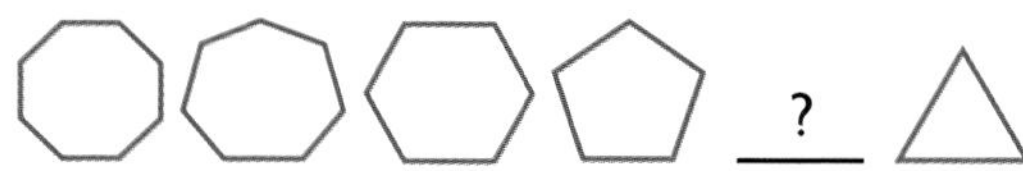

Rule: Decrease the number of sides by 1.

So, the missing figure is [square].

Check

1. Draw a geometric pattern that uses a rectangle.

Write a rule for the pattern. Then draw the next two figures.

2.

3. 

Practice and Problem Solving

Extra Practice, page 414, Set E

Write a rule for the pattern. Then draw the next two figures.

4. 

5. 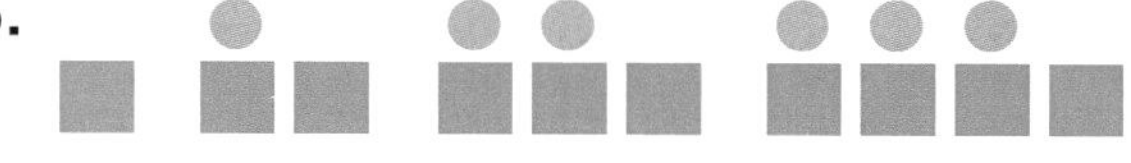

6. 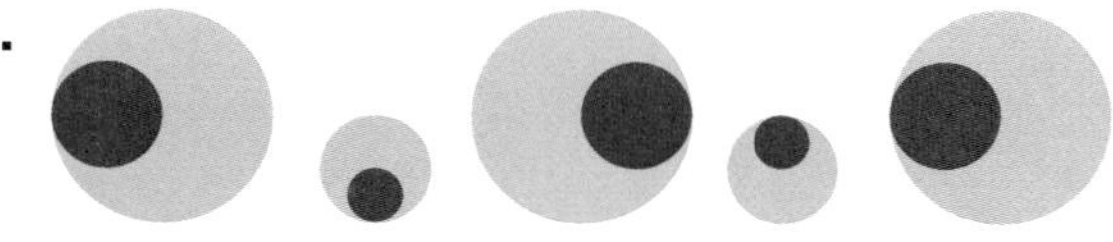

7. 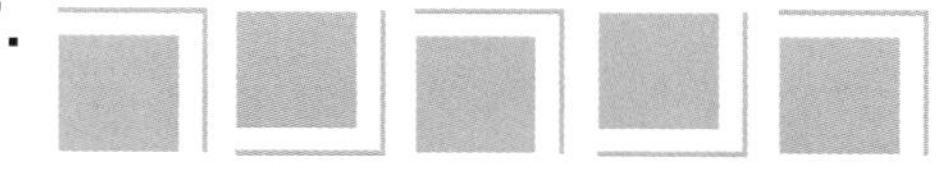

Write a rule for the pattern. Then draw the missing figures.

8. 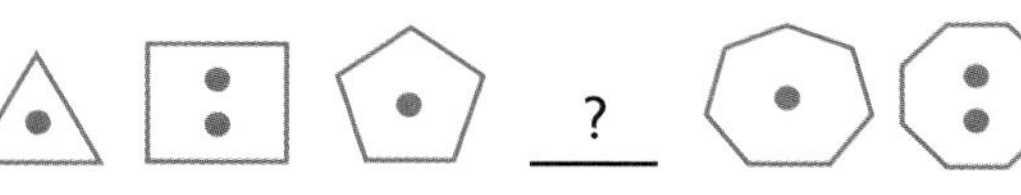

9. 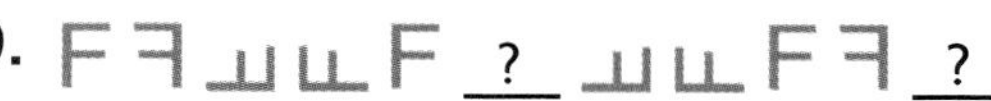

10. Phil made this design for a tabletop. Describe his pattern. Then copy the pattern and add three pieces to extend his pattern.

11. Caro used this rule for a pattern: Add 2 more dots to each rectangle to make the next figure. Draw a pattern she might have made.

12. **NUMBER SENSE** 75 is the product of 2 factors. One factor is 3 times the other factor. What are the factors?

13. Draw a geometric pattern for a wallpaper border. Ask a classmate to describe and extend your pattern.

Mixed Review and Test Prep

For 14–16, tell whether the number is divisible by 2, 3, 5, 9, or 10. (p. 336)

14. 75 **15.** 210 **16.** 1,386

17. Jennifer's soccer practice begins at 4:15 P.M. and lasts 1 hour and 20 minutes. At what time does her practice end? (p. 98)

18. **TEST PREP** Over 4 months, the library spent \$125, \$240, \$176, and \$235 for new books. What is the average amount it spent each month? (p. 328)

A \$176 **C** \$294
B \$194 **D** \$776

Extra Practice

Set A (pp. 398–401)

Tell whether the figure has *line symmetry, rotational symmetry,* or *both.*

1. 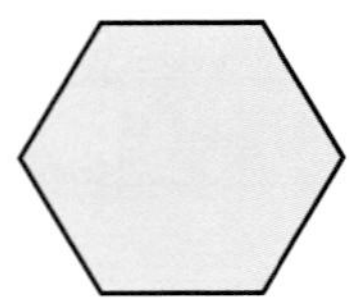

2. 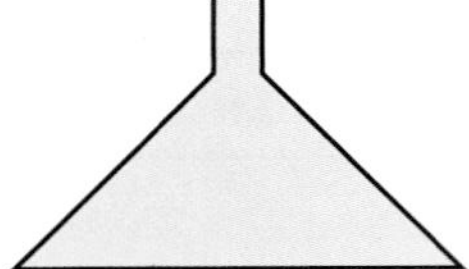

3. 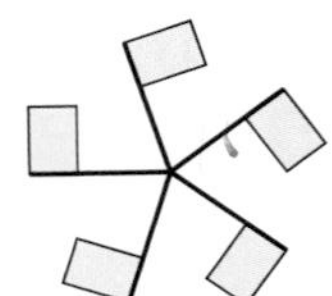

4. 

Set B (pp. 402–403)

Tell whether the two figures appear to be *congruent, similar, both,* or *neither.*

1. 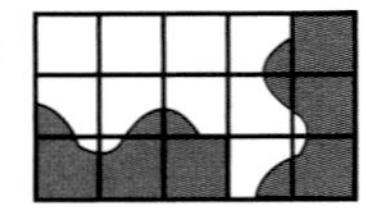

2. 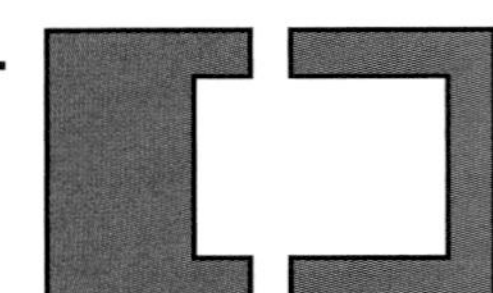

3. 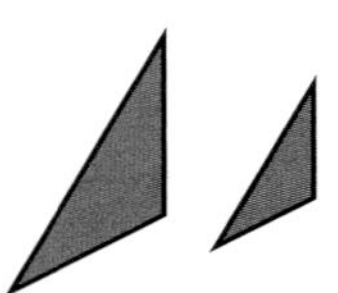

4. 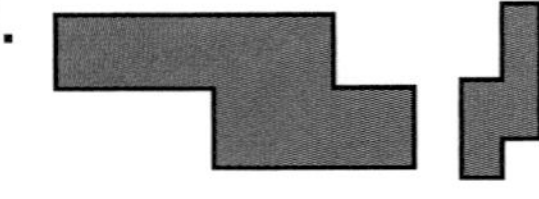

Set C (pp. 406–409)

Tell how each figure was moved. Write *translation, reflection,* or *rotation.*

1. 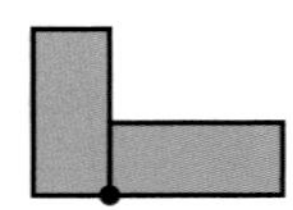

2. 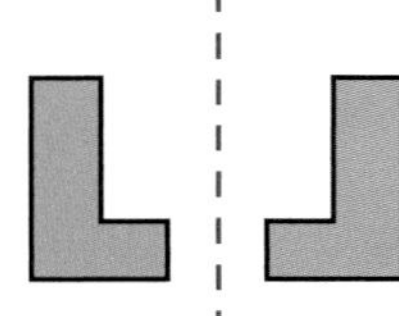

3. 

4. 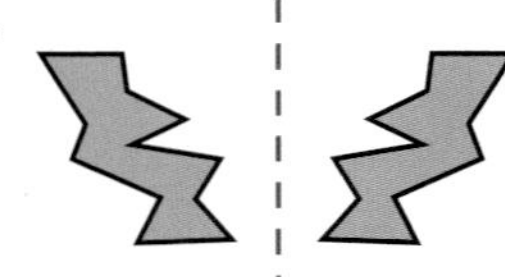

Set D (pp. 410–411)

Trace and cut out several of each figure. Tell if the figure will tessellate. Write *yes* or *no*.

1. 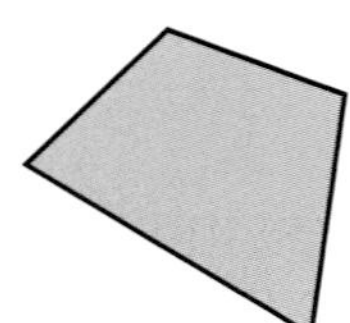

2. 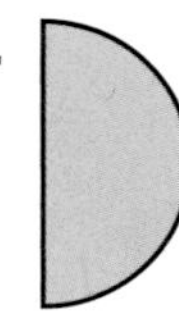

3. 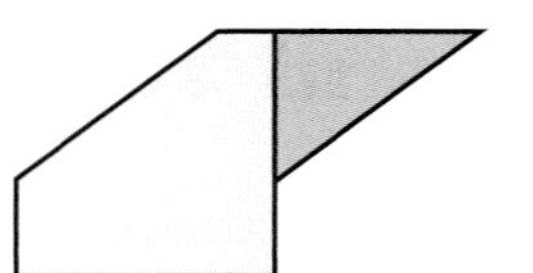

4. 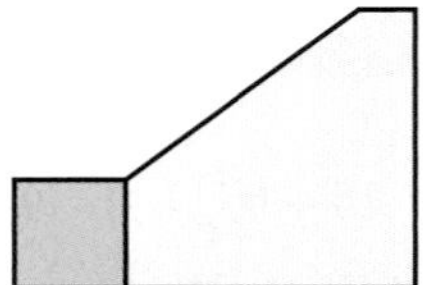

Set E (pp. 412–413)

Write a rule for the pattern. Then draw the next two figures.

1. 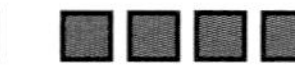

2. 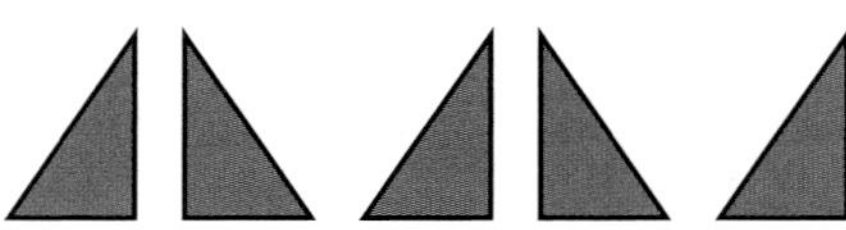

Review/Test

CHECK VOCABULARY AND CONCEPTS

Choose the best term from the box.

congruent complete turn half turn similar

1. The angle measure of a _?_ is 180°. (p. 398)
2. Figures that have the same shape but may have different sizes are _?_. (p. 402)

CHECK SKILLS

Tell whether each figure has *line symmetry, rotational symmetry,* or *both*. (pp. 398–401)

3. 
4. 
5. 
6. 

Tell whether the two figures appear to be *congruent, similar, both,* or *neither*. (pp. 402–403)

7. 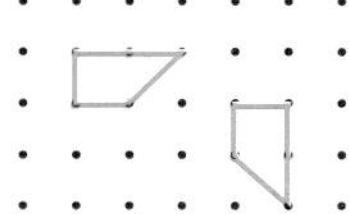
8. 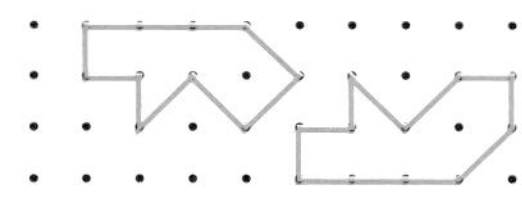
9. 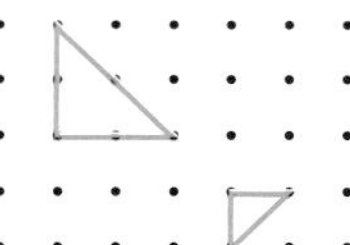
10. 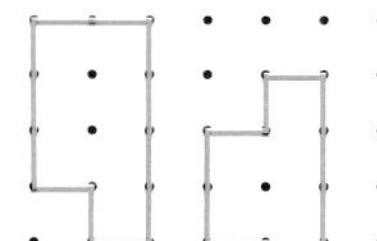

Tell how each figure was moved. Write *translation, reflection,* or *rotation*. (pp. 406–409)

11. 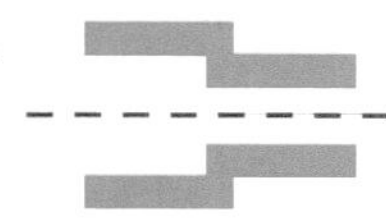
12. 
13. 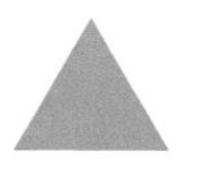
14. 

Write a rule for the pattern. Then draw the next two figures. (pp. 412–413)

15. 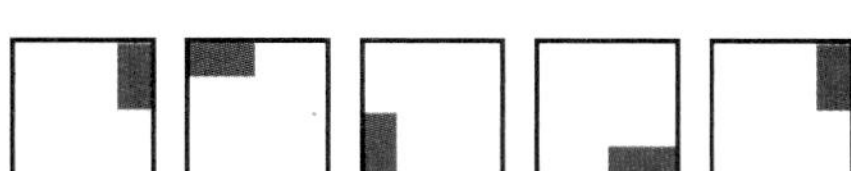
16. 
17. 
18. 

CHECK PROBLEM SOLVING

Solve. (pp. 404–405)

19. Fred has a map of Kansas in his textbook. There is also a map of Kansas in a dictionary. Are the maps similar? Why or why not?
20. Lucy chose a drawing on 1-cm grid paper to reduce in size. Should she choose 0.5-cm or 2-cm grid paper? Explain.

Standardized Test Prep

MEASUREMENT

1. Which is the measure of $\angle ABC$?

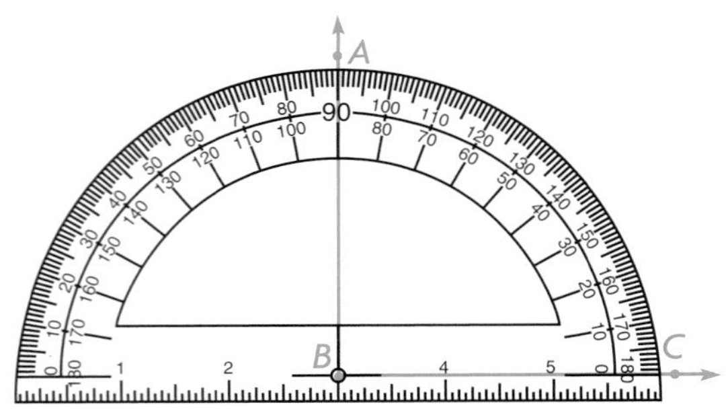

A $45°$ C $120°$

B $90°$ D $180°$

2. Dan has been mowing the lawn for 20 minutes. The present time is 2:15. At what time did Dan start mowing?

F 1:45 H 2:00

G 1:55 J 2:35

3. **Explain It** Salina bought 3 large pizzas and 5 bottled waters.

PIZZA PRICE LIST	
Item	**Cost**
Large pizza	\$9.95
Small pizza	\$7.95
Salad	\$2.49
Bottled water	\$0.89

She paid for her items with the bills and coins below.

ESTIMATE the amount of change Salina should receive to the nearest \$1.00. Explain your thinking.

GEOMETRY AND SPATIAL SENSE

4. Which figure has been turned 180°?

A
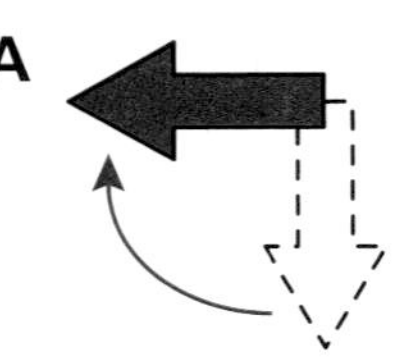

B
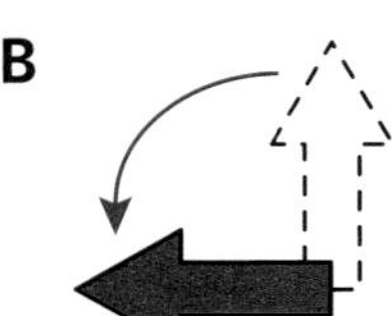

C
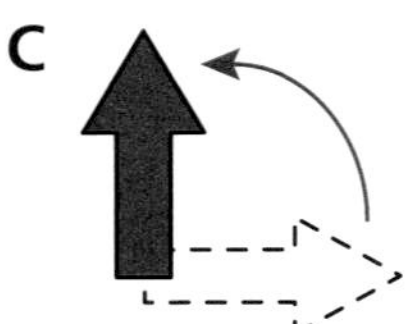

D
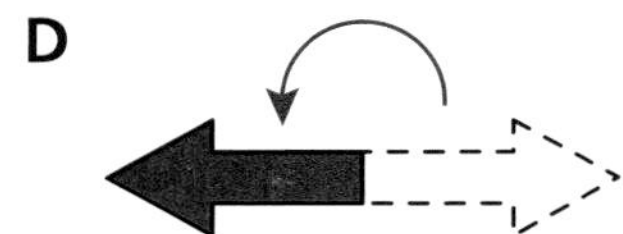

5. Which figure will NOT tessellate?

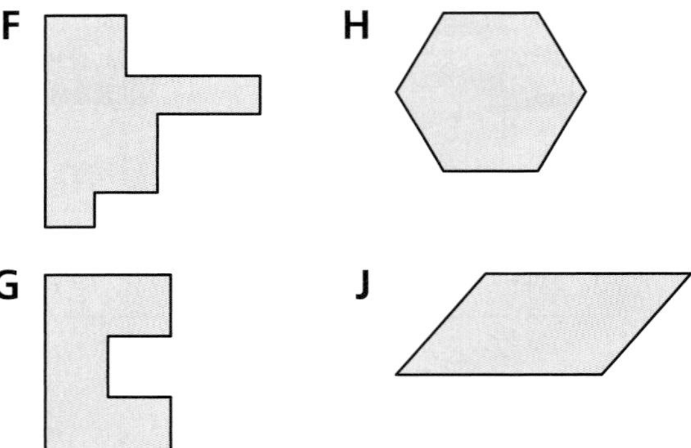

6. **Explain It** Draw a quadrilateral that has 2 pairs of parallel sides, 4 congruent sides, and 4 right angles. Is your quadrilateral a *rhombus,* a *rectangle,* a *square,* or a *trapezoid*? Explain how you decided.

 ALGEBRAIC THINKING

TIP **Decide on a plan.** See item 7. Find the number of black dots in the first four figures. Think about how the number of black dots changes from one figure to the next. Identify the pattern. Then use the pattern to find the number of black dots in the sixth figure.

7. How many black dots will the sixth figure in the pattern have?

   A 9

   B 11

   C 25

   D 36

8. Bob wrote a number pattern. The next number in his pattern is 320. Which pattern could be the one Bob wrote?

   F 1, 4, 16, 64, 256, 512

   G 800, 400, 200, 100, 50, 25

   H 10, 40, 20, 80, 40, 160, 80

   J 7, 14, 7, 14, 7, 14, 7, 14

9. **Explain It** A packing company packs 5 boxes with the same number of cans in each box. Write an expression that represents the total number of cans packed. Use c for the number of cans in each box. Explain why you wrote the expression you did.

 DATA ANALYSIS AND PROBABILITY

10. The table below shows the number of tickets sold for a movie.

MAIN STREET THEATER	
Day	**Tickets Sold**
Wednesday	28
Thursday	25
Friday	30
Saturday	42
Sunday	25

Which statement is true for the set of tickets sold?

A The median is 22.

B The median is 25.

C The mode is 25.

D The mode is 28.

11. Look at the graph below.

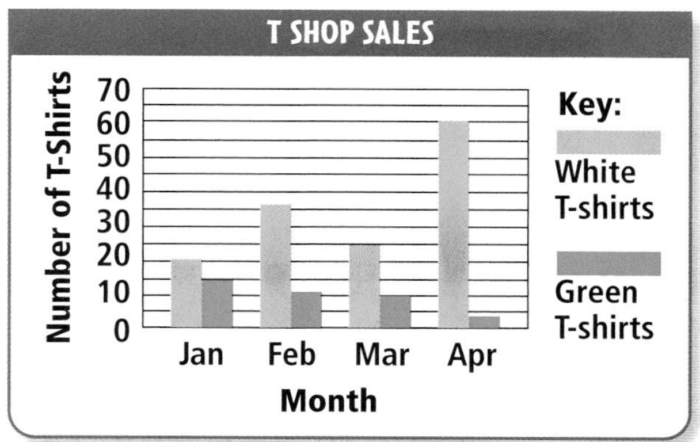

How many white T-shirts did the T Shop sell in March?

F 10 H 25

G 20 J 30

12. **Explain It** Look at the graph above. The owner of the T Shop thinks he should stock up on green T-shirts. Do you agree? Explain your thinking.

20 Algebra: Explore Negative Numbers and Graphing

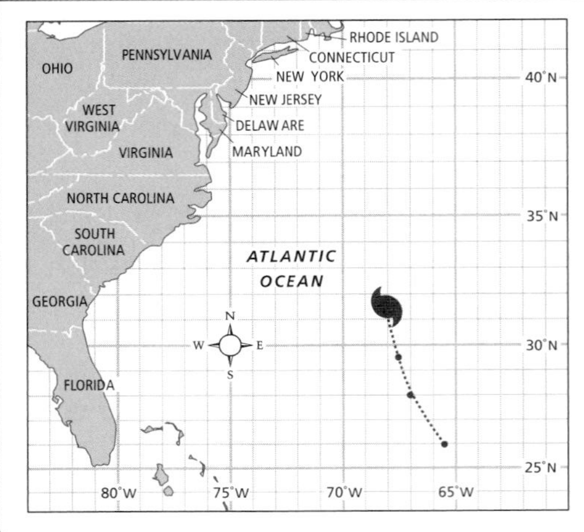

FAST FACT • **SCIENCE** The National Hurricane Center, in Coral Gables, Florida, has tracked and monitored Atlantic hurricanes since 1967. The position of a storm is given using longitude and latitude, and can be tracked on a map with a coordinate grid.

PROBLEM SOLVING Use the table of positions to the right and the map above to tell whether hurricane Humberto hit the United States in 2001. Describe how you can tell.

TRACK OF HURRICANE HUMBERTO, 2001

Latitude	Longitude
32.5° N	67.5° W
33.0° N	67.0° W
34.5° N	66.5° W
35.5° N	66.5° W
36.5° N	65.0° W
37.0° N	64.0° W
38.0° N	63.0° W
39.0° N	62.0° W
39.5° N	61.0° W

CHECK WHAT YOU KNOW

Use this page to help you review and remember important skills needed for Chapter 20.

ORDER NUMBERS ON A NUMBER LINE

Write the numbers in order from *least* to *greatest*. Use the number line to help you.

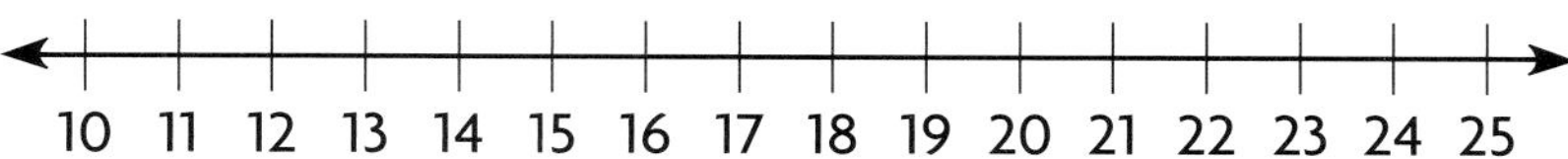

1. 15, 20, 13 **2.** 24, 18, 17 **3.** 21, 23, 14

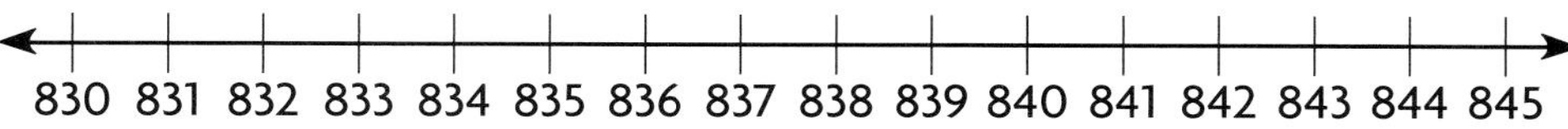

4. 842, 832, 845 **5.** 840, 838, 830 **6.** 831, 836, 839

IDENTIFY POINTS ON A GRID

Look at the map of Hamilton. Name the place you find at each point.

7. (3,5) **8.** (2,3) **9.** (1,1)

10. (1,3) **11.** (3,1) **12.** (2,2)

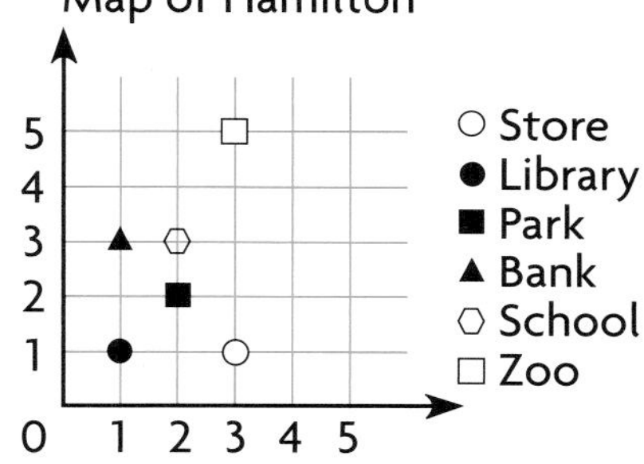

VOCABULARY POWER

REVIEW

zero [zē′rō] *noun*

In mathematics, *zero* means "none." In everyday life, there are other words people use to mean *zero*, such as *love* in tennis or *a duck* in the British game of cricket. Ask your friends and family what words they use for *zero,* and make a list of those words.

PREVIEW

degrees Fahrenheit (°F)
degrees Celsius (°C)
positive numbers
negative numbers
opposites
ordered pair
inequality
***x*-axis**
***x*-coordinate**
***y*-axis**
***y*-coordinate**

www.harcourtschool.com/mathglossary

LESSON 1

Temperature: Fahrenheit

Learn

BELOW ZERO **Degrees Fahrenheit (°F)** are customary units for measuring temperature.

Read 68°F as "68 degrees Fahrenheit."

Some temperatures are less than 0°F. These are negative temperatures. The lowest temperature marked on the thermometer at the right is ⁻10°F.

Read ⁻10°F as "10 degrees below zero Fahrenheit."

Example

Look at the table. How much would the temperature change if it dropped from the normal high to the normal low?

MINNEAPOLIS-ST. PAUL, MINNESOTA, IN JANUARY	
Normal High: 16°F	**Normal Low:** ⁻2°F

STEP 1 First find the change in temperature from 16°F to 0°F.

The change in temperature is 16°F.

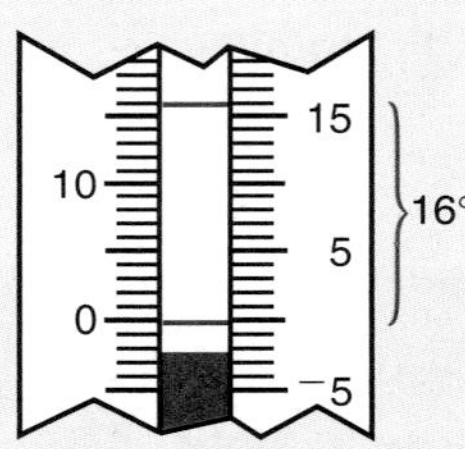

STEP 2 Then, find the change in temperature from 0°F to ⁻2°F.

The change in temperature is 2°F.

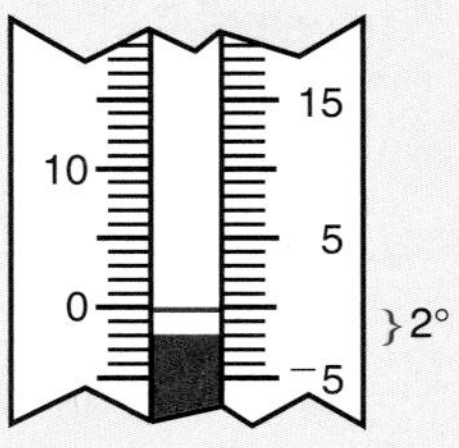

STEP 3 Add the two changes.
16°F + 2°F = 18°F

So, the change in temperature from 16°F to ⁻2°F is 18°F.

Quick Review

Write the temperature that is 20°F warmer.

1. 60°F
2. 15°F
3. 0°F
4. 49°F
5. 192°F

VOCABULARY

degrees Fahrenheit (°F)

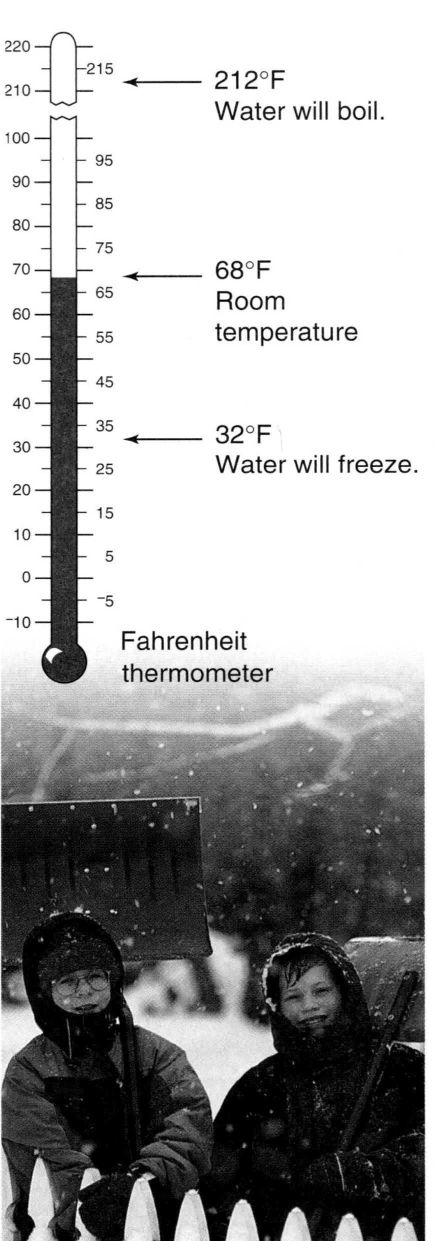

Fahrenheit thermometer

Check

1. **Explain** how you would estimate the temperature change of a day that starts out warm and becomes cool.

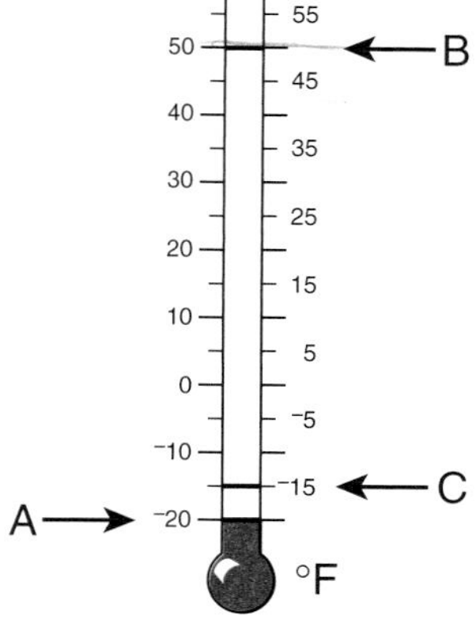

Use the thermometer to find the temperature each letter represents.

2. A
3. B
4. C
5. Use the thermometer to order the temperatures A, B, and C from *lowest* to *highest*.

Practice and Problem Solving

Extra Practice, page 432, Set A

Use the thermometer to find the temperature, in °F.

6. 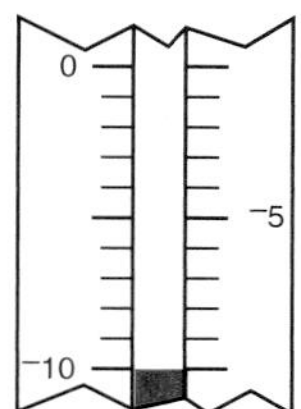

7. 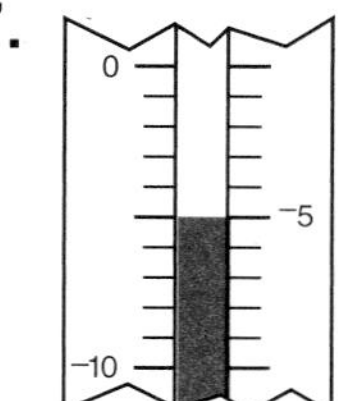

8. 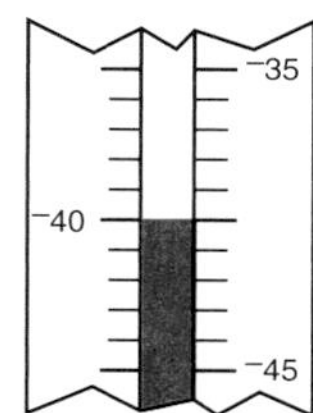

9. Order the temperatures in Exercises 6–8 from *lowest* to *highest*.

Use a thermometer to find the change in temperature.

10. $^{-}10$°F to 20°F
11. 40°F to 115°F
12. 25°F to 82°F
13. 45°F to 90°F
14. $^{-}5$°F to 20°F
15. $^{-}5$°F to $^{-}30$°F

Choose the temperature that is a better estimate.

16. a bowl of hot soup
85°F or 185°F
17. an ice cube
30°F or 100°F
18. a classroom
75°F or 125°F
19. The temperature Monday afternoon was 55°F, and it dropped 12°F that night. The temperature Wednesday afternoon was 52°F, and it dropped 8°F that night. Which night was colder?

Mixed Review and Test Prep

20. Divide. 375 ÷ 15 (p. 320)
21. \$3,640 − \$2,891 (p. 48)
22. Multiply. 5,000 × 12 (p. 236)
23. 2,435 + 7,892 (p. 48)
24. **TEST PREP** Find the median.
36, 42, 85, 18, 24 (p. 118)
A 24 **B** 36 **C** 41 **D** 42

LESSON 2

Temperature: Celsius

Learn

BRRR . . . Degrees Celsius (°C) are metric units for measuring temperature.

Read 20°C as "20 degrees Celsius."

Some temperatures are less than 0°C. The lowest temperature marked on the thermometer at the right is $^{-}50$°C.

Read $^{-}50$°C as "50 degrees below zero Celsius."

Quick Review

Write the temperature that is 20°C cooler.

1. 40°C
2. 20°C
3. 36°C
4. 100°C
5. 23°C

VOCABULARY

degrees Celsius (°C)

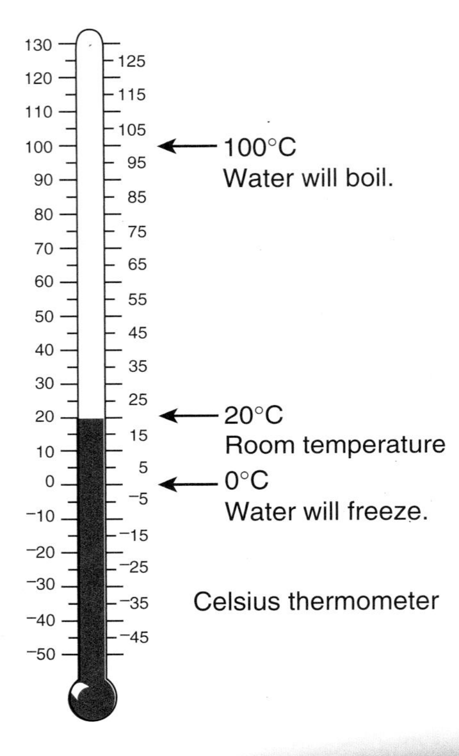

Celsius thermometer

Example

From February to April, the average temperature in Moline, Illinois, rises from about $^{-}4$°C to 10°C. How many degrees does the temperature rise?

STEP 1 First find the change in temperature from $^{-}4$°C to 0°C.

The change in temperature is 4°C.

STEP 2 Then, find the change from 0°C to 10°C.

The change in temperature is 10°C.

STEP 3 Add the two changes.
4°C + 10°C = 14°C

So, the rise in temperature from $^{-}4$°C to 10°C is 14°C.

- What is the change in temperature from $^{-}10$°C to 23°C?

Check

1. **Compare** $^{-}15$°C and $^{-}5$°C to determine which is warmer. What is the difference in temperature?

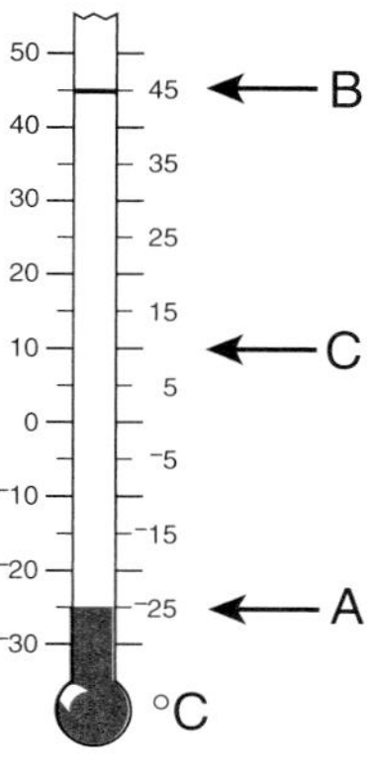

Use the thermometer to find the temperature for each letter.

2. A
3. B
4. C
5. Use the thermometer to order temperatures A, B, and C from *lowest* to *highest*.

Practice and Problem Solving

Extra Practice, page 432, Set B

Use the thermometer to find the temperature, in °C.

6. 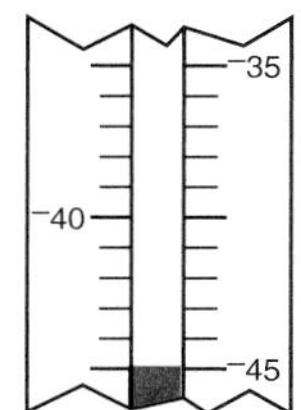

7. 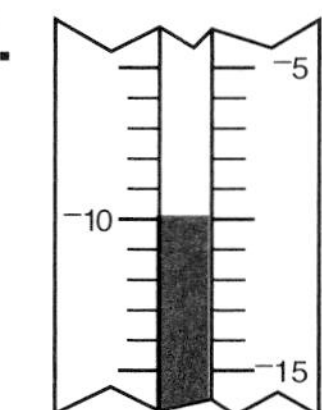

8. 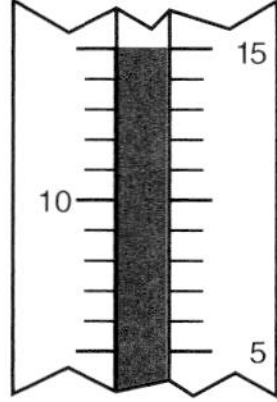

9. Order the temperatures in Exercises 6, 7, and 8 from *highest* to *lowest*.

Use a thermometer to find the change in temperature.

10. $^{-}12$°C to 5°C
11. 0°C to $^{-}30$°C
12. 5°C to 82°C
13. 40°C to 90°C
14. 5°C to $^{-}2$°C
15. $^{-}20$°C to 11°C

Order the temperatures from *highest* to *lowest*.

16. **a.** cup of hot cocoa **b.** glass of milk **c.** inside a library
17. **a.** swimming pool **b.** summer day in Florida **c.** snow ball
18. Which temperature is closer to 5°C, 17°C or $^{-}4$°C?
19. **What's the Question?** The difference in temperatures is 32°.

Mixed Review and Test Prep

20. 7 + (72 ÷ 6) (p. 184)
21. Order from *least* to *greatest*. (p. 24)
88,404; 84,808; 88,040
22. Find the missing number. (p. 104)
6 weeks = ■ days
23. Divide. 597 ÷ 5 (p. 300)
24. **TEST PREP** Which is one thousand less than 5,679? (p. 2)

A 4,679 **B** 5,579 **C** 5,669 **D** 6,679

LESSON 3

Explore Negative Numbers

Quick Review

Compare. Write $<$, $>$, or $=$ for each ●.

1. 32 ● 42 **2.** 12 ● 12.0

3. 119 ● 109 **4.** 400 ● 40

5. 1,231 ● 1,230

VOCABULARY

negative numbers

positive numbers

opposites

Learn

COUNTDOWN At 9 minutes before a shuttle launch, or $^{-}9$ minutes, crews check to make sure the weather conditions are good for liftoff.

Look at the number line. All numbers to the left of 0 are called **negative numbers**. So $^{-}9$, read as "negative nine," is a negative number. All numbers to the right of 0 are called **positive numbers**. The number 0 is neither positive nor negative.

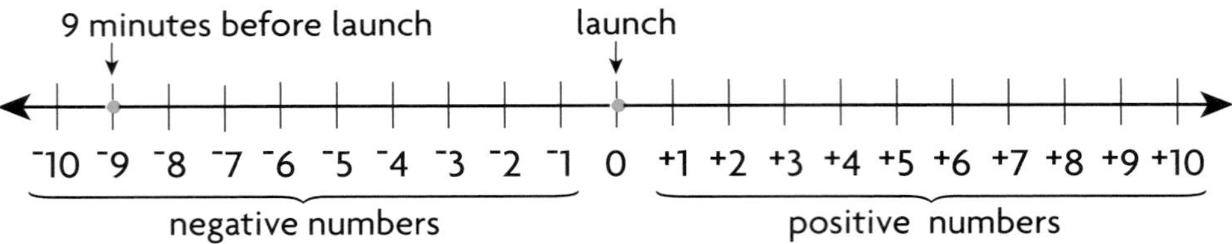

- How do you know that a negative number is always less than a positive number?

On a thermometer, negative numbers are below 0. The thermometer shows $^{-}5$°F.

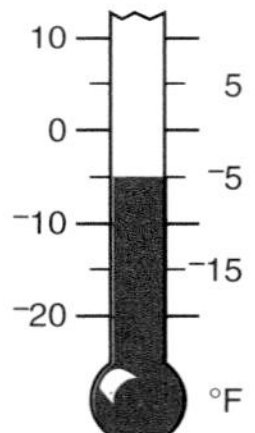

For every positive number, there is an opposite, negative number. Numbers that are **opposites** are the same distance from 0 on a number line, but in opposite directions.

Example

These pairs of numbers are opposites on the number line.

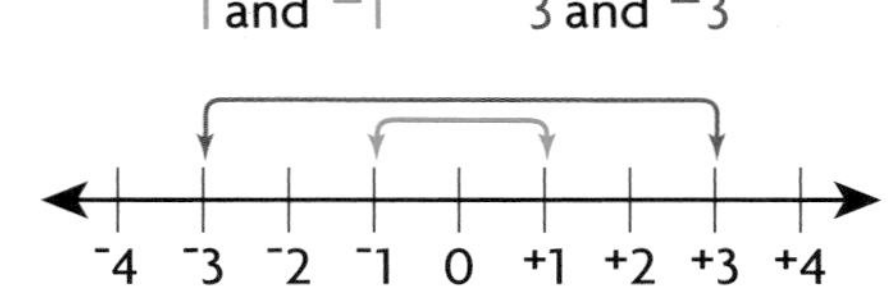

Check

1. **Explain** how a thermometer is like a number line.

Use the number line to name the number each letter represents.

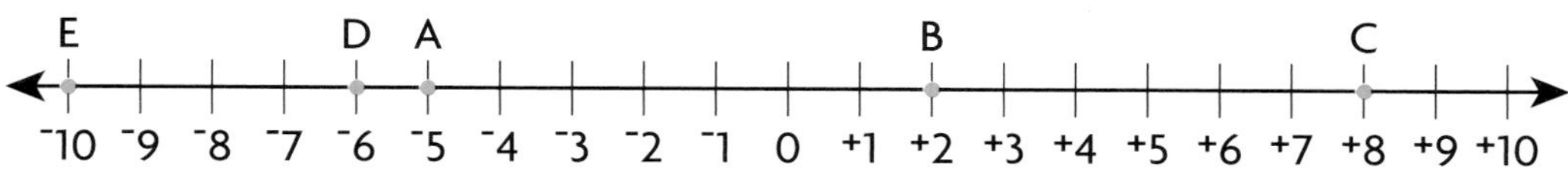

2. A **3.** B **4.** C **5.** D **6.** E

Draw a number line and graph each number and its opposite.

7. $^{+}5$ **8.** $^{-}2$ **9.** $^{-}10$ **10.** $^{+}8$ **11.** $^{-}4$

Practice and Problem Solving

Extra Practice, page 432, Set C

Use the number line to name the number each letter represents.

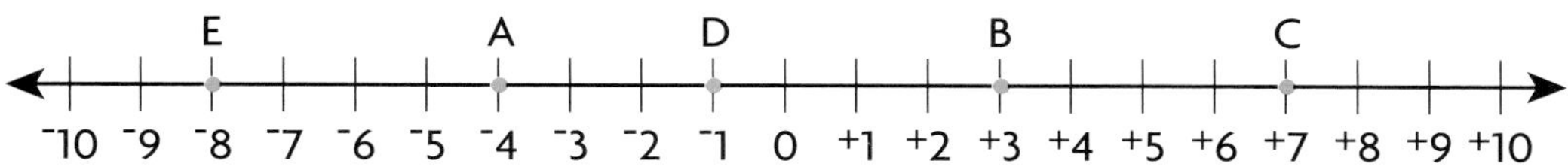

12. A **13.** B **14.** C **15.** D **16.** E

Draw a number line and graph each number and its opposite.

17. $^{-}6$ **18.** $^{+}7$ **19.** $^{+}9$ **20.** $^{-}1$ **21.** $^{-}5$

Compare. Write <, >, or = for each ●.

22. $^{-}10$ ● $^{+}3$ **23.** $^{-}4$ ● $^{+}1$ **24.** $^{+}10$ ● $^{-}9$ **25.** $^{+}2$ ● $^{-}3$

26. At 3 minutes before launch, the shuttle's oxygen tank is pressurized. Five minutes later, the solid rocket boosters separate from the shuttle. How long after launch do the boosters separate?

27. Vocabulary Power The root *thermo* means "heat" and the root *meter* means "to measure." Use these root words to explain what a thermometer does.

Mixed Review and Test Prep

28. List the factors of 27. (p. 338)

29. Multiply. 51 × 244 (p. 256)

30. Find the mean. (p. 328)

53, 57, 53, 55, 62

31. Divide. 580 ÷ 4 (p. 302)

32. TEST PREP Which of these letters does NOT have a line of symmetry? (p. 398)

A T B S C W D E

LESSON 4

Problem Solving Skill
Make Generalizations

UNDERSTAND · PLAN · SOLVE · CHECK

Quick Review

Name the next possible number for each pattern.

1. 3, 6, 9, 12, ▒

2. 10, 20, 30, ▒

3. 480, 240, 120, ▒

4. $^-20$, $^-15$, $^-10$, ▒

5. $^-10$, $^-5$, 0, ▒

WIND-BREAKER When the wind blows, the outside air feels colder than the actual temperature. The table below gives the windchill temperature. That is what the temperature feels like with the wind blowing.

Suppose that it is 30°F and the wind is blowing at 15 miles per hour. What temperature does it feel like? How do the two temperatures compare?

WINDCHILL TABLE

Wind Speed (mph)	Actual Temperature (°F) 35	30	25	20	15	10
5	32	27	22	16	11	6
10	22	16	10	3	$^-3$	$^-9$
15	16	9	2	$^-5$	$^-11$	$^-18$
20	12	4	$^-3$	$^-10$	$^-17$	$^-24$
25	8	1	$^-7$	$^-15$	$^-22$	$^-29$

Find the column with the actual temperature. Find the row with the wind speed. The number shown where the column and row meet tells what the temperature feels like.

So, when the wind is blowing at 15 miles per hour and the actual temperature is 30°F, the windchill temperature is 9°F.

Talk About It

- What is the windchill temperature when it is 20°F and the wind is blowing at 25 miles per hour?
- What generalizations can you make about what the temperature feels like as the wind blows harder?

Problem Solving Practice

1. Darcy wants to walk to a store 1 mile from her house. The actual temperature is 20°F and the wind is blowing at 10 mph. What is the windchill temperature?

2. Krista is getting ready to walk to school. The actual temperature is 0°C and the wind is blowing at 11 mph. Will it feel warmer or cooler than the actual temperature? Explain.

In the summer when the humidity is high, the temperature can feel hotter than the actual temperature.

USE DATA For 3–4, use the heat index table below.

HEAT INDEX TABLE

Relative Humidity	Actual Temperature (°F) 70	75	80	85	90	95	100
60%	70	76	82	90	100	114	132
70%	70	77	85	93	106	124	144
80%	71	78	86	97	113	136	157
90%	71	79	88	102	122	150	170

3. Find the heat index for an actual temperature of 85°F with relative humidity of 80%.
   A 86°F **B** 93°F **C** 97°F **D** 102°F

4. What would be the relative humidity if it is 90°F with a heat index of 106°F?
   F 70% **H** 90%
   G 80% **J** 95%

Mixed Applications

5. Claude practiced piano for 15 minutes on Monday, 20 minutes on Tuesday, 45 minutes on Wednesday, and an hour on Thursday. What is the mean number of minutes Claude practiced?

6. Mrs. Sloan bought a stereo for $280. She made a down payment of $100 and paid the rest in equal payments of $60 each month. How many months did it take to pay for the stereo?

USE DATA For 7–8, use the heat index table above.

7. What generalization can you make about the heat index when the outside temperature is at or above 75°F and the relative humidity is greater than 70%?

8. **? What's the Error?** The relative humidity was 90% and the actual temperature was 80°F. Kaley said the heat index was 113°F. Describe and correct her error.

9. **Write a problem** that shows a change between typical high and low temperatures on your birthday. Compare the change with your classmates' changes.

LESSON 5

Explore Inequalities

Quick Review

Write $<$, $>$, or $=$ for each ●.

1. $^{+}5$ ● $^{+}2$
2. $^{-}5$ ● $^{+}2$
3. $^{+}5$ ● $^{-}2$
4. $^{+}5$ ● $^{-}10$
5. $^{+}5$ ● 0

VOCABULARY

inequality

Learn

I'M TIRED! All students in your class sleep more than 5 hours every night. Most sleep for fewer than 10 hours every night. What are the possible numbers of hours that students in your class sleep?

An **inequality** shows a relationship between two quantities that are not equivalent.

Remember

$\leq$ means "is less than or equal to."
$\geq$ means "is greater than or equal to."

Activity **MATERIALS:** Equabeam™ balance

Use a balance to show all the numbers greater than 5 and less than 10.

- Put a weight on 5 on the left side.
- Put a weight on 10 on the right side. What happens to your balance?
- Move the weight on the left side to a number greater than 5. Repeat until you find all whole numbers that are greater than 5 and less than 10. What numbers did you find?

Examples

A Which of the numbers 5 and 6 make this inequality true?

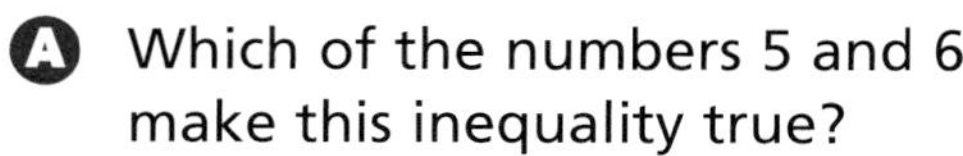

$c > 5$

Try 5. → $5 > 5$ No

Try 6. → $6 > 5$ Yes

So, 6 makes the inequality true.

B Which of the numbers 14 and 15 make this inequality true?

$g - 3 \leq 11$

Try 14. → $14 - 3 \leq 11$ Yes

Try 15. → $15 - 3 \leq 11$ No

So, 14 makes the inequality true.

More Examples

You can graph an inequality using points on a number line to show whole numbers that make it true.

C $d < 6$

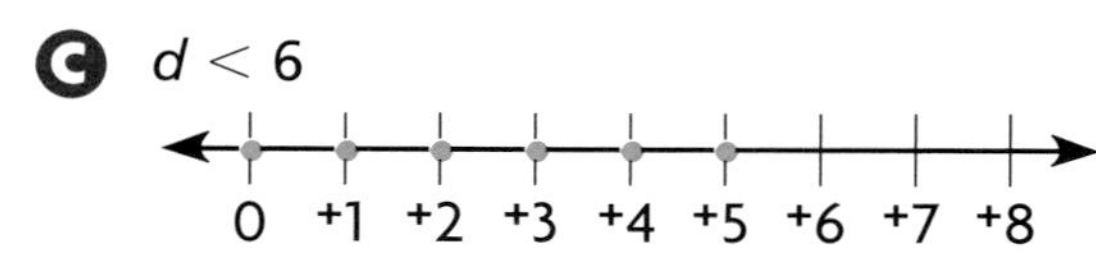

D $m + 4 \geq 2$

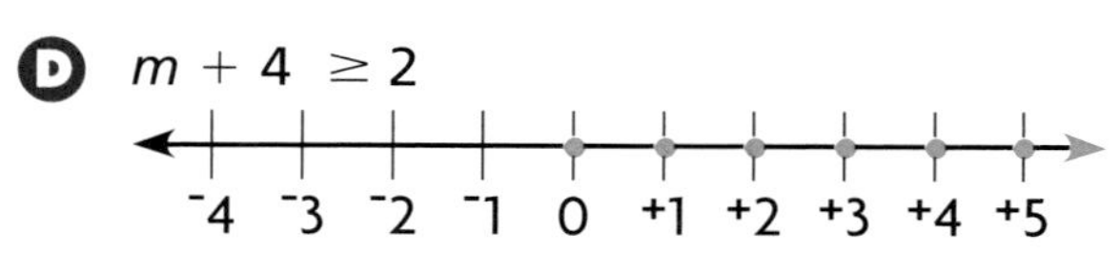

Check

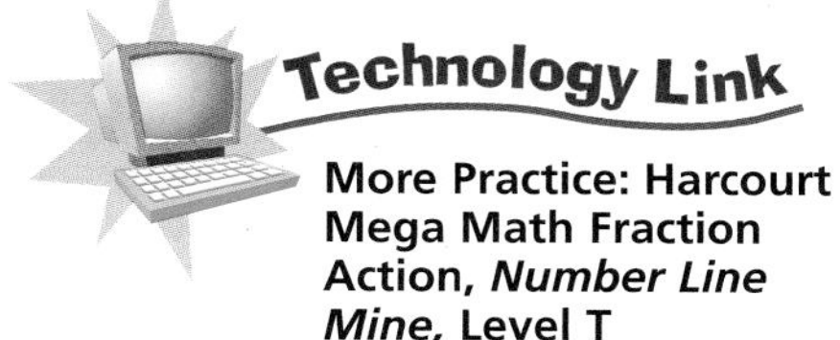

More Practice: Harcourt Mega Math Fraction Action, *Number Line Mine,* Level T

1. **Explain** how you know whether a number makes an inequality true.

Which of the numbers 1, 2, 4, and 5 make each inequality true?

2. $k < 3$
3. $n \geq 4$
4. $x + 4 \leq 5$
5. $y - 0 > 4$

Draw a number line and graph three whole numbers that make each inequality true.

6. $b \geq 2$
7. $z < 6$
8. $f - 2 > 2$
9. $p - 3 \leq 0$

Practice and Problem Solving

Extra Practice, page 432, Set D

Which of the numbers 5, 7, and 12 make each inequality true?

10. $a < 7$
11. $h > 10$
12. $c < 6$
13. $m \geq 12$
14. $d - 12 = 0$
15. $g + 6 > 12$
16. $4 + r \geq 7$
17. $w - 5 < 7$

Draw a number line and graph three whole numbers that make each inequality true.

18. $q \geq 2$
19. $7 - r > 1$
20. $k \leq 4$
21. $4 < n + 3$
22. $5 + p > 5$
23. $8 \leq z + 7$
24. $b + 1 \geq 3$
25. $2 < x - 6$

26. **? What's the Error?** Riders on the roller coaster must be at least 48 inches tall. John wrote the inequality $48 \geq t$ to show who may ride. Describe and correct his error.

27. ***FAST FACT*** **• SCIENCE** Koalas sleep an average of 22 hours per day. Write an inequality using k to show the amount of sleep a koala gets if it sleeps less than the average.

Mixed Review and Test Prep

28. Find the median and mode. (p. 118)

    34, 32, 22, 28, 28, 30, 35

29. $11 \times \$3.50$ (p. 260)

30. Michael took 40 minutes to ride to the park, and arrived at 12:30 P.M. What time did he leave for the park? (p. 98)

31. $4{,}267 + 3{,}493$ (p. 48)

32. **TEST PREP** Susan is putting her rock collection of 146 rocks into egg cartons. Each carton can hold 12 rocks. How many cartons does she need? (p. 308)

    A 10 **C** 12
    B 11 **D** 13

LESSON

6 Use a Coordinate Grid

Learn

Use an **ordered pair** (x,y) to locate points on a coordinate grid. A coordinate grid has an ***x*-axis** (a horizontal line) and a ***y*-axis** (a vertical line).

In an ordered pair such as (x,y), the ***x*-coordinate** tells how far to move horizontally along the *x*-axis. The ***y*-coordinate** tells how far to move vertically along the *y*-axis.

(5,9)

x-coordinate ↑ ↑ *y*-coordinate

Quick Review

1. $3 + x$ if $x = 6$
2. $7 \times y$ if $y = 3$
3. $a - 4$ if $a = 12$
4. $b \div 7$ if $b = 14$
5. $(5 \times c) - 8$ if $c = 4$

VOCABULARY

ordered pair

***x*-axis** ***x*-coordinate**

***y*-axis** ***y*-coordinate**

Example 1 A gardener used a coordinate grid to map where she planted each type of flower. What did she plant at (7,3)?

STEP 1

Start at 0. Count 7 units horizontally.

STEP 2

Then count 3 units vertically.

So, the gardener planted tulips at (7,3).

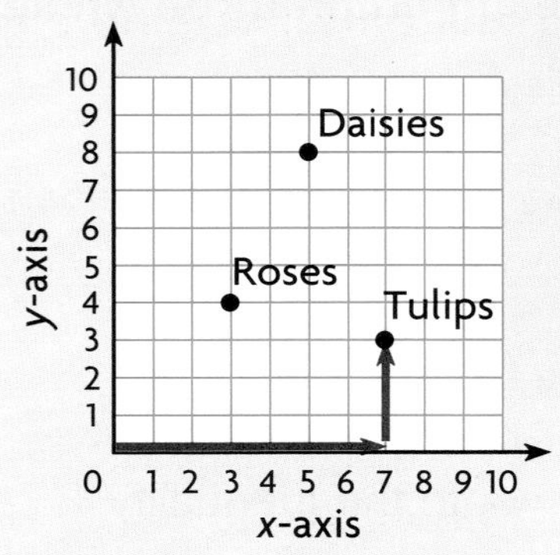

Example 2 What ordered pair tells where the roses are?

STEP 1

Start at the point labeled Roses. Look down at the *x*-axis. It is 3 units to the right of 0. The *x*-coordinate is 3.

STEP 2

Then look across at the *y*-axis. It is 4 units up from 0. The *y*-coordinate is 4.

So, the ordered pair (3,4) tells where the roses are.

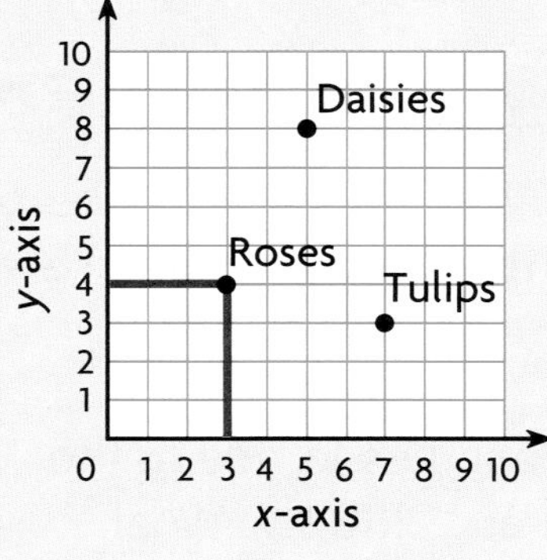

• What plane figure is shown if the points on the grid are connected?

Check

1. **Explain** how to locate a point at (6,5).
2. **Name** the ordered pair that locates the daisies in the garden map on page 430.

Graph each ordered pair on a coordinate grid.

3. (2,2) 4. (6,5) 5. (3,4) 6. (8,1) 7. (10,10) 8. (1,8)

Write the ordered pair for each object on the map.

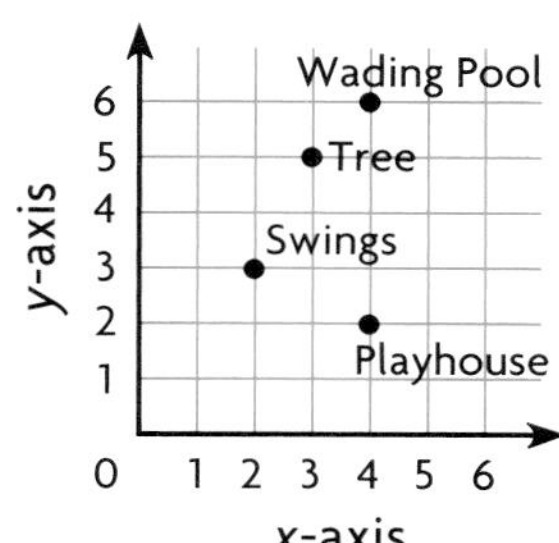

9. tree
10. playhouse
11. swings
12. wading pool

Practice and Problem Solving

Extra Practice, page 432, Set E

Graph each ordered pair on a coordinate grid.

13. (1,5) 14. (1,3) 15. (5,1) 16. (4,9) 17. (0,7) 18. (4,1)

Write the ordered pair for each point on the coordinate grid.

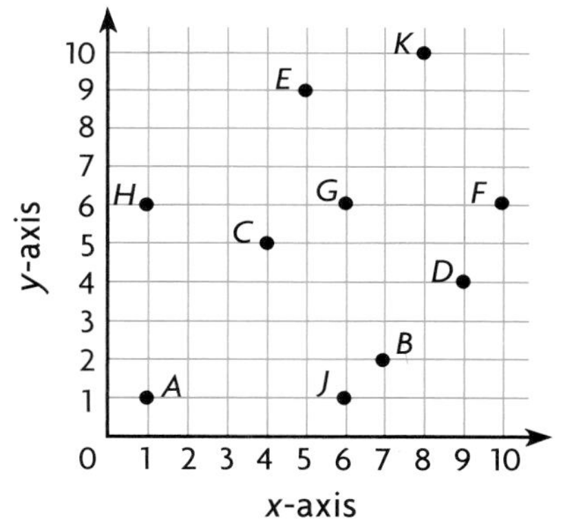

19. point *A* 20. point *B*
21. point *C* 22. point *D*
23. point *E* 24. point *F*
25. Which lettered points on the coordinate grid form a square when connected? Which points form an isosceles triangle?
26. Susan graphed the points (2,1), (2,4), and (4,4) on a coordinate grid. What point should she plot next if she wants the points to be the vertices of a rectangle?

Mixed Review and Test Prep

27. What is the value of the blue digit? 2,390,410 (p. 6)
28. What temperature is 8°C warmer than $^{-}5$°C? (p. 422)
29. 1,396 + ■ = 1,404 (p. 48)
30. ■ − 13 = 2,977 (p. 48)
31. **TEST PREP** Which is the mean of this set of numbers? 1, 3, 5, 7, 9 (p. 118)
   - **A** 3
   - **B** 4
   - **C** 5
   - **D** 8

Extra Practice

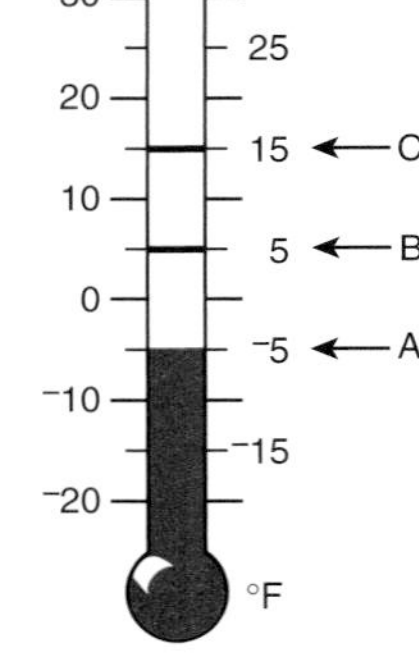

Set A (pp. 420–421)

Use the thermometer to find the temperature for each letter.

1. A
2. B
3. C

Choose the temperature that is a better estimate.

4. ice cream
   31°F or 55°F
5. glass of orange juice
   45°F or 100°F
6. banana
   34°F or 68°F

Set B (pp. 422–423)

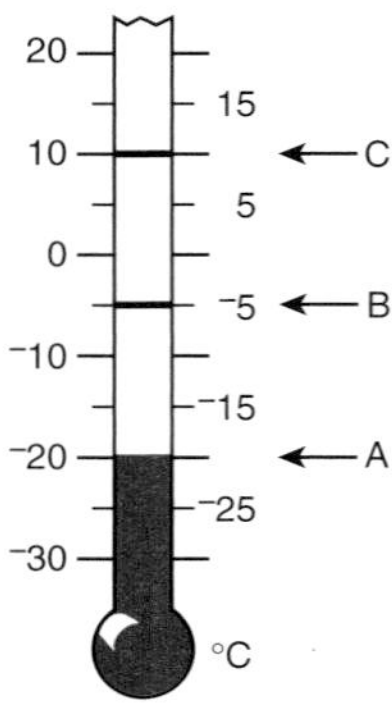

Use the thermometer to find the temperature for each letter.

1. A
2. B
3. C

Use the thermometer to find the change in temperature.

4. $^-20$°C to 5°C
5. $^-11$°C to $^-26$°C

Set C (pp. 424–425)

Use the number line to name the number for each letter.

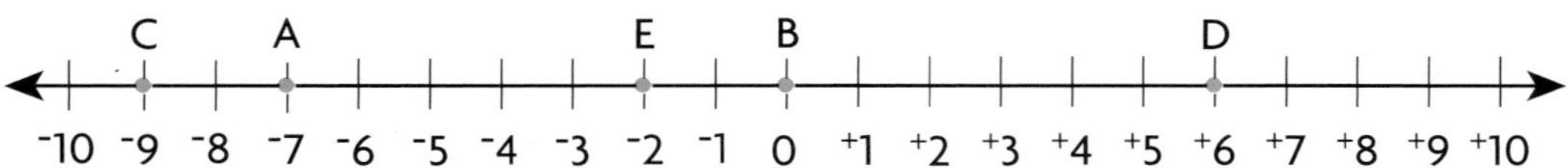

1. A
2. B
3. C
4. D
5. E

Set D (pp. 428–429)

Which of the numbers 4, 6, and 8 make each inequality true?

1. $c < 8$
2. $m + 7 > 12$
3. $5 - g \geq 1$
4. $2 + d \leq 8$

Set E (pp. 430–431)

Write the ordered pair for the point on the coordinate grid.

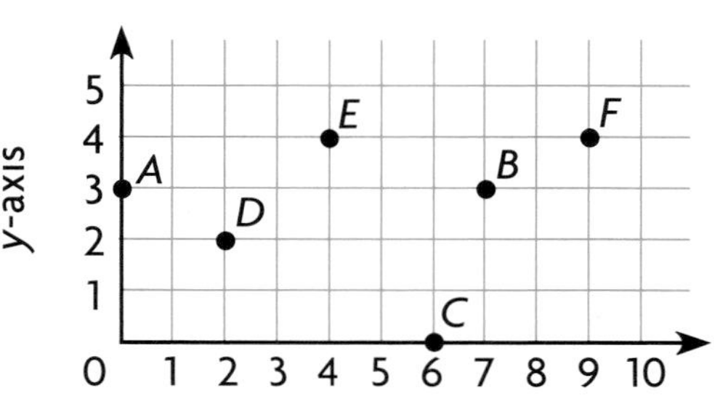

1. point A
2. point B
3. point C
4. point D
5. point E
6. point F

Review/Test

CHECK VOCABULARY AND CONCEPTS

Choose the best term from the box.

negative numbers
positive numbers
degrees Celsius (°C)
degrees Fahrenheit (°F)

1. The metric units for measuring temperature are ? . (p. 422)
2. The customary units for measuring temperature are ? . (p. 420)
3. Numbers to the left of 0 on the number line are called ? . (p. 424)

CHECK SKILLS

Use the thermometer to find the temperature. (pp. 420–423)

4. 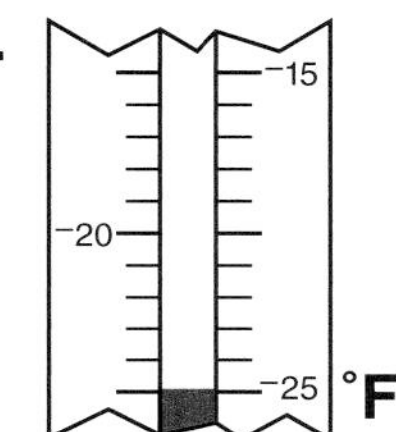

5. 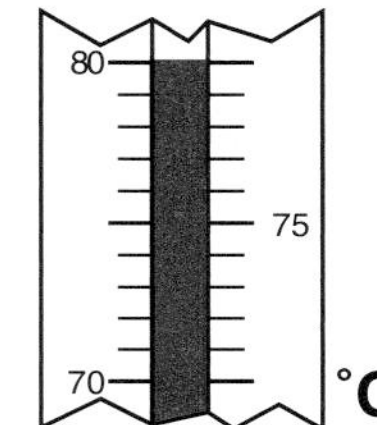

6. 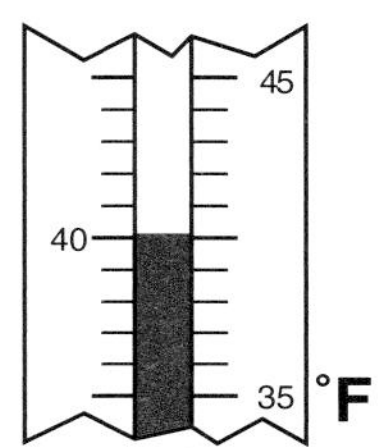

Use a thermometer to find the change in temperature. (pp. 420–423)

7. 40°F to ⁻3°F
8. ⁻5°C to 13°C
9. 17°C to 32°C
10. ⁻11°F to ⁻2°F

Which of the numbers 1, 2, and 3 make each inequality true? (pp. 428–429)

11. $x \leq 2$
12. $y - 1 < 2$
13. $5 + z \geq 8$
14. $3 - p \geq 1$

Write the ordered pair for each point on the coordinate grid. (pp. 430–431)

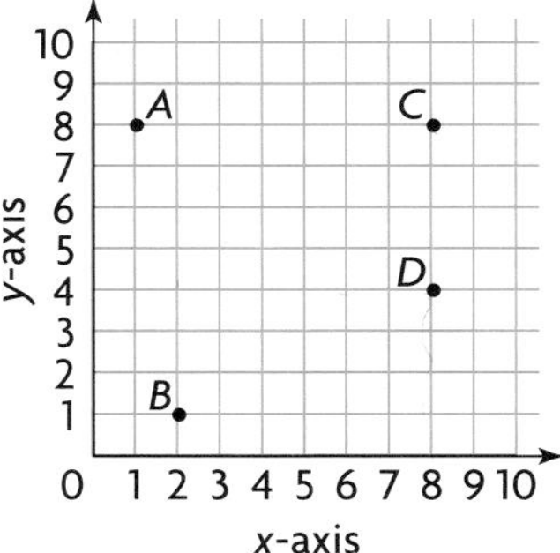

15. point *A*
16. point *B*
17. point *C*
18. point *D*

CHECK PROBLEM SOLVING

Solve. (pp. 420–421, 426–427)

19. Using the heat index table on page 427, find the relative humidity if it is 80°F with a heat index of 86°F.

20. When Fran left her house, the outside temperature was 12°F. When she arrived back home, the temperature was ⁻7°F. What was the change in temperature?

Standardized Test Prep

NUMBER SENSE, CONCEPTS, AND OPERATIONS

1. Which is NOT true?

A $^{-}8 < 0$

B $^{-}8 > 0$

C $7 > {}^{-}9$

D $^{-}9 < 7$

2. The director of the science museum made the following table to keep track of the number of people who visited over a period of four days.

SCIENCE MUSEUM VISITORS	
Day	**Number of Visitors**
Saturday	1,942
Sunday	2,086
Monday	854
Tuesday	651

Which of the following statements is true?

F The total attendance for the four days was greater than 8,000.

G The total attendance for the four days was less than 4,000.

H The total attendance for the four days was greater than 5,000.

J The total attendance for the four days was greater than 7,000.

3. Explain It A concert hall has 48 rows with 28 seats in each row. ESTIMATE the number of programs that should be printed for a show in this concert hall. Explain which strategy you used to estimate.

MEASUREMENT

4. Which temperature does the letter W represent?

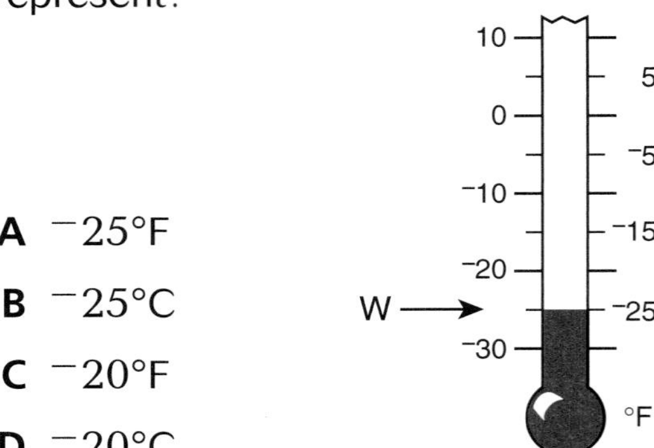

A $^{-}25°F$

B $^{-}25°C$

C $^{-}20°F$

D $^{-}20°C$

5. Which is the length of the leaf, to the nearest $\frac{1}{2}$ inch?

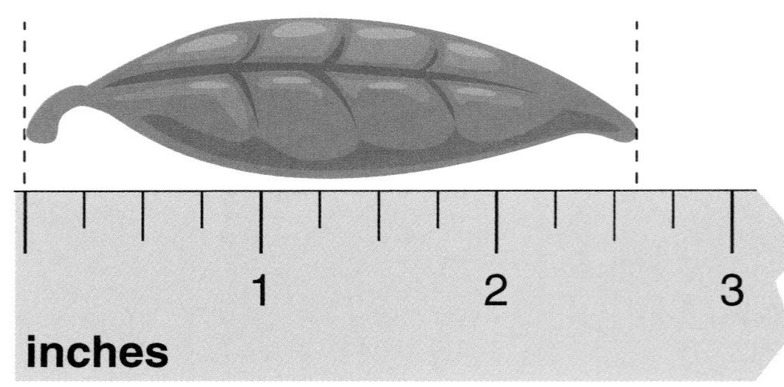

F $1\frac{1}{2}$ inches

G 2 inches

H $2\frac{1}{2}$ inches

J 3 inches

6. Explain It ESTIMATE the elapsed time. Explain how you got your answer.

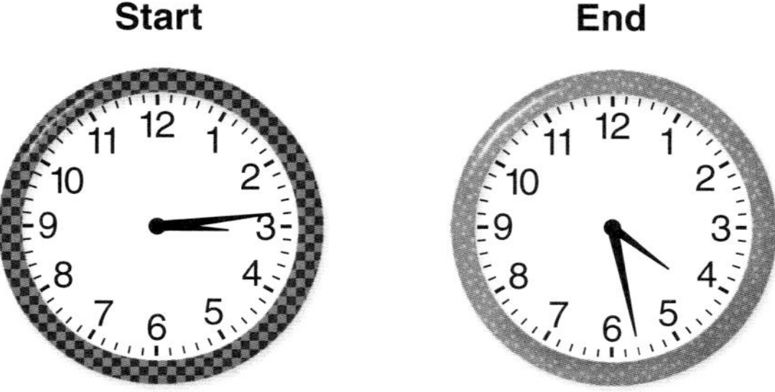

GEOMETRY AND SPATIAL SENSE

7. Which is the ordered pair for point C on the coordinate grid?

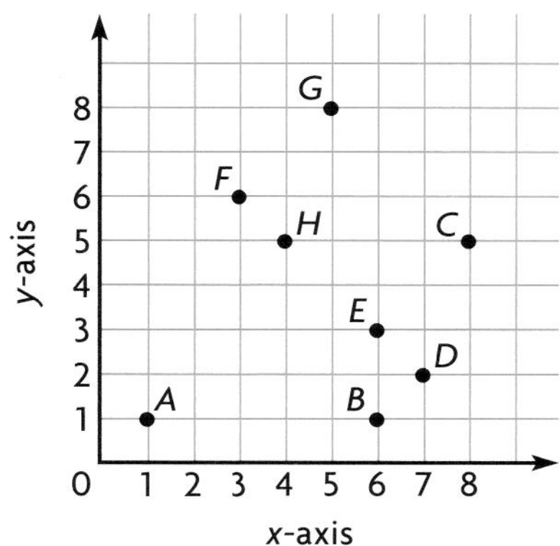

A (5,8)

B (8,5)

C (3,6)

D (6,3)

8. The Smiths had a sign hanging by their front door.

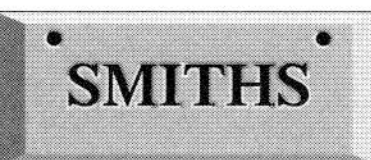

One of the nails at the top of the sign came out so the sign rotated 90° clockwise. Which shows how the sign looks now?

F 

H 

G 

J 

9. **Explain It** Compare a rectangle and a square. Identify one way they are alike and one way they are different.

ALGEBRAIC THINKING

10. Which number makes this sentence true?

$$n - 2 = 8$$

A 2

B 6

C 8

D 10

TIP **Get the information you need.** See item 11. Look for a relationship of p to r that is the same for each pair of numbers in the table. Find the equation that matches this relationship.

11. Which equation describes a rule in this table?

INPUT	OUTPUT
p	r
45	31
39	25
33	19
27	13

F $r - 14 = p$

G $p + 14 = r$

H $r - p = 14$

J $p - 14 = r$

12. **Explain It** Before the movie started, there were 57 people in the theater. Some people arrived after the movie started. Write an expression, using n, to show the total number of people in the theater after the movie started. Explain your thinking.

IT'S IN THE BAG

Coordinate Treasures

PROJECT Make a coordinate-grid "treasure map" to draw and classify plane figures.

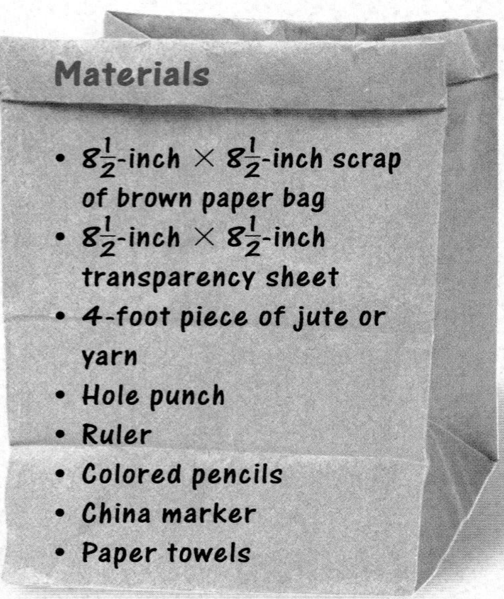

Materials

- $8\frac{1}{2}$-inch × $8\frac{1}{2}$-inch scrap of brown paper bag
- $8\frac{1}{2}$-inch × $8\frac{1}{2}$-inch transparency sheet
- 4-foot piece of jute or yarn
- Hole punch
- Ruler
- Colored pencils
- China marker
- Paper towels

Directions

1. Fold the scrap of brown paper in half. Then fold it in half, lengthwise, in half, and in half again. Unfold. *(Picture A)*

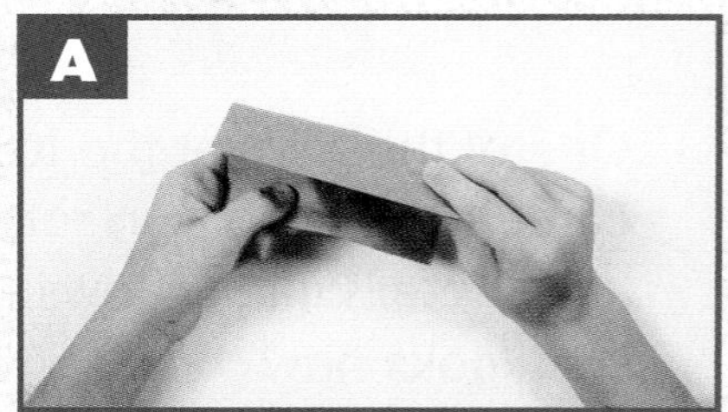
A

2. Turn the paper $90°$ and repeat Step 1. *(Picture B)*

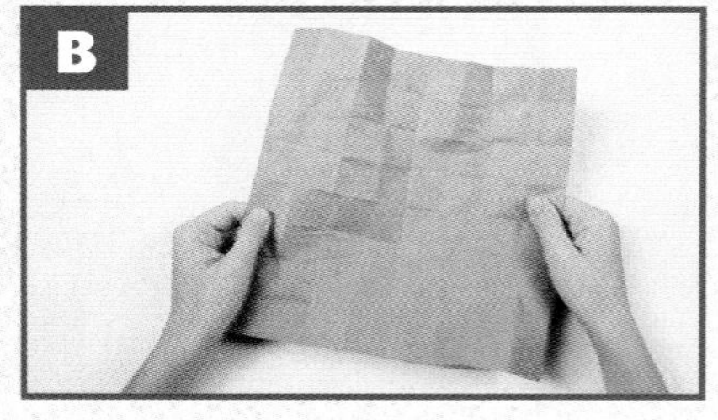
B

3. Using a ruler, draw a 6×6 coordinate grid along the folds. Label the left side *y-axis*. Label the bottom *x-axis*. Label each scale from 0 to 6. *(Picture C)*

C

4. Place the transparency sheet over the grid. Hold the two sheets together. On each edge, punch a row of holes about $1\frac{1}{2}$ inches apart. Thread the yarn through the holes and tie a bow.

5. Use a marker to draw a plane figure by connecting points on the grid. Name the ordered pairs for a classmate. He or she should draw the figure on his or her grid, identify the figure, and classify it in as many ways as possible. Then wipe the treasure map clean and switch roles with your classmate.

Challenge

Explore the Coordinate Plane

A **coordinate plane** is formed by two intersecting and perpendicular number lines. The lines intersect each other at a point called the **origin**, or (0,0).

The coordinates of point *A* are $(^{+}4,^{-}5)$.

The first number describes the distance left or right of the origin. The numbers left of the origin are negative.

The second number describes the distance above or below the origin. The numbers below the origin are negative.

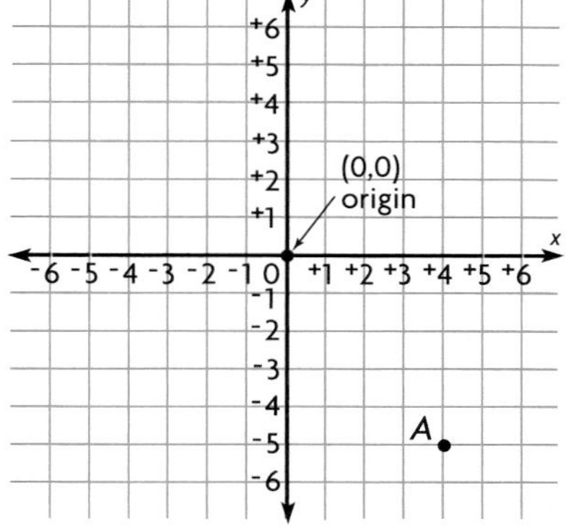

Examples

A 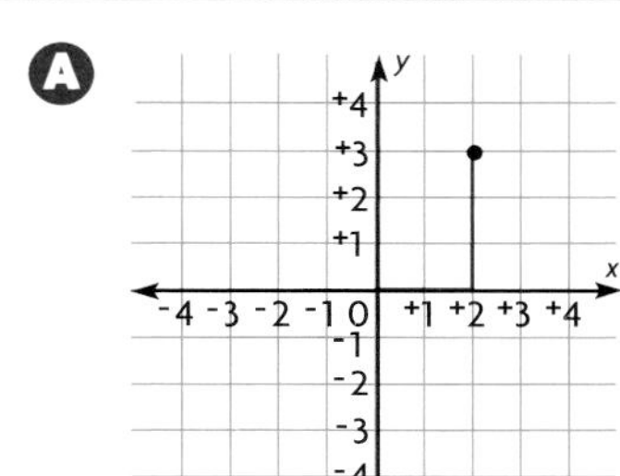

$(^{+}2,^{+}3)$ tells you to move 2 spaces to the right and 3 spaces above the origin.

B 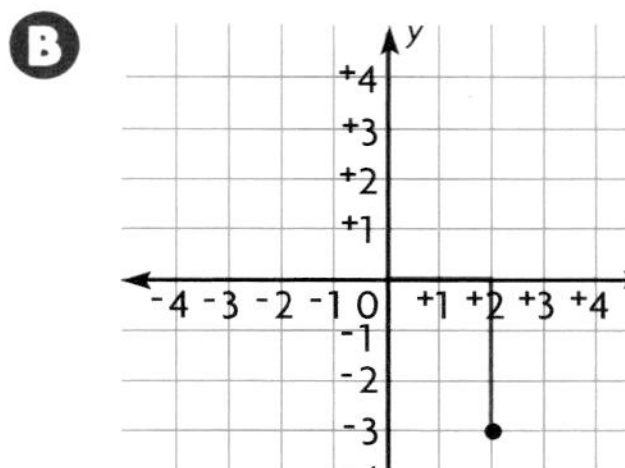

$(^{+}2,^{-}3)$ tells you to move 2 spaces to the right and 3 spaces below the origin.

C 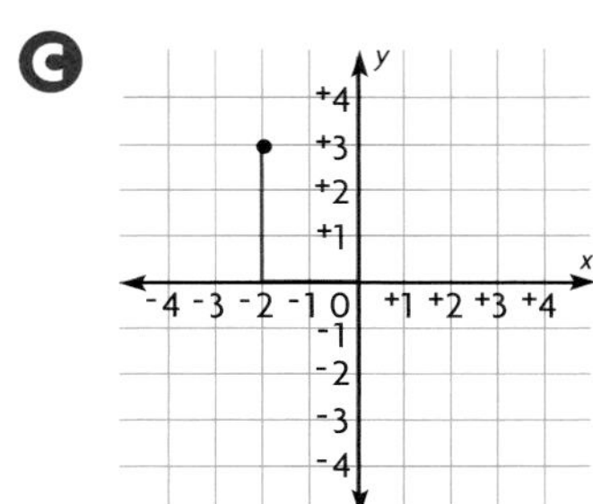

$(^{-}2,^{+}3)$ tells you to move 2 spaces to the left and 3 spaces above the origin.

D 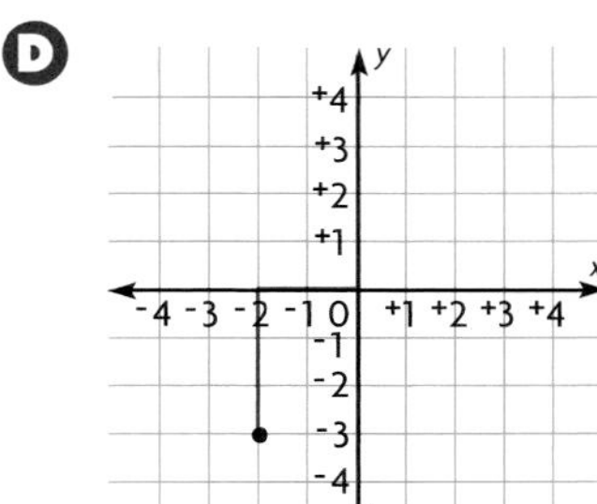

$(^{-}2,^{-}3)$ tells you to move 2 spaces to the left and 3 spaces below the origin.

Try It

Write the ordered pair for each point.

1. point *F* **2.** point *C* **3.** point *E* **4.** point *A*

Name the point for each ordered pair.

5. $(^{-}5,^{-}4)$ **6.** $(^{-}2,0)$ **7.** $(^{+}4,^{+}4)$ **8.** $(^{+}3,^{-}6)$

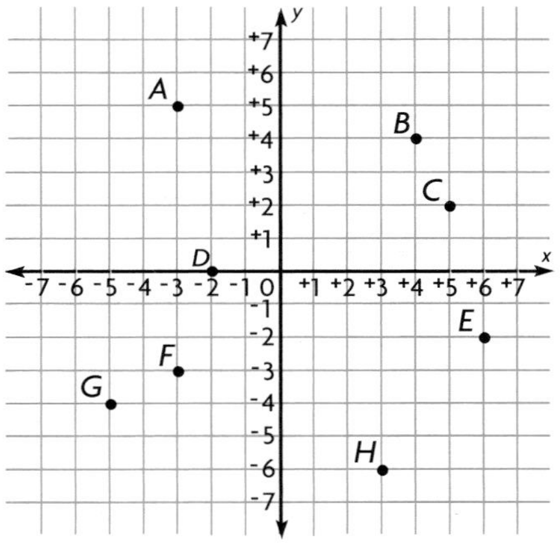

Study Guide and Review

VOCABULARY

Choose a word from the list to complete each sentence.

1. A figure has ? if it can be turned about a point and still look the same in at least two different positions. (p. 399)
2. A ? is the movement of a figure by a translation, a reflection, or a rotation. (p. 406)
3. An ? shows a relationship between two quantities that are not equivalent. (p. 428)

transformation
inequality
equation
rotational symmetry
line symmetry

STUDY AND SOLVE

Chapter 17

Identify lines, rays, angles, and line relationships.

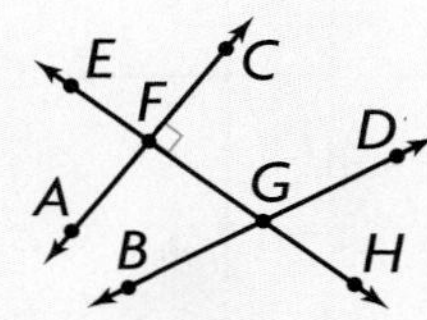

Name 2 acute angles in the figure above.

Both $\angle BGF$ and $\angle DGH$ measure greater than 0° and less than 90°.

So, $\angle BGF$ and $\angle DGH$ are acute angles.

For 4–9, use the drawing at the left. (pp. 364–371)

4. Name 4 line segments.
5. Name 3 lines.
6. Name a ray.
7. Name 2 obtuse angles.
8. Name 2 perpendicular lines.
9. Name 2 intersecting lines.

Chapter 18

Classify triangles.

Classify the triangle. Write *isosceles, scalene,* or *equilateral.* Then write *right, acute,* or *obtuse.*

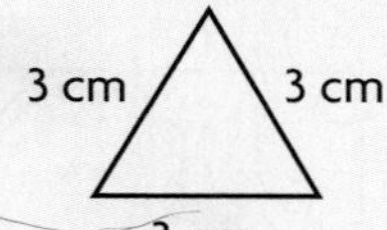

The triangle is equilateral and acute.

Classify each triangle. Write *isosceles, scalene,* or *equilateral.* Then write *right, acute,* or *obtuse.* (pp. 382–383)

10. 5 cm, 5 cm, 5 cm

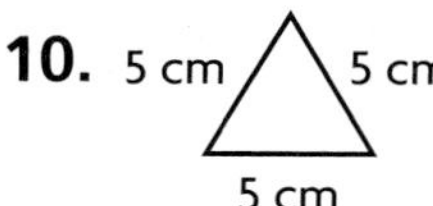

11.

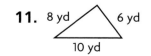

Classify quadrilaterals.

Classify the figure in as many ways as possible. Write *quadrilateral, parallelogram, rhombus, rectangle, square,* or *trapezoid.*

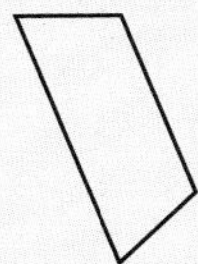

4 sides, 1 pair of parallel sides

So, this figure is a quadrilateral and a trapezoid.

Classify each figure in as many ways as possible. Write *quadrilateral, parallelogram, rhombus, rectangle, square,* or *trapezoid.* (pp. 384–387)

12.

13.

Chapter 19

Identify congruent and similar figures.

Tell whether the two figures appear to be *congruent, similar, both,* or *neither.*

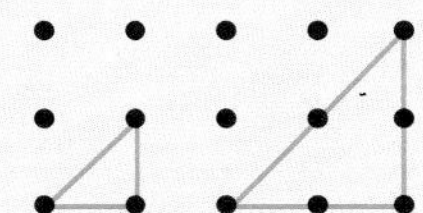

Since the figures have the same shape, they are similar.

Tell whether the two figures appear to be *congruent, similar, both,* or *neither.* (pp. 402–403)

14. 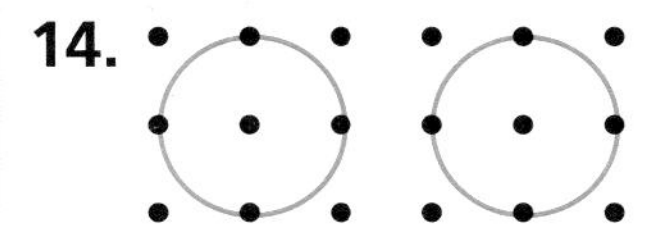

15. 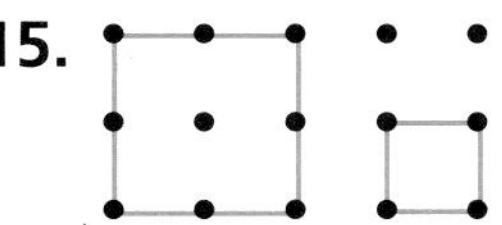

16. 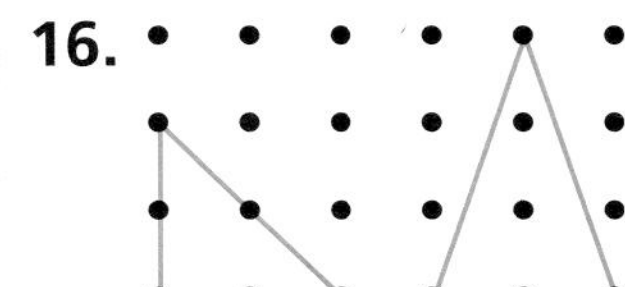

17. 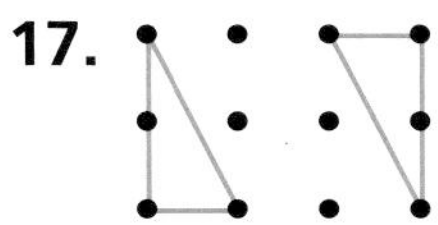

Chapter 20

Write ordered pairs for points on a coordinate grid.

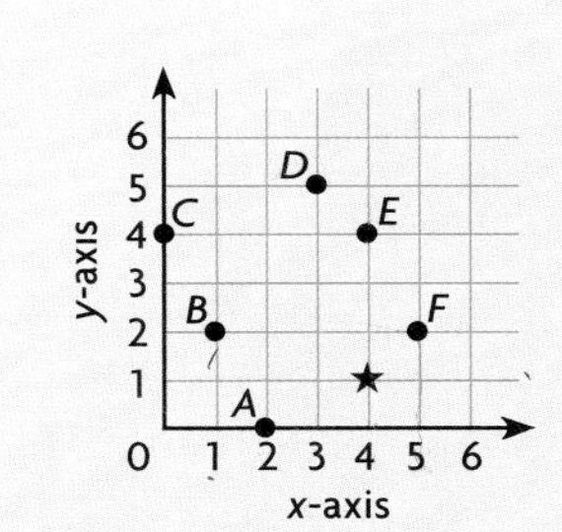

Start at 0.

Count 4 units horizontally. Then count 1 unit vertically.

The ★ is at (4,1).

Write the ordered pair for each point on the coordinate grid at the left. (pp. 430–431)

18. point *A*

19. point *B*

20. point *C*

21. point *D*

22. point *E*

23. point *F*

PROBLEM SOLVING PRACTICE

Solve. (pp. 388–389, 404–405)

24. Tracy drew a square with sides of 6 units on 1-cm grid paper. How long would each side of the square be if Tracy used 0.5-cm grid paper?

25. Sort the numbers 2–20 into a Venn diagram showing *Prime* and *Composite.*

PERFORMANCE ASSESSMENT

TASK A • PICTURE THIS

The Rodriquez family visited the Museum of Modern Art in New York City. They saw plane figures in many of the paintings and drawings.

a. Draw a picture that includes the plane figures in List A.

b. Write a description of your picture using the terms in List B.

c. Tell if your picture has line symmetry or rotational symmetry.

List A	List B
right angle	line segment
acute angle	ray
obtuse angle	plane
intersecting lines	vertex
parallel lines	congruent
perpendicular lines	

TASK B • WHAT AM I?

Jamie found this riddle in a book.

I have 4 congruent sides.
All of my angles are right angles.
What am I?
I am a square.

He wants to have a collection of riddles like this.

a. Write three different riddles for Jamie. Make the answer to each riddle the name of a plane figure.

b. Tell if there is more than one answer to any of your riddles. Explain.

Transform Plane Figures

Morgan is making a design for his book report cover using a drawing program. For his design, he is planning to transform a triangle.

Step 1
Click *Shapes* or *Polygon* on the drawing toolbar. Choose the shape you want. In the page, click where you want the shape to begin. Drag the pointer to the size you want.

Step 2
Select the shape.
Click *Copy.*
Then click *Paste.*
Translate the copy.

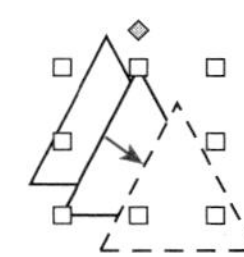

Step 3
Select the copy. Click *Copy.* Then click *Paste.* Click *Draw* or *Transform* on the drawing toolbar. Select *Reflect* or *Flip Vertical.* Translate the copy.

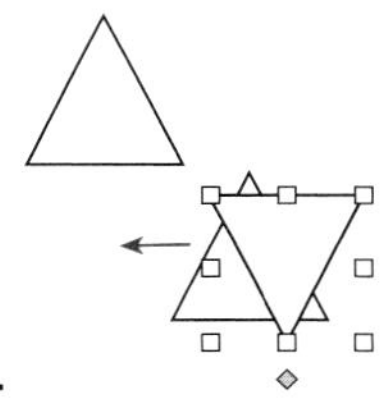

Step 4
Select the copy. Click *Copy.* Then click *Paste.* Click *Draw* or *Transform* on the drawing toolbar. Select *Rotate Right.* Translate the copy.

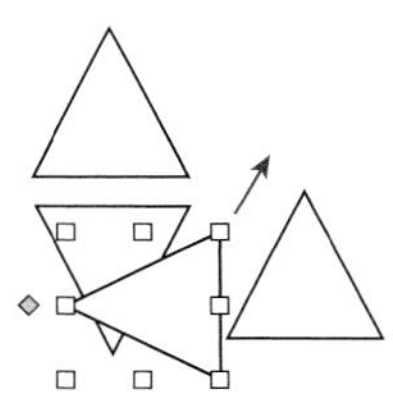

Step 5
To complete the design, select a shape. Click *Fill Color* and select the color you want. Repeat this step for each shape.

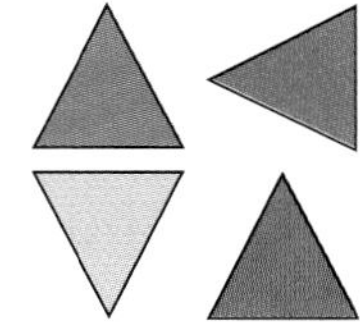

Practice and Problem Solving

Draw and transform each plane figure.

1. Draw and rotate a rectangle.
2. Draw and translate a parallelogram.
3. Draw and reflect a rhombus.
4. Draw and translate a trapezoid and then reflect it.
5. Make your own design. Describe the transformations you used.

GO ON-LINE **Multimedia Math Glossary**
www.harcourtschool.com/mathglossary
Vocabulary Power Look up *transformation* in the Multimedia Math Glossary. Draw a figure and use it to show examples of each type of transformation.

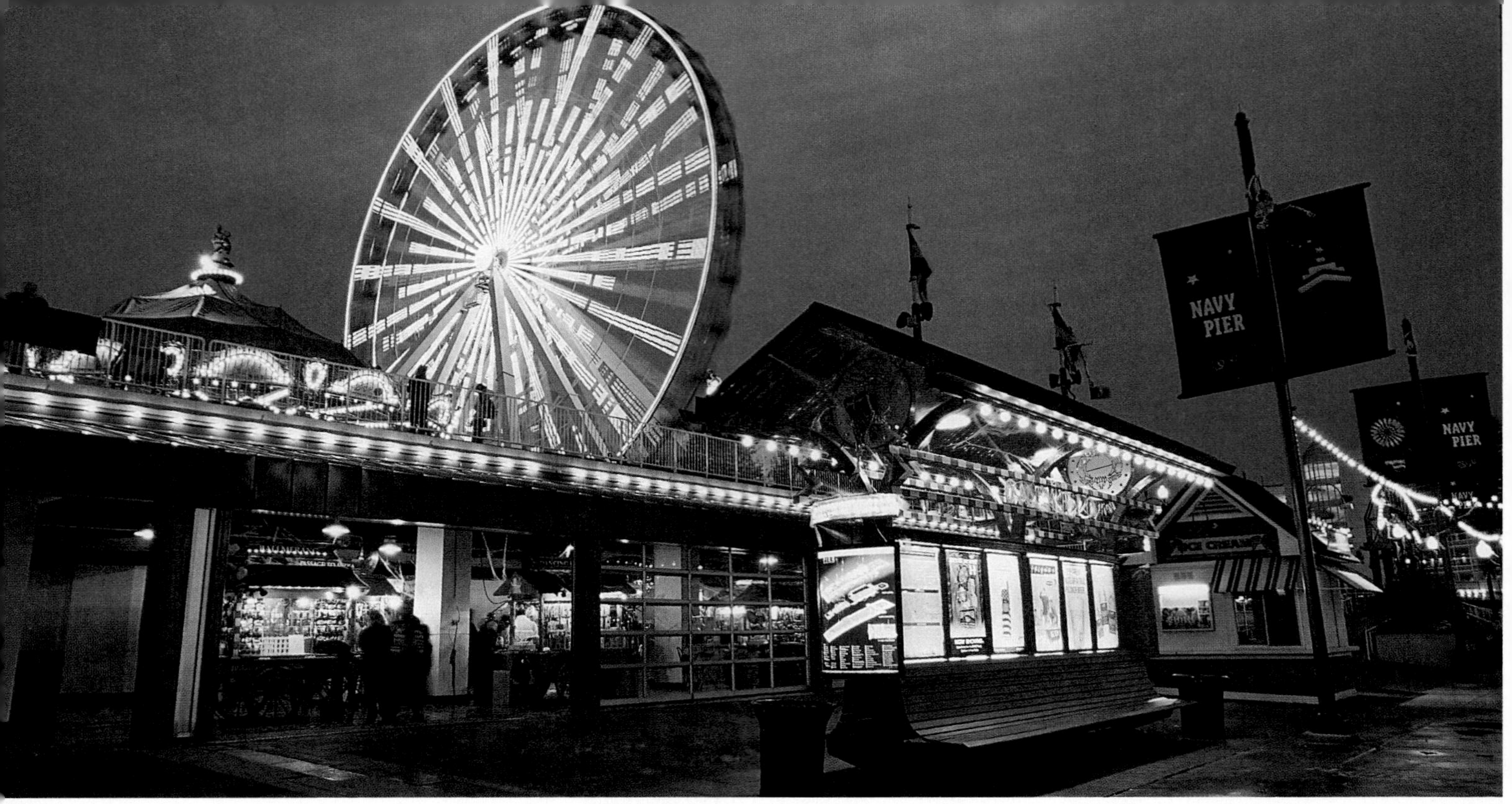

▲ The Ferris wheel at Navy Pier is 150 feet tall and holds up to 240 people.

PROBLEM SOLVING ON LOCATION

in Illinois

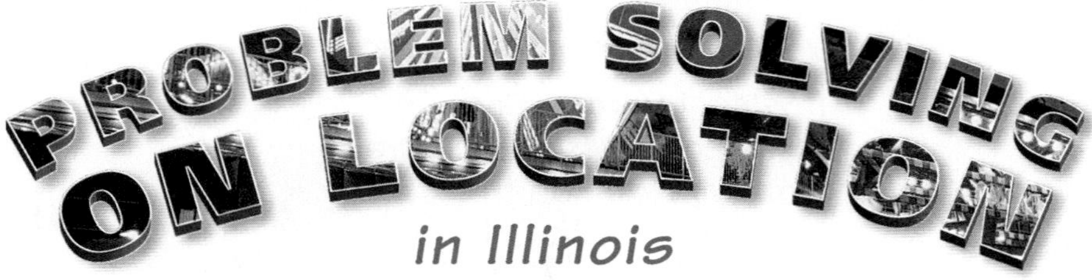

NAVY PIER

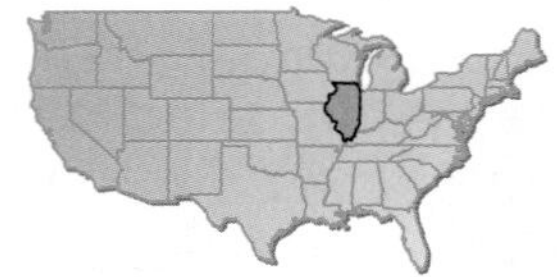

Navy Pier is a popular tourist destination in Chicago on Lake Michigan. It offers many attractions including rides, museums, theaters, and shopping. Built in 1916, Navy Pier was originally a commercial-shipping pier.

1. The screen in a theater at Navy Pier is six stories tall and measures 60 feet by 80 feet. Erika says the screen is shaped like a rectangle. Ian says the screen is shaped like a parallelogram. Who is correct? Explain.

2. At the Smith Museum of Stained Glass Windows, there is a window made up of equilateral, isosceles, and scalene triangles. Draw a picture of what the window might look like. Label each type of triangle.

3. Along Lake Michigan, the lake breeze can make the temperature feel as much as 10°F cooler. Suppose the temperature is 22°F. What might the temperature feel like with a breeze?

4. The diameter of the carousel at Navy Pier is 44 feet. How long is the radius of the carousel?

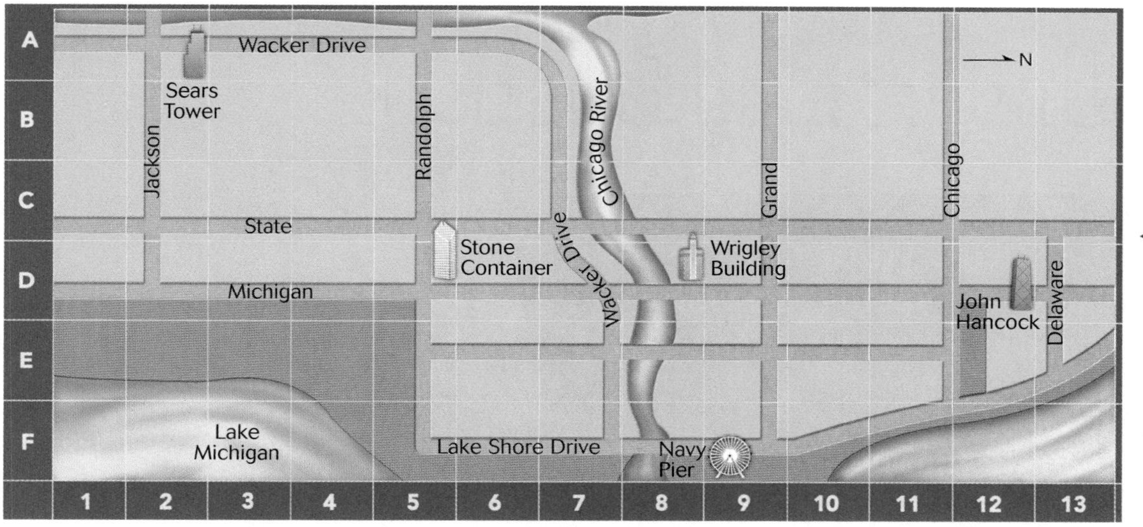

◀ Downtown Chicago

OTHER CHICAGO SIGHTS

Chicago also has an aquarium, a planetarium, and many museums and unique buildings.

▼ The John Hancock Center is one of the 10 tallest buildings in the world.

1. What line relationships can you identify in the photograph of the John Hancock Center? What types of angles do you see? What types of triangles can you find? Draw a diagram with labels to show your answer.

2. Trace one of the triangles shown on the photograph of the John Hancock Center.
   a. Draw a triangle that is congruent to the triangle you traced.
   b. Make a drawing in which you translate, reflect, and rotate the triangle. Label each move.

3. Suppose the frame for a painting in the Museum of Contemporary Art is described as having 4 congruent sides, 2 pairs of parallel sides, and no right angles.
   a. Draw a picture to show the shape of the frame.
   b. Write a name for the quadrilateral you drew.

4. You can identify locations of places on a map much as you identify points on a coordinate grid. On the map above you can find the Sears Tower at A2.
   a. What is the location of the Navy Pier on the map?
   b. What is the location of the John Hancock Center on the map?

CHAPTER 21

Understand Fractions

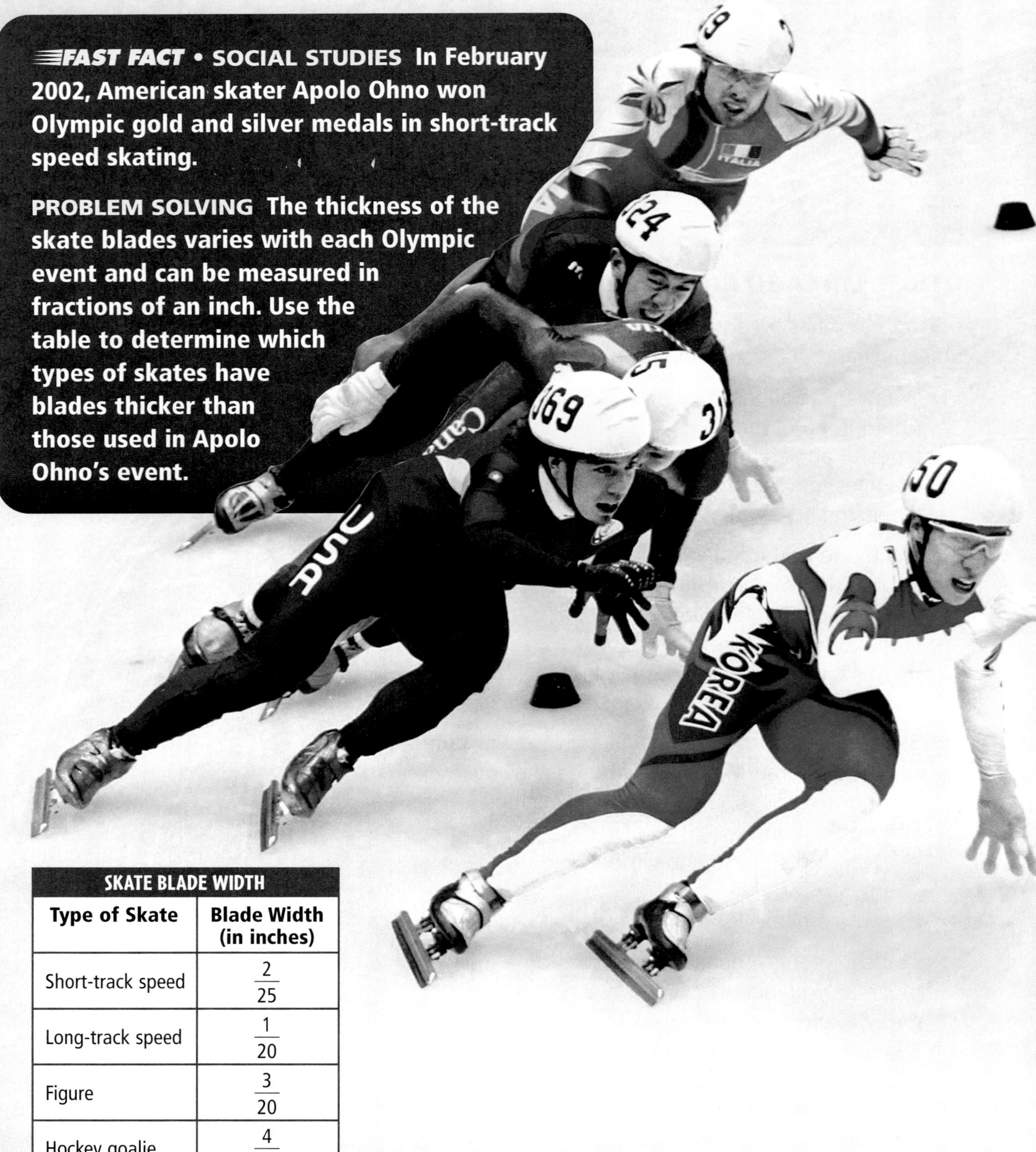

FAST FACT • SOCIAL STUDIES In February 2002, American skater Apolo Ohno won Olympic gold and silver medals in short-track speed skating.

PROBLEM SOLVING The thickness of the skate blades varies with each Olympic event and can be measured in fractions of an inch. Use the table to determine which types of skates have blades thicker than those used in Apolo Ohno's event.

SKATE BLADE WIDTH

Type of Skate	Blade Width (in inches)
Short-track speed	$\frac{2}{25}$
Long-track speed	$\frac{1}{20}$
Figure	$\frac{3}{20}$
Hockey goalie	$\frac{4}{25}$

CHECK WHAT YOU KNOW

Use this page to help you review and remember important skills needed for Chapter 21.

PARTS OF A WHOLE

Choose the word to name the equal parts in each whole.

halves thirds fourths sixths

1. 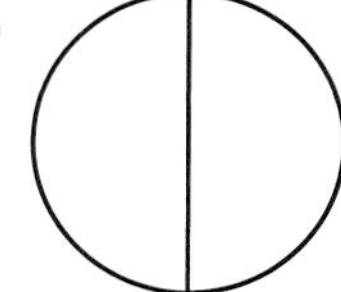
2. 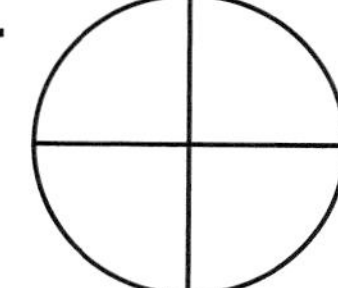
3. 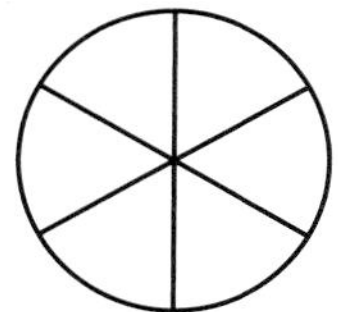
4. 

Write a fraction for each shaded part.

5. 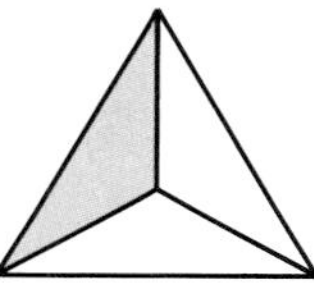
6. 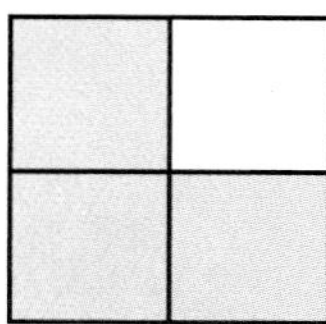
7. 
8. 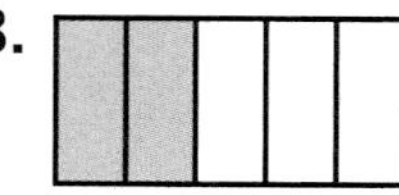

PARTS OF A GROUP

Write a fraction for the shaded part.

9.
10. 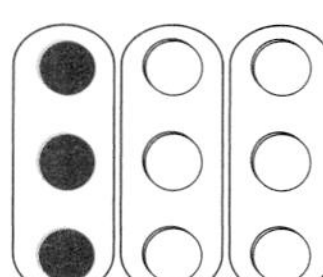
11. 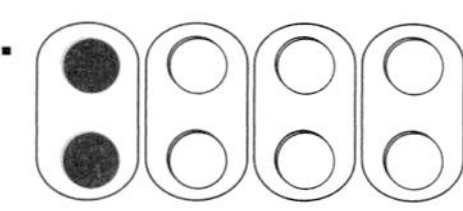
12. 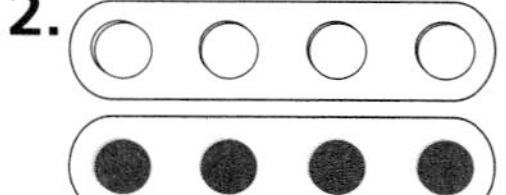

VOCABULARY POWER

REVIEW

equivalent [i•kwiv′ə•lənt] *adjective*

The word *equivalent* comes from the Latin words *aequus,* meaning "equal," and *valere,* meaning "to be strong." What does the origin of the word *equivalent* tell you about two quantities that are equivalent?

PREVIEW

fraction
numerator
denominator
equivalent fractions
simplest form
mixed number

www.harcourtschool.com/mathglossary

LESSON 1

Read and Write Fractions

Quick Review

1. $20 \div 5 = \blacksquare + 1$
2. $4 \times \blacksquare = 10 \times 2$
3. $\blacksquare \div 6 = 7 - 4$
4. $\blacksquare \times 3 = 12 \div 2$
5. $30 - 2 = 4 \times \blacksquare$

VOCABULARY

fraction

numerator

denominator

Learn

BOW WOW BISCUITS Mario wants to cut the dog treats recipe in half. What fraction shows the amount of oats he needs?

A **fraction** is a number that can name a part of a whole. One whole can be divided into 2 equal parts.

each part → $\frac{1}{2}$ ← numerator
total equal parts → ← denominator

Read: one half
one divided by two

Write: $\frac{1}{2}$

So, Mario needs $\frac{1}{2}$ cup of oats.

Mario baked 8 treats on one tray. He fed 2 treats to his puppy. What fraction of the treats were eaten?

A fraction can also name a part of a group.

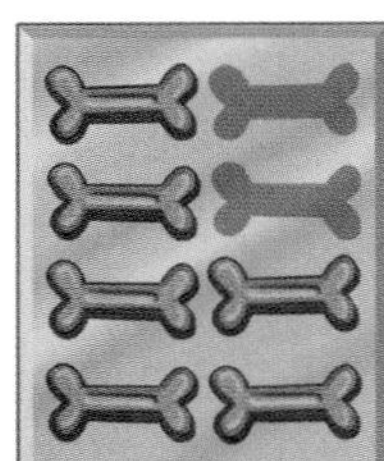

number eaten → $\frac{2}{8}$ ← numerator
number in the group → ← denominator

Read: two eighths
two out of eight

Write: $\frac{2}{8}$

So, $\frac{2}{8}$ of the treats were eaten.

Dog Treats

2 cups flour
6 tablespoons oil
2 eggs, beaten
2 packages yeast
1 teaspoon salt
1 cup oats
1 cup bran
1 cup hot water

Mix ingredients. Spoon onto greased cookie sheet. Bake at 350° for 25 minutes.

Check

1. **Explain** how to find what fraction of the treats were **not** eaten.

Write a fraction for the shaded part. Write a fraction for the unshaded part.

2. 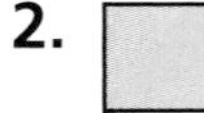 

3.

4.

5.  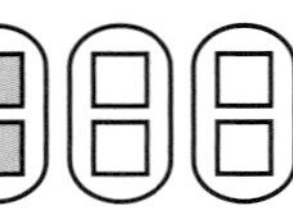

Practice and Problem Solving

Extra Practice, page 462, Set A

Write a fraction for the shaded part. Write a fraction for the unshaded part.

6. 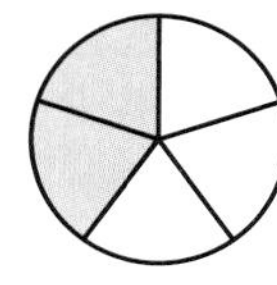

7. 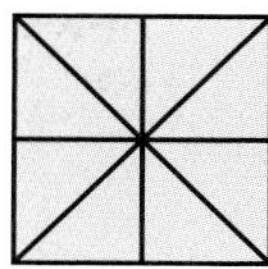

8. 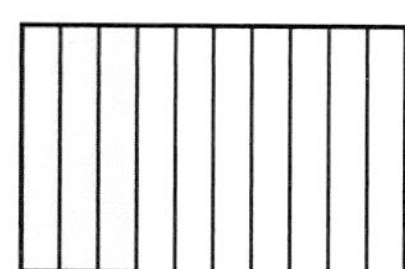

9. 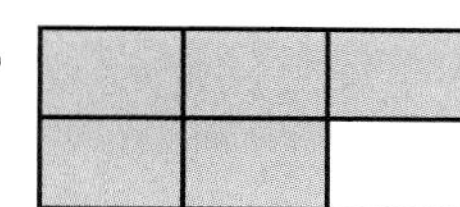

10. 

11. 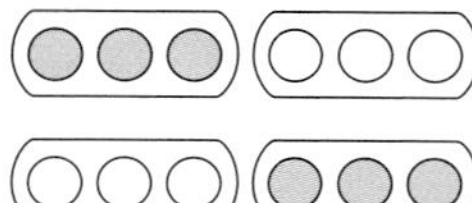

12. 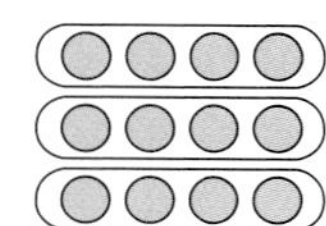

13. 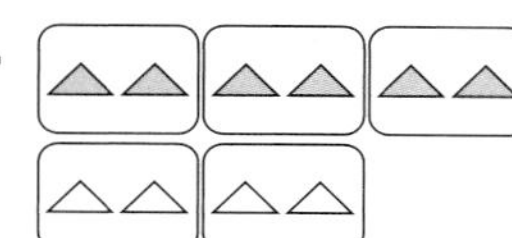

Draw a picture and shade part of it to show the fraction. Write a fraction for the unshaded part.

14. $\frac{3}{5}$ 15. $\frac{1}{2}$ 16. $\frac{4}{6}$ 17. $\frac{6}{8}$ 18. $\frac{1}{8}$ 19. $\frac{3}{10}$

20. $\frac{2}{7}$ 21. $\frac{4}{4}$ 22. $\frac{2}{3}$ 23. $\frac{10}{12}$ 24. $\frac{6}{6}$ 25. $\frac{1}{5}$

Write the fraction for each.

26. one out of nine **27.** two divided by four **28.** eight twentieths **29.** one fourth

For 30–32, use the figure at the right. Write a fraction for each part of the figure.

30. green **31.** red **32.** not yellow or red

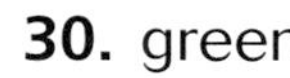

33. How much money can Mr. Drew save by buying 1 large box of dog biscuits for $0.96 rather than the same number of dog biscuits in 2 small boxes for $0.59 each?

Mixed Review and Test Prep

34. $\begin{array}{r} 3,456 \\ -\ 2,785 \\ \hline \end{array}$ (p. 48)

35. $\begin{array}{r} 921 \\ \times\ 45 \\ \hline \end{array}$ (p. 258)

36. $4 \times 4 \times 2$ (p. 174)

37. Thomas arrived at the library at 11:45 A.M. He left 1 hour 40 minutes later. At what time did Thomas leave the library? (p. 98)

38. TEST PREP Which term best describes a triangle with only 2 sides of the same length? (p. 382)

A equilateral
B scalene
C acute
D isosceles

LESSON 2

Equivalent Fractions

Quick Review

Find the missing number.

1. $\frac{0}{6}, \frac{1}{6}, \frac{2}{6}, \frac{\square}{6}$
2. $\frac{3}{2}, \frac{2}{2}, \frac{\square}{2}, \frac{0}{2}$
3. $\frac{1}{4}, \frac{2}{4}, \frac{3}{4}, \frac{4}{\square}$
4. $\frac{1}{5}, \frac{2}{5}, \frac{\square}{5}, \frac{4}{5}$
5. $\frac{4}{8}, \frac{5}{8}, \frac{\square}{\square}, \frac{7}{8}$

VOCABULARY

equivalent fractions

simplest form

Learn

GO FOR THE GOLD U.S. short-track and speed skaters won 8 medals in the 2002 Winter Olympics. Of these, 2 were gold medals. What fraction of the medals is this?

$\frac{2}{8}$ → gold medals / → total medals

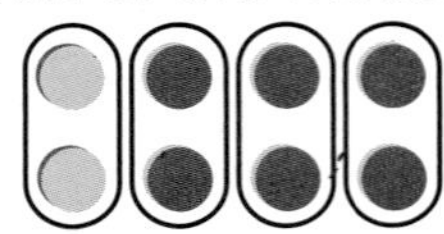

$\frac{1}{4}$ → gold medal group / → all groups

So, $\frac{2}{8}$, or $\frac{1}{4}$, of the medals were gold. $\frac{2}{8}$ and $\frac{1}{4}$ are called **equivalent fractions** because they name the same amount.

Activity Find an equivalent fraction for $\frac{3}{4}$.

MATERIALS: fraction bars

One Way Use fraction bars.

Line up fraction bars to show $\frac{3}{4}$.

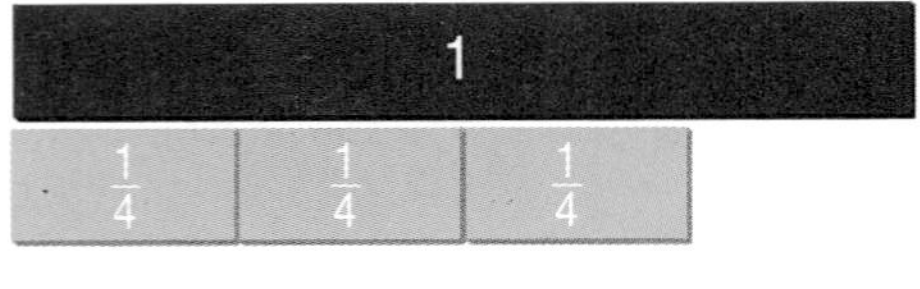

STEP 2

Then line up other fraction bars of the same type that show the same amount as $\frac{3}{4}$.

1

$\frac{1}{4}$ $\frac{1}{4}$ $\frac{1}{4}$

$\frac{1}{8}$ $\frac{1}{8}$ $\frac{1}{8}$ $\frac{1}{8}$ $\frac{1}{8}$ $\frac{1}{8}$

$\frac{1}{12}$ $\frac{1}{12}$ $\frac{1}{12}$ $\frac{1}{12}$ $\frac{1}{12}$ $\frac{1}{12}$ $\frac{1}{12}$ $\frac{1}{12}$ $\frac{1}{12}$

Another Way Use number lines.

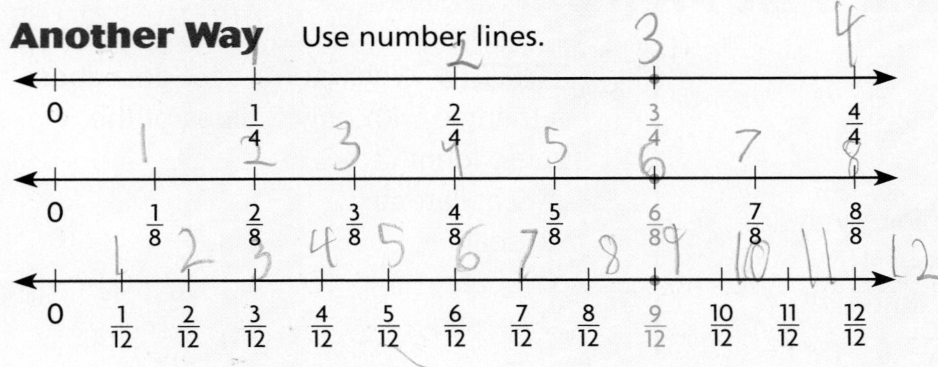

Fractions that line up with $\frac{3}{4}$ are equivalent to $\frac{3}{4}$.

So, $\frac{6}{8}$ and $\frac{9}{12}$ are equivalent to $\frac{3}{4}$.

Multiply or Divide

You also can multiply the numerator and the denominator by any number except zero to find equivalent fractions. Sometimes you can divide to find equivalent fractions.

Find equivalent fractions for $\frac{4}{6}$.

One Way Multiply the numerator and denominator by the same number.

Try 3. $\frac{4}{6} = \frac{4 \times 3}{6 \times 3} = \frac{12}{18}$

So, $\frac{4}{6}$ is equivalent to $\frac{12}{18}$.

Another Way Divide the numerator and denominator by the same number.

Try 2. $\frac{4}{6} = \frac{4 \div 2}{6 \div 2} = \frac{2}{3}$

So, $\frac{4}{6}$ is equivalent to $\frac{2}{3}$.

If you continue to divide until 1 is the only number that can be divided into the numerator and the denominator evenly, you find the fraction in **simplest form**. So, $\frac{4}{6}$ in simplest form is $\frac{2}{3}$.

Technology Link

More Practice: Harcourt Mega Math Fraction Action, *Fraction Flare-Up,* Levels D and E

Example

Find the simplest form of $\frac{45}{60}$.

Try 5. Divide the numerator and denominator by 5. $\frac{45}{60} = \frac{45 \div 5}{60 \div 5} = \frac{9}{12}$

Next try 3. Divide the numerator and denominator by 3. $\frac{9}{12} = \frac{9 \div 3}{12 \div 3} = \frac{3}{4}$

Now the only number that can be divided into the numerator and denominator of $\frac{3}{4}$ evenly is 1.

So, the simplest form of $\frac{45}{60}$ is $\frac{3}{4}$.

You can also write equivalent fractions for whole numbers.

$1 = \frac{1}{1} = \frac{1 \times 2}{1 \times 2} = \frac{2}{2}$

So, $\frac{2}{2}$ is equivalent to 1.

$3 = \frac{3}{1} = \frac{3 \times 3}{1 \times 3} = \frac{9}{3}$

So, $\frac{9}{3}$ is equivalent to 3.

Check

1. **Explain** how you can find the simplest form of $\frac{18}{24}$.

Write two equivalent fractions for each picture.

2. 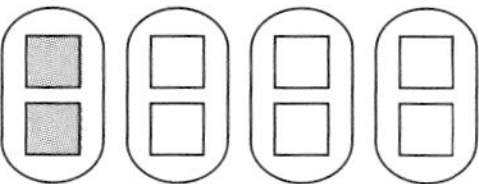

3. 

4.

LESSON CONTINUES

Practice and Problem Solving

Extra Practice, page 462, Set B

Write two equivalent fractions for each picture.

5. 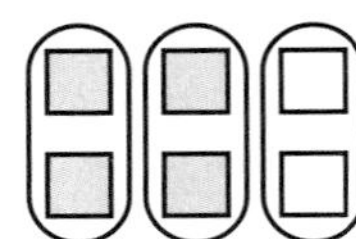

6. 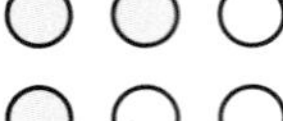

7. 

Use the number lines to write an equivalent fraction for each.

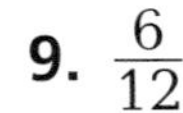

8. $\frac{2}{3}$

9. $\frac{6}{12}$

10. $\frac{4}{12}$

11. $\frac{6}{6}$

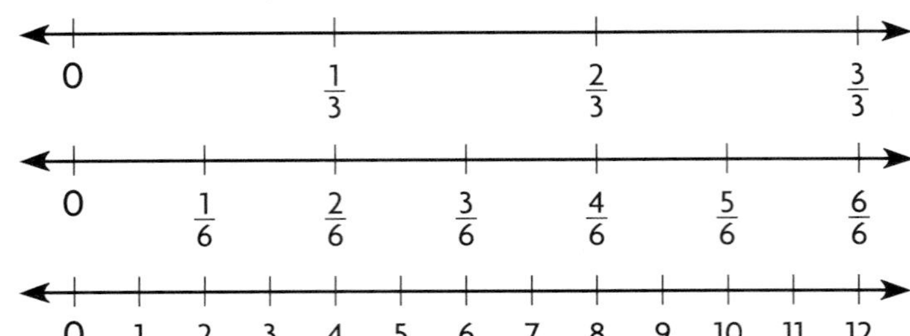

Write two equivalent fractions for each.

12. $\frac{8}{12}$ 13. $\frac{4}{10}$ 14. $\frac{4}{2}$ 15. $\frac{1}{2}$ 16. $\frac{2}{4}$ 17. $\frac{3}{9}$

18. $\frac{5}{6}$ 19. $\frac{3}{5}$ 20. $\frac{2}{8}$ 21. $\frac{9}{3}$ 22. $\frac{3}{3}$ 23. $\frac{6}{10}$

Tell whether each fraction is in simplest form. If not, write it in simplest form.

24. $\frac{2}{4}$ 25. $\frac{1}{3}$ 26. $\frac{6}{9}$ 27. $\frac{3}{4}$ 28. $\frac{1}{4}$ 29. $\frac{15}{5}$

30. $\frac{13}{20}$ 31. $\frac{9}{21}$ 32. $\frac{12}{32}$ 33. $\frac{11}{44}$ 34. $\frac{10}{25}$ 35. $\frac{18}{27}$

ALGEBRA Find the missing numerator or denominator.

36. $\frac{2}{3} = \frac{\square}{18}$ 37. $\frac{\square}{10} = \frac{2}{5}$ 38. $\frac{9}{3} = \frac{18}{\square}$ 39. $\frac{3}{\square} = \frac{9}{12}$ 40. $\frac{4}{4} = \frac{\square}{8}$

41. $\frac{3}{\square} = \frac{6}{10}$ 42. $\frac{\square}{9} = \frac{4}{18}$ 43. $\frac{3}{7} = \frac{12}{\square}$ 44. $\frac{5}{8} = \frac{\square}{56}$ 45. $\frac{5}{6} = \frac{20}{\square}$

46. Find a possible missing fraction. Explain your pattern.

a. $\frac{1}{2}, \frac{2}{4}, \frac{3}{6}, \frac{4}{8}, \frac{\square}{\square}$

b. $\frac{5}{15}, \frac{4}{12}, \frac{3}{9}, \frac{2}{6}, \frac{\square}{\square}$

47. **Write About It** Write a rule that you can use to tell whether a fraction is in simplest form.

48. **What's the Error?** Babs says that $\frac{3}{4}$ and $\frac{3}{8}$ are equivalent fractions based on the model she made. Describe and correct her error.

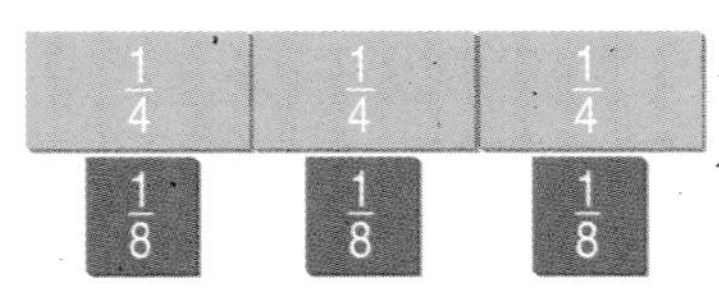

49. James and his friends picked oranges in a grove. James picked 19 oranges, Sal picked 22, Tara picked 12, and Pam picked 11 oranges. If they share the oranges equally, how many oranges will each person get?

50. **FAST FACT • SOCIAL STUDIES** The United States won a total of 34 medals in the 2002 Winter Olympics. Of these, 10 were gold medals. Write two equivalent fractions that show how many of the medals were gold.

51. Sally's dog ate 2 out of 6 dog treats. What fraction of the dog treats was left? Write the fraction in simplest form.

52. **REASONING** Is the product of a 4-digit number and a 2-digit number always a 6-digit number? Explain.

Mixed Review and Test Prep

Which quotient is greater? (p. 300)

53. $160 \div 2$ or $180 \div 3$

54. $295 \div 5$ or $312 \div 6$

55. **TEST PREP** $8{,}924 + 3{,}452$ (p. 48)

A 11,276
B 11,376
C 12,276
D 12,376

56. **Find the value of n.** (p. 214)

$n \times 46 = 2{,}300$

57. **TEST PREP** Which polygon has five sides and five angles? (p. 380)

F hexagon
G pentagon
H octagon
J quadrilateral

Problem Solving

In music, one whole note is equivalent to two $\frac{1}{2}$ notes, four $\frac{1}{4}$ notes, or eight $\frac{1}{8}$ notes. The diagram shows how the notes are related.

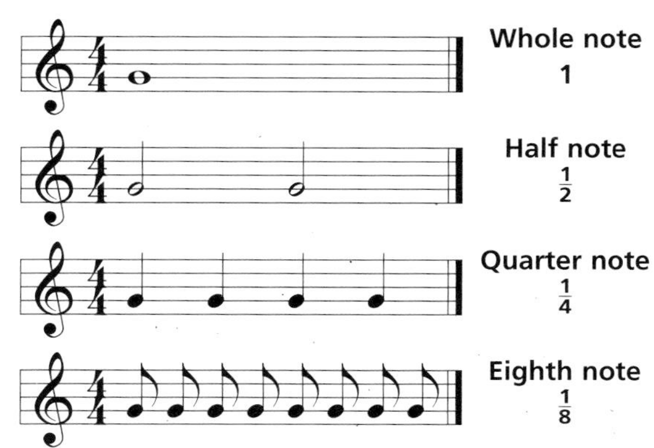

Copy and complete.

1. __?__ $\frac{1}{4}$ notes equal two $\frac{1}{2}$ notes.

2. Two $\frac{1}{8}$ notes equal one __?__ note.

3. One whole note equals one $\frac{1}{2}$ note and __?__ $\frac{1}{4}$ note(s).

LESSON 3

Compare and Order Fractions

Quick Review

Find an equivalent fraction for each.

1. $\frac{2}{3}$ **2.** $\frac{4}{16}$ **3.** $\frac{4}{5}$

4. $\frac{14}{28}$ **5.** $\frac{6}{8}$

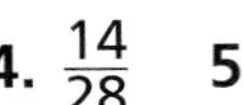

Learn

LET IT SNOW! Eva Marie took a survey of her classmates to find out what winter activities they have tried. Have more of her classmates gone ice skating or built a snowman?

Winter Activities

Ice Skating $\frac{1}{3}$ of the class

Snowman $\frac{2}{3}$ of the class

Sledding $\frac{1}{2}$ of the class

Activity 1

MATERIALS: two-color counters, fraction bars

Compare Fractions with Like Denominators

A Compare $\frac{1}{3}$ and $\frac{2}{3}$.

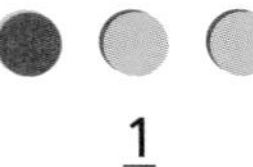

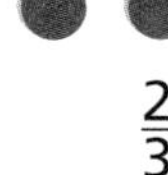

$\frac{1}{3}$ $\frac{2}{3}$

Compare the number of red counters. $1 < 2$, so $\frac{1}{3} < \frac{2}{3}$.

So, more of her classmates have built a snowman.

MATH IDEA When comparing fractions with like denominators, you need to compare only the numerators.

Compare Fractions with Unlike Denominators

B Have more of her classmates gone sledding or built a snowman?

Compare $\frac{1}{2}$ and $\frac{2}{3}$, using fraction bars.

Start with the bar for 1.

Line up the fraction bars for $\frac{1}{2}$ and $\frac{2}{3}$.

Compare these two rows of fraction bars. The longer row represents the greater fraction.

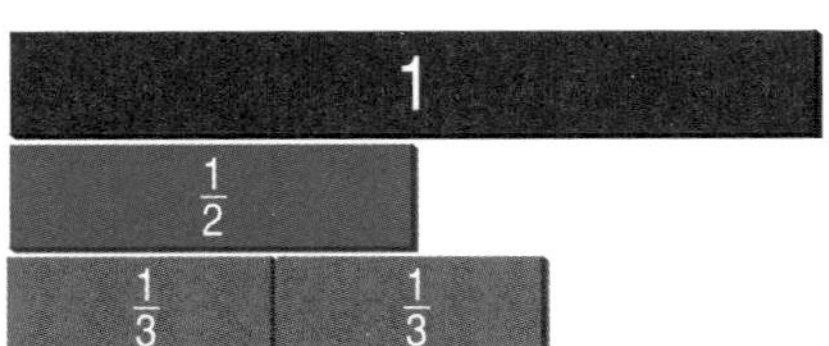

$\frac{2}{3} > \frac{1}{2}$, so more of her classmates have built a snowman.

C Have more of her classmates gone ice skating or sledding?

Compare $\frac{1}{3}$ and $\frac{1}{2}$, using a number line.

Draw a number line. Place $\frac{1}{3}$ and $\frac{1}{2}$ on the number line.

The fraction farther to the right is the greater fraction.

$\frac{1}{2}$ is closer to 1 on the number line, so $\frac{1}{2} > \frac{1}{3}$. More of her classmates have gone sledding.

Order Fractions

You can use a number line or fraction bars to order three or more fractions.

Activity 2 MATERIALS: fraction bars

A Order $\frac{1}{2}$, $\frac{1}{6}$, and $\frac{2}{3}$ from *least* to *greatest*.

Draw a number line.

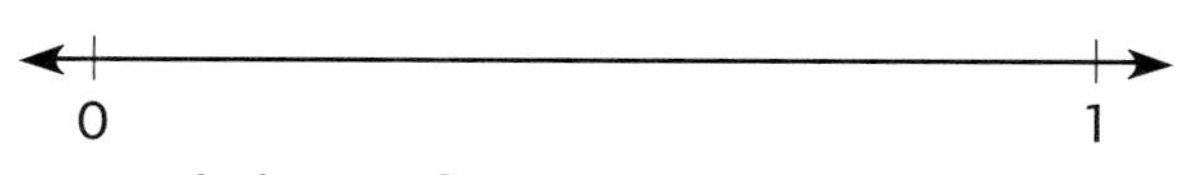

Place $\frac{1}{2}$, $\frac{1}{6}$, and $\frac{2}{3}$ on the number line. The fraction farthest to the right is the greatest. The fraction farthest to the left is the least.

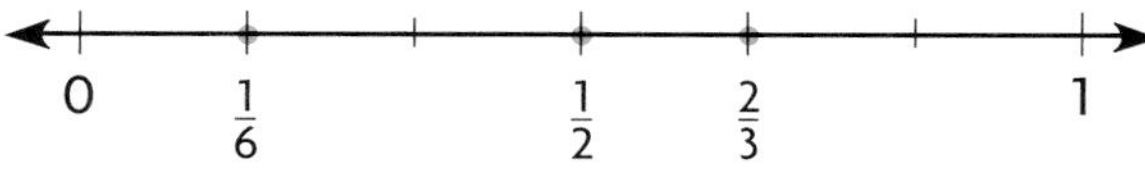

$\frac{2}{3}$ is farthest to the right, so it is the greatest of these fractions.

$\frac{1}{6}$ is farthest to the left, so it is the least of these fractions.

So, the order from least to greatest is $\frac{1}{6}$, $\frac{1}{2}$, $\frac{2}{3}$.

B Order $\frac{1}{4}$, $\frac{5}{12}$, and $\frac{1}{3}$ from *greatest* to *least*.

Start with the bar for 1.

Line up the fractions bars for $\frac{1}{4}$, $\frac{5}{12}$, and $\frac{1}{3}$ below it.

Compare these rows of fraction bars. The longest row represents the greatest fraction.

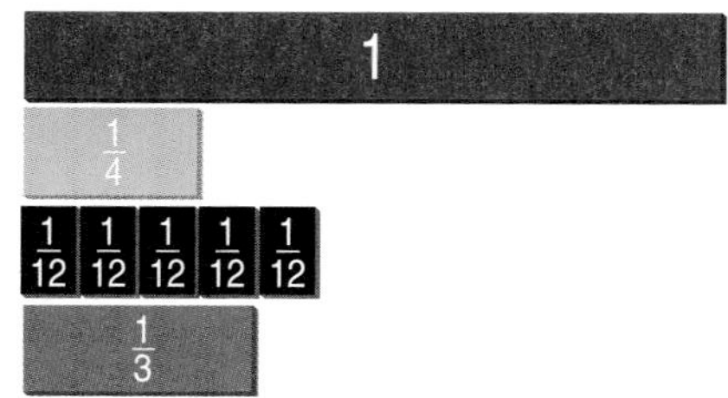

So, the order from greatest to least is $\frac{5}{12}$, $\frac{1}{3}$, $\frac{1}{4}$.

Use <, >, or = when comparing and ordering fractions. So, for the fractions in Activity 2A, you can write $\frac{1}{6} < \frac{1}{2} < \frac{2}{3}$.

- Order the fractions in Activity 2B from *least* to *greatest,* using symbols.

Check

1. **Explain** how you can compare fractions that have the same denominators, but different numerators, such as $\frac{2}{5}$ and $\frac{3}{5}$.

Compare the fractions. Write <, >, or = for each ●.

2. $\frac{2}{5}$ ● $\frac{1}{5}$

3. $\frac{3}{4}$ ● $\frac{3}{8}$

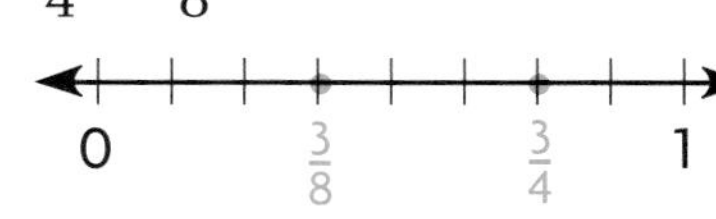

4. $\frac{2}{6}$ ● $\frac{1}{3}$

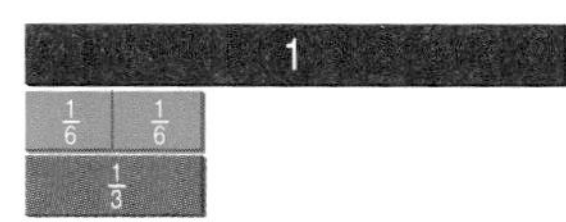

LESSON CONTINUES

Practice and Problem Solving

Extra Practice, page 462, Set C

Compare the fractions. Write <, >, or = for each ●.

5. $\frac{2}{8}$ ● $\frac{5}{8}$

6. $\frac{4}{8}$ ● $\frac{1}{4}$

7. $\frac{6}{10}$ ● $\frac{2}{3}$

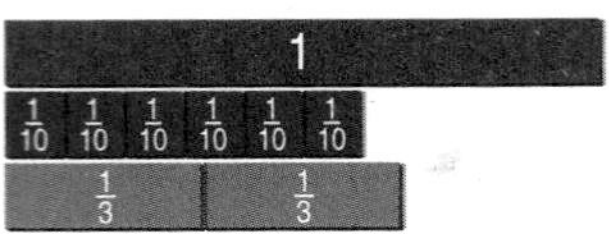

Write <, >, or = for each ●.

8. $\frac{7}{8}$ ● $\frac{3}{8}$
9. $\frac{2}{6}$ ● $\frac{1}{3}$
10. $\frac{5}{8}$ ● $\frac{5}{6}$
11. $\frac{10}{3}$ ● 4
12. $\frac{5}{7}$ ● $\frac{4}{7}$
13. $\frac{16}{8}$ ● 2
14. $\frac{6}{12}$ ● $\frac{7}{14}$
15. $\frac{3}{9}$ ● 3

Order the fractions from *least* to *greatest*.

16. $\frac{1}{2}, \frac{1}{3}, \frac{1}{4}$

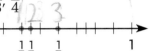

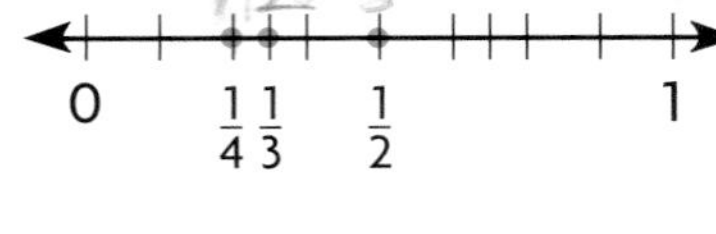

17. $\frac{3}{5}, \frac{3}{8}, \frac{4}{6}$

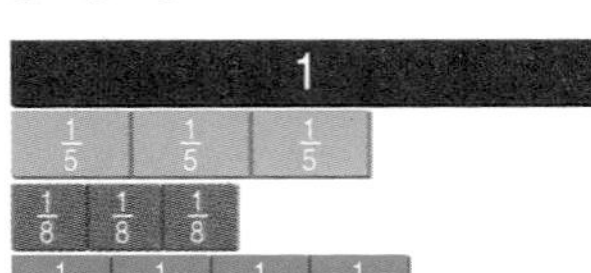

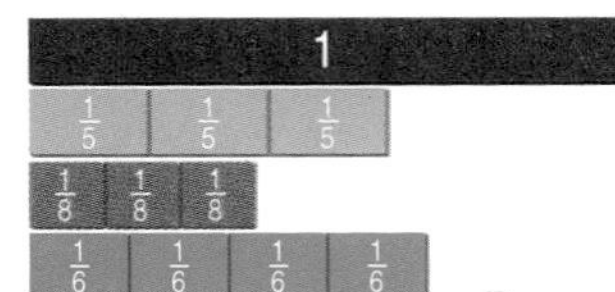

18. $\frac{1}{10}, \frac{2}{3}, \frac{4}{12}$

19. $\frac{3}{4}, \frac{3}{6}, \frac{3}{5}$
20. $\frac{7}{8}, \frac{1}{4}, \frac{5}{8}$
21. $\frac{2}{12}, \frac{3}{6}, \frac{2}{3}$
22. $\frac{2}{4}, \frac{9}{12}, \frac{1}{8}$
23. $\frac{2}{4}, \frac{2}{7}, \frac{2}{6}$
24. $\frac{5}{6}, \frac{5}{9}, \frac{5}{10}$
25. $\frac{3}{8}, \frac{4}{16}, \frac{3}{4}$
26. $\frac{5}{6}, \frac{5}{12}, \frac{2}{3}$

Order the fractions from *greatest* to *least*.

27. $\frac{1}{4}, \frac{3}{4}, \frac{2}{4}$
28. $\frac{2}{6}, \frac{1}{12}, \frac{3}{4}$
29. $\frac{1}{4}, \frac{1}{2}, \frac{1}{3}$
30. $\frac{5}{10}, \frac{4}{5}, \frac{2}{5}$

31. **ALGEBRA** Name all possible whole number values for n when $\frac{1}{2} > \frac{n}{3}$.

USE DATA For 32–33, use the price list.

32. **REASONING** If Jane buys $\frac{1}{2}$ pound of the deluxe mix, will she pay more or less than $1.35? Explain.

33. **Write a problem** using the fractions in the price list.

34. **Vocabulary Power** When we say that one thing is *like* another, we mean that it is the same or similar. How does this help you understand the term *like denominator*?

PRICE LIST

Item	Price
$\frac{1}{3}$ pound almonds	$1.95
$\frac{1}{2}$ pound cashews	$3.15
$\frac{1}{4}$ pound deluxe mix	$1.35

35. Jordan ate $\frac{1}{3}$ of the pizza. James ate $\frac{7}{15}$ of it, and Matthew ate $\frac{1}{5}$ of it. Who ate the most pizza? Who ate the least?

36. Michelle had $\frac{1}{3}$ cup of raisins and $\frac{1}{2}$ cup of sunflower seeds left from her bird seed mix. Which is the greater amount?

37. Lee scored 91 points on a math test. On the next test, she scored 13 fewer points. On the third test, she scored 92. What is the difference between Lee's highest and lowest scores?

Mixed Review and Test Prep

For 38–39, write each fraction in simplest form. (p. 448)

38. $\frac{9}{12}$

39. $\frac{5}{10}$

40. $2{,}422 \times 4$ (p. 222)

41. $29{,}000 - 13{,}752$ (p. 50)

42. Find the mean for 59, 63, 53, 75, 65, 81, 73. (p. 328)

43. Maria bought 2 bags of popcorn for \$1.05 each. Felipe bought 2 drinks for a total of \$2.25. Who spent more money? How much more? (p. 262)

44. $64 \div 4$ (p. 282)

45. $521 \div 3$ (p. 300)

46. **TEST PREP** What are the missing numbers in the pattern? (p. 346)

23, 38, 53, 68, ■, ■, ■, 128

A 78, 83, 93
B 83, 98, 113
C 88, 93, 103
D 98, 108, 113

47. **TEST PREP** Mr. Edwards drives a total of 25 miles to and from work each day. He works 6 days each week. How many miles is this in 4 weeks? (p. 222)

F 200 miles
G 400 miles
H 500 miles
J 600 miles

Problem Solving Thinker's Corner

FUN WITH FRACTIONS Solve each problem. Then match each answer to the missing fraction bar. The letters on the fraction bars will spell the answer to the riddle below. The first problem is done for you.

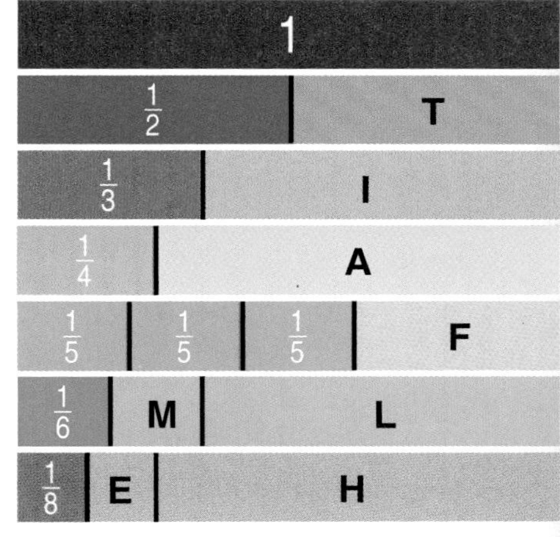

Which fraction is greater?

1. $\frac{3}{4}, \frac{4}{6}$ 

2. $\frac{1}{6}, \frac{1}{2}$ ■

3. $\frac{1}{8}, \frac{6}{8}$ ■

4. $\frac{1}{2}, \frac{3}{4}$ ■

5. $\frac{4}{6}, \frac{2}{5}$ ■

Which fraction is least?

6. $\frac{2}{3}, \frac{2}{5}, \frac{1}{2}$ ■

7. $\frac{2}{3}, \frac{3}{4}, \frac{1}{2}$ ■

8. $\frac{3}{4}, \frac{2}{3}, \frac{6}{8}$ ■

9. $\frac{1}{6}, \frac{3}{4}, \frac{6}{8}$ ■

10. $\frac{1}{2}, \frac{2}{5}, \frac{1}{8}$ ■

Riddle: When can you hear the band play?

LESSON 4

Problem Solving Strategy
Make a Model

Quick Review

Compare. Write <, >, or = for each ●.

1. $\frac{3}{5}$ ● $\frac{2}{5}$ **2.** $\frac{1}{2}$ ● $\frac{3}{6}$

3. $\frac{3}{10}$ ● $\frac{3}{8}$ **4.** $\frac{1}{2}$ ● $\frac{7}{8}$

5. $\frac{1}{2}$ ● $\frac{3}{4}$ ● $\frac{7}{8}$

PROBLEM Sammy, Henry, and Jeb are gopher tortoises. They are training for a 1-yard race. In the first week, who ran the greatest distance? Who ran the least distance?

TORTOISE TRAINING

Name	Yards Run First Week
Sammy	$\frac{1}{2}$
Henry	$\frac{3}{4}$
Jeb	$\frac{2}{3}$

UNDERSTAND

- What are you asked to do?
- What information will you use?
- Is there information you will not use? If so, what?

PLAN

- What strategy can you use to solve the problem?

  Make a model by using a number line. Locate and mark points to represent $\frac{1}{2}$, $\frac{3}{4}$, and $\frac{2}{3}$ yards.

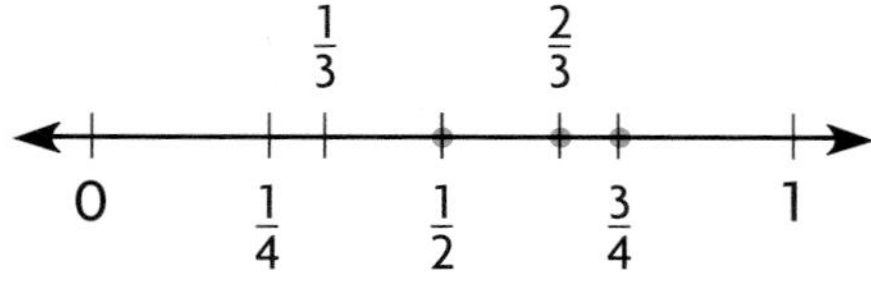

SOLVE

- How can you use the model to solve the problem?

  $\frac{3}{4}$ is farthest to the right, so it is the greatest fraction.

  $\frac{1}{2}$ is farthest to the left, so it is the least fraction.

  So, Henry ran the greatest distance and Sammy ran the least distance.

CHECK

- What other strategy can you use?

Problem Solving Practice

Make a model to solve.

1. **What if** Sammy ran 1 yard the first week? Would he have run more than Henry ran the first week? Explain.

A spinner has 12 equal sections. Two of the sections are blue, 3 sections are yellow, 2 sections are red, and 5 sections are green.

2. Which color covers $\frac{1}{4}$ of the spinner?
   A red **C** green
   B blue **D** yellow

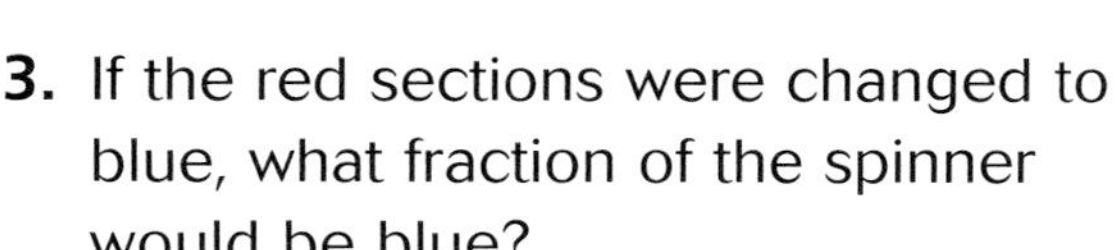

3. If the red sections were changed to blue, what fraction of the spinner would be blue?
   F $\frac{2}{12}$ **G** $\frac{1}{8}$ **H** $\frac{1}{3}$ **J** $\frac{1}{4}$

Strategies

Draw a Diagram or Picture
Make a Model or Act It Out
Make an Organized List
Find a Pattern
Make a Table or Graph
Predict and Test
Work Backward
Solve a Simpler Problem
Write an Equation
Use Logical Reasoning

Problem Solving

Mixed Strategy Practice

4. Ty's tomato sauce has $\frac{1}{4}$ teaspoon basil, $\frac{1}{2}$ teaspoon oregano, and $\frac{1}{8}$ teaspoon pepper. Order the amounts from greatest to least.

5. **REASONING** Explain how you know whether Ty used more or less than 1 teaspoon of seasonings in the tomato sauce.

6. Beatrice read 3 pages of her book on Monday, 6 pages on Tuesday, 12 pages on Wednesday, and 24 pages on Thursday. If this pattern continues, how many pages might she read on Friday?

7. Jon and his sister made cupcakes. They each ate 2 cupcakes. Jon took 12 cupcakes to school and left 8 cupcakes at home. What fraction of the cupcakes did Jon take to school?

USE DATA For 8–10, use the table.

MORNING ASSEMBLY SCHEDULE	
Kindergarten and First Grade	8:45–9:15
Second Grade and Third Grade	9:30–10:15
Fourth Grade and Fifth Grade	10:30–11:20

8. How long will each assembly last?

9. Which assembly will be the longest? Which will be the shortest?

10. How much longer will the longest assembly last than the shortest?

11. Cindy is making a square design with 16 tiles. The 4 corner tiles are red, and the rest of the outside border tiles are blue. She puts 4 green tiles in the middle. Show what Cindy's design will look like.

LESSON 5

Mixed Numbers

Quick Review

1. 8×7
2. 3×6
3. $13 \div 4$
4. $27 \div 5$
5. 12×11

VOCABULARY

mixed number

Learn

HOP TO IT Susan gave one and one-fourth cups of rabbit food to Whiskers, her pet rabbit.

A **mixed number** is made up of a whole number and a fraction. Look at the picture that represents one and one-fourth cups of food.

Read: one and one fourth

Write: $1\frac{1}{4}$

Example 1 Write a mixed number for each picture.

A

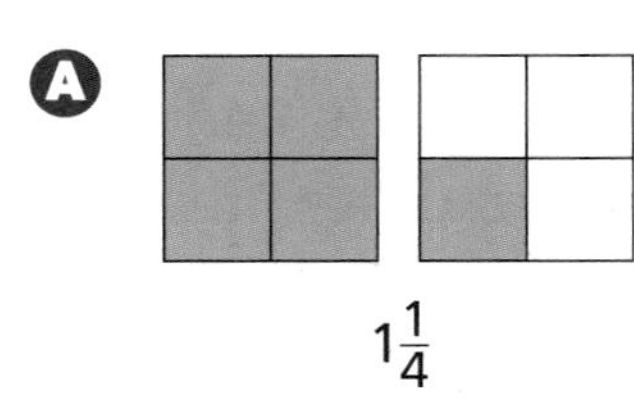

$1\frac{1}{4}$

B

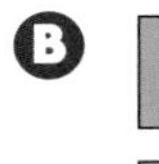
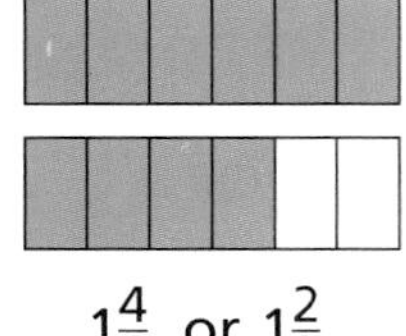

$1\frac{4}{6}$, or $1\frac{2}{3}$

C

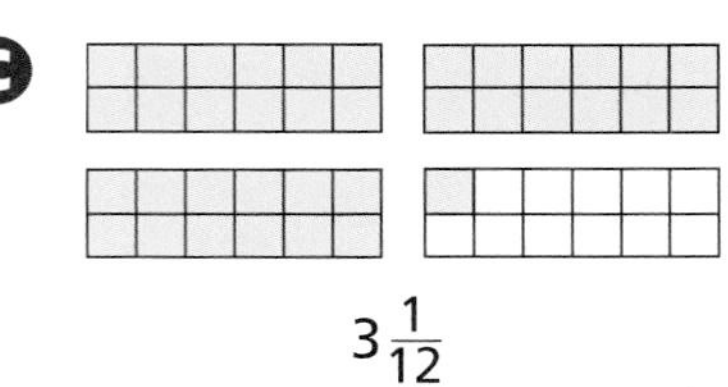

$3\frac{1}{12}$

- Look at Example 1A. How many fourths does it take to make two wholes?

You can compare mixed numbers like you compare fractions.

Example 2

A Compare $2\frac{1}{2}$ and $2\frac{1}{3}$, using fraction bars.

Model $2\frac{1}{2}$, then line up the bars for $2\frac{1}{3}$ below it.

1	1	$\frac{1}{2}$
1	1	$\frac{1}{3}$

Compare the two rows of fraction bars. The longer row represents the greater mixed number.

So, $2\frac{1}{2} > 2\frac{1}{3}$.

B Compare $6\frac{1}{4}$ and $5\frac{1}{2}$, using a number line.

Place $6\frac{1}{4}$ and $5\frac{1}{2}$ on a number line.

The mixed number farther to the right on the number line is greater.

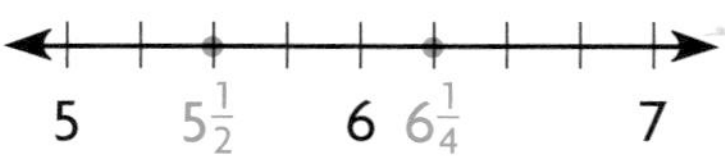

$6\frac{1}{4}$ is farther to the right on the number line, so $6\frac{1}{4} > 5\frac{1}{2}$.

Rename Fractions and Mixed Numbers

Sometimes the numerator of a fraction is greater than the denominator. These fractions have a value greater than 1. They can be renamed as mixed numbers.

Example 3

A Rename $\frac{15}{4}$ as a mixed number.

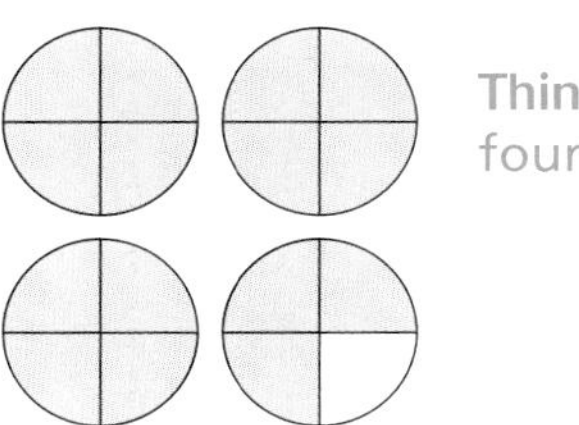

Think: How many fourths are shown?

Since $\frac{15}{4}$ means $15 \div 4$, you can use division to rename a fraction greater than 1 as a mixed number.

$$\begin{array}{r} 3 \text{ r}3 \\ 4\overline{)15} \\ -12 \\ \hline 3 \end{array}$$

denominator → 4; 15 ← numerator; 3 ← number of fourths left over

Write the quotient as the whole-number part. Then write the remainder as the numerator and the divisor as the denominator.

So, $\frac{15}{4}$ renamed as a mixed number is $3\frac{3}{4}$.

B Rename $1\frac{3}{5}$ as a fraction.

Use fraction bars to rename the mixed number as a fraction.

Model $1\frac{3}{5}$, using fraction bars.

Put $\frac{1}{5}$ bars under the 1 bar.

1					1/5	1/5	1/5
1/5	1/5	1/5	1/5	1/5	1/5	1/5	1/5

The total number of $\frac{1}{5}$ bars is the numerator of the fraction. The numerator of the fraction is 8.

So, $1\frac{3}{5}$ renamed as a fraction is $\frac{8}{5}$.

A fraction greater than 1 is sometimes called an *improper fraction.*

So, $\frac{15}{4}$ and $\frac{8}{5}$ are examples of improper fractions.

Check

1. **Explain** how you can tell that a fraction is greater than 1.

Write a mixed number for each picture.

2. 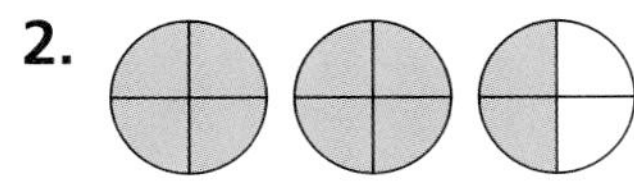

3.

4. 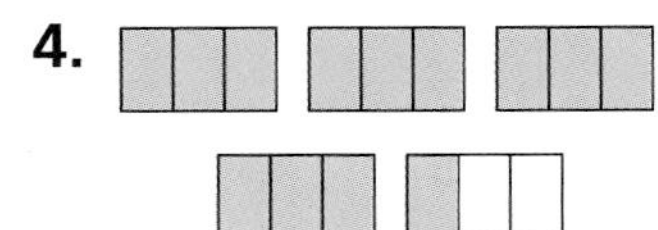

Compare. Write <, >, or = for each ●.

5. $3\frac{1}{2}$ ● $3\frac{2}{3}$
6. $5\frac{1}{3}$ ● $5\frac{2}{6}$
7. $8\frac{1}{4}$ ● $7\frac{3}{4}$
8. $\frac{12}{7}$ ● $\frac{3}{2}$

Rename each fraction as a mixed number and each mixed number as a fraction. You may wish to draw a picture.

9. $\frac{4}{3}$
10. $4\frac{3}{4}$
11. $\frac{13}{4}$
12. $9\frac{1}{6}$
13. $\frac{5}{2}$

LESSON CONTINUES

Practice and Problem Solving

Extra Practice, page 462, Set D

Write a mixed number for each picture.

14. 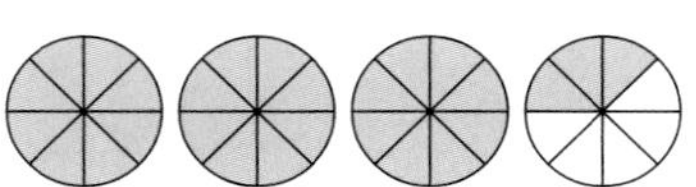

15. 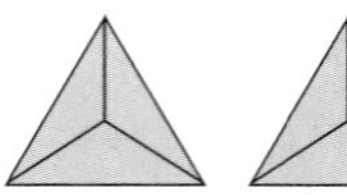

16. 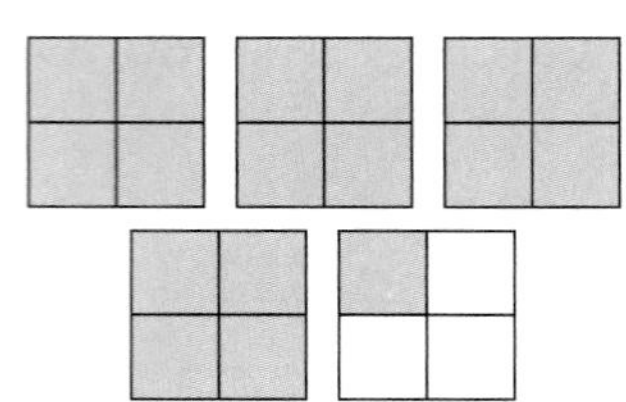

Compare. Write <, >, or = for each ●.

17. $\frac{10}{6}$ ● 3

18. $\frac{13}{4}$ ● $\frac{5}{2}$

19. $4\frac{2}{6}$ ● $4\frac{1}{3}$

20. $\frac{17}{8}$ ● $\frac{22}{7}$

21. $3\frac{3}{4}$ ● $6\frac{1}{2}$

22. 6 ● $\frac{37}{7}$

23. $\frac{19}{3}$ ● $9\frac{1}{2}$

24. $\frac{10}{8}$ ● $1\frac{1}{4}$

25. $3\frac{3}{4}$ ● $\frac{25}{9}$

Rename each fraction as a mixed number and each mixed number as a fraction. You may wish to draw a picture.

26. $\frac{5}{2}$

27. $9\frac{1}{3}$

28. $\frac{10}{8}$

29. $5\frac{1}{4}$

30. $4\frac{5}{12}$

31. $\frac{21}{8}$

32. $7\frac{4}{7}$

33. $\frac{25}{9}$

For 34–38, use the figures at the right.

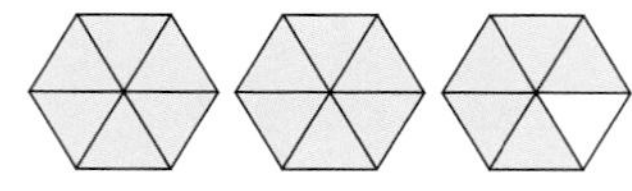

34. Write a fraction for the shaded part in the third figure.

35. How many whole figures are shaded in the picture?

36. What fraction and mixed number can you write for the picture?

37. How can you change the picture to show 3 wholes?

38. How can you change the picture to show $1\frac{4}{6}$?

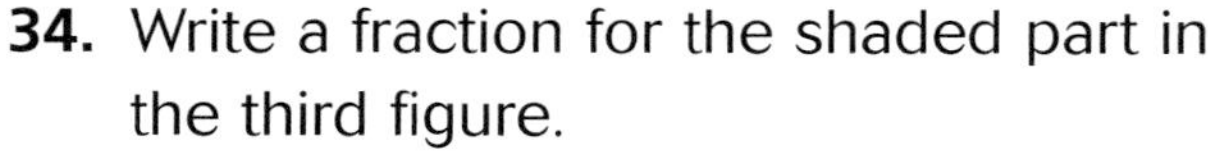

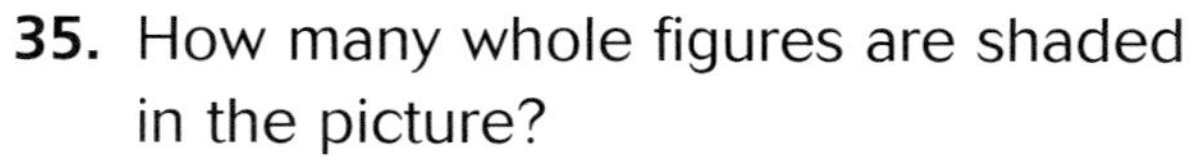

39. A cup holds 8 ounces of liquid. Mary used 24 ounces of milk to make waffles. How many cups of milk did she use?

40. At snack time, Tim drank $\frac{1}{2}$ cup of juice and Cory drank $\frac{3}{4}$ cup of juice. Who drank more than $\frac{5}{8}$ cup of juice?

41. **ESTIMATION** Mrs. James cut some grapefruit into quarters. She used 9 quarters to make juice. Is that closer to 2 or 3 whole grapefruit?

42. **Write About It** When you compare $4\frac{5}{8}$ and $5\frac{4}{8}$, do you need to compare the fraction parts of each mixed number? Explain.

43. In 1940, a man set a world record by riding his bike about 200 miles each day for 500 days. About how many miles did he ride?

44. A serving of rabbit food is $1\frac{1}{4}$ cups. If you have $\frac{3}{2}$ cups of food, do you have enough for a full serving? Explain.

Mixed Review and Test Prep

45. $\begin{array}{r} 3,524 \\ +\ 1,524 \\ \hline \end{array}$ (p. 48)

46. $\begin{array}{r} 67,004 \\ -\ 9,386 \\ \hline \end{array}$ (p. 52)

47. Round 2,316,790 to the nearest thousand. (p. 30)

Write <, >, or = for each ●.

48. 5,236,909 ● 5,237,987 (p. 20)

49. $\frac{3}{8}$ ● $\frac{6}{5}$ (p. 452)

50. $98.02 × 6 (p. 260)

51. **TEST PREP** How many zeros are in the product of 65 and 40,000? (p. 236)

A 2 **C** 4
B 3 **D** 5

52. **TEST PREP** Which product is different from the others? (p. 174)

F 3 × 3 × 2 **H** 3 × 2 × 4
G 2 × 2 × 2 × 3 **J** 2 × 2 × 6

Problem Solving Thinker's Corner

RATIO Double Dutch is a jump rope game that often is played on city streets. In tournaments, teams of 4 jumpers do several stunts. Each team of 4 jumpers uses 2 jump ropes.

A **ratio** compares two amounts. There are three ways to write a ratio comparing the number of jumpers to the number of jump ropes they will use:

4:2 $\frac{4}{2}$ 4 to 2

All of these ratios are read "4 to 2."

The ratio of the number of jumpers to the number of jump ropes will be equivalent to 4:2 no matter how many teams there are.

Write a ratio to compare the number of jumpers to the number of jump ropes. Write each ratio in three ways.

1. 8 jumpers **2.** 6 ropes **3.** 16 jumpers **4.** 10 ropes

Extra Practice

Set A (pp. 446–447)

Write a fraction for the shaded part.

1. 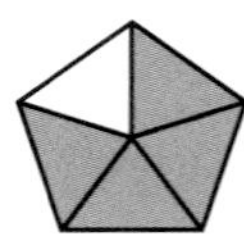
2. 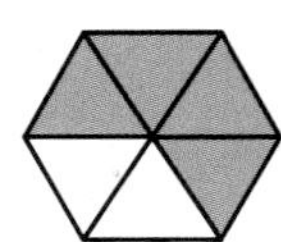
3. 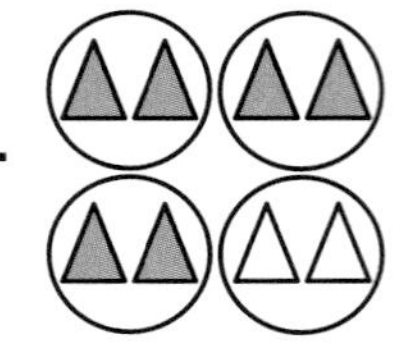
4. 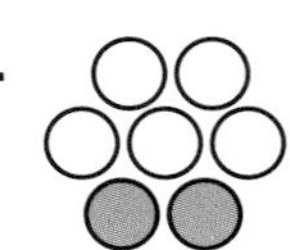

Draw a picture and shade part of it to show the fraction. Write a fraction for the unshaded part.

5. $\frac{1}{3}$
6. $\frac{8}{8}$
7. $\frac{5}{12}$
8. $\frac{3}{3}$
9. $\frac{2}{6}$

Set B (pp. 448–451)

Write two equivalent fractions for each.

1. $\frac{2}{4}$
2. $\frac{4}{4}$
3. $\frac{6}{10}$
4. $\frac{4}{12}$
5. $\frac{6}{9}$

Tell whether each fraction is in simplest form. If not, write it in simplest form.

6. $\frac{1}{5}$
7. $\frac{2}{12}$
8. $\frac{2}{5}$
9. $\frac{6}{8}$
10. $\frac{5}{7}$

Set C (pp. 452–455)

Order the fractions from *greatest* to *least*.

1. $\frac{2}{3}, \frac{2}{5}, \frac{1}{2}$
2. $\frac{3}{4}, \frac{1}{2}, \frac{2}{3}$
3. $\frac{1}{6}, \frac{3}{4}, \frac{2}{5}$
4. $\frac{1}{5}, \frac{1}{3}, \frac{1}{2}$
5. $\frac{4}{12}, \frac{1}{10}, \frac{3}{5}$
6. $\frac{5}{6}, \frac{1}{2}, \frac{2}{3}$
7. $\frac{1}{8}, \frac{3}{5}, \frac{1}{2}$
8. $\frac{3}{8}, \frac{1}{4}, \frac{3}{4}$

Set D (pp. 458–461)

Write a mixed number for each picture.

1. 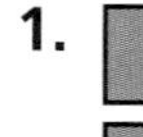 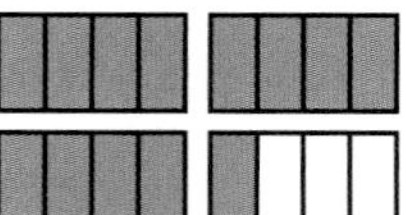
2. 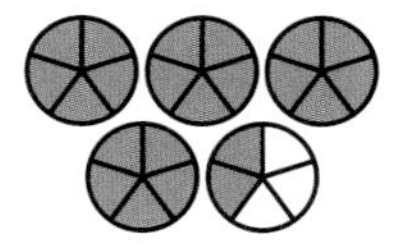
3. 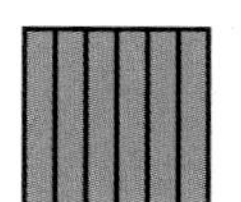 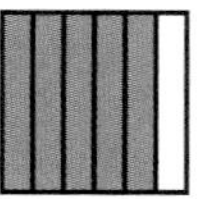

Rename each fraction as a mixed number and each mixed number as a fraction.

4. $\frac{7}{2}$
5. $\frac{13}{8}$
6. $\frac{11}{5}$
7. $\frac{14}{6}$
8. $2\frac{3}{4}$
9. $5\frac{1}{2}$
10. $4\frac{11}{12}$
11. $7\frac{6}{7}$

Review/Test

CHECK VOCABULARY AND CONCEPTS

Choose the best term from the box.

equivalent fractions
mixed number
simplest form

1. Different fractions that name the same amount are called __?__. (p. 448)

2. A __?__ is made up of a whole number and a fraction. (p. 458)

CHECK SKILLS

Write the fraction or mixed number for the shaded part. (pp. 446–447, 458–461)

3. 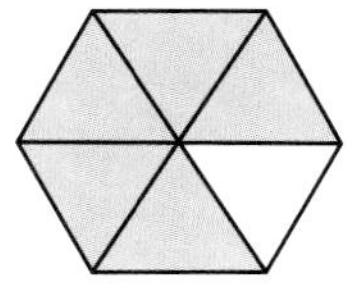

4. 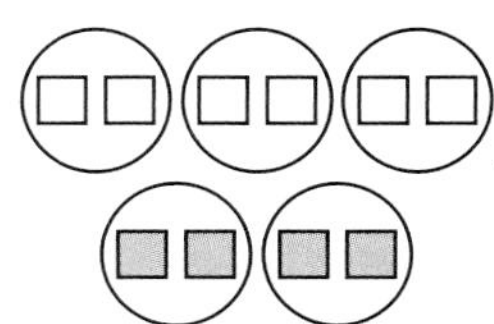

5. 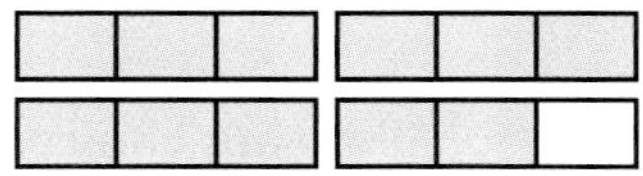

Write two equivalent fractions for each. (pp. 448–451)

6. $\frac{1}{2}$ 7. $\frac{3}{4}$ 8. $\frac{7}{8}$ 9. $\frac{4}{10}$ 10. $\frac{2}{5}$

Write each fraction in simplest form. (pp. 448–451)

11. $\frac{9}{12}$ 12. $\frac{6}{10}$ 13. $\frac{4}{6}$ 14. $\frac{10}{12}$ 15. $\frac{6}{4}$

Write <, >, or = for each ●. (pp. 452–455)

16. $\frac{3}{8}$ ● $\frac{5}{8}$ 17. $\frac{3}{6}$ ● $\frac{4}{8}$ 18. $\frac{2}{3}$ ● $\frac{1}{4}$ 19. $\frac{11}{12}$ ● $\frac{5}{6}$

Rename each fraction as a mixed number and each mixed number as a fraction. (pp. 458–461)

20. $\frac{7}{2}$ 21. $8\frac{1}{3}$ 22. $\frac{16}{3}$ 23. $1\frac{1}{12}$

CHECK PROBLEM SOLVING

Make a model to solve. (pp. 456–457)

24. Tom made $\frac{1}{3}$ of his free throws and Maria made $\frac{4}{6}$ of hers. Who made a greater part of his or her free throws?

25. Sue has a set of wrenches. Three of the sizes are $\frac{1}{2}$, $\frac{3}{4}$, and $\frac{5}{8}$ inch. Put the sizes in order from *least* to *greatest*.

Standardized Test Prep

NUMBER SENSE, CONCEPTS, AND OPERATIONS

1. John ate $\frac{3}{8}$ of a pizza. Which model shows how much pizza John ate?

A 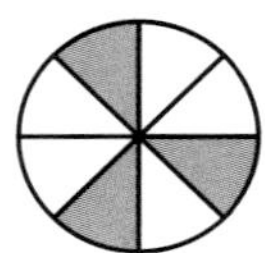

C 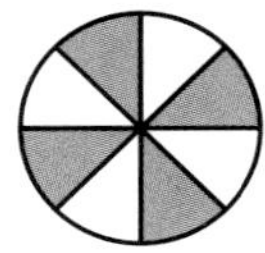

B 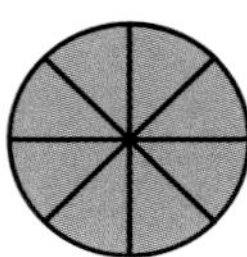

D 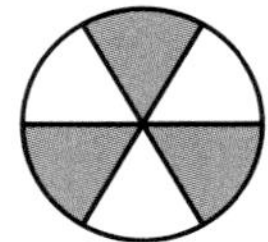

TIP **Eliminate choices.** See item 2. Think about a fraction that names the part of the group. Eliminate the choices with an incorrect denominator.

2. What fraction of this group of balloons has dots?

F $\frac{5}{2}$

G $\frac{2}{3}$

H $\frac{3}{5}$

J $\frac{2}{5}$

3. **Explain It** Last Saturday 3,921 people attended a baseball game. This Saturday 4,210 people attended. Marge ESTIMATED that about 5,000 people attended on the two days. Was she correct? Explain how you decided.

MEASUREMENT

4. When Cy checked the temperature at 9:00 A.M., it was $^-3$°C. By 10:00 A.M. the temperature had dropped by 5°. What was the temperature at 10:00 A.M.?

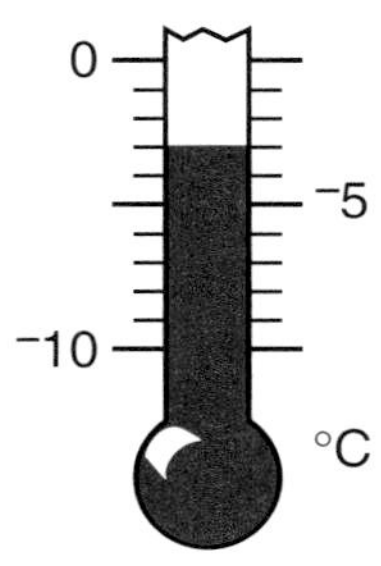

A 8°C

B 2°C

C $^-5$°C

D $^-8$°C

5. The temperature was $^-18$°F at 1:00 P.M. By 3:00 P.M. the temperature had risen by 8°. What was the temperature at 3:00 P.M.?

F 26°F

G 10°F

H $^-10$°F

J $^-26$°F

6. **Explain It** Suzanne made the following schedule for her plane trip from Baltimore to Houston.

SUZANNE'S FLIGHT SCHEDULE	
Baltimore to Jacksonville	
Leaves 9:00 A.M.	Arrives 11:38 A.M.
Jacksonville to Houston	
Leaves 1:50 P.M.	Arrives 3:36 P.M.

To the nearest 5 minutes, about how long will Suzanne wait between flights? Explain your thinking.

ALGEBRAIC THINKING

7. Jared wrote these fractions.

$$\frac{2}{4}, \frac{3}{6}, \frac{4}{8}, \frac{5}{10}$$

He noticed a pattern in his list. If he continues to follow the same pattern, which fraction would he write next?

A $\frac{6}{11}$

B $\frac{6}{12}$

C $\frac{7}{10}$

D $\frac{7}{12}$

8. Which is NOT a value for n in the inequality below?

$$\frac{2}{5} > \frac{n}{10}$$

F 1

G 2

H 3

J 4

9. Explain It Look at the table below.

INPUT	OUTPUT
$\frac{1}{3}$	$\frac{2}{3}$
$\frac{3}{7}$	$\frac{6}{7}$
$\frac{2}{12}$	$\frac{4}{12}$
$\frac{1}{9}$	$\frac{2}{9}$
$\frac{4}{10}$	$\frac{8}{10}$
$\frac{2}{5}$	■

Write a rule. What is the missing fraction? Explain how you decided.

DATA ANALYSIS AND PROBABILITY

10. The graph shows the favorite movies of a class of fourth graders.

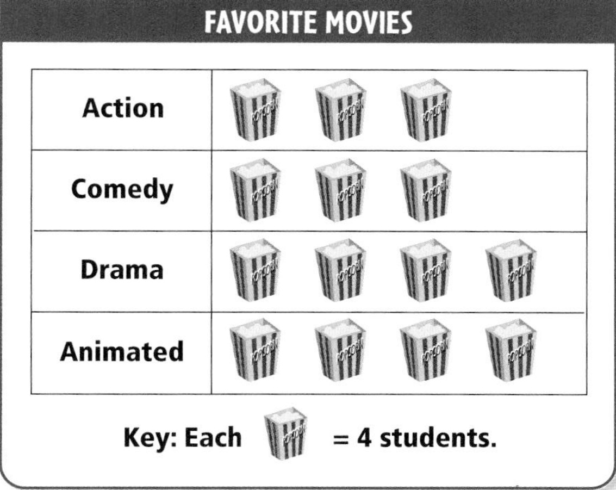

How many more students chose animated movies than chose action movies?

A 1

B 4

C 5

D 6

11. Which is the fraction of numbers that are even on a number cube labeled 1 to 6?

F $\frac{3}{4}$

G $\frac{2}{3}$

H $\frac{1}{2}$

J $\frac{1}{3}$

12. Explain It The Pizza Palace sells small pizzas and large pizzas. Toppings include pepperoni, sausage, and peppers.

How many different one-topping pizza combinations are possible using these three toppings and two sizes? Make a list to show how you decided.

CHAPTER 22 Add and Subtract Fractions and Mixed Numbers

FAST FACT • SCIENCE Lemurs are primates that are native to the island of Madagascar. The Duke University Primate Center in Durham, North Carolina, is home to over 250 lemurs, representing 21 different species.

PROBLEM SOLVING The pictograph shows the amounts of dry food that researchers feed some species of lemurs each day. How much more dry food is a ring-tailed lemur given each day than a grey gentle lemur?

LEMURS' DAILY DIETS

Mongoose lemur	🥣🥣🥣
Ring-tailed lemur	🥣🥣🥣🥣
Crowned lemur	🥣🥣🥣
Grey gentle lemur	🥣

Key: Each 🥣 = $\frac{1}{4}$ cup of dry food.

CHECK WHAT YOU KNOW

Use this page to help you review and remember important skills needed for Chapter 22.

EQUIVALENT FRACTIONS

Write two equivalent fractions for each picture.

1.  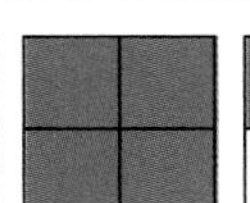 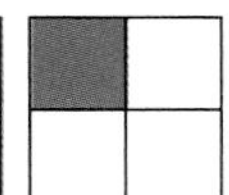

2. 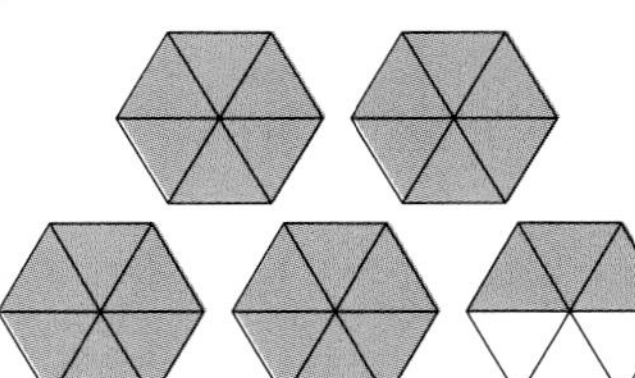

3. 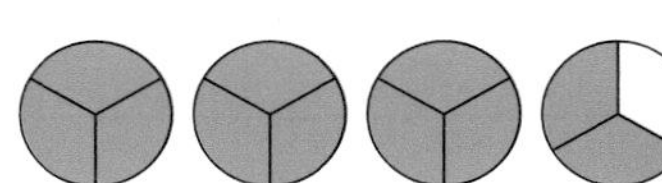

SIMPLEST FORM

Tell whether each fraction is in simplest form. If not, write it in simplest form.

4. $\frac{2}{4}$

5. $\frac{3}{5}$

6. $\frac{8}{12}$

7. $\frac{16}{4}$

8. $\frac{3}{7}$

9. $\frac{15}{3}$

MIXED NUMBERS

Write a mixed number for each picture.

10.

11.

12.

VOCABULARY POWER

REVIEW

fraction [frak′shən] *noun*

The word *fraction* comes from the Latin word *frangere,* which means "to break." Another English word with the same root is *fractured,* which means "broken." Explain how a *fraction* can represent a piece of a "broken" whole.

PREVIEW

like fractions

unlike fractions

www.harcourtschool.com/mathglossary

Add Like Fractions

Quick Review

Write an equivalent fraction for each.

1. $\frac{12}{15}$ 2. $\frac{9}{18}$ 3. $\frac{4}{6}$

4. $\frac{6}{24}$ 5. $\frac{7}{28}$

VOCABULARY

like fractions

Learn

A STEP AT A TIME Pam walked $\frac{1}{4}$ mile to Lori's house. Then, the two girls walked together $\frac{2}{4}$ mile to pottery class. Did Pam walk more than or less than 1 mile?

Like fractions are fractions with the same denominator. You can add like fractions by using fraction bars or drawings.

One Way Use fraction bars.

Find $\frac{1}{4} + \frac{2}{4}$ and compare to 1.

STEP 1

Line up one of the $\frac{1}{4}$ fraction bars under the bar for 1.

STEP 2

Line up two more $\frac{1}{4}$ fraction bars. Count the $\frac{1}{4}$ fraction bars. $\frac{1}{4} + \frac{2}{4} = \frac{3}{4}$

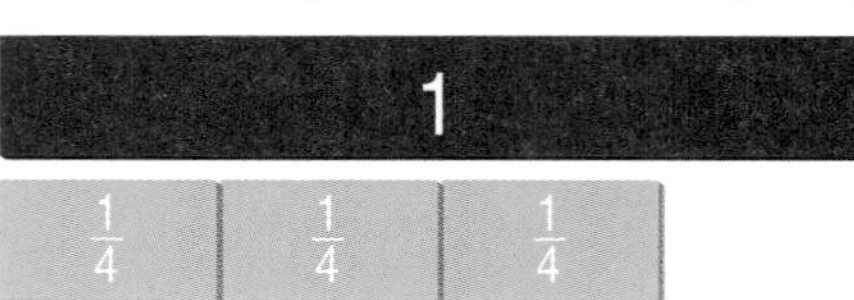

Compare. $\frac{3}{4} < 1$

So, Pam walked less than 1 mile.

Another Way Use drawings.

At pottery class, Pam and Lori divided a block of clay into 8 equal pieces. Pam used 2 pieces of the clay, and Lori used 3 pieces. What fraction of the block of clay did they use?

STEP 1

Draw a rectangle divided into 8 equal parts. Model $\frac{2}{8}$ by shading 2 of the parts.

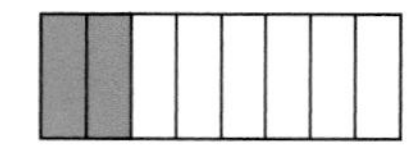

STEP 2

Add $\frac{3}{8}$ by shading 3 more of the parts. There are 5 parts shaded.

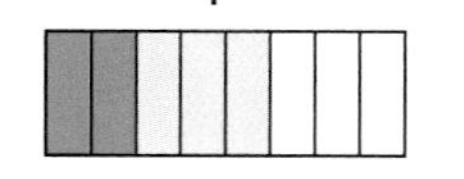

$\frac{2}{8} + \frac{3}{8} = \frac{5}{\square}$

STEP 3

There are 8 equal parts, so the denominator stays the same. Write the sum of the numerators over the denominator.

$\frac{2}{8} + \frac{3}{8} = \frac{5}{8}$

So, Pam and Lori used $\frac{5}{8}$ of the block of clay.

Add Numerators

What if Pam walked $\frac{3}{10}$ mile from class to the library and $\frac{7}{10}$ mile home? How far did Pam walk?

You also can add fractions with like denominators by adding the numerators.

Distance to the library ↓		Distance home ↓		Total distance ↓	
$\frac{3}{10}$	+	$\frac{7}{10}$	=	$\frac{10}{10}$	← Add the numerators. ← The denominator stays the same.

So, Pam walked a total of 1 mile.

Examples

$\frac{2}{10} + \frac{6}{10}$

$\frac{2}{10} + \frac{6}{10} = \frac{8}{10}$

Write the sum in simplest form.

$\frac{8}{10} = \frac{8 \div 2}{10 \div 2} = \frac{4}{5}$

B

$\frac{3}{8} + \frac{5}{8}$

$\frac{3}{8} + \frac{5}{8} = \frac{8}{8}$

Write the sum as a whole number.

$\frac{8}{8} = 1$

C

$\frac{2}{6} + \frac{5}{6}$

$\frac{2}{6} + \frac{5}{6} = \frac{7}{6}$

Write the sum as a mixed number.

$\frac{7}{6} = \frac{6}{6} + \frac{1}{6} = 1\frac{1}{6}$

MATH IDEA To add like fractions, add the numerators. Use the same denominator as in the like fractions.

Check

1. **Explain** why you add only the numerators when adding like fractions.

Find the sum.

2. 

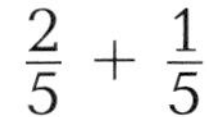

$\frac{2}{5} + \frac{1}{5}$

3. 

$\frac{4}{10} + \frac{3}{10}$

4. $\frac{1}{12}$ | $\frac{1}{12}$ $\frac{1}{12}$ $\frac{1}{12}$ $\frac{1}{12}$

$\frac{1}{12} + \frac{4}{12}$

5. $\frac{1}{2} + \frac{1}{2}$

6. $\frac{3}{4} + \frac{1}{4}$

7. $\frac{4}{8} + \frac{2}{8}$

8. $\frac{1}{3} + \frac{1}{3}$

LESSON CONTINUES

Practice and Problem Solving

Extra Practice, page 484, Set A

Find the sum.

9. $\frac{1}{8}$ $\frac{1}{8}$ $\frac{1}{8}$ $\frac{1}{8}$

$\frac{1}{8} + \frac{3}{8}$

10. $\frac{1}{10}$ $\frac{1}{10}$ $\frac{1}{10}$ $\frac{1}{10}$ $\frac{1}{10}$

$\frac{1}{10} + \frac{4}{10}$

11. $\frac{1}{6}$ $\frac{1}{6}$ $\frac{1}{6}$ $\frac{1}{6}$ $\frac{1}{6}$ $\frac{1}{6}$ $\frac{1}{6}$

$\frac{4}{6} + \frac{3}{6}$

12. $\frac{2}{6} + \frac{4}{6}$ **13.** $\frac{3}{4} + \frac{2}{4}$ **14.** $\frac{3}{7} + \frac{4}{7}$ **15.** $\frac{2}{3} + \frac{2}{3}$

16. $\frac{3}{12} + \frac{5}{12}$ **17.** $\frac{9}{12} + \frac{10}{12}$ **18.** $\frac{3}{10} + \frac{7}{10}$ **19.** $\frac{3}{3} + \frac{1}{3}$

Compare. Write <, >, or = for each ●.

20. $\frac{1}{4} + \frac{2}{4}$ ● $\frac{1}{2}$ **21.** $\frac{1}{6} + \frac{3}{6}$ ● $\frac{2}{3}$ **22.** $\frac{4}{8} + \frac{3}{8}$ ● 1 **23.** $\frac{1}{5} + \frac{1}{5}$ ● $\frac{3}{10}$

24. $\frac{1}{3} + \frac{1}{3}$ ● $\frac{1}{2}$ **25.** $\frac{1}{12} + \frac{6}{12}$ ● $\frac{1}{2}$ **26.** $\frac{4}{10} + \frac{1}{10}$ ● $\frac{2}{5}$ **27.** $\frac{2}{8} + \frac{4}{8}$ ● $\frac{3}{4}$

ALGEBRA For 28–35, find the value of *n*.

28. $\frac{7}{10} + \frac{2}{n} = \frac{9}{10}$ **29.** $\frac{5}{n} + \frac{3}{n} = 1$ **30.** $\frac{5}{n} + \frac{3}{n} = \frac{8}{12}$ **31.** $\frac{4}{n} + \frac{3}{n} = \frac{7}{9}$

32. $\frac{n}{4} + \frac{n}{4} = \frac{2}{4}$ **33.** $\frac{1}{7} + \frac{2}{n} = \frac{3}{n}$ **34.** $\frac{3}{8} + \frac{3}{8} = \frac{n}{4}$ **35.** $\frac{4}{n} + \frac{3}{n} = \frac{7}{11}$

36. Vocabulary Power The word *denominator* comes from a Latin word meaning "to name." Explain how the denominator helps to name a fraction.

37. Write About It Describe how you could make a model from an egg carton to find the sum $\frac{3}{12} + \frac{5}{12}$. Solve.

38. REASONING The three identical jars at the right have pottery glaze. Will all the pottery glaze fit into one of the jars? Explain.

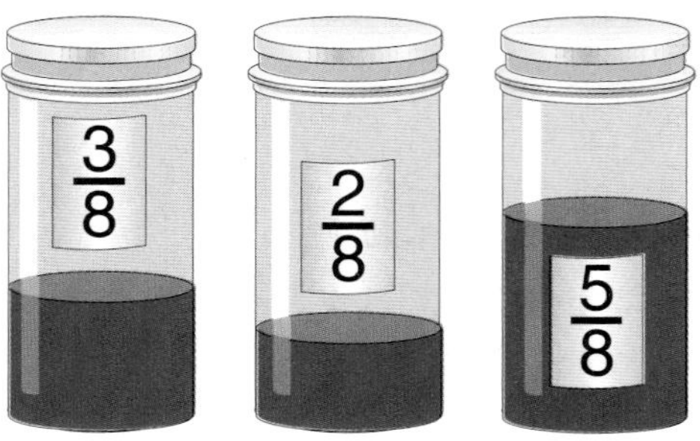

39. What's the Error? Allen says the sum $\frac{3}{5} + \frac{2}{5}$ is $\frac{5}{10}$. Describe his error. Write the correct answer.

40. Each lap around a track is $\frac{1}{4}$ mile. Leslie walked 1 lap around the track on Saturday and walked 2 laps around the track on Sunday. How far did Leslie walk on Saturday and Sunday, in miles?

41. During cooking class, a loaf of bread was sliced into 9 equal pieces. Wendy, Peter, and Jack each got $\frac{1}{9}$ of the loaf. What fraction of the total loaf did they get altogether? How many pieces is this?

Mixed Review and Test Prep

42. Order $\frac{1}{2}$, $\frac{1}{4}$, and $\frac{2}{3}$ from greatest to least. (p. 452)

43. 983×6 (p. 222)

44. $1,820 \times 54$ (p. 258)

45. School starts at 8:15 A.M. and ends at 2:50 P.M. How long is the school day? (p. 98)

46. 82×51 (p. 252)

47. $275 \div 8$ (p. 300)

48. TEST PREP Which fraction is in simplest form? (p. 448)

A $\frac{2}{10}$ **B** $\frac{3}{6}$ **C** $\frac{2}{3}$ **D** $\frac{6}{8}$

49. TEST PREP Evie had 3 packages of pens with 10 pens in each pack. She gave Toby *n* pens. Choose an expression that shows how many she had left. (p. 188)

F $(3 \times 10) + n$ **H** $(3 + n) \times 10$

G $(3 \times 10) - n$ **J** $(3 - n) \times 10$

Problem Solving Thinker's Corner

ESTIMATE FRACTION SUMS You can use benchmarks to estimate fraction sums.

Estimate the sum $\frac{3}{8} + \frac{7}{8} + \frac{1}{8}$.

Use a number line to round fractions to a benchmark of 0, $\frac{1}{2}$, or 1.

$$\frac{3}{8} + \frac{7}{8} + \frac{1}{8}$$
$$\downarrow \quad \downarrow \quad \downarrow$$
$$\frac{1}{2} + 1 + 0 = 1\frac{1}{2}$$

So, $\frac{3}{8} + \frac{7}{8} + \frac{1}{8}$ is about $1\frac{1}{2}$.

Benchmarks

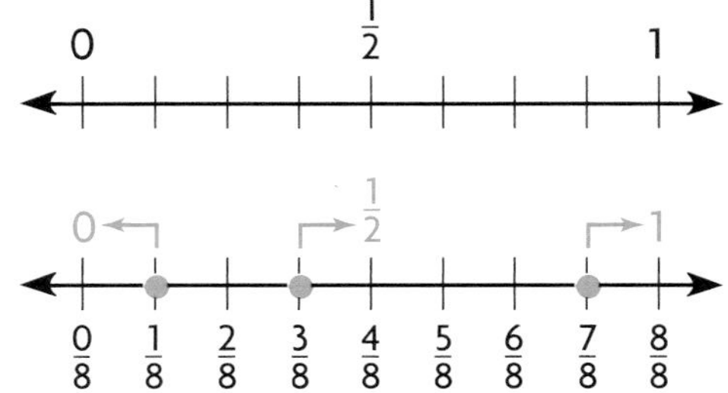

Round each fraction to its nearest benchmark.

Estimate each sum and give the benchmarks you used. Then find the actual sum and compare it to the estimate to determine whether your answer is reasonable.

1. $\frac{1}{6} + \frac{4}{6}$
2. $\frac{3}{8} + \frac{5}{8}$
3. $\frac{7}{12} + \frac{4}{12} + \frac{1}{12}$
4. $\frac{5}{6} + \frac{1}{6} + \frac{3}{6}$

LESSON 2

Subtract Like Fractions

Quick Review

Write in simplest form.

1. $\frac{3}{6}$
2. $\frac{14}{21}$
3. $\frac{6}{24}$
4. $\frac{8}{40}$
5. $\frac{8}{12}$

MATERIALS fraction bars

Explore

How can you subtract two fractions with like denominators?

Activity Use fraction bars to find $\frac{5}{6} - \frac{3}{6}$.

One Way Take away fraction bars.

STEP 1

Line up 5 of the $\frac{1}{6}$ bars.

STEP 2

Take away 3 of the $\frac{1}{6}$ bars.

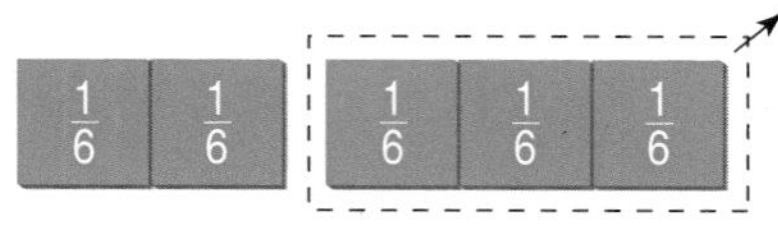

STEP 3

Count the $\frac{1}{6}$ bars left.

There are two $\frac{1}{6}$ bars left.

Another Way Compare two groups of fraction bars.

STEP 1

Line up 5 of the $\frac{1}{6}$ bars.

STEP 2

Line up 3 of the $\frac{1}{6}$ bars.

$\frac{1}{6}$ $\frac{1}{6}$ $\frac{1}{6}$ $\frac{1}{6}$ $\frac{1}{6}$

$\frac{1}{6}$ $\frac{1}{6}$ $\frac{1}{6}$

STEP 3

Compare the rows of bars. Find the difference.

The difference is two $\frac{1}{6}$ bars.

So, $\frac{5}{6} - \frac{3}{6} = \frac{2}{6}$, or $\frac{1}{3}$.

Try It

Find the difference.

a. $\frac{7}{8} - \frac{2}{8}$

b. $\frac{8}{12} - \frac{6}{12}$

c. $\frac{5}{10} - \frac{2}{10}$

d. $\frac{3}{4} - \frac{2}{4}$

I am comparing $\frac{7}{8}$ and $\frac{2}{8}$. What is the difference?

Connect

You can draw pictures to subtract like fractions.

Example Use a drawing to find $\frac{7}{8} - \frac{3}{8}$.

STEP 1

Draw a rectangle divided into 8 equal parts. Model $\frac{7}{8}$ by shading 7 of the parts.

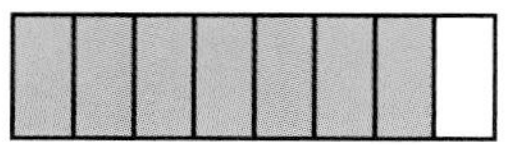

STEP 2

Subtract $\frac{3}{8}$ by crossing out 3 of the shaded parts. There are 4 shaded parts not crossed out.

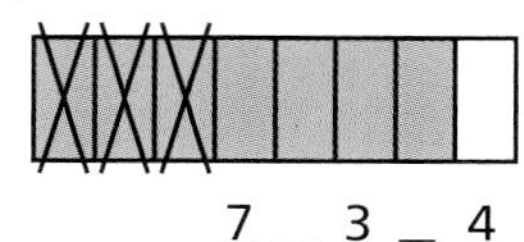

$\frac{7}{8} - \frac{3}{8} = \frac{4}{\blacksquare}$

STEP 3

The denominator stays the same. Write the difference over the denominator.

$\frac{7}{8} - \frac{3}{8} = \frac{4}{8}$

Write the answer in simplest form.

$\frac{4}{8} = \frac{1}{2}$

So, $\frac{7}{8} - \frac{3}{8} = \frac{1}{2}$.

- Find the difference in the numerators of $\frac{7}{8} - \frac{3}{8}$. How does this answer compare to the numerator of the difference, $\frac{4}{8}$, found in the Example?

MATH IDEA To subtract like fractions, use fraction bars, draw a picture, or subtract the numerators. Use the same denominator as in the like fractions.

Practice and Problem Solving

Use fraction bars or draw a picture to find the difference.

1. $\frac{3}{5} - \frac{1}{5}$
2. $\frac{8}{10} - \frac{1}{10}$
3. $\frac{9}{9} - \frac{1}{9}$
4. $\frac{11}{12} - \frac{5}{12}$

Find the difference.

5. $\frac{5}{8} - \frac{4}{8}$
6. $\frac{6}{10} - \frac{2}{10}$
7. $\frac{4}{6} - \frac{1}{6}$
8. $\frac{5}{8} - \frac{2}{8}$
9. In a survey, $\frac{4}{10}$ of the students chose an animal as a mascot. The rest chose a cartoon character. Which type of mascot received more votes? Explain.

Mixed Review and Test Prep

10. List the factors of 36. (p. 338)
11. Write the first five multiples of 7. (p. 338)
12. $595 \div 5$ (p. 300)
13. $438 \div 2$ (p. 300)
14. **TEST PREP** Hannah can fit 32 names on each page of the school directory. She has 416 names. How many pages does she need? (p. 320)

    A 12 **B** 13 **C** 14 **D** 17

LESSON 3

Add and Subtract Mixed Numbers

Quick Review

1. $\frac{1}{4} + \frac{2}{4}$
2. $\frac{1}{3} + \frac{2}{3}$
3. $\frac{2}{5} + \frac{1}{5}$
4. $\frac{4}{6} - \frac{1}{6}$
5. $\frac{5}{8} - \frac{3}{8}$

Learn

DINNER TIME Susan is helping prepare fruit for the animals at the primate center. She has mixed $2\frac{2}{4}$ cups of banana slices with $1\frac{1}{4}$ cups of apple slices. How much fruit has she prepared?

Example 1

Add. $2\frac{2}{4} + 1\frac{1}{4}$

STEP 1

Draw a picture for each mixed number. Add the fractions first.

$$\begin{array}{r} 2\frac{2}{4} \\ +1\frac{1}{4} \\ \hline \frac{3}{4} \end{array}$$

STEP 2

Then add the whole numbers.

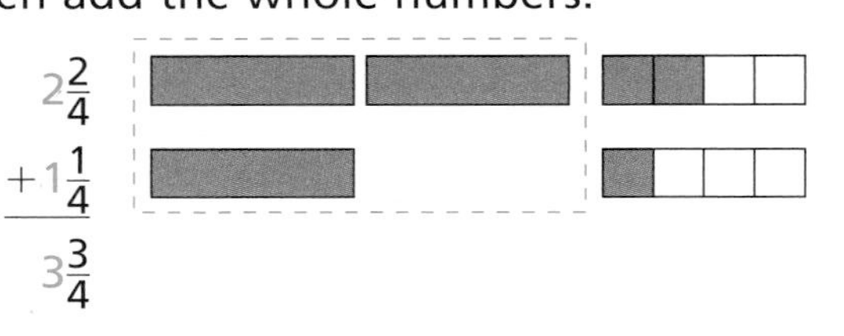

$$\begin{array}{r} 2\frac{2}{4} \\ +1\frac{1}{4} \\ \hline 3\frac{3}{4} \end{array}$$

So, Susan has prepared $3\frac{3}{4}$ cups of fruit.

More Examples

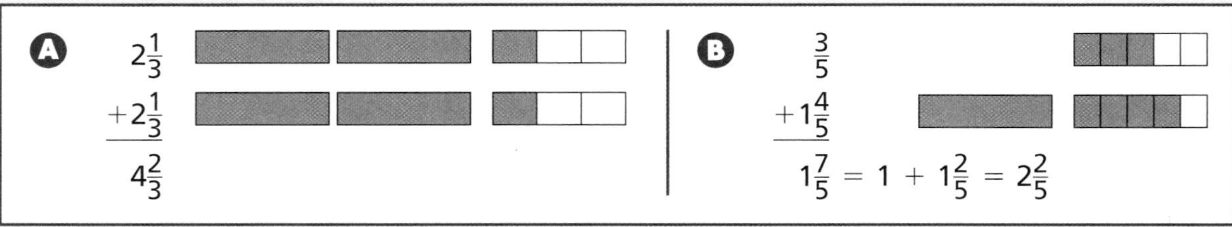

A

$$\begin{array}{r} 2\frac{1}{3} \\ +2\frac{1}{3} \\ \hline 4\frac{2}{3} \end{array}$$

B

$$\begin{array}{r} \frac{3}{5} \\ +1\frac{4}{5} \\ \hline 1\frac{7}{5} \end{array}$$

$1\frac{7}{5} = 1 + 1\frac{2}{5} = 2\frac{2}{5}$

MATH IDEA When you add mixed numbers, add the fractions first, and then add the whole numbers.

Subtract Mixed Numbers

Subtracting mixed numbers is similar to adding mixed numbers.

Susan has $3\frac{5}{8}$ cups of dry food. She gives $2\frac{1}{8}$ cups to a group of ring-tailed lemurs. How much dry food does she have left?

Example 2

Subtract. $3\frac{5}{8} - 2\frac{1}{8}$

STEP 1

Draw a model for the first mixed number. Subtract the fractions first.

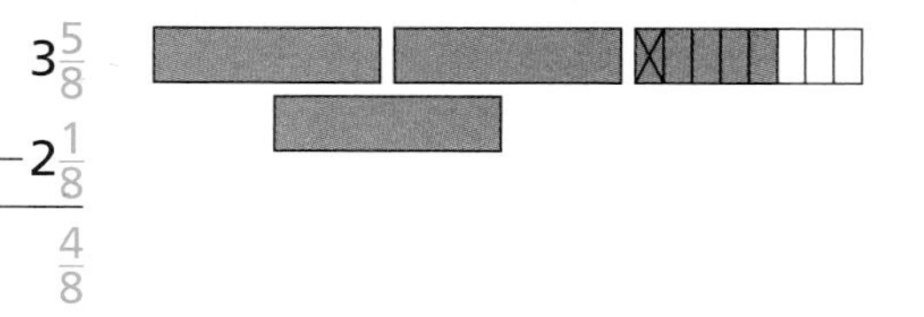

$$\begin{array}{r} 3\frac{5}{8} \\ -2\frac{1}{8} \\ \hline \frac{4}{8} \end{array}$$

STEP 2

Then subtract the whole numbers.

$$\begin{array}{r} 3\frac{5}{8} \\ -2\frac{1}{8} \\ \hline 1\frac{4}{8} \end{array}\text{, or } 1\frac{1}{2}$$

So, Susan has $1\frac{1}{2}$ cups of dry food left.

More Examples

A

$$\begin{array}{r} 5\frac{3}{4} \\ -2\frac{2}{4} \\ \hline 3\frac{1}{4} \end{array}$$

B

$$\begin{array}{r} 2\frac{9}{12} \\ -2\frac{3}{12} \\ \hline \frac{6}{12} \end{array}\text{, or } \frac{1}{2}$$

Check

1. **Explain** how you can check whether your answer to a subtraction problem is correct.

Find the sum or difference.

2. $\begin{array}{r} 2\frac{1}{4} \\ +3\frac{3}{4} \\ \hline \end{array}$

3. $\begin{array}{r} 4\frac{3}{5} \\ +1\frac{3}{5} \\ \hline \end{array}$

4. $\begin{array}{r} 2\frac{3}{5} \\ -1\frac{1}{5} \\ \hline \end{array}$

5. $\begin{array}{r} 2\frac{5}{6} \\ -1\frac{3}{6} \\ \hline \end{array}$

LESSON CONTINUES

Practice and Problem Solving

Extra Practice, page 484, Set B

Find the sum or difference.

6. $3\frac{1}{3} + 2\frac{1}{3}$

7. $4\frac{3}{4} - 1\frac{1}{4}$

8. $5\frac{1}{4} + 1\frac{2}{4}$

9. $3\frac{5}{6} - 2\frac{2}{6}$

10. $6\frac{10}{12} - 2\frac{4}{12}$

11. $8\frac{1}{6} + 1\frac{5}{6}$

12. $5\frac{8}{10} - 3\frac{3}{10}$

13. $7\frac{2}{9} + 4\frac{8}{9}$

14. $4\frac{3}{6} + 2\frac{4}{6}$

15. $4\frac{2}{2} - 3\frac{1}{2}$

16. $8\frac{7}{10} + 7\frac{2}{10}$

17. $4\frac{6}{8} - 1\frac{2}{8}$

18. $3\frac{5}{6} - 1\frac{4}{6}$

19. $5\frac{3}{8} + 1\frac{5}{8}$

20. $6\frac{5}{8} - 3\frac{2}{8}$

21. $7\frac{9}{12} + 4\frac{2}{12}$

Compare. Write <, >, or = for each ●.

22. $1\frac{2}{8} + 3\frac{3}{8}$ ● $4\frac{1}{2}$

23. $5\frac{3}{5} + 4\frac{2}{5}$ ● 10

24. $7\frac{2}{4} + 9\frac{1}{4}$ ● $16\frac{7}{8}$

25. $4\frac{5}{6} - 2\frac{2}{6}$ ● $2\frac{1}{2}$

26. $12\frac{8}{10} - 8\frac{2}{10}$ ● $4\frac{4}{5}$

27. $12\frac{4}{5} - 7\frac{2}{5}$ ● $5\frac{3}{10}$

28. $5\frac{2}{3} - 3\frac{1}{3}$ ● $8\frac{2}{3}$

29. $6\frac{5}{6} - 1\frac{2}{6}$ ● $5\frac{1}{2}$

30. $4\frac{3}{8} + 6\frac{1}{8}$ ● $10\frac{1}{4}$

ALGEBRA For 31–33, find the value of n.

31. $3\frac{6}{8} + 5\frac{2}{8} = n$

32. $9\frac{6}{10} + 11\frac{n}{10} = 20\frac{9}{10}$

33. $7\frac{4}{6} - 4\frac{1}{6} = 3\frac{3}{6}$, or $3\frac{1}{n}$

USE DATA For 34–35, use the table.

AREAS OF ANIMAL ENCLOSURES	
Animals	**Area (in acres)**
Giraffes	$5\frac{1}{6}$
Zebras	$9\frac{4}{6}$
Lions	$3\frac{2}{6}$

34. What is the total area of the enclosures for the zebras and the giraffes?

35. How much larger is the zebras' enclosure than the lions' enclosure?

36. **What's the Question?** Two mixed numbers are $1\frac{1}{4}$ and $2\frac{1}{4}$. The answer is $3\frac{1}{2}$.

37. **FAST FACT • SCIENCE** A ring-tailed lemur's tail is about $15\frac{1}{8}$ inches long. Its head and body are about $11\frac{6}{8}$ inches long. How long is a ring-tailed lemur in all?

38. Draw pictures to represent the mixed numbers $3\frac{1}{4}$ and $1\frac{1}{2}$. Explain how to redraw the second mixed number so you could add them together.

Mixed Review and Test Prep

39. $\begin{array}{r} 5{,}463 \\ \times \quad 8 \\ \hline \end{array}$ (p. 222)

40. $\begin{array}{r} \$7{,}492 \\ \times \quad 28 \\ \hline \end{array}$ (p. 258)

41. Mrs. Troy had 6 cans of apple juice. Keisha, Geoffry, and Latika each drank 1 can. Mr. Troy drank 2 cans. What fraction of the apple juice is left? (p. 472)

42. $(\blacksquare \times 6) - 13 = 35$ (p. 188)

43. **TEST PREP** If a water cooler bottle holds 12 gallons of water, how many gallons do 150 bottles hold? (p. 256)

A 180 C 18,000
B 1,800 D 180,000

44. **TEST PREP** Find the elapsed time from 12:45 P.M. to 5:18 P.M. (p. 98)

F 3 hr 40 min H 4 hr 33 min
G 4 hr 5 min J 5 hr 20 min

Problem Solving Thinker's Corner

ESTIMATE WITH FRACTIONS You can use fraction models to estimate whether fractions are greater than or less than $\frac{1}{2}$.

A pizza is cut into eighths. Ty and Ron eat $\frac{3}{8}$ of the pizza. Is the part that is left *greater than* or *less than* $\frac{1}{2}$ of the whole?

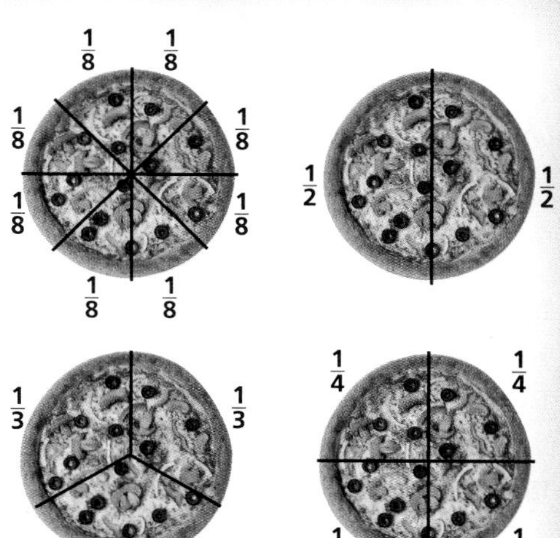

Look at the picture. Compare $\frac{5}{8}$ with $\frac{1}{2}$. You can see that $\frac{5}{8} > \frac{1}{2}$.

Compare. Write < or > for each ●.

1. $\frac{3}{4}$ ● $\frac{1}{2}$
2. $\frac{1}{3}$ ● $\frac{1}{2}$
3. $\frac{3}{8}$ ● $\frac{1}{2}$
4. $\frac{3}{5}$ ● $\frac{1}{2}$

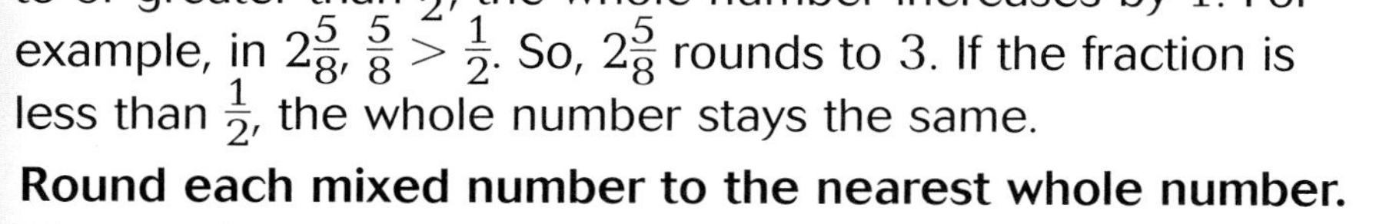
You can round fractions and mixed numbers to the nearest whole number. If the fractional part of a mixed number is equal to or greater than $\frac{1}{2}$, the whole number increases by 1. For example, in $2\frac{5}{8}$, $\frac{5}{8} > \frac{1}{2}$. So, $2\frac{5}{8}$ rounds to 3. If the fraction is less than $\frac{1}{2}$, the whole number stays the same.

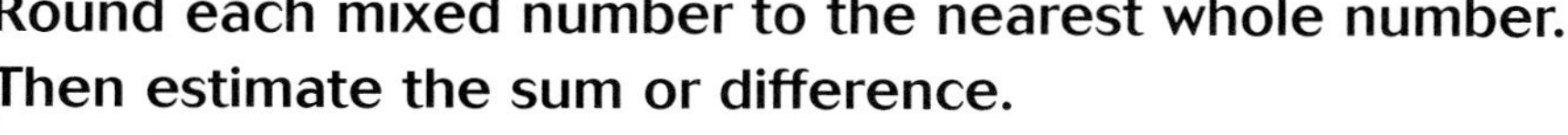
Round each mixed number to the nearest whole number. Then estimate the sum or difference.

5. $1\frac{1}{4} + 4\frac{3}{4}$
6. $3\frac{1}{5} + 5\frac{1}{5}$
7. $2\frac{4}{5} - 2\frac{3}{5}$
8. $2\frac{3}{4} + 5\frac{1}{4}$
9. $4\frac{1}{3} - 1\frac{2}{3}$
10. $3\frac{1}{8} + 6\frac{5}{8}$

LESSON 4

Problem Solving Skill
Choose the Operation

Quick Review

1. $\frac{2}{4} + \frac{1}{4}$
2. $\frac{3}{7} + \frac{4}{7}$
3. $\frac{4}{9} + \frac{2}{9}$
4. $\frac{5}{8} + \frac{4}{8}$
5. $\frac{3}{4} - \frac{2}{4}$

UNDERSTAND PLAN SOLVE CHECK

WANT SOME FLIES WITH THAT? Gorillas and chimpanzees have similar diets in the wild. These circle graphs show the makeup of each animal's diet.

Study the data. Then read Problems A and B.

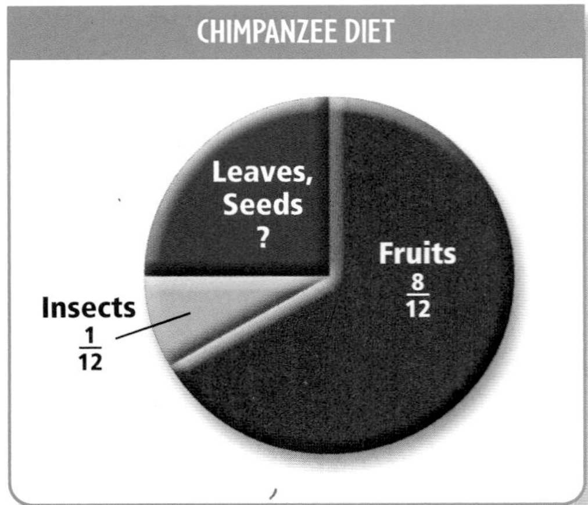

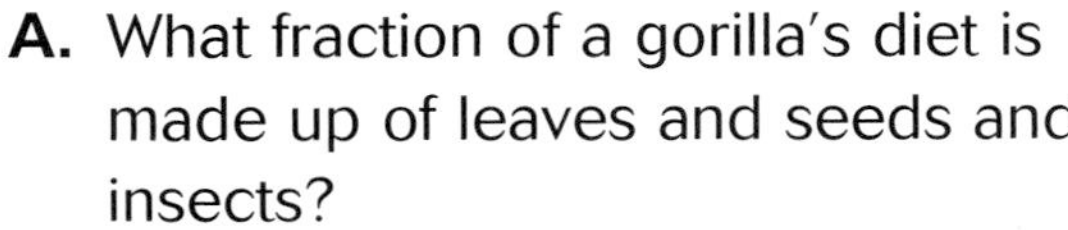

A. What fraction of a gorilla's diet is made up of leaves and seeds and insects?

B. How much more of a chimpanzee's diet is made up of fruits than insects?

MATH IDEA Before you solve a problem, read it carefully and think about how the numbers are related. Then decide which operation is needed to solve the problem.

Talk About It

- Discuss how you would solve Problems A and B. Then solve.
- What operation would you use to find the fraction of a chimpanzee's diet that is made up of fruits or leaves and seeds? Explain how you know.
- What operation would you use to find out how much greater a fraction of its diet insects are for a gorilla than for a chimpanzee? Explain how you know.
- What fraction of a gorilla's diet is made up of fruits? What fraction of a chimpanzee's diet is made up of leaves and seeds? Copy and complete the circle graphs.

Problem Solving Practice

Write the operation. Then solve the problem.

1. Mei ate $\frac{1}{12}$ of the watermelon and Billy ate $\frac{2}{12}$. What fraction of the watermelon did they eat?
2. Michelle practiced the piano for $\frac{5}{6}$ hour and Seth practiced for $\frac{3}{6}$ hour. How much longer did Michelle practice than Seth?

For a science report on apes, Lloyd says that he wrote $\frac{2}{4}$ page more than Mary and Bob combined. Mary wrote $\frac{3}{4}$ page and Bob wrote $1\frac{1}{4}$ pages. How many pages did Lloyd write?

3. Which expression could you use to solve the problem?

   A $\left(\frac{5}{4} - \frac{3}{4}\right) - \frac{2}{4}$ **C** $\left(\frac{5}{4} - \frac{3}{4}\right) + \frac{2}{4}$

   B $\left(\frac{3}{4} + \frac{5}{4}\right) + \frac{2}{4}$ **D** $\left(\frac{5}{4} + \frac{3}{4}\right) - \frac{2}{4}$

4. Which is NOT an answer to the question?

   F $\frac{10}{4}$ **H** $2\frac{2}{4}$

   G $\frac{6}{4}$ **J** $2\frac{1}{2}$

Mixed Applications

USE DATA For 5–7, use the graph.

Mr. Smith measured the amount of rainfall for five days. The measurements are shown on the graph.

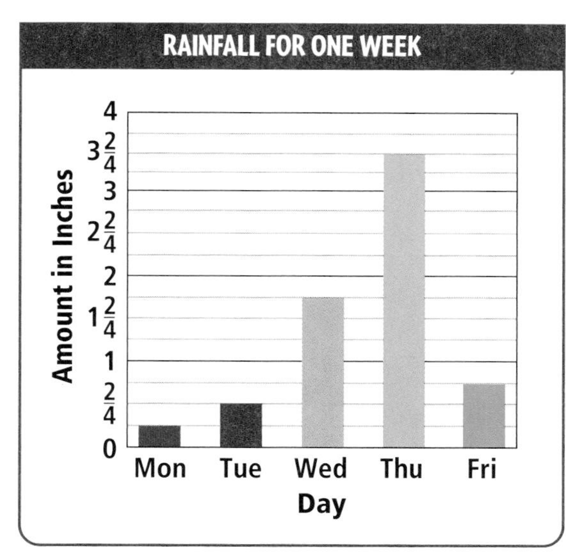

5. What was the difference in the rainfall amounts on Friday and on Monday?
6. Find the total amount of rainfall for the five days.
7. Was the total rainfall for the first two days greater than the rainfall amount on Friday? Explain.
8. Arjun spent 3 of his 8 quarters at the store. He gave a friend 2 quarters. What fraction of his quarters does he have left?
9. **Write About It** Explain how you know what operation to use when solving a word problem.
10. **REASONING** Find a number that could come next in the sequence. $0, \frac{1}{2}, 1, \frac{3}{2}, 2, \frac{5}{2}, ■$. Write a rule.
11. Find the value for ▲ that makes the equation true.

    $▲ \times 3{,}000 = 360{,}000$

LESSON 5

Add Unlike Fractions

Quick Review

1. $\frac{7}{8} + \frac{2}{8}$
2. $\frac{2}{6} + \frac{3}{6}$
3. $\frac{3}{5} + \frac{1}{5}$
4. $\frac{10}{12} + \frac{3}{12}$
5. $\frac{9}{18} + \frac{2}{18}$

VOCABULARY

unlike fractions

MATERIALS fraction bars

Explore

Unlike fractions are fractions with different denominators. When you add fractions, you need to have the same denominators. This activity shows how to use fraction bars to add unlike fractions.

Activity 1

Find $\frac{1}{2} + \frac{1}{4}$.

STEP 1

Model with fraction bars. Place one $\frac{1}{2}$ bar and one $\frac{1}{4}$ bar together under the bar for 1.

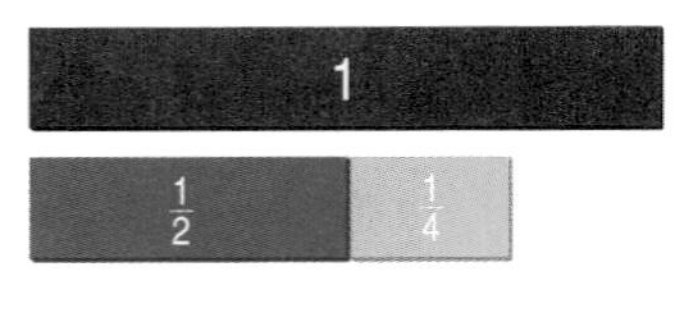

STEP 2

Find the like fraction bars that together are equivalent to $\frac{1}{2} + \frac{1}{4}$ in length.

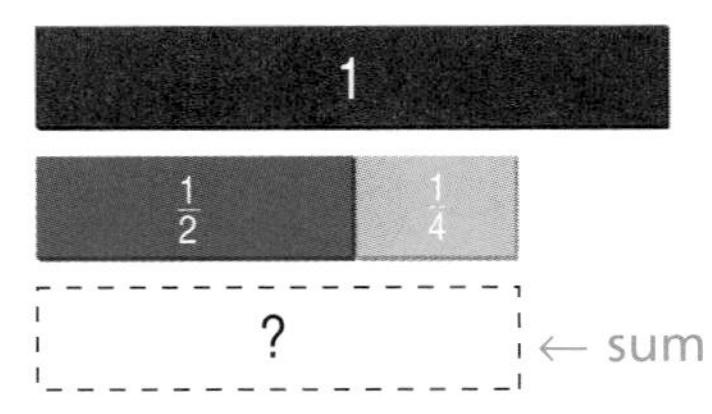

STEP 3

Since $\frac{1}{2} = \frac{2}{4}$, three $\frac{1}{4}$ fraction bars are equal in length to $\frac{1}{2} + \frac{1}{4}$.

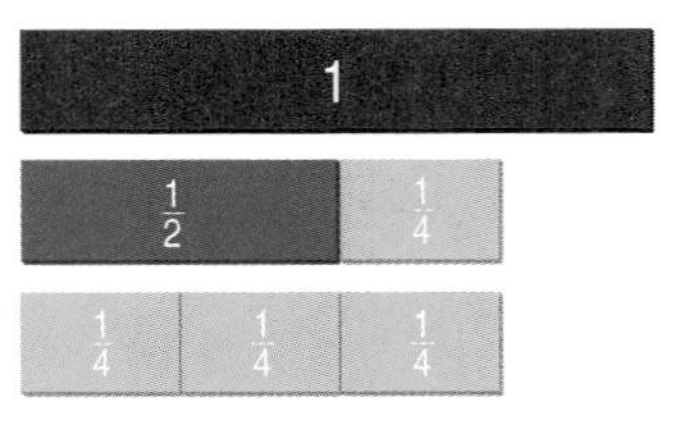

So, $\frac{1}{2} + \frac{1}{4} = \frac{3}{4}$.

- What would your answer have been if you had used $\frac{1}{8}$ fraction bars instead of $\frac{1}{4}$ fraction bars? How is that number related to $\frac{3}{4}$?

Try It

Use fraction bars to find the sum. Draw a picture of your model.

a. $\frac{1}{4} + \frac{3}{8}$

b. $\frac{1}{3} + \frac{1}{6}$

c. $\frac{1}{6} + \frac{5}{12}$

d. $\frac{3}{4} + \frac{1}{6}$

How many $\frac{1}{8}$ bars are needed to show an equivalent fraction for $\frac{1}{4}$?

Connect

When you add fractions with unlike denominators, you need to find equivalent fractions with like denominators.

Activity 2

Find $\frac{2}{3} + \frac{1}{2}$.

STEP 1

Place two $\frac{1}{3}$ fraction bars under a bar for 1. Then place one $\frac{1}{2}$ fraction bar beside the two $\frac{1}{3}$ bars.

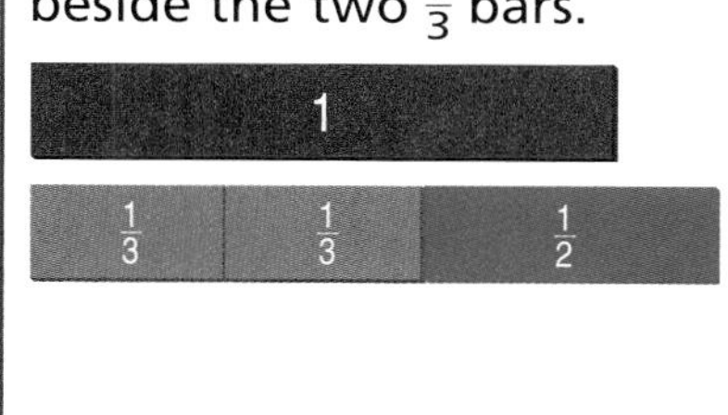

STEP 2

Find like fraction bars that are equivalent to $\frac{2}{3}$ and $\frac{1}{2}$.

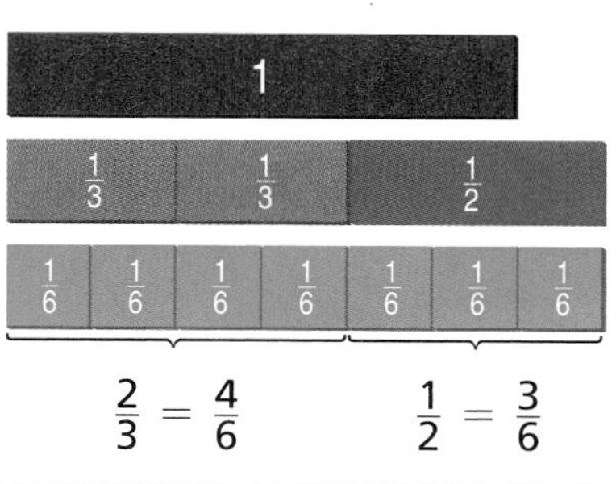

$\frac{2}{3} = \frac{4}{6}$ $\frac{1}{2} = \frac{3}{6}$

STEP 3

Add the like fractions. Write the answer as a mixed number.

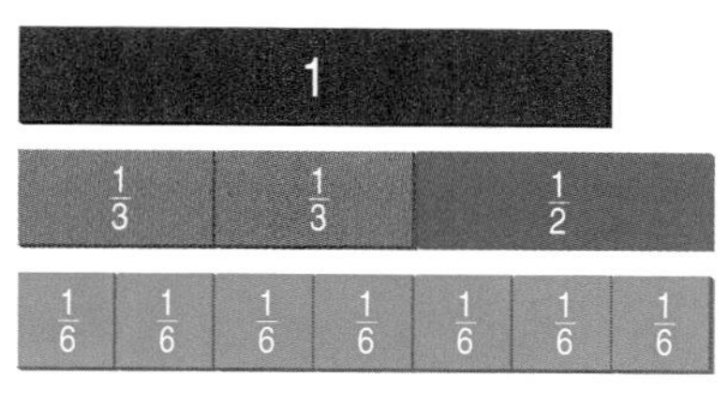

So, $\frac{2}{3} + \frac{1}{2} = \frac{4}{6} + \frac{3}{6} = \frac{7}{6}$, or $1\frac{1}{6}$.

Practice and Problem Solving

Use fraction bars to find the sum. Draw a picture of your model.

1. $\frac{1}{10} + \frac{3}{5}$ **2.** $\frac{1}{3} + \frac{2}{6}$ **3.** $\frac{2}{4} + \frac{1}{6}$

4. $\frac{2}{5} + \frac{1}{2}$ **5.** $\frac{2}{3} + \frac{1}{4}$ **6.** $\frac{1}{12} + \frac{3}{4}$ **7.** $\frac{1}{5} + \frac{3}{10}$

8. Lisa is making a layered bow and has $9\frac{7}{12}$ yards of ribbon. If she needs $5\frac{2}{3}$ yards for the large bow and $2\frac{3}{4}$ yards for the small bow, how many yards will she have left?

9. **What's the Question?** Kathy ran $2\frac{2}{10}$ miles on Saturday and $4\frac{7}{10}$ miles on Sunday. The answer is $2\frac{1}{2}$ miles.

Mixed Review and Test Prep

Order from *least* to *greatest*. (p. 452)

10. $\frac{1}{3}, \frac{1}{2}, \frac{1}{10}$ **11.** $\frac{3}{6}, \frac{2}{8}, \frac{3}{9}$

12. $24\overline{)369}$ (p. 320) **13.** $32\overline{)512}$ (p. 320)

14. **TEST PREP** Eric ate $\frac{4}{3}$ apples. What mixed number represents how many apples Eric ate? (p. 458)

A $1\frac{4}{3}$ **B** $1\frac{3}{3}$ **C** $1\frac{1}{3}$ **D** 1

LESSON 6

Subtract Unlike Fractions

Quick Review

1. $\frac{6}{10} - \frac{2}{10}$
2. $\frac{10}{12} - \frac{3}{12}$
3. $\frac{6}{14} - \frac{2}{14}$
4. $\frac{10}{15} - \frac{9}{15}$
5. $\frac{8}{9} - \frac{2}{9}$

MATERIALS fraction bars

Explore

Use fraction bars to find $\frac{5}{8} - \frac{1}{4}$.

Activity 1

STEP 1

Place five $\frac{1}{8}$ fraction bars under the bar for 1. Then place one $\frac{1}{4}$ fraction bar under the five $\frac{1}{8}$ bars.

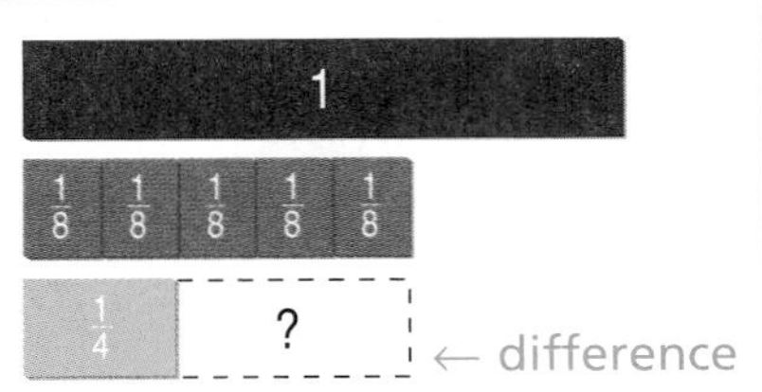

STEP 2

Compare the bars. Find like fraction bars that fit exactly under the difference $\frac{5}{8} - \frac{1}{4}$.

Three $\frac{1}{8}$ bars fit under → the difference.

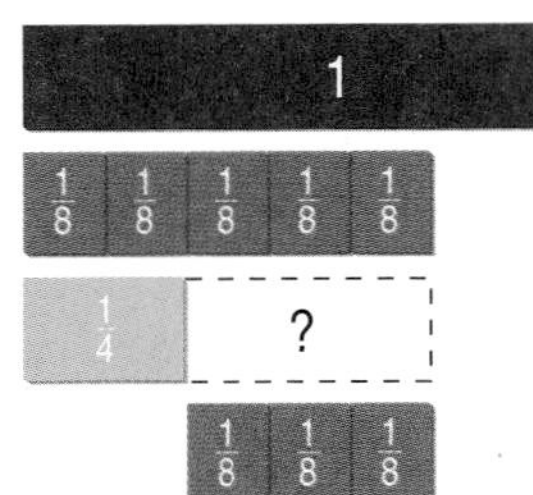

So, $\frac{5}{8} - \frac{1}{4} = \frac{3}{8}$.

- **REASONING** Suppose the problem is $\frac{6}{8} - \frac{1}{4}$. What is the difference?

Technology Link

More Practice: Harcourt Mega Math Fraction Action, *Fraction Flare-Up*, Levels J and K

Try It

Use fraction bars to find the difference. Draw a picture of your model.

a. $\frac{5}{6} - \frac{1}{3}$ b. $\frac{7}{8} - \frac{1}{4}$

c. $\frac{1}{2} - \frac{1}{4}$ d. $\frac{9}{10} - \frac{2}{5}$

How many $\frac{1}{6}$ fraction bars are needed to show the difference $\frac{5}{6} - \frac{1}{3}$?

Connect

When you subtract unlike fractions, you need to find equivalent fractions with like denominators.

Activity 2

Find $\frac{2}{3} - \frac{1}{4}$.

STEP 1

Place two $\frac{1}{3}$ fraction bars under a bar for 1. Then place one $\frac{1}{4}$ fraction bar under the two $\frac{1}{3}$ bars.

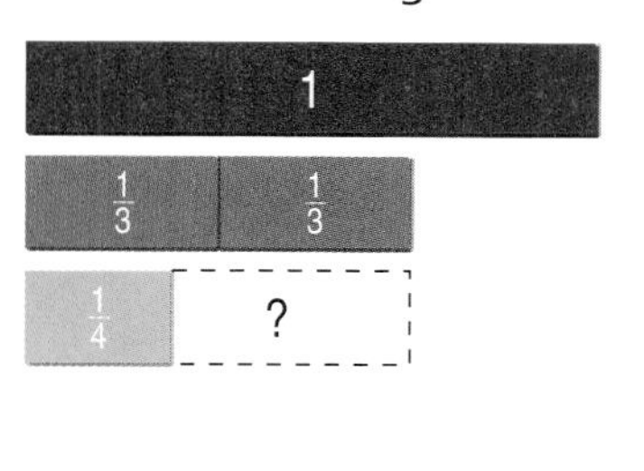

STEP 2

Find like fraction bars that are equivalent to $\frac{2}{3}$ and $\frac{1}{4}$.

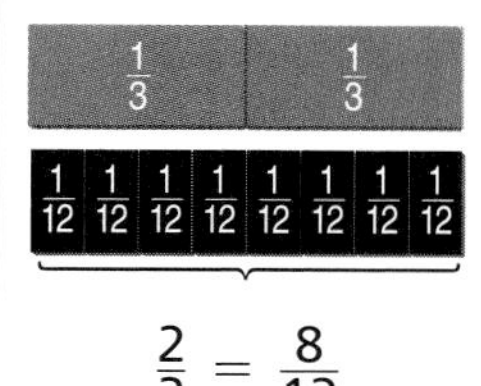

$\frac{2}{3} = \frac{8}{12}$ $\quad$ $\frac{1}{4} = \frac{3}{12}$

STEP 3

Compare the rows of bars. Find the number of $\frac{1}{12}$ bars that fit exactly under the difference $\frac{2}{3} - \frac{1}{4}$.

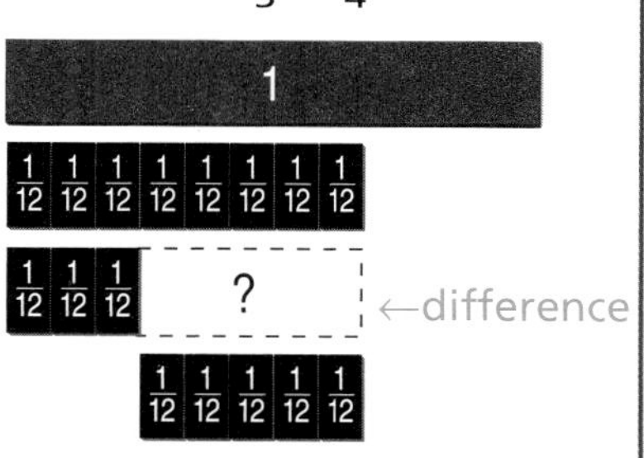

So, $\frac{2}{3} - \frac{1}{4} = \frac{8}{12} - \frac{3}{12} = \frac{5}{12}$.

Practice and Problem Solving

Use fraction bars to find the difference. Draw a picture of your model.

1. $\frac{3}{4} - \frac{1}{3}$ $\quad$ **2.** $\frac{6}{8} - \frac{1}{4}$ $\quad$ **3.** $\frac{9}{10} - \frac{3}{5}$ $\quad$ **4.** $\frac{7}{12} - \frac{1}{4}$

5. Crystal has $\frac{11}{12}$ cup of sugar to make two cakes. The first cake needs $\frac{2}{3}$ cup of sugar and the second needs $\frac{1}{4}$ cup of sugar. Does she have enough sugar to make both cakes? Explain.

6. Find the distance, in miles, from York to Camden.

19 mi — 43 mi — 28 mi

York — Clermont — Athens — Camden

Mixed Review and Test Prep

7. List the factors of 7. Is 7 prime or composite? (p. 342)

Rename as mixed numbers. (p. 458)

8. $\frac{11}{4}$ $\quad$ **9.** $\frac{10}{3}$ $\quad$ **10.** $\frac{8}{5}$

11. **TEST PREP** John and his brother ate $\frac{3}{8}$ of a cake. His sisters ate $\frac{1}{4}$ of the same cake. How much cake was eaten in all? (p. 480)

A $\frac{1}{8}$ $\quad$ **B** $\frac{3}{4}$ $\quad$ **C** $\frac{1}{2}$ $\quad$ **D** $\frac{5}{8}$

Extra Practice

Set A (pp. 468–471)

Find the sum.

1. $\frac{1}{8} + \frac{5}{8}$
2. $\frac{2}{6} + \frac{1}{6}$
3. $\frac{4}{12} + \frac{5}{12}$
4. $\frac{3}{10} + \frac{4}{10}$
5. $\frac{1}{4} + \frac{2}{4}$
6. $\frac{2}{7} + \frac{3}{7}$
7. $\frac{2}{10} + \frac{5}{10}$
8. $\frac{4}{10} + \frac{6}{10}$
9. $\frac{4}{8} + \frac{2}{8}$
10. $\frac{7}{12} + \frac{5}{12}$
11. $\frac{4}{5} + \frac{3}{5}$
12. $\frac{8}{12} + \frac{2}{12}$
13. $\frac{4}{5} + \frac{2}{5}$
14. $\frac{6}{7} + \frac{1}{7}$
15. $\frac{5}{8} + \frac{1}{8}$
16. $\frac{3}{4} + \frac{3}{4}$
17. $\frac{3}{10} + \frac{2}{10}$
18. $\frac{5}{12} + \frac{8}{12}$
19. $\frac{5}{6} + \frac{5}{6}$
20. $\frac{2}{3} + \frac{2}{3}$

21. There was $\frac{2}{3}$ cup of milk left in the refrigerator after Robbie used $\frac{1}{3}$ cup of milk in his oatmeal. How much milk was in the refrigerator before Robbie ate his oatmeal?

22. On Monday $\frac{3}{10}$ inch of snow fell in Leigh's yard. On Tuesday $\frac{7}{10}$ inch of snow fell. How much snow fell in all?

Set B (pp. 474–477)

Find the sum or difference.

1. $4\frac{2}{5} + 3\frac{1}{5}$
2. $3\frac{2}{4} + 3\frac{3}{4}$
3. $2\frac{1}{3} + 4\frac{1}{3}$
4. $3\frac{5}{9} + 4\frac{4}{9}$
5. $3\frac{2}{10} + 6\frac{3}{10}$
6. $8\frac{1}{2} + 7\frac{1}{2}$
7. $5\frac{2}{3} - 4\frac{1}{3}$
8. $8\frac{8}{12} - 5\frac{3}{12}$
9. $5\frac{4}{6} - 1\frac{3}{6}$
10. $7\frac{4}{5} - 3\frac{2}{5}$
11. $4\frac{5}{10} - 3\frac{2}{10}$
12. $3\frac{3}{4} - 1\frac{1}{4}$

13. Joseph fed his dogs. Brewster got $2\frac{1}{4}$ cups of dry dog food, and Beatrice got $1\frac{1}{4}$ cups of dry dog food. How much dry dog food was used altogether?

14. Sam's book report is $3\frac{4}{8}$ pages long. Mary's book report is $2\frac{2}{8}$ pages long. Whose report is longer? How many pages longer?

Review/Test

CHECK VOCABULARY AND CONCEPTS

Choose the best term from the box.

like fractions
unlike fractions
numerators
denominators

1. Fractions with different denominators are __?__. (p. 480)
2. Fractions that have the same denominator are __?__. (p. 468)
3. Add like fractions by adding the __?__ and using the same denominator. (p. 468)

CHECK SKILLS

Find the sum. (pp. 468–471; 474–477)

4. $\frac{2}{8} + \frac{5}{8}$
5. $\frac{2}{3} + \frac{1}{3}$
6. $\frac{1}{12} + \frac{4}{12}$
7. $\frac{2}{10} + \frac{6}{10}$
8. $\begin{array}{r} 3\frac{1}{4} \\ +12\frac{3}{4} \\ \hline \end{array}$
9. $\begin{array}{r} 2\frac{2}{3} \\ +1\frac{2}{3} \\ \hline \end{array}$
10. $\begin{array}{r} 2\frac{1}{4} \\ +8\frac{2}{4} \\ \hline \end{array}$
11. $\begin{array}{r} 7\frac{6}{8} \\ +5\frac{3}{8} \\ \hline \end{array}$

Find the difference. (pp. 472–477)

12. $\frac{5}{8} - \frac{2}{8}$
13. $\frac{3}{4} - \frac{1}{4}$
14. $\frac{5}{5} - \frac{2}{5}$
15. $\frac{10}{12} - \frac{3}{12}$
16. $\begin{array}{r} 5\frac{8}{12} \\ -2\frac{5}{12} \\ \hline \end{array}$
17. $\begin{array}{r} 3\frac{3}{5} \\ -\ \frac{2}{5} \\ \hline \end{array}$
18. $\begin{array}{r} 9\frac{5}{8} \\ -7\frac{3}{8} \\ \hline \end{array}$
19. $\begin{array}{r} 2\frac{11}{12} \\ -2\frac{5}{12} \\ \hline \end{array}$

Use fraction bars to find the sum or difference. (pp. 480–483)

20. $\frac{1}{4} + \frac{1}{3}$
21. $\frac{3}{8} + \frac{3}{4}$
22. $\frac{7}{8} - \frac{1}{4}$
23. $\frac{1}{2} - \frac{2}{5}$

CHECK PROBLEM SOLVING

Write the operation(s). Then solve the problem. (pp. 478–479)

24. Justin ate $\frac{1}{2}$ of the pizza, and Julie ate $\frac{1}{3}$ of the pizza. How much of the pizza is left?
25. Ed worked $2\frac{3}{4}$ hours and Tom worked $3\frac{1}{4}$ hours. Find the total time they worked.

Standardized Test Prep

NUMBER SENSE, CONCEPTS AND OPERATIONS

1. Allison read $\frac{1}{4}$ of her book on Friday, $\frac{1}{10}$ of her book on Saturday, and $\frac{1}{2}$ of her book on Sunday. Which operations could you use to find what fraction of her book she has left to read?

A addition and then subtraction

B subtraction and then addition

C addition and then addition

D subtraction and then subtraction

2. The platypus can hold its breath for 10 minutes. The sea otter can hold its breath for $\frac{5}{10}$ the time that the platypus can hold its breath. Which fraction is equivalent to $\frac{5}{10}$?

F $\frac{1}{4}$

G $\frac{3}{8}$

H $\frac{1}{2}$

J $\frac{3}{4}$

3. **Explain It** Zack spent $\frac{1}{6}$ hour reading, $\frac{4}{6}$ hour on his computer, and $\frac{5}{6}$ hour helping his father.

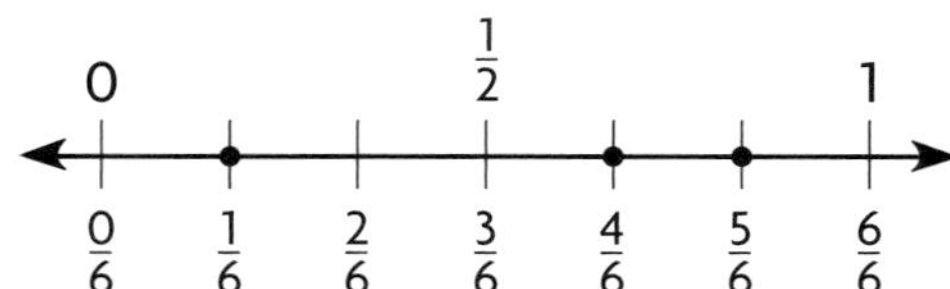

Explain how you can use the number line to ESTIMATE the amount of time Zack spent on all these activities.

MEASUREMENT

4. Fred made the table below to show the lengths of several objects in his home.

OBJECTS IN MY HOME	
Object	**Length**
Microwave oven	2 feet
Towel	38 inches
Rug	1 yard
Computer	1 foot 5 inches

Which object is the **longest**?

A microwave oven

B towel

C rug

D computer

5. Which of the following is the **best** estimate for the measure of $\angle DEF$?

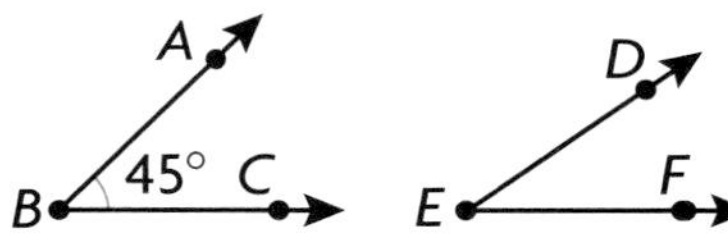

F 90°

G 65°

H 35°

J 5°

6. **Explain It** Explain how you can ESTIMATE the perimeter of the square below if you know that the pencil is about 7 inches long.

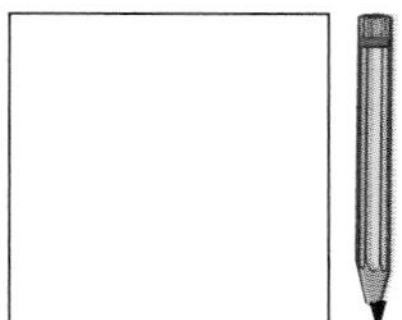

ALGEBRAIC THINKING

TIP **Eliminate choices.** See item 7. Think about the word *increased*. Eliminate the choices that use operations that do not increase amounts. Then determine which of the remaining choices is the answer.

7. Which expression describes the situation below? Let s represent the original number of stickers in Sally's collection.

The number of stickers, s, in Sally's sticker collection increased by 7.

A $s + 7$

B $s - 7$

C $s \times 7$

D $s \div 7$

8. Which is probably the next shape in the pattern?

F 

G

H 

J

9. **Explain It** Use the variable n to write an expression that means "four times a number." Explain why you wrote the expression you did.

DATA ANALYSIS AND PROBABILITY

10. Which **best** describes the probability that the pointer will land on 3?

A certain

B likely

C unlikely

D impossible

11. In May, 7 dogs were adopted from Pet Pals. In June, 3 dogs were adopted. In July, 6 were adopted. Which graph shows this information?

F

H

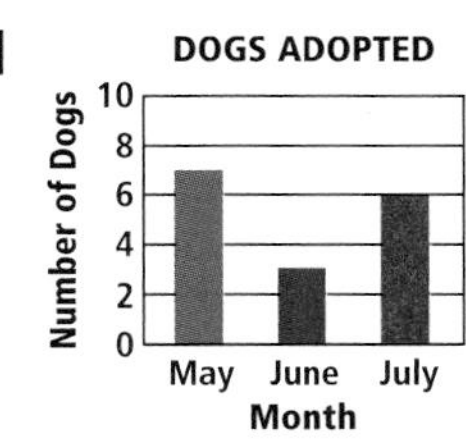

G

J

DOGS ADOPTED

May	🐾🐾🐾🐾
June	🐾🐾
July	🐾🐾🐾

Key: Each 🐾 = 2 dogs.

12. **Explain It** Billy made this list to record the numbers of goals he scored in 3 hockey games.

Game 1	2
Game 2	3
Game 3	4

If the trend in his scoring continues, will Billy score **more than** or **fewer than** 4 goals in Game 4? Explain your thinking.

Outcomes and Probability

FAST FACT • SOCIAL STUDIES The piñata (pēn•yä′tə) has been used in many traditional Latin American celebrations since the early 1500s. Blindfolded children try to break open the piñata with a stick to get the treats inside.

PROBLEM SOLVING The circle graph shows the contents of one piñata. What is the probability of getting a piece of hard candy from this piñata when it breaks?

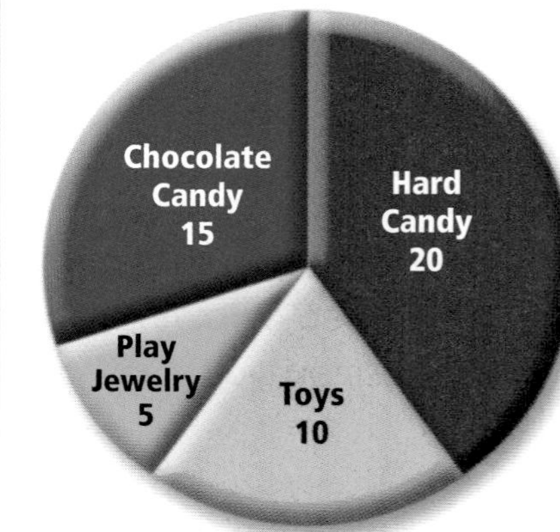

CHECK WHAT YOU KNOW

Use this page to help you review and remember important skills needed for Chapter 23.

IDENTIFY POSSIBLE OUTCOMES

List the possible outcomes for each event.

1. spinning the pointer of this spinner

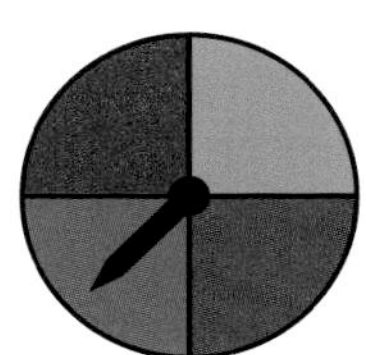

2. pulling a marble from this bag

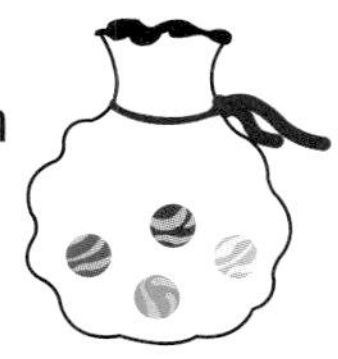

3. pulling a marble from this bag

CERTAIN AND IMPOSSIBLE

Tell whether each event is *certain* or *impossible*.

4. pulling a red pencil from a box of blue pencils

5. pulling a quarter from a bag full of quarters

6. tossing a number less than 7 on a number cube labeled 1 to 6

7. spinning a number less than 10 on a spinner labeled 9, 2, 8, 4, and 6

PARTS OF A GROUP

Write a fraction for the part of the group named.

8. circles

9. squares

10. triangles or squares

11. green marbles

12. red marbles

13. blue or green marbles

VOCABULARY POWER

REVIEW

experiment [ik•sper′ə•mənt] *noun*

The word *experiment* comes from the Latin word *experior,* meaning "to try" or "to prove." Give an example of an experiment you have done in math or science *to try* or *to prove* something.

PREVIEW

outcomes
event
predict
likely
unlikely
equally likely
mathematical probability
tree diagram

www.harcourtschool.com/mathglossary

LESSON 1

Record Outcomes

Quick Review

1. ■ × 2 = 8 + 2
2. 6 × 6 = ■ × 4
3. 63 ÷ 9 = ■ × 7
4. 320 ÷ 8 = 10 × ■
5. 7 × 6 = ■ ÷ 2

VOCABULARY

outcomes **event**

MATERIALS coin; 4-part spinner colored red, blue, yellow, and green; 3-part spinner colored blue, green, and red; number cube labeled 1 to 6

Explore

You can use a table to record the **outcomes**, or results, of an experiment. An **event** can be one outcome or a set of outcomes.

Do an experiment in which you toss a coin and spin the pointer on a spinner with four equal parts.

Activity 1

STEP 1

Make a table to show all the possible outcomes. There are 8 possible outcomes:

- The coin lands heads up (H) and the pointer stops on red, blue, yellow, or green: H red, H blue, H yellow, H green.
- The coin lands tails up (T) and the pointer stops on red, blue, yellow, or green: T red, T blue, T yellow, T green.

STEP 2

Toss the coin and spin the pointer. Record the outcome in your table.

Repeat for a total of 20 times, recording the outcome after each toss and spin.

Coin	Color			
	red	blue	Yellow	green
heads	I		I	I
tails		II	I	

More Practice: Harcourt Mega Math Fraction Action, *Last Chance Canyon*, Level C

Try It

- Make a table to record the outcomes of tossing a coin and spinning the pointer on a spinner with three equal parts colored blue, yellow, and red. Record 20 outcomes.

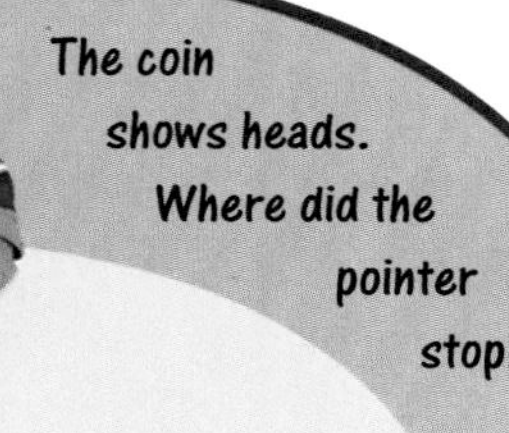

The coin shows heads. Where did the pointer stop?

Connect

It is important to include all the possible outcomes in your table.

How can you organize the outcomes of an experiment in which you use a spinner with 3 equal parts colored red, blue, and green and toss a cube labeled 1 to 6?

Activity 2

STEP 1

Make a table. Use the 18 possible outcomes of the experiment to name the parts of the table. 18 possible outcomes:

- The pointer stops on red, blue, or green, and the cube shows 1, 2, 3, 4, 5, or 6.

STEP 2

Spin the pointer and toss the cube 20 times. After each spin and toss, record the outcome in the table.

EXPERIMENT RESULTS						
	Number					
Color	**1**	**2**	**3**	**4**	**5**	**6**
red	|				|	
blue			|			
green		|				

- **REASONING** Will there be more than 1 tally mark for any of the outcomes in your table? Explain how you know.

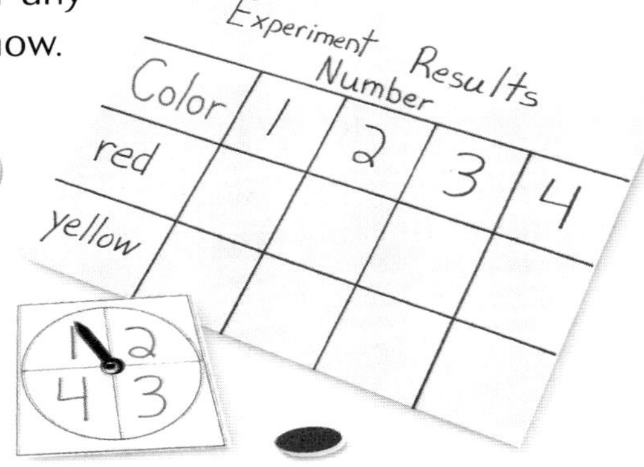

Practice and Problem Solving

USE DATA For 1–3, use the table.

Bernadette and Charles organized their outcomes in this table. They tossed a counter and used a spinner labeled 1, 2, 3, and 4.

1. Name the possible outcomes for this experiment.
2. How many possible outcomes are there?
3. How many outcomes would there be if they had used a spinner with 6 different numbers?
4. A plane left at 10:02 A.M. The flight arrived 3 hr 17 min after it took off. If the flight should have arrived at 12:45 P.M., how late was the plane?

Mixed Review and Test Prep

5. 6 weeks = ■ days (p. 104)
6. 48 months = ■ years (p. 104)
7. How many sides does a hexagon have? (p. 380)
8. Find the value of $58 - (3 + 9)$. (p. 64)
9. **TEST PREP** Which is the solution for $14 - c = 6$? (p. 70)

   A $c = 20$
   B $c = 9$
   C $c = 8$
   D $c = 6$

LESSON 2

Predict Outcomes of Experiments

Quick Review

Compare. Write <, >, or = for each ●.

1. 17 ● 15
2. 31 ● 301
3. 42 ● 42
4. 1,001 ● 1,100
5. 7,546 ● 7,564

VOCABULARY

predict **likely**
unlikely **equally likely**

Learn

WHAT'S POSSIBLE? Bag A has 28 red marbles and 2 blue marbles. Bag B has 15 red marbles and 15 blue marbles. If you pull a marble from each bag, what colors do you think you will pull?

Before doing an experiment, you can **predict** what probably will happen.

Bag A

Bag A has many more red marbles than blue marbles.

So, it is **likely**, but not certain, that you will pull a red marble from Bag A.

It is **unlikely**, but not impossible, that you will pull a blue marble from Bag A.

Bag B

Bag B has the same number of red marbles as blue marbles.

So, it is **equally likely** that you will pull a red or a blue marble. Each color has the same chance of being pulled.

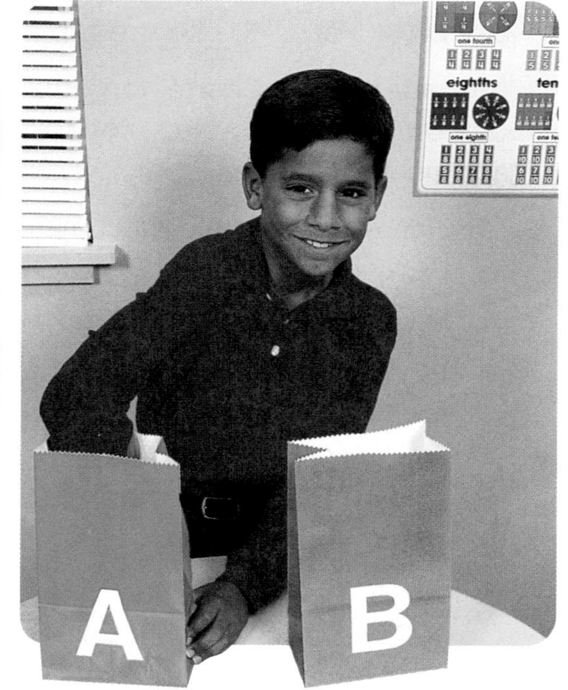

Examples

Look at the number cube labeled 1 to 6. Tell whether the events are *likely, unlikely,* or *equally likely.*

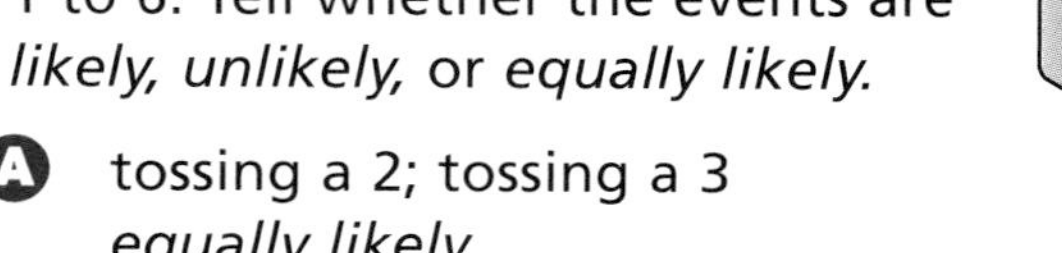

A tossing a 2; tossing a 3
equally likely

B tossing a composite number
unlikely

C tossing a number greater than 5
unlikely

D tossing a number less than 6
likely

Predicted vs. Actual Outcomes

In the activity below, there are six possible outcomes: blue, blue, blue, red, red, yellow. You can make predictions based on the likelihood of each outcome.

Activity

MATERIALS: 6-part spinner; marker; blue, red, and yellow crayons; paper clip; brad

STEP 1 Color 3 parts of the spinner blue, 2 parts red, and 1 part yellow.

STEP 2 Copy the table. Predict the outcomes for spinning the pointer 30 times. Use tally marks to show the number of times you think the pointer will land on each color.

Color	Predicted Outcomes	Actual Outcomes
red		
blue		
yellow		

STEP 3 Now spin the pointer 30 times. Record the actual outcomes in your table. Compare your predictions from Step 2 to your actual outcomes here.

- Which outcome is more likely: blue or red? How do you know?

Check

1. **Explain** how you made your predictions in the activity.

Write *likely, unlikely,* or *equally likely* for the events.

2. tossing a prime number on a cube labeled 3, 5, 7, 9, 11, 13
3. tossing a 1; tossing a 3; on a number cube labeled 1 to 6
4. pulling a green marble from a bag that has 1 green, 6 yellow, and 5 red marbles
5. spinning an even number on a spinner with 6 equal parts labeled 1, 3, 5, 7, 9, 10

 Extra Practice, page 504, Set A

Write *likely, unlikely,* or *equally likely* for the events.

6. pulling a green marble

7. spinning a 5

8. a student in your class has a first name beginning with *S*, *T*, or *N*

9. tossing a 6; tossing a 1; number cube labeled 1 to 6

For 10–12, look at the spinner.

10. Which sum for 2 spins is more likely, 2 or 3, or are they equally likely?

11. What sum are you most likely to get if you spin the pointer 2 times?

12. Make a spinner like the one shown. Spin the pointer twice and record the sum. Do this 11 more times. Explain how your results compare with your answers above.

For 13–14, look at the bag of marbles.

13. Which color are you most likely to pull from the bag? Why?

14. Which color marble are you least likely to pull? Why?

15. Describe a number cube that would make tossing an even number unlikely.

16. **What's the Question?** Scott had some stamps. He gave away 5 stamps and then arranged the rest in 6 rows of 12. The answer is 77 stamps.

17. **What's the Error?** Sally has a number cube labeled 3, 5, 7, 8, 9, and 11. She says it is certain that she will toss an odd number. Describe her error.

18. **Write About It** Are you *likely* or *unlikely* to get rain on a day when the forecast calls for a 90% chance of rain? Explain.

19. Angela has 1 nickel, 2 dimes, and 3 quarters in her pocket. Is it *certain* or *impossible* that she will pull less than \$0.20 if she pulls out 3 coins at the same time?

20. **Vocabulary Power** Look up the definitions of the words *"prediction"* and *"guess."* Compare the two words. How are they alike? How are they different?

Mixed Review and Test Prep

21. Write $\frac{35}{50}$ in simplest form. (p. 448)

For 22–23, compare. Write <, >, or = for each ●. (p. 424)

22. $^-3$ ● 2

23. 5 ● $^-7$

24. $\frac{3}{4} - \frac{1}{3}$ (p. 482)

25. 14×25 (p. 252)

26. **TEST PREP** Which has only one pair of parallel sides? (p. 384)

A trapezoid
B square
C rhombus
D rectangle

27. **TEST PREP** Which is a prime number? (p. 342)

F 4
G 6
H 7
J 9

Problem Solving LINKUP . . . to Reading

STRATEGY • CLASSIFY AND CATEGORIZE
To *classify* information is to group information that is alike. To *categorize* information is to label the classified groups, or categories.

Daisy is choosing a clown outfit. She has a polka-dot suit, a rainbow wig, and a striped suit. She also has black boots, a pink wig, and red floppy shoes.

Categorize → WIGS, SUITS, SHOES; Classify ↓

WIGS	SUITS	SHOES
pink	?	?
?	?	?

1. Copy and complete the table using the information above.

2. How many outfits (1 wig, 1 suit, 1 pair of shoes) does she have?

3. Daisy is making party favors. She had blue, white, and green balloons and gold ribbon. She bought red balloons and silver ribbon. How can you classify and categorize the information? How many kinds of favors can she make?

LESSON

Probability as a Fraction

Learn

COLOR WHEEL The spinner has six equally likely color outcomes: blue, green, yellow, orange, red, and purple. What is the probability of the pointer stopping on red?

Mathematical probability is a comparison of the number of favorable outcomes to the number of possible outcomes. The probability of an event can be written as a fraction.

Probability of red $= \frac{1}{6}$ ← **one favorable outcome (red)** / ← **total possible outcomes (blue, green, yellow, orange, red, purple)**

So, the probability of the pointer stopping on red is $\frac{1}{6}$, or 1 out of 6.

The probability of an event occurring can be expressed as 0, 1, or a fraction between 0 and 1.

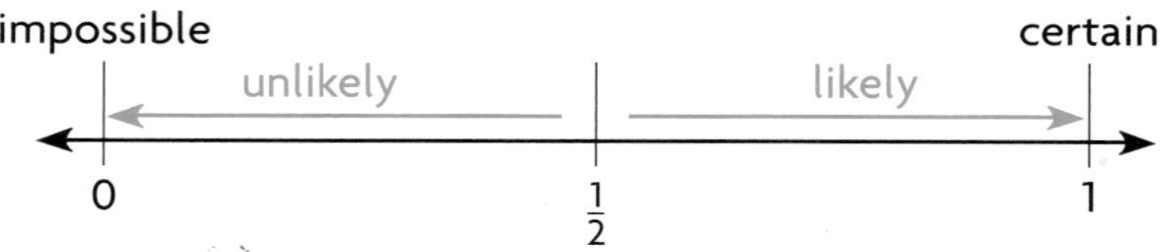

The closer a probability is to 1, the more likely the event is to occur. The closer it is to 0, the more unlikely. A probability of $\frac{1}{2}$ means that the event is just as likely to happen as not to happen.

Quick Review

Write an equivalent fraction for each.

1. $\frac{1}{2}$
2. $\frac{2}{3}$
3. $\frac{8}{10}$
4. $\frac{2}{6}$
5. $\frac{10}{30}$

VOCABULARY

mathematical probability

Technology Link

More Practice: Harcourt Mega Math Fraction Action, *Last Chance Canyon,* Levels F and G

Example

Use the spinner to find the probability of the pointer stopping on 3 or 4.

Probability of 3 or 4 $= \frac{2}{6}$ ← favorable outcomes (3 or 4) / ← total possible outcomes (1, 2, 3, 4, 5, 6)

An equivalent fraction for $\frac{2}{6}$ is $\frac{1}{3}$. So, the probability of the pointer stopping on a 3 or 4 can be written as $\frac{2}{6}$, or $\frac{1}{3}$.

Check

1. **Explain** which event is more likely, one with a probability of $\frac{1}{4}$ or one with a probability of $\frac{3}{4}$.

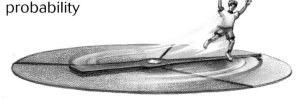

Look at the spinner on page 496. Find the probability of each event.

2. the number 7
3. *not* 3 or 4
4. a number greater than 3
5. a prime number

Practice and Problem Solving

Extra Practice, page 504, Set B

Look at the spinner on page 496. Find the probability of each event.

6. blue
7. orange or red
8. black
9. *not* brown

Look at the bag of marbles. Write *impossible, likely, unlikely,* or *certain* for each event, and find the probability.

10. a marble that is *not* blue
11. a blue marble
12. a green marble
13. a red, blue, or yellow marble
14. a marble that is *not* yellow
15. an orange marble
16. **What's the Error?** Rita says that an event with a probability of $\frac{1}{2}$ is more likely to occur than an event with a probability of $\frac{3}{5}$. Explain her error.
17. **FAST FACT • SOCIAL STUDIES** Machines for making glass marbles were introduced around 1895. How many years ago was this?
18. **GEOMETRY** A spinner has 6 equal sections. Two sections have a triangle, and three have a square. One section has a pentagon. What is the probability the pointer will stop on a figure with fewer than 5 sides?

Mixed Review and Test Prep

19. Write 3 out of 6 as a fraction. (p. 446)
20. $3{,}202 - 476$ (p. 48)
21. Which has a greater measure, an acute angle or a right angle? (p. 366)
22. $739 \div 8$ (p. 300)
23. **TEST PREP** Which event is impossible when you toss a number cube labeled 1 to 6? (p. 490)
    - **A** an even number
    - **B** an odd number
    - **C** a number greater than 6
    - **D** a number less than 2

LESSON 4

More About Probability

Quick Review

Write each fraction in simplest form.

1. $\frac{4}{12}$
2. $\frac{3}{9}$
3. $\frac{10}{20}$
4. $\frac{8}{10}$
5. $\frac{6}{8}$

MATERIALS number cube labeled 1 to 6

Explore

The mathematical probability of tossing each number on a number cube labeled 1 to 6 is $\frac{1}{6}$. When you do an experiment, your results may not match this probability.

Mary tossed a number cube labeled 1 to 6 twelve times. Look at the table. Mary's results show that she tossed a 5 in her experiment 3 out of 12 times. You can also write $\frac{3}{12}$, or $\frac{1}{4}$.

MARY'S EXPERIMENT

Number	1	2	3	4	5	6
Frequency	3	2	2	1	3	1

Technology Link

More Practice: Harcourt Mega Math Fraction Action, *Last Chance Canyon,* Level I

Activity

STEP 1

Make a tally table. Toss the number cube 12 times and record the outcomes in the tally table.

STEP 2

Make a frequency table like Mary's. Use your tally table to complete the frequency table.

- Using your results, write a fraction that shows the results for getting each number. How do your results compare to the mathematical probability of getting each number?

Talk About It

- You spin the pointer of this spinner 10 times. The pointer stops on yellow 4 times and on blue 6 times. Based on this experiment, what fraction of times does the pointer stop on blue? What fraction of times does it stop on yellow?

Connect

As the number of tries increases, the fraction for each event in the experiment comes closer to the mathematical probability of the event.

Kiley combined her 10 tosses with those of nine of her classmates.

- Look at the table. Which fraction for heads is closer to the mathematical probability of $\frac{1}{2}$?

Think: Is $\frac{40}{100}$ or $\frac{52}{100}$ closer to $\frac{50}{100}$?

COIN TOSS EXPERIMENT				
	Heads	Fraction	Tails	Fraction
Kiley	4	$\frac{4}{10}$, or $\frac{40}{100}$	6	$\frac{6}{10}$, or $\frac{60}{100}$
Total	52	$\frac{52}{100}$	48	$\frac{48}{100}$

Practice and Problem Solving

1. Toss a coin 50 times. Record your results. Write the fraction of tosses that showed heads and the fraction that showed tails based on your experiment.

2. **REASONING** Think of a spinner with equal parts numbered 1 to 5. Is it reasonable that the pointer will stop on 4 twice in 10 spins? Explain.

USE DATA For 3–5, use the spinner and the table.

SPINNER EXPERIMENT (100 SPINS)				
Outcome	Red	Blue	Yellow	Green
Tally	卌 卌 卌 卌 卌 III	卌 卌 卌 卌 II	卌 卌 卌 卌 卌 IIII	卌 卌 卌 卌 I

3. What is the mathematical probability of the pointer stopping on each color on the spinner?

4. Use the table to find the fraction of spins when the pointer stopped on green. How does this compare to the mathematical probability?

5. **Write About It** How does the fraction of spins in which the pointer stopped on green or yellow compare to the mathematical probability of that event?

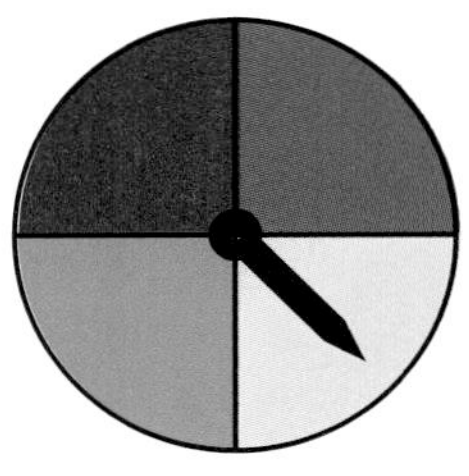

Mixed Review and Test Prep

For 6–7, find the value if $c = 8$. (p. 64)

6. $c - (5 + 2)$
7. $14 + c - 6$
8. What is the mean of this set of numbers? (p. 118)

   8, 8, 9, 7, 3

9. 6,904 − 5,826 (p. 48)
10. **TEST PREP** Which is the probability of tossing an even number on a number cube labeled 3, 4, 6, 7, 9, 11? (p. 496)

    A 0
    B $\frac{1}{3}$
    C $\frac{1}{2}$
    D $\frac{2}{3}$

LESSON 5

Combinations

Quick Review

1. 36 ÷ 3 = 3 × ■
2. 640 ÷ 8 = ■ × 8
3. 19 + 8 = ■ × 9
4. 1,200 ÷ 40 = ■ × 5
5. 4 × 4 × 3 = 24 × ■

VOCABULARY

tree diagram

Learn

DECISIONS, DECISIONS Betsy will choose a frozen yogurt flavor and a topping for her sundae. She can choose lemon, vanilla, or peach yogurt and cherry or nut topping. How many different sundaes can Betsy make? List the different sundaes.

A **tree diagram** shows all the possible combinations or outcomes.

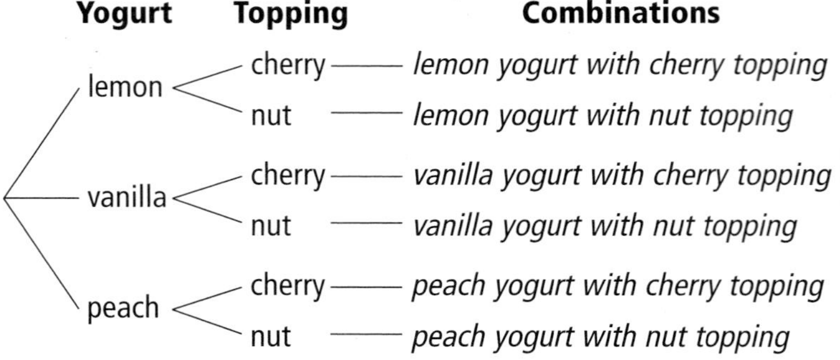

So, Betsy can make 6 different sundaes.

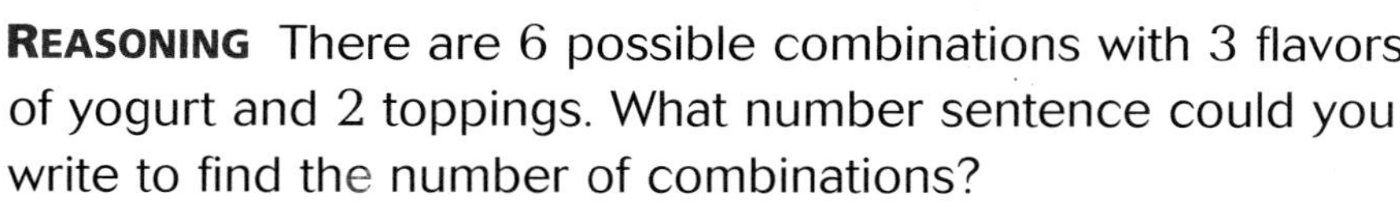

REASONING There are 6 possible combinations with 3 flavors of yogurt and 2 toppings. What number sentence could you write to find the number of combinations?

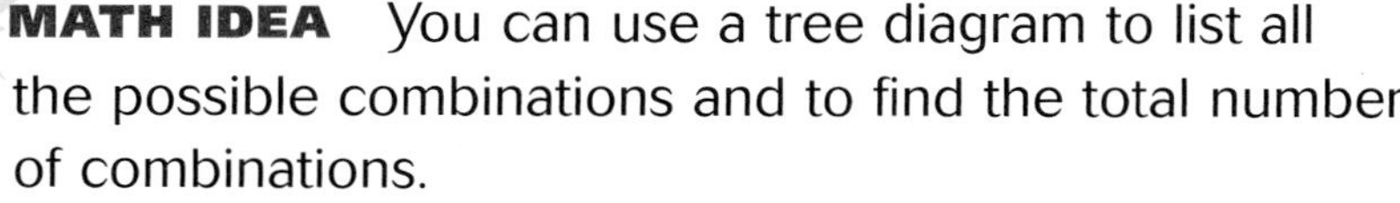

MATH IDEA You can use a tree diagram to list all the possible combinations and to find the total number of combinations.

Check

1. **Explain** how you know how many different peach sundaes Betsy can make.

Find the number of possible combinations by making a tree diagram.

2. You can plant one type of flower in one location.
   Type: tulips, roses, or irises
   Location: front yard, back yard, or side yard

Practice and Problem Solving

Extra Practice, page 504, Set C

For 3–5, choose one of each. Find the number of possible combinations by making a tree diagram.

3. Event choices
Event: play, movie, zoo, or concert
Day: Friday, Saturday, or Sunday

4. Clothing choices
Pants: blue, black, or tan
Shirt: red or green

5. Sandwich choices
Meat: ham, turkey, roast beef, or pastrami
Cheese: American, Swiss, Jack, or Colby

6. Bill has 8 different sets of 1 shirt and 1 tie. This means he could have 1 shirt and 8 ties. List 3 other possibilities for the number of shirts and ties Bill could have.

7. Julie can choose from three types of pasta: rigatoni, linguini, and fettucine. She can make either marinara, meat, alfredo, or vegetable sauce. How many different combinations are possible?

USE DATA For 8–11, use the table.

BIKE SHOP PRICE LIST			
Helmet:	$18	Water Bottle:	$2
Horn:	$4	Reflector:	$2
T-shirt:	$12	Snack:	$1

8. Nick bought a helmet and a snack. Joan bought 2 reflectors, a T-shirt, and a water bottle. Who spent more? How much more?

9. Josh has $16. He buys a T-shirt and wants to buy 2 more items. What items can he buy?

10. **Write a problem** using two or more items from the Bike Shop Price List.

11. How many combinations of 2 different items have a total price for the 2 items of not more than $6?

Mixed Review and Test Prep

For 12–14, give the probability of each event using the spinner. (p. 496)

12. 1

13. 1, 2, or 3

14. 4 or 5

15. $4\frac{5}{8} - 2\frac{1}{8}$ (p. 474)

16. TEST PREP Find the elapsed time between 10:35 A.M. and 4:17 P.M. (p. 98)

A 5 hr 18 min
B 5 hr 42 min
C 6 hr 18 min
D 6 hr 42 min

LESSON 6

Problem Solving Strategy
Make an Organized List

Quick Review

1. 7 × 8 = ▪ − 4
2. 14 − 9 = ▪ ÷ 5
3. 36 ÷ 4 = ▪ × 9
4. 8 × ▪ = 28 − 4
5. ▪ × 6 = 12 × 2

PROBLEM Winnie is playing a game at the fair using a 3-part spinner labeled 1, 2, and 3. If her total for two spins is greater than 4, she wins a prize. Show all the possible outcomes of the two spins and find the ways that Winnie can win a prize.

UNDERSTAND

- What are you asked to find?
- What information will you use?
- Is there any information you will not use? Explain.

PLAN

- What strategy can you use to solve the problem?

Make an organized list.

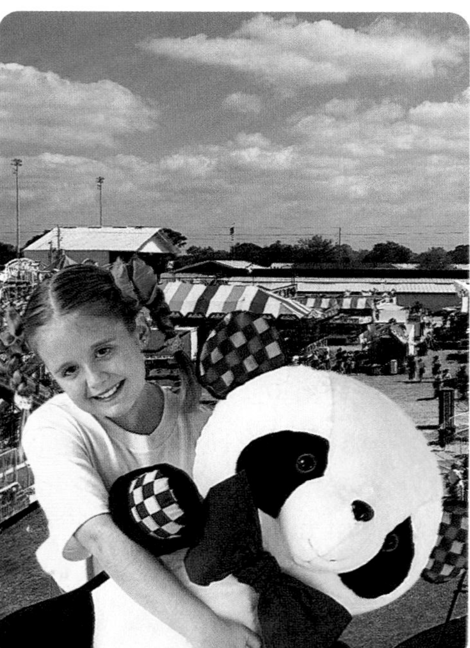

SOLVE

- How can you use the strategy to solve the problem?

Make a list of the 9 possible outcomes. Three outcomes have a total greater than 4.

Possible Outcomes		
1, 1	2, 1	3, 1
1, 2	2, 2	3, 2
1, 3	2, 3	3, 3

So, she can win a prize if her spins are 2, 3; 3, 2; or 3, 3.

CHECK

- What other strategy could you use?

Problem Solving Practice

Make an organized list to solve.

1. **What if** the spinner on page 502 were labeled 3, 4, 5? List the possible outcomes of spinning the pointer two times. Write the total number of outcomes.

2. Gwen is choosing a computer project. She can make a card, a calendar, a postcard, or a banner. She can use black or red ink. In how many ways can she do the project?

Strategies

- Draw a Diagram or Picture
- Make a Model or Act It Out
- **Make an Organized List**
- Find a Pattern
- Make a Table or Graph
- Predict and Test
- Work Backward
- Solve a Simpler Problem
- Write an Equation
- Use Logical Reasoning

Problem Solving

For 3–4, find the possible outcomes of spinning each pointer one time.

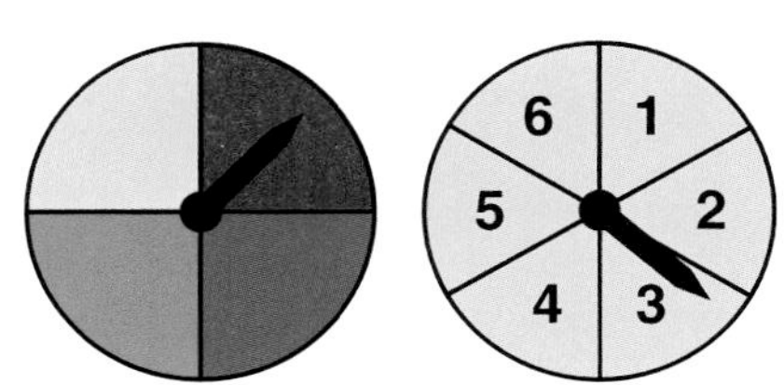

3. How many possible outcomes are there?
   A 6 **B** 10 **C** 12 **D** 24

4. How many of the possible outcomes include red?
   F 1 **G** 3 **H** 6 **J** 12

Mixed Strategy Practice

5. A furniture store sells sofas made of vinyl, leather, or cloth. Each kind of sofa comes in green, blue, or black. Make an organized list. How many sofa choices are there?

6. Mr. Johnson counted his change. He had 4 quarters, 8 dimes, 9 nickels, and 19 pennies. What was the total amount of money?

7. Mrs. Landry wants to use string to show where the sides of her garden will be. Use the diagram to find the number of feet of string she needs.

   10 yd

   3 yd 3 yd

   10 yd

8. Five students played basketball. Bob, Mike, and Jill scored 8 points each. Lynn scored half as many points as Chris. The total number of points scored was 54. How many points were scored by Lynn and Chris?

9. Kathy has 23 flowers. She places an equal number of flowers in some vases and has 2 left over. Each vase can hold up to 6 flowers. How many vases does she use?

10. Each side of a square patio is 10 feet long. Starting at one corner, there is a plant every 2 feet around the border of the patio. How many plants are around the patio?

Extra Practice

Set A (pp. 492–495)

For 1–3, look at the bag of marbles and the spinner at the right.

1. Which colors are you unlikely to pull from the bag?
2. Is it likely or unlikely that the pointer will land on blue?
3. Which two colors are you equally likely to spin?

Write *likely, unlikely,* or *equally likely* for the events.

4. tossing a 4; tossing a 6; on a cube labeled 1 to 6
5. spinning an odd number on a 6-part spinner labeled 1, 3, 6, 9, 12, 15
6. pulling a quarter from a bag of 10 quarters and 4 dimes
7. pulling a white sock from a drawer with 10 black socks and 2 white socks

Set B (pp. 496–497)

Look at the spinner. Find the probability of each event.

1. yellow
2. an odd number
3. 6
4. an even number
5. yellow or even
6. a number less than 6
7. A spinner has 8 equal sections. Two are purple, $\frac{1}{2}$ are green, and the remaining sections are blue. What is the probability of getting blue?
8. On a cube, two sides have an 8, $\frac{1}{3}$ of the sides have a 5, $\frac{1}{6}$ have a 3, and $\frac{1}{6}$ have a 4. What is the probability of tossing a 5?

Set C (pp. 500–501)

For 1–4, choose one of each. Find the number of possible combinations by making a tree diagram.

1. Decorations
   Type: balloons, streamers
   Color: blue, gold, silver, white, purple
2. Activities
   Sport: soccer, tennis, football
   Day: Mon, Tue, Wed, Thu
3. Outfits
   Tops: sweater, blouse, T-shirt
   Bottoms: jeans, skirt, shorts
4. Lunch
   Main: meatloaf, sandwich, taco
   Side: salad, fruit
5. The Smiths are taking a vacation. They can go to the beach, mountains, or lake. They can go in June, July, or August. How many choices do they have?
6. Sam can buy either milk or orange juice. Each comes in a pint, quart, or gallon. How many choices does Sam have?

Review/Test

✓ CHECK VOCABULARY AND CONCEPTS

Choose the best term from the box.

outcome
mathematical probability
event

1. You can use a table to record each __?__, or result, of an experiment. (p. 490)
2. A comparison of the number of favorable outcomes to the number of possible outcomes is __?__. (p. 496)

✓ CHECK SKILLS

3. Tonia tosses a coin and spins the pointer on a spinner colored red, white, blue, and gold. Name all the possible outcomes. (pp. 490–491)

For 4–5, look at the spinner. Write *likely* or *unlikely* for the events. (pp. 492–495)

4. spinning a number greater than 10
5. spinning an odd number

Use the spinner to find the probability of each event. (pp. 496–497)

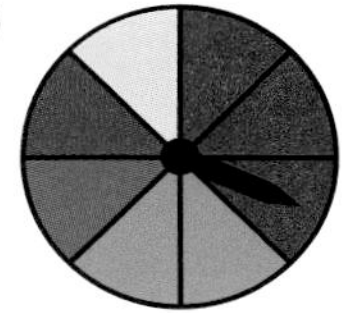

6. red
7. *not* green
8. red or blue
9. yellow
10. purple or green
11. brown

Find the number of possible outcomes by making a tree diagram. (pp. 500–501)

12. Winter sports
    Sport: skiing, skating, sledding
    Day: Friday, Saturday, Sunday

13. Guitars
    Type: electric, acoustic
    Color: tan, brown, black

✓ CHECK PROBLEM SOLVING

For 14–15, make an organized list to solve. (pp. 502–503)

14. Claire had chicken, beef, broccoli, and carrots. She bought corn, white bread, and wheat bread. How many choices of 1 meat, 1 vegetable, and 1 bread are there?
15. Anna is ordering a skirt. She can choose black, white, green, blue, or gray, and short or long length. How many choices are there?

Standardized Test Prep

MEASUREMENT

1. David made a patio using concrete squares as shown below. Each concrete square is 1 foot on each side. What is the perimeter of his patio?

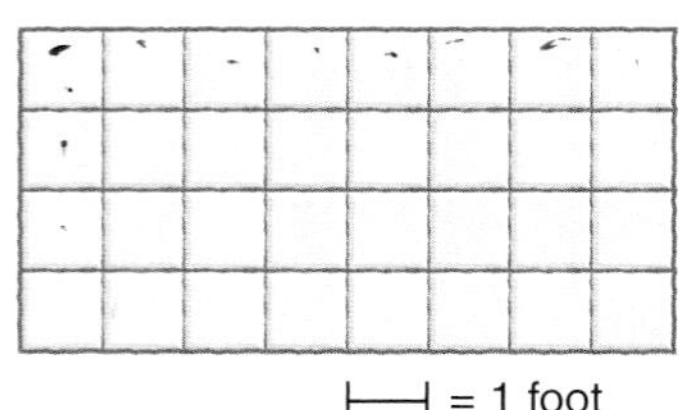

A 12 feet
C 24 feet
B 16 feet
D 32 feet

2. Which solid has the **greatest** volume?

F 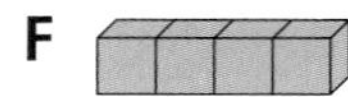

G 

H 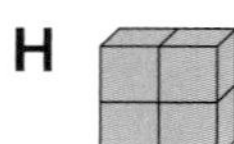

J 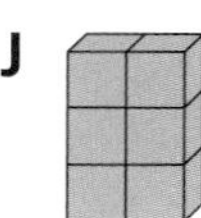

3. Which is the **best** unit for measuring the distance between Miami, Florida, and New York City, New York?

A inch
C yard
B foot
D mile

4. **Explain It** Susan took $30 to the mall and bought a CD for $13.95, lunch for $6.12, and a hair clip for $3.79. About how much money did Susan have left? Explain how you got your answer.

GEOMETRY AND SPATIAL SENSE

5. What term **best** describes the motion shown by the letter N below?

F reflection

G tessellation

H rotation

J translation

6. Which figure has no lines of symmetry?

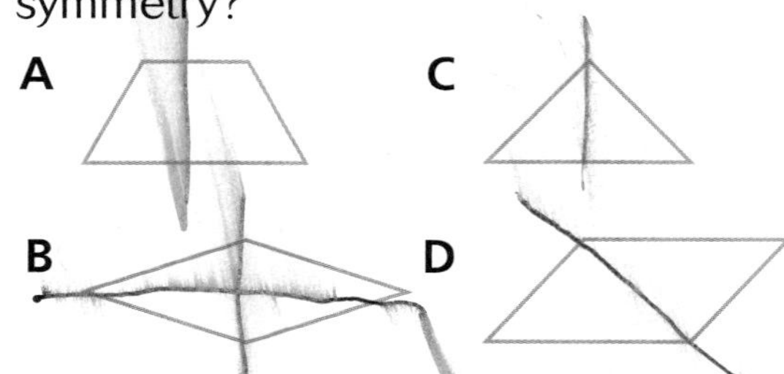

7. **Explain It** Miguel made the table below to classify some polygons.

POLYGONS		
Name	**Sides**	**Angles**
Triangle	3	3
Square	4	4
Rectangle	4	4
Pentagon	5	5
Hexagon	6	6

Based on the data in Miguel's table, how many angles does a seven-sided polygon have? Explain how you decided.

ALGEBRAIC THINKING

TIP **Choose the answer.** See item 8. Determine a rule that applies to the pattern in the table. Relate each answer choice to the rule one by one and choose the best answer.

8. Which is the missing fraction in the table below?

INPUT	$\frac{2}{7}$	$\frac{4}{10}$	$\frac{1}{3}$	$\frac{3}{5}$	■	$\frac{9}{12}$
OUTPUT	$\frac{2}{6}$	$\frac{4}{9}$	$\frac{1}{2}$	$\frac{3}{4}$	$\frac{6}{7}$	$\frac{9}{11}$

F $\frac{5}{7}$

G $\frac{5}{8}$

H $\frac{6}{8}$

J $\frac{7}{8}$

9. Which sentence comes next in this pattern?

$$1 \times 2 = 2$$
$$10 \times 20 = 200$$
$$100 \times 200 = 20{,}000$$
$$1{,}000 \times 2{,}000 = 2{,}000{,}000$$

A $1{,}000 \times 2{,}000 = 2{,}000{,}000$

B $1{,}000 \times 20{,}000 = 20{,}000{,}000$

C $10{,}000 \times 2{,}000 = 20{,}000{,}000$

D $10{,}000 \times 20{,}000 = 200{,}000{,}000$

10. Explain It Brett drew the pattern below.

He said that the second shape is the first shape rotated 180°. Do you agree? Explain how you decided.

DATA ANALYSIS AND PROBABILITY

11. Which is the probability of the pointer stopping on either 10 or 20 on this spinner?

F $\frac{1}{8}$

G $\frac{1}{4}$

H $\frac{3}{8}$

J $\frac{1}{2}$

12. This number cube is labeled 7 to 12.

Pauline tosses the cube once. Which event is **unlikely** to happen?

A even number

B number less than 12

C number greater than 7

D prime number

13. Explain It Kathy tossed a coin 20 times. This table shows the results of her experiment.

COIN TOSS EXPERIMENT		
Outcome	Heads	Tails
Tally	𝍸 𝍸 ||	𝍸 |||

What fraction of tosses showed tails? Explain your thinking.

IT'S IN THE BAG

Fraction Pizza Plates

PROJECT Make model pizzas to practice operations with fractions.

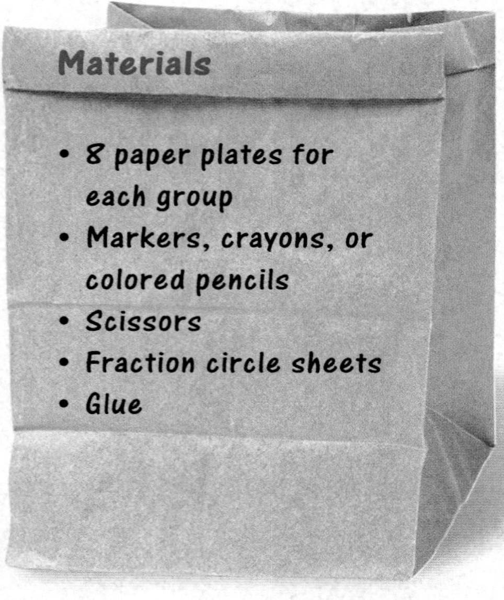

Materials
• 8 paper plates for each group
• Markers, crayons, or colored pencils
• Scissors
• Fraction circle sheets
• Glue

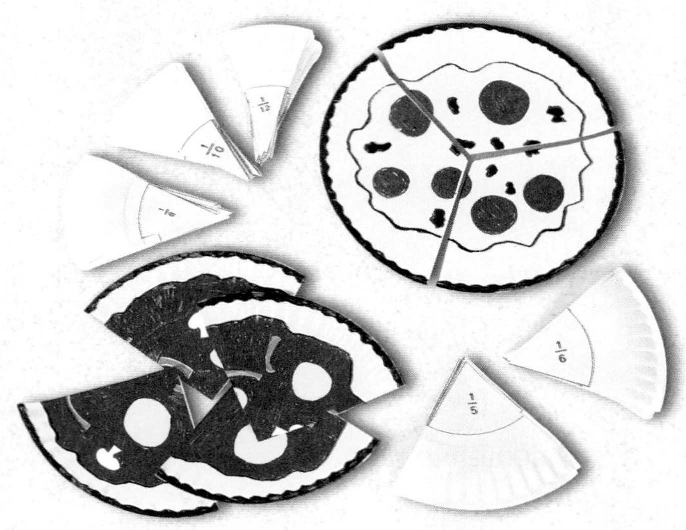

Directions

1. Color the tops of the paper plates to look like pizzas with your favorite toppings. *(Picture A)*
2. Cut out a different fraction circle for each of your group's pizzas, and glue the circles on the backs of the paper plates. *(Picture B)*
3. Cut your pizzas into slices by cutting along the lines of the fraction circles. *(Picture C)*
4. Place all of your group's pizza slices together, face-up, on a table.
5. Take different-size slices from the table, and try to put them together to form a whole pizza. Once you have made a whole pizza, turn the slices over. Write an equation that shows the sum of the fractions.
6. Take two different-size slices from the table, turn them over, and compare the two fractions. Then find the sum and the difference of the fractions.

A

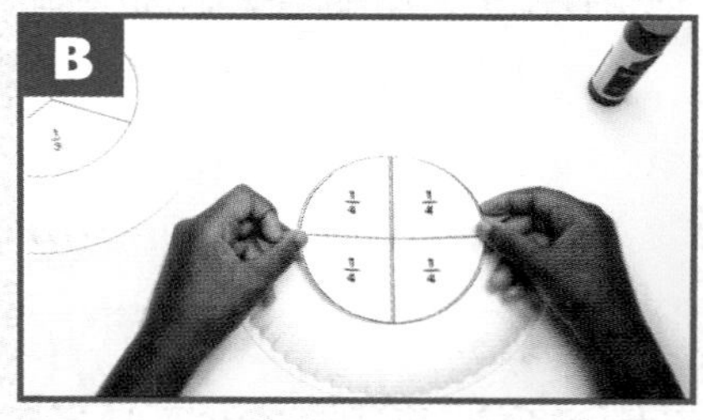
B

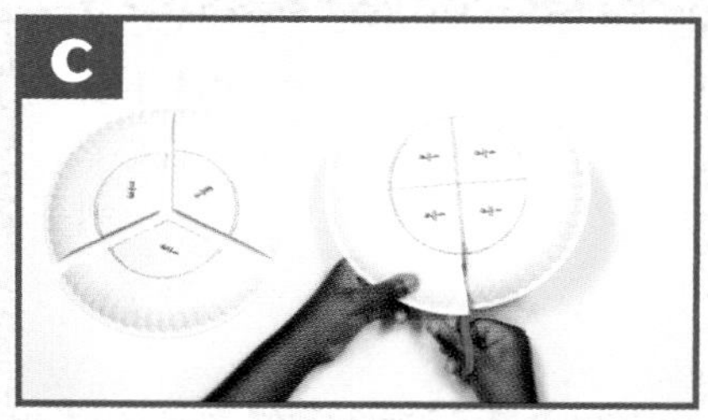
C

Challenge

Test for Fairness

Victor and Brian are playing a game. They take turns using a spinner. Victor scores 1 point when he spins an odd number. Brian scores 1 point when he spins an even number. Which of the spinners should be chosen so that the game is fair?

Fairness in a game means that one player is as likely to win as another. So, each player has an equal chance of winning.

Spinner A

13 10 18 17

Spinner B

Spinner C

Example

STEP 1

Find the probability of getting an odd number on each spinner.

Spinner A: $\frac{1}{2}$

Spinner B: $\frac{1}{3}$

Spinner C: $\frac{3}{4}$

STEP 2

Find the probability of getting an even number on each spinner.

Spinner A: $\frac{1}{2}$

Spinner B: $\frac{2}{3}$

Spinner C: $\frac{1}{4}$

STEP 3

Find the spinner with equal probabilities for an odd number and an even number.

	ODD	EVEN
Spinner A:	$\frac{1}{2}$	$\frac{1}{2}$
Spinner B:	$\frac{1}{3}$	$\frac{2}{3}$
Spinner C:	$\frac{3}{4}$	$\frac{1}{4}$

There is the same probability of getting an odd number as an even number on Spinner A. So, in order for the game to be fair, Spinner A should be chosen.

Try It

Look at the spinner. Each player scores 1 point when the pointer stops on his or her choice. Write *yes* or *no* to tell if each game is fair. Explain.

1. Player A: number between 8 and 15
   Player B: number greater than 10

2. Player A: prime number
   Player B: number that can be divided evenly by 4

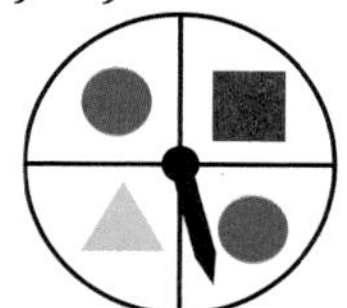

Each player chooses a different shape on the spinner. Each player scores 1 point when the pointer stops on his or her choice.

3. What is the probability of the pointer stopping on each shape?

4. How could you change the game to make it fair?

Study Guide and Review

VOCABULARY

Choose the best term from the box.

1. A number that names a part of a whole is a ? (p. 446)
2. Fractions that name the same amount are ? . (p. 448)
3. If you continue to divide until 1 is the only number that can be divided into the numerator and the denominator evenly, you find the fraction in ? . (p. 449)
4. Fractions with different denominators are ? . (p. 480)
5. When you compare the number of favorable outcomes to the number of possible outcomes, you are finding the ? . (p. 496)

mathematical probability
fraction
equivalent fractions
unlike fractions
simplest form
mixed numbers

STUDY AND SOLVE

Chapter 21

Find equivalent fractions.

Find equivalent fractions by multiplying or dividing.

Multiply the numerator and denominator by 2.

$\frac{6}{12} = \frac{6 \times 2}{12 \times 2} = \frac{12}{24}$

So, $\frac{6}{12}$ is equivalent to $\frac{12}{24}$.

Divide the numerator and denominator by 6.

$\frac{6}{12} = \frac{6 \div 6}{12 \div 6} = \frac{1}{2}$

So, $\frac{6}{12}$ is equivalent to $\frac{1}{2}$.

Write an equivalent fraction for each. (pp. 448–451)

6. $\frac{2}{3}$
7. $\frac{3}{4}$
8. $\frac{2}{5}$
9. $\frac{1}{6}$
10. $\frac{4}{8}$
11. $\frac{6}{10}$
12. $\frac{6}{9}$
13. $\frac{4}{12}$
14. $\frac{10}{12}$
15. $\frac{7}{14}$
16. $\frac{6}{8}$
17. $\frac{4}{6}$

Chapter 22

Add and subtract fractions and mixed numbers.

Subtract.

$2\frac{3}{5} - 1\frac{1}{5}$

$$\begin{array}{r} 2\frac{3}{5} \\ -1\frac{1}{5} \\ \hline 1\frac{2}{5} \end{array}$$

- Subtract the fractions first.
- Then subtract the whole numbers.

Find the sum or difference. (pp. 468–479)

18. $\frac{7}{12} + \frac{6}{12}$
19. $\frac{7}{8} - \frac{3}{8}$
20. $9\frac{6}{9} - 4\frac{3}{9}$
21. $1\frac{3}{5} + 7\frac{2}{5}$
22. $2\frac{3}{8} + 3\frac{1}{8}$
23. $5\frac{4}{6} - 4\frac{3}{6}$

Chapter 23

Write the probability of a simple event.

Find the probability of the pointer stopping on the color red.

Probability of red = $\frac{2}{6}$, or $\frac{1}{3}$

So, the probability of the pointer stopping on red is $\frac{1}{3}$.

A bag of marbles contains 7 blue, 3 green, 5 purple, and 3 red marbles. Find the probability of each event. (pp. 496–497)

24. a green marble

25. a blue marble

26. a purple marble

27. a marble that is not purple

Record outcomes of an experiment in different forms.

Meat: Turkey, Roast Beef
Vegetable: Carrots, Corn, Broccoli

Meat	Vegetable	Outcomes
Turkey	Carrots	Turkey with carrots
	Corn	Turkey with corn
	Broccoli	Turkey with broccoli
Roast Beef	Carrots	Roast Beef with carrots
	Corn	Roast Beef with corn
	Broccoli	Roast Beef with broccoli

Find the number of possible combinations by making a tree diagram. (pp. 500–501)

28. Activity Choices
Activity: volleyball, tennis, or basketball
Day: Saturday or Sunday

29. Sundae choices
Ice Cream: vanilla or chocolate
Toppings: chopped walnuts or pecans

PROBLEM SOLVING PRACTICE

Solve. (pp. 456–457, 478–479, 502–503)

30. Jim and Brianna each ate $\frac{5}{12}$ of the pizza. What fraction of the pizza is left? Name the operation or operations you used.

31. Ling has a set of measuring cups. Three of the sizes are $\frac{3}{4}$, $\frac{1}{3}$, and $\frac{1}{2}$ cup. Put the sizes in order from least to greatest.

32. Andy is designing a shirt for his soccer team. The shirt can be green, blue, purple, or red. It can be either striped or a solid color. How many different design combinations are there?

33. A spinner has 8 equal sections. Two of the sections are orange, 4 sections are green, and 2 sections are blue. Which two colors together cover $\frac{1}{2}$ of the spinner?

PERFORMANCE ASSESSMENT

TASK A • SHARE YOUR PIZZA

Curtis, Joe, Sara, and Laura have a coupon for one free pizza at the Pizza Palace. They all want the same number of slices.

a. Tell which size pizza they should order. Explain your answer.

b. Write a fraction that names how much of the pizza will be left after each person eats 1 slice. Write an equivalent fraction for that amount.

c. Should the friends order the same size pizza if Laura decides she does not want any pizza? Explain.

PIZZA PALACE MENU

Size	Servings
Personal	4 slices
Small	6 slices
Medium	8 slices
Large	12 slices
Jumbo	16 slices

TASK B • VISIT TO GRANDMOTHER

Robyn is planning a one-week visit with her grandmother. She wants to pack enough shorts and shirts so that she has enough different outfits to wear during the week.

a. Robyn wants to take more shirts than shorts. How many of each should she pack? Make a tree diagram to show that your answer is correct.

b. Suppose Robyn packs her favorite red shirt. If she reaches into her suitcase and pulls out a shirt without looking, is it likely or unlikely that she will pull out the red shirt?

c. Robyn buys one more shirt during her visit. How many different outfits will she be able to make now?

Technology Linkup

Calculator • Add and Subtract Mixed Numbers

Kathy uses $3\frac{1}{8}$ cups of semolina flour and $3\frac{5}{8}$ cups of white flour to make her pasta dough. How much flour does she use in all?

You can use a calculator to add and subtract mixed numbers.

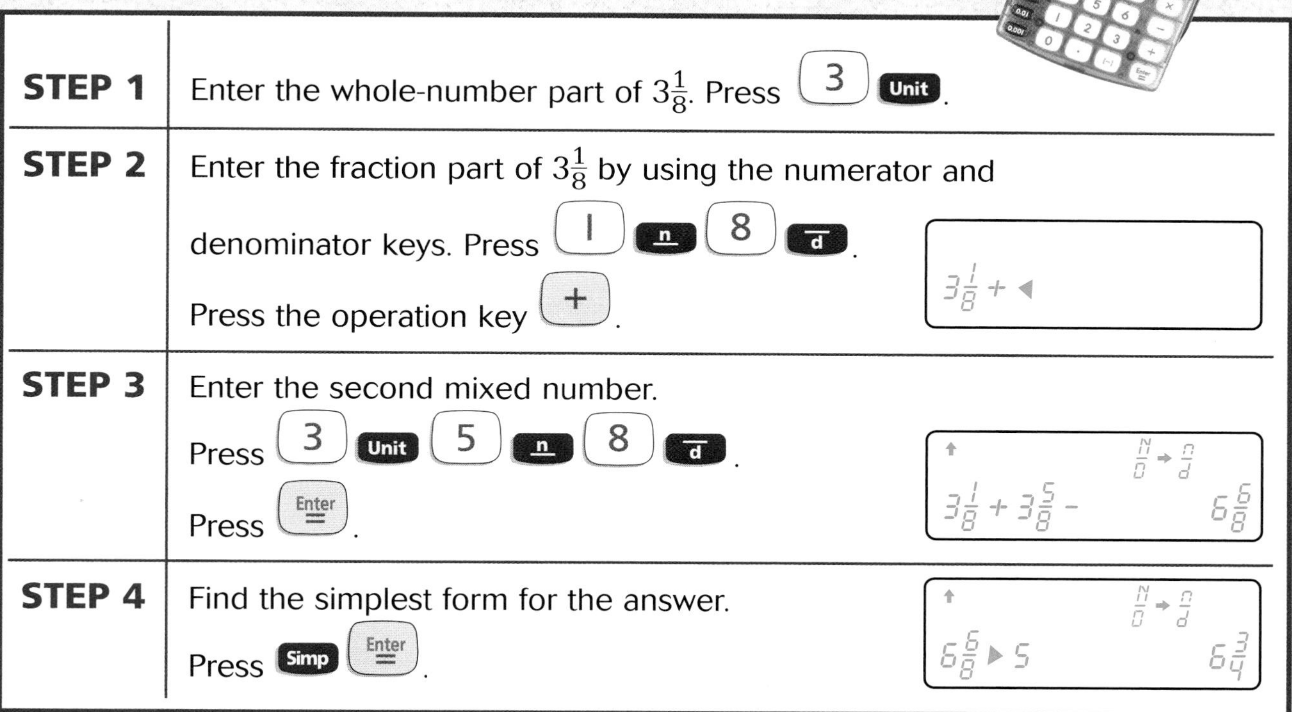

STEP 1	Enter the whole-number part of $3\frac{1}{8}$. Press 3 Unit.	
STEP 2	Enter the fraction part of $3\frac{1}{8}$ by using the numerator and denominator keys. Press 1 n 8 d. Press the operation key +.	$3\frac{1}{8}$ + ◄
STEP 3	Enter the second mixed number. Press 3 Unit 5 n 8 d. Press Enter.	$3\frac{1}{8} + 3\frac{5}{8}$ – $6\frac{6}{8}$
STEP 4	Find the simplest form for the answer. Press Simp Enter.	$6\frac{6}{8}$ ► 5 $6\frac{3}{4}$

So, she uses $6\frac{3}{4}$ cups of flour in all.

Practice and Problem Solving

Use a calculator to find each sum or difference. Write the answer in simplest form.

1. $4\frac{1}{2} + 3\frac{1}{2}$

2. $5\frac{5}{8} - 3\frac{1}{8}$

3. $8\frac{1}{6} + 5\frac{2}{6}$

4. $10\frac{3}{4} - 7\frac{1}{4}$

5. $14\frac{2}{3} - 13\frac{2}{3}$

6. $12\frac{3}{5} + 20\frac{4}{5}$

GO ON-LINE **Multimedia Math Glossary**
www.harcourtschool.com/mathglossary

Vocabulary Power Look up *mixed number* and *simplest form* in the Multimedia Math Glossary. Give an example of a mixed number that is not in simplest form. Then write the mixed number in simplest form.

▲ **The Idaho state capitol building in Boise, completed in 1920, was patterned after the U.S. Capitol.**

DOWNTOWN BOISE

Boise, the state capital, is located on the Boise River in southwest Idaho. The downtown area is a cultural center and is home to many parks and museums.

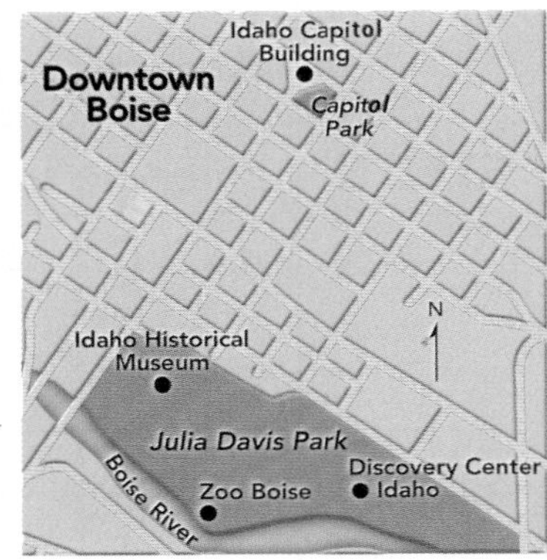

1. On her visit to Boise, Susan walked $\frac{3}{4}$ mile from the capitol building to Julia Davis Park and then $\frac{1}{2}$ mile through the park. If she walked back to the capitol building along the same route, how far did she walk?

2. The central section and dome of the capitol building took about 8 years to build. The two wings for the building took about 2 years to build. Write a fraction that shows how much of the total construction time was spent on the wings.

3. While at the park, Maria spent 2 hours at the Idaho Historical Museum, 3 hours at Zoo Boise, and 3 hours at Discovery Center Idaho. What fraction of her total time at the park did Maria spend at the discovery center or the historical museum?

4. The Boise Greenbelt offers a 25-mile-long pathway along the Boise River for walking, running, biking, and in-line skating. Michael skated $7\frac{3}{5}$ miles along the path, and Pauline skated $8\frac{4}{5}$ miles. Who skated farther, and by how much?

5. Lynda has time before lunch to visit the capitol building or walk along the river. After lunch she can go to the historical museum, the zoo, or the discovery center. List all of her possible combinations of activities for the day.

LUCKY PEAK STATE PARK

Lucky Peak State Park is located along the Boise River only about 18 miles east of Boise. The park is made up of three areas around the Lucky Peak Reservoir and is a popular location for boating, swimming, hiking, and fishing.

1. Chris and his family rode their bikes to the park from Boise along the Boise Greenbelt. They rode $11\frac{3}{4}$ miles before stopping for a break. How much farther did they have to ride to get to the park?

2. The Lucky Peak Reservoir has about 45 miles of shoreline. Katie rode in a boat along about 18 miles of the shoreline. What fraction of the total shoreline did Katie travel along?

3. The marina at the park has spots for about 200 boats. Of the spots, about 125 are for small boats, 50 for medium boats, and 25 for large boats. What fraction of the total number of spots at the marina is for small or medium boats?

4. The reservoir is stocked with rainbow trout and cutthroat trout. Bull trout also live there. If there are equal numbers of each type of trout, what is the probability that a trout you catch there will be either a rainbow or cutthroat trout?

5. Mac spent $\frac{1}{4}$ of his time at the park swimming, $\frac{1}{3}$ of his time hiking, and $\frac{5}{12}$ of his time fishing. On which activity did he spend the greatest amount of time?

6. The Sandy Point part of the park is about $\frac{2}{12}$ the size of the Spring Shores part. Write two equivalent fractions for $\frac{2}{12}$.

▲ **Lucky Peak State Park recently was chosen as one of the northwest's top 25 parks.**

Customary Measurement

FAST FACT • SPORTS Each Memorial Day weekend, the roar of racing cars fills the air at the Indianapolis Motor Speedway. The Indy 500 has taken place there since 1911. Cars in this race go more than 200 miles an hour around the oval track.

PROBLEM SOLVING Four laps around the track equal 10 miles. What is the total distance for the Indy car race? for the stock car race?

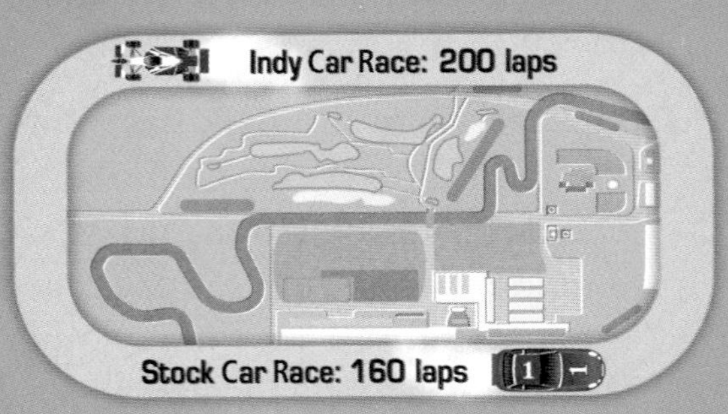

Indianapolis Motor Speedway Track, Indianapolis, Indiana

CHECK WHAT YOU KNOW

Use this page to help you review and remember important skills needed for Chapter 24.

MEASURE TO THE NEAREST INCH AND HALF INCH

Measure the length of each to the nearest inch.

1. 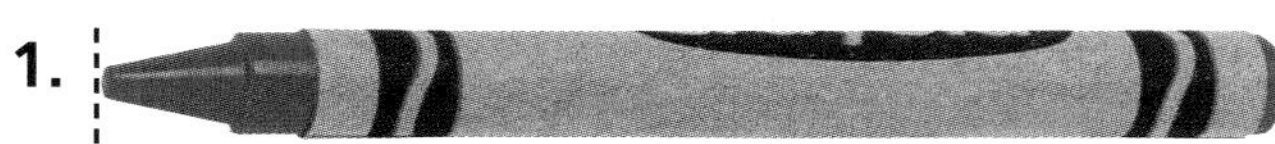

2. 

Measure the length of each to the nearest $\frac{1}{2}$ inch.

3. 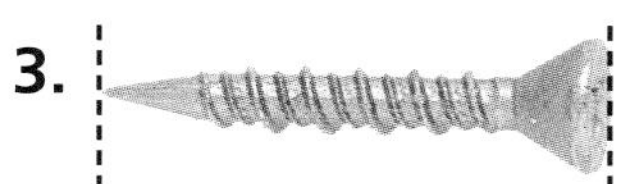

4. 

MULTIPLICATION

Find the product.

5. 16×3
6. 36×3
7. 12×4
8. 16×4
9. 12×7
10. 12×2
11. $1{,}760 \times 3$
12. $5{,}280 \times 2$
13. 12×12
14. $2{,}000 \times 9$

DIVISION

Divide.

15. $27 \div 3$
16. $36 \div 12$
17. $33 \div 3$
18. $60 \div 2$
19. $525 \div 7$
20. $702 \div 6$
21. $72 \div 4$
22. $84 \div 12$

VOCABULARY POWER

REVIEW

length [len(k)th] *noun*

The word *length* comes from the Old English word *lang,* which means "long." What customary units of length can you use to measure how long something is?

PREVIEW

linear units
yard (yd)
mile (mi)
capacity
teaspoon (tsp)
tablespoon (tbsp)
gallon (gal)
ounce (oz)
pound (lb)
ton (T)

www.harcourtschool.com/mathglossary

LESSON 1

Length: Choose the Appropriate Unit

Learn

MEASURE UP! Have you ever wondered just how far you rode your bike or walked? You can use nonstandard units such as one rotation of the bike pedals and the length of your shoe, or you can use standard units such as miles and yards.

Quick Review

Compare. Write <, >, or = for each ●.

1. 12 ● 8
2. 24 ● 26
3. $9\frac{1}{2}$ ● $9\frac{2}{4}$
4. $2\frac{3}{5}$ ● $2\frac{1}{3}$
5. 2 min ● 60 sec

VOCABULARY

linear units
inch (in.)
foot (ft)
yard (yd)
mile (mi)

HANDS ON

Activity 1 MATERIALS: tape measure or yardstick

- Estimate and measure the distance from your desk to the classroom door, using your foot as the unit of measure. Record your estimate and the actual distance. Compare your results with your classmates' results.
- Estimate and measure the same distance in feet, using a tape measure or yardstick. Record your estimate and the actual distance. Compare your results with your classmates' results.
- How does your estimate compare to the distance you found by using a tape measure or yardstick?

Linear units are used to measure length, width, height, and distance. Understanding the sizes of different standard linear units will help you choose the appropriate units of measure to use.

Examples

A An **inch (in.)** is about the length of your thumb from the first knuckle to the tip.

1 in.

Smaller objects, such as pencils or nails, are measured in inches.

B A **foot (ft)** is about the length of a sheet of paper.

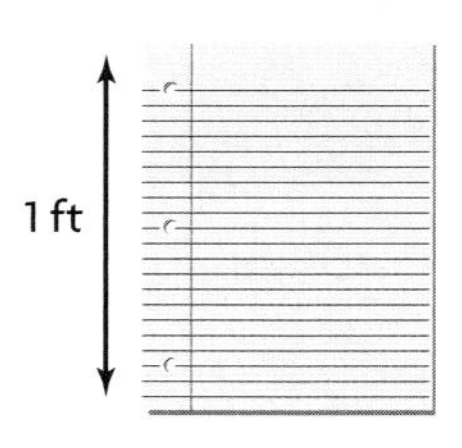

A person's height or the length of a room is measured in feet.

C A **yard (yd)** is about the length of a baseball bat.

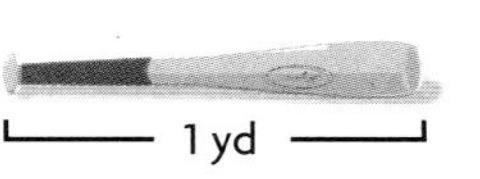

The length of a football field is measured in yards.

D A **mile (mi)** is about the distance you can walk in 20 minutes.

The distance a person travels in a car is measured in miles.

1 mi

More About Linear Units

At the Minnesota State Fair, large vegetables are lined up so judges can decide which vegetable is biggest. The judges use string to compare the large vegetables.

You can use indirect measurement to compare the length of one object to the length of another.

Activity 2

MATERIALS: 2 apples, 2 pieces of string, scissors

- Use a string to find the distance around the first apple. Measure horizontally around the apple at its largest part.
- Cut or mark the string to show the distance around the apple.
- Then measure the second apple, using another piece of string.
- Compare the strings. How do the two apples compare?

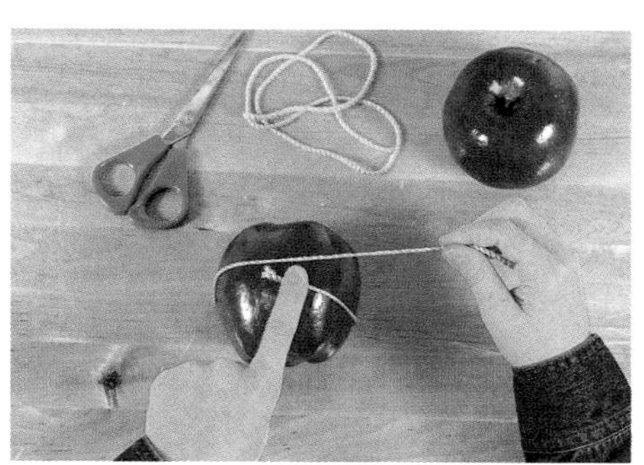

Check

1. **Explain** how you can decide what linear unit to use.

Choose the most reasonable unit of measure. Write *in., ft, yd,* or *mi*.

2. The width of a book is about 8 ? .
3. The length of a car is about 14 ? .
4. Yesterday Jordan ran 3 ? .
5. The length of a license plate is about 1 ? .
6. The width of my thumb is about 1 ? .
7. The length of 15 football fields is about 1 ? .

Name the greater measurement.

8. 2 yd or 2 mi
9. 16 ft or 16 in.
10. 32 in. or 32 yd
11. 24 in. or 24 mi
12. 3 ft or 3 yd
13. 56 mi or 56 yd

LESSON CONTINUES 

Practice and Problem Solving

Extra Practice, page 534, Set A

Choose the most reasonable unit of measure.
Write *in., ft, yd,* or *mi.*

14. The distance from New York to Los Angeles is 2,794 __?__.

15. The length of the playground is 22 __?__.

16. The length of a goldfish is about 3 __?__.

17. The door of your classroom is about 1 __?__ wide.

18. The width of my notebook is about 10 __?__.

19. The height of a desk is about 2 __?__.

Name the greater measurement.

20. 400 ft or 400 yd

21. 10 in. or 10 ft

22. 20 yd or 20 mi

Name the lesser measurement.

23. 10 yd or 10 ft

24. 128 in. or 128 yd

25. 30 in. or 30 ft

USE DATA For 26–29, use the table.

26. Compare the lengths of the cars. Write the types of cars in order from shortest to longest.

27. How many inches longer is the longest car compared to the shortest car? What is the median car length?

28. The garage in Jim's house is 228 inches long. If Jim buys a sedan, will his car fit in his garage? Explain.

AVERAGE CAR LENGTHS (from bumper to bumper)	
Type of Car	**Length (in inches)**
Coupe	175
Sedan	215
SUV	206
Station Wagon	198

29. **Write About It** Explain why you think car makers describe the lengths of their cars in inches rather than in feet or yards.

30. Karen bought 3 yards of lace for $2 per yard and 2 yards of fabric for $6 per yard. She gave the clerk a $20 bill. How much change did she receive?

31. Liz took a trip from Baltimore, Maryland, to Huntsville, Alabama. Which unit of measure would you use to describe the distance between these two cities?

32. Measure the length of your math book by using the length of your thumb from the first knuckle to the tip. How many thumb lengths is it? How many inches is it?

33. Think about how long a yard is. Then estimate in yards the distance from the school office to your classroom. Choose a tool and a unit, and measure the distance. Record your estimate and measurement.

34. **Write a problem** about choosing a customary unit of measure to solve a problem.

Mixed Review and Test Prep

35. $\frac{3}{6} + \frac{2}{6}$ (p. 468)

36. $\frac{7}{8} - \frac{3}{8}$ (p. 472)

37. $4\frac{3}{8} + 7\frac{1}{8}$ (p. 474)

38. $512 \div 8$ (p. 300)

39. **TEST PREP** Which shows an equivalent fraction to $\frac{12}{20}$? (p. 448)

A $\frac{3}{5}$ **B** $\frac{72}{100}$ **C** $\frac{2}{4}$ **D** $\frac{2}{5}$

40. **TEST PREP** Bradley is packing for a vacation. He packed 5 different T-shirts and 4 different pairs of jeans. How many different outfits can Bradley make? (p. 500)

F 9 **G** 10 **H** 20 **J** 24

Problem Solving Thinker's Corner

MEASURING TOOLS Whenever you need to measure an object or a distance, you should choose the appropriate tool according to the size of the object or the distance.

What tools could you use to measure the distance from your house to your school?

TOOLS
Distances greater than 1 yard:
• Odometer: mile
• Pedometer: foot, mile
• Measuring wheel: foot
Lengths less than 1 foot:
• Ruler: inch
Lengths greater than 1 foot:
• Tape measure: inch, foot, yard
• Yardstick: inch, foot, yard
• Folding rule: inch, foot, yard

pedometer

measuring wheel

odometer

You could use a pedometer, a measuring wheel, or an odometer.

Give an example of an object or a distance you would measure by using the tool.

1. ruler **2.** tape measure **3.** odometer

4. measuring wheel **5.** pedometer **6.** yardstick

LESSON 2
Measure Fractional Parts

Quick Review

Compare. Write <, >, or = for each ●.

1. $\frac{1}{2}$ ● $\frac{1}{4}$ **2.** $9\frac{2}{8}$ ● $9\frac{1}{4}$

3. $9\frac{1}{2}$ ● $9\frac{3}{4}$ **4.** $9\frac{5}{8}$ ● $9\frac{1}{4}$

5. 1 ● $\frac{4}{4}$

Learn

LEAF LESSON Mary collected and classified leaves for her science project. Part of her assignment was to measure each leaf to the nearest $\frac{1}{4}$ inch and $\frac{1}{8}$ inch.

Fractional units, such as $\frac{1}{2}$ inch, $\frac{1}{4}$ inch, and $\frac{1}{8}$ inch, are used to measure lengths that are between two whole units.

Measuring to the nearest fractional unit is like rounding a number.

Examples

A Measure to the nearest $\frac{1}{4}$ inch.

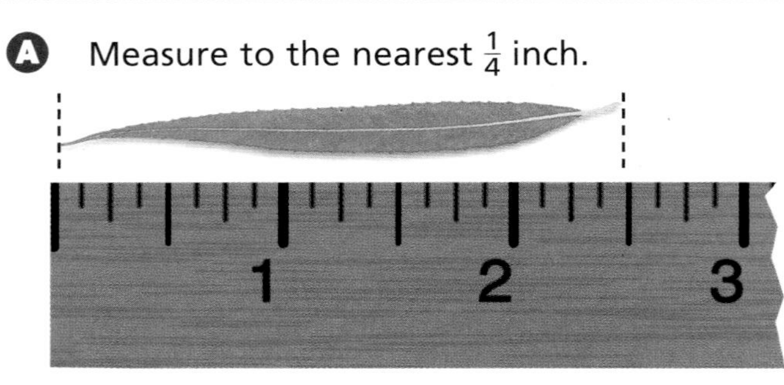

The length is closer to $2\frac{2}{4}$ in. than to $2\frac{1}{4}$ in. So, the leaf's length is about $2\frac{2}{4}$ in., or $2\frac{1}{2}$, in.

B Measure to the nearest $\frac{1}{8}$ inch.

The length is closer to $1\frac{6}{8}$ in. than to $1\frac{7}{8}$ in. So, the leaf's length is about $1\frac{6}{8}$, or $1\frac{3}{4}$, in.

Technology Link

More Practice: Harcourt Mega Math Ice Station Exploration, *Linear Lab*, Level F

Activity

MATERIALS: 5 objects, ruler, yardstick

OBJECT	ESTIMATE	ACTUAL MEASUREMENT TO THE NEAREST:			
		1 in.	$\frac{1}{2}$ in.	$\frac{1}{4}$ in.	$\frac{1}{8}$ in.
?	■	■	■	■	■

STEP 1

Make a table like the one shown. Estimate the lengths of 5 objects to the nearest inch, and record the estimates in your table.

STEP 2

Measure the length of each object to the nearest inch, $\frac{1}{2}$ inch, $\frac{1}{4}$ inch, and $\frac{1}{8}$ inch. Record the measurements in your table.

- For each object, which measurement is the closest to the actual length?
- Suppose you wanted to measure the height of a book to decide whether it would fit on a bookshelf. Is an actual measurement or an estimate needed to decide whether the book would fit on the bookshelf?

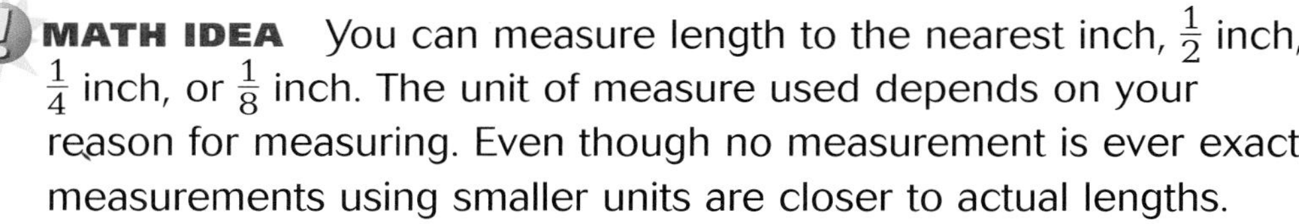

MATH IDEA You can measure length to the nearest inch, $\frac{1}{2}$ inch, $\frac{1}{4}$ inch, or $\frac{1}{8}$ inch. The unit of measure used depends on your reason for measuring. Even though no measurement is ever exact, measurements using smaller units are closer to actual lengths.

Check

1. **Explain** how to find the $\frac{1}{2}$-inch marks and the $\frac{1}{4}$-inch marks on a ruler.

Estimate to the nearest inch. Then measure to the nearest $\frac{1}{4}$ inch.

2\.

3\.

Estimate to the nearest $\frac{1}{2}$ inch. Then measure to the nearest $\frac{1}{8}$ inch.

4\.

5\. 

Order the measurements from *least* to *greatest*.

6\. $2\frac{1}{2}$ in., $1\frac{7}{8}$ in., $2\frac{3}{8}$ in., $2\frac{3}{4}$ in.

7\. $5\frac{1}{4}$ in., $5\frac{1}{8}$ in., $5\frac{1}{2}$ in.

LESSON CONTINUES

Practice and Problem Solving

Extra Practice, page 534, Set B

Estimate to the nearest inch. Then measure to the nearest $\frac{1}{4}$ inch.

8. 

9. 

Estimate to the nearest $\frac{1}{2}$ inch. Then measure to the nearest $\frac{1}{8}$ inch.

10. 

11. 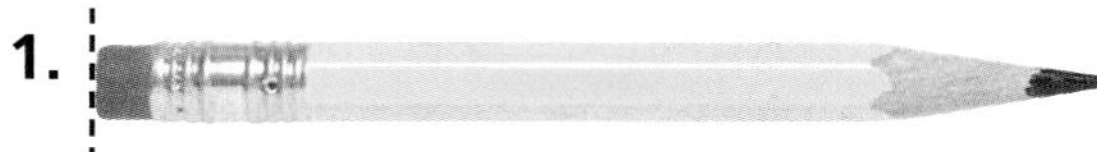

Order the measurements from *least* to *greatest*.

12. $1\frac{3}{4}$ in., $2\frac{3}{8}$ in., 1 in., $2\frac{1}{2}$ in.

13. $\frac{3}{4}$ in., $\frac{2}{8}$ in., $\frac{1}{2}$ in., $\frac{7}{8}$ in.

Order the measurements from *greatest* to *least*.

14. $\frac{5}{8}$ in., $1\frac{1}{4}$ in., $1\frac{1}{8}$ in., 1 in.

15. $2\frac{7}{8}$ in., 2 in., $2\frac{1}{2}$ in., $2\frac{3}{4}$ in.

Use a ruler. Draw a line for each length.

16. 2 in.
17. $1\frac{1}{2}$ in.
18. $3\frac{3}{4}$ in.
19. $\frac{5}{8}$ in.
20. $4\frac{3}{8}$ in.
21. $5\frac{1}{4}$ in.
22. $2\frac{7}{8}$ in.
23. $6\frac{6}{8}$ in.

USE DATA For 24–25, use the picture.

24. Find the length of the rock to the nearest inch and nearest $\frac{1}{2}$ inch.

25. Find the length of the fossilized leaf in the rock to the nearest inch.

26. Vocabulary Power *Inch* comes from the Latin word *uncia.* A uncia was a unit of length $\frac{1}{12}$ of the length of the Roman unit called a *pes.* How is the uncia similar to the inch?

27. Your class wants to take a tour of the Natural History Museum at 1:15 P.M. It is 11:38 A.M. now. How long is it until the tour begins?

28. What's the Error? Max says that his measurement of $2\frac{3}{8}$ in. is closer to 2 in. than to $2\frac{1}{2}$ in. Describe and correct his error.

29. Write About It Could you measure an object to the nearest $\frac{1}{4}$ in. and get a measurement that is a whole number? Explain.

30. **FAST FACT • SCIENCE** A horse's height is measured in a unit called hands. A hand is 4 inches, or about the width of an adult's hand. The average height of an Arabian horse is 15 hands. What is the average height in inches?

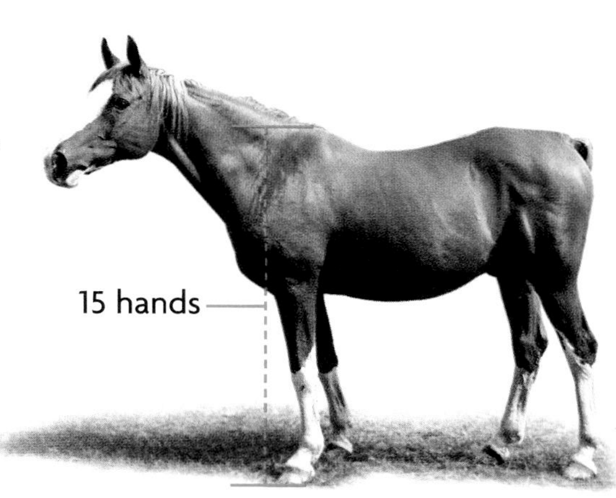

31. Ken's project included a maple leaf $5\frac{3}{4}$ in. long, a dogwood leaf $5\frac{1}{2}$ in. long, and a poplar leaf $5\frac{3}{8}$ in. long. Order the lengths from shortest to longest.

Mixed Review and Test Prep

32. Compare. Write $<$ or $>$ for the ●. (p. 424)
$^{-}7$ ● $^{+}9$

33. $6\frac{2}{3} - 2\frac{1}{3}$ (p. 474)

34. Write 23 minutes before twelve as it would appear on a digital clock. (p. 96)

35. Round 214,568 to the nearest hundred thousand. (p. 30)

36. Write $\frac{10}{12}$ as a fraction in simplest form. (p. 448)

37. **TEST PREP** 12×345 (p. 256)

A 3,000 C 4,060
B 3,600 D 4,140

38. **TEST PREP** $816 \div 34$ (p. 320)

F 20 G 24 H 28 J 30

Problem Solving Thinker's Corner

ESTIMATE OR MEASURE Sometimes an estimate is all you need to answer a problem, and sometimes you need to find an accurate measurement. Choosing whether to estimate or to measure is based on the situation.

Examples

Decide whether you need an estimate or an accurate measurement.

A The hardware store sells chain by the foot.

accurate measurement

B The coach wonders if the water is too cold for swimming.

estimate

C The nurse gives her patient cough syrup.

accurate measurement

Decide whether you need an estimate or an accurate measurement. Write *estimate* or *measure*.

1. length of boards to make a fence
2. distance from home to a store
3. amount of water needed to fill a pool

LESSON 3

Algebra: Change Linear Units

Quick Review

1. 3×16
2. $72 \div 3$
3. 5×12
4. $96 \div 12$
5. $180 \div 3$

Learn

TALL ENOUGH? In order to ride the roller coaster, Renee must be at least 48 inches tall. Renee is 5 feet tall. Is she tall enough to ride the roller coaster?

Equivalent Measures
1 foot (ft) = 12 inches (in.)
1 yard (yd) = 3 feet
1 mile (mi) = 1,760 yards, or 5,280 feet

You must be as tall as my tail to ride the roller coaster.

Example 1 5 feet = ■ inches

A foot is a larger unit than an inch. When you change larger units to smaller units, you need more of the smaller units, so multiply.

feet	×	inches in 1 foot	=	total inches
↓		↓		↓
5	×	12	=	60

60 inches is greater than 48 inches.
So, Renee is tall enough to ride the roller coaster.

Example 2 How many yards are 10,560 feet?

Think: 10,560 feet = ■ yards

When you change smaller units to larger units, you need fewer of the larger units, so divide.

You can divide 10,560 by 3 with a calculator.

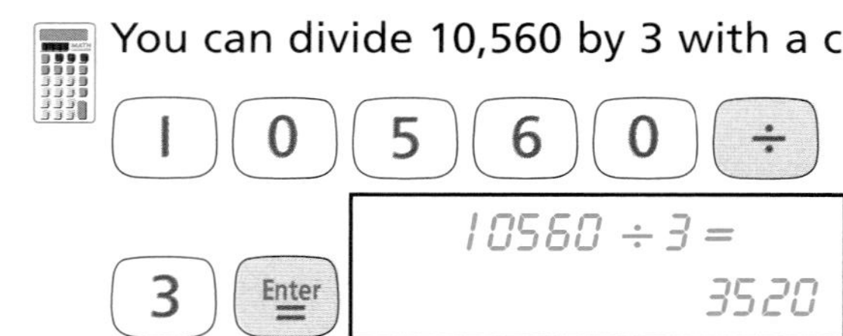

So, 10,560 feet is the same as 3,520 yards.

You can use an equation to change units.

Example 3 Use $y = f \div 3$ to complete the table.

Feet, f	Yards, y
24	■
30	■
36	■

$y = f \div 3$
$y = 24 \div 3$, so $y = 8$.
$y = 30 \div 3$, so $y = 10$.
$y = 36 \div 3$, so $y = 12$.

Feet, f	Yards, y
24	8
30	10
36	12

Check

1. **Explain** whether you would multiply or divide to change miles to yards.

Complete. Tell whether you multiply or divide.

2. 36 in. = ■ ft
3. 2 mi = ■ ft
4. 5 yd = ■ ft

Practice and Problem Solving

Extra Practice, page 534, Set C

Complete. Tell whether you multiply or divide.

5. 8 ft = ■ in.
6. 1,200 ft = ■ yd
7. 3 mi = ■ ft
8. 48 in. = ■ ft
9. 432 in. = ■ yd
10. 2 mi = ■ yd

USE DATA For 11–12, write an equation that can be used to complete each table. Copy and complete the table.

11.

Feet, f	2	3	4	5	7	9
Inches, i	■	36	■	60	84	■

12.

Inches, i	36	72	108	144	252	324
Yards, y	1	2	■	■	■	9

Compare. Write <, >, or = for each ●.

13. 144 in. ● 5 yd
14. 1,820 yd ● 1 mi
15. 525 ft ● 6,300 in.
16. 22 in. ● 2 ft
17. 16 yd ● 45 ft
18. 6 ft ● 72 in.

19. Use a yardstick to measure the length of your classroom in yards. Record the measurement. What is the length of your classroom in feet? Explain how you changed yards to feet.

20. **REASONING** To make a bench for their playhouse, the children need a board 80 inches long. They have a board that is $6\frac{1}{2}$ feet long. Is the board long enough? Explain.

21. The *Raven*, a roller coaster at Holiday World in Indiana, requires riders to be 46 inches tall. If Fernando is 4 feet tall, can he ride the *Raven*? Explain.

22. Russ bought 3 feet of rope. He then cut off 7 inches of rope to glue around the edge of a pot. How many inches of rope does Russ have left?

Mixed Review and Test Prep

23. $4 \times (25 + 4)$ (p. 186)

Compare. Write <, >, or = for each ●.

24. $\frac{5}{8}$ ● $\frac{4}{6}$ (p. 452)

25. $5\frac{3}{4}$ ● $\frac{23}{4}$ (p. 458)

26. 250 + ■ = 532 (p. 40)

27. **TEST PREP** Which unit would you use to measure the length of a room? (p. 518)

A quart
B foot
C mile
D pound

LESSON 4

Capacity

Quick Review

Multiply each number by 4.

1. 8
2. 9
3. 12
4. 7
5. 20

VOCABULARY

capacity
teaspoon (tsp)
tablespoon (tbsp)
cup (c)
pint (pt)
quart (qt)
gallon (gal)

MATERIALS 1-cup, 1-pint, 1-quart, and 1-gallon containers, water

Explore

The **capacity** of a container is the amount it can hold when it is filled. The customary units for measuring capacity are **teaspoon**, **tablespoon**, **cup**, **pint**, **quart**, and **gallon**.

Activity

How many cups fill a pint? a quart? a gallon?

STEP 1

Copy the table. Estimate the number of cups needed to fill each container. Record your estimate.

CONTAINER	NUMBER OF CUPS	
How many cups are in each?	Estimate	Actual
Pint	■	■
Quart	■	■
Gallon	■	■

STEP 2

Fill the measuring cup with water to the 1-cup line.

STEP 3

Pour the water into each of the containers. In your table, record the actual number of cups. Then compare your measurements with those of your classmates.

- **REASONING** Suppose you wanted to find the capacity of a child's wading pool. Which would be the more appropriate unit to use, a small bucket or a paper cup? Explain.

There is 1 pint of water in the gallon container. How many more pints do we need to make a gallon?

Try It

Estimate. Then measure.

a. How many pints fill a gallon container?

b. How many cups fill 2 quart containers?

c. How many cups fill 3 pint containers?

d. How many quarts fill 4 gallon containers?

Connect

You can change units of capacity from one unit to another. Use the table of measures and multiply or divide.

Customary Units for Measuring Liquids	
1 tablespoon (tbsp)	= 3 teaspoons (tsp)
1 pint (pt)	= 2 cups (c)
1 quart (qt)	= 2 pints
1 gallon (gal)	= 4 quarts

Examples

A How many quarts are in 2 gallons?

2 gal = ■ qt

gallons ↓ 2 × quarts in 1 gallon ↓ 4 = quarts ↓ 8

So, 2 gallons equals 8 quarts.

B How many pints are equal to 6 cups?

6 c = ■ pt

cups ↓ 6 ÷ cups in 1 pint ↓ 2 = pints ↓ 3

So, 6 cups equals 3 pints.

Practice and Problem Solving

Copy and complete the tables. Change the units.

1.

Cup	2	8	14
Pint	■	■	■

2.

Pint	8	24	■
Gallon	■	■	8

3.

Teaspoon	3	■	15
Tablespoon	■	4	■

Choose the most reasonable unit of capacity. Write *a*, *b*, or *c*.

4. 

a. cup
b. tablespoon
c. gallon

5. **a.** gallon
b. cup
c. quart

6. **a.** quart
b. cup
c. teaspoon

7. Alice bought 5 half gallons of orange juice, 2 quarts of pineapple juice, and 2 gallons of lemonade to make fruit punch. How many gallons of drink did she buy altogether?

8. ALGEBRA Use the equation $c = 16 \times g$ to find the number of cups in 7 gallons.

c = number of cups
g = number of gallons

Mixed Review and Test Prep

9. 4 ft = ■ in. (p. 526) **10.** 6 yd = ■ ft (p. 526)

11. Write $\frac{12}{16}$ in simplest form. (p. 448)

12. 4,008 − 1,992 (p. 50)

13. TEST PREP Which is equal to 36? (p. 184)

A $2 \times 2 \times 3$
B $2 \times 2 \times 9$
C $2 \times 3 \times 4$
D 2×8

LESSON 5

Weight

Quick Review

Multiply each number by 16.

1. 8
2. 10
3. 6
4. 5
5. 14

VOCABULARY

ounce (oz) **pound (lb)** **ton (T)**

MATERIALS spring scale, 5 classroom objects

Explore

How would you describe the weight of a toy car? the weight of a real car?

The customary units for measuring weight are **ounce (oz)**, **pound (lb)**, and **ton (T)**.

One toy car weighs about 1 oz.

One remote-control car weighs about 1 lb.

One real car weighs about 1 T.

Activity

Choose 5 classroom objects that you can weigh with your scale.

STEP 1

Make a table. Estimate the weight of each object in ounces or pounds. Record the object and estimated weight.

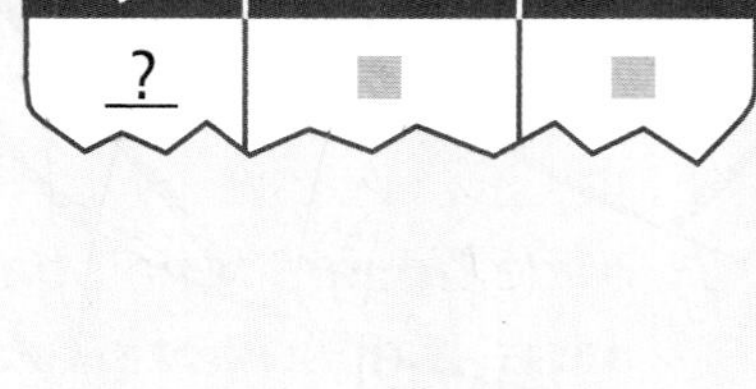

OBJECT	ESTIMATE	ACTUAL
?	■	■

STEP 2

Weigh each object. Record each actual weight in your table. Compare your actual measurement to your estimate.

- Are your estimates reasonable?
- What tool do you think is used to measure the weight of a car?

Try It

Choose *ounce* or *pound* for each object. Then measure the weight.

a. a stapler **b.** a box of crayons

We have a spring scale. Will the stapler weigh more than or less than 1 pound?

Connect

You can multiply or divide to change units of weight.

Equivalent Weights		
16 ounces (oz)	=	1 pound (lb)
2,000 pounds (lb)	=	1 ton (T)

Examples

A How many ounces are in 7 pounds?

7 lb = ▒ oz

pounds		ounces in 1 pound		ounces
↓		↓		↓
7	×	16	=	112

So, 7 pounds equals 112 ounces.

B How many tons are equal to 4,000 pounds?

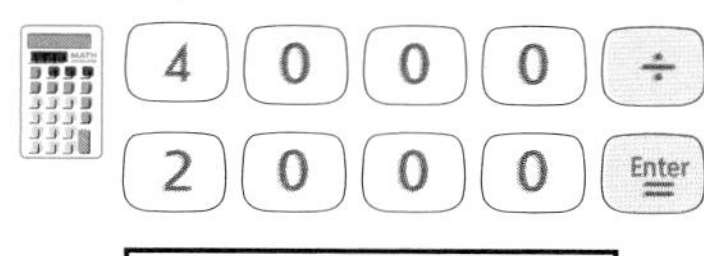

4000 ÷ 2000 = 2

So, 4,000 pounds equals 2 tons.

Practice and Problem Solving

Choose the more reasonable measurement.

1. 15 oz or 15 lb

2. 1 lb or 1 T

3. 14 oz or 14 lb

Complete. Tell whether you multiply or divide.

4. 3 lb = ▒ oz

5. 5 T = ▒ lb

6. 160 oz = ▒ lb

Change to pounds.

7. 32 oz

8. 2 T

9. 3 T

10. 96 oz

11. Tamika weighed 7 lb 6 oz at birth. Her weight doubled in three months. How much did she weigh at the end of three months?

12. **? What's the Error?** Byron needs 2 lb of snack mix. He bought two 8-oz packages. Describe his error. Tell what Byron should have bought.

13. Which is less, 3,000 lb or 2 T? Explain.

14. Which is greater, 5 lb or 88 oz? Explain.

Mixed Review and Test Prep

15. Round 213,467 to the nearest ten. (p. 30)

16. $5\frac{4}{5} - 3\frac{1}{5}$ (p. 474)

17. $\begin{array}{r} 4{,}306 \\ -2{,}987 \\ \hline \end{array}$ (p. 48)

18. 5 ft = ▒ in. (p. 526)

19. **TEST PREP** How many inches are in 8 yards? (p. 526)

A 24 in. **B** 96 in. **C** 288 in. **D** 324 in.

LESSON 6

Problem Solving Strategy
Compare Strategies

Quick Review

Name the next possible number for each pattern.

1. 16, 32, 48, 64, ■

2. 2, 4, 6, 8, ■

3. 12, 24, 36, 48, ■

4. 4, 8, 12, 16, ■

5. 3, 6, 9, 12, ■

PROBLEM Carol's mom is making punch for 8 children. If she mixes 5 pints of pineapple juice and 2 quarts of orange juice, will each child be able to have 2 cups of punch?

UNDERSTAND

- What are you asked to find?
- What information will you use?
- Is there any information you will not use?

PLAN

- What strategy can you use?

Often you can use more than one strategy to solve a problem. Use *draw a picture* or *make a table*.

SOLVE

- How will you solve the problem?

Draw a Picture Show how to find the total cups of punch.

Pineapple Juice
1 pt = 2 c

Orange Juice
1 qt = 2 pt

2 qt = 4 pt

5 pt = 10 c

4 pt = 8 c

10 + 8 = 18, or 18 cups

Make a Table Show the relationships between cups, pints, and quarts.

1 pt = 2 c

1 qt = 2 pt

PINEAPPLE JUICE					
pints	1	2	3	4	5
cups	2	4	6	8	10

ORANGE JUICE		
quarts	1	2
pints	2	4
cups	4	8

5 pints of pineapple juice equals 10 cups, and 2 quarts of orange juice equals 8 cups.

10 + 8 = 18, or 18 cups

Carol's mom needs 2 × 8, or 16, cups of punch. Since 18 > 16, there will be enough punch for each child to have 2 cups.

CHECK

- What other strategy could you use?

Problem Solving Practice

Choose a strategy to solve. Explain your choice.

1. **What if** Carol's mom mixed 2 quarts of orange juice and 1 quart of pineapple juice? Would there be enough for each child to have 2 cups of punch? Explain.

2. Deborah is making punch. One cup of concentrated juice makes 1 quart of punch. If Deborah buys 3 pints of concentrated juice, how many quarts of punch can she make?

Strategies

- **Draw a Diagram or Picture**
- Make a Model or Act It Out
- Make an Organized List
- Find a Pattern
- **Make a Table or Graph**
- Predict and Test
- Work Backward
- Solve a Simpler Problem
- Write an Equation
- Use Logical Reasoning

Problem Solving

Luisa is sewing doll clothes and uses lace for the trim. Each dress needs 1 foot of lace. Luisa buys 2 yards of lace.

3. **ALGEBRA** Which equation represents the number of dresses Luisa can trim?
   y = yards, d = number of dresses
   A $y = 3 + d$
   B $d = 3 \div y$
   C $d = 3 + y$
   D $d = y \times 3$

4. How many doll dresses can Luisa trim?
   F 5
   G 6
   H 11
   J 12

Mixed Strategy Practice

5. Angelo caught a fish that was 2 feet long. Mitch caught a fish that was 5 inches shorter than the fish Angelo caught. How long was the fish that Mitch caught?

6. The test scores for four students were 85, 93, 77, and 92. Jackie's score was 8 points higher than Mark's but 7 points lower than Mary's. Nick had the highest score. What was each student's test score?

USE DATA **For 7–8, use the graph.**

7. Maria kept a record of how many miles she walked around a track each school day. It takes 4 laps around the track to equal 1 mile. How many laps around the track did Maria walk in one week?

8. **What's the Error?** Anna says that the distance Maria walked for the week was over 16,000 yards. Describe and correct her error.

Extra Practice

Set A (pp. 518–521)

Choose the most reasonable unit of measure. Write *in., ft, yd,* or *mi.*

1. The length of my foot is about 8 ?.
2. The height of my dog is about 3 ?.
3. The width of my room is 4 ?.

Name the greater measurement.

4. 15 ft or 15 yd
5. 300 mi or 300 ft
6. 39 in. or 39 yd
7. 72 in. or 72 ft
8. 4 ft or 4 mi
9. 93 yd or 93 ft

Set B (pp. 522–525)

Estimate to the nearest inch. Then measure to the nearest $\frac{1}{4}$ inch.

1. 

2.

Estimate to the nearest $\frac{1}{2}$ inch. Then measure to the nearest $\frac{1}{8}$ inch.

3.

4.

Order the measurements from *least* to *greatest*.

5. $7\frac{1}{2}$ in., $7\frac{5}{8}$ in., $7\frac{1}{4}$ in.
6. $4\frac{1}{8}$ in., $4\frac{3}{4}$ in., $3\frac{7}{8}$ in.
7. $2\frac{1}{2}$ in., $2\frac{3}{8}$ in., $2\frac{5}{8}$ in.

Set C (pp. 526–527)

Complete. Tell whether you multiply or divide.

1. 60 in. = ■ ft
2. 12 yd = ■ in.
3. 5 mi = ■ yd
4. 900 ft = ■ yd

Compare. Write <, >, or = for each ●.

5. 7 ft ● 80 in.
6. 4 mi ● 2,200 ft
7. 108 in. ● 2 yd
8. 36 in. ● 1 yd
9. 210 ft ● 75 yd
10. 3 ft ● 36 in.
11. 144 in. ● 3 yd
12. 3,520 yd ● 3 mi
13. 20 ft ● 60 yd

Review/Test

CHECK VOCABULARY AND CONCEPTS

Choose the best term from the box.

capacity
cup
foot
linear
mile
ounce
pound
ton
yard

1. The _?_ of a container is the amount it can hold when it is filled. (p. 528)
2. Units used to measure length, width, height, and distance are _?_ units. (p. 518)
3. The customary units for weight are _?_, _?_, and _?_. (p. 530)

CHECK SKILLS

Choose the most reasonable unit of measure.
Write *in., ft, yd,* or *mi.* (pp. 518–521)

4. The height of a desk is about 3 _?_.
5. The length of a bus route is about 10 _?_.
6. The width of a door is about 36 _?_.

Name the greater measurement. (pp. 518–521, 528–529, 530–531)

7. 300 yd or 300 ft
8. 3 c or 3 pt
9. 4 T or 4 lb
10. 64 oz or 3 lb

11. Measure to the nearest $\frac{1}{4}$ inch. (pp. 522–525)

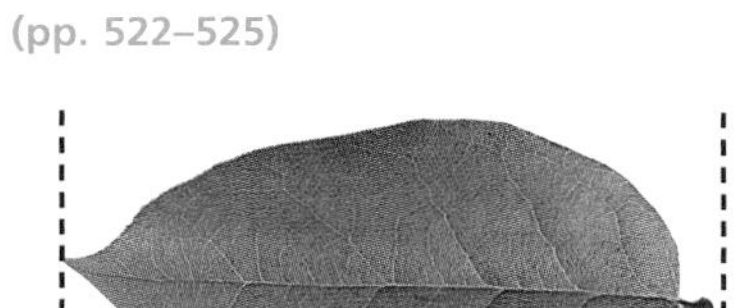

12. Measure to the nearest $\frac{1}{8}$ inch. (pp. 522–525)

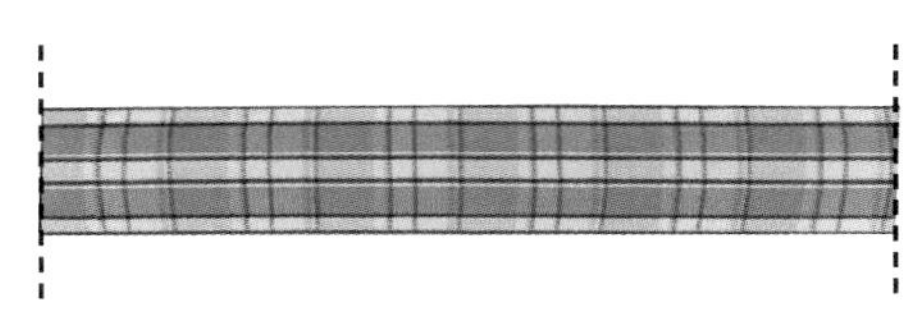

Complete. Tell whether you multiply or divide. (pp. 526–527, 528–529, 530–531)

13. 2 lb = ■ oz
14. 2 yd = ■ in.
15. 48 in. = ■ ft
16. 2 mi = ■ yd
17. 3 T = ■ lb
18. 4 pt = ■ qt

CHECK PROBLEM SOLVING

Choose a strategy to solve. Explain your choice. (pp. 532–533)

19. There are 22 students in the class. If each student will drink 1 cup of punch, how many pints are needed?
20. Karl's grandmother needs 72 inches of lace for her quilt. Lace costs $3 per yard. How much will she pay?

Standardized Test Prep

NUMBER SENSE, CONCEPTS, AND OPERATIONS

TIP **Check your work.** See item 1. Check your work by dividing your answer by one of the factors. The quotient should be the other factor.

1. The table below shows the number of some books in Mr. Duran's fourth-grade classroom.

MR. DURAN'S CLASS LIBRARY	
Type of Book	**Number**
Science	34
History	19
Poetry	12

The school library has 5 times as many poetry books as Mr. Duran has in his class library. How many poetry books are in the school library?

A 50 **C** 60
B 55 **D** 70

2. Which pair of fractions are equivalent?

F $\frac{1}{4}$ and $\frac{1}{8}$ **H** $\frac{2}{4}$ and $\frac{3}{8}$
G $\frac{1}{4}$ and $\frac{3}{8}$ **J** $\frac{2}{4}$ and $\frac{4}{8}$

3. **Explain It** Which is a more reasonable number of coins in the full jar: 120 or 1,200?

12 coins

Explain your thinking.

MEASUREMENT

4. Rosa has a Great Dane that is 2 feet 6 inches tall. How many inches tall is Rosa's Great Dane?

1 foot = 12 inches

A 24 inches
B 30 inches
C 36 inches
D 42 inches

5. Gallons would be the **best** unit for measuring the capacity of which object?

F

G

H

J

6. **Explain It** Which object weighs about 10 ounces: a stuffed animal, a cat, or a tiger? Explain how you decided.

GEOMETRY AND SPATIAL SENSE

7. Which two figures below appear to be congruent?

A

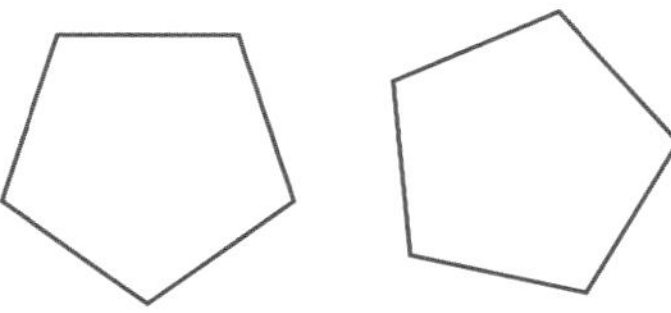

B

C

D

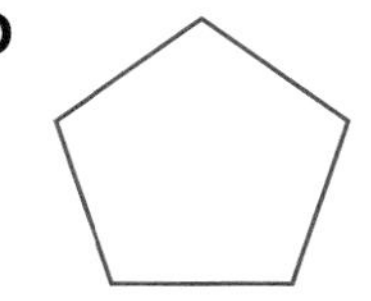
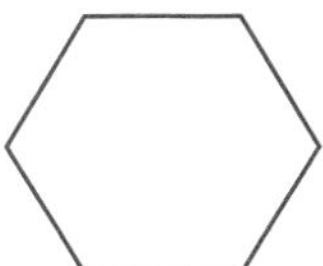

8. Which lines are parallel?

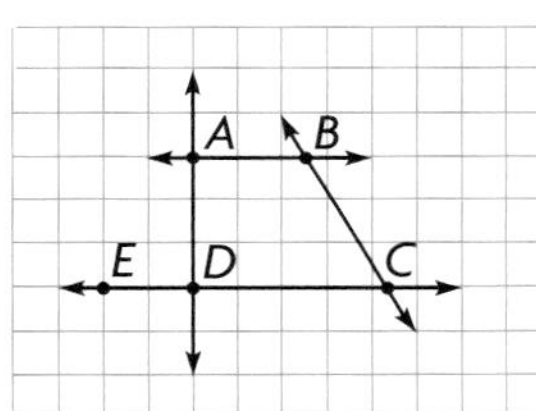

F $\overleftrightarrow{AB}$ and $\overleftrightarrow{BC}$ **H** $\overleftrightarrow{AD}$ and $\overleftrightarrow{BC}$

G $\overleftrightarrow{AB}$ and $\overleftrightarrow{EC}$ **J** $\overleftrightarrow{AD}$ and $\overleftrightarrow{EC}$

9. Explain It Find the sum of the numbers inside all the quadrilaterals.

1

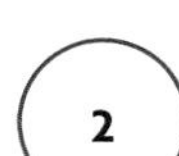

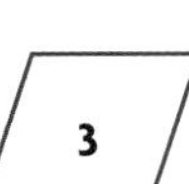

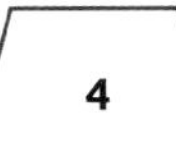

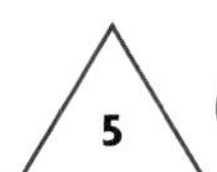

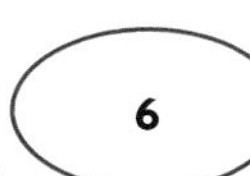

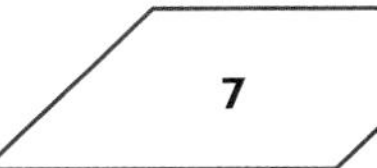

Explain your thinking.

DATA ANALYSIS AND PROBABILITY

10. George surveyed several friends to find out their favorite sport that they watch on television. The graph below shows the results.

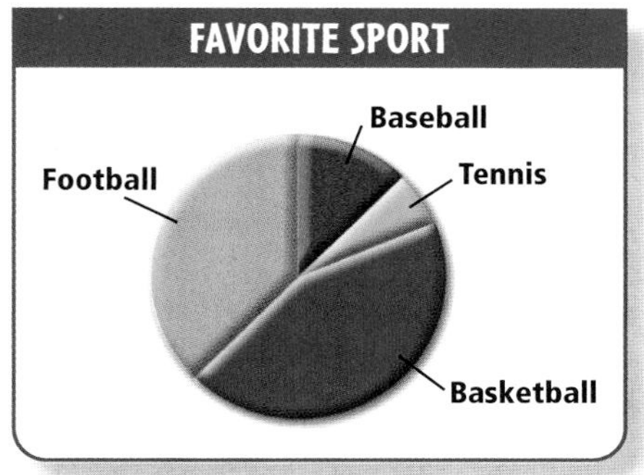

Which is the **least** popular sport?

A tennis **C** baseball

B basketball **D** football

11. What is the probability of picking an orange marble from the bag below without looking?

F $\frac{1}{6}$ **H** $\frac{5}{12}$

G $\frac{1}{3}$ **J** $\frac{1}{2}$

12. Explain It John recorded the time he spent at the gym for four days.

TIME SPENT AT THE GYM	
Day	**Time (in minutes)**
Thursday	40
Friday	65
Saturday	90
Sunday	30

What is the range for his times? Explain how you decided.

CHAPTER 25 Metric Measurement

Grizzly Bear

Cardinal

Raccoon

Ostrich

FAST FACT • SCIENCE When animals walk through soft soil, they often leave tracks. People can look at the tracks and tell what kind of animal has been there. For example, tracks with four toes on the front foot and five on the hind foot were made by a rodent.

PROBLEM SOLVING Look at the drawings of the animal tracks. Which animal has the largest track? the smallest? Measure your foot. How does it compare to the tracks?

ANIMAL TRACKS

Track	Animal	Length
	Ostrich	14 cm
	Grizzly Bear	18 cm
	Cardinal	3 cm
	Raccoon	8 cm

CHECK WHAT YOU KNOW

Use this page to help you review and remember important skills needed for Chapter 25.

MEASURE TO THE NEAREST CENTIMETER

Measure the length of each object to the nearest centimeter.

1. 

2. 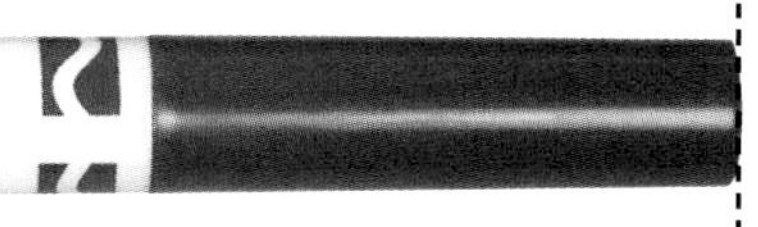

3.

MENTAL MATH: MULTIPLICATION PATTERNS

Use a pattern to find each product.

4. 3×10
3×100
$3 \times 1{,}000$

5. 6×10
6×100
$6 \times 1{,}000$

6. 8×10
8×100
$8 \times 1{,}000$

7. 12×10
12×100
$12 \times 1{,}000$

MENTAL MATH: DIVISION PATTERNS

Use a pattern to find each quotient.

8. $70 \div 10$
$700 \div 10$
$7{,}000 \div 10$

9. $40 \div 10$
$400 \div 10$
$4{,}000 \div 10$

10. $90 \div 10$
$900 \div 10$
$9{,}000 \div 10$

11. $50 \div 10$
$500 \div 10$
$5{,}000 \div 10$

VOCABULARY POWER

REVIEW

measure [mezh′ər] *noun*

When *measure* is used as a noun, it means "a unit used for comparison." When used as a verb, it means "to find the size, quantity, amount, time, or degree of." Name some tools used for measuring.

PREVIEW

millimeter (mm)
centimeter (cm)
decimeter (dm)
meter (m)
kilometer (km)
milliliter (mL)
kilogram (kg)
liter (L)
mass
gram (g)

www.harcourtschool.com/mathglossary

LESSON 1

Metric Length

Learn

HOW LONG? HOW SHORT? The western pygmy-blue butterfly is one of the smallest butterflies. Measure the width of its wingspan to the nearest centimeter using a metric ruler.

Quick Review

1. 10 × 10
2. 10 × 7
3. 100 × 3
4. 800 × 100
5. 10 × 100

VOCABULARY

millimeter (mm) **centimeter (cm)**
decimeter (dm) **meter (m)**
kilometer (km)

The wingspan of this butterfly is between 2 and 3 centimeters. To the nearest centimeter, the wingspan is 2 centimeters.

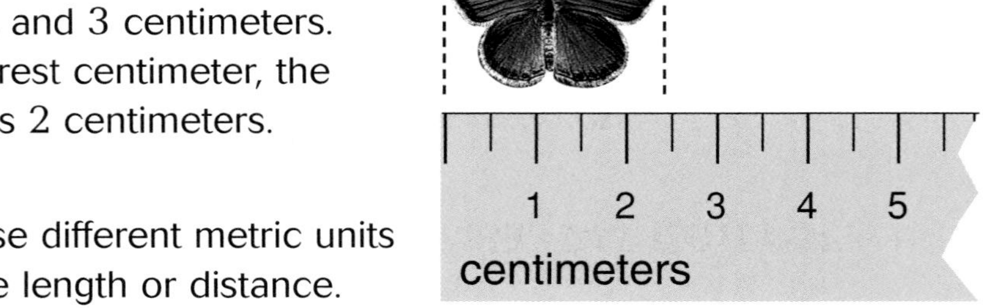

You can use different metric units to measure length or distance.

A **millimeter (mm)** is about the thickness of a dime.

A **centimeter (cm)** is about the width of your index finger.

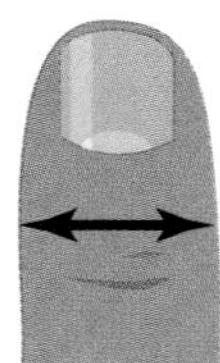

A **decimeter (dm)** is about the width of an adult's hand.

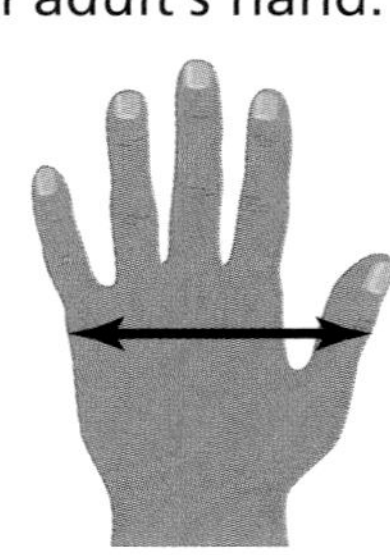

A **meter (m)** is about the width of a door.

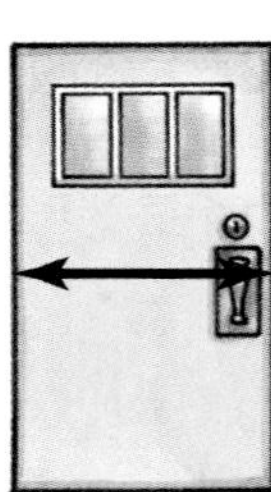

HANDS ON

Activity 1 **MATERIALS:** centimeter ruler, meterstick

- Estimate and then measure the lengths of 5 objects in your classroom to the nearest millimeter, centimeter, decimeter, or meter. Record the estimates and actual measurements in a table.
- How did you estimate the length of each object?
- Order the objects you measured from least to greatest length.

	Object	Unit of Measure	Estimate	Measurement
1.				
2.				
3.				

Greater Lengths

Activity 2

MATERIALS: centimeter ruler, meterstick

Now measure your desktop.

- Choose a unit of measure. Record all the linear measurements of your desktop to the nearest centimeter, decimeter, or meter.
- Compare your results to your classmates' results. Are the measurements of your desktops the same? If not, why not?

Mrs. Chen's class is taking a bus to the zoo. She wants to know how far the zoo is from the school. What unit of measure should she use?

Longer distances and lengths can be measured in kilometers. A **kilometer (km)** is about the length of 10 football fields.

So, Mrs. Chen should measure the distance from the school to the zoo in kilometers.

Technology Link

More Practice: Harcourt Mega Math Ice Station Exploration, *Linear Lab,* Levels I and J

MATH IDEA The millimeter, centimeter, decimeter, meter, and kilometer are metric units of length or distance.

Check

1. **Estimate** and measure the length of a poster or bulletin board in your classroom. Then explain how you decided what unit of measure to use.

Use a centimeter ruler or a meterstick to measure each item. Write the measurement and unit of measure used.

2. length of a thumbtack
3. length of a stapler
4. length of a classroom

Choose the most reasonable unit of measure. Write *mm, cm, dm, m,* or *km*.

5. 

The length of an airport runway is about 3 ?.

6. 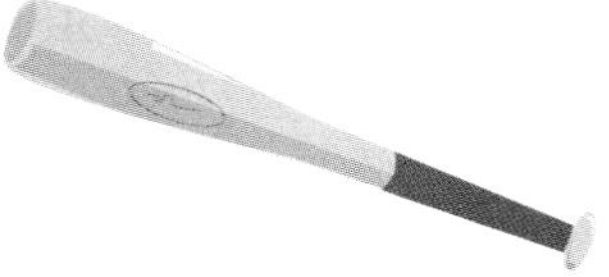

The length of a baseball bat is about 1 ?.

7. 

The length of a key is about 5 ?.

LESSON CONTINUES 

Practice and Problem Solving

Extra Practice, page 554, Set A

Use a centimeter ruler or a meterstick to measure each item. Write the measurement and unit of measure used.

8. length of a pencil

9. width of a poster

10. length of a chalkboard

Choose the most reasonable unit of measure. Write *mm, cm, dm, m,* or *km*.

11.

The height of the table is about 76 __?__.

12.

The length of the worm is about 10 __?__.

13.

The length of the car is about 4 __?__.

14. distance between two cities

15. height of a maple tree

16. thickness of a string

Compare. Write $<$ or $>$ for each ●.

17. 98 cm ● 98 m

18. 100 dm ● 100 km

19. 87 mm ● 87 cm

Use a metric ruler. Draw a line for each length.

20. 20 centimeters

21. 35 millimeters

22. 2 decimeters

For 23–24, use the ruler to find the distance.

23. between point A and point B

24. between point B and point D

25. Hudson ran a 5-kilometer race. Use the table to find how many minutes he ran in all. If the race began at 7:35 A.M., when did he cross the finish line?

HUDSON'S RACE

Kilometer	Time (each kilometer)
1 and 2	5 min 30 sec
3, 4, and 5	6 min

26. Tell whether the width of your notebook, your teacher's desk, and your desk are *about a meter, less than a meter,* or *more than a meter*. Then order the widths from greatest to least.

27. **REASONING** Cary's broken ruler begins at the 16-cm mark. If she draws a 7-cm line beginning at the 16-cm mark, at which mark will she stop?

28. Five students are 149 centimeters, 151 centimeters, 139 centimeters, 152 centimeters, and 144 centimeters tall. What is their average height?

29. In the first 3 weeks of their science project, Lea's plant grew 197 millimeters and Stacy's plant grew 211 millimeters. How much more did Stacy's plant grow than Lea's?

Mixed Review and Test Prep

30. Evaluate $5 \times (2 + 3)$. (p. 186)

31. Find the mean of 14, 16, 17, 17, 18, 19, 22, 23, 25. (p. 328)

32. What are the factors of 36? (p. 338)

33. Order $\frac{1}{3}$, $\frac{5}{6}$, $\frac{4}{9}$, and $\frac{1}{6}$ from least to greatest. (p. 452)

34. **TEST PREP** How many inches are in 3 feet? (p. 526)

   A 9 in. **B** 12 in. **C** 32 in. **D** 36 in.

35. **TEST PREP** Which fraction is equivalent to $\frac{8}{12}$? (p. 448)

   F $\frac{2}{6}$ **G** $\frac{2}{4}$ **H** $\frac{4}{8}$ **J** $\frac{2}{3}$

Problem Solving LINKUP . . . to Reading

STRATEGY • USE GRAPHIC AIDS Some maps show distances with metric units. In many countries distances from one city to another city are measured in kilometers. A map scale shows how distances on a map compare to actual distances. This scale shows 1 centimeter = 32 kilometers.

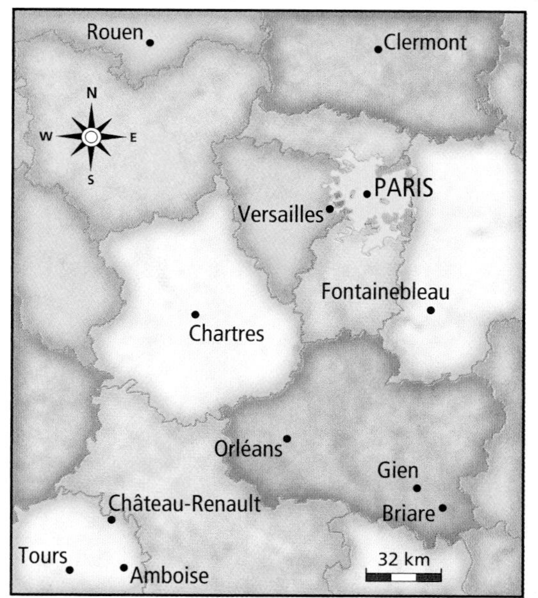

Use the scale to find the actual distance from Paris to Clermont.

Using a centimeter ruler, measure the length between the cities on the map. The length is about 2 centimeters. Since there are 32 kilometers in each centimeter, multiply 2 by 32.

So, 2 lengths $\times$ 32 kilometers = 64 kilometers.

Estimate the distances in centimeters. Then use the scale to find the actual distances.

1. Tours to Versailles
2. Gien to Paris
3. Chartres to Château-Renault
4. Briare to Tours

LESSON 2

Algebra: Change Linear Units

Quick Review

1. 60 × 10
2. 9,000 ÷ 10
3. 4 × 1,000
4. 600 ÷ 10
5. 300 × 10

Equivalent Measures

1 centimeter (cm) = 10 millimeters (mm)
1 decimeter (dm) = 10 centimeters
1 meter (m) = 1,000 millimeters
1 meter = 10 decimeters
1 kilometer (km) = 1,000 meters

Learn

ANIMAL ENGINEER In five hours, a mole can dig a tunnel 500 decimeters long. How many centimeters long would the tunnel be?

Think: 500 dm = ■ cm

A decimeter is a larger unit than a centimeter. When you change larger units to smaller units, you need more of the smaller units, so multiply by 10, 100, or 1,000.

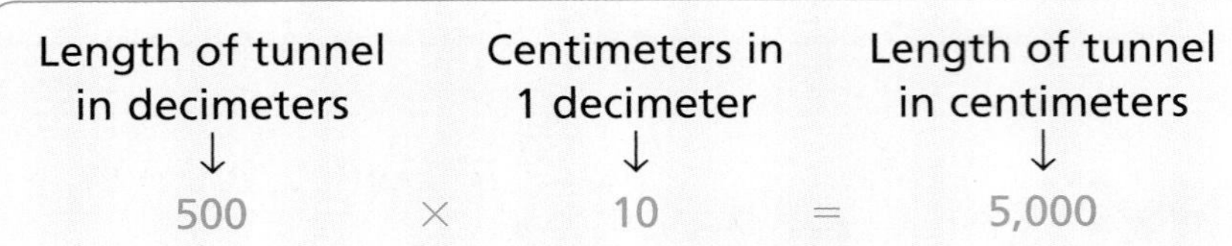

Length of tunnel in decimeters
Centimeters in 1 decimeter
Length of tunnel in centimeters
500 × 10 = 5,000

So, the tunnel would be 5,000 centimeters long.

When you change smaller units to larger units, you need fewer of the larger units, so divide by 10, 100, or 1,000.

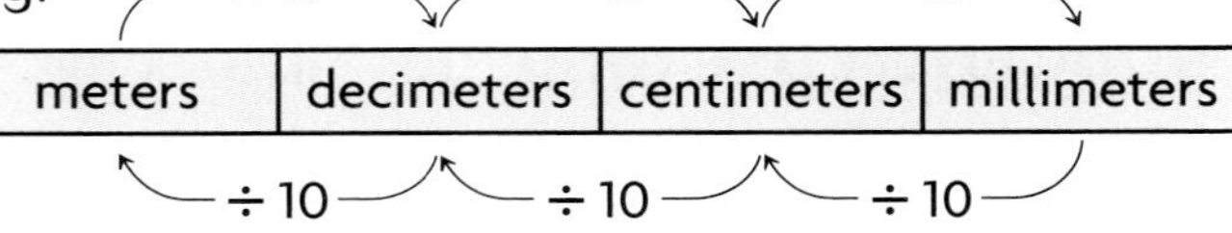

Examples

 300 millimeters = ■ centimeters

Since a millimeter is a smaller unit than a centimeter, divide.

millimeters		millimeters in 1 centimeter		centimeters
↓		↓		↓
300	÷	10	=	30

So, 300 millimeters = 30 centimeters.

B 7,000 millimeters = ■ meters

Since a millimeter is a smaller unit than a meter, divide.

You can divide 7,000 by 1,000 with a calculator.

7 0 0 0 ÷ 1 0 0 0 = 7

So, 7,000 millimeters = 7 meters.

Check

1. **Explain** whether you would multiply or divide by 100 to change meters to centimeters.

Complete. Tell whether you multiply or divide by 10, 100, or 1,000.

2. 5 m = ■ dm
3. 16 m = ■ cm
4. 900 mm = ■ cm

Practice and Problem Solving

Extra Practice, page 554, Set B

Complete. Tell whether you multiply or divide by 10, 100, or 1,000.

5. 500 dm = ■ mm
6. 35 m = ■ cm
7. 10 mm = ■ cm
8. 10 m = ■ dm
9. 8,000 m = ■ km
10. 2 km = ■ m

Write the correct unit.

11. 20 dm = 200 _?_
12. 40 cm = 400 _?_
13. 6 _?_ = 60 dm
14. 8 _?_ = 80 cm
15. 500 _?_ = 50 m
16. 14 m = 1,400 _?_

Compare. Write <, >, or = for each ●.

17. 8 m ● 400 cm
18. 40 cm ● 10 dm
19. 900 m ● 9 km
20. 2,000 cm ● 20 m
21. 10 dm ● 1,000 mm
22. 1 km ● 500 m

Order from least to greatest.

23. 3 dm; 120 cm; 18 dm; 1m
24. 20 m; 2 km; 2,100 dm; 2,000 mm

For 25–26, use this information. A beaver's dam can reach 300 m long. Some beavers dig canals so they can move sticks to their dams. These canals are about 40 cm deep and 50 cm wide and can be 210 m long.

25. Write how long a beaver canal and a beaver dam are in cm. How many cm is this in all?
26. Write the width and depth of a beaver canal in millimeters.
27. The top of one beaver's lodge is 130 cm above the water. Is this *more than* or *less than* 2 m? Explain.
28. **? What's the Error?** Ed is 2 m tall with shoes. Without shoes, Ed is 3 cm shorter. He wrote his height without shoes as 1,997 cm. Describe his error. Write the correct height.

Mixed Review and Test Prep

29. 2,000 − 876 (p. 50)
30. Write an expression for 2 more than some number. Use the variable *n*. (p. 64)
31. $\frac{3}{4} + \frac{5}{8}$ (p. 480)
32. 2 ft = ■ in. (p. 526)
33. **TEST PREP** Choose the most reasonable measurement for the height of the front door of a house. (p. 518)
    A 7 inches
    B 7 feet
    C 7 yards
    D 7 miles

LESSON 3

Capacity

Quick Review

1. ■ dm = 10 cm
2. 100 cm = ■ dm
3. ■ dm = 1 m
4. ■ cm = 3 m
5. 2 km = ■ m

VOCABULARY

milliliter (mL) **liter (L)**

MATERIALS 1-liter container, metric measuring cup, small plastic cup, bucket, tall plastic cup, dropper

Explore

To stay healthy, most people should drink more than $1\frac{1}{2}$ liters of water every day.

A **milliliter (mL)** and a **liter (L)** are metric units of capacity.

1 mL

1 L

1 L = 1,000 mL

What is the capacity of a plastic cup? of a bucket? You can measure the capacity of a container by using water.

Activity

STEP 1 Copy the table. Write an estimate of the capacity of each container in your table.

STEP 2 Measure the actual capacity of each container by using the dropper, metric measuring cup, or 1-liter container. Record the actual measurements to the nearest milliliter or liter in your table.

CONTAINER	ESTIMATE	ACTUAL
small cup		
tall cup		
bucket		

- Compare your estimates to the actual measurements. Are your estimates reasonable? Explain.
- Order the actual measurements from least to greatest.

Try It

Choose *mL* or *L* for each. Then measure the capacity.

a. small spoon
b. water pitcher
c. small cup
d. beaker

Which should we use to measure the capacity of the spoon?

Connect

You can use multiplication to change liters to milliliters.
You can use division to change milliliters to liters.

Capacity Equivalent
1 L = 1,000 mL

Examples

A 2 L = ▓ mL

Think: There are 1,000 mL in 1 L.

2 L = 2 × 1,000 = 2,000 mL

So, 2 L = 2,000 mL.

B 4,000 mL = ▓ L

Think: There are 1,000 mL in 1 L.

So, 4,000 mL = 4 L.

Practice and Problem Solving

Choose the more reasonable unit of measure. Write *mL* or *L*.

1. a raindrop

2. water in a pool

3. juice in a punch bowl

Choose the best estimate. Write *a, b,* or *c*.

4. 
a. 25 mL
b. 250 mL
c. 25 L

5. 

a. 6 mL
b. 600 mL
c. 6 L

6.
a. 2 mL
b. 20 mL
c. 2 L

Estimate and tell whether each object has a capacity of *about a liter, less than a liter,* or *more than a liter*.

7. 

8. 

9. 

Complete. Tell whether you multiply or divide.

10. 3 L = ▓ mL

11. 5,000 mL = ▓ L

12. 10 L = ▓ mL

13. Eric drinks 8 glasses of water each day. Each glass contains 300 milliliters. Anna drinks 2 liters of water each day. Who drinks more water? How much more?

14. **Write About It** Explain how two different containers can have the same capacity. Give an example.

Mixed Review and Test Prep

15. 82 × 63 (p. 252)

16. 216 ÷ 12 (p. 320)

17. $\frac{9}{10} - \frac{2}{10}$ (p. 472)

18. 78 × 43 (p. 252)

19. **TEST PREP** Which shows $\frac{20}{100}$ written in simplest form? (p. 448)

A $\frac{1}{5}$ **B** $\frac{2}{10}$ **C** $\frac{1}{2}$ **D** $\frac{5}{10}$

LESSON 4

Mass

Quick Review

1. $3 \times 1{,}000$
2. 10 cm = 1 __?__
3. $1{,}000 \times 2$
4. 100 __?__ = 1 m
5. $5{,}000 \div 10$

VOCABULARY

mass **gram (g)** **kilogram (kg)**

MATERIALS balance, gram and kilogram masses

Explore

Matter is what all objects are made of. **Mass** is the amount of matter in an object. Metric units of mass are the **gram (g)** and the **kilogram (kg)**.

The mass of a dollar bill or a small paper clip is about 1 gram.

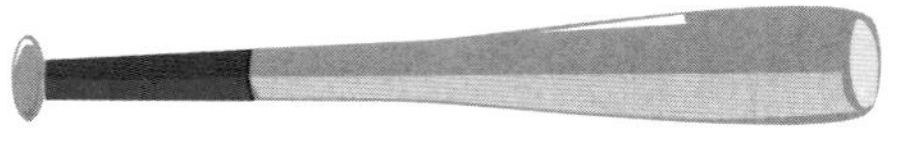

The mass of a baseball bat is about 1 kilogram.

Activity

Use a balance to find the mass of other objects.

STEP 1

Find the mass of each of 5 objects. Make a table. Estimate the mass of each object in grams or kilograms. Record the object and the estimated mass in the table.

STEP 2

Place each object on the balance. Record the actual measurements to the nearest gram or kilogram in your table.

OBJECT	ESTIMATE	ACTUAL
1.		
2.		
3.		
4.		
5.		

- Explain how to order the items you measured from least to greatest in mass.

We have gram and kilogram masses. Which should we use to measure the mass of the stapler?

Try It

Choose *g* or *kg* for each mass. Then measure the mass.

a. the mass of a stapler
b. the mass of a book

Connect

You can use multiplication to change kilograms to grams.
You can use division to change grams to kilograms.

Mass Equivalent
1 kg = 1,000 g

Examples

A 6 kg = ▒ g
Think: There are 1,000 g in 1 kg.
6 kg = 6 × 1,000 = 6,000 g

So, 6,000 g = 6 kg.

B 5,000 g = ▒ kg
Think: There are 1,000 g in 1 kg.

5 0 0 0 ÷ 1 0 0 0 = 5

So, 5,000 g = 5 kg.

Practice and Problem Solving

Choose the more reasonable measurement.

1. 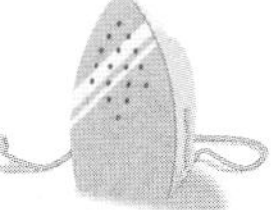
1 g or 1 kg

2. 
20 g or 200 g

3. 
10 g or 10 kg

4. 

40 kg or 4,000 kg

Complete. Tell whether you multiply or divide.

5. 4 kg = ▒ g **6.** 7,000 g = ▒ kg **7.** 3,000 g = ▒ kg **8.** 10 kg = ▒ g

USE DATA For 9–10, use the bar graph.

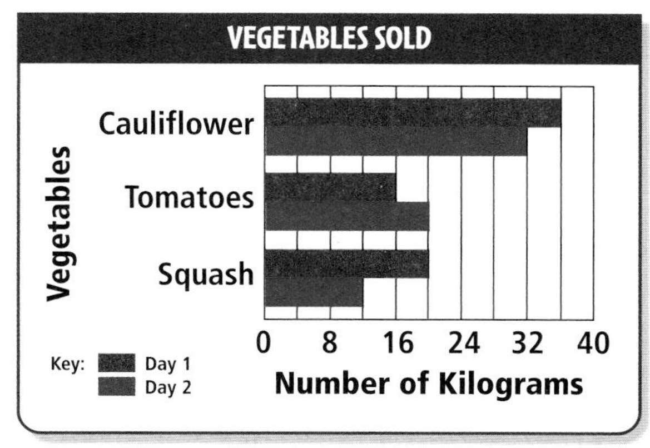

9. Find the vegetable whose sales increased from Day 1 to Day 2. How many more kilograms of vegetables were sold on Day 2?

10. Find the total mass of the vegetables sold on the two days.

11. ALGEBRA Write an equation that can be used to change kilograms to grams. Use *g* for the number of grams and *k* for the number of kilograms.

Mixed Review and Test Prep

12. 6,580 − 2,461 (p. 48)

13. 18 × 35 (p. 252)

Find the missing number.

14. 3,000 − ▒ = 1,284 + 254 (p. 70)

15. TEST PREP There are 256 cookies to be placed on 8 platters. How many cookies will be on each platter? (p. 300)

A 22 **B** 23 **C** 32 **D** 37

LESSON 5

Problem Solving Strategy
Draw a Diagram

Quick Review

1. 3 dm = 30 ?
2. 4 ? = 400 cm
3. 100 cm = 10 ?
4. 15 m = 1,500 ?
5. 800 cm = 8 ?

PROBLEM Darrell and Charles each caught a fish while deep-sea fishing. The two fish have a mass of 10 kilograms. The mass of Charles's fish is 1 kilogram more than twice the mass of Darrell's fish. What is the mass of each fish?

UNDERSTAND

- What are you asked to find?
- What information will you use?
- Is there any information you will not use? If so, what?

PLAN

- What strategy can you use to solve the problem?
  You can *draw a diagram.*

SOLVE

- How can you use the strategy to solve the problem?
  Draw a diagram showing the relationship between the masses of the two fish.

Charles's	▒ kg	▒ kg	1 kg
Darrell's	▒ kg		

Total mass is 10 kilograms.

Subtract 1 kilogram from 10 kilograms to find the sum of the three equal parts. $10 - 1 = 9$

Divide the sum by 3 to find the value of each part. $9 \div 3 = 3$

Each part is 3 kilograms, so Darrell's fish has a mass of 3 kilograms and Charles's fish has a mass of $3 + 3 + 1$, or 7 kilograms.

CHECK

- What other strategy could you use?

Problem Solving Practice

Draw a diagram to solve.

1. Val, Brent, and Don caught a total of 24 fish. Val caught 4 more fish than Brent. Don caught twice as many fish as Brent. How many fish did each catch?

For 2–3, use this information. Matt's dog is 15 centimeters longer than Michael's dog. Derek's dog is 9 centimeters longer than twice the length of Michael's dog. Michael's dog is 3 decimeters long.

2. What should you do to change the unit of length of Michael's dog from decimeters to centimeters?
   A divide by 100
   B divide by 10
   C multiply by 100
   D multiply by 10

3. What are the lengths of Matt's, Michael's, and Derek's dogs in centimeters?
   F 18 cm; 30 cm; 15 cm
   G 45 cm; 30 cm; 69 cm
   H 45 cm; 30 cm; 60 cm
   J 180 cm; 30 cm; 150 cm

Strategies

- **Draw a Diagram or Picture**
- Make a Model or Act It Out
- Make an Organized List
- Find a Pattern
- Make a Table or Graph
- Predict and Test
- Work Backward
- Solve a Simpler Problem
- Write an Equation
- Use Logical Reasoning

Problem Solving

Mixed Strategy Practice

USE DATA For 4–5, use the table.

4. The Martins went fishing for the weekend. They rented a fishing boat for 4 hours. They also rented 3 fishing poles and bought one bucket of bait. How much money did the Martins spend?

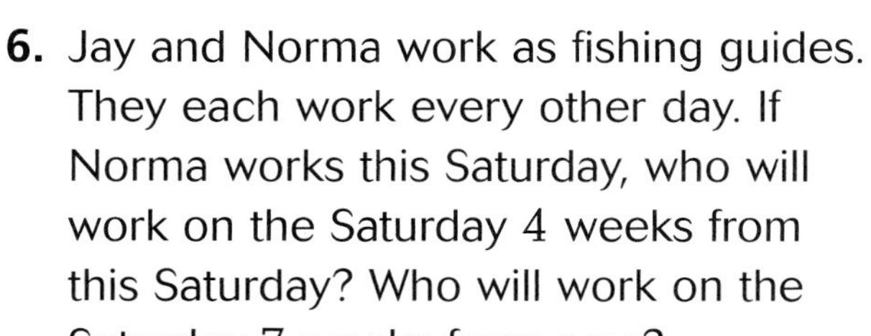

Lakeside Fish Camp

Open Daily at 10 A.M.

Boat Rental..............	$25 per hour
Fishing Pole Rental.....	$4 per day
Bucket of Bait............	$5 each

5. The Kells arrived at the Lakeside Fish Camp when it opened. They spent $4\frac{1}{2}$ hours fishing, 30 minutes eating lunch, and 90 minutes driving home from the camp. At what time did they get home?

6. Jay and Norma work as fishing guides. They each work every other day. If Norma works this Saturday, who will work on the Saturday 4 weeks from this Saturday? Who will work on the Saturday 7 weeks from now?

7. Felipe has a piece of bamboo that is 3 meters long. To make a fishing pole, he shortened it by 60 centimeters. How long is his fishing pole?

8. **Write a problem** that can be solved by drawing a diagram. Exchange problems with a classmate and solve.

LESSON 6

Relate Benchmark Measurements

Learn

RELATED The American Black Bear can weigh up to 500 pounds. About how many kilograms can the American Black Bear weigh?

You can use benchmark measurements to relate metric and customary measurements to each other.

Think: 1 kg is a little more than 2 lb.

1 kg ≈ 2 lb
↑
≈ means "is approximately equal to."

500 lb ≈ ▒ kg
$500 \div 2 = 250$

So, the American Black Bear can weigh up to about 250 kilograms.

Quick Review

1. $2\frac{1}{2} + 2\frac{1}{2} + 2\frac{1}{2}$
2. $1,600 + 1,600 + 1,600$
3. $\frac{1}{2} + \frac{1}{2} + \frac{1}{2} + \frac{1}{2}$
4. $1,200 \div 2$
5. $112 \div 28$

TABLE OF CONVERSIONS

Linear

- 1 inch is about $2\frac{1}{2}$ centimeters.
- 1 meter is a little longer than 1 yard.
- 1 kilometer is a little longer than $\frac{1}{2}$ mile.
- 1 mile is about 1,600 meters.
- 1 mile is a little longer than $1\frac{1}{2}$ kilometers.

Capacity

- 1 liter is a little more than 1 quart.

Mass/Weight

- 1 ounce is about 28 grams.
- 1 kilogram is a little more than 2 pounds.

Examples

Use the table of related benchmarks to estimate conversions.

A 4 oz ≈ ▒ g

Think: 1 oz is about 28 g.
$4 \times 28 = 112$

So, 4 oz is about 112 g.

B 1 gal ≈ ▒ L

Think: 1 L is a little more than 1 qt.
There are 4 qt in 1 gal.

So, 1 gal is about 4 L.

C 5 in. ≈ ▒ cm

Think: 1 in. is about $2\frac{1}{2}$ cm.
$2\frac{1}{2} + 2\frac{1}{2} + 2\frac{1}{2} + 2\frac{1}{2} + 2\frac{1}{2} = 12\frac{1}{2}$

So, 5 in. is about $12\frac{1}{2}$ cm.

D 2 yd ≈ ▒ m

Think: 1 m is a little longer than 1 yd.

So, 2 yd is a little less than or about the same as 2 m.

Check

1. **Explain** how you can find the number of ounces an object weighs by using paper clips. A paper clip weighs about 1 gram.

Estimate the conversion.

2. 15 mi ≈ ▢ m

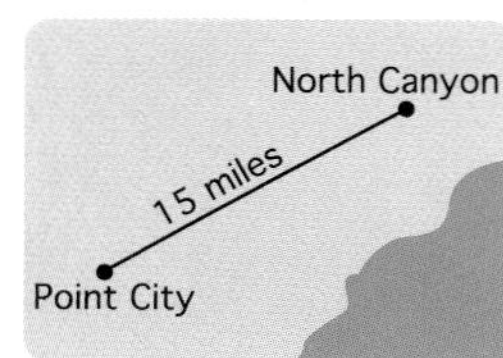

3. 7 kg ≈ ▢ lb

4. 6 oz ≈ ▢ g

Practice and Problem Solving

Extra Practice, page 554, Set C

Estimate the conversion.

5. 2 in. ≈ ▢ cm
6. 56 g ≈ ▢ oz
7. 2 mi ≈ ▢ m
8. 9 ft ≈ ▢ m
9. 3 kg ≈ ▢ lb
10. 8 L ≈ ▢ qt
11. 10 lb ≈ ▢ kg
12. 14 qt ≈ ▢ L
13. 2 mi ≈ ▢ km

Compare. Write $<$ or $>$ for each ●.

14. 5 km ● 2 mi
15. 4 oz ● 100 g
16. 5 cm ● 4 in.
17. 2 kg ● 2 lb
18. 1 m ● 4 ft
19. 1 L ● 3 qt
20. Is one mile greater than or less than a kilometer? Explain.
21. Which is heavier, 20 pounds or 20 kilograms? Explain.
22. ALGEBRA Using the variables *i* for *inch* and *c* for *centimeter,* write an equation to convert inches to centimeters.
23. The length of a paper clip is about an inch. What is the length of a paper clip in centimeters?
24. **Vocabulary Power** The prefix *kilo-* comes from the Greek word *chilioi,* meaning "thousand." A kilogram is 1,000 grams and a kilometer is 1,000 meters. How many watts do you think are in a kilowatt? Explain.
25. **FAST FACT • SCIENCE** The African elephant can weigh up to 7,000 kilograms and grow to $7\frac{3}{10}$ meters in length. Estimate the weight of the African elephant in pounds.

Mixed Review and Test Prep

26. 592 × 16 (p. 256)
27. 276 ÷ 21 (p. 320)
28. What is the mean of 75, 82, 90, 86, and 72? (p. 328)
29. Is the angle shown a right angle, an acute angle, or an obtuse angle? (p. 366)

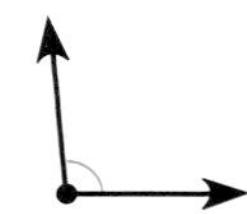

30. **TEST PREP** Anton bought $1\frac{1}{8}$ pounds of tangerines, $\frac{5}{8}$ pound of grapes, and $2\frac{3}{8}$ pounds of apples. How many pounds of fruit did Anton buy? (p. 474)

A 4 pounds
B $4\frac{1}{8}$ pounds
C $5\frac{1}{8}$ pounds
D $5\frac{5}{8}$ pounds

Extra Practice

Set A (pp. 540–543)

Choose the most reasonable unit of measure.
Write *mm, cm, dm, m,* or *km*.

1. The width of a book is about 22 __?__.
2. The length of a marker is about 13 __?__.
3. The height of a desk is about 10 __?__.
4. length of a peanut
5. thickness of a CD
6. height of a building

Compare. Write < or > for each ●.

7. 750 m ● 750 dm
8. 20 cm ● 20 dm
9. 2 cm ● 2 mm
10. 70 dm ● 70 m
11. 500 m ● 500 km
12. 200 m ● 200 cm

Set B (pp. 544–545)

Complete. Tell whether you multiply or divide by 10, 100, or 1,000.

1. 3 m = ■ dm
2. 7 m = ■ mm
3. 500 cm = ■ m
4. 150 cm = ■ dm
5. 28 dm = ■ cm
6. 3 km = ■ m

Write the correct unit.

7. 5 __?__ = 50 cm
8. 40 mm = 4 __?__
9. 3 __?__ = 300 cm

Compare. Write <, >, or = for each ●.

10. 45 cm ● 4 dm
11. 60 mm ● 3 cm
12. 30 dm ● 3 m
13. 72 m ● 95 cm
14. 9,000 cm ● 6,400 dm
15. 70 km ● 700 m

Set C (pp. 552–553)

Estimate the conversion.

1. 5 cm ≈ ■ in.
2. 10 lb ≈ ■ kg
3. 56 g ≈ ■ oz

Compare. Write < or > for each ●.

4. 1 lb ● 1 kg
5. 5 L ● 4 qt
6. 5,000 m ● 10 mi
7. In a relay race, 4 people ran 3,000 meters each. In a distance race, John ran 15 kilometers. Who ran farther, the whole relay team or John? How much farther?
8. Josh ran 1,600 meters on Saturday and 3,200 meters on Sunday. How many meters did he run in all? Is that *more than* or *less than* 5 kilometers?

Review/Test

CHECK VOCABULARY AND CONCEPTS

Choose the best term from the box.

milliliter
mass
decimeter
meter

1. Metric units of capacity are _?_ and liter. (p. 546)
2. The amount of matter in an object is the _?_. (p. 548)
3. The width of an adult's hand is about a _?_. (p. 540)

CHECK SKILLS

Complete. Tell whether you multiply or divide by 10, 100, or 1,000. (pp. 544–545, 546–547, 548–549)

4. 6 L = ■ mL
5. ■ cm = 8 m
6. 30 m = ■ cm
7. 800 mm = ■ cm
8. 20 kg = ■ g
9. 12 m = ■ dm
10. 90 dm = ■ m
11. ■ g = 2 kg

Compare. Write <, >, or = for each ●. (pp. 544–545)

12. 16 cm ● 12 dm
13. 4 m ● 40 cm
14. 90 dm ● 10 m

Choose the most reasonable unit of measure. Write *mm, cm, dm, m, km, mL, L, g,* or *kg*. (pp. 540–543, 546–547, 548–549)

15. the mass of a pin
16. the height of a door
17. the capacity of a mug

Estimate the conversion. (pp. 552–553)

18. 84 oz ≈ ■ g
19. 6 mi ≈ ■ m
20. 15 qt ≈ ■ L

Compare. Write <, >, or ≈ for each ●. (pp. 552–553)

21. 5 yd ● 6 m
22. 12 kg ● 10 lb
23. 4 km ● 3 mi

CHECK PROBLEM SOLVING

Solve. (pp. 544–545, 550–551)

24. Vince is building a table. Each leg will be 75 centimeters long. He has a piece of wood that is 3 meters long. Can he make 4 table legs? Explain.

25. The mass of a box of cookies is 60 grams. The mass of a box of crackers is 3 grams more than twice the mass of the box of cookies. What is the mass of the box of crackers?

Standardized Test Prep

MEASUREMENT

1. Milliliters would be the **best** unit for measuring the capacity of which object?

A 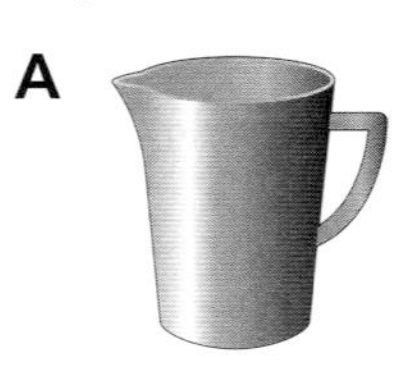

C 

B 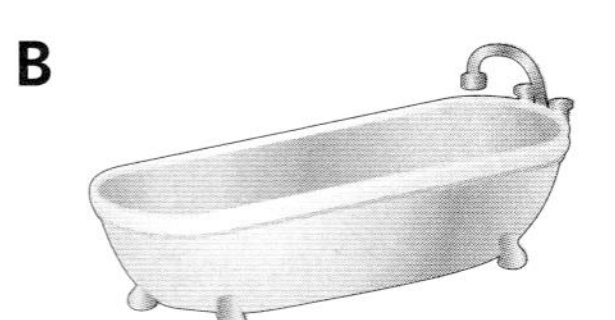

D 

2. Ellen wants to make a rectangular picture frame like the one shown below. What is the **shortest** length of wood she needs to buy?

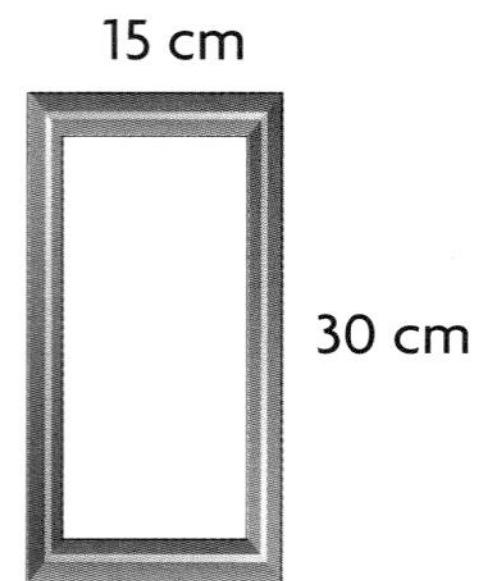

F 45 centimeters

G 90 centimeters

H 1 meter

J 90 meters

3. **Explain It** Which object has a mass of about 10 grams: *a pen, a brick,* or *a shoe*? Explain your thinking.

GEOMETRY AND SPATIAL SENSE

4. Which figure will tessellate?

A

C 

B 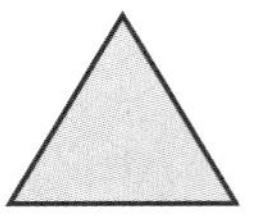

D 

5. Which figure has been turned 90° clockwise from the original figure?

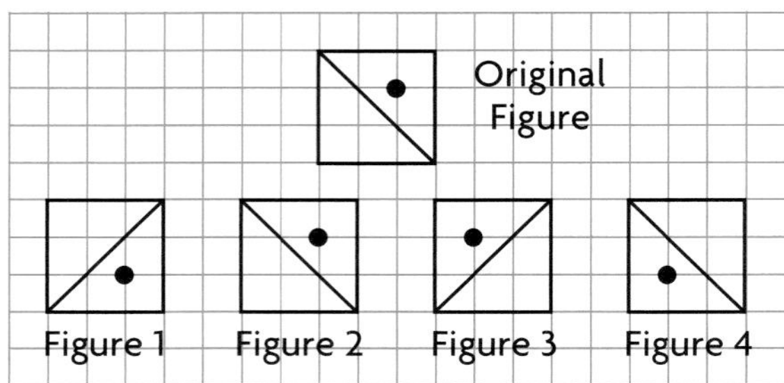

F Figure 1

G Figure 2

H Figure 3

J Figure 4

 **Look for important words.**

See item 6. The important words are *face* and *rectangular prism.* Think about what a rectangular prism looks like and how many faces, or flat surfaces, it has.

6. **Explain It** Tom is painting each face of a rectangular prism with a different color. How many different colors will he use? Explain how you decided.

ALGEBRAIC THINKING

7. Which equation can be used to convert pounds to kilograms? Let k represent the number of kilograms and p represent the number of pounds.

1 kilogram $\approx$ 2 pounds

A $k \approx 2 \times p$

B $k \approx 5 \times p$

C $k \approx p \div 2$

D $p \approx 2 + k$

8. Which equation describes a rule for the pattern in this table?

INPUT	OUTPUT
a	***m***
2	6
7	21
1	3
9	27

F $a + 3 = m$

G $a - 3 = m$

H $a \times 3 = m$

J $m \times 3 = a$

9. Explain It Use the variable c to write an expression that means "3 milliliters less than the capacity, c, of some container."

Explain why you wrote the expression you did.

DATA ANALYSIS AND PROBABILITY

10. From which set of cards would you **most likely** pick a 2?

A

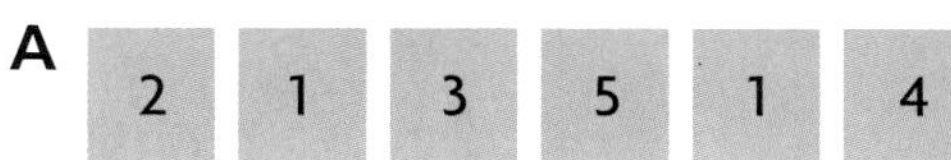

B

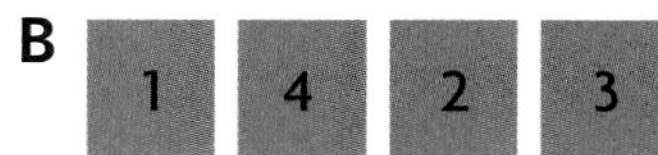

C

D

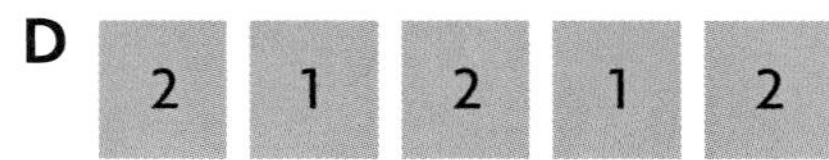

11. The table shows the heights of several basketball players.

BASKETBALL PLAYERS	
Player	**Height (in centimeters)**
Allan Alvarez	204
Brian Johnson	210
Larry Fox	201
Joe Peters	205
Norm O'Hara	201

What is the mode of the heights?

F 9 **H** 204

G 201 **J** 210

12. Explain It Karol made the list below to show the temperature at noon for five days.

Monday	67°F
Tuesday	71°F
Wednesday	70°F
Thursday	73°F
Friday	73°F

Make a graph to display the data. Tell why you used the graph you did.

CHAPTER 26 Understand Decimals

FAST FACT • SOCIAL STUDIES In July 1968, Chicago hosted 1,000 athletes in the first international Special Olympics Games. Now the Special Olympics reaches more than 1.5 million children and adults with disabilities, in over 180 countries.

PROBLEM SOLVING The table lists the times in a 100-meter dash at a recent Special Olympics competition. Which was the fastest time? Which was the slowest?

100-METER DASH TIMES (in seconds)			
20.18	21.35	22.40	21.03
23.86	20.88	20.07	21.63

CHECK WHAT YOU KNOW

Use this page to help you review and remember important skills needed for Chapter 26.

MODEL FRACTIONS

Write the fraction for the shaded part.

1.

2. 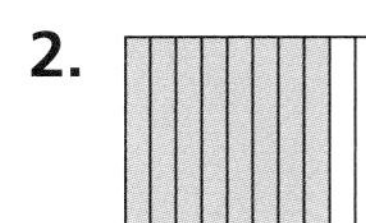

3. 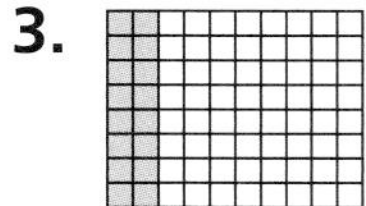

4. 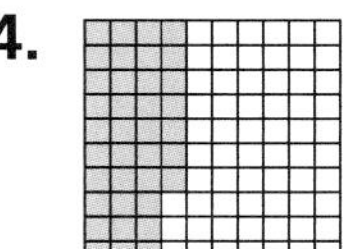

DECIMALS AND MONEY

Write the name of the coin that is described.

5. 0.1 of a dollar is a __?__.

6. 0.01 of a dollar is a __?__.

Write a decimal for the money amount.

7. two dollars and fifteen cents

8. three dollars and twelve cents

FRACTIONS WITH DENOMINATORS OF 10 AND 100

Write a fraction for each.

9. five tenths

10. nine hundredths

11. fifty-three hundredths

Complete to show equivalent fractions.

12. $\frac{6}{10} = \frac{■}{100}$

13. $\frac{1}{10} = \frac{■}{100}$

14. $\frac{9}{10} = \frac{■}{100}$

VOCABULARY POWER

REVIEW

greater than (>) [grā•tər t͟han] *adjective*

The symbol > first was used in a mathematics publication in 1631. Other symbols also were used to show "greater than," even into the 1700s. Make up your own symbol for "greater than." Explain how the symbol could be useful in comparing two numbers.

PREVIEW

decimal

decimal point

thousandth

equivalent decimals

www.harcourtschool.com/mathglossary

LESSON 1

Relate Fractions and Decimals

Learn

BATTER UP! A **decimal** is a number with one or more digits to the right of the **decimal point**.

Understanding fractions that have a denominator of 10 or 100 will help you understand decimals.

Gina plays on a Little League team. Gina scored 14 of her team's 100 runs this year. In the past three games, she was at bat 10 times and had 6 hits.

Quick Review

Draw a model for each.

1. $\frac{3}{10}$
2. $\frac{7}{10}$
3. $\frac{9}{10}$
4. $\frac{15}{100}$
5. $\frac{4}{100}$

VOCABULARY

decimal **decimal point**

Example

Gina had 6 hits out of 10 tries at bat.

Model	Fraction	Decimal
	Write: $\frac{6}{10}$ **Read:** six tenths	**Write:** 0.6 **Read:** six tenths

Gina scored 14 of her team's 100 runs this year.

Model	Fraction	Decimal
	Write: $\frac{14}{100}$ **Read:** fourteen hundredths	**Write:** 0.14 **Read:** fourteen hundredths

Gina got a hit $\frac{6}{10}$, or 0.6, of her times at bat recently and scored $\frac{14}{100}$ or 0.14, of her team's runs this year.

More Examples

A

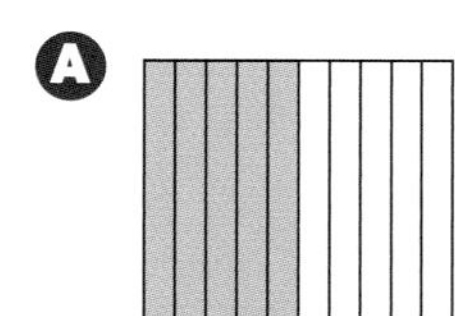

Write: $\frac{5}{10}$, or 0.5
Read: five tenths

B

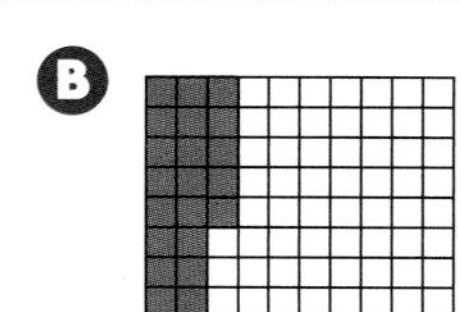

Write: $\frac{25}{100}$, or 0.25
Read: twenty-five hundredths

Read and Write Decimals

Decimals, like whole numbers, can be written in standard form, word form, and expanded form. Look at these numbers on the place-value chart.

Examples

Ones	.	Tenths	Hundredths
0	.	8	
0	.	1	2

Standard Form	Word Form	Expanded Form
0.8	eight tenths	0.8
0.12	twelve hundredths	0.1 + 0.02

You can write a decimal for a fraction that has a denominator other than 10 or 100. First write the fraction using a denominator of 10 or 100.

Example

What decimal shows the same amount as $\frac{1}{2}$?

$\frac{1}{2} = \frac{1 \times 5}{2 \times 5} = \frac{5}{10}$ $\qquad \frac{5}{10} = 0.5$

So, $\frac{1}{2}$ shows the same amount as 0.5.

A number line divided into 100 equal parts can be used to model fractions and decimals that show the same amount in tenths or hundredths.

$\frac{0}{100}$ $\frac{10}{100}$ $\frac{20}{100}$ $\frac{25}{100}$ $\frac{30}{100}$ $\frac{40}{100}$ $\frac{50}{100}$ $\frac{60}{100}$ $\frac{70}{100}$ $\frac{80}{100}$ $\frac{90}{100}$ $\frac{100}{100}$

0 0.1 0.2 0.25 0.3 0.4 0.5 0.6 0.7 0.8 0.9 1

So, the decimal 0.25 shows the same amount as $\frac{25}{100}$, or $\frac{1}{4}$.

LESSON CONTINUES

Check

1. **Explain** how the tenths model is different from the hundredths model.

Write the decimal and fraction shown by each model or number line.

2. 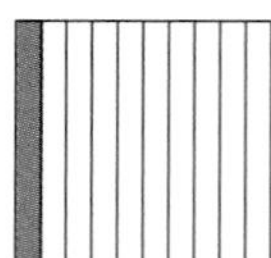

3. 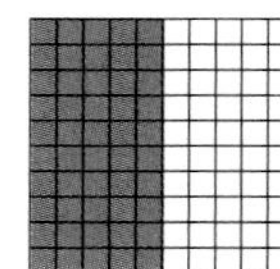

4. 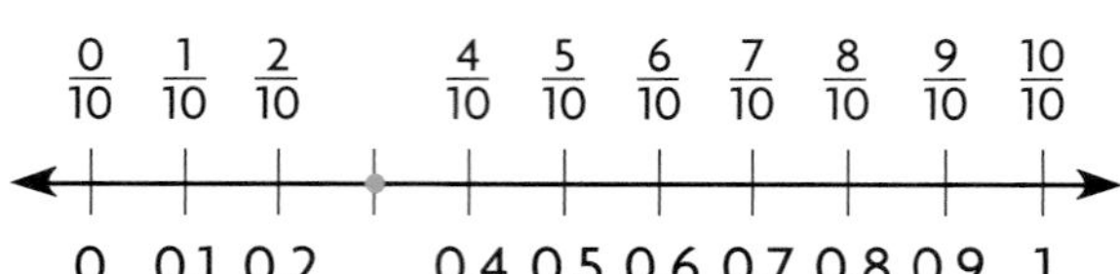

Practice and Problem Solving

Extra Practice, page 578, Set A

Write the decimal and fraction shown by each model or number line.

5. 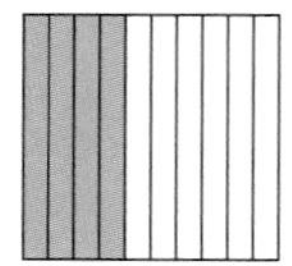

6. 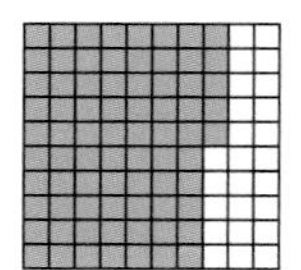

7. 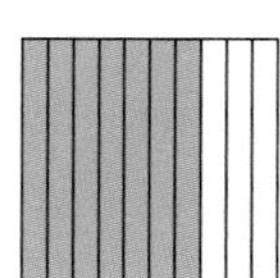

8. 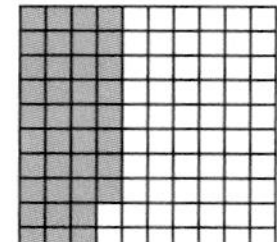

9. 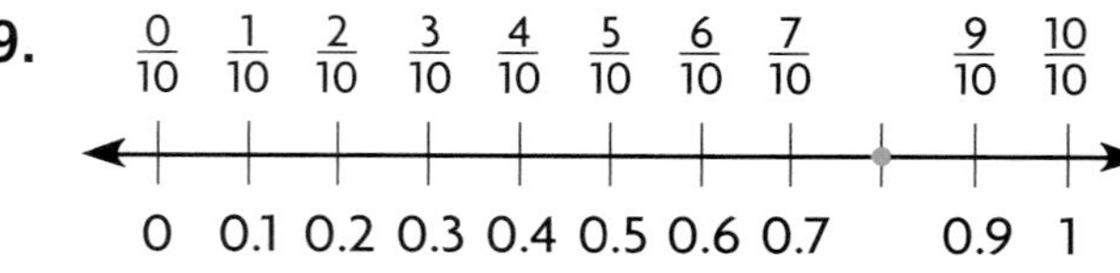

10. 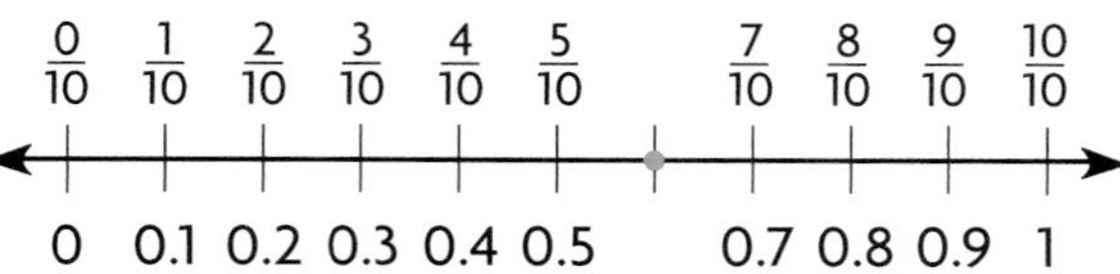

Write each fraction as a decimal. Use a model to help you.

11. $\frac{8}{10}$ 12. $\frac{7}{10}$ 13. $\frac{60}{100}$ 14. $\frac{25}{100}$ 15. $\frac{4}{100}$

16. $\frac{32}{100}$ 17. $\frac{1}{5}$ 18. $\frac{2}{100}$ 19. $\frac{2}{4}$ 20. $\frac{4}{5}$

21. $\frac{5}{10}$ 22. $\frac{3}{5}$ 23. $\frac{47}{100}$ 24. $\frac{7}{100}$ 25. $\frac{9}{10}$

ALGEBRA Find the missing number or digit to write each fraction as a decimal.

26. $\frac{■}{10} = 0.70$ 27. $\frac{3}{■} = 0.75$ 28. $\frac{■}{4} = 0.50$ 29. $\frac{■}{5} = 0.40$ 30. $\frac{1}{■} = 0.25$

Write the decimal two other ways.

31. 0.1 32. 0.4 + 0.07 33. 0.4 34. 8 tenths

35. For three weeks a theater sold $9,500 worth of tickets per week. For each of the next 2 weeks, the theater sold $7,200 worth of tickets per week. What were the total ticket sales?

36. **Write About It** Aline walked $\frac{3}{4}$ mile to school. Dave walked 0.75 mile to school. Aline said she walked farther than Dave. Is she correct? Explain.

USE DATA For 37–39, use the graph.

37. The graph shows how Pepe spends 100 minutes of baseball practice. He spends $\frac{28}{100}$ of the time running bases. What decimal is this?

38. Write a decimal to show what part of the total time is spent on warm-ups.

39. **Write a problem** about the time Pepe spends fielding and throwing.

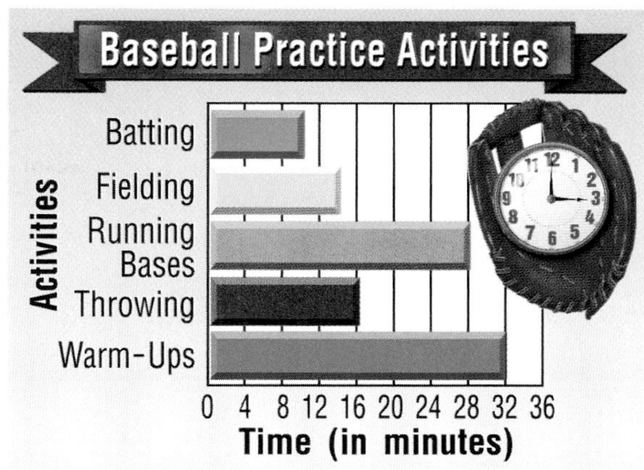

Mixed Review and Test Prep

40. Round 23,425 to the nearest hundred. (p. 30)

41. 398×11 (p. 256)

42. $\$5.21 \times 8$ (p. 222)

43. $\frac{2}{3} + \frac{1}{3}$ (p. 468)

44. 543×23 (p. 256)

45. TEST PREP What is $\frac{6}{10}$ in simplest form? (p. 448)

A $\frac{1}{4}$ **B** $\frac{2}{5}$ **C** $\frac{1}{2}$ **D** $\frac{3}{5}$

46. TEST PREP Which number does NOT divide into 210 evenly? (p. 300)

F 2 **G** 3 **H** 4 **J** 5

Problem Solving Thinker's Corner

REASONING You can use a meterstick to model decimal numbers.

meter (m)	decimeter (dm) *Deci* means "tenths."	centimeter (cm) *Centi* means "hundredths."
1.0 meter	1 decimeter = 0.1, or $\frac{1}{10}$, meter.	1 centimeter = 0.01, or $\frac{1}{100}$, meter.

Write 3.26 meters as meters + decimeters + centimeters.

0.2 meter = 2 decimeters 0.06 meter = 6 centimeters

So, 3.26 meters = 3 meters + 2 decimeters + 6 centimeters.

Complete.

1. $\frac{4}{10}$ m = ■ dm

2. 0.23 m = ■ cm

3. $\frac{9}{100}$ m = ■ cm

4. 4.52 m = 4 m + ■ dm + ■ cm

5. 0.51 m = ■ m + ■ dm + ■ cm

LESSON 2
Decimals to Thousandths

Quick Review

Write each fraction as a decimal.

1. $\frac{4}{10}$ 2. $\frac{34}{100}$ 3. $\frac{1}{10}$
4. $\frac{61}{100}$ 5. $\frac{50}{100}$

VOCABULARY

thousandth

Learn

TINY PARTS Thousandths are even smaller parts than hundredths. If one hundredth were divided into ten equal parts, each part would represent one **thousandth**.

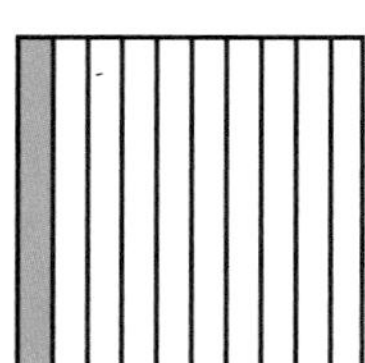
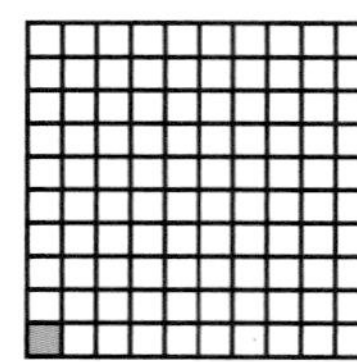
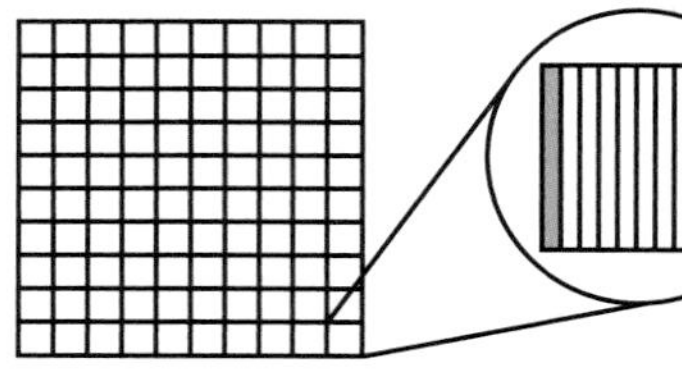

Fraction:	$\frac{1}{1}$	$\frac{1}{10}$	$\frac{1}{100}$	$\frac{1}{1,000}$
Decimal:	1	0.1	0.01	0.001
Read:	one	one tenth	one hundredth	one thousandth

Examples You can use a place-value chart to help you understand thousandths.

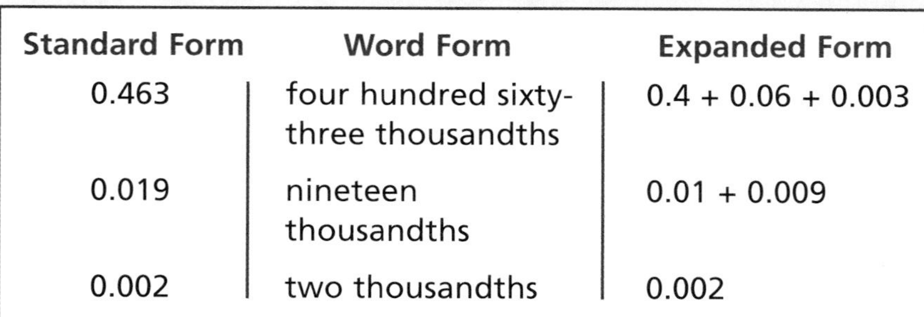

Ones	.	Tenths	Hundredths	Thousandths
0	.	4	6	3
0	.	0	1	9
0	.	0	0	2

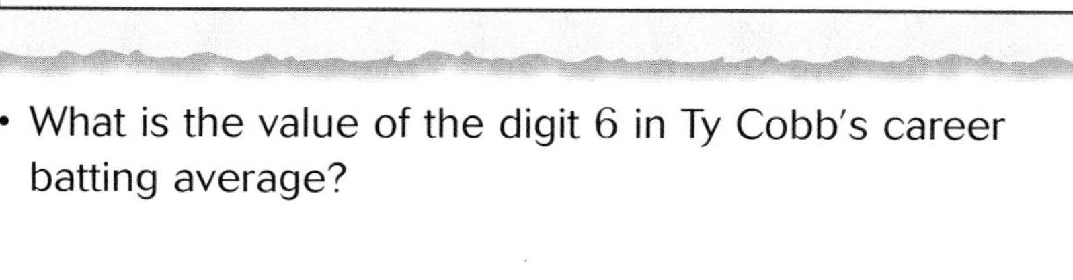

Standard Form	Word Form	Expanded Form
0.463	four hundred sixty-three thousandths	0.4 + 0.06 + 0.003
0.019	nineteen thousandths	0.01 + 0.009
0.002	two thousandths	0.002

Ty Cobb has the all-time highest career batting average of .367. ▼

- What is the value of the digit 6 in Ty Cobb's career batting average?

Check

1. **Explain** how many thousandths are in one hundredth. How many thousandths are in one?

Write each decimal as a fraction.

2. 0.095 3. 0.418 4. 0.639 5. 0.002 6. 0.007

Practice and Problem Solving

Extra Practice, page 578, Set B

Write each decimal as a fraction.

7. 0.005 8. 0.749 9. 0.038 10. 0.001 11. 0.634

Write each fraction as a decimal.

12. $\frac{6}{1,000}$ 13. $\frac{134}{1,000}$ 14. $\frac{56}{1,000}$ 15. $\frac{785}{1,000}$ 16. $\frac{10}{1,000}$

Use a place-value chart to write the value of the digit 5 in each decimal.

17. 0.025 18. 0.519 19. 0.153 20. 0.465 21. 0.593

Write the decimal two other ways.

22. 0.025
23. forty-two thousandths
24. 0.451
25. one hundred five thousandths

Complete.

26. $0.36\blacksquare = 0.3 + 0.06 + 0.004$
27. 0.903 = nine ? three thousandths
28. $0.408 = 0.4 + \blacksquare$
29. 0.072 = seventy-two ?
30. $0.8\blacksquare6 = 0.8 + 0.02 + \blacksquare$
31. 0.184 = ■ hundred ■ thousandths
32. A 1-hour piano lesson costs $18. Students receive 1 free lesson for every 8 paid lessons. How much will 36 lessons cost?
33. Pam practiced the piano for $\frac{1}{6}$ hr on Wednesday and $\frac{1}{3}$ hr on Friday. How many minutes did she practice in all?

Mixed Review and Test Prep

34. Write the word form of 0.14. (p. 560)
35. $4 \times (25 \times 2)$ (p. 184)
36. $427 \div 7$ (p. 300)
37. $4\frac{2}{3} + 5\frac{2}{3}$ (p. 474)
38. **TEST PREP** Which is five million, two thousand, eight hundred sixteen written in standard form? (p. 6)

A 502,816 **C** 5,020,816
B 5,002,816 **D** 5,028,160

LESSON 3

Equivalent Decimals

Quick Review

1. $3.\square = 3\frac{2}{10}$
2. $2.6 = 2\frac{\square}{10}$
3. $7\frac{41}{\square} = 7.41$
4. $8.9 = 8\frac{9}{\square}$
5. $6.\square = 6\frac{49}{100}$

VOCABULARY

equivalent decimals

MATERIALS tenths and hundredths models; markers

Explore

Equivalent decimals are decimals that name the same number.

Use models and paper folding to find equivalent decimals. Are 0.2 and 0.20 equivalent decimals?

Activity

STEP 1

Shade 0.2 of the tenths model and 0.20 of the hundredths model.

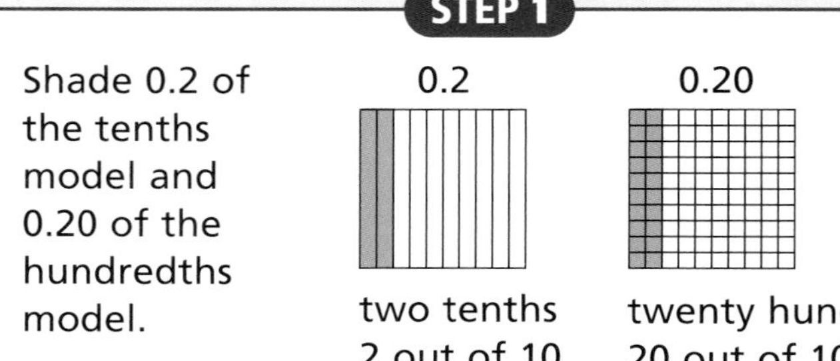

STEP 2

Fold 0.2 of the tenths model and 0.20 of the hundredths model. Then compare the models.

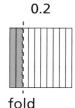

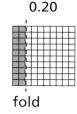

0.2 0.20

fold fold

The folded parts of the models are the same size.

So, 0.2 and 0.20 are equivalent decimals.

Technology Link

More Practice: Harcourt Mega Math Fraction Action, *Fraction Flare-Up*, Level M

Try It

Use a tenths model and a hundredths model. Are the two decimals equivalent? Write *equivalent* or *not equivalent*.

a. 0.50 and 0.6 **b.** 0.3 and 0.30

c. 0.70 and 0.75 **d.** 0.8 and 0.80

How do these models show whether 0.50 and 0.6 are equivalent?

Connect

Felipe said that $0.30 is 3 tenths of a dollar. Lea said that $0.30 is 30 hundredths of a dollar. Who was correct?

Example Compare the models.

Felipe used a tenths model to show $0.30 = 3 tenths.

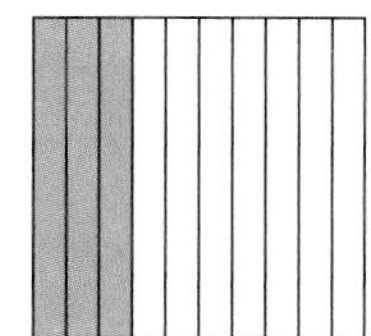

Each column is equal to 0.1, or one tenth, of a dollar.

0.3 of a dollar

Lea used a hundredths model to show $0.30 = 30 hundredths.

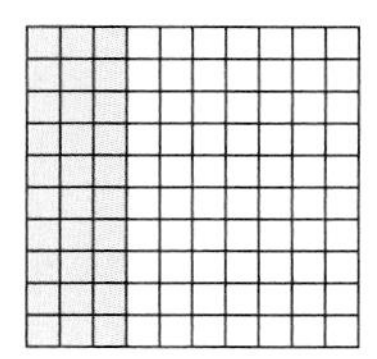

Each square is equal to 0.01, or one hundredth, of a dollar.

0.30 of a dollar

The two models show that 3 tenths of a dollar is equal to 30 hundredths of a dollar. So, both Felipe and Lea are correct.

- How else can $0.30 be read?

Practice and Problem Solving

Are the two decimals equivalent? Write *equivalent* or *not equivalent*.

1. 0.7 and 0.70 **2.** 0.04 and 0.4 **3.** 0.9 and 0.09

4. 0.28 and 0.82 **5.** 0.17 and 0.07 **6.** 0.1 and 0.10

Write an equivalent decimal for each. You may use decimal models.

7. 0.8 **8.** 0.7 **9.** 0.90 **10.** 0.2

11. 0.5 **12.** 0.10 **13.** 0.40 **14.** 0.6

15. **MENTAL MATH** Erin's family plants a garden on 0.5 acre of their land. Write an equivalent decimal for this amount.

16. **Write About It** Make a model to show that 0.8 and 0.80 are equivalent. Explain your model.

Mixed Review and Test Prep

17. $\frac{4}{5} + \frac{4}{5}$ (p. 468)

18. $5\frac{5}{7} - 2\frac{2}{7}$ (p. 474)

19. $4\overline{)580}$ (p. 300)

20. 785 ÷ 7 (p. 300)

21. **TEST PREP** Which number is NOT a factor of 320? (p. 338)

A 4 **B** 6 **C** 8 **D** 10

LESSON 

Relate Mixed Numbers and Decimals

Quick Review

Write each as a mixed number.

1. $\frac{4}{3}$ 2. $\frac{7}{2}$ 3. $\frac{11}{4}$
4. $\frac{15}{4}$ 5. $\frac{27}{5}$

Learn

ANNA'S BANANAS Plantains, a variety of banana, grow in Mexico. Anna bought two and three tenths pounds of plantains at the store. How can you write this weight as a mixed number and as a decimal?

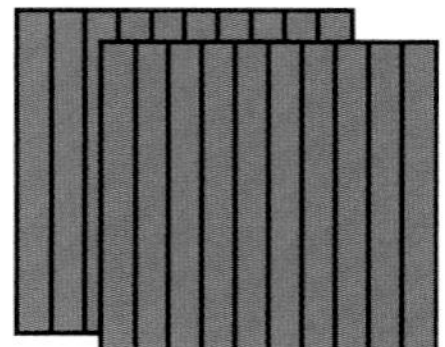

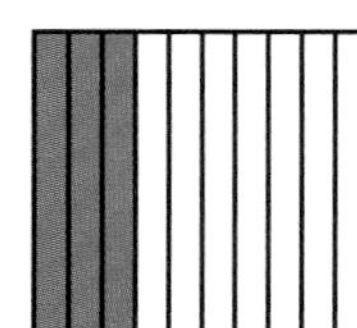

Mixed Number: $2\frac{3}{10}$

Decimal: 2.3

Read: two and three tenths

So, write the weight as $2\frac{3}{10}$, or 2.3, pounds.

- **What if** Anna also bought $3\frac{4}{10}$ pounds of peanuts? What decimal will a decimal scale show if she has the correct amount?

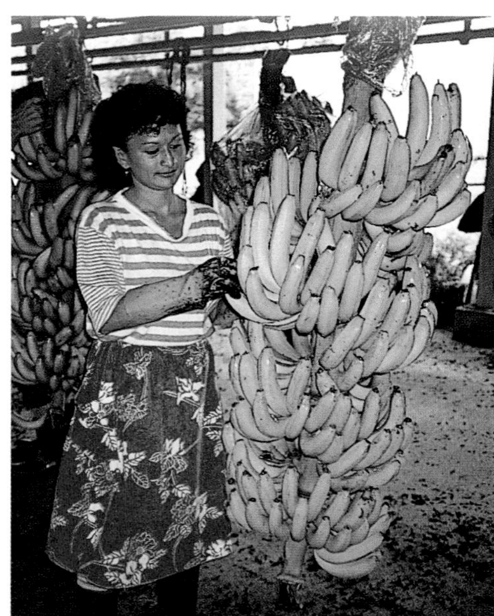

▲ There are 300 varieties of bananas worldwide.

Examples

A

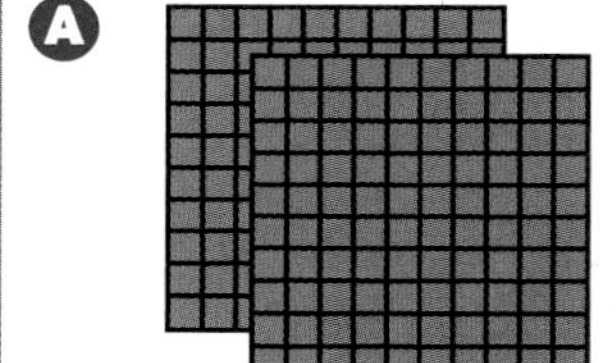

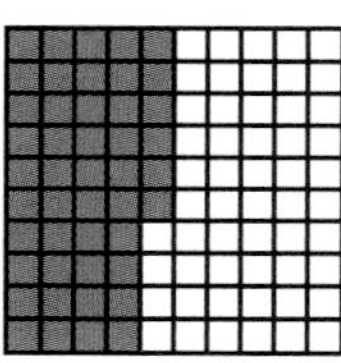

Mixed Number: $2\frac{46}{100}$

Decimal: 2.46

Read: two and forty-six hundredths

B

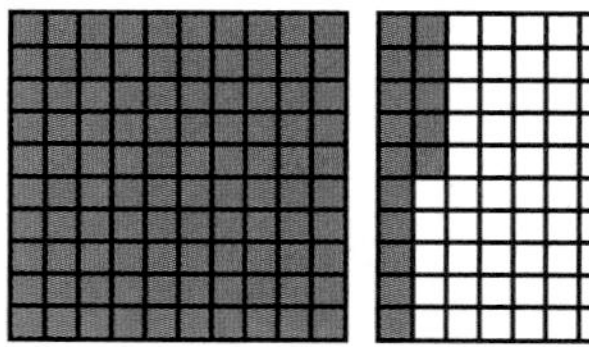

Mixed Number: $1\frac{15}{100}$

Decimal: 1.15

Read: one and fifteen hundredths

- **REASONING** How can you write four and fifty-one thousandths as a mixed number and as a decimal?

Technology Link

More Practice: Harcourt Mega Math Fraction Action, *Number Line Mine*, Level O

Decimal Equivalents

Sandy and Bill brought $2\frac{1}{2}$ pounds of bananas to the class picnic. The decimal equivalent for $2\frac{1}{2}$ can be found by using a number line or a decimal model.

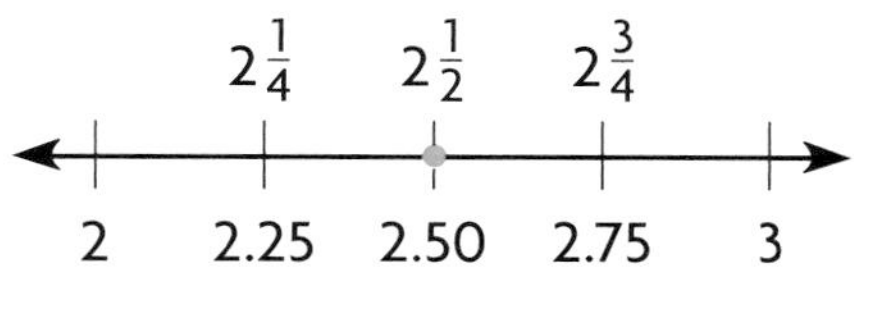

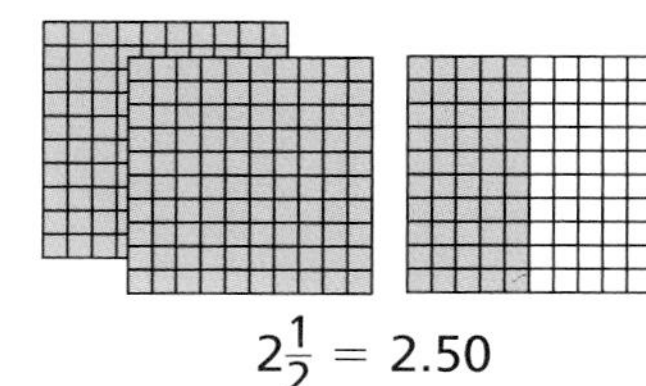

$2\frac{1}{2} = 2.50$

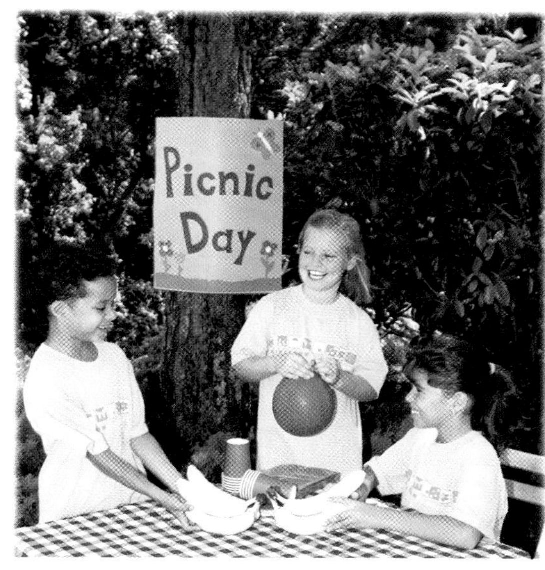

The number line and the decimal model both show that $2\frac{1}{2}$ and 2.50 name the same amount.

More Examples You can use decimal models to show other mixed numbers and decimals that are equivalent.

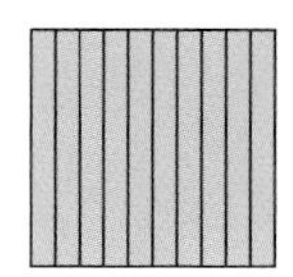

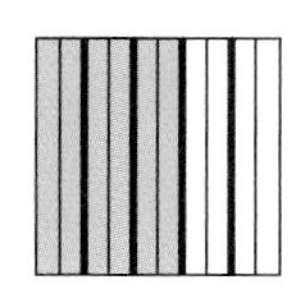

$1.60 = 1\frac{6}{10} = 1\frac{3}{5}$

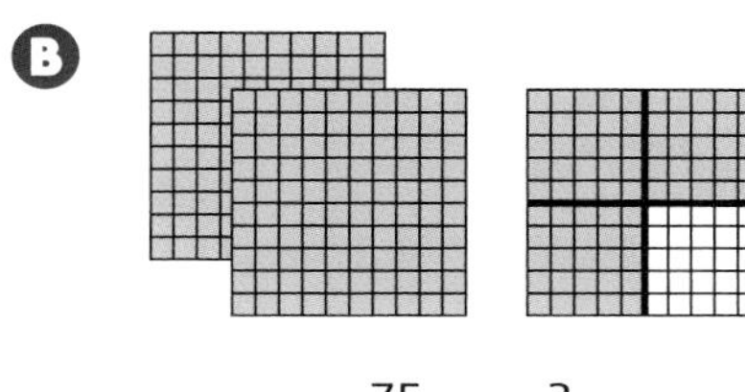

$2.75 = 2\frac{75}{100} = 2\frac{3}{4}$

- Are $2\frac{1}{4}$ and 2.25 equivalent? Explain.

Check

1. **Explain** how you can use a number line or a decimal model to relate mixed numbers and decimals.

Write an equivalent decimal and mixed number for each decimal model. Then write the word form.

2. 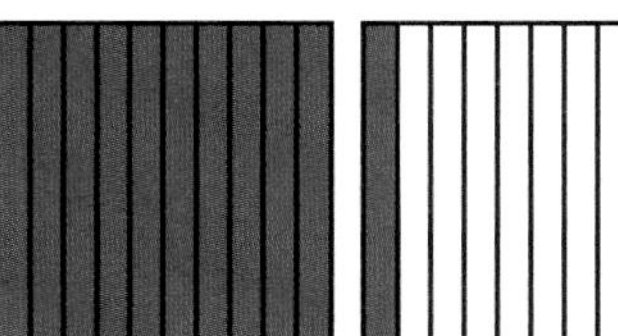

3. 

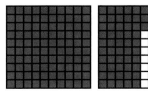

4. 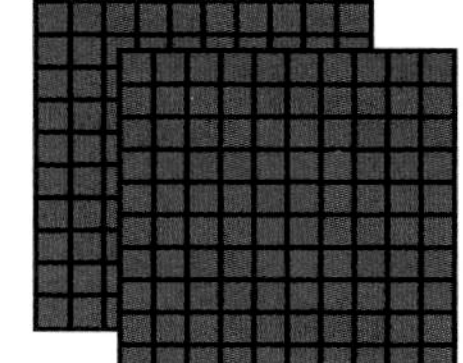 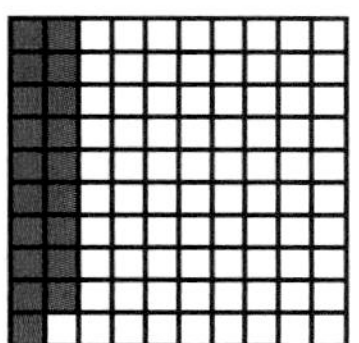

LESSON CONTINUES

Practice and Problem Solving

Extra Practice, page 578, Set C

Write an equivalent decimal and mixed number for each decimal model. Then write the word form.

5. 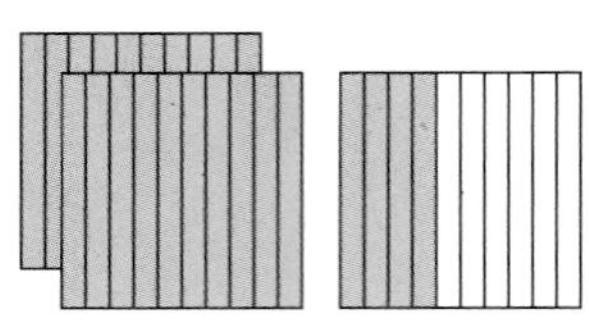

6. 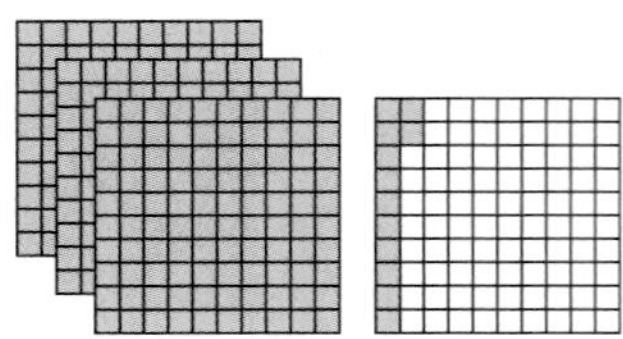

7. 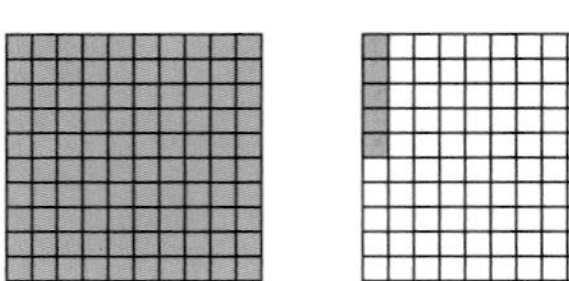

8. 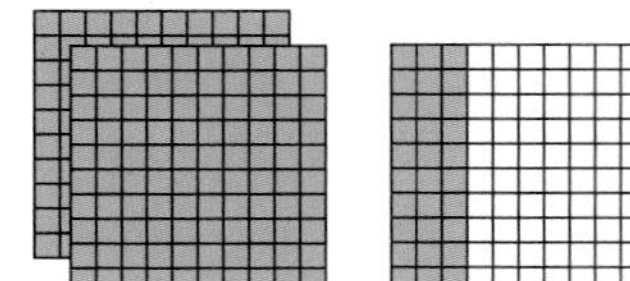

Write an equivalent mixed number or decimal.

9. 11.50 **10.** $9\frac{1}{4}$ **11.** 7.25 **12.** $4\frac{1}{5}$ **13.** 7.7

14. $4\frac{2}{5}$ **15.** 8.06 **16.** 16.3 **17.** $27\frac{3}{5}$ **18.** $6\frac{1}{2}$

Use the number line to write an equivalent mixed number or decimal for each letter.

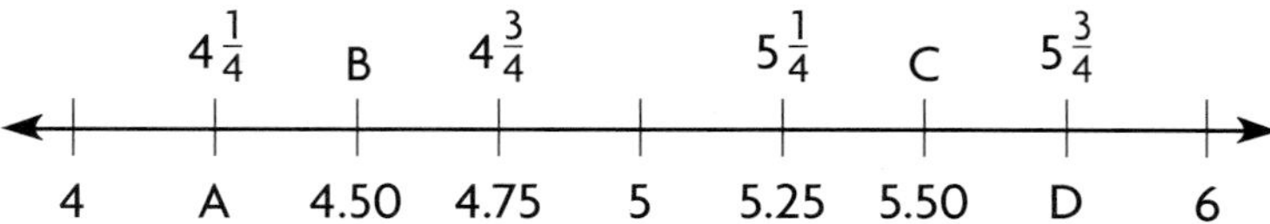

19. C **20.** B **21.** A **22.** D

23. Kerri went to the store with \$100. She spent \$22 on a shirt, \$12 on a hat, and \$45 on a pair of lawn chairs for her parents. How much money did Kerri have left?

24. Lance said that he had spent twenty-four dollars and eighteen cents on a lock for his bike. Write this amount in standard form.

25. Vocabulary Power Numbers such as $1\frac{1}{2}$ and $2\frac{3}{5}$ are called *mixed numbers*. In what way is a mixed number "mixed"?

26. Use the number line above to name two mixed numbers and two decimals between 4.25 and 4.50.

27. **What's the Error?** Kris wrote the mixed number $2\frac{7}{10}$ in two ways, shown at the right. Describe her error. Write the correct answer.

28. Tasha buys 16 posters. Each poster costs $\$3$. If she gives the cashier $\$60$, how much is her change?

29. Sumi ran 10.75 miles. Larry ran $10\frac{4}{5}$ miles. Who ran farther? Explain.

Mixed Review and Test Prep

30. Order from least to greatest: 27,654; 26,654; 27,754; 27,652 (p. 24)

31. Kara recorded these temperatures each day for a week: 65°F, 72°F, 74°F, 68°F, 67°F, 62°F, 65°F. What is the median? (p. 118)

32. List the factors of 21. (p. 338)

33. $\$2.17 \times 5$ (p. 222)

34. $3{,}425 \times 9$ (p. 222)

35. 26×24 (p. 252) 36. $441 \div 9$ (p. 300)

37. Write $\frac{6}{9}$ in simplest form. (p. 448)

38. **TEST PREP** Which fraction is the greatest? (p. 452)

A $\frac{2}{3}$ B $\frac{3}{4}$ C $\frac{4}{5}$ D $\frac{5}{6}$

39. **TEST PREP** Which is equivalent to 2.4? (p. 568)

F 2.04 G $2\frac{4}{10}$ H $2\frac{4}{100}$ J 2.41

Problem Solving Thinker's Corner

PERCENT A sewing store sells 100 buttons on a card. One half of the buttons are green. What percent is this?

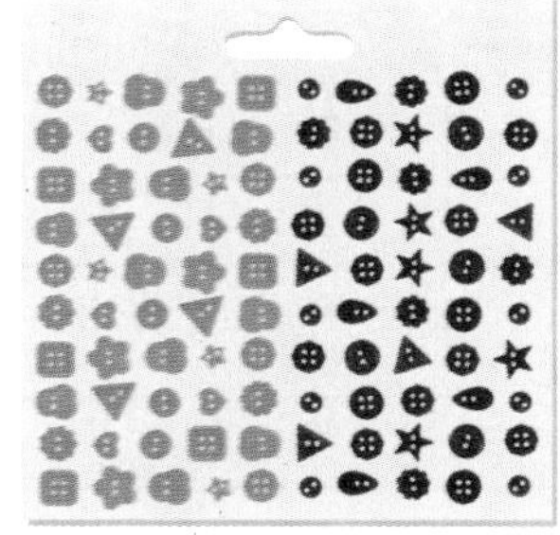

You have seen how decimals and fractions are related. Let's explore how they are related to percents.

Percent (%) means "per hundred." So, you can write a percent as a fraction or a decimal.

$100\% = \frac{100}{100} = 1.0$

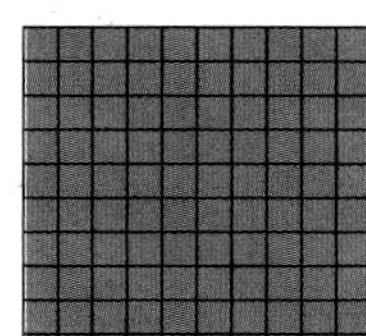

Think: 100 out of 100 squares are shaded.

$50\% = \frac{50}{100} = 0.50$

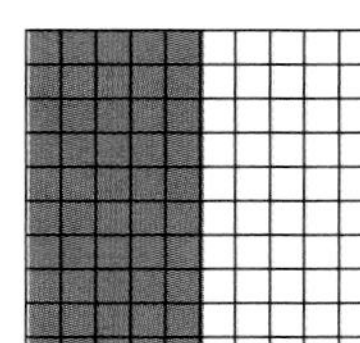

Think: 50 out of 100 squares are shaded.

$25\% = \frac{25}{100} = 0.25$

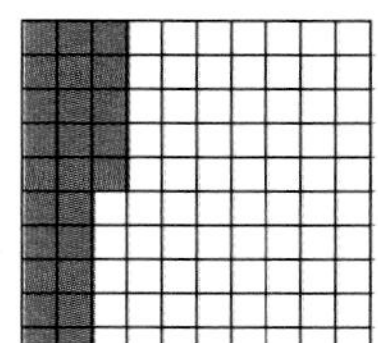

Think: 25 out of 100 squares are shaded.

So, 50% of the buttons on a card are green.

Write the following decimals or fractions as percents.

1. 0.10 2. $\frac{40}{100}$ 3. 0.80 4. $\frac{33}{100}$ 5. 0.30

LESSON 5

Compare and Order Decimals

Quick Review

Write an equivalent decimal for each.

1. 0.50 **2.** 0.60

3. 0.1 **4.** 0.20

5. 0.9

Learn

TUNNEL TRAVEL The Brooklyn-Battery Tunnel in New York is 1.73 miles long. The E. Johnson Memorial Tunnel in Colorado is 1.70 miles long. Which tunnel is longer?

Example You can use a number line, a place-value chart, or a decimal model to compare decimals.

Use a number line.

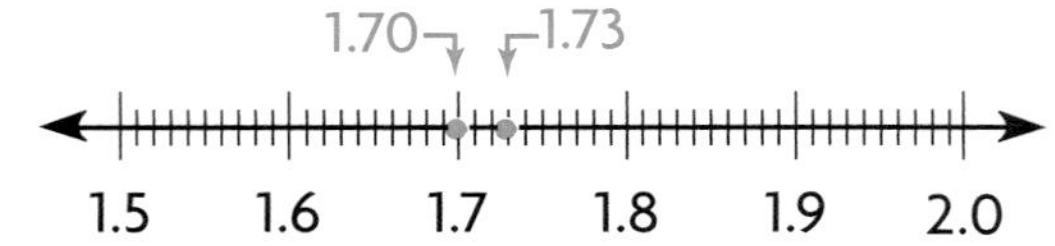

Since 1.73 is to the right of 1.70, 1.73 > 1.70.

Use a place-value chart.

ONES	.	TENTHS	HUNDREDTHS
1	.	7	3
1	.	7	0

1 = 1   7 = 7   3 > 0

Think: Line up the decimal points. Compare the digits, beginning with the greatest place value.

Since 3 > 0, 1.73 > 1.70.

Use a decimal model.

Think: Compare the number of shaded squares.

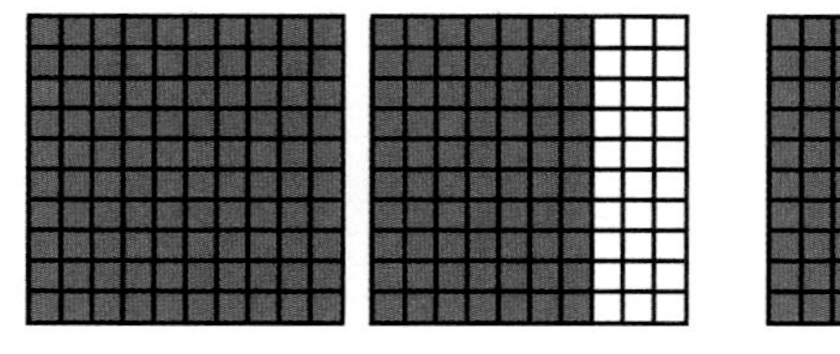
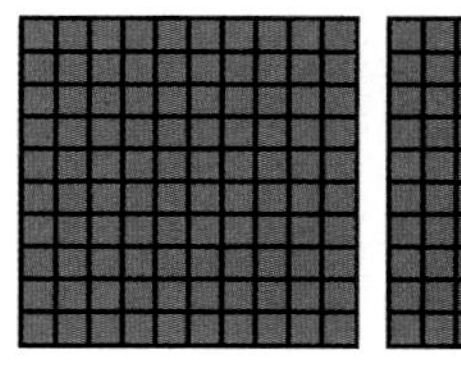
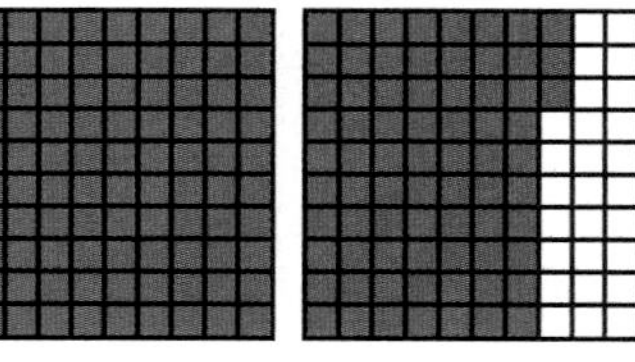

1.70   1.73

Since the model for 1.73 has 3 more shaded squares, 1.73 > 1.70.

So, the Brooklyn-Battery Tunnel is longer.

Remember

On a number line, the numbers to the right are greater than the numbers to the left.

Order Decimals

One Way Use a number line to order decimals. Order 9.4, 9.63, and 9.27 from greatest to least.

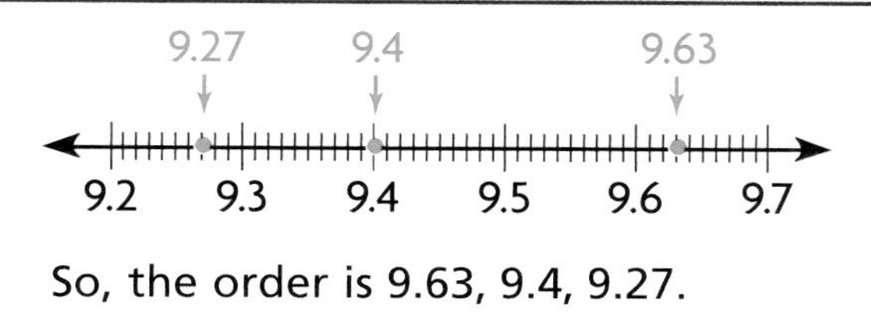

So, the order is 9.63, 9.4, 9.27.

Another Way Use place value to order decimals. Order 1.23, 0.98, and 1.28 from least to greatest.

STEP 1

Line up the decimal points. Compare the digits in the greatest place.

1.23
↓
0.98 $0 < 1$
↓
1.28

Since $0 < 1$, 0.98 is the least.

STEP 2

Compare the tenths.

1.23
↓ $2 = 2$
1.28

There are the same number of tenths.

STEP 3

Compare the hundredths.

1.23
↓ $3 < 8$
1.28

So, the order from least to greatest is 0.98, 1.23, 1.28.

- **What if** you wanted to write the decimals from greatest to least? How would this change the order?

Example

Order 0.813, 0.6, 0.65 from least to greatest.

0.813		**Think:** $8 > 6$, so 0.813 is the greatest.
↓		
0.6	0.600	0.6 is equivalent to 0.600.
↓	↓	0.65 is equivalent to 0.650.
0.65	0.650	$0 < 5$, so 0.6 is the least.

The order from least to greatest is 0.6, 0.65, 0.813.

LESSON CONTINUES

Check

1. **Explain** how you can use decimal models to help you compare decimals.

Compare. Write <, >, or = for each ●.

2. 0.45 ● 0.35 **3.** 0.5 ● 0.7 **4.** $0.03 ● $0.30 **5.** 5.4 ● 5.243 **6.** 1.036 ● 1.308

Use the number line to order the decimals from *least* to *greatest*.

7. 2.01, 2.10, 2.2, 2.02

8. 2.7, 2.67, 2.76, 2.6

Practice and Problem Solving

Extra Practice, page 578, Set D

Compare. Write <, >, or = for each ●.

9. 0.82 ● 0.93 **10.** $0.81 ● $0.18 **11.** 0.5 ● 0.51 **12.** 0.20 ● 0.02

13. 1.0 ● 1.029 **14.** 0.600 ● 0.6 **15.** $2.31 ● $2.63 **16.** 0.74 ● 0.53

Use the number line above to order the decimals from *least* to *greatest*.

17. 2.01, 2.11, 2.13, 2.10 **18.** 2.23, 2.45, 2.32, 2.5 **19.** 2.94, 2.49, 2.4, 3.00

Order the decimals from *greatest* to *least*.

20. $1.04, $4.11, $0.41, $1.40

21. 0.96, 1.06, 0.9, 1.6

22. 4.08, 4.3, 4.803, 4.038

23. 2.007, 2.714, 2.09, 2.97

24. 0.086, 8.6, 8.069, 0.006

25. 1.703, 1.037, 1.37, 1.073

26. **What's the Question?** Wes has $4 more than June. Debbie has $7 less than Wes. June has $5. The answer is $2.

27. Compare the decimals 0.8 and 0.2 using < or >. Then explain how you can use a number line to find the difference between them.

28. **REASONING** Which of these numbers has the same value as the digit 7 in the number 136.074?

70, 7, 0.7, 0.07, 0.007

29. **REASONING** List all the possible digits for the missing digit.

12.34 < 12.■6 < 12.77

USE DATA For 30–32, use the table.

30. What was the time for the fastest runner? What was the time for the slowest runner?
HINT: The least time is the fastest.

31. Mia also ran the 50-yard dash. Her time was 6.48 seconds. Order the times from least to greatest.

32. Keisha ran the 50-yard dash in 6.43 seconds. Compare her time to Jessica's time. Who was faster?

50-YARD DASH

Runner	Time (in seconds)
Lisa	6.50
Jessica	6.45
Kelly	6.40

Mixed Review and Test Prep

33. Write $\frac{9}{12}$ in simplest form. (p. 448)

34. $3{,}618 \div 9$ (p. 306)

35. List the factors of 36. (p. 338)

36. 32×100 (p. 236)

37. Write a fraction equivalent to 0.73. (p. 560)

38. Write a decimal equivalent to 5.4. (p. 566)

39. **TEST PREP** Choose the letter of the fraction equivalent to 1.06. (p. 568)

A $1\frac{6}{10}$ **C** $1\frac{60}{10}$

B $1\frac{6}{100}$ **D** $1\frac{60}{100}$

40. **TEST PREP** Choose the letter of the greatest fraction. (p. 452)

F $\frac{1}{3}$ **H** $\frac{1}{2}$

G $\frac{1}{6}$ **J** $\frac{1}{8}$

Problem Solving Thinker's Corner

A-MAZE-ING REASONING

MATERIALS: Decimal Maze worksheet

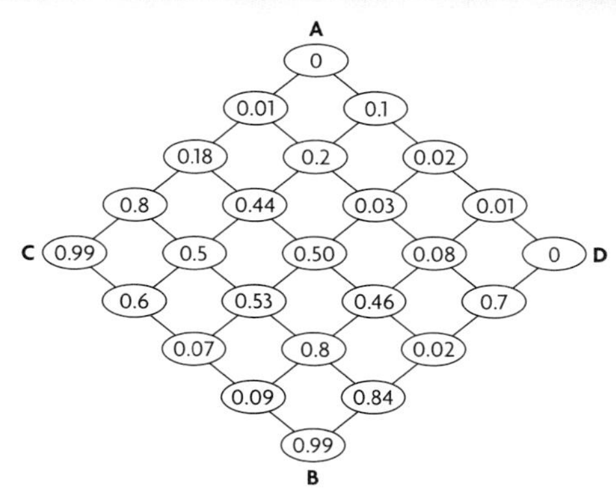

1. On the worksheet, trace a path through the maze from A to B. For each step, move to a number of greater value.
2. On the worksheet, trace a path through the maze from C to D. For each step, move to a number of lesser value.
3. Then, using the blank maze on the worksheet, make your own maze. Try to make your path the only possible way to get across the maze. Give your maze to a partner to solve.

LESSON 6

Problem Solving Strategy
Use Logical Reasoning

Quick Review

Which is greater?

1. 0.5 or 0.9 **2.** 0.12 or 0.21

3. 3.1 or 2.5 **4.** 5.50 or 5.35

5. 37.0 or 37.10

PROBLEM Miss Epps used a stopwatch to time Max, Jenna, and Dalia in a race. The times were 25.15 sec, 30.50 sec, and 34.10 sec. Jenna was slower than Dalia. A boy came in second. Who received first, second, and third places?

▲ This stopwatch shows thirteen and fifteen hundredths seconds.

UNDERSTAND

- What are you asked to find?
- What information will you use?
- Is there any information you will not use?

PLAN

- What strategy can you use to solve the problem?

  Use *logical reasoning* to determine the order in which the students finished.

SOLVE

- How can you use the strategy?

  Organize what you know in a table. Show all the possibilities.

A A boy came in second.

Max is the only boy, so he must have the middle time. No two people have the same time, so there can be only one *yes* in each row and column.

	25.15	30.50	34.10
Max	NO	YES	NO
Dalia		NO	
Jenna		NO	

B Jenna was slower than Dalia.

Since 34.10 sec is slower than 25.15 sec, Dalia's time must be 25.15 sec.

	25.15	30.50	34.10
Max	NO	YES	NO
Dalia	YES	NO	NO
Jenna	NO	NO	YES

So, Dalia was first, Max was second, and Jenna was third.

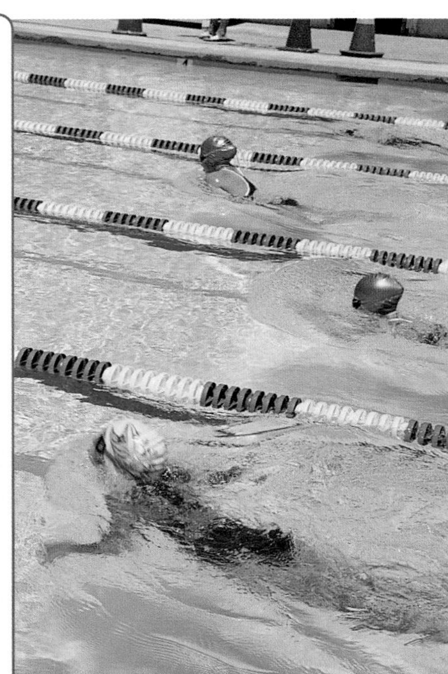

CHECK

- What other strategy could you use?

Problem Solving Practice

Use logical reasoning and solve.

1. **What if** after the race, Max, Dalia, and Jenna were thirsty? One person had a sports drink. The winner chose juice, and another person had water. Max does not like sports drinks. What did each person drink?

Strategies

- Draw a Diagram or Picture
- Make a Model or Act It Out
- Make an Organized List
- Find a Pattern
- Make a Table or Graph
- Predict and Test
- Work Backward
- Solve a Simpler Problem
- Write an Equation
- **Use Logical Reasoning**

Problem Solving

The temperatures last week were 85°F, 75°F, 77°F, 83°F, and 81°F. Monday was the hottest day, and Thursday was the coolest. Wednesday was cooler than Friday but warmer than Tuesday.

2. On which day was the temperature 83°F?
   A Monday
   B Tuesday
   C Wednesday
   D Friday

3. On which day was the median temperature recorded?
   F Monday
   G Tuesday
   H Wednesday
   J Friday

Mixed Strategy Practice

4. Tim earns $4.00 an hour mowing lawns. He worked from 12:00 P.M. to 5:00 P.M. How much did he earn?

5. What two numbers come next in this pattern? Explain.

   32, 28, 23, 17, ■, ■

6.  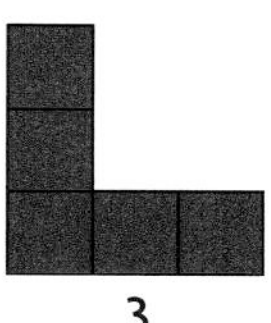

   1 2 3

   If this pattern continues, how many squares will be in the 7th figure? Explain.

7. 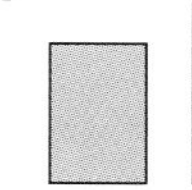 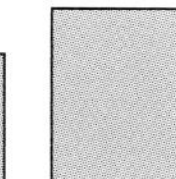 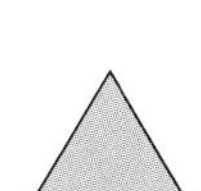 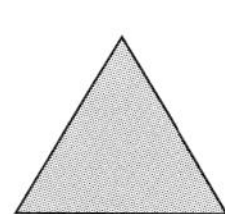 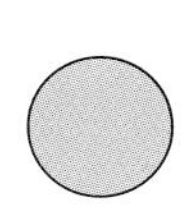 ?

   Look at the pattern. Describe the pattern. Draw the next figure.

8. A spinner is divided into 3 equal parts: one white, one blue, and one orange. List the possible outcomes of spinning the pointer two times. Write the total number of outcomes.

9. Bruno, David, and Zack are out for breakfast. The waiter brings eggs and bacon, pancakes, and cereal to their table. Bruno needs syrup and David does not like meat. Who gets which order?

10. Write the greatest and least four-digit decimals expressed to hundredths without a zero in the hundredths place.

Extra Practice

Set A (pp. 560–563)

Write the decimal and fraction shown by each model or number line.

1. 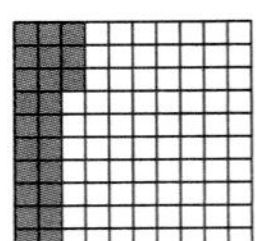

2. 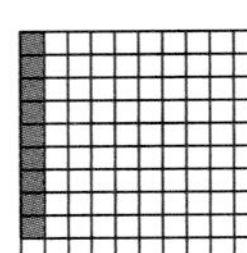

3. 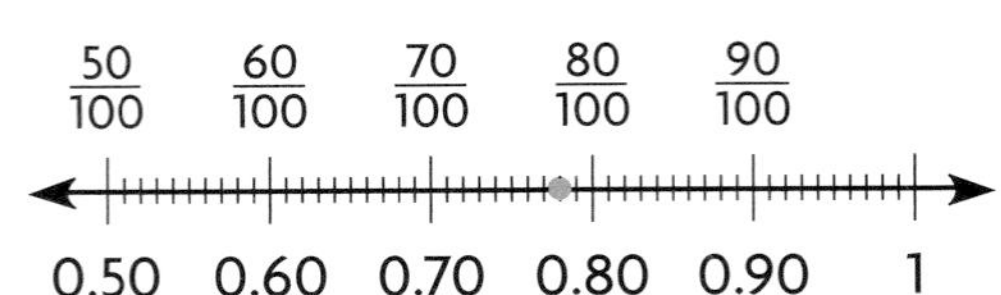

Write each fraction as a decimal.

4. $\frac{2}{10}$ **5.** $\frac{33}{100}$ **6.** $\frac{8}{100}$ **7.** $\frac{9}{10}$ **8.** $\frac{84}{100}$

9. Patty has $\frac{3}{4}$ of a dollar. How much money does she have?

Set B (pp. 564–565)

Write each decimal as a fraction.

1. 0.372 **2.** 0.025 **3.** 0.009 **4.** 0.461 **5.** 0.073

Write the decimal two other ways.

6. 0.548 **7.** 0.029 **8.** 0.004 **9.** 0.473 **10.** 0.081

11. eighty-three thousandths **12.** $0.7 + 0.01 + 0.006$ **13.** 8 thousandths

Set C (pp. 568–571)

Write an equivalent mixed number or decimal.

1. 6.5 **2.** $7\frac{1}{4}$ **3.** $\frac{6}{4}$ **4.** 3.75 **5.** 8.25

6. 9.75 **7.** $5\frac{1}{2}$ **8.** $\frac{8}{3}$ **9.** $\frac{61}{7}$ **10.** $\frac{73}{9}$

Set D (pp. 572–575)

Compare. Write <, >, or = for each ●.

1. 0.30 ● 0.3 **2.** 5.67 ● 6.75 **3.** 3.60 ● 3.06 **4.** 1.2 ● 1.20

Order the decimals from *least* to *greatest*.

5. 0.19; 0.21; 0.91; 0.12; 1.69 **6.** 4.35; 3.45; 5.43; 4.53; 3.54

7. Juan ran 1.65 miles during track practice and Evan ran 1.68 miles. Who ran the greater distance?

Review/Test

CHECK VOCABULARY AND CONCEPTS

Choose the best term from the box.

decimal decimal point equivalent decimals

1. A number with one or more digits to the right of the decimal point is a ? . (p. 560)
2. Decimals that name the same number are ? . (p. 566)

CHECK SKILLS

Write each fraction as a decimal. (pp. 560–565)

3. $\frac{6}{10}$
4. $\frac{1}{100}$
5. $\frac{9}{25}$
6. $\frac{48}{1,000}$
7. $\frac{2}{5}$

Write an equivalent decimal for each. (pp. 566–567)

8. 0.60
9. 0.9
10. 0.4
11. 0.50
12. 0.70

Write an equivalent mixed number or a decimal. (pp. 568–571)

13. $6\frac{79}{100}$
14. $1\frac{67}{1,000}$
15. $3\frac{5}{100}$
16. 8.16
17. 4.002

Compare. Write <, >, or = for each ●. (pp. 572–575)

18. 0.71 ● 0.63
19. 0.56 ● 0.837
20. 2.603 ● 2.61
21. 1.4 ● 1.40

Order the decimals from *greatest* to *least*. (pp. 572–575)

22. 1.23, 2.23, 1.32, 0.89, 2.03
23. 3.06, 3.97, 3.614, 3.8

CHECK PROBLEM SOLVING

Solve. (pp. 576–577)

24. May, Peg, Lon, and Tim each bought a gift. The gifts cost $9.57, $8.64, $9.32, and $8.97. May's gift cost more than Tim's but less than Lon's. Lon's cost more than Peg's. Tim's gift cost $8.97. Name each child and the amount of his or her gift.
25. Four runners ran a mile in 6.52 min, 7.20 min, 6.59 min, and 7.16 min. Elena finished after Lara but before Nick. Jan ran the fastest. List the runners with their times, from first through fourth place.

Standardized Test Prep

NUMBER SENSE, CONCEPTS, AND OPERATIONS

1. Martha writes a number sentence on the board. Then she covers up one of the numbers with an eraser.

$8 \times$ ERASER $= 40$

What number is under the eraser?

A 3

B 4

C 5

D 6

2. Which of the following is **true**?

F $0.53 > 0.55$

G $0.03 > 0.019$

H $0.072 < 0.059$

J $0.02 = 0.2$

3. **Explain It** ESTIMATE the number of oil changes the Oil Change Shop completed from Monday to Friday. Explain your thinking.

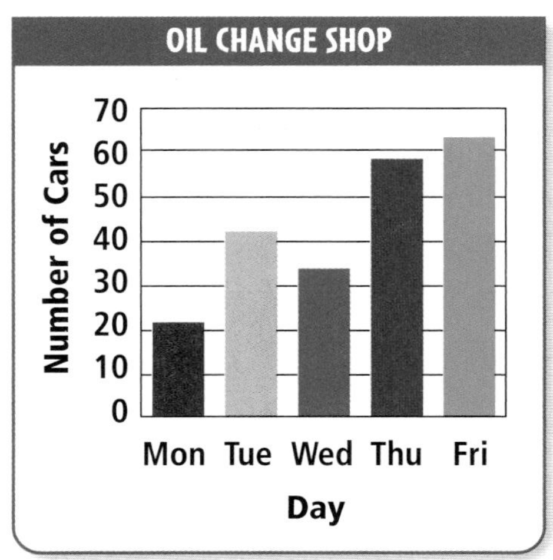

MEASUREMENT

4. Hayley buys 6 one-liter bottles of water. How many milliliters is that?

1 liter = 1,000 milliliters

A 60 milliliters **C** 6,000 milliliters

B 600 milliliters **D** 6,500 milliliters

TIP **Decide on a plan.** See item 5. Find the information you need in the table. Then use the relationship between ounces and pounds to solve the problem.

5. The table shows serving sizes of Liam's favorite foods.

FAVORITE FOODS

Food	Serving Size (in ounces)
Peanut butter	3
Chicken	5
Cereal	4
Muffin	6

Liam buys a 1-pound box of cereal. How many servings are in it?

1 pound = 16 ounces

F 2 **H** 4

G 3 **J** 5

6. **Explain It** Allison left school at 3:23. It took her 9 minutes to walk home. Then Allison talked to her friend on the phone for 37 minutes. To the nearest 5 minutes, ESTIMATE what time it was when Allison got off the phone with her friend. Explain your thinking.

ALGEBRAIC THINKING

7. The table below shows the regular and sale prices of several furniture items.

FURNITURE STORE SALE		
Item	**Price**	**Sale Price**
Sofa	\$875	\$875 − s
Chair	\$630	\$630 − s
Table	\$599	\$599 − s

If $s = \$75$, which is the sale price of a chair?

A \$705

B \$555

C \$525

D \$75

8. José scored some points in his first basketball game. In his second game, he scored 8 more points than in the first. Let p represent the number of points José scored in the first game. Which expression shows how many points he scored in the second game?

F $p + 8$

G $p - 8$

H $p \times 8$

J $p \div 8$

9. **Explain It** David picked 6 times as many strawberries as Matthew. Matthew picked 52 strawberries. How many strawberries did David pick? Let d stand for the number of strawberries David picked. Write an equation for the problem. Explain your thinking.

DATA ANALYSIS AND PROBABILITY

10. A gymnast scored 6 on his first exercise and 8 on his second exercise. His mean score for three exercises was 7. What did he score on his third exercise?

A 21

B 8

C 7

D 2

11. What is the probability of rolling an even number with a number cube that is labeled 1 through 6?

F $\frac{1}{6}$

G $\frac{1}{3}$

H $\frac{1}{2}$

J $\frac{2}{3}$

12. **Explain It** Plant A was in a sunny window. Plant B was in the corner of a room and received less sunlight. Greta measured the heights of the two plants once a week. The results are shown in the table.

PLANT HEIGHT		
Week	**Plant A**	**Plant B**
Week 1	4 inches	4 inches
Week 2	5 inches	$4\frac{1}{2}$ inches
Week 3	6 inches	5 inches
Week 4		

Predict the heights of Plant A and Plant B in week 4. Explain your thinking.

Add and Subtract Decimals

FAST FACT • SCIENCE The first weather station in Alaska was established in Anchorage in 1915. December is the snowiest month in Anchorage, with an average snowfall of 14.8 inches.

PROBLEM SOLVING The graph below shows the annual snowfall for 5 years in Anchorage. What is the range of the amounts shown?

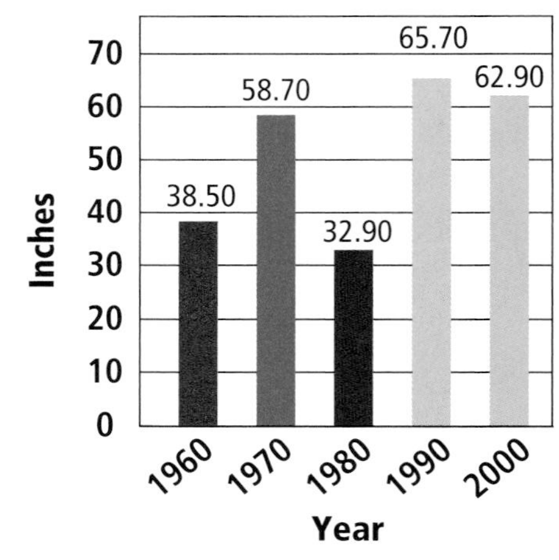

Owl snow sculpture in Alaska

CHECK WHAT YOU KNOW

Use this page to help you review and remember important skills needed for Chapter 27.

MODEL DECIMALS

Write the decimal for the shaded part.

1. 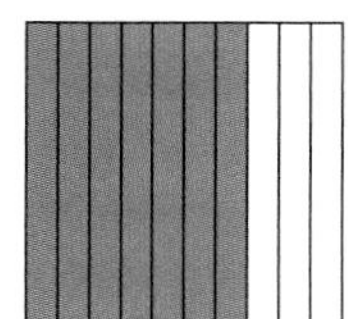

2. 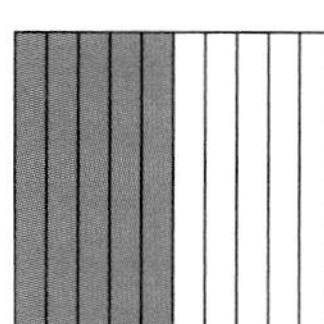

3. 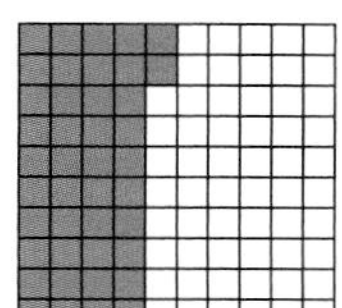

4. 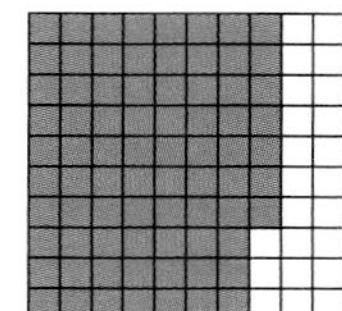

DECIMAL PLACE VALUE

Write the value of the blue digit in each decimal.

5. 0.13	**6.** 0.45	**7.** 0.137	**8.** 0.689
9. 0.101	**10.** 0.748	**11.** 0.56	**12.** 0.352

ROUND WHOLE NUMBERS

Round to the nearest hundred and the nearest ten.

13. 145	**14.** 281	**15.** 764	**16.** 115
17. 405	**18.** 327	**19.** 575	**20.** 391

REVIEW

decimal [de′sə•məl] *noun*

Decimal begins with the prefix *deci-,* which means "one tenth." Based on what you know about decimals, explain why the prefix *deci-* helps you understand what a decimal is.

www.harcourtschool.com/mathglossary

LESSON 

Round Decimals

Learn

SNOW TREK Lisa and some friends went cross-country skiing. They covered 4.2 miles.

Round 4.2 to the nearest whole number.

One Way Use a number line.

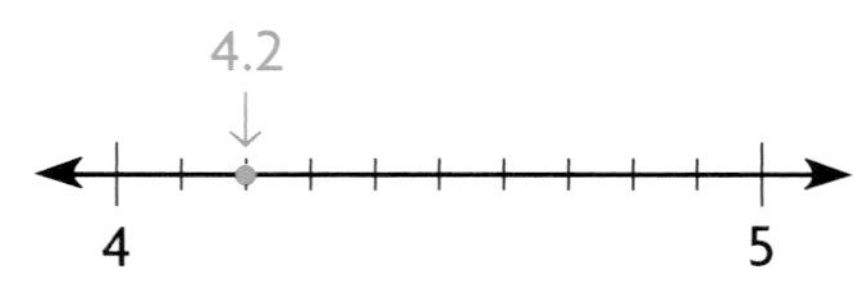

4.2 is between 4 and 5, but it is closer to 4.

Another Way Use the rounding rules.

Look at the tenths place. 4.2

Since 2 < 5, the digit 4 stays the same.

So, 4.2 rounded to the nearest whole number is 4.

Examples

A Round 6.48 to the nearest tenth. Look at the number line.

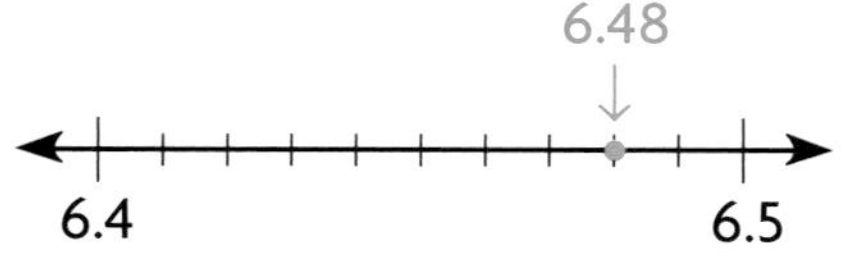

6.48 is closer to 6.5 than to 6.4. So, 6.48 rounds to 6.5.

B Round 5.076 to the nearest hundredth.

Use the rounding rules.

Look at the thousandths place. 5.076

Since 6 > 5, the digit 7 is increased by 1.

So, 5.076 rounds to 5.08.

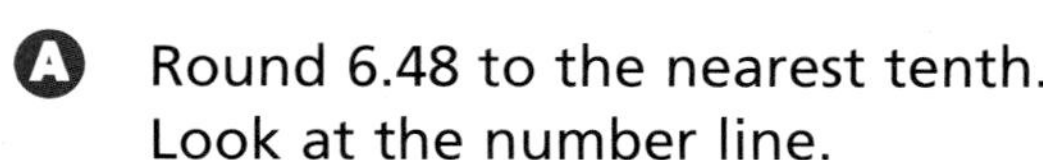

Quick Review

Round each number to the nearest ten.

1. 56 **2.** 84 **3.** 938

4. 4,892 **5.** 15,284

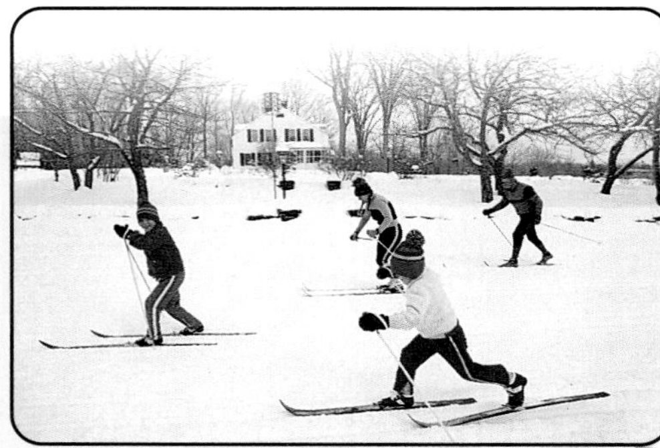

Remember

Rounding Rules:
- Find the place to which you want to round.
- Look at the digit to its right.
- If that digit is less than 5, the digit in the rounding place stays the same.
- If that digit is 5 or more, the digit in the rounding place is increased by 1.

MATH IDEA Decimals can be rounded using a number line or the rounding rules.

Check

1. **Explain** how to use a number line to round 3.4 to the nearest whole number.

Round each number to the place of the blue digit.

2. 2.2 3. 1.8 4. $16.98 5. 7.305 6. 6.327

Round to the nearest tenth. Use the number lines or the rounding rules.

9.5 9.6 9.7

7. 4.50 8. 4.55 9. 4.61 10. 9.67 11. 9.52

Practice and Problem Solving

Extra Practice, page 598, Set A

Round each number to the place of the blue digit.

12. 5.84 13. 3.18 14. $1.43 15. $7.71 16. $36.52

17. 13.68 18. 49.274 19. 27.643 20. $83.54 21. $54.91

Round to the nearest hundredth.

22. 10.076 23. 61.349 24. 5.181 25. 9.413 26. 24.259

27. Round 5.261 and 5.19 to the nearest tenth, and compare.

28. **REASONING** For what digits will 43.9▢5 round to 43.9?

29. David bought a jacket on sale for $32.49. To the nearest ten dollars, how much did David's jacket cost?

30. What is two and fifty-one thousandths rounded to the nearest hundredth? to the nearest tenth?

31. **REASONING** James paid $5.82 for a paint set. He told Pete the cost was about $6.00. Was $6.00 a reasonable rounded amount? Explain.

32. **What's the Question?** Ted has half as many marbles as Joel and 25 fewer marbles than Spencer. Spencer has 60 marbles. The answer is 70 marbles.

Mixed Review and Test Prep

33. Write an equivalent decimal for 8.3. (p. 566)

34. Write 235,617 in expanded form. (p. 4)

35. Round 217,627 to the nearest ten thousand. (p. 30)

36. Find the value of $n + 8$ if $n = 16$. (p. 64)

37. **TEST PREP** Which number is NOT a multiple of 9? (p. 338)

A 3
B 9
C 18
D 90

LESSON 2

Estimate Decimal Sums and Differences

Quick Review

1. 58 + 72
2. 130 + 45
3. 216 + 194
4. 125 − 32
5. 1,089 − 59

Learn

PACK YOUR BAGS! The table shows the three countries that had the most visitors in 2000. Altogether, about how many people traveled to these countries?

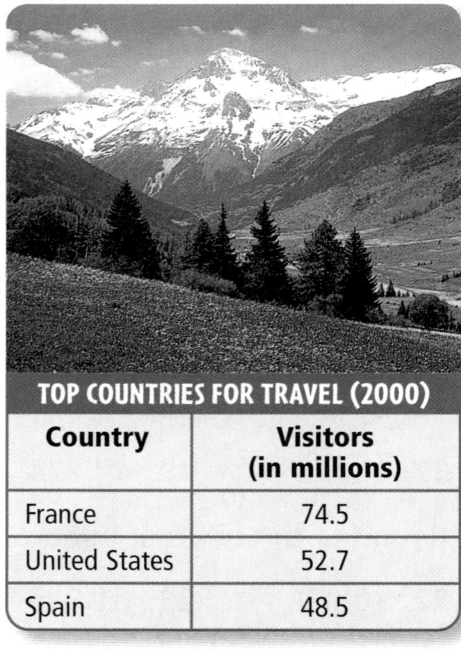

TOP COUNTRIES FOR TRAVEL (2000)	
Country	**Visitors (in millions)**
France	74.5
United States	52.7
Spain	48.5

▲ **Spring Meadow, France**

Estimate by rounding to the nearest ten.

$$\begin{array}{r} 74.5 \\ 52.7 \\ +48.5 \\ \hline \end{array} \quad \begin{array}{c} \rightarrow \\ \rightarrow \\ \rightarrow \\ \end{array} \quad \begin{array}{r} 70 \\ 50 \\ 50 \\ \hline 170 \end{array}$$

- Line up the decimal points.
- Round to the nearest ten.

So, altogether about 170 million travelers visited France, the United States, and Spain in 2000.

A travel magazine showed that in New Orleans, Louisiana, each traveler spent an average of $82.98 per day. In Paris, France, it was an amount equal to $97.55. About how much more did each traveler spend in Paris per day?

Estimate by rounding to the nearest dollar.

$$\begin{array}{r} \$97.55 \\ -\$82.98 \\ \hline \end{array} \quad \begin{array}{c} \rightarrow \\ \rightarrow \\ \end{array} \quad \begin{array}{r} \$98 \\ -\$83 \\ \hline \$15 \end{array}$$

- Line up the decimal points.
- Round to the nearest dollar.

So, each traveler spent about $15 more per day in Paris.

- Name some situations in which you might need only an estimated sum or difference.

Check

1. **Explain** how you would determine if a total cost of $19.48 is reasonable for a travel book that costs $12.99 and a poster that costs $6.49.

Estimate the sum or difference.

2. $\begin{array}{r} \$24.76 \\ +\$\ \ 5.21 \\ \hline \end{array}$

3. $\begin{array}{r} 5.25 \\ +7.06 \\ \hline \end{array}$

4. $\begin{array}{r} 2.314 \\ -1.238 \\ \hline \end{array}$

5. $\begin{array}{r} \$7.80 \\ -\$2.07 \\ \hline \end{array}$

6. $\begin{array}{r} 17.136 \\ +19.785 \\ \hline \end{array}$

Practice and Problem Solving

Extra Practice, page 598, Set B

Estimate the sum or difference.

7. 2.8 − 0.5 **8.** \$21.06 − \$4.11 **9.** 1.07 + 1.54 **10.** 2.903 + 2.541

11. 3.59 − 3.37 **12.** 7.99 − 1.93 **13.** 7.126 + 7.719 **14.** \$11.99 + \$10.58

Estimate to compare. Write < or > for each ●.

15. 12.853 − 8.021 ● 15.95 − 9.99 **16.** 82.85 + 3.70 ● 96.20 − 11.04

USE DATA **For 17–20, use the graph.**

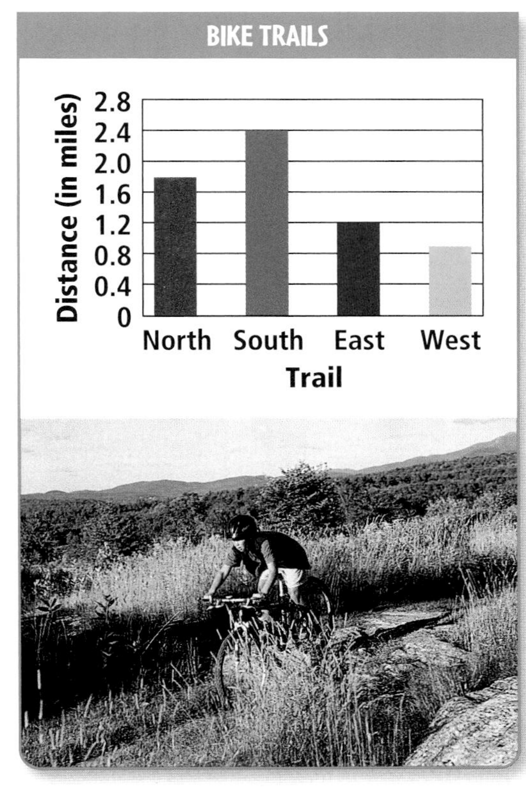

17. Ann rode the north and south trails. Carly rode the east and west trails. To the nearest mile, about how many more miles did Ann ride than Carly?

18. Brett and Rob rode all four bike trails. To the nearest mile, how far did each ride?

19. **REASONING** Trudy wants to ride a bike trail with a distance greater than $1\frac{1}{2}$ miles. Which trails could Trudy choose?

20. Sandy rode a total of 2.1 miles. Becky rode 0.9 mile more than Sandy. Which bike trails did Becky ride? Which bike trails did Sandy ride?

21. **Vocabulary Power** When you *round* a number such as 5.28 to the nearest tenth, you change the number. Explain how rounding a number changes it.

22. Pam bought a bike helmet for \$22.29, a light for \$21.79, and a backpack for \$21.99 including tax. Estimate the total cost and the change she should receive from \$70.00.

Mixed Review and Test Prep

Compare. Write < or > for each ●. (pp. 20, 572)

23. 3,980 ● 3,907 **24.** 5.32 ● 5.03

25. 4 × 50 = 200. So, 40 × 50 = ■. (p. 214)

26. 30 × 6 = 180. So, 30 × 60 = ■. (p. 214)

27. **TEST PREP** What is the average of the test scores 98, 72, 84, and 86? (p. 328)

A 98 **B** 85 **C** 80 **D** 70

LESSON 3

Add Decimals

Quick Review

1. $1.10 + $0.25
2. $0.85 + $0.20
3. $3.05 + $0.45
4. $7.03 + $0.05
5. $0.75 + $0.25

Learn

SLIGHT CHANCE OF RAIN The Marco family will be in Tucson, AZ, in November and December. The average rainfall is 0.62 in. for November and 0.94 in. for December. How many inches of rainfall can the Marco family expect while in Tucson?

▲ Tucson, Arizona

Activity

HANDS ON

MATERIALS: decimal models, colored pencils

Add. 0.62 + 0.94 Estimate. 1 + 1 = 2

Use decimal models to find 0.62 + 0.94.

STEP 1

Shade 0.62 red.

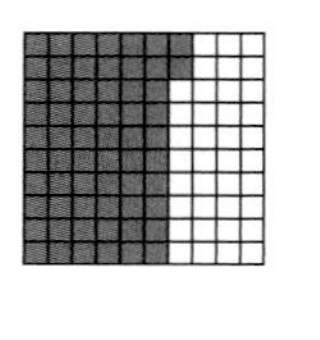

STEP 2

Shade 0.94 blue. Find the sum.

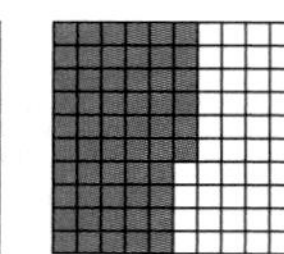

0.62 + 0.94 = 1.56

The answer of 1.56 is close to the estimate of 2, so the answer is reasonable.

So, the total amount of expected rainfall is 1.56 inches.

MATH IDEA You can add decimals the same way you add whole numbers if you line up the decimal points first.

Examples

A

$$\begin{array}{r} 0.41 \\ +\ 0.36 \\ \hline 0.77 \end{array}$$

Line up the decimal points.

Place the decimal point in the sum.

B

$$\begin{array}{r} \scriptstyle 1 \\ \$4.26 \\ +\ \$0.54 \\ \hline \$4.80 \end{array}$$

C

$$\begin{array}{r} \scriptstyle 1\ 11 \\ 5.076 \\ +\ 3.928 \\ \hline 9.004 \end{array}$$

- Which examples can be solved using mental math? Explain.

Check

1. Make a model to find the sum $1.42 + 0.55$. Draw a picture of your model.

Find the sum. Estimate to check.

2. $0.8 + 0.1$
3. $0.6 + 2.5$
4. $3.72 + 5.03$
5. $0.695 + 4.231$

Practice and Problem Solving

Extra Practice, page 598, Set C

Find the sum. Estimate to check.

6. $0.9 + 0.5$
7. $1.66 + 0.32$
8. $0.364 + 2.289$
9. $\$5.61 + \$2.69$
10. $0.73 + 0.49$
11. $\$7.05 + \$0.95$
12. $1.89 + 1.54$
13. $24.918 + 21.703$
14. $\$49.99 + \$71.99$

Write the letter of the model that matches each problem. Solve.

a. 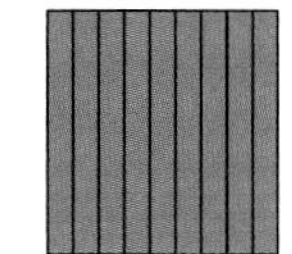

b. 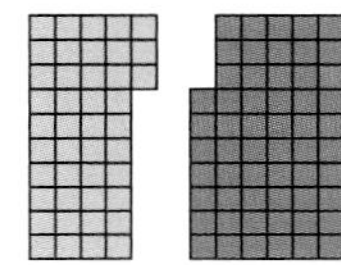

c. 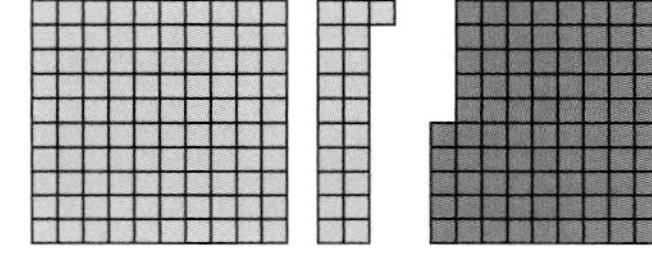

15. $1.21 + 0.85 = n$
16. $0.4 + 0.9 = n$
17. $0.43 + 0.57 = n$

Use mental math to find the missing addend.

18. ■ $+ 5.25 = 9.5$
19. $1.1 + 0.6 +$ ■ $= 1.8$
20. $1.111 +$ ■ $= 2.222$

USE DATA For 21–22, use the table.

21. How many more inches of snow fell in the first three months of 2001 than in 2002?
22. **FAST FACT • SCIENCE** The record snowfall for January in Pittsburgh is 40.2 inches. Is this amount greater than or less than the total amount of snowfall for the first 3 months of 2001 and 2002? by how much?

SNOWFALL IN PITTSBURGH, PA (in inches)

	2001	2002
January	13.7	10.0
February	2.7	6.4
March	8.0	4.0

Mixed Review and Test Prep

23. Write the first five multiples of 8. (p. 338)
24. Write a decimal equivalent for $\frac{21}{100}$. (p. 560)
25. Round 3.27 to the nearest tenth. (p. 584)
26. List the factors of 8. (p. 338)
27. **TEST PREP** $5 \times (20 + 2) =$ ■ (p. 184)
   A 30 **B** 102 **C** 110 **D** 200

LESSON 4 Subtract Decimals

Quick Review

1. \$3.50 − \$1.00
2. \$0.85 − \$0.25
3. \$1.20 − \$0.90
4. \$5.25 − \$0.75
5. \$0.89 − \$0.10

Learn

SMALL SITES One of the smallest countries in the world is Monaco with an area of 1.8 square kilometers. Central Park in New York City has an area of 3.2 square kilometers. How much larger is Central Park than Monaco?

Activity

MATERIALS: decimal models, colored pencils, scissors

Subtract. 3.2 − 1.8 Estimate. 3 − 2 = 1

Take-Away Model Use decimal models.

STEP 1

Show 3.2 by shading decimal models.

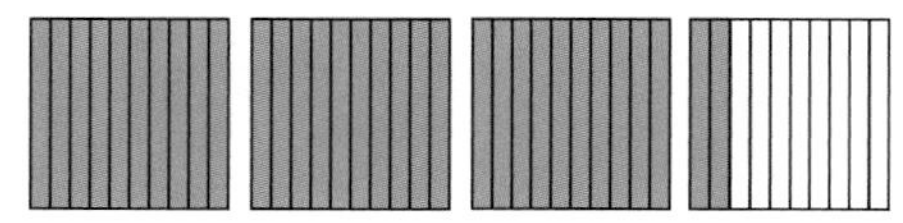

STEP 2

Take away 18 tenths. 14 tenths are left.

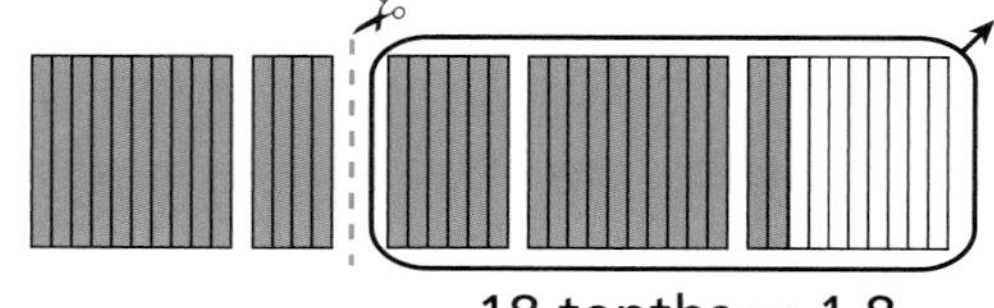

18 tenths = 1.8

3.2 − 1.8 = 1.4

The answer of 1.4 is close to the estimate of 1, so the answer is reasonable. So, the area of Central Park is 1.4 square kilometers larger than the area of Monaco.

▲ The Principality of Monaco

Technology Link

More Practice: Harcourt Mega Math The Number Games, *Tiny's Think Tank*, Level L

Examples

A 2.3 − 1.4

$$\begin{array}{r} \overset{1}{\cancel{2}}.\overset{13}{\cancel{3}} \\ -1.4 \\ \hline 0.9 \end{array}$$

Line up the decimal points.

Place the decimal point in the difference.

B \$18.56 − \$4.93

$$\begin{array}{r} \$1\overset{7}{\cancel{8}}.\overset{15}{\cancel{5}}6 \\ -\$\ \ 4.93 \\ \hline \$13.63 \end{array}$$

C 84.063 − 26.057

$$\begin{array}{r} \overset{7}{\cancel{8}}\overset{14}{\cancel{4}}.0\overset{5}{\cancel{6}}\overset{13}{\cancel{3}} \\ -26.057 \\ \hline 58.006 \end{array}$$

Check

1. **Explain** how regrouping to subtract decimals is like regrouping to subtract whole numbers.

Find the difference. Estimate to check.

2. $0.8 - 0.5$
3. $\$20.82 - \$7.71$
4. $22.3 - 11.9$
5. $3.426 - 0.249$
6. $2.914 - 1.685$

Practice and Problem Solving

Extra Practice, page 598, Set D

Find the difference. Estimate to check.

7. $0.9 - 0.2$
8. $\$6.93 - \$0.54$
9. $1.6 - 0.8$
10. $41.97 - 10.38$
11. $\$52.72 - \$21.28$
12. $2.453 - 2.386$
13. $3.517 - 1.274$
14. $4.768 - 2.993$
15. $16.702 - 5.178$
16. $5.083 - 2.226$
17. $\$7.89 - \$4.37$
18. $9.84 - 3.87$
19. $8.2 - 6.9$
20. $\$29.53 - \$18.98$
21. $9.124 - 3.076$
22. $4.237 - 2.819$
23. $13.207 - 11.496$
24. $9.532 - 4.107$

ALGEBRA Use mental math to find the missing digits.

25. $2.\blacksquare - \blacksquare.1 = 1.2$
26. $\blacksquare.5 - 4.\blacksquare = 0.2$
27. $6.\blacksquare - \blacksquare.6 = 5.1$
28. $\blacksquare.8 - 7.\blacksquare = 3.5$

29. **REASONING** The difference of two 3-digit decimal numbers is 1.34. One number has a 6 in the ones and hundredths places. The other has a 6 in the tenths place. What are the two numbers?

30. 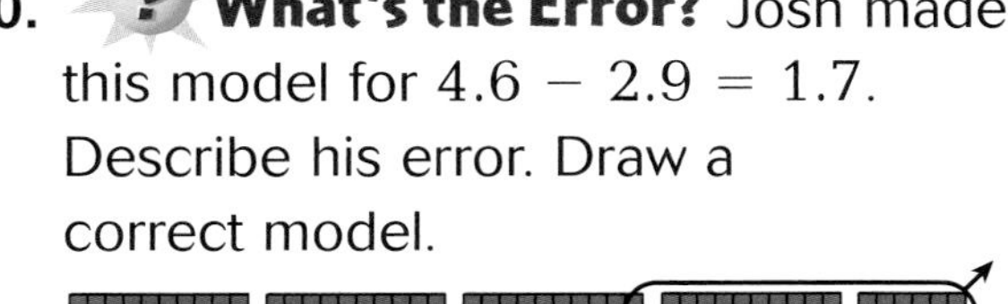
What's the Error? Josh made this model for $4.6 - 2.9 = 1.7$. Describe his error. Draw a correct model.

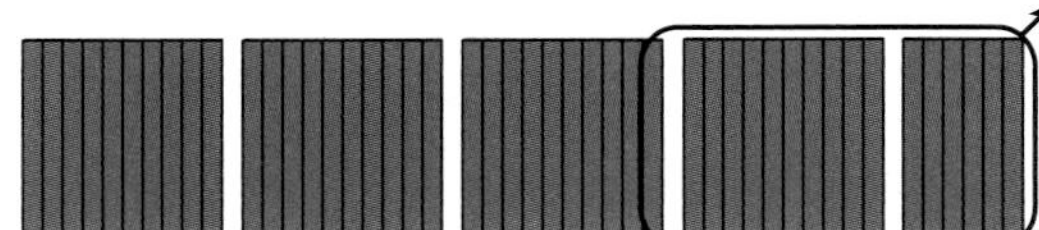

31. Molly has saved \$600 for a trip to France with the French Club. She needs twice that amount plus \$50 more. How much does the trip cost?

Mixed Review and Test Prep

32. List the factors of 18. (p. 338)
33. Order 5.82, 4.95, and 5.89 from *least* to *greatest*. (p. 572)
34. 8×136 (p. 222)
35. $156 \div 4$ (p. 300)
36. **TEST PREP** Find 5×13. (p. 218)
   A 55 **B** 60 **C** 65 **D** 70

LESSON 

Add and Subtract Decimals and Money

Quick Review

Compare. Write <, >, or = for each ●.

1. 47.5 ● 4.81
2. 3.2 ● 2.3
3. 0.75 ● 0.72
4. 2.8 ● 2.84
5. 9.9 ● 9.90

Learn

RAIN, RAIN, GO AWAY! Danny is doing a report on Iowa weather. Des Moines receives about 33 inches of rain each year. Use the table to find the total average rainfall from April through June.

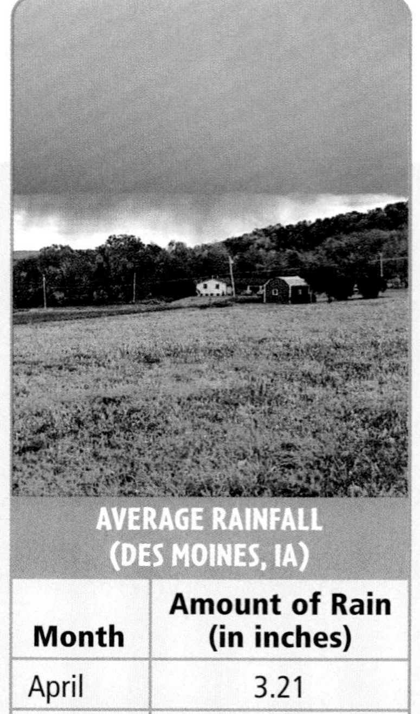

AVERAGE RAINFALL (DES MOINES, IA)

Month	Amount of Rain (in inches)
April	3.21
May	3.96
June	4.18

Example 1

Add. 3.21 + 3.96 + 4.18

Estimate. 3 + 4 + 4 = 11

STEP 1

Line up the decimal point and place value of each number.

```
  3.21
  3.96
+ 4.18
```

STEP 2

Add as you do with whole numbers. Place the decimal point in the sum.

```
  1 1
   3.21
   3.96
+  4.18
  11.35
```

Since the answer of 11.35 is close to the estimate of 11, the answer is reasonable. So, the total average rainfall is 11.35 inches.

Example 2

What if Danny wanted to compare the average rainfall for April and June? On average, how many more inches are received in June?

Subtract. 4.18 − 3.21

Estimate. 4 − 3 = 1

```
  3 11
  4̸.1̸8
− 3.21
  0.97
```

Line up the decimal points.

Since the answer of 0.97 is close to the estimate of 1, the answer is reasonable. So, the average rainfall is about 0.97 inch more in June than in April.

Equivalent Decimals

Sometimes one number has more decimal places after the decimal point than the other. Write equivalent decimals with the same number of decimal places before adding or subtracting.

Andrea goes to the store to buy a sun visor that costs $12.56. She gives the cashier $20. How much change should she receive?

Example

Subtract. $20 − $12.56 Estimate. $20 − $13 = $7

STEP 1

Line up the decimal points. Place zeros to the right of the decimal point so each number has the same number of digits after the decimal point.

```
  $20.00
 −$12.56
```

STEP 2

Subtract as you do with whole numbers. Place the decimal point in the difference.

```
    9  9
   1 10  1010
  $20.00
 −$12.56
  $ 7.44
```

So, Andrea will receive $7.44 in change.

- How much change should Andrea get back if she gives the cashier $20.01? Why would she do this?

More Examples

A $25 − $16.33

```
    14  9
   1 4  1010
  $25.00
 −$16.33
  $ 8.67
```

B $32 + $57.89

```
  $32.00
 +$57.89
  $89.89
```

C 57.68 − 38.567

```
  4 17   7 10
  57.680
 −38.567
  19.113
```

You can also use a calculator to add and subtract decimals.

   1 6  3 3 

2 5 − 1 6 • 3 3 Enter

25 − 16.33 =
8.67

LESSON CONTINUES

Check

1. **Explain** why zeros are sometimes placed to the right of the decimal points of numbers.

Find the sum or difference. Estimate to check.

2. $\$21 - \$10.20$ 3. $5.4 + 0.39$ 4. $\$13 + \$9.12$ 5. $15.03 - 9.647$

Practice and Problem Solving

Extra Practice, page 598, Set E

Find the sum or difference. Estimate to check.

6. $\begin{array}{r} 9.5 \\ +2.52 \\ \hline \end{array}$
7. $\begin{array}{r} 6.4 \\ -2.26 \\ \hline \end{array}$
8. $\begin{array}{r} \$3 \\ -\$1.39 \\ \hline \end{array}$
9. $\begin{array}{r} 3.8 \\ +4.073 \\ \hline \end{array}$
10. $\begin{array}{r} \$21.28 \\ -\$\ 8 \quad \\ \hline \end{array}$
11. $\begin{array}{r} 43.8 \\ +\ 1.73 \\ \hline \end{array}$
12. $\begin{array}{r} \$7 \\ -\$3.18 \\ \hline \end{array}$
13. $\begin{array}{r} 5.3 \\ -2.87 \\ \hline \end{array}$
14. $\begin{array}{r} 56.123 \\ -\ 8 \quad \\ \hline \end{array}$
15. $\begin{array}{r} 16.2 \\ +\ 9.5 \\ \hline \end{array}$
16. $\begin{array}{r} \$19 \\ -\$\ 4.37 \\ \hline \end{array}$
17. $\begin{array}{r} 79.142 \\ -\ 3.861 \\ \hline \end{array}$
18. $\begin{array}{r} 7.9 \\ -2.58 \\ \hline \end{array}$
19. $\begin{array}{r} 74.68 \\ +\ 8.3 \\ \hline \end{array}$
20. $\begin{array}{r} 43 \\ -\ 6.507 \\ \hline \end{array}$

21. $\$6.99 + \$2.09$ 22. $1.3 - 0.4$ 23. $18.7 - 5.941$ 24. $\$65 - \$30.50$

25. $56.83 - 0.67$ 26. $\$1.34 + \$12.09$ 27. $41.36 - 7.89$ 28. $69.4 + 7.802$

29. $4.5 + 19 + 6.032$ 30. $14.4 + 19 + 7.74$ 31. $\$45 + \$31.50 + \$20$

ALGEBRA **Find the missing number.**

32. $2.51 - 0.8 = \blacksquare$ 33. $2.32 - 1.6 = \blacksquare$ 34. $\blacksquare - 0.90 = 0.2$

35. $3.02 - \blacksquare = 1.31$ 36. $0.9 + 2.25 = \blacksquare$ 37. $\blacksquare + 0.52 = 1.12$

38. $4.76 - \blacksquare = 2.93$ 39. $15.86 + 3.79 = \blacksquare$ 40. $\blacksquare - 6.5 = 21.89$

41. Find two 3-digit decimals whose difference is 7.09.

42. Find three 3-digit decimals whose sum is 16.5.

43. **What's the Error?** Maria added 3.16, 1.04, and 0.07 and got a sum of 42.7. Describe her error. Write the correct answer.

44. **Write a problem** using addition or subtraction in which the answer is $9.21.

45. Alex went to the store with $10 and left the store with $5.98. He bought milk, eggs, and bread. The milk was $1.49 and the eggs were $0.89. How much was the bread?

46. Trevor scored 2 home runs in a college baseball game. Use the diagram to find how many feet Trevor ran to score the 2 home runs.

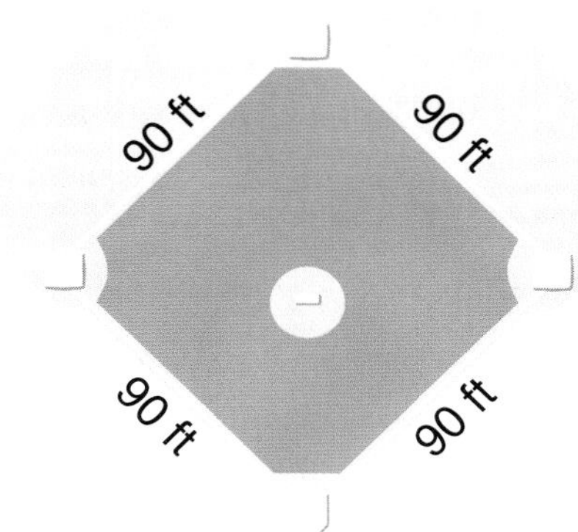

47. Will is walking to the ball field, which is 2.3 kilometers from his home. He has walked 0.8 kilometer. How much farther must he walk?

Mixed Review and Test Prep

48. $\frac{5}{6} - \frac{1}{6}$ (p. 472)

49. $40 \times 8{,}000$ (p. 236)

50. 9×367 (p. 222)

51. $\frac{3}{5} + \frac{1}{10}$ (p. 480)

52. Round 9.81 to the nearest whole number. (p. 584)

53. Find the value of $(17 - 8) \times 7$. (p. 184)

54. **TEST PREP** Which is $456 \div 7$? (p. 300)
A 46 r1 **B** 65 r1 **C** 65 **D** 65 r4

55. **TEST PREP** Which is equivalent to 9.1? (p. 568)
F $\frac{9}{10}$ **G** $\frac{91}{100}$ **H** $9\frac{1}{10}$ **J** $9\frac{9}{10}$

Problem Solving Thinker's Corner

BENCHMARK DECIMALS

Rounding decimals to benchmarks such as 0, 0.5, and 1 on a number line can help you estimate sums and differences.

Josh and Maya went on a nature walk to collect different kinds of leaves for science class. The first hour they walked 0.46 mi. The second hour they went 0.85 mi. About how many miles did they walk?

Estimate. 0.46 + 0.85

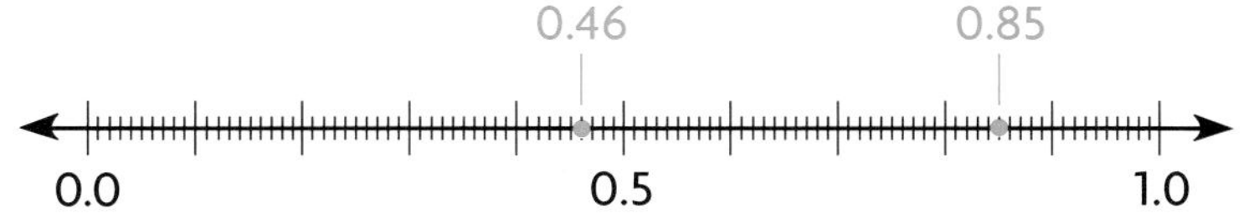

$0.46 \rightarrow 0.5$ 0.46 is between 0 and 0.5, but closer to 0.5.

$+0.85 \rightarrow 1.0$ 0.85 is between 0.5 and 1, but closer to 1.

1.5

So, Josh and Maya walked about 1.5 miles.

Use a number line and benchmark decimals to estimate each sum or difference.

1. 0.55 + 0.32
2. 0.79 − 0.53
3. 0.33 + 0.55
4. 0.89 − 0.41
5. 0.08 + 0.64

LESSON 6

Problem Solving Skill
Evaluate Reasonableness of Answers

UNDERSTAND · PLAN · **SOLVE** · CHECK

Quick Review

Write each mixed number as a decimal.

1. $3\frac{1}{10}$
2. $1\frac{28}{100}$
3. $9\frac{7}{10}$
4. $4\frac{2}{5}$
5. $7\frac{1}{4}$

ROAD TRIP Mrs. Pate drives a bus three days a week. The table shows the Virginia cities she went to last week. How many miles did Mrs. Pate drive last week if she made one round trip to each city?

MILES FROM RICHMOND, VA	
City	**Distance**
Charlottesville	70.5
Danville	162.7
Norfolk	91.4
Roanoke	192.0

Which is a more reasonable answer?

a. Joe got an answer of 516.6 miles.
b. Jane got an answer of 1,033.2 miles.

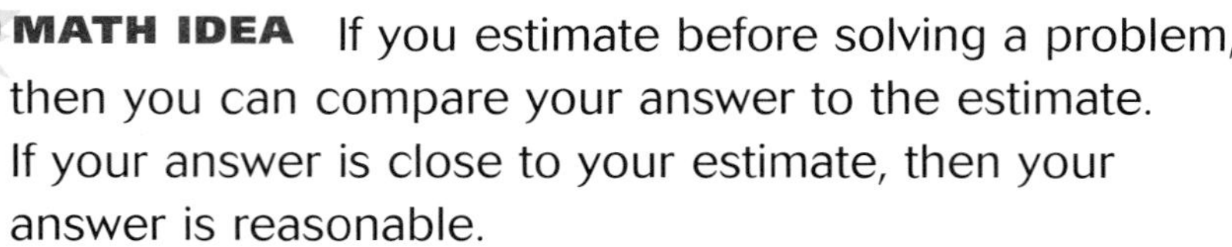

MATH IDEA If you estimate before solving a problem, then you can compare your answer to the estimate. If your answer is close to your estimate, then your answer is reasonable.

Estimate by rounding to the nearest 10.

$$70.5 + 162.7 + 91.4 + 192.0$$
$$\downarrow \quad \downarrow \quad \downarrow \quad \downarrow$$
$$70 + 160 + 90 + 190 = 510$$

$510 + 510 = 1{,}020$ **Think:** 510 miles is the estimate for one-way trips.

You can add to see that Jane answered the problem correctly.

$70.5 + 162.7 + 91.4 + 192.0 = 516.6$
$516.6 + 516.6 = 1{,}033.2$

1,033.2 miles is close to the estimate of 1,020 miles.

So, Jane's answer is reasonable. Mrs. Pate drove 1,033.2 miles last week.

Talk About It

- Why is it helpful to estimate to see if an answer is reasonable?
- Why is Joe's answer not reasonable for the problem?

Problem Solving Practice

1. Mark ran 3 miles on Friday, 4.4 miles on Saturday, and 3.5 miles on Sunday. Which of the following is reasonable? Explain.
   a. Mark ran a total of 10.9 miles.
   b. Mark ran a total of 6.5 miles.

2. Joe is buying a notebook that costs $2.25, an eraser that costs $0.99, and a pen that costs $1.25. Which of the following is reasonable? Explain.
   a. Joe's supplies cost $11.74.
   b. Joe's supplies cost $4.49.

Problem Solving

Tim has 3 hours to drive to his grandmother's house, which is 129.5 miles away. He drove 52.3 miles the first hour and 47.7 miles the second hour.

3. Which is the best estimate of the number of miles Tim drove in 2 hours?
   A 75 miles
   B 100 miles
   C 130 miles
   D 180 miles

4. Which is a reasonable answer for the number of miles Tim must travel in the last hour?
   F 10 miles
   G 30 miles
   H 60 miles
   J 230 miles

Mixed Applications

5. Jodie swam 2.8 miles on Monday. She swam 0.5 mile more on Tuesday than Monday. If she swam a total of 8 miles Monday through Wednesday, how many miles did she swim on Wednesday?

6. Katie completed the first half of a race in 8.6 minutes and the second half in 11.1 minutes. Is it reasonable to say that Katie finished the race in about 20 minutes?

USE DATA For 7–10, use the table of Amy Chow's 2000 Olympics All-Around Finals scores.

7. What was Amy's total score?

8. Write Amy's scores in order from least to greatest.

9. On which event did Amy receive her highest score? her lowest score?

10. Find the difference between Amy's highest and lowest scores.

11. **Write About It** Why is estimating a good way to check the reasonableness of your answer?

AMY CHOW'S SCORES

Event	Result
Vault	9.443
Bars	9.737
Beam	9.225
Floor	9.187

Extra Practice

Set A (pp. 584–585)

Round each number to the place of the blue digit.

1. 9.301 **2.** $5.79 **3.** $8.65 **4.** 4.531 **5.** $3.49

6. $8.93 **7.** 4.57 **8.** 16.895 **9.** 39.472 **10.** $7.65

Set B (pp. 586–587)

Estimate the sum or difference.

1. $2.80 + $2.30 **2.** 2.356 + 1.192 **3.** 2.356 − 0.918 **4.** $23.47 − $14.96 **5.** 18.92 + 39.45

Set C (pp. 588–589)

Find the sum. Estimate to check.

1. 10.29 + 33.46 **2.** $15.98 + $12.04 **3.** 6.419 + 7.234 **4.** 7.98 + 2.31 **5.** 6.29 + 8.88

6. 0.31 + 4.57 **7.** 4.875 + 8.136 **8.** 7.5 + 8.3 **9.** 5.76 + 2.18

10. Bob went to the store. He bought oranges for $1.32, juice for $1.48, and eggs for $1.10. How much money did he spend?

Set D (pp. 590–591)

Find the difference. Estimate to check.

1. 2.56 − 1.38 **2.** 13.287 − 3.534 **3.** $11.27 − $ 7.55 **4.** $75.43 − $18.63 **5.** 67.30 − 31.72

6. $0.78 − $0.51 **7.** 5.94 − 5.76 **8.** $9.49 − $6.23 **9.** $7.65 − $1.85

Set E (pp. 592–595)

Find the sum or difference. Estimate to check.

1. $13.95 + $21.76 **2.** 22.49 + 14.3 **3.** $26.00 − $18.94 **4.** 74.3 − 6.794 **5.** 14.28 + 8.5

6. 16.3 + 1.094 **7.** $8 − $3.78 **8.** 3.7 − 1.99 **9.** 46 − 3.059

Review/Test

CHECK VOCABULARY AND CONCEPTS

Choose the best term from the box.

decimal points
equivalent decimals
tenths

1. When adding or subtracting decimals, first line up the __?__. (pp. 588, 590)

2. 0.6 and 0.60 are __?__ since they are different names for the same amount. (p. 593)

CHECK SKILLS

Round each number to the place of the blue digit. (pp. 584–585)

3. 8.294 4. $4.68 5. $9.76 6. 3.49

Round to the nearest hundredth. (pp. 584–585)

7. 7.695 8. 3.504 9. 1.635 10. 14.839

Estimate the sum or difference. (pp. 586–587)

11. $1.29 + 3.46$

12. $\$5.98 + \$9.04$

13. $16.104 + 87.259$

14. $14.337 - 4.652$

Find the sum or difference. Estimate to check. (pp. 588–595)

15. 5.7 + 8.4
16. $9.61 + $0.81
17. 16.309 + 9.743
18. $3.67 − $0.59
19. 23.107 − 5
20. $78.41 − $42.83
21. 1.94 + 0.8
22. 42.51 + 22.4
23. 20 − 8.684

CHECK PROBLEM SOLVING

Solve. (pp. 596–597)

24. Dave earned $8.00 from his garage sale. The items for sale were a chair for $2.50, a radio for $1.25, 3 shirts for $2.75, and an old television set for $5.25. Is it reasonable to say that Dave sold all of the items? Explain.

25. Joanna has $5.50. She needs to buy eggs for $0.98, bread for $1.19, and milk for $2.69. Is it reasonable to say that Joanna has enough money to buy all of these items? Explain.

Standardized Test Prep

NUMBER SENSE, CONCEPTS, AND OPERATIONS

1. Which number sentence matches the model below?

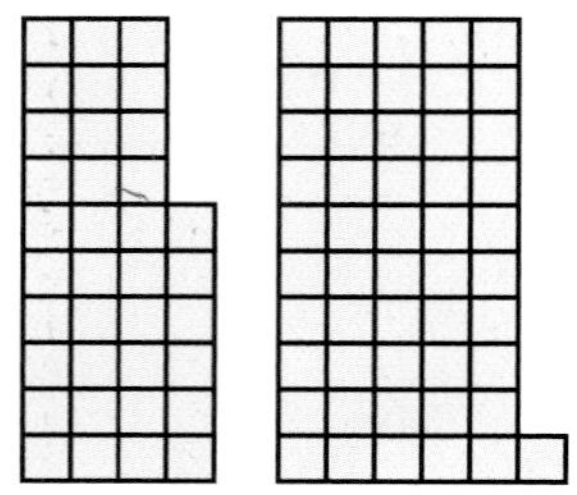

A $0.36 + 0.2 = 0.56$

B $0.36 + 0.51 = 0.87$

C $0.46 + 0.52 = 0.98$

D $0.46 + 0.62 = 0.87$

Look for important words.
See item 2. NOT is an important word. A number that is NOT a multiple of a number is a number that is NOT a product of that number and a counting number.

2. Which number is NOT a multiple of 8?

F 40

G 32

H 8

J 4

3. **Explain It** Evan bought a CD for $14.89, a skateboard for $39.29, and a baseball cap for $7.99 including tax. ESTIMATE the total cost and the change he should receive from $65.00. Explain your thinking.

GEOMETRY AND SPATIAL SENSE

4. A folded napkin looks like this drawing.

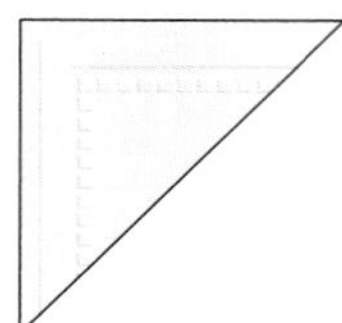

Which types of angles does the folded napkin have?

A 2 acute angles and 1 right angle

B 2 obtuse angles and 1 right angle

C 2 right angles and 1 obtuse angle

D 2 acute angles and 1 obtuse angle

5. Which dashed line shows a line of symmetry for this figure?

F

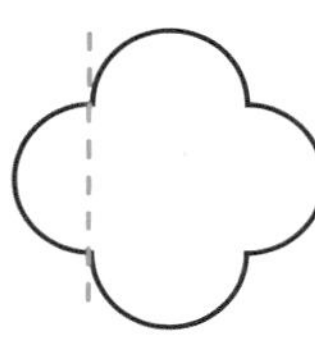

H

G

J

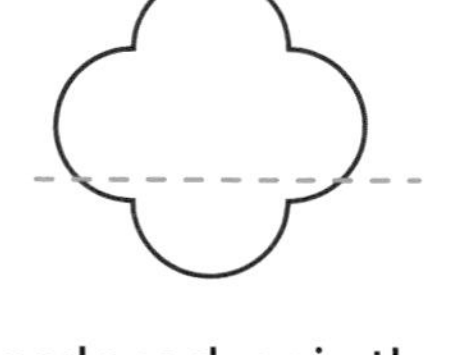

6. **Explain It** Write the ordered pair that describes the location of Claudia's house. Explain your answer.

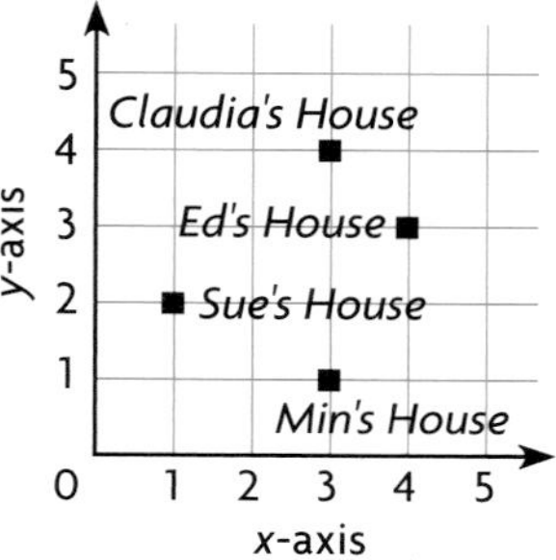

ALGEBRAIC THINKING

7. What could the eighth number be in the pattern below?

3, 7, 11, 15, . . .

A 16 **C** 31

B 19 **D** 32

8. When a number is put into the number machine below, a different number comes out.

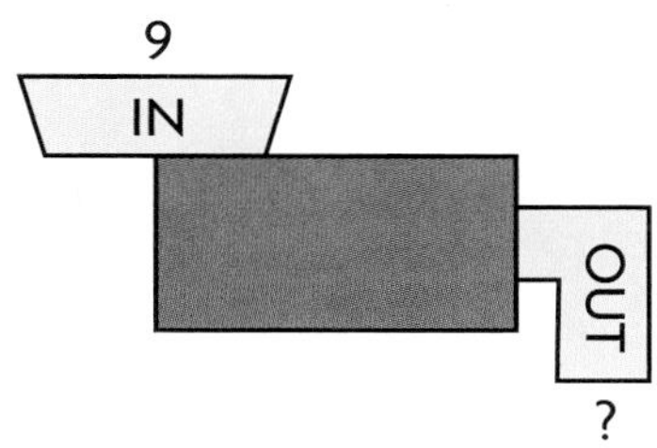

If a 1 goes in, a 5 comes out.

If a 3 goes in, a 15 comes out.

If a 7 goes in, a 35 comes out.

If a 9 goes in, which number will come out?

F 90 **H** 18

G 45 **J** 0

9. Mrs. Summers bought 8 packs of pencils. Each pack has 48 pencils. How many pencils did Mrs. Summers buy?

A 6 **C** 330

B 56 **D** 384

10. **Explain It** Let *a* represent Alan's age today. Write an expression to show Alan's age 4 years ago. Explain your thinking.

DATA ANALYSIS AND PROBABILITY

11. Jared scored the following points in the first four games he played: 3 points, 5 points, 6 points, and 4 points. Which graph shows this information?

F

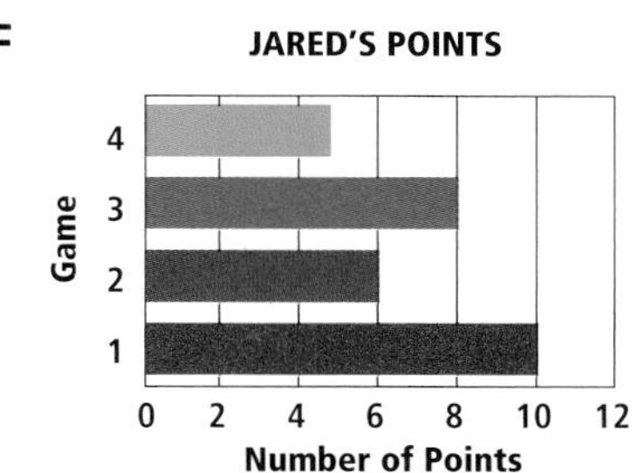

G

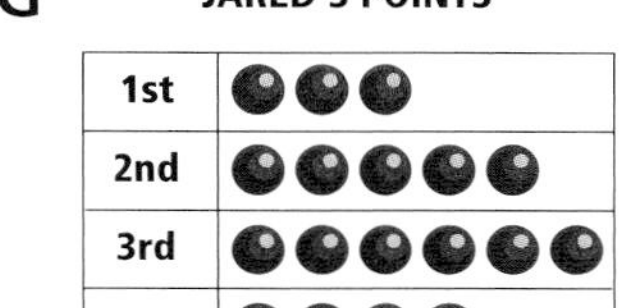

H

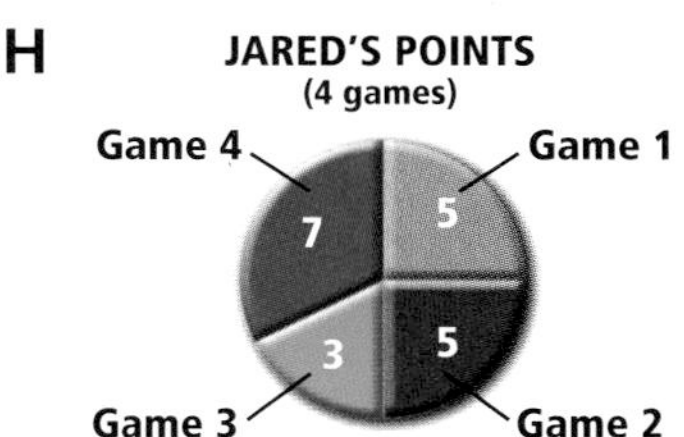

J

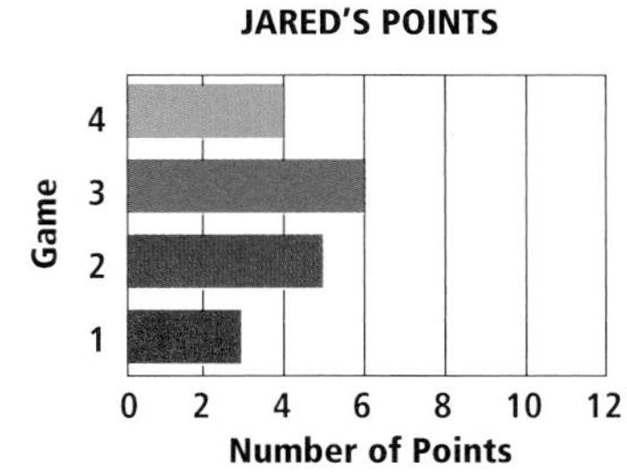

12. **Explain It** The following letter tiles are face down on a table.

Write a fraction to tell the probability of picking an *M*. Explain your thinking.

IT'S IN THE BAG

Two-Faced Views

PROJECT Make a two-faced accordion picture.

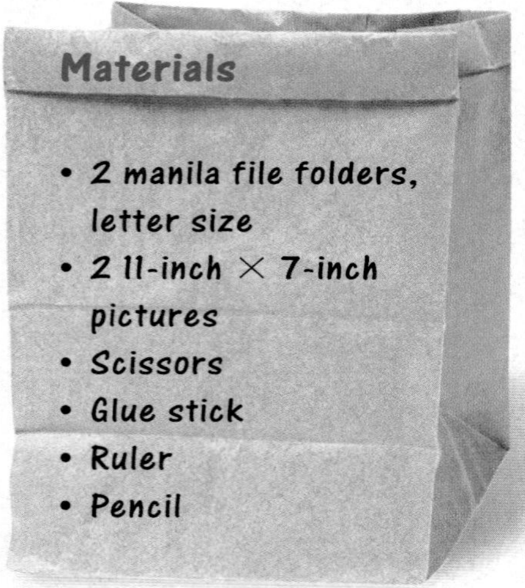

Directions

1. Place one picture face down. Using a ruler, measure and draw seven 1-inch vertical strips on the picture. Label the strips *7A, 6A, 5A, 4A, 3A, 2A,* and *1A*. Cut the strips apart. *(Picture A)*

A

2. Repeat Step 1 with the second picture. Label the strips *7B, 6B, 5B, 4B, 3B, 2B,* and *1B*. Cut the strips apart.

3. Cut off the tab edges of one folder to make a 16-inch × $11\frac{3}{4}$-inch rectangle when the folder is opened. Draw 15 lines down the folder, 1 inch apart. Label the strips, starting at the second strip from the left edge, as *1A, 1B, 2A, 2B, 3A, 3B, 4A, 4B, 5A, 5B, 6A, 6B, 7A,* and *7B*. Accordion fold. *(Picture B)*

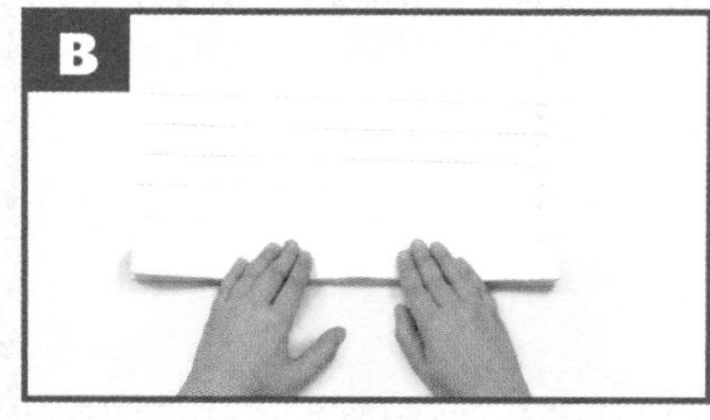
B

4. Glue the picture strips to the correct folder strips. Fold back the left and right edges of the folder, and glue them to an 8-inch × $11\frac{3}{4}$-inch rectangle cut from the second folder. *(Picture C)*

C

5. You will see a different view from the right and from the left side. What fraction of the whole accordion picture is one of your pictures? Write a decimal for the fraction.

Challenge

Change Quantities

Hannah's mom is planning to serve hot chocolate at Hannah's slumber party. For 2 servings, she needs 12 ounces of milk and 4 tablespoons of chocolate syrup. How many ounces of milk will she need for 8 servings?

You can use ratios to solve the problem. A **ratio** is a comparison of two amounts. The recipe makes 2 servings for every 12 ounces of milk. The ratio of servings to ounces is 2 to 12. You can write a ratio as a fraction.

servings → / ounces → $\frac{2}{12} = \frac{8}{■}$ ← servings / ← ounces

One Way Use a ratio table.

Servings, s	2	4	6	8
Ounces, m	12	24	36	48

← increases by 2 (servings)
← increases by 12 (ounces)

So, $\frac{2}{12} = \frac{8}{48}$.

Another Way Find an equivalent ratio.

You can find equivalent ratios the same way you find equivalent fractions.

$\frac{2}{12} = \frac{2 \times 4}{12 \times 4} = \frac{8}{48}$

Think: $2 \times 4 = 8$
Multiply the numerator and the denominator by the same number.

So, 48 ounces of milk are needed to make 8 servings.

- How many tablespoons of chocolate syrup will she need? Explain how you decided.

Try It

Copy and complete the ratio table.

1.

Servings, s	2	4	6	8
Cups, c	3	6	■	■

2.

Servings, s	5	10	15	■
Pounds, m	10	20	■	40

3. Karen has all the ingredients she needs to make animal crackers except for oatmeal. For 6 servings, she needs 2 cups of oatmeal. How many cups of oatmeal will she need for 18 servings?

Study Guide and Review

VOCABULARY

Choose the best term from the box.

1. Units that are used to measure length, width, height, and distance are ? . (p. 518)
2. The amount a container can hold is its ? . (p. 528)
3. The amount of matter in an object is its ? . (p. 548)

capacity
mass
equivalent decimals
linear units

STUDY AND SOLVE

Chapter 24

Use multiplication and division to change units within the customary system.

4 ft = ■ in.

feet
↓
4 × 12 = ■
↑
inches in 1 foot

4 × 12 = 48
So, 4 ft = 48 in.

- When you change larger units to smaller units, you need more of the smaller units, so multiply.

Complete. Tell whether you multiply or divide. (pp. 526–531)

4. 5 ft = ■ in.
5. 32 oz = ■ lb
6. 2 mi = ■ ft
7. 2 T = ■ lb
8. 3 gal = ■ pt
9. 8 qt = ■ pt
10. 16 c = ■ qt
11. 4 gal = ■ c
12. 6 tsp = ■ tbsp
13. 21 ft = ■ yd
14. 48 in. = ■ ft
15. 6 qt = ■ pt

Chapter 25

Use multiplication and division to change units within the metric system.

30 dm = ■ m

decimeters
↓
30 ÷ 10 = ■
↑
decimeters in 1 meter

30 ÷ 10 = 3
So, 30 dm = 3 m.

- When you change smaller units to larger units, you need fewer of the larger units, so divide.

Complete. Tell whether you multiply or divide by 10, 100, or 1,000. (pp. 544–549)

16. 200 cm = ■ dm
17. 7 m = ■ cm
18. 7 km = ■ dm
19. 9,000 mL = ■ L
20. 480 cm = ■ mm
21. 500 dm = ■ m
22. 5 kg = ■ g
23. 3 km = ■ m
24. 6 L = ■ mL

Chapter 26

Compare and order decimals.

Tell which number is greater, 3.45 or 3.46. Begin with the digits to the left of the decimal point.

ONES	.	TENTHS	HUNDREDTHS
3	.	4	5
3	.	4	6

3 = 3 4 = 4 6 > 5

Since 6 > 5, 3.46 > 3.45.

- Line up the decimal points.
- Compare the digits, beginning with the greatest place value.

Compare. Write <, >, or = for each ●. (pp. 572–575)

25. 3.65 ● 3.54

26. 6.89 ● 7.32

27. 1.059 ● 1.127

Order the decimals from *least* to *greatest*.

28. 3.48, 3.79, 3.02

29. 8.43, 5.62, 8.47

30. 1.928, 1.849, 1.959

Chapter 27

Add and subtract decimals.

Subtract. 4.53 − 3.47

```
   4 13
  4.5̸ 3̸
− 3.4 7
  1.0 6
```

- Line up the decimal points.
- Subtract.
- Place the decimal point.

Find the sum or difference. Estimate to check. (pp. 588–595)

31. 2.4 + 5.1

32. 5.87 − 4.72

33. 9.62 + 3.79

34. 2.76 − 1.68

35. 6.273 − 3.864

36. 3.825 + 7.519

PROBLEM SOLVING PRACTICE

Solve. (pp. 532–533, 550–551, 576–577, 596–597)

37. Margaret needs 30 cups of juice. She bought a gallon of orange juice, 2 pints of grape juice, and 3 quarts of cranberry juice. Did she buy enough? Explain.

38. Heidi, Debbie, Frank, and Carrie painted pictures. Carrie painted a sun. Someone painted a house. A boy painted a farm. Heidi did not paint the cat. Who painted which picture?

39. Members of the gymnastics team had the following scores: 8.75, 9.20, 8.60, and 9.55. Is it reasonable to say that the total score was 50? Explain.

40. Jean's two dogs, Nicky and Alex, together have a mass of 23 kilograms. Nicky's mass is 2 kilograms more than twice Alex's mass. What is the mass of each dog?

PERFORMANCE ASSESSMENT

TASK A • CLASS PARTY

You are on a committee for the class party. You need to be sure there will be enough juice for everyone at the party. There will be 24 students and 2 teachers attending the party.

The table shows the kind of juice and the amount of each kind available.

Juices	Amounts
Grapefruit	1 quart
Pineapple	4 pints
Orange	1 gallon
Kiwi	2 quarts 1 pint
Apple	1 gallon 1 quart
Grape	3 quarts
Cherry	2 pints
Strawberry	2 gallons 1 pint

a. How much juice will be needed for each person to have 2 cups?

b. How many cups can everyone have if all the juice on the list is used?

c. Decide on the amount of juice needed for the party. Tell how you made the decision. Choose at least 4 different kinds and amounts of juice you could use to make that amount.

TASK B • ON THE EDGE

Tina earns extra money in the spring by putting lawn edging around her neighbors' gardens. The table shows how many feet of edging she will need for each neighbor.

The garden center sells edging in rolls of 10.5 feet and 15 feet.

a. Tina decided to buy the 10.5-foot rolls of edging. How many rolls will she need to buy? Explain how you know.

b. How could Tina buy the edging in different-sized rolls to have the least amount left over?

c. Suppose Tina sends you to the garden center to buy 22 feet of edging. How many of each size roll would you buy?

EDGING FOR NEIGHBORS

Neighbor	Length
Mrs. Jones	9 ft
Mr. Morgan	6.5 ft
Mr. Rodriguez	11.25 ft
Ms. O'Donnell	8.75 ft

Calculator • Fractions and Decimals

Olivia walked along a nature trail that is 0.85 mile long. What fraction of a mile did Olivia walk?

 **You can use a calculator to change a decimal to an equivalent fraction and a fraction to an equivalent decimal.**

Use F↔D to find out what fraction of a mile Olivia walked.

- Change 0.85 to a fraction.

So, Olivia walked $\frac{17}{20}$ mile.

To change a fraction to an equivalent decimal, you can divide. Write the fraction as a division problem. Use the ÷ to divide.

- Change $\frac{7}{8}$ to a decimal.

$\frac{7}{8}$ = 7 ÷ 8 = 0.875

So, $\frac{7}{8}$ is equivalent to 0.875.

Practice and Problem Solving

Use the F↔D key to write each decimal as a fraction.

1. 0.64 **2.** 0.35 **3.** 0.6 **4.** 0.36 **5.** 0.125

Use the ÷ key to write each fraction as a decimal.

6. $\frac{1}{20}$ **7.** $\frac{3}{8}$ **8.** $\frac{4}{5}$ **9.** $\frac{16}{25}$ **10.** $\frac{7}{80}$

11. REASONING Explain how to use a calculator to help you compare 0.58 and $\frac{2}{5}$. Then use > to compare 0.58 and $\frac{2}{5}$.

GO ON-LINE **Multimedia Math Glossary** www.harcourtschool.com/mathglossary

Vocabulary Power Look up *equivalent* in the Multimedia Math Glossary. Write a problem that can be solved by finding a fraction equivalent to a decimal.

▲ "Thru-hikers" can hike the entire Trail in 5 to 6 months.

in New York

THE APPALACHIAN NATIONAL SCENIC TRAIL

The Appalachian National Scenic Trail is a 2,167-mile (3,488-kilometer) footpath along the Appalachian Mountain ridgelines and across valleys from Katahdin in Maine to Springer Mountain in Georgia. The Trail passes through 14 states, including New York.

USE DATA For 1–3 and 6, use the table.

APPALACHIAN TRAIL IN NEW YORK	
Trail	**Length (in miles)**
Bear Mountain—East	12.7
Bear Mountain—West	5.7
Bear Mountain Bridge and Anthony's Nose	6.7
Corbin Hill and Pawling Nature Reserve	9.5
Fahnestock State Park	10.4
Hosner Mountain to Cat Rocks	16.8
Sterling Forest	12.3

1. Order the trails by length from least to greatest. Which trail is the longest? Which is the shortest?
2. Mike has hiked all three Bear Mountain trails. What is the total length of these trails?
3. One week, Calvin hiked the Hosner Mountain to Cat Rocks trail. The same week, Kelsey hiked the Sterling Forest and the Bear Mountain West trails. Who hiked the greater distance? How much farther did that person hike?
4. About 88 miles of the Trail go through New York. How many feet are there in 88 miles?
5. In New York, the highest point along the Trail is 1,433 feet. As the Trail passes through Bear Mountain, it drops to its lowest point of 124 feet. Find the difference between the lowest point and the highest point.
6. **Write a problem** about the hiking trails, using the data in the table.

▲ A footbridge takes hikers over a stream west of Taconic Parkway.

THE BIG CHAIR BATTLE

Not far from the Appalachian Trail is Wingdale, New York, the site of two very tall chairs. Over the years, several towns have battled for the honor of having the world's largest chair. Wingdale's first big chair, the World's Largest Fireside Chair, was built in 1978. It was 25 feet high and 14 feet wide. Torn down in 1980, it was rebuilt in 1996. The new chair was 30 feet high!

SOME VERY TALL CHAIRS!		
Place	**Type**	**Height**
Gardner, MA	Mission	15 ft
Washington, D.C.	Duncan Phyfe	19 ft 6 in.
Thomasville, NC	Duncan Phyfe	18 ft
Anniston, AL	Office	33 ft
Binghamton, NY	Ladderback	24 ft 9 in.
Wingdale, NY	Fireside	30 ft

▼ **The World's Largest Fireside Chair, in Wingdale, New York used 2 tons of wood. In 2001, it was destroyed by a spring storm.**

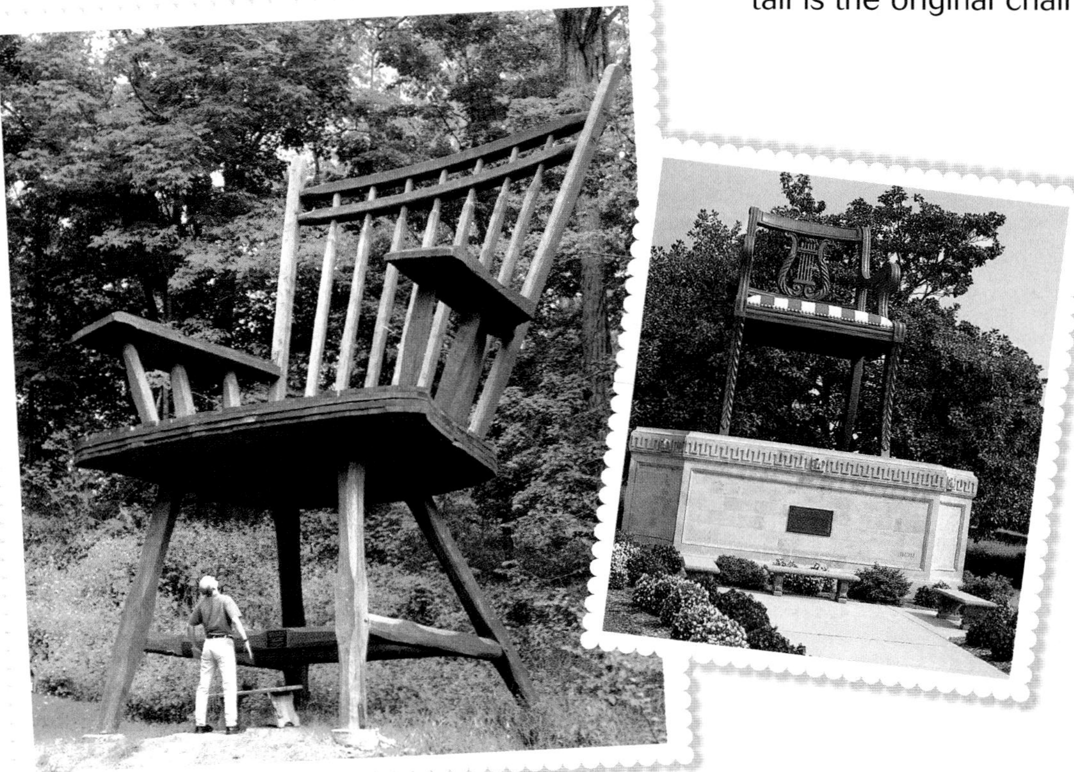

◀ **While many chairs have come and gone, Thomasville, North Carolina, still boasts they have the remaining "World's Largest Chair!"**

USE DATA For 1–4 and 7, use the table.

1. How many yards tall was the Wingdale chair?
2. How many inches tall is the Thomasville chair?
3. Which chairs are more than 8 yards tall? Explain.
4. How much taller was the Wingdale chair than the Binghamton chair?
5. Darrell traveled 81.6 miles to see the chair in Thomasville. Rosa traveled $81\frac{3}{4}$ miles to see the chair. Who drove the greater distance? Explain.
6. **STRETCH YOUR THINKING** The first World's Largest Fireside Chair was made out of more than a ton and a half of wood! About how many pounds of wood were used to make this chair?
7. The height of the big chair in Thomasville is 6 times as great as the height of the original Duncan Phyfe chair located in the Smithsonian. How tall is the original chair in inches?

Perimeter of Plane Figures

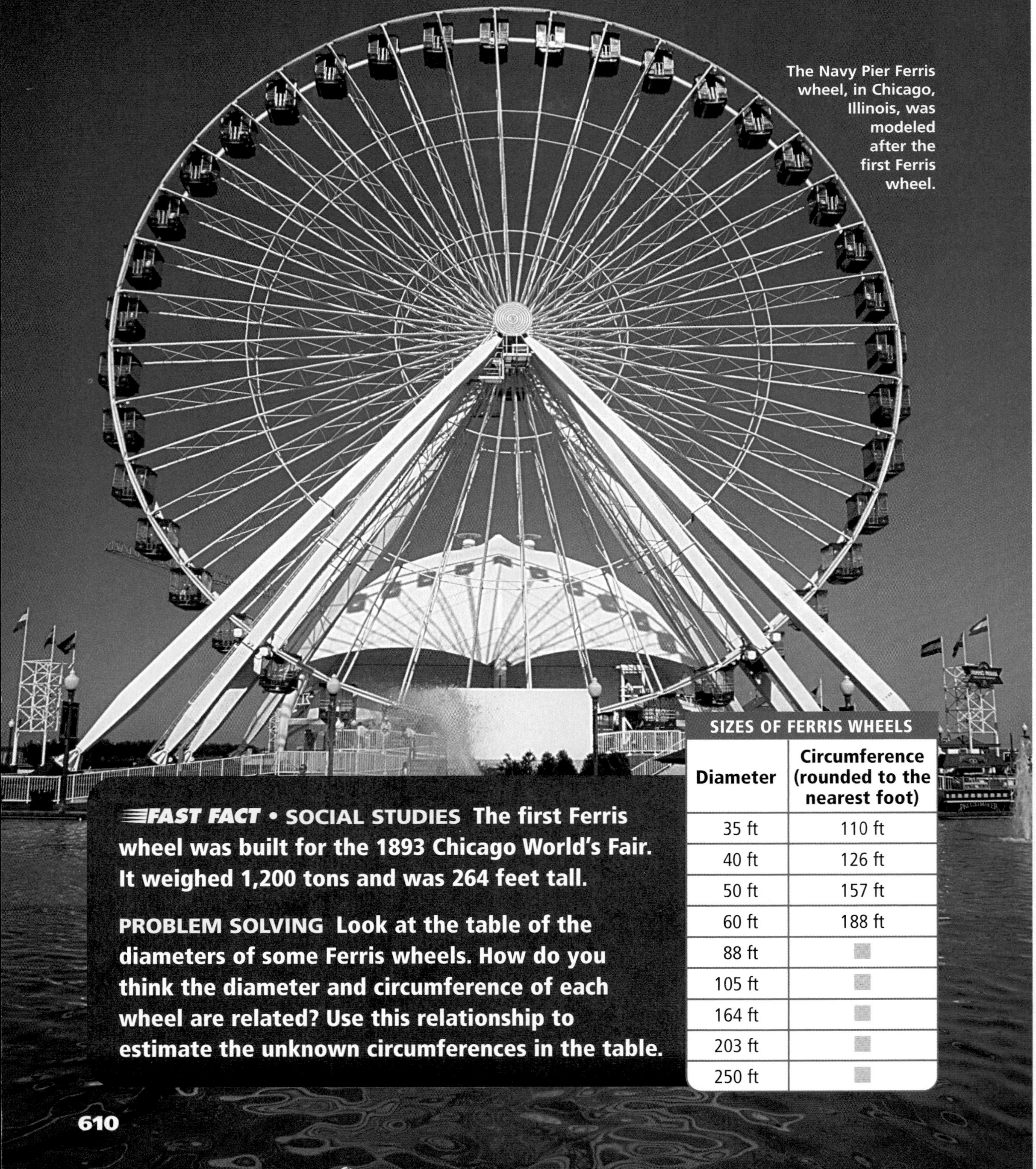

The Navy Pier Ferris wheel, in Chicago, Illinois, was modeled after the first Ferris wheel.

FAST FACT • SOCIAL STUDIES The first Ferris wheel was built for the 1893 Chicago World's Fair. It weighed 1,200 tons and was 264 feet tall.

PROBLEM SOLVING Look at the table of the diameters of some Ferris wheels. How do you think the diameter and circumference of each wheel are related? Use this relationship to estimate the unknown circumferences in the table.

SIZES OF FERRIS WHEELS

Diameter	Circumference (rounded to the nearest foot)
35 ft	110 ft
40 ft	126 ft
50 ft	157 ft
60 ft	188 ft
88 ft	■
105 ft	■
164 ft	■
203 ft	■
250 ft	■

CHECK WHAT YOU KNOW

Use this page to help you review and remember important skills needed for Chapter 28.

ADDITION

Find the sum.

1. $5 + 2 + 5$ **2.** $3 + 7 + 6$ **3.** $1 + 5 + 9$ **4.** $4 + 4 + 6$

5. $9 + 8 + 2$ **6.** $8 + 8 + 3$ **7.** $7 + 8 + 3$ **8.** $5 + 7 + 5$

FIND PERIMETER

Count to find the perimeter of each figure.

9.

10. 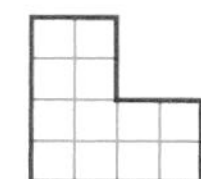

11. 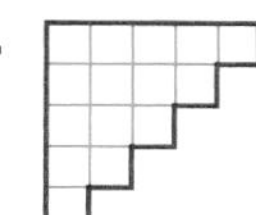

12. 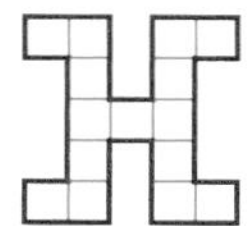

EXPRESSIONS WITH VARIABLES

Find the value of the expression.

13. $6 + 2 + x$ if $x = 6$ **14.** $3 + a + 5$ if $a = 4$ **15.** $y + 16 + 8$ if $y = 7$

16. $4 + b + 4 + 8$ if $b = 8$ **17.** $3 + 3 + 2 + x$ if $x = 2$ **18.** $5 + a + 3 + 6$ if $a = 9$

19. $5 + 5 + 5 + 5 + x$ if $x = 5$ **20.** $8 + 5 + 3 + b + 2$ if $b = 3$ **21.** $3 + 8 + 4 + 2 + y$ if $y = 2$

REVIEW

polygon [pä′lē•gän] *noun*

Polygon comes from the Greek root words *poly* meaning "many" and *gonos* meaning "knees" or "angles." How is the number of angles in a polygon related to the number of sides?

PREVIEW

perimeter

formula

circumference

www.harcourtschool.com/mathglossary

Explore Perimeter

Quick Review

1. 4 + 9 + 4 + 9
2. 23 + 15 + 23 + 15
3. 34 + 18 + 22
4. 16 + 16 + 16 + 16
5. 24 + 6 + 24 + 6

VOCABULARY

perimeter

MATERIALS small paper clips, large paper clips, Triangles worksheet, geoboard, dot paper

Explore

Have you ever wondered how long the fence is around a playground? **Perimeter** is the distance around a figure. To measure perimeter, you can use nonstandard units such as paper clips, toothpicks, and string or standard units such as inches, feet, miles, centimeters, meters, and kilometers. For example, to measure the perimeter of a playground, you could find the number of fence panels used.

Activity

STEP 1

Use small paper clips to measure the perimeter of your triangle. Record the number of small paper clips you used.

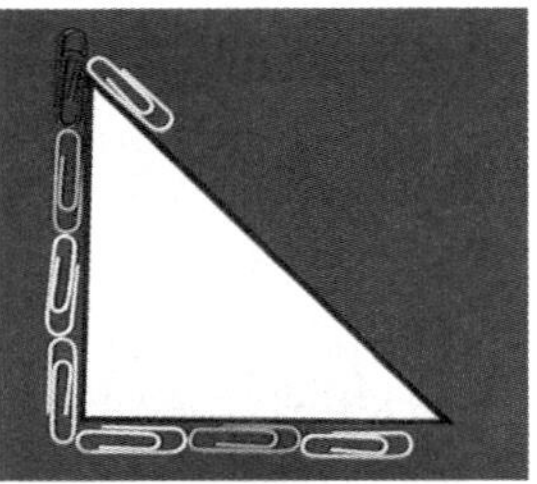

STEP 2

Use large paper clips to measure the perimeter of your triangle. Record the number of large paper clips you used.

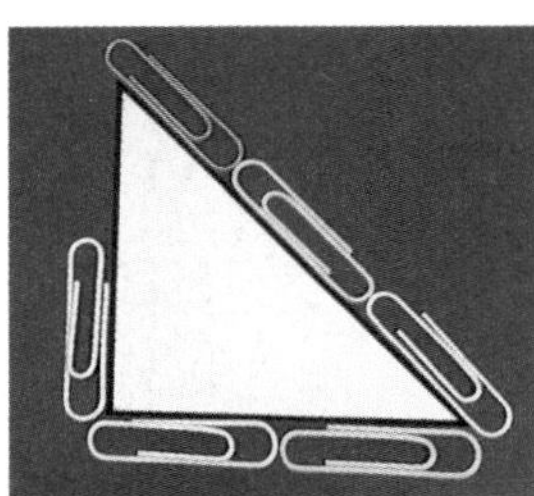

- How does the perimeter you found with small paper clips compare to the perimeters your classmates found?
- Did you need more small paper clips or more large paper clips to measure the perimeter of the triangle? Explain.
- Describe some situations in which you might need to find perimeter.

Will I need more paper clips to measure the perimeter of the sheet of notebook paper or the index card?

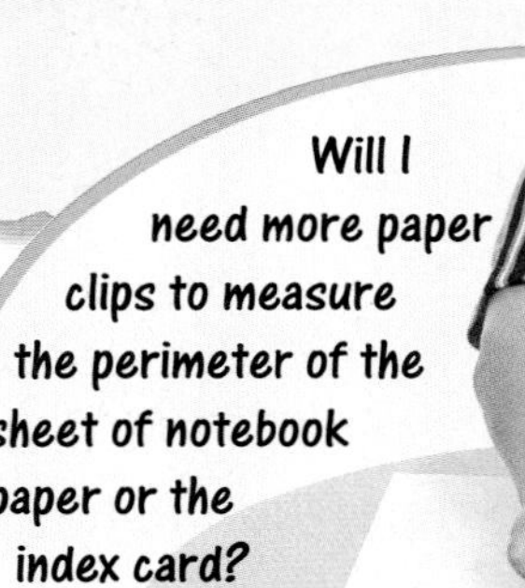

Try It

Use paper clips to measure the perimeter of each object.

a. a sheet of notebook paper

b. an index card

Connect

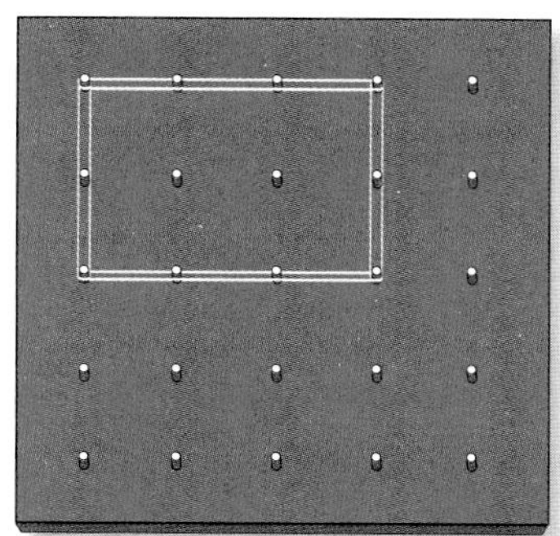

You can find the perimeters of rectangles constructed on a geoboard or on dot paper by counting the number of units on each side.

This rectangle is 3 units long and 2 units wide. So, the perimeter of the rectangle is 3 units + 2 units + 3 units + 2 units, or 10 units.

Practice and Problem Solving

Find the perimeter of each figure.

1. 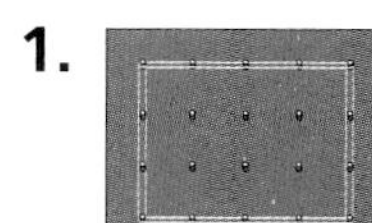

2.  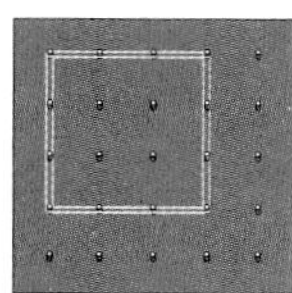

3. 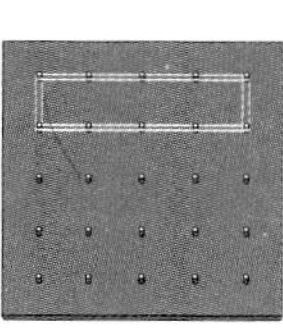

4. 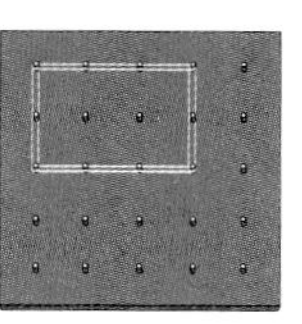

5. 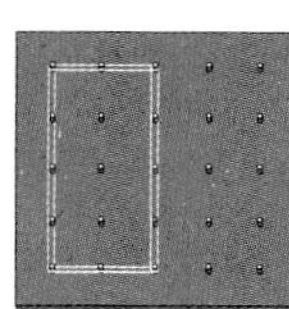

6. 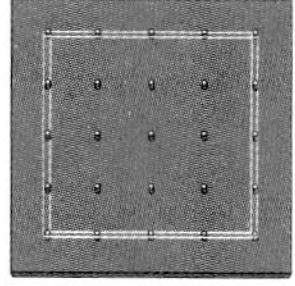

Use dot paper to draw a rectangle with the given perimeter. Then record the lengths of the sides.

7. 8 units **8.** 16 units **9.** 10 units

Sophie wants to make a rectangular rabbit hutch that has a perimeter of 36 units.

10. On dot paper, draw the different hutches Sophie can make. Label the length of each side.

11. If each side is measured in whole units, how many different rectangular shapes can Sophie make for the hutch?

Mixed Review and Test Prep

12. $\begin{array}{r} 1{,}096 \\ \times \quad 8 \\ \hline \end{array}$ (p. 222)

13. $24\overline{)372}$ (p. 320)

14. Subtract 1.38 from 3.07. (p. 590)

15. Find the median for this set of numbers: 60, 62, 64, 64, 64, 68, 68, 68, 68 (p. 118)

16. **TEST PREP** Traci wants to buy a stereo that costs $130. She saves $14 each week. How many weeks will it take Traci to save enough money to buy the stereo? (p. 320)

A 8 weeks **C** 10 weeks

B 9 weeks **D** 11 weeks

LESSON 2

Estimate and Find Perimeter

Quick Review

1. 2 × 12
2. 4 × 8
3. 24 + 16
4. 20 + (9 × 2)
5. (2 × 7) + 12

VOCABULARY

formula

Learn

MEASURING MATH You can use what you know about units of length to help you estimate and measure perimeter.

HANDS ON

Activity **MATERIALS:** customary and metric rulers

STEP 1

Copy the table. Estimate the perimeter of the cover of your math book in centimeters. Record your estimate.

STEP 2

Measure the length of each side to the nearest centimeter. Then add the lengths of the sides to find the perimeter.

STEP 3

Choose two other objects in your classroom to measure. Choose the most appropriate unit of measure for each object. Estimate the perimeter and then measure it.

PERIMETER			
Object	**Units**	**Estimate**	**Measure**
math book	cm		

- How do your measurements compare to your estimates?
- How did you decide which unit to use to measure each object?

Examples Find the perimeter.

A Add the lengths of the sides.

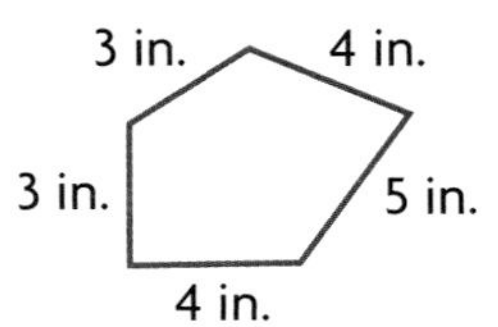

3 in. + 4 in. + 5 in. + 4 in. + 3 in. = 19 in.
The perimeter is 19 inches.

B Add the lengths of the sides.

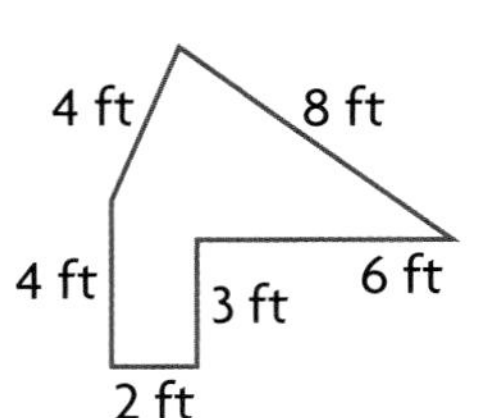

4 ft + 4 ft + 8 ft + 6 ft + 3 ft + 2 ft = 27 ft
The perimeter is 27 feet.

Use a Formula to Find Perimeter

The amusement park has a safety fence around its carousel. What is the perimeter of the fence?

You can use a **formula**, or mathematical rule, to find perimeter. Since the carousel's safety fence has 5 sides, use a formula that has 5 variables.

P = sum of the length of the sides

$P = a + b + c + d + e$ Use a variable to represent the length of each side.

$P = 14 + 17 + 13 + 15 + 16$

$P = 75$

So, the perimeter of the safety fence is 75 feet.

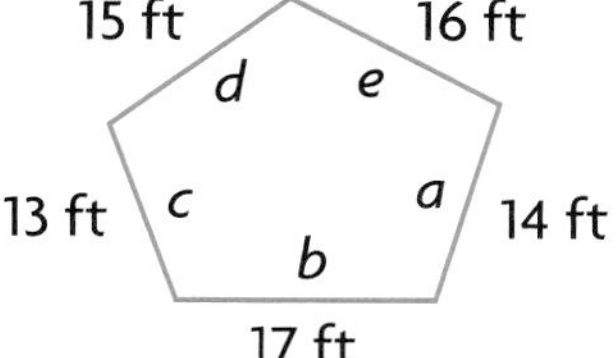

You can use a formula to find the perimeter of a rectangle and of a square.

Polygon	Perimeter	Formula
rectangle (l, w, w, l)	Perimeter = length + width + length + width or Perimeter = 2 × length + 2 × width	$P = l + w + l + w$ or $P = (2 \times l) + (2 \times w)$
square (s, s, s, s)	Perimeter = side + side + side + side or Perimeter = 4 × side	$P = s + s + s + s$ or $P = 4 \times s$

More Examples

C

7 in. / 5 in. / 5 in. / 7 in.

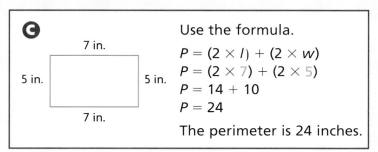

Use the formula.

$P = (2 \times l) + (2 \times w)$
$P = (2 \times 7) + (2 \times 5)$
$P = 14 + 10$
$P = 24$

The perimeter is 24 inches.

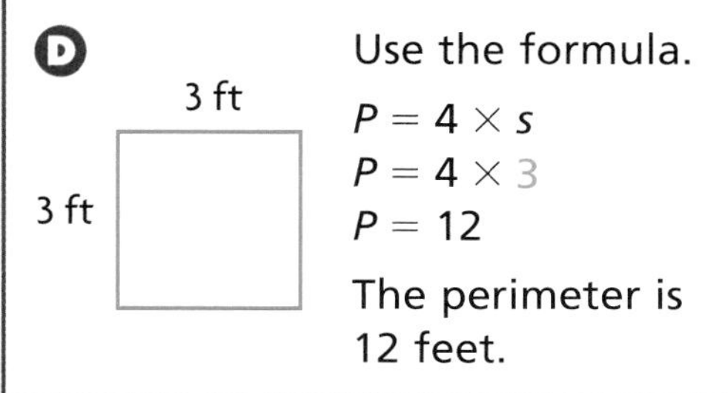

D

3 ft / 3 ft

Use the formula.

$P = 4 \times s$
$P = 4 \times 3$
$P = 12$

The perimeter is 12 feet.

Check

1. **Estimate** the perimeter of your desk in inches. Then measure the perimeter to the nearest $\frac{1}{4}$ inch, and compare the measurement to your estimate.

LESSON CONTINUES

Find the perimeter.

2.
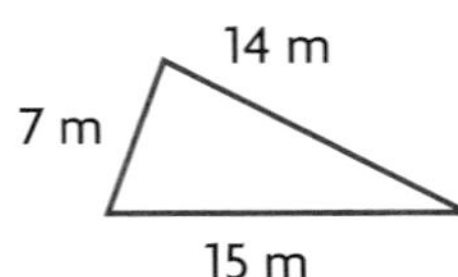

3.
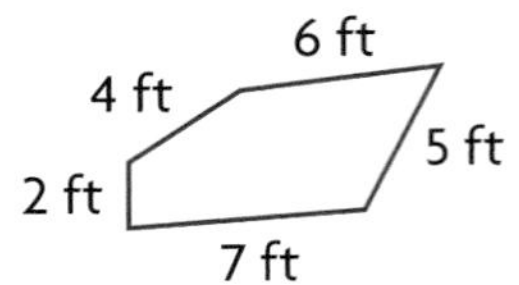

4. 12 in. 3 in.

5.
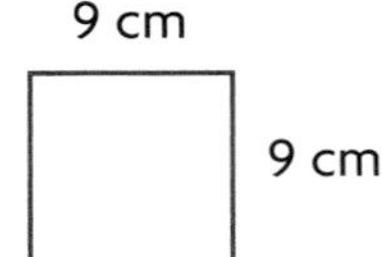

Practice and Problem Solving

Extra Practice, page 622, Set A

Find the perimeter.

6.
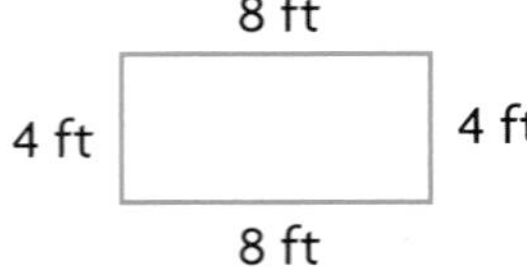

7.
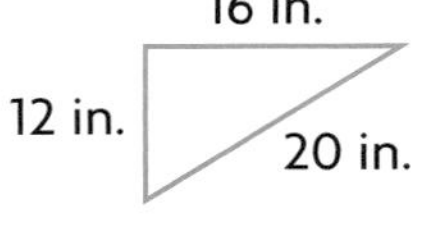

8.
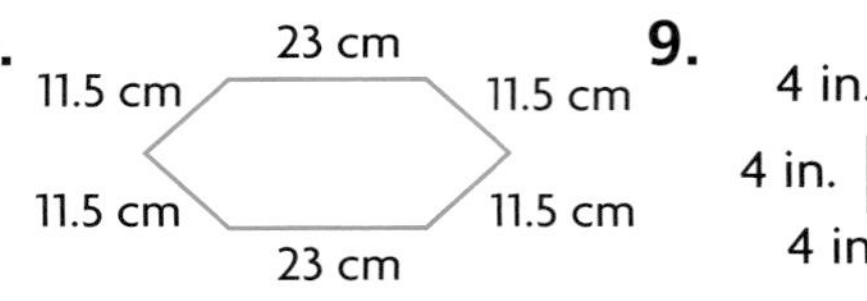

9.
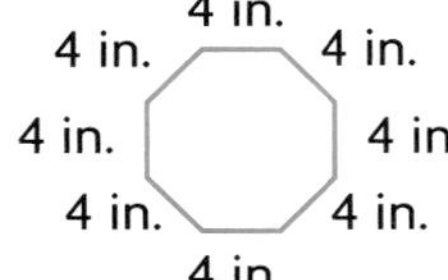

10.
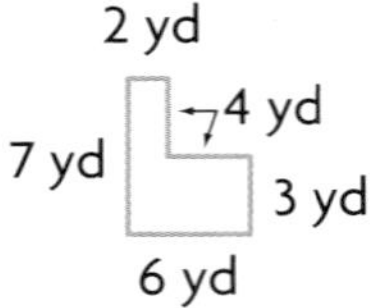

11. 11 m, 4 m, 5 m, 15 m, 10 m, 15 m

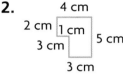

12. 4 cm, 2 cm, 1 cm, 5 cm, 3 cm, 3 cm

13.
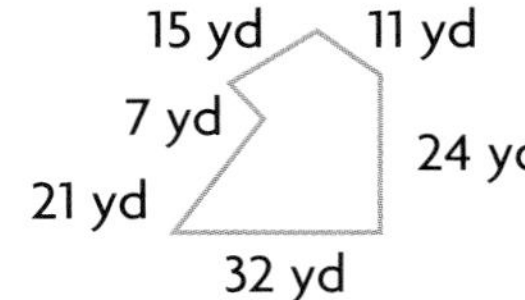

Use a formula to find the perimeter.

14. 12 yd, 9 yd

15. 11 cm, 11 cm

16.
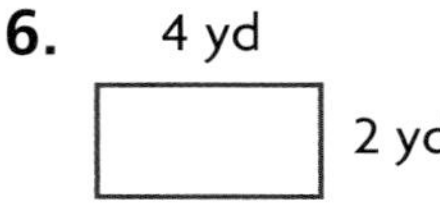

17. 13 m, 13 m

Measure with a ruler to find the perimeter.

18.
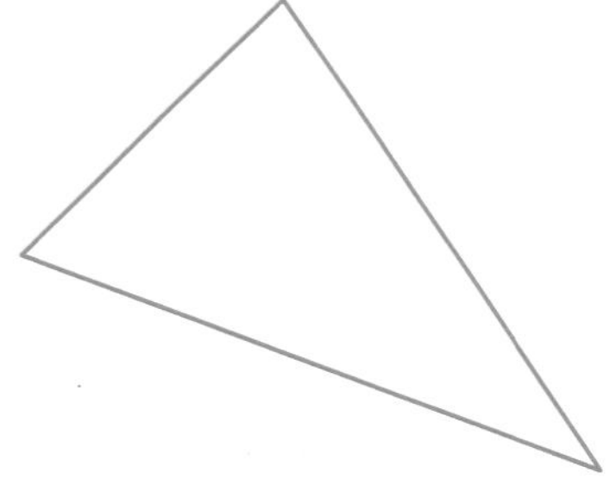

19.

20.
 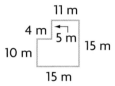

21. **REASONING** An equilateral triangle and a square each have a perimeter of 24 inches. Draw each figure.

22. **Write About It** Explain how you could write a perimeter formula for an equilateral triangle.

23. **What's the Question?** A quadrilateral has sides with lengths of 4 feet, 5 feet, 8 feet, and 10 feet. The answer is 27 feet.

24. **REASONING** The perimeter of a rectangle is 26 centimeters. The length is 8 centimeters. What is the width?

25. The Wegners are putting a fence around their yard. Their rectangular yard is 60 feet wide by 24 feet long. If each 6-foot panel costs $21, how much will the fence cost?

26. **Vocabulary Power** *Perimeter* comes from the Greek root words *peri* meaning "around" and *metron* meaning "measure." In your own words, write a definition for *perimeter*.

Mixed Review and Test Prep

27. $\frac{3}{8} + \frac{1}{4}$ (p. 480)

28. $\frac{2}{3} - \frac{1}{6}$ (p. 482)

29. $356 \div 67$ (p. 320)

30. List 6 multiples of 3. (p. 172)

31. Round 2.35 to the nearest tenth. (p. 584)

32. Write 24,607 in expanded form. (p. 4)

33. **TEST PREP** Mike bought a flashlight for $6.95 and a CD for $10.99. How much change did he get from a $20 bill? (p. 592)

A $13.05 **C** $3.06
B $9.01 **D** $2.06

34. **TEST PREP** The bandstand in the park has 5 sides. What is another name for a polygon with 5 sides? (p. 380)

F quadrilateral **H** hexagon
G pentagon **J** octagon

Problem Solving LINKUP . . . to Architecture

Interior designers use wallpaper to decorate rooms. This table can be used to estimate the number of rolls of wallpaper needed to cover the walls of a room.

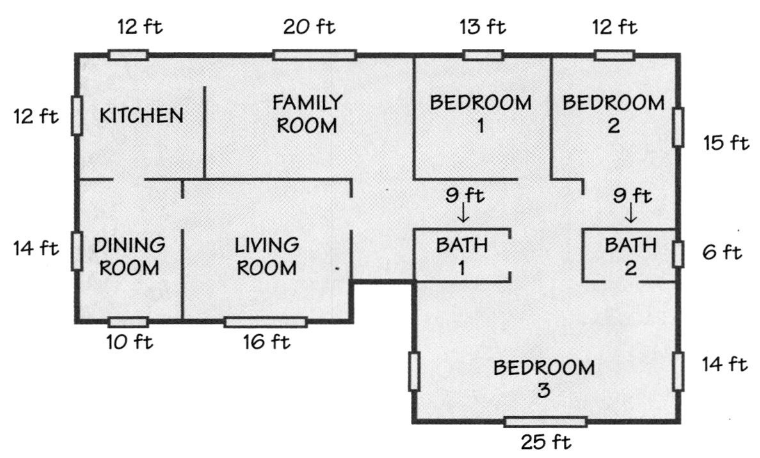

WALLPAPER TO COVER WALLS

Room Perimeter (in feet)	Rolls Needed 8-ft walls	Rolls Needed 10-ft walls
25–32	4	5
33–40	5	7
41–48	6	8
49–56	7	9
57–64	8	10
65–72	9	11
73–80	10	13

USE DATA For 1–4, use the floor plan and the wallpaper table to find the number of rolls of wallpaper needed for each room.

1. bedroom 1 with 8-foot walls
2. dining room with 10-foot walls
3. kitchen with 8-foot walls
4. family room with 10-foot walls

LESSON 3

Circumference

Quick Review

Measure to the nearest centimeter.

1. ____
2. ____
3. ____
4. ____
5. ____

VOCABULARY

circumference

MATERIALS string, metric ruler, circular object, can, jar, scissors

Explore

The **circumference** of a circle is the distance around the circle.

Activity

Use a ruler and a string to find the circumference and diameter of a circular object such as a lid.

STEP 1

Wrap string around a circular object. Mark and cut the string to show the distance around.

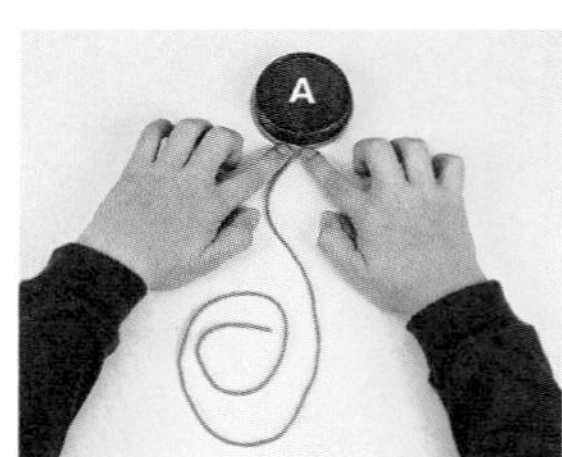

STEP 2

Measure the string in centimeters. The length of the string is the circumference of the circle.

STEP 3

Trace your object. Draw the diameter, and then measure it. Record the circumference and the diameter.

Remember

A **diameter** is a chord that passes through the center of a circle.

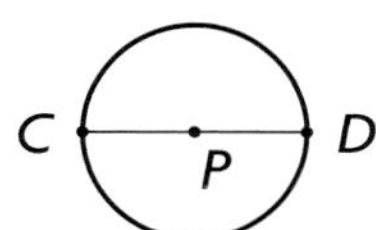

diameter: $\overline{CD}$

Try It

Use a string and a metric ruler to find the circumference and diameter of each object to the nearest centimeter.

a. can **b.** jar

I wrapped the string around the can. What do I do next to find the circumference?

Connect

Look at the data for each circle in the table. About how many times as great as the diameter is each circle's circumference?

CIRCLE	DIAMETER	ESTIMATED CIRCUMFERENCE
A	2 cm	about 6 cm
B	3 cm	about 9 cm
C	4 cm	about 12 cm
D	5 cm	about 15 cm

The circumference of a circle is about 3 times the diameter of the circle. If you know the diameter of a circle, you can estimate its circumference.

Estimate the circumference of a circle with a diameter of 6 centimeters.

Think: $6 \times 3 = 18$

So, the circumference is about 18 centimeters.

Practice and Problem Solving

Estimate the circumference.

1. 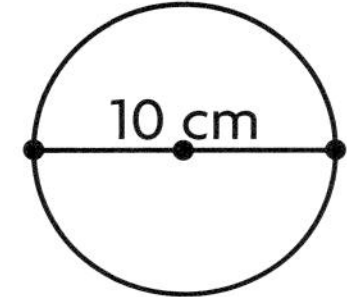

2. 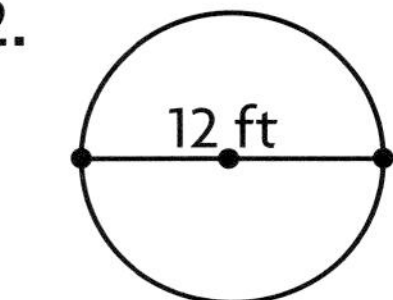

3. 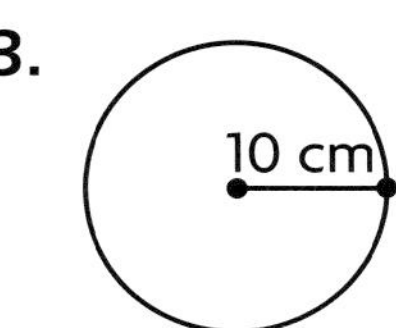

4. Diameter: 38 feet

5. Diameter: 19 miles

6. Diameter: 42 meters

USE DATA For 7–8, use the graph.

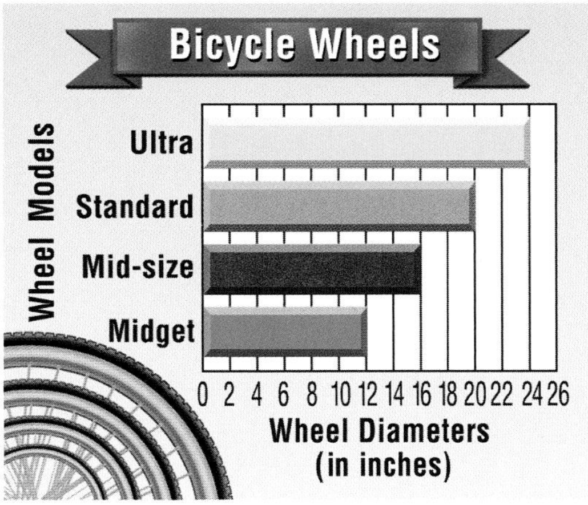

7. About how much shorter is the circumference of the Mid-size wheel than the circumference of the Ultra wheel?

8. Estimate the circumference of the Standard wheel.

9. **? What's the Error?** The diameter of a circle that Nina measured is 18 inches. Nina estimated the circumference to be about 6 inches. Describe and correct her error.

Mixed Review and Test Prep

10. $46 \div 3$ (p. 278)

11. $79 \div 5$ (p. 278)

12. Write five hundred thousand, thirty in standard form. (p. 4)

13. Write five thousand, two hundred thirty-four in expanded form. (p. 4)

14. **TEST PREP** Which term best describes the line relationship of the hands on the clock? (p. 370)

A perpendicular
B parallel
C obtuse
D acute

LESSON 4

Problem Solving Skill
Use a Formula

UNDERSTAND PLAN SOLVE CHECK

Quick Review

1. $4 + \square = 20$
2. $3 + \square + 2 = 10$
3. $4 + \square = 13$
4. $\square + 2 + 6 = 15$
5. $54 = 12 + 18 + \square$

CITY PARK Aboussie Park, Saint Louis's smallest city park, is in the shape of a triangle and has a perimeter of 942 feet. One of its sides is 80 feet and another side is 426 feet. What is the length of the third side of the park?

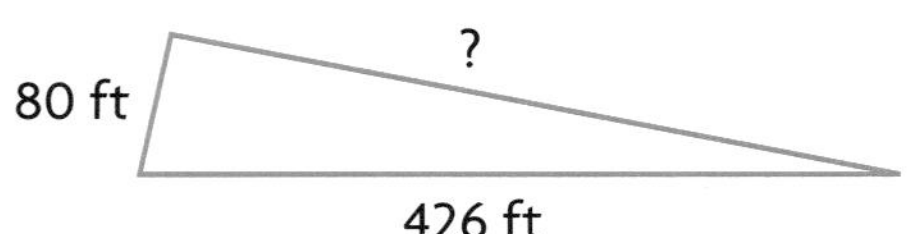

You can use a formula to find the length of a side of a triangle if you know the perimeter and the lengths of two of the sides.

$P = a + b + c$

$942 = 80 + 426 + c$ — Replace P with 942, a with 80, and b with 426.

$942 = 506 + c$ — Add.

$942 - 506 = c$ — Since subtraction is the inverse of addition, subtract 506.

$436 = c$

So, the third side of Aboussie Park is 436 feet long.

▲ Aboussie Park in St. Louis, Missouri

Examples Find the unknown length.

A The perimeter is 24 meters.

8 m, 6 m, ?

$P = a + b + c$

$24 = 6 + 8 + c$

$24 = 14 + c$

$24 - 14 = c$

$10 = c$

The length is 10 meters.

B The perimeter is 42 centimeters.

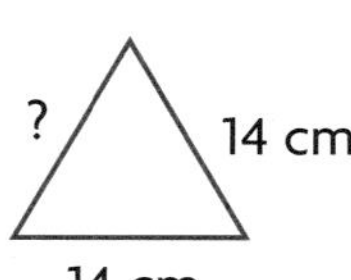

$P = a + b + c$

$42 = 14 + 14 + c$

$42 = 28 + c$

$42 - 28 = c$

$14 = c$

The length is 14 centimeters.

- **REASONING** Explain how to find the length of a side of a square whose perimeter is 36 inches. What is the length of each side?

Problem Solving Practice

Use a formula to solve.

1. **What if** the perimeter of another triangular park is 2.25 miles. If one of its sides is 0.75 mile, and another is 1.2 miles, what is the length of the third side?

2. Nancy is jogging around the perimeter of a triangular park. The park's perimeter is 2.5 miles. So far she has jogged around two sides that are 0.5 mile and 0.75 mile. How far does she have left to jog?

A triangular playground has a perimeter of 120 feet. One of its sides is 30 feet, and another is 40 feet.

3. Which formula would you use to find the length of the unknown side?

   A $P = a + b + c + d + e$
   B $P = a + b + c + d$
   C $P = a + b + c$
   D $P = a + b$

4. Which is the unknown length?

   F 30 feet
   G 40 feet
   H 50 feet
   J 60 feet

Mixed Applications

5. A rectangle has a width 7 inches less than its length. The perimeter is 26 inches. What are its length and width?

6. The mean of Brad's scores on three tests is 89. His last two scores were 94 and 78. What was his first score?

7. Olivia asked 24 students to name their favorite type of music. Two like rock, 12 like jazz, 4 like country, and 6 like pop music. Make a graph of the data.

8. Jon gave the clerk $20.00 to pay for a flat of 12 plants that cost $14.52 including tax. How much change did Jon receive?

9. Find the unknown length. The perimeter is 160 centimeters.

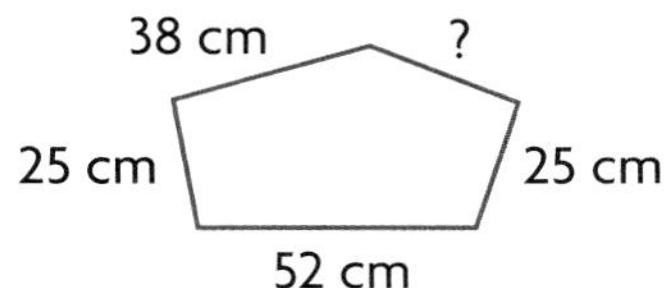

10. **Write About It** Explain how to find the length of one side of a triangle if you know that its perimeter is 41 feet, and one of its sides is 11 feet, and another side is 14 feet. What is the length of the unknown side?

11. **FAST FACT • SOCIAL STUDIES** Boston's Public Garden is the first public botanical garden in the United States. In about 1862 an iron fence was placed around the perimeter for a cost of $25,000. Find the perimeter.

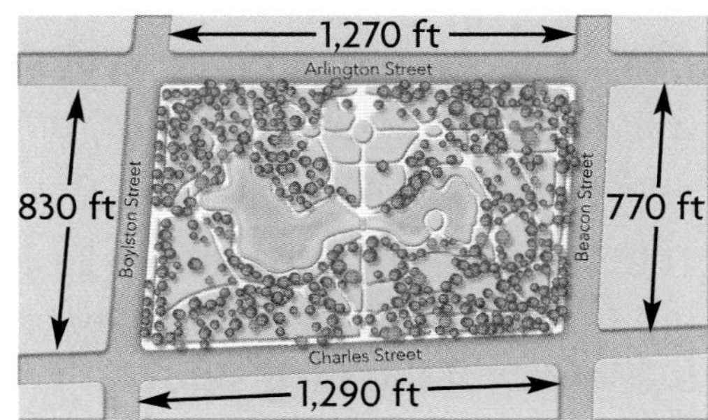

Extra Practice

Set A (pp. 614–617)

Find the perimeter.

1. 4 in., 2 in., 3 in., 3 in., 7 in., 5 in.

2. 5 cm, 2 cm, 2 cm, 2 cm, 5 cm, 6 cm

3. 9 cm, 3 cm, 4 cm, 1 cm, 3 cm, 3 cm, 8 cm, 7 cm

4. 14 in., 9 in., 14 in., 9 in.

5. 3 m, 3 m, 3 m, 3 m, 3 m

6. 9 yd, 2 yd, 7 yd, 6 yd

7. 8.9 mm, 8 mm, 4 mm

8.

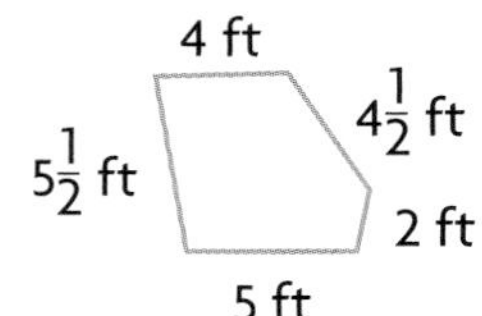

Use a formula to find the perimeter.

9. 11 mm, 11 mm

10. 9 in., 3 in.

11. 15 in., 6 in.

12. 9 cm, 9 cm

13. 15 ft, 9 ft

14. 24 yd, 6 yd

15. 8 m, 4 m

16. 20 cm, 20 cm

17. Write a perimeter formula for a hexagon.

18. At lunch time, Jaco walked around the perimeter of the field at the right. Use the measurements in the drawing to find the perimeter of the field.

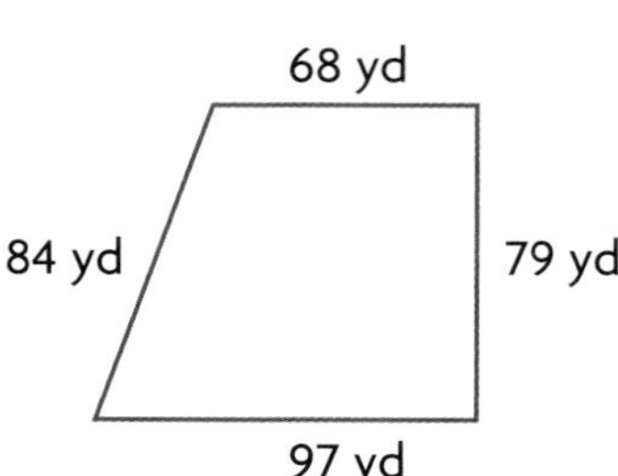

19. Mai walked around the perimeter of the playground 3 times. The rectangular playground is 25 meters long and 15 meters wide. How far did Mai walk?

20. The perimeter of a triangle is 24 inches. Two sides of the triangle measure 10 inches and 6 inches. What is the length of the third side?

Review/Test

CHECK VOCABULARY AND CONCEPTS

Choose the best term from the box.

circumference
formula
perimeter
polygon

1. The distance around a figure is its ?. (p. 612)
2. You can use a mathematical rule, or ?, to find the perimeter of a figure. (p. 615)
3. The distance around a circle is its ?. (p. 618)

CHECK SKILLS

Find the perimeter. (pp. 612–617)

4. 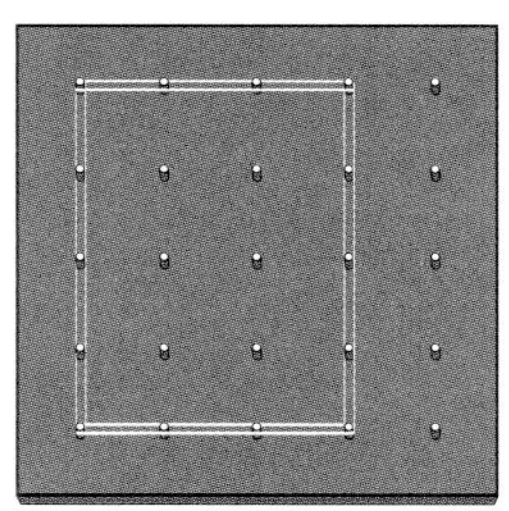

5.

6. 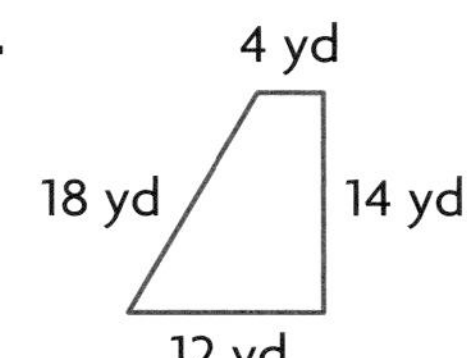

7. 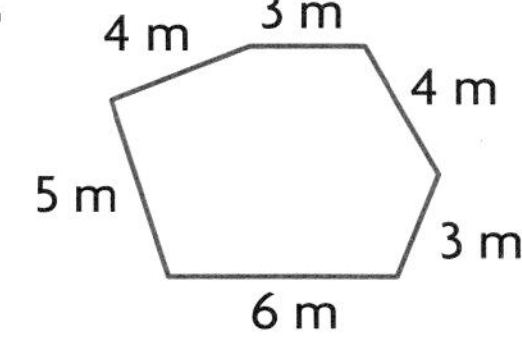

Use a formula to find the perimeter. (pp. 614–617)

8. 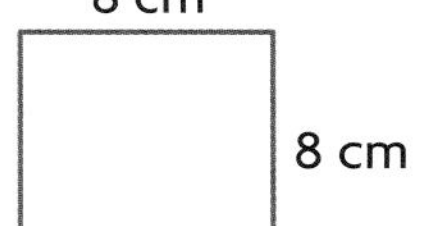

9. 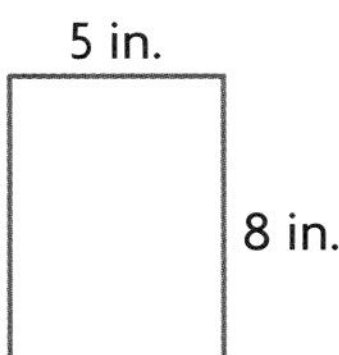

10.

Estimate the circumference. (pp. 618–619)

11. 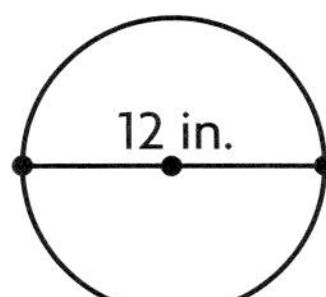

12. 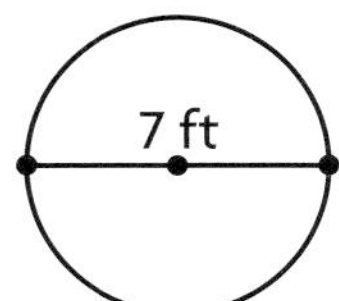

13. 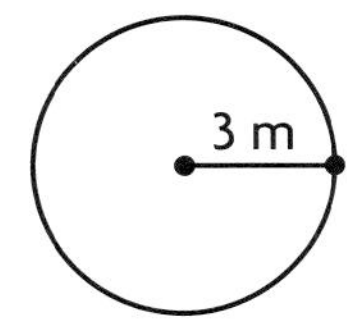

CHECK PROBLEM SOLVING

Solve. (pp. 620–621)

14. The perimeter of a triangle is 36 inches. Two sides of the triangle measure 9 inches and 12 inches. What is the length of the third side?

15. The perimeter of a rectangle is 24 meters. The length of the rectangle is 2 times the width. What are the length and width of the rectangle?

CHAPTERS 1–28

Standardized Test Prep

MEASUREMENT

1. Each square on the grid is 1 square inch. What is the area of the shaded figure?

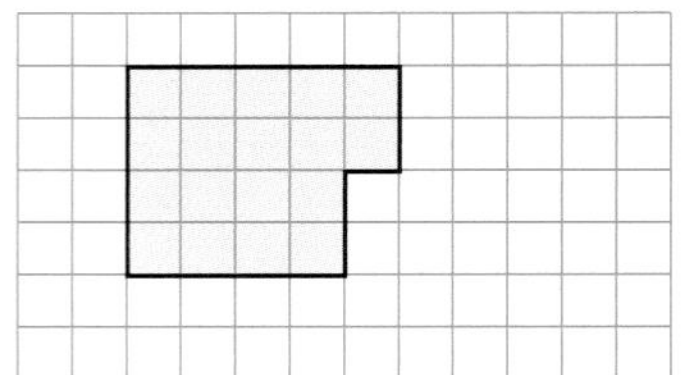

   A 16 square inches

   B 17 square inches

   C 18 square inches

   D 19 square inches

2. The table below shows the perimeters of several items in Sue's linen closet.

LINEN CLOSET ITEMS	
Item	**Perimeter (in yards)**
Blanket	15
Sheet	10
Beach towel	6
Quilt	12

   Sue's quilt is a square. What is the length of one of its sides?

   F 3 yards   H 6 yards

   G 4 yards   J 48 yards

3. **Explain It** ESTIMATE in centimeters the perimeter of an envelope such as the one below.

10 centimeters 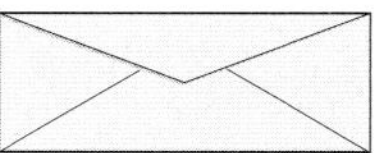

   Explain your thinking.

GEOMETRY AND SPATIAL SENSE

TIP **Eliminate choices.** See item 4. Look for shapes that are the same size. Eliminate those that are not.

4. Which two figures below appear to be congruent?

   A

   B 

   C 

   D 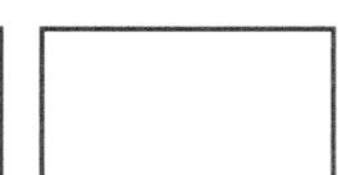

5. Which term **best** describes a pattern of closed figures that covers a surface with no gaps and no overlaps?

   F round

   G symmetrical

   H tessellation

   J similar

6. **Explain It** How would you classify this triangle? Write *scalene*, *isosceles*, or *equilateral*.

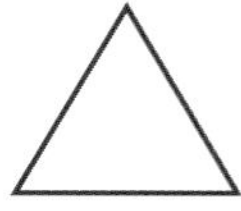

   Explain how you decided.

ALGEBRAIC THINKING

7. Which equation describes a rule for the pattern in this table?

INPUT	OUTPUT
f	z
3	30
17	170
25	250
30	300
48	480
61	610
77	770
83	830

A $f \div z = 10$

B $f \times z = 10$

C $f \div 10 = z$

D $f \times 10 = z$

8. Which is the value of x for $8.7 - 6.9 = x$?

F 1.86

G 1.8

H 1.6

J 1.46

9. **Explain It** Allie wrote the number pattern below.

2, 6, 18, 54, 162

She said that a rule for her pattern is add 3. Do you agree? Explain your thinking.

DATA ANALYSIS AND PROBABILITY

10. What is the probability of picking a green crayon from the box below?

A $\frac{1}{10}$

B $\frac{3}{10}$

C $\frac{2}{5}$

D $\frac{7}{10}$

11. Marla made a stem-and-leaf plot showing the weights of several dogs in her neighborhood.

Weight of Dogs (in pounds)

Stem	Leaves
1	0 1 7 7 8
2	2 2 8
3	1 4 5 5

How many dogs weigh **less than** 30 pounds?

F 4

G 8

H 12

J 28

12. **Explain It** Draw a tree diagram to show the outcomes for choosing an outfit of jeans or shorts with either a white, black, or red shirt. How many different outfits are possible? Explain how you decided.

CHAPTER 29

Area of Plane Figures

FAST FACT • ART You're flying in an airplane over fields in Eudora, Kansas. You look down and see a huge vase filled with sunflowers! This image was made by artist Stan Herd. Using materials such as crops, rocks, and mounds of soil, he designs huge pictures that cover from $\frac{1}{4}$ acre to 160 acres. To make the *Sunflower Field,* he planted 10,000 sunflowers.

PROBLEM SOLVING Use the grid to estimate the area of just the vase. Each square stands for 1 acre.

SUNFLOWER FIELD BY STAN HERD

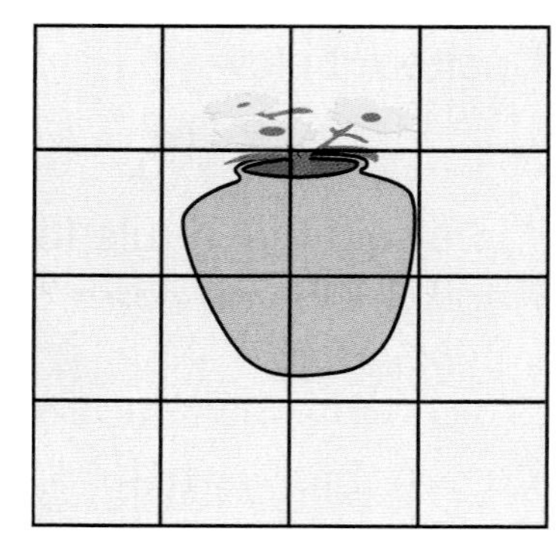

CHECK WHAT YOU KNOW

Use this page to help you review and remember important skills needed for Chapter 29.

MULTIPLICATION FACTS

Find the product.

1. 5×5
2. 6×8
3. 11×4
4. 8×3
5. 3×4
6. 12×10
7. 7×7
8. 9×2

FIND AREA

Count to find the area of each figure in square units.

9. 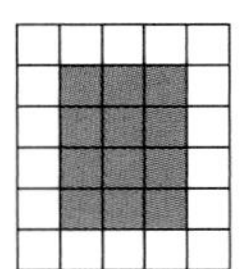
10. 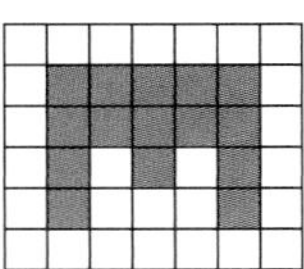
11. 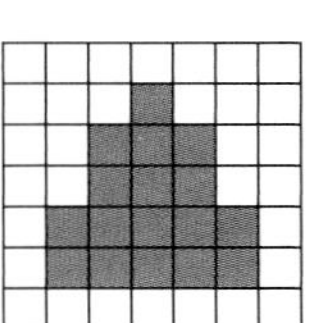
12. 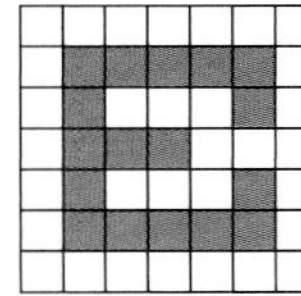
13. 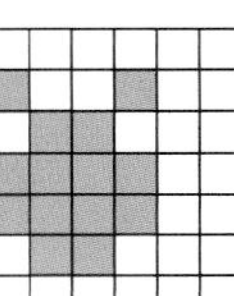
14. 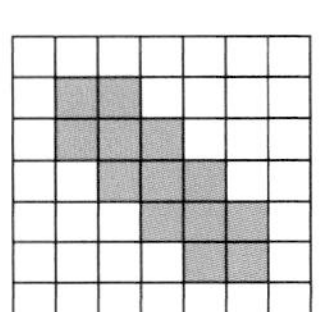
15. 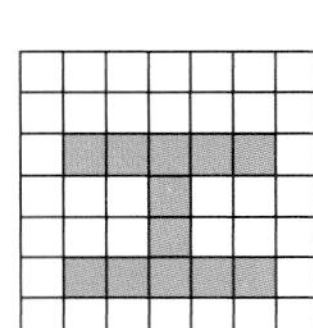
16. 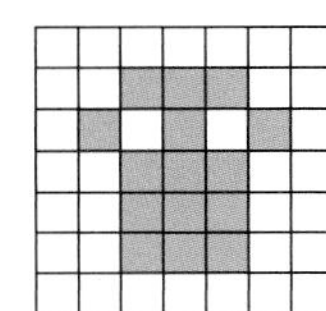

EXPRESSIONS WITH VARIABLES

Find the value of the expression.

17. $4 \times y$ if $y = 5$
18. $7 \times n$ if $n = 3$
19. $y \times 6$ if $y = 2$
20. $2 \times n$ if $n = 12$
21. $3 \times n$ if $n = 2$
22. $6 \times y$ if $y = 7$
23. $y \times 5$ if $y = 8$
24. $9 \times n$ if $n = 11$

VOCABULARY POWER

REVIEW

square [skwâr] *noun*

Square is the root of the word *squadron,* which originally meant "a square array of soldiers." How does this help you understand the term, *square unit*?

PREVIEW

area

www.harcourtschool.com/mathglossary

LESSON 1

Estimate Area

Quick Review

1. 48 ÷ 2
2. 88 ÷ 2
3. 22 ÷ 2
4. 36 ÷ 2
5. 50 ÷ 2

VOCABULARY

area

MATERIALS grid paper, three different colored pencils

Explore

Area is the number of square units needed to cover a surface.

Mr. Luu used grid paper to draw a diagram showing part of his house, sidewalk, and flower bed. He wants to estimate the area of his flower bed. Each square on his grid equals 1 square foot. How can Mr. Luu use the grid to estimate the area of his flower bed?

Activity

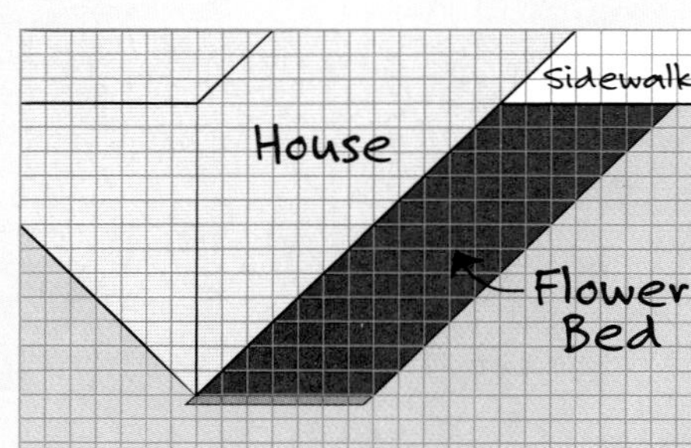

STEP 1

Copy the flower bed shown at the right on grid paper.

STEP 2

Shade all the full squares in one color and count them.

red full squares: 72

STEP 3

Shade all the half-full squares in another color and count them. Two half-full squares equal one full square.

blue half-full squares: 24

24 ÷ 2 = 12 full squares

STEP 4

Find the sum of the squares counted. 72 + 12 = 84

So, the area of Mr. Luu's flower bed is about 84 sq ft.

Try It

Estimate the area of each figure. Each square is 1 sq m.

a. 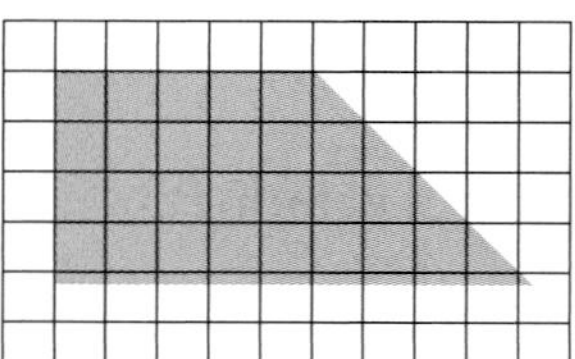

b. 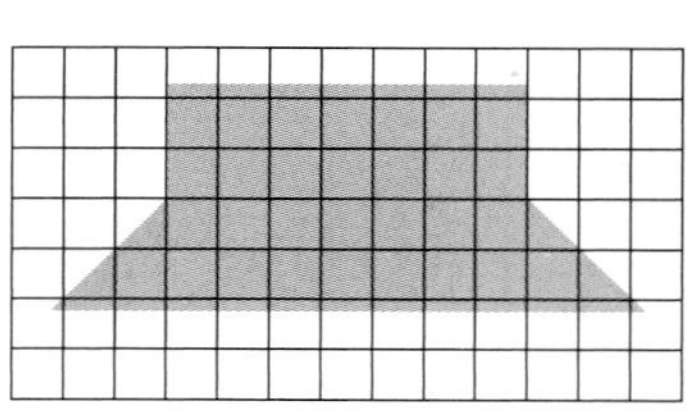

I am estimating the area of figure a. I shaded and counted 26 full squares. What is my next step?

Connect

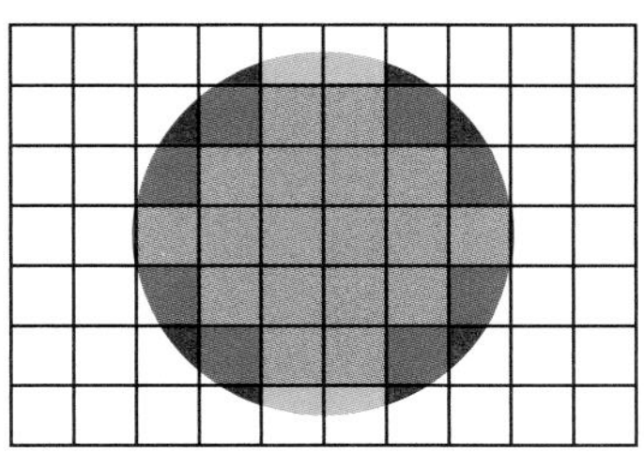

Sometimes a figure on a grid has square units that are almost full or less than half full. To estimate the area, you will need to count each square that is full, almost full, and half full. Estimate the area of the circle. Each square is 1 square inch.

Count the full squares.	orange full squares: 18
Count the almost-full squares.	blue almost-full squares: 8
Count the half-full squares.	green half-full squares: 4 $4 \div 2 = 2$ full squares
Do not count squares that are less than half full.	
Find the sum of the squares counted.	$18 + 8 + 2 = 28$

So, the area of the circle is about 28 sq in.

Practice and Problem Solving

Estimate the area of each figure. Each square is 1 sq yd.

1. 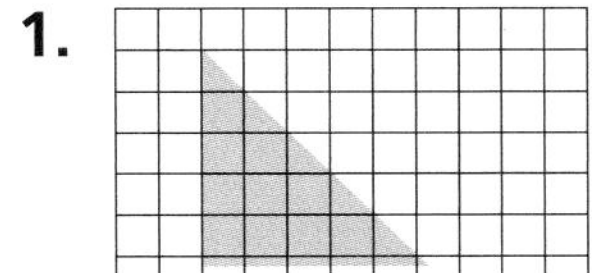

2. 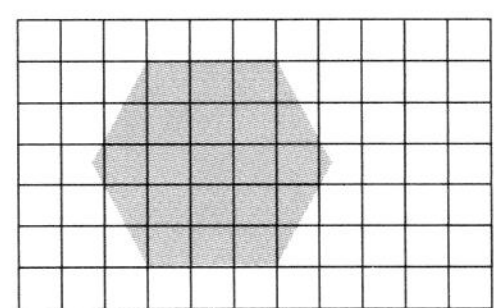

3. 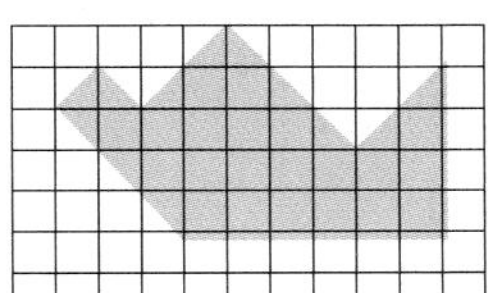

4. 

5. Draw a circle on grid paper. Then estimate the area in square units.

6. Draw a triangle on grid paper. Then estimate the area in square units.

7. A baseball field is divided into two congruent triangles. If the area of one triangle is 50 sq m, what is the area of the baseball field?

8. **Write About It** Explain how to estimate the area of a figure shown on grid paper.

Mixed Review and Test Prep

9. $\frac{2}{3} + \frac{5}{6}$ (p. 480)

10. $\frac{7}{8} - \frac{1}{4}$ (p. 482)

11. What number is represented by the letter M on the number line? (p. 424)

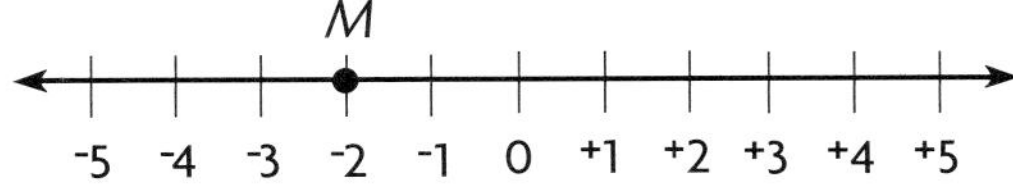

12. $3,892 \div 2$ (p. 306)

13. **TEST PREP** Amy decides on April 1 to have a flower garden. The seed packets say to plant on May 10. How many days must Amy wait to plant? (p 104)

A 20 days
B 25 days
C 32 days
D 40 days

Find Area

Quick Review

1. 4×9
2. 5×6
3. 8×7
4. 7×7
5. 6×8

Learn

ROW BY ROW Mr. Jones is putting 1-square-foot tiles on the shower wall of his bathroom. Estimate the number of tiles he needs to cover the wall.

Think: How many squares are in each row? about 6 squares
How many rows are needed? about 8 rows

$6 \times 8 = 48$

So, Mr. Jones needs about 48 1-square-foot tiles to cover the area of the shower wall.

Example

One Way You can count square units to find the area.

STEP 1

Using a centimeter ruler and grid paper, draw a rectangle 7 cm long and 5 cm wide.

STEP 2

Count the number of squares.

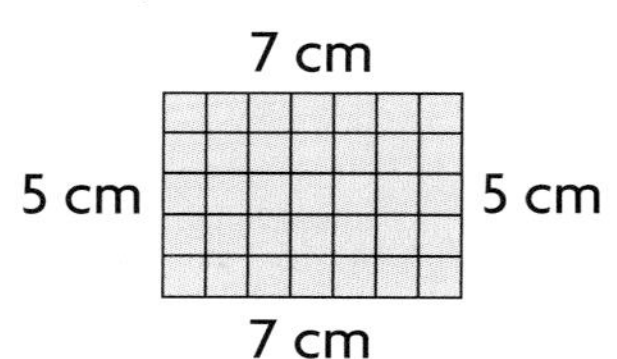

STEP 3

Record your answer in square units.

$A = 35$

Another Way You can also use a formula.

The formula for the area of a rectangle is Area = length × width, or $A = l \times w$.

Use the formula to find the area.

$A = l \times w$
$A = 7 \times 5$
$A = 35$

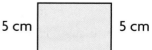

So, the area is 35 sq cm.

- How is using an array like using the formula to find the area of the rectangle above?
- Describe situations in which someone might need to find area.

Divide Figures into Parts

What is the area of this figure?

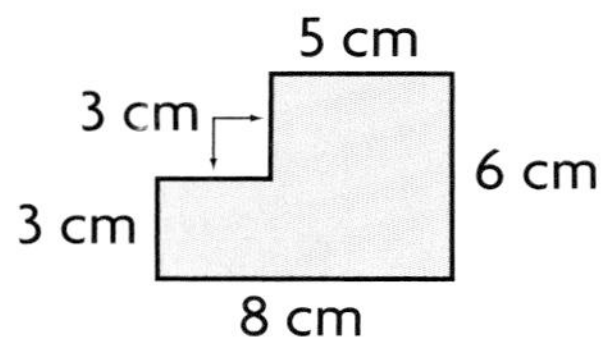

It is easier to find the area of some figures by dividing them into rectangles first.

Example

STEP 1

Divide the figure into two rectangles.

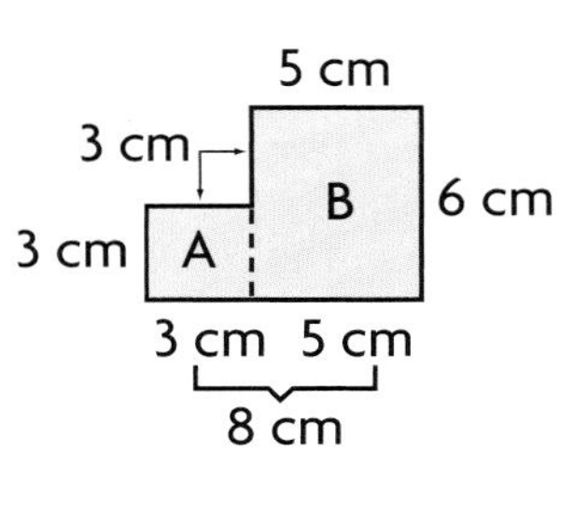

STEP 2

Find the area of each part.

Figure A

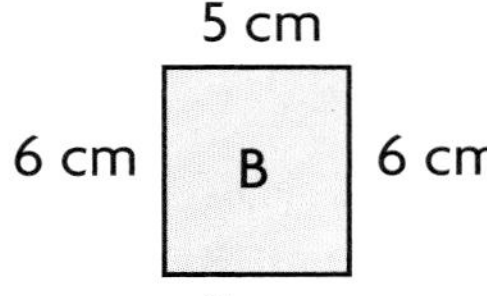

$A = l \times w$

$A = 3 \times 3$

$A = 9$

The area is 9 sq cm.

Figure B

5 cm

6 cm B 6 cm

5 cm

$A = l \times w$

$A = 5 \times 6$

$A = 30$

The area is 30 sq cm.

STEP 3

Add the areas together to find the total area of the figure.

$9 + 30 = 39$

So, the total area is 39 sq cm.

- Discuss why you can use the formula $A = s \times s$ for the area of a square.

Technology Link

More Practice: Harcourt Mega Math Ice Station Exploration, *Polar Planes*, Level R

Check

1. **Draw** this figure and show one way to divide it into rectangles so you can find the area.

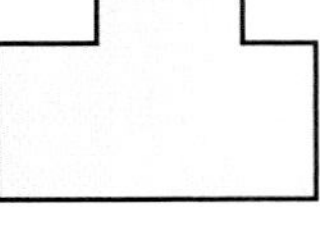

Find the area.

2.

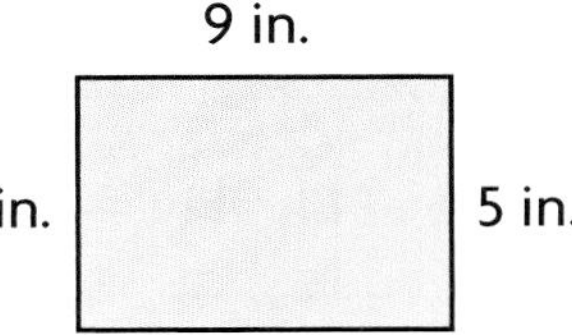

3.

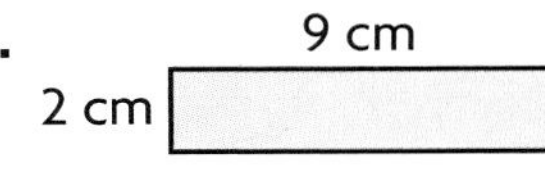

4.

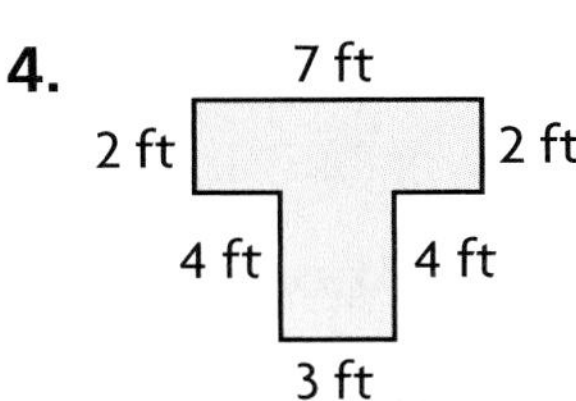

LESSON CONTINUES

Practice and Problem Solving

Extra Practice, page 638, Set A

Find the area.

5. 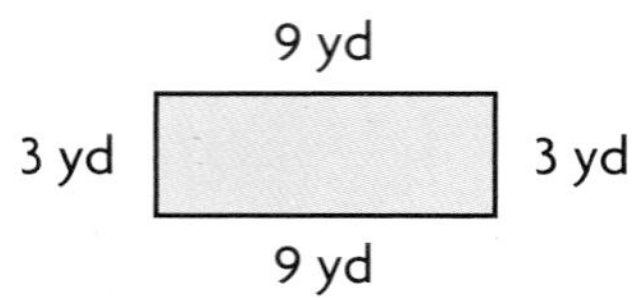

6. 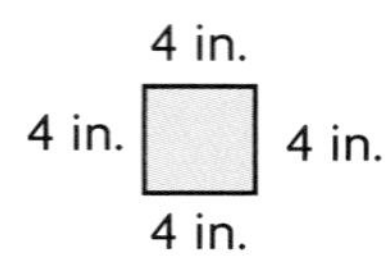

7. 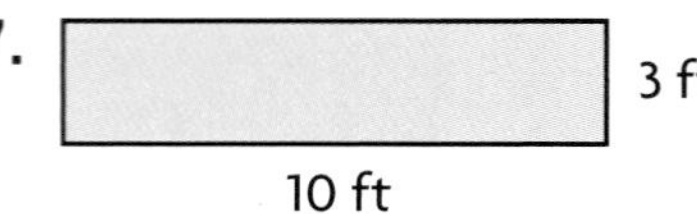

8. 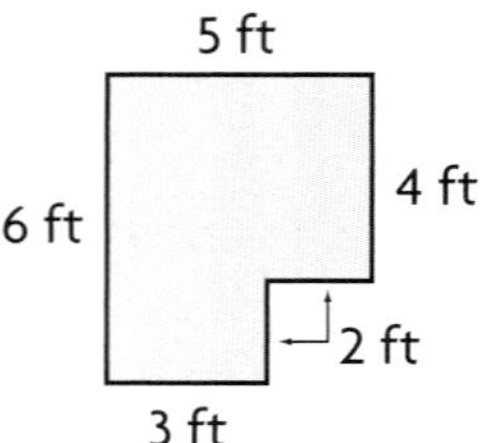

9. 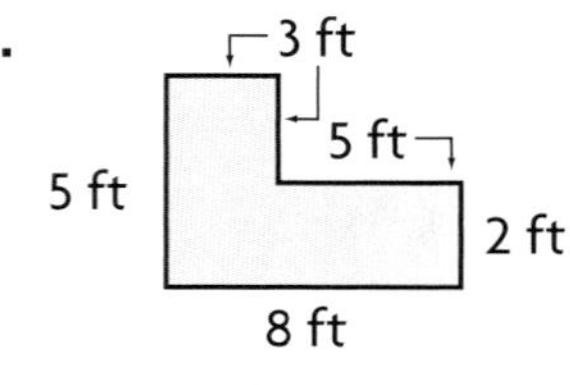

10. 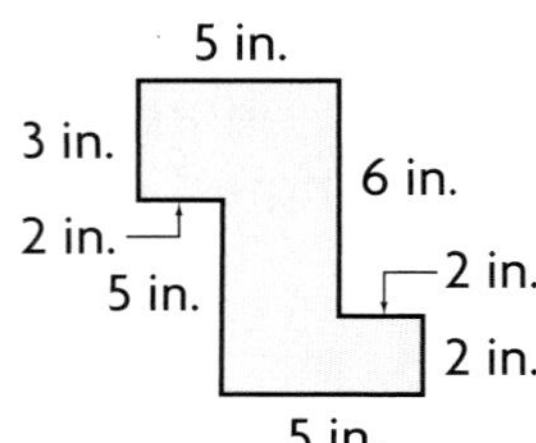

ALGEBRA Find the unknown length.

11. 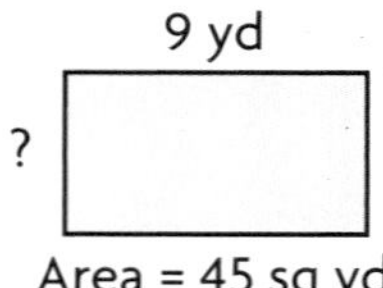

12. 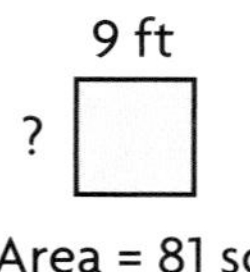

13. 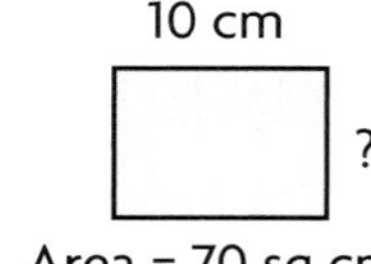

Use a centimeter ruler to measure each figure. Find the area and perimeter.

14. 

15. 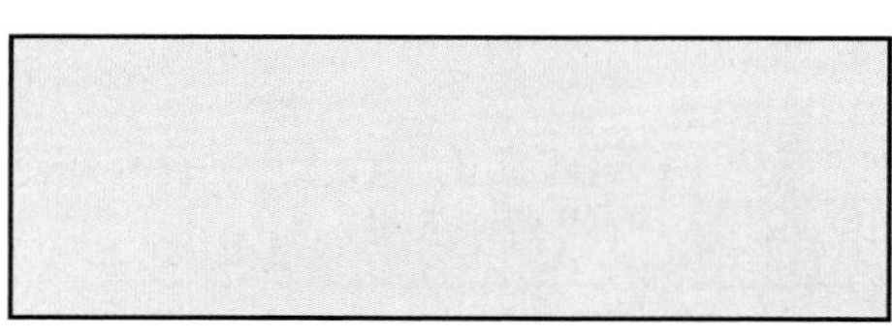

USE DATA For 16–17, use the bar graph. The length of each blanket is 90 inches.

16. What is the difference in the area of a full blanket and a twin blanket?

17. What is the difference in the area of a king blanket and a queen blanket?

18. **What's the Question?** The school yard has an area of 90 sq ft set aside for hopscotch. The length of the section is 10 ft. The answer is 9 ft.

19. **Write About It** One bulletin board is a rectangle. Another is a square. Explain how 16 square pictures could cover either one.

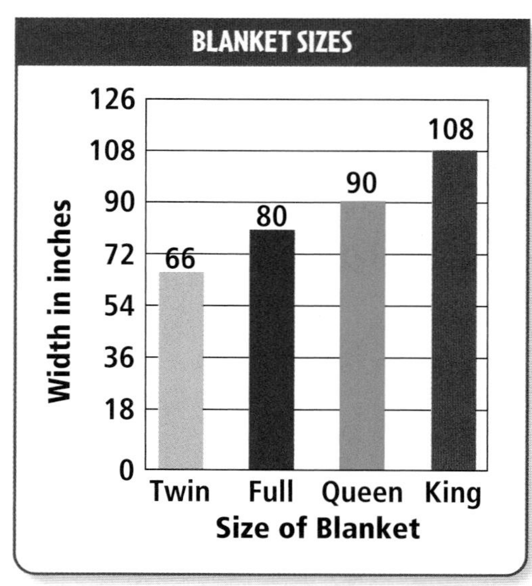

20. Andrea's living room is 4 yards wide. The perimeter is 20 yards. What is the area?

21. Don is putting carpet in a room that measures 14 ft by 12 ft. How many square feet of carpet does he need?

22. **Vocabulary Power** The word *formula* can mean "form" or "recipe." A recipe tells how to make a certain food. How is the formula for area of a rectangle like a recipe?

23. **FAST FACT • SOCIAL STUDIES** The largest U.S. flag, the Superflag, is 505 ft by 255 ft. It travels to events around the country. It takes at least 700 people to unfurl the flag. What is its area?

Mixed Review and Test Prep

24. $\begin{array}{r} 7{,}218 \\ -2{,}643 \\ \hline \end{array}$ (p. 48)

25. $\begin{array}{r} 5{,}207 \\ -1{,}958 \\ \hline \end{array}$ (p. 48)

26. $3\frac{3}{8} + 7\frac{1}{8}$ (p. 474)

27. $2\frac{2}{5} + 4\frac{1}{5}$ (p. 474)

Find the value of each expression. (p. 64)

28. $(36 - 12) + 8$

29. $36 - (12 + 8)$

30. **TEST PREP** Which number shows $\frac{30}{6}$ in simplest form? (p. 448)

A $\frac{1}{6}$ **B** 5 **C** 24 **D** 180

31. **TEST PREP** Which number is equivalent to 0.7? (p. 566)

F 0.0007 **H** 0.07
G 0.007 **J** 0.70

Problem Solving Thinker's Corner

COMBINED FIGURES Look at the drawing of Carl's farm. It is divided into a rectangle and a square. Will he need more fencing to enclose the two fields separately or to enclose the combined field? How does the total area of the two fields compare to the area of the combined field?

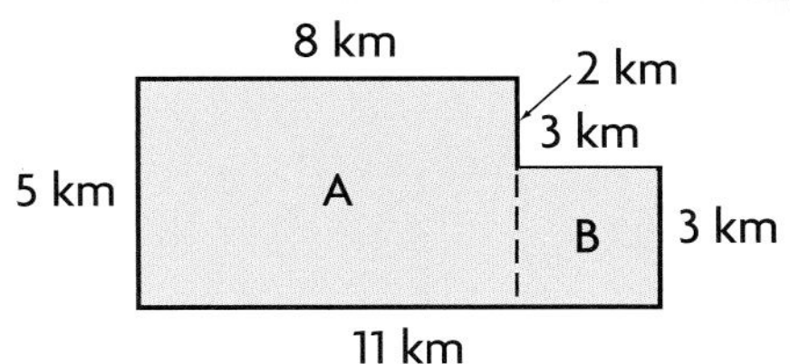

TWO FIELDS		COMBINED FIELD
Field A	**Field B**	
$P = 8 + 5 + 8 + 5 = 26$ The perimeter is 26 km.	$P = 3 + 3 + 3 + 3 = 12$ The perimeter is 12 km.	$P = 8 + 2 + 3 + 3 + 11 + 5 = 32$ The perimeter is 32 km.
$A = 8 \times 5 = 40$ The area is 40 sq km.	$A = 3 \times 3 = 9$ The area is 9 sq km.	Add the areas together to find the area of the combined field. $A = 40 + 9 = 49$
Total Area = 40 + 9 = 49 sq km		The area is 49 sq km.

Since 26 km + 12 km, or 38 km, is greater than 32 km, he will need more fencing to enclose the two fields separately than the combined field. The areas are equal.

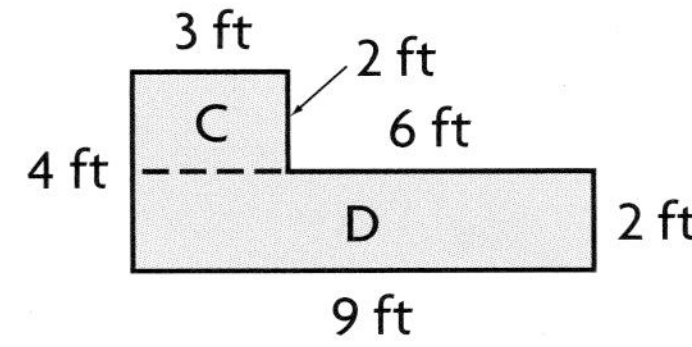

1. Use the figure at the right. Find the combined and divided perimeters and areas.

LESSON

3 Relate Area and Perimeter

Learn

AREA VS. PERIMETER Two figures can have the same area but different perimeters, or different areas but the same perimeter.

Quick Review

Compare. Use <, >, or = for each ●.

1. 3 × 4 ● 8 + 3
2. 34 ● 9 × 4
3. 9 + 8 ● 4 × 4
4. 9 × 2 ● 29 − 11
5. 25 + 19 ● 7 × 7

MATERIALS: square tiles, grid paper

Activity 1

Copy each figure using square tiles. Use grid paper to record your work. Then find the area and perimeter of each figure.

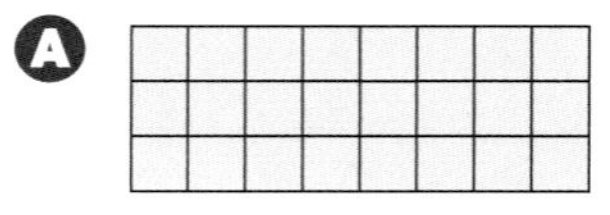

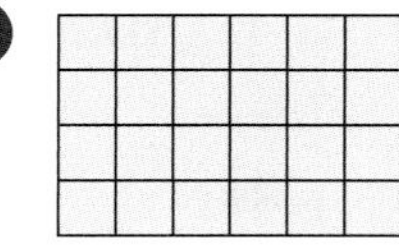

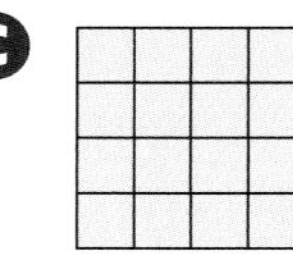
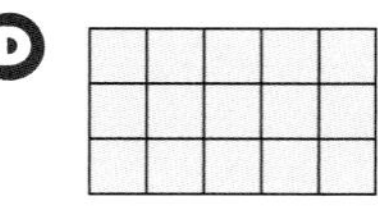

- Compare and contrast figures A and B.
- Compare and contrast figures C and D.

Activity 2 Show a rectangle that has the same area as rectangle R but a different perimeter. You can use square tiles to model.

6 ft

6 ft

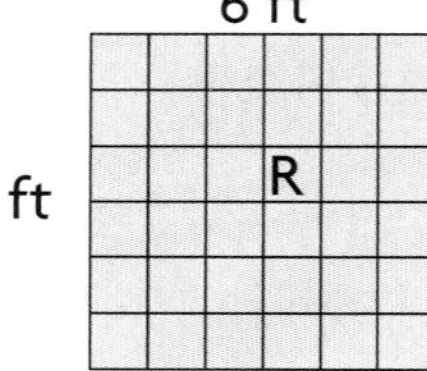

Area = 36 sq ft
Perimeter = 24 ft

One possible rectangle:

9 ft

4 ft

Area = 36 sq ft
Perimeter = 26 ft

- Describe the difference between area and perimeter.

Check

1. **Draw** two figures that have different perimeters but the same area. Use grid paper.
2. **Draw** two figures that have different areas but the same perimeter. Use grid paper.

Practice and Problem Solving

Extra Practice, page 638, Set B

For 3–8, find the area and perimeter of each figure. Then draw another figure that has the same perimeter but a different area.

3.

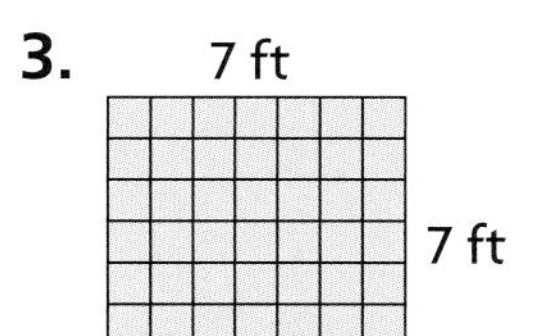

4. 10 cm, 4 cm, 4 cm, 10 cm

5. 5 cm, 5 cm

6.

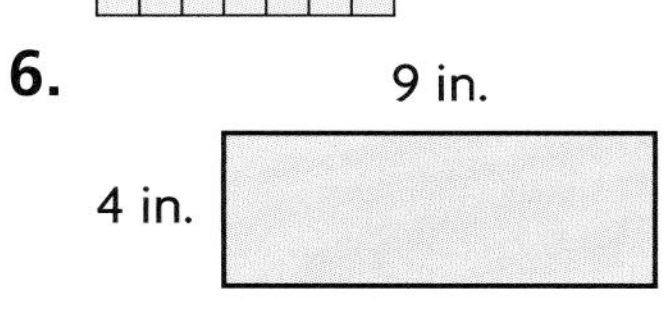

7. 9 cm, 10 cm, 10 cm, 9 cm

8.

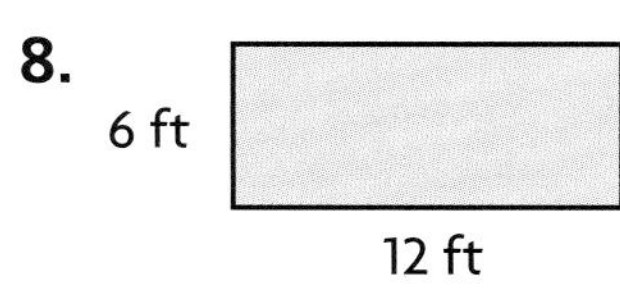

For 9–12, find the area and perimeter of each figure. Then draw another figure that has the same area but a different perimeter.

9.

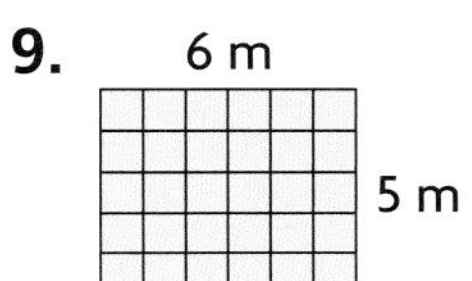

10.

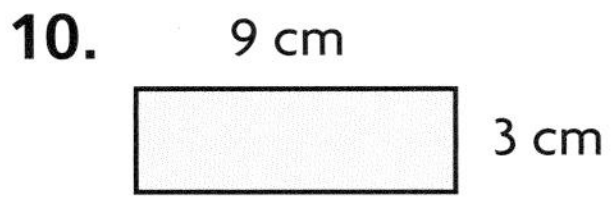

11.

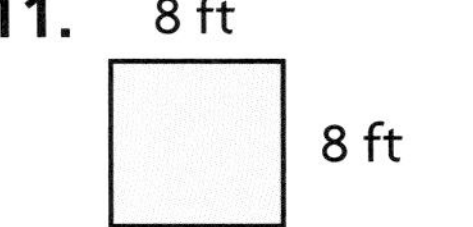

12.

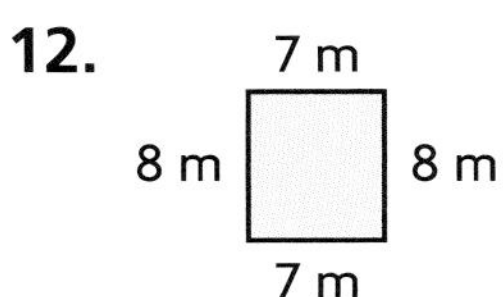

For 13–14, use figures a–d.

13. Which of the figures below have the same area but different perimeters?

14. Which of the figures below have the same perimeter but different areas?

a.

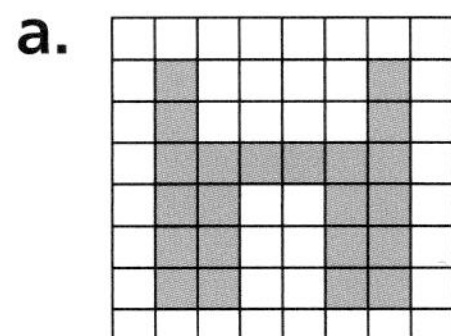

b.

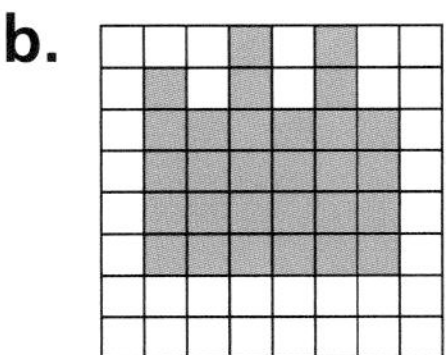

c.

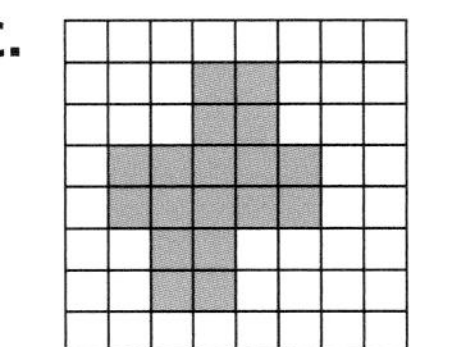

d.

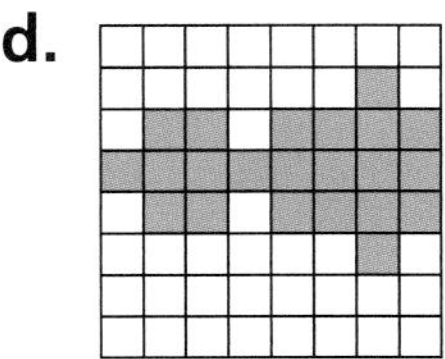

15. **Write a problem** about the square floor of a tree house that is 8 feet on each side.

16. **REASONING** The area of a rectangular garden is 24 square feet. Give four possible perimeters of the garden.

Mixed Review and Test Prep

17. 47×22 (p. 252)

18. 71×18 (p. 252)

19. $938 \div 31$ (p. 320)

20. Order from least to greatest. (p. 572)
29.6, 23.2, 29.5, 25.78

21. **TEST PREP** Cindy had 416 trading cards. She gave 72 to her sister and got 37 for her birthday. How many cards did she have then? (p. 262)

A 109 **B** 344 **C** 379 **D** 381

LESSON 4

Problem Solving Strategy
Find a Pattern

Quick Review

1. 99 ÷ 11 2. 360 ÷ 15
3. 504 ÷ 14 4. 132 ÷ 12
5. 700 ÷ 35

PROBLEM Mr. Jiminez wants to build different-size storage buildings, so he drew plans for the buildings. Some of the buildings will be twice as long as others but with the same width. He wants to know how the areas of the buildings are related. How do the areas change?

JIMINEZ STORAGE BUILDINGS

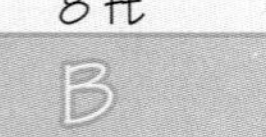

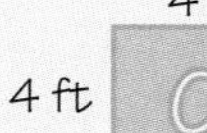

UNDERSTAND

- What are you asked to find?
- What do you know?

PLAN

- What strategy can you use to solve the problem?

You can *find a pattern* to solve the problem.

SOLVE

- How can you use *find a pattern* to solve the problem?

Look for a pattern in the areas.

	LENGTH	WIDTH	AREA		LENGTH	WIDTH	AREA
Building A	4	3	12	Building C	4	4	16
Building B	8	3	24	Building D	8	4	32
Building E	4	5	20	Building G	4	6	24
Building F	8	5	40	Building H	8	6	48

The areas change from 12 to 24, 16 to 32, 20 to 40, and 24 to 48.

So, as the length of one side doubles, the area also doubles.

CHECK

- Explain how you can check your answer.

Problem Solving Practice

Use *find a pattern* and solve.

1. **What if** Mr. Jiminez wants to know how the areas of his storage buildings change when both sides are doubled? Make a table to show how the areas change. Explain.
2. Mr. Jiminez also wants to know what happens to the perimeters of his storage buildings when both sides are doubled. Make a table to show how the perimeters change. Explain.

Strategies

- Draw a Diagram or Picture
- Make a Model or Act It Out
- Make an Organized List
- **Find a Pattern**
- Make a Table or Graph
- Predict and Test
- Work Backward
- Solve a Simpler Problem
- Write an Equation
- Use Logical Reasoning

Problem Solving

Rectangular swimming pools come in different sizes. Use the table to find how the perimeters of the swimming pools are related.

SWIMMING POOL SIZES

Pool	Length	Width	Perimeter
A	12 ft	20 ft	64 ft
B	12 ft	30 ft	84 ft
C	12 ft	40 ft	104 ft
D	12 ft	50 ft	124 ft

3. How do the widths of the swimming pools change?
   A decrease by 20 ft
   B decrease by 30 ft
   C increase by 10 ft
   D increase by 20 ft
4. What pattern do you see in the perimeters of the swimming pools?
   F increase by 20 feet **G** double in size **H** decrease by 10 ft **J** decrease by half

Mixed Strategy Practice

5. On a coordinate grid, graph a rectangle with vertices (1,2), (6,2), (1,5), and (6,5). Then find the perimeter and area of the rectangle.
6. Three stickers cost 15¢. Six stickers cost 30¢ and 9 stickers cost 45¢. How much will 15 stickers cost? How much will 30 stickers cost?
7. Mark travels 14.75 miles to soccer practice. First, he travels 5.25 miles to pick up John, then 3.75 miles to pick up Harold, and finally 2.25 miles to pick up Frank. How many miles does he have left to travel to soccer practice?
8. **Write About It** Explain how to find the unknown length.

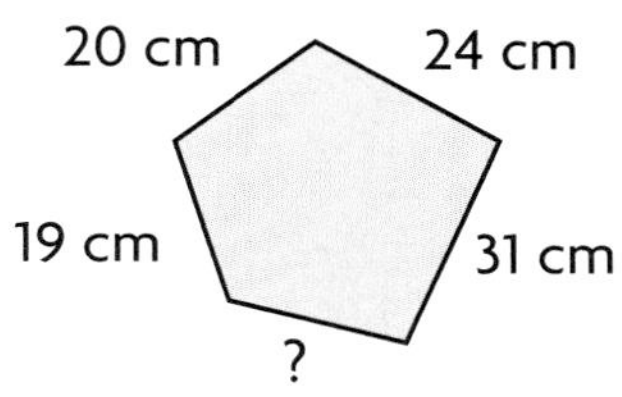

Perimeter = 115 cm

Extra Practice

Set A (pp. 630–633)

Find the area.

1. 6 m, 3 m, 3 m, 6 m

2. 7 m, 4 m, 4 m, 7 m

3. 9 cm, 9 cm, 9 cm, 9 cm

4. 15 in., 6 in., 6 in., 15 in.

5. 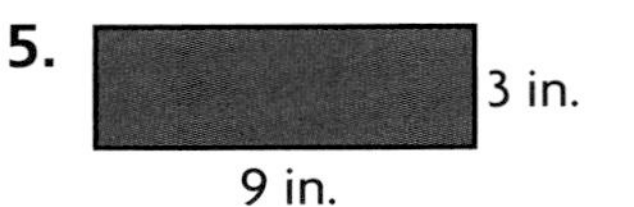

6. 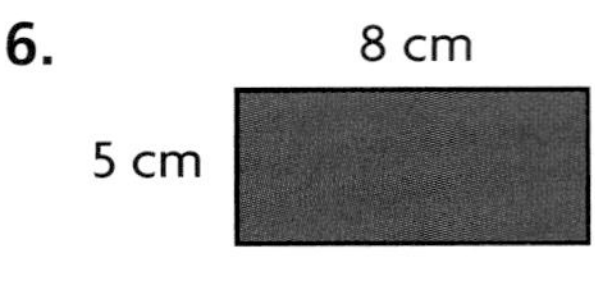

7. 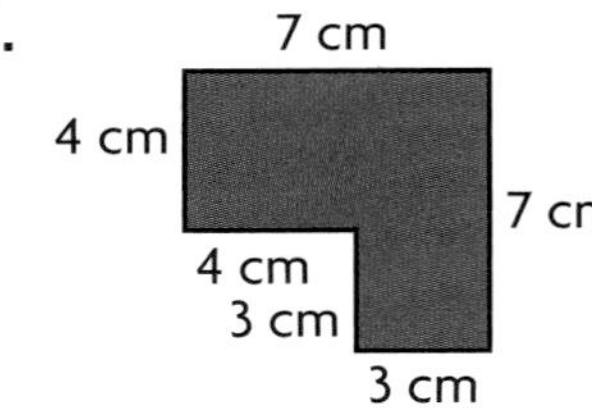

8. 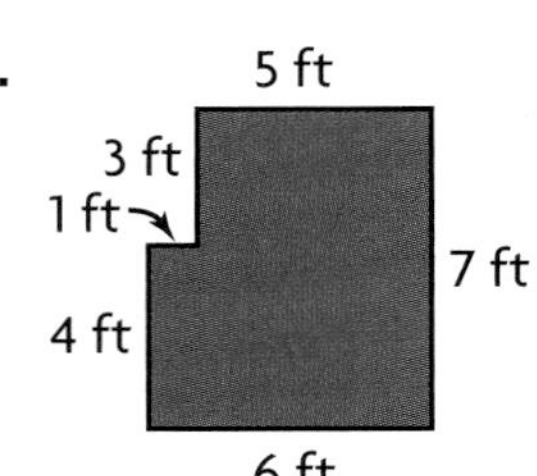

9. Mandy's class is painting a mural on a wall. The wall is 6 feet high and 4 feet wide. What is the area of the wall?

10. Ivonne wants to know how many quilt blocks are in her quilt. It is 12 blocks long and 6 blocks wide. How many blocks are in her quilt?

Set B (pp. 634–635)

Find the area and perimeter of each figure. Then draw another figure that has the same area but a different perimeter.

1.

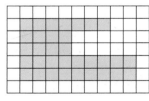

2. 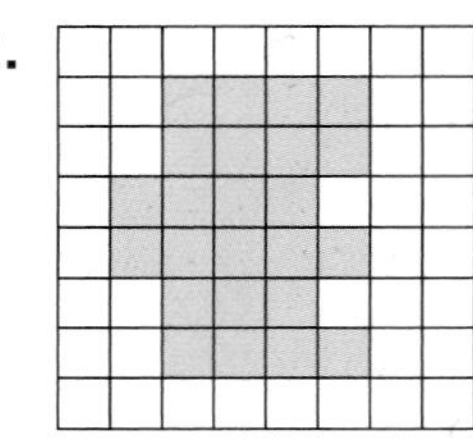

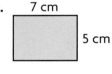

3. 7 cm, 5 cm

4. 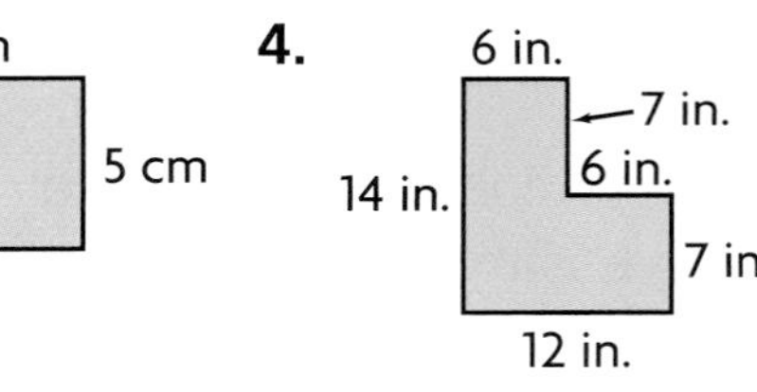

5.

6. 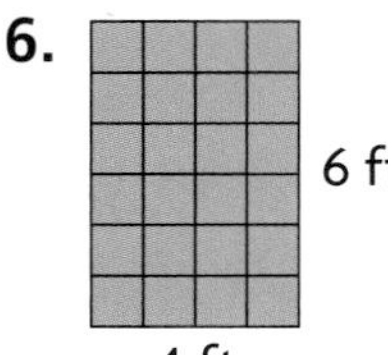

7. 4 m, 4 m

8. 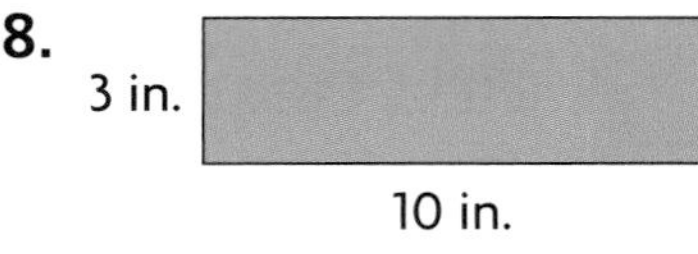

9. The floor of Ben's tree house is a square measuring 6 feet on each side. What are the area and perimeter of the floor?

10. Debbie's living room ceiling measures 16 feet by 14 feet. What are the area and perimeter of the ceiling?

Review/Test

✓ CHECK VOCABULARY AND CONCEPTS

Choose the best term from the box.

area
formula
length
perimeter

1. The formula for the area of a rectangle is *Area* = ? × *width.* (p. 630)
2. The number of square units needed to cover a surface is its ? . (p. 628)
3. Two figures can have different areas but the same ? . (p. 634)

Estimate the area of each figure. Each square is 1 sq cm. (pp. 628–629)

4. 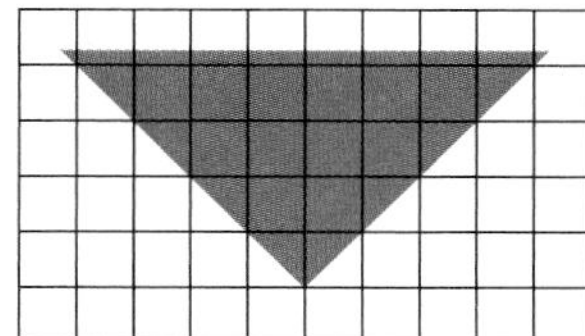

5. 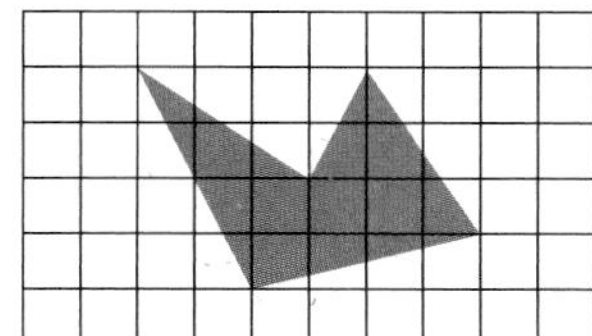

6. 

✓ CHECK SKILLS

Find the area. (pp. 630–633)

7. 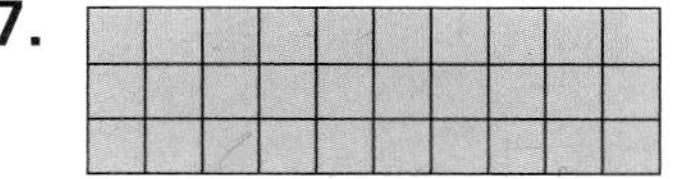

8. 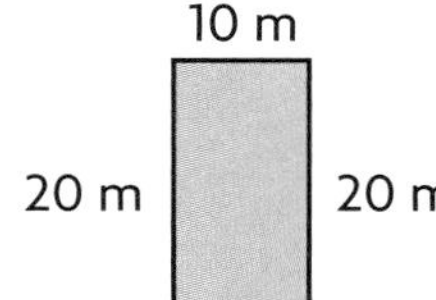

9. 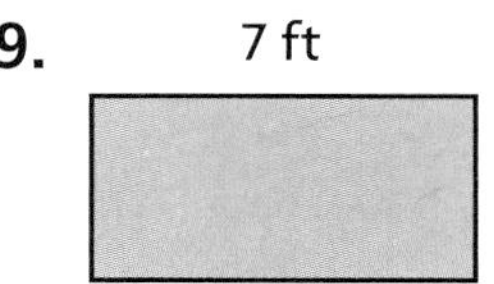

10. 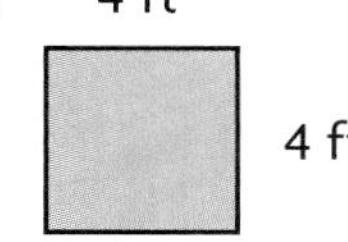

Find the area and perimeter of each figure. Then draw another figure that has the same perimeter but a different area. (pp. 634–635)

11. 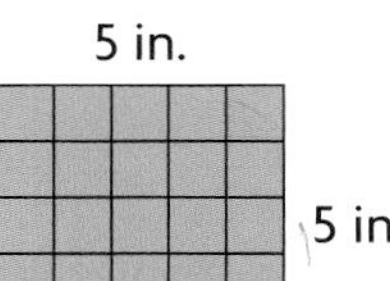

12. 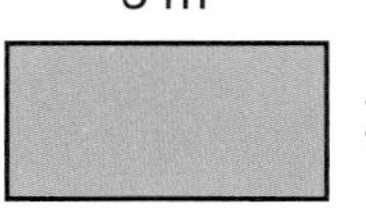

13. 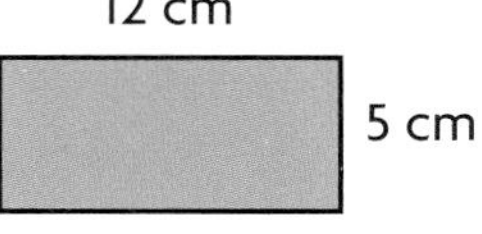

✓ CHECK PROBLEM SOLVING

Solve. (pp. 636–637)

14. Mr. Walker's front porch is 6 feet by 8 feet. He wants to double the length and the width of his porch. How will the area of the porch change?

15. A stone wall has 28 stones on the first layer, 24 stones on the second layer, and 20 stones on the third layer. How many stones are on the fifth layer?

Standardized Test Prep

MEASUREMENT

1. What is the area of the shaded figure?

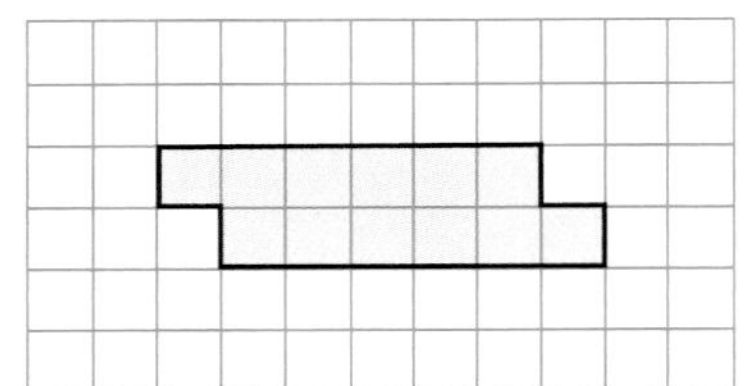

A 8 square units

B 10 square units

C 12 square units

D 20 square units

2. Which city has the warmest average temperature?

TEMPERATURES FOR MARCH (in degrees Fahrenheit)

City	Temperatures for 5 Days				
Atlanta	68	62	65	62	67
New York	40	45	50	48	48
Raleigh	77	71	68	70	67
Miami	72	70	75	73	77

F Atlanta

G New York

H Raleigh

J Miami

3. **Explain It** Suppose you wanted to find the length of the ribbon below to the nearest $\frac{1}{2}$ inch.

Explain the steps you would take to measure the length of the ribbon.

ALGEBRAIC THINKING

4. Grady practices the piano for 12 hours each week.

Let p represent the number of weeks Grady practices. Which expression can you write to show the total number of hours he practices in a number of weeks?

A $12 + p$

B $12 \times p$

C $12 \div p$

D $12 - p$

5. Which equation describes a rule in this table?

Input	Output
a	***b***
2	11
16	25
21	30
34	43
42	51

F $a - 9 = b$

G $b + 9 = a$

H $a + 9 = b$

J $a - b = 9$

6. **Explain It** Which number makes this sentence true?

$$n + 6 = 10$$

Explain your thinking.

DATA ANALYSIS AND PROBABILITY

7. If you spin the pointer, which fraction tells how likely you are to land on 2?

A $\frac{5}{6}$ **C** $\frac{1}{3}$

B $\frac{1}{2}$ **D** $\frac{1}{6}$

8. Look at the line graph below.

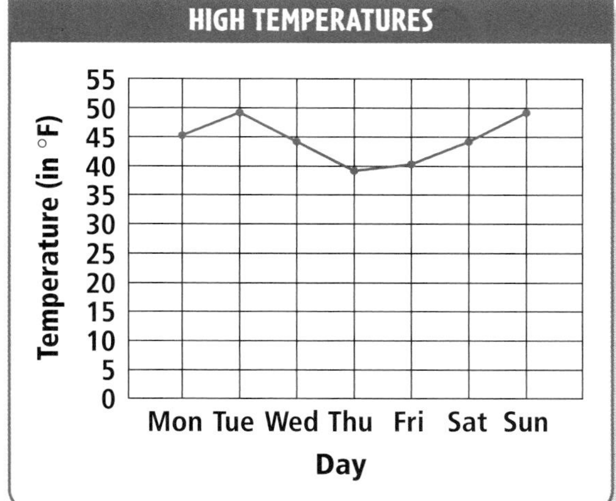

Which of the following is true?

F Monday was cooler than Saturday.

G Wednesday was cooler than Sunday.

H Friday was warmer than Tuesday.

J Sunday was cooler than Thursday.

9. Explain It Martin had a nickel, 2 dimes, and a quarter in his pocket. He chose 1 coin without looking. Use a fraction to show whether it is likely or unlikely that the value of the coin was greater than 5 cents. Explain your answer.

GEOMETRY AND SPATIAL SENSE

10. Which two figures below appear to be congruent?

A

B

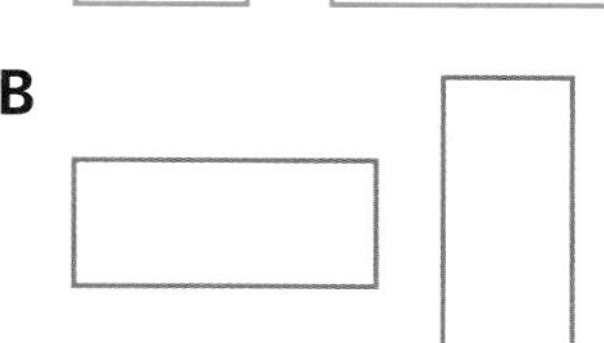

C

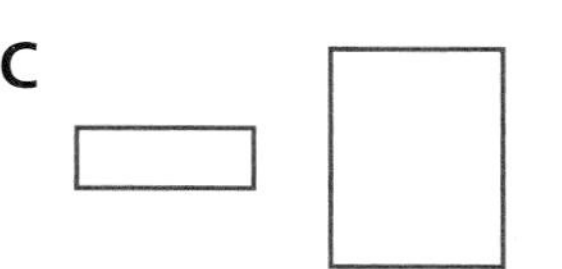

D

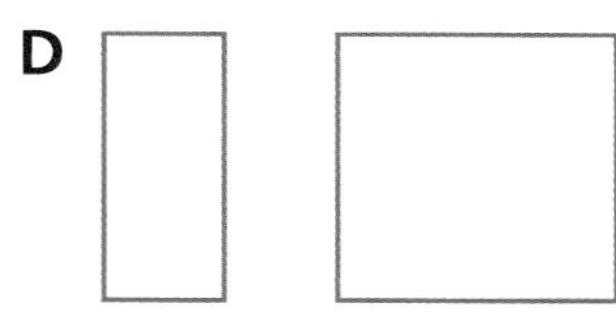

TIP **Understand the problem.** See item 11. Hold your hand in the same position as the drawing. Move your hand in the same way the figure was moved over the dotted line. Look for the term that describes this motion.

11. Which term best describes the motion shown by the figure?

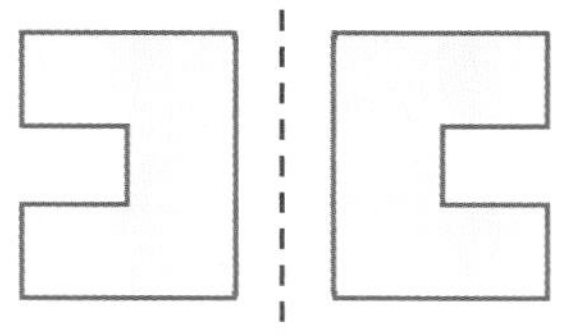

F translation **H** rotation

G reflection **J** not congruent

12. Explain It Explain the following statement.

"Perpendicular lines are always intersecting, but intersecting lines are not always perpendicular."

CHAPTER 30 Solid Figures and Volume

FAST FACT • SCIENCE Do shrubs naturally grow like the ones in this photograph? The answer is no. Gardeners carefully clip and train these shrubs to grow into geometric and animal shapes called topiaries. It takes 3 to 10 years to form each shrub into the desired shape.

PROBLEM SOLVING The topiaries in this garden have 20 different shapes, including cones, cubes, spirals, and birds. What solid figures are used to make the topiary in the diagram?

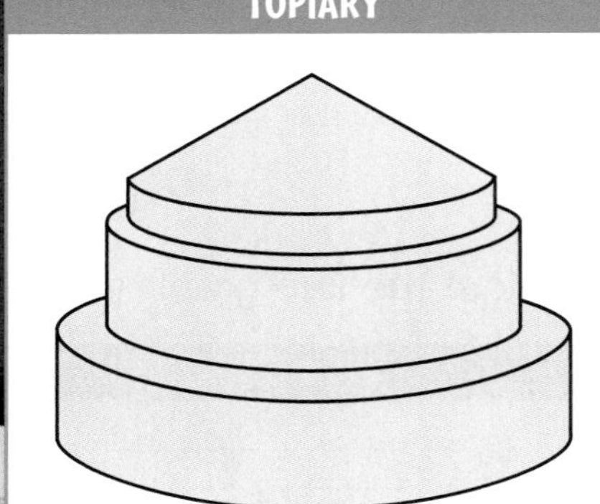

Topiary Garden in Longwood Gardens, Kennett Square, Pennsylvania

CHECK WHAT YOU KNOW

Use this page to help you review and remember important skills needed for Chapter 30.

IDENTIFY SOLID FIGURES

Choose a name from the list for each solid shape.

cube	cone
sphere	cylinder
square pyramid	
rectangular prism	

1. 

2. 

3. 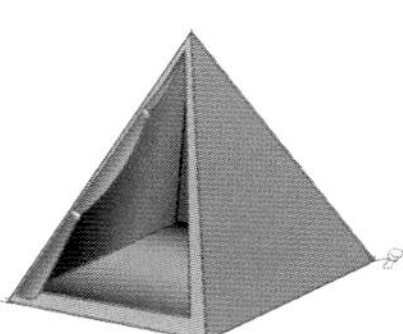

4. 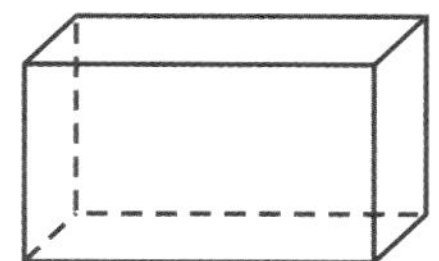

5. 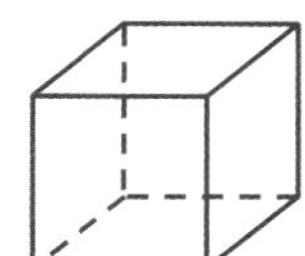

6. 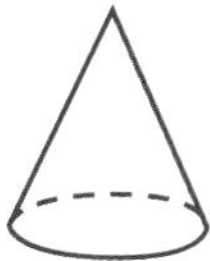

DRAW POLYGONS

Use dot paper to draw each polygon.

7. triangle **8.** square **9.** rectangle **10.** pentagon

MULTIPLY THREE FACTORS

Show two ways to group by using parentheses. Find the product.

11. $4 \times 2 \times 2 = \blacksquare$ **12.** $5 \times 2 \times 1 = \blacksquare$ **13.** $2 \times 5 \times 5 = \blacksquare$

14. $7 \times 2 \times 3 = \blacksquare$ **15.** $8 \times 5 \times 2 = \blacksquare$ **16.** $9 \times 5 \times 2 = \blacksquare$

VOCABULARY POWER

REVIEW

dimension [də•men′shən] *noun*

Dimension is from the Latin words *dis* and *meteri* which, when combined, mean "to measure out." The glossary definition of *dimension* is "a measure in one direction." Which dimensions of a prism do you think you would measure?

PREVIEW

two-dimensional	**edge**
three-dimensional	**vertex**
triangular prism	**net**
triangular pyramid	**volume**
face	**cubic units**

www.harcourtschool.com/mathglossary

LESSON 1

Faces, Edges, and Vertices

Quick Review

Tell the number of sides.

1. square **2.** triangle
3. rectangle **4.** pentagon
5. hexagon

VOCABULARY

two-dimensional **face**
three-dimensional **edge**
triangular prism **vertex**
triangular pyramid

Learn

ANOTHER DIMENSION Polygons have only length and width, so they are **two-dimensional** figures.

Solid figures have length, width, and height, so they are **three-dimensional** figures.

Study these solid figures. A polygon that is a flat surface of a solid figure is a **face**. Look for polygons that are faces of each solid figure.

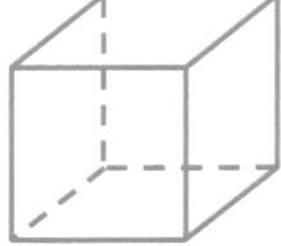
cube

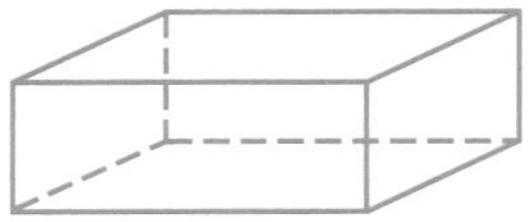
rectangular prism

triangular prism

triangular pyramid

square pyramid

▲ Pyramids at Giza, Egypt

• Name the plane figures found in the faces of each solid above.

Look carefully at the faces of the square pyramid below. The faces of a square pyramid are triangles and a square.

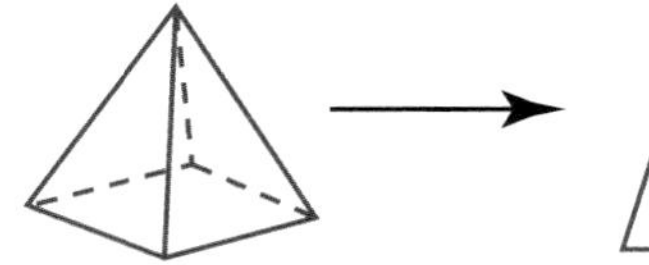
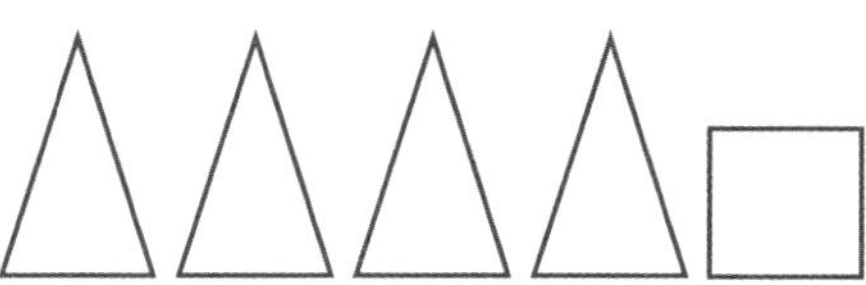

Technology Link

More Practice: Harcourt Mega Math Ice Station Exploration, *Frozen Solids*, Levels F and G

Some solid figures have curved surfaces and no faces.

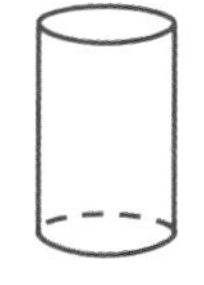
cylinder

cone

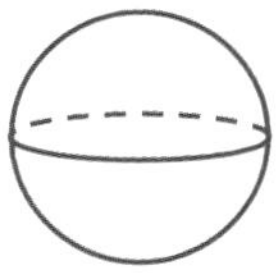

sphere

Activity

Find the number of faces, edges, and vertices of the solid figures in the table below.

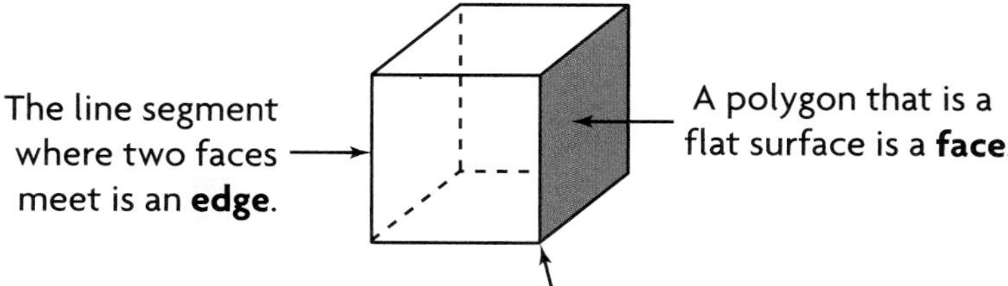

The line segment where two faces meet is an **edge**.
A polygon that is a flat surface is a **face**.

The point where three or more edges meet is a **vertex**. The plural of vertex is vertices.

Copy and complete the table.

FIGURE	NAME OF FIGURE	NUMBER OF FACES	NUMBER OF EDGES	NUMBER OF VERTICES
	Cube	6	12	8
	Rectangular prism	■	■	■
	Triangular prism	■	■	■
	Triangular pyramid	■	■	■
	Square pyramid	■	■	■

▲ **David Smith's sculpture *Cubi XX* is made of a cylinder and rectangular prisms.**

- Look at the table. Find a relationship between the number of faces and the number of edges of a rectangular prism.

Check

1. **Name** three solid figures that have no faces or straight edges.

Name a solid figure that is described.

2. 9 edges
3. 5 vertices
4. more than 5 faces

LESSON CONTINUES

Practice and Problem Solving

Extra Practice, page 656, Set A

Name a solid figure that is described.

5. some or all triangular faces

6. some or all rectangular faces

7. curved surfaces

8. 8 vertices, 12 edges, 6 faces

Which solid figure do you see in each?

9. 

10. 

11. 

12. 

Write the names of the plane figures that are the faces of each solid figure.

13. 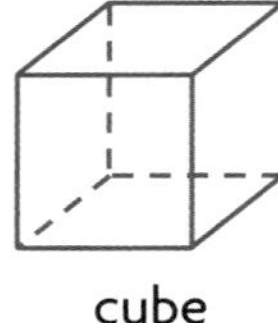

cube

14. 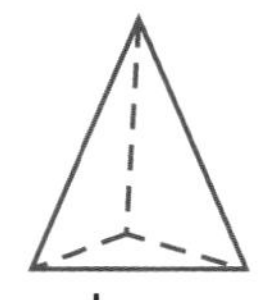

triangular pyramid

15. 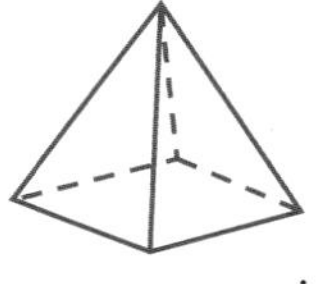

square pyramid

16. 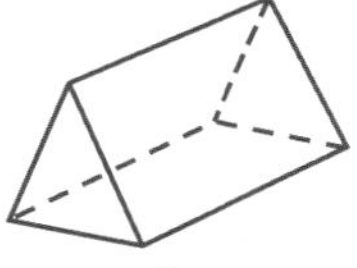

triangular prism

Copy the drawings. Circle each vertex, outline each edge in red, and shade one face in yellow.

17. 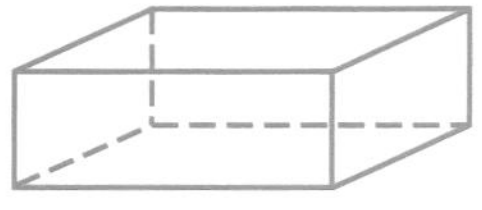

18. 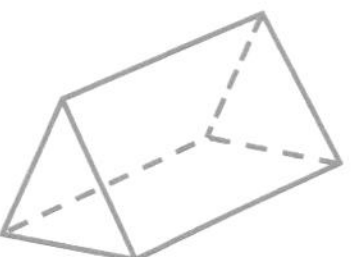

19. 

20. 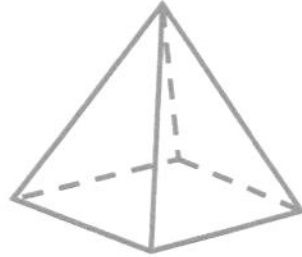

Write the names of the faces and the number of each kind of face of the solid figure.

21. cube

22. square pyramid

23. triangular prism

24. **What's the Question?** The answer is 4 triangular faces.

25. **REASONING** What plane figure is always found in a pyramid?

26. Explain how circles and spheres are alike. How are they different?

27. Explain how squares and cubes are alike. How are they different?

28. Look at the edges of the cube at the right. $\overline{AB}$ and $\overline{CD}$ are parallel line segments. $\overline{AC}$ and $\overline{AE}$ are perpendicular line segments. List two other pairs of parallel line segments and two other pairs of perpendicular line segments.

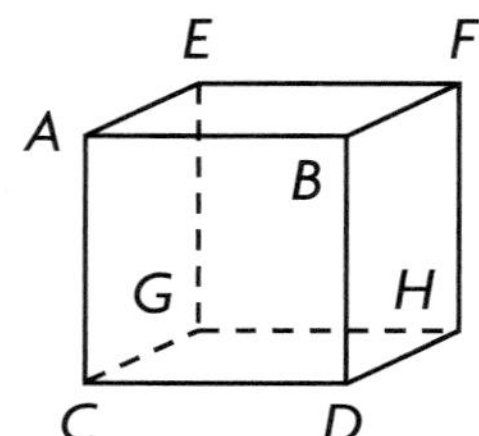

29. Laura has 1 dog and 2 cats. Laura hung 7 drawings of cats in her room. She hung 10 drawings of dogs. She has 8 more drawings to hang. How many drawings does Laura have in all?

30. Brandon and Joe played a number game. Joe chose a number and subtracted 3. Then, he added 7 and subtracted 5. The answer was 27. What number did Joe choose?

Mixed Review and Test Prep

Write whether each number is prime or composite. (p. 342)

31. 28
32. 31
33. 59
34. 56

List the factors of each number. (p. 338)

35. 6
36. 15
37. 18
38. 20

39. Holly is baking a double batch of cookies. For a single batch, $2\frac{1}{3}$ cups of flour are needed. How much flour does Holly need for the double batch? (p. 474)

40. **TEST PREP** Jane rode her bike 4 miles from her house to school. How many yards did she ride her bike? (HINT: 1 mile = 1,760 yards) (p. 526)

A 440 yards
B 1,760 yards
C 6,940 yards
D 7,040 yards

41. **TEST PREP** One insect is $\frac{1}{2}$ inch long and a second insect is $\frac{1}{4}$ inch long. How much longer is the first insect than the second insect? (p. 482)

F $\frac{1}{4}$ inch
G $\frac{1}{2}$ inch
H $\frac{3}{4}$ inch
J 1 inch

Problem Solving Thinker's Corner

VISUAL THINKING Solid figures can look different when viewed from different directions. Here are some different ways of looking at the figure at the right.

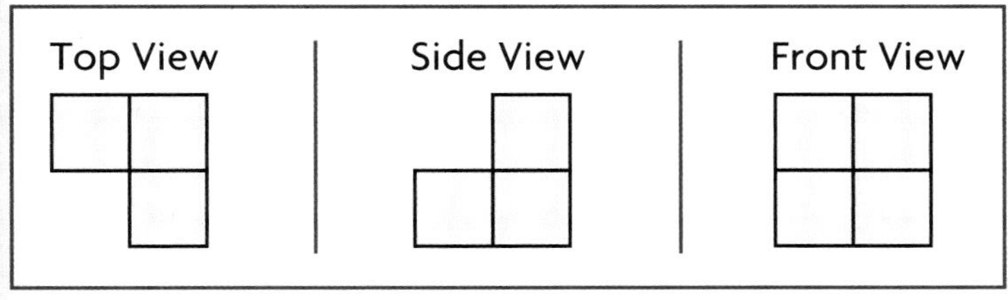

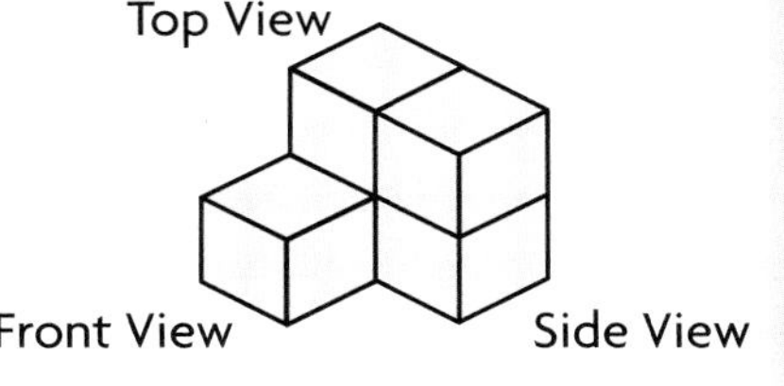

Write the letter of the figure that shows the correct view of the figure at the right.

1. top view
2. side view
3. front view

a. 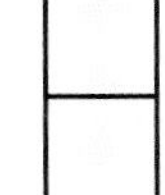

b. 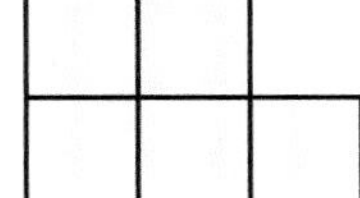

c. 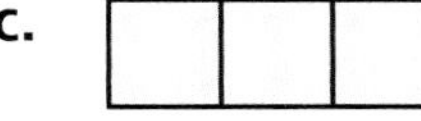

LESSON

2 Patterns for Solid Figures

Learn

SHAPE OF THINGS A **net** is a two-dimensional pattern of a three-dimensional figure. It can be folded to make a model of a solid figure.

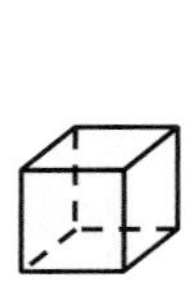

cube

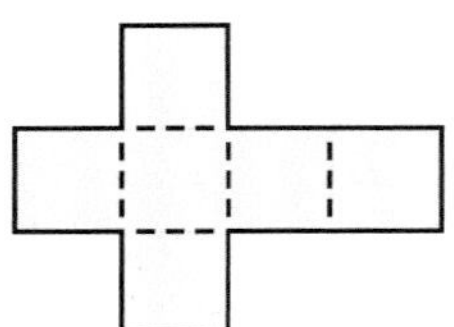

a net for a cube

You can cut apart a three-dimensional box to make a two-dimensional pattern, or net.

HANDS ON

Activity **MATERIALS:** empty container, such as a cereal box; scissors and tape

STEP 1	Cut along some of the edges until the box is flat. Be sure that each face is connected to another face by at least one edge.
STEP 2	Trace the flat shape on a piece of paper. This shape is a net of the box.
STEP 3	Cut out the net. Fold it into a three-dimensional box. Use tape to hold it together.

- How is the net for a rectangular prism different from the net for a cube?

Quick Review

Tell the number of faces for each.

1. cube

2. square pyramid

3. triangular prism

4. rectangular prism

5. triangular pyramid

VOCABULARY

net

Technology Link

More Practice: Harcourt Mega Math Ice Station Exploration, *Frozen Solids,* Levels H and I

Check

1. **Explain** how the net for a square pyramid is different from the net for a rectangular prism.
2. **Look** at the figure and the net at the right. Tell whether the figure can be made from the net.

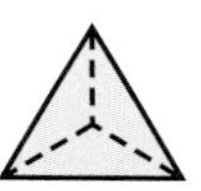

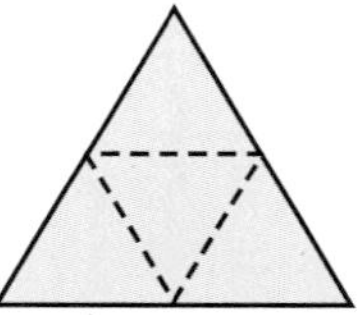

Practice and Problem Solving

Extra Practice, page 656, Set B

Write the letter of the figure that is made with each net.

3. 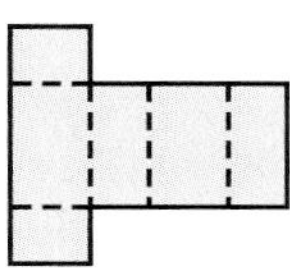

4. 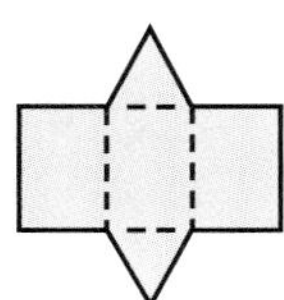

5. 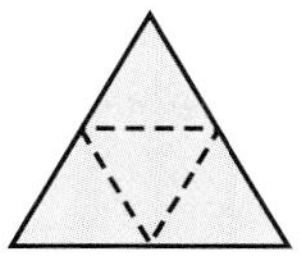

6. 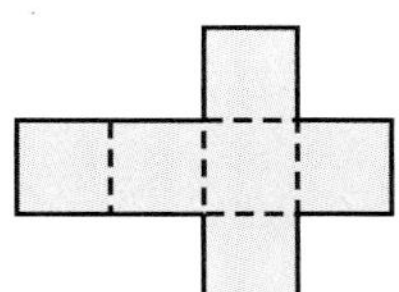

a. 

b. 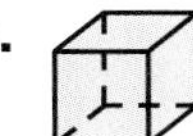

c. 

d. 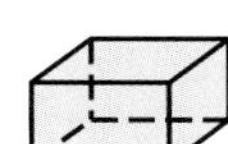

Draw a net that can be cut and folded to make a model of the solid figure shown.

7. 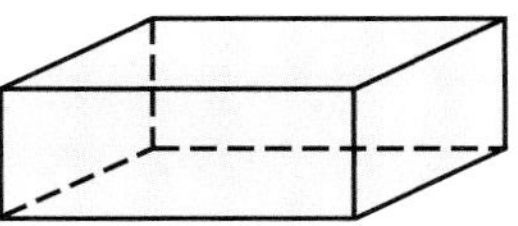

8. 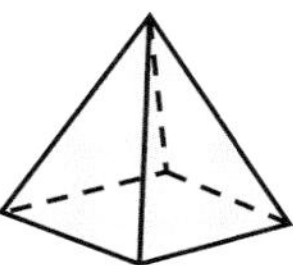

9. 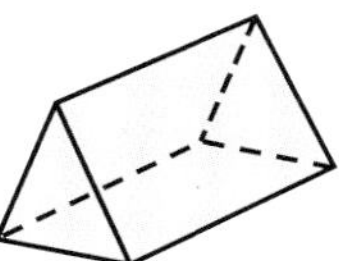

10. 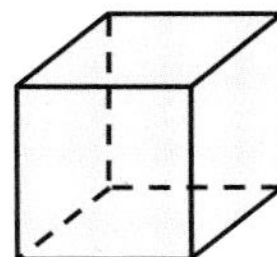

Would the net make a cube? Write *yes* or *no*.

11. 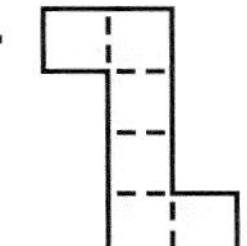

12. 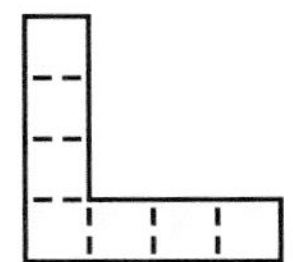

13. 

14. 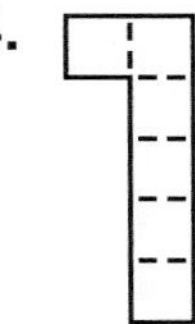

For 15–16, use the net.

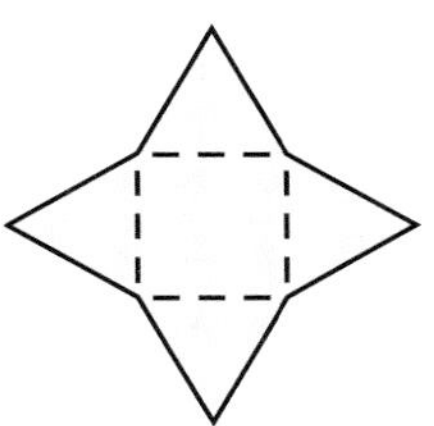

15. Juanita drew the net at the right. What solid figure can she make?

16. Ernest folded Juanita's net into a model of a solid figure. How many faces, edges, and vertices did the model have?

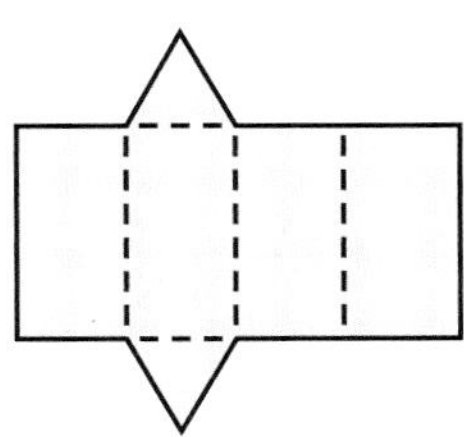

17. **What's the Error?** Nina says the net at the right can be folded to make a triangular prism. Explain Nina's error. Then draw a net for a triangular prism.

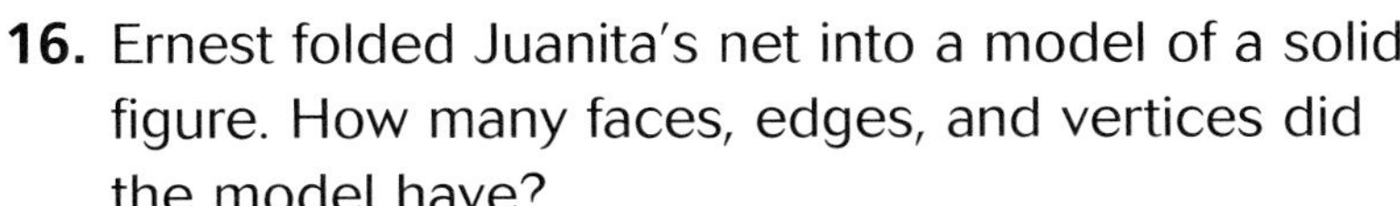

Mixed Review and Test Prep

18. 11×4 (p. 172)

19. 12×7 (p. 172)

20. $60 \div 5$ (p. 172)

21. $99 \div 9$ (p. 172)

22. 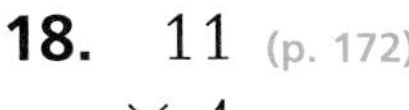 TEST PREP Rename $2\frac{1}{4}$ as a fraction. (p. 458)

A $\frac{3}{4}$

B $\frac{7}{4}$

C $\frac{9}{4}$

D $\frac{21}{4}$

LESSON 3

Estimate and Find Volume of Prisms

Quick Review

1. $4 \times 4 \times 4$
2. $6 \times 2 \times 3$
3. $4 \times 3 \times 2$
4. $5 \times 5 \times 2$
5. $3 \times 6 \times 5$

VOCABULARY

volume **cubic units**

Learn

ORNAMENTAL SHAPES Sarah wants to estimate the amount of sphagnum moss she will need to stuff a wire topiary frame. To estimate, she can think about the volume of the frame.

The measure of the space that a solid figure occupies is called **volume**. Volume is measured in **cubic units**.

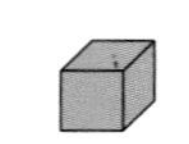

1 cubic unit

Activity

MATERIALS: prism net, scissors, tape, centimeter cubes

Estimate the volume of a box.

STEP 1

Cut out the net. Fold along the lines and tape the sides to make an open box.

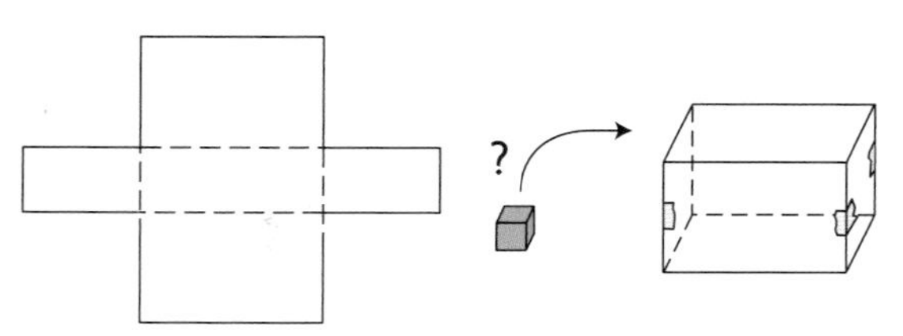

STEP 2

Estimate how many cubes will fit in the box. Record your estimate.

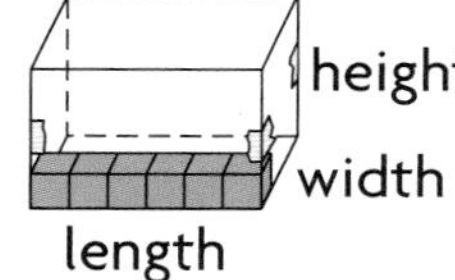

STEP 3

Place as many cubes as you can in the box. Count the cubes you use. Record the number.

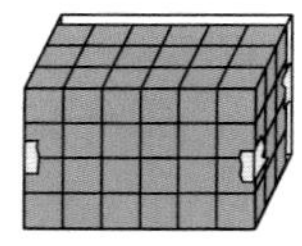

To help you estimate volume, you can picture the number of cubes that will fit along the length, the width, and the height of a prism.

Example Use the centimeter cube to estimate the volume.

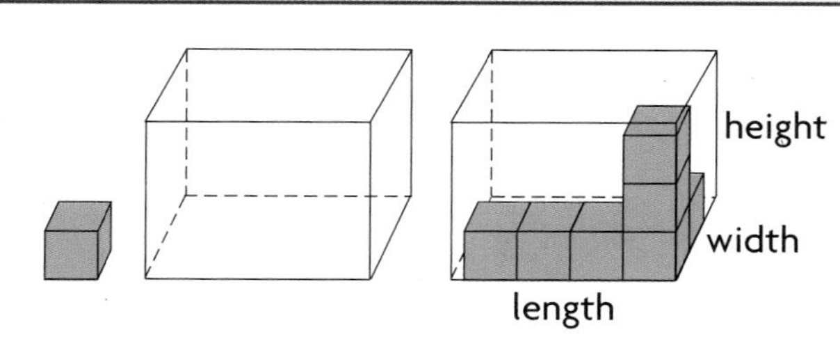

Think: About 4 cubes fit along the length and about 2 cubes fit along the width. So, the bottom layer has about 8 cubes. There are about 3 layers of about 8 cubes each.

3 layers × 8 cubes = 24 cubes

So, the volume is about 24 cubic centimeters.

Find the Volume

Here are two ways to find volume.

One Way

Count the number of cubic units as you build a 6-cube × 2-cube × 3-cube rectangular prism.

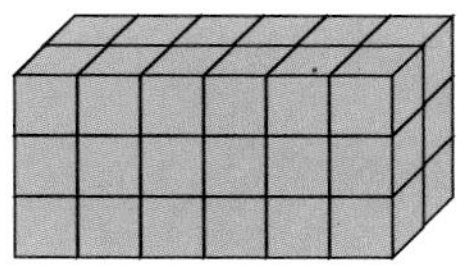

Another Way

Multiply the length, width, and height of the rectangular prism to find the volume in cubic units.

STEP 1

Find the length. Count the number of cubes in one row.

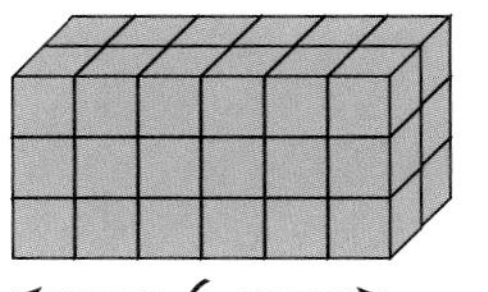

The length is 6 cubes.

STEP 2

Find the width. Count the number of rows in one layer.

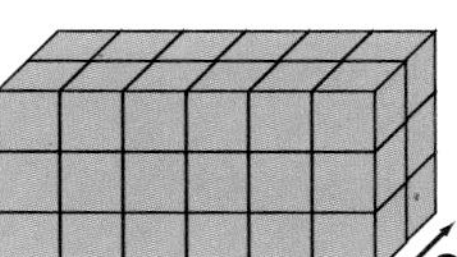

The width is 2 cubes.

STEP 3

Find the height. Count the number of layers in the prism.

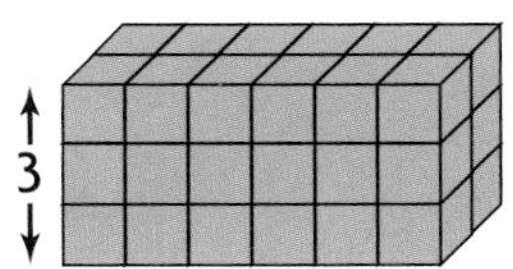

The height is 3 cubes.

STEP 4

Multiply length × width × height to find the volume.

$6 \times 2 \times 3 = 36$

So, the volume is 36 cubic units.

- Does a 2-cube × 1-cube × 3-cube rectangular prism have the same volume as a 3-cube × 2-cube × 1-cube rectangular prism? Build models to explain.

Check

1. **Explain** how you would estimate the number of centimeter cubes you would need to fill a shoebox.
2. **Name** the solid figure that is 2 cubes × 2 cubes × 2 cubes. What is its volume?

Count or multiply to find the volume.

3. 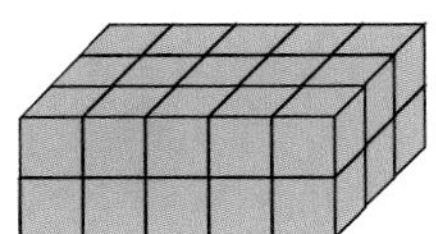
4. 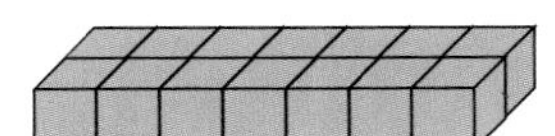
5. 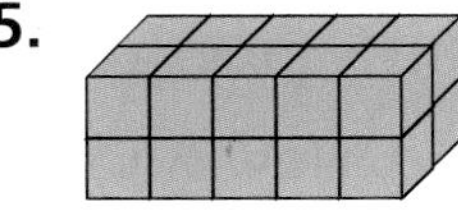

LESSON CONTINUES

Practice and Problem Solving

Extra Practice, page 656, Set C

Find the volume.

6. 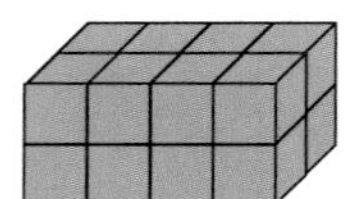

7. 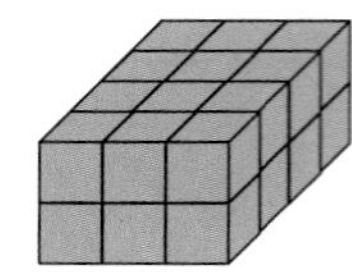

8. 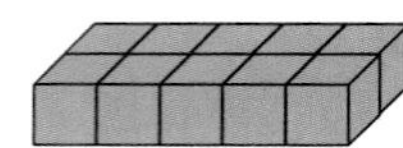

9. 

10. 

11. 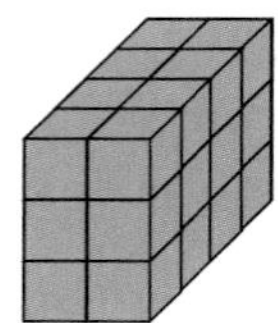

12. 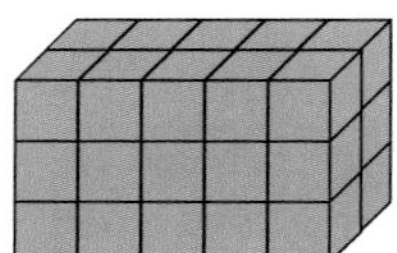

13. 

14. 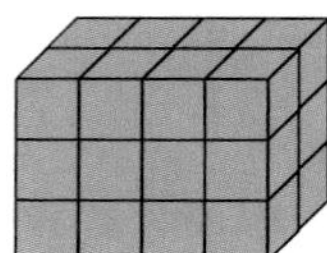

Copy and complete the table.

	LENGTH	WIDTH	HEIGHT (number of layers)	VOLUME (cubic units)
15.	2 in.	6 in.	4 in.	■
16.	10 cm	3 cm	3 cm	■
17.	3 m	7 m	2 m	■
18.	4 ft	■	5 ft	60 cu ft
19.	5 cm	2 cm	■	80 cu cm

20. Maria used centimeter cubes to build a prism that was 3 cubes long, 4 cubes wide, and 5 cubes high. Tyler built a prism that was 5 cubes long, 4 cubes wide, and 3 cubes high. Who used more cubes? Explain.

21. ***FAST FACT*** • **SCIENCE** The weight of 1 cubic yard of sand is about 1.25 tons. Suppose you used 2 cubic yards of sand to make a giant sand castle. About how many tons of sand would you have used?

22. **REASONING** Describe the different ways you can build a rectangular prism with a volume of 8 cubic units.

23. **REASONING** How will the volume change if the height of the prism in Exercise 6 is doubled?

24. **Vocabulary Power** A *cube* is a prism with each side the same length, width, and height. Use this definition to give the dimensions of a cube that has a volume of 1 *cubic yard.*

25. Box A is 3 feet long, 2 feet wide, and 2 feet high. Box B is 2 feet long, 4 feet wide, and 1 feet high. Which box has the greater volume? Explain.

26. **REASONING** How will the volume change if all the dimensions of the prism in Exercise 8 are doubled?

27. Deborah's keepsake trunk is 40 inches long, 19 inches wide, and 17 inches high. What is the volume of her trunk?

28. There were 368 red cubes and 274 blue cubes in a box. Yong used 450 of the cubes to build a prism. How many cubes are left?

29. **REASONING** Explain the difference between a square inch and a cubic inch. Draw a picture of each.

Mixed Review and Test Prep

30. 12×13 (p. 252)

31. 51×32 (p. 252)

32. $45.61 - 43.39$ (p. 592)

33. $278 \div 43$ (p. 320)

34. TEST PREP Hannah divided 456 pennies into 3 equal groups. How much money is in each group? (p. 300)

A $0.52 C $1.52
B $1.18 D $4.53

35. 5,000 cm = ■ m (p. 544)

36. 3 kg = ■ g (p. 548)

37. $45.72 + $2.82 (p. 592)

38. $14.5 + 13 + 5.62$ (p. 588)

39. TEST PREP Which is greater than 5.5? (p. 572)

F 5.16 H 5.61
G 5.09 J 5.49

Problem Solving LINKUP . . . to Science

There are different ways to measure the space inside an object. Look at this fish tank. You can measure its volume and its capacity.

Volume Use centimeter cubes to measure the volume of the fish tank.

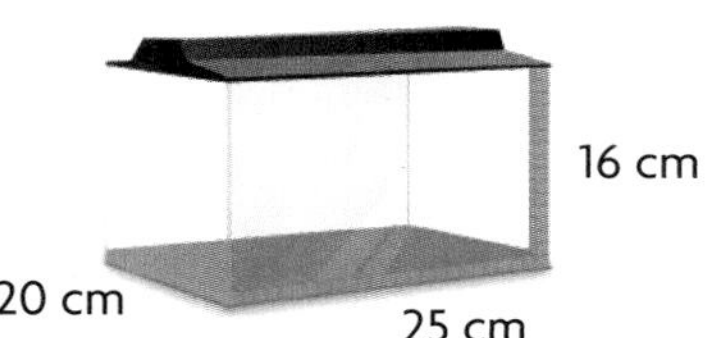

The bottom layer has 500 cubes. There are 16 layers. So, the fish tank has a volume of about 8,000 cubic centimeters.

Capacity Use water in a 1-liter container to measure the capacity of the fish tank.

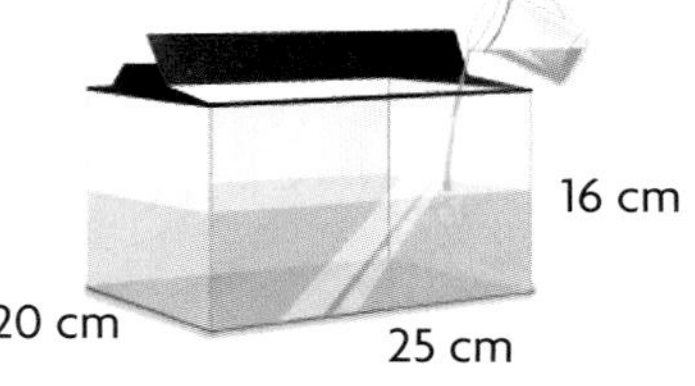

There are about 4 liters of water in the fish tank. It is half full. So, the fish tank has a capacity of about 8 liters.

1. How might you measure the volume of a cake pan? How might you measure its capacity?
2. Describe a situation in which you might need to find the volume of a rectangular prism.
3. Describe a situation in which you might need to find the capacity of a rectangular prism.

Problem Solving Skill
Too Much/Too Little Information

Quick Review

1. $5 \times 8 \times 4$
2. $5 \times 2 \times 6$
3. $3 \times 4 \times 9$
4. $2 \times 1 \times 4$
5. $6 \times 5 \times 4$

UNDERSTAND PLAN SOLVE CHECK

HOW SWEET IT IS! The Sweets Factory packs individually wrapped caramel candies in a 12-inch by 9-inch by 2-inch box. Each box sells for \$2.35, and there are 24 boxes to a case. What is the volume of one box?

- **Decide what the problem asks you to find.**
  The problem asks you to find the volume of one box.
- **Decide what information you need to solve the problem.**
  The length, width, and height of the box are needed.

  volume = length × width × height
- **Read the problem again carefully. Decide if there is too much information or not enough information in the problem.**
  There is too much information. The price of each box and how many boxes in a case are not needed.
- **Solve the problem, if possible.**
  Multiply.
  volume = length × width × height
  volume = $12 \times 9 \times 2$
  volume = 216

So, the volume of the box is 216 cubic inches.

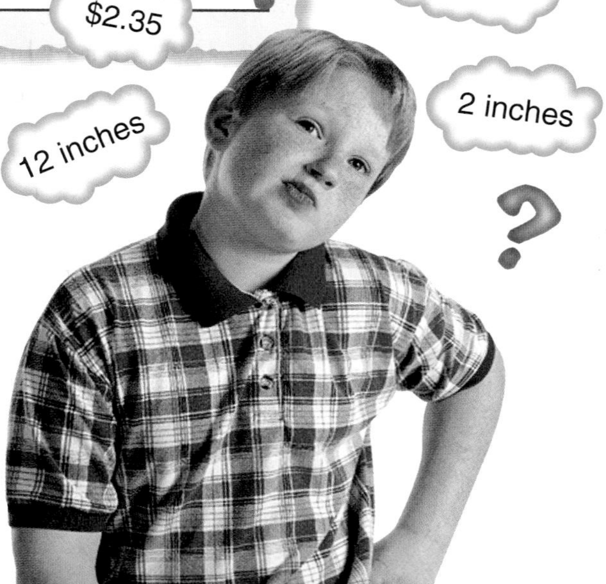

Talk About It

- **What if** the width of the box was not given in the problem above? Would you have too much or too little information to solve the problem? Explain.
- What can happen if there is too much information in a problem?

Problem Solving Practice

Decide if the problem has *too much* or *too little information*. Then solve the problem, if possible.

1. Allison has a drawer that is 33 inches long, 11 inches wide, and 8 inches high. She can fit 10 T-shirts in the drawer. What is the volume of the drawer?

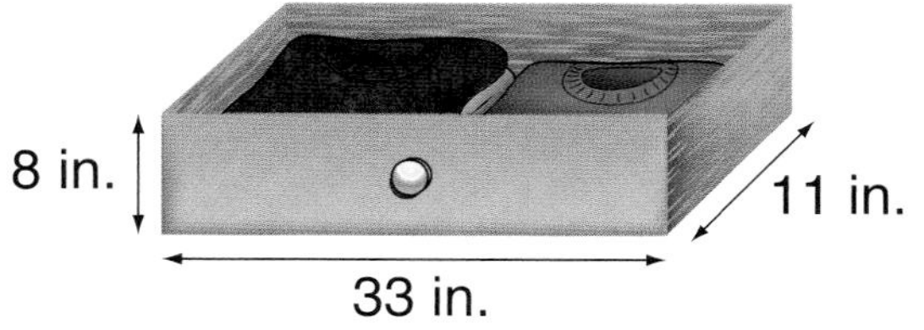

2. Rosa bought 3 CDs for $32.65. She also bought a sweater for $25.50 and a skirt for $19.95. How much did Rosa spend on clothes?

3. Kirk has a suitcase that is 40 inches long and 32 inches wide. What is the volume of his suitcase?

A 5-sided figure has one side that is 12 inches, a second side that is 29 inches, a third side that is 17 inches, and a fourth side that is 35 inches.

4. This problem contains _?_ to find the perimeter of the figure.
   - **A** too much information
   - **B** too little information
   - **C** just enough information
   - **D** none of the above

5. What information do you need to find the perimeter?
   - **F** length of the fifth side
   - **G** length of the sixth side
   - **H** area of the figure
   - **J** None; no information is missing.

Mixed Applications

6. Kim scored 8 goals, and Leticia scored 10 goals. Hillary scored twice as many goals as Kim. How many goals did the three girls score?

7. Together, Terrence and Mike took 24 apples to a picnic. Mike took 6 more apples than Terrence. How many apples did they each take?

8. Austin built a storage box using 5 pieces of wood. It was 2 feet high, 3 feet wide, and 5 feet long. What is the volume of his storage box?

9. The Springside Cafe has 16 tables outside on the patio and 25 tables inside. Each table seats 4 people. How many people can eat at the cafe?

10. Mrs. Fearn has $22.50. She wants to buy 4 pies that each cost $5.65. Does she have enough money? Explain.

11. **Write a problem** that contains too much information.

12. Mr. Kemp wanted to buy a horse for his farm. He drove 125 miles to Florence and then 98 miles to Camden to look at horses. When he returned home he had driven 380 miles. How far did he drive from Camden to his home?

CHAPTER 30

Extra Practice

Set A (pp. 644–647)

Which solid figure do you see in each?

1. 
2. 
3. 
4. 

Write the names of the plane figures that are the faces of each solid figure.

5. 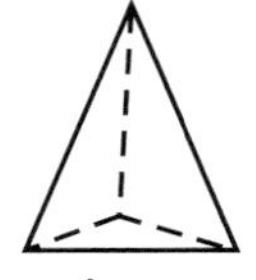
triangular pyramid
6. 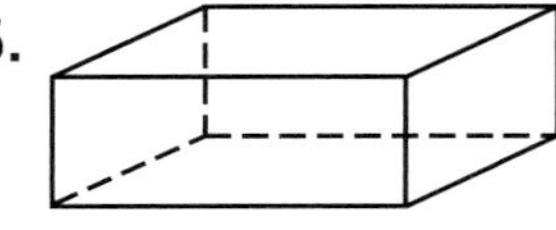
rectangular prism
7. 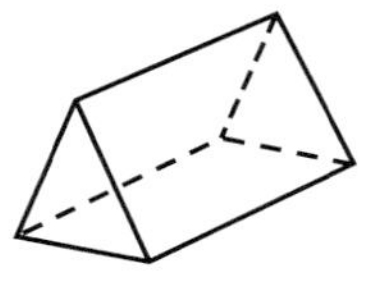
triangular prism
8. 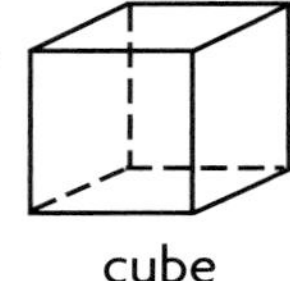
cube

Set B (pp. 648–649)

Write the letter of the figure that is made with each net.

1. 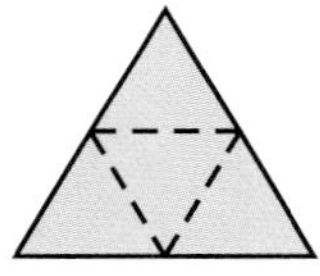
2. 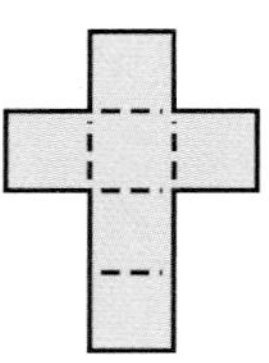
3. 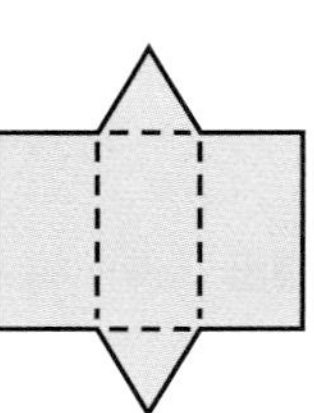
4. 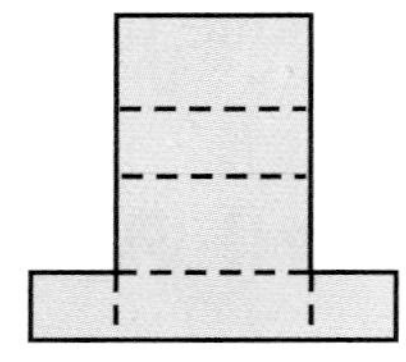

a. 
b. 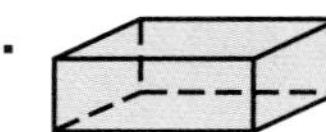
c. 
d. 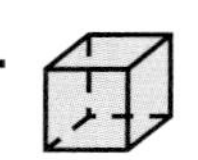

5. Draw a net that when cut and folded will form a square pyramid.

Set C (pp. 650–653)

Find the volume.

1. 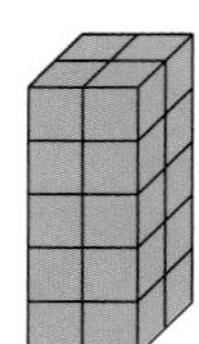
2. 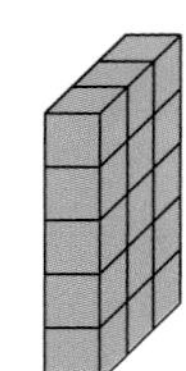
3. 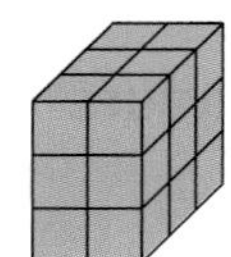
4. 

5. The volume of a rectangular prism is 12 cubic units. Its length is 2 units and its width is 2 units. What is its height?

Review/Test

CHECK VOCABULARY AND CONCEPTS

Choose the best term from the box.

cube
area
volume
square pyramid

1. The measure of the space that a solid figure occupies is called __?__. (p. 650)
2. A __?__ has 5 faces, 8 edges, and 5 vertices. (p. 645)

CHECK SKILLS

Write the letter of the figure that is made with each net. (pp. 648–649)

3. 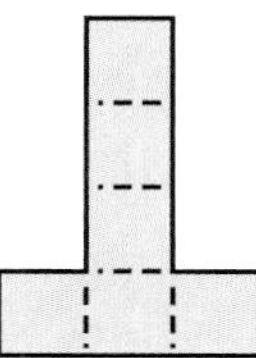

4. 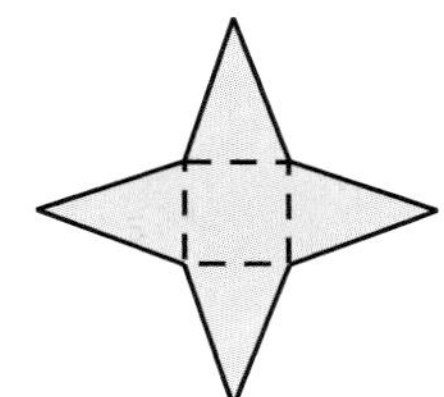

5. 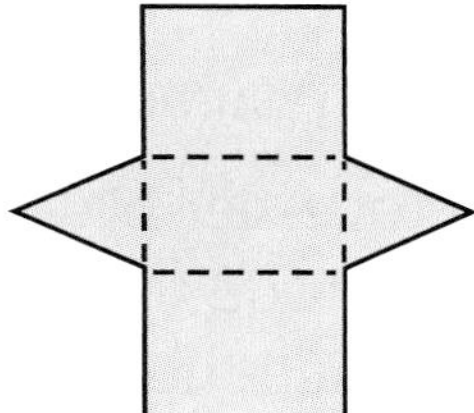

a. 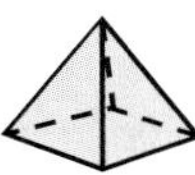

b. 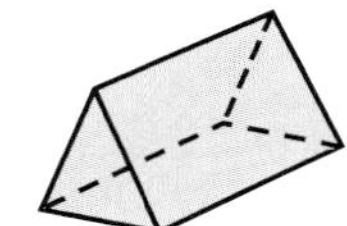

c. 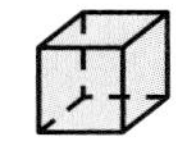

Find the volume. (pp. 650–653)

6. 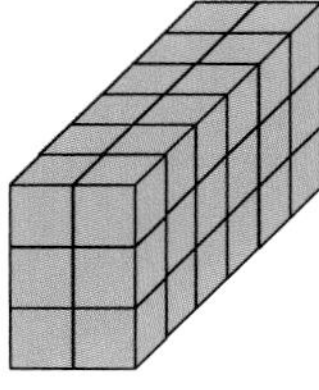

7. 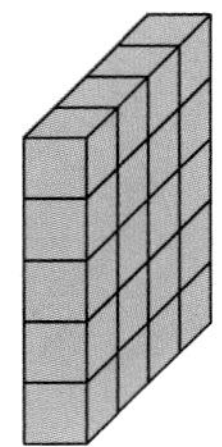

8. 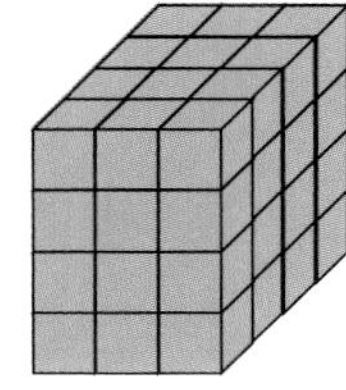

CHECK PROBLEM SOLVING

Decide if the problem has *too much* or *too little information*. Then solve the problem, if possible. (pp. 654–655)

9. Jill has $10.00. She buys a picture frame that is 8 in. long and 5 in. wide for $6.78. How much change does she receive?

10. The delivery truck can hold 2,560 cardboard boxes. The height of the box is 62 cm, and the width of the box is 75 cm. What is the volume of the box?

Standardized Test Prep

NUMBER SENSE, CONCEPTS, AND OPERATIONS

1. Bradley and Erica each ate $\frac{3}{10}$ of a large pizza. Which operations can be used in the circles below to find out how much pizza is left?

$\frac{3}{10} \bullet \frac{3}{10} = \frac{6}{10}$ $\frac{10}{10} \bullet \frac{6}{10} = \frac{4}{10}$

A subtraction, addition

B subtraction, subtraction

C addition, addition

D addition, subtraction

2. Nancy rode her bike 1.8 miles to the park. She rode her bike another 2.5 miles around the bike trail and then she rode back home. Which shows how many miles Nancy rode her bike?

F $1.8 + 1.8 = 3.6$

G $1.8 + 2.5 = 4.3$

H $1.8 + 2.5 + 1.8 = 6.1$

J $1.8 + 2.5 + 2.5 = 6.8$

3. **Explain It** The table below shows the lengths of 3 pieces of string.

LENGTHS OF STRINGS	
String	**Length (in inches)**
A	$1\frac{1}{4}$
B	$2\frac{3}{4}$
C	$3\frac{3}{4}$

Suppose the three pieces of string are laid next to each other, end to end. ESTIMATE the total length of the strings to the nearest inch. Explain how you decided.

MEASUREMENT

4. Which rectangular prism has a volume of 12 cubic units?

A

C

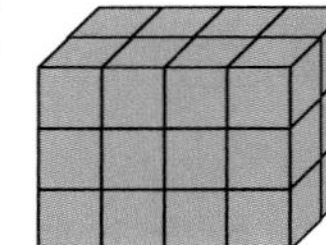

B

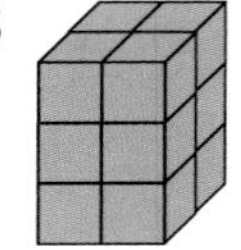

D

5. Conley is helping his little brother put away his building blocks. Each block is 1 cubic inch. How many building blocks will fit in the box shown?

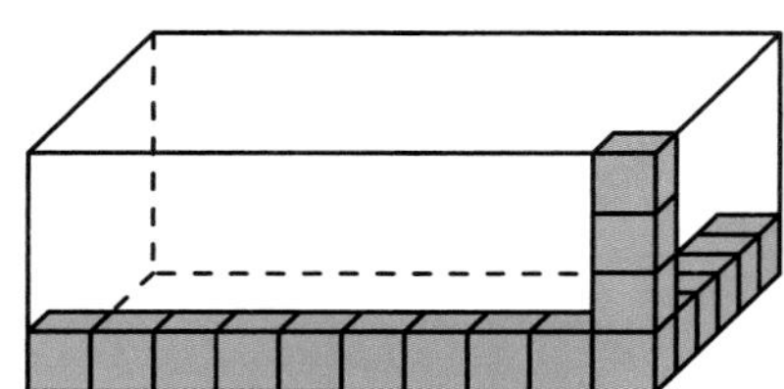

F 60

G 150

H 240

J 320

6. **Explain It** The tissue box has the shape of a cube. ESTIMATE in cubic centimeters the volume of the tissue box.

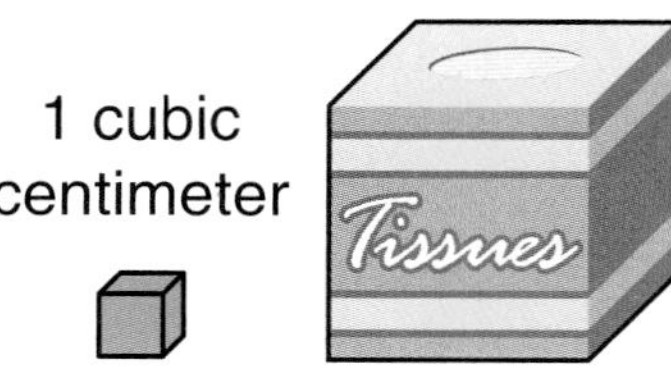

Explain how you decided.

GEOMETRY AND SPATIAL SENSE

7. How many vertices does this square pyramid have?

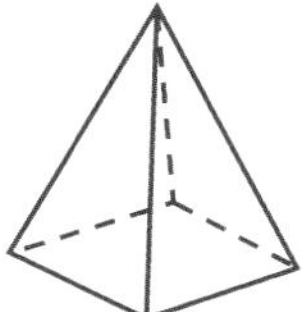

A 8

B 6

C 5

D 4

TIP **Decide on a plan.** See item 8. Study the solid figure. Then use what you know about nets of solid figures to solve the problem.

8. Which of these groups of plane figures shows all the faces of the solid figure below?

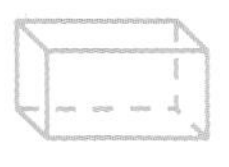

F

G

H

J

9. Explain It Draw a solid figure that has no faces. Explain why you drew the solid figure you did.

ALGEBRAIC THINKING

10. The fourth-grade class is having a party. Alex volunteered to bring plastic cups. Which equation shows the relationship of the number of packages to the number of cups shown in the table below?

Number of Packages, p	1	2	3	4	5
Number of Cups, c	12	24	36	48	60

A $c \times 12 = p$

B $p \times 12 = c$

C $c + 12 = p$

D $p + 12 = c$

11. What is the solution of the equation $7 + p = 9$?

F 1

G 2

H 3

J 4

12. Explain It This table represents the cost of pizzas at Pizza Palace.

PRICE LIST	
Number	**Cost**
1	$9
2	$18
3	$27
4	■
5	■

Copy and complete the table. Explain how the cost of pizzas changes as the number of pizzas changes.

IT'S IN THE BAG

Matchbook Solid Figures

PROJECT Make a "matchbook" holder to show different views of a solid figure.

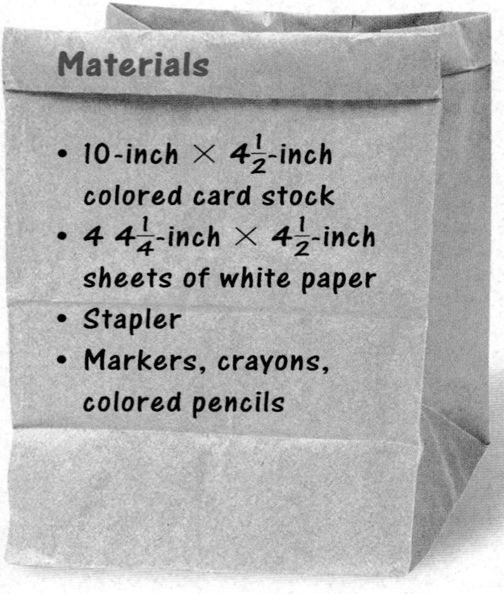

Materials
• 10-inch × $4\frac{1}{2}$-inch colored card stock
• 4 $4\frac{1}{4}$-inch × $4\frac{1}{2}$-inch sheets of white paper
• Stapler
• Markers, crayons, colored pencils

Directions

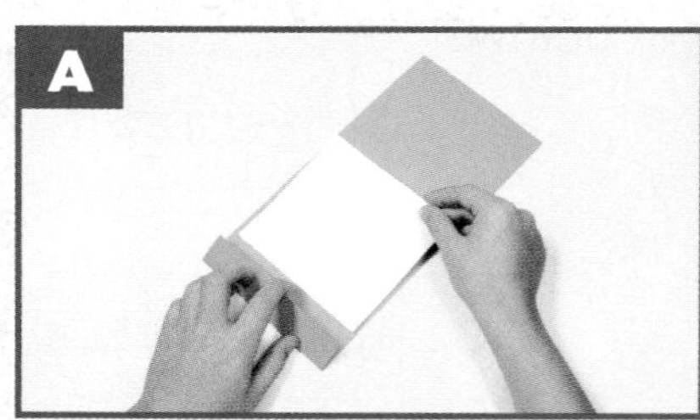

1. Hold the card stock vertically and fold up the bottom 1 inch. Slide the sheets of white paper into the folded edge. Staple the edge, close to the bottom. *(Picture A)*

2. Fold the top down to about $\frac{1}{2}$ inch from the bottom. To close, tuck the top into the folded pocket. *(Picture B)*

3. Draw a different view of a solid figure on three sheets of white paper. Draw a top view, front view, and side view. On the fourth sheet, draw the solid figure. *(Picture C)*

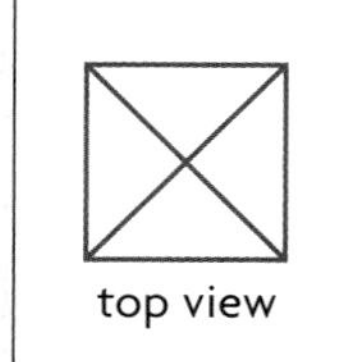

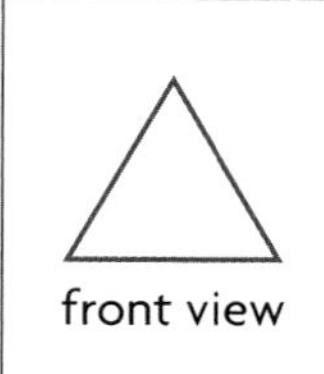

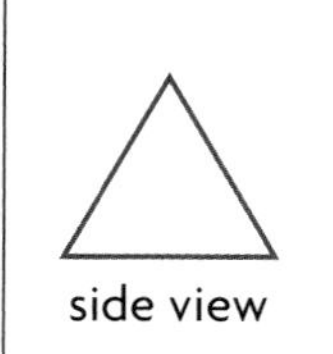

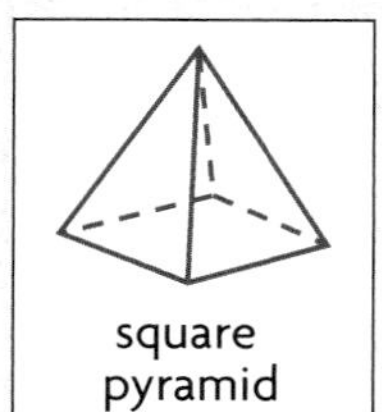

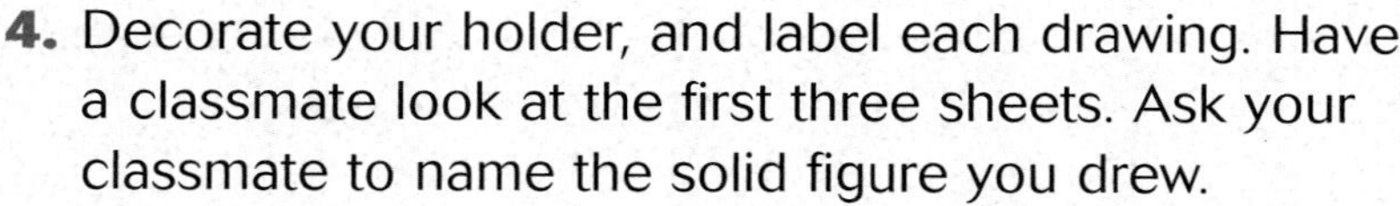

4. Decorate your holder, and label each drawing. Have a classmate look at the first three sheets. Ask your classmate to name the solid figure you drew.

Challenge

Explore Surface Area of Prisms

Ashley and Antonio are painting a box to use as scenery for their class play. The box is 4 feet long, 3 feet wide, and 6 feet high. The directions on the can of paint say it will cover 40 square feet. How many cans of paint will they need?

They can find the surface area of the box to decide how many cans of paint to buy. **Surface area** is the sum of the areas of the faces of a solid figure. Because surface area measures two dimensions, it is measured in square units.

STEP 1

Draw a net on grid paper. Label the faces *A*–*F*.

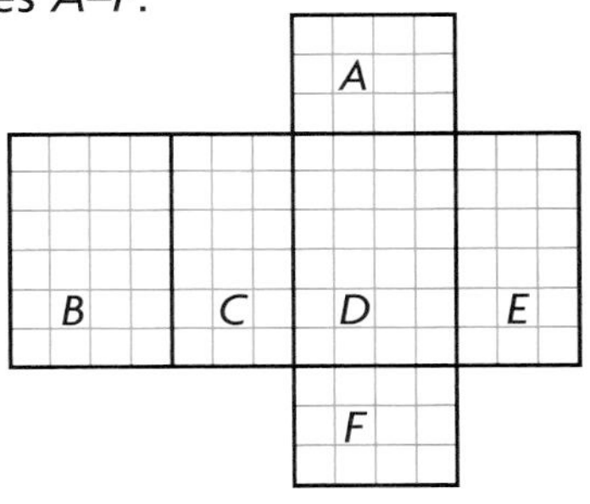

STEP 2

Use the formula for the area of a rectangle to find the area of each face.

$A = l \times w$

face A: $A = 4 \times 3 = 12$
face B: $A = 4 \times 6 = 24$
face C: $A = 3 \times 6 = 18$
face D: $A = 4 \times 6 = 24$
face E: $A = 3 \times 6 = 18$
face F: $A = 4 \times 3 = 12$

STEP 3

Add the areas of the faces to find the total surface area.

$12 + 24 + 18 + 24 + 18 + 12 = 108$

STEP 4

Divide the total surface area by the area each can of paint will cover.

$108 \div 40 = 2$ r28

Since 2 cans of paint will not cover 108 square feet, 1 more can is needed to cover the remaining 28 square feet. So, Ashley and Antonio need 3 cans of paint.

Try It

Use the net to find the area of each face. Then find the surface area of each prism.

1.

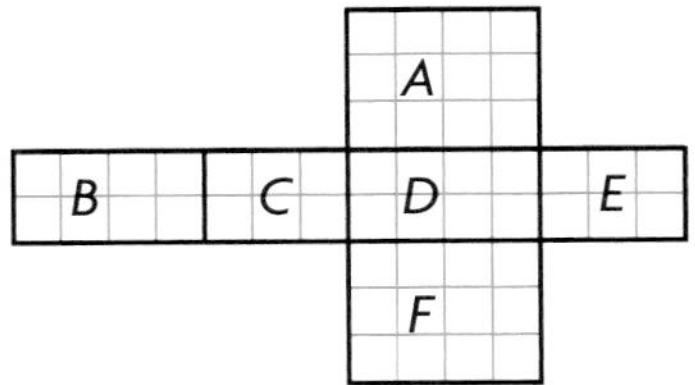

2.

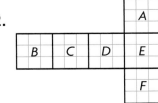

A
B C D E
F

UNIT 9

Study Guide and Review

VOCABULARY

Choose the best term from the box.

perimeter
area
solid figure
volume

1. When you find the distance around a figure, you are finding the ?. (p. 612)
2. When you find the number of square units needed to cover a surface, you are finding the ?. (p. 628)
3. The measure of the space a solid figure occupies is called ?. (p. 650)

STUDY AND SOLVE

Chapter 28

Find the perimeter.

Find the perimeter.

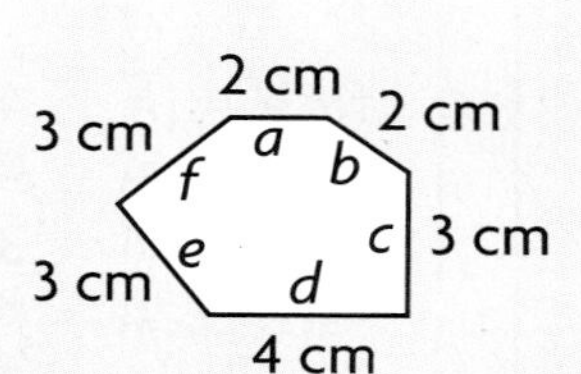

P = sum of the length of the sides

$P = a + b + c + d + e + f$

$P = 2 + 2 + 3 + 4 + 3 + 3$

$P = 17$

So, the perimeter is 17 cm.

Find the perimeter. (pp. 612–617)

4.

5. 22 in. 11 in.

6.

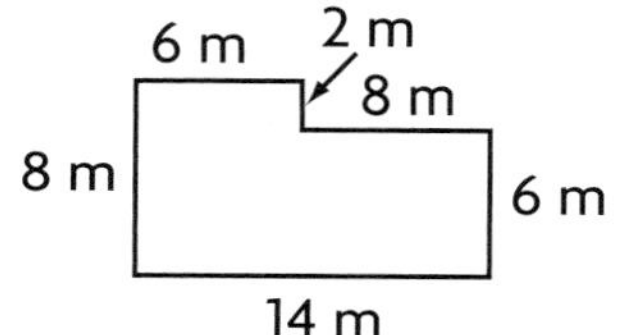

Estimate circumference.

The circumference of a circle is about 3 times the diameter of the circle.

8 yd

Diameter: 8 yd

THINK: $8 \times 3 = 24$

So, the circumference is about 24 yd.

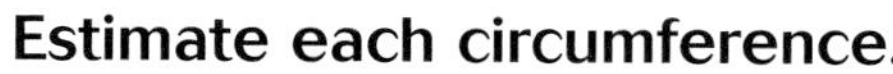

Estimate each circumference. (pp. 618–619)

7.

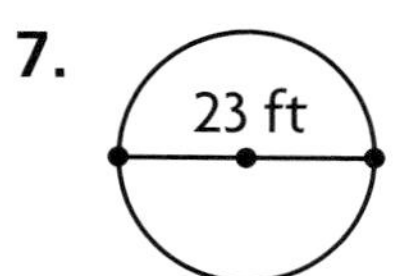

8.

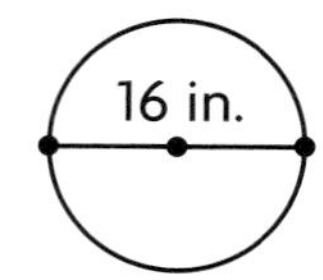

9. Diameter: 33 m

10. Diameter: 12 mi

Chapter 29

Find the area.

Area = length × width

Use the formula to find the area.

$A = l \times w$

$A = 12 \times 9$

$A = 108$

So, the area is 108 sq ft.

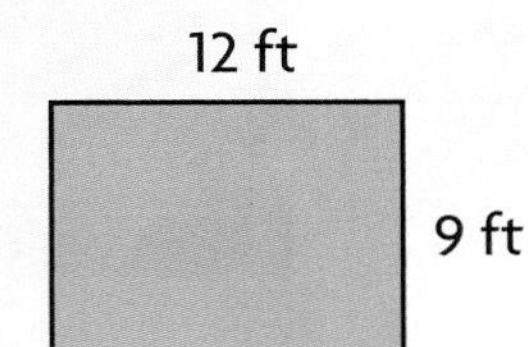

Find the area. (pp. 630–633)

11.

12.

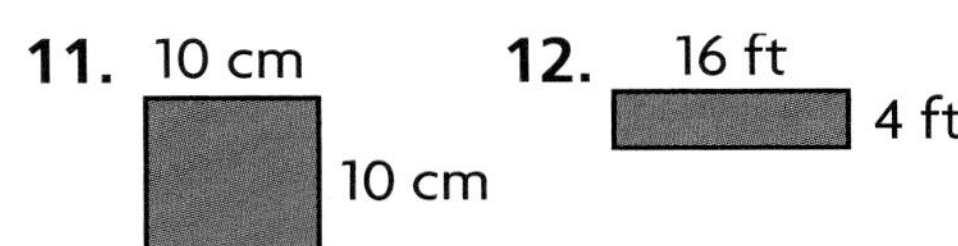

13.

14.

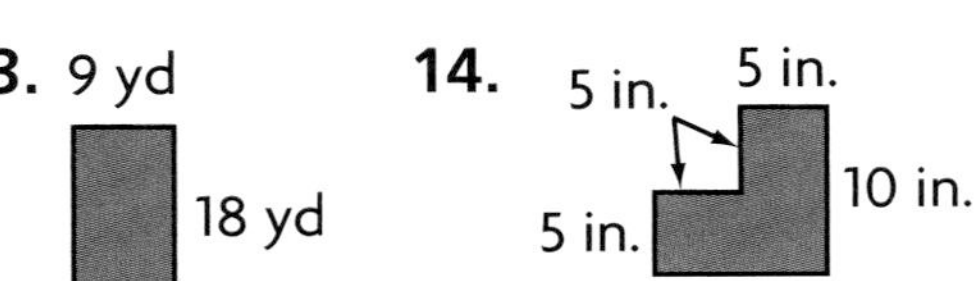

Chapter 30

Find the volume of rectangular prisms.

Find the volume.

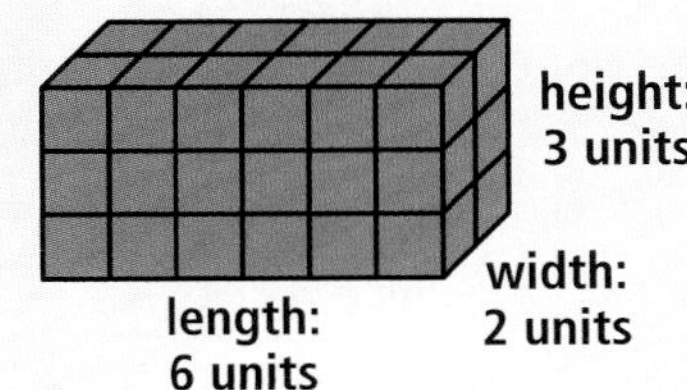

Method 1: Count the number of cubic units in the prism: 36 cubic units.

Method 2: Multiply length × width × height.
6 cubes × 2 cubes × 3 cubes = 36
Volume: 36 cubic units

For 15–17, use the figure.

(pp. 644–647, 650–653)

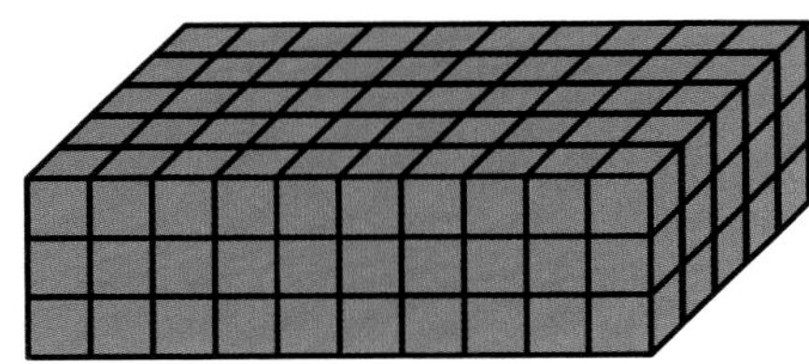

15. Name the solid figure.

16. How many faces, edges, and vertices does this solid figure have?

17. What is the volume?

18. Mrs. Jost has a box that is 12 inches by 8 inches by 14 inches. What is the volume of her box?

PROBLEM SOLVING PRACTICE

Solve. (pp. 620–621, 636–637)

19. John wants to make a triangle that has a perimeter of 26 inches. He drew two sides of the triangle as 8 inches and 10 inches. What is the length of the third side of John's triangle?

20. Elisa has a deck that is 20 feet long by 7 feet wide on the back of her house. If she doubles the width of her deck, how will the perimeter and area of her deck change?

PERFORMANCE ASSESSMENT

TASK A • HOUSE ADDITION

The Millers plan to build an addition onto their home. The addition will be 12 feet by 18 feet and will include a bedroom, bath, and closet.

a. Decide how large the bedroom, bath, and closet could be. Then draw a diagram of this floor plan. Write the lengths and widths in feet of the three rooms on your diagram.

b. The Millers will put carpet in the bedroom and in the closet. How many square feet of carpet will they need for these two rooms of your floor plan?

c. In the bedroom and the bath, they will put a wallpaper border on the walls just below the ceiling. How many feet of border will they need for your floor plan?

TASK B • BOX IT!

MATERIALS: centimeter cubes, 1-centimeter grid paper

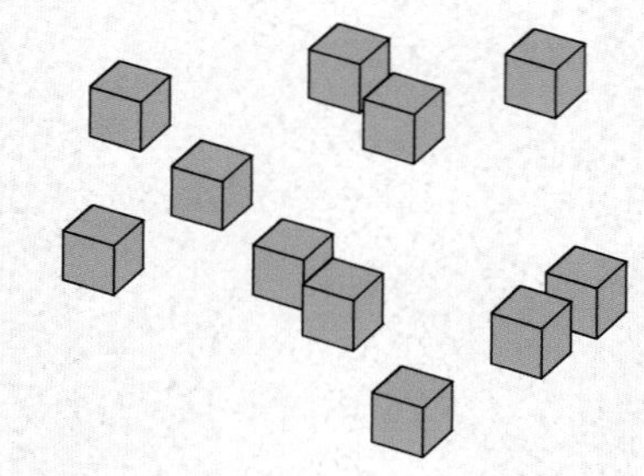

Marta wants a rectangular-shaped box that will hold exactly 12 centimeter cubes.

a. On grid paper, draw a net for a rectangular prism that would hold 12 centimeter cubes. Cut it out and tape it together to make a box. What are the length, width, and height of the box?

b. Draw nets and make boxes for different rectangular prisms that can hold exactly 12 centimeter cubes. Copy and complete the table at the right.

c. Suppose Marta wants to fill a box that will hold exactly 16 centimeter cubes. If each side is measured in whole centimeters, how many different boxes can she make? Give the length, width, and height of each box.

BOXES THAT HOLD EXACTLY 12 CENTIMETER CUBES		
Length	Width	Height

Find Perimeter and Area of Rectangles

You can use formulas in a spreadsheet program to find the perimeter and area of different rectangles. The lengths and widths of three rectangles are shown in the spreadsheet below.

- Enter in a spreadsheet the data shown.

	A	B	C	D
1	Length (in cm)	Width (in cm)	Perimeter (in cm)	Area (in sq cm)
2	4	3		
3	6	9		
4	8	12		

- Click in cell C2 under Perimeter, and enter this formula: =2*A2+2*B2. On a spreadsheet, * means multiplication.
- Press *Enter* on your keyboard to move to the next cell to the right. The perimeter will then appear in cell C2.
- Click in cell D2, under Area, and enter this formula: =A2*B2.
- Press *Enter*. The area will then appear in cell D2.
- Highlight each of the perimeter and area cells one at a time, click on *Edit* in the toolbar, select *Fill*, and then select *Down*.

	A	B	C	D
1	Length (in cm)	Width (in cm)	Perimeter (in cm)	Area (in sq cm)
2	4	3	14	12
3	6	9	30	54
4	8	12	40	96

Practice and Problem Solving

Use a spreadsheet program to find the perimeter and area.

1. Length = 16 in.
Width = 7 in.

2. Length = 7 in.
Width = 6 in.

3. Length = 12 in.
Width = 5 in.

4. Length = 8 in.
Width = 9 in.

5. Length = 4 in.
Width = 9 in.

6. Length = 14 in.
Width = 6 in.

Multimedia Math Glossary www.harcourtschool.com/mathglossary

Vocabulary Power Look up *formula* in the Multimedia Math Glossary. Explain how to use the formula $A = l \times w$ to find the area of a rectangle.

▲ Mound B has a steep ramp that is 58 feet high.

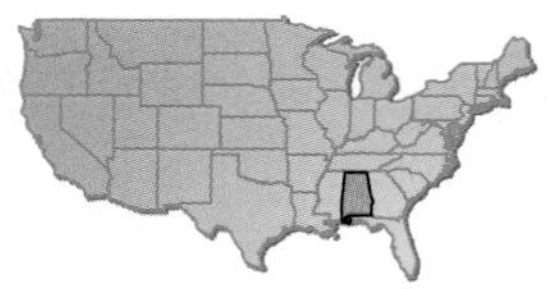

MOUNDVILLE ARCHAEOLOGICAL PARK

About 800 years ago, the town of Moundville in Alabama was the largest city in North America. Today, archaeologists are learning about the Indians who lived there by digging for things that give clues about their past.

USE DATA For 1–2, use the map of Moundville.

1. Estimate the area of the site. Each square unit equals about 48,400 sq ft.
2. **STRETCH YOUR THINKING** The town was almost square. Fences protected it on three sides. The fourth side overlooked the Black Warrior River. Estimate the perimeter of the site. Explain how you decided.
3. Mound A is almost in the center of the great plaza. It measures about 110 feet by 55 feet. Find the perimeter and area of Mound A.
4. Look at the photograph of Mound B. The mound looks like what solid figure? Name the plane figures found in the faces of the solid figure.

▼ This map shows the locations of more than 20 mounds. The nobles' homes were on the larger mounds.

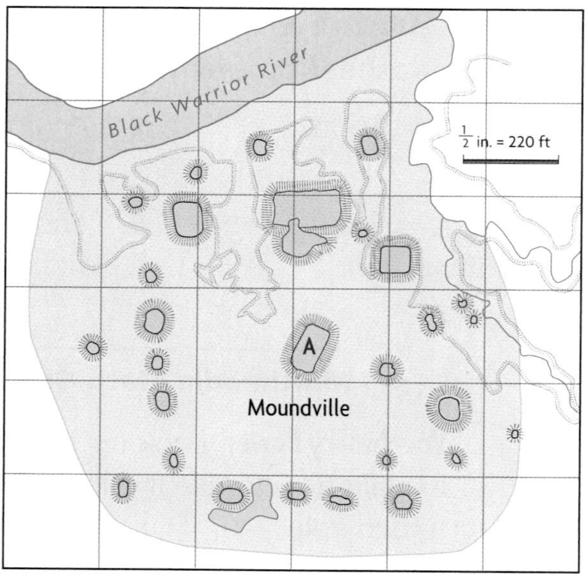

ARTIFACTS FOUND AT MOUNDVILLE

Many types of artifacts, including animal bones and pottery, have been discovered at Moundville. The people of Moundville were famous for their skill in making pottery and in working with stone and copper.

USE DATA For 1–2, use the photograph of the ear spool.

1. Use a string and a ruler to find the diameter and the circumference of the ear spool.
2. Suppose a museum worker wants to store the ear spool in a box.
   a. What size will the box need to be? Explain.
   b. Draw a net of the box.
   c. Find the volume of the box.
3. A museum worker has a collection of artifacts. He would like to keep the collection together in the same box. Look at his diagram of the box he designed. Each section is 2 inches high.
   a. What size artifact can he store in section A? in section B? in section C?
   b. What is the volume of the box?

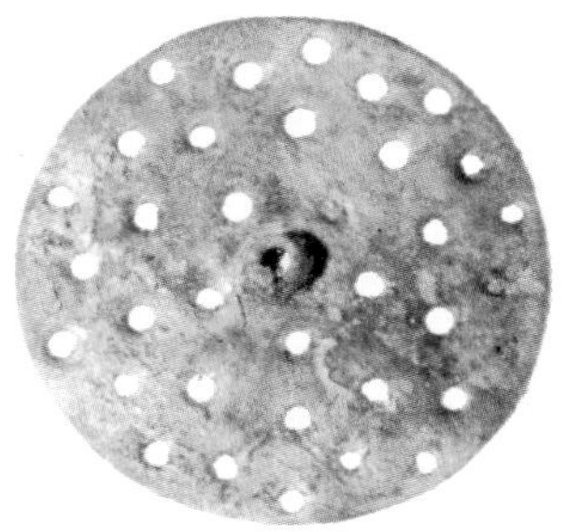

▲ **This piece of copper jewelry is called an ear spool.**

$4\frac{1}{2}$ in. $4\frac{1}{2}$ in. 9 in.
3 in. A
3 in. C
3 in. B
3 in.

▼ **These artifacts of pottery, stoneware, and copper are from Moundville.**

▲ **Visitors can walk along a half-mile nature trail. The boardwalk trail rises from ground level to the tops of the trees!**

STUDENT HANDBOOK

PREREQUISITE SKILLS REVIEW Do you have the math skills needed to start a new chapter? Use this list of skills to review and remember your skills.

USA
Spay
Neuter
37
Teddy Bears USA 37

TROUBLESHOOTING

BENCHMARK NUMBERS

Numbers that help you estimate a number of objects without counting are **benchmark numbers**. Any useful number can be a benchmark.

Example

The first box contains 100 straws. Choose the best estimate for the number of straws in the second box.

Think: The number of straws in the second box is a little less than in the first box.

So, a good estimate is 60.

▶ Practice

Choose the best estimate for the second set of objects.

1. 20

10 40 70

2. 60

30 50 90

READ AND WRITE NUMBERS TO THOUSANDS

Use a place-value chart to read and write numbers to thousands. Numbers can be written in word form and in standard form.

Example

Write nine thousand, forty-eight in standard form.

Thousands	Hundreds	Tens	Ones
9,	0	4	8

- Write 9 in the thousands place.
- Write a 0 in the hundreds place.
- Write 4 in the tens and 8 in the ones place.

So, the number is 9,048 in standard form.

▶ Practice

Write each number in standard form.

1. six thousand, one hundred forty-four

2. eight hundred three

3. seven thousand, fifty-one

4. nine hundred ninety-nine

PLACE VALUE TO THOUSANDS

The value of a digit depends on its place in a number.
A place-value chart can help you to find the value.

Example

Tell the value of the digits 4 and 5 in 4,325.

Thousands	Hundreds	Tens	Ones
4,	3	2	5

- The 4 is in the thousands place. So, it has a value of $4 \times 1{,}000$, or 4,000.
- The 5 is in the ones place. So, it has a value of 5×1, or 5.

▶ Practice

Write the value of the blue digit.

1. 2,317 **2.** 8,002 **3.** 5,681 **4.** 1,947

5. 2,508 **6.** 7,095 **7.** 9,462 **8.** 4,723

PLACE VALUE TO MILLIONS

You can use a place-value chart to find the value of a digit in a greater number.

Example

Write the value of the digits 3 and 8 in 3,682,901.

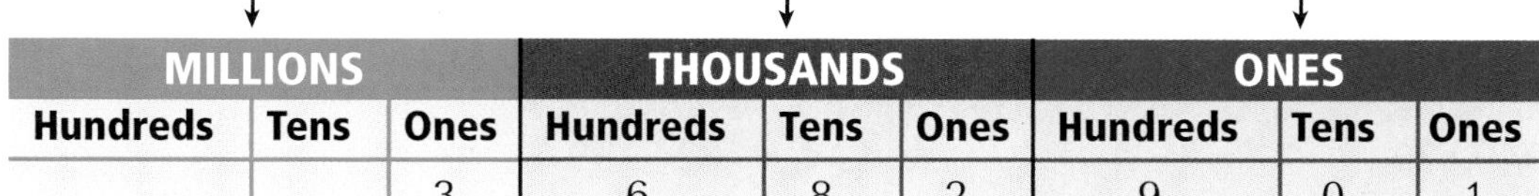

MILLIONS			THOUSANDS			ONES		
Hundreds	Tens	Ones	Hundreds	Tens	Ones	Hundreds	Tens	Ones
		3,	6	8	2,	9	0	1

- The 3 is in the millions place.
  So, it has a value of $3 \times 1{,}000{,}000$, or 3,000,000.
- The 8 is in the ten-thousands place.
  So, it has a value of $8 \times 10{,}000$, or 80,000.

▶ Practice

Write the value of the blue digit.

1. 75,340 **2.** 1,892,300 **3.** 524,160 **4.** 92,450

5. 6,000,910 **6.** 924,750 **7.** 3,928,325 **8.** 4,592,023

TROUBLESHOOTING

ROUND TO TENS AND HUNDREDS

To round to the tens or hundreds place, look at the digit to the right of the rounding place. If the digit is less than 5, the digit in the rounding place stays the same. If the digit is 5 or more, the digit in the rounding place increases by 1.

Examples

A Round 724 to the nearest ten.

Think: The digit in the rounding place is 2. The digit to its right is 4. Since $4 < 5$, the tens digit stays the same.

So, 724 rounds to 720.

B Round 2,851 to the nearest hundred.

Think: The digit in the rounding place is 8. The digit to its right is 5. Since $5 = 5$, the hundreds digit increases by 1.

So, 2,851 rounds to 2,900.

▶ Practice

Round each number to the nearest ten.

1. 694 **2.** 126 **3.** 439 **4.** 322

Round each number to the nearest hundred.

5. 9,127 **6.** 1,035 **7.** 2,665 **8.** 7,251

ROUND TO MILLIONS

To round greater numbers, follow the same steps you use to round lesser numbers.

Rounding Rules

- Look at the digit to the right of the digit in the rounding place.
- If the digit is less than 5, the digit in the rounding place stays the same.
- If the digit is 5 or more, the digit in the rounding place increases by 1.

Examples

Round each number to the place value of the blue digit.

A 68,340,570

Think: The digit in the rounding place is 8. The digit to its right is 3. Since $3 < 5$, the digit in the millions place stays the same.

So, 68,340,570 rounds to 68,000,000.

B 824,799

Think: The digit in the rounding place is 4. The digit to its right is 7. Since $7 > 5$, the digit in the thousands place increases by 1.

So, 824,799 rounds to 825,000.

▶ Practice

Round each number to the place value of the blue digit.

1. 32,750 **2.** 926,533 **3.** 8,235 **4.** 1,340,816

5. 43,504,900 **6.** 7,825,392 **7.** 8,283,293 **8.** 28,929,830

ORDER NUMBERS TO THOUSANDS

You order numbers by comparing digits in the same place-value position.

Write the numbers in order from *least* to *greatest*. 3,962; 3,978; 3,899

STEP 1	STEP 2	STEP 3
Compare the thousands.	Compare the hundreds.	Compare the tens.
3,962 3,978 3,899	3,962 3,978 3,899	3,962 3,978
same number of thousands	8 < 9, so 3,899 is least.	6 < 7, so 3,978 is greatest.

So, the order from *least* to *greatest* is 3,899; 3,962; 3,978.

▶ Practice

Write the numbers in order from *least* to *greatest*.

1. 5,478; 5,576; 4,589 **2.** 3,275; 2,854; 3,189 **3.** 1,746; 978; 1,066

Write the numbers in order from *greatest* to *least*.

4. 6,734; 6,546; 6,874 **5.** 743; 7,341; 7,431 **6.** 3,601; 3,610; 3,106

2-DIGIT ADDITION AND SUBTRACTION

The **sum** is the total of two or more addends. The **difference** is the amount left after one number is subtracted from another.

Find the sum. 87 + 46 = ▢

STEP 1

Add the ones. 7 + 6 = 13

Regroup 13 ones as 1 ten 3 ones.

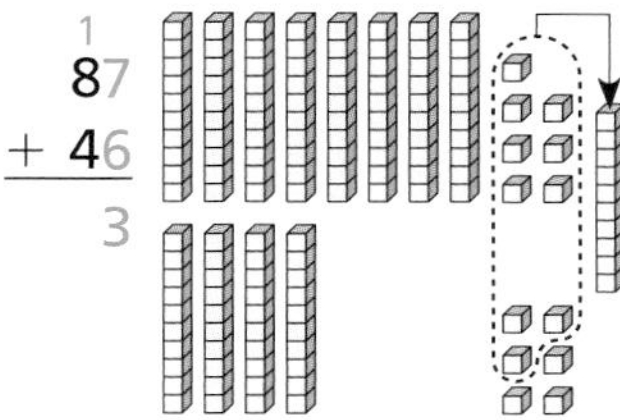

STEP 2

Add the tens. 1 + 8 + 4 = 13

Regroup 13 tens as 1 hundred 3 tens.

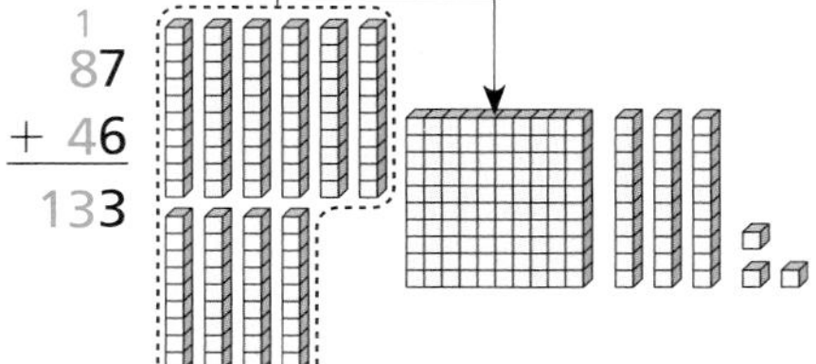

▶ Practice

Find the sum or difference.

1. 31 + 79

2. 92 − 24

3. 55 + 85

4. 40 + 16

5. 73 − 37

TROUBLESHOOTING

✓ MISSING ADDENDS

A missing addend can be found when one addend and the sum are known.

Examples

Find the missing addend.

A 9 + ■ = 16
Think: 9 + [What number?] = 16
So, the missing addend is 7.

B ■ + 6 = 14
Think: [What number?] + 6 = 14
So, the missing addend is 8.

▶ Practice

Find the missing addend.

1. 7 + ■ = 11 **2.** ■ + 5 = 12 **3.** ■ + 8 = 13 **4.** 2 + ■ = 8

5. 2 + ■ = 20 **6.** ■ + 17 = 23 **7.** ■ + 13 = 22 **8.** 5 + ■ = 18

✓ ADDITION WITH THREE ADDENDS

To find the sum of more than two addends, look for ways to group the addends so that the addition is easier.

Examples

Find the sum.

A 4 + 8 + 6
(4 + 6) + 8 — Look for a 10. 4 + 6 = 10
10 + 8 — Add.
18
So, 4 + 8 + 6 = 18.

B 5 + 7 + 7
(7 + 7) + 5 — Look for a double. 7 + 7 = 14
14 + 5 — Add.
19
So, 5 + 7 + 7 = 19.

▶ Practice

Find the sum.

1. 8 + 2 + 3 **2.** 3 + 3 + 9 **3.** 6 + 3 + 7 **4.** 6 + 4 + 4

5. 5 + 6 + 5 **6.** 6 + 5 + 6 **7.** 8 + 9 + 2 **8.** 1 + 8 + 9

9. 8 + 8 + 9 **10.** 1 + 9 + 9 **11.** 2 + 7 + 2 **12.** 2 + 8 + 4

ADDITION AND SUBTRACTION FACT FAMILIES

The fact families for addition and subtraction can have either two or four number sentences.

Examples

A An addition family with two different addends has four related facts. This fact family is for 3, 4, and 7.

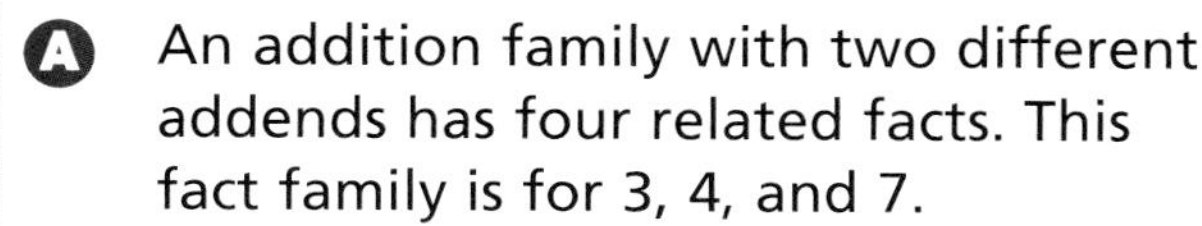

$3 + 4 = 7$ $7 - 3 = 4$

$4 + 3 = 7$ $7 - 4 = 3$

B An addition family with the same addends has only two related facts. This fact family is for 5, 5, and 10.

$5 + 5 = 10$

$10 - 5 = 5$

▶ Practice

Find the missing numbers.

1. 2 + 6 = 8
6 + 2 = ■
8 − 2 = ■
8 − ■ = 2

2. 5 + 7 = 12
7 + 5 = ■
12 − 7 = ■
■ − 5 = 7

3. 8 + 8 = ■
16 − 8 = ■

4. 9 + 4 = 13
4 + ■ = 13
13 − 4 = ■
13 − 9 = ■

5. 5 + 9 = 14
14 − 9 = ■

6. 3 + 8 = 11
11 − 3 = ■

7. 6 + 8 = 14
14 − 6 = ■

8. 9 + 9 = 18
18 − ■ = ■

NUMBER PATTERNS

A list of numbers can show a number pattern.

Examples

Write the next three possible numbers in the pattern.

A 14, 24, 34, 44, ■, ■, ■

Think: Skip-count by tens.

$44 + 10 = 54$ $54 + 10 = 64$ $64 + 10 = 74$

So, the next three numbers could be 54, 64, and 74.

B 20, 18, 16, 14, ■, ■, ■

Think: Count back by twos.

$14 - 2 = 12$ $12 - 2 = 10$ $10 - 2 = 8$

So, the next three numbers could be 12, 10, and 8.

▶ Practice

Write the next three possible numbers in the pattern.

1. 17, 20, 23, 26, ■, ■, ■

2. 14, 21, 28, 35, ■, ■, ■

3. 15, 21, 27, 33, ■, ■, ■

4. 78, 74, 70, 66, ■, ■, ■

5. 37, 32, 27, 22, ■, ■, ■

6. 34, 37, 40, 43, ■, ■, ■

TROUBLESHOOTING

✓ READ PICTOGRAPHS

Pictographs show data by using pictures. The **key** at the bottom of a pictograph tells how many items each picture stands for. This pictograph shows the numbers of bushels of apples picked.

Example

How many more bushels of Granny Smith apples were picked than of Delicious apples?

Think: Skip-count by 5s to find the number of Granny Smith apples and Delicious apples. Then subtract.

35 − 25 = 10

So, 10 more bushels of Granny Smith apples were picked.

BUSHELS OF APPLES	
Cortland	
Delicious	
Granny Smith	

Key: Each [apple] = 5 bushels.

▶ Practice

For 1–2, use the pictograph.

1. In all, how many bushels of Cortland and Granny Smith apples were picked?
2. Were there two more bushels of Delicious apples picked than Cortland apples? Explain.

✓ TALLIES TO FREQUENCY TABLES

Tally marks show numbers of things counted in groups of five. You can skip-count to find a total.

KINDS OF SHIRTS	
Kind	**Number**
Striped	𝍸 𝍸 II
Solid	𝍸 𝍸 𝍸 I
Flowered	𝍸 I

A **frequency table** uses numbers to show how often something happens.

KINDS OF SHIRTS	
Kind	**Number**
Striped	12
Solid	16
Flowered	6

▶ Practice

Use the tally table to complete the frequency table at the right.

	FLOWER SALES	
	Type	**Number**
1.	Irises	𝍸 𝍸 𝍸 𝍸 II
2.	Lilies	𝍸 𝍸 𝍸 III
3.	Roses	𝍸 𝍸 𝍸 𝍸 𝍸 𝍸 𝍸 𝍸 III

FLOWER SALES	
Type	**Number**
Irises	■
Lilies	■
Roses	■

4. Were more roses sold than irises and lilies together? Explain.

PARTS OF A GRAPH

A **graph** is used to compare information. A bar graph should have a title, a label for the scale, and a label for the data.

Example

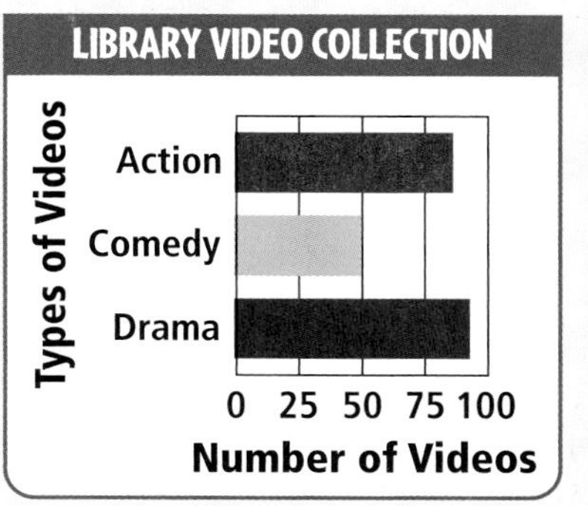

What is the label for the scale? Look at the bottom of the graph.

The label for the scale is Number of Videos.

What is the label for the data? Look along the left side of the graph.

The label for the data is Types of Videos.

▶ Practice

For 1–2, use the bar graph. It shows the number of fourth graders who went on each field trip.

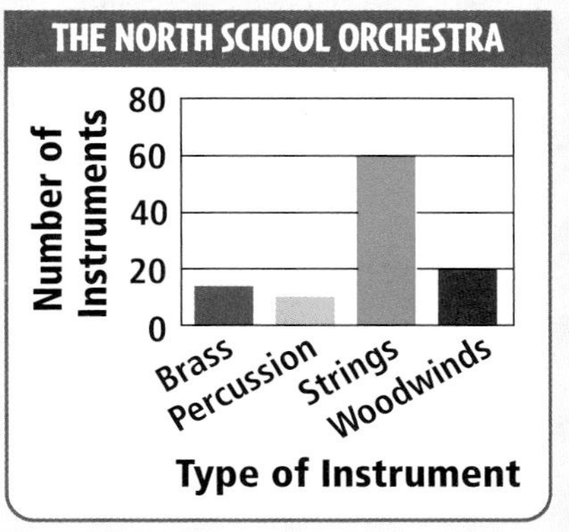

1. What would you label the scale?
2. What would you label the data?

READ BAR GRAPHS

Bar graphs help to compare information, or data. The graph below shows the number of instruments in each section of the orchestra.

Example

Which section has the fewest instruments?

Think: The section that has the shortest bar has the fewest instruments.

So, the percussion section has the fewest instruments.

▶ Practice

For 1–2, use the bar graph.

1. Which section has the most instruments?
2. Which section has more instruments than the other three sections combined?

TROUBLESHOOTING

IDENTIFY POINTS ON A GRID

An **ordered pair** of numbers locates a point on a grid. The first number in an ordered pair tells how many units to the right of zero the point is. The second number tells how many units above zero it is.

Example

What is the ordered pair for point M?

Think: Point M is 4 units to the right of zero and 1 unit up from zero.

So, the ordered pair is (4,1).

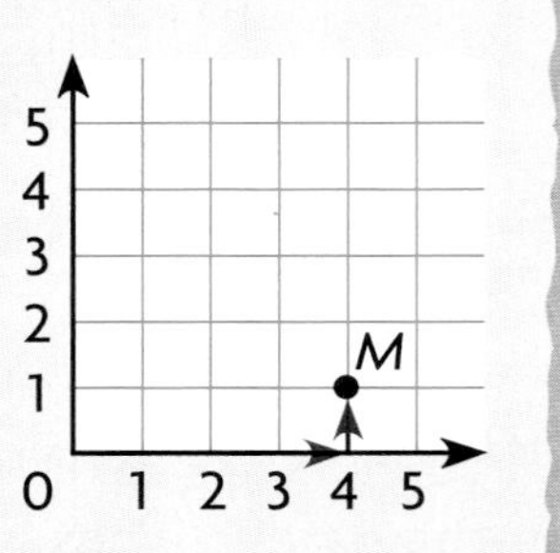

▶ Practice

For 1–6, use the grid. Write the ordered pair for each fruit or vegetable.

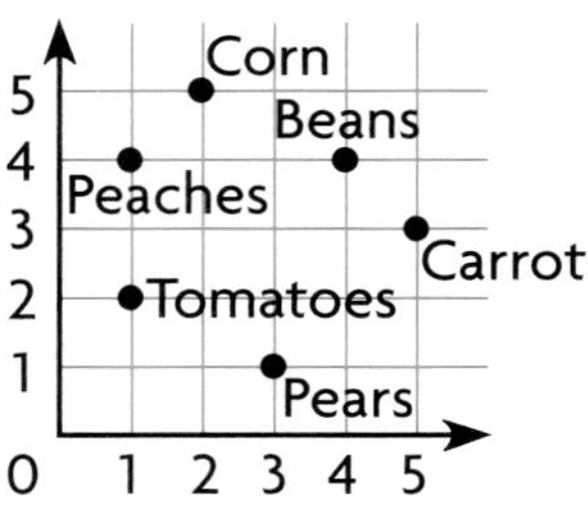

1. Tomatoes **2.** Pears **3.** Carrots

4. Peaches **5.** Beans **6.** Corn

EXPRESSIONS WITH VARIABLES

To find the value of an expression, replace the variable with the given value and then compute.

Examples

Find the value of the expression.

A $5 + 4 + g$ if $g = 5$ Replace the variable with the given value. Add.

$5 + 4 + 5 = 14$

So, the value of the expression is 14.

B $3 \times a$ if $a = 10$ Replace the variable with the given value. Multiply.

$3 \times 10 = 30$

So, the value of the expression is 30.

▶ Practice

Find the value of the expression.

1. $3 + 8 + y$ if $y = 2$ **2.** $5 + z + 4$ if $z = 3$ **3.** $n + 6 + 2$ if $n = 5$

4. $9 + c + 3 + 5$ if $c = 7$ **5.** $3 + 5 + 6 + p$ if $p = 4$ **6.** $a + 2 + 4 + 7$ if $a = 7$

7. $2 \times b$ if $b = 8$ **8.** $4 \times r$ if $r = 6$ **9.** $h \times 5$ if $h = 9$

10. $d \times 10$ if $d = 10$ **11.** $8 \times w$ if $w = 7$ **12.** $v \times 7$ if $v = 4$

TIME TO THE MINUTE

The minute hand on an analog clock moves 60 minutes each hour. A digital clock shows time as the hour and the number of minutes after the hour.

Examples

A Write the time after the hour.

Think: Skip-count by fives to the number 2. Then count one more minute.

So, the time is 4:11.

B Write the time before the hour, or as it is shown on a digital clock.

Think: Count back by fives starting with 12. Then count by ones to the mark where the minute hand is pointing.

So, the time is nine minutes before eight, or 7:51.

▶ Practice

Write the time.

1. 
2. 
3. 
4. 

USE A CALENDAR

Calendars show the months and days in a year.

Example

Use the calendar. What is the date of the second Sunday in February?

Think: The first column is Sunday. The second number in the column is 10.

So, the second Sunday is February 10.

FEBRUARY						
Sun	Mon	Tue	Wed	Thu	Fri	Sat
					1	2
3	4	5	6	7	8	9
10	11	12	13	14	15	16
17	18	19	20	21	22	23
24	25	26	27	28		

▶ Practice

1. Presidents' Day is the third Monday in February. What is the date?
2. What day of the week is February 28?
3. The fourth graders have music on Wednesdays and Fridays. How many days in February will they have music?

TROUBLESHOOTING

✓ MEANING OF MULTIPLICATION AND DIVISION

When you **multiply**, you put equal groups together. When you **divide**, you separate into equal groups.

Examples

A Find the product.
$3 \times 4 = ■$

This array shows 3 rows of 4, or 12.
So, $3 \times 4 = 12$.

B Find the quotient.
$12 \div 3 = ■$

12 counters in all
3 equal groups
4 in each group
So, $12 \div 3 = 4$.

▶ Practice

Find the product or quotient. You may wish to draw arrays or groups.

1. $2 \times 5 = ■$	**2.** $21 \div 3 = ■$	**3.** $3 \times 9 = ■$	**4.** $3 \times 5 = ■$
5. $45 \div 5 = ■$	**6.** $4 \times 7 = ■$	**7.** $2 \times 10 = ■$	**8.** $40 \div 5 = ■$
9. $24 \div 3 = ■$	**10.** $4 \times 6 = ■$	**11.** $50 \div 5 = ■$	**12.** $15 \div 3 = ■$

✓ MULTIPLICATION AND DIVISION FACTS

The answer to a multiplication fact is the **product**.
The answer to a division fact is the **quotient**.

Examples

A Find the product. $5 \times 7 = ■$

Skip-count to find a product. Starting with 0, count by fives 7 times. So, the product is 35.

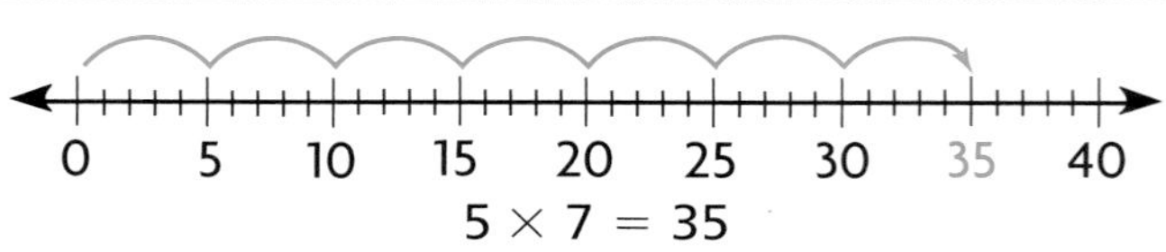

$5 \times 7 = 35$

B Find the quotient. $35 \div 5 = ■$

Count back to find a quotient. Starting with 35, count back by fives to 0. So, the quotient is 7.

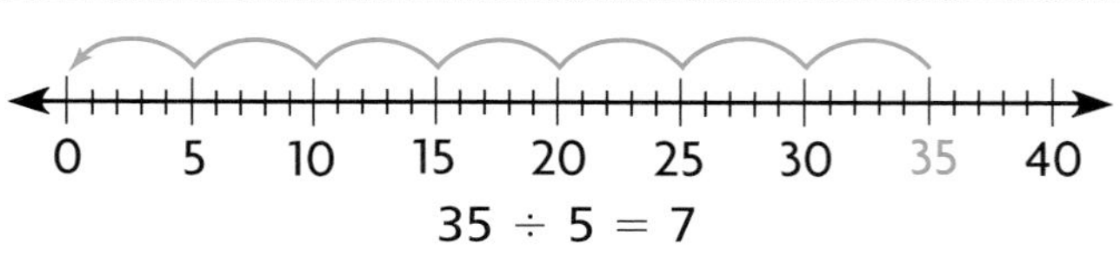

$35 \div 5 = 7$

▶ Practice

Find the product or quotient. You may wish to use number lines.

1. $6 \times 8 = ■$	**2.** $28 \div 7 = ■$	**3.** $8 \times 9 = ■$	**4.** $6 \times 6 = ■$
5. $56 \div 8 = ■$	**6.** $7 \times 7 = ■$	**7.** $9 \times 10 = ■$	**8.** $35 \div 7 = ■$

MISSING FACTORS

You can find a missing factor by recalling basic facts.

Examples

A 7 × ■ = 28

Think: 7 × [What number?] = 28

So, the missing factor is 4.

B ■ × 5 = 30

Think: [What number?] × 5 = 30

So, the missing factor is 6.

▶ Practice

Find the missing factor.

1. 6 × ■ = 24	**2.** ■ × 7 = 28	**3.** 9 × ■ = 27	**4.** ■ × 8 = 64
5. ■ × 5 = 35	**6.** 7 × ■ = 14	**7.** 4 × ■ = 32	**8.** ■ × 5 = 0
9. ■ × 6 = 30	**10.** 10 × ■ = 30	**11.** ■ × 7 = 63	**12.** 6 × ■ = 18
13. 9 × ■ = 63	**14.** 8 × ■ = 32	**15.** ■ × 5 = 45	**16.** ■ × 4 = 48

MODEL MULTIPLICATION

Use base-ten blocks to find the product. 3 × 16 = ■

STEP 1

Model 3 groups of 16.

3 × 16 = ■

STEP 2

Combine the tens and ones.
Regroup 10 ones as 1 ten.

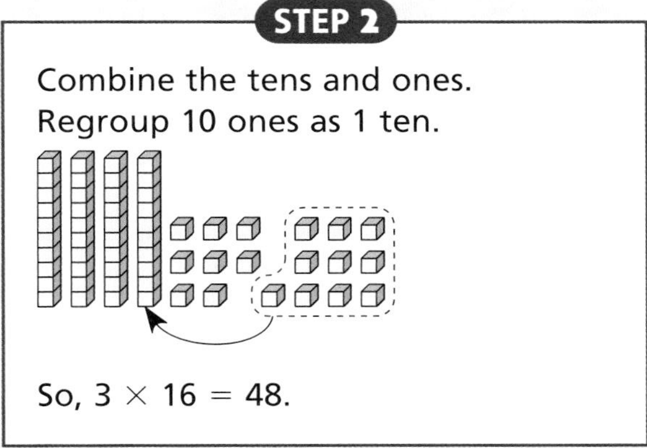

So, 3 × 16 = 48.

▶ Practice

Use base-ten blocks to find each product.

1. 23 × 8	**2.** 17 × 5	**3.** 26 × 3	**4.** 32 × 4	**5.** 56 × 2
6. 13 × 7	**7.** 43 × 6	**8.** 21 × 9	**9.** 44 × 6	**10.** 65 × 3

TROUBLESHOOTING

MULTIPLY BY TENS, HUNDREDS, AND THOUSANDS

To multiply by tens, hundreds, and thousands, look for a basic fact and a pattern.

Examples

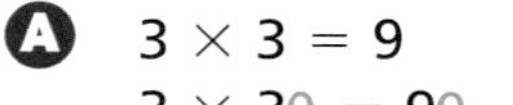

A	B	C
$3 \times 3 = 9$	$2 \times 6 = 12$	$10 \times 1 = 10$
$3 \times 30 = 90$	$2 \times 60 = 120$	$10 \times 10 = 100$
$3 \times 300 = 900$	$2 \times 600 = 1{,}200$	$10 \times 100 = 1{,}000$
$3 \times 3{,}000 = 9{,}000$	$2 \times 6{,}000 = 12{,}000$	$10 \times 1{,}000 = 10{,}000$

▶ Practice

Multiply. Use a basic fact and a pattern.

1. 10×8 **2.** 10×80 **3.** 10×800 **4.** $10 \times 8{,}000$

5. 10×4 **6.** 10×40 **7.** 100×40 **8.** $1{,}000 \times 400$

FRACTION MODELS

A fraction names a part of a whole. You can write a fraction for a model that shows part of a whole shaded.

Example

Write the fraction for the shaded part.

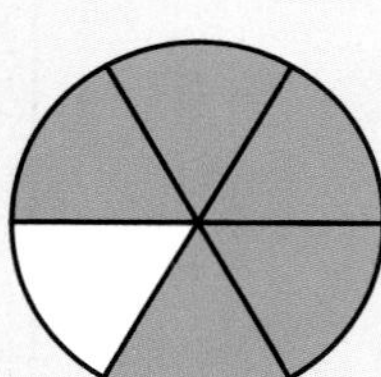

Count the number of shaded parts, 5.

Count the total number of equal parts, 6.

Write a fraction that shows the number of shaded parts over the total number of equal parts.

5 ← number of shaded parts
6 ← total number of equal parts

So, $\frac{5}{6}$ names the shaded part in the model.

▶ Practice

Write the fraction for the shaded part.

1. 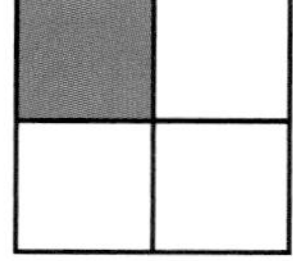

2. 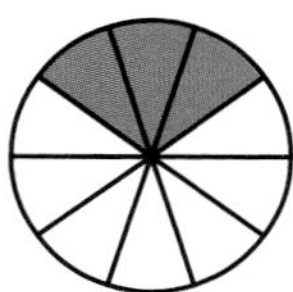

3. 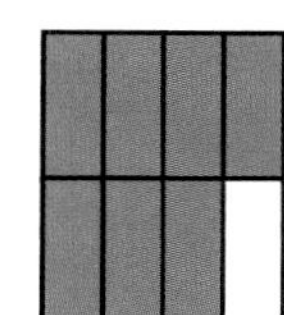

4. 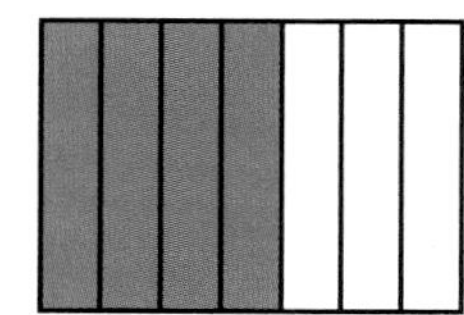

MULTIPLY BY 1-DIGIT NUMBERS

An understanding of place value can help you find products.

Find the product. $8 \times 43 = \blacksquare$

STEP 1

Multiply the ones.

8×3 ones $= 24$ ones

Regroup 24 ones as 2 tens 4 ones.

$$\begin{array}{r} {}^{2} \\ 43 \\ \times\ 8 \\ \hline 4 \end{array}$$

STEP 2

Multiply the tens.

8×4 tens $= 32$ tens

Add the regrouped tens.

2 tens + 32 tens = 34 tens

Record the product. So, $8 \times 43 = 344$.

$$\begin{array}{r} {}^{2} \\ 43 \\ \times\ 8 \\ \hline 344 \end{array}$$

▶ Practice

Multiply.

1. $\begin{array}{r} 15 \\ \times\ 6 \\ \hline \end{array}$
2. $\begin{array}{r} 27 \\ \times\ 3 \\ \hline \end{array}$
3. $\begin{array}{r} 59 \\ \times\ 2 \\ \hline \end{array}$
4. $\begin{array}{r} 86 \\ \times\ 5 \\ \hline \end{array}$
5. $\begin{array}{r} 63 \\ \times\ 8 \\ \hline \end{array}$
6. $7 \times 48 = \blacksquare$
7. $4 \times 143 = \blacksquare$
8. $5 \times 483 = \blacksquare$

ESTIMATE PRODUCTS

You can round one factor to estimate products.

Examples

A $6 \times 87 = \blacksquare$

6×87 — Round 87 to the nearest 10.

↓

$6 \times 90 = 540$ — Use a basic fact and patterns.

So, 6×87 is about 540.

B $4 \times 329 = \blacksquare$

4×329 — Round 329 to the nearest 100.

↓

$4 \times 300 = 1{,}200$ — Use a basic fact and patterns.

So, 4×329 is about 1,200.

▶ Practice

Round the blue number. Estimate the product.

1. $\begin{array}{r} 23 \\ \times\ 9 \\ \hline \end{array}$
2. $\begin{array}{r} 46 \\ \times\ 6 \\ \hline \end{array}$
3. $\begin{array}{r} 73 \\ \times\ 8 \\ \hline \end{array}$
4. $\begin{array}{r} 91 \\ \times\ 7 \\ \hline \end{array}$
5. $\begin{array}{r} 68 \\ \times\ 5 \\ \hline \end{array}$
6. $4 \times 145 = \blacksquare$
7. $9 \times 589 = \blacksquare$
8. $6 \times 358 = \blacksquare$

TROUBLESHOOTING

FIND A RULE

You can find a pattern in a table, write a rule, and then use the rule to find a missing number in the table.

Example

Write a rule for the table. Then complete the table.

Teams	1	2	3	4	5	6
Players	6	12	18	24	30	■

Look for a pattern.

Pattern: The number of players is equal to the number of teams times 6.

Rule: Multiply by 6.

So, when there are 6 teams, the number of players is 6 × 6, or 36 players.

▶ Practice

Write a rule for each table. Copy and complete each table.

1.

Tickets	1	2	3	4	5
Cost	\$7	\$14	\$21	\$28	■

2.

Books	2	3	4	5	6
Stamps	40	60	80	100	■

3.

Nickels	2	3	4	5	6
Pennies	10	15	20	25	■

4.

Hours	3	4	5	6	7
Dollars	\$27	\$36	\$45	\$54	■

MENTAL MATH: MULTIPLICATION AND DIVISION PATTERNS

You can use basic facts and patterns to multiply and divide.

Examples

A Use a pattern to find each product.

16 × 1 = 16 ←basic fact
16 × 10 = 160
16 × 100 = 1,600
16 × 1,000 = 16,000

B Use a pattern to find each quotient.

7 ÷ 1 = 7 ←basic fact
70 ÷ 10 = 7
700 ÷ 10 = 70
7,000 ÷ 10 = 700

▶ Practice

Use a pattern to find each product or quotient.

1. 60 ÷ 10
   600 ÷ 10
   6,000 ÷ 10
2. 9 × 10
   9 × 100
   9 × 1,000
3. 30 ÷ 10
   300 ÷ 10
   3,000 ÷ 10
4. 27 × 10
   27 × 100
   27 × 1,000

DIVIDE WITH REMAINDERS

When you divide into equal groups, you may have some left over. The leftover amount is called a **remainder.**

Example

Find the quotient and remainder. 23 ÷ 4

20 ÷ 4 = 5	Find the greatest number of 4s in 23.
23 − 20 = 3	Subtract to find how many are left over.
23 ÷ 4 = 5 r3	Write the quotient and remainder.

So, 23 ÷ 4 = 5 r3.

▶ Practice

Write the quotient and remainder.

1. 27 ÷ 4	**2.** 82 ÷ 9	**3.** 60 ÷ 8	**4.** 22 ÷ 3	**5.** 26 ÷ 6
6. 68 ÷ 8	**7.** 37 ÷ 5	**8.** 46 ÷ 8	**9.** 45 ÷ 7	**10.** 70 ÷ 9
11. 49 ÷ 5	**12.** 58 ÷ 9	**13.** 81 ÷ 4	**14.** 94 ÷ 7	**15.** 83 ÷ 6

DIVIDE BY 1-DIGIT DIVISORS

In a division problem such as 40 ÷ 5 = 8, the **dividend** is 40 and the **divisor** is 5. The answer, 8, is the **quotient.**

Examples

A Divide. 108 ÷ 4

```
   27
4)108
 - 8↓
   28
 - 28
    0
```

Divide the hundreds. 1 ÷ 4 There are not enough hundreds.

Divide the 10 tens. 10 ÷ 4 Multiply 2 and 4. Subtract. Bring down the 8.

Divide the 28 ones. 28 ÷ 4 Multiply 7 and 4. Subtract.

So, the quotient is 27.

B Divide. 82 ÷ 3

```
  27 r1
3)82
 - 6↓
  22
 -21
   1
```

So, the quotient is 27 r1.

▶ Practice

Divide.

1. 96 ÷ 8	**2.** 126 ÷ 3	**3.** 51 ÷ 6	**4.** 40 ÷ 7	**5.** 120 ÷ 8
6. 21 ÷ 2	**7.** 74 ÷ 7	**8.** 87 ÷ 4	**9.** 85 ÷ 5	**10.** 172 ÷ 4

TROUBLESHOOTING

✓ USE COMPATIBLE NUMBERS

Compatible numbers can be used to estimate quotients mentally. **Compatible numbers** are in a fact family close to the numbers you need to divide.

Estimate the quotient. $50 \div 6$

STEP 1

Name the fact families close to $50 \div 6$.

$48 \div 6$ $\quad$ $50 \div 10$ $\quad$ $54 \div 6$

STEP 2

Determine which fact family is closest to the actual dividend and divisor. The fact family with the closest numbers is $48 \div 6$.

So, a good estimate is $50 \div 6 = 8$.

▶ Practice

Estimate the quotient. Tell the compatible numbers you used.

1. $5\overline{)27}$
2. $7\overline{)65}$
3. $6\overline{)29}$
4. $8\overline{)61}$
5. $12\overline{)45}$
6. $73 \div 9$
7. $58 \div 11$
8. $67 \div 7$
9. $87 \div 9$
10. $59 \div 7$

✓ PARTS OF A WHOLE

Fractions can describe parts of a whole.

The **numerator**, or top number, tells how many of the parts are being used.

The **denominator**, or bottom number, tells the total number of equal parts in the whole.

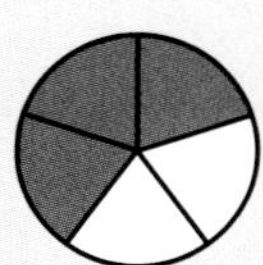

$\frac{3}{5} \leftarrow \frac{\text{number of red parts}}{\text{total number of equal parts}}$

▶ Practice

Write a fraction for the shaded part.

1. 
2. 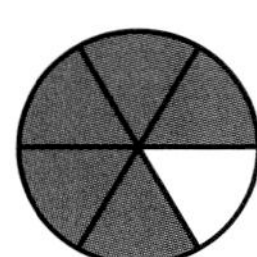
3. 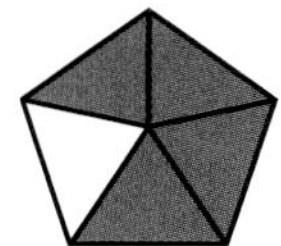
4. 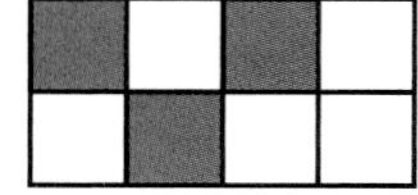

Draw a picture for each description.

5. A rectangle with three parts shaded out of four parts.
6. A square with one part shaded out of two parts.
7. A triangle with two parts shaded out of three parts.

PARTS OF A GROUP

Fractions can describe parts of a group.

The **numerator**, or top number, tells how many of the parts are being used.

The **denominator**, or bottom number, tells the total number of equal parts in the group.

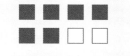

$\frac{6}{8} \leftarrow \frac{\text{number of blue squares}}{\text{total number of squares}}$

▶ Practice

Write a fraction for the shaded part.

1. 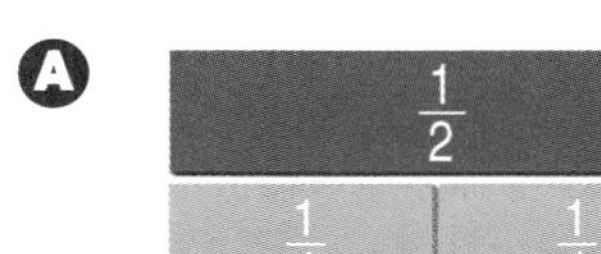

2. 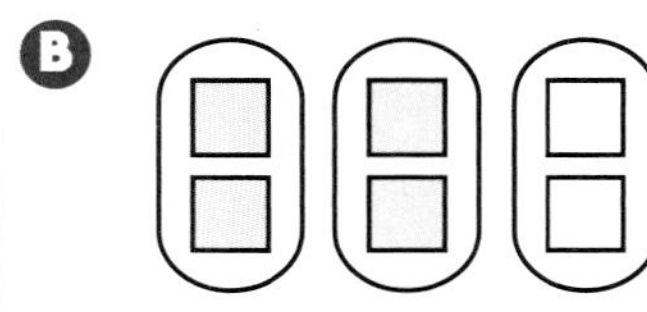

3. 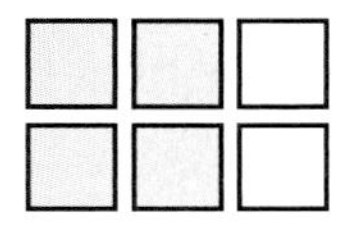

Draw a picture for each description.

4. Two out of three triangles are shaded.

5. Two out of five squares are shaded.

6. Seven out of ten circles are shaded.

EQUIVALENT FRACTIONS

Equivalent fractions are fractions that name the same amount.

Examples

Write two equivalent fractions for each picture.

A

$\frac{1}{2}$

$\frac{1}{4}$ $\frac{1}{4}$

The top bar shows $\frac{1}{2}$.
The bottom bars show $\frac{2}{4}$.

The bars for $\frac{1}{2}$ and $\frac{2}{4}$ are the same length.

So, $\frac{1}{2}$ and $\frac{2}{4}$ are equivalent fractions.

B

$\frac{2 \text{ shaded groups}}{3 \text{ groups in all}}$ $\frac{4 \text{ shaded squares}}{6 \text{ squares in all}}$

Both fractions name the same amount.

So, $\frac{2}{3}$ and $\frac{4}{6}$ are equivalent fractions.

▶ Practice

Write two equivalent fractions for each picture.

1. 

$\frac{1}{3}$

$\frac{1}{6}$ $\frac{1}{6}$

2. 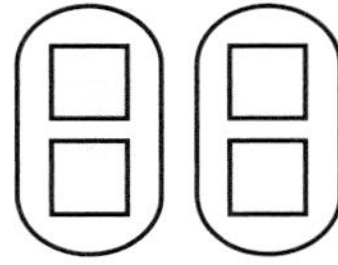   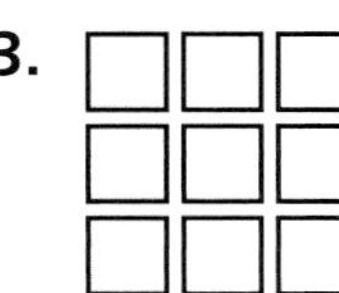

3.

TROUBLESHOOTING

MODEL DECIMALS

You can write a decimal for a model that shows tenths or hundredths.

Examples

Write a decimal for the shaded part.

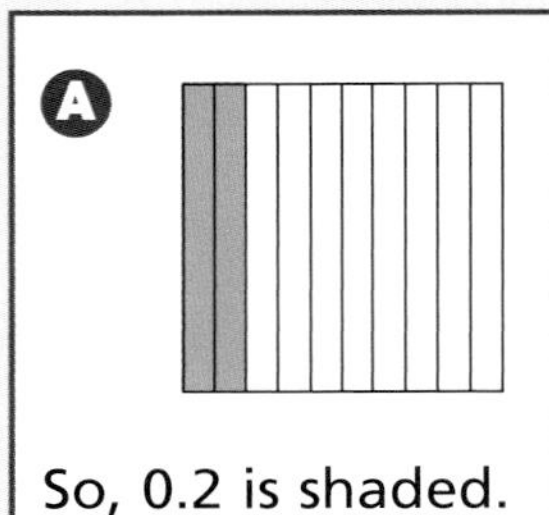

So, 0.2 is shaded.

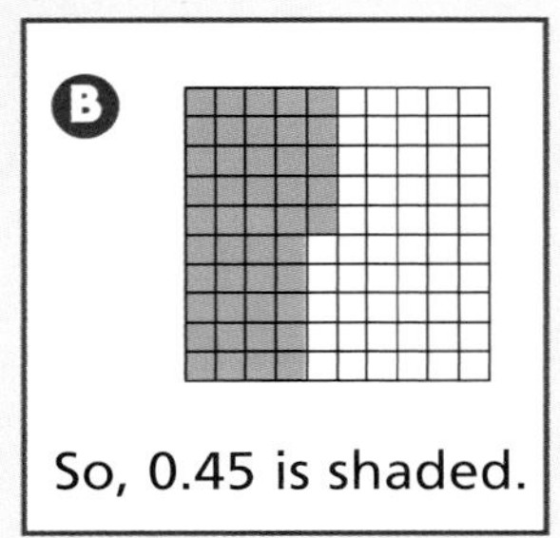

So, 0.45 is shaded.

▶ Practice

Write the decimal for the shaded part.

1. 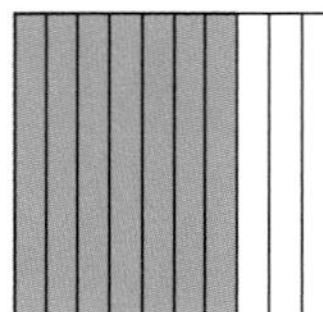

2. 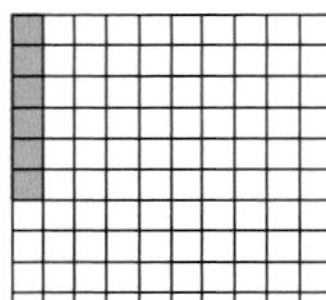

3. 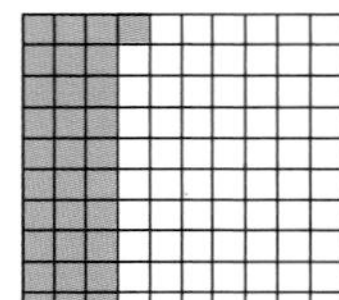

RELATE DECIMALS TO MONEY

The number before a decimal point shows the number of dollars. The number after the decimal point shows hundredths of dollars, or cents.

Example

Write three dollars and fifty-eight cents as a decimal.

- Write the whole number of dollars. $3
- Write the cents as hundredths. $0.58

So, write $3.58.

▶ Practice

Write a decimal for each money amount.

1. six dollars and forty-five cents

2. ninety-eight cents

3. ten dollars and two cents

4. one dollar and fifty-four cents

5. twenty dollars and ten cents

6. two dollars and fifty-one cents

FRACTIONS WITH DENOMINATORS OF 10 AND 100

You can use decimal models to write equivalent fractions.

Example

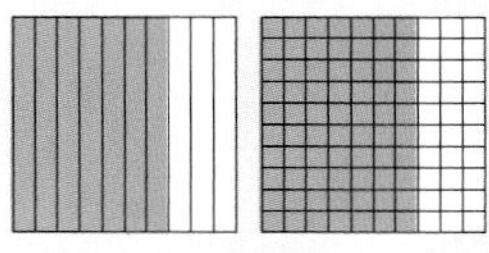

The first square shows 7 out of 10 parts shaded.

The second square shows 70 out of 100 parts shaded.

Both have the same amount shaded.

So, $\frac{7}{10} = \frac{70}{100}$.

▶ Practice

Complete to show equivalent fractions.

1. 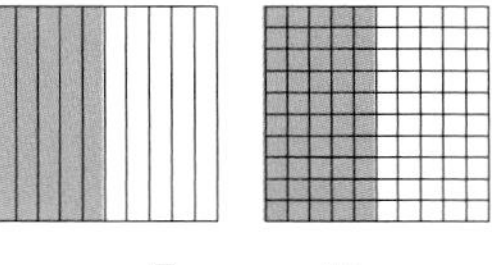

$\frac{5}{10} = \frac{\blacksquare}{100}$

2. 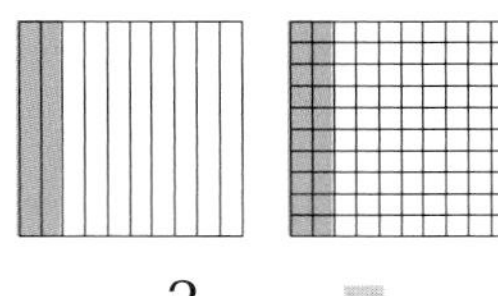

$\frac{2}{10} = \frac{\blacksquare}{100}$

3. 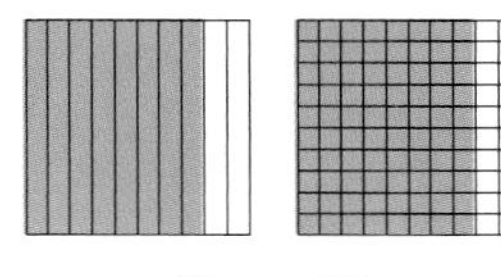

$\frac{8}{10} = \frac{\blacksquare}{\blacksquare}$

SIMPLEST FORM

A fraction is in **simplest form** when 1 is the only number that will divide evenly into the numerator and the denominator.

Examples

Tell whether each fraction is in simplest form. If not, write it in simplest form.

A $\frac{3}{5}$

Factors of 3: 1, 3
Factors of 5: 1, 5

The only number that divides evenly into the numerator and denominator of $\frac{3}{5}$ is 1.

So, $\frac{3}{5}$ is in simplest form.

 $\frac{3}{9}$

Factors of 3: 1, 3
Factors of 9: 1, 3, 9

The numerator and denominator of $\frac{3}{9}$ can be divided by 1 or 3 evenly.

$\frac{3 \div 3}{9 \div 3} = \frac{1}{3}$ 1 is the only factor.

So, $\frac{3}{9}$ in simplest form is $\frac{1}{3}$.

▶ Practice

Tell whether each fraction is in simplest form. If not, write it in simplest form.

1. $\frac{4}{8}$ 2. $\frac{5}{7}$ 3. $\frac{9}{12}$ 4. $\frac{8}{2}$ 5. $\frac{3}{8}$ 6. $\frac{6}{15}$

TROUBLESHOOTING

MEASURE TO THE NEAREST INCH AND HALF INCH

Linear units are used to measure length, width, height, and distance.

Example

Measure the length to the nearest inch.

- Line up one end of the eraser with the 0 mark on the ruler.
- Find the inch mark that is nearest the eraser's length.
- The length is closest to the 2-inch mark.

So, the eraser is about 2 inches long.

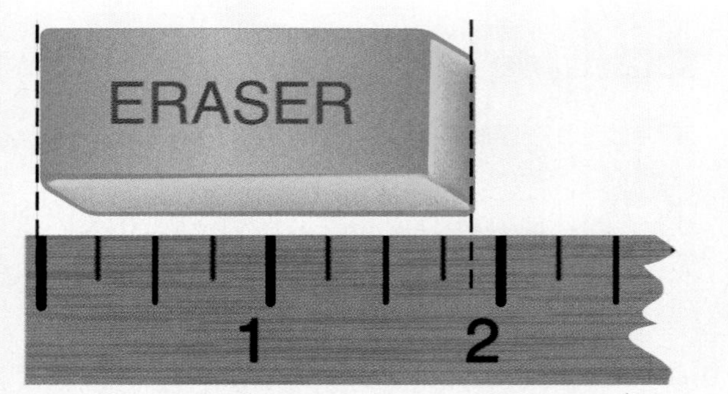

▶ Practice

Measure the length to the nearest inch.

1. 

2. 

Measure the length to the nearest half inch.

3.

MIXED NUMBERS

A **mixed number** is made up of a whole number and a fraction.

Examples Write a mixed number for each picture.

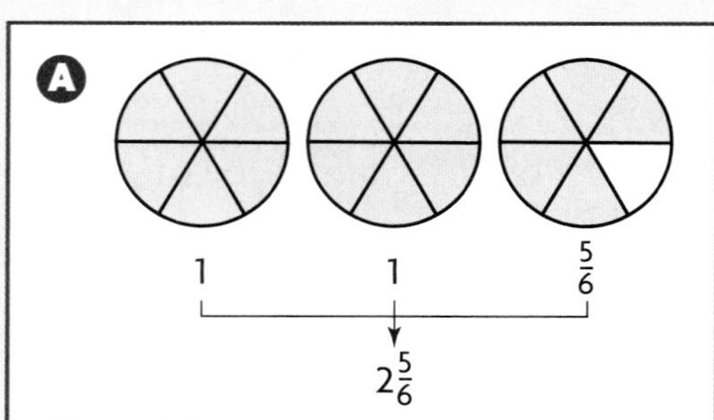

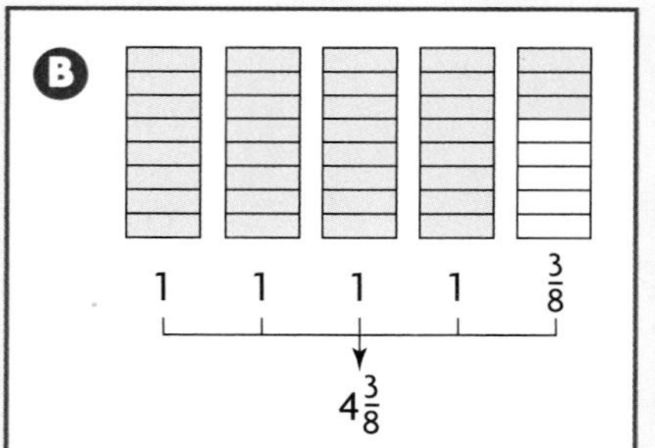

▶ Practice

Write a mixed number for each picture.

1. 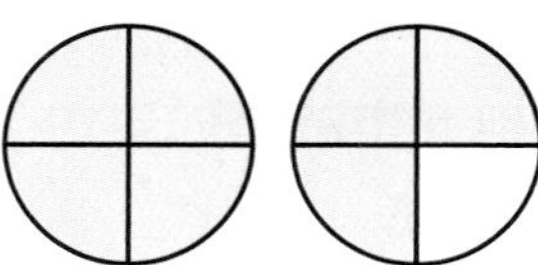

2. 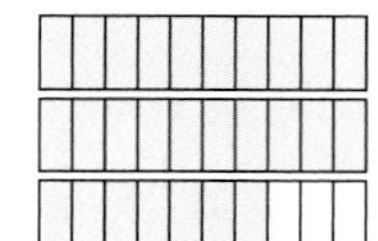

3. 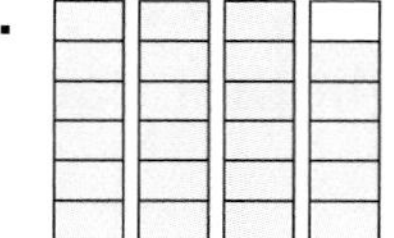

MEASURE TO THE NEAREST CENTIMETER

You can use centimeters to measure length and distance.

Example

Measure to the nearest centimeter.

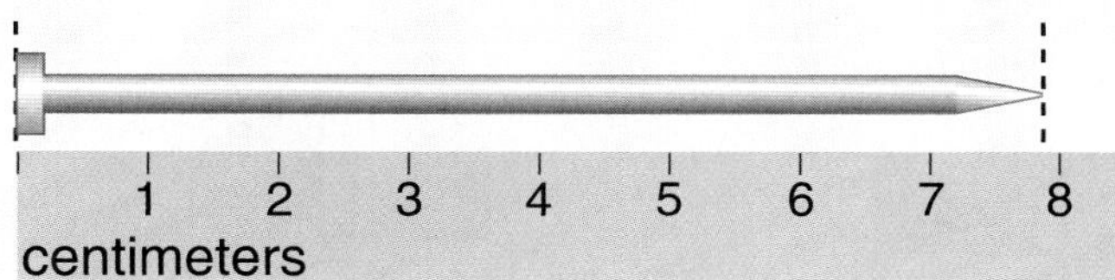

- Line up one end of the nail with the 0 mark on the ruler.
- Find the centimeter mark that is nearest to the nail's length.
- The nail's length is closest to 8 cm.

So, to the nearest centimeter, the nail is about 8 cm long.

▶ Practice

Measure the length to the nearest centimeter.

1.

2. 

3.

DECIMAL PLACE VALUE

You can use a place-value chart to find the value of each digit in a decimal.

Example Write the value of the blue digit in the number 0.257.

ONES	TENTHS	HUNDREDTHS	THOUSANDTHS
0 .	2	5	7

The blue digit, 5, is in the hundredths place. So, the value of the blue digit is 5 hundredths, or 0.05.

▶ Practice

Write the value of the blue digit in the decimal.

1. 0.57 **2.** 0.741 **3.** 0.48 **4.** 0.917

5. 0.742 **6.** 0.803 **7.** 0.396 **8.** 0.425

9. 0.825 **10.** 0.45 **11.** 0.634 **12.** 0.721

TROUBLESHOOTING

✓ SLIDES, FLIPS, AND TURNS

Here are three ways to move a figure.

You can **slide** a figure by moving it to a new position without turning or flipping it.	You can **flip** a figure by flipping it across a line. The new figure is a mirror image of the first figure.	You can **turn** a figure by rotating it around a point.
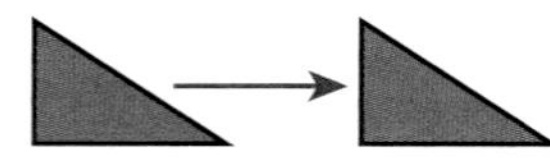	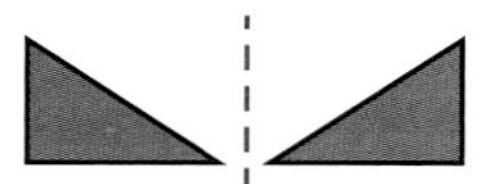	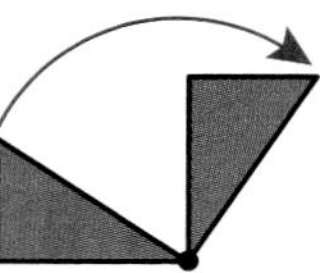

▶ Practice

Tell what kind of motion was used to move each figure.
Write *slide, flip,* or *turn*.

1. 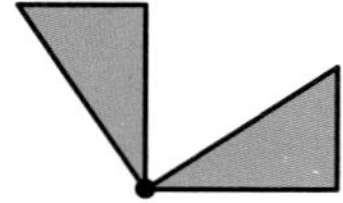

2. 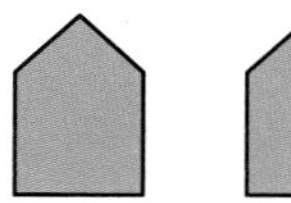

3. 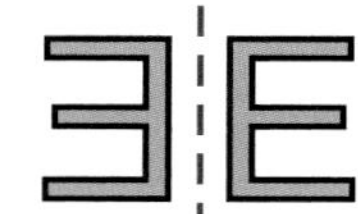

✓ ORDER NUMBERS ON A NUMBER LINE

To order numbers on a number line, graph a point for each number, and then write the numbers in order from least to greatest by reading the numbers you graphed from left to right. On a number line the numbers to the left are least and the numbers to the right are greatest.

Write 89, 95, and 82 in order from *least* to *greatest*.

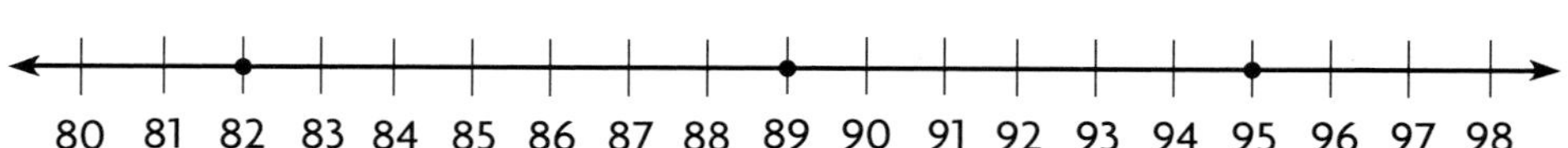

Graph a point for each number. Then, start at the left and write the numbers you graphed in order.

So, from least to greatest, you would write 82, 89, 95.

▶ Practice

Write the numbers in order from *least* to *greatest*. Use the number line to help you.

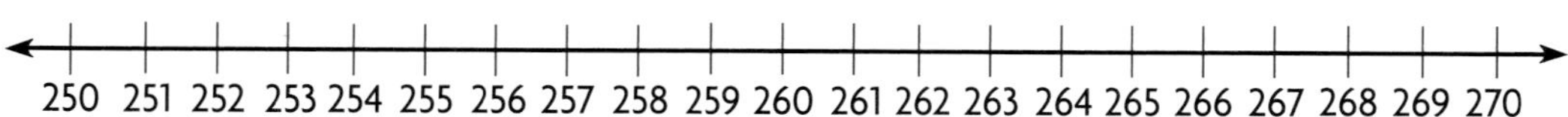

1. 262, 252, 259 **2.** 255, 254, 253 **3.** 267, 250, 259 **4.** 270, 250, 260

IDENTIFY GEOMETRIC FIGURES

Here are some types of geometric figures.

FIGURE	READ	SYMBOL
• A	point A	
A B (line)	line AB or line BA	$\overleftrightarrow{AB}$ or $\overleftrightarrow{BA}$
C D (line segment)	line segment CD or line segment DC	$\overline{CD}$ or $\overline{DC}$
E F (ray)	ray EF	$\overrightarrow{EF}$
G, H, I, vertex (angle)	angle GHI, angle IHG, or angle H	$\angle GHI$, $\angle IHG$, or $\angle H$

▶ Practice

Name each figure. Write *point, line, line segment, ray,* or *angle*.

1. M N

2. • Z

3. X Y

4. J K L

IDENTIFY ANGLES

You can use the size of a right angle to determine whether another angle is less than or greater than a right angle.

right angle

Examples

Tell if the angle is a *right* angle, *greater than* a right angle, or *less than* a right angle.

A 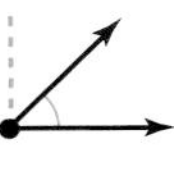

The dashed line shows where the ray would be if the angle were a right angle.

So, the angle is *less than* a right angle.

B 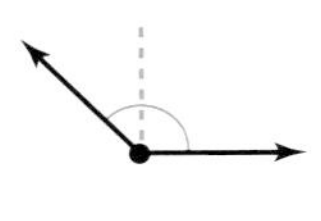

The dashed line shows where the ray would be if the angle were a right angle.

So, the angle is *greater than* a right angle.

▶ Practice

Tell if each angle is a *right* angle, *greater than* a right angle, or *less than* a right angle.

1.

2. 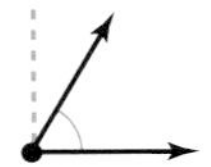

3. 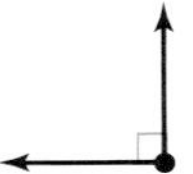

4.

TROUBLESHOOTING

✓ COMPARE FIGURES

Congruent figures have the same size and shape.

Examples Are the figures congruent?

A

Think: The figures are the same shape but not the same size.

So, the figures are not congruent.

B

Think: The figures are the same shape and the same size.

So, the figures are congruent.

▶ Practice

Are the figures congruent? Write *yes* or *no*.

1. 
2. 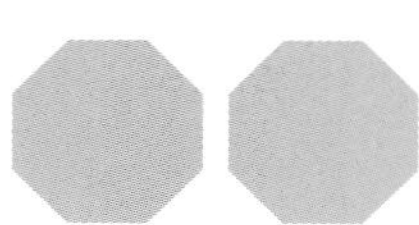
3. 

✓ IDENTIFY SYMMETRIC FIGURES

A figure has **line symmetry** if you can fold it on the line and the two parts match.

Examples Is the blue line a line of symmetry?

A

If you fold the circle on the line, the two parts are identical.

So, the blue line is a line of symmetry.

B

If you fold the circle on the line, the two parts are not identical.

So, the blue line is not a line of symmetry.

▶ Practice

Is the blue line a line of symmetry? Write *yes* or *no*.

1. 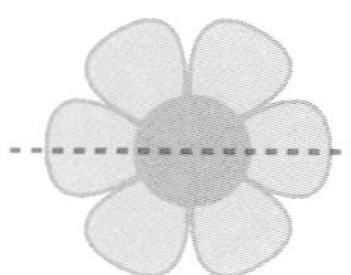
2. 
3. 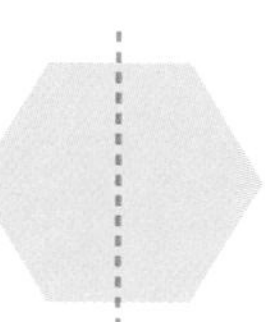
4. 

IDENTIFY PLANE FIGURES

A **plane figure** is flat and is all in one plane. It can be closed or open.

These are types of closed plane figures.

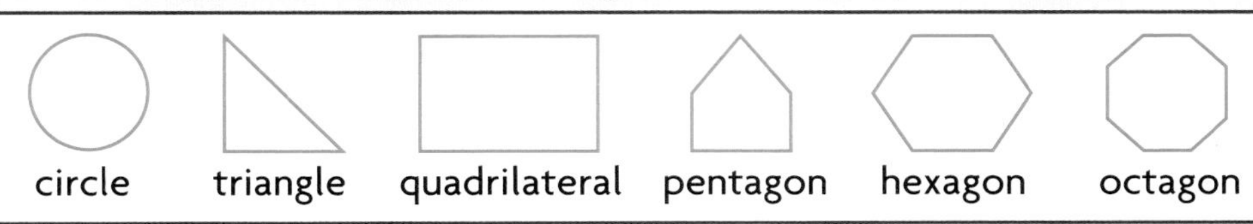

▶ Practice

Write a name for each figure.

1. 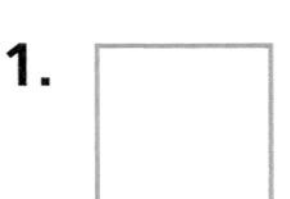

2. 

3. 

4. 

5. 

6. 

7. 

8. 

IDENTIFY QUADRILATERALS

A **quadrilateral** has four sides and four angles.

Examples

Tell if the polygon is a *quadrilateral* or *not a quadrilateral.*

A 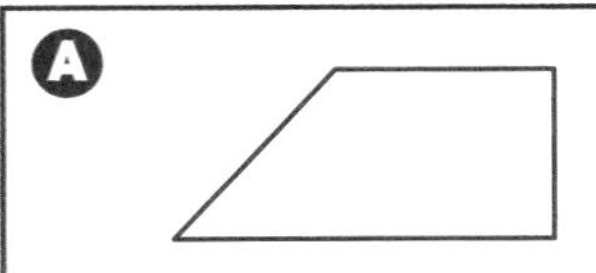

This figure has 4 sides and 4 angles.

So, this figure is a *quadrilateral.*

B 

This figure has 5 sides and 5 angles.

So, this figure is a *not a quadrilateral.*

▶ Practice

Tell if the polygon is a *quadrilateral* or *not a quadrilateral*.

1.

2. 

3. 

4. 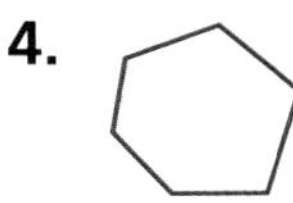

5.

6. 

7. 

8. 

TROUBLESHOOTING

✓ FIND PERIMETER

Perimeter is the distance around a figure. You can find the perimeter of a polygon by counting or adding the lengths of its sides.

Example

Count to find the perimeter of the figure.

STEP 1

Count to find the length of each side. The sides are each 3 units in length.

STEP 2

Add the lengths of the sides.
$3 + 3 + 3 + 3 = 12$

So, the figure has a perimeter of 12 units.

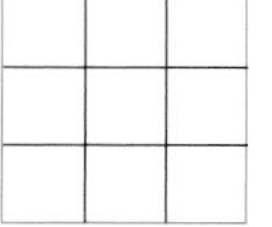

▶ Practice

Count to find the perimeter of each figure.

1. 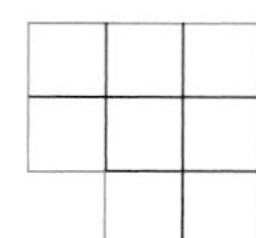

2. 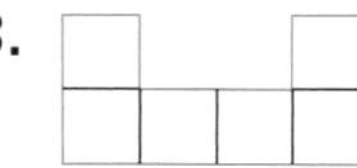

3. 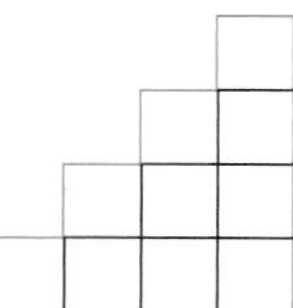

4. 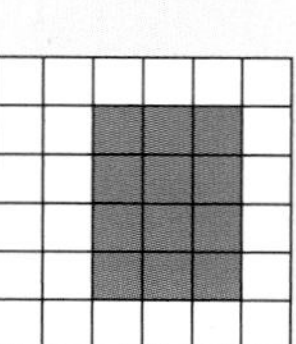

✓ FIND AREA

Area is the number of square units that cover a closed figure. To find the area of the figure, you can count the number of square units.

Example

Count to find the area of the blue figure.

The blue figure covers exactly 12 squares.

So, the area is 12 square units.

▶ Practice

Count to find the area of each blue figure.

1. 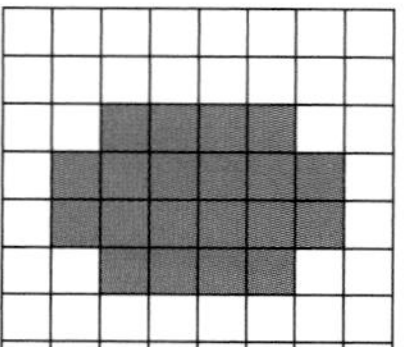

2. 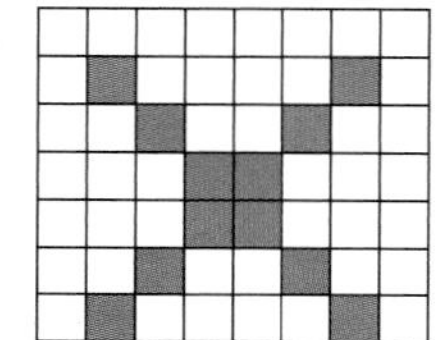

3. 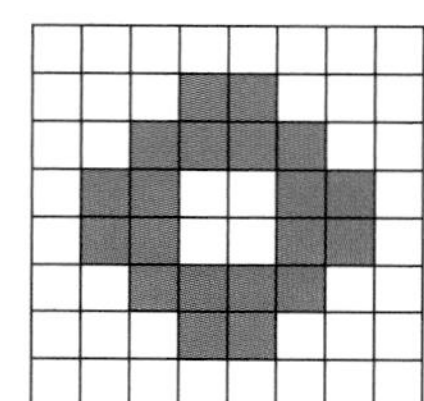

4. 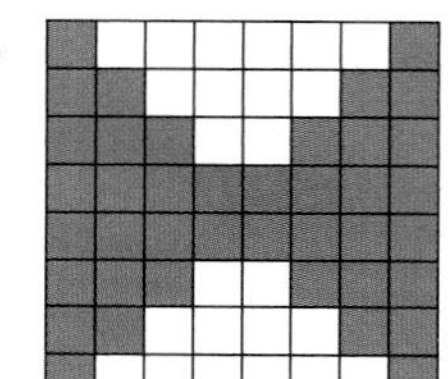

IDENTIFY SOLID FIGURES

Solid figures have three dimensions: length, width, and height.

These figures are called solid figures.

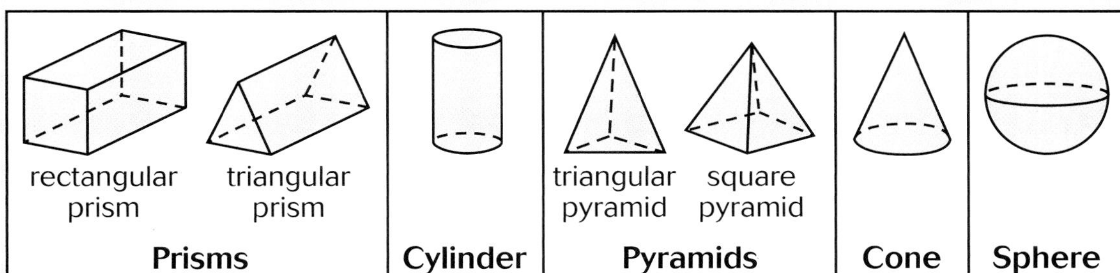

▶ Practice

Name the solid figure that the object looks like.

1. 

2. 

3. 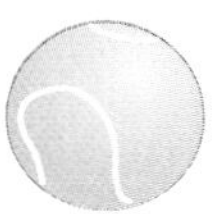

Name the solid figure.

4. 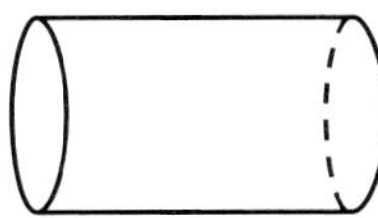

5. 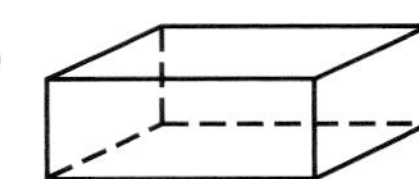

6. 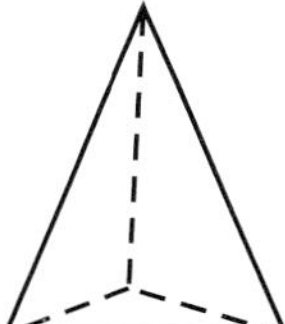

DRAW PLANE FIGURES

When you draw a plane figure, think about the properties of the figure.

Example

Draw a triangle.

Think: A triangle has 3 sides.

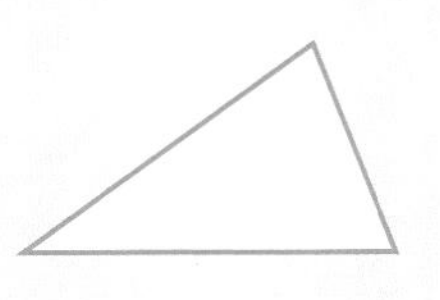

▶ Practice

Draw the plane figure named.

1. pentagon **2.** rectangle **3.** octagon **4.** hexagon **5.** circle

TROUBLESHOOTING

✓ MULTIPLY 3 FACTORS

When you multiply three factors, you can use the **Associative Property** to group them so that it is easy to multiply mentally.

Example

Find the product. $6 \times 8 \times 5$

One Way

Multiply the first two factors.

$(6 \times 8) \times 5$

48×5

240

Another Way

Multiply the last two factors.

$6 \times (8 \times 5)$

6×40

240

Either way you group the factors, the product is the same.
So, the product is 240.

▶ Practice

Group the factors two different ways. Find the product.

1. $6 \times 4 \times 2 = \blacksquare$
2. $5 \times 3 \times 4 = \blacksquare$
3. $5 \times 6 \times 7 = \blacksquare$
4. $10 \times 3 \times 5 = \blacksquare$
5. $27 \times 9 \times 0 = \blacksquare$
6. $14 \times 1 \times 7 = \blacksquare$
7. $12 \times 3 \times 4 = \blacksquare$
8. $20 \times 5 \times 5 = \blacksquare$
9. $6 \times 2 \times 30 = \blacksquare$

✓ CLASSIFY ANGLES

An angle is formed by two rays that have the same endpoint.

A **right angle** measures 90°. A right angle forms a square corner.

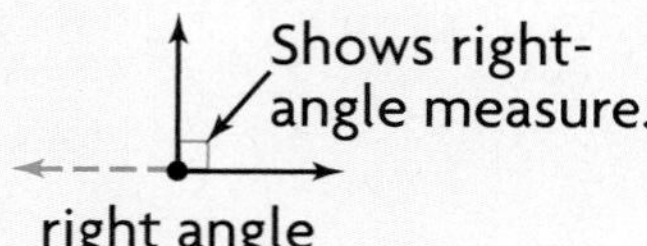
Shows right-angle measure.

right angle

An **acute angle** measures greater than 0° and less than 90°.

acute angle

An **obtuse angle** measures greater than 90° and less than 180°.

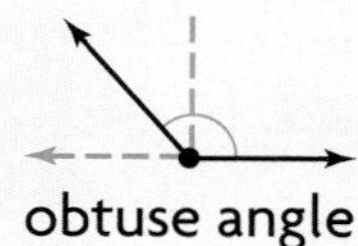

obtuse angle

▶ Practice

Tell if each angle is acute, right, or obtuse.

1. 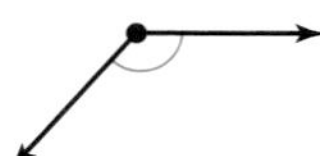
2. 
3. 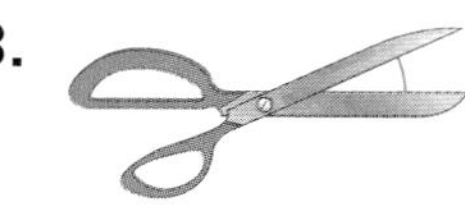

CERTAIN AND IMPOSSIBLE

An event that is sure to happen is **certain**. An event that will never happen is **impossible**.

Examples

Write *certain* or *impossible* for the event.

A ice melting on a warm summer day

Ice will always melt at temperatures above freezing.

So, this event is certain.

B snow from a cloudless day

It cannot snow without clouds.

So, this event is impossible.

▶ Practice

Write *certain* or *impossible* for the event.

1. tossing a number less than 7 with a number cube labeled 1 to 6
2. making change for a $5 bill when you have only three $1 bills
3. drawing a 4-sided triangle
4. drawing a 4-sided square

IDENTIFY POSSIBLE OUTCOMES

Some events can happen in only a few ways. You can list the ways, or **possible outcomes**, of the event.

Examples

Write the possible outcomes for the event.

A tossing a counter with one red side and one blue side

The 2 possible outcomes are red side up and blue side up.

B pulling a coin from a bag of one dime, one nickel, and one penny

The 3 possible outcomes are pulling a dime, pulling a nickel, and pulling a penny.

▶ Practice

Write the possible outcomes for the event.

1. pulling a balloon out of the bag

2. spinning the pointer of this spinner

3. tossing a number cube labeled 1–6
4. tossing two coins

Tips for Taking Math Tests

Being a good test-taker is like being a good problem solver. When you answer test questions, you are solving problems. Remember to **UNDERSTAND, PLAN, SOLVE,** and **CHECK.**

UNDERSTAND

Read the problem.

- Look for math terms and recall their meanings.
- Reread the problem and think about the question.
- Use the details in the problem and the question.

1. Twenty students signed up for a new club. Six more girls than boys signed up. How many boys signed up?

A 16 **C** 7
B 13 **D** 4

TIP! Understand the problem.
Six more girls than boys **is the difference between the number of girls and boys. So find two numbers with a difference of 6 whose sum is 20. The number of boys will be the lesser number. The answer is C.**

- Each word is important. Missing a word or reading it incorrectly could cause you to get the wrong answer.
- Pay attention to words that are in **bold** type, all CAPITAL letters, or *italics* and words like *round, best,* or *least to greatest.*

2. Skates cost $219. Kent rounded the price to the nearest hundred dollars. Abby rounded to the nearest ten dollars. Which statement is true?

F Kent's amount and Abby's amount are the same.

G Kent's amount is $20 less than Abby's amount.

H Kent's amount is $10 less than Abby's amount.

J Kent's amount is $10 more than Abby's amount.

TIP! Look for important words.
The words *rounded* and *true* are important words. Kent and Abby each rounded the price to a different place value. Round the price as Kent and Abby did. Then compare your rounded amounts to each answer choice to determine which one is true. The answer is G.

PLAN

Think about how you can solve the problem.

- Can you solve the problem with the information given?
- Pictures, charts, tables, and graphs may have the information you need.
- You may need to recall information not given.
- The answer choices may have information you need.

3. Trains run from New York to Washington, D.C., every 30 minutes. Which train takes the least amount of time to reach Washington, D.C.?

Train Number	Leaves New York	Arrives in Washington
15	9:00 A.M.	11:54 A.M.
26	9:30 A.M.	12:30 P.M.
86	10:30 A.M.	1:03 P.M.
127	10:00 A.M.	12:44 P.M.

A Train 15 **C** Train 86

B Train 26 **D** Train 127

TIP! **Get the information you need.** Use the schedule to find how much time it takes each train to reach Washington, D.C. Then compare the times to find the one that is less than the others. The answer is **C**.

- You may need to write a number sentence and solve it.
- Some problems have two steps or more.
- You may need to look at relationships rather than compute.
- If the path to the solution isn't clear, choose a problem solving strategy and use it to solve the problem.

4. Roberto has $38, which is $2 more than twice the amount Janet has. How much money does Janet have?

F $14 **H** $40

G $18 **J** $78

TIP! **Decide on a plan.** Use the strategy *work backward.* Start with Roberto's $38. When you work backward, each operation will be opposite to what is in the problem. *$2 more* means add $2, so you would subtract $2. *Twice the amount* means multiply by 2, so you would divide by 2. The answer is **G**.

SOLVE

Follow your plan, working logically and carefully.

- Estimate your answer. Are any answer choices unreasonable?
- Use reasoning to find the most likely choices.
- Make sure you solved all steps needed to answer the problem.
- If your answer does not match any of the answer choices, check the numbers you used. Then check your computation.

5. 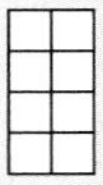

Which figure has the same area as the one above but a different perimeter?

A 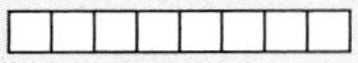

B 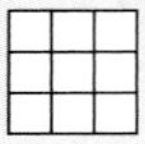

C 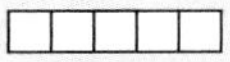

D 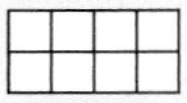

TIP! Eliminate choices.
You can eliminate choices B and C because they do not have the same area. Only answer choices A and D have an area of 8. Since D is congruent to the figure but in a different position, its perimeter will be the same. The answer is A.

- If your answer still does not match, look for another form of the number such as a decimal instead of a fraction.
- If answer choices are given as pictures, look at each one by itself while you cover the other three.
- Read answer choices that are statements and relate them to the problem one by one.
- Change your plan if it isn't working. Try a different strategy.

6. Which statement is true?

F All circles are congruent.
G All squares are similar.
H All rectangles are similar.
J All squares are congruent.

TIP! Choose the answer.
Read each statement to decide if it is true. If you aren't sure which is true, think about the properties of circles, squares, and rectangles. The answer is G.

CHECK

Take time to catch your mistakes.

- Be sure you answered the question asked.
- Check that your answer fits the information in the problem.
- Check for important words you might have missed.
- Be sure you used all the information you needed.
- Check your computation by using a different method.
- Draw a picture when you are unsure of your answer.

7. What number is inside the triangle, inside the square, and is an even number?

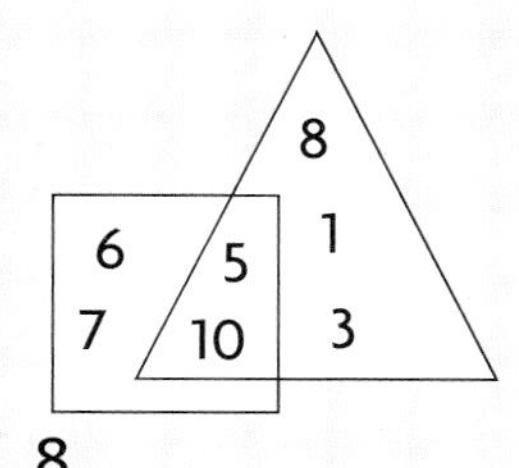

A 5 **C** 8

B 6 **D** 10

TIP! Check your work.

Look at your answer choice. Does it match all the descriptions given in the problem? If not, look for important words you might have missed. The answer is D.

Don't Forget!

Before the test

- Listen to the teacher's directions and read the instructions.
- Write down the ending time if the test is timed.
- Know where and how to mark your answers.
- Know whether you should write on the test page or use scratch paper.
- Ask any questions you may have before the test begins.

During the test

- Work quickly but carefully. If you are unsure how to answer a question, leave it blank and return to it later.
- If you cannot finish on time, look over the questions that are left. Answer the easiest ones first. Then go back to answer the others.
- Fill in each answer space carefully. Erase completely if you change an answer. Erase any stray marks.
- Check that the answer number matches the question number, especially if you skip a question.

ADDITION FACTS TEST

	K	L	M	N	O	P	Q	R
A	6 + 7	9 + 6	3 + 5	8 + 9	0 + 7	2 + 8	6 + 4	7 + 7
B	1 + 6	8 + 4	5 + 1	2 + 7	3 + 3	8 + 2	4 + 5	2 + 6
C	6 + 6	3 + 7	7 + 8	4 + 6	9 + 0	4 + 2	10 + 4	3 + 8
D	6 + 1	5 + 9	10 + 6	5 + 7	3 + 9	9 + 8	8 + 7	8 + 1
E	7 + 6	7 + 1	6 + 9	4 + 3	5 + 5	8 + 0	9 + 5	2 + 9
F	9 + 1	8 + 5	7 + 0	8 + 3	7 + 2	4 + 7	10 + 5	4 + 8
G	5 + 3	9 + 9	3 + 6	7 + 4	0 + 8	4 + 4	7 + 10	6 + 8
H	8 + 6	10 + 7	0 + 9	7 + 9	5 + 6	8 + 10	6 + 5	9 + 4
I	9 + 7	8 + 8	1 + 9	5 + 8	10 + 9	6 + 3	6 + 2	9 + 10
J	9 + 2	7 + 5	6 + 0	10 + 8	5 + 4	4 + 9	9 + 3	10 + 10

SUBTRACTION FACTS TEST

	K	L	M	N	O	P	Q	R
A	13 − 4	7 − 1	9 − 7	9 − 9	11 − 5	6 − 3	12 − 7	8 − 5
B	8 − 8	16 − 8	15 − 6	10 − 2	6 − 5	8 − 7	14 − 4	11 − 9
C	9 − 5	12 − 8	15 − 8	11 − 7	14 − 8	18 − 9	15 − 5	8 − 1
D	10 − 4	16 − 10	13 − 9	9 − 1	7 − 2	7 − 0	13 − 8	6 − 4
E	10 − 9	9 − 6	17 − 9	7 − 3	6 − 0	11 − 8	8 − 6	9 − 4
F	8 − 4	13 − 6	11 − 2	15 − 7	19 − 10	12 − 3	17 − 8	7 − 5
G	9 − 8	13 − 7	7 − 4	15 − 9	8 − 2	10 − 6	14 − 7	12 − 5
H	10 − 7	6 − 6	8 − 0	12 − 4	14 − 6	11 − 4	6 − 2	17 − 7
I	13 − 5	12 − 9	16 − 7	7 − 6	10 − 5	11 − 3	12 − 6	14 − 9
J	10 − 8	11 − 6	14 − 5	16 − 9	9 − 3	5 − 4	18 − 10	20 − 10

MULTIPLICATION FACTS TEST

	K	L	M	N	O	P	Q	R
A	5 × 6	5 × 9	7 × 7	9 × 10	7 × 5	12 × 2	10 × 6	6 × 7
B	6 × 6	0 × 6	2 × 7	12 × 8	9 × 2	3 × 5	5 × 8	8 × 3
C	7 × 0	5 × 1	4 × 5	9 × 9	6 × 8	8 × 11	11 × 7	10 × 5
D	1 × 7	9 × 4	0 × 7	2 × 5	9 × 7	10 × 9	3 × 3	12 × 7
E	5 × 7	1 × 9	4 × 3	7 × 6	11 × 3	3 × 8	4 × 2	10 × 10
F	10 × 12	5 × 5	6 × 4	9 × 8	0 × 8	9 × 6	11 × 2	12 × 6
G	5 × 3	4 × 6	6 × 3	7 × 9	12 × 5	0 × 9	5 × 4	12 × 11
H	7 × 1	6 × 9	1 × 6	4 × 4	3 × 7	11 × 11	4 × 8	12 × 9
I	7 × 4	2 × 4	8 × 6	3 × 4	11 × 5	2 × 9	8 × 9	7 × 8
J	8 × 0	3 × 9	12 × 12	8 × 5	4 × 7	6 × 2	9 × 5	8 × 8

	K	L	M	N	O	P	Q	R
A	$7\overline{)56}$	$5\overline{)40}$	$6\overline{)24}$	$6\overline{)30}$	$6\overline{)18}$	$7\overline{)42}$	$8\overline{)16}$	$9\overline{)45}$
B	$3\overline{)9}$	$10\overline{)90}$	$1\overline{)1}$	$1\overline{)6}$	$10\overline{)100}$	$3\overline{)12}$	$10\overline{)70}$	$8\overline{)56}$
C	$6\overline{)48}$	$12\overline{)60}$	$4\overline{)32}$	$6\overline{)54}$	$7\overline{)0}$	$3\overline{)18}$	$9\overline{)90}$	$11\overline{)55}$
D	$2\overline{)16}$	$3\overline{)21}$	$5\overline{)30}$	$3\overline{)15}$	$11\overline{)110}$	$9\overline{)9}$	$8\overline{)64}$	$9\overline{)63}$
E	$4\overline{)28}$	$2\overline{)10}$	$9\overline{)18}$	$1\overline{)5}$	$7\overline{)63}$	$8\overline{)32}$	$2\overline{)8}$	$9\overline{)108}$
F	$8\overline{)24}$	$4\overline{)4}$	$2\overline{)14}$	$11\overline{)66}$	$8\overline{)72}$	$4\overline{)12}$	$7\overline{)21}$	$6\overline{)36}$
G	$12\overline{)36}$	$5\overline{)20}$	$7\overline{)28}$	$7\overline{)14}$	$4\overline{)24}$	$11\overline{)121}$	$9\overline{)36}$	$11\overline{)132}$
H	$9\overline{)27}$	$3\overline{)27}$	$7\overline{)49}$	$4\overline{)20}$	$9\overline{)72}$	$5\overline{)60}$	$8\overline{)88}$	$10\overline{)80}$
I	$4\overline{)44}$	$8\overline{)48}$	$5\overline{)35}$	$8\overline{)40}$	$5\overline{)10}$	$2\overline{)12}$	$10\overline{)60}$	$9\overline{)54}$
J	$10\overline{)120}$	$12\overline{)72}$	$9\overline{)81}$	$4\overline{)16}$	$1\overline{)7}$	$12\overline{)60}$	$12\overline{)96}$	$12\overline{)144}$

ADDITION AND SUBTRACTION FACTS TEST

	K	L	M	N	O	P	Q	R
A	15 + 4	9 − 3	6 + 5	10 − 7	13 − 9	5 + 8	11 − 4	0 + 9
B	12 − 4	9 + 9	16 − 9	8 − 6	12 + 5	11 − 6	5 + 3	16 − 9
C	8 + 6	0 + 8	9 − 6	7 + 7	19 − 9	3 + 6	11 − 8	7 + 4
D	6 + 3	14 − 6	8 + 8	4 − 4	16 − 8	7 + 9	9 + 7	12 − 3
E	6 + 8	17 − 9	7 − 3	6 + 6	8 − 4	1 + 9	8 + 7	12 − 9
F	8 + 5	3 + 9	11 − 3	3 + 7	10 − 2	9 + 0	12 − 8	7 + 2
G	5 + 7	13 − 4	4 + 6	20 − 10	7 − 0	6 + 9	14 − 7	10 + 8
H	6 + 7	7 − 4	9 − 9	9 + 8	13 − 5	8 + 10	17 − 10	10 − 5
I	8 + 4	14 − 9	3 + 3	9 + 10	10 − 6	4 + 7	9 − 7	7 + 6
J	11 − 2	9 + 5	15 − 7	10 + 10	18 − 9	7 + 8	11 − 5	13 − 7

MULTIPLICATION AND DIVISION FACTS TEST

	K	L	M	N	O	P	Q	R
A	$3\overline{)21}$	9×6	$6\overline{)30}$	10×7	10×1	$4\overline{)32}$	$7\overline{)63}$	5×4
B	8×3	$7\overline{)56}$	$8\overline{)88}$	12×2	8×11	$1\overline{)8}$	$9\overline{)90}$	10×5
C	$12\overline{)36}$	7×8	5×7	$10\overline{)90}$	$5\overline{)45}$	12×4	$8\overline{)16}$	5×5
D	7×7	$4\overline{)48}$	$9\overline{)99}$	11×3	12×3	$9\overline{)108}$	$11\overline{)88}$	10×2
E	7×10	12×9	$12\overline{)84}$	$2\overline{)20}$	12×0	10×11	$3\overline{)36}$	$10\overline{)110}$
F	$4\overline{)44}$	$12\overline{)72}$	7×11	12×6	$7\overline{)56}$	$9\overline{)45}$	10×3	9×7
G	$12\overline{)108}$	$6\overline{)60}$	9×2	8×12	$12\overline{)144}$	$6\overline{)24}$	4×4	$7\overline{)84}$
H	4×9	8×8	$11\overline{)44}$	$7\overline{)77}$	6×11	12×5	$11\overline{)132}$	$6\overline{)42}$
I	$8\overline{)96}$	$8\overline{)56}$	12×11	12×12	$5\overline{)60}$	3×6	10×10	$4\overline{)40}$
J	11×5	9×9	$10\overline{)80}$	$7\overline{)35}$	11×4	$10\overline{)120}$	9×8	10×9

TABLE OF MEASURES

METRIC	CUSTOMARY
Length	
1 centimeter (cm) = 10 millimeters (mm)	1 foot (ft) = 12 inches (in.)
1 decimeter (dm) = 10 centimeters	1 yard (yd) = 3 feet, or 36 inches
1 meter (m) = 10 decimeters	1 mile (mi) = 1,760 yards, or 5,280 feet
1 kilometer (km) = 1,000 meters	
Capacity	
1 liter (L) = 1,000 milliliters (mL)	1 tablespoon (tbsp) = 3 teaspoons (tsp)
1 metric cup = 250 milliliters	1 cup (c) = 8 fluid ounces (fl oz)
	1 pint (pt) = 2 cups
	1 quart (qt) = 2 pints
	1 gallon (gal) = 4 quarts
Mass/Weight	
1 gram (g) = 1,000 milligrams (mg)	1 pound (lb) = 16 ounces (oz)
1 kilogram (kg) = 1,000 grams	1 ton (T) = 2,000 pounds

TIME

1 minute (min) = 60 seconds (sec)
1 hour (hr) = 60 minutes
1 day = 24 hours
1 week (wk) = 7 days
1 year (yr) = 12 months (mo), or about 52 weeks
1 year = 365 days
1 leap year = 366 days

MONEY

1 penny = 1 cent (¢)
1 nickel = 5 cents
1 dime = 10 cents
1 quarter = 25 cents
1 half dollar = 50 cents
1 dollar ($) = 100 cents

SYMBOLS

$\perp$	is perpendicular to	$<$	is less than	$^\circ$	degree
$\parallel$	is parallel to	$>$	is greater than	$^\circ$F	degrees Fahrenheit
$\overleftrightarrow{AB}$	line *AB*	$\leq$	is less than or equal to	$^\circ$C	degrees Celsius
$\overrightarrow{AB}$	ray *AB*	$\geq$	is greater than or equal to	$^{+}8$	positive 8
$\overline{AB}$	line segment *AB*	$\approx$	is approximately equal to	$^{-}8$	negative 8
$\angle ABC$	angle *ABC*	$=$	is equal to	1:2	ratio of 1 to 2
$\triangle ABC$	triangle *ABC*	$\neq$	is not equal to	(2,3)	ordered pair (x,y)
				%	percent

FORMULAS

Perimeter of polygon = sum of length of sides
Perimeter of rectangle $P = (2 \times l) + (2 \times w)$
Perimeter of square $P = 4 \times s$
Area of rectangle $A = l \times w$
Volume of rectangular prism $V = l \times w \times h$

Pronunciation Key

a	add, map	f	fit, half	n	nice, tin	p	pit, stop	yo͞o	fuse, few
ā	ace, rate	g	go, log	ng	ring, song	r	run, poor	v	vain, eve
â(r)	care, air	h	hope, hate	o	odd, hot	s	see, pass	w	win, away
ä	palm, father	i	it, give	ō	open, so	sh	sure, rush	y	yet, yearn
b	bat, rub	ī	ice, write	ô	order, jaw	t	talk, sit	z	zest, muse
ch	check, catch	j	joy, ledge	oi	oil, boy	th	thin, both	zh	vision, pleasure
d	dog, rod	k	cool, take	ou	pout, now	t͟h	this, bathe		
e	end, pet	l	look, rule	o͝o	took, full	u	up, done		
ē	equal, tree	m	move, seem	o͞o	pool, food	û(r)	burn, term		

ə the schwa, an unstressed vowel representing the sound spelled *a* in above, *e* in sicken, *i* in possible, *o* in melon, *u* in circus

Other symbols:
• separates words into syllables
ʹ indicates stress on a syllable

A.M. [ā•emʹ] The time between midnight and noon (p. 98)

acute angle [ə•kyo͞otʹ angʹəl] An angle that measures greater than 0° and less than 90° (p. 367)
Example:

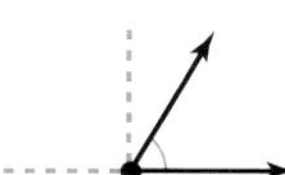

acute triangle [ə•kyo͞otʹ trīʹang•əl] A triangle with three acute angles (p. 382)
Example:

addend [aʹdend] A number that is added to another in an addition problem
Example: 2 + 4 = 6;
2 and 4 are addends.

addition [ə•diʹshən] The process of finding the total number of items when two or more groups of items are joined; the opposite operation of subtraction

analog clock [aʹnəl•ôg kläk] A device for measuring time by moving hands around a circle for showing hours, minutes, and sometimes seconds.
Example:

angle [angʹəl] A figure formed by two line segments or rays that share the same endpoint (p. 366)
Example:

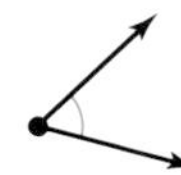

area [ârʹē•ə] The number of square units needed to cover a surface (p. 628)
Example:

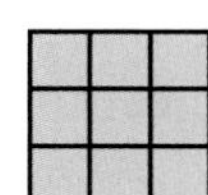

area = 9 square units

array [ə•rāʹ] An arrangement of objects in rows and columns

Associative Property of Addition [ə•sōʹshē•ə•tiv präʹpər•tē əv ə•diʹshən] The property that states you can group addends in different ways and still get the same sum (p. 68)
Example: 3 + (8 + 5) = (3 + 8) + 5

Associative Property of Multiplication [ə•sōʹshē•ə•tiv präʹpər•tē əv mul•tə•plə•kāʹshən] The property that states you can group factors in different ways and still get the same product (p. 174)
Example: 3 × (4 × 2) = (3 × 4) × 2

average [avʹrij] See *mean.*

bar graph [bär graf] A graph that uses bars to show data (p. 136)

benchmark [bench′märk] A known number of things that helps you understand the size or amount of a different number of things (p. 10)

calendar [ka′lən•dər] A table that shows the days, weeks, and months of a year (p. 104)

capacity [kə•pa′sə•tē] The amount a container can hold when filled (p. 528)

center [sen′tər] The point inside a circle that is the same distance from each point on the circle (p. 390)
Example:

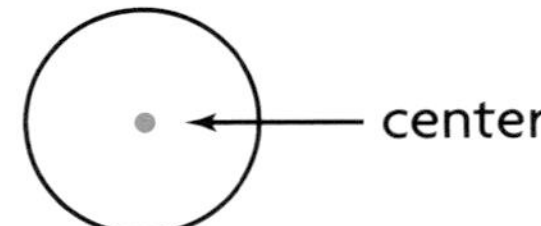

Word History

The word *center* comes from a Greek root, *kentrus*, meaning "spur or sharp, pointed object." A sharp point was made at a center point to fix the spot and a duller object was dragged around the center to form the circle.

centimeter (cm) [sən′tə•mē•tər] A metric unit for measuring length or distance (p. 540)
100 centimeters = 1 meter
Example:

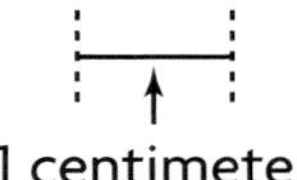

1 centimeter

century [sen′chə•rē] A measure of time equal to 100 years (p. 105)

certain [sər′tən] An event is certain if it will always happen (p. 496)

chord [kôrd] A line segment with endpoints on a circle (p. 390)
Example:

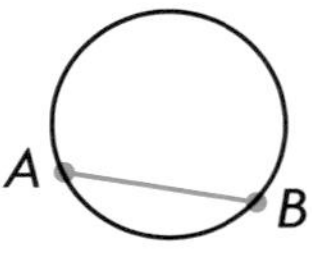

$\overline{AB}$ is a chord.

circle [sûr′kəl] A closed figure made up of points that are the same distance from the center (p. 390)
Example:

circle graph [sûr′kəl graf] A graph in the shape of a circle that shows data as a whole made up of different parts (p. 142)
Example:

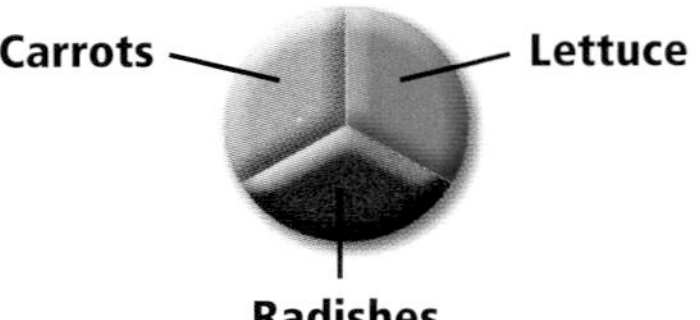

circumference [sər•kum′fər•əns] The distance around a circle (p. 618)

closed figure [klōzd fi′gyər] A figure that begins and ends at the same point
Examples:

Commutative Property of Addition [kə•myōō′tə•tiv prä′pər•tē əv ədi′shən] The property that states that when the order of two addends is changed, the sum is the same (p. 68)
Example: $4 + 5 = 5 + 4$

Commutative Property of Multiplication [kə•myōō′tə•tiv prä′pər•tē əv mul•tə•plə•kā′shən] The property that states that when the order of two factors is changed, the product is the same (p. 174)
Example: $4 \times 5 = 5 \times 4$

compass [kəm′pəs] A tool used to construct circles (p. 390)

compatible numbers [kəm•pa′tə•bəl num′bərz] Numbers that are easy to compute mentally (p. 216)

composite number [kəm•pä′zət num′bər] A whole number that has more than two factors (p. 342)
Example: 9 is composite since its factors are 1, 3, and 9.

cone [kōn] A solid, pointed figure that has a flat, round base (p. 644)
Example:

congruent [kən•gro͞o′ənt] Having the same size and shape (p. 402)
Example:

coordinate grid [kō•ôr′də•nət grid] A grid formed by a horizontal line called the *x*-axis and a vertical line called the *y*-axis (p. 430)
Example:

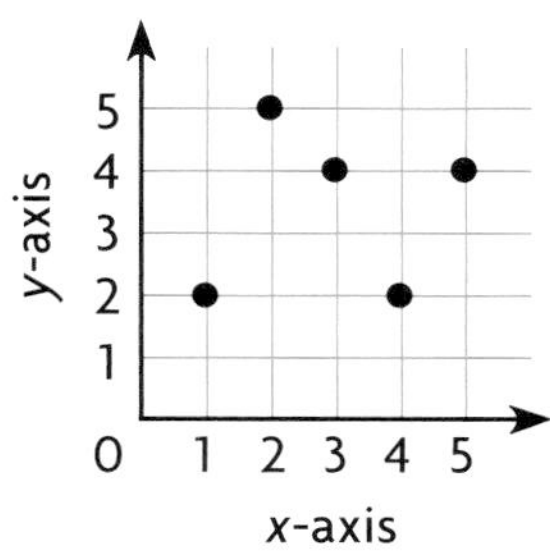

coordinate plane [kō•ôr′də•nət plān] A plane formed by two intersecting and perpendicular number lines called axes (p. 437)
Example:

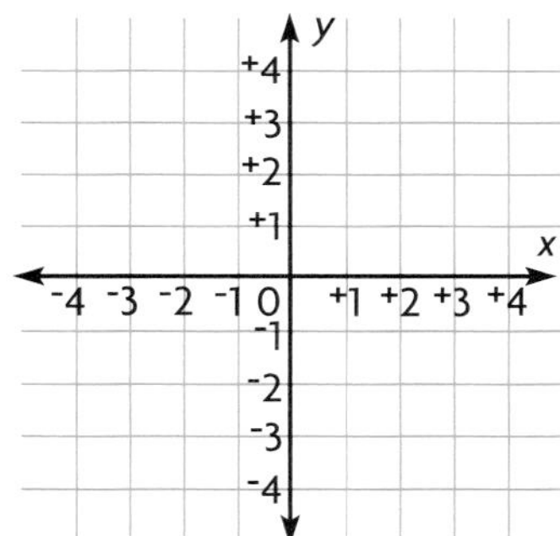

corner [kôr′nər] See *vertex.*

cube [kyo͞ob] A solid figure with six congruent square faces (p. 644)
Example:

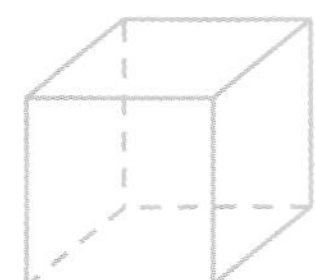

cubic unit [kyo͞o′bik yo͞o′nət] A unit of volume with dimensions of 1 unit × 1 unit × 1 unit (p. 650)

cumulative frequency [kyo͞o′myə•lə•tiv frē′kwən•sē] A running total of items being counted (p. 115)

cup (c) [kup] A customary unit used to measure capacity (p. 528) 8 ounces = 1 cup

cylinder [si′lən•dər] A solid figure that is shaped like a can (p. 644)
Example:

D

data [dā′tə] Information collected about people or things

decade [de′kād] A measure of time equal to 10 years (p. 105)

decimal [de′sə•məl] A number with one or more digits to the right of the decimal point (p. 560)

decimal point [de′sə•məl point] A symbol used to separate dollars from cents in money amounts and to separate the ones and the tenths places in a decimal (p. 560)
Example: 6.4
↑ decimal point

decimeter (dm) [de′sə•mē•tər] A metric unit for measuring length or distance (p. 540)
10 decimeters = 1 meter

degree (°) [di•grē′] The unit used for measuring angles and temperatures (pp. 366, 420)

degree Celsius (°C) [di•grē′ sel′sē•əs] A metric unit for measuring temperature (p. 422)

degree Fahrenheit (°F) [di•grē′ fâr′ən•hīt] A standard unit for measuring temperature (p. 420)

denominator [di•nä′mə•nā•tər] The number below the bar in a fraction that tells how many equal parts are in the whole (p. 446)
Example: $\frac{3}{4}$ ← denominator

diameter [dī•am′ə•tər] A line segment that passes through the center of a circle and has endpoints on the circle (p. 390)
Example:

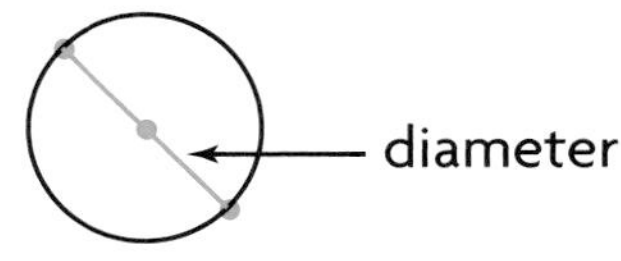

difference [di′fər•əns] The answer to a subtraction problem (p. 45)

digit [di′jət] Any one of the ten symbols 0, 1, 2, 3, 4, 5, 6, 7, 8, or 9 used to write numbers (p. 2)

digital clock [di′jə•təl kläk] A clock that shows time to the minute using digits
Example:

dimension [də•men′shən] A measure in one direction

Distributive Property [di•stri′byə•tiv prä′pər•tē] The property that states that multiplying a sum by a number is the same as multiplying each addend by the number and then adding the products (p. 238)
Example: $5 \times (10 + 6) = (5 \times 10) + (5 \times 6)$

dividend [di′və•dend] The number that is to be divided in a division problem (p. 164)
Example: $36 \div 6$; $6\overline{)36}$; the dividend is 36.

divisible [də•vi′zə•bəl] Capable of being divided so that the quotient is a whole number and the remainder is zero (p. 336)
Example: 21 is divisible by 3.

division [də•vi′zhən] The process of sharing a number of items to find how many groups can be made or how many items will be in each group; the opposite operation of multiplication

divisor [də•vi′zər] The number that divides the dividend (p. 164)
Example: $15 \div 3$; $3\overline{)15}$; the divisor is 3.

double-bar graph [du′bəl bär graf] A graph used to compare similar kinds of data (p. 136)
Example:

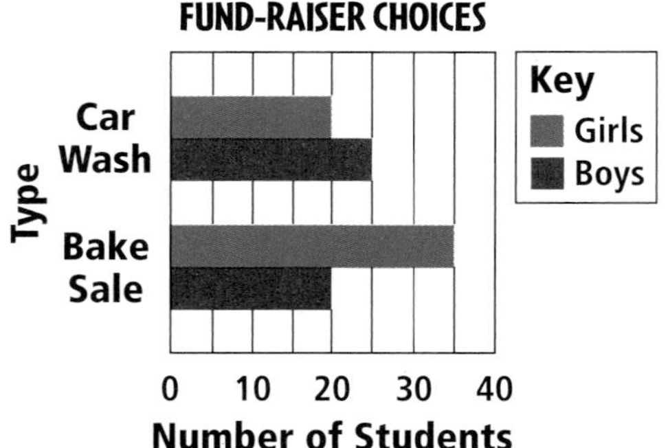

doubles [du′ bəlz] Two addends that are the same number

edge [ej] The line segment where two or more faces of a solid figure meet (p. 645)
Example:

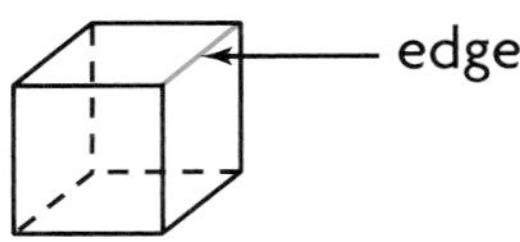

elapsed time [i•lapst′ tīm] The time that passes from the start of an activity to the end of that activity (p. 98)

equally likely [ē′kwə•lē lī′klē] Having the same chance of happening (p. 492)

equation [i•kwā′zhən] A number sentence which shows that two quantities are equal (p. 70)
Example: $4 + 5 = 9$

equilateral triangle [ē•kwə•la′tə•rəl trī′ang•əl] A triangle with 3 equal, or congruent, sides (p. 382)
Example:

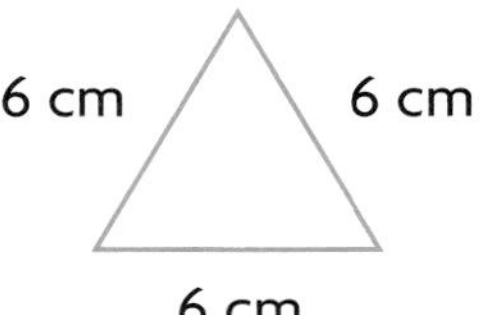

equivalent [ē•kwiv′ə•lənt] Having the same value or naming the same amount

equivalent decimals [ē•kwiv′ə•lənt de′sə•məlz] Two or more decimals that name the same amount (p. 566)

equivalent fractions [ē•kwiv′ə•lənt frak′shənz] Two or more fractions that name the same amount (p. 448)
Example: $\frac{2}{4}$ and $\frac{1}{2}$ name the same amount.

estimate [es′tə•māt] *verb* To find an answer that is close to the exact amount (p. 44)

estimate [es′tə•mət] *noun* A number close to an exact amount

event [i•vent′] One outcome or a combination of outcomes in an experiment (p. 490)

expanded form [ik•span′dəd fôrm] A way to write numbers by showing the value of each digit (p. 4)
Example: $253 = 200 + 50 + 3$

expression [ik•spre′shən] A part of a number sentence that has numbers and operation signs but does not have an equal sign (p. 64)

face [fās] A polygon that is a flat surface of a solid figure (p. 644)
Example:

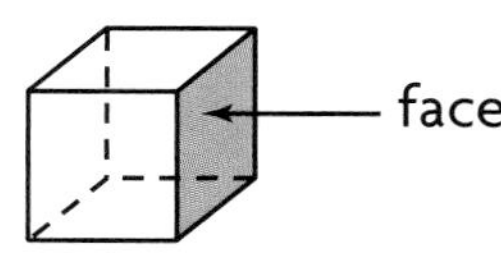

fact family [fakt fam′ə•lē] A set of related multiplication and division, or addition and subtraction, equations (p. 164)
Example: $7 \times 8 = 56$; $8 \times 7 = 56$;
$56 \div 7 = 8$; $56 \div 8 = 7$

factor [fak′tər] A number that is multiplied by another number to find a product (p. 164)

factor tree [fak′tər trē] A diagram that shows the prime factors of a number (p. 355)
Example:

30
/ \
5 × 6
/ / \
5 × 2 × 3

fairness [fâr′nəs] Fairness in a game means that one player is as likely to win as another; each player has an equal chance of winning. (p. 509)

flip [flip] See *reflection.*

foot (ft) [fo͝ot] A customary unit used for measuring length or distance (p. 518)
1 foot = 12 inches

formula [fôr′myə•lə] A set of symbols that expresses a mathematical rule (p. 614)
Example: $A = l \times w$

fraction [frak′shən] A number that names a part of a whole or part of a group (p. 446)

frequency [frē′kwen•sē] The number of times an event occurs (p. 115)

frequency table [frē′kwen•sē tā′bəl] A table that uses numbers to record data about how often something happens (p. 115)

gallon (gal) [ga′lən] A customary unit for measuring capacity (p. 528)
4 quarts = 1 gallon

gram (g) [gram] A unit for measuring mass (p. 548)
1,000 grams = 1 kilogram

greater than (>) [grā′tər than] A symbol used to compare two quantities, with the greater quantity given first (p. 24)
Example: $6 > 4$

greater than or equal to (≥) [grā′tər than ər ē•kwəl to͞o] A symbol used to compare two quantities when the first is greater than or equal to the second (p. 428)
Example: $4 + 5 \geq 7$

grid [grid] Evenly divided and equally spaced squares on a figure or flat surface

Grouping Property of Addition [gro͞o′ping prä′pər•tē əv ə•di′shən] See *Associative Property of Addition.*

Grouping Property of Multiplication [gro͞o′ping prä′pər•tē əv mul•tə•plə•kā′shən] See *Associative Property of Multiplication.*

hexagon [hek′sə•gän] A polygon with six sides (p. 380)
Examples:

hour (hr) [our] A unit used to measure time; 60 minutes = 1 hour

hour hand [our hand] The short hand on an analog clock

hundredth [hən′drədth] One of one hundred equal parts (p. 560)
Example:

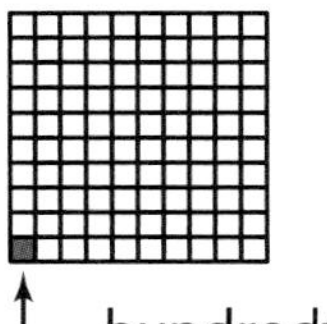

Identity Property of Addition [ī•den′tə•tē prä′pər•tē əv ə•di′shən] The property that states that when you add zero to any number, the sum is that number (p. 68)
Example: 0 + 16 = 16

Identity Property of Multiplication [ī•den′tə•tē prä′pər•tē əv mul•tə•plə•kā′shən] The property that states that the product of any number and 1 is that number (p. 174)
Example: 9 × 1 = 9

impossible [im•pä′sə•bəl] Never able to happen (p. 496)

improper fraction [im•prä′pər frak′shən] A fraction greater than 1 (p. 459)

inch (in.) [inch] A customary unit used for measuring length or distance (p. 518)
Example:

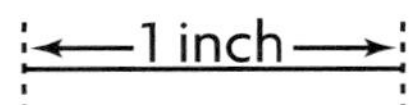

inequality [in•i•kwol′ə•tē] A mathematical sentence that shows two expressions do not represent the same quantity (p. 428)
Example: 4 < 9 − 3

intersecting lines [in•tər•sek′ting līnz] Lines that cross each other at exactly one point (p. 370)
Example:

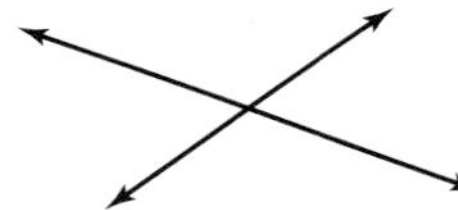

interval [in′tər•vəl] The distance between two numbers on the scale of a graph (p. 126)

inverse operations [in′vərs ä•pə•rā′shənz] Operations that undo each other. Addition and subtraction are inverse operations. Multiplication and division are inverse operations. (p. 164)
Example: 6 × 8 = 48 and 48 ÷ 6 = 8

is approximately equal to (≈) [iz ə•präk′sə•mət•lē ē•kwəl to͞o] A symbol that indicates one amount, size, or value is about the same as another (p. 552)
Example: 1 kg ≈ 2 lb

isosceles triangle [ī•sä′sə•lēz trī′ang•əl] A triangle with two equal, or congruent, sides (p. 382)
Example:

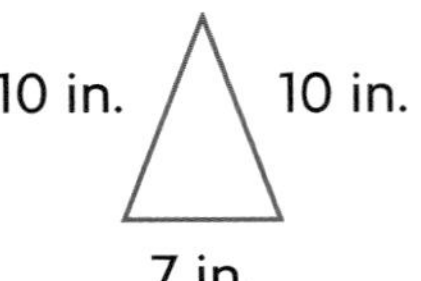

Word History

When you look at the sides on an *isosceles* triangle, you see that the two sides are equal in length. The Greek root *iso-* means "same or equal," and *skelos* means "legs."

key [kē] The part of a map or graph that explains the symbols

kilogram (kg) [ki′lə•gram] A metric unit for measuring mass (p. 548)
1 kilogram = 1,000 grams

kilometer (km) [kə•lä′mə•tər] A metric unit for measuring length or distance (p. 541)
1,000 meters = 1 kilometer

leaf [lēf] A ones digit in a stem-and-leaf plot (p. 124)

less than (<) [les th̶an] A symbol used to compare two numbers, with the lesser number given first (p. 24)
Example: 3 < 7

less than or equal to (≤) [les th̶an ər ē′kwəl to͞o] A symbol used to compare quantities, when the first is less than or equal to the second (p. 428)
Example: 8 ≤ 14 − 5

like fractions [līk frak′shənz] Fractions with the same denominator (p. 468)

likely [līk′lē] Having a greater than even chance of happening (p. 492)

line [līn] A straight path of points in a plane that continues without end in both directions with no endpoints (p. 364)
Example:

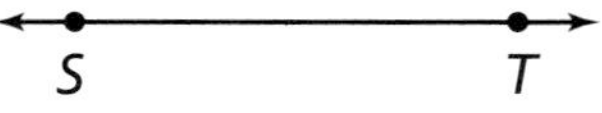

line graph [līn graf] A graph that uses a line to show how data changes over a period of time (p. 138)
Example:

line plot [līn plät] A graph that shows the frequency of data along a number line (p. 122)
Example:

line segment [līn seg′mənt] A part of a line that includes two points called endpoints and all the points between them (p. 364)
Example:

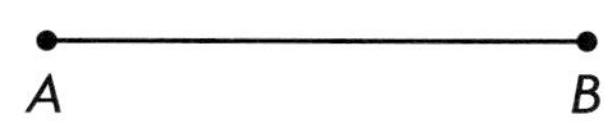

line symmetry [līn si′mə•trē] What a figure has if it can be folded about a line so that its two parts match exactly (p. 399)
Example:

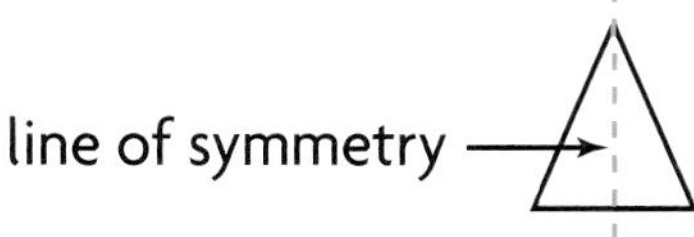

linear units [li′nē•ər yo͞o′nəts] Units that measure length, width, height, or distance (p. 518)

liter (L) [lē′tər] A metric unit for measuring capacity (p. 546)
1 liter = 1,000 milliliters

M

mass [mas] The amount of matter in an object (p. 548)

mathematical probability [math•ma′ti•kəl prä•bə•bi′lə•tē] A comparison of the number of favorable outcomes to the number of possible outcomes of an event (p. 496)

mean [mēn] The number found by dividing the sum of the set of numbers by the number of addends (p. 118)

median [mē′dē•ən] The middle number in an ordered set of data (p. 119)

meter (m) [mē′tər] A metric unit for measuring length or distance (p. 540)
100 centimeters = 1 meter

mile (mi) [mīl] A customary unit for measuring length or distance (p. 518)
5,280 feet = 1 mile

milliliter (mL) [mi′lə•lē•tər] A metric unit for measuring capacity (p. 546)
1,000 milliliters = 1 liter

millimeter (mm) [mi′lə•mē•tər] A metric unit for measuring length or distance (p. 540)
1 centimeter = 10 millimeters

millions [mil′yənz] The period after thousands (p. 6)

minute (min) [mi′nət] A unit to measure short amounts of time used
60 seconds = 1 minute

minute hand [mi′nət hand] The long hand on an analog clock

mixed number [mikst nəm′bər] An amount given as a whole number and a fraction (p. 458)

mode [mōd] The number(s) or item(s) that occur most often in a set of data (p. 119)

multiple [mul′tə•pəl] The product of a given whole number and another whole number (p. 173)

multiplication [mul•tə•plə•kā′shən] A process to find the total number of items in equal-sized groups, or to find the total number of items in a given number of groups when each group contains the same number of items; multiplication is the inverse of division

multistep problem [mul′ti•step prä′bləm] A problem requiring more than one step to solve (p. 262)

negative numbers [ne′gə•tiv num′bərz] All the numbers to the left of zero on the number line; negative numbers are less than zero (p. 424)

net [net] A two-dimensional pattern that can be folded to make a three-dimensional figure (p. 648)
Example:

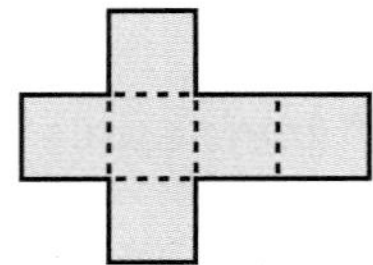

not equal to (≠) [nät ē′kwəl to͞o] A symbol that indicates one quantity is not equal to another
Example: $12 \times 3 \neq 38$

number line [num′bər līn] A line with equally spaced tick marks named by numbers
Example:

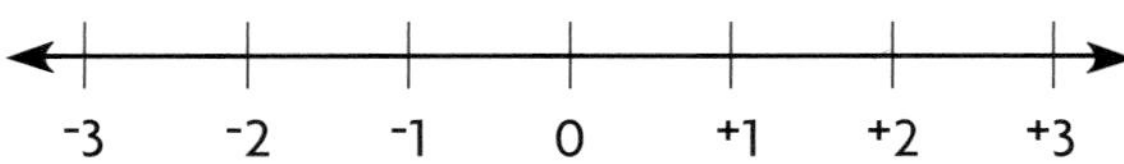

numerator [no͞o′mə•rā•tər] The number above the bar in a fraction that tells how many parts of the whole or group are being considered (p. 446)

Example: $\frac{2}{3}$ ← numerator

obtuse angle [äb•to͞os′ ang′əl] An angle that measures greater than 90° and less than 180° (p. 367)
Example:

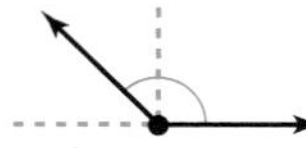

Word History

The Latin prefix *ob-* means "against." When combined with *-tuse* meaning "to beat," the word *obtuse* means "to beat against." This makes sense when you look at an obtuse angle because the angle is not sharp or acute. The angle has been beaten against and become blunt and rounded.

obtuse triangle [äb•to͞os′ trī′ang•əl] A triangle with one obtuse angle (p. 382)
Example:

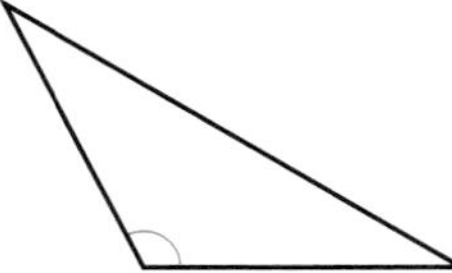

octagon [äk′tə•gän] A polygon with eight sides (p. 380)
Example:

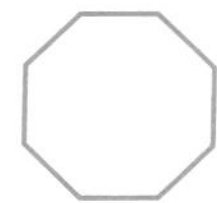

open figure [ō′pən fi′gyər] A figure that does not begin and end at the same point
Examples:

opposites [ä′pə•zəts] Numbers that are the same distance from zero, but in opposite directions from zero (p. 424)

order of operations [ôr′dər əv ä•pə•rā′shənz] A special set of rules that can be used to solve an expression with more than one operation (p. 186)

Order Property of Addition [ôr′dər prä′pər•tē əv ə•di′shən] See *Commutative Property of Addition.*

Order Property of Multiplication [ôr′dər prä′pər•tē əv mul•tə•plə•kā′shən] See *Commutative Property of Multiplication.*

ordered pair [ôr′dərd pâr] A pair of numbers used to locate a point on a coordinate grid. The first number tells how far to move horizontally, and the second number tells how far to move vertically. (p. 430)

origin [ôr′ə•jən] The point where the *x*-axis and the *y*-axis in the coordinate plane intersect, (0,0) (p. 437)

ounce (oz) [ouns] A customary unit for measuring weight (p. 530)
16 ounces = 1 pound

outcome [out′kum] A possible result of an experiment (p. 490)

outlier [out′lī•ər] A value separated from the rest of the data (p. 122)

P

P.M. [pē•em′] The time between noon and midnight (p. 98)

parallel lines [par′ə•lel līnz] Lines in the same plane that never intersect and are always the same distance apart (p. 370)
Example:

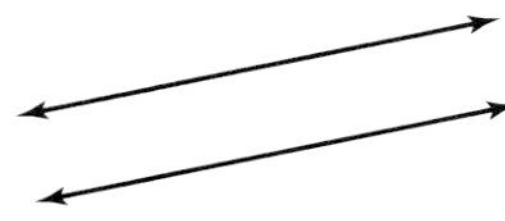

Word History

Euclid, an early Greek mathematician, was one of the first to explore the idea for parallel lines. The prefix *para-* means "beside or alongside." This prefix helps you understand the meaning of the word *parallel*.

parallelogram [par•ə•lel′ə•gram] A quadrilateral whose opposite sides are parallel and equal, or congruent (p. 385)
Example:

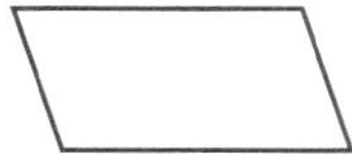

parentheses [pə•ren′thə•sēz] The symbols used to show which operation or operations in an expression should be done first (p. 64)

partial product [pär′shəl prä′dəkt] A method of multiplying in which the ones, tens, hundreds, and so on are multiplied separately and then the products are added together (p. 238)

pentagon [pen′tə•gän] A polygon with five sides (p. 380)
Examples:

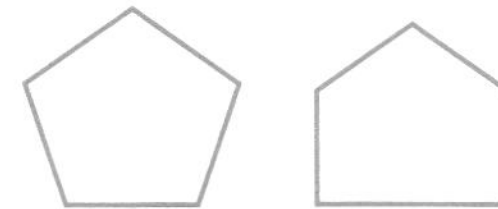

perimeter [pə•ri′mə•tər] The distance around a figure (p. 612)

period [pir′ē•əd] Each group of three digits separated by commas in a multidigit number (p. 4)
Example: 85,643,900 has three periods.

perpendicular lines [pər•pən•di′kyə•lər līnz] Two lines that intersect to form four right angles (p. 370)
Example:

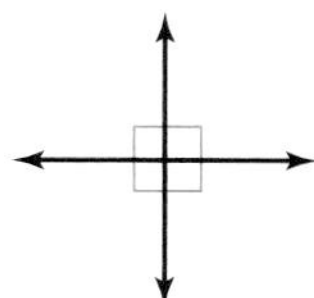

pictograph [pik′tə•graf] A graph that uses pictures to show and compare information (p. 128)
Example:

HOW WE GET TO SCHOOL

Walk	❀ ❀ ❀
Ride a Bike	❀ ❀ ❀ ❀
Ride a Bus	❀ ❀ ❀ ❀ ❀ ❀
Ride in a Car	❀ ❀

Key: Each ❀ = 10 students.

pint (pt) [pīnt] A customary unit for measuring capacity (p. 528)
2 cups = 1 pint

place value [plās val′yo͞o] Place value determines the value of a digit in a number, based on the location of the digit

plane [plān] A flat surface that extends without end in all directions (p. 364)
Example:

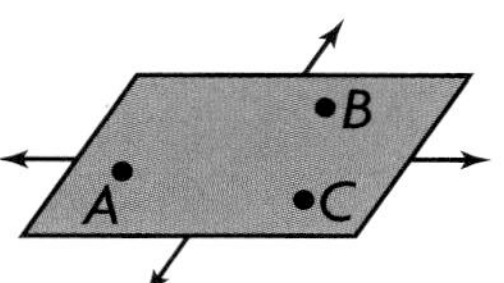

plane figure [plān fi′gyər] A figure in a plane that is formed by lines that are curved, straight, or both

point [point] An exact location in space (p. 364)

polygon [pä′lē•gän] A closed plane figure with straight sides; each side is a line segment. (p. 380)
Examples:

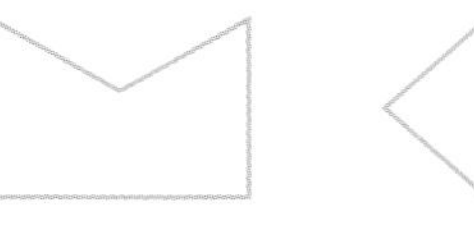

positive numbers [pä′zə•tiv num′bərz] All the numbers to the right of zero on the number line; positive numbers are greater than 0 (p. 424)

pound (lb) [pound] A customary unit for measuring weight (p. 530)
16 ounces = 1 pound

predict [pri•dikt′] To make a reasonable guess about what will happen (p. 492)

prime factor [prīm fak′tər] A factor that is a prime number (p. 355)

prime number [prīm num′bər] A number that has only two factors: 1 and itself (p. 342)
Examples: 5, 7, 11, 13, 17, and 19 are prime numbers.

probability [prä•bə•bi′lə•tē] The likelihood that an event will happen (p. 494)

product [prä′dəkt] The answer to a multiplication problem (p. 164)

protractor [prō′trak•tər] A tool for measuring the size of an angle (p. 366)

pyramid [pir′ə•mid] A solid figure with a polygon base and triangular sides that meet at a single point
Example:

quadrilateral [kwä•drə•la′tə•rəl] A polygon with four sides (p. 380)

quart (qt) [kwôrt] A customary unit for measuring capacity (p. 528)
2 pints = 1 quart

quotient [kwō′shənt] The number, not including the remainder, that results from dividing (p. 164)
Example: 8 ÷ 4 = 2; 2 is the quotient.

radius [rā′dē•əs] A line segment with one endpoint at the center of a circle and the other endpoint on the circle (p. 390)
Example:

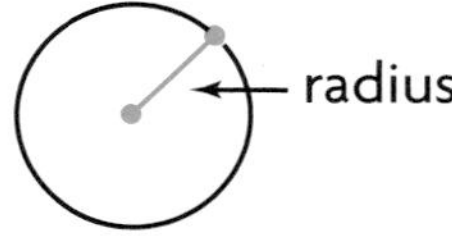

range [rānj] The difference between the greatest and the least number in a set of data (p. 122)

ratio [rā′shē•ō] The comparison of two numbers by division (p. 603)

ray [rā] A part of a line; it has one endpoint and continues without end in one direction (p. 364)
Example:

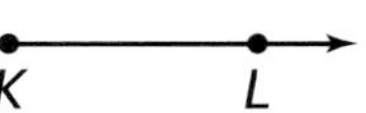

rectangle [rek′tang•əl] A parallelogram with opposite sides that are equal, or congruent, and with four right angles (p. 385)
Example:

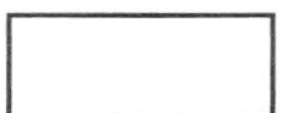

rectangular prism [rek•tang′yə•lər pri′zəm] A solid figure in which all six faces are rectangles (p. 644)
Example:

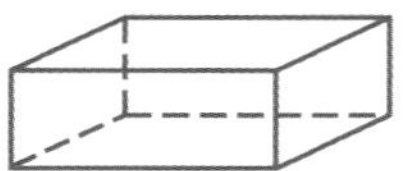

reflection (flip) [rē•flek′shən] A movement of a figure to a new position by flipping the figure over a line (p. 406)
Example:

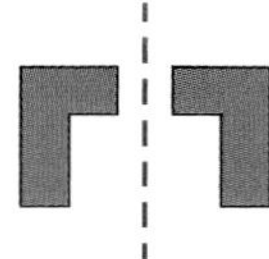

regroup [rē•groop′] To exchange amounts of equal value to rename a number
Example: 5 + 8 = 13 ones or 1 ten 3 ones

regular polygon [reg′yə•lər pä′lē•gän] A polygon that has sides that are the same length (p. 380)
Examples:

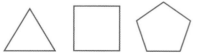

remainder [ri•mān′dər] The amount left over when a number cannot be divided equally (p. 278)

rhombus [räm′bəs] A parallelogram with four equal, or congruent, sides (p. 385)
Example:

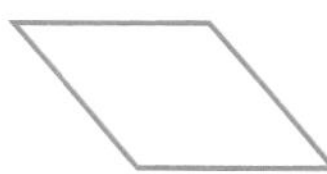

right angle [rīt ang′əl] An angle that forms a square corner and has a measure of 90° (p. 367)
Example:

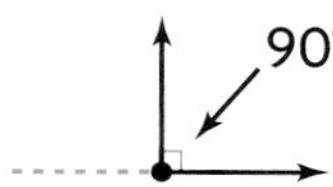

right triangle [rīt trī′ang•əl] A triangle with one right angle (p. 382)
Example:

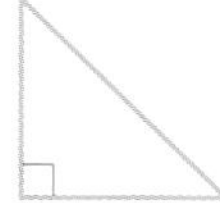

rotation (turn) [rō•tā′shən] A movement of a figure to a new position by rotating the figure around a point (p. 406)
Example:

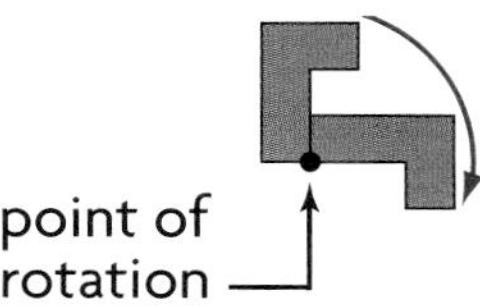

rotational symmetry [rō•tā′shən•əl si′mə•trē] What a figure has if it can be turned about a central point and still look the same in at least two positions (p. 399)

round [round] To replace a number with another number that tells about how many or how much (p. 30)

scale [skāl] A series of numbers placed at fixed distances on a graph to help label the graph (p. 126)

scalene triangle [skā′lēn trī′ang•əl] A triangle with no equal, or congruent, sides (p. 382)
Example:

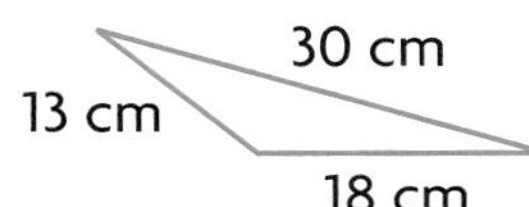

schedule [ske′jo͞ol] A table that lists activities or events and the times they happen

second (sec) [se′kənd] A small unit of time (p. 96)
60 seconds = 1 minute

similar [si′mə•lər] Having the same shape but possibly different in size (p. 402)
Example:

simplest form [sim′pləst fôrm] A fraction is in simplest form when 1 is the only number that can divide evenly into the numerator and the denominator (p. 449)

slide [slīd] See *translation.*

solid figure [sä′ləd fi′gyər] A three-dimensional figure

sphere [sfēr] A round object whose curved surface is the same distance from the center to all its points (p. 644)
Example:

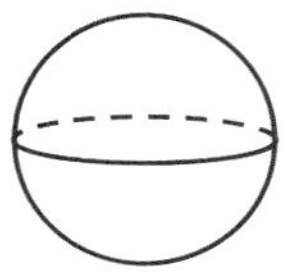

square [skwâr] A parallelogram with 4 equal, or congruent, sides and 4 right angles
Example:

square number [skwâr num′bər] The product of a number and itself (p. 348)
Example: $2 \times 2 = 4$, so 4 is a square number.

square pyramid [skwâr pir′ə•mid] A pyramid with a square base and with four triangular faces (p. 644)
Example:

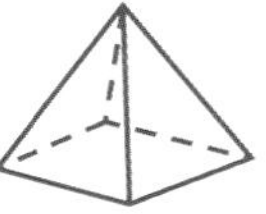

square root [skwâr ro͞ot] One of two equal factors of a number (p. 348)

square unit [skwâr yo͞o′nət] A unit of area with dimensions of 1 unit × 1 unit

standard form [stan′dərd fôrm] A way to write numbers by using digits (p. 7)
Example: 3,540 ←standard form

stem [stem] A tens digit in a stem-and-leaf plot (p. 124)

stem-and-leaf plot [stem ənd lēf plät] A data display that shows groups of data arranged by place value (p. 124)
Example:

Number of Sit-Ups

Stem	Leaves
1	1 3 4
2	0 1 2 3
3	3 4 6
4	0 5 9

straight angle [strāt ang′əl] An angle whose measure is 180° (p. 367)
Example:

subtraction [səb•trak′shən] The process of finding how many are left when a number of items are taken away from a group of items; the process of finding the difference when two groups are compared; the opposite operation of addition

sum [sum] The answer to an addition problem (p. 44)

surface area [sər′fəs âr′ē•ə] The sum of the areas of all the faces of a solid figure (p. 661)

survey [sûr′vā] A method of gathering information to record data (p. 114)

tablespoon (tbsp) [tā′bəl•spo͞on] A customary unit used for measuring capacity (p. 528)
3 teaspoons = 1 tablespoon

tally table [ta′lē tā′bəl] A table that uses tally marks to record data (p. 114)

Word History

Some people keep score in card games by making marks on paper (IIII). These marks are known as tally marks. The word *tally* is related to *tailor*, from the Latin *talea*, meaning "one who cuts." In early times, a method of keeping count was by cutting marks into a piece of wood or bone.

teaspoon (tsp) [tē′spo͞on] A customary unit used for measuring capacity (p. 528)
1 tablespoon = 3 teaspoons

tenth [tenth] One of ten equal parts (p. 560)
Example:

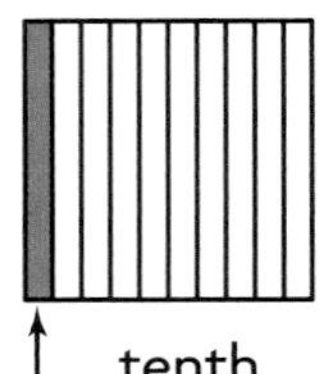

tessellation [tes•ə•lā′shən] A repeating pattern of closed figures that covers a surface with no gaps and no overlaps (p. 410)
Example:

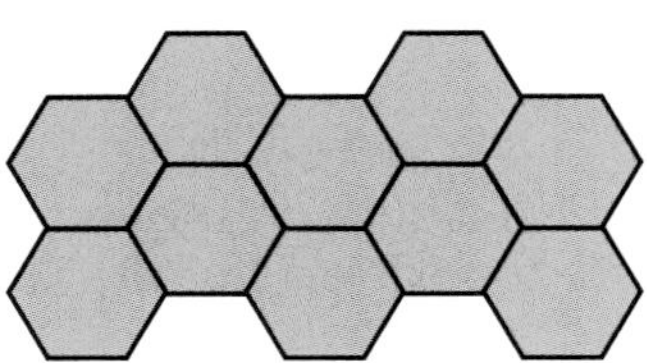

thousandth [thou′zəndth] One of one thousand equal parts (p. 564)

three-dimensional [thrē•də•men′shən•əl] Measured in three directions, such as length, width, and height (p. 644)
Example:

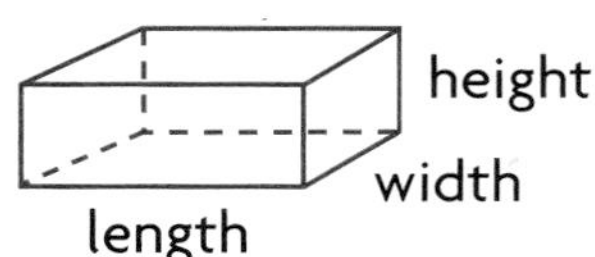

time line [tīm līn] A schedule of events or an ordered list of historic moments

ton (T) [tun] A customary unit for measuring weight (p. 530)
2,000 pounds = 1 ton

transformation [trans•fər•mā′shən] The movement of a figure by a translation, reflection, or rotation (p. 406)

translation [trans•lā′shən] A movement of a figure to a new position along a straight line (p. 406)
Example:

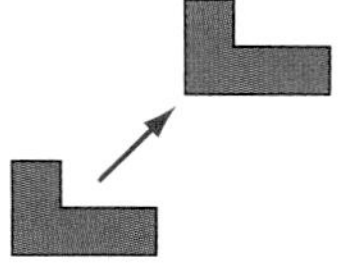

trapezoid [tra′pə•zoid] A quadrilateral with exactly one pair of parallel sides (p. 385)
Example:

tree diagram [trē dī′ə•gram] An organized list that shows all possible outcomes of an event (p. 500)

trends [trendz] On a graph, areas where the data increase, decrease, or stay the same over time (p. 138)

triangle [trī′ang•əl] A polygon with three sides (p. 380)
Example:

triangular prism [trī•an′gyə•lər pri′zəm] A solid figure that has two triangular bases and three rectangular faces (p. 644)
Example:

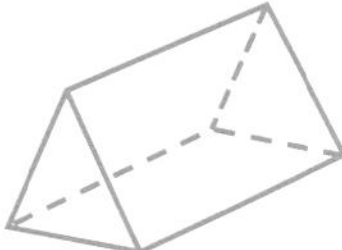

triangular pyramid [trī•an′gyə•lər pir′ə•mid] A pyramid that has a triangular base and three triangular faces (p. 644)
Example:

turn [tûrn] See *rotation.*

two-dimensional [to͞o•də•men′shən•əl] Measured in two directions, such as length and width (p. 644)
Example:

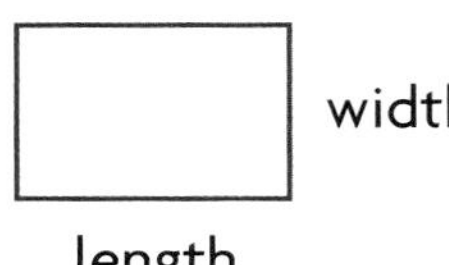

unlike fractions [un′līk frak′shənz] Fractions with different denominators (p. 480)

unlikely [un•lī′klē] Having a less than even chance of happening (p. 492)

variable [vâr′ē•ə•bəl] A letter or symbol that stands for a number or numbers (p. 65)

Venn diagram [ven dī′ə•gram] A diagram that shows relationships among sets of things (p. 388)
Example:

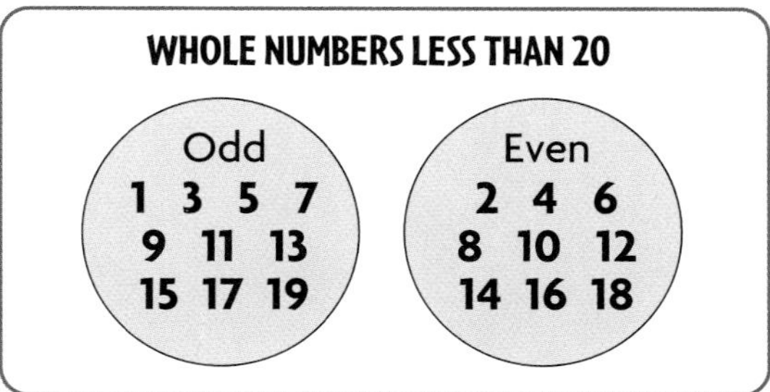

vertex [vûr′teks] The point at which two rays of an angle or two or more line segments meet in a plane figure, or where three or more edges meet in a solid figure; the top point of a cone (pp. 366, 645)
Example:

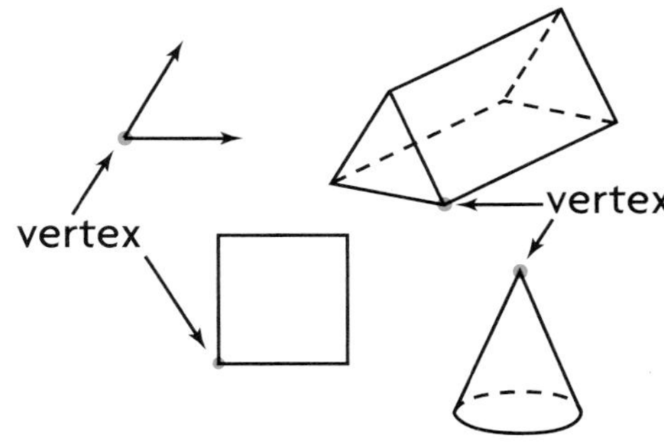

volume [väl′yəm] The measure of the amount of space a solid figure occupies (p. 650)

weight [wāt] How heavy an object is (p. 530)

whole number [hōl num′bər] One of the numbers 0, 1, 2, 3, 4...; the set of whole numbers goes on without end

word form [wûrd fôrm] A way to write numbers by using words (p. 7)
Example: Sixty-two million, four hundred fifty-three thousand, two hundred twelve

***x*-axis** [eks′ak′səs] The horizontal line on a coordinate grid or plane (p. 430)

***x*-coordinate** [eks′kō•ôr′də•nət] The first number in an ordered pair; it tells the distance to move horizontally (p. 430)

***y*-axis** [wī′ak′səs] The vertical line on a coordinate grid or plane (p. 430)

***y*-coordinate** [wī′kō•ôr′də•nət] The second number in an ordered pair; it tells the distance to move vertically (p. 430)

yard (yd) [yärd] A customary unit for measuring length or distance (p. 518)
3 feet = 1 yard

Zero Property of Multiplication [zē′rō prä′pər•tē əv mul•tə•plə•kā′shən] The property that states that the product of 0 and any number is 0 (p. 174)
Example: $0 \times 8 = 0$

B

C

D

E

F

G

H

N

O

P

S

T

PHOTO CREDITS

Photography Credits: Page Placement key: (t) top, (b) bottom, (c) center, (l) left, (r) right, (bg) background, (i) inset.

Page: v S.I. Epperson/Index Stock; xi David Stoecklein/The Stock Market; xvii (t) NASA; xvii (b) Jeff Schultz/Alaska Stock Images; Chip Henderson/Picturesque Stock Photo; xxi David B. Fleetham/Natural Selection; xxvii (t) Barbara Reed/Animals Animals; xxviii Russell D. Curtis/Photo Researchers; xxviii (i) Elsa Peterson/The Stock Market; 4 Kyodo News International; 6 Index Stock; 7 NASA; 8 Mark E. Gibson; 9 www.roadsideamerica.com, Kirby, Smith, Wilkins; 10 NASA; 11 Ann Purcell/Words and Pictures; 12 Ariel Skelley/The Stock Market; 16 Craig Tuttle/The Stock Market; 21 Lee Snider/Corbis; 24 S.I. Epperson/Index Stock; 26 Dembinsky Photo Associates; 28 Elliott Varner Smith/International Stock; 29 J.C. Carton/Bruce Coleman, Inc.; 32 Charles Sleicher/Stone; 34 (t) Ron Kimball; 34 (b) G.K. & Vikki Hart/The Image Bank; 40 Corbis; 42 David B. Fleetham/Natural Selection; 43 Bill Hickey/The Image Bank; 45 David Muench/Corbis; 46 Wyman Meinzer/Texas Panhandle Heritage Foundation; 48 Superstock; 54 David Young Wolff/PhotoEdit; 79A,79B (t) John Elk III; 79B (b) Richard Hamilton Smith; 80 Fred Bavendam/Minden Pictures; 88 Index Stock; 89 Richard Hutchings/PhotoEdit; 91 Chuck Savage/The Stock Market; 94 Alan Thornton/Stone; 98 Jim Nilsen/Stone; 102 Gerard Fritz/International Stock; 103 Roy Engelbrecht; 106 (b) Leonard Lee Rue III/Animals Animals; 106 (t) Johnny Johnson/Animals Animals; 109 (l to r) #1 Wolfgang Kaehler/Corbis; 109 (l to r) #2 Mitsuaki Iwago/Minden Pictures; 109 (l to r) #3 Roland Seitre/Peter Arnold, Inc.; 109 (l to r) #4 Manfred Danegger/Peter Arnold, Inc.; 109 (l to r) #5 Trevor Bararett/Animals Animals; 109 (l to r) #6 Rick Edwards/Animals Animals; 110 Biological Photo Service; 111 Bradley Simmons/Bruce Coleman, Inc.; 114 Richard Cummins/Corbis; 116 Ernest H. Robl; 118 Todd Gipstein/National Geographic Image Collection; 121 A. Ramey/Stock, Boston; 122 (t) Charles Thatcher/Stone; 122 (b) Sports Illustrated; 124 (b) Superstock; 125 The Purcell Team/Corbis; 127 John Skowronski; 129 NASA; 137A Mark E. Gibson; 137B (t) Phil Shermeister/Corbis; 137B (b) Dean Dunson/Corbis; 138 Rafael Macia/Photo Researchers; 147 George Holton/Photo Researchers; 150 Underwood & Underwood/Corbis; 151 Paul Barton/The Stock Market; 152 Bob Daemmrich/Stock, Boston; 153 Owen Franken/Stock, Boston; 156 Christies Images; 166 Steven Needham/Envision; 168 Brian Bailey/Stone; 182 (t) Daemmrich/Stock, Boston; 183A (t) LaFOTO/H. Armstrong Roberts, Inc.; 183A (br) E.R. Degginger/Bruce Coleman, Inc.; 183A (bl) Thom Lang/The Stock Market; 183A (bc) Eastcott/Momatiuk/Animals Animals; 183B Doug Perrine/Innerspace Visions; 184 Dale O'Dell/The Stock Market; 188 Andre Jenny/International Stock; 208 Index Stock; 210 Index Stock; 212 AGStock USA; 222 David R. Frazier/Photo Researchers; 224 Lowell Georgia/Corbis; 225 Flip Chalfant/The Image Bank; 227 J. C. Carton/Bruce Coleman, Inc.; 223 Larry Lefever/Grant Heilman Photography; 228 Ed Young/AGStock USA; 232 Michael Newman/PhotoEdit; 243A (t) P. Degginger/H. Armstrong Roberts, Inc.; 243A (b) Annie Griffiths Belt/Corbis; 243B (b) Jack Olson; 244 Dave Fleetham/Tom Stack & Associates; 250 Jeff Simon/Bruce Coleman, Inc.; 251 Jose Luis G. Grande/Photo Researchers; 254 (t) Rex A. Butcher/Stone; 256 David Madison/Bruce Coleman, Inc.; 258 Renee Lynn/Stone; 262 Phil Kramer/The Stock Market; 266 Philip Rosenburg/Pacific Stock; 268, 269 United States Postal Service; 272 Jon Feingersh/The Stock Market; 277 Paul Barton/The Stock Market; 280 Myrleen Ferguson/PictureQuest; 288 Alan Schein/The Stock Market; 291 Johnny Stockshooter/International Stock; 293 Carl Purcell/Words and Pictures; 296 Peter Dean/Grant Heilman Photography; 299 John M. Roberts/The Stock Market; 317A (t), 317A (b) Chuck Dresner/Saint Louis Zoo; 317B (bg) Philip Roullard; 317B Chuck Keeler/The Stock Market; 318 Cliff Hollenbeck/International Stock; 320 Mark E. Gibson; 330 Adam Peiperl/The Stock Market; 331 (tr) John Watkins/Photo Researchers; 331 (trc) Peter Steiner/The Stock Market; 331 (bl) D and J Heaton/Stock, Boston; 333 Gregory G. Dimijian/Photo Researchers; 336 Joseph Sohm/ChromoSohm/Corbis; 348, 349 Christie's Images; 361A Richard Cummins/The Viesti Collection; 361B (i) Dembinsky Photo Associates; 361B R. Krubner/H. Armstrong Roberts; 362 (t) Manuel Denner/Internatonal Stock; 362 (c), 362 (b) Bob Firth/International Stock; 364 Noble Stock/International Stock; 368 (r) Barbara Reed/Animals Animals/Earth Scenes; 371 David Young-Wolff/PhotoEdit; 372 C.C.Lockwood/Animals Animals; 374 Laurie Campbell/Stone; 378 Robert Maier/Animals Animals; 381 Mark Downey/Lucid Images/PictureQuest; 389 David Muench Photography; 409 (t) NASA; 409 (b) Zeva Oelbaum/Envision; 410 Associated Press File/Wide World Photos; 414 Gary Braasch Photography; 415 Len Rue, Jr./Bruce Coleman, Inc.; 421 (b) Ed Wheeler/The Stock Market; 422 Mark E. Gibson; 426 Ken Graham/Bruce Coleman, Inc.; 428 Bruce Curtis/Peter Arnold, Inc.; 430 Hubertus Kanus/Photo Researchers; 431 Rose McNulty; 432 D. Boone/Corbis; 433 George Disario/The Stock Market; 434 J.C. Carton/Bruce Coleman, Inc.; 436 Richard Cummins/Corbis; 440 David Muench/Corbis; 441 Craig Jones/Allsport; 449A Carr Clifton/Minden Pictures; 449B (l) Raymond Gehman/Corbis; 449B (r) Tim Fitzharris/Minden Pictures; 456 E. R. Degginger/Bruce Coleman, Inc.; 468 (bg) Mark J. Thoms/Dembinsky Photo Associates; 468 (ti) Johnny Johnson/Stone; 468 (ci) Stephen J. Krasemann/DRK; 468 (bi) Marty Cordano/DRK; 470 (t) Ray Coleman/Photo Researchers; 472 D. Young-Wolff/PhotoEdit; 474 Index Stock; 475 J. Swedberg/Bruce Coleman, Inc.; 480 Index Stock; 484 Larry West/FPG International; 487 Tom Edwards/Animals Animals; 501 Federal Clip Art/One Mile Up; 506 Kevin Hart/International Stock; 508 Jean Kugler/FPG International; 509 Tom McHugh/Photo Researchers; 510 (cl) Peter Aaron/Esto; 510 Frederica Georgia/Picturesque; 510 Ezra Stoller/Esto; 511 Alex S. Maclean/Landslides; 515 Richard Barnet/Omni-Photo Communications; 521 Spencer Grant/PhotoEdit; 524 Superstock; 525A, 525B H. Abernathy/H. Armstrong Roberts; 525B (br) Ty Smedes Nature Photography; 540 Marc Romanelli/The Image Bank; 552 Roland Seitre/Peter Arnold, Inc.; 554 Bob Krist/ Stone; 555 (l) Rita Maas/The Image Bank; 555 (r) Jose L. Pelaez/The Stock Market; 556 Jeff Schultz/Alaska Stock Images; 558, 559, 560 NASA; 562 Color Day/The Image Bank; 563 Ken Levinson/International Stock; 564 (c) Mark E. Gibson; 564 (l) Envision(c)Overseas; 566 NASA/Science Photo Library/Photo Researchers; 566 (i) American Red Cross/NOAA; 568 T & D McCarthy/The Stock Market; 573 David R. Frazier; 587A Michael Evans/The Image Finders; 587A (t) (bi) 587B (t) John Gillmoure/The Stock Market; 587B (b) Lance Beeny; H1 David Madison/Bruce Coleman, Inc.; H58 (r) John Margolies/Esto; H58 (cl) William Johnson/Stock, Boston; H58 (r) Ezra Stoller/Esto; H58 (cr) Frederica Georgia/Picturesque.

All other photography by Harcourt photographers listed below, © Harcourt: Weronica Ankarorn; Victoria Bowen; Richard Haynes; Ken Kinzie; Ron Kunzman; Ed McDonald; Sheri O'Neal; Terry Sinclair, Sonny Spenser.

Chapter Opener Photography Credits by Chapter: 1 Phil Degginger/Animals Animals/Earth Scenes; 2 Chuck Summers/Contemplative Images; 3 Charles Sleicher/Stone; 4 Sonny Senser/Harcourt; 5 Jim Nilsen/Stone; 6 Fred Bavendam/Minden Pictures; 7 Dale O'Dell/The Stock Market; 8 AP Photo/Tina Fineberg; 9 Harcourt; 10 Dan Bailey;11 Index Stock Photography; 12 Harcourt; 13 Dave Fleetham/Tom Stack & Associates; 14 Phil Kramer/The Stock Market; 15 Stock Image/Image State; 16 Doug Sudduth; 16 Billie Ruth Sudduth; 17 Cliff Hollenbeck/International Stock Photography; 18 Ken Laffal; 19 Susie Leavines; 19(inset) Ken Laffal; 20 NASA/Science Photo Library/Photo Researchers; 21 AFP/Corbis; 22 David Haring/Duke University Primate Center; 23 Marc Romanelli/The Image Bank; 24 Abbot/Mercury Press.com; 25 Mark J. Thomas/Dembinsky Photo Associates; 26 Lawrence Migdale; 27 Ken Graham/Bruce Coleman, Inc.; 28 Joseph Sohm/Chromosohm/Corbis; 29 Larry Fleming/AgStock USA; 30 Pat & Chuck Blackley.

Problem Solving On Location Pages: Page 160(both), Marilyn "Angel" Wynn / Nativestock.com; 161(both), courtesy, Red Earth Museum; 360(t) Michael Evans / The Image Finders; 360(bl), Len Rue, Jr. / Leonard Rue Enterprises; 360(br), Michael Evans / The Image Finders; 514, Patti McConville / Dembinsky Photo Associates; 515(all), David R. Frazier Photo Library; 608(both), Mike Warren / Appalachian Trail Conference; 609, RoadsideAmerica.com; 609 John Elk III; 666-667, The University of Alabama Museums.